11th Edition

Warman's

Americana & Collectibles

Identification and Price Guide

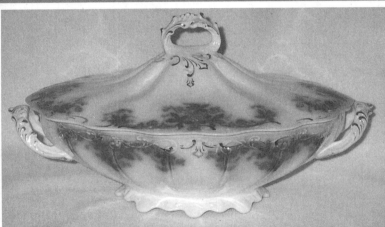

Edited by **Ellen T. Schroy**

©2004 KP Books
Published by

Our toll-free number to place an order or obtain
a free catalog is (800) 258-0929.

kp books

An imprint of F+W Publications, Inc.

700 East State Street • Iola, WI 54990-0001
715-445-2214 • 888-457-2873

On the cover: Mickey Mouse PEZ, **$5**; baseball program, Yankees vs. Pirates, 1927, **$125**;
Shirley Temple doll, 20" h, Ideal, original dress, box and pinback button, **$2,000**;
McCoy sunflower vase, 1950s, unusual airbrush decoration, unmarked, **$450-$550**.

On the title page: Flow Blue vegetable tureen with lid, LaFrancaise, floral ivy pattern,
$325; Mickey Mouse figural telephone, push-button dial, **$20**; early 20th century
wood brisé souvenir fan from Florida, imported from Austria and marked "Austria"
in fine print on back, **$22**; railroad lantern, D.L. & W.R.R., Adams Westlake Co.
frame, clear globe embossed P.R.R., **$225**.

Library of Congress Catalog Number: 0739-6457

ISBN: 0-87349-685-X

Designed by Kay Sanders
Edited by Kris Manty

Printed in United States of America

Contents

Part 1

Part 2

Part 3

A new category in this edition is Carnival Glass, Modern, featured on P. 92.

Another new category is Tobaccoania, which starts on P. 469.

Acknowledgments

Since its creation in 1984, *Warman's Americana & Collectibles* has grown and changed with the shifts of the antiques and collectibles marketplace. New categories are included that show what folks are collecting as we embrace a new century. New collectibles are drawing folks to antiques shows, shops, flea markets, and browsing the Internet. Perhaps it's living in a country and society where you are free to decide what to collect, how to spend your money, or perhaps my aging baby-boomer philosophy, but I believe every dedicated collector brings their own unique dedication and enthusiasm to the hobby. Thankfully there are collectors for almost every type of object, keeping the hobby lively.

Reflecting back on the 20 years this particular book has been part of my life causes me to stop and smile and remember wonderful folks, such as Stanley and Katherine Greene, who saw the wisdom of creating the very first edition of *Warman's Americana & Collectibles*. I remember the long hours it took to carefully write down all the pricing research that we gathered for the new book. Back in 1984, the information was gathered, written on 3-inch x 5-inch cards and then filed until enough data was generated to compile a category. Then the cards were sorted, analyzed, and finally typed into lists on real paper, using a typewriter. Now the information is sorted, analyzed and typed into large databases that are maintained on computers.

When work was completed on the first edition, we had much too much information, so together, Stanley, former editor Harry L. Rinker, and I sat at the printer's office and cut out sections with a scissors. Today, it's a few e-mails back and forth to my editor Kris Manty at KP Books, a few buttons are pushed and the information is deleted. Back in 1984, we spent hours finding objects to be photographed at flea markets, antiques shows, private collectors, etc. Film was developed into prints. Notes were taken about the objects, hand written labels were affixed to prints and photos were filed. Today, some of that tedious work is replaced by digital photography, allowing advisers and collectors from all over the country to send images to be used in this edition. This edition also repre-sents some changes that are occurring in the collectible word in respect to terminology. Today collectors who specialize in beer, its manufacture, and advertising, prefer the name "Breweriana." Collectors who look for items related to the tobacco industry prefer "Tobaccoania," rather than the former headings of "Cigar Collectibles" or "Cigarette Collectibles." Soakies were also simply bubble bath containers we played with as kids, not hot collectibles. Other collecting categories, such as Star Wars, have been expanded in this 11th edition to show how interest has grown over the past few years.

No edition of *Warman's* would ever be complete without a special thanks to the members of the Board of Advisers, a wonderful, dedicated group. Some new names have been added, helping to give this edition a very up-to-date and wide-geographical flavor, while providing some solid information about some hot topics. Through the mail, telephone, and e-mail, I've been in contact with each and every one, and heard about what's important to their collecting interests as well as what's new in their lives. Through these conversations and their warm wishes of support, we've created an even better *Warman's Americana & Collectibles*.

The fine staff of KP Books continues its nurturing support of *Warman's*. Perhaps you have noticed some of the additional books that now include "Warman's" in their titles, like *Warman's Advertising, Warman's Country, Warman's Sports,* and *Warman's Depression Glass.* Collectors should be assured every title that contains that familiar Warman's name is full of good information as well as solid, up-to-date pricing. So with a special thanks to Kris Manty and her talented co-workers in production and design, we'll now offer you a new edition of *Warman's Americana & Collectibles*.

Here's hoping you enjoy it as much as we enjoy creating it for collectors and dealers like you.

Ellen Tischbein Schroy
April 15, 2004

Introduction

Welcome to *Warman's Americana & Collectibles*. In 1984, the first edition of *Warman's Americana & Collectibles* introduced the collecting community to category introductions featuring collecting hints, histories, references, periodicals, and reproduction and copycat information complemented by detailed, accurate listings and values. As a result of the enthusiastic acceptance of this format, it was extended to *Warman's Antiques and Collectibles Price Guide* and ultimately to other Warman's books.

Warman's Americana & Collectibles was a pioneering work, the first general price guide to mass-produced 20th-century objects. It helped define and solidify the modern collectibles market. As the collectibles market has matured, so has *Warman's Americana & Collectibles*. If you have a copy of the first edition, compare the categories listed in it to those found in this 11th edition. Times have changed. Perhaps this is why so many individuals find the collectibles market exciting.

Collectibles are the things your parents, you, and your children have played and lived with. The things that belonged to your grandparents are now *antiques*. The evolution of an object from new to desirable to collectible to antique within one's lifetime, i.e., an approximately 50-year span, is difficult for some to accept. However, it is reality.

Warman's Americana & Collectibles takes you on a nostalgic trip down memory lane. Sometimes it's sad to think back about things that have been passed on to others, perhaps have been broken or discarded. However, it's better to be thrilled by the value of the things that were saved. Do not hesitate to buy back the things from your childhood that evoke pleasant memories. As you do, you will find that the real value of objects is not monetary, but the joy that comes from collecting, owning, and, most importantly, playing and living with them once again.

As we celebrate the 20th anniversary of Warman's Americana & Collectibles, it's our philosophy that collectors should enjoy what they treasure so passionately and take the time to learn more about their specialties. Warman's Americana & Collectibles is based on the premise that it is acceptable to collect anything you wish. Remember one simple fact: All of today's antiques were collectibles in the past.

What is a collectible?

As this edition represents the 20th anniversary of *Warman's Americana & Collectibles*, the definition of an antique remains clear, while what constitutes a collectible has become more confusing.

For the purpose of this book, an antique is anything made before 1945. A great many individuals in the antiques and collectibles field disagree with this definition, but with each passing year it becomes harder and harder to deny this premise. The key is the war years of 1942-1945. During this period, production switched from domestic to wartime products. When the war ended, things were different. American life and expectations were very different in 1948 than in 1938. New war technology modified for productive civilian use was partially responsible. However, the most-telling fact of all is that well over half the population living in America today was born after 1945 and approximately two-thirds grew up in the post-1945 era.

Keeping this in mind and seeking technical definitions, a collectible then becomes an object made between 1945 and 1965, and a "desirable" an object made after 1965. The difference between a collectible and a desirable is that a collectible has a clearly established secondary market, while a desirable exists in a market rampant with speculation.

Actually, the post-1945 era is broken down into three distinct collecting periods: 1945-1965, 1965-1980, and post-1980. Goods from 1965-1980 period are moving out of their speculative mode into one of price stability.

Within the Warman's Encyclopedia of Antiques and Collectibles, *Warman's Americana & Collectibles* is the volume designed to deal with objects from the

20th century. Three criteria are applied when preparing the book: Was the object mass produced? Was it made in the 20th century, preferably after 1945? Do the majority of the items in the category sell for less than $200? The ideal collectible fits all three qualifications.

Since collecting antiques became fashionable in the early 20th century, there have been attempts to define certain groups of objects as the "true" antiques, worthy of sophisticated collectors, and to ignore the remaining items. Most museums clearly demonstrate this attitude. Where do early 20th-century tin toys, toy soldiers, or dolls fit? Those made before 1915 are antique. No one argues this any longer. Those made between 1920 and 1940 are in transition. We designate them "prestige" collectibles, objects changing in people's minds from collectible to antique.

In some collecting areas, such as advertising, dolls, and toys, *Warman's Americana & Collectibles* offers readers descriptions and values for 20th century items that might not be covered in *Warman's Antiques & Collectibles*. Other topics covered in *Warman's Americana & Collectibles* expand on the information found in that companion book. Areas like costume jewelry and Star Wars can better be addressed in *Warman's Americana & Collectibles*. When *Warman's Americana & Collectibles* was initially launched, it was hoped that this book could capture that segment of the market place that was missing from other price guides. Today, that fine tradition continues as *Warman's Americana & Collectibles* evolves again to respond to the collectibles marketplace.

To clarify the distinction between antique and collectible, consider Webster's definition of collectible: "an object that is collected by fanciers, especially one other than such traditionally collectible items as art, stamps, coins, and antiques."

International market

Collectibles began to draw worldwide interest at the end of the 1980s. All of a sudden, American buyers found themselves competing with buyers from Europe and Japan on their home turf. In head-to-head competition, the American buyers frequently lost. How can this be explained?

The largest portion of the 2000's collectibles market is made up of post-World War II material. During this period, the youth of the world fell under three dominant American influences: movies, music, and television. As the generations of the 1950s, 1960s, and even 1970s reached adulthood and started buying back their childhood, many of the things they remember and want have American associations.

America is the great mother lode of post-war collectibles. At the moment it is packages and boxes of American collectibles that are being sent abroad. It will not be too much longer before the volume reaches container loads.

American collectors also are expanding their horizons. They recognize that many objects within their favorite collectible category were licensed abroad. They view their collections as incomplete without such examples. Objects are obtained by either traveling abroad or by purchasing from foreign sources through mail or auction.

The addition of the Internet and its auctions, dealer Web sites, and collector club Web sites has created additional buying opportunities. Collectors no longer have to set aside time to travel to their favorite haunts and search for hours for something to add to their collection. Sometimes it's as easy as sitting down at their computer and reading what's posted for sale. Some collecting areas are also benefiting from chat rooms dedicated to their specialties, allowing collectors to explore and learn from each other in ways and with speed only now available. This new openness is creating more savvy collectors and allowing information to flow globally.

Price notes

Prices in the collectibles field are not as firmly established as in the antiques area. Nevertheless, we do not use ranges unless we feel they are absolutely necessary.

Our pricing is based on an object being in very good condition. If otherwise, we note this in our description. It would be ideal to suggest that mint, or unused, examples of all items do exist. In reality, objects from the past were used, whether they be glass, china, dolls, or toys. Because of this, some normal wear must be expected.

The biggest problem in the collectibles field is that an object may have more than one price. A George Eastman bubble gum card may be worth $1 to a bubble gum card collector but $35 to a collector of photographic memorabilia. I saw the same card marked both ways. In preparing prices for this guide we have considered the object in terms of the category in which it is included. Hence, a girlie matchcover may be valued at 25¢ to 50¢ in the matchcover category and $2 to $5 in pinup art. However, for purposes of making a sale, if all you can find are matchcover collectors, take the quarter and move on.

Organization of the book

Listings: We have attempted to make the listings descriptive enough so the specific object can be identified. Most guides limit their descriptions to one line, but not *Warman's*. We have placed emphasis on those items actively being sold in the marketplace. Nevertheless, some harder-to-find objects are included in order to demonstrate the market spread. A few categories in this book also appear in *Warman's Antiques and Collectibles Price Guide*. The individual listings, however, seldom overlap except for a few minor instances. We've tried to include enough objects to give readers a good base for comparison. After all, that is what much of the collectibles marketplace uses to establish prices: comparables. To properly accomplish this task, some overlapping between books is unavoidable. It is our intention to show objects in the low to middle price range of a category in *Warman's Americana & Collectibles* and the middle to upper range in our main antiques guide, *Warman's Antiques and Collectibles Price Guide*, thus creating two true companion lists for the general dealer or collector.

History: Here we discuss the category, describe how the object was made, who are or were the leading manufacturers, and the variations of form and style. In many instances, a chronology for the object is established. Finally, we place the object in a social context—how it was used, for what purpose, etc.

Collecting Hints: This section calls attention to specific hints as they relate to the category. We note where cross-category collecting and nostalgia are critical in pricing. Clues are given for spotting reproductions. In most cases, we just scratch the surface. We encourage collectors to consult specialized publications.

Collectors' Clubs: In past editions of *Warman's Americana & Collectibles* we listed collectors' clubs, along with their addresses. Yes, the large number of collectors' clubs adds vitality to the collectibles field. Their publications and conventions produce knowledge, which often cannot be found anywhere else. However, many of these clubs are short-lived, while others are so strong that they have regional and local chapters. Many collector clubs are now going online, offering chat rooms and other benefits to their members. We have mentioned collecting clubs where they are important to the category. We urge readers of this edition to consult David J. Maloney Jr.'s marvelous reference work, *Maloney's Antiques & Collectibles, Resource Directory*, 7th edition, KP Books, for up-to-date information about collector clubs, experts, etc.

Periodicals: In respect to the collectibles field, there are certain general monthly periodicals to which the general collector should subscribe:

Antiques & Collecting Hobbies, 1006 South Michigan Ave., Chicago, IL 60605.

AntiqueWeek, P.O. Box 90, Knightstown, IN 46148; http://www.antiqueweek.com.

Maine Antique Digest, P.O. Box 358, Waldoboro, ME 04572; http://www.maineantiquedigest.com.

Several excellent periodicals relating to the collectibles marketplace are published by KP Books, 700 East State St., Iola, WI 54990-0001; http://www.krause.com. Check out these interesting publications:

Antique Trader Weekly

Coin Prices

Coins

Goldmine

Numismatic News

Postcard Collector

Sports Collectors Digest

Toy Shop

Many of the categories included in Warman's Americana & Collectibles have listings of specialized periodicals and newsletters. Please refer to your specific collecting interest for these additional references.

Museums: The best way to study any field is to see as many documented examples as possible. Collectors are urged to visit and support museums where significant collections are on display. Special attention must be directed to the Margaret Woodbury Strong Museum in Rochester, New York, and the Smithsonian Institution's Museum of American History in Washington, D.C.

Reproduction Alert: Reproductions are a major concern, especially with any item related to advertising. Most reproductions are unmarked; the newness of their appearance is often the best clue to uncovering them. Where the words "Reproduction Alert" alone appear, a watchful eye should be kept on all objects in the category. Serious collectors should invest in a subscription to Antique & Collectors Reproduction News, P.O. Box 12130, Des Moines, IA 50312-9403, www.repronews.com. Learning about what new reproductions are surfacing every month might just save a collector from making a bad investment.

Reproductions are only one aspect of the problem; outright fakes are another. Unscrupulous manufacturers make fantasy items that never existed, e.g., a Depression glass Sharon butter dish reproduced in Mayfair blue.

Research

Collectors of objects in the categories found in this book deserve credit for their attention to scholarship and the skill with which they have assembled their collections. This book attests to how strong and encompassing the collectibles market has become through their efforts.

We obtain our prices from many key sources—dealers, publications, auctions, collectors, the Internet, and field work. The generosity with which dealers have given advice is a credit to the field. Everyone recognizes the need for a guide that is specific and has accurate prices. We study newspapers, magazines, newsletters, and other publications in the collectibles and antiques fields, as well as spending more and more time on-line. All of them are critical to understanding what is available in the market. Special recognition must be given to those collectors' club newsletters and magazines that discuss prices.

Our staff is constantly monitoring the field and paying attention to all parts of the country. We accomplish this by reading trade publications and using the Internet and its vast resources to reach many places. Frequent visits to several different Web sites yield valuable information as to what is being offered for sale and what people are looking for, as well as insights into collecting clubs and new collecting interests. Our Board of Advisers provides regional, as well as specialized, information. More than 100 specialized auctions are held annually, and their results provided to our office. Finally, private collectors have worked closely with us, sharing their knowledge of price trends and developments unique to their specialties.

Buyer's guide, not seller's guide

Warman's Americana and Collectibles is designed to be a buyer's guide, a guide to what you would have to pay to purchase an object on the open market from a dealer or collector. **It is not a seller's guide to prices.** People frequently make this mistake and are deceiving themselves by doing so.

If you have an object mentioned in this book and wish to sell it, you should expect to receive approximately 35-40 percent of the value listed. If the object cannot be resold quickly, expect to receive even less. The truth is simple: Knowing to whom to sell an object is worth 50 percent or more of its value. Buyers are very specialized; dealers work for years to assemble a list of collectors who will pay top dollar for an item.

Examine your piece as objectively as possible. If it is something from your childhood, try to step back from the personal memories in evaluating its condition. As an antiques appraiser, I spend a great deal of my time telling people their treasures are not "gold," but items readily available in the marketplace.

In respect to buying and selling, a simple philosophy is that a good purchase occurs when both the buyer and seller are happy with the price. Don't look back. Hindsight has little value in the collectibles field. Given time, things tend to balance out.

Sometimes small items are displayed together on a ribbon. This collection features several patriotic pins, firemen badges, World War II remembrance badges, a gold caddie's ID button, and a religious medallion.

Where to buy collectibles

The collectible has become standard auction house fare in the new millenium. Christie's East, Sotheby's Arcade, and Skinner's conduct collectibles sales several times each year. Specialized auction firms, e.g., James Julia, Inc. and Bill Bertoia Auctions in advertising, toys, and a host of other categories, have proven the viability of the collectible as a focal point.

The major collectibles marketing thrust has changed from the mail auction to Internet auctions. Hake's Americana & Collectibles is the leader in mail auctions. More and more collectible Internet auctions are sprouting up all across the country. The excitement of buying and selling online keeps collectors interested. It is easy to see why so many expand their collections using these venues.

It is becoming easier and easier to buy and sell collectibles on-line. There are numerous auction sites, including e-bay.com, Collectoronline.com, TIAS.com, etc. The same excitement of buying collectibles at a real auction can be achieved. However, this arena is growing quickly and is not yet regulated. Buyers need to be cautious, know what they are buying and learn to set limits on what to spend. Buyers should feel comfortable with the venue before jumping in on the bidding and should feel free to ask questions of the seller, just as they would in a

These colorful large sized displays were exhibited at the March 2004 Atlantique City: lollipop tree display; Ronald McDonald and his very own bench, **$1,800**; a large RCA Victor Nipper neon sign; and Mother Goose store display.

This booth, by W Chourney Antiques & Collectibles, at the March 2004 Atlantiques City Antiques Show featured quality advertising pieces and other interesting memorabilia.

more traditional selling setting. With online services and live auctioneers merging and forming new alliances, it is now possible to live bid on objects being auctioned off at a major auction house. This is a brand new area to explore and hopefully it will bring excitement and energy to the antiques and collectibles market as we begin the new millennium.

Direct-sale catalogs abound. Most major categories have one or more. These dealers and many more advertise in periodicals and collectors' clubs' newsletters. Most require payment of an annual fee before sending their catalogs.

Of course, there are an unlimited number of flea markets, estate and country auctions, church bazaars, and garage sales. However, if you are a specialized collector, you may spend days looking for something to add to your collection. If you add in your time, the real cost of an object will be much higher than the purchase price alone.

All of which brings us to the final source—the specialized dealer. The collectibles field is so broad that dealers do specialize. Find the dealers who handle your material and work with them to build your collection.

Board of Advisers

Our Board of Advisers are dealers, authors, collectors, and leaders of collectors' clubs throughout the United States. All are dedicated to accuracy in description and pricing. If you wish to buy or sell an object in their field of expertise, drop them a note. Please include a stamped, self-addressed envelope with all correspondence. E-mail addresses and Web-sites are now also included as an additional way to contact an adviser. If time permits, they will respond.

We list the names of our advisers at the end of their respective categories. Included in the list here are the mailing address for each adviser and, when available, phone number and/or e-mail address.

Lorie Cairns
Cairns Antiques
P.O. Box 44026
Lemon Cove, CA 93244
(559) 597-2242
Labels

Barry L. Carter
Knightstown Antique Mall
136 West Carey St.
Knightstown, IN 46148
(765) 345-5665
E-mail: Indytoysoldier@hotmail.com
Soldiers, Dimestore; Soldiers, Toy

Cynthia Fendel
5128 Spyglass Drive
Dallas, TX 75287
(972) 931-1025
Web site: www.handfanpro.com
Fans

David J. and Deborah G. Folckemer
RR2, Box 394
Hollidaysburg, PA 16648-9200
(814) 696-0301
Royal China

Ted Hake
Hake's Americana & Collectibles
P.O. Box 1444
York, PA 17405
(717) 848-1333
Web site: Auction@hakes.com
Disneyana; Political & Campaign Items

Doris and Burdell Hall
B & B Antiques
210 West Sassafras Drive
Morton, IL 61550
(309) 263-2988
Morton Potteries

Mary Hamburg
20 Cedar Ave.
Danville, IL 61832
(217) 446-2323
Pig Collectibles

Jon Haussler
1806 Brownstone Ave., SW
Decatur, AL 35603
(256) 351-8567
E-mail: jhaus23985@aol.com
Griswold

George A. Higby
Sutton Place, #205
1221 Minor Ave.
Seattle, WA 98101
Treasure Craft/Pottery Craft

Tom Hoepf
c/o Antique Week
P.O. Box 90, 27 North Jefferson
Knightstown, IN 46148
(800) 876-5133
E-mail: antiqueth@aol.com
Cameras & Accessories

Tim Hughes
P.O. Box 3636
Williamsport, PA 17701-8636
(570) 326-1045
(570) 326-7606 fax
E-mail timothy@rarenewspapers.com
Web site: www.rarenewspapers.com
Newspapers, Headlines

Joan Hull
1376 Nevada
Huron, SD 57350
(605) 352-1685
Hull Pottery

David and Sue Irons
Irons Antiques
223 Covered Bridge Road
Northampton, PA 18067
(610) 262-9335
Web site: Ironsantiques.com
E-mail: dave@ironsantiques.com
Irons

Auction Houses

The following auction houses cooperate with *Warman's* by providing catalogs of their auctions and price lists. This information is used to prepare *Warman's Antiques and Collectibles Price Guide*, volumes in the Warman's Encyclopedia of Antiques and Collectibles. This support is truly appreciated.

Absolute Auction & Realty, Inc.
P.O. Box 1739
#45 South Ave.
Pleasant Valley, NY 12569-1739
(845) 635-3169
Web site: www.absoluteauctionrealty.com

Albrecht & Cooper Auction Services
3884 Saginaw Road
Vassar, MI 48768
(517) 823-8835

Sanford Alderfer Auction Company
501 Fairgrounds Road
Hatfield, PA 19440
(215) 393-3000
Web site: www.alderfercompany.com

American Bottle Auctions
1507 21st St., Suite 203
Sacramento, CA 95814
(800) 806-7722
Web site: www.americanbottle.com

American Social History and Social Movements
4025 Saline St.
Pittsburgh, PA 15217
(412) 421-5230

Andre Ammelounx
The Stein Auction Company
P.O. Box 136
Palantine, IL 60078
(847) 991-5927

Antique Bottle Connection
147 Reserve Road
Libby, MT 59923
(406) 293-8442

Apple Tree Auction Center
1616 W. Church St.
Newark, OH 43055
(704) 344-4282
Web site: www.appletreeauction.com

Arthur Auctioneering
563 Reed Road
Hughesville, PA 17737
(570) 584-3697

Auction Team Köln
Jane Herz
6731 Ashley Court
Sarasota, FL 34241
(941) 925-0385

Auction Team Köln
Postfach 501168 D 5000
Köln 50, W. Germany

Noel Barrett Antiques & Auctions, Ltd
P.O. Box 300
Carversville, PA 18913-0201
(215) 297-5109
Web site: www.noelbarret.com

Robert F. Batchelder
1 W. Butler Ave.
Ambler, PA 19002
(610) 643-1430

Bear Pen Antiques
2318 Bear Pen Hollow Road
Lock Haven, PA 17745
(717) 769-6655

Bertoia Auctions
2141-F Demarco Dr.
Vineland, NJ 08360
(856) 692-1881

Brunk Auctions
117 Tunnel Ave.
Asheville, NC 28805
(828) 254-6846
Web site: www.brunkauctions.com

Buffalo Bay Auction Co.
5244 Quam Circle
Saint Michael MN 55376
(763) 428-8440
Web site: www.buffalobayauction.com

Bonham & Butterfield
220 San Bruno Ave.
San Francisco, CA 94103
(415) 861-7500
Web site: www:bonhams.com

W. E. Channing & Co., Inc.
53 Old Santa Fe Trail
Santa Fe, NM 87501
(505) 988-1078

Chicago Art Galleries
5039 Oakton St.
Skokie, IL 60077
(847) 677-6080

Childers & Smith
1415 Horseshoe Pike
Glenmoore, PA 19343
(610) 269-1036
E-mail: harold@smithauctionco.com

Christie's
502 Park Ave.
New York, NY 10022
(212) 546-1000
Web site: www.christies.com

Cincinnati Art Galleries
635 Main St.
Cincinnati, OH 45202
(513) 381-2128
Web site: www.cincinnatiartgalleries.com

Mike Clum, Inc.
7795 Cincinnati Zanesville Road
Rushville, OH 43150
(740) 536-7421
Web site: www.clum.com

Cobb's Doll Auctions
1909 Harrison Road
Johnstown, OH 43031-9539
(740) 964-0444
Web site: www.cobbsdolls.com

Cohasco Inc.
P.O. Drawer 821
Yonkers, NY 10702-0821
(914) 476-8500
Web site: www.cohasodpc.com

**Collection Liquidators
Auction Service**
341 Lafayette St.
New York, NY 10012
(212) 505-2455
Web site: www.rtam.com/coliq/bid.html

Collector's Sales and Service
P.O. Box 6
Pomfret Center, CT 02659
(860) 974-7008
Web site: www.antiquechina.com

Conestoga Auction Co.
768 Graystone Road
P.O. Box 1
Manheim, PA 17545
(717) 898-7284
Web site: www.conestogaauction.com

Coole Park Books and Autographs
P.O. Box 199049
Indianapolis, IN 46219
(317) 351-8495
E-mail: cooleprk@indy.net

Copake Auction
P.O. Box H, 226 Route 7A
Copake, NY 12516
(518) 329-1142
Web site: www.copakeauction.com

Cottone Auctions
15 Genesee St.
Mt. Morris, NY 14510
(716) 583-3119
Web site: www.cottoneauctions.com

C. Wesley Cowan Historic Americana
673 Wilmer Ave.
Cincinnati, OH 45226
(513)-871-1670
Web site: info@HistoricAmericana.com
E-mail: wescowan@fuse.net

Craftsman Auctions
1485 W. Housatoric
Pittsfield MA 01202
(413) 442-7003
Web site: hwww.artsncrafts.com

Decoys Unlimited, Inc.
P.O. Box 206
West Barnstable, MA 02608
(508) 362-2766
Web site: www.decoysunlimited.inc.com

Marlin G. Denlinger
RR3, Box 3775
Morrisville, VT 05661
(802) 888-2775

Dixie Sporting Collectibles
1206 Rama Road
Charlotte, NC 28211
(704) 364-2900
Web site: www.sportauction.com

Dorothy Dous, Inc.
1261 University Drive
Yardley, PA 19067-2857
(888) 548-6635

Dotta Auction Company, Inc.
330 W Moorestown Road
Nazareth, PA 18064
(610) 759-7389
Web site: www.dottaauction.com

William Doyle Galleries, Inc.
175 E. 87th St.
New York, NY 10128
(212) 427-2730
Web site: www.doylegalleries.com

Early Auction Co.
123 Main St.
Milford, OH 45150
(513) 831-4833

Eldred's
P.O. Box 796
East Dennis, MA 02641-0796
(508) 385-3116
Web site: www.eldreds.com

Fain & Co.
P.O. Box 1330
Grants Pass, OR 97526
(888) 324-6726

Ken Farmer Realty & Auction Co.
105 Harrison St.
Radford, VA 24141
(703) 639-0939
Web site: www.kauctions.com

Fine Tool Journal
27 Fickett Road
Pownal, ME 04069
(207) 688-4962
Web site: www.wowpages.com/FTJ/

Steve Finer Rare Books
P.O. Box 758
Greenfield, MA 01302
(413) 773-5811

Fink's Off The Wall Auctions
108 E. 7th St.
Lansdale, PA 19446
(215) 855-9732
Web site: www.finksauctions.com

Flomaton Antique Auction
P.O. Box 1017
320 Palafox St.
Flomaton, AL 36441
(334) 296-3059

Fontaine's Auction Gallery
1485 W. Housatonic St.
Pittsbfield, MA 01201
(413) 488-8922

William A. Fox Auctions Inc.
676 Morris Ave.
Springfield, NJ 07081
(201) 467-2366

Freeman's Auction Gallery
1808 Chestnut St.
Philadelphia, PA 19103
(215) 563-9275
Web site: www.freemansauction.com

Garth's Auction, Inc.
2690 Stratford Road
P.O. Box 369
Delaware, OH 43015
(740) 362-4771
Web site: www.garths.com

Green Valley Auction Inc
2259 Green Valley Lane
Mt. Crawford, VA 22841
(540) 434-4260
Web site: www.greenvalleyauctions.com

Guersney's Auction
108 E. 73rd St.
New York, NY 10021
(212) 794-2280
Web site: www.guersneys.com

Hake's Americana & Collectibles
P.O. Box 1444
York, PA 17405
(717) 848-1333
Web site: www.hakes.com

Gene Harris Antique Auction Center, Inc.
203 South 18th Ave.
P.O. Box 476
Marshalltown, IA 50158
(515) 752-0600
Web site: www.harrisantiqueauction.com

Norman C. Heckler & Company
79 Bradford Corner Road
Woodstock Valley, CT 06282-2002
(860) 974-1634
Web site: www.hecklerauction.com

High Noon
9929 Venice Blvd
Los Angeles CA 90034
(310) 202-9010
Web site: www.High Noon.com

Leslie Hindman, Inc.
122 N Aberdeen St.
Chicago, IL 60607
(312) 280-1212
Web site: www.lesliehindman.com

Historical Collectibles Auctions
24 NW Court Sq. #201
Graham NC 27253
(336) 570-2803
Web site: www.hcaauctions.com

Randy Inman Auctions, Inc.
P.O. Box 726
Waterville, ME 04903
(207) 872-6900
Web site: www.inmanauctions.com

Michael Ivankovich Auction Co.
P.O. Box 2458
Doylestown, PA 18901
(215) 345-6094
Web site: www.nutting.com

Jackson's Auctioneers & Appraisers
2229 Lincoln St.
Cedar Falls, IA 50613
(319) 277-2256
Web site: www.jacksonauction.com

James D. Julia Inc.
Rt. 201 Skowhegan Road
P.O. Box 830
Fairfield, ME 04937
(207) 453-7125
Web site: www.juliaauctions.com

J. W. Auction Co.
54 Rochester Hill Road
Rochester, NH 03867
(603) 332-0192

Gary Kirsner Auctions
P.O. Box 8807
Coral Springs, FL 33075
(954) 344-9856
Web site: www.garykirsnerauctions.com

Lang's Sporting Collectables, Inc.
31 R Turthle Cove
Raymond, ME 04071
(207) 655-4265

Joy Luke Auction Gallery
300 E. Grove St.
Bloomington, IL 61701-5232
(309) 828-5533
Web site: www.joyluke.com

Mapes Auctioneers & Appraisers
1729 Vestal Pkwy
Vestal, NY 13850
(607) 754-9193
Web site: www.maplesauction.com

Maynards Auctioneers
415 West 2nd Ave.
Vancouver, British Columbia, V5Y 1E3
Canada
(604) 876-6787
Web site: www.maynards.com

McMasters Harris Doll Auctions
P.O. Box 1755
Cambridge, OH 43725-1755
(740) 432-7400
Web site: www.mcmastersharris.com

William Frost Mobley
P.O. Box 10
Schoharie, NY 12157
(518) 295-7978

William Morford
RD #2
Cazenovia, NY 13035
(315) 662-7625

Neal Auction Company
4038 Magazine St.
New Orleans, LA 7015
(504) 899-5329
Web site: www.nealauction.com

New England Auction Gallery
P.O. Box 764
Middleton, MA 01949
(978) 304-3140
Web site: www.old-toys.com

New Orleans Auction Galleries, Inc.
801 Magazine St.
New Orleans, LA 70130
(504) 566-1849
Web site: www.neworleansauction.com

New Hampshire Book Auctions
P.O. Box 460
92 Woodbury Road
Weare, NH 03281
(603) 529-7432

Norton Auctioneers of Michigan Inc.
50 West Pearl at Monroe
Coldwater, MI 49036
(517) 279-9063

Nostalgia Publications, Inc.
21 S. Lake Dr.
Hackensack, NJ 07601
(201) 488-4536
Web site: www.nostalgiapubls.com

Old Barn Auction
10040 St. Rt. 224 West
Findlay, OH 45840
(419) 422-8531
Web site: www.oldbarn.com

Richard Opfer Auctioneering Inc.
1919 Greenspring Dr.
Timonium, MD 21093-4113
(410) 252-5035
Web site: www.opferauction.com

Pacific Book Auction Galleries
133 Kerney St., 4th Floor
San Francisco, CA 94108
(415) 989-2665
Web site: www.nbn.com/~pba/

Past Tyme Pleasures
PMB #204, 2401 San Ramon Valley
Blvd, #1
San Ramon, CA 94583
(925) 484-6442
Fax: (925) 484-2551
Web site: www.pasttyme.com

Pook and Pook, Inc.
463 East Lancaster Ave., P.O. Box 268
Downington, PA 19335
(610) 269-4040
Web site: www.pookandpookinc.com

Poster Auctions International
601 W. 26th St.
New York, NY 10001
(212) 787-4000
Web site: www.posterauction.com

Profitt Auction Company
684 Middlebrook Road
Staunton VA 24401
(540) 885-7369

Provenance
P.O. Box 3487
Wallington, NJ 07057
(201) 779-8725

David Rago Auctions, Inc.
333 S. Main St.
Lambertville, NJ 08530
(609) 397-9374
Web site: www.ragoarts.com

Lloyd Ralston Toy Auction
350 Long Beach Blvd
Stratford, CT 06615
(203) 375-9399
Web site: www.lloydralstontoys.com

James J. Reeves
P.O. Box 219
Huntingdon, PA 16652-0219
(814) 643-5497
Web site: www.JamesJReeves.com

Mickey Reichel Auctioneer
1440 Ashley Road
Boonville, MO 65233
(816) 882-5292

Remmen Auction & Appraisals
P.O. Box 301398
Portland, OR 97294
(503) 256-1226
Web site: www.remmenauction.com

Roan Inc. Auction Gallery
RR 3, Box 118
Cogan Station, PA 17728
(570) 494-0170
Web site: www.roaninc.com/roan

Sandy Rosnick Auctions
15 Front St.
Salem, MA 01970
(508) 741-1130

Thomas Schmidt
7099 McKean Road
Ypsilanti, MI 48197
(313) 485-8606

Seeck Auctions
P.O. Box 377
Mason City, IA 50402
(515) 424-1116
Web site: www.willowtree.com/~seeck-auctions

L. H. Selman Ltd
761 Chestnut St.
Santa Cruz, CA 95060
(408) 427-1177
Web site: www.selman.com

Skinner, Inc.
The Heritage on the Garden
63 Park Plaza
Boston, MA 02116
(617) 350-5400
Web site: www.skinnerinc.com

Sky Hawk Auctions
P.O. Box 55
Sellersville, PA 18960
(215) 257-6986
Web site: www.skyhawkauctions.com

Sloans & Kenyon
4605 Bradley Blvd
Bethseda, MD 20815
(301) 634-2330
Web site: www.sloansandkenyon.com

Joseph P. Smalley Jr. Auctions
2400 Old Bethlehem Pike
Quakertown, PA 18951
(215) 529-9834

Smith & Jones, Inc., Auctions
12 Clark Lane
Sudbury MA 01776
(508) 443-5517

R. M. Smythe & Co.
26 Broadway
New York, NY 10004-1710
(212) 943-1880
Web site: www.rm-smythe.com

Sotheby's
1334 York Ave.
New York, NY 10021
(212) 606-7000
Web site: www.sothebys.com

Southern Folk Pottery Collectors Society
220 Washington St.
Bennett, NC 27208
(336) 581-4246

Stanton's Auctioneers
P.O. Box 146
144 South Main St.
Vermontville, MI 49096
(517) 726-0181

Stout Auctions
11 W. Third St.
Williamsport, IN 47993-1119
(765) 764-6901

Michael Strawser
200 N. Main St., P.O. Box 332
Wolcottville, IN 46795-0332
(219) 854-2859
Web site: www.strawserauctions.com

Swann Galleries Inc.
104 E. 25th St.
New York, NY 10010
(212) 254-4710
Web site: www.swanngalleries.com

Swartz Auction Services
2404 N. Mattis Ave.
Champaign, IL 61826-7166
(217) 357-0197
Web site: www.SwartzAuction.com

The House In The Woods
S91 W37851 Antique Lane
Eagle, WI 53119
(414) 594-2334

Theriault's
P.O. Box 151
Annapolis, MD 21401
(301) 224-3655
Web site: www.theriaults.com

Toy Scouts
137 Casterton Ave.
Akron, OH 44303
(216) 836-0668

Tradewind Antiques & Auctions
P.O. Box 249
Manchester-by-the-Sea, MA 01944-0249
(987) 526-4085
Web site: www.tradewindsantiques.com

Treadway Gallery, Inc.
2029 Madison Road
Cincinnati, OH 45208
(513) 321-6742
Web site: www.a3c2net.com/treadway gallery

Unique Antiques & Auction Gallery
449 Highway 72 West
Collierville, TN 38017
(901) 854-1141

Venable Estate Auction
423 West Fayette St.
Pittsfield, IL 62363
(217) 285-2560

Victorian Images
P.O. Box 284
Marlton, NJ 08053
(609) 985-7711
Web site: www.tradecards.com/vi

Victorian Lady
P.O. Box 424
Waxhaw, NC 28173
(704) 843-4467

Vintage Cover Story
P.O. Box 975
Burlington, NC 27215
(919) 584-6900

Bruce and Vicki Waasdorp
P.O. Box 434
10931 Main St.
Clarence, NY 14031
(716) 759-2361
Web site: www.antiques-stoneware.com

Waddington's
111 Bathurst St.
Toronto, Ontario M5V 2R1 Canada
(416) 504-9100
Web site: www.waddingtonsauctions.com

Wiederseim Associates, Inc.
P.O. Box 470
Chester Springs, PA 19425
(610) 827-1910
Web site: www.wiederseim.com

Winter Associates, Inc. Auctioneers & Appraisers
21 Cooke St.
P.O. Box 823
Plainville, CT 06062
(860)-793-0288
Web site: www.winterassociatesinc.com

Woody Auction
P.O. Box 618
317 S Forrest St.
Douglass, KS 67039-9800
(316) 746-2694
Web site: www.woodyauction.com

Jim Wroda Auction Co.
5239 St. Rt 49 South
Greenville, OH 45331
(937) 548-2640
Web site: www.jimwrodaauction.com

York Town Auction, Inc.
1625 Haviland Road
York, PA 17404
(717) 751-0211
Web site: www.yorkauction.com

Abbreviations

The following are standard abbreviations used throughout this edition of *Warman's*.

3D = three dimensional
ADS = Autograph Document Signed
adv = advertising
ALS = Autograph Letter Signed
approx = approximately
AQS = Autograph Quotation Signed
bw = black and white
C = century
c = circa
cov = cover
CS = Card Signed
d = diameter or depth
dec = decorated
dj = dust jacket
DS = Document Signed
ed = edition, editor
emb = embossed
ext. = exterior
ftd = footed
gal = gallon
ground = background
h = height
horiz = horizontal
hp = hand painted
illus = illustrated, illustration, illustrator
imp = impressed
int. = interior
irid = iridescent
j = jewels
K = karat
l = length
lb = pound
litho = lithograph
LS = Letter Signed
MBP = mint in bubble pack
mfg = manufactured

MIB = mint in box
MIP = mint in package
MISB = mint in sealed box
mkd = marked
MOC = mint on card
MOP = mother of pearl
n.d. = no date
No. = number
NOB = no original box
NRFB = never removed from box
NRFP = never removed from package
OB = orig box
opal = opalescent
orig = original
oz = ounce
pat = patent
pc = piece
pcs = pieces
pg = page
pgs = pages
pr = pair
PS = Photograph Signed
pt = pint
qt = quart
rect = rectangular
Soc = Society
sgd = signed
SP = silver plated
SS = sterling silver
sq = square
TLS = Typed Letter Signed
vol = volume
w = width
yg = yellow gold
# = numbered

Grading Condition

The following numbers represent the standard grading system used by dealers, collectors, and auctioneers:

C.10 = Mint
C.9 = Near Mint
C.8.5 = Outstanding
C.8 = Excllent
C.7.5 = Fine+
C.7 = Fine
C. 6.5 = Fine – (good)
C.6 = Poor

A

Abingdon Pottery

History: The Abingdon Sanitary Manufacturing Company, Abingdon, Illinois, was founded in 1908 for the purpose of manufacturing plumbing fixtures. Sometime between 1933 and 1934, Abingdon introduced a line of art pottery. In 1945, the company changed its name to Abingdon Potteries, Inc. Production of the art pottery line continued until 1950 when fire destroyed the art pottery kiln.

After the fire, the company once again placed its emphasis on plumbing fixtures. Eventually, Abingdon Potteries became Briggs Manufacturing Company, a firm noted for its sanitary fixtures.

Collecting Hints: Like wares from many contemporary potteries, Abingdon Pottery pieces are readily available in the market. The company produced more than 1,000 shapes and used more than 150 colors to decorate its wares. Because of this tremendous variety, it is advisable to collect Abingdon Pottery with particular forms and/or colors in mind.

Abingdon art pottery, with its vitreous body and semi-gloss and high-gloss glazes, is found at all levels of the market, from garage sales to antiques shows. For this reason, price fluctuations for identical pieces are quite common. Black (gunmetal), a semi-gloss dark blue, a metallic copper brown, and several shades of red are the favored colors. Decorated pieces command a premium of 15 to 20 percent.

Ashtray, #456.. **35.00**
Bookends, pr, horse head, black, 6-1/2" h
.... **65.00**
Bowl, 14" d, blue, molded as aster flower, detailed petals and leaves, blue ink stamp mark...................................... **70.00**
Candleholders, pr, 3-1/2" w, 4" h, #505, Shell, slightly opened shells with places for two candles in each, pink, stamped #505, Abingdon, USA **20.00**

Centerpiece bowl
11-1/4" l, 8" w, #533, Shell, sea-green, interior with emb shell-like veins, marked "Abingdon U.S.A." **35.00**

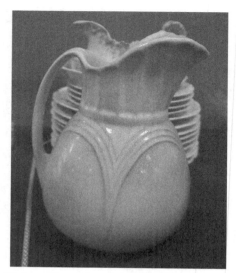

Pitcher, white, slight crazing, $35.

13-1/2" l, 5-1/2" w, 3-1/2" h, pink, semi-gloss, raised acanthus leaf handles, box mark **35.00**
14-1/2" l, 3-3/4" h, #532, blue, Scroll, marked "Scroll/MD/14.5SL/1941," c1941-50.. **25.00**
14-1/2" l, 4" h, #5-11, semi-gloss white, blue oval ink stamp, incised 5-11 .. **48.00**
Compote, 5-1/2" d, 4" h, tan, rect stamp mark **27.50**

Cookie jar
Cookie Time, #653, 9" h, 7" w....... **185.00**
Cooky Little Girl, 9-1/2" h, 7-1/4" w
.... **150.00**
Little Bo Peep, 12" h, 8" w............ **330.00**
Little Miss Muffet, #662, 11" h, hand painted, blond hair, blue eyes, blue bow, red, blue, and green flowers, blue diagonal stripes, black spider, flake on interior rim **135.00**
Pineapple, 10-1/2" h, naturalistic coloring, marked, chip on top of leaf **90.00**
Train engine **95.00**
Figure, #416, peacock, 6-1/8" l, 7" h, blue, marked "Abingdon USA" in box, diamond mark with "A #416" **85.00**

Planter
6-1/2" l, 3" w, #484, fan-shape, bow trim, ivory.. **20.00**
7-1/2" h, 2-3/4" w, star-shape, blue, emb clouds and stars, rect stamp mark .. **20.00**
7-1/2" l, 3" w, 4-1/4" h, #462, bow-shape, pink.. **20.00**
Tile, 5" sq, titled "Coolie," molded relief of Asian man sitting among bamboo, yellow majolica glaze, c1937 .... **185.00**

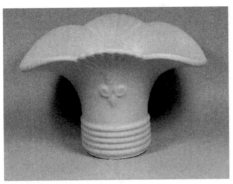

Vase, #491, flared, pink matte, fan and molded ring trim, flower frog type opening, blue ink stamp mark, embossed #491, 7-1/2" d, 5" h, $65.

Vase

5" h, 10-3/4" w, double, ivory matte glaze, blue rect stamp mark **25.00**
6-1/4" h, 6-1/4" d, #560, Special B, cameo, pink and white star flower, dated 4-16-42, rect stamp mark **125.00**
7" h, #515, white, handles, blue ink stamp mark, incised #515 .... **30.00**
8-1/2" h, 5-7/8" d, #156, rect stamp mark **27.50**
8-3/4" h, 5" d, #538, pink, imp number, blue ink stamp mark........................ **20.00**
9" h, Boyne pattern, pale peach, rect stamp mark...................................... **40.00**
9-1/2" h, #101, delphite blue, handles, orig paper label............................... **45.00**
9-5/8" h, 6-3/8" d, #114, white, rect stamp mark.. **55.00**
9-3/4" h, #117, dusty blue, handles. **45.00**
10" h, 6" d, #103, soft Chinese red, molded relief Shou pattern, buttressed handles, high gloss glaze, ink stamp mark, incised #103, 1930s **150.00**
10-1/4" h, two small beaded handles, dec with yellow and pink flowers and pair of blue parakeets, gold rim and accents **30.00**
11" l, #482, double cornucopia, white, c1939-50 .... **35.00**

Wall Pocket

#601, butterfly **70.00**
#377, flower, gray sticker, imp "377" **40.00**
Window box, 10" l, 3-3/4" w, 3" h, #437, matte aqua, blue ink stamp mark, incised #437, c1934-50 .... **35.00**

Action Figures

History: An action figure is a die-cast metal or plastic posable model with flexible joints that portrays a real or fictional character. In addition to the figures themselves, clothing, personal equipment, vehicles, and other types of accessories are also collectible.

Collectors need to be aware of the following attempts to manipulate the market: 1) limited production—a deliberate act on the part of manufacturers to hold back on production of one or more figures in a series; 2) variations—minor changes in figures made by manufacturers to increase sales (previously believed to be mistakes, but now viewed as a deliberate sales gimmicks), and 3) prototypes—artists' models used during the planning process. Any prototype should be investigated thoroughly—there are many fakes.

The earliest action figures were the hard-plastic Hartland figures of popular television Western heroes of the 1950s. Louis Marx also included action figures in a number of playsets during the late 1950s. Although Barbie, who made her appearance in 1959, is posable, she is not considered an action figure by collectors.

G.I. Joe, introduced by Hassenfield Bros. in 1964, triggered the modern action figure craze. In 1965, Gilbert introduced action figures for James Bond 007, The Man from U.N.C.L.E., and Honey West. Bonanza figures arrived in 1966 along with Ideal Toy Corporation's Captain Action. Ideal altered the figures by simply changing heads and costumes. Captain Action and his accessories were the hot collectible of the late 1980s.

In 1972, Mego introduced the first six super heroes in what would become a series of 34 different characters. Mego also established the link between action figures and the movies when the company issued series for Planet of the Apes and Star Trek: The Motion Picture. Mego's television series figures included CHiPs, Dukes of Hazzard, and Star Trek. When Mego filed for bankruptcy protection in 1982, the days of eight- and twelve-inch fabric-clothed action figures ended.

The introduction of Kenner's Star Wars figure set in 1977 opened a floodgate. Action figures enjoyed enormous popularity, and manufacturers rushed into the market, with Mattel quickly following on Kenner's heels. Before long, the market was flooded, not only with a large selection but also with production runs in the hundreds of thousands.

Not all series were successful; just ask companies such as Colorform, Matchbox, and TYCO. Some sets were not further produced when initial sales did not justify the costs of manufacture. These sets have limited collector value. Scarcity does not necessarily equate with high value in the action figure market.

Collecting Hints: This is one of the hot, trendy collecting categories. While there is no question that action figure material is selling—and selling well—much of the pricing is highly speculative. Trends change from month to month as one figure or group of figures becomes hot and another cools off.

The safest approach is to buy only objects in fine or better condition and, if possible, with or in their original packaging. Any figure that has been played with to any extent will never have long-term value. This is a category with off-the-rack expectations.

Be extremely cautious about paying premium prices for figures less than 10 years old. During the past decade, dealers have made a regular practice of buying newly released action figures in quantity, warehousing them, and releasing their stash slowly into the market once production ceases.

Also examine packaging very closely. A premium is placed on a figure in its original packaging, i.e., the packaging used when the figure was introduced into the market. Later packaging means a lower price.

Additional Listings: G.I. Joe Collectibles, Super Heroes, Star Wars, Star Trek.

Addams Family, Playmates Toys, 1992, NRFP
Lurch	25.00
Pugsley	25.00
Uncle Fester	30.00

Alien
Arachnid	20.00
Bull	20.00
Gorilla	20.00
Night Cougar	12.00
Panther	12.00

Cu –Angela, Todd McFarlane's Spawn, Deluxe Edition, Ultra-Action Figure, NRFP, $8.

Scorpion	20.00
Snake	15.00
Wild Boar	12.00

A-Team, Galoob, 6" h
Amy Allen, MOC	30.00
Hannibal, MOC	20.00
Mr. T, © 1983, MIB	38.00
Murdock, MOC	25.00
Templeton Peck, MOC	20.00
Villians, four-pack	45.00

Baseball, Starting Lineup
Belle, Albert, 1997, MBP	10.00
Caminiti, Ken, 1996, MBP	5.00
Gordero, Will, 1996, MBP	5.00
Guillen, Ozzie, 1996, MBP	7.50
McGriff, Fred, 1996, MBP	5.00
O'Neill, Paul, 1996, MBP	5.00
Piazza, Mike, 1996, Phillies All Star Game, Veterans Stadium, MBP	40.00
Ripkin, Cal, 1992, loose, fair	20.00
Sosa, Sammy, 1996, MBP	7.50
Thomas, Frank, 1996, MBP	5.00
Williams, Matt, 1996, MBP	5.00

Basketball, Starting Lineup
Dumars, Joe, and Grant Hill, Classics Doubles, 1997, MBP	25.00
Duncan, 1997, MBP	50.00
Ewing, Patrick, 1998, NRFP, package plastic damaged	10.00
Hill, Grant, Kings Detroit Pistons, 1997, MBP	25.00

Battlestar Galactica
Baltar, loose	35.00
Laserscope Fighter, Italy, loose	195.00

Beetlejuice, Showtime Beetlejuice with Rotten Rattler, 1989, wear to 3" x 5" box
	32.00

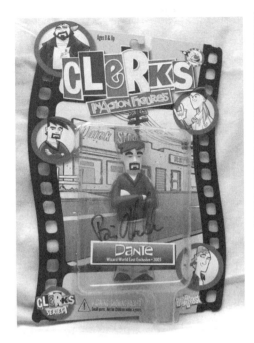

Clerks, Series 1: Dante, Wizard World East Exclusive 2003, autographed by Brian O'Halloran, who played Dante in the movie "Clerks," **$45**.

Star Trek, Capt. James T. Kirk, space suit, 1994, Playmates, MOC, **$20**.

Buck Rogers in the 25th Century,
12-1/2" h, Mego, ©1979, MIB **45.00**
Charlie's Angels, Jill, Farah Fawcett, MIB
.... **75.00**
Clash of the Titans, Mattel, 1980, Charo,
3-3/4" h, MOC **35.00**

Comic Book
Joker, Legends of Batman **15.00**
Mercy, Hobby Exclusive, gold edition,
7" h **17.50**
Pandora, Bolt, MOC **15.00**

DC Direct
Supergirl, animated, Kenner exclusive,
5" h **12.00**
Superman, animated, Kenner exclusive,
12" h **25.00**
Usage Yojimbo, Antartic Press, 5" h **12.00**
Xena, 6-1/2" h, Series II, Harem **9.00**
Defenders of the Earth, Galoob, 1985
Flash Gordon, MOC **35.00**
Garax, MOC.................................... **35.00**
Garax Swordship, MIB **45.00**
Lothar, MOC................................... **35.00**
Ming the Merciless, MOC.............. **35.00**
Phantom, MOC............................... **35.00**
Fantastic Four, Invisible Woman, Invisible
Force Shield, 1995, MOC.............. **18.00**
Football, Starting Line Up
Bledsoe, Drew, 1995, NRFP.......... **25.00**
Marino, Dan, 1988, number coming off
jersey, fair **20.00**
Walker, Herschel, 1988, jersey
discolored, fair **20.00**

Happy Days, Mego
Fonzie, loose.................................. **35.00**
Potsie, MOC................................... **65.00**
Ralph, MOC **65.00**
Ritchie, MOC.................................. **65.00**
MAD Magazine, 6" h
Alfred E. Neuman **12.00**
Spy vs Spy, white or black, each ... **12.00**
Masters of the Universe, Mattel, loose
Clawful, 1981 .... **5.00**
Mekanek, 1983 .... **5.00**
Motu Battle Armor Skeletor, 1983 .... **5.00**
Monster, Universal, 8" h, Mego
Frankenstein **90.00**
Mummy **90.00**
Wolfman **90.00**
Planet of the Apes, Kenner
Cornelius.. **30.00**
Dr. Zauis **25.00**
General Ursus................................. **25.00**
Raiders of the Lost Ark, Kenner
German Mechanic, MOC.............. **60.00**
Streets of Cairo Adventure set, Monkey
Man, Monkey, Marion Ravenwood, MIB
.... **75.00**
Star Com, 2" h, Coleco, 1986, MOC
Col John Griffin **17.50**
General Vondar............................... **20.00**
Pfc John Jefferson **15.00**

Sgt Hector Morales **17.50**
Sgt Red Baker **15.00**
Star Trek, see Space Adventurers and Exploration Category
Star Wars, see Star Wars Category
Super Powers, Kenner, Canada, 1985
Batman, MOC................................. **65.00**
Cyclotron, MOC.............................. **75.00**
Darkside Destroyer, MIB................. **45.00**
Delta Probe One, MIB..................... **30.00**
Golden Pharoh, MOC **125.00**
Penguin, mint in orig bag............... **65.00**
Superman, MOC **45.00**
Windsock, mail-in premium, MIP.... **25.00**
S.W.A.T., Hondo, LIN Toys, © 1975, MOC
.... **35.00**
Visionaires, Hasbro, 1987
Arzon, MOC.................................... **35.00**
Cryotec, MOC **35.00**
Darkstorm, MOC **35.00**
Lexor, MOC **40.00**
Witterquick, MOC............................ **35.00**
X-Men, Toy Biz, Apocalypse, 2nd edition, 1993, MOC **10.00**

Advertising

History: The earliest advertising in America is found in colonial newspapers and printed broadsides. By the mid-19th century, manufacturers began to examine how a product was packaged. The box could convey a message and help identify and sell more of the product. The advent of the high-speed, lithograph printing press led to regional and national magazines, resulting in new advertising markets. The lithograph press also introduced vivid colors into advertising.

Simultaneously, the general store branched out into specialized departments or individual specialty shops. By 1880, advertising premiums such as mirrors, paperweights, and trade cards, arrived on the scene. Through the early 1960s, premiums remained popular, especially with children.

The advertising character developed in the early 1900s. By the 1950s, endorsements by the popular stars of the day became a firmly established advertising method. Advertising became a lucrative business as firms, many headquartered in New York City, developed specialties to meet manufacturers' needs. Advertising continues to respond to changing opportunities and times.

Collecting Hints: Many factors affect the price of an advertising collectible—the product and its manufacturer, the objects or people used in the advertisement, the period and aesthetics of design, the designer and illustrator of the piece, and the form the advertisement takes. In addition, advertising material was frequently used to decorate bars, restaurants, and other public places. Interior decorators do not purchase objects at the same price level as collectors.

In truth, almost every advertising item is sought by a specialized collector in one or more collectible areas. The result is diverse pricing, with the price quoted to an advertising collector usually lower than that quoted to a specialized collector.

Most collectors seem to concentrate on the period prior to 1940, with special emphasis on the decades from 1880 to 1910. New collectors should examine the advertising material from the post-1940 period. Much of this material is still very inexpensive and likely to rise in value as the decorator trends associated with the 1950s through the 1970s gain importance.

Reproduction Alert.

Grading Condition. The following numbers represent the standard grading system used by dealers, collectors, and auctioneers.

C10	=	Mint
C9	=	Near Mint
C8.5	=	Outstanding
C8	=	Excellent
C7.5	=	Fine +
C7	=	Fine
C6.5	=	Fine – (good)
C6	=	Poor

Ashtray

Blue Diamond Coal Co., metal, 6" d
.... **20.00**
Evinrude, brass, circular, 1950s..... **65.00**
Firestone Tires, copper **20.00**
Modern Radio & Television, 114 N 8th St., Reading, PA, glass **4.50**
Parkside Café George St., York, PA, glass
.... **3.00**

Bank, Boscul Coffee, W.S. Scull Co., 2-1/2" d, 2-1/4", **$17.50**.

Bag, cloth, Arbuckle's Cane Sugar, 18" x 33", blue text, NRA logo with eagle and slogan, image of Brooklyn Bridge .. **20.00**

Bank, Campell Soup, Dinosaur Vegetable Soup, plastic lid, C-8 .... **5.00**

Blotter
Eagle White Lead, York Hardware, 3" x 6" **7.50**
Lancaster Iron Works, Proclamation of Emancipation painting, list of services, ruler at top, 8-1/2" x 3-1/2" **10.00**
Levi's, full-color art, black and white imprint of local dealer store, unused, 1960s, 2-3/4" x 6-1/4" **20.00**
Morton's Salt, 3-1/2" x 6-1/8" **7.50**
The Soap Suds Blues, dog being bathed in tub, Harry N. Johnson, Real Estate & Insurance, Highlands, NJ **12.00**

Box
Argo Starch, unopened, 1930s **12.00**
King Brand Rolled Oats, unopened **45.00**
Kirkman, 4-3/4" h, red, white, dark blue, and light blue, paper label over cardboard, metal top and bottom, label with three ladies and three gentlemen dressed in Swiss Alps attire, mountains in background, unused **12.00**
Regal Underwear, cardboard **20.00**
Rama Hindu Incense 22 Cones 15¢ Wisteria, 2" x 3-1/2", cardboard, blue, black, white, red, and yellow, slides open, back panel with text for use, copyright 1934, back reads "Made Expressly For S. S. Kresge Co." **10.00**
Vantine's Temple Incense Sandalwood And Patchouli A Fragrant Oriental Burning Powder For Use Indoors and Outdoors, 2-3/4" w, 4" h, turtle with text "A. A. Vantine & Co., New York," top lithographed with Vantine logo, 1930s **12.00**

Box, Fairy Soap, Gold Dust Corp., 2-3/8" x 3-7/8", **$24**.

Box, Armour's Cloverbloom, White American Process Cheese, wooden, red and blue lettering, worn, **$10**.

Cake pan, Swans Down Cake Flour Makes Better Cakes, metal tube pan, text in raised letters on bottom, side panels "Swans Down Cake Pan Pat Dec18-23 E Katzinger Co. Chicago Licensed Mfgrs" **10.00**

Charm, Pet Evaporated Milk, 11/16" h, figural can, red, white, and white label wrapped around celluloid, small loop on top, c1940 .... **12.00**

Clip
Frank Fehr Cold Storage Co., Louisville, 1-3/4" d white on dark green celluloid button on 2-1/4" w metal spring clip **35.00**
Golden Blend Coffee, black, white, and red waiter bringing coffee cup, "Here You are Sir!" **48.00**
Thomas A. Edison Cement Co., Edison Portland Cement Co., New Village, N.J., 1-3/4" d black on bright yellow celluloid button on 2-1/4" w metal spring clip, C-7.5... **40.00**

Coffee tin, 1 lb, orig lid
Comrade, 3-1/2" h, 5" d, J. A. Folger & Co., keywind **170.00**
Eight O'Clock Coffee, 6" sq, 7" h, red, white, black, and gold **40.00**

Eureka Blend Coffee, 4-1/4" x 6-3/4",
green, gold, and black, Ross W. Weir &
Co., NY, wooden knob on lid, c1920
.... **35.00**
Folger's Coffee, 5" x 6", keywind,
copyright 1950 .... **35.00**
Gold Metal Coffee, 4-1/4" x 6" h, blue,
white, gold, and red, "Roasted and
Packed For Consumers, Sanitary Coffee
& Butter Stores, Chicago, Ill," 1930s
.... **45.00**
Hatchet Brand Coffee, 4" d, 6" h, red,
blue, white, and gold, "Roasted and
Packed By The Twitchell-Champlin Co.,
Portland, Me & Boston, Mass"........ **40.00**
Hills Bros Vacuum Packed Coffee, 3-3/4"
x 5", black, white, red, gold, and yellow,
orig silver lid marked "Steel Cut," 1930s
.... **45.00**
Hostess Brand Coffee, 4" d, 6" h, orange,
black, white, and blue, "In A Class By
Itself, McInnes Bros Inc, Milwaukee, Wis,"
c1930... **40.00**
Latouraine Coffee, 4-1/4" x 6", paper label
on tin, copyright 1938 .... **35.00**
Zat Zit Brand Steel Cut Coffee Sells Like
Lightning, 3-1/2" x 5-1/4", black, yellow,
blue, and white, packed by Biston
Coffees, Teas, and Spices, St. Louis, MO,
1920s **35.00**

Counter jar, electric, Heinz Oven Baked Beans
57, brown glazed ceramic base, aluminum lid,
toggle switch at top, **$125**.

Display

Boston Garter, diecut tin, five orig boxes
of garters, man examining garter on his
left as he reads from back of box, 9" h,
4" w, C-9... **425.00**
Diamond Dye, wood cabinet, emb tin
front showing children playing with
Maypole, rusting and staining to fair
condition tin panel, 30" h, 22-3/4" w,
10-1/4" d, C-6 .... **550.00**
Door push, Nelson's Ice cream, 3-1/2" x
9-1/2", enameled metal, red and black on
white, red text "Ask For, Richer-Tastier,"
1940s **45.00**

Diecut, stiff paper, multicolored scene of little
girl holding teddy bear, puppy and kitten,
marked "Compliments of C.A. Steely, Fancy
Groceries, Etc.," 20" h, **$85**.

Counter display sign, "Look Better In A
Mademoiselle Fifth Ave Sweater," cardboard, self
frame, pretty blond wearing black and white
tweed jacket, deep pink sweater, black and
white plaid skirt, **$40**.

Display stand, Take Home Green Spot Orange Drink, tin litho top, white, green, orange, and black, steel rack, **$45**.

Miller Lock, diecut cardboard, shows ship going through Panama Canal, actual examples of Gatun Locks, easel back, patent 1905 Breüker & Kessler Co. litho, 16" h, 13" w **50.00**

Egg, Fleischmann's Egg Beaters, wood, red, wear to paint **10.00**

Flipper pin, diecut thin celluloid. 1-3/4" h

Fansteel Electric Iron, gold pocket watch image on one side, inscribed "See The Woman In The Case," reverse black and white illus of woman using iron **20.00**

Golden Orangeade, orange fruit, red and black inscription, slogan on back "Everybody Likes It-What?" **30.00**

Schaeffer Pianos, full-color image of upright piano, inscribed "Schaeffer, Best in the West," black and white logo on reverse, ad text, 1905 patent date .. **30.00**

Sunset Coffee, canister shape, sponsored by International Coffee Co. **12.00**

Ward's Bread, turkey shape, slogan on back "Serve Ward's Bread With Your Thanksgiving Dinner" **18.00**

Key fob

Bell Atlantic, Your Equipment Connection, combination key ring and bottle opener **7.50**

Lion Milk, celluloid disk, metal ring, product illus on one side, other with holly sprig and "Compliments of Lion Brand Condensed Milk" **25.00**

New York Edison Co., silvered metal circular clip, black, white, red, and gold celluloid disk on both sides............ **20.00**

Ozonite, For Pure Sweet Clean Linen, 1-3/4" l, celluloid, product barrel on left end, maker's name "Wm Waltke, St. Louis," reverse with company and product name in blue and red, cream ground, c1915 .... **24.00**

Spradling's, St. Louis, MO, 2-1/4" l, celluloid, ivory, one side printed with black doorway, young child, one boot on, one boot in hand, pale blue shirt, flexible silver link chain, 1930s **20.00**

Lapel stud

Ceresota Flour, 7/8" d, orange and cream, black text "The Northwestern Consolidated Milling Co.," c1898 .. **15.00**

Garland Stoves and Ranges, 7/8" d, white text on blue center, color border with ribbon "The World's Best," c1896 .. **15.00**

Remington UMC, 1/2" d, white on red, metal back, c1904.......................... **60.00**

Letter opener, Uneeda Biscuit, 8-1/4" l, flat diecut metal, silver luster blade below diecut handle, young man wearing yellow rain hat and slicker, product in one arm, black boots, wear, 1920s, C-6 .... **28.00**

Lunch box, tin litho

Fashion Cut Plug Tobacco, 7-3/4" l, 5-1/4" w, 4" d, image of couple **95.00**

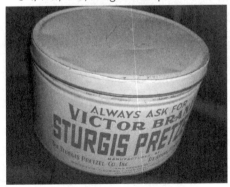

Tin, Always Ask For Victor Brand, Sturgis Pretzels, tan, red lettering, The Sturgis Co., Reading, PA, **$10**.

Hand Bag Tobacco, figural **75.00**

Round Trip Tobacco, 6-1/2" h, 5" l, 3-1/2" d **100.00**

Memo booklet

Libby's Food Products, Libby, McNeill & Libby, celluloid cover, full-color view of Chicago factory, six examples of packaged products, 14 pages, printed by Whitehead & Hoag Co., 2-1/2" x 4-1/2" **55.00**

Sunbeam, celluloid cover with young lady, swirling hair, sheer fabric, pale yellow sun rays, published by Bastian Bros. Co., 2-1/2" x 4-3/4" **40.00**

Mirror, pocket

Alcazar Ranges and Heaters, 2-1/4" d, gold lettering on blue panel surrounded by red background, gold wreath, blue ribbon, gold text "The Housekeeper's Delight," outer edge with blue text on white adv Milwaukee dealer **40.00**

A Picture of Health After Treatment At The Ladies' St. Botolph St. Turkish Bath, Swimming Pool And Gymnasium, Boston, c1910, black text, black and white photo on cream ground........................... **40.00**

Auditorium Cream, 2-3/4" h, Art Nouveau styling, cream text on light green ground, text for benefits of product............. **45.00**

Berry Brothers, Luxeberry White Enamel Paint, 2" d, red, white, and blue...... **30.00**

Carmen Adjustable Bracelet, sepia photo of young woman against shaded brown ground, holding bracelet in hands, early 1900s **50.00**

Columbia Tool Steel Co., 2" d, red, white, and blue shield with gold stars and outlining on white, red text above, company name below in blue **40.00**

Compliments of Golden Pheasant Inn, 2-3/4" h oval, gold and red pheasant on white, light blue text, Chicago address **55.00**

Sign, litho tin, "Now Cascade Club Coffee at Your Grocers," white lettering with blue accents on bright red, **$95**.

Compliments of McArthur Piano Co., 2-3/4" h, shaded black and white image of young girl next to woman seated at piano, text has three locations in S. Dakota, bottom reads "High Grade Pianos Easy Terms Write Us".......... **45.00**

Crème Oil The Cream Of Olive Oil Soaps, 1-3/4" d, blue package, white text, white ground, brown text "Peet Bros Mfg Co. Kansas City, San Francisco"........... **40.00**

Daily Mirror, 2" d, tin frame, red on off-white paper label, extensive center text with newspaper name describes contest, hold to light to find questions, Sept. 11, 1933... **40.00**

Harry Mitchell Fine Tailoring, Minneapolis, 2-3/8" d, sepia real photo **40.00**

Kleinert's Dress Shield Guimpe, 2" d, black and white, illus of product, text "A Garment With Shields Always In Place" **45.00**

Lucky Tiger Dandruff Cure, 2" d, black and white on bright red, white text, pretty girl with flowing hair next to large tiger, c1930 .... **95.00**

M. J. Carr, St. Paul, Minn, 2" d, black and white, center edge designed as if business owner is looking through a burst, bottom slogan "When You Get It At Carr's It's Right".............................. **40.00**

Navarre Indestructable Pearls, 2-1/4" d, logo in purple, gold, and white on white ground, outer rim designed as white pearls accented in purple, text "Whaler's, The Oldest Jewelry Store in Miami" **40.00**

Newbro's Herpicide Mirror, 2-3/4" h oval, printed in red and black on cream, cartoon illus of man with hair on both head and comb, second cartoon with less hair on head, more on comb, third with no hair on either head or comb **60.00**

Pacific Shoe, Friedman Shelby, 2-1/2" d, product name in red lettering outlined in black, black and white photo of woman's high top shoe, lower half with company logo in two shades of blue outlined in gold **65.00**

Peifer's Restaurant, Reading, PA, 2-3/4" h, black on cream, proprietor with caption "I Aim To Please" **40.00**

Pioneer For Your Money's Worth, 2-1/8" d, dark blue and cream, bold text for Cincinnati business **45.00**

Queen's Quality Shoes, Howland's 2-3/4" h, shaded black and white queen posed on flight of steps................. **50.00**

Rattan Trunkdom Trunk Co., Lightest and Strongest Made, 2-3/4" h, gold text, image of scale holding suspended trunk in air, Los Angeles address, early 1900s **50.00**

Shaw's Giant Cement-Mends Everything And Liquid Lightning Cleans Everything, Agents Wanted, H. B. Shaw Alfred Me, emb lettering on brass cover, c1880 .... **45.00**

The Ideal Means Perfection In Loose Leaf Albums, 2-1/2" d, whit text on fabric like black textured covering with albums titled "Our Baby, Automobile Trips, My Vacation Days, My Memory Book, Photographs," c1920 .... **65.00**

The Lennox Torrid Zone Furnace With Casing, 2-1/4" d, black on cream, cut-away furnace view in center, Marshalltown, IA, dealer................ **40.00**

The Most Handsome Music House In The State, A (square) Deal For Everybody, 2-3/4" h, cream on white, shows tall thin building in Allentown, PA............... **40.00**

The Silver State Music Co., Pueblo, CO, Pianos, Organs, Victor Talking Machines, 2-1/4" h, 2-3/4" w, dark blue text on cream **45.00**

Whitehead & Hoag Co., 2-1/8" d, sample type, multicolored Victorian lady in pale green dress, light blue hair ribbon, brown text "This Mirror Is A Novelty That Will Be Appreciated And Used By Both Ladies And Gentlemen-This Is A Sample Of One Of A Thousand Advertising Novelties Made By The Whitehead & Hoag Company, Newark, NJ, USA" **50.00**

William Frank, Paris, Texas, 1905, 2-1/4" d, colored portrait of young woman, background shading from yellowish-green to dark green, gold text **40.00**

Zona Face Pomade, The Zona Toilet Company, Wichita, 2-1/2" d, black and white, fabric-like textured covering with glamours woman looking into hand mirror with text "The Result" **45.00**

Pail, Sweet Home Brand Pure Lard, 6" d, 6-1/2" h, 4 lb size, graphics of house, children playing, red text "Luer Brothers Packing & Ice Company, Alton, Illinois," 1940s **20.00**

Paperweight

Bon Ami, glass, color ad, 3" w, 4-1/4" l **85.00**

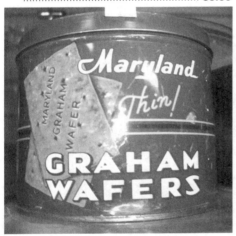

Tin, Maryland Graham Wafers, green, gold, white, and black decoration, round, $25.

Chelten Trust Company, 2-1/2" d, red, white, green, and light green, perpetual calendar, shamrock in center with "Sigiilum Germanopolitanum-1691," red border with Philadelphia address, text "Insures Titles To Real Estate, Prompt And Courteous Service," orig box. **24.00**

Derby & Kilmer Desk Co., Boston and New York, glass, black and white illus of roll-to desk and flat-top desk, 7/8" x 2-1/2" x 4" **40.00**

Fink, Bodenheimer & Co., Diamond Importers and Cutters, glass, chart listing prices for single and multiple sale units, 1" x 3-1/4" x 4-1/2" l, slight scratching to top **35.00**

J. K. Larkin & Co., New York, Brooklyn, Immediate Delivery From Stock, Pipe All Sizes, Steel and Iron **20.00**

Kall-Zimmers Mfg. Co., Milwaukee, WI, Children's Shoes, glass, real photo of toddler in striped shirt, bib overalls, shoes, 1900s, 1" x 2-1/4" x 4" l **50.00**

Leatherbee Lumber, Co., Boston, glass, two black and white lumber processing facilities, inscribed "Established 1821" and "Incorporated 1897," made by J. N. Abrams, New York City, early 1900s, 3/4" x 2-1/2" x 4" l **50.00**

Niagara Falls Lumber & Coal, glass, black and white engraved style scenic falls from US side, black inscriptions, red lettering, early 1900s, 3/4" x 2-1/4" x 4" l **45.00**

Oriental Silk Co. Limited, Montreal, white metal bull dog figure, black luster finish, name and slogan "Never Loses Its Grip On The Seam," British empire motto "What We Have We Hold," maker name, Whitehead & Hoad Co., Montreal on underside, 4" l, 2-1/2" h, 3-1/2" d base **75.00**

Tins, El Producto Blunt, white, multicolored lady, $20; Grimes Chicken Livers, blue and white, Grimes Poultry Processing, Lebanon, PA, $10; Tip-Top Coffee, blue and gold, $25; Prince Albert, Father's Day tin, $25; Fluffy Flour, Your Mother's Choice Since 1837, green, $20.

Wall pocket, embossed multicolored stiff paper, woodland scene, text on pocket "Compliments of L. F. Harpel, General Merchandise, Richlandtown, Pa," $45.

Parisian Novelty Company, 3-1/2" d, celluloid front shows color graphic of factory, white cursive lettering "Advertising Specialities," Lindbergh style type of plane circles overhead, words "The Spirit of Good Will" are seen over plane's wing, blue border with white letters "Western Ave. at 35th Street, Chicago," late 1920s........................ **45.00**

S. F. Fatzinger Painting, Paper Hanging, Decorating, The Best Equipped Shop in Town, Watch Us Grow, Allentown, PA **25.00**

S Slotnick Building Material Masons And Plasterers Supplies, Artificial Stone, Chelsea, Mass, printed in tan on cream **15.00**

United States Asbestos Division of Raybestos-Manhattan, Inc., solid brass eagle position on 4-3/4" x 6" rounded oval steel tray, maker Hubley Mfg. Co., Lancaster, PA, on underside, 1920s, 6" w, 3" h **65.00**

Pen, Bell Atlantic, Wild Things Are Happening, black barrel, gold trim, cartoon-like forest scene inside clear barrel **7.50**

Pie pan, Enjoy Py-O-Ice Box Pie, raised letters in bottom, wear from use **5.00**

Pinback button

Bear Brand Hosiery, 7/8" d, brown bear, white text, dark red rim, c1910 .... **18.00**

Big Horn Coal, Vote For The Housewife's Delight, 1-1/4" d, black and white, center coal lump, ram's head above, St. Louis back paper, c1950 .... **15.00**

Chas D. Griffith Shoe Co., 7/8" d, black and white high top shoe, red initial "G," tiny text "Griffith's Queen City Shoe," Whitehead & Hoag back paper, c1910 .... **18.00**

Drink Peter Pan Delicious Refreshing, 1-1/2" d, red on cream, oval portrait of Peter Pan in feathered hat, reverse covered tin with horizontal pin, c1930 .... **45.00**

Educator Shoes, 1-1/4" d, cream ground, young boy seated at black chalkboard outlined in red, one shoe sole complete, other open to show foot, signboard "Educator Shoes Let The Child's Foot Grow As It Should," red text "Rice & Hutchins Boston Mass," back paper with offer for illus booklet........................ **35.00**

Fairbanks Fairy Soap, The Two Best Things That Float, 1-1/4" d, black and white bar of Fairy soap, on bluish-green ocean waves, red, white, and blue flag, Whitehead & Hoag on curl, late 1890s **18.00**

Fearman Ham, 1-1/4" d, dark brown ham, company white star logo, letter "F," yellow carrying cord at top, light blue ground, dark blue rim with white text "Who Put The Ham In Hamilton? Fearman," Bastian back paper, 1910 .... **20.00**

Gimme H O Oats For Breakfast, 1-1/4" d, multicolored package, light blue ground, dark blue text, Bastian back paper, 1920s **12.00**

Hawk Eye Boiler Compound, Chicago, Ill, 7/8" d, yellow brick on white, black text, Whitehead & Hoag, c1910............. **12.00**

Heron Ballbearing Wool Casters, 7/8" d, black and white caster frame, yellow accents, Whitehead & Hoag back paper, c1910 .... **12.00**

Wall pocket, embossed multicolored stiff paper, doves and water pump, text on pocket "Compliments of H. B. Schanley, 212 W Broad St, Quakertown, Pa," $35.

Hill's Bread, Alone in Quality-Every Loaf Has The Seal of Approval, 7/8" d, dark red on cream, Whitehead & Hoag back paper, c1910................................. **10.00**

I Eat Rockville Cheese Do You, 7/8" d, bright red and yellow, black text, covered metal back, vertical pin, c1910...... **15.00**

Norbest Mountain Grown Turkeys, 1-1/2" d, black, white, orange, and dark blue mountain logo, 1940s........................ **15.00**

Ocean Soap, 7/8" d, full-color ship, pale yellow sails, greenish-blue ocean, cream ground, Whitehead & Hoag back paper, 1896 .... **24.00**

Patton's Sun-Proof Paints 5 Year, 1-1/4" d, smiling sun face, shades of yellow, blue text, brown rim edge, Whitehead & Hoag back paper, c1910 .... **24.00**

Quaker Oats, 7/8" d, full color, trademark character holding product **30.00**

Quaker Ranges, 1-1/4" d, shaded green image of Quaker man on cream, red text, maker's name "Ehrman, Boston" on curl, early 1900s **24.00**

RCA Victor Magic Brain Radio, 1-1/4" d, dark blue on white, pinktone center human head with radio mechanism in brain, 1930s **30.00**

Red Seal Lye, Disinfectant-Cleanser-Soap Maker Sold By Storekeepers, 7/8" d, multicolored product, blue text on cream, c1904 .... **18.00**

Remember Wonder Bread, It's Slo-Baked, 1-1/2" d, blue text on white, 1930s ... **12.00**

Ritz Crackers, 7/8" d, red, white, and blue litho, name in large yellow letters, text on back "National Biscuit Company, 2-36" **15.00**

Stiletto Tools Cutlery, 7/8" d, black, white, red design on bright yellow, c1930 **30.00**

Sunny Monday Bubbles Will Wash Away Your Troubles, 1-1/4" d, dark red and dark blue, white text, trace of Whitehead & Hoag back paper, c1910 .... **24.00**

Turkeys That Satisfy, The Shearer Farm, Vinemont, Pa, 1-1/2" d, red, white, and blue, Keystone Badge back paper, 1930s **15.00**

United States Express Co., 7/8" d, black and white strongbox, pair of brown wings at sides, black horseshoe, shaded light red and yellow blending to cream, top of horseshoe reads "Security Dispatch," below "1854" **24.00**

Vote for Fergusons Honey Bread, 7/8" d, colored loaf in center, bright yellow ground, Whitehead & Hoag back paper **18.00**

Widow Jones Suits Me, 1-1/4" d, multicolored, women in gray high collar dress, black headpiece, trailing veil, black gloves, pale blue ground, Whitehead & Hoag back paper, c1910 .... **75.00**

Wilbur's Cocoa, 7/8" d, multicolored, cherub using spoon to stir cup labeled "Wilbur" **25.00**

Wool Soap, 7/8" d, blue on white, young child in shrunken night shirt looking at companion in proper length night shirt, text "Use Wool Soap for Toilet & Bath" on back, Whitehead & Hoag back paper **18.00**

Worth's Hats, 1" oval, black and white photo center of naked young baby in adult-sized hat, red rim with product name and "Harris-Polk Hat Co.," Whitehead & Hoag back paper, c1910 .... **18.00**

Radio, figural

Crayola Rocks, AM **35.00**
Heinz 57 .... **85.00**
Kraft Macaroni & Cheese, Dinomac carton **35.00**
Oreo Cookie, Amico **35.00**

Many dealers offered vintage advertising objects at the March 2004 Atlantique City Antiques Show. Shown here is part of the Signs of the Tymes booth, which was filled with quality advertising items.

Record brush, celluloid top, soft tufted bristles, c1925
Ellis Bookkeeping Machine, black and white image of bookkeeping machine, red lettering, 3-1/2" d **20.00**
Liberty State Bank, bluetone image of Wilkes-Barre, PA, bank building, dark blue inscriptions, 1924 patent date, maker Parisian Novelty Co., Chicago, 4" d **15.00**

Ruler, Whitehead & Hoag Co., ivory white celluloid, printed with emblem of button maker and five inch markings, reverse with Philadelphia office and manager name **20.00**

Salesman portfolio, Saleswinner Line Pencils, 11" x 14" closed brown leather zippered display case, brown vinyl sleeve pouch, tab indexed sales brochure titled "Nobody Ever Threw A Pencil Away," 32-page glossy paper catalog with dozens of pencils in full color, several paper items dated 1957 .... **90.00**

Sign

Butternut Bread, Gee! But It's Dandy Bread, 7" x 10", cardboard diecut, repairs, C-5 .... **20.00**
Carter's Union Suits, tin, young man in only his union suit, framed, 10-3/4" h, 6-3/4" l, C-8 .... **200.00**

Sign, litho tin, yellow, red, white, and black, Columbia Records, Accredited Dealer, **$125**.

Whistle, celluloid, "Visit Penny's Toyland," 1920s, **$20**.

G. E. Fans Buy Them Here, two sided flanged tin, shows table top rotating fan, 12" h, 16" l **300.00**

Gooch's Sarsaparilla - for the Blood, paper, showing upper Thames River scene, artist sgd "Bowers," framed, 7-1/2" h, 9-1/2" l **200.00**

Kramer's Full Flavored Beverages, 9" x 20", tin, red, black, and green on white, c1960.. **40.00**

Merkle's Blu-J Brooms, emb tin, shows Blu-J sitting atop broom, framed, some damage, 13" h, 9-1/2" w............... **175.00**

Monarch Paint, two sided flanged porcelain, hand holding paint brush, 17" h, 15-1/2" l, C-8........................ **225.00**

Niagara Shoe, beveled tin over cardboard, American Art Works litho, 19" h, 8-3/4" w.............................. **150.00**

Nichol Kola, 14" x 14-1/2", emb tin, bottle cap shape, red, white, gray, and black, 1940s.. **45.00**

Occident Flour, tin over cardboard, actual examples as it goes through cleaning, washing, and scouring process, 9" h, 13-3/4" w.. **75.00**

Park Lane Frocks, 7-1/2" x 15", reverse glass, gold, brown, green, white, light green, Price Brothers, Inc., Chicago-NY **20.00**

Purity Butter Pretzels, diecut cardboard, easel back, smiling blond boy carrying giant pretzel against black background, white lettering, early 1930s, 22" h, 12-1/4" w.. **70.00**

Rainbow Is Good Bread, 2-1/2" x 18", emb tin... **15.00**

Royal Baking Powder, paper, Gingerbread Man pointing to can with one hand, pointing to book titled The Little Gingerbread Man with other hand, small tear at center, 30" h, 20-1/2" l **125.00**

Simon Pure Baking Powder, reverse painting on mirror, showing Simon Pure, framed, some loss of paint and silvering, 17" h, 14" l **225.00**

Vegetaline, En Vente Ici, Grand Prix, Exposition Universelle, Paris, 1900, 7-1/4" x 16", tin, c1910 .... **40.00**

Wells Fargo Lamont Gloves, 9-1/2" x 23-1/2", 1950s **25.00**

Stamp case, Scarritt Seats, book shape, horizontal formal, black, white, and red sides, illus of Scarritt Car Chairs & Seats, black cover reads 'For Steam and Streetcar," early 1900s **55.00**

Stickpin, Old Dutch Cleanser, enameled figure, brass pink, reverse "Old Dutch Cleanser Chases Dirt" slogan, 1920s **35.00**

Tape measure, celluloid canister

Hawk Work Clothes, full-color brown half holding red, white, and blue sign from beak, yellow background, blue rim, blue letter on reverse "Miller Co.," 1920s **35.00**

Plate, The Rufe-Gussman Co., Department Store, Quakertown, Pa., shaded pink border, pink roses, green leaves, gold letter, c1910, **$45**.

Indian Head National Bank, blue lettering, white ground, one side with Indian profile, other side with slogan text, 1920s **30.00**

Telephone, figural

Heinz, catsup bottle **45.00**

Raid Bug **120.00**

Tetley Tea **50.00**

Stegmaier Brewing Co., factory scene, early railroad and automobilia, minor scratching and rubbing, C-6 .... **70.00**
Woodward's The Candy Man, 5" x 7", litho, black and white center image of midget couple holding box of chocolates, red and white peppermint sticks on sides, text with name, statistics, selling slogans, bottom rim printed "Made by John G. Woodward & Co. (The Candy Man), Council Bluffs, Iowa," 1920s, C-8 .... **45.00**

Whistle

Butter-Krust Bread, red and white celluloid, tin backing panel, 1930s. **20.00**
Endicott Johnson Shoes, green litho tin, biplane shape, red lettering, marked "Made in Germany," c1930 .... **25.00**
Golden Royal Milk, yellow and black **12.50**
Old Reliable Coffee, tin litho **15.00**
Poll Parrot Shoes, tin litho, yellow, red, and green trademark, made by Kilchof Co., 1930s **40.00**

Advertising Characters

History: Americans learned to recognize specific products by their particular advertising characters. In the early 1900s, many immigrants could not read but could identify the colorful characters. Thus, the advertising character helped to sell the product.

Some manufacturers developed similar names for inferior-quality products, like Fairee Soap versus the popular Fairy Soap. Trade laws eventually helped protect companies by allowing advertising characters to be registered as part of a trademark.

Trademarks and advertising characters are found on product labels, in magazines, as premiums, and on other types of advertising. Popular cartoon characters also were used to advertise products.

Some advertising characters, such as Mr. Peanut and the Campbell Kids, were designed to promote a specific product. The popular Campbell Kids first appeared on streetcar advertising in 1906. The illustrations of Grace G. Drayton were originally aimed at housewives, but the characters were gradually dropped from Campbell's advertising

until the television industry expanded the advertising market. In 1951, Campbell redesigned the kids and successfully reissued them. The kids were redesigned again in 1966. Other advertising characters (e.g., Aunt Jemima) also have enjoyed a long life; some, like Kayo and the Yellow Kid, are no longer used in contemporary advertising.

Collecting Hints: Concentrate on one advertising character. Three-dimensional objects are more eagerly sought than two-dimensional ones.

Reproduction Alert.

Additional Listings: Advertising, Black Memorabilia, Cartoon Characters, Fast Food, Planter's Peanuts.

Alka Seltzer, Speedy

Figure, 5-1/2" h, plastic, 1960s **20.00**
Sign, 10" w **65.00**

Aunt Jemima

Cookbook, *Aunt Jemima's Album of Secret Recipes*, 1935, 33 pgs **35.00**
Place mat, paper, full color, Story of Aunt Jemima, "Story of Aunt Jemima and her Pancake Days...has devoted her time to working with service clubs...on her community Pancake Day Festivals...," unused, 1950s, 10-1/2" x 13-1/2" ... **45.00**

Borden's, Elsie and Family

Badge, white ground, blue lettering, 1-1/2" d **10.00**
Cookie cutter, Buelah, hard plastic, emb face, 2-1/14" d **48.00**
Drinking glass, Elsie the Cow, Elmer, and Beauregard, 1776 garb, red, white, and blue **25.00**
Fun book, *Elsie Fun Book*, coloring pages, dot games, safety games, etc., 20 pgs, unused, 1940s **75.00**
Postcard, Elsie and Elmer, color, traveling scene **25.00**
Poster, *Borden's Egg Nog*, portrait of Elsie, 20" x 14" **30.00**
Ring, dark gold luster plastic, center clear plastic dome over multicolored Elsie image, 1950 .... **35.00**
Salt and pepper shakers, pr, Elsie and Elmer, china, c1940 .... **125.00**

Buster Brown

Box, *Buster Brown Stockings*, c1905, 11" x 4" x 3" **150.00**
Game, Buster Brown Game and Play Box, Andy Devine photo, unused .. **80.00**
Pinback button, 7/8" d
Buster Brown Hose Supporters A Jolly Pair, multicolored Buster and Tige doing a jig, c1920 .... **24.00**

Buster Brown, plate, multicolored transfer, gold rim, 5-1/4" d, $45.

Resolved That If It Busted, It Wasn't A Buster Brown Hose Supporter, Buster using pen to print his name on resolution message **28.00**
You Can't Buster Brown Hose Supporter, winking Buster, Whitehead & Hoag back paper, c1910 .... **24.00**
Playing cards, copyright 1906, each card 1-3/4" x 2-1/4" **160.00**
Pocket mirror, Buster Brown Shoes, multicolored portrait of Buster and Tige, lighted aged collet, traces of scratching **175.00**

Cadbury Bunny, stuffed rabbit, talking **125.00**

Campbell Kids, Campbell's Artist Apron, MIB, $25.

Campbell Kids
Christmas ornament, MIB **25.00**
Doll, boy and girl, vinyl, orig clothes, pr **150.00**
Radio, MIB **48.00**
Soup bowl, Campbell Girl on inside, alphabet and "Christine" on bottom, c1940 .... **35.00**

California Raisins, sticker album, slide O-scope animation viewer **5.00**

Chiquita Banana
Recipe book, 1950 .... **5.00**
Record, 78 RPM, Auravision, 1950 .. **7.50**

Dutch Boy Paint, Dutch Boy
Hand puppet, 11" h, vinyl head, fabric body, orig cellophane bag, 1960s . **45.00**
Paint book, Dutch Boy illus, 1907, unused **25.00**
Pinback button, multicolored trademark, red and blue rim inscription **12.00**

Esso, Tiger
Bank, tiger, figural, plastic **35.00**
Drinking glass, Put a Tiger in Your Tank, slogan printed on back in eight different languages, 5" h **18.00**

Fairy Soap, tip tray, Have You A Little Fairy In Your Home? 4-1/2", tin, color graphic of little girl wearing purple coat, bloomers, and blue bonnet, holding flowers and sitting on oval bar of Fairy Soap, made by Passaic Metal Ware Co., Litho, Passaic, NJ, back with text in oval "Sense-Cents-Scents, People With Common Sense Play But Five, Common Cents For A Soap With No Common Scents-That's Fairy Soap. Fairy Soap The Floating Oval Cake Is White and Pure, With No Scents or Dyes to Disguise Alternations, It Costs But 5 Cents, Avoid Dyed Soaps, The N. K. Fairbanks Co., Chicago" **70.00**

Flintstones, cup, plastic, Yabba Dabba Doo Flintstones Multiple Vitamins Are Good For You, 1975 .... **8.00**

Frito Bandito, eraser, figural **15.00**

Gold Dust Twins, "The Many Purpose Cleaner, Fairbank's Gold Dust Washing Powder," box, 6-1/4" h, $35.

Gold Dust Twins, Gold Dust Washing Powder
Box, 4-1/2" x 6-1/2", Washing Powder, Twins cleaning dishes, woodwork, clothes, glassware, etc. on top and sides, full **35.00**

Can, 3" d, 4-3/4" h, Scouring Cleanser, cardboard sides, metal top and bottom, full.. **12.00**
Pinback button, 7/8" d, twins seated in yellow wash tub, cream ground, black text, orig Whitehead & Hoag back paper, c1896... **32.00**

Green Giant
Figure, Sprout, vinyl.......................... **24.00**
Telephone, Little Sprout, 14" h **65.00**
Heinz 57, Mr. Aristocrat, figure, 5-1/2" h, painted hard latex rubber, 2-1/2" x 2-1/2" base, red head, green leaf hair sprigs, black top hat, "57" circle symbol on 3 sides of base, name "Heinz" in raised white lettering **75.00**
Hush Puppy, Hush Puppies Shoes, figure, composition, 8-1/4" h **40.00**

Kebbler, Elf
Bank, figural, ceramic..................... **65.00**
Cookie jar, cookie tree, raised figures
.... **95.00**
Doll, Ernie, plush, talking **65.00**
Kellogg's, Tony The Tiger
Bank, figural, vinyl........................... **40.00**
Doll, cloth.. **25.00**
Radio **30.00**
Spoon, SP, emb "Kellogg's"............ **10.00**

Kool Cigarettes
Drinking glass, 5-1/2" h, frosted, black image of Willie, four-line verse below
.... **45.00**
Figure, Dr. Kool, 4-1/2" h, black and white, painted plaster, full figure walking along carrying satchel with name on side, wearing stethoscope, late 1930s . **165.00**
Pin, 1-1/8" h, Millie, figural white metal, brass luster, black and white painted body, 1950s..................................... **18.00**
Pinback button, 1" d, multicolored, Willie smoking cigarette, each wing draped over seated glaring donkey and elephant, white text "In Either Case, Keep Kool" on green, 1944 or 1948........ **24.00**
Lee Jeans, Lee Boy, bank, ceramic, 8" h, MIB... **150.00**
Magic Chef Kitchen Ranges, Magic Chef, bank, 7" h, painted vinyl, fleshtone head, white chef's hat, black bow tie, jacket, and trousers, white shirt front and cuffs, 1980s... **25.00**
Michelin Man, figure, plastic, 12" h .. **100.00**
Mr. Bubble, figure, plastic **25.00**
Mr. Clean, figure, plastic..................... **65.00**

Oscar Mayer Meats
Toy, Oscar Mayer Weinermobile, pop-up Oscar figure................................. **155.00**
Whistle, Oscar Meyer Weiner **15.00**

Oscar Mayer Weinermobile, stuffed toy, $5.

Pepto Bismol 24 Hour Bug, bank, soft vinyl, 4" x 6", green, dark green spots, four legs, two crossed arms, white eyes, orange closure marked "Niagara Plastics, Erie, Pa" **25.00**
Peter Pan Peanut Butter, Peter Pan, lunch box, plastic, 1980s **20.00**

Philip Morris, Johnny
Box, 3-1/2" x 5-1/4" x 10-1/2", plastic, hinged lid with molded logo........... **35.00**
Pinback button, black, white, red, and fleshtone, 1930s **35.00**
Place card, figural **17.50**
Sign, emb tin, well worn, 12" x 14" . **95.00**

Philip Morris, sign, tin litho "Call for Philip Morris," yellow, red, black, and white, $95.

Pillsbury Co., Dough Boy
Cookie jar **25.00**
Doll, 7-1/4" h, vinyl, smiling full figure boy, blue accent eyes, button on cap, copyright 1971 Pillsbury Co. Minneapolis
.... **18.00**
Salt and pepper shakers, 4" h Poppin Fresh, 3-1/4" h Poppie, names on bases, blue accents, copyright 1974 .... **28.00**

RCA Victor, Nipper
Coffee mug, plastic **8.00**
Pinback button, 1-1/4" d, diecut celluloid, red, white, and blue, dealer's name on back **40.00**
Snowdome.................................... **40.00**

Red Goose Shoes
Bank **150.00**
Egg layer, 27" h, 22" w, plastic red goose sitting atop cardboard box, slight paint loss **200.00**

Child's rocking chair, oak, pressback design of Yellow Kid blowing horn, repair to back support, **$650**.

Ring, secret compartment, glow, photo **150.00**
String holder, 15" h, 11" w, cast iron, wing emb "Red goose Shoes" **150.00**

Reddy Kilowatt

Badge, 4" d, Reddy Kilowatt, The People's Choice, cello, red on white **35.00**
Cookie cutter **25.00**
Figure, 5" h plastic, 1/4" x 1-1/2" x 3" black plastic base, translucent pink body and white plastic heat, hands and boots glow after being exposed to bright light, name on base, mid-1930s **300.00**
Identification badge, 3-3/4" sq, red and white paper envelope, 3" d still paper peel-off "E-Z Stick-On" badge with yellow upper and lower bands, red and white Reddy portrait, 1950s, unused **20.00**
Magic gripper, 5-1/4" sq red and white paper envelope, 4-3/4" d thin textured dark yellow rubber disk, printed on one side with title and image of Reddy the Chef, c1950 .... **20.00**
Pin, 1" h brass and red enamel figure, orig 2-1/4" x 2-3/4" diecut card with clear plastic window, c1950 .... **40.00**

Purple Cow, Pick-Ohio Hotel, Youngstown, OH, mustard jar, Shenango China, **$10**.

Plate, 9" d, white china, 2-1/2" h smiling full figured Reddy at left, dark red accent rim, early 1950s **60.00**
Potholder, MIP **30.00**
7-Up, Fresh-Up Freddy, ruler **15.00**
Sinclair Oil, Dinosaur, booklet, 1960s **20.00**
Sunkist, Charlie Tuna
Alarm Clock, 1969 .... **85.00**
Doll, talking, Mattel **120.00**

Trix Rabbit

Cereal breakfast set, plastic bowl with Trix Rabbit on sides, plastic figural mug, two vinyl placements with Trix Rabbit antidotes, orig mailing box, 1960s. **75.00**
Figure, vinyl **45.00**
Tropicana, Orange Bird
Bank, 4-3/4" h orange vinyl, yellow accent, green leaf petal hair and wings, Hong Kong, c1960 .... **35.00**
Child's ring **5.00**
Radio **30.00**
Serving plate, 10-3/4" d **8.00**

Aluminum, Hand Wrought

History: During the late 1920s aluminum was used to make many decorative household accessories. Although manufactured by a variety of methods, the hammered aluminum with repoussé patterns appears to have been the most popular.

At one time many companies were competing for the aluminum giftware market. In order to be more competitive, numerous silver manufacturers added aluminum articles to their product lines during the Depression. Some of these aluminum objects were produced strictly as promotional items; others were offered as more affordable options to similar silver objects. Many well-known and highly esteemed metalsmiths contributed their skills to the production of hammered aluminum. With the advent of mass-production and the accompanying wider distribution of aluminum giftware, the demand began to decline, leaving only a few producers who have continued to turn out quality work using the age-old and time-tested methods of metal crafting.

Collecting Hints: Some manufacturers' marks are synonymous with quality, e.g., "Continental Hand Wrought Silverlook." However, some quality pieces are not marked and should not be overlooked. Check carefully for pitting, deep scratches, and missing glassware.

Silent butler, Chrysanthemum pattern, Continental Silverlook, #505, pierced handle, 12" l, 7-1/2" d, **$28**.

Ashtray, 3-1/4" d, Stanhome, Stanley Home Product, house dec in center **5.00**

Basket

10-1/2" l, 6" w, 5" h, chrysanthemum in center, ribbed handle with leaves, marked "Continental Trade Mark (minuteman soldier) Hand Wrought Silverlook 510" **40.00**

11" d, 6" h, pierced, chrysanthemum center design, elaborate handle, marked "Forman 4 Family" **30.00**

Bowl

5-3/4" d, 4" h, floral pattern, serrated rim, hammered handle riveted to edge, marked "Continental Trademark Hand Wrought 783" **10.00**

10" d, 3-1/2" h, flared, sgd "Don Drumm" **90.00**

12" d, 4" h, marked "Continental 765" **38.00**

Bracelet, four 1" x 1-3/4" l sections of hammered aluminum, each with dogwood dec, Wendell August Forge, #101 .... **75.00**

Bread tray, 13-1/4" l, 7-3/4" w, chrysanthemum dec, marked "Continental #572" **27.50**

Breakfast set, Tulip pattern, 8-1/2" l, x 3-3/4" w x 3" h toast rack, marked "Hand Wrought Creations Rodney Kent 405"; 16-1/2" l x 11-1/2" w x 2" h double handled serving tray with scalloped edges, bouquet of tulips tied with a ribbon dec, marked "Hand Wrought Creations Rodney Kent 408" with Knight in Armor hallmark; set of six scalloped 3-1/4" d butter pats **75.00**

Butter dish, cov, round, domed cover, double-loop finish, glass insert, marked "Handwrought Buenilum" **35.00**

Candleholder, rolled metal handle, imp floral design, marked "Farber & Shlevin Inc., Hand Wrought 1702" **35.00**

Candlesticks, pr, 4" w, 3" h, Pine Cone pattern, advertising premium for Triangle Springs CO., DuBois, PA, marked "Wendell August Forge" **30.00**

Candy dish

7" d, 4" l curled handle, center china dish with Japanese floral dec, hand wrought aluminum edge with floral design, marked "Farber and Shlevin" **40.00**

12" l x 4-3/4" w, two glass inserts, applied ribbon and floral design handles, marked "Hand Wrought Creations by Rodney Kent #462," one rivet replaced on handle **42.00**

Casserole, cov

10" d, rose finial with leaves, marked "Continental Trade Mark, Silverlook 557" **50.00**

10-1/2" d, 5" d, twisted vine handles and finial, marked "IC-2, Made in Italy" **18.00**

Cigarette box, cov, 5-1/4" l, 3-1/2" w, 1-1/2" h, ducks flying over marsh scene, two compartments, marked "Wendell August Forge #275," late 1930s or early 1940s **75.00**

Coaster

Flying ducks and cattails, set of six **12.00**

State of Texas, various state symbols **7.50**

Cocktail shaker, 11-1/4" h, 4" w, Art-Deco style, Buenilum **140.00**

Compote, 13-1/4" d, 2" h, entwined dogwood blossoms **30.00**

Creamer and sugar, Chrysanthemum pattern, grooved handles, applied leaves, matching tray, marked "Continental Hand Wrought Silverlook" **35.00**

Crumb catcher set, plain, unmarked. **10.00**

Desk set, Bali Bamboo pattern, Everlast Forge, three pcs **45.00**

Dish

6" d, coiled handle, fluted edge with poinsettia design, marked "Farber & Shlevin Hand Wrought 1702" **15.00**
10" w, 9" l, Sea Shell pattern, four cone feet, marked "Bruce Fox," c1940 ... **85.00**
11-3/4" w, 1-1/2" h, two handles, marked "Handwrought Buenlium" **30.00**

Fruit basket, 11-1/8" w, 10" h, grapes, apples, cherries, pears, iris, poppy, and other floral dec, marked "Cromwell"
.... **20.00**

Fruit bowl, 13-1/2" d, 2-3/4" h, serrated rolled edge, marked "Hand Wrought Aluminum" **30.00**

Ice bucket, cov, orig tongs, marked "Cromwell Hand Wrought Aluminum"
.... **25.00**

Ladle, 14-1/2" l, Argental Cellini Craft . **25.00**

Lazy Susan, 16" d, Rodney Kent, covered glass dish, ribbon and flower trim .. **35.00**

Pin, 2" w, 1-1/2" h, rect, bittersweet design, marked "Wendell August Forge #101"
.... **50.00**

Pitcher

Buenilum, ovoid, slender neck, twisted handle **35.00**
Regal, some scratches and wear .. **15.00**

Relish, 10" d, three divided sections, crimped rim, handles, intaglio fruit, Cromwell **15.00**

Sandwich tray, 11-1/2" d, tulip pattern, serrated edges, marked "Hand Wrought Creations Rodney Kent 421" **40.00**

Scoop, 6-1/2" l, handle curled under **6.00**

Serving dish

10-1/2" sq, center figural lobster handle, four serving areas, marked "Bruce Fox"
.... **60.00**
12-5/8" l, 8" w, center bouquet of three tulips, marked "Hand Wrought Creations Rodney Kent 404" **24.00**
13" w x 8" l oval, marked "Hand Wrought Creations Rodney Kent 406" **20.00**

Silent butler, from page 20, with lid down. $20.

Tray, Oriental tea house design, unmarked, 10" d, $20.

Serving piece, 11" l, 5" w, figural lobster claw, three cone feet, dark matte patina, marked "Bruce Fox," 1960s **32.00**

Silent butler

Flower design, unmarked **18.00**
Moon and star design, 6-1/2" x 11" **24.00**

Tid-bit tray, three tiers, 8-1/4" d, 11-1/4" d, and 14-1/4" d trays, 13" h, ornate floral design, ruffled rims, handle with pineapple at top **40.00**

Tray

10-1/2" d, round, flying geese handles, marked "Shup Laird Hand Wrought Argental Number 713" **55.00**
11-3/4" l, 7-7/8" w, 5/8" h, North Fork Lodge, Wendell August Forge **85.00**
13" d, leaf shape, handle, marked "Buenilum Hand Wrought Aluminum"
.... **18.00**
13-1/4" l, 7-3/4" w, chrysanthemum in center, two raised decorative leaves on handles, marked "Continental Trade Mark (minuteman soldier) Hand Wrought Silverlook 572" **35.00**
18-1/2" l, 12-1/2" w, etched deer scene in center, marked "Continental Trade Mark (minuteman soldier) Hand Wrought Silverlook" **75.00**

American Bisque

History: The American Bisque Company was founded in Williamstown, West Virginia, in 1919. Although the pottery's original product was china-head dolls, it quickly expanded its inventory to include serving dishes, cookie jars, ashtrays, and various other decorative ceramic pieces. B. E. Allen, founder of the Sterling China Company, invested heavily in the company and eventually purchased the remaining stock. In 1982, the plant was sold and operated briefly under the name American China Company. The plant closed in 1983.

Sequoia Ware and Berkeley are two trademarks used by American Bisque, the former used on items sold in gift shops, and the latter found on products sold through chain stores. Cookie jars produced by this company are marked "ABC" inside blocks.

Collecting Hint: When searching for American Bisque products, look for a mark consisting of three stacked baby blocks with the letters "A," "B," and "C." This common mark is readily found.

Ashtray, Sequoia, marked................. **18.00**
Bank, elephant, 6" h............................ **95.00**
Clothes sprinkler, figural, cat, marbles for eyes **175.00**

Cookie jar

Baby elephant, bonnet **175.00**
Bear with cookie, marked "USA"... **90.00**
Beehive, 11-3/4" h, marked "USA" **175.00**
Cat, 5" w, 8-7/8" h **300.00**
Churn, raised USA mark on back, 8" w, 11" h, faint all-over crazing.............. **60.00**
Dutch boy with sailboat................. **175.00**
Jack-in-the-Box, imp "USA" on back, 12" h... **195.00**
Feed Sack, words "Cookie Jar" cold painted on front with decorative flowers, some slight age crazing, wear to paint **85.00**
Flintstones, Fred and Dino, imp "USA" on back, 14-1/2" h, well done repairs to Dino's neck **550.00**
Flying Bluebirds, 7" w, 9" h.............. **95.00**
Ludwig Von Drake, name incised on graduate cap, back incised "copyright Walt Disney Productions, USA 1961," 9" h **985.00**
Saddle without blackboard, marked "USA," 12" h................................... **350.00**
Wooden soldier, 10-1/2" h............ **100.00**

Creamer

Chicken, pink highlights, gold trim . **30.00**
Pig, red bow, red and black paint dec, 5-3/4" w, 5" h, hairline at handle, pinpoint glaze skips **20.00**

Food mold

Fish, 10" l, white, red trim, ring for hanging, incised "ABC" **20.00**
Set, hand painted, round, red and white, rings for hanging, set of four, incised "ABC".. **70.00**

Planter, baby carriage with lamb, pink and blue flowers with yellow centers, **$12.50**.

Planter

Bear leaning on edge of hollow stump, brown bear, black eyes, red mouth, green stump, 6-3/4" l, 2-1/2" h **20.00**
Cockatoo, glazed bottom, 6-1/2" l, 3" w, 5" h.. **25.00**
Horn of plenty, gold, marked "American Bisque Co. 28 kt gold," 4-1/2" h..... **25.00**
Lamb, colorful glaze, marked, 6-1/2" l, 3-3/4" w, 5" h................................. **15.00**
Salt and pepper shakers, pr, churn ... **65.00**
Sugar bowl, pig, red and black paint dec, 5-3/4" w, 3" h, rim hairline, slight discoloration inside...................................... **20.00**
Teapot, Red Rose, 6-1/2" h, gold trim **55.00**
Vase

5" h, 7" l, running deer, running, stepped base **36.00**
6" h, white heart, blue bow **30.00**
6-1/2" h, standing deer, Art-Deco style **20.00**

Aviation Collectibles

History: Most of the income for the first airlines in the United States came from government mail-carrying subsidies. The first non-Post Office Department flight to carry mail was in 1926 between Detroit and Chicago. By 1930, there were 38 domestic and five international airlines operating in the United States. A typical passenger load was 10. After World War II, four-engine planes with a capacity of 100 or more passengers were introduced.

The jet age was launched in the 1950s. In 1955, Capitol Airlines used British-made turboprop airliners for domestic service. In 1958, National Airlines began domestic jet passenger service. The giant Boeing 747 went into operation in 1970 as part of the Pan American fleet. The Civil Aeronautics Board, which regulates the airline industry, ended control of routes in 1982 and fares in 1983.

Major American airlines included American, Delta, Northwest, Pan Am, TWA, United, and USAir. There are many regional lines as well. As a result of deregulation, new airlines are forming, with some lasting longer than others.

Collecting Hints: This field developed in the 1980s and is now firmly established. The majority of collectors focus on personalities, especially Charles Lindbergh and Amelia Earhart. New collectors are urged to look at the products of airlines, especially those items related to the pre-jet era.

Bank, Harley-Davidson Lockheed Vega 5B Highwing airplane, diecast metal replica, MIB, **$15**.

Commercial

Book, *Dan Dunn Meets Chang Loo*, 3-1/2" x 5-3/4", Whitman, Stephen Slesinger, based on comic strip by Norman Marsh, copyright 1938, Pan-Am premium **150.00**

Bowl, Delta Airlines, for VIP International flights, Mayer China **20.00**

Cup and saucer, Delta Airlines, for VIP International flights, Mayer China... **25.00**

Dinner plate, Delta Airlines, for VIP International flights, Mayer China... **20.00**

Cigar cutter, pocket, Pan Am, 1901 ... **70.00**

Figure, Air-India, 4-1/2" h, painted plastic statuette, green flying carpet base, traditional red, white, and blue striped turban, green clasp, red jacket, white

harem trousers, curled red shoes, orig label "Ameya Industries/Bombay, India," c1970 .... **35.00**

Napkin holder, American Airlines, 1" h, 1-1/2" d, open ended metal clasp, center with "AA" soaring eagle symbol, c1930 .... **15.00**

Playing cards, 3/4" x 2-1/4" x 3-1/2" box, c1960-80
American Airlines, US mail plane .. **12.00**
Delta Airlines, white pyramid design **10.00**
Eastern/Ryder, text with logo design **10.00**
Ozark, snow covered Rockies design **12.00**

Postcard, unused
Aerolineas Argentinas, 1950s, Carrasco Airport, Montevideo Uruguay, black and white **10.00**
Air Transat, Lockheed L1011, color, oversized **6.00**
Alitalia, Caravelle III S.E. 210, radio print on back **8.00**
Eastern, Constellation, color **6.00**
Lufthansa DC10, airline issued **5.00**
Piedmont Airlines, Boeing 737-300 series, color, oversized **6.00**
Trans-Canada Airlines, airline issued, Viscount at Windsor Airport, Windsor, Ontario, Canada **10.00**

Candy container, figural, glass, Army bomber, **$35**.

Stand-up display, TWA Flight Attendant, 1960s **45.00**

Stewardess wings, United Airlines, 2-1/2" x 3-1/4" orig black and white card, 2" w silver accent wings, red, white, and blue center logo, c1960, unused **24.00**

Stock certificate, Pan American World Airways, Inc., NY, 1960s, red, 100 shares, common, large eagle with spread wings over twin world hemispheres, flanked by two allegorical men, issued, perforation cancel, American Bank Note Co. .. **10.00**

Toy car, TWA Airlines, airport service car, tin friction, 11" l **120.00**

Toy plane

Bristol Beinhem, Dinky, 1956-63..... **20.00**
Corvair Inter-continental Jet, friction, 14" l,
MIB.. **145.00**
Douglas DC3, Dinky, silver, #60t, 1937-41
.... **125.00**
Pan Am Boeing 747, friction, 7" l, MIB
.... **225.00**
Royal Dutch Airlines, KLM Corvair jet,
friction, 14" l **95.00**

Travel bag, Pan Am World **10.00**

General

Ashtray, Naval Aviation Museum,
Pensacola, Florida, figural airplane,
souvenir decal, gold lettering, incised
"Japan," 7" l **24.00**
Big Little Book, Whitman, minor wear
*Barney Baxter In The Air With The Eagle
Squadron,* #1458, 1938 .... **30.00**
Jimmie Allen In The Air Mail Robbery,
#1143, 1939................................. **30.00**
Pat Nelson-Ace Of Test Pilots, #1445,
1937 .... **30.00**
Skyroads With Hurricane Hawk, #1127,
1936 .... **30.00**

Book

Fighter Planes, Colby Book, 1966
copyright, used library stock **5.00**
Jets of the World, used library stock **5.00**
*Wings Around The World, The American
Flight of 1924,* K. C. Tessendorf,
hardcover, dj................................. **10.00**
Catalog, *Merchandising Dynamics,* Detroit,
MI, 1964, 150 pgs, 8-1/2" x 11", aviation
supplies, engine accessories, pilot's
supplies, safety equipment, propellers,
etc. **20.00**
Cigarette lighter, chrome plated, desk type,
propeller, lighter compartment in wing,
c1937 .... **95.00**
Comic book, *Jim Ray's Aviation
Sketchbook,* No. 2, 1946, ink stain on
front cov, wear, yellowing, 64 pgs .. **18.00**

Game, Lindy, The New Flying Game, Parker
Bros., $75.

Game, Wings, The Air Mail Game, Parker
Brothers, 4" x 5-1/2", flying Air Mail plane,
set of 99 cards, orig instruction sheet,
copyright 1928 .... **35.00**

Magazine tear sheet, Bendix Aviation Corp,
1947, *Saturday Evening Post*........... **4.00**
Palm puzzle, silvered rim, plastic cover, full
color paper playing surface, Vosin box
aircraft in flight, inscription "1908 80
Kahen/Frankreich," German, c1970
.... **35.00**
Paperweight, copper colored metal, Sphere
and Trylon, orange tag on each end reads "Aviation Bldg, N.Y.W.F."
.... **95.00**

Pinback button

50th Anniversary of Powered Flight,
1-5/8" d, dark blue on bright yellow, text
on banner dividing images of biplane
and jet plane, out rim "Solar Celebrates,
San Diego, Calif" **18.00**
National Air Mail Week, 1-1/2" d, blue and
white text on panels of bright orange,
white, and dark blue "May 15 to 21st
1938 San Francisco, Calif"............ **25.00**
Pin, enamel, Air and Space Bicentennial,
text on orig 1-1/2" x 1-3/4" white card,
blue inscription, 7/8" tall silver luster pin
with red, white, and blue enamel accents
outline balloon, dates 1783-1983 .. **18.00**
Plate, Martin Aviation, Vernon Kilns, brown
illus of five aircraft, titles, c1940, 10-1/2" d
.... **50.00**
Postcard, Friendship Airport, Baltimore, MD,
textured paper, tinted art, C. T. Art-
Colortone, mid-1950s, 3-1/2" x 5-1/2",
unused, set of four......................... **20.00**
Sign, Texaco Aviation, enameled porcelain
.... **30.00**
Tin, Aeroplane View of Manhattan Island,
11" x 12-1/2" x 6" h, full-color aerial view of
Manhattan Island, Manhattan skyline on
front panel, total of 25 scenes around
sides... **95.00**

Personalities

Autograph

Earhart, Amelia, clipped signature from
letter, June 1928, 1-1/2" x 6-1/2"... **350.00**
Lindbergh, Charles A., TLS, Nov. 17,
1930, NY, sgd to C. B. Whittelsey,
declining invitation to banquet, one pg,
single 4to sheet, personal stationery,
folds.. **675.00**
Lindbergh, Charles A., photo sgd
"Charles A. Lindbergh," silver print of
Lindbergh shaking hands with Charles
Lawrance, Pres of Wright Aeronautical
Corp, standing in front of Spirit of St. Louis,
also sgd by Lawrance, Acme News-
pictures stamp on verso, 7" x 9". **2,760.00**
Wright, Orville, photo sgd, silver bust
portrait by Underwood & Underwood,
name and "Kitty Hawk, 17 December
1928" sgd under portrait, orig
Underwood folder, 9" x 7" image on
13-1/2" x 10-1/4" sheet.............. **2,990.00**

Wright, Orville, sgd on selvage of block of six two-cent International Civil Aeronautics Conference commemoratives, c1928 .... **635.00**

Big Little Book, *Hall of Fame of the Air,* by Captain Eddie Rickenbacker, drawings by Clayton Knight, Whitman #1159, 1936, first edition **65.00**

Photo, Charles Lindbergh standing in front of Spirit of St. Louis, matted, framed, **$125**.

Book

Alone, account of Richard Byrd in Antarctica, 1934, autographed..... **125.00**

That's My Story, Douglas Corrigan, published by E P Dutton & Co, 1938, 5-1/2 x 8-1/4", hard cover, 221 pgs, 56 sepia photos.................................... **20.00**

Twelve Seconds To the Moon, Rosamond Young and Catharine Fitzgerald, US Air Force Museum, 1983, hard cover .. **14.00**

Booklet, *Highlights of the Smithsonian Museum,* photos include Spirit of St. Louis and Wright Bros plane, as well as others **10.00**

Character mug, *Wright Brothers,* ceramic, hand painted, Avon, 1985 .... **20.00**

Children's book, *Boy's Story of Charles Lindbergh,* hard cover **5.00**

Christmas ornament, *Flight at Kitty Hawk,* #1, Hallmark, 1997 .... **10.00**

Doll, Precious Moments, Famous Women Series, Amelia Earhart, #1584 .... **30.00**

Film, "Lindbergh's Paris Flight," Pathex Motion Pictures................................ **50.00**

First day cover, *Wright Brothers 100th Anniversary,* canceled at Kill Devil Hills, NC... **3.50**

Game, Howard Hughes Game, 11" x 17" x 3", Family Games, Inc., thick brown plastic box designed as attaché case, orig cardboard label and shrink wrap, copyright 1972............................ **100.00**

Limited edition plate, Wright Bros at Kitty Hawk, #4 in Man's Dream of Flight Series by Ghent, by artist August Frank, 1983, MIB.. **50.00**

Money clip, Spirit of St. Louis, silvered brass, spring clip, finely detailed illus of Lindbergh aircraft, Anson Co....... **125.00**

Pendant, bronze, high relief bust portrait of Amelia Earhart, goldtoned chain ... **45.00**

Pinback button

Bond Bread, red, white, and black, illus of Amelia Earhart's plane, 1-1/4" d..... **70.00**

Gordon Bennett 1930 International Balloon Race And Aerial Carnival Cleveland, 2" d, red and blue on white, employee's red serial number, horizontal bar pin on back **45.00**

Howard Hughes Around The World In 4 Days, 1-1/4" d, black and white photo, black text, circle of bue and white stars, segmented red and white striped rim, 1930s **25.00**

Lindbergh, 1-1/4" d, smiling black and white photo on white, shadow silhouette of flying Spirit of St. Louis **40.00**

Orville Wright, 2" d, black, white, and buff litho, "Orville Wright-American/First Man To Fly," 1930s................................. **24.00**

Wright Aeronautical Employees Ass'n, 1-1/4" black text on dark green, "Dues Paid for June 1938," back paper from Eagle Regalia **15.00**

Photograph, 31" x 41", Wright Bros first flight, 1903, framed **195.00**

Toy, airmail airplane, pressed steel, made by Keystone Toys, **$400**.

Plate, 8-1/2" d, yellow glazed china, color graphics of smiling Lindy, plane over ocean between Statue of Liberty and Eiffel Tower, text "First To Navigate The Air In Continuous Flight From New York To Paris-1927," Limoges China Co., Ohio, Golden Glove stamp **24.00**

Pocket mirror, 2-1/4" x 3-1/2", celluloid, Lindbergh and plane in flight, maroon and white **125.00**

Postcard, 3-3/4" x 5-1/2", air mail, black and white, issued to welcome Lindbergh, Milwaukee, Aug, 1927, back text endorses air mail **30.00**

Sheet music, 9-1/4" x 12-1/4", Lindy, Lindy, Wolfe Gilbert and Abel Baer, 1927 copyright, black, white, and orange cov **25.00**

Teddy bear, Steiff, light brown mohair, commemorates 100th anniversary of Wright Brothers flight, limited North American edition of 1903 pcs **250.00**

Avon Collectibles

History: David H. McConnell founded the California Perfume Co. in 1886. He hired saleswomen, a radical concept for that time. They used a door-to-door technique to sell their first product, "Little Dot," a set of five perfumes; thus was born the "Avon Lady," although by 1979 they numbered more than one million.

In 1929, California Perfume Co. became the Avon Company. The tiny perfume company grew into a giant corporation. Avon bottles began attracting collector interest in the 1960s. Today's catalogs offer many interesting products, many of which may become collectibles.

Collecting Hints: Avon collectibles encompass a wide range of objects, including California Perfume Company bottles, decanters, soaps, children's items, jewelry, plates, and catalogs. Another phase of collecting focuses on Avon Representatives' and Managers' awards. Avon products are well marked with one of four main marks. There is a huge quantity of collectibles from this company; collectors should limit their interests. Although they may be harder to find, do include some foreign Avon collectibles. New items take longer to increase in value than older items. Do not change the object in any way; this destroys the value.

Aftershave, station wagon, Wild Country after shave, description of 1923 car on back, NRFB, $5.

Beauty products

After shave or cologne decanter, figural Coleman Lantern, Deep Woods cologne, 5-1/2" h, MIB **28.00**
Country Vendor, Wild Country after shave, 7" l, MIB **20.00**
First Volunteer, fire engine, 6" l **50.00**
Stagecoach, Oland after shave, 5-1/2" l **30.00**
Station Wagon, Tai Winds after shave, 7" l, MIB **15.00**
Steamboat Natchez, Spicy after shave, 7-1/2" l, MIB **18.00**
Volkswagen, Oland after share, 6" l, MIB **50.00**

Bath salts, Ariel, California Perfume Co., ribbed glass jar, 1903 .... **135.00**

Body splash, tennis ball, 3 oz, light green flocking, green cap, 1977 .... **4.00**

Bubble bath
Christmas Sparkler, red, 1969 .... **10.00**
Mickey Mouse, figural plastic container, 4-1/2" fl oz, MIB **12.00**

Cologne
Betsy Ross, glass, white, 1976 ...... **15.00**
Moodwind, dogwood flower design, paper label, 3" h **15.00**

Decanter, Skin So Soft, 5-3/4 oz, cylindrical carton, 1962 .... **18.00**

Foaming bath oil, cruet, amber, ribbed, 1973 .... **6.50**

Guest soap set, Winter Frolics, 6 oz, orig box, 1972 .... **18.00**

Hair trainer set, 6 oz bottle, blue cap, red and white label, plastic comb, 1967 .... **25.00**

Hand lotion, rooster, 6 oz, milk glass, red plastic head, 1973 .... **6.00**

Lip gloss, Lucky Penny, 2" d compact type, 1978 .... **4.50**

Hand lotion, coffee pot, 10 oz, full, $4.

Perfume, White Rose, California Perfume Co., clear glass jar, orig neck ribbon, 1918... **115.00**

Sachet, cream type
Petit Point, purple glass base, cloth insert, 1 oz **4.00**

Salt Shaker, milk glass, yellow and white buttercups, yellow plastic cap, 1974 **4.50**

Shampoo, child's, Jet Plane, red, white, and blue plastic tube, white plastic wings, 1965.. **3.00**

Soap
Artistocat Kitten Soap, orig box, 1970s
.... **65.00**
Christmas Children, girl holds doll, boy holds toy rocking horse, 1983 .... **9.00**

Stein, pewter lid, marked "Hand Crafted in Brazil," MIB
At Point, Wild Country after share, 1978, 8-1/2" h.. **50.00**
Car Classics, Trazzara cologne, 1979, 8" h... **40.00**
Flying Classics, 1981, 9" h............. **50.00**
Winner's Circle, 1992, 10" h **50.00**

Talcum, California Rose, California Perfume Co., 3-1/2 oz, 1921....................... **100.00**

Toothpaste, Toofie, 3-1/2 oz, white tube, raccoon, pink cap, pink toothbrush, 1968
.... **6.50**

Wash bowl and pitcher, miniature, blue and white swirled opaque slag glass, 5-1/2" h, 1978... **60.00**

Glassware

Cape Cod pattern, red
Butter dish, cov, MIB...................... **65.00**
Candleholder, MIB **27.50**

Hair lotion, radio, dark amber, gold cap, paper dials, Wild Country hair lotion, $4.50.

Candy jar, cov, 6" w, 3" h **40.00**
Coffee cup **12.00**
Creamer, orig scented candle, MIB **37.50**
Cruet... **20.00**
Dessert plate, 7-3/8" d, set of four.... **35.00**
Goblet **8.00**
Hurricane lamp, ruby base, clear chimney.. **65.00**
Luncheon plate............................. **10.00**
Napkin rings, 1-3/4" d, 1-1/2" h, set of four **45.00**
Salad plate, 7-1/2" d **8.00**
Salt and pepper shakers, pr, MIB.. **42.00**
Saucer.. **6.00**
Serving bowl, #98-363-364, MIB, price for pr **25.00**
Tumbler, 5-1/2" h **20.00**
Vase, 8" h **30.00**
Water pitcher, 48 oz, 7-1/2" h, MIB. **90.00**
Wine decanter **36.00**
Wine goblet, 4-1/2" h **18.00**

Mount Vernon pattern, cobalt blue, Fostoria
Creamer, orig scented candle, MIB
.... **12.00**
Salt and pepper shakers, orig perfume and labels, no box........................... **10.00**

Jewelry

Bracelet, bangle, goldtone, ivory colored flowers... **20.00**

Necklace
Chain, goldtone, five graduated sized gold balls **22.00**
Cross, goldtone, 3" l filigree cross with ruby red center stone, sgd............ **35.00**
Cross, silvertone, 24" l, 2-3/4" x 2" filigree cross with ruby red center stone, four multicolored stones, sgd................ **30.00**

Jewelry, pin, ceramic, pink, blue, and white flowers with yellow centers, and green leaves, tan ground, marked "Avon" on back, $5.

Heart, silvertone, three goldtone puffed hearts in center, sgd **20.00**

Pendant, 3" l brown plastic and goldtone pendant, 23" l goldtone chain, sgd **20.00**

Perfume pendant, swirl dec, 26" l thick goldtone chain, perfume intact, sgd, orig box... **35.00**

Ring, cameo, Perfume Glace, 1970, MIB **20.00**

Suite

Necklace and earrings, Heart of My Heart, faux pearl heart clip earrings surrounded by crystals, matching 18-1/2" l necklace, orig box **50.00**

Necklace and ring, Pale Fire, 23" l silvertone chain, faux peach skin coral cabochon, matching ring, 1975, sgd **75.00**

Tie tac, telephone, gold tone, 1981 .... **15.00**

Miscellaneous collectibles

Bank, Humpty Dumpty, 5" h, ceramic, 1982 .... **18.50**

Barbie

Spring Blossom Barbie, first edition, MIB **40.00**

Strawberry Sorbet Barbie, 1998, shoe replaced, orig stand and box **30.00**

Bride and groom figures, 11-1/2" h, 1992, MIB.. **50.00**

Candle, Gingerbread House, brown and white, 1977 .... **8.00**

Canister set, set of four ceramic house containers, roofs as lids **55.00**

Collector's plate

Cardinal, North America Songbird, 1974, 10-1/2" d **12.50**

Gentle Moments, Wedgwood, 1975, 8-1/2" d **15.00**

Silver Jubilee, stamped "Enoch

Wedgwood (Tunstall) Ltd. England," 8" d **55.00**

Comb and brush set, Hot Dog, yellow and red plastic, 1975 .... **5.00**

Convention bottle, 1973, certificate, 6-1/2" w, 6-1/4" h **60.00**

Doll, Colorsnaps, Courtney, dated 1987, 14" h **30.00**

Egg dish, cov, multicolored flowers and butterflies, gold trim, marked "Produced Exclusively for Avon Products, Inc., Fine Porcelain decorated with 24k gold trim, Avon 1974 1979R"........................ **12.00**

Figurine, Images of Hollywood series, MIB Dorothy, Wizard of Oz, 5-3/4" h, 1985 .... **75.00**

Elvis Presley, 7" h, marked "Copyright 1967 Elvis Presley Productions, Inc." **95.00**

Scarlett O'Hara and Rhett Butler, 1985 .... **115.00**

John Wayne, 7-1/2" h, 1985 .... **90.00**

Nail brush, Happy Hippo, 3" l, pink, 1973 .... **2.50**

Pomander

Bountiful Harvest, spiced apple fragrance, orig box, c1973............. **25.00**

Heart, Wedgwood blue and white, plastic, white tassel, 1973 .... **5.00**

Picture Hat, yellow and pink, plastic, yellow cord and tassel, 1975 .... **5.00**

Radio, 1-1/2" x 3" x 7-1/4", Avon Skin So Soft, AM/FM, aqua on white, bottle shape, orig box and instructions **20.00**

Sachet, pin cushion, Sweet Shoppe, ice cream chair shape **20.00**

Thimble, porcelain, blue and red flowers, marked "Avon"............................... **6.00**

Valet, maroon and ivory box, 4 oz after shave, shaving cream tube, talc can, smoker's tooth powder, 1945 .... **85.00**

Writing paper set, Fragrance Notes, writing paper, sealing wax, goldtone seal, 1977 .... **6.50**

Sales awards and ephemera

Catalog, Christmas issue, 1953, 24 pgs **10.00**

Magazine, *Avon Outlook*, 1953, 20 pgs **5.00**

Pin, manager's, diamond crown, guard, 1961 .... **175.00**

Plate, For Avon Representatives Only, 1977 .... **5.00**

President's Club, Albee Award, 1992 **90.00**

President's Club, Albee Award, 1993 .... **110.00**

Sign, tin, Avon Polish for Boots & Leggings, 8" x 3"... **30.00**

Tea set, Superior Sales Award, teapot, creamer, and cov sugar, 1977 .... **55.00**

Vase, Christmas, 1998 President Club Holiday Gift, 4" d, 9" h.................... **55.00**

B

Banks, Still

History: Banks with no mechanical action are known as still banks. The first still banks were made of wood or pottery or from gourds. Redware and stoneware banks, made by America's early potters, are prized possessions of today's collectors.

Still banks reached their golden age with the arrival of the cast-iron bank. Leading manufacturing companies include Arcade Mfg. Co., J. Chein & Co., Hubley, J. & E. Stevens, and A. C. Williams. The banks often were ornately painted to enhance their appeal. During the cast-iron era, banks and other businesses used the still bank as a form of advertising.

The tin lithograph bank, again frequently a tool for advertising, was at its zenith between 1930 to 1955. The tin bank was an important premium, whether a Pabst Blue Ribbon beer can bank or a Gerber's Orange Juice bank. Most tin advertising banks resembled the packaging of the product.

Almost every substance has been used to make a still bank—die-cast white metal, aluminum, brass, plastic, glass, etc. Many of the early glass candy containers also converted to a bank after the candy was eaten. Thousands of varieties of still banks were made, and hundreds of new varieties appear on the market each year.

Collecting Hints: The rarity of a still bank has much to do with determining its value. Common banks, such as tin advertising banks, have limited value. The Statue of Liberty cast iron bank by A. C. Williams sells in the hundreds of dollars. See Long and Pitman's book for a rarity scale for banks.

Banks are collected by maker, material, or subject. Subject is the most prominent, focusing on categories such as animals, food, mailboxes, safes, transportation, and world's fairs. There is a heavy crossover of buyers from other collectible fields.

Banks are graded by condition. Few banks are truly rare. Therefore, only purchase examples in very good to mint condition—those which retain all original paint and decorations.

Clown, tin litho, Chein, dents and wear, $12.

Advertising, metal

Atlas Storage, litho tin **24.00**
Citizens Federal Savings, cable car, orig key **27.50**
Fulton Savings Bank Kings County, steel, 1" x 3" x 3-1/2", brass plaque with name on front, late 1930s **25.00**
Harris Trust and Savings, Chicago, lion, pot metal **30.00**
Lucas Paint, litho tin **24.00**
Nipper, cast iron, 8" w, paint flaking ... **75.00**
Ocean Spray Cranberry Juice, litho tin **24.00**
Old Dutch Cleanser, litho tin **28.00**
Schlitz Beer, can shape, 1960s, 3" d, 7-3/4" h **5.00**

Ceramic

Dry Dock Savings Bank, 5" x 5-1/4", ship's wheel, rope, seashells, 1950s **20.00**
Snoopy, figural
    Italy, c1969, 6" h **75.00**
    With Woodstock, 40th Anniversary, orig hang-tag, unused **30.00**
Chalkware, clown, 12-1/2" h **65.00**

Lewis Bros. Home Dressed Meats delivery truck, metal, red body, black trim, white lettering, **$35**.

Composition

Barrel, yellow, marked "Sunny Future," made by Broadhaven Mfg Co., NY, some damage to orig label, metal lid slightly bent.. **20.00**

Buffalo, brown and black, green grassy base marked "Buffalo Savings," late 1940s **48.00**

Collectors type, Brookfield Collectors Guild, Inc., Chevy Suburban, blue, NRFB, **$10**.

Metal

Atomic, litho and diecut tin, Hobbyville Toy Co., 1950s, 10" h **110.00**

Building, "Bank," 2" w, 3" h, orig silver paint flaking **70.00**

Boxer, cast iron, orig gold paint, A. C. Williams, c1912-28, 4-1/2" h **250.00**

Elephant, cast iron, red blanket, wheels **90.00**

Horse, cast iron, black, emb "Beauty" . **65.00**

Jack and Jill, diecast, dark bronze finish, holding pail, 5" h............................... **35.00**

Lion, cast iron, orig gold paint, Arcade, c1910-13, 4" h **95.00**

Pig, pot metal, painted gold, seated... **65.00**

Prancing horse, orig gold paint, Arcade, c1910, 7-1/4" h **185.00**

Safe, cast iron, marked "Security/Safe Deposit," letter and number combination dial, 2-1/2" w x 3" d, 3-1/2" h, door hinge broken, unknown combination **75.00**

Schoolhouse, tin, red, snow covered green roof, arched windows and doorway, teacher ringing hand held bell, children coming, marked "School PS 23," marked "US Metal Toy Mfg Co., Made in USA," 5-1/8" l, 4-1/2" d, 4-1/2" h................ **40.00**

Metal, treasure chest, embossed tin, pistol, pirate, sword, and lock motif on one side, sword and anchor on reverse, 3-3/4" w, 3" h, **$15**.

Superman, litho tin, dime register, opens at $5, DC Publications **85.00**

Tank, cast iron, marked "Tank Bank U.S.A.," 1918, 4-1/2" l **275.00**

Thrifty Pig, cast iron, sq base inscribed "The wise pig, save a penny yesterday, another save today, tomorrow save another, to keep the wolf away," 6-5/8" h **95.00**

Top Hat, cast iron, emb "Pass Around The Hat" **90.00**

Plastic and vinyl

Barney Rubble, with bowling ball **45.00**

Bozo the Clown, Larry Harmon Productions, Play Pal Plastic Inc., 1972, 7-1/2" h **25.00**

Bullwinkle, 1973 .... **85.00**

Bus, Greyhound Amercruiser, Jimson, Hong Kong, 10" l, MIB **60.00**

Mickey Mouse, Walt Disney Productions, 6-1/2" h **35.00**

Tweety Bird, animated, holding large hammer behind his back, 8-1/4" h. **10.00**

Underdog, Play Pal Plastics, Inc., 1973, 10-1/2" h **35.00**

Wonder Bread Fresh Guy, orig paper label and closure **125.00**

Diecast, Ertl, 1905 Ford, True Value, red, white, gold, and blue, NRFB, **$15**.

Barbershop and Beauty Collectibles

History: The neighborhood barbershop was an important social and cultural institution during the 19th century and first half of the 20th century. Men and boys gathered to gossip, exchange business news, and check current fashions. "Girlie" magazines and comic books, usually forbidden at home, were available for browsing, as were adventure magazines and police gazettes.

In the 1960s, the number of barbershops dropped by half in the United States. Unisex shops broke the traditional men-only barrier. In the 1980s, several chains began running barber and hairdressing shops on a regional and national basis.

Collecting Hints: Many barbershop collectibles have a porcelain finish. If chipped or cracked, the porcelain is difficult, if not impossible, to repair. Buy barber poles and chairs in very good condition or better. A good appearance is a key consideration. Many old barbershops are still in business. Their back rooms often contain excellent display pieces. Collectors are also starting to appreciate the products used in early beauty parlors. Some collectors now include home beauty products in their collections. Watch for attractive packaging and endorsements by famous people.

Advertising paperweight, Coates Clipper, Coates Clipper Mfg. Co., Worcester, Mass, glass, slogan "For Barbers and Horseman," 1" x 2-1/2" x 4", early 1900s
.... **50.00**

Barber bottle, glass
Bristol, white, enamel and gold trim, 7" h
.... **60.00**
Hobnail, amber, 7" h **95.00**
Paneled, colorless, band of gold trim, 8-1/4" h **75.00**
Satin, white, emb florals, cartouche for paper label, marked "56 (triangle over oval) 4", Federal Law Forbids Sale or Re-Use of This Bottle," 9-3/4" h **35.00**

Barber chair, Koken, wood, emb filigree on sides, imitation leather reupholster, head rest, child's seat, 46" h to top of head rest, restored **850.00**

Barber bottles, both personalized for Frank Lambert, left: "Bay Rum," pink banding, light house scene, marked "W.T. & Co.," 9-1/2" h, **$650**; right: Tonic, gray banding, cabin scene, marked "W.T. & Co.," 9-1/2" h, **$650**.

Catalog, *Success Barber Supply,* Moravia, IA, c1933, Illustrated Catalog No. 8, 30 pgs, 5-3/4" x 8-3/4" **25.00**

Comb holder
Barbicide Germicide & Disinfectant, glass jar, aluminum lid and drain caddy, rubber base, base marked "King Research Inc., Glass Made in Canada, 4764," 11-1/2" h **35.00**
Jeris Disinfecting System, heavy glass jar, turquoise plastic lid and strainer, 11-1/4" h **48.00**
Counter mat, 9" x 8", Wardonia Razor Blades, rubber **20.00**

Hair net, orig envelope, 4-1/2" x 6-1/2"
Sensation **12.00**
Venida's **10.00**

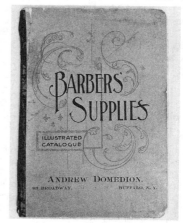

Catalog, *Barbers' Supplies,* Andrew Domedion, Buffalo, NY, illustrated, 140 pages, **$60**.

Pole

31-1/4" to top of porcelain, wall mounted, red and white striped glass, porcelain top and mount, heavy soiling, oxidation to aluminum **550.00**

37" to top of porcelain, floor standing, porcelain, disassembled, glass cylinder, red and white insert, top globe missing, warped insert **375.00**

91" h, floor standing, porcelain, beige, green, red, and white, top cylinder rotates, round white top globe... **1,200.00**

Razor, straight

Bakelite, Sheffield, brown Bakelite handle, celluloid separator, marked "Non-XXL, Sheffield, England, No. 309, Finest Hollow Ground, Joseph Allen & Sons" **35.00**

Bone, English, Dyer, marked "Dyer, Plymouth" **35.00**

Bone, English, marked "Hopkins/22 New Bond St".. **45.00**

Celluloid, Geneva, cream colored handle, marked "Geneva Cutlery Corp, Geneva, NY, USA," stamped pyramid mark with "7N"... **35.00**

Celluloid, Sheffield, England, Art Nouveau emb dec on black celluloid handle, c1892 .... **40.00**

Scuttle shaving mug, floral transfer dec, cobalt blue rim and handle, 6" l, 4-1/4" h **50.00**

Child's barber chair, white carousel-type pony with green, black, and rose trim, green seat, white base with chrome trim, restored, **$3,800**.

Shaving mug, hand painted

C. Lemmon, gold name and laurel wreath, 3-1/2" h **50.00**

Floral dec, marked "Ironstone China," c1890 .... **65.00**

Floral dec in three panels, embossed, fancy handle, 3-1/2" h, wear to gold trim **50.00**

Horseman, sgd "Sparta," late 1950s **35.00**

Leaves and berries, rect cartouche with scene of birds flying over mountains, worn gold on rim, illegible backstamp, 3-5/8" h **65.00**

Sign, Barber, Bastian Bros, NY Allied Printing, Rochester, 15" x 6" **165.00**

Razor, Gillette, gold-plated, original case and blades, $35.

Tin

Gem Cutlery Co, 5-3/8" h, 1-3/8" d, image of gentleman shaving on front, adv on back **300.00**

Yankee Blades, 1-1/4" w, 2-1/4" l, tin litho, eagles and center image of man shaving, red ground **200.00**

Barbie

History: In 1945, Harold Matson (MATT) and Ruth and Elliott (EL) Handler founded Mattel. Initially the company made picture frames but became involved in the toy market when Elliott Handler began to make doll furniture from scrap material. When Harold Matson left the firm, Elliott Handler became chief designer and Ruth Handler principal marketer. In 1955, Mattel advertised its products on "The Mickey Mouse Club," and the company prospered.

In 1958, Mattel patented a fashion doll. The doll was named "Barbie" and reached the toy shelves in 1959. By 1960, Barbie's popularity was assured.

Development of a boyfriend for Barbie, named Ken after the Handlers' son, began in 1960. Over the years, many other dolls were added. Clothing, vehicles, room settings, and other accessories became an integral part of the line.

From September 1961 through July 1972, Mattel published a Barbie magazine. At its peak, the Barbie Fan Club was second only to the Girl Scouts as the largest girls' organization in the United States.

Barbie has now become a billion-dollar baby, the first toy in history to reach this prestigious mark—that's a billion dollars per year, just in case you're wondering.

Collecting Hints: Never forget that a large quantity of Barbie dolls and related material has been manufactured. Because of this easy availability, only objects in excellent to mint condition with original packaging (also in very good or better condition) have significant value. If items show signs of heavy use, their value is probably minimal.

Collectors prefer items from the first decade of production. Learn how to distinguish a Barbie #1 doll from its successors. The Barbie market is one of subtleties.

Some collectors have shifted their focus from the dolls themselves to the accessories. There have been rapid price increases in early clothing and accessories.

Bob Mackie, Moon Goddess, NRFB, $40.

Activity book, Skipper and Scott Beauty Sticker Fun, 1980 .... **5.00**
Bed, Starlight, canopy and bed linens, lamp, orig box, 1991, played-with condition **18.00**
Book
  Barbie Solves A Mystery, Random House, 1963 .... **20.00**
  Barbie's Hawaiian Holiday, Random House, 1963 .... **20.00**
  Barbie's New York Summer, Random House, 1962 .... **25.00**
Box
  Barbie, for issue No. 850, brunette ponytail, 1962 .... **115.00**
  Ken, for issue No. 750, 1961 .... **115.00**
Car
  Corvette, 1968, MIB **60.00**
  Hot Rod, #1460, 1963 .... **195.00**
Carrying case
  Barbie and Francie, light blue vinyl, white vinyl handle, 1965 .... **80.00**
  Barbie and Midge, pink, 1964 .... **30.00**
  Fashion Queen Barbie, red, 1963 **215.00**
  Ken, vinyl, 1962 .... **35.00**
Christmas ornament, Hallmark, 1993, red dress, 1st edition **125.00**
  Colorforms set **15.00**
Cookbook, *Barbie's Easy-As-Pie Cookbook,* Cynthia Lawrence, 1964, 1st printing, 114 pgs **15.00**
Diary, 1963, unused **20.00**

Barbie, summertime Coca-Cola theme, holding glass in one hand, Coca-Cola advertising fan in other, red and white striped outfit, NRFB, $48.

Doll, Barbie
  American Girl Barbie, ash blonde, side part, bendable legs, replaced ribbon, orig one-pc swimsuit, turquoise open toe shoes, NM **1,200.00**

Bubble cut, platinum blond, straight legs, one pc red nylon swimsuit, red open toe shoes, orig box with black wire stand, orig box, VG **175.00**

Color Magic Barbie, lemon yellow hair, yellow metal barrette, undressed, no box, VG **365.00**

Happy Holidays, orig box, 1988, #1, NRFB **230.00**

Happy Holidays, 1989, NRFB **70.00**

Happy Holidays, 1994, NRFB, box slightly scuffed, sticker residue on plastic window.. **35.00**

Pink Splendor, limited edition, 1996, NRFB **255.00**

Ponytail, #2, blond, straight legs, black and white striped swimsuit, hoop earrings, white rimmed glasses with blue lenses, black open toe shoes, pedestal stand with black plastic base, wire top, pink cover booklet, orig box, VG, hair retied **2,500.00**

Ponytail, #3, blond, orig set, black and white striped swimsuit, black open toe shoes, white glasses with blue lenses, G **500.00**

Ponytail, #5, brunette, orig set, black and white striped swimsuit, white rimmed glasses with blue lenses, pink cover booklet, black wire stand, NMIB... **275.00**

Ponytail, #6, blond, red nylon one-pc swimsuit, red open toe shoes, orig box with cardboard liner, black wire stand, light blue cover booklet, VG **215.00**

Quick Curl Barbie, blond, T'N'T waist, bent legs, pink and white gingham dress, white nylon sleeves, black ribbon accents, VG.................................... **95.00**

Russell Stover Candies, © 1996, blond, multicolored dress, MIB.................. **30.00**

Solo In the Spotlight, porcelain, limited edition, 1989, orig shipping box, MIB **45.00**

Sun Luvin Malibu Barbie, © 1978 Mattel, mirrored sunglasses, tan lines, MIB **25.00**

Swirl Ponytail, platinum hair, yellow ribbon tie, red nylon swimsuit, attached wrist tag, white cover booklet, orig box, VG, some strands of hair loose..................... **550.00**

Teen Talk Barbie, #1612, © 1991 Mattel, Black, NRFB **55.00**

Twist 'n' Turn, blond, pink lips, bent legs, orig multicolored diamond checked knit swimsuit, booklet, paper label, NRFB **300.00**

Twist 'n' Turn, brunette, dark pink lips, hot pink and white tricot swimsuit, wrist tag, NRFB, box age discolored **375.00**

Water Lily Barbie, limited edition, Claude Monet, first in series, 1997, NRFB .. **45.00**

Jewel Princess Barbie, red plaid skirt, NRFB, $60.

Doll, Barbie's family and friends

Allan, painted red hair, straight legs, blue swim trunks, wrist tag, cork sandals, black wire stand, booklet, orig box, VG **65.00**

Christie, Twist 'n' Turn, dark reddish-brown hair, orig one-pc pink and yellow tricot swimsuit, wrist tag, clear plastic stand, NRFB.................................. **275.00**

Francie, black, brown hair, bent leg, orig two-pc multicolored print swimsuit, attached nylon cover-up, wrist tag, NRFB, box age discolored **1,900.00**

Francie, blond, straight leg, orig two-pc red and white swimsuit, red soft pointed toe heels, white comb, gold wire stand, orig pamphlet, replaced box insert, orig box, G **175.00**

Francie, brunette, two-pc yellow nylon swimsuit, orig clear plastic bag, cardboard hanger, NRFP, orig price sticker... **250.00**

Francie, Growing Hair, 1970 .... **75.00**

Julia, Twist 'n' Turn, two-pc uniform, 1969 .... **35.00**

Ken, painted blond hair, straight legs, red swim trunks, red and white striped jacket, wrist tag, cork sandals, black wire stand, partial box insert, orig box, MIB... **120.00**

Ken, painted brunette hair, bent legs, red swim trunks, blue jacket, booklet, cork sandals, black wire stand, NRFB, box in F condition, age discolored, scuffed **125.00**

Ken, painted brunette hair, straight legs, red swim trunks, red and white striped jacket, VG...................................... **50.00**

Midge, ash blond, pink lips, bent legs, orig one-pc striped knit swimsuit, wrist tag, gold wire stand, booklet, orig box, NRFB **550.00**

Midge, ash blond, pink lips, straight legs, two-pc blue nylon swimsuit, VG **70.00**

Skipper, Camp Barbie, #11076, © 1993, Mattel, NRFB **25.00**

Skipper, Pose'n Play, blond, blue and white outfit, wrist tag, orig clear plastic bag, cardboard hanger, NRFP **85.00**

Skipper, blond, straight leg, one-pc red and white swimsuit, red flats, metal head band, partial wrist tag, white plastic comb and brush, booklet, orig box **95.00**

Skooter, straight leg, lavender dress, attached slip, matching purse and shoes, cross necklace, played-with condition **40.00**

Stacey, talking, blond, green ribbon, blue and silver lame swimsuit, wrist tag, clear plastic stand, non-working, NRFB **325.00**

Grooming set, Hi-Fashion, Barbie Foaming Bath Oil, Barbie Cologne, two bars of soap, orig cardboard box insert, partially used, age discoloration, wear and damage to orig box....................... **465.00**

Knitting case, purple vinyl, butterfly print canister, matching lid, metal closure, dark pink braided handle, VG................ **60.00**

Lunch box, The World of Barbie, vinyl, blue, multicolor images of Barbie, copyright 1971 Mattel, King-Seeley, used, 6-3/4" x 8-3/4" x 4" d...................................... **50.00**

Magazine, Mattel Barbie Magazine, March-April, 1969 .... **15.00**

Outfit

American Airlines Stewardess, #984, blue jacket with white trim, silver wings, blue skirt, white body blouse, blue hat with metal insignia, blue flight bag with white insignia, black open toe shoes **90.00**

Arabian Nights, #0874, Ken, 1963, NRFC **125.00**

Barbie Learns to Cook, #1634, print dress, toaster, tea kettle, three pots with lids, pot holder, VG, some discoloration **85.00**

Benefit Performance, #1667, red velvet tunic, flared skirt, red open toe shoes, VG **145.00**

Bride's Dream, #0947, NRFB **265.00**

Bride's Maid Dress, hat and lace leggings, tagged, played-with condition **12.00**

Campus Sweetheart, #1616, white satin gown, gloves, pink pearl necklace, red shoes, silver trophy, NM **255.00**

Career Girl, #954, black and white tweed, VG **80.00**

Coat, Francie, vinyl, tagged, 1965, loose **25.00**

Coat, Ken, blue felt, double breasted, played-with condition **22.00**

Dog 'n' Duds, #1613, wooly gray poodle, red velvet coat, VG **70.00**

Fur stole, 1960s **20.00**

Garden Tea Party, #1606, 1964 ..... **30.00**

Going Huntin', #1409, Ken, NRFB **115.00**

Golden Elegance, #992, brocade, VG **115.00**

Midnight Princess Barbie, NRFB, **$55**.

Winter Princess Barbie, NRFB, **$65**.

Junior Prom, #1614, red gown, white fur stole, gloves, pearl on chain necklace, red open toe shoes, NM **165.00**
Ken in Switzerland, #0776, NRFB **155.00**
Land & Sea, #1917, Skipper, NRFB **125.00**
Learning to Ride, #1935, Skipper, NRFB **155.00**
Let's Dance, #978, VG **55.00**
Masquerade, #944, NRFB............ **265.00**
Midnight Blue, #1617, NM-VG...... **150.00**
Mr. Astronaut, #1641, Ken, NRFB. **285.00**
Orange Blossom, #987, yellow, NM **50.00**
Plantation Belle, #966, pink sheer, VG **150.00**
Registered Nurse, #991, white uniform, NM **85.00**
Saturday Matinee, #1615, NM/VG **310.00**
School Teacher Dress, played-with condition **6.00**
Ship Ahoy, #1918, 1964 .... **27.50**
Shirt, Skipper, hot pink, orig hanger, tagged **5.00**
Solo in the Spotlight, #982, VG....... **85.00**
Sweater, Ken, red, orig card, black hanger, yellow cover booklet, orig cellophane...................................... **35.00**
Sweatshirt, Ken, orange, white cord, orig card, black hanger, yellow cover booklet, orig cellophane **30.00**
Tennis Tunic, #1221, Francie, NRFB **95.00**
The Combination, #1234, Francie, NRFB **125.00**
Theatre Date, green, G **60.00**
Time for Tennis, #790, Ken, NRFB **115.00**

Spiegel Shopping Chic Barbie, NRFB, **$40**.

Paper doll book, Whitman, uncut
Barbie and Ken Cut-Outs, #1986, dated 1970, NM **35.00**
Barbie's Boutique, #1954, dated 1973, NM **85.00**

Barbie Dolls and Clothes, #1976, dated 1969, NM **50.00**
Pencil case, Skipper and Skooter, Standard Plastic, 1966 .... **15.00**
Pendant, Sweet 16............................ **20.00**
Perfume set, Kiddle Kolognes Sweet Three Boutique, violet, sweet pea, and lily of the valley, Mattel, NRFB...................... **250.00**

Playset

Barbie Pool Party, Mattel, 1973, orig box and contents, some wear to box and accessories.................................... **50.00**
Barbie Teen Dream Bedroom, dated 1970, MIB, discoloration to orig box **65.00**
Fashion Plaza, 1976 .... **80.00**
Record, 12-1/2" x 12-1/2", 33-1/3 rpm, sealed
Birthday Album **6.50**
Sing-Along **6.00**

Barbie Screen Styler, computer program, NRFB, **$5**.

Carrying case, The World of Barbie, red dress, **$10**.

Barbie Action Scooter, ARCO, MIB, **$15**.

Refrigerator, 11-3/4" h, Mattel, 1987, played-with condition **12.00**
Ring, 1962, MOC **175.00**
Scarf, Hair Fair, lavender linen, Hair Fair graphics, 1986 .... **50.00**
Stand, black wire, mid 1960s **15.00**
Stickers, complete set of 216 stickers, album, display box, Topps, 1983 ... **80.00**
Viewmaster, talking, MIB **72.00**
Wallet, red vinyl, Barbie graphics, vinyl strap, snap closure, 1962 .... **40.00**

Baseball Cards

History: Baseball cards were first printed in the late 19th century. By 1900, the most common cards, known as "T" cards, were those made by tobacco companies such as American Tobacco Co. The majority of the tobacco-related cards were produced between 1909 and 1915. During the 1920s, American Caramel, National Caramel, and York Caramel candy companies issued cards identified in lists as "E" cards.

During the 1930s, Goudey Gum Co. of Boston (from 1933-1941) and Gum Inc. (in 1939) were prime producers of baseball cards. Following World War II, Bowman Gum of Philadelphia (B.G.H.L.I.), the successor to Gum, Inc., lead the way. Topps, Inc., (T.C.G.) of Brooklyn, New York, followed. Topps bought Bowman in 1956 and enjoyed almost a monopoly in card production until 1981 when Fleer of Philadelphia and Donruss of Memphis became competitive. All three companies now produce annual sets numbering 600 cards or more.

Collecting Hints: Condition is a key factor—collectors should strive to obtain only cards in excellent to mint condition.

Concentrate on the superstars; these cards are most likely to increase in value. Buy full sets of modern cards. In this way, you have the superstars of tomorrow on hand. When a player becomes a member of the Baseball Hall of Fame, the value of his cards and other memorabilia will increase significantly.

The price of cards fluctuates rapidly, often changing on a weekly basis. Spend time studying the market before investing heavily.

Reproduced cards and sets have become a fact of life. Novice collectors should not buy cards until they can tell the difference between the originals and reproductions.

The latest, highly speculative trend is collecting rookie cards, i.e., those from a player's first year.

Reproduction Alert: The 1952 Topps set, except for five cards, was reproduced in 1983 and clearly marked by Topps. In addition, a number of cards have been illegally reprinted including the following Topps cards:

1963 Peter Rose, rookie card, #537
1971 Pete Rose, #100
1971 Steve Garvey, #341
1972 Pete Rose, #559
1972 Steve Garvey, #686
1972 Rod Carew, #695
1973 Willie Mays, #100
1973 Hank Aaron, #305
1973 Mike Schmidt, rookie card, #615

Notes: The prices below are for cards in excellent condition. The number of cards in each set is indicated in parentheses.

Bowman Era

1950 Bowman, color

Complete set (252) **2,850.00**
Common player (1-72) **12.00**
Common player (72-252) **8.00**
18 E Robinson **10.00**
248 Sam Jethroe **6.50**

1951 Bowman, color

Complete set (324) **8,350.00**
Common player (1-252) **9.50**
Common player (253-324) **6.50**
32 Elliott **60.00**
134 W Spahn **80.00**
143 T Kluszewski **36.00**

1952 Bowman, color

Complete set (252) **900.00**
Common player (1-216).................. **2.50**
Common player (217-252)............. **4.00**
4 R Roberts...................................... **24.00**
8 Pee Wee Reese........................... **80.00**
22 W Ranmsdell **8.00**
44 R Campanella **55.00**
100 S Sisty **8.00**
159 D Leonard **12.00**

1953 Bowman, black and white,
4 Pat Mullin **8.00**

1953 Bowman, color

Complete set (160) **4,500.00**
Common player (1-96)................... **15.50**
Common player (97-112)............... **16.50**
Common player (113-128)............. **24.00**
Common player (129-160)............. **18.00**
69 Charlie Grimm **12.00**
90 Joe Nuxhall................................ **8.00**
95 Wally Moses **10.00**

1954 Bowman

Complete set (224) **850.00**
Common player (1-128)................... **4.00**
Common player (129-224)............. **4.50**
1 P Rizzulo...................................... **60.00**
73 Mueller....................................... **25.00**
135 Pesky **55.00**

1955 Bowman, color

Complete set (320) **2,900.00**
Common player (1-96)..................... **6.50**
Common player (97-224)................. **7.50**
Common player (225-320)............. **14.00**
10 Rizzuto....................................... **13.00**
29 Schoendienst **18.00**
156 Hughes **6.00**
201 Reynolds **7.50**
252 Smalley **50.00**

1991 Bowman

Factory set...................................... **65.00**
569 Chipper Jones........................... **5.00**

1992 Bowman

Complete set **320.00**
549, R. Klesko **10.00**
1993 Bowman, complete set **65.00**
1994 Bowman, complete set **100.00**
1995 Bowman, complete set **300.00**
1996 Bowman, complete set **120.00**
1997 Bowman, complete I set **75.00**
1997 Bowman, complete II set **60.00**
1998 Bowman, complete I and II set, BB
.... **115.00**

Donruss

1984
151 Wade Boggs **8.00**
311 Ryne Sandberg......................... **8.00**
1989
42 Randy Johnson, rookie **6.00**
548 Ken Griffey, Jr., rookie **6.00**
635 Curt Schilling, rookie............... **10.00**
1990, 489 Sammy Sosa, rookie **12.00**

Fleer

1989
548 Ken Griffey, Jr........................... **6.00**
602 John Smoltz **10.00**
1990, Sammy Sosa, rookie.................. **8.00**

Goudey

1939, 4-3/4" x 7-5/16", NM
Luke Appling.................................. **40.00**
Joe Cronin...................................... **40.00**
Bill Dickey **45.00**
Bob Feller....................................... **60.00**
Mell Ott.. **40.00**

Leaf

1990, 25 Greg Maddux **8.00**
1998, 6 Cal Ripkin, Jr....................... **15.00**
2001, 161 Will Ohman, rookie **10.00**

Topps, 1965, Jackie Robinson, #30, **$12**.

Topps Era

1951 Topps, blue backs
Complete set (52)........................ **725.00**
Common player (1-52) **12.00**
3 R Ashburn.................................. **22.00**
50 J Mize....................................... **25.00**
1951 Topps, red backs
Complete set (52)........................ **350.00**
Common player (1-52) **3.10**
1 Y Berra....................................... **27.50**
31 G Hodges **10.00**
38 D Snider **20.00**

1952 Topps
Complete set (407).................... **4,850.00**
Common player (1-80) **14.00**
Common player (81-252)................ **6.50**
Common player (253-310)............. **12.00**
Common player (311-407)............. **25.00**
33 W Spahn **20.00**
48 J Page, error **45.00**
88 B Feller..................................... **20.00**

1953 Topps
Archives set **60.00**
Complete set (280) **5,000.00**
Common player (1-165)................. **11.50**
Common player (166-220)............. **7.50**
Common player (221-280)............. **42.50**

89 Chuck Stobbs **8.00**
92 Paul Minner **12.00**
98 Cal Abrams **10.00**
103 Joe Astroth **10.00**
108 Bob Porterfield **8.00**
124 Sibby Sisti............................... **10.00**
153 Andy Seminick **10.00**

1954 Topps

Archives set................................. **85.00**
Complete set (250) **7,900.00**
Common player (1-50)................. **7.00**
Common player (51-75)................ **8.00**
Common player (76-250)............. **5.00**
3 Irvin **10.00**
32 Snider **925.00**
63 Pesky **10.00**
94 Banks....................................... **175.00**
177 Milliken.................................. **4.00**
248 Smith...................................... **10.00**

1955 Topps

Complete set (210) **7,300.00**
Common player (1-160)............... **6.00**
Common player (161-210)............ **7.50**
6 Hack **6.50**
31 Spah **30.00**
40 Don Hoak **10.00**
120 Kluszewski............................. **20.00**
177 Robertson-High...................... **145.00**

1956 Topps

Complete set (340) **3,000.00**
Common player (1-180)............... **2.50**
Common player (181-260)............ **3.50**
20 Kaline....................................... **875.00**
33 R Clemente............................... **265.00**
180 R Roberts **15.00**
181 Martin..................................... **695.00**
226 Giants Team **12.00**

1957 Topps

Complete set (407) **3,500.00**
Common player (1-88)................... **3.50**
Common player (89-176).............. **3.00**
Common player (177-264)............ **6.00**
Common player (265-352)............ **8.50**
Common player (353-407)............ **2.50**
20 H Aaron **85.00**
30 Pee Wee Reese......................... **30.00**
120 B Lemon **10.00**
366 Lehman **50.00**

1958 Topps

Complete set (495) **2,600.00**
Common player (1-110)............... **3.50**
Common player (111-440)............ **3.00**
Common player (441-495)............ **2.00**
52 Clemente **165.00**
70 Kaline....................................... **50.00**
440 Matthews **10.00**
485 Williams **50.00**

1959 Topps

Complete set (572) **4,150.00**
Common player (1-10)................... **3.50**
Common player (11-198)............... **2.75**

Common player (199-506).............. **2.50**
Common player (507-572).............. **7.50**
8 Phillies Team **8.00**
315 Adcock.................................... **55.00**
462 Colavito's Catch...................... **75.00**
467 H Aaron HR............................. **7.00**
478 Clemente **365.00**
480 Schoendienst........................... **45.00**

1960 Topps

Complete set (572).................... **3,350.00**
Common player (1-506) **2.50**
Common player (507-572) **2.00**
132 F Howard **70.00**
136 Kaat.. **20.00**
464 Braves Coaches...................... **6.00**
564 Willie Mays, All Star **65.00**

1961 Topps

Complete set (589).................... **4,650.00**
Common player (1-522)................. **1.00**
Common player (523-589)............. **7.00**
35 R Stato RC **15.00**
42 AL Batting Leaders **50.00**
47 NL Pitching Leaders................. **50.00**
98 Checklist **7.50**
388 Clemente **225.00**
405 Gehrig Benched.................... **100.00**

1962 Topps

Complete set (598).................... **4,600.00**
Common player (1-370)................. **3.50**
Common player (371-446)............. **5.00**
Common player (447-522)............. **7.50**
Common player (553-598)............ **20.00**
18 Mickey Mantle and William Mays
.... **45.00**
73 N Fox.. **3.50**
470 Kaline **75.00**
490 C Boyer **40.00**
530 B Gibson................................. **85.00**

1963 Topps

Complete set (576).................... **4,200.00**
Common player (1-196)................. **2.50**
Common player (197-446)............. **2.00**
Common player (447-506)............. **2.00**
Common player (507-576)............. **1.50**
10 Leaders.................................... **4.00**
128 Alou **6.00**
138 Pride of NL............................. **35.00**
439 Zimmer................................... **19.00**
492 Wickersham............................ **85.00**
542 St Louis Team **135.00**

1964 Topps

Complete set (587).................... **2,550.00**
Common player (1-370)................. **.50**
Common player (371-522)............. **.75**
Common player (523-587)............. **1.25**
5 Koufax/Drysdale **5.00**
125 P Rose.................................... **55.00**
155 Duke Snider **15.00**
243 H Aaron.................................. **35.00**

1965 Topps

Complete set (598).................... **3,350.00**
Common player (1-506) **1.00**

Common player (507-598)............... **1.50**
10 NL Pitching Leaders **28.00**
138 Bob Gibson, World Series **6.00**
481 Cleveland Indians Team **7.00**

1966 Topps
Complete set (598) **3,500.00**
Common player (1-506).................. **1.00**
Common player (507-598)............... **3.50**
70 Yastrzemski **20.00**
420 Marichal................................. **11.00**
428 Alomar................................... **65.00**
590 Skowron................................. **95.00**

1967 Topps
Complete set (609) **4,450.00**
Common player (1-533)..................... **.75**
Common player (534-609)............... **2.00**
103 Mantle Checklist #2, SGS 96-9
.... **295.00**
215 Banks, SGC 92-8.5 .... **200.00**
480 W McCovey............................. **20.00**
609 T John.................................... **25.00**

1968 Topps
Complete set (598) **2,750.00**
Common player (1-457).................... **.75**
Common player (458-598)................. **.50**
45 Seaver, SGC 92-8.5 .... **250.00**
144 Morgan **5.00**
408 Carlton, SGC 96-9................. **195.00**
460 Lonborg, SGC 88-8 .... **25.00**
497 Cardinals Team **7.00**

1969 Topps
Complete set (664) **2,200.00**
Common player (1-218)..................... **.50**
Common player (219-327)................. **.30**
Common player (328-512)................. **.25**
Common player (513-664)................. **.30**
7 Leaders **6.00**
75 Aparicio **90.00**
100 Hank Aaron **25.00**
410 Al Kaline **20.00**
564 Hodges................................... **45.00**

1970 Topps
Complete set (720) **1,150.00**
Common player (1-132)..................... **.20**
Common player (133-459)................. **.20**
Common player (460-546)................. **.25**
Common player (547-633)................. **.35**
Common player (634-720)................. **.60**
140 R Jackson............................... **15.00**
210 Juan Marichal.......................... **2.50**
537 Joe Morgan **6.00**

1971 Topps
Complete set (752) **2,000.00**
Common player (1-523)..................... **.25**
Common player (524-643)................. **.35**
Common player (644-752)................. **.75**
180 A Kalkine **10.00**
709 D Maylor **50.00**

1972 Topps
Complete set (787) **1,500.00**
Common player (1-394)..................... **.20**
Common player (395-525)................. **.20**

Common player (526-656)................. **.25**
Common player (657-787)................. **.65**
433 Johnny Bench.......................... **10.00**
595 N Ryan................................... **75.00**
588 Cardinals Team......................... **3.50**
777 Wilhelm SGC 92-8.5 .... **45.00**

1973 Topps
Complete set (660)...................... **700.00**
Common player (1-396).................... **.20**
Common player (397-528)................. **.40**
Common player (529-660)................. **.45**
31 B Bell..................................... **1.75**
193 C Fisk................................... **1.75**
245 C Yastrzemski.......................... **5.00**

1974 Topps
Complete set (660)...................... **500.00**
Common player (1-660).................... **.15**
Team checklist set **60.00**
Traded set **40.00**
50 R Carew **2.75**
456 D Winfield **30.00**

1975 Topps
Complete set (660)...................... **750.00**
Common player (1-660).................... **.50**
61 D Winfield................................ **25.00**
370 T Seaver................................. **7.00**

1976 Topps
Complete set (660)...................... **300.00**
Common player (1-660).................... **.10**
Traded set **40.00**
19 G Brett.................................... **6.00**
341 Lou Gehrig.............................. **10.00**

1977 Topps
Complete set (660)...................... **250.00**
Common player (1-660).................... **.10**
6 Nolan Ryan and Tom Seaver **8.00**
400 S Garvey................................ **1.75**
473 Rookies Outfielders **9.00**

1978 Topps
Complete set (726)...................... **235.00**
Common player (1-726).................... **.10**
6 Nolan Ryan **8.00**
36 Eddie Murray, rookie **30.00**
360 M Schmidt............................... **2.50**

1979 Topps
Complete set (726)...................... **180.00**
Common player (1-726).................... **.10**
25 Paul Molitor **12.00**
39 D Murphy **4.00**
650 P Rose................................... **2.50**

1980 Topps
Complete set (726)...................... **165.00**
Common player (1-726).................... **.10**
270 Mike Schmidt............................ **10.00**
393 Ozzie Smith............................. **8.00**
540 Pete Rose **9.00**

1981 Topps
Complete set (726)...................... **145.00**
Common player (1-726).................... **.10**
240 Nolan Ryan **6.00**
315 K Gibson................................. **2.50**
700 G Brett................................... **1.75**

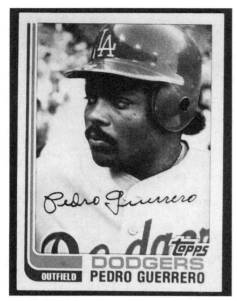

Topps, Pedro Guerrero, #247, 1982, $.25.

1982 Topps
Complete set (792) 100.00
Common player (1-792).................... .05
254 J Bell... 9.00
668 D Murphy.................................. 1.50

1983 Topps
Complete set (792) 115.00
Common player (1-792)..................... .05
Traded set....................................... 35.00
163 C Ripken.................................... 4.50
251 A Wiggins .... .50

1984 Topps
Complete set 40.00
Traded set....................................... 40.00
8 Don Matingley, rookie 7.50

1985 Topps
Complete set 200.00
Traded set....................................... 12.00
181 Roger Clemens 10.00
536 Kirby Puckett, rookie................ 5.00

1986 Topps
Complete set 30.00
Traded set....................................... 18.00

1987 Topps
Complete set 18.00
Factory set 25.00
Traded set....................................... 10.00
366 Mark McGwuire........................ 8.00

1988 Topps
Complete set 18.00
Factory set...................................... 20.00
Traded set....................................... 12.00

1989 Topps
Complete set.................................. 18.00
Factory set 20.00
Traded set...................................... 30.00

1990 Topps
Factory set 25.00
Traded set....................................... 5.00
692 Sammy Sosa............................ 8.00

1991 Topps
Factory set 25.00
Traded set 12.00
45T Jason Giami............................. 8.00
48T Luis Gonzalez.......................... 6.00

1992 Topps
Gold factory set 120.00
Gold traded set........................... 290.00
Traded set.................................... 120.00

1993 Topps
Factory set 50.00
Traded set....................................... 50.00

1994 Topps
Factory set 60.00
Traded set....................................... 80.00

1995 Topps
Factory set 90.00
Traded set....................................... 65.00

1996 Topps
Factory set 60.00
Traded set....................................... 40.00

Upper Deck
1989
Factory set, BB 280.00
25 Randy Johnson, rookie............ 20.00
652 Pat Sheridan, error card.......... 15.00
1990
17 Sammy Sosa, rookie................. 12.00
156 Ken Griffey, Jr........................... 5.00
1991, SP1 Michael Jordon 5.00
1993, complete Set, SP BB.......... 160.00
1996, complete set, BB................. 80.00
1997, complete set, BB (550) 200.00
2000, Victory, factory set 25.00

Baseball Collectibles

History: Baseball had its beginnings in the mid-19th century and by 1900 had become the national pastime. Whether sandlot or big league, baseball was part of most every male's life until the 1950s, when leisure activities expanded in a myriad of directions.

The superstar has always been the key element in the game. Baseball greats were popular visitors at banquets, parades, and, more recently, at baseball autograph shows. They were subjects of extensive newspaper coverage and, with heightened radio and TV exposure, achieved true celebrity status. The impact of baseball on American life has been enormous.

Collecting Hints: Baseball memorabilia spans a wide range of items that have been produced since baseball became the national pastime more than 100 years ago. This variety has made it more difficult to establish reliable values, leaving it to the individual to identify and determine what price to pay for any particular item. This "value in the eye of the beholder" approach works well for the experienced collector. Novices should solicit the advice of a reliable dealer or an advanced collector before investing heavily. Fluctuating market trends are compounded by the emerging interest in—and inordinately high prices paid for—unique pieces, especially items associated with superstars such as Cobb, Ruth, and Mantle.

Because of the unlimited variety of items available, it is virtually impossible to collect everything. Develop a collecting strategy, concentrating on particular player(s), team(s), or type of collectible(s). A special emphasis allows the collector to become more familiar with the key elements effecting pricing within that area of interest, such as condition and availability, and permits building a collection within a prescribed budget.

Reproduction Alert: Autographs and equipment.

Autographed baseball, plastic case, wood base, autographs pale and hard to read, **$15**.

Action figure, Starting Line Up, Kenner
   Johnson, Randy, rookie, 1994 .... **35.00**

McGwuire, Mark, 1998, MOC **100.00**
Olerud, John, 1995, MOC **10.00**
Ruth, Babe, Cooperstown Collection,
   1995, MOC **10.00**
Autographed baseball, Rawlings ball,
   certificate of authenticity
   Buhner, Jay, plastic holder **20.00**
   Johnson, Randy, name and #51 in blue
   ink, holder, wooden base **80.00**
   Wolcott, Bob, #33, sgd in blue ink, holder,
   wooden base **25.00**

Autographed baseball card
   Fernandez, Sid, Donruss, 2002, sgd in
   front in blue sharpie **15.00**
   Fisk, Carlton, Donruss Diamond Kings,
   sgd in blue sharpie **12.00**
   Horton, Willie, Pacific 1990 Baseball
   Legends, #83, sgd in black sharpie, with
   certificate of authenticity **10.00**
   Torre, Joe, #502, Topps, 1984, sgd in
   black sharpie **10.00**

The booth of Empire State Sports Collectibles, found at the March 2004 Atlantique City Antiques Show, was filled with vintage baseball collectibles.

Autographed photo
   Bench, Johnny, Baseball Photo from
   Focus Sports, sgd in red sharpie .. **25.00**
   Dawson, Andre, color photo, sgd in blue
   sharpie **12.00**
   Gaetti, Gary, Topps Baseball Talk #91,
   1991, sgd in black sharpie **10.00**
   Glavine, Tom, color 4" x 6" Disney Wide
   World of Sports card, sgd in black
   sharpie **30.00**
   Johnson, Randy, black and white photo,
   sgd in black sharpie **65.00**
   Lea, Charlie, color photo, sgd in blue
   sharpie **5.00**
   Reardon, Jeff, color photo, sgd in blue
   sharpie **5.00**
   Robinson, Frank, color photo, sgd in blue
   pen **20.00**
   Rose, Pete, sgd on 1977 photo from
   Focus Sports, black sharpie **20.00**

Ryan, Nolan, 3" x 5" black and white promotional Texas Rangers photo, sgd in front in blue sharpie **12.00**
Schmidt, Mike, Donross Champion #11, 3-1/2" x 5", color, blue sharpie **45.00**
Stargell, Willie, sgd on black and white photo, blue pen **20.00**

Badge, Mets 1973 World Series Souvenir, 1-1/8" diecut brass shaped like world globe, orange and blue logo in center **18.00**

Cake decorating set, set of seven plastic figures, ball, and glove, orig card, 1970s **5.00**

Coin

Bobby Shantz, Salada Tea & Junket, 1-3/8" d, blue plastic frame holds full-color cardboard insert with coin, 188 from set of 221, 1962............................. **15.00**
Frank Robinson, Topps, 1971, 1-1/2" d, blue metallic rim surrounds full color photo... **15.00**
Jim Fregosi, Topps, 1964, 1-1/2" d, metal coin, #98 from set of 164 .... **15.00**

Glove, first base mitt, Wilson, right handed, early 1940s, stamped patent number **55.00**

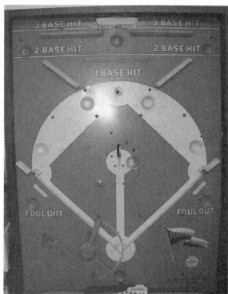

Game, litho tin back, wooden sides, as found, $10.

Hartland figurine, Ruth, 2 .... **175.00**
Matchbook, 2" h, orig matches intact
Philadelphia National League Baseball Club, Home Games of the Phillies for 1940, schedule printed on int. **24.00**
World Famous DiMaggio's Restaurant and Cocktail Lounge, black, white, blue, and orange portrait **24.00**

Big League Baseball, game, tin litho, red, yellow, blue, and green, **$67.50.**

Media guide, Minnesota Twins, Gary Gaetti and Kirby Puckett, 1987 .... **10.00**
Miniature plaque, Authentic Images, limited edition, facsimile 24 kt gold signature, certificate of authenticity
Jeter, Derek and the NY Yankees, Oct. 23, 2000 *Sports Illustrated* cover, MIB **15.00**
Mcgwire, Mark, recreation of Sept. 8, 1998 *Sports Illus Extra Edition*, MIB **12.00**
Nesting dolls, Hideki Matsui, NY Yankees, 2003, MIB.. **15.00**
Pennant, California Angels, red, white, and navy blue, Wincraft, 1980s, 29-1/2" l **10.00**
Pin, New York Mets 1988 National East Champions, 1-1/4" w diecut metal, brass luster, orange, dark red, green, and blue enamel accents, needle post and clutch back **15.00**

The booth of Empire State Sports Collectibles, found at the March 2004 Atlantique City Antiques Show, was filled with vintage baseball collectibles.

Pinback button

Ames New York Giants, 7/8" d brown-tone photo, Sweet Caporal Cigarettes back paper, c1900-1911 .... **18.00**

Champions Wisconsin State League 1905-1906, red, white, and blue pennant on cream, additional red and blue text "New Process Rubber Stamps Are Pennant Winners," red and blue address text for La Crosse, WI dealer, Parisian Novelty name on curl **90.00**

Charlie Grimm Eats Ward's Sporties, 1-1/4" d, blue-tone photo on white, white text on red rim "Good Sports Enjoy…" **42.00**

I Love Mickey, 1-3/4" d, black on cream, Mickey Mantle in sports short, holding black bat, Teresa Brewer in NY uniform holding white bat **135.00**

Irvin, Monte, NY Giants, 1-3/4" d, black and white center photo **20.00**

Leach Pittsburg Pirates, 7/8" d brown-tone photo, Sweet Caporal Cigarettes back paper, c1900-1911 .... **18.00**

Leroy (Satchel) Paige, 1-3/4" d, black and white stadium button, 1940s **115.00**

Moran Phila Phillies, 7/8" d brown-tone photo, Whitehead & Hoag back paper, c1900-1911 .... **18.00**

National League Champions, Phillies World Series, 1983, 2-1/4" d, burgundy and white **5.00**

Rookie Of The Year 1947 Jackie Robinson, 1-3/4" d, brown-tone photo on white, white text on deep red rim . **145.00**

Sam White, 1-3/4" d, real photo, black and cream stadium button **25.00**

St Louis Cardinals 1968 National League Champs, 2" d..................................... **9.00**

White Chicago White Sox, 7/8" d brown-tone photo, Sweet Caporal Cigarettes back paper, c1900-1911 .... **18.00**

Program

All Star Game '99, Boston, 208 pgs **20.00**

Reading Phillies, 1978 .... **10.00**

Pennant, Whiz Kids, Philadelphia Phillies Champions, Eddie Sawyer, Mgr, black felt, white lettering, $25.

Reprint porcelain Topps card, limited edition, Mickey Mantle, 1952, certificate of authenticity................................. **12.00**

Team photo, Elmira Pioneer Red Sox, AAA Minor League team, President Joe Buzzas, Wade Boggs, 1976 .... **18.00**

Top, 2" d, litho tin, slugger in dark blue uniform, swinging yellow bat, background designed as baseball, yellow rim shades to orange, cream text, center black wooden handle, Japan, late 1930s **30.00**

Trash can, metal, black ground, pennants of college teams, 1960s, 10-1/2" w, 12" h **15.00**

Whistle, 2" l, silvered brass, Rawlings, Mfrs of High Grade Athletic Goods St. Louis, USA," 1930s, worn from use **18.00**

Yearbook, Orioles, 1993, third edition, "Go To Cooperstown, Mr. Thompson!" . **10.00**

Basketball Collectibles

History: The game of basketball originated in Springfield, Massachusetts, in 1891, under the direction of Dr. James Naismith of the YMCA. Schools and colleges soon adopted the game, and it began to spread worldwide.

Basketball was added to the Olympic games in 1936. The National Basketball Association was founded in 1949 after professional teams became popular. Today the NBA consists of 27 teams in two conferences, each having two divisions.

Basketball is generally considered to be an indoor game, but almost every town in America has some place where locals gather to shoot a few hoops. Regulation games have two teams with five players each. Courts are 92 feet long and 50 feet wide and have a hoop attached to a backboard at each end.

Collecting Hints: The NBA is trying hard to make collectors out of all their fans. Enjoy the hoopla as more and more collectibles are being generated. Save those programs, promotional pieces, and giveaways. Collectors should pay careful attention to the growing interest in women's collegiate basketball and the enthusiasm it's creating.

Action figure, Starting Line-up, Kenner
Anderson, Kenney, 1993, MOC...... **10.00**
Johnson, Larry, 1993, MOC........... **10.00**
Jordon, Michael, 1998, MOC........ **100.00**
Kemp, Shawn, 1994, MOC.............. **8.00**
Mourning, Alonzo, MOC................ **10.00**
Robinson, David, 1991, MOC......... **15.00**

Playmate Toys Inc., talking Michael Jordan figure,
from the movie "Space Jam," **$45**.

Autograph, basketball
Auerbach, Red, official Spaulding NBA
leather ball..................................... **150.00**
Bird, Larry, sgd and numbered limited
edition, Spaulding leather all-star game
ball **400.00**
Boston Celtics, 20 team autographs,
official Spaulding NBA leather ball,
numbered................................. **2,500.00**
Erving, Julius and Connie Hawkins, ABA
30th-Year Reunion ball.................. **400.00**
Grant Hill, Christian Laettner, Bobby
Hurley, Duke University, Final four ball
.... **275.00**
Pitting, Rick, official Spaulding indoor/
outdoor NBA ball............................ **85.00**
Autograph, card, Kobe Bryant, #7, sgd on
front of Topps Heritage card, 2000-01,
sgd in blue sharpie **45.00**
Autograph, photograph, 8" x 10"
Anderson, Kenny **20.00**
Baker, Vic.. **15.00**

Carr, Kenny **15.00**
Chamberlain, Wilt, 100-point game
.... **125.00**
Gervin, George **35.00**
Grant, Brian..................................... **20.00**
Howard, Juwan, Univ of Michigan... **7.50**
Jones, K.C. **8.00**
Lucas, J.. **25.00**
Malone, Moses **18.00**
Meadowlark Lemon........................ **25.00**
Ratliff, Theo, Wyoming..................... **5.00**
Traylor, Robert, Univ of Michigan... **12.00**
Autograph, press pass
Gadzuric, Dan, 2002 .... **8.00**
Stevenson, Deshaun, 2002 .... **10.00**
Williams, Roy, 2002......................... **10.00**
Autograph, uniform, Wilt Chamberlain, LA
Lakers, double tagged, home **450.00**

Card, Fleer
Allen, Ray, jersey **6.00**
1988-89, complete set, 132 cards,
11-card sticker set........................ **100.00**
1990-91, complete set, 198 cards. **10.00**

Card, Topps
#81, Vladimir Radmanovic, rookie, 2001-
02 .... **25.00**
#87, Zach Randolph, rookie, 2001-02
.... **6.00**
#96, Loren Woods, rookie, 2001-02. **5.00**

Card, Upper Deck
#CM, Cuttino Mobley, jersey, 2001-02
.... **15.00**
#GA-J, Gilbert Arenas, game jersey,
2003-04... **6.00**
#JR-AF, Jalen Rose, autograph, 2003-04
.... **12.00**
#LB4, Lebron James, 2003-04 ...... **40.00**
#TD-F, Tim Duncan, 2003-04 .... **15.00**
#99, Reece Gaines, rookie, 2003-04 **2.00**
#106, Zoran Planinic, rookie, 1999 .. **2.00**
#107, Travis Outlaw, rookie, 1999 .... **3.00**
#110, Dahntay Jones, rookie, 2003-04
.... **8.00**
#185 Tony Parker, rookie, 2001-02. **10.00**
#224, Eddie Griffin, rookie, 2001-02
.... **10.00**
#226, Shareef Abdur Rahim, 2001-02
.... **8.00**
1992-93, complete set, All-Star Weekend,
celloed box **10.00**
Photograph, Grove City, OH, team, 5" x 7",
1930s **40.00**
Press pass, game used, Dan Gadzuric,
jersey, 2003-04 .... **8.00**

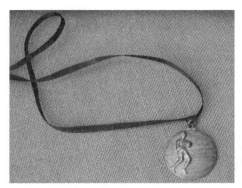

Medallion, basketball player on basketball, marked "E.H.H.S. 1934-35" on back, $20.

T-shirt, St. Joe's Hawk's, red and white
.... **10.00**

Wire service photo, Los Angeles Lakers, 1989
Magic Johnson................................. **7.50**
Magic Johnson and Seattle's Jerry Reynolds... **7.50**
Kareem Abdul Jabbar, A.C. Green, and Magic Johnson............................... **12.50**
Magic Johnson and Phoenix Suns' Tyrone Corbin **5.00**

Beatles

History: The fascination with the Beatles began in 1964. Soon the whole country was caught up in Beatlemania. The members of the group included John Lennon, Paul McCartney, George Harrison, and Ringo Starr. The group broke up in 1970, after which the members pursued individual musical careers. Beatlemania took on new life after the death of John Lennon in 1980.

Collecting Hints: Beatles collectibles date from 1964 to the present. The majority of memorabilia items were produced from 1964 to 1968. The most valuable items are marked "NEMS." Most collectors are interested in mint or near-mint items only, although some items in very good condition, especially if scarce, have considerable value.

Major auction houses have auctions which include Beatles memorabilia, primarily one-of-a-kind items such as guitars and stage costumes. The average collector can participate in these sales now in person or online.

Reproduction Alert: Records, picture sleeves, and album jackets have been counterfeited. Sound quality may be poorer on the records, and printing on labels and picture jackets usually is inferior to the original. Many pieces of memorabilia have been reproduced, often with some change in size, color, or design.

Autographed photo, signed by all four, matted and framed, $300.

Air bed, The Beatles Li Lo Air Bed, 23-1/2" x 58", inflatable, vinyl, Li-Lo, England, 1964, portraits, facsimile signatures, yellow front, blue back............................ **450.00**

Bag, 9-1/2" x 10", textured vinyl, red, portraits, black inscription and signatures, cord carrying strap, 1964....... **150.00**

Bank, 3" x 4-1/2" x 7-3/4", painted composition, Yellow Submarine, Ringo, base marked "Pride Creations, copyright 1968 King Features-Suba Films, Ltd."
.... **250.00**

Blanket, 62" x 80", wool, tan, printed black and red bust figures and instruments, "The Beatles" center, mfg by Whitney
.... **150.00**

Bubble gum cards, Topps, 1964
#12 .... **5.00**
#22 .... **5.00**
#50 .... **9.00**
#59 .... **9.00**

Cake decorating kit, figurals, playing instruments, set of four, MIB......... **175.00**

Coat hangers, Yellow Submarine, set
.... **265.00**

Diary, 1964... **15.00**

Fabric panel, 25" x 46", black and white cotton fabric panel used to produce Beatles dress, Holland, 1964, with Beatles portraits, text, copyrighted............. **250.00**
Handkerchief, 11" x 11", silk like fabric, c1964... **120.00**
Limited edition collector plate, Delphi
  Sgt. Pepper, 25th Anniversary, 1992, orig box.. **35.00**
  The Beatles Live in Concert, first edition, 1991, orig box **45.00**
  The Beatles Rubber Soul, 1992, orig box **25.00**
Lunch box
  Blue, rim wear............................... **225.00**
  Yellow Submarine, some edge wear **125.00**

Metal tray, color litho of four Beatles, each with facsimile signature, marked "Worcester Ware," **$75**.

Magazine cover and story
  Life, Nov. 7, 1969, Paul McCartney and family... **18.00**
  Life, Aug. 6, 1981, Yoko story **15.00**
  Pop Pics Super, 1964...................... **12.00**
  Time, Dec. 22, 1980, John Lennon **20.00**
Mug, 4" h, 3" d, ceramic, bust photos of group wearing blue jackets, England, c1964... **65.00**
Notebook, three-ring binder, red vinyl cov, Standard Plastic Products **95.00**
Pencil drawing, Yellow Submarine, 12-1/2" x 16" sheet of animation paper, 3-1/2" x 7" lead pencil image of group of people looking forward, from numbered sequence, 1968 .... **120.00**
Pennant, 23" l, felt, white, red, and black, printed illus and facsimile signatures, red trim and streamers, "Official Licensee" copyright, c1964 .... **40.00**
Pinback button, 3-1/2" d, set of four buttons for Yellow Submarine, 1968 .... **30.00**
Poster, 39" x 55", life size, full band photo against orange background, black facsimile signatures, orig 13-1/2" x 20" clear plastic bag with orange printing "Beatles Giant-Size Pin-Up Panel, Printed in England," neatly opened **150.00**

Program, tour, Beatles pictured in playing cards, 1964 British tour, minor folds **200.00**
Puzzle, Yellow Submarine, MIB **55.00**
Record album, LP, orig cover
  Love Songs, Capital SEBX 11844, gold vinyl **45.00**
  Magical Mystery Tour, Capitol 2835, stereo **25.00**
  Sgt Pepper, Toshiba, LF-95014...... **35.00**
  The American Tour with Ed Rudy, Radio Pulsebeat News............................. **25.00**
  The Beatles Story, Capitol STBO 2222 .... **25.00**
  The World's Best, EMI Electrola 27-408-4 .... **30.00**

Notebook, white, black letters, sepia-toned figures, NEMS Enterprises, **$40**.

Sales sheet, 8-1/2" x 11", for "The Beatles" vending machine buttons, text "Here's The Hottest Vending Item Yet," price for 1,000 is $12.50, price further reduced for greater quantities, 1964 .... **150.00**
Scarf, 26" sq, white silk-like fabric, silk-screened image in one corner, 1964, NEMS Enterprises, Ltd. Copyright **100.00**
School bag, 12" x 9" x 3-1/2", tan, "The Beatles" printed on flap, handle, and shoulder strap............................... **195.00**
Scrapbook, NEMS, 1964................... **20.00**
T-Shirt, Beatles '65, size large, unused **20.00**
Wallet, 3-1/2" x 4-1/2" tan vinyl, browntone photo, black facsimile signatures, Standard Plastics Products, © Ramat & Co., Ltd., 1964...................................... **65.00**

Beswick

History: Beswick characters are well known to collectors and include figures from children's literature, as well as animals and other subjects. The firm was created by James Wright Beswick and his sons, John and Gilbert Beswick, in 1894. Initial production was plain and decorated wares. By 1900, they were producing jugs, tea ware, dinnerware, flowerpots, pedestals, figurines, vases, bread trays, and other household items. The factory was a family-run organization for decades. Gilbert Beswick is credited with creating the company's shape numbering system and shape book in 1934 while he was sales manager and his nephew, John Ewart Beswick, was chairman and managing director.

The first full-time modeler, Arther Gredington, was hired in 1939. Many of the designs he created are still in production. James Hayward was an outstanding decorator and created many new patterns and shapes. He also is credited with experimenting and perfecting glazes used on Beswick wares.

By 1969, the family members were nearing their retirement years and had no successors, so the company was sold to Royal Doulton Tableware, Ltd. Many of the Beswick animals are still being continued by Royal Doulton, but several have been discontinued. In August of 1989, the animal line was renamed as "Doulton Animals" and numbering system instituted that includes DA numbers rather than the Beswick backstamp.

Collecting Hints: Collectors have shortened the name of these interesting ceramics from House of Beswick to simply Beswick. There are five common marks that consist of "Beswick, England." Some include shape numbers and other information.

Creamer and sugar, Pecksniff, 3-1/2" h
.... **85.00**

Character jug

Mr. Micawber, second version, #310, backstamp and orig sticker, 8-1/2" h
.... **125.00**
Old Mr. Brown, BP-4 John Beswick mark, c1987-1992, 3" h, MIB **215.00**

Kitten, white, green trim, $50.

Peter Rabbit, BP-4 stamp, c1987-89
.... **150.00**
Tony Weller, second version, #281, 7" h
.... **150.00**
Child's bowl, Walt Disney characters, Goofy, Bambi, and Thumper, 6-1/8" d
.... **140.00**
Decanter set, decanter, four mugs, tray, Friar Monk, head as stopper, marked "Beswick" **265.00**

Figure

Alice in Wonderland, 2-7/8" w, 4-5/8" h
.... **125.00**
Amiable Guinea Pig, brown backstamp
.... **425.00**
Barnaby Rudge **60.00**
Benjamin Bunny, Royal Albert, marked "Beswick, Made in England, Beatrix Pottery, F. Warne & Co., 1948, 1989 Royal Doulton" **45.00**
Cardinal, #927, pink, 6-1/4" h **160.00**
Cat orchestra, four pcs, dark gray, 1940-50s, 2" h **235.00**
Cecily Parsley, 2nd gold mark **270.00**
Cheshire Cat, 3-1/4" w, 3-1/2" h.... **125.00**
Clydesdale, marked, 9" l, 5-3/4" h, repairs to ears **100.00**
Fierce Bad Rabbit, first version, 4-3/4" h
.... **165.00**
Foxy Whiskered Gentleman, marked "Beswick, Made in England, Beatrix Potter, F. Warne & Co., 1954, 1989 Royal Doulton," 4-3/4" h **48.00**
Gentlemen Pig, suit and tie, 5-3/4" d
.... **110.00**
Girl, holding doll behind her back, designed by Joan Walsh Anglund, 4-3/4" h **175.00**
Hereford Bull, 4-3/4" h, 7-1/2" l **185.00**
Horse, #915, 4-7/8" l, 3-1/8" h......... **90.00**

Jemima Puddleduck, marked in gold "Beswick Ware, Made in England, Jemima"
Miss Moppet, 1954-78, BP-2 backstamp, 3" h **225.00**
Kanga, Winnie The Pooh series, Beswick and Disney Productions marks, 3-1/4" h **150.00**
Labrador Retriever, black, brown and white eyes, 5-3/4" h **85.00**
Little Pig Robinson, first version, blue stripes, gold backstamp **395.00**
Mr. Benjamin Bunny and Peter Rabbit, Beatrix Potter, BG-3b stamp, 4" h, orig box **165.00**
Mr. Jeremy Fisher, first version, spotted legs, lilac coat, green frog, gold backstamp **290.00**
Mrs. Tittlemouse, first gold mark, 3-1/2" h **325.00**
Old Mr. Brown, Beatrix Potter character, 1955-72, 3-1/4" h **125.00**
Owl, Winnie the Pooh series, 1968-90, 3" h **125.00**
Palomino Horse, #1261, 6-3/4" h.... **165.00**
Peter Rabbit, first gold mark, 4-5/8" h **295.00**
Puddleduck, Beatrix Potter, F. Warne & Co., 1997 Royal Doulton, #33, #15, #29, MIB **65.00**
Racehorse, #1564, Palomino, 11-1/4" h **265.00**
Ribby, Beatrix Potter, gold mark BP-2 .... **195.00**
Samuel Whiskers, BP2 .... **250.00**
Scottie, 3" w, 6-3/4" l, 4-1/2" h **115.00**
Siamese cat, 7-1/4" l, 4-1/2" h **115.00**
Squirrel Nutkin, Beatrix Potter, gold mark **220.00**
Swish Tail Horse, #1182, orig Beswick sticker, 8-1/2" h, 10" l **225.00**
Thomasita Tittlemouse, Beatrix Potter, BP-3b stamp, 3-1/4" h **100.00**
Top Cat and Choo Choo, Hanna-Barbera, 1996, designed by Andy Moss, 4-1/2" h **160.00**
Teapot, squirrel, holding nut, reddish-brown, 7" h **115.00**
Wall vase, beige, blue spots, palm trees, #1063, 8-1/2" h **110.00**

Bicycle Collectibles

History: In 1818, Baron Karl von Drais, a German, invented the Draisienne, a push scooter, that is viewed as the "first" bicycle. In 1839, Patrick MacMillan, a Scot, added a treadle system; a few years later Pierre Michaux, a Frenchman, revolutionized the design by adding a pedal system. The bicycle was introduced in America at the 1876 Centennial.

Early bicycles were high wheelers with a heavy iron frame and two disproportionately sized wheels with wooden rims and tires. The exaggerated front wheel was for speed, the small rear wheel for balance.

James Starley, an Englishman, is responsible for developing a bicycle with two wheels of equal size. Pedals drove the rear wheels by means of a chain and sprocket. By 1892, wooden rim wheels were replaced by pneumatic air-filled tires, and these were followed by standard rubber tires with inner tubes.

The coaster brake was developed in 1898. This important milestone made cycling a true family sport. Bicycling became a cult among the urban middle class—as the new century dawned, more than four million Americans owned bicycles.

The automobile challenged the popularity of bicycling in the 1920s. Since that time, interest in bicycling has been cyclical although technical advances continued. The 1970s was the decade of the ten speed.

The success of American Olympiads in cycling and the excitement of cycle racing, especially the Tour d'France, have kept the public's attention focused on the bicycle.

Collecting Hints: Collectors divide bicycles into two groups—antique and classic. The antique category includes early high wheelers through safety bikes made into the 1920s and 1930s. Highly stylized bicycles from the 1930s and 1940s represent the transitional step to the classic period, beginning in the late 1940s and running through the end of the balloon-tire era.

Restoration is an accepted practice, but never pay a high price for a bicycle that is rusted, incomplete, or repaired with non-original parts. Replacement of leather seats or rubber handlebars does not affect value since these have a short life. Make certain to store an old bicycle high (hung by its frame to protect the tires) and dry (humidity should be no higher than 50 percent).

Do not forget all the secondary material that features bicycles, e.g., advertising premiums, brochures, catalogs, and posters. This material provides important historical data for research, especially for restoration.

Advertising

Brochure, Schwinn-Built Bicycles, 3-1/4" x 6", illus of nine bicycles, c1948....... **55.00**

Lapel stud

Miller's 97 Bicycle Lamp, black and white, red accents on lamp, red rim text for Meriden, CT, company, Cheshire..... **24.00**
Road King, 7/8" d, dark blue bike, cream ground, bright red text and accents, Baldwin & Gleason on reverse stud, c1895.. **45.00**
Tanner Special $85, 7/8" d, black on cream, Whitehead & Hoag, c1896. **20.00**
The Bl Gear Syracuse, 7/8" d, red, blue, and cream, interlocking blue and red gears, red test, Gleason, c1896..... **20.00**
The P & F Bicycle Seat, black and white, red text, Whitehead & Hoag, c1896 **24.00**

Pinback button

7/8" d, Bellis Cycles, white text on blue, Whitehead & Hoag back paper, c1896 .... **18.00**
7/8" d, Corbin Brake, black and white brake in center on dark green, initial "C" against pale green shaded ground, Whitehead & Hoag back paper, c1901-12... **18.00**
7/8" d, Crawford Cycles, blue text, lightly printed floral and cream ground, Whitehead & Hoag back paper, c1896 .... **15.00**
7/8" d, League Bicycles, overlapping wing logo in dark yellow against black and white spoke design, bright red circle, "Mnf'd by League Cycle Mf'g Co. Milwaukee" on bottom edge, Whitehead & Hoag back paper, c1896 .... **35.00**
7/8" d, League of American Wheelmen, bike rider, multicolored, cream ground, green and yellow accents, blue text, was tobacco giveaway by American Pepsin Gum Co., orig back paper, Whitehead & Hoag **18.00**
7/8" d, Member Fisk Bicycle Club, name in white, red text, dark blue ground, Pilgrim back paper, c1920............. **15.00**
7/8" d, New Clipper Business Bicycles, ship with 10 sails positioned against bicycle spoke design, Whitehead & Hoag, c1896................................... **30.00**
7/8" d, Tiger Bicycle, bright red text, head of growling tiger, red eyes, maker's name "Stoddard Mfg Co." on collar, text "Ride A (tiger) Bicycle Dayton, O," Whitehead & Hoag back paper, c1896............... **45.00**
1" d, Safety First Ride A Morrow, dark red and cream, gold brake hub in center, Whitehead & Hoag back paper **18.00**

Sign, Roadfinder Cycle Tires, porcelain **20.00**

This high-wheeler went home with a new owner for **$1,600** at the March 2004 Atlantique City Antiques Show.

Bicycle

Ace Cycle and Motor Works, metal label reading "George Tenby-Cycling Champion of Wales- retired, 1879-1889," as-found orig condition **150.00**
AMF Roadmaster........................... **500.00**
Bronco, boy's **5,500.00**
Cleveland, lady's drive shaft model, 20" frame... **290.00**

Columbia

Fire Arrow..................................... **300.00**
5 Star Superb, 75th Anniversary edition **375.00**
Standard, 1883, 48" front wheel, restored condition **2,700.00**
Twinbar....................................... **3,200.00**
Dayton Champion........................ **4,620.00**
Dursley-Pederson, English, No. 4, 1903, British racing green, restored.... **4,050.00**
Eagle, Roadster, 1890, high wheel, rotary crank, orig unrestored condition **10,000.00**
Elgin, Black Hawk, 1934................ **2,200.00**
Elliot, hickory safety, wooden spokes and fellows, c1898, as-found condition, needs retiring **470.00**
Fox, companion side by side, 1896, red, restored **3,200.00**
Gendron, tricycle, c1900, tiller steering, 20" wheel, restored **370.00**
High Wheeler, Scottish, 42" h front wheel, primitive, excellent condition..... **3,100.00**
Homer Benedict, tricycle, invalid type **325.00**
Huffy, Radiobike........................... **2,000.00**
Monarch, Silver King, hex tube **825.00**

Pope Mfg Co, Columbia Model #50, drive-shaft, orig condition....................... **400.00**
Roadmaster, Luxury Liner................ **600.00**
Rollfast, Custom Built, Model V200
.... **2,750.00**
Schwinn
  Autocycle, B-107....................... **1,750.00**
  Corvette **300.00**
  Green Phantom, lady's, orig parts including Schwinn Typhoon white wall tires, replaced horn and interior light assembly, restored **550.00**
  Hornet.. **400.00**
  Mark II Jaguar **750.00**
  Panther, Model D-77, girl's............ **900.00**
  Starlet, Model D0-67 .... **500.00**
  Whizzer, restored US Army trim, 1945
  .... **2,500.00**
Seaman, wood frame **3,630.00**
Sears, Elgin
  Bluebird **7,000.00**
  Robin **3,500.00**
  Sklark **2,000.00**
  Twin 30... **700.00**
Shelby, Donald Duck..................... **2,000.00**
Springfield Roadster, c1888, 50" to 100" ratchet drive, orig condition....... **5,100.00**
TRB Alenax, ratchet drive, nice condition
.... **110.00**
Unknown maker
  Boy's, tricycle, butterfly handlebar, leather padded seat...................... **190.00**
  Girl's, tricycle, tiller steering, 28" rear wheels, front treadle drive............ **270.00**
  Hopalong Cassidy **660.00**
  Lady's, hard tired safety type, 1891, good unrestored condition **3,600.00**
Victor, tricycle, 25" wheels, c1890 . **1,000.00**

Two Schwinn bicycles, left: Schwinn Sting-Ray, yellow, original owner's manual; left: Schwinn, Apple Krate, red, $425.

Equipment

Bike horn, Hopalong Cassidy, orig handlebar clamp.......................... **150.00**
Lamp, oil lamp, 19th C **1,100.00**

Nameplate, early 1900s
  2-1/2" h, aluminum, Bloomingdale's Lexington, New York..................... **18.00**
  3" h, curled brass, Roamer........... **20.00**
Spoke reflectors, 7/8" x 3", flat plastic, relief image of Garfield on top, copyright United Features Syndicate, 1978, blue with serious expression, yellow with smiling expression........................... **8.00**

Miscellaneous

Book

  Around the World on a Bicycle, Fred A. Birchmore, autographed **30.00**
  Patterson, 150 line drawings.......... **70.00**
  Riding High, A. Judson Palmer, autographed **85.00**
  The Complete Book of Bicycling, Eugene A. Sloane, Trident Press, 1970, 342 pgs, illus **6.50**

Catalog

  Eclipse, Elmira, NY **40.00**
  Flying Merkel, 1916 .... **250.00**
  G. W. Stevens Bike Suits, orig fabric swatches...................................... **100.00**
  Indian Bicycle **90.00**
  Iver Johnson, 1914 .... **120.00**
  Mead Cycle Co., Chicago, IL, c1923
  .... **12.00**
  Pope Mfg Co., Westfield, MA, 1907, Crescent Bicycles, illus, 16 pgs, 5" x 7-3/4"... **75.00**
  Rollfast.. **70.00**
  Springfield Roadster.................... **110.00**
  White Flyer, 1890 .... **880.00**
Medal, loop at top
  ABL of America, 1-3/8" d, brass, octagonal, shield design with winged wheel at center, surrounded by wreath, curved ribbon design "Competitor's Award 1923," image of man on racing bike, additional text "Amateur Bicycle League Dela. State Championship," reverse with letter "T" inscribed with "Chicago Tribune," maker's mark "Wm Schridde, Chicago" **80.00**
  Cycle Trades of America Award, 1-1/2" d, brass, high relief image of bicycle racer going down country road, maker's stamp "Newark, NJ" on back with company name, first two letters unreadable "...eandheur," c1920..................... **75.00**
  Sterling, 1-1/2" d, silver luster metal, rider on country road, tree in background on left, fence on right, back inscribed "The Robbins Co., Attleboro, Mass," ribbon with "Cycle Trades of America Award," 1920s **85.00**
Photo, Hartford Wheel Club, First Connecticut Century Run, showing 20 uniformed wheelman posed indoors, c1885-86
.... **400.00**

Black Memorabilia

History: The term "Black memorabilia" refers to a broad range of collectibles that often overlap other collecting fields, e.g., toys and postcards. It also encompasses African artifacts, items created by slaves or related to the slavery era, modern Black cultural contributions to literature, art, etc., and material associated with the Civil Rights Movement and the Black experience throughout history.

The earliest known examples of Black memorabilia include primitive African designs and tribal artifacts. Black Americana dates back to the arrival of African natives upon American shores.

The advent of the 1900s saw an incredible amount and variety of material depicting Blacks, most often in a derogatory and dehumanizing manner that clearly reflected the stereotypical attitude held toward the Black race during this period. The popularity of Black portrayals in this unflattering fashion flourished as the century wore on.

As the growth of the Civil Rights Movement escalated and aroused public awareness of the Black plight, attitudes changed. Public outrage and pressure during the early 1950s eventually put a halt to these offensive stereotypes.

Black representations are still being produced in many forms, but no longer in the demoralizing designs of the past. These modern objects, while not as historically significant as earlier examples, may become the Black memorabilia of tomorrow.

Collecting Hints: Black memorabilia was produced in vast quantities and variations. As a result, collectors have a large field from which to choose and should concentrate on one type of item or a limited combination of types.

Outstanding examples or extremely derogatory designs command higher prices. Certain categories, e.g., cookie jars, draw more collectors, resulting in higher prices. Regional pricing also is a factor.

New collectors frequently overpay for common items because they mistakenly assume all Black collectibles are rare or of great value. As in any other collecting field, misinformation and a lack of knowledge leads to these exaggerated values. The Black memorabilia collector is particularly vulnerable to this practice since so little documentation exists.

New collectors should familiarize themselves with the field by first studying the market, price trends, and existing reference material. Seeking out other collectors is especially valuable for the novice. Black memorabilia has developed into an established collecting field and continues to experience increasing public attention and interest.

Reproduction Alert: The number of Black memorabilia reproductions has increased during the 1980s. Many are made of easily reproducible materials and generally appear new. Collectors should beware of any item offered in large or unlimited quantities.

Note: The following price listing is based on items in excellent to mint condition. Major paint loss, chips, cracks, fading, tears, or other extreme signs of deterioration warrant a considerable reduction in value, except for very rare or limited-production items. Collectors should expect a certain amount of wear on susceptible surfaces.

Advertising trade card, Perry Davis Pain Killer, two panels, black boy eating watermelon in one panel, sick in bed in second panel, Henderson, Achert, Krebs Litho Co., Cincinnati, price for pair, $45.

Advertising card, 4-1/4" x 7-1/4", diecut, Hudson's Soap, detailed face of black child, bright eyes, red lips, black text "Mercifulness. Hudson's Extract of Soap Is Merciful To The Clothes, It Only Removes The Dirt, Grease, and Stains, Leaving The Linen Behind-Spotlessly White, Wholesome and Pure," additional text on back, c1890 .... **65.00**

Ashtray, 3" d, bisque, boy in outhouse while other boy waits, marked "Japan" ... **35.00**

Badge, Aunt Jemima Breakfast Club, 4" d, litho tin, sepia face, pink lips, yellow and red checkered bandanna, red ground, white letters "Eat A Better Breakfast," bar pin fastener, c1960............................ **50.00**

Bank, still, cast iron
4-1/2" h, Mammy **95.00**
5-1/8" x 4-7/16", Pickanny, painted red shirt, blue bow tie, England **440.00**
5-1/4" h, Darkey Sharecropper, painted, AC Williams, c1901 .... **150.00**

Bean bag game, Three Black Crows, 24" l, painted wooden standing frame, swing out targets.................................... **195.00**

Bell, Mammy **45.00**

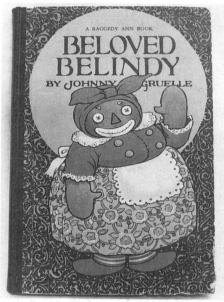

Children's book, *Beloved Belindy,* Johnny Gruelle, 1926, **$25**.

Children's book
Little Black Sambo, 1932 .... **75.00**
Turkey Trot and the Black Santa, 1940s
.... **75.00**

Cigar box
6-1/4" l, Sir Jonathon Brand **45.00**
11" l, Old Plantation Brand, emb **60.00**

Cigarette holder, 5-1/2" l, ceramic, boy with melon, melon bowl for ashes.......... **35.00**

Comics page, Kemple Duke of Dahomey, 1911.. **45.00**

Cookbook, *Dixie Southern Cookbook* **50.00**

Cookie jar, Mammy
Mosaic Tile, yellow **495.00**
Pearl China **650.00**

Creamer and sugar, Black Clown, stacking type **75.00**

Cut-out sheet, 8" x 10-1/2", stiff paper, full-color printed caricatures of jazz band members, intended to be used as table place cards, band members have brown faces, matching red, blue, and yellow marching band uniforms, each playing different instrument, Mayfair Novelty Co, c1930, unused................................ **60.00**

Dart board, 23" h, 14" w, tin over cardboard, Sambo, name on straw hat, Wyandotte Toy Mfg., some denting and scratching **80.00**

Doll, 18" h, Cream of Wheat, chef, stuffed cloth, 1960s **60.00**

Doorstop, 13-1/2" h, cast iron, Mammy, painted, Littco label **265.00**

Egg timer, 2-3/4" h, 0ceramic, chef, white outfit, blue necktie, bright red lips, marked "Germany"........................ **48.00**

Fan, cardboard, Jamup and Honey, black and white illus **40.00**

Figure

2" h, diecut painted metal, porter, carrying suitcase, bird cage, golf clubs, and bat, 1930s................................ **65.00**
4-1/2" h, plastic and wire, black figure wearing red plastic pants, cuffs, bellhop cap, brown plastic head with highlighted eyes, red lips, black hair, single piece of black cloth forms body, arms and feet cloth-covered wire, left hand holds plastic container with two dice, c1930 ...... **60.00**

Game, board

Chocolate Splash, 7" x 10" x 1-1/2", cardboard box, paper label, target game, Willis G Young Mfg, Chicago, 1916 copyright...................................... **150.00**
The Game of Hitch Hiker, 13" x 13" x 1-1/2", Whitman, 1937 copyright.... **75.00**

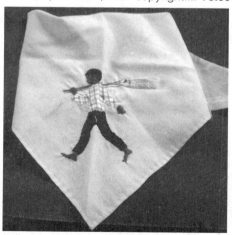

Neckerchief, bright yellow, embroidered young Black boy, carrying brooms over his shoulder, **$15**.

Hair care bottle, High Life Perfume, Valmor Products Co., 3-1/4" h, glass bottle, black lid, label with white man in tux, light skinned Black woman with slick wavy hair, bright red lips, wearing diamond earrings and necklace, orange low cut dress, c1940 .... **25.00**

Letter opener, 5-1/2" l, celluloid, alligator eating black boy, marked "Made in Japan," 1930s **60.00**

Magazine, *Life*, Dec. 8, 1972, featuring Diana Ross on cover **18.00**

Menu, 12-1/2" h, Coon Chicken Inn, 1949, price insert **300.00**

Nodder

   Girl, hp, porcelain, marked "Japan" **300.00**

   Mammy **125.00**

Palm puzzle, tin rim holding glass over emb glossy paper image

   Caricature black face, blue shirt, green ground, dark red mouth slot, five tiny balls serve as teeth, German, c1920 .... **150.00**

   Caricature black youngster eating slice of watermelon, two tiny balls serve as eyes, 1930s **85.00**

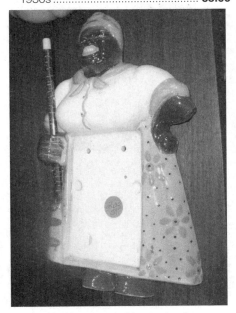

Note pad holder, ceramic, Mammy, head, shoulder, and arms, pink, brown, green, and white, blue flowers on green dress, marked "Ciasa," $65.

Pinback button

   1-1/8" d, I Raise You, black man in uniform holding cable with word "elevator" net to him, art by Goldberg **30.00**

   1-1/2" d, Free Angela, photo of Angela Davis overprinted in day-glo yellow, black text **25.00**

   1-3/4" d, All Power To The People, portrait of Huey Newton overprinted in dark blue, black text **35.00**

   1-3/4" d, Decatur Corn Carnival and Exposition, yellow and black, Negro youngsters enjoying ears of corn, Oct 1899, Decatur, IL **225.00**

   1-3/4" d, Free Bobby, black photo, text overprinted in green, Seale in beret **35.00**

   2-13/16" d, For City Council Florence Lucas, black text on yellow-cream ground, pair of eagles, 1940s NY City council candidate **20.00**

Pipe rack, 12" l, figural, male head with large hat, brass **225.00**

Poster, paper mounted on linen cloth, titled "Girl Chicken Melon Dice Horse Oh What a Dream!," illus good things of life, only bottle of Ripple missing, Quigley litho, poor condition **175.00**

Puzzle, Amos and Andy, Peposdent, 1932 .... **90.00**

Recipe booklet, Knox Gelatin, black child on cov, 1915 .... **10.00**

Recipe holder, Mammy, wood **45.00**

Menu, Mammy's Shanty, Atlanta, Georgia, youngster enjoying watermelon slice, red, black, and white, $25.

Record

   Josephine Baker Chansons Americanes, Columbia Records, 1951, black and white 10-1/4" sq cover, 9-3/4" d record **50.00**

   Paul Robeson, Bass, Ballad For Americans, RCA Victor, 10-1/2" x 12", pair of 78 rpm records **50.00**

Reserve card, Coon Chicken Inn **100.00**

Salt and pepper shakers, pr

Chef holding cleaver in one hand, touches his face with finger of other hand, white outfit, four red buttons, marked "Japan," 1930s, 2-3/4" h.... **20.00**

Jemima & Uncle Mose, F & F **75.00**

Jonah and Whale **85.00**

Leapfrog Boys **90.00**

Mammy & Chef, 8" h, ceramic, Japan, 1940s **115.00**

Native and alligator **70.00**

Salty and Peppy, Pearl China **225.00**

Trainer and Seal **90.00**

Smoking Sambo, cigarette holder, black, white, and red, diecut cardboard, $20.

Print, framed, "Color Man Is No Slacker," young woman saying goodbye to Black soldier, WWI vintage uniforms, newspaper backing on frame dated 1949, $150.

Sign, diecut cardboard

7" d, Hambone Sweets, diecut cardboard, color graphics on both sides, black caricature aviator smiling and puffing on cigar while seated in aircraft, titled "Going Over," orig string loop handle, late 1920s **38.00**

24" h, 12" w, Golliwogg, porcelain **275.00**

24" h, 33" w, Red Cross Cotton, framed cardboard, illus of blacks' picking season on cotton plantation, copyright 1894 .... **200.00**

Stove pipe vent cover, 9-1/2" d, multi-colored, black youngster with straw hat, holding banjo, looking at two others driving car made out of corn ear, watermelon wheels, passenger with pink plumed hat, brass frame and hanging chain, asbestos backing, c1900 .. **125.00**

Tin

3-3/4" h, Delites Cocoa, paper label **50.00**

7-1/4" h, Sunny South Peanuts **75.00**

11" h, CD Kenney, Mammy's Favorite Brand Coffee, Mammy carrying coffeepot and cup **195.00**

Tip tray, 4" d, Cottolene Shortening, litho tin **65.00**

Toy

Dancing Dan, in front of lamp post on stage, microphone remote attached to stage, 13" h, MIB **375.00**

Strutting Sam, tap dancer on pedestal, tin, battery operated, 11" h, MIB .. **475.00**

Transfers, Pickannies, orig envelope, unused **30.00**

Tray, 12" d, Green River Whiskey, black man and horse **95.00**

Wall plaque, 5" l, 5" h, plaster, couple, smiling, each holds one end of large slice of watermelon, two hooks on bottom, c1950 .... **45.00**

Weather forecaster and thermometer, 2-1/4" x 4" x 6", Diaper Dan, brown, red, and yellow, text on orig box "Watch Ma Diaper Change Color, Blue 'Em Fo' Sunny Days, Pink Am Fo' Rain," additional similar text, copyright 1949 .... **75.00**

Blue Ridge Pottery

History: In 1917, the Carolina Clinchfield and Ohio Railroad, in an effort to promote industry along its line, purchased land along its right-of-way and established a pottery in Erwin, Tennessee. Erwin was an ideal location because of the availability of local white kaolin and feldspar, two of the chief ingredients in pottery. Workers for the new plant were recruited from East Liverpool and Sebring, Ohio, and Chester, Virginia.

In 1920, J. E. Owens purchased the pottery and received a charter for Southern Potteries, Incorporated. Within a few years, the pottery was sold to Charles W. Foreman. Foreman introduced hand painting under glaze and trained girls and women from the nearby hills to do the painting. By 1938, Southern Potteries, Incorporated, was producing Blue Ridge "Hand Painted under the Glaze" dinnerware. The principal sales thrust contrasted the Blue Ridge hand-painted ware with the decal ware produced by most other manufacturers. Blue Ridge maintained a large national sales organization with eleven showrooms scattered nationwide. Few catalogs were issued and trade advertising was limited. As a result, researching Blue Ridge is difficult.

Most of the patterns used on Blue Ridge originated at the plant. Lena Watts, an Erwin native, was chief designer. Eventually, Watts left Blue Ridge and went to Stetson China Company. Blue Ridge also made limited-production patterns for a number of leading department stores.

As the 1930s came to a close, Southern Potteries was experiencing strong competition from inexpensive Far Eastern imports, but World War II intervened and changed the company's fortune. Southern Potteries' work force increased tenfold, production averaged more than 300,000 pieces per week, and the company experienced a period of prosperity that lasted from the mid-1940s into the early 1950s.

By the mid-1950s, however, imports and the arrival of plastic dinnerware once again threatened Southern Potteries' market position. The company tried half-time production, but the end came on Jan. 31, 1957, when the stockholders voted to close the plant.

Collecting Hints: Blue Ridge patterns are among the most established of the collectible American dinnerwares. Collectors pay a premium for artist-signed pieces. The Talisman Wallpaper dinnerware pattern, because of its original failure to attract buyers, is the most difficult dinnerware pattern to find. Among the harder to find shapes are the China demi-pot and the character jugs.

Patterns and forms made in the 1940s are the most popular. As in most dinnerware patterns, hollowware pieces command higher prices than flat pieces. Demi-sets that include the matching tray are considered a real find. Blue Ridge collectors must compete with children's dish collectors for miniature pieces.

Because the wares were hand decorated, identical pieces often contain minor variations. Develop a practiced eye to identify those that are most aesthetically pleasing. Minor color variations can change a pleasing pattern into one that is ordinary.

Alice, pitcher, hand painted, 8-1/2" d, 6" h **275.00**
Apple, spoon rest **45.00**
Applejack, Skyline shape
    Bread and butter plate, 6" d **10.00**
    Coffeepot, Ovide **235.00**
    Platter **38.00**
    Vegetable bowl, divided **46.00**
Appleyard, teapot, cov **95.00**
Becky
    Dinner plate, 10" d **20.00**
    Luncheon plate, 8" d **12.00**
Big Blossom, pitcher, Grace shape, mark #5, 5-3/4" h **125.00**
Black Edge
    Bonbon **90.00**
    Chicken Shakers **85.00**
    Chocolate pot **190.00**
    Powder box **135.00**

Plate, red, pink, and blue florals, green leaves, marked "Blue Ridge, Hand Painted, Underglaze, Southern Potteries, Inc., Made in USA," **$10.**

Bluebell Bouquet
Bowl, 9" d, some crazing **20.00**
Dinner plate, 9" d **15.00**
Gravy boat **35.00**
Bud Top, salt and pepper shakers, pr, 6" h
.... **95.00**

Calico
Candy box **175.00**
Teapot, colonial shape **190.00**

Carnival
Mixing bowl, 9 1/2" d **20.00**
Platter, 13" l, oval **48.00**
Carol's Roses, vegetable bowl, open, oval
.... **18.00**
Cassandra, pie plate, maroon border
.... **25.00**
Champagne Pinks, teapot, cov **95.00**

Character jug
Daniel Boone **750.00**
Pioneer Woman **850.00**

Cherry Bounce
Platter, 11" l, oval **38.00**
Vegetable bowl, open, round **25.00**
Chevron, teapot **165.00**
Chick, pitcher, figural, 6" h, all white, vitreous china **75.00**
Chickory, teapot, colonial shape, crazed inside **45.00**

Chintz
Bonbon **85.00**
Chocolate pot **295.00**
Christmas Tree, plate, 10-1/4" d **120.00**
Chrysanthemum, platter **28.50**

Cock O' the Morn
Cup and saucer **25.00**
Dinner plate, 10" d **35.00**
Fruit bowl **20.00**
Snack set, plate and cup **36.00**

Crab Apple
Bread and butter plate, 6" d **7.50**
Platter, 11" l, oval **35.00**

Set, 40 pcs, six each: 5" d berry bowls, 6" d bread and butter plates, cups and saucers, 10" d dinner plates; creamer, cov sugar, platter, round vegetable bowl
.... **425.00**

Platter, red and blue florals, green leaves, marked "Blue Ridge, Hand Painted, Underglaze, Southern Potteries, Inc., Made in USA," 12" l, **$20.**

Cumberland, platter, 13" l, oval **45.00**
Daffodil
Bread and butter plate, 6" d **10.00**
Dinner plate, 10" d **20.00**
Set, 45 pcs, eight each: 6" d cereal bowls, 6" d bread and butter plates, 10" dinner plates, cups and saucers; creamer, sugar, gravy boat, 9" l oval bowl, 9" d round vegetable bowl, 12" l platter, 14" l platter, two pcs with under rim chips
.... **575.00**
Delicious, starter set, 29 pcs, Candlewick edge, four each: 5" berry bowls, 6" d bread and butter plates, cups and saucers, 9-1/4" d luncheon plates, 10" d dinner plates; creamer, cov sugar, gravy boat, round vegetable bowl, oval vegetable bowl **425.00**
Delphine
Cigarette box **75.00**
Vase **95.00**

Duck in Hat
Child's feeding dish **65.00**
Teapot, child size **125.00**
Dutch Bouquet, Colonial shape
Bread and butter plate, 6" d **18.00**
Cereal bowl, 6" d **15.00**
Cup and saucer **18.00**
Dinner plate, 9-3/8" d **22.00**

Easter Parade
Celery tray, leaf shape **95.00**
Creamer and sugar, open **95.00**
Relish dish, round **85.00**
Floral, teapot, 8-3/4" w, 9-1/4" h **280.00**
French Peasant
Bonbon **165.00**
Candy box, cov **250.00**

Chocolate pot, 7-1/2" w, 9" h......... **500.00**
Creamer.. **75.00**
Dinner plate, 10" d....................... **100.00**
Pitcher, 5-1/4" w, 8-1/4" h.............. **200.00**
Soup bowl, two handles................ **135.00**
Fruit Fantasy, cake plate, maple leaf-shape, loop handle, molded grape cluster, 10" l
.... **50.00**
Fruit Punch, dinner plate, 10-1/2" d, Colonial shape **25.00**
Gloriosa, set, 20 pcs, four each: 5" d berry bowls, cups, saucers, 6" d bread and butter plates, 10" dinner plates; creamer, cov sugar...................................... **250.00**
Grape Wine, teapot, snub nose........ **225.00**
Harvest Time, set, Modern shape, 50 pcs, eight each: 5" d berry bowls, 6" d cereal bowls, 6" bread and butter plates, cups and saucers, 9" d dinner plates; 12" platter, round vegetable bowl....... **475.00**
Helen, pitcher, mark #5, 4-1/2" h....... **120.00**

Vegetable dish, Dogwood, yellow and brown floral decoration, 9-1/2" x 7", **$24.**

Hibiscus, Milady pitcher **175.00**
Iris, relish tray, four sections, center handle
.... **150.00**
Irresistible, snack tray, Martha shape
.... **100.00**
King's Ransom, vegetable bowl, cov **85.00**
Mallard
Box, cov.. **675.00**
Salt and pepper shakers, pr........ **395.00**
Mardi Gras
Creamer... **15.00**
Dinner plate, 9" d, Colonial shape... **8.00**
Pie baker, Candlewick shape......... **25.00**
Teapot, cov.................................. **175.00**
Millie's Pride, chocolate pot **275.00**
Mexican, bowl.................................. **150.00**
Miscellaneous, hand painted multicolored floral dec
Lamp, 4-1/2" w, 8" h pottery segment with floral dec................................... **190.00**
Teapot, 8-1/4" w, 7-3/4" h.............. **260.00**
Urn, 4-1/2" d, 7-3/4" h................... **150.00**
Vase, 10" h, boot shape................ **95.00**

Mum Spray, vase, stamped "Blue Ridge China," numbered, 8-1/2" h.......... **95.00**
Nocturne, plate, sq......................... **24.50**
Normandy, platter, Skyline shape, 13" l
.... **125.00**
Nova Rose
Bonbon, flat shell-shape **55.00**
Teapot, cov **295.00**
Orinda
Cereal bowl, 6" d, Colonial shape.. **10.00**
Cup and saucer, Colonial shape ... **22.00**
Pansy Trio, pitcher, 7" h, Spiral shape **95.00**
Petit Point
Child's tea set............................... **300.00**
Coffeepot, cov **145.00**
Petunia Party
Cup... **20.00**
Plate **20.00**
Pixie, bonbon **165.00**
Poinsettia
Bread and butter plate, 6" d........... **9.00**
Cup and saucer, Colonial shape ... **10.00**
Fruit bowl, 5" d **5.00**
Luncheon plate, Colonial shape, 8-1/2" d
.... **15.00**
Queen's Lace, dinner plate, 10-1/2" d
.... **40.00**
Ridge Daisy
Sugar, cov **26.50**
Vegetable, round **28.50**
Ridge Rose, snack tray, Martha shape
.... **120.00**
Rock Rose, batter set tray, Astor shape, single large pink flower with yellow center, four buds, green shaded leaves in each of the four compartments, mauve border, underglaze "Hand Painted Made in U.S.A." logo, 8" w, 13-1/4" l, 1-1/2" h
.... **120.00**
Rooster
Cigarette box, 4" x 4" **195.00**
Egg plate, holds 12 eggs, marked "PV" in circle, 9" d **125.00**
Plate, motto, 6-1/8" d **250.00**
Roseanna, demitasse cup and saucer
.... **35.00**
Rose Marie, chocolate pot **175.00**
Rustic Plaid, snack set, plate and cup, price for set of six **60.00**
Rutledge, dinner service, Candlewick shape, service for four plus serving pieces, price for 22-pc set **250.00**
Sculptured Fruit, pitcher, 7-1/8" h ... **125.00**
Seaside, box, cov, 3-1/2 x 4-1/2" **120.00**
Shell, dish, deep, marked "Blue Ridge China Hand Painted Underglaze Southern Pottery, Inc., Made in U.S.A."
.... **135.00**
Sherman Lily, box, cov, raised figural lily on cov... **995.00**

Song Bird, salad plate, 8-1/2" d........ **140.00**
Specialty plate

Christmas Doorway....................... **115.00**
Christmas Mistletoe......................... **95.00**
Country Home, 9-1/2" d, mark #6 . **140.00**
Flower Cabin, artist sgd "Mildred T.
Broyles" **650.00**
Ham and Eggs, 9" d, jobbers mark "PV"
on back.. **175.00**
Provincal Farm, 6" sq **95.00**
Quail scene, artist sgd "Mildred T.
Broyles".. **900.00**
Thanksgiving Turkey, 10-1/2" d..... **200.00**

Spiderweb, pink and charcoal gray

Bread and butter plate, 6" d **15.00**
Cereal bowl **12.00**
Cup and saucer **20.00**
Dinner plate **20.00**
Fruit bowl **16.00**

Vegetable Bowl

Oval.. **28.00**
Round **28.00**

Spindrift, pie baker **48.00**
Spring Blossom, creamer, crimped rim
.... **20.00**
Spring Hill Tulip, teapot, cov **140.00**
Square Danish, snack set, plate and cup
.... **125.00**

Stanhouse Ivy

Dinner plate, 9 1/2" d, dinner, Skyline
shape.. **18.00**
Set, 45 pcs, Skyline shape, eight each:
5" d berry bowls, 6" d bread and butter
plates, cups and saucers, 9" d dinner
plates; creamer, cov sugar, gravy boat,
13" l platter, round vegetable bowl
.... **425.00**

Strawberry Patch

Bread and butter plate, 6".............. **15.00**
Creamer.. **20.00**
Cup and saucer **20.00**
Dinner plate, 10" d **24.00**
Luncheon plate, 8" d **20.00**
Soup plate, flanged rim **30.00**
Sugar bowl, cov **20.00**

Strawberry Sundae, vegetable bowl, open,
round... **35.00**
Summertime, celery tray, leaf-shape, 11" l,
6-1/2" w **95.00**
Sunfire, creamer, Colonial shape, teal edge
.... **25.00**

Sunflower, Colonial shape

Creamer... **25.00**
Soup plate, 8" d, flat....................... **35.00**

Sweet Clover, dinner plate................. **18.00**
Tic-Tac

Set, 22-pc set **275.00**
Teapot, cov **150.00**
Vegetable, round............................ **20.00**

Tropical, dinner plate, 9" d, Skyline shape
.... **18.00**

Turkey with Acorns, platter, oval, Skyline
Clinchfield shape.......................... **165.00**
Verna, cake tray, maple leaf shape, mark #6,
9-1/2" x 10" **115.00**
Vintage, dinner plate, 11-1/2" d, Colonial
shape **38.00**

Weathervane

Bread and butter plate, 6" d.......... **65.00**
Dinner plate, 10-1/2" d.................. **42.00**
Fruit bowl....................................... **28.00**
Luncheon plate, 9" d **48.00**
Saucer.. **18.00**

Wild Rose, pitcher, 7" h, Spiral shape **75.00**
Winnie, set, Skyline shape, six each: 5" d
berry bowls, 6" d bread and butter plates,
cups and saucers, 9-1/4" d dinner plates;
9" vegetable bowl **325.00**

Bookends

History: No formal history of bookends is available, but it is not too difficult to imagine those eager for knowledge that began to accumulate books searching for something to hold them in an orderly fashion. Soon decorators and manufacturers saw the need and began production of bookends. Today bookends can be found in almost every type of material, especially metal and heavy ceramics, which lend their physical density to keep those books standing straight. Bookends range from artistic copies of famous statuary to simple wooden blocks, offering collectors an endless adventure.

Collecting Hints: Since bookends were originally designed to be used in pairs, make sure you've got the proper set. Check for matching or sequential numbers as well as damage or loss of decoration. Single bookends are sometimes marketed as doorstops or shelf sitters, and a careful eye is needed to find one-of-a-kind items.

Anchors, 8" h, brass, mounted to faux stone
.... **48.00**
B.P.O.E., bronzed cast iron, elk in high relief
.... **75.00**
Cathedrals, 5-1/4" h, 4" w, 3 Gothic doorways, cast metal, copper-colored plating **32.00**
Dolphins, 7-1/2" h, jumping, bronze, verdigris finish................................. **80.00**
Eagles, Frankart, bronzed metal finish **50.00**
Elephants, ivory, teakwood base **165.00**
End of the Trail, cast iron **115.00**

Carnival glass, figural duck heads, dark blue, $20.

Hummel look-alikes, girl with red dress sitting on fence, unmarked, chips, $5.

Globes, 7" h, brass, hardwood base **115.00**

Indians, painted cast metal, K & O Co., 1935 .... **150.00**

Kissing Children, Hubley, cast iron . **185.00**

Liberty Bell, 5" h, bronze **35.00**

Lincoln Memorial, plaster, bronze finish **40.00**

Lyres, 7" h, enameled brass, green shading to black at edges, stamped "Made in Israel" **48.00**

Mandolin Players, 7-1/2" h, bronzed, cold painted spelter, celluloid faces, two-tier marble bases **475.00**

Monks, reading books, cathedral shape, "Solitude" written on base, Art Pottery **150.00**

Peonies, Roseville, yellow floral dec.. **135.00**

Peterborough Cathedral, bronzed cast iron, inscribed "C" inside triangle inside circle, copyright 1928, 5" h **120.00**

Puppies, bronzed pot metal, three puppies resting their heads together, felt base **70.00**

Race Horse and Jockey, bronzed white metal, Art Deco **90.00**

Sailboats, 7" h, solid polished brass.. **45.00**

Sailing Ships, Constitution, chalkware, 5-1/2" **15.00**

Scotties, brass-tone, detailed casting **245.00**

Shells, 5" h, solid polished brass **37.50**

Tom and Jerry, 8" h, Gorham, 1980... **45.00**

Wagon Train, painted cast iron, American Hardware Co., dated 1931, some loss to paint **90.00**

Books

History: Before the advent of television and the remote control, people more frequently read books for enjoyment and personal fulfillment, traveling around the world from the comfort of their favorite armchair. Others enjoyed reading about the lives of famous people, while others escaped into the fantasy world of fiction.

Collecting Hints: Many types of books can be found in the antiques and collectibles marketplace. Watch for well-illustrated, complete, and clean copies. Condition is always a key to prices. Keep an eye open for autographed copies, as well as first editions.

Today's book collectors now have a wealth of Web sites, which cater to locating vintage titles. Just as in the real world, it pays to shop around in this new cyber market.

Eden: Book 1, by Frank Cho, Liberty Meadows, **$20**

A Japanese Nightengale, Onoto Watanna, illus by Genjiro Yeto, Harper & Bros, 1901, 225 pgs **12.00**

Americans-The Democratic Experience, The, Daniel Boorstin, Random House, 1973, 1st ed, dj worn **8.75**

An Eye for the Dragon, Southeast Asia Observed: 1954-1970, Dennis Bloodworthl, Farrar Strass & Giroux, 1970, 1st ed, Book of the Month Club, 188 pgs **8.75**

Aunt Emma's Cope Book-How To Get From Monday to Friday…in 12 Days, Erma Bombeck, McGraw-Hill, 1979, 1st ed., 180 pgs.. **8.50**

Back Roads of New England, Conn., Mass., Maine, RI, UT, NH, Earl Hollander, Clarkson Patten, 1974, 1st ed., 224 pgs, ex-lib **7.50**

Beauties and Antiquities of Ireland, T. O. Russell, 1897, 399 pgs, illus, gold emb front board **25.00**

Ben Hur, Lew Wallace, Harper & Bros, 1908 .... **10.00**

Benjamin Franklin: Envoy Extraordinary-His Secret Missions & Open Pleasures in London and Paris, R. Burlingame, 1967, 1st ed, dj... **12.00**

Bermuda Triangle-An Incredible Saga of Unexplained Disappearances, The, Charles Berlitz, Doubleday, 1974, 203 pgs **8.75**

Black Majesty. The Life of Christophe, King of Haiti, Harper & Bros, 1928, 207 pgs, illus... **25.00**

Bulfinch's Mythology, The Age of Fable, forward by Robert Graves, illus by Joseph Popin, Doubleday, 1968, dj **6.50**

Captain Caution, A Chronicle of Arundel, Kenneth Roberts, Doubleday, 1943, orig map, stain on back cover................ **5.00**

Cold Harbor, Jack Higgins, 1990, 1st ed., dj **8.00**

Court Belisarius, Robert Graves, c1938, 564 pgs **9.00**

Dear Sir, Humorous Letters To Draft Boards, Juliet Lowell, Duell, Sloane, Pierce, 1944 .... **4.50**

Dollmaker, The, Hariette Amo, MacMillian Co., 1954, 5th printing................... **18.00**

Edgar Allen Poe, The Man, M. E. Phillips, 1926, two volumes, 1,683 pgs, illus **22.00**

Eight Bells and All's Well, Daniel V. Gallery, Rear Admiral USN, 1965................. **8.00**

Esther Waters, George Moore, London, 1920, limited, sgd, dj **30.00**

Fake Your Own Antiques, P. Knott, North Light Books, 1996, 128 pgs, photos **10.00**

Fares, Please! John Anderson, Mioller D. Appleton, 1941, 204 pgs, photos .. **14.00**

Five Victorian Ghost Novels, E. F. Bieler, Dover, 1971, 420 pgs, illus.............. **7.00**

Fur, Feathers and Steel – Of Feathers, Hackles, Fishhooks & Other Materials used in Tying Trout Flies, R. Cross, Dodd, Mead & Co., NY, 1940, 2nd printing, 78 pgs, photos.................................... **15.00**

Gandhi, Peter Rhe, Phaidon, **$35**.

Good Night Sweet Prince, G. Fowler, Blakiston Co., 1944, book of the month club edition, 474 pgs, dj................ **12.00**

Griti's Children, Johanna Spyri, 1924, large paste on picture cover, 256 pgs **9.00**

Happiness Hill, Grace Livingston Hill, G&D, 1912, illus... **6.00**

Heart of the Hills, The, John Fox, Jr., Schribners, 1913, 1st ed, illus........ **10.00**

Heroes of American Discovery, N D'Anvers, George Routledge & Son, 1885, 281 pgs, illus **20.00**

Holy Terror, Andy Warhol Close Up, Bob Colacello, Harper Collins, 1990, photos **12.00**

Hoosier Book of Riley Verse, The, James Whitcomb Riley, Bobbs-Merrill, 1906, 598 pgs **20.00**

I'll Die Before I'll Run-Story of the Great Fueds of Texas, C. L. Sonnichsen, 1951, illus, 300 pgs **45.00**

Jack London Stories, The Call of the Wild, The Cruise of the Dazzler and Others, Platt & Munk Publishers, 1980, 528 pgs **8.00**

Journals of Lewis and Clark, The, Devoto, 1953, 500 pgs, maps **45.00**

Knowing, Collecting, & Restoring Early American Furniture, forward by E. Keyes, 59 illus, 22 line drawings, Lippencott, 1931, 156 pgs **10.50**

Know Your Woods: Their Identification, Properties, and Uses, A. Constantine, Jr., 1959, 384 pgs **13.00**

Life of Colonel Paul Revere, The, Henry Goss, 2 vols, 1902, 5th ed., portraits, facsimiles, gilt dec **30.00**

Life Story of the Lewis & Clark Guide, Sacagawea of the Shoshones, Emmon, 1943, 300 pgs, photos, maps **45.00**

The Life and Adventures of Santa Claus, by L. Frank Baum, **$45**.

Look Down That Winding River, An Informal Profile of the Mississippi, Ben L. Burman, illus by Alice Caddy, David & Chas, 1973, 192 pgs, dj **7.00**

Lore of the Lakes, Told In Story & Picture, Dana Thomas Bowen, Freshwater Press, 1969, 9th printing, 314 pgs, photos **15.00**

Marcus Aurelius, A Birley, 1966, 354 pgs **10.00**

Meet General Grant, W. E. Woodward, Garden City, 1928, 524 pgs, illus..... **7.50**

Mountain Man, Jim Bridger, Rocky Mountain Fur Co., 1946, 323 pgs **35.00**

Mr Skeffington, Elizabeth, Doubleday, 1940, 322 pgs, dj **10.00**

Narrative of the Life of David Crockett of the State of Tennessee, Paul Hutton, originally written by David Crockett 1834, copyright 1987, 200 pgs **35.00**

Nature in Miniature, Knopf, 1989, 400 pgs, illus, 1st ed **9.00**

New Structures in Flower Arrangement, Frances Bode, Heartside press, 1968, 1st ed., 128 pgs, dj **8.75**

Now We Are Enemies, Story of Bunker Hill, Thomas J. Fleming, St John's Press, 1960, book club edition, maps, dj ... **7.00**

Ohio Archaeological and Historical Publ., volume 2, 1900, 582 pgs **15.00**

Old Saratoga and the Burgoyne Campaign, Wm S Ostrander, chipped **15.00**

Origami Safari, Steve and Megumi Biddle, Tupelo Books, 1994, 1st ed. **7.00**

Origins and Annals of 'The Old South, First Presbyterian Church in Newburyport, MA, 1746-1896, H. C. Hewey, 1896, 221 pgs, illus **10.00**

Our Forgotten Past-Seven Centuries of Life on the Land, Jerome Blum, Thames & Hudson, 1982, 1st ed., dj **8.75**

Riding the Red Rooster By Train Through China, Paul Theroux, Putnams, 1988, 1st ed, maps, dj **7.00**

River to the West, Three Centuries of the Ohio, Walter Havighurst, Putnams, 1970, 1st ed. **18.00**

Panama and the Canal, In Pictures and Prose, Willis J. Abbot, Syndicate Publishing, 1913, **$20**.

Sandy MacDonald's Man, R. Clyde Ford
.... **8.00**
Singing an Indian Song, A Biography of D'Arcy McNickle, D R Parker, 1993, 316 pgs... **12.00**
Soo Canal!, Wm Ratigan, WE Eerdmans Pub, Grand Rapids, MI, 1954, 186 pgs, maps, dj.. **22.00**
Stillmeadow Calendar: A Countrywoman's Journal, Gladys Taber, 1967, 25 pgs, illus by Sidonie Coryn, dj......................... **8.00**
Washington and the Pamlico, V. F. Loy, P. M. Worthy, Bicentennial History Washington-Beaufort County, NC, 1976, 591 pgs
.... **15.00**
Washington, the Indispensable Man, James Thomas Flexner, Little Brown, 1974, ex-lib
.... **12.00**
White Savage, the Case of John Dunn Hunter, R Drinnon, 1972, 282 pgs, maps
.... **18.00**
Wild Places, Superior's North Shore, photography by Jay Steinke.......... **10.00**

Boyd Crystal Art Glass

History: The Boyd Crystal Art Glass Company was founded in Cambridge, Ohio, on Oct. 10, 1978, by father and son Bernard C. Boyd and Bernard F. Boyd. Today, Bernard F.'s son, John Bernard, has joined the firm and it continues to produce glass collectibles, using 300 uniquely colored formulas.

In 1964, Elizabeth Degenhart asked glassmaker Zachery Boyd to assume the management of her company, Degenhart Glass. Upon Zachery's death in 1968, his brother Bernard C. Boyd assumed the leadership of the Degenhart Glass. Bernard C. and his son, Bernard F., purchased the Degenhart Company in 1978 and changed the name to Boyd Crystal Art Glass. Their initial production used the 50 Degenhart molds. They started issuing new colors in these moulds. Over the years, additional molds were added, now numbering more than 200. Some were purchased from other glass companies, such as Imperial, creating some items in colored Candlewick.

Collecting Hints: Boyd Crystal Art Glass objects are usually made in a specific run of colors. The mark used has changed over the years. The first mark was a "B" in a diamond. Starting in 1983, an embossed line was added, and an additional line was added every five years thereafter. Counting the lines around the diamond will give the collector a clue as to the year of production. The latest mark includes an embossed "R," meaning the mould has been retired.

Animal-covered dish

Produced for National Milk Glass Collectors Society, marked "NMGCS" inside lid
Frog, Columbia Green, 5" **45.00**
Lamp, light blue slag, 5" d, with "B" in diamond and 4 lines mark **40.00**
Turtle, Columbia Green, 5" **45.00**

Box, cov
Candlewick, 5" l, 4" w, 2-1/2" h, vaseline, "B" in diamond with lines mark............ **25.00**
Capri, ftd, 5" l, 4" w, 2-3/4" h, "B" in diamond with lines mark
Aruba Slag **28.00**
Vaseline... **25.00**

Salt, bird with cherry in beak, carnival iridescent, $8.

Figurine

Airplane, 3-1/4" l, 4" l, 1-3/4" h, emb "BOYD" across wings, "B" in diamond with lines on side
Black carnival **25.00**
Blue carnival **25.00**
Angel, introduced 1995
Fantasia... **19.00**
Rosie Pink **18.00**
Bernie the Eagle, introduced 1992
Alexandrite..................................... **9.00**
Capri Blue **9.00**
Cardinal Red Carnival **10.00**
Cobalt Carnival **10.00**
Columbus White **9.00**
Lemon Custard **9.00**
Mint Julep....................................... **9.00**
Rosie Brown.................................... **9.00**
Waterloo **9.00**
Brian the Bunny, introduced 1986, retired 1988
Alpine Blue...................................... **8.00**
Nutmeg Carnival............................. **9.00**

C

Calendars

History: Calendars were a popular advertising giveaway in the late 19th century and during the first five decades of the 20th. Recently, a calendar craze has swept bookstores throughout America. These topic-oriented calendars contain little or no advertising.

Collecting Hints: Value increases if all monthly pages are attached. Collectors who are interested in the subject illustrated on the calendar, rather than the calendar per se, buy most calendars.

Additional Listings: Pinup Art.

Reproduction Alert.

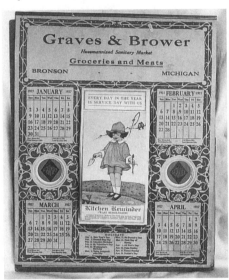

1927, Graves & Brower Hussmannized Sanitary Market, Groceries and Meats, Bronson, MI, shopping-list style, young boy in center, multicolored, **$27.50**.

1890, Hoyt's German Cologne, E. W. Hoyt & Col, Lowell, MA, advertising trade card with calendar on back.................... **60.00**
1899, C. I. Hood Co., Lowell, MA, titled "The American Girl," orig pad and cover sheet **100.00**

1908, Antimamnia Tablets, 7-3/4" w, 10" h
.... **150.00**
1909, American Clay Machinery Co., pocket size, bound in leather-type material, world maps, populations of US states, 2-1/2" w, 4-1/2" h... **120.00**
1918, Swifts Premium, Haskell Coffin art, titled "The Girl I Leave Behind Me," soldier saying goodbye to lady, bottom pieces missing, 8-1/2" w, 15" h **100.00**
1937, Dr. Miles Products, Alka-Seltzer ad, 6 pages, 10" w, 12-3/4" h.................. **48.00**

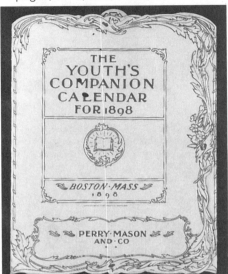

1898, *Youth Companion Magazine*, company give-away, foldout type, 8" x 11" closed, **$45**.

1941, Peoples Drug Company, Tulsa, OK, two cute twins eating ice cream cones
.... **75.00**
1946, Esso, Russell Sambrook prints, 8-1/2" w, 15" l.................................. **25.00**
1947, Petty, pin-up, minor soiling on January page, 9" x 12".............................. **155.00**
1951, Coronet Kiddies, Butler's Sunoco adv
.... **10.00**
1952, William Boyd, Hopalong Cassidy, Mobil Gas, Portland, OR, each page with different Hoppy picture, copyright Brown & Bigelow..................................... **110.00**
1954, Esquire Girl, pin-up, orig envelope with few tears around edge, 9" x 12"
.... **145.00**
1954, Jayne Mansfield, pin-up pose, 10-1/2" w, 12" h **85.00**
1956, Travelers, Hartford, CT, Currier & Ives prints, double-sided **75.00**
1958, Esso Family, Dec. 1957 to Dec. 1958
.... **10.00**
1959, Ramco Piston Rings, tin, stand-up type **12.00**

1961, International Edition, Best magazine, in English, French, and Spanish..... **30.00**
1968, Grove Funeral Home, Christian Home illus.. **8.00**
1969, Kennedy Brothers United, Alton S. Tobey, some personal notations on pages, right corner damaged, thumbtack holes, 12" w, 14" h **20.00**

Left: 1936, *Liberty A Weekly For Everyone*, real estate agent advertisement, Ginger Rogers and Fred Astaire, **$20**; 1930, *Liberty A Weekly For Everyone*, two children, titled "Wash your face" as little girl smooshes snowball into face of little boy, Thresher illustration, real state agent advertisement, **$15**.

1970, Hummel figures, Goebel.............. **8.00**
1974, Marilyn Monroe, orig envelope.. **30.00**
1977, hunting scene, Weaver & Son Food Market, Merriam, KS **12.00**
1978, Arizona Highways **7.00**
1984, dollhouse illus, 9" x 12".............. **10.00**
1992, Pop Tarts, Dweezil Twins, from October 1991 to Dec. 1992 .... **10.00**
1996, Quakertown National Bank, local scenes **5.00**

Cameras and Accessories

History: Of all the antique and classic cameras available, the most prized are those that took the earliest photographs known as daguerreotypes. The process was successfully developed by Louis-Jacques-Mandé Daguerre of Paris in 1839. These photographic images, made of thinly coated silver on copper plate, have a legion of collectors all their own. However, few of the cameras that photographed daguerreotypes have survived.

Edward Anthony became America's first maker of cameras and photographic equipment by founding E. Anthony in 1842. The company later became Ansco. Stereoscope photos were shown at London's Great Exhibition in 1851 and soon became the rage in Britain and Europe. Stereo cameras are recognized by their horizontally mounted twin lenses. Tintype photographs were introduced in 1856.

George Eastman's introduction of the Kodak camera in 1888 made photography accessible to the general public. Made by Frank Brownell for the Eastman Dry Plate & Film Co., it was the first commercially marketed roll-film camera. The original Kodak camera was factory loaded with 100 exposures. The finished pictures were round and 2-1/2 inches in diameter. Eastman Kodak's No. 2 Brownie, a box camera made of cardboard, became a best seller shortly after it was introduced in 1902.

After manufacturing microscopes and optical equipment for 75 years, Ernst Leitz of Wetzlar, Germany, introduced the first Leica 35mm camera in 1925. Japanese companies entered the photography market with Minolta (Nifca) cameras circa 1928, Canon (Kwanon) in 1933, and Nippon Nogaku's Nikon range-finder cameras in 1948.

Collecting Hints: Because of the sheer numbers of antique and classic cameras available, collectors often concentrate on specific eras, types, models, manufacturers, or country of origin.

Leica has been the top name in 35mm photography since the German company of Ernst Leitz introduced its landmark camera in 1925. Although prices are relatively stable, Leica cameras are generally expensive. Demand for them exists worldwide.

Kodak has been American's favorite camera since the introduction of the low-cost Brownie in 1900. As a result of the company's mass production and marketing, there is a surplus of many common models, both antique and modern.

The commercial success of Polaroid's instant-picture cameras has resulted in a surplus in the marketplace. Introduced in 1948, Polaroid cameras are not widely collected, and prices for most models remain low. The few exceptions are Polaroid cameras outfitted with superior optics.

Condition is of utmost importance unless the camera in question is particularly scarce. Shutters should function properly. Minimal wear is generally acceptable. Avoid cameras that have missing parts, damaged bellows, or major cosmetic problems.

In addition to precision instruments, camera collectors look for the odd and unusual models. Examples run the gamut from an inexpensive plastic camera that looks like a can of soda to a rare antique camera disguised to look like three books held together by a leather strap.

Adviser: Tom Hoepf.

Kodak, Brownie Hawkeye Flash Model, black and white case, c1950-61, **$5**.

Bell & Howell, Chicago, Ill.
Foton, 35mm rangefinder camera, spring-powered automatic film advance, Amotal f2.2 50mm lens, c1948..... **700.00**
Stereo Colorist I, 35mm camera by Three Dimension Co., division of Bell & Howell, c1954, f 3.5 Rodenstock Trinar lenses, made in Germany **80.00**

Busch Camera Corp., Chicago, Ill, Verascope F40 stereo camera, c1946, made in France by Jules Richard, Berthiot f3.5 40mm lens, considered scarce.. **430.00**

Coronet Camera Co. Birmingham, Great Britain
Coronet Portrait Box Camera, c1930s, blue, Coronet meniscus lens, 3" w x 4" h x 4-5/8" d box **35.00**
Midget, novelty camera, black or colored bakelite, 2-1/2" h, f10 Taylor Hobson meniscus lens

    Black **70.00**
    Blue...................................... **200.00**

Green **175.00**
Red.. **150.00**

Argus, Seventy-Five, twins lens reflex-style, Bakelite body, original carrying case, c1958-75, **$5**.

Eastman Kodak, Rochester, NY
Kodak Boy Scout Camera, folding vest-pocket folding camera, c1929, 127 roll film, olive color, official Boy Scout emblem, "Be Prepared" motto on front, orig green bellows and matching case **170.00**
Kodak Ektra, 35mm rangefinder camera, c1944, interchangeable lenses, Ektra f3.5 50mm lens **1,200.00**
Kodak No. 4, string-set box camera, 4" x 5" film factory-loaded, Bausch & Lomb Unversal lens and sector shutter . **400.00**
Kodak 35 35mm rangefinder camera **27.00**
Kodak Stereo Camera, 35mm, c1954, Kodak Anaston 35mm f3.5 lenses **120.00**

Franke & Heidecke, Braunschweig, Germany
Rolleiflex I, original model, circa 1930, twin lens reflex camera, Zeiss Tessar f3.8 7.5cm lens, Compur shutter, 1-300 speeds in addition to time and bulb, clean lens and viewfinder, excellent condition **190.00**
Rolleiflex Automat, circa 1950, twin lens camera, Carl Zeiss Tessar f3.5 75mm taking lens, Synchro-Compur shutter, 1-500 and bulb setting **230.00**

Herbert George Co., Chicago, Ill, Roy Rogers & Trigger camera, bakelite box camera, c1954, aluminum faceplate pictures Roy Rogers on his horse, 620 film **50.00**

Kodak, Hawkeye, Instamatic, R4, green plastic case, wrist strap, basic model, introduced 1963, **$5**.

Houghton, London, Ensign Greyhound, folding camera, c1931, metal body with gray crackle finish **18.00**

Leitz, Wetzlar, Germany, Leica Model II, 35mm camera, c1932, built-in coupled rangefinder, Elmar f3.5 50mm lens, body in very good condition showing normal wear **360.00**

Minolta, Japan, Minolta A, 35mm rangefinder camera, c1955, Rokkor f3.5 45mm lens **45.00**

Minox, Wetzlar, Germany, Minox III-S subminiature spy-type camera, c1954, chrome finish, push-pull film advance, attached beaded silver chain measures camera to subject for close focusing **165.00**

Ray Camera Co., Rochester, NY, Ray No. 7, folding plate camera, c1897, 6-1/2" x 8-1/2" format, leather-covered exterior, polished mahogany and brass interior with maroon bellows, brass-cased Unicum shutter and large rapid rectilinear lens **400.00**

Sign, Ansco Film #620, bathing beauty with large hat, red, white, yellow, and black, cardboard, diecut sunburst shape, **$35**.

Rochester Optical Co., Rochester, NY No. 6 Pony Premo folding plate camera, 1903, 4" x 5" format, black leather-covered exterior, red leather bellows, polished wood interior, nickel-plated hardware, Bausch & Lomb Planatograph lens, Automatic shutter **305.00**

Cyko Reko folding plate camera, 4" x 5" format, circa 1900, similar to Pony Premo D, polished hardwood and brass interior with red bellows, Cyko shutter **175.00**

Riken Optical, Japan, Steky II, 16mm subminiature camera, c1950, Stekinar Anastigmat f3.5 25mm lens **95.00**

Universal Camera Corp., New York, NY, Univex Minicam AF, compact strut-type folding miniature camera, No. 00 rollfilm, various colors................................. **50.00**

Unknown maker, Diana camera, plastic novelty camera having with lens noted for causing distorted images, 120 roll film, in original box with instructions **75.00**

Zeiss Ikon, Jena Germany
Contax III, 35mm rangefinder camera, c1936, leather-covered body with chrome top and trim, built-in uncoupled exposure meter (often nonfunctioning), Sonnar f2 5cm lens.. **160.00**
Contessa 35, folding 35mm camera, round rangefinder window mounted above lens, Tessar f2.8 45mm lens **135.00**

Cap Guns

History: Although the first toy gun patents date from the 1850s, toy guns did not play an important part in the American toy market until after the Civil War. In the 1870s, the toy cap gun was introduced.

Cast-iron cap pistols reached their pinnacle between 1870 and 1900, with J. & E. Stevens and Ives among the leading manufacturers. Realism took second place to artistic imagination. Designs ranged from leaf and scroll to animal and human heads. The use of cast iron persisted until the advent of World War II, although guns made of glass, lead, paper, rubber, steel, tin, wood, and zinc are known from the 1920 to 1940 period.

In the 1950s, die-cast metal and plastic became the principal material from which cap guns were manufactured. Leading manufacturers of die-cast guns were Hubley, Kilgore, Mattel, and Nichols. Many of the guns were associated with television cowboys and detective heroes. Often the guns were part of larger sets that consisted of a holster and numerous other accessories.

Collecting cap and other toy guns began in the 1930s with the principal emphasis on cast-iron examples made between 1875 to 1915. In the mid-1980s, the collecting emphasis shifted to the cap pistols of the post-World War II period.

Collecting Hints: Condition is crucial to pricing. A broken spring that can be replaced is far less critical than a crack that cannot be repaired. Many older cast-iron cap pistols rusted and suffered other ravages of time. While restoration is acceptable, an unrestored gun in fine condition is more valuable than a restored example.

Beware of restrikes, reproductions, and new issues. Recasts often have a sandy or pebbled finish and lack the details found on the original pieces. Several of the molds for cast-iron cap pistols have survived. Owners have authorized restrikes as a means of raising money. New issues are frequently made with the intention of deceiving, and the restrikes are sold to the unknowing as period examples. Two prime examples are the Liberty Bell cap bomb and the Deadshot powder keg cap bomb.

It is important to know the full history of any post-World War II cap pistol, especially if it is one of a pair. Toy guns associated with a character or personality sell better than their generic counterparts. Some of the price difference is negated for products from leading manufacturers, e.g., Hubley. The presence of the original box, holster, and/or other accessories can add as much as 100 percent to the value of the gun.

Assorted cap pistols, including Hubley Midget Flintlock, Colt Pat'd June 17, 1890; Jax S & W Pat'd Sept. 11, 1923, and cast iron cowboy cap gun with holster, **$350**.

Dynamite, MIB **85.00**
Hamilton, Cheyenne Shooter **70.00**
Hubley
    Cowboy, gold plated, black grips
    .... **200.00**
    Disintigrator, diecast, space gun
    .... **600.00**
    Rodeo Patrol, cowboy on bucking hose, red, white, and blue, orig box **150.00**
    Western Cap Pistol, white grips, black steer **50.00**
Kilgore
    Border Patrol, cast iron **70.00**
    Deputy, single holster, 2-1/4" wide fancy felt **200.00**
    Derringer, sealed, MOC **70.00**
    Eagle **40.00**
    Roy Rogers, illus **185.00**
Leslie-Henry
    Gene Autry, gold tone, MIB **500.00**
Lone Ranger, cast iron **350.00**
Lone Star/Wicke, dueling pistol, 1970s, all metal, 8" l **35.00**
Mattel
    Fanner 50, orig holster **75.00**
    Winchester Saddle Gun, orig box
    .... **500.00**

Hopalong Cassidy, 1952, **$95**.

Nichols, Stallion .45 Mark II, black grips
.... **175.00**
Pony Boy, celluloid handle, 10" x 4-1/2"
.... **50.00**
Roy Rogers
    Classy, Model R50, all metal diecast, single shot **110.00**
    Double holster and gun set, Kilgore
    .... **225.00**
Schmidt, Buck n' Bronc Deputy, unfired
.... **225.00**
Stevens, J & E, cast iron, Buffalo Bill, repeating, 1920s, orig box **320.00**
Unidentified Maker
    Big Scout, cast iron, white grips .. **100.00**
    Hero, cast iron, cowboy on grips... **45.00**
    Western **50.00**
Wyandotte, Red Ranger, dragoon style
.... **175.00**

Carnival Glass, Modern

History: Vintage carnival glass began to be produced by American makers from 1900 to the early 1920s. Many of the original molds used to produce this glassware were sold to other companies. Companies like Imperial Glass, Westmoreland, and Fenton began to produce new carnival glass items using these molds in the 1970s. Usually they developed new color formulas, but some original colors were also re-created. Some new patterns have been created. New forms in old patterns have also been created by the contemporary carnival glass makers.

As in vintage carnival glass, color dictates value as much as pattern or form. To determine the true color of a piece of carnival glass, it is necessary to find the part that has not been iridized, showing the true color of the base glass. When the base glass is clear and the iridized coloring is orange to rust, the color is known as marigold, reflecting on the carnival coloration.

Collecting Hints: Several of the major carnival glass collecting societies have commissioned new carnival glass forms to be made as souvenirs for the conventions. These souvenirs are now becoming very collectible and commanding high prices. Because the secondary market for modern carnival glass is still in its infancy, price fluctuations exist. Collectors should concentrate on purchasing perfect pieces of contemporary carnival glass and saving original sales documentation and labels.

Plate, chicks center, dark blue, Westmoreland, $17.50.

Adam & Eve, Fenton, plate, blue, 8" d **10.00**
Cactus, Fenton, six-pc set, red, cracker jar, creamer, cruet, spittoon, sugar, toothpick holder **150.00**
Cardinal, Westmoreland, water set, 7 pc, white, hand painted red birds, green branches **125.00**
Cherry Chain, Fenton, candy dish, purple **30.00**
Cherry Lattice, creamer and sugar, purple **20.00**
Christmas, Imperial, limited edition plate, purple, 9" d **10.00**
Covered animal dish, figural animal lid, nest or basketweave base, Westmoreland
  Chicken, red **25.00**
  Chicken, slag, white **20.00**
  Dove, purple **25.00**
  Pigeon, slag **40.00**
  Rooster, amethyst slag **35.00**
  Swan, slag, white **20.00**
  Turtle, slag **40.00**
Dahlia, water set, seven-pc, purple ... **75.00**
Diamond Block & Scroll, platter, marigold **10.00**
Fan Tail, Fenton
  Bowl, blue **20.00**
  Bowl, red **25.00**
  Plate, lavender **20.00**
Farm Yard, plate, 11" d, purple **25.00**
Fashion, punch set, 10-pc, amethyst **65.00**
Fenton Flower, Fenton, nut bowl, aqua opalescent **30.00**
Field Flower, Imperial, water set, seven-pc
  Ice blue **200.00**
  Red **100.00**
Frolicking Bears, commissioned by International Carnival Glass Association
  Creamer, 1981, aqua opalescent **675.00**
  Jack in the pulpit vase, 1998, purple **115.00**
  Mug, 1997, plum opalescent, hand painted hummingbirds and floral dec **225.00**
  Rose bowl, 1986, green opalescent **75.00**
  Spittoon, 1982, red **65.00**
  Spittoon, 1982, red, satin finish **85.00**
  Tumbler, 1993, amber **85.00**
  Tumbler, 2001, pink opalescent ... **125.00**
Golden Harvest, wine set, seven-pc, purple **75.00**
Grape, Westmoreland
  Juice set, five-pc, purple **50.00**
  Water set, seven-pc, blue **60.00**
  Water set, seven-pc red **95.00**
Grape & Cable, Fenton
  Bowl, ice blue **35.00**
  Pitcher, purple **30.00**
  Spittoon, purple **25.00**
  Vase, ice blue **30.00**
Grapevine Lattice, water set, tankard pitcher, six tumblers, purple **80.00**

Candy dish, covered, heart shaped, purple, Fenton, **$65**.

Hobstar, punch bowl set
Nine-pc, purple **100.00**
Fourteen-pc set, red, limited edition, large bowl **225.00**

Punch bowl set, Grape pattern, purple, 13 pieces, Summit, **$65**.

Hobstar & Leaves, Imperial, compote
Amethyst **20.00**
Blue **25.00**
Imperial Grape, Imperial
Bowl, ruffled, 11" d, purple **40.00**
Goblet, stemmed, smoke **25.00**
Punch bowl set, 12-pc, ice blue **95.00**
Sandwich plate, center handle, smoke
.... **25.00**
Water pitcher, smoke **35.00**
Water set, seven-pc, marigold **65.00**
Inverted Strawberry, Fenton
Bell, purple **15.00**
Compote, aqua opalescent **60.00**
Iris, Gibson, water set, red, 1989 ...... **150.00**

Lewis, punch bowl set, 15 pcs, purple
.... **75.00**
Loganberry, Imperial, vase
Green **30.00**
Smoke **35.00**
Lustre Rose, Imperial
Bowl, ftd, ruffled, smoke **30.00**
Bowl, white **20.00**
Breakfast set, three-pc, white **85.00**
Mother & Child, Fenton
Bell, red **30.00**
Compote, marigold **45.00**
Pansy, Imperial
Bowl, amethyst **30.00**
Relish, marigold **12.50**

Lady bell and figurine, amber and teal, each **$15**.

Peacock, Westmoreland, bowl, purple, 11" d
.... **35.00**
Persian Medallion, Fenton, compote, purple **25.00**
Poppy, lamp, Gone with the Wind-style, purple **100.00**
Robin, Imperial, water set, seven-pc, white
.... **70.00**
Roses, Fenton, compote, purple **30.00**
Stork, Westmoreland, water set, seven-pc, amethyst **65.00**
Strawberry, Westmoreland, spittoon, stemmed, aqua opalescent **35.00**
Three Fruits, plate, 14" d, purple **27.50**
Tiger Lily, water set, seven-pc, pink **100.00**
Water Lily, Fenton, Gone with the Wind, red, 30" h **125.00**
Whirling Star, Fenton, compote, purple
.... **30.00**
Windmill, Imperial
Bowl, small, smoke **15.00**
Plate, blue **7.50**

Cartoon Characters

History: The first daily comic strip was Bud Fisher's Mutt and Jeff, which appeared in 1907. By the 1920s, the

Sunday comics became an American institution. One of the leading syndicators was Captain Joseph Patterson of the News-Tribune. Patterson, who partially conceived and named Moon Mullins and Little Orphan Annie, worked with Chester Gould to develop Dick Tracy in the early 1930s.

Walt Disney and others pioneered the movie cartoon, both as shorts and full-length versions. Disney and Warner Brothers characters dominated the years from 1940 to 1960. With the advent of television, the cartoon characters of Hanna-Barbera, e.g., the Flintstones, added a third major force. Independent studios produced cartoon characters for television, and characters multiplied rapidly. By the 1970s, the trend was to produce strips with human characters, rather than the animated animals of the earlier period.

Successful cartoon characters create many spin-offs, including comic books, paperback books, Big Little Books, games, dolls, room furnishings, and other materials which appeal to children. The secondary market products may produce more income for the cartoonist than the drawings themselves.

Collecting Hints: Many collectible categories include objects related to cartoon characters. Cartoon characters appeared in advertising, books, comics, movies, television, and as a theme in thousands of products designed for children.

Concentrate on one character or the characters from a single comic or cartoon. Most collectors tend to focus on a character that was part of their childhood. Another collecting concentrates on the work of a single artist. Several artists produced more than one cartoon character.

The most popular cartoon characters of the early period are Barney Google, Betty Boop, Dick Tracy, Gasoline Alley, Li'l Abner, Little Orphan Annie, and Popeye. The movie cartoons produced Bugs Bunny, Felix the Cat, Mighty Mouse, Porky Pig, and a wealth of Disney characters. The popular modern cartoon characters include Garfield, Peanuts, and Snoopy.

Additional Listings: Disneyana; also see the index for specific characters.

Andy Panda, Walter Lantz

Cartoon, Apple Andy, #493, Castle Films, 8mm, headline edition, orig box **10.00**

Figure, 4-3/4" h, Miranda Panda, Don Roberto, Los Angeles, mkd "Lantz Productions," orig foil label **95.00**

Viewmaster reel, Andy Panda in Mystery Tracks, Sawyer, #822 .... **4.00**

Archie

Character drinking glass, Welch's, 1971, Hot Dog Goes to School **6.50**

Comic book, Vol. 1, #97, December 1958 .... **27.50**

Doll, Archie, Jughead, Betty, and Veronica, 1975, Marx, NRFB, price for set... **200.00**

Paper dolls, orig box, played with condition **45.00**

Barney Google

Comic book, *Barney Google & Snuffy Smith*, four colors **120.00**

Pep pin, Kellogg's, Barney, 1946 .... **18.00**

Betty Boop

Alarm clock, metal, 8" w **38.00**

Bathroom set, toothbrush holder, soap dish, and mug, purple, black, and silver, three-pc set **55.00**

Character drinking glass, 6" h, frosted, Betty Boop on Motorcycle............. **20.00**

Doll, 14" h, all cloth, orig tag "Play by Play Toys & Novelties" **15.00**

Perfume bottle, figural, glass bottle, wooden head, painted features, stamped "P.E.F.5" **30.00**

Wall light, figural, 10" x 24" **30.00**

Bringing Up Father

Doll, Schoenhut, carved jointed wood, orig paper label with 1924 copyright, price for pr **600.00**

Movie poster, "Jiggs and Maggie in Society," Monogram Pictures, 1948, 22" w, 27-1/2" h **60.00**

Bugs Bunny

Advertising counter display, Sunoco promotion, six different 3"-4" rubber Looney Tunes figures, 1989, 17" x 15" **60.00**

Character drinking glass, Happy 50th Birthday Bugs, copyright 1990 .... **4.50**

Comic book, *Bugs Bunny*, Dell
No. 59, Feb-March, 1958 .... **20.00**
No. 72, April-May, 1960 .... **18.00**

Cookie jar **40.00**

Hand puppet, plush, tag "Bugs Bunny 50th Birthday Celebration," 1990, 14" h. **12.00**

Limited Edition Collector's Plate, Mother's Day, 1977, Dave Grossman design, licensed Warner Brothers Products, copyright 1977, orig box, 7-1/2" d . **10.00**

Little Golden Book, *Bugs Bunny At The Easter Party,* Warner Bros. Cartoons, Inc., 1953, 28 pgs **12.00**

Lunch box, tin, 6" x 5-1/2" x 2" **18.00**

Planter, Evan K. Shaw, 1940s, 4" w, 5" h **90.00**

Toy, jack-in-the-box, Matty Mattel Presents, Mattel Toymakers, 1951-53, does not play **65.00**

The booth of What A Character offered many different types of cartoon and vintage characters at the March 2004 Atlantique City show.

Casper and Friends, Harvey Comics

Premium ring, thin copper luster metal band joined to circular copper luster frame which holds convex metal insert with color image of character against white background, mkd "copyright 1979 Harvey Comics," seven of Casper, two of Wendy, one horse Nightmare, set of 10, some wear **65.00**

Push puppet, Casper **100.00**

Radio, figural, MIB **130.00**

Daffy Duck

Character drinking glass, Pepsi, Warner Brothers Looney Tunes, copyright 1980 .... **8.00**

US Postal Service, stamped card book of 10 postal cards, 1999, orig packaging **9.00**

Dick Tracy, Chester Gould

Box, Dick Tracy image, for transistor radio **15.00**

Camera dart gun, Larami, 1971 .... **60.00**

Christmas tree light bulb, figural Dick Tracy, 1930s **90.00**

Doll, Bonny Braids, Ideal, 1952, 8" h, crawls **170.00**

Pin, Bonny Braids, Charmore, 1951, MOC **60.00**

Play set, Ideal, orig box **150.00**

Police station, Marx, tin litho, 1950s **800.00**

Pop-on ring, dark green plastic base, stamped in letters on top, 3-D pale blue full figure of Tracy pointing gun **40.00**

Soap, Sparkle Plenty, figural, c1950, diecut dec box **95.00**

Statue, Dick Tracy, full color, 15" h.... **150.00**

Elmer Fudd

Figure, Dakin, red hat, black jacket, white shirt, yellow pants, red necktie, red shoes, plastic, 1968, 8" h **25.00**

Felix the Cat, King Features

Cookie jar **50.00**

Figure, cast lead, c1920 .... **385.00**

Record, Peter Pan, 45 rpm, ©1959 King Features Syndicate, Inc................. **30.00**

Flintstones, comic book, Charlton Comics, No. 6, October, *All New Flintstones, Starring Dino,* Hanna-Barbera, $5.

Flintstones, Hanna-Barbera

Character drinking tumbler, plastic Arthur Treacher's Fish & Chips, Betty, 1974, yellow .... **5.00** Don Penotti, Fred, Betty, and Wilma on beach, orig lid **8.00**

Coloring book, Flintstones Color by Number, Whitman **24.00**

Cookie jar, Fred, plastic, yellow **30.00**

Figure, Dino, Dakin, blue, moveable arms and tail, 1970, 8" h **35.00**

Mug, 5-1/2" h, glass, Bedrock U, Grand Canyon, Arizona **12.00**

Playset, #4672, copyright 1961, 15" x 24" x 4" orig box, played-with condition **165.00**

Plush toy, Barney Rubble, 14" h, felt hat, shirt, and pants, tag "NANCO/Country of Origin: Thailand, copyright 1989 Hanna-Barbera Productions, Inc." **22.00**

Pop-on ring, Bam-Bam, black plastic base, lime green character, c1966.......... **24.00**

Premium ring, Betty Rubble, off-white plastic, expansion band, diecut portrait, c1960... **25.00**

Video storage case, full-color Fred and Dino... **25.00**

Heckle and Jeckle

Children's book, Whitman, wear.......... **5.00**

Premium ring, thin copper luster metal band joined to circular copper luster frame which holds convex metal insert with color image of black crow against white background, mkd "Copyright Terrytoons," c1977, set of three...... **18.00**

Huckleberry Hound, Hanna Barbera **Lamp**, 20" h, plastic **30.00**

Jetsons, Hanna-Barbera

Character drinking glass, 1990, Kraft

George... **40.00**

Jane... **40.00**

Word Search puzzle book, 64 pgs, 1978, unused, 5-1/8" w, 7-1/2" h **10.00**

Lil Abner, Al Capp

Bank, Smoo, blue plastic...................... **50.00**

Big little book, *Lil Abner, Among the Millionaires,* Whitman Publishing, 1939, spine missing, cover detached **10.00**

Cartoon strip, from Boston Sunday Globe, Sept. 27, 1942 .... **5.00**

Flicker ring, 1" h, blue square............ **10.00**

Hand puppet, Baby Barry, 1957, played with condition **65.00**

Magazine ad, Cream of Wheat Breakfast Food, Rastus on front of Cream of Wheat box, 5" x 11".................................... **20.00**

Pin, Shmoo, 1-1/2" h, brass tone......... **15.00**

Mighty Mouse, child's puzzle, 100 pieces, Whitman, **$10**.

Moon Mullins, Frank Willard

Salt and pepper shakers, pr, figural, glass, black hard plastic hats, red painted ties and shoes, mkd "Made in Japan" . **95.00**

Toothbrush holder, bisque, incised "Moon Mullins & Kayo, copyright F.A.S.". **135.00**

Mutt and Jeff, Bud Fisher

Cartoon strip from Boston Sunday Globe, Sept. 13, 1942.................................. **5.00**

Comic book, Mutt & Jeff, #44.............. **8.00**

Doll, jointed, felt clothing, cotton shirts, Buchere, Switzerland, price for pr **500.00**

Sheet music, *Moonlight,* 1911, caricature cover, pages separated **12.00**

Peanuts, Charles Schultz

Address book, Peanuts, United Feature Syndicate, Inc., 3-3/4" x 2-1/2" **6.00**

Boots, child's, plastic, blue, Peanuts cartoon on each, one reads "Good," the other "Grief"... **18.00**

Coin, "The Great Pumpkin," 30th anniversary, silver, limited edition of 1,996 pcs, black case, certificate of authenticity......... **80.00**

Cookbook, *Peanuts Cook Book,* Scholastic Book Services, January, 1970, 1st printing... **25.00**

Figure, Charlie Brown and Peggy Jean, sitting on grass, orig box with graphics of whole Peanuts gang, 4" l................ **18.00**

Lunch box and thermos, plastic, red ground, some loss to graphics, 1965 .... **65.00**

Sculpture, Snoopy kissing Lucy, orig certificate of authenticity **75.00**

Soakie, Camping Snoopy, 9-3/4" h..... **12.00**

Telephone, Snoopy and Woodstock, Western Electric, rotary, 1970s, 8" sq base, 14" h **125.00**

Pogo, Walt Kelly

Children's book

Pogo Peek-A-Book, Walt Kelly, Simon & Schuster, 1955, 6-5/8" x 9-3/4" **40.00**

The Pogo Papers, Walt Kelly, Simon & Schuster, 1951, 5-1/4" x 8", 192 pgs **38.00**

Poster, 17" x 11", "The World of Pogo, Walt Kelly's menagerie of characters from Okefenokee Swamp," made for exhibit held at the Museum of Fine Arts, Springfield, MA, 1971..................... **55.00**

Tin, Popeye Daily Dime Bank, original closure, **$85**.

Popeye, E. C. Segar

Bubble pipe, plastic, train-shape, Popeye as conductor, 3" w, 1960s **10.00**

Chalkboard, 17" h, Popeye holding his pipe, copyright King Features Syndicate, 1978 .... **10.00**

Child's record and coloring book, Popeye & Becky in Wimpy's Sunken Treasure, 45 rpm record, 17 pg coloring book, 1980, unused **15.00**

Doll, 10-1/2" h, rubber head, cloth stuffed body, play-with condition **135.00**

Flicker ring, Popeye and Sweet Pea, plastic, 1960s **15.00**

Game, 1983, unused **45.00**

Pencil sharpener, figural, Bakelite, copyright 1929 King Features Syndicate, 1-3/4" h **75.00**

Ring toss, Popeye Pipe Toss, 1939, thick cardboard and wood, copyright King Features Syndicate, Inc. and Rosebud Art Company, NY, Sole Licensee.. **110.00**

Tin, Popeye Yellow Popcorn, packed by Pure Mills, Inc., Dixon, Ill, pry-top lid, litho "Just a Better POP," image of Popeye on both sides, King Features Syndicate, copyright 1943, 3-1/4" w, 4-3/4" h. **200.00**

Porky Pig, Leon Schlesinger, Warner Bros.

Big Little Book, *Porky Pig and His Gang*, Whitman #1404 .... **50.00**

Character drinking glass, Pepsi, Warner Brothers Looney Tunes, copyright 1966 .... **7.50**

Figure, Dakin, vest, blue and white polka dotted bow tie, 1970s, 8" h **20.00**

Soakie, 9-1/2" h, molded vinyl, plastic body, hard plastic removable head, 1960s **28.00**

Rocky and Bullwinkle, Jay Ward

Bendie, MOC **20.00**

Character drinking glass, Pepsi logo, Bullwinkle, circus, balloons, Ward Brocking, 1970s **16.00**

Character drinking mug, 3" h, milk glass, yellow panel with brown dec **18.00**

Charm, figural **15.00**

Musical instruments, set of three plastic toy instruments, 1969, MOC **50.00**

Simpsons

Character drinking glass

Bart and Homer golfing, Amora **12.00**

Bart, metal emblem on front, frosted glass, Australian, 5-3/4" h **25.00**

Lisa et Maggie, eating sundae, Amora **15.00**

Comic book play set **35.00**

Figure, poseable, Mattel

Homer, nuke gear, NRFP **7.50**

Nelson, trash can, NRFP.................. **5.00**

Lunch box.. **25.00**

Toy, Pool Hall, MIB **35.00**

Game, pin ball, Poosh-M-Up Jr., wooden case, colorful tin litho back, glass front, PTPT, #2314, US patents, **$45**.

Sylvester, Warner Bros.

Character drinking glass, Sylvester, Pepsi, Warner Brothers Looney Tunes, copyright 1966 .... **6.00**

Character drinking glass, Tweety Bird, Pepsi, Warner Brothers Looney Tunes, copyright 1973................................. **6.00**

Cookie jar, Sylvester and Tweety, Applause **55.00**

Figure

Sylvester, Dakin, moveable arms and tail, 1969, 8-3/4" h................................. **20.00**

Tweety, Dakin, 1969, 6-1/2" h **15.00**

Hot water bottle, Sylvester holding Tweety, Warner Brothers, Inc., Duarry, Spain, 12-1/4" h **75.00**

Spinning ring, silvered metal frame, thin expansion band, clear acrylic cover over shaded color portrait, 1990s **10.00**

Tom and Jerry, Hanna-Barbera

Bendable figure, MOC **20.00**

Character drinking glass, Pepsi, Jerry, name in black letters, 1975, some small scrapes to decals **8.00**

Comic book, #240, Gold Key............. **2.00**

Mug, scenes of Tom and Jerry, Staffordshire, 1970, mkd "MGM," 3-1/4" h **36.00**

Pinback button, Sunbeam Bead, 1-1/4" d **10.00**

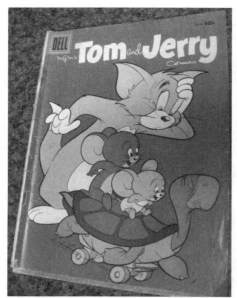

Tom & Jerry, comic book, Dell, May, **$3.50.**

Sculpture, ceramic, musical, Tom & Jerry as Musketeers on revolving wedge of cheese **30.00**

Stereoview film card, *The Two Mouse-keteers,* #T-32, 1956, Lowe's Inc., Tru-Vue Co., Beavertown, OR **10.00**

Wile E. Coyote, mug, plastic, embossed "G B Des. No. 2023013, © Promotional Partners, 1992, Made in China," **$5.**

Wile E Coyote/Road Runner

US Postal Service, 2000 stamped card book, orig packaging **9.00**

Woody Woodpecker, Walter Lantz

Bank, 7" h, ceramic, figural, red, yellow, blue, white, black, and brown, plastic stopper **40.00**

Children's book, *Woody Woodpecker Pogo Stick Adventures,* Tell-A-Tale, 1954 **10.00**

Doll, 13" h, plush **20.00**

Game, Travel with Woody Woodpecker, Walter Lantz, Cadaco, lids detached from two containers, all pieces present, played-with condition **115.00**

Harmonica, 5-1/2" h, nodding head, red plastic, Lantz copyright on chest, some decal missing from eyes **25.00**

Little Golden Book, *Woody Woodpecker,* Walter Lantz, copyright 1952 .... **12.50**

Ring, thin brass adjustable band, diecut brass Woody facing right, black, white, red, and yellow enamels, mkd "Walter Lantz Productions 1977" **20.00**

Salt and pepper shakers, pr, Woody and Winnie, paper label "W. Lantz, 1990"
.... **50.00**

Spoon, child's, mkd "W.L.P.," stamped "IS," c1950 .... **8.00**

Toothbrush holder, 3-3/4" h, 1940s, unmarked **125.00**

Winnie the Pooh, original cel and sketch, matted and framed, sold with certificate of authenticity, **$795.**

Yellow Kid, R. F. Outcault

Cigar box, 5-1/2" x 9" x 4", wood, hinged lid with lightly engraved portrait of Kid, other images, orig red label "Smoke Yellow Kid Cigars, Manuf'd by DR Fleming, Curwensville, PA," early 1900s **345.00**

Ice cream mold, 4-3/4" h, hinged, full figure
.... **215.00**

Pinback button, High Admiral Cigarettes
No. 3, Kid standing in barrel, Mrs. Murphy mends clothes **35.00**
No. 14, Kid with large white collar, dressed to go to ball **45.00**
Yogi Bear, Hanna-Barbera

Lamp, 20" h, mkd "Hanna Barbera Productions" **30.00**

Premium ring, non-adjustable plastic base with gold luster, black plastic top, portrait and character name along studio initials "H-B"
Dixie, wear to gold luster **45.00**
Huck **48.00**
Mr. Jinks, some scratches **45.00**
Yogi Bear **48.00**

Yosemite Sam, Warner Bros.

Figure, Dakin, removable black cowboy hat, orange shirt, blue jeans, boots, and gun belt, 1970s, 8" h **25.00**

Ring, wide brass expansion band, diecut figure with multicolored enamel, foil tag "J.R.S./Warner Bros./1970/Hand-Painted" **20.00**

Cat Collectibles

History: The popular view of cats has been a roller coaster of opinion, from peaks of favoritism to valleys of superstition. Cats were deified in ancient Egypt and feared by Europeans in the Middle Ages. Customs and rituals resulted in brutal treatment of felines. Cats became associated with witchcraft, resulting in tales and superstitions that linger to the present. This lack of popularity adds to the scarcity of antique cat items.

Collecting Hints: Cat-related material can be found in almost all collecting categories—advertising items, dolls, figurines, folk art, fine art, jewelry, needlework, linens, plates, postcards, and stamps, to name just a few. Antique cats are scarce but modern objects d'feline are plentiful. The better ones, the limited editions and pieces created by established artists, are future collectibles.

The cat collector competes with collectors from other areas. Chessie, the C & O Railroad cat, is collected by railroad and advertising buffs; Felix, Garfield, and other cartoon characters, plus cat-shaped toys and cat-related games, are loved by toy collectors. Postcard collectors collect cat postcards in general.

Because cat collectors are attracted to all cat items, all breeds, and realistic or abstract depictions, they tend to buy many items. It is best to specialize. Popular categories are fine art, antique porcelain cats, stamps, advertising, postcards and unique or unusual pieces. Up-and-coming collecting categories include first day covers, jewelry, and dolls. Kliban's cats, especially the ceramic examples, art by Louis Wain, good Victorian paintings, and

cartoon cats are best sellers in the secondary market.

Reproduction Alert.

Stuffed toy, Dakin, Siamese, original tag marked "R. Dakin, San Francisco, Made in Korea," 14" l, **$15**.

Book, *Old Possum's Book of Practical Cats,* T. S. Eliot, Faber & Faber, Ltd., London, 1957 .... **42.00**

Bookends, pr, ceramic

Black cats, gold trim, mkd "Japan," c1950 .... **30.00**

One with black and white cat stretching his paw through to other bookend, second bookend has gray mouse with mallet, ready to strike extended cat's paw, incised "© 1983" and ceramist's initials **35.00**

Bookmark, figural cat face, celluloid, reverse mkd "don't kiss me," 22" l green cord, c1920, 1-3/4" w x 1-3/4" h **65.00**

Chalkware, figure, 7-1/2" h, Persian Cat, sitting up, pale yellow head, darkens to black chin and tail **55.00**

Child's cup and saucer, cat on twig of pussy willows, mkd "Made in Japan" **15.00**

Clock, 9" h, Sessions Clock Co., white ceramic cat holding clock, plastic cat as second hand, 1950s **50.00**

Figure

4" h, pottery, pair, white with yellow and black spots, blue bases, stamped in blue "Staffordshire, England" **35.00**

4" h, 2-3/4" l, three pink kittens, attached and seated on blue Victorian-style sofa with gold trim, stamped "© 1959 Bradley Onimco" **25.00**

8" h, Siamese, ceramic, model #4693, paper label "Lefton Japan" **28.00**

10-1/2" h, Egyptian cat, museum repro, incised mark "© Austin production © 1965" **75.00**

Child's mug, white porcelain, pink rim, green, blue, and tan decal of little girl holding cat, gold trim, unmarked, **$15**.

Lamp, ceramic, shape of two Siamese cats, incised "© 1958 Lane & Co., Van Nys, CA, U.S.A." **85.00**

Letter opener, 9" l, solid brass, arched back cat atop, incised "England" **55.00**

Mug, 3-1/4" h, ceramic, cat face, white, dark blue floral collar and handle, incised "Avon" **18.00**

Paperweight, glass, rect, multicolored scene of cats playing with yarn **25.00**

Pitcher, 8-1/4" h, glass, cat shape, tail forms handle, incised "WMF Germany" ... **25.00**

Planter

6" l, composition, laying down cat holds balls of yard from sewing basket, incised "Pompadour 1984" **6.50**

6" l, 5" h, pottery, stylized laughing cat, aqua, script "Weller Pottery" mark . **75.00**

Planter, light aqua-green glaze, marked "USA," **$20**.

Plate

6" d, china, cream colored, gold pattern around border, long-haired golden tabby cat fore transfer, Mount Clemens Pottery hallmark, c1935 .... **25.00**

8" d, 1985 series, titled "Minou-ettes" by Vista Allegra, C. Pradalie, series includes various breeds, all with lacy curtain backgrounds **20.00**

Postcards, full color, Clivette, white long-hair cats, neck ribbons of various colors, short verse of inspiration or sentimental nature, used, c1906, set of six, 3-1/2" x 5-1/2" **30.00**

Print, French artist, H. Gobin, titled "Le Tigre," 1840 .... **80.00**

Puzzle, 10-1/2" x 14", cardboard, yellow cat in blue pants and white sailor hat, playing concertino **10.00**

Salt and pepper shaker sets, ceramic

Garfield with Fishburger sandwich **60.00**

Hello Kitty, three-pc set **60.00**

Mr. and Mrs. Black Cats, stamped "Japan" **15.00**

Sylvester and Tweety Bird with mallet **60.00**

Puzzle, Comical Animals Picture Puzzle, Parker Bros, **$85**.

Cat covered dish, white milk glass, ribbed base, **$65**.

Scrapbook, greeting and note cards, some with envelopes, approx 125 cards, c1940 to present...................................... **200.00**

Serving tray, 15" x 21", metal, painted gold, aqua border, two Siamese cats in center, sgd "Alexander" **65.00**

Tape measure, celluloid case, pictures of playing cats, tape mkd "Made in U.S.A." **35.00**

Teapot, figural, Norcrest **40.00**

Tea towel, linen................................. **10.00**

Thermometer, hammered aluminum, white metal cat on base........................... **45.00**

Toy

Cat with shoe, wind-up, off-white celluloid cat, orange accents, red neck bow, tin litho shoe, mkd "Made in Japan," 1950s **65.00**

Kitten with ball, celluloid, wind-up, of-white kitten, pink shirt and bow, pink and green ball attached to one paw by string, orig key, mkd "Made in Occupied Japan," 1940s **35.00**

Wall plaque, 6-1/2" h, chalkware, Tabby cat face, red ears and big bow, green eyes **45.00**

Character and Promotional Glasses

History: Character and promotional drinking glasses date to the movie premier of "Snow White and the Seven Dwarfs" in December of 1937. Libbey Glass and Walt Disney designed tumblers with a safety edge and sold them through variety stores and local dairies. The glasses proved extremely popular. Today collector glasses can be found for almost every Disney character, cartoon, and movie theme.

In 1953, Welch's began to package its jelly in decorated tumblers that featured Howdy Doody and his friends. Once again, the public's response was overwhelming. Welch's soon introduced tumblers with other cartoon characters, such as Mr. Magoo.

In the late 1960s, fast food restaurants and gasoline stations started to use drinking glasses as advertising premiums. Soft drink manufacturers like Coke and Pepsi saw the advertising potential and developed marketing plans focused on licensed characters and movies. Sport's team licensing also entered the picture. By the early 1980s, hundreds of new glasses were being issued each year.

As the 1980s drew to a close, plastic drinking cups replaced glasses, although the use of licensed images continued. While most collectors still prefer to collect glass, a few far-sighted individuals are stashing away pristine plastic examples.

Collecting Hints: Contemporary character and promotional glasses are usually produced in series. It is important to collect the full series, including any color variations. This is not as easy as it sounds. Sports team glasses are frequently issued regionally, i.e., Philadelphia Eagles glasses may appear just in the Philadelphia market while San Diego Charger glasses may be available only in the area around San Diego. Before paying a great deal of money for a recent glass, ask yourself if what may be rare in your area is common somewhere else. Any serious collector needs this sense of perspective.

Some early examples were decorated with lead-based paint. They should not be used for drinking purposes.

Collectors place a premium on glasses with never-out-of-the-box luster. The mere act of washing a glass, in a dishwasher or even by hand, can lessen its value. Avoid examples with any evidence of fading.

Because of their wide availability, character and promotional drinking glasses should be collected only if they are in excellent to mint condition. Pay premium prices only for glasses that pre-date 1980. After that, distributors, dealers, and collectors hoarded glasses in quantity.

Amazing Spider-Man, Marvel Comics, 1977 .... **5.00**

Animal Crackers, 1978

Dodo **8.50**

Lyle **9.00**

Arby's

BC Ice Age, riding on wheel, 1981.. **9.00**

Bullwinkle, Crossing the Delaware, 11 oz, 1976 .... **9.00**

Charlie Chaplin, Movie Star series... **7.50**

Little Rascals.................................... **8.00**

Monopoly, Just Visiting.................. **18.00**

Rocky, In The Dawn's Early Light, 11 oz, 1976 .... **9.00**

Wizard of Id, 1983 .... **12.00**

Zodiac, Scorpio **10.00**

Archies, 1971, 8 oz

Betty and Veronica Fashion Show ... **4.00**

Hot Dog Goes To School................. **4.50**

Battlestar Galactica, 16 oz, Universal Studios, Inc, 1979

Commander Adama **15.00**
Cylon Warriors **15.00**
Starbuck **15.00**

Brockway, Al Capp, 1975

Daisy Mae....................................... **65.00**
Lil Abner **55.00**
Mammy... **55.00**
Sadie Hawkins............................... **55.00**

Burger Chef

Endangered Species, 1978.............. **6.50**
Jefferson, President Series **6.00**
Washington, Bicentennial Series **7.00**

Burger King

Burger King, 1989............................ **10.00**
Denver Broncos, Riley Odomos **5.00**
Have It Your Way, two drummers, piper,
1976... **10.00**
Shake A Lot, 1979............................ **9.00**

Burger King and Coca-Cola, Star Wars

Empire Strikes Back, 16 oz, copyright
Lucasfilm, 1980

Darth Vadar......................... **15.00**
Lando Calrissian **18.00**
Luke Skywalker **15.00**
R2-D2 and C-3PO **15.00**

Return of the Jedi, 16 oz, copyright Lucasfilm, 1983

C-3PO at the Ewok Village.............. **15.00**
Luke & Han, Fighting on Tatooine .. **15.00**
Luke Fighting Darth in the Throne Room
.... **20.00**

Coca Cola

Bag of French Fries, 1992, 6" **8.00**
Betty, tray girl................................... **12.00**
Christmas Tour, 1999, German Derichs,
W. S. Woche, Himmericks, Santa on front,
5-1/4" h... **3.00**
Dinosaurs, Triceratops, European,
6-7/8" h... **12.00**
Disney on Parade.............................. **5.00**
Happy Chef, stained glass design... **5.00**
Harry Potter, German, coat of arms,
6-1/4" h... **15.00**
Heritage Collector Series, Washington,
Revere, Jones, and Henry **12.00**
Holly Hobbie and Robbie, Deck the Hall
with Holly series, 1980, #2 of four..... **5.00**
Kollect-A-Set, Popeye....................... **6.00**
Mickey's Christmas Carol, complete set
of three... **12.00**
National Flag Foundation.................. **9.00**
Santa and Elves **7.50**
75th Anniversary, fountain, 1977, Buffalo,
NY, 5" h... **7.50**
Sign of Good Taste Around the World,
Quebec, Canada **7.00**
Winter Wonderland, 5-3/4" h............. **5.00**

Davy Crockett, brown decoration, ice tea size, $10.

DC Comics, Pepsi

Aquaman, 16 oz, 1978.................... **15.00**
Batman, 1966 .... **7.50**
Green Lantern.................................. **8.50**

Disney

Donald Duck and Daisy **9.00**
Mickey Mouse Club, Donald Duck
building brick wall............................ **3.00**
Peter Pan, keyhole with Peter and Hook
on plant **26.00**
World on Ice, Snow White Kissing
Dopey's head.................................. **14.00**

Domino's Pizza, 1988, Avoid the Noids,
complete set of four....................... **25.00**

Dr Pepper

Happy Days, Pizza Hut, The Fonz . **10.00**
Hot Air Balloon................................ **9.00**
Star Trek, Dr Spock, 1976 .... **8.00**

Garfield, 100% Cattitude, frosted, 6" h **8.00**

Hanna Barbera Productions, Inc., Larosa
Pizzaria Parlor, 16 oz, Fred and Wilma,
Yogi and Mr Ranger, Scooby, Luigi, 1973
.... **30.00**

Hardee's, Flintstones, The First 30 Years -
1964, 16 oz, 1991

Going to the Drive-In **5.00**
The Blessed Event........................... **6.50**
The Snorkasaurus Story **6.00**

Marvel Comics

Howard the Duck, 1977 .... **4.00**
Hulk, 1978.. **3.50**

McDonalds

Big Mac, 1983, emb arches around base
.... **25.00**
Canadian, Disney Movie Series, Peter
Pan **20.00**

Disneyland, Adventureland **3.00**
Disney World 25th Anniversary, set of four
.... **30.00**
Garfield, Are We Having Fun Yet, 5-7/8" h
.... **5.00**
Mayor McCheese Taking Pictures.... **5.00**
McDonald Action Series, 16 oz, 1977
.... **5.00**
Ronald McDonald Saves The Falling Star,
1977 .... **6.00**
Seattle Seahawks, Beeson Eller/Beamon
.... **10.00**
Mobil, football, 10 different logos, price for
set **20.00**

National Periodical Publications

Batman **15.00**
Robin, 6 oz, 1960s **25.00**
Superman, Fighting the Dragon, 5-1/4" h,
1965 .... **12.00**
Wonder Woman **10.00**

Paramount Pictures

Gulliver's Travels, 1939 .... **40.00**
Happy Days - Fonze, "Hey!" 16 oz, 1977
.... **15.00**

Pepsi

Batgirl, 1976 .... **45.00**
Bugs Bunny and Martian, ray gun, 1976
.... **48.00**
Bullwinkle **30.00**
Chilly Willy, 16 oz **38.00**
Cool Cat, black letters, 1973 .... **5.00**
Daffy Duck and Tasmanian Devil, 1976
.... **15.00**
Dudley Do-Right, black lettering, 16 oz
.... **30.00**
Flash, 16 oz, 1976, minor mispaint. **15.00**
Foghorn Leghorn, 16 oz, 1973 .... **12.00**
Green Arrow, 1976 .... **40.00**
Happy Birthday Mickey, 1978 .... **4.00**
Harvey Cartoons, Wendy, black letters
.... **50.00**
Leonardo TTV, Underdog, 16 oz **14.00**
M.G.M. Barney Bear, 1975 .... **10.00**
Natasha, 12 oz, copyright P.A.T. Ward,
slight fading **35.00**
Pepsi can, plastic lid with tab, 1970s **5.00**
Rescuers, Brutus & Nero **3.00**
Road Runner, black letters, 1973 ..... **3.00**
Simon Bar Sinister, 12 oz **40.00**
Speedy Gonzales, black letters, 1973
.... **6.00**
Springfield Restaurant Group, red logo,
6" h **11.00**
Super Action Baseball, Count on
Schmidt, 1981 .... **8.00**
Superman, 1975, slightly faded **15.00**
Tim Horton Doughnuts, Yosemite Sam,
1978 .... **8.00**
Tweety, 16 oz, thin glass, white lettering,
1973 .... **15.00**
United Oil Baseball, Babe Ruth **15.00**

Pizza Hut

All-Time Greatest Denver Broncos, #4 of
four **10.00**
Buffalo Bills Historic Logo, mug, 1960
.... **12.00**
CB Lingo, blue truck **38.00**
Denver Broncos, 25th Anniversary, #3 of
four **3.00**
Dudley Do-right, helicopter **8.00**
Utah State Collectors Series, David Keith
Mansion **5.00**

Popeye's Fried Chicken, 1979 Popeye Pals

Brutus **20.00**
Olive Oyl **28.00**
Popeye **25.00**

7-Up, Marvel Comics

Captain America **15.00**
Fantastic Four **20.00**
Howard the Duck **18.00**
Incredible Hulk **12.00**

Sunbonnet Sue, blue Sunbonnet Sue with
watering can, lower border of red flowers, **$12**.

Sunday Funnies

Gasoline Alley, 16 oz, copyright Chicago
Tribune, Uncle Walt, Nina, Judy, Skeezix,
1976, slight paint loss **15.00**
Little Orphan Annie, 16 oz, copyright New
York News, Orphan Annie, Sandy, Daddy
Warbucks, ASP, Punjab, 1976 .... **15.00**
Moon Mullins, 16 oz, copyright New York
News, Lord Plushbottom, Kayo, Willie,
Lady Plushbottom, and Moon Mullins,
1976 .... **18.00**
Terry and the Pirates **7.00**
Taco Bell, Star Trek III, 16 oz, copyright
Paramount Pictures Corp, 1984
Lord Kruge **12.00**
The Search for Spock Enterprise
Destroyed **15.00**

Walt Disney
> Goof, 1937 .... **140.00**
> Goofy, Goofy and Pluto on back, 16 oz,
> Pepsi, copyright Walt Disney
> Productions, 1978 .... **12.00**
> Minnie Mouse **30.00**

Warner Bros, Pepsi
> Beaky Buzzard, 16 oz, thin glass, 1973
> **15.00**
> Cool Cat and Beaky Buzzard, 16 oz,
> 1976 .... **15.00**
> Daffy Duck, 4 oz, 1976 .... **15.00**
> Elmer Fudd, 6 oz, 1976 .... **15.00**
> Marriots Great America, 1975, pedestal
> milk glass mug, 5-1/2" h **20.00**
> Speedy/Slo Poke, hammer, orig
> Brockway sticker on base, 1976 .. **175.00**
> Taz and Bugs, #4 of eight **10.00**

Welch's, 8 oz
> Archies, Betty & Veronica Give a Party,
> 1971 .... **5.00**
> Archies, Betty & Veronica Fashion Show,
> Jughead, 1971 .... **9.00**
> Archies, Sabrina cleans her room, 1971,
> orig label **15.00**
> Davy Crockett, Fought the War, orange
> and white **17.50**
> Flintstones **6.00**
> Howdy Doody, Doodyville Circus, Flub-A-
> Dub **10.00**
> Speedy Snaps up the Cheese, Sylvester,
> 1974 .... **4.00**
> That's All Folks, Elmer, 1974 .... **6.00**
> Warner Bros, Bugs Bunny, Tweety
> bottom, 1976 .... **12.00**
> Warner Bros, Porky Pig, 1976 .... **10.00**

WWF, Swarts Peanut Butter, orig lid
> Hulkamania **9.00**
> Jake the Snake **5.00**
> Macho Man **6.50**
> The Ultimate Warrior **8.00**

Children's Books

History: William Caxton, a printer in England, is considered the first publisher of children's books. *Aesop's Fables*, printed in 1484, was one of his early publications. Other very early books include John Cotton's *Spiritual Milk for Boston Babes* in 1646, *Orbis Pictis* translated from the Latin about 1657, and *New England Primer* in 1691.

Early children's classics were *Robinson Crusoe* (1719), *Gulliver's Travels* (1726), and Perrault's *Tales of Mother Goose* (translated into English in 1729). The well-known "A Visit from St. Nicholas" by Clement C. Moore appeared in 1823. Some of the best-known children's works were published between 1840 and 1900, including Lear's *Book of Nonsense*, Andersen's and Grimm's *Fairy Tales*, *Alice in Wonderland*, *Hans Brinker*, *Little Women*, *Tom Sawyer*, *Treasure Island*, *Heidi*, *A Child's Garden of Verses*, and *Little Black Sambo*.

During the late 1800s, novelty children's books appeared. Lothar Meggendorfer, Ernest Nister, and Raphael Tuck were the best-known publishers of these fascinating pop-up and mechanical, or movable, books. The popularity of this type of book has continued to the present, and some of the early movable books are being reproduced.

Series books for boys and girls were introduced around the turn of the century. The Stratemeyer Syndicate, established about 1906, became especially well known for series such as Tom Swift, the Bobbsey Twins, Nancy Drew, and the Hardy Boys.

After the turn of the century, biographies, poetry, and educational books became popular. Van Loon's *Story of Mankind* received the first Newbery Medal in 1922. This award, given for the year's most distinguished literature for children, was established to honor John Newbery, an English publisher of children's books.

Picture books became a major part of the children's book field as photography and new technologies for reproducing illustrations developed. The Caldecott Medal, given for the most distinguished picture book published in the United States, was established in 1938. Dorothy Lathrop's *Animals of the Bible* was the first recipient of this award, which honors Randolph Caldecott, an English illustrator from the 1800s.

Collecting Hints: Most collectors look for books by a certain author or illustrator. Others are interested in books from a certain time period, such as the 19th century. Accumulating the complete run of a series, such as Tom Swift, Nancy Drew, or the Hardy Boys, is of interest to some collectors. Subject categories are popular, too, and include ethnic books, mechanical books, first editions, award-winning books, certain kinds of animals, rag books, Big Little Books, and those with photographic illustrations.

A good way to learn about children's books is to go to libraries and museums where special children's collections have been developed. Books on various aspects of children's literature are a necessity. You also should read a general reference on book collecting to provide you with background information. Eventually, you will want to own a few reference books most closely associated with your collection.

Although children's books can be found at all the usual places where antiques and collectibles are for sale, also seek out book and paper shows. Get to know dealers who specialize in children's books; ask to receive their lists or catalogs. Some dealers will try to locate books for your collection. Most stores specializing in used and out-of-print books have a section with children's books. Regular bookstores may carry the most recent works of authors or illustrators who are still working.

When purchasing books, consider the following: presence of a dust jacket or box, condition of the book, the edition, quality of illustrations and binding, and prominence of the author or illustrator. Books should be examined very carefully to make sure that all pages and illustrations are present. Missing pages will reduce the value of the book. Significant bits of information, particularly details of the book's edition, can be found on the title page and verso of the title page.

Try to buy books in the best condition you can afford. Even if your budget is limited, you can still find very nice inexpensive children's books if you keep looking.

Reprints: A number of replicas are now appearing on the market, most having been published by Evergreen Press and Merrimack. A new Children's Classics series offers reprints of books illustrated by Jessie Willcox Smith, Edmund Dulac, Frederick Richardson, and others.

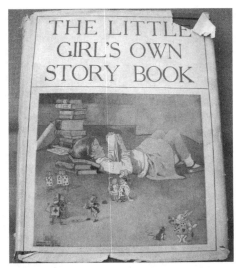

The Little Girl's Own Story Book, Frederick A. Stokes Co., 1924, hard bound, six color illustrations, 176 pages, original dust jacket, $20.

A Child's Life of Christ, 1920s, 167 pgs, illus **7.00**
Adventures of Galloping Gas Stove, Howard Garis, Grossett & Dunlap, 1926, illus by Lang Campbell **20.00**
Aesop's Fables, illus by Nora Fry, eight color plates, Longmeadow Press, 1988 . **10.00**
And To Think I Saw It On Mulberry Street, Dr. Seuss, Vanguard Press, 1937, 3rd printing **35.00**
Animal Stories For Little People, illus by Henry Altemus Co., 1902, 192 pgs **14.00**
Around the Mulberry Bush, color illus by Fern Bisel Peat, Saalfield, 1933 ..... **55.00**
A Treasury of Verses, six color plates by Willy Pogany, black and white dwgs, MacMillian, 1900 .... **15.00**
Assignment In Space With Rip Foster, Blake Savage, illus by Denny McManis, Whitman #1576, hardbound, 1958 .. **9.00**
Black Beauty, Anna Sewell, Whitman Classic, 1951, illus by Robert Doremus, dj **12.00**
Captain June, Alice Hegan Rice, illus by C. D. Weldon, Century 1907 .... **8.25**
Cherry Ames Senior Nurse, Helen Wells, 1944 .... **10.00**
Children of the Dust Bowl, The True Story Of The School At Weekpatch Camp, Jerry Stanley, illus, 1st ed, dj **12.00**
Christmas At The Little Zoo, pop-up, 1950s, 22 pgs **12.00**
Combat: the Counterattack, Whitman Authorized TV Adventure Series, hardbound, 1966 .... **8.00**

Curious George, H. A. Rey, Hough Mifflin, 1969.. **6.50**

Daniel Boone, Wilderness Scout, Stewart Edward White, 1948.......................... **8.00**

Dolly and Molly At The Seashore, Elizabeth Gordon, color illus by Frances Breen, Rand McNally, 1904........................ **50.00**

Don Sturdy on the Desert of Mystery, Victor Appleton, illus by Walter S. Rogers, Grossett & Dunlap, 1925 .... **8.00**

This Is The House That Jack Built, Cinderella Series, McLoughlin Bros, New York, no date, hand-stitched repair to spine, **$10**.

Fairy Tales From Grimm, Christmas Stocking Series, introduction by L. Frank Baum, Reilley & Britton, Chicago, 1905..... **12.00**

Five Little Peppers & How They Grew, Margaret Sidney, 1948, illus by Wm Sharp, 275 pgs................................. **7.50**

Floppy In Santa Land, pop-up, use wear **5.00**

F Troop, Whitman TV edition, William Johnston, illus by Larry Pelini, 1967 . **5.00**

Good Stories, Easy Growth in Reading, 1st Reader, Level 2, Gertrude Felton, John Winston, 1940.................................. **10.00**

Heidi, Johanna Spyri, illus Jessie Wilcos Smith, 10 color plates, Longmeadow Press, 1986...................................... **10.00**

Hope Laura Lee, 1960 .... **6.00**

Huckleberry Hound, Hanna Barbera, Giant Story Book, 192 pgs, illus **9.00**

Johnny Crow's Party, picture book drawn by L. Leslie Brooke, Frederick Warne & Co., 1959, ex-lib.................................... **12.00**

Joyful Poems for Children, James W. Riley, 1946, 1st ed.................................... **28.00**

Kitty's Class Day and Other Stories, Louisa M. Alcott, 1908, 334 pgs **8.00**

Little Women, Louisa May Alcott, John Winston, 1926, embossed picture cover **25.00**

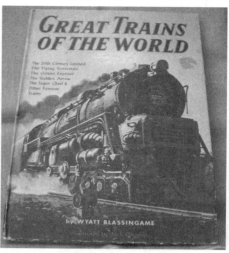

Great Trains of the World, Wyatt Blassingame, illustrations by Jack Coggins, Random House, 1953, **$15**.

Lullaby Land, Eugene Field, Schribner, 1911, illus by Charles Robinson **15.00**

More All-Of-A-Kind Family, Sydney Taylor Follett Publ., illus by Mary Stevens, 1954, 159 pgs, ex-lib................................. **9.00**

Mother Goose in Silhouettes, cut by Katherine Buffum, Hough-Mifflin, 1907, 1st ed **40.00**

Pinocchio, the Adventures of a Marionette, C. Collodi, six color plates by Charles Copeland, 1904 .... **45.00**

Pinocchio, The Story of A Puppet, C. Collodi, eight color plates by Marie Kirk, 1916 .... **22.50**

Pollyanna Grows Up, E. H. Porter, illus by H. W. Taylor, The Page Co., 1915, 1st ed **22.00**

RacKetty PacKetty House, Frances H. Burnett, Century, 1906, 1st ed., 20 color plates by Harrison Cady **85.00**

Raggedy Ann and Andy And the Camel With The Wrinkled Knees, Johnny Gruelle, Volland, 1924, 1st ed.................... **85.00**

Rick Brant Adventure #16, The Egyptian Cat Mystery, John Blaine, Grossett & Dunlap, 1961, illus **15.00**

Rip Van Winkle, Washington Irving, McKay Publishing, 1921, nine color illus by N. C. Wyatt, black and white drawings... **45.00**

Silver Pennies, A Collection of Modern Poems For Boys And Girls, Blanche Thompson, illus by Winifred Bromhall, MacMill, 1938.............................. **15.00**

Son of the Black Stallion, Walter Farley, black and white illus by Milton Manasco, Randon House, 21st printing, 1947 **12.00**

Stocky, Boy of West Texas, Elizabeth W. Baker, illus by Chars. Hargens, John Winson & Co., 3rd printing, 1946 ..... **8.00**

Tarzan And The Golden Lion, Edgar Rice Burroughs, 1928, 1st ed., scuff on cov **18.50**

Tarzan, Lord of the Jungle, Edgar Rice Burroughs, 1928, 1st ed **24.50**

The Adventures of Holly Hobbie, Richard Dubelman, Delacourt Press, 1980, 1st ed., wear to dj................................. **15.00**

Guess Who, Dick and Jane Jr. Primer, 1962, $95.

The Adventures of Tom Sawyer, color plates by Tom Hurd, Winston, 1931 .... **22.50**

The Big Book of Burgess Nature Stories, T. Burgess, H. Cady, Grossett & Dunlap, 1945 .... **24.00**

The Big Trick & Puzzle Book, 1929, 208 pgs, color litho on soft cover of three young people, back cover missing **5.00**

The Bobbsey Twins And The Baby May, Laure Lee Hope, 1924, Grossett & Dunlap, 242 pgs.............................. **12.00**

The Bobbsey Twins In The Mystery Cave, 1960 .... **8.00**

The Bobbsey Twins, Merry Days Indoors and Out, Laura Lee Hope, Whitman **5.75**

The Bobbsey Twins On A Houseboat, Laura Lee Hope, Grossett & Dunlap, 1915, 244 pgs, green cover, top and bottom edges rough... **10.00**

The Cat In The Hat Beginner Book, Dictionary in French, Random House, 1965 .... **10.00**

The Christopher Robin Reader, Dutton, 1929, dj... **75.00**

The Christopher Robin Verses, A. A. Milne, Dutton, 1932, 1st printing, 12 color plates **65.00**

The Green Hornet, The Case of the Disappearing Doctor, Whitman TV edition, hardbound, 1966................ **5.00**

Our New Friends, Dick and Jane, hard cover, 1946, for grades 1 and 2, $135.

The Hardy Boys, The Missing Churn, Franklin Dixon, Grossett & Dunlap, 1928, dj taped to cover **12.50**

The Hardy Boys, The Secret of the Old Mill, Franklin Dixon, Grossett & Dunlap, 1927, dj taped to cover **12.50**

The Lennon Sisters, The Secret of Holiday Island, Doris Schroeder, Whitman Authorized TV edition, 1960 .... **12.00**

The Mouse and the Motorcycle, Beverly Cleary, illus by Louis Darling, Wm Morrow, 1963, Weekly Readers Club, wear to cover **6.00**

The Outdoor Girls On Cape Cod, Laura Lee Hope, Grossett & Dunlap, 1924..... **20.00**

The Secret World of Teddy Bears, A Privileged Glimpse into Their Lives When You're Not There, Pamela Prince, photos by Elaine Faris Kennan, Harmony Books, 1983, 1st ed., dj............................. **15.00**

The Surprising Adventure of the Man in the Moon, Ray M. Steward, Lee & Shepard, Boston, August 1903, 12 full page color illus **50.00**

The Tale of Little Pig Robinson, story and illus by Beatrix Potter, Frederick Wayne, 1930, six color plates, black and white illus **18.00**

The Tale of the Good Cat Jupie, Neely McCoy, author and illus, MacMillian, 1926, 1st edition **10.00**

Tim and Lucy Go To Sea, Edward Ardizzone, Henry Z. Walck, Inc., 1958, ex-lib.... **9.00**

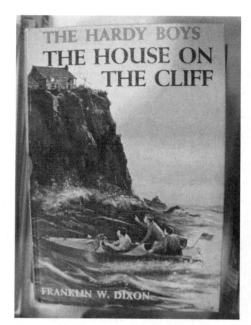

Hardy Boys, The House on the Cliff, Franklin W. Dixon, **$12.50**.

Tough Enough and Sassy, Ruth and Latrobe Carroll, Henry Z. Walck, Inc., 1958, 63 pgs, ex-lib **9.00**
Travels of Babar, Jean De Brunhoff, Randon House, 1962 .... **12.00**
Upside-Down Town, F. Emerson Andrews, illus by Louis Slobodkin, Little, Brown & Co., 1958, 2nd printing, ex-lib **9.00**
Wizard of Oz Picture Book, Whitman, #865, 1939 copyright, 8-1/2" x 12" **28.00**
The Yearling, Marjorie Kinnan Rawlings, Scribner's, 1947, school set **12.00**
When We Were Very Young, A. A. Milne, Dutton, 1948 .... **8.00**

Children's Dishes

History: Dishes for children to play with have been popular from Victorian times to the present and have been made in aluminum, tin, china, and glass.

Many glass companies made small child-size sets in the same patterns as large table sets. This was especially true during the period when Depression glass was popular, and manufacturers made child-size pieces to complement the full-size lines.

Collecting Hints: Children's dishes were played with, so a bit of wear is to

be expected. Avoid rusty metal dishes and broken glass dishes.

Additional Listings: Akro Agate.

Aluminum

Coffeepot, black wooden handle and knob
.... **25.00**
Cook set, The Griddlette, three pcs, orig red card, 1950s **25.00**
Measuring cup, graduated, handle... **10.00**
Silverware set, four spoons, two forks, knife, pie server **10.00**
Teapot, black wooden knob, swing handle
.... **20.00**
Tumbler set, 2-1/4" h, two green, silver, and gold, Japan, 1950s, set of six **28.00**

Punch bowl set, File and Fan pattern, blue carnival glass, contemporary, **$45**.

Cast iron

Skillet, 5" from handle to edge, mkd "8"
.... **15.00**

China

Blue Willow
Creamer **18.00**
Cup and saucer, 2-1/4" cup, 2-3/4" saucer **15.00**
Plate, 3-3/4" d **9.00**
Plate, 4-1/2" d **8.75**
Platter, 6-1/4" x 3-3/4", oval **25.00**
Set, 26 pc **485.00**
Sugar, cov **25.00**
Teapot, cov, 4" **50.00**

Moss Rose
Cup and saucer **7.50**
Plate **5.00**
Platter, oval **10.00**
Tea set **125.00**

Occupied Japan
Set, 26 pcs **350.00**
Teapot, cov **85.00**

Cereal bowl, Rub-A-Dub Dub, Three Men In A Tub, multicolored illustration, $5.

Depression-era glass

Bowl, Little Deb, ribbed 15.00
Creamer, Cherry Blossom, pink **45.00**

Cup and saucer
   Cherry Blossom.............................. **45.00**
   Diana, pink 45.00
   Doric and Pansy, pink 40.00
   Moderntone, beige.......................... 20.00
Mixing bowl, Glassbake, three ftd...... **40.00**

Plate
   Cherry Blossom, Delfite Blue.......... **16.75**
   Doric and Pansy, pink **15.00**
   Homespun, pink.............................. **15.00**
   Laurel, red trim **15.00**
   Moderntone, blue, green, pink, or yellow
   .... **12.00**

Set
   Cherry Blossom, 14 pcs, blue delphite
   .... **265.00**
   Diana, crystal, gold trim, rack, 12 pcs
   .... **175.00**

Little Lady Refreshment Set, Banner Plastics Corp., NY, box marked "RS100," original box and contents, $25.

Pattern glass

Butter, cov, Doyle's 500, amber **100.00**

Creamer
   Fernland... 18.00
   Hawaiian Lei 15.00
Cup and saucer, Lion 20.00
Mug, Fighting Cats 35.00
Pitcher, Nursery Rhyme...................... 80.00
Punch bowl set, punch bowl and six cups
   Flattened Diamond and Sunburst.. **65.00**
   Tulip and Honeycomb **80.00**
Spooner, Menagerie Fish, amber..... **115.00**
Sugar, cov
   Hawaiian Lei 35.00
   Nursery Rhyme.............................. 48.00
Table set, four pcs
   Arrowhead in Oval......................... 75.00
   Beaded Swirl.................................. 115.00

Tumbler
   Nursery Rhyme............................... 20.00
   Sandwich Ten Panel, sapphire blue
   .... **145.00**

Tea set, 17 pieces, white ground, boy in blue shirt, girl in orange dress, marked "Made in Japan," 8-3/4" x 10-3/8" original box, $65.

Plastic

Chocolate set, Banner, service for four, napkin holder, silverware................ **85.00**

Dinnerware set
   Nine pcs, Tinkerbelle, Walt Disney **25.00**
   Eleven pcs, Plasco, Queen of Hearts with rabbit, Plasco.................................. **18.00**
   Seventeen pcs, Alice in Wonderland, Plasco, beige................................. **35.00**
   Seventeen pcs, Tupperware, multicolored
   .... **55.00**

Silverware set
   Six pcs, two knives, forks, and spoons, Plasco, pink, orig cardboard........... **9.00**
   Eight pcs, serving set, two knives, forks, and spoons, Bestmade, red, orig cardboard **12.50**

Christmas Collectibles

History: In the 1800s, the Christmas tree, popularized by Queen Victoria, and the Christmas village or Moravian putz became integral to the American celebration of Christmas. The first Christmas decorations and ornaments were homemade and trees were decorated with fruits and candies. With the increase in popularity of the holiday a glass ornament developed in Germany. By 1870, glass ornaments were being sold in major cities such companies as F. W. Woolworth and Sears Roebuck and Company.

Collecting Hints: Beware of reproduction ornaments and other Christmas collectibles, especially candy container figures. The ornaments are usually brighter in color and have shinier paint than the originals. It is common to find tops replaced on ornaments. Older decorations should show some signs of handling.

Reproduction Alert.

Additional Listings: Santa Claus.

Advisers: Lissa Bryan-Smith and Richard Smith.

Figures, carolers, papier-mâché, nodder heads, set of three, Germany, 6" to 6-1/2" h, **$120.** All Christmas photos courtesy of advisers Richard Smith and Lissa Bryan-Smith.

Christmas village/garden/putz

Animal, celluloid

Cow, 3-1/2" h **12.00**
Duck, 1-1/2" h, metal feet **10.00**
Ram, 3-1/2" h **8.00**
Reindeer, 3" h, brown **8.00**

Animal, composition

Camel, 6" h, flocked, wood legs, mkd "Germany" **45.00**
Chick, 1" h, metal feet **15.00**
Dog, 1-1/2" h, white and brown, wood legs and feet **12.00**
Elephant, 5" h, bone tusks, mkd "Germany" **75.00**
Goat, 4" h, wool covering, wood legs, metal horns **30.00**
Horse, 5" h, wood legs, mkd "Germany" **35.00**
Reindeer, 5" h, brown, glass eyes, wood legs, mkd "Germany" **60.00**
Sheep, 5" h, wool covering, wood legs, paper collar, mkd "Germany" **45.00**
Swan, 2" h, composition body, feather covering **15.00**

Animal, glass, penguin, 2-1/2" h, glass, black and white, orange feet **8.00**

Animal, plaster, lamb, 1-1/2" h, standing, grassy base, mkd "Germany" **5.00**

Animal, plastic

Horse, 3" h, gray, USA **2.50**
Reindeer, 3-3/4" h, white, USA **4.00**

Building

Cardboard, lithographed, assorted homes or business, USA, 5" h **8.00**
Cardboard, painted with mica, bulb hole in back, Japan, multicolored, 3-1/2" h **5.00**
Plaster, solid, multicolored, 4" h **10.00**
Plastic, assorted homes or business, multicolored, 6" h **7.00**

Fence

Plastic, 2" h, white, Plasticville, six sections **24.00**
Wood, 3" h, folding fence, 6" sections, red and green **40.00**
Wood, 5" h, picket, white, wired for Christmas lights on each post, four sections, 24" l **55.00**

People, composition, mkd "Germany"

Goose girl, 4" h, metal staff **15.00**
Nativity, Joseph, 6" h **12.00**
Shepherd, 4" h, European dress **17.00**

People, metal

Couple, 2" h, sitting on park bench, metal, USA **20.00**
Skater, 2-1/2" h, metal, USA **10.00**
Skier, 2" h, two poles, USA **12.00**

People, plaster, mkd "Japan"

Angel, 3-12" h **4.00**
Nativity figure, Mary, kneeling, 3" h .. **3.00**

People, plastic
    Cowboy on horse, 3" h...................... **2.00**
    Train figures, 1-1/4" h, set of six **15.00**
People, wood, angel, painted, East
    Germany, 2" h.................................... **3.00**

Tree
    Brush, green, white flocking, red wood
    base, 6" h... **8.00**
    Brush, white, glass bead decorations,
    red base, 12" h **18.00**
    Metal, green, semi-flat, 3-1/2" h...... **15.00**
    Plastic, green, brown base, flat, USA, 4" h
    .... **3.00**

Ornament, cotton batting, fruit, Japan, 3-1/2" h, $40.

Decorations

Bank, 5" h, snowman, white, black bowler
    hat, red scarf, orig box................... **15.00**
Book
    Christmas Carols, Little Golden Book,
    Simon & Schuster, 1946................. **10.00**
    Merry Christmas, Happy New Year,
    Phyllis McGinley, Viking Press, 1968 **7.00**
    The Night Before Christmas, color
    painting by Grandma Moses, published
    by Random House, 1961................ **35.00**
Boot
    Papier-mâché, 10" h, white, mica trim
    .... **18.00**
    Plastic, 4" h, red, USA **4.00**
Candleholders, pr, 2-1/2" w, 6" l, 1-1/8" h,
    iron, poinsettias **35.00**
Candy box, cardboard
    4-1/2" l, string handle, nativity scene,
    1950s **6.00**
    10-1/2" l, paper label, red background,
    three wise men scene.................... **12.00**
Candy container, pressed cardboard,
    opening in base, USA
    Christmas tree, 10" h, green and white
    .... **75.00**
    Snowman, 7-1/2" h, black hat......... **40.00**

Ornament, glass, clip-on bird, Germany, $35.

Figure, hard plastic
    Angel, 4" h, white, silver halo **5.00**
    Choir Boy, 3-1/2" h, red and white.... **4.50**
Nativity, cardboard
    Barn, brightly painted chalk figures glued
    to base, Japan................................ **12.00**
    Boxed set, 14" h, 20" l, fold-out, USA,
    1950s **24.00**
Postcard, 3" x 5"
    A Hearty Christmas Greeting, sledding
    Victorian children **4.00**
    Wishing You A Very Happy Christmas,
    dog with riding crop in mouth, toy horse
    .... **5.00**
Record, orig record in orig cover
    33 .... **3.00**
    45 .... **3.00**
    78 .... **5.00**
Sheet music
    "Christmas in Killarney," Remick Music
    Corp., NY, 1950 .... **5.00**
    "Santa Claus is Coming to Town," Leo
    Feist, Inc., NY, 1934......................... **6.00**
    "Silent Night, Holy Night," Calumet Music
    Co., Chicago, 1935 .... **5.00**
    "Twelve Days of Christmas," Leeds Music
    Corp, NY, 1948 .... **5.00**
Stocking
    Flannel, 12" l, red, stenciled Santa and
    sleigh... **15.00**
    Oil cloth, 8" l, blue and white, cowboy
    boot shape, red cloth loop **22.00**
Tree
    3" h, feather, green, red painted wood
    base **18.00**
    12" h, feather, white sq red base, mkd
    "West Germany" **72.00**
    36" h, feather, green, candle clips, round
    wood base, mkd "Germany"........ **300.00**
    42" h, plastic, green, wood column, metal
    base **25.00**
    48" h, aluminum, metal tripod base **45.00**
    48" h, viscose, white, white painted wood
    base **40.00**
Tree stand
    Cast iron, silver paint, three legs.... **60.00**
    Tin litho, lighted.............................. **48.00**
Wreath, cellophane, 10" d, red, silver foil
    trim, electric candle inside **15.00**

Tree decorations

Beads, 60" l, glass, multicolored, Japan
.... **12.00**
Candy cane, 6" l, chenille, red and white
.... **4.00**
Icicle, 4" h, metal, twisted, color or silver
.... **2.00**
Light bulb, working
    Bubble, Noma, set **24.00**
    Japanese lantern, 4" h, milk glass.. **14.00**
    Santa head, 2" h, milk glass........... **24.00**
    Snowman, 3" h, milk glass **20.00**
Ornament, **beaded**, 4" l, airplane, double-sided, Czechoslovakian.................. **20.00**
Ornament, **chromolithograph**, tinsel trim, German
    Angel, 10" h, chorus of three **22.00**
    Fish, 6" l, several on a string, crepe paper trim **30.00**
    Child, 5" h, winter clothes............... **14.00**

Ornament, glass

    Clown, 3" h, standing on ball **40.00**
    Doll's head, 2-1/2" d **60.00**
    Heart, 3-1/2" h, red **10.00**
    Pinecone, 3-1/2" l, red, tinsel inside **12.00**
    Round, 2-1/2" d, plain, red, pink, green, gold, or silver..................................... **3.00**
    Round, 3" d, striped, unsilvered, paper cap.. **6.00**
    Tree, 3-1/2" h, clip-on base, red and white
.... **30.00**

Ornament, wax, drummer boy, metal hook, USA, 3" h, $7.

Ornament, plastic

    Bell, 2-1/2" h, red **2.00**
    Cat, 3-1/2" h, white and red, annealed hook, USA **7.00**
    Icicle, semi-clear, glow in the dark, annealed hook, set of six **12.00**
    Reflector, 3" d
        Foil, set of six........................ **6.00**
        Metal, pierced tin **5.00**
Tree topper
    5" d, foil star with hole in center for light bulb **15.00**
    6" h, angel, cardboard and spun glass
.... **25.00**
    9" h, silvered glass, multicolored ... **12.00**

Circus Items

History: The 18th-century circus was a small traveling company of acrobats and jugglers, and the first record of an American troupe is from that time. Washington is known to have attended a circus performance.

By the mid-19th century, the tent circus with accompanying side shows and menagerie became popular throughout America. P. T. Barnum was one of the early circus promoters. His American Museum in New York featured live animal acts in 1841. Other successful Barnum promotions included Jenny Lind in 1850, Tom Thumb from 1843 to 1883, and Jumbo, who was purchased from the London Zoo in 1883.

The Ringlings and Barnum and Bailey brought a magical quality to the circus. The golden age of the tent circus was the 1920s to the 1940s, when a large circus consisted of more than 100 railroad cars.

As television challenged live entertainment, the tent circus fell on hard times. Expenses for travel, food, staff, etc., mounted. A number of mergers took place, and many smaller companies simply went out of business. There are a few tent circuses remaining. However, most modern circuses now perform inside large convention centers.

Collecting Hints: Circus programs are one of the most popular items in this category. Individuals have collected them since the 1920s. Programs prior to the 1930s are hard to find; post-1930 material is readily available.

Model building plays an active part in collecting. Some kits are available, however, most collectors like to build models from scratch. Great attention is placed on accurate details.

There are many books published about the circus. These are sought by collectors for intrinsic, as well as research, value.

Baraboo Script, 50th Anniversary 1883-1933, Celebration of the Founding of Ringling Bros. Shows at Baraboo, Wisconsin, pictures and names of different brother, different script value on each, expiration date of Nov 1, 1933, 2" x 4", set of three.................................. **12.00**

Calendar, Circus World Museum, 1974 **5.00**

Child's book

The Jolly Jump-Ups Book, See The Circus, Ringling Bros, The Greatest Show, McLaughlin Bros., 1944, six pop-up scenes... **95.00**

Toby Tyler or Ten Weeks With A Circus, James Otis, G & D, 1923, dj, some wear **9.00**

Tom & Jerry and the Toy Circus, Whitman, 1953... **12.00**

Christmas card

Clyde Beatty-Cole Bros, black, white, blue, and yellow, holiday dates on back, 8" x 9-1/2"... **20.00**

Seasons Greetings from Ringling Brothers and Barnum & Bailey, cartoon elephant family enjoying Christmas in tropical setting, 1954 pencil date, 6" x 7-1/2" paper folder............................. **20.00**

Circus pass

Circus Hall of Fame, Sarasota, FL.... **3.50**

Covina, California Jr. Chamber of Commerce... **3.50**

Garden Grove Breakfast Lions Club **3.50**

King Bros, sponsored by fire company **3.50**

United Nations Circus, Bridgeport ... **3.50**

Wallace & Clark Trained Animal Circus **3.50**

Letterhead, Ringling Bros, multicolored, five brothers with crest, 1909 .... **18.00**

Model, 1" scale

Bareback riders, man and woman, two horses... **800.00**

Clarke Bros Circus, two wheel hitch **150.00**

Hay wagon and harness, blue and red **300.00**

Railroad flat car **200.00**

Side show paraphernalia, fourteen set-ups **1,120.00**

Poster, Ringling Bros and Barnum & Bailey, Panto's Paradise, 16" x 28", **$125**.

Newspaper, The Circus News, 15" x 23" four page newspaper, Sixteenth Year, Volume 70, 1970, Carson and Barnes Circus, top half of front features Sky King's appearance at circus, black and white illus and photo of Kirby Grant, orig fold lines... **30.00**

Noisemaker, tin, black, white, and red clown, gray ground, red wood handle **5.00**

Original art prototype, prepared for Topps, 1930s, 8" x 10" artist tracing paper, "Big Top Circus Gum/A Clyde Beatty Action Animal Snapper," art in lead and colored pencil, 6" x 8" image showing Clyde Beatty holding whip and taming lion, text "Snapper Open and Close Mouth, Free In Each Package of Circus Gum" **95.00**

Pinback button

Barnum '76 Festival, red, white, and blue **10.00**

Cole Bros, Clyde Beatty, 1930s **25.00**

King Reid Shows, black and white clown, red, yellow, and green accents, light blue ground, c1950 .... **30.00**

Little Hip And His Owner Prof Andre, trained elephant, c1910 .... **45.00**

Setlin & Wilson Shows, 1-3/4" d, black and white clown, red, yellow, and green accents, light blue ground, dark blue rim border, c1940................................. **50.00**

Playing cards, Ringling Bros and Barnum & Bailey Circus, miniature size **12.00**

Playset, Marx, played-with condition **475.00**

Poster

Arthur Bros, 1940, Big Railroad Show, arrival parade with showgirls on horses and elephants................................. **90.00**

Barnum & Bailey, 1913, Lion and Tiger, reclining jungle cats, circus logo, Strobridge Litho **275.00**

Clyde Beatty Circus, holds reign over field of wild jungle cats, date tag "July 4, Glendale Speedway" **50.00**

Cole Bros, All the Marvels, animal sin cages, Erie Litho........................... **210.00**

Hagenbeck-Wallace, 1925, Capt. Clyde Beatty, World's Most Daring Trainer, posing with lions, tigers, and leopards pyramid **270.00**

King Bros, 1946, clown face, red and
yellow, advertising arrival.............. **210.00**
Ringling Bros and Barnum & Bailey, army
of 50 clowns, Logansport, Friday, July 29
.... **175.00**

Program

Barnum & Bailey, 1953 .... **12.00**
Cole Bros Clyde Beatty, 1969, 24 pgs, 40
photos.. **8.00**
Gentry Bros & James Patterson, 1924
.... **15.00**
Hamid-Morgan, 1948...................... **12.00**
New York Hippodrome, Archie Gunn
orange and blue cover art.............. **15.00**
Ringling Bros Barnum & Bailey, 1962, 53
pgs, 10 articles, 90 photos............. **18.00**

Puzzle, Milton Bradley, early 1900s, worn
10" x 11" x 1" box............................ **20.00**

Record, Old Time Circus Calliola, Wurlitzer,
Calliola, Paul Eakin's Gay 90s Village
.... **5.00**

Route book

Barnum & Bailey, 1906 .... **225.00**
Cristiani Bros Circus, 1958 .... **25.00**
Forepaugh, Adam, shows, 1891 .. **225.00**

Poster, Ringling Bros and Barnum & Bailey,
Madison Sq Garden, 108th Edition, **$55**.

Sign, 43" x 65", Aqua Circus, wood, painted,
scallop border, woman in 1890s garb
with parachute............................... **140.00**

Souvenir book, Ringling Bros and Barnum
& Bailey Circus, 1939..................... **15.00**

Ticket booklet, Von Bros 3 Ring Circus,
1940s, 2" x 5"................................... **6.00**

Ticket

Ringling Bros, 4-14-56 .... **20.00**
Tom Mix's Circus, child, 1-3/4" x 4",
attached to 2" x 5-1/2" card, black text on
red ticket... **75.00**

Toy

Circus drumming monkey, litho tin wind-
up, Yoneya, Japan, 1950s **65.00**
Clown motorcycle rider, litho tin wind-up,
Sato, Japan, 1950s **300.00**
Clown with cane, litho tin wind-up, sad
face, mkd "Made in Occupied Japan,"
1940s... **45.00**
Elephant circus parade, litho tin wind-up,
TPS, Japan, 1950s **150.00**
Monkey with ball, litho tin wind-up, mkd
"Made in US Zone, Germany," 1950s
.... **75.00**

Wagon wheel, wood, metal rim, red, white,
and blue painted spokes **250.00**

Clocks

History: The clock always has served a
dual function: decorative and utilitarian.
Beginning in the late 19th century, the
clock became an important advertising
vehicle, a tradition that continues today.
As character and personality recognition became part of the American
scene, clocks, whether alarm or wall
models, were a logical extension.
Novelty clocks, especially figural ones,
were common from 1930 to the 1960s.
Since digital wristwatches and clocks
became popular in the 1970s, clocks
have been less commonly used as
promotional items.

Collecting Hints: Many clocks of the
20th century were reproductions of
earlier styles. Therefore, dates should
be verified by checking patent dates on
the mechanism, makers' labels, and
construction techniques. The principal
buyers for the advertising and figural
clocks are not the clock collectors, but
the specialists with whose area of
interest the clock overlaps. For example, the Pluto alarm clock is of far
greater importance to a Disneyana
collector than to most clock collectors.
Condition is critical. Rust and non-
working parts have a major affect on
prices.

Additional Listings: See *Warman's
Antiques and Collectibles Price Guide.*

Vaseline glass, Daisy & Button pattern, case
made by McKee Glass Co., clock face marked
"Made in USA," **$295**.

Advertising

Busch Beer, electrical, horse and rider
scene, crossing valley near mountains of
Busch... **35.00**

Cincinnati Reds, logo, wood frame, electric, 1940s **60.00**

Coca-Cola, "Drink Coca-Cola in Bottles," sq. wood case, electric, Selected Devices Co. NY **215.00**

Four Roses Whiskey, 14" sq, lights up, orig wiring, metal, glass front, 1950s ... **250.00**

Frostie Root Beer, metal, fluorescent bulb **150.00**

General Electric, peach, mirror, electric **55.00**

John Deere, 14" d, round, electric **85.00**

Kodak, "Pictures Are Priceless-Use Kodak Film," 15-1/2", sq, lights up **35.00**

Lord Calvert, "Custom Distilled for Men of Distinction," black wood case, 11" x 12", 1940s **70.00**

Piels Beer, 15" x 11" **85.00**

Schlitz, lights, 1959 .... **60.00**

St. Joseph's Aspirin, neon **300.00**

Tetley, Tea Time, 13", blue and gray, tin, Art Deco **85.00**

Warren Telephone Co., Ashland, MA, oak **80.00**

Wise Potato Chip, owl, electric **75.00**

Cottage, quartz clock, molded resin body, white, green, brown, and yellow painted decoration, $5.

Alarm

Bradley, brass, double bells, Germany **35.00**

Garfield, painted metal case, double bells **40.00**

Hello Kitty, MIB **65.00**

Mickey Mouse, metal, Phinney-Walker, West German **40.00**

Peter's Shoes, New Haven Clock Co., 4" x 4", Art Deco, c1930 .... **50.00**

Purina Poultry Chows, electric, three dials, red, white, and blue checkerboard bag **40.00**

Trix The Rabbit, alarm, c1960 .... **15.00**

Tweety, Looney Tunes, talking, Janex, battery operated, 1978 .... **65.00**

Animated

Fish punching hole in side of boat with moving hammer, Hero Clock Co., wind-up, mkd "Made in China" **40.00**

Fish swimming around dial, Art Deco style, Sessions **250.00**

Haddon, rocking grandmother **175.00**

Mastercrafter's, fireplace **115.00**

United, ballerina, music box **150.00**

United, boy, gold fishing, 1950s **175.00**

Character

Bugs Bunny **90.00**

Davy Crockett, wall, pendulum **75.00**

Donald Duck, 9" h, wall, glazed china, 2-1/4" d case inscribed "Blessings," blue outfit, green glazed ground, orig gold sticker marked "Waechtersbach," inscribed "Walt Disney Productions, J.A. Sural Hanua/Main-Made in Germany," c1950 ... **175.00**

Howdy Doody, talking **75.00**

Mickey Mouse, Bradley animated hands **45.00**

Pluto, 4" x 5" x 9", electric, black, white, and red plastic, bone hands, moving eyes and tongue, c1940 .... **100.00**

Sesame Street, schoolhouse shape.. **25.00**

Raggedy Ann and Andy, talking alarm clock, Equity Clock Co., $45.

Figural

Artist's Palette, bakelite **35.00**

Chef, 10-1/2" h, electric, wall, white, Sessions Clock Co, Forestville **24.00**

Doghouse, 11" h, iron, dog looking out, flowers **80.00**

Donut, 8-3/4" h, dark herbal green glaze, Clifton Art Pottery **85.00**

Refrigerator, 8-1/2" h, metal, painted white, GE label, Warren Telechron Co, Ashland, MA **185.00**

Spinning Wheel, Lux, animated **80.00**

Wall

Smiley Face, "Have A Happy Day," 7" d hard plastic, Robertshaw Controls Co., Lux Time Division, some wear **25.00**

Clothing and Clothing Accessories

History: Clothing is collected and studied as a reference for learning about fashion, construction, and types of materials used. New collectors to this segment of the market are being attracted by designer label accessories, such as compacts and handbags. Other buyers of collectible clothing are looking for costumes for theater or other events, such as re-enactors.

Collecting Hints: Vintage clothing should be clean and in good repair. Designer labels and original boxes can add to the value.

Jacket, lady's, black knit, original tag "Castleberry," military-style gold trim, **$15**.

Apron, red, white, and green printed cotton, poinsettias **15.00**
Baby bonnet, cotton, tatted, ribbon rosettes **15.00**

Bed jacket, satin, pink, lavish ecru lace, labeled "B Altman & Co, NY," 1930s **30.00**
Belt, Kenneth Jay Lane, woven goldtone, alternating sizes of coral cabochons, hook clasp, 1" w, 30" l, mkd "KJL" on back **125.00**
Bloomers, wool, cream **25.00**

Blouse

Chiffon, green, child's, multiple rows of ruffles.. **15.00**
Cotton, white, cutwork, Victorian.... **20.00**
Lace, ecru, evening style, gathered waist, 1950s **18.00**
Poplin, white, middy style, c1910 .. **15.00**
Silk, cream, embroidered, 1900s... **65.00**
Silk damask, ivory, floral design, fabric covered buttons, late 1950s.......... **45.00**

Bonnet

Beaded, jet beads, 19th C............. **95.00**
Silk, hand crocheted lace **36.00**
Straw, finely woven, worn silk lining **135.00**

Book, *The Sharpness of Steele,* Julian Street, A. E. Little & Co., Lynn, MA, c1919, mystery, cuts of men's and women's shoes, 32 pgs, 4-3/4" x 7".............. **15.00**
Brochure, Willard's Wear Best, H Willard, Son & Co., Marshalltown, IA, c1930, furs for men, women, and children, four pgs, 4" x 8-3/4" **6.00**
Bustle, canvas and woven wire **30.00**

Child's dress, white lawn, lace trim, deep hem, $10.

Cape

Girl's, flannel wool, ivory, silk cord
embroidery **45.00**
Lady's, mohair, black, ankle length,
c1930 .... **75.00**
Lady's, velvet, black, pockets
embroidered with rhinestones, large
black beads, black satin lining, single
button closure at neck, early 1950s **80.00**

Catalog

A. E. Little & Co., Lynn, MA, 1901, 36 pgs,
4-3/4" x 7", The Story of Sorosis, cuts of
12 factories, 47 cuts of shoes **16.00**
Arlington Works, Wilmington, DE, 1917,
16 pgs, Arlington Cleanable Collars, cuts
of men's collars, 5-1/2" x 8-1/2" **24.00**
Copper, Wells & Co., St Joseph, MI,
1934, 50 pgs, hosiery, 6" x 5-1/2" ... **24.00**
Henry Arthur & Co., New York, NY, 1883,
62 pgs, 5-1/2" x 8", Spring Price List of
Leather & Findings, Boots and Shoe
Uppers with Listings of Items and Prices,
16 cuts of ladies shoes, 28 men's shoes,
spats, etc. **28.00**
N. B. Holden, Inc., Chicago, IL, 1915, 64
pgs, 5-1/4" x 7-1/2", Holden's Shoes for
Spring & Summer for Men and Women,
illus **18.00**
Sears, Roebuck & Co., Chicago, IL,
1919, 32 pgs, Made to Measure Clothes
for Men & Boys, Spring & Summer, 81
material swatches tipped in, 8-1/2" x 11"
.... **35.00**
Shanedling Dept. Store, Minneapolis,
MN, c1929, 32 pgs, 7" x 10-1/4", mail
order work clothes, gloves, house
dresses, lingerie, etc. **18.00**

Change purse, cut steel beads, ecru
crochet, push bottom clasp, fringe, leaf
dec, 2-1/2" x 3-1/2", inscribed "B Cottle,
1847" **65.00**

Christening gown, white

Cotton, matching bonnet, 47" l **100.00**
Cutwork embroidery bodice, tuck pleats
around ruffled skirt **65.00**
Machine sewn, lace, hand embroidery,
42" l **50.00**
Net, embroidered, silk slip, 44" l ... **150.00**

Coat

Baby's, cotton, gathered yoke and
capelet, embroidery, flannel lining . **25.00**
Boy's, linen, hand stitched, dec cuffs
.... **35.00**
Lady's, evening, black velour, brown
highlights, satin lining, large cuffs and
stand-up collar, frog closure at neck
.... **275.00**
Lady's, light tan plush, lined with tan,
brown, peach, and blue striped taffeta,
swing style, labeled "Borgana, A Borg
Fabric," mid-1950s **65.00**
Lady's, muskrat, bell shaped sleeves,
c1940 .... **90.00**

Evening dress, cream silk, beaded plume
decoration, sleeveless, **$45**.

Lady's, wool, blue, beaver collar and cuffs,
blouson, drop waist style, c1920... **100.00**

Collar

Beaded, white, 1930s **12.00**
Cotton, white, embroidered, wide,
scalloped **20.00**
Rabbit fur, white, pearl trim **15.00**

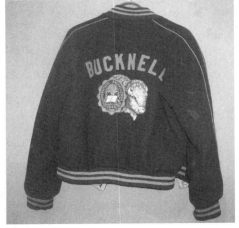

Jacket, blue wool, orange trim, embroidered
"Bucknell" with collegiate symbol on back, **$65**.

Compact

Avon, oval, lid dec with blue and green checkerboard pattern **35.00**
Evans, goldtone and mother -of-pearl, compact and lipstick combination . **45.00**
Hudnut, Richard, Deauville, blue, cloisonné tango-chain vanity, metal mirror, compartments for power and rouge, lipstick attached to finger ring chain **200.00**
K & K, brass, colored engine tooled dec basket compact, multicolored silk flowers enclosed in plastic dome lid, emb swinging handle **125.00**
Rowanta, brown enamel, oval petit point compact **65.00**
Unknown Maker, goldtone, heart shape, brocade lid **50.00**
Unknown Maker, plastic, red, white, and blue, Naval Officer's cap shape **85.00**
Volupt, USA, Adam and Eve, under apple tree **50.00**
Whiting and Davis, CO, Piccadilly, gilded mesh, vanity bag, compact incorporated in front lid, carrying chain **250.00**
Woolworth, Karess, polished goldtone, corset shaped, vanity case, powder and rouge compartments **45.00**
Yardley, goldtone, vanity case, red, white, and blue emb design no lid, powder and rouge compartments **75.00**

Dress, child's

Cotton, day type, gold, net trim, c1900 .... **20.00**
Georgette, pink, many layers of georgette and chiffon, c1920 .... **75.00**
Gingham, blue and white, hand and machine sewn, white embroidery trim, 25" h **50.00**
Knit, two pcs, 1930.......................... **25.00**
Lawn, white, lace, drop waist, c1910 .... **60.00**
Linen, embroidered wisteria inserts, Irish lace trim **150.00**
Net, silk lining, ruffles at neck, sleeves, pink rosette trim **120.00**
Velvet, red, white nylon, Shirley Temple style, Cinderella tag **20.00**

Dress, lady's

Batiste, white, lace, high neck, full skirt, long sleeves, c1900 .... **150.00**
Chiffon, blue, edges trimmed with braided fabric, 1925 .... **40.00**
Crochet, navy blue cotton, long fringe, deep scoop neckline, satin fringe hem, mid-1940s.. **35.00**
Lawn, drop waist **60.00**
Satin, black, 1920s.......................... **85.00**
Taffeta, blue, embossed dec, 1950s, dinner-type **10.00**

Handbag, beaded, silver and white beads with floral motif, original lining and beaded fringe, **$45**.

Viscose/polyester/nylon, red, circular skirt, fitted bodice, scoop neckline, puff sleeves, ribbed knit midriff, labeled "Zandra Rhodes, at Fifth Avenue," mid-1980s **45.00**
Wool jersey, black, long sleeves, wrap style hem trimmed with red wool jersey, patch pocket, black silk lining, labeled "Bill Blass, Made in U.S.A," late 1970s **40.00**

Evening gown, lady's

Crepe, brown, matching velvet capelet with feather trim, c1930 .... **40.00**
Net and taffeta, black, lace flowers, c1940 .... **48.00**
Organza, white, shirred, rhinestones, c1940 .... **45.00**
Silk, black, embroidered all over with black glass beads, halter style neckline, single strap on low back, labeled "Lillie Rubin, 100% silk, Made in China," 1970s **60.00**
Silk crepe, black, sheer, pleated ruffled detailing, straight skirt, black sequin embroidered wrap style jacket, long sleeves, labeled "Pierre Cardin, Paris, New York," late 1960s **65.00**
Velvet, blue, silver brocade, sequins on collar, blue feather hem trim extends up one side and on back drape, label "Edtyhe, Original Designs By Mr. Ben," early 1960s **35.00**

Three advertising boxes: Phoenix Muffler, **$8**;
Black Cat Hosiery box, red and yellow, **$12**;
Shirley President Suspenders, litho of peasant on
cover, **$10**; tan wool felt spats, **$20**.

Evening jacket, crepe, pink, floral patterned
sequins, lined, 1940 .... **58.00**

Gloves

Lady's, kid, white, long.................... **20.00**
Men's, driving, leather, black, c1910
.... **25.00**

Handbag

Alligator, suede lining...................... **18.00**
Beaded, Abstract design, white and gray,
milk glass beads, beaded handle, zipper,
5", marked "Czechoslovakia" **20.00**
Florals, pink and blue, shiny beads, gold
frame.. **45.00**
Lucite, pearlized, round lid, lunch box
clasp, twisted handle, seashell dec **17.50**
Mesh, enameled, white ground, floral dec
.... **55.00**
Pearl, envelope, Hong Kong label . **15.00**
Plastic, child's, red, imitation leather, three
Scotties dec, silver frame and chain, int.
mirror... **20.00**
Sequins, irid multicolored, silver and
seed pearl dec, rhinestone clasp, fancy
frame, Belgium **30.00**
Silk, clutch, black, cut steel beads,
marked "France," c1930................. **42.00**

Kimono, silk, coral, satin embroidered birds and
flowers in gold, white, and green, white rayon
lining, labeled "Excellent Quality, Made in Japan,"
1960s, **$65**.

Hand fan, see Fans

Handkerchief, see Handkerchiefs

Hat, lady's

Felt, cloche, black **15.00**
Satin, black, stitched pattern covers
upper crown, design of small glass
beads and metallic thread on lower
crown, rose taffeta lining, label "The
Margate Chapeau, Paris, New York,"
c1916 .... **95.00**
Satin, pillbox, black, netting **18.00**
Straw, black, Victorian **95.00**
Hat, man's, Stetson, orig box, some wear
.... **150.00**

Muff

Marabou, white **45.00**
Rabbit fur, white, child's.................. **25.00**
Sable, brown, tails **100.00**

Necktie, men's

Bow-tie, white polka dots on black **10.00**
Fish, 1940s...................................... **5.00**
Striped, rayon, 1930s **3.00**

Nightgown

Rayon, pale blue, lace and blue satin
embroidery, 1940s.......................... **10.00**

Silk crepe, pale peach, lace insertion, drawn work, floral embroidery on bodice, early 1900s **30.00**
Silk or silk blend, pale pink, cut on bias, beige lace trim, matching long sleeved robe, early 1940s **45.00**
Voile, black sheer, cut on bias, black lace straps and trim, early 1940s **20.00**
Pajama's, girl's, baby-doll style, cotton, pink hearts, 1960s..................................... **7.00**
Pajama's, lady's, lounging, aqua brocade jacket, black satin detailing and frogs, long sleeves, black satin pants, labeled "Fukubon," 1960s........................... **40.00**
Petticoat, cotton, white
Crocheted insert, wide crocheted hem **45.00**
Three rows crochet trim **40.00**

Shirt, man's, cotton, long sleeved, green, pale, blue, and black print with figural images, unworn, $20.

Prom gown

Georgette, yellow, embroidered bodice, strapless, c1960............................. **25.00**
Net and Taffeta, pink, layered skirt, bow trim, c1950..................................... **35.00**
Scarf, Maggie Rouff, Paris, black, fuchsia, rose, pink, and off-white, black borders with geometric-style flowers, 1930s, 30" sq **30.00**

Shawl

Cotton, mint green, fully embroidered, fringed edges, 1925...................... **35.00**
Paisley, printed design, 66" x 128" . **90.00**
Woven design, 68" x 69", minor damage **165.00**
Shoes, children's
Faux crocodile and suede, side buckle, rust, 1930s..................................... **36.00**

Leather, Mary Jane, two strap style, camel kid, side buttons, Buster Brown brand, 1930s................................. **42.00**
Leather, Oxford, black kid, Buster Brown brand, 1930s................................. **40.00**
Leather, T-strap style, brown leather, black, rust, and tan suede, Red Goose brand, 1930s................................. **40.00**

Sweater, hand knit, green, yellow "V," $35.

Shoes, lady's
Leather, boots, brown or black, lace up, pointed toes **125.00**
Leather, brown, high button top **40.00**
Low heels, black kid, black patent toes, Buster Brown brand **145.00**
Shoes, men's
Boots, work type, leather, early, 11" h, pr **25.00**
Tennis, high top, c1920 .... **20.00**
Skirt
Linen, gore style, Edwardian type . **40.00**
Polished Cotton, floral print, full, c1950 .... **24.00**
Wool, black, Victorian **40.00**
Socks, men's, rayon and silk, cotton toe and heel, black, colored arrow, 1950s.... **5.00**
Sport coat, men's, green, purple, blue, and white floral print on mustard yellow ground, mkd "Camelot Brothers Co.," mid-1960s **35.00**
Suit, boy's, wool
Blazer, short pants, navy, 26" chest, Tom Sawyer brand **42.00**
Herringbone, lined, Amish, c1920 . **40.00**
Sweater, cashmere, cream, fur collar, embroidered silk lining, labeled "Hadley Cashmere," crocheted buttons at cuffs, late 1950s................................... **65.00**
Teddy, yellow, pink emb trim on bodice, 1920s **25.00**
Wedding gown, satin, ivory, padded shoulders, sweetheart neckline, waist swag, self train, c1940 .... **125.00**
Wedding headpiece, pearls and net, 1940s, needs new veiling........................... **65.00**

Coca-Cola Collectibles

History: The originator of Coca-Cola was John Pemberton, a pharmacist from Atlanta, Georgia. In 1886, Dr. Pemberton introduced a patent medicine to relieve headaches, stomach disorders, and other minor maladies. Unfortunately, his failing health and meager finances forced him to sell his interest.

In 1888, Asa G. Candler became the sole owner of Coca-Cola. Candler improved the formula, increased the advertising budget, and widened the distribution. Accidentally, a patient was given a dose of the syrup mixed with carbonated water instead of the usual still water. The result was a tastier, more refreshing drink.

As sales increased in the 1890s, Candler recognized that the product was more suitable for the soft drink market and began advertising it as such. From these beginnings a myriad of advertising items have been issued to invite all to "Drink Coca-Cola."

Dates of interest: "Coke" was first used in advertising in 1941. The distinctively shaped bottle was registered as a trademark on April 12, 1960.

Collecting Hints: Most Coca-Cola items were produced in large quantity; the company was a leader in sales and promotional materials. Don't ignore the large amount of Coca-Cola material printed in languages other than English. Remember, Coke has a worldwide market.

Reproduction Alert: Coca-Cola trays.

Clock, electric, square, "Things go better with Coke" in red, green numerals, white ground, working, **$275**.

Ashtray, 4" d, bright red, white logo, 1980s
.... **12.00**

Bank
 Battery operated, red Coke machine
 shape **175.00**
 Coke Year of the Tiger, cute tiger beside
 large bottle, MIB **40.00**
Banner, 11" x 22", printed paper, c1951
.... **15.00**

Battery operated toy, polar bear, reading, head moves back and forth between bottle of Coke and penguin server, Christmas tree in background, 1994, orig instructions and box, 8-1/2" w, 11" h
.... **60.00**

Binder cover, *Advertising Price List,* 13" x 15-1/2", rigid cardboard under textured red oilcloth cover, four-ring metal binder, c1950 .... **45.00**

Blotter, 3-1/2" x 7-1/2"
 Full-color graphics of smiling Coca-Cola
 Sprite elf digging bottle of Coke out of
 snow bank, copyright 1953 Coca-Cola
 Co. **10.00**
 Full color ski scene, copyright 1947,
 unused **18.00**

Book, *Portrait of a Business,* 1961, autographed by W. G. Kurtz **75.00**

Book cover, 10" x 14", dark green stiff paper, advertising "Safety A.B.C.'s" motif in brown and red, copyright 1940, unfolded
.... **5.00**

Booklet, 2" x 6-1/4", paper fold-out, diecut bottle shape, front and back covers with image, inside 12 pages printed in red and green with info about plant tour, equipment, etc., 1950s **24.00**

Calendar, 1997, Travel Refreshed Collection, titled: Compiled from post card collection of John Baeder, spiral bound, **$15**.

Bottle, commemorative
 Cincinnati Reds, World Champs, 1994
 .... **5.00**
 Colorado Rockies, 1993 MLB Record
 Season **6.00**
 Dallas Cowboy Superbowl,
 commemorative six-bottle set **30.00**
 Denver Broncos 1st Team logo........ **5.00**
 Detroit Red Wings, 70th anniversary **6.50**

Florida Aquarium................................ **4.00**
Ft Worth Stock Show......................... **4.50**
Graceland, 1995 .... **10.00**
Houston Rockets, Back to Back Champs, 1995.. **3.50**
Kentucky Derby 122 .... **4.50**
Oriole Park at Camden Yards **4.00**
Texas Tech Lady Red Raiders.......... **3.50**
Bottle carrier, shopping cart.............. **50.00**
Bottle opener, wall-mount, Starr X type, cast iron, some rust................................. **22.00**
Box, wooden..................................... **65.00**
Bridge, score pad.............................. **12.00**
Calendar, 1955 .... **50.00**
Chalkboard, diner menu **45.00**
Charm, loop at top
1" h, figural metal replica of glass stamped "Sterling," reverse with "To P. V. Cochran, Commemorating The 500,000,000th Gallon of Coca-Cola Fountain Syrup June 1953" **60.00**
1-1/4" h, figural metal replica of bottle, brass luster, 1950s **30.00**
Check, used
1946, May 3, bottle logo **14.00**
1961, April 14, bottle logo.............. **12.00**

Diecut, Santa and little boy with poodle on top of crate, **$125**.

Cigarette lighter, miniature **10.00**
Clock, 15" sq, electric, metal............. **115.00**
Coaster, Santa Claus, set.................... **15.00**
Cookie jar, jug-shaped, red label with Coca-Cola logo, McCoy **85.00**
Cuff links, pr, bottle shape................. **45.00**
Dart board, 1950s **40.00**
Doll, 18" h, porcelain and cloth, boy with scooter, Franklin Mint **35.00**
Door push, 11" x 4", porcelain, 1930s **85.00**
Dry-server, unused............................. **5.00**

Folder, 8-1/2" x 11", black, white, and red, four pgs plus overleaf, "More Profit Per Patron," Coca-Cola refreshment counter in movie house lobbies or vending machines, back text describes average weekly gross profits from lobby sales, late 1930s **65.00**
Game, board
India Game, Milton Bradley, 9-1/2" x 18-1/2" hinged cardboard, bottle cap kid, early 1950s.................................... **35.00**
Steps to Health, Coca-Cola of Canada, 11-1/4" x 13-1/4", folded cardboard, color playing surface, copyright 1938.... **60.00**
Winko Baseball, Milton Bradley, 9-1/2" x 18-1/2" hinged cardboard, instructions on back panel, c1945.......................... **30.00**
Glass, set, 8 glasses
10 oz size, sealed in orig carton, Libbey, c1960 .... **125.00**
16 oz size, Polar Bear, "Always Cool, Always Coca-Cola," Indiana Glass, 1992 .... **30.00**

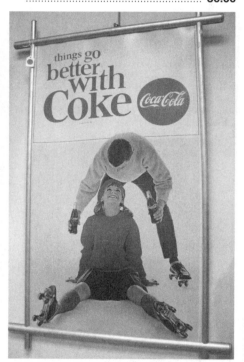

Sign, double-sided, "Things go better with Coke," roller skating couple, tubular aluminum frame, 1950s, **$165**.

Ice chest, airline cooler..................... **400.00**
Ice pick, with opener.......................... **90.00**
Kite, High Flyer, six ounce bottle illus, 1930s **45.00**

Another Mickey Mouse Coloring Book, Saalfield Publishing, copyright 1935, 10-3/4" x 15", 28 pgs, used, some signs of aging **40.00**

Astro Boy **75.00**

Banana Splits.. **48.00**

Battlestar, set **75.00**

Beetle Bailey.. **25.00**

Ben Casey **20.00**

Ben Hur... **20.00**

Black Hole, Whitman, Walt Disney Productions, 1979 .... **8.00**

Bob Hope, oversized **25.00**

Brenda Starr **25.00**

Car 54 Where Are You.......................... **60.00**

Chilly Willy **40.00**

Christmas Cut-Out and Coloring Book, illus by Florence Sarah Winship, Santa wearing flocked hat on cover, 1954, 15" x 11".. **35.00**

Choo Choo, Top Cat.............................. **45.00**

Dick Tracy Paint Book, Saalfield, 1930s, 96 pgs... **200.00**

Dick Van Dyke Show............................. **75.00**

Dutch Boy Disneyland Coloring Book, copyright 1957, 8-1/2" x 11", premium from Dutch Boy paints **15.00**

Family Affair, Whitman, 1969............... **48.00**

Frankenstein Jr. **38.00**

Red Skelton's Story Coloring Book, Clown Alley, Gravette Giant, unused, **$15**.

Gilligan's Island **65.00**

Hanna Barbera Sampson and Goliath **30.00**

Happy Hooper.. **25.00**

Jeanette MacDonald, Costume Parade theme, Merrill Publishing, copyright 1941, 68 pgs, some crayoned **18.00**

Krazy Kat.. **25.00**

Laugh-In... **20.00**

Leave It To Beaver............................... **40.00**

Muskie, Deputy Dwag **25.00**

My Mother The Car............................... **30.00**

Peanuts featuring Charlie Brown, Rats!, Saalfield, authorized edition........... **10.00**

Raggedy Ann, 1945 .... **28.00**

Range Rider, Lowe, 1956, Jack Mahoney **40.00**

Robin Hood Color and Color, spiral bound, orig crayons, wipe-off pages **7.50**

Ronald McDonald Goes to the Moon, 9" x 12-1/4", 1967, 12 pgs, black and white story.. **125.00**

Sgt. Bilko... **60.00**

Space 1999, Saalfield, 1975 .... **20.00**

Stokley's Jolly Jingles of Vegetable Land, 10" x 13-1/4", 1938, slight use **24.00**

Superboy, 1960s................................. **25.00**

Terry and the Pirates, Saalfield, 1940s **75.00**

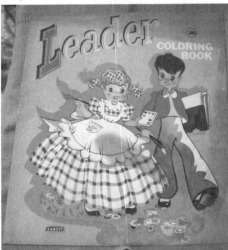

Leader Coloring Book, Abbott, some pages neatly colored, cover faded, **$5**.

Thunderbirds.. **30.00**

Top Cat.. **25.00**

Walter Lantz Color Parade, Woody and other Lantz characters............................. **10.00**

Wizard of Oz, Whitman, 1975, some pages colored **15.00**

Woodsy Owl.. **15.00**

Comic Books

History: Who would ever believe that an inexpensive, disposable product sold in the 1890s would be responsible for a current multimillion-dollar industry? That 2-cent item—none other than the Sunday newspaper—has its modern counterpart in flashy comic books and related spin-offs.

Improved printing techniques helped 1890s newspaper publishers change from a weekly format to a daily one that included a full page of comics. The rotary printing press allowed the use of color in the "funnies," and comics soon became the newest form of advertising.

It wasn't long before these promotional giveaways were reprinted into books and sold in candy and stationery stores for 10 cents each. They appeared in various formats and sizes, many with odd shapes and cardboard covers. Others were printed on newsprint and resembled the comic books sold today. Comics printed prior to 1938 have value today only as historical artifacts or intellectual curiosities.

From 1939 to 1950, comic book publishers regaled readers with humor, adventure, Western, and mystery tales. Super heroes such as Batman, Superman, and Captain America first appeared in books during this era. This was the "Golden Age" of comics—a time for expansion and growth.

Unfortunately, the bubble burst in the spring of 1954 when Fredric Wertham published his book *Seduction of the Innocent,* which pointed a guilt-laden finger at the comic industry for corrupting youth, causing juvenile delinquency, and undermining American values. This book forced many publishers out of business, while others fought to establish a "comics code" to assure parents that comics complied with morality and decency mores. Thus, the "Silver Age" of comics is marked by a decline in the number of publishers, caused by the public uproar surrounding Wertham's book and the increased production costs of an inflationary economy.

The period starting with 1960 and continuing to the present has been marked by a resurgence of interest in comic books. Starting with Marvel's introduction of "The Fantastic Four" and "The Amazing Spiderman," the market has grown to the extent that many new publishers are now rubbing elbows with the giants and the competition is keen!

Part of the reason for this upswing must be credited to that same inflationary economy that spelled disaster for publishers in the 1950s. This time, however, people are buying valuable comics as a hedge against inflation. Even young people are aware of the market potential. Today's piggy-bank investors may well be tomorrow's Wall Street tycoons.

Collecting Hints: Remember, age does *not* determine value! Prices fluctuate according to supply and demand. Collectors should always buy comic books in the best possible condition. While archival restoration is available, it's frequently costly and may involve a certain amount of risk.

Comic books should be stored in an upright position away from sunlight, dampness, and insect infestations. Avoid stacking comic books because the weight of the uppermost books may cause acid and oils to migrate. As a result, covers on books near the bottom of the stack may become stained with material that is difficult or impossible to remove.

Golden Age (1939-1950s) Marvel and D.C. first issues and key later issues continue to gain in popularity as do current favorites such as Marvel's X-Men and D.C.'s New Teen Titans.

Reproduction Alert: Publishers frequently reprint popular stories, even complete books, so the buyer must pay strict attention to the title, not just the portion printed in outsized letters on the front cover. If there's ever any doubt, look inside at the fine print on the bottom of the inside cover or first page. The correct title will be printed there in capital letters.

Buyers also should pay attention to the size of the comic they purchase. The comics offered are exact replicas of Golden Age D.C. titles which normally sell for thousands of dollars. The seller offers the large, 10-by-13-inch copy of Superman #1 in mint condition for $10 to $100. The naive collector jumps at the chance since he knows this book sells for thousands on the open market. When the buyer gets his "find" home and checks further, he discovers that he's paid way too much for the treasury-sized "Famous First Edition" comic printed in the mid-1970s by D.C. These comics originally sold for $1 each and are exact reprints except for the size. Several came with outer covers that announced the fact they were reprints, but it didn't take long for dishonest dealers to remove these and sell the comic at greatly inflated prices.

Notes: Just like advertising, comic books affect and reflect the culture that nurtures them. Large letters, bright colors, and pulse-pounding action hype this product. Since good almost always triumphs over evil, many would say comics are as American as mom's apple pie. Yet there's truly something for every taste in the vast array of comics available today. There are underground (adult situation) comics, foreign comics, educational comics, and comics intended to promote the sale of products or services.

The following listing concentrates on mainstream American comics published between 1938 and 1985. Prices may vary from region to region due to excessive demand in some areas. Prices given are for comic books in fine condition; that is, comics that are like new in most respects, but may show a little wear. Comics should be complete; no pages or chunks missing.

Adventures Into The Unknown, #37 .... **25.00**
Adventures Into Weird Worlds, #28 ... **175.00**
Adventures of Superman #500, Direct Edition **12.00**
After Dark, #8 .... **30.00**
Airboy Comics, Vol. 8, #2 .... **80.00**
Alice in Wonderland, #49 .... **95.00**
All American Comics, #100, first Johnny Thunder **125.00**
All American Men of War, DC, #19 ...... **65.00**
Amazing Adventures, Ziff Oavis, #4 .... **30.00**
Amazing Spider-Man, #299, Cameo Venom **20.00**
Annette's Life Story, Annette Funicello, #1100, Dell, 1960 .... **80.00**
Astonishing, #33 .... **25.00**
A-Team, Marvel, #2 .... **25.00**
Baby Huey, Harvey, #14 .... **8.00**
Batman Chronicles, #1-3, NM **10.50**
Batman Legends of the Dark Knight, #6 **8.00**
Beagle Boys, Gold Key, #28, VF **5.00**
Beetle Bailey, Dell, #552 .... **15.00**

The Man of Steel, Special Collector's Edition, DC, No. 1, six-part mini-series by Bryne & Giordano, **$20**.

Bewitched, #51 .... **18.00**
Black Arrow, Classics Illustrated, 1946 **28.00**
Black Beauty, #60 .... **80.00**
Black Cat Mystery, #38 .... **155.00**
Black Magic, Vol. 2, #5 .... **160.00**
Blue Beetle, #49 .... **75.00**
Blue Bolt Weird Tales, #114 .... **70.00**
Bold Stories, #1 .... **76.00**
Bugs Bunny Christmas Funnies, Dell, #3
.... **20.00**
Bugs Bunny Vacation Funnies, Dell Giant, #4, glossy **40.00**
Candy, #60 .... **15.00**
Captain America, #1-4, mini series, 2002, NM **12.00**
Casper Strange Ghost Stories, #13, VG **7.50**
Chamber of Chills, #15 .... **135.00**
Chastity, #1, NM **10.00**
Cheyenne, #734 .... **35.00**
Chip 'N' Dale, Gold Key, #1, fine **8.00**
Cisco Kid, Dell, #10 .... **8.00**
Classics Illustrated
    Les Miserables, #9, second print, VG **70.00**
    Oliver Twist, #23, second print, VG **65.00**
Comics Greatest World, Week 3, Arccadia Ghost, NM **10.00**
Crime & Punishment, #89 .... **20.00**
Crime Does Not Pay, #102 .... **18.00**
Crime Reporter, #2 .... **100.00**
Crimes by Women, #54 .... **150.00**

Crimson Nun, Antartic Press, 1997,
  #1-4, NM... **15.00**
Cyblade/Shi, #1, NM **12.00**
Daredevil, #227 .... **10.00**
Darker Image, #1, mint in bag **12.00**
David Copperfield, #48........................ **50.00**
Deathblow, #1, NM............................... **15.00**
Dell Giants, #49 .... **40.00**
Detective Comics, #140...................... **150.00**
Dick Tracy, Harvey, #86 .... **18.00**
Dick Tracy, Popped Wheat Cereal
  premium, 1947 .... **10.00**
Doctor Solar, Dell, #9........................... **25.00**
Donald Duck, Dell, #31 .... **12.00**
Eerie, #15... **50.00**
Elmer Fudd, Dell, #558 .... **8.00**
Eternals, #1, VF.................................... **8.00**
Evil Ernie: Resurrection #0, NM **18.00**
Fantastic Fears, #7 .... **370.00**
Fantastic Four, #301, NM **5.00**
Felix the Cat, #4................................... **18.00**
Fighting America, #3, glossy **220.00**
Fighting Fronts, Harvey, #5 .... **8.00**

X-Force, #66, March 1997, Wish You Were Here,
Marvel, **$3.50.**

Flintstones, Gold Key, #60 .... **20.00**
Funky Phantom, #4, fine......................... **5.00**
Forbidden Worlds, #29 .... **20.00**
Gene Autry, Dell, #85 .... **8.00**
Girls Love Stories, DC, #174, VF **15.00**
Goofy, Dell, #562 .... **20.00**
Green Arrow, #4, 2nd series, 1988,
  NM **12.00**
Green Hornet, Gold Key, #2................. **25.00**
Green Mansions, #90............................ **20.00**
Gypsy Colt, Dell, #568 .... **12.00**

Hector Heathcote, #1 .... **25.00**
Hopalong Cassidy, DC, #88............... **30.00**
Huckleberry Hound, #42, VF............. **15.00**
I Love Lucy, Dell, 1954, #26, fine **25.00**
Infinity War, #1-6, complete, NM **15.00**
Inspector, The, #7 .... **5.00**
Jace Pearson of the Texas Rangers, Dell,
  #6 .... **12.00**
Jet Fighters, #5 .... **15.00**
Jetsons, #1 .... **40.00**
Johnny Mack Brown, Dell, #618 .... **35.00**
Journey Into Fear, #4......................... **190.00**
Judge Dredd, Crimefile, #4, NM......... **12.50**
Jughead, #149, fine................................ **5.00**
Jungle #78 .... **50.00**
Konga, #16... **30.00**
Law Breakers Suspense, #11 .... **100.00**
Lawman, #1035 .... **20.00**
Little Iodine, Dell, #15 .... **5.00**
Little Lulu, French................................. **15.00**
Little Stooges, #2, fine **6.00**
Lone Ranger, French **35.00**
Lone Ranger's Famous Horse, Hi Yo
  Silver, Dell, #10 .... **12.00**
Looney Tunes/Merry Melodies, Dell,
  #139 .... **6.00**
Love Confessions, #47 .... **10.00**

Classics Illustrated, *Treasure Island*, No. 64, **$7.**

Love Letters, #150, fine **5.00**
Magnus Robot Fighter, Dell, #5........... **55.00**
Man from U.N.C.L.E., #4 .... **12.00**
Manhunt, #14 .... **100.00**
Man in Iron Mask, Classics Illustrated,
  #54 .... **10.00**
Mannix, French **25.00**
Marvel Spotlight, #29........................... **25.00**
Marvel Tales, #112............................. **230.00**

Maverick, #945 .... **20.00**
Mickey Mouse Birthday Party, Dell, #1 **25.00**
Mighty Samson, Dell, #8 .... **10.00**
Moby Dick, Classics Illustrated, #5 ..... **45.00**
Murder Inc, #1 .... **75.00**
Mysteries Weird & Strange, #6 .... **18.00**
Mystery Comics, #2G........................... **40.00**
Mystery In Space, DC, #3 .... **130.00**
Mystic Tales, #7 .... **80.00**
Navy Combat, #14 .... **30.00**
Oregon Trail, Classics Illustrated, #72. **16.00**
Our Army At War, DC, #4 .... **90.00**
Our Love Story, #23............................... **5.00**
Perfect Crime, #30 .... **50.00**
Peter Panda, DC, #5 .... **25.00**
Petticoat Junction, #4, VG..................... **6.00**
Phantom Lady, #22 .... **125.00**
Popeye, Dell, #29 .... **22.00**
Porky Pig, Dell, #285 .... **10.00**
Prairie, #58.. **70.00**
Punch, #12... **100.00**
Quest of Zorro, Dell, #617................... **60.00**

Beetle Bailey, Dell, June-July, $4.

Rangers, #14 .... **75.00**
Real Heroes, #2................................... **75.00**
Rex Allen, Dell, #2 .... **80.00**
Richie Rich and His Girl Friends, #1, NM
.... **10.00**
Rifleman... **15.00**
Rin Tin Tin, Dell, #12............................ **15.00**
Rootie Kazootie, Dell, #4..................... **12.00**
Rusty Riley, Dell, #554.......................... **8.00**
Sabretooth, #1-4, complete, NM **16.00**
Savage Dragon, #1-3, complete **12.00**
Scooby Doo, Charlton, #2, fine............. **6.50**
Scoop, #2 .... **125.00**
Sea Wolf, Classics Illustrated, #85 ...... **10.00**
Sharp Comics, #2................................. **75.00**

She-Hulk, The Sensational, #2, NM **6.50**
Silver Streak, #7 .... **250.00**
Song of Hiawatha, #57 .... **70.00**
Spawn, the Dark Ages, #4, NM.............. **5.00**
Spectacular Spiderman, #111, NM **20.00**
Squadron Supreme, #12, NM **18.00**
Starling, #40.. **75.00**
Star Wars, #3, NM............................... **10.00**
Strange Adventures, DC, #13 .... **45.00**
Strange Fantasy, #11 .... **25.00**
Strange Stories of Suspense, #6........ **135.00**
Summer Love, #47............................... **45.00**
Superman, #61 .... **125.00**
Swiss Family Robinson, #42............... **10.00**
Tarzan, Dell, #113 .... **10.00**
Taskmaster, Marvel, 2002, #1-4,
    complete, NM **15.00**
Tell It To The Marines, #7 .... **5.00**
Teen Confessions, #81 .... **4.00**
The Crow #2 Image, NM **20.00**
The Undertaker, #1, NM **12.00**
Thieves and Kings, #1, NM **12.00**
Thrilling Crime, #49............................. **50.00**
Thunder Agents, Dell, #17 .... **24.00**
Tom & Jerry Summer Fun, Dell, #1 ..... **20.00**
Tom Brown's School Days, #45 .... **85.00**
Tonto, Dell, #15 .... **6.00**
Top Cat, #27.. **20.00**

X-Men, Marvel, December, $4.50.

Torchy, #1 .... **150.00**
Turok, Son of Stone, #66, fine.............. **15.00**
Tweety and Sylvester, Dell, #524.......... **6.50**
Uncanny X-Men Annual, #16, NM **25.00**
Uncle Scrooge, Dell, #495 .... **60.00**
Underworld Crime, #7 .... **75.00**
Unexpected, #144................................. **7.00**
Wacky Races, #1, VF........................... **30.00**

Walt Disney Comics and Stories, Dell,
　#148 .... **10.00**
Wanted, #52 .... **50.00**
War Birds, #2 .... **16.00**
War Front, Harvey, #20 .... **5.00**
War Fury, #1 .... **50.00**
War Stories, #3 .... **6.00**
Web of Spider-Man, #1-9, VF **85.00**
Weird Mysteries, #2 .... **75.00**
Witching Hour, #19, VF **20.00**
Wolverine, #2, NM **20.00**
Woody Woodpecker, Dell, #16 .... **5.00**
X-Factor, #3, NM **15.00**
X Files, #4, NM **10.00**
X-Force, #10, NM **15.00**
Yosemite Sam and Bugs Bunny, #1, fine
　... **12.00**
Young Love, DC, #101 .... **10.00**

Cookbooks

History: Among the earliest American
cookbooks are *Frugal Housewife or
Complete Woman Cook* by Susanna
Carter, published in Philadelphia in
1796, and *American Cookery* by Amelia
Simmons, published in Hartford,
Connecticut, in 1796. Cookbooks of this
era were crudely written, for most cooks
could not read well and measuring
devices were not yet refined.

　Collectible cookbooks include those
used as premiums or advertisements.
This type is much less expensive than
the rare 18th-century books.

Collecting Hints: Look for books in
good, clean condition. Watch for special interesting notes in margins.

Leaflet, *Gourmet & Entertaining Guide*,
Christian Brothers, 1974, **$5**.

American Woman's Cook Book, Ella
Blackstone, Chicago, 1910, 384 pgs
　... **35.00**
Amy Vanderbilt's Complete Cookbook, 1961,
811 pgs **15.00**
Anyone Can Bake, Royal Baking Power Co.,
1929, hardback, 1st ed **10.00**
*A Place Called Sweet Apple-Country Living
& Southern Recipes*, Clestine Sibley,
1967, dj **10.00**
Arm & Hammer Good Things to Eat, Church
& Dwight Co., 3" x 5", 1925, 32 pgs. **5.00**
Armour's Star Ham, Armour & Co., Chicago,
IL, c1933, 28 pgs, 5" x 6-1/2" **10.00**
*Betty Crocker's Baking Classics, Best
Recipes of 100 Years*, Random House,
1979, dj **10.00**
Betty Crocker Do-Ahead Cookbook, Golden
Press, 1974, 4th printing, spiral bound
　... **10.00**
Blueberry Hill Menu Cookbook, Elsie
Msterson, Crowell, 1966, 1st printing, 373
pgs **7.50**
Classic Cooking with Coca-Cola **5.00**
Cook's Tour of San Francisco, Doris
Muscatine, Scribners, 1963, lower back
edge bumped **9.50**
Dinners Long & Short, A. H. Adair, Knopf,
1929, illus by J. E. Labourer, 257 pgs
　... **32.00**
Favorite Foods of Famous Stars, Norge
Corp., 8" x 10", 1934 copyright, 32 pgs
　... **10.00**
*Favorite Recipes From Our Best Cooks
Cookbook*, Women's Club of Batavia,
Ohio, Circulation Service, 1981 .... **4.00**

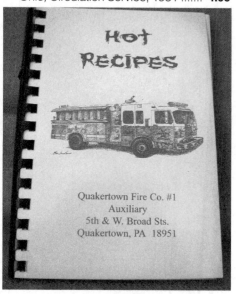

Cookbook, *Hot Recipes*, Quakertown Fire Co. #1
Auxiliary, Walter's Publishing, Minnesota, 1995, **$15**.

Food & Fun for the Invalid, Florence Harris and Dorothy Rider, 1942, 2nd printing, 255 pgs, dj **9.00**

Forty Delightful Ways to Serve, Green & Green Co., Dayton, OH, 1928, 16 pgs, 5" x 7" **9.00**

From Amish and Mennonite Kitchens, Phylis Pell and Good & Rachel Pellman, Good Books Publishing, 1984, 420 pgs... **10.00**

Game Cookery, E. N. & Edith Sturdivant, Outdoor Life, 1967, 166 pgs............. **6.00**

Gebhardt's Mexican Cookery for American Homes, San Antonio, TX, 1932, 35 pgs, 4-5/8" x 7-1/4" **12.00**

Green on Greens, Vegetable Cookbook, Bert Greene, Workmans, NY, 1984, paperback, 432 pgs, 450 recipes, illus **9.00**

Heal Thyself Cookbook, A Guide to Natural Living Through Vegetarian Cooking and Holistic Juicing, Diane Ciccone, A&B Books, 1993, 2nd printing................. **7.00**

Helen Corbitt's Cookbook, Houghton Mifflin, 1957, 29th printing, dj **8.00**

How To Cook a Wolf, MFK Fisher, Duel Sloane & Pearce, 1942-43, 5th printing **25.00**

Jell-O, Rose O'Neill illus, 5-1/4" x 6-7/8" **50.00**

Kate Smith's Collection of Famous Dishes from Famous Places/Authentic Recipes from New York's Foremost Eating Places, issued by Diamond Crystal Salt Co., Inc., copyright 1939 .... **10.00**

Kraft Mini Marshmallows, mini booklet.. **3.00**

Magic in Herbs, Leonie de Sounin, Gramercy, 1941................................ **9.50**

Martha Washington Log Cabin Cookbook, Philadelphia, 1924, 132 pgs........... **38.00**

Mastering the Art of French Cooking, Julia Child, 1961, 14th printing................ **15.00**

Maxwell House, How to Make Good Coffee, 1931, black and white illus **12.00**

Metropolitan Cook Book, Feb, 1948, red, white, and blue cover...................... **12.00**

Mexico Through My Kitchen Window, Maria A. de Carbia, printed in Mexico, 1937, 215 pgs.. **22.00**

Midwestwern Home Cookery, Suggested Recipes by L Szathmary, Promontory Press, 1974...................................... **14.50**

Mrs. Miller's Amish Cook Book, Favorite Recipes From the Family of Miller's Home Cooking, Berlin, OH, Dutch Home Products, 1973, 111 pgs **7.50**

Mrs Rorer's Philadelphia Cook Book, Mrs. S T Rover, Arnold & Co, 1885, 1st edition, 8vo, 581 pgs, 16 pgs of ads........... **20.00**

My Better Homes & Gardens Cook Book, Meredith Publishing, 1935, 10th printing, tabs... **7.00**

New Ideas For Kraft Oil, mini booklet.... **3.00**

Peanuts Cook Book, Scholastic Books, 1970, cartoon illus by Charles Schultz **5.00**

Secrets of Fat-Free Baking, Sandra Woodruff, Avery Publ, 1994 .... **8.00**

Southern Food & Plantation Houses, Lee Bailey, 1990, dj................................ **26.00**

Southern Sideboards Recipe Book, Junior League of Jackson, MS, 1980, 5th printing, spiral bound, 414 pgs...... **10.00**

The Art of Cooking with Herbs and Spices...A Handbook of Flavors and Savors, Milo Miloradovich, 1950, 304 pgs **12.50**

Breads from Amish and Mennonite Kitchens, Pennsylvania Dutch Cookbooks, Good Books, Lancaster, PA, 1982, $5.

The Art of Creole Cookery, Wm Kaufman & Sister Mary Ursula Cooper, illus by Margot Tomes, Double Day, 1962, 1st edition, sgd by Sister Mary **10.00**

The Blender Cookbook, Seranne & Gaden, Doubleday, 1961, 288 pgs, dj.......... **5.00**

The California Heritage Cookbook, Jr. League of Pasadena, Double Day, 1976 .... **8.50**

The Carbondale (PA) Cookbook, Scranton, PA, 1924, 7th ed., 203 pgs............. **38.00**

The Chef's New Secret Cookbook, Louis Szathmary, Hen Regmery, 1975, dj **12.00**

The Cookie Jar, Josephine Perry, Gramercy, 1951 .... **14.50**

The Home Book of French Cookery, Mme Germaine Carter, Doubleday, 1950 **18.00**

The New Butterick Cook Book, Revised and Enlarged, Flora Rose, Butterick Pub Co., NY, 1925, 34th ed **36.00**

The New Cookery, Lenna Frances Cooper, Battle Creek, MI, 1916, 5th ed., 472 pgs, illus **45.00**

The Philadelphia Cook Book of Town and Country, Anna Wetherill Reed, Bramhall House, 1963, 346 pgs, dj **15.00**

The Rocky Mountain Cookbook, Menus & Recipes for a Hearty Country Cuisine, Connie Chesnel, Clarkson Potter, 1989, 1st edition, dg **10.00**

The Soup and Sandwich Handbook, Campbell Soups, thermal mug on cover, 1971 .... **12.00**

Pennsylvania Dutch Cookbook, *Fine Old Recipes*, Culinary Arts Press, 1979, **$7.50**.

The Vegetarian Cook Book, E. P. Dutton, Pacific Press, 1914, 271 pgs **50.00**

The Williamsburg Art of Cookery...or...Accomplished Gentlewoman's Companion...5000 Recipes Virginia Cookery, Helen Bullick, Colonial Williamsburg/Holt Rinehart Winston, 1990, 1961 .... **19.50**

365 Ways to Cook Hamburger, Doyne Nickerson, Doubleday, 1960, 189 pgs **9.00**

White Trash Cooking, Ernest Matthew Mickler, The Jargon Society, Berkleley, CA, 1986, 134 pgs, spiral bound ... **28.75**

Cookie Jars

History: The date the first cookie was made is unknown. However, early forms of cookie jars can be found in several mediums, including glass and pottery. Perhaps it was the Depression that caused people to bake more cookies at home, coupled with the pretty Depression-era glass jars that created the first real interest in cookie jars. A canister, complete with matching lid, was made in the popular Kolorkraft line by Brush Pottery Company in Roseville, Ohio, in the 1920s. By embossing the word "Cookies" on it, the piece became one of the first such documented cookie jars. By 1931, McKee Glass Company, Jeannette, Pennsylvania, was advertising a cookie jar that consisted of a 5-1/2 inch with a lid, and by 1932 Hocking Glass was advertising a large glass jar with a wide screw-on metal lid. These products were additions to canister sets.

The clever figural jars so often associated with cookie jars were introduced by several companies during the early 1940s. Soon apples, animals, and comic characters were added to more colorful kitchens. Production of American cookie jars flourished until the mid- or late 1970s, when foreign competition became too great for several companies. However, a resurgence in the cookie jar collecting market has helped spur new companies to develop interesting jars, and production is starting to increase. As Americans fall in love with new characters, from Sesame Street to Star Wars, cookie jar manufacturers eagerly fill orders.

Collecting Hints: It is not unusual to find two cookie jars made by the same company which have been decorated differently. These variations add some interest to cookie jar collections.

Reproduction Alert: Reproduction cookie jars are starting to plague the market. Oddly enough, it's not only the old cookie jars being reproduced. The cute blue Cookie Monster made by California Originals in 1970 has been copied. California Originals are clearly marked "© Muppets, Inc. 1970" along the base. Brayton Pottery's Mammy has been reproduced. Unmarked copies have been found in addition to well-made copies with a date on the bottom and new-looking decals on the apron.

Other reproductions include American Bisque: Casper; Brush: elephant with an ice cream cone and Peter Pumpkin Eater; California Originals: Count and Cookie Monster; McCoy: Davy Crockett; Regal China: Davy Crockett; Robinson-Ransbottom: World War II soldier and Oscar.

After School Cookies, large rectangular body, roof shaped lid, **$45**.

Abingdon Pottery
    Jack-In-Box, ABC on front, incised mark "611" **125.00**
    Money Sack..................................... **95.00**

Advertising
    Blue Bonnet Sue.............................. **40.00**
    Cookie Bandit, Hallmark **190.00**
    Keebler Tree House, Brush-McCoy **100.00**
    Quaker Oats, 120th Anniversary **70.00**

American Bisque
    Cat in a Basket, 12-1/2" h **60.00**
    Chef **90.00**
    Cowboy Boots............................... **235.00**
    Churn Boy....................................... **225.00**
    Ernie... **95.00**
    Milk and Cookies........................... **225.00**
    Mr. Rabbit **185.00**
    Poodle, gold trim........................... **275.00**

Avon
    African Village **35.00**
    Spatter Bear **30.00**
    Townhouse, small, MIB **15.00**

Brush
    Bobby Baker.................................... **75.00**
    Clock **185.00**
    Humpty Dumpty, cowboy hat....... **350.00**
    Night Owl **75.00**
    Panda, black and white............... **325.00**

California Originals
    Koala on Stump **275.00**
    Seated Turtle................................... **45.00**
    Superman in Phone Booth **525.00**
    Tigger... **150.00**
    Winnie-the-Pooh **95.00**

Cardinal, French Chef....................... **225.00**

Certified International
    Barney Rubble................................ **65.00**
    Bugs Bunny **85.00**
    Christmas Bugs **95.00**
    Christmas Tweety, in stocking...... **125.00**
    Dino and Pebbles........................... **65.00**
    Fred Flintstone **65.00**
    Talking Taz...................................... **95.00**

Clay Art
    Humpty Dumpty **125.00**
    Toaster... **60.00**
    Wizard of Oz **90.00**

French Chef, blue hat with black lettering "Petits Gateaux (Cookies)," marked "Cardinal," **$225**.

Cleminsons, Card King, gold trim on hearts **400.00**

Doranne
    Coca-Cola Bottle **150.00**
    Dragon **275.00**
    Hound Dog, yellow **30.00**
    Mailbox.. **90.00**

Enesco

Garfield **90.00**
Sugar Town General Store **60.00**

Fitz and Floyd

Autumn Woods Rabbit **70.00**
Busy Bunnies Tree **145.00**
Christmas Wreath Santa **150.00**
Cotton Tailors Hat Box **95.00**
English Garden Wheelbarrow **145.00**
Father Christmas **270.00**
Herb Garden Rabbit **95.00**
Hydrangea Bears **150.00**
Rocking Horse **265.00**
Rose Terrace Rabbit **80.00**
Santa in airplane **195.00**
Santa's Magic Workshop **165.00**
Unicorn **85.00**

McCoy

Clyde Dog **165.00**
Coffee Grinder, 10" h **60.00**
Football Boy **225.00**
Friendship Space Ship **195.00**
Hamm's Bear **300.00**
Mammy **90.00**
Pepper, yellow **95.00**
Raggedy Ann, mkd "USA 741" **150.00**
Traffic Light **75.00**
Woodsy Owl **325.00**

Metlox

Apple Barrel **75.00**
Ballerina Bear **120.00**
Chef Pierre **65.00**
Cookie Bandit **215.00**
Francine **95.00**
Frosty **65.00**
Hen **325.00**
Mammy, polka dot dress **450.00**
Miss Cutie Pie **250.00**
Mona-Monocionius Rose **150.00**
Panda Bear **95.00**
Puddles, yellow coat **35.00**
Raggedy Andy **165.00**
Roller Skating Bear, 13" h **75.00**
Squirrel, pine cone **95.00**
Wally Walrus, 1976, 9-3/4" h **200.00**

Pottery Guild

Elsie the Cow, 12-1/2" h **615.00**
Little Red Riding Hood **225.00**

Redwing Pottery

Dutch Girl, two shades of blue, cracked
brown base, faded Redwing symbol and
"Redwing Pottery, Hand Painted,"
10-1/2" h, 6-3/4" w **190.00**
Friar Tuck, old nicks **95.00**

Jukebox selector shape, pages open to Coca-Cola sign, silvered top and sides, modern, **$35**.

Regal

Humpty Dumpty **300.00**
Quaker Oats **150.00**
Jim Beam, cylinder **90.00**
Quaker Oats **145.00**
RRP CO, Roseville, OH, Peter, Peter
Pumpkin Eager, 9" w, 8" w **210.00**

Shawnee

Dutch Girl, mkd "USA," 11-1/2" h, 7-1/2" w
.... **200.00**
Jill, 12" h **95.00**
King Corn, 10-1/2" h **355.00**
Mugsey **495.00**
Puss N Boots **275.00**
Sailor Boy, Shawnee Commemorative,
limited to 100 jars, designed by S. A.
Corl, produced by Mark Supnick, 1992,
black hair **495.00**
Smiley, blue collar and black hooves
.... **270.00**
Winnie, combination bank and cookie jar,
10-1/2" h **475.00**

Treasure Craft

Bart Simpson, holding cookie **75.00**
Baseball **75.00**
Bird House **45.00**
Buzz Lightyear **225.00**
Cactus, wearing bandana and cowboy
hat **50.00**
Dinosaur, large purple spots, gray body,
blue spines, 11-1/2" h **65.00**
Dorothy and Toto, Wizard of Oz, 1994
.... **350.00**
Flop Ear Rabbit **50.00**
Mickey Mouse **75.00**
Nanna, Mammy-type, USA, 1989 .. **95.00**
Noah's Ark **65.00**
Peter Pumpkin Eater **45.00**
Pink Panther **175.00**
Slot Machine **125.00**

House shape, figural, complete with picket fence and flowers, unmarked, **$25**.

Twin Winton

Elf, Collector Series **175.00**
Friar Tuck **85.00**
Gunfighter Rabbit, Collector Series
.... **250.00**
Magilla Gorilla................................. **275.00**
Ranger Bear with Badge, mkd "Code
#84"... **60.00**
Vandor, Popeye **400.00**

Warner Brothers

Bugs Bunny...................................... **40.00**
Olympics, 1996 .... **75.00**
Superman.. **95.00**
Sylvester & Tweety Bird **40.00**
Tweety on Flour Sack **85.00**
Yosemite Sam.................................. **35.00**

Cowboy Heroes

History: The era when the cowboy and longhorn cattle dominated the Great Western Plains was short, lasting only from the end of the Civil War to the late 1880s. Dime novelists romanticized this period and created a love affair in America's heart for the Golden West.

The cowboy was a prime entertainment subject in motion pictures. William S. Hart developed the character of the cowboy hero—often in love with his horse more than the girl. He was followed by Tom Mix, Ken Maynard, Tim McCoy, and Buck Jones. The "B" movie, the second feature of a double bill, was often of the cowboy genre.

In 1935, William Boyd starred in the first of the Hopalong Cassidy films.

Gene Autry, "a singing cowboy," gained popularity over the airwaves, and by the late 1930s, Autry's Melody Ranch was a national institution on the air, as well as on the screen. Roy Rogers replaced Autry as the featured cowboy at Republic Pictures in the mid-1940s. Although the Lone Ranger first starred in radio shows in 1933, he did not appear in movies until 1938.

The early years of television enhanced the careers of the big three—Autry, Boyd, and Rogers. The appearance of the Lone Ranger in shows made specifically for television strengthened the popularity of the cowboy hero. "Gunsmoke," "Wagon Train," "Rawhide," "The Rifleman," "Paladin," and "Bonanza" were just a few of the shows that followed.

By the early 1970s, the cowboy hero had fallen from grace, relegated to reruns or specials. In early 1983, the Library of Congress in Washington, D.C., conducted a major show on the cowboy heroes, perhaps a true indication that they are now a part of history.

Collecting Hints: Cowboy hero material was collected and saved in great numbers. Don't get fooled into thinking an object is rare—check carefully. Roy Rogers and Dale Evans material currently is the most desirable, followed closely by Hopalong Cassidy, Tom Mix, and Gene Autry memorabilia.

Additional Listings: Western Americana.

Annie Oakley

Autographed poster, 16" x 20", inscribed "Best Wishes Gail Davis, TV's Annie Oakley" in blue marker, 1995 .... **50.00**
Comic book, #1 .... **25.00**
Dixie cup picture, Barbara Stanwyck **50.00**
Game, board, Milton Bradley.............. **45.00**
Holster set box, Daisy, 10-1/2" x 12-1/2" box
.... **175.00**
Puzzle, frame tray, Milton Bradley, 10-1/2" x 14-1/4", 1950s **25.00**
Record, 45 rpm, mint in sleeve.......... **20.00**

Bobby Benson

Map, 18-1/2" x 24-1/2", Bobby Benson and the H-O Rangers in Africa, full color, paper, copyright Hecker H-O Co., Inc., 1930s **95.00**

Record, Bobby Benson's B-Bar-B Riders, 10-1/8" x 10-1/8" illus picture sleeve, 78 rpm record, white and white label, "The Story of the Golden Palomino," Decca #88036, copyright 1950 .... **12.00**

Bonanza

Card game, Bonanza Michigan Rummy, Parker Brothers, 14-1/2" x 14-1/2" x 1-1/4" box, color cover with photo of Purnell Roberts, Michael Landon, Lorne Green, and Dan Blocker playing card game at round table in front of fireplace, c1963 .... **30.00**

Charm bracelet, c1970s, six charms, gold-colored metal, MIB **65.00**

Coloring book, unused **30.00**

Gun set, Marx **550.00**

Magazine
  Parade **15.00**
  Police Gazette **20.00**

Playing cards, shows orig cast, sealed deck of 54 cards, orig plastic box, 1970s **18.00**

Poster, Ponderosa, 22-1/2" x 17", c1967, facsimile autographs of cast **12.00**

Buck Jones

BB gun, 36", wood stock with printed sundial, metal side with name, metal compass insert, Daisy **90.00**

Better Little Book, *Buck Jones and The Two-Gun Kid*, Whitman, #1404, 1937 .... **30.00**

Big Little Book, *The Fighting Code*, #1104, Columbia Pictures, artists, Pat Patterson, author, 1934, 160 pgs, hard cover, soft spine **35.00**

Book
  Rocky Rhodes, Five Star Library Series, #15, Engel-Van Wiseman, Universal Pictures, artist, adapted by Harry Ormiston, 1935, 160 pgs, hard cover **35.00**
  Songs of the Western Trails, 60 pgs, words and music, 9" x 12", 1940 copyright **40.00**

Magazine, *Remember When Magazine*, 8-1/2" x 11", Jones on cov, story and black and white photos inside, 1974 .... **7.50**

Pinback button, Bucks Jones Club, enamel on brass, horseshoe, picture in center, 1930s **15.00**

Buffalo Bill

Cabinet photo, 4-1/4 x 6-1/2", black and white close-up portrait, c1890 .... **75.00**

Figurine, 2-1/8", metal, Blenheim **20.00**

Cisco Kid

Bowl **40.00**

Bread label, 2-3/4" x 5-1/2", black and white, red stars and stripes, Cisco Kid's Choice Tip Top Bread, Cisco and Pancho, uncut sheet of two, early 1950s **30.00**

Gun, premium, red, white, and blue cardboard, Cisco's picture on handle, clicker mounted inside, advertises TV show and Tip-Top Bread **45.00**

Membership kit, Triple S Club, Cotton's Wholesome Bread, 3-1/2" x 6-1/2" envelope with logo, return address, postage cancellation, 5-1/2" x 8-1/2" folded letter with facsimile signature, 2-1/2" x 7-3/8" membership card, 1-1/2" litho red, white, and yellow button. **115.00**

Ring, saddle **450.00**

Snack set, plate and mug **50.00**

Davy Crockett

Bath mat, chenille **50.00**

Bow tie, Tennessee Colonel, 4-7/8" x 8-3/8" black and white store car, yellow accents, image of Davy in center, 1-1/2" x 4" x 6-1/2" clip-on dark thin brown suede-like tie, mid 1950s, MOC **25.00**

Doll, 22-1/2" h, plush, vinyl clothing, belt, and tag, "Official Frontierland Doll inspired by Walt Disney's Davy Crockett," c1950, Gund, hat missing **45.00**

Frontier suitcase **60.00**

Game, Davy Crockett Rescue Game, compass, 1955 .... **45.00**

Night light, 1-3/4" x 2-1/4" x 3-1/4" orig box, figural 2" h night light of Davy wearing red coonskin cap, c1955 .... **65.00**

Puzzle, frame tray, Fess Parker **35.00**

Record, Crockett Meets Woody Wood-pecker, 78 rpm **125.00**

Ring, brass frame, thin expansion bands, clear sheet of plastic over paper insert with color portrait, c1955 .... **48.00**

Sheet music, Fess Parker, for accordion **25.00**

Shirt, boy's, unused, orig tags **40.00**

Tru-Vue cards, MIP **60.00**

Water gun, 5" x 10" diecut display card, c1964 .... **75.00**

Wristwatch, arrows as hands, orig band **85.00**

Gabby Hayes

Child's book, *Jack In Box*, hardcover **125.00**

Coloring book, 8" x 10-1/2", Magic Dial Funny coloring book, diecut television screen opening in front with disk wheel, Samuel Lowe Co, c1950 .... **50.00**

Comic book, Quaker Oats giveaway. **25.00**

Dixie cup picture, color, Bill Elliott and Gabby **50.00**

Ring, cannon **185.00**

Rocking horse **200.00**

Gene Autry

Autographed photo, 8" x 10" black and white glossy, bold signature across white hat "To Peggy Ann From Your Pal Gene Autry" **50.00**

Comic book, *Gene Autry Comics Outlaw Roundup*, Vol 1 #6, March 10, 1943 7 .... **25.00**
Gun and holster set, cast iron **500.00**
Movie slide, *Gene Autry And Champion In The Old West*, 3-1/4" x 4" white cardboard mount, hand colored art slide, 1952 .... **20.00**
Pennant, Gene Autry & Champ, from rodeo show, 1949 .... **60.00**
Souvenir program, 20 pgs, c1950, five full-page ads for Autry merchandise.... **25.00**
Sweater, child's **65.00**
Writing tablet.................................... **55.00**

Gunsmoke

Annual, 1975 .... **45.00**
Board game, photo cover with James Arness, British **70.00**
Comic book, #720, four-color **20.00**
Doll, Matt Dillon, limited edition, MIB .. **30.00**
Hartland figure, with horse, no accessories **65.00**
Little Golden Book, 1958 .... **20.00**
Magazine, *TV Guide*........................... **25.00**
Notepad, Amanda Blake, unused **45.00**
Pencil box, Hasbro, 1961................... **18.00**

Hopalong Cassidy, advertising broad sheet, "Made This Christmas A Hoppy Holiday," 12-3/4" x 19-1/4", **$25**.

Hopalong Cassidy, bedspread, chenille, twin size, pair, **$800**.

Hopalong Cassidy

Bag, Jo Mar Ice Cream **50.00**
Bedspread, chenille.......................... **400.00**
Book
    Hopalong Cassidy Returns, Clarence E. Mulford, Triangle Books, July 1943, 310 pgs, front of dj partially missing..... **10.00**
    Hopalong Cassidy Television Book, 1950, glossy hardcover, mechanical dial moves images around small TV screen on cover, 30-page story, *Hoppy and Lucky at Copper Gulch,* full-color photo on front and back...................................... **100.00**
    Trail Dust, A. L. Burt edition, dust jacket **75.00**
Chow set, small, dish, plate, and glass **280.00**
Comic book, Bond Bread
    The Mad Barber **80.00**
    The Strange Legacy...................... **80.00**
Drinking glass, black image, breakfast **45.00**
Game, board **65.00**
Good luck coin, silver-colored metal, 1-1/4" d **15.00**
Greeting card, 4-1/2" x 5-1/4", *Hello Hopalong Cassidy,* 1" x 1-3/4" pistol attached to front, full-color image of Hoppy, 1950s................................. **40.00**
Hair bow, girl's, hairpin, orig card....... **40.00**
Ice cream container, 4" d, 6" h........... **45.00**
Little Golden Book, *Hopalong Cassidy & Bar 20*... **25.00**
Lobby card, *Mystery Man,* set of eight, mint in envelope **375.00**
Lunch box, red, cloud decal, no thermos **90.00**
Magazine
    Time.. **90.00**
    TV Guide, 1949............................ **200.00**
Manual, Film Exploration.................... **30.00**
Neckerchief slide, steer head, red eyes **35.00**
Paperback book, *Hopalong Cassidy Returns*.. **30.00**
Pencil box **60.00**
Pennant, felt, 28" l **45.00**
Puzzle, frame tray............................... **45.00**
Record, double set
    Hopalong Cassidy and the Singing Bandit.. **55.00**
    Hopalong Cassidy and the Square Dance Hold Up.............................. **55.00**
Ring, brass, adjustable bands with initials and "XX" brand, loss to black enamel accents **50.00**
Sign, Hopalong Cassidy Rides Again, The Knickerbocker News, cardboard, 11" x 21" **225.00**
Soap, Topper, Castile **125.00**
Spurs, Olympia **200.00**
Wallet, child's, special agent pass **45.00**

Wallpaper section, 3-1/2' x 18'......... **175.00**
Wooden nickel, Hopalong on front with "Bar 20 Ranch," stagecoach on back, 1-1/2" d
.... **10.00**
Wrist cuffs, small, black, pr **220.00**

John Wayne

Arcade card, c1950............................. **4.00**
Clock plaque, wooden **45.00**
Coin, metal, gold, c1979 .... **7.50**
Coloring book, 11" x 15", 32 pgs, 10 colored pages, Saalfield, #2354-15, 1951 copyright.. **50.00**
Doll, Horse Soldier, Effanbee, MIB.... **185.00**
Holster set, leather belt, two holsters with name on side, orig box, early 1950s
.... **45.00**
Knife, memorial, metal and plastic, "The Duke—John Wayne (1907-1979)".. **10.00**
Movie still, 8" x 10", black and white **4.00**
Paper dolls, 1980, unused................. **30.00**
Pinback button, 2-1/2" d, In Memory of a Great American............................... **5.00**
Record album, Horse Soldiers, soundtrack, 1959...................................... **50.00**
Sheet music, *Put Your Arms Around Me, Honey,* 9 x 12", four pgs, black and white photo, of Wayne, Martha Scott and Dale Evans, 1937 copyright.................... **15.00**
Standee, cardboard **35.00**

Ken Maynard

Autograph, 8" x 10" black and white glossy photo, black inked signature "Ken Maynard 1941".............................. **125.00**

Big Little Book

Ken Maynard in Western Justice, Whitman, #1430, Irwin Myers, artist, Rex Loomis, author, 1938, standard size, 432 pgs, hard cover.............................. **22.00**
Strawberry Roan, Saalfield, Universal Pictures, artist, Grace Mack, author, 1934, 4-3/4" x 5-1/4", 160 pgs, hard cover
.... **22.00**
Premium, photo, 9" x 11", color, black and white "In Old Santa Fe" scenes on back, Dixie.. **30.00**

Kit Carson

Gun and holder set **500.00**

Lone Ranger

Badge, deputy, secret compartment, secret folder.. **150.00**
Belt, glow-in-the-dark **85.00**
Belt buckle, Pyramid Belt Co., 1973... **12.00**
Book, *The Lone Ranger Tells The Story of Branding*... **45.00**
Caps, repeating roll, 1940s, orig box of 20 rolls, MIB.. **35.00**
Child's outfit, red shirt, 1940s **100.00**
Dish set, four pcs, premium, 8-5/8" d plate, 5-3/8" d bowl, 2-1/2" h cup, 6" d saucer, copyright T.L.R. Inc., 1938, red on white milk glass, bowl mkd "Vitrock"...... **175.00**

Lone Ranger, comic book, *Hi-Yo Silver,* Dell, **$7.50**.

Flashlight, pistol gun **45.00**
Game, horseshoes **75.00**
Gum wrapper, 4-1/2" x 6", Bowman, color illus, official Lone Ranger Gum picture card promotional text, 1940s **225.00**
Gun, pressed steel............................. **60.00**
Holster, double, no guns **250.00**
Insert, Bond Bread, 10¢ insert, uncut sheet, 1938 .... **85.00**
Keychain, solid silver bullet............... **65.00**
Lunch box, metal, no thermos, 1980, some rust **20.00**
Membership kit, letter, certificate, card, orig mailer, Merita Bread, 1939 .... **125.00**
Model, comic scenes, Aurora, MIB
  Lone Ranger **45.00**
  Tonto, orig sealed box.................... **75.00**
  Ped-O-Meter 30.00
Pencil sharpener, bullet shape, Merita Bread.. **40.00**
Photo, 8" x 10", color, Lone Range and Tonto, facsimile autograph of Clayton Moore **25.00**
Ring, gold plastic base, full-color portrait against yellow background, sticker mounted on top, clear plastic cover missing, 1950s............................... **20.00**

Sign, 9" x 12", black, white, bight orange, *Boys and Girls Listen Monday-Wednesday-Friday,* Williams Bread, Wilkes-Barre and Scranton, PA, stations, c1938.. **265.00**

Sleeping bag, 31" x 62" cloth, color image and text "Good Luck Always The Long Ranger and Tonto," copyright 1978 **50.00**

Socks, pr, striped socks in 7-3/4" x 10-1/4" orig colorful box with Lone Ranger and Silver galloping, text "Manufactured Exclusively By Sportwear Hoisery Mills, Inc., T.L.R. Inc."copyright, 1940s . **200.00**

Star, tin, Merita Bread **50.00**

Toothbrush holder, figural, 1930s ... **115.00**

Toy, litho tin, Marx, Lone Ranger riding Silver, MIB.. **725.00**

Water pistol, hard plastic, Durham, 1974, figural, MOC **75.00**

Maverick

Eras-O Picture Book, 1960, unused, sealed, MIB **100.00**

Magazine, *TV Guide*, James Garner cover **30.00**

Rawhide

Television storybook, 1962 .... **60.00**

Red Ryder, children's book, *Red Ryder and The Thunder Trail,* Jerry McGill, illus by Fred Harman,Whitman, 1956, **$15**.

Red Ryder

Autograph letter signed, artist Fred Harmon, typed letter on personal stationery, orig envelope, dated June 1, 1977 .... **40.00**

BB Gun, Daisy, 50th Anniversary........ **90.00**

Handbook, *Daisy,* 4-1/2" x 5-1/4", wrap around cover art with Red Ryder and Little Beaver on front on horseback, stagecoach behind them on back cover fighting off Indian attack as Buck Rogers flies above firing his zap gun, Daisy Mfg Co., 1946.................................... **75.00**

Pocket knife **400.00**

Restless Gun

Book, Whitman, 1959......................... **15.00**

Comic, Dell, #1146............................. **20.00**

Game, board **60.00**

Rin Tin Tin

Big Little Book, *Rin Tin Tin & The Hidden Treasure* **18.00**

Button, "Official Rin Tin Tin Button," orig envelope and mailer, "Name the Puppy Contest," Nabisco Shredded Wheat **50.00**

Comic book, Dell, #12....................... **15.00**

Drinking glass, 8" h, pilsner shape, gold and black design, c1958 .... **50.00**

Paint by number, large...................... **60.00**

Ring, magic, instructions **450.00**

Stuffed toy, large **45.00**

Walkie-Talkie, Nabisco Shredded Wheat, 9-1/2" x 11-1/2" box...................... **150.00**

Roy Rogers

Autograph, 8" x 10" color photo
  Roy Rogers **65.00**
  Roy Rogers and Dale Evans.......... **75.00**

Bandana, 18" sq, Roy and Trigger **65.00**

Camera, Herbert George Co., orig instructions, orig box **250.00**

Cereal bowl, ceramic, 6-1/4" d.......... **85.00**

Child's book

  Roy Rogers and the Desert Treasure, Alice Sankey, color ills by Paul Souza, Whitman Cozy Corner Book, 1954 **20.00**
  Roy Rogers and the Outlaws of Sundown Valley, Snowden Miller, Whitman Pub., 1950, 250 pgs............................. **13.50**
  Trigger to the Rescue **25.00**
  Dixie ice cream pictureDale Evans
  .... **50.00**
  Roy Rogers, 1938........................... **60.00**

Flyer, 5-3/4" x 8-3/4" folds out to 17-1/2" x 23-1/2", full color, *Roy Rogers Schwinn Bicycles,* shows 18 models............ **70.00**

Gloves, pr **150.00**

Lunch box, thermos, metal, used **75.00**

Magazine cover, Roy, Dale and Trigger, *New York News*, 1958............................ **48.00**

Membership card, photo, Del Comics, orig mailer.. **210.00**

Mug, Quaker Oats, head shape **50.00**

Pinback button

  Bullet **25.00**
  Pat Brady **15.00**
  Roy's Brands.................................. **20.00**
  Roy's Guns..................................... **20.00**
  Sheriff **20.00**
  Trigger **25.00**

Pocket knife **100.00**

Pop gun, *Roy Rogers Cookies*, 5-1/2" x 8" pr of diecut cardboard panels, c1951 **45.00**

Punch-out book, *Roy Rogers and Dale Evans*, 10" x 14-3/4", 12 pgs, copyright 1952, three full-color heavy pages, unused **295.00**

Ring

Branding iron **225.00**
Hat, sterling **675.00**
Magnifying **120.00**
Microscope **125.00**
Saddle, silver **450.00**

Tie slide, metal, 2" l, 1950s **30.00**

Straight Arrow, board game, Selchow & Righter CO., Trademark of the National Biscuit Co., copyright 1950 by National Biscuit Co., **$45**.

Straight Arrow

Headband, 2" x 10-1/2" thin cardboard, two orig red feathers, Nabisco premium, copyright 1949 .... **65.00**

Manual, 4" x 7", Straight Arrow Injun-uity Manual, 72 pgs, copyright 1951 National Biscuit Co., red, white, and blue cover, black and white illus **35.00**

Membership card, 3" x 11-5/8", green stiff cardboard, black text and artwork of sign language, copyright 1949 National Biscuit Co. **35.00**

Patch, shoulder, 3" d, black, red, and yellow, profile, Nabisco cereal premium, c1950 .... **20.00**

Premium card, Straight Arrow Injun-uity Index, 4" x 7-1/4" gray stiff paper, Nabisco Shredded Wheat

Announcement card, replacement for card #19, Book #2, Poisonous Snake Recognition **5.00**
Book #1, 29 cards, blue accent art and text, 1949 copyright, some age discoloration **35.00**
Book #2, copyright 1950 .... **40.00**
Book #4, copyright 1952 .... **35.00**

Ring

Arrow **65.00**
Face **90.00**
Nugget Cave **180.00**

The Rifleman

Autographed photograph, 8" x 10", pen inscription "To My Pal Best Wishes Chuck Conners" **35.00**

Book, *The Rifleman Chuck Conners TV Adventure*, copyright 1959, 5-3/4" x 7-3/4" **20.00**

Game, board **85.00**

Magazine, *Guns,* Chuck Connors on cover, article **55.00**

Notepad, cover photo of Connors and Crawford **45.00**

Jack Ingram, arcade card, green, **$10**.

Tim McCoy

Autograph, 8" x 10" glossy black and white photo, purple inked signature "Best Wishes Tim McCoy," c 1940 .... **75.00**

Better Little Book, *Tim McCoy And The Sandy Gulch Stampede*, Whitman, #1490, 1939 .... **40.00**

Big Little Book, *The Prescott Kid*, Whitman, #1152, Columbia Pictures, artist, adapted by Eleanor Packer, 1935, 4-5/8" x 5-1/4", 160 pgs, hard cover, soft spine **25.00**

Lobby poster, 11" x 14", set of eight, 1930s
Fighting Renegade **100.00**
Straight Shooter **125.00**

Premium, photo, 9" x 11", color, black and white movie scenes on back, Dixie **15.00**

Tom Mix

Arrowhead, Lucite **85.00**

Badge

Straight Shooters, orig mailer **150.00**
Wrangler's **150.00**

Big Little Book, *Tom Mix In The Fighting Cowboy*, #1144, copyright 1935 .... **25.00**

Decoder badge, Six Shooter, 1930s radio show premium **150.00**

Fob, gold ore **65.00**

Manual, secret writing **100.00**

Pocket knife, Straight Shooters, slight use **40.00**
Poster, *Tom Mix In Broncho Twister*, 21-1/2" x 28", stiff card stock, 1927, black and white image of Tom in fight with man, cowgirl cowering **400.00**

Ring
    Look Around, instructions, orig mailer **225.00**
    Magnet, 1930s Ralston Radio show premium... **95.00**
    Mystery Picture, photo missing **75.00**
    Siren, red TV film, instructions, orig mailer **500.00**
    Sliding whistle, 1930s Ralston Radio show premium............................... **135.00**
    Straight Shooter........................... **100.00**
Sheet music, *Tom Mix Fox Trot*, 4 pgs **90.00**
Telescope and bird call, Golden Bullet **75.00**
Television set, film, orig mailer **100.00**

Wagon Train

Magazine, *Look*, cast on cover **20.00**
Target game, English, illus box **195.00**

Wild Bill Hickok

Game, Built-Rite **45.00**
Gun and holster, double.................. **500.00**

Wyatt Earp

Badge, Marshall's, illus of Hugh O'Brien on card, 1957 .... **40.00**
Book, *Wyatt Earp, U. S. Marshall*, Stewart Holbrook, E. Richardson illus, Hale Landmark Books, Random House, 1956, 180 pgs.. **7.00**
Hartland figure, 1958, played with condition **100.00**
Magazine, *TV Guide*........................... **18.00**
Paint box... **35.00**
Postcard, facsimile signature "Best Wishes Hugh O'Brian," mailed **15.00**
Record, Wyatt Earp Sings, Hugh O' Brien **35.00**
Shirt, child's...................................... **40.00**

Cracker Jack

Collecting Hints: Most collectors concentrate on the pre-plastic era. Toys in the original packaging are very rare. One possibility for specializing is collecting toys from a given decade, for example World War II soldiers, tanks, artillery pieces, and other war-related items.

Many prizes are marked "Cracker Jack" or carry a picture of the Sailor Boy and Bingo, his dog. Unmarked prizes can be confused with gumball machine novelties or prizes from Checkers, a rival firm.

History: F. W. Rueckheim, a popcorn store owner in Chicago, introduced a mixture of popcorn, peanuts, and molasses at the World's Columbian Exposition in 1893. Three years later the name Cracker Jack was applied to it. It gained popularity quickly and by 1908 appeared in the lyrics of "Take Me out to the Ball Game."

In 1910, Rueckheim included on each box coupons which could be redeemed for prizes. In 1912, prizes were packaged directly in the boxes. The early prizes were made of paper, tin, lead, wood, and porcelain. Plastic prizes were introduced in 1948.

The Borden Company's Cracker Jack prize collection includes more than 10,000 examples; but this is not all of them. More examples are still to be found in drawer bottoms, old jewelry boxes, and attics.

Items currently included in the product boxes are largely paper, the plastic magnifying glass being one exception. The company buys toys in lots of 25 million and keeps hundreds of prizes in circulation at one time. Borden's annual production is about 400 million boxes.

Reference: Alex Jaramillo, *Cracker Jack Prizes*, Abbeville Press, 1989.

Collectors' Club: Cracker Jack Collectors Association, 108 Central St, Rowley, MA 01969.

Museum: Columbus Science Museum, Columbus, OH.

Premium, truck, tin, red, black, and white graphics, name on door, "The More You Eat The More You Want" on roof, one side shows box of Cracker Jr., the other side shows Angelus Marshmallows, 1/2" w, 1-3/4" l, **$85**.

Badge, stud-type, Cracker Jack Junior Detective, dark charcoal luster finished metal, shield shape, c1920-30 ...... **90.00**
Baseball score counter, 3-1/2" **150.00**
Bendee figure, MOC **6.00**
Book, *Cracker Jack Painting & Drawing Book*, Saalfield, 1917, 24 pgs **40.00**
Booklet
Chicago Expo, 1-1/2" x 2-1/2", 12 pgs, red, white, and blue Cracker Jack box illus, views of 1933 fair **120.00**
Cracker Jack In Switzerland, four pgs, 1926 copyright **50.00**
Cracker Jack Riddles, red, white, and blue, cov, 42 pgs, 1920s **60.00**
Bookmark, 2-3/4" h, diecut litho tin, printed on one side with brown dog, solid gold flashing on back, 1930s **24.00**
Box, 7" h, red, white, and blue cardboard, 1930s **40.00**
Cereal cup, Ralston **5.00**
Clicker, aluminum, pear-shaped, 1949 .... **35.00**
Coin, 1" d, Mystery Club, emb aluminum, presidential profile, back emb "Join Cracker Jack Mystery Club/Save This Coin," 1930s **20.00**
Doll, 12" h, vinyl, Vogue Dolls, orig unopened display card, 1980 copyright **35.00**
Fortune wheel, still paper, two disk wheels joined by center grommet, red, white, and blue art and instructions, "Jack the Sailor Boy Says To Spell Your Name And Red Your Fortune," 1930s **35.00**
Game, Cracker Jack Toy Surprise Game, Milton Bradley, orig box, 1976 .... **35.00**
Lapel stud
Cracker Jack Air Corps, very dark luster, metal wings, 1930s **45.00**
Cracker Jack Police, dark finish, metal, star badge shape, 1930s **30.00**
Lunch box, metal, Aladdin Industries, c1979 .... **30.00**
Pencil, 3-1/2" l, red name **15.00**
Pin, Angelus Delivery Wagon, diecut, red, white, and blue litho, horse-drawn wagon, one side with Cracker Jack box, other side with Angelus Marshmallows box, roof inscribed "The More You Eat The More You Want," c1920 .... **95.00**
Pinback
Cracker Jack 5 Cents Candied Popcorn and Roasted Peanuts, multicolored portrait illus of young lady, 1-1/4" d, early 1900s **60.00**
Junior Jackie Club, blue sailor boy, white ground, red lettering, Chicago Sunday Herald, 1930s **40.00**
Junior Jackie Club, Little Sisters, blue sailor girl, white ground, red lettering, Chicago Sunday Herald, 1930 .... **40.00**

Pin, Cracker Jack sailor, bouquet and heart, tin, 1-1/2" x 1-3/4", $45.

Portrait of Lady, Cracker Jack back paper, multicolored, early 190s **85.00**
Sailor Jack and Bingo, rim inscription for maker Cosmos Mfg Co., Chicago, 1920s **140.00**
Pinball game, MOC **6.00**
Postcard, 3" x 5-1/2" d, Cracker Jack Bears #7, bears greeting President Roosevelt, 1907 postmark **25.00**
Prize toy
Battleship, red enameled white metal, portholes on both sides **17.50**
Binoculars, dark finish white metal **12.00**
Carnival barker, black, white, and red litho, stand-up turning chance wheel **50.00**
Gun, Smith & Wesson .38 replica, black finish white metal **20.00**
Magic Dots, Game No. 2, 1930s, red, white, and blue paper, 1-1/2" x 2-1/2" **15.00**
Magnet, silvered wire horseshoe magnet, orig red and white marked "Made in Japan" paper wrapper **15.00**
Man's shoe, dark finish white metal, hobnail sole design **30.00**
Model T Touring Car, dark finish white metal **35.00**
Owl, red, blue, and yellow emb stiff paper stand-up, marked "Cracker Jack" . **40.00**
Pocket watch, dark silver luster white metal, ornate back, 9:27 time **30.00**
Pocket watch, dark silver luster white metal, plain back, 4:00 time **35.00**
Rocking chair, yellow enameled litho tin doll furniture chair, curved slat back **20.00**
Rocking horse, dark blue wash tint **20.00**
Scottie, bright silver luster white metal **25.00**
Spinner top, red, white, and blue litho, Cracker Jack mystery toy box **35.00**

Tank Corps No. 57, diecut, dark olive green, black litho tin tank, c1930-40 .... **40.00**

Envelope, red and blue box of Cracker Jack, name written on front, postally used, one end torn open, 6-3/4" x 3-5/8", $40.

Train engine, dark white metal, engine and joined coal car **20.00**

Train passenger car, litho tin, black and yellow, 1930s, some rust **25.00**

Watch, litho tin, pocket watch, gold flashing, black and white dial, 1930s **50.00**

Whistle, green enameled tin, top side inscribed "Close End with Fingers" **35.00**

Stand-up, litho tin

Lion, green and black, unmarked, 1930s **70.00**

Sailboat Prize, red, white, and blue, mkd "DM 38," and "Dowst Mfg, Chicago, U.S.A.," unmarked, lightly rubbed, 1930s **40.00**

Smitty, full color, white background, dark green rim, 1930s **80.00**

Tilt card, sq cardboard, flicker image of sailor passing ball from one hand to the other, back mkd "Tilt Card To And Fro" and Cracker Jack marking, Borden, Inc., Columbus, 1950s **12.00**

Watch, litho, 1940s, near mint **75.00**

D

Depression Glass

History: Depression glass was made from 1920 to 1940. It was an inexpensive machine-made glass and was produced by several companies in various patterns and colors. The number of forms made in different patterns also varied.

The colors varied from company to company. The number of items made in each pattern also varied. Knowing the proper name of a pattern is the key to collecting. Collectors should be prepared to do research.

Collecting Hint: Many collectors specialize in one pattern; others collect by a particular color.

Reproduction Alert: Reproductions of Depression glass patterns can be a real problem. Some are easy to detect, but others are very good. Now that there are reproductions of the reproductions, the only hope for collectors is to know what they are buying and to buy from reputable dealers and/or other collectors. Most of the current Depression glass reference books have excellent sections on reproductions. The following items marked with † have been reproduced, but beware that they are more reproductions being brought into the marketplace.

Adam, cup and saucer, pink, **$38**

Adam

Manufactured by Jeannette Glass Company, Jeannette, Pennsylvania, from 1932 to 1934. Made in crystal, Delphite blue, green, pink, some topaz and yellow.

Reproductions: † Butter dish in pink and green.

Note: Crystal prices would be approximately 50 percent of the prices listed for green.

Item	Green	Pink
Ashtray, 4-1/2" d	28.00	32.00
Berry bowl, small	20.00	18.50
Bowl, 9" d, cov	95.00	80.00
Bowl, 9" d, open	45.00	30.00
Butter dish, cov †	400.00	145.00
Cake plate, 10" d, ftd	38.00	35.00
Candlesticks, pr, 4" h	125.00	100.00
Candy jar, cov, 2-1/2" h	120.00	115.00
Casserole, cov	95.00	80.00
Cereal bowl, 5-3/4" d	50.00	48.00
Coaster, 3-1/4" d	25.00	35.00
Creamer	30.00	32.00
Cup	28.00	30.00
Dessert bowl, 4-3/4" d	25.00	25.00
Iced tea tumbler, 5-1/2" h	70.00	75.00
Lamp	500.00	500.00
Pitcher, 32 oz, round base	-	125.00
Plate, 6" d, sherbet	15.00	18.00
Plate, 7-3/4" d, salad, sq	20.00	24.00
Platter, 11-3/4" l, rect	38.00	35.00
Relish dish, 8" l, divided	27.00	20.00
Salt and pepper shakers, pr, 4" h	130.00	95.00
Saucer, 6" sq	12.00	10.00
Sherbet, 3"	40.00	35.00
Sugar, cov	48.00	42.00

Tumbler, 4-1/2" h	35.00	38.00
Vase, 7-1/2" h	60.00	250.00
Vegetable bowl, 7-3/4" d	30.00	30.00

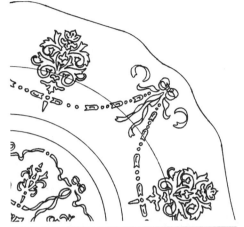

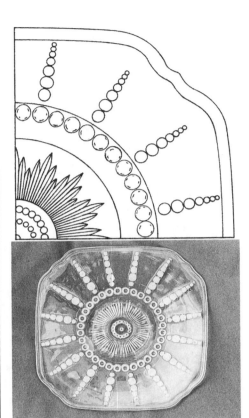

Columbia, saucer, crystal, $4.50.

Bowknot, tumbler, green, footed, $20.

Bowknot

Unknown maker, late 1920s. Made in green.

Item	Green
Berry bowl, 4-1/2" d	25.00
Cereal bowl, 5-1/2" d	30.00
Cup	20.00
Plate, 7" d, salad	15.00
Sherbet, low, ftd	25.00
Tumbler, 10 oz, 5" h, flat	20.00
Tumbler, 10 oz, 5" h, ftd	20.00

Columbia

Manufactured by Federal Glass Company, Columbus, Ohio, from 1938 to 1942. Made in crystal and pink. Several flashed (stained) colors are found and some decaled pieces are known.

Reproductions: † The 2-7/8" h juice tumbler has been reproduced. Look for the "France" on the base to clearly identify the reproductions.

Item	Crystal	Flashed	Pink
Bowl, 10-1/2" d, ruffled edge	24.00	20.00	-
Butter dish, cov	20.00	25.00	-
Cereal bowl, 5" d	18.00	-	-
Chop plate, 11" d	17.00	12.00	-
Crescent-shaped salad	27.00	-	-
Cup	9.50	10.00	25.00
Juice tumbler, 4 oz, 2-3/4" h †	30.00	-	-
Plate, 6" d, bread and butter	5.00	4.00	14.00

Plate, 9-1/2" d, luncheon	22.00	12.00	32.00
Salad bowl, 8-1/2" d	20.00	-	-
Saucer	4.50	4.50	10.00
Snack tray, cup	35.00	-	-
Soup bowl, 8" d, low	25.00	-	-
Tumbler, 9 oz	42.50	-	-

Early American Prescut

Manufactured by Anchor Hocking Glass Corporation, Lancaster, Ohio, from 1960 to 1999. Made in crystal with some limited production in colors.

Item	Crystal
Ashtray, 5" d	8.00
Basket, 6" x 4-1/2"	20.00
Bowl, 4-1/4" d, plain rim	20.00
Bowl, 4-1/4" d, scalloped	7.50
Bud vase, 5" h, ftd	475.00
Butter, cov, 1/4 lb	7.50
Cake plate	25.00
Candlesticks, pr, 2-lite	28.50
Candy, cov, 7-1/4"	14.50
Chip and dip, 10-1/4" bowl, metal holder	25.00
Coaster	6.00
Cocktail shaker, 30 oz	300.00
Console bowl, 9" d	15.00
Creamer	3.50
Creamer and sugar tray	3.00
Cruet, os	9.50
Dessert bowl, 5-3/8" d	3.00
Deviled egg plate, 11-3/4" d	42.00
Gondola dish, 9-1/2" l	7.50
Hostess tray, 6-1/2" x 12"	14.00
Iced tea tumbler, 15 oz, 6" h	20.00
Juice tumbler, 5 oz, 4" h	5.00

Lamp, oil	315.00
Lazy Susan, 9 pcs	60.00
Pitcher, 18 oz	15.00
Pitcher, 60 oz	20.00
Plate, 6-3/4" d, salad	55.00
Punch cup	3.00
Punch set, 15 pcs	35.00
Relish, three-part, 8-1/2" l, oval	6.50
Salad bowl, 10-3/4" d	15.00
Salt and pepper shakers, pr, individual size	72.00
Serving plate, 11" d, four parts	90.00
Sherbet, 6 oz	90.00
Snack cup	3.00
Sugar, cov	4.50
Syrup pitcher, 12 oz	24.00
Tumbler, 10 oz, 4-1/2" h	6.50
Vase, 10" h	15.00

Floral, butter dish, covered, round, pink, $95.

Floral, Poinsettia

Manufactured by Jeannette Glass Company, Jeannette, Pennsylvania, from 1931 to 1935. Made in amber, crystal, Delphite, green, Jadite, pink, red, and yellow. Production in amber, crystal, red, and yellow was very limited. A crystal 6-7/8" h vase would be valued at $295.

Reproductions: † Reproduction salt and pepper shakers have been made in cobalt blue, dark green, green, pink, and red.

Item	Green	Jadite	Pink
Berry bowl, 4" d	25.00	-	25.00
Butter dish, cov	95.00	-	90.00
Candlesticks, pr, 4" h	90.00	-	95.00
Candy jar, cov	80.00	-	45.00
Canister set	-	60.00	-
Casserole, cov	45.00	-	28.00
Coaster, 3-1/4" d	15.00	-	-
Comport, 9"	875.00	-	795.00
Cream soup, 5-1/2" d	735.00	-	735.00
Creamer, flat	24.00	-	24.00
Cup	15.00	-	15.00
Dresser set	1,350.00	-	-
Dresser tray, 9-1/4" l, oval	200.00	-	-
Flower frog	695.00	-	-
Ice tub, 3-1/2" h, oval	850.00	-	825.00
Juice tumbler, ftd	28.00	-	27.50
Juice tumbler, 5 oz, 4" h, flat	35.00	-	35.00
Lamp	295.00	-	260.00
Lemonade pitcher, 48 oz, 10-1/4" h	295.00	-	350.00
Pitcher, 23 or 24 oz, 5-1/2" h	595.00	-	-
Plate, 6" d, sherbet	8.50	-	8.50
Plate, 9" d, dinner	30.00	-	27.50
Platter, 11" l	30.00	-	30.00
Refrigerator dish, cov, 5" sq	-	15.00	-
Relish, two-part oval	24.00	-	20.00
Rose bowl, three legs		500.00	- -
Salad bowl, 7-1/2" d, ruffled		125.00	- 120.00
Salt and pepper shakers, pr, 6" flat	-	-	60.00
Saucer	12.50	-	12.50
Sherbet	20.00	-	20.00
Sugar, cov	32.00	-	35.00
Sugar, open	-	-	-
Tray, 6" sq, closed handles	195.00	-	-
Tumbler, 7 oz, 4-1/2", ftd	25.00	-	25.00
Vase, 6-7/8" h	475.00	-	-
Vegetable bowl, 8" d, cov	50.00	-	65.00

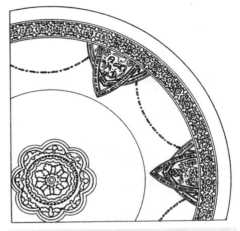

Georgian, sugar bowl, green, footed, 4" h, **$15**.

Georgian, Lovebirds

Manufactured by Federal Glass Company, Columbus, Ohio, from 1931 to 1936. Made in green. A crystal hot plate is valued at $25.

Item	Green
Berry bowl, 7-1/2" d, large	65.00
Bowl, 6-1/2" d, deep	65.00
Butter dish, cov	80.00
Cereal bowl, 5-3/4" d	30.00
Cold cuts server, 18-1/2" d, wood, seven openings for 5" d coasters	875.00

Creamer, 3" d, ftd	16.00
Cup	10.00
Hot plate, 5" d, center design	48.00
Plate, 6" d, sherbet	6.50
Plate, 9-1/4" d, center design only	25.00
Platter, 11-1/2" l, closed handle	70.00
Saucer	4.50
Sherbet, ftd	16.00
Sugar cover, 3" d	12.00
Sugar, 4" d, ftd	15.00
Tumbler, 9 oz, 4" h, flat	80.00
Vegetable bowl, 9" l, oval	65.00

Princess, pitcher, pink, **$80**.

Princess

Manufactured by Hocking Glass Company, Lancaster, Ohio, from 1931 to 1935. Made in apricot yellow, blue, green, pink, and topaz yellow.

Reproductions: † The candy dish and salt and pepper shakers have been reproduced in blue, green, and pink.

Item	Green	Pink	Topaz Yellow
Ashtray, 4-1/2" d	72.00	90.00	110.00
Berry bowl, 4-1/2" d	40.00	32.00	55.00
Butter dish, cov	110.00	115.00	700.00
Cake plate, 10" d, ftd	37.50	100.00	-
Candy dish, cov †	-	75.00	85.00 -
Cereal bowl, 5" d	48.00	9.00	-
Coaster	65.00	65.00	100.00
Cookie jar, cov	65.00	75.00	-
Creamer, oval	15.00	17.50	22.50
Cup	14.00	15.50	10.00
Hat-shaped bowl, 9-1/2" d	45.00	50.00	125.00
Iced tea tumbler, 13 oz, 5-1/2" h	125.00	115.00	40.00
Juice tumbler, 5 oz, 3" h	25.00	28.00	28.00
Pitcher, 37 oz, 6" h	60.00	62.00	775.00
Pitcher, 60 oz, 8" h	65.00	80.00	95.00
Plate, 8" d, salad	15.00	15.00	10.00
Plate, 9-1/2" d, dinner	33.50	45.00	25.00
Plate, 10-1/2" d, grill, closed handles	15.00	15.00	10.00
Platter, 12" l, closed handles	25.00	25.00	60.00
Relish, 7-1/2" l, plain	195.00	195.00	225.00
Salad bowl, 9" d, octagonal	55.00	40.00	125.00
Sandwich plate, 10-1/4" d, to closed handles	30.00	35.00	175.00
Saucer, 6" sq	10.00	10.00	3.75

Sherbet, ftd

| | 28.00 | 25.00 | 40.00 |

Spice shakers, pr,

| 5-1/2" h | 20.00 | - | - |

| Sugar, cov | 35.00 | 65.00 | 30.00 |

Tumbler, 9 oz, 4" h

| | 28.00 | 25.00 | 25.00 |

Tumbler, 10 oz,

| 5-1/4" h, ftd | 35.00 | 32.00 | 30.00 |
| Vase, 8" h | 45.00 | 50.00 | - |

Vegetable bowl,

| 10" l, oval | 30.00 | 30.00 | 65.00 |

Diecast Vehicles

History: The history of collectible diecast vehicles goes back to right after World War II. At this time, the baby boomers wanted more cars to play with and toy makers decided to meet the demand by creating miniature vehicles that would be durable and inexpensive. Corgi created its Castoys line from 1948 to 1958. By the 1960s, character diecasts had become popular as toy makers like Corgi went into licensing agreements with the entertainment industry. Some companies, like Meccano, later to become Dinky Toys, created Model Miniatures, 1:48 scale vehicles as early as 1933, but war time material shortages had a negative effect on the overall toy industry.

One of the largest diecast manufacturers is Ertl. Its attention to detail when creating scale models is outstanding. Its standardized Replica series began in 1982 at a scale of 1:64. In 2000, Ertl teamed with Ford to release a high quality 1:18 scale diecast series of important Ford vehicles, the line known as Precision 1000.

Manufacturers, such as Ertl, Kyosho, and Matchbox, retire their vehicles, helping to create collector demand for their precision made 1:43 and 1:18 scale models.

The miniature version of Queen Elizabeth II's coronation coach that toy makers John Odell and Leslie Smith made in 1953 got Matchbox toys really started. The company followed the coach with three diecasts: a road roller, a cement mixer, and a dump truck. Every year after that it added models to the line while some existing ones were retired, producing 75 different vehicles by 1960. Matchbox was challenged in 1965 when Corgi introduced its Husky line of cars. To meet that challenge, it started a Collector's Club, published a quarterly newsletter, and tried to unite collectors in America and Great Britain.

Collecting hints: Diecast vehicles are made in large quantities, so collectors can afford to be particular when searching for examples to add to their collections. Ertl made more than 20 million Dukes of Hazzard vehicles in 1981. This is a rather speculative market at the present time and collectors should remember that when investing in diecast items. Collecting the ephemera, such as catalogs and associated advertising, is an interesting way to help document a collection.

Additional listings: Hot Wheels, NASCAR, Toys.

Anson, 1:18 scale

Ferrari Dino 246GT, deep green, MIB
.... **25.00**
Lamborghini Muira, blue, MIB........ **25.00**
Porsche 911 Carrera, purple, removable top, MIB.. **20.00**

Burango, 1:18 scale

Chevrolet Corvette, 1957, white, red int. and stripe, MIB **25.00**
Diamonds Chevrolet Corvette, 1957, red, MIB.. **25.00**
Diamonds Dodge Viper GTS Coupe, red convertible, MIB............................. **30.00**
Diamonds Ferrari 456GT, blue, MIB **25.00**
Diamonds Jaguar E coupe, 1961, green, MIB.. **30.00**
Ferrari 360 Modena, bright red, MIB
.... **30.00**
Porsche 356B Cabriolet, 1961, MIB
.... **25.00**

Corgi

Beach buggy and sailboat, #26-A, 1971-76, purple, NM............................. **45.00**
Bedford milk tanker, 1962-65, NM **150.00**
Bell Rescue Helicopter, #924-A, 1976-80, blue body, yellow plastic floats, black rotors, MIP....................................... **50.00**
BRM racing car, #152-A, 1958-65, dark green body, MIP **140.00**
Chevrolet Caprice classic, #341-B, 1981, white upper body, red sides, red, white, and blue stripes, #43 decals, STP labels, MIP **60.00**
Chevrolet Impala Fire Chief Car, #482-A, 1965-69, red on white body, decals on doors, MIP................................. **130.00**
Decca airfield radar van, 1959-60, cream body, rotating scanner and aerial, NM
.... **180.00**
Ferrari Daytona and racing car, 1975-77, yellow trailer, MIP **85.00**

Ferrari 206 Dino, #344-A, 1969-73, yellow body, #23 label, gold hubs, MIP..... **60.00**
Ford Aral tank truck, 1977-90, light blue cab, white tanker body, Aral labels, MIP **50.00**
Ford Esso tank truck, 1976-81, white cab and tank, red tanker chassis, chrome wheels, Esso labels, NM................ **30.00**
Hillman Hunter, #302-B, 1969-72, blue body, gray int., kangaroo figure, MIP **125.00**
Military set, #17-B, 1975-80, #904 tiger tank, #920 Bell helicopter, #906 Saladin armored car, MIP........................... **150.00**
RAF Land Rover, 1957-62, blue body, NM **90.00**
Renault 5 Turbo, #381-B, 1983, white body, red roof, red and blue trim, NM **18.00**
Silver Streak jet dragster, #169-A, 1973-76, metallic blue body, Firestone and flag labels, silver engine, orange plastic jet and nose cone, NM **25.00**
Super Karts, 1982, one orange, one blue, Whizz Wheels in front, slicks on rear, silver and gold drivers, MIP **30.00**
Volkswagen, racing tender and Cooper, 1967-69... **50.00**
White Wheelie Motorcycle, #172-A, 1982, white body, black and white police decals, MIP..................................... **35.00**

Ertl, 1957 Chevy Tanker, Goodwrench, silver and black, NRFB, **$15**.

Ertl, Mack Bulldog, 1926 delivery van, white and green, green "Produce" on side, some writing on original box, **$8**.

Danbury Mint, 1957 Studebaker Golden Hawk, 1:24 1995, MIB..................... **80.00**
Ertl, 1:18 scale
American Graffiti, 1932 Ford Duece

Coupe, American Muscle Street Rods, 1999, MIB...................................... **40.00**
Chevy 3100 Stepside, 1955, white, red bed liner, American Muscle Street Rods, 1994, MIB...................................... **35.00**
Cobra 427 Roadster, 1957, American Muscle Street Rods, 1999, yellow, black stripes, MIB...................................... **30.00**
Corvette Stingray, 1963, black, American Muscle Street Rods, 1993, MIB **35.00**
Dodge Airflow, 1939, Texaco on sides, bank, MIB.. **15.00**
Ford Newstalgia, 1939, American Muscle Street Rods, 1998, canary yellow, MIB **25.00**
Ford Street Rod, 1940, American Muscle Street Rods, 1998, blue, orange and red flames on hood, broken bumpers, orig box **15.00**

Guiloy
Aston Martin D87, 1:18 scale, metal, plastic parts, burgundy, MIB.......... **25.00**
Aston Martin D87, 1:18 scale, metal, plastic parts, green, MIB................ **25.00**
Hershey, truck, "Reese's" on yellow cap, litho "Reese's Peanut Butter Cups, They're Peanutritous Enjoy Them Today," 1994, 1:64, MIB **20.00**
Hot Wheels – see separate listing under "H" for Hot Wheels.
Kyosho, 1:18 scale
Austin Martin Countryman, light blue, wood trim, MIP.............................. **25.00**
Lotus Europa Special, dark metallic blue body, 1:43 scale, MIP.................... **30.00**
Mazda Miata MX-5, 2001, red, MIP **80.00**
Mercedes Benz 300SL, 2001, red, MIP **80.00**
Morris Mini Cooper, blue, white roof, MIP **25.00**
Morris Mini Traveler, green, wood trim, MIP **20.00**
Nissan 300XZ Turbo, 2001, red, MIP **80.00**
Porsche 356 Speedster, red, MIP**..** **25.00**
Shelby Cobra Daytona, blue, white stripe, 1:43 scale, MIP **30.00**
Shelby Cobra 427S/C, silver body, black int., MIP **75.00**
Triumph TR3-A, MIP **60.00**
Maistro, 1:18 scale, Special Edition series
Cadillac Eldorado Biarritz, red, red and white int., MIB **40.00**
Chevrolet Fleetmaster, 1948, gray, woodgrain sides, MIB **30.00**
Dodge Concept, orange metallic, MIB **25.00**
Ferrari F50, red, MIB...................... **25.00**
Hummer, red, cream int., MIB........ **25.00**
Jaquar S-type, 1999, gold, MIB **30.00**
Jaquar SJ220, green, broken side mirrors, orig box............................ **10.00**
Lamborghini SE, metallic purple, MIB

.... **25.00**
Porsche Boxster, black convertible, MIB
.... **25.00**
Porsche Boxster, red convertible, MIB
.... **25.00**
Porsche 911 Carrera Cabriolet, red
convertible, broken side mirror, orig box
.... **12.00**

Matchbox, 1:64 scale
Cement mixer, #3-1RW, 1953, NM . **50.00**
Dodge stake truck, #4-4RW, 1967, yellow
cab and body, green plastic stakes,
played with **6.50**
Foden concrete truck, #21, reg wheels,
1968, 80% paint **12.00**
Iso Grifo, #14, chrome hubs **18.00**
Quarry truck, #6-2RW, 1959, yellow,
black plastic wheels, NM................ **30.00**
Skoal Bandit, racing car hauler, car,
Kenny Schrader, MIB...................... **42.00**
Triumph Motorcycle with sidecar, #4-
3RW, 1960, MIP............................. **85.00**
Mira, 1:18 scale, Calidad Golden Line
Collection
Chevrolet Corvette, 1953, white, MIB
.... **30.00**
Chevrolet 3100 pickup, 1953, maroon,
orig box... **25.00**

Revell, 1:18 scale
BWM Jsetta 250, light blue, MIB **25.00**
BWM Jsetta 250, two tone yellow and
cream, MIB **25.00**
Chevrolet Monte Carlo, Jeff Green, #29,
Cartoon Network, Tom & Jerry, 1997,
driver's name on bottom, MIB......... **20.00**
Chevrolet Monte Carlo, Wally
Dallenbbach, #46, Universal Studios,
Woody Woodpecker, 1997, driver's name
on base, MIB **20.00**
Corvette Convertible Stingray, 1969, blue,
MIB.. **25.00**
Corvette Convertible Stingray, 1969,
orange, MIB..................................... **25.00**
Corvette Convertible Stingray, 1969, red,
MIB.. **25.00**
Goggomobile T250, red, MIB......... **25.00**
Pontiac Grand Prix, Ernie Irvan, #36,
M&M's, MIB **20.00**
Porsche 911 Turbo, 1991, yellow, black
removable hardtop, missing mirror .. **8.00**
Thunderbird, '56, Pink Dream, MIB **30.00**
Road Legends, 1:18 scale
Cadillac Couple Deville, 1949, deep red,
ran leather seats, MIB **25.00**
Ford F-1 pickup, 1949, F-series, red, MIB
.... **18.00**
Solido, 1:12 scale, Prestige series, Citroen
HY #8060, yellow, red roof, red lettering
on sides "Pinder"............................ **25.00**
Team Caliber, 1:64 scale, CVS Pharmacy,
Tony Raines Busch car, 2001, MIB. **10.00**

Disneyana

History: Walt Disney and the creations of the famous Disney Studios hold a place of fondness and enchantment in the hearts of people throughout the world. The 1928 release of "Steamboat Willie," featuring Mickey Mouse, heralded an entertainment empire.

Walt and his brother, Roy, were shrewd businessmen. From the beginning they licensed the reproduction of Disney characters on products ranging from wristwatches to clothing.

The market in Disneyana has been established by a few determined dealers and auction houses. Hake's Americana and Collectibles has specialized in Disney material for more than three decades and Disney offerings on eBay are prolific, although the vast majority of the material is post-1960.

Walt Disney characters are popular throughout the world. Belgium is a leading producer of Disneyana along with England, France, and Japan. The Disney characters often take on the regional characteristics of the host country; don't be surprised to find a strange-looking Mickey Mouse or Donald Duck. Disney has opened theme parks in Japan and France, Disney retail stores in America, and holds company sponsored collector conventions, all resulting in ever increasing Disney collectibles.

Collecting Hints: The products from the 1930s command the most attention. Disneyana is a popular subject, with items for most characters available in many price ranges depending on age and rarity.

Condition should be a prime consideration before purchasing any item. An incomplete toy or game should sell for 40 percent to 50 percent less than one in mint condition. Hundreds of Disney items from the earliest years through 2004 are pictured and evaluated in *Hake's Price Guide To Character Toys,* 5th edition, Gemstone Publishing, Inc., 2004, available on Hake's Auction Web site, www.hakes.com.

Adviser: Ted Hake.

Bambi, Flower, holding flower between paws, pair salt and pepper shakers, ceramic, Goebel, 1950s, 2-1/2" h, **$65**.

Bambi

Bank, 3" x 4" x 7-1/4" h, painted and glazed figural ceramic, shades of brown, black accents on face, pink inner ears, pink and green flowers and leaves on base, Leeds, 1949 .... **40.00**

Book, *Bambi Flocked Press Out Book*, 8-1/2" x 11-3/4", Whitman #1920, copyright 1966, full color, card stock cover, unused **40.00**

Comic book, *Walt Disney's Bambi*, 7-3/4" x 10-1/4", KK Publications, Inc., 1941 copyright, 32 pgs, glossy cover, large story art and text, used as premium by various stores, room for advertising on back **75.00**

Figure, painted and glazed ceramic
3" h, Thumper, shades of gray, black, pink, and brown accents, American Pottery, foil sticker, 1940s **40.00**
3-1/4" h, Owl, brown and yellow, black accents on eyes and feet, American Pottery/Shaw, 1940s **195.00**

Lamp, figural, 4" x 4-1/2" x 6", Thumper, painted and glazed ceramic, incised name and copyright on back of base, orig electric cord, 1940s **90.00**

Poster, 14-1/4" x 20", Prevent Forest Fires, issued by US Dept. of Agricultural Forest Service, 1943, reads "Please Mister, Don't Be Careless. Prevent Forest Fires/Greater Danger Than Ever!" **200.00**

Salt and pepper shakers, pr, Flower, 2-1/2" h, ceramic, Flower holding flower between paws, Goebel, 1950s **65.00**

Studio Fan Card, 7-1/8" x 9-1/4", stiff tan paper, brown design, facsimile Walt Disney signature, 1942 .... **35.00**

Cinderella

Figure, 5-1/4", painted and glazed ceramic, blue and white dress, 1970s **25.00**

Flip book, *Moving Picture Flip Book*, 1-3/4" x 3", full color, actual photo scenes from movie, Merrimack Publishing Co, c1970 .... **26.00**

Magazine, 8-1/4" x 11, *Newsweek*, Feb. 13, 1950, three-page article, color cover **25.00**

Paint book, *Cinderella Paint Book*, 8-1/2" x 10-3/4", Whitman, copyright 1950, 192 pgs, some colored **35.00**

Watch, Bradley, 2-3/4" x 6-1/2" deep blue hard plastic case, hinged lid, 1" dia. goldtone case, white vinyl straps, 1973, full-color case insert **45.00**

Davy Crocket, record album, *Three Adventures of Davy Crockett*, 33-1/3 romp record with Disneyland label, "Fess Parker as Davy Crockett, Buddy Epsen Narrates as George Russell," full-color photo on front, black and white photo scenes on back, 12-1/4" x 12-1/4" cardboard cover, **$25**.

Davy Crockett

Film card, Tru-Vue, 3-3/4" x 5-1/2", black and white card, full-color film scenes, copyright 1955 .... **20.00**

Pinback button, 1-1/4" d, black and white photo of Fess Parker, coonskin cap accented by his name in red text and "Star Cinemas" in blue, pair of blue star accents, Australian issue, c1955 . **165.00**

Record album, *Three Adventures of Davy Crockett,* 12-1/4" x 12-1/4" cardboard cover, 33-1/3 rpm record with Disneyland label, "Fess Parker as Davy Crockett, Buddy Epsen Narrates as George Russell," full-color photo on front, black and white photo scenes on back ... **25.00**

Wallet, Davy Crockett Indian Fighter, 4" x 4-1/2", stiff "Real leather," red and white braid trim, zippered sides, black, white, blue, and brown image of Davy with animal skin map behind him........... **25.00**

Disneyland, cookie jar, 40th anniversary, Sleeping Beauty's castle, numbered limited edition by Nestle, 1955, original certificate and box, 7" x 9", **$50.**

Disneyland

Cookie jar, 7" x 9" x 11" h, 40th anniversary, Sleeping Beauty's castle, numbered limited edition by Nestle, copyright 1995, certificate, orig box **50.00**

Figure, Mickey's 60th Birthday, 3" x 6" x 4-1/2", bisque, mkd "Designed and Made For Disneyland/Walt Disney World," orig $45 price sticker............................. **55.00**

Map, 30" x 40" stiff paper, full color, overhead view, copyright 1974, American Sings illus at lower left corner, folds to 7-1/2" x 15".. **25.00**

Mug, It's A Small World, 3-3/4" h, ceramic, wrap around high relief design, copyright on bottom, c1966 .... **15.00**

Pamphlet, Your Guide To Disneyland, 3-1/2" x 8", issued by Bank of America, 1955 copyright, opens to 13-1/2" x 16" with map on one side, other side with text and Bank of America CA locations........ **30.00**

Pinback button, 4" d, Main Street Commemorative, blue text, 3,000th Performance Sept. 4, 1991, color photo of Main Street Electrical Parade, castle in background **35.00**

Plate, 9-1/2" d, white china, gold trim, six large color illus, pierced for hanging, c1950 .... **60.00**

Playing cards, 2-1/2" x 3-3/4", orig box, 52 cards and two jokers, abstract green and silver foil design, Western Printing Co., 1950s **30.00**

Postcard, 5-1/4" x 6-3/4" d, glossy stiff paper, postmark 1959, full-color front with Donald Duck, Chip and Dale riding on Sante Fe train, "All Aboard for Disneyland," pr of diecut windows, attached wheel turns to change portrait of Donald and sign names, designed by Disney Studio artists exclusively for Art Corner, pencil and ink marks on back **35.00**

Punch-Out Book, *Disneyland Punch-Out Book,* Gold Press Inc., copyright 1963, 7-1/2" x 13", unpunched **150.00**

Record, Disneyland Haunted House, 12-1/4" sq colorful cardboard album cover, 33-1/3 rpm record, Disneyland label, c1964 .... **50.00**

Scarf, 27" x 28", white silk-like fabric, orange, yellow, and brown designs, flowers and fruit borders, center outline of California covered by illus of attractions, and landmarks, Mickey Mouse holding Disneyland sign in lower right corner **25.00**

Donald Duck, pair bookends, painted plaster, red, white, blue, and yellow Donald, red books slung over his shoulder, metallic green grass base, incised Disney copyright and "U.S.A." on each, very fine condition, 3" x 5" x 7-1/4", **$250.**

Donald Duck

Bank, dime register, 2-1/2" x 2-1/2" x 3/4", tin litho, late 1930s............................. **250.00**

Big Little Book, *Silly Symphony Featuring Donald Duck,* Whitman, #1169, copyright 1937, angry Donald on back cover, very fine.. **75.00**

Blotter, 4" x 7", Sunoco, color illus of Donald pinning "Quick Starting" medal on gas pump, early 1940s.......................... **40.00**

Book, *Story of Donald Duck,* 4-3/4" x 5-1/2", Whitman 1066 series, copyright 1938, 96 black and white pages, full-page story illus on ever other page, full-color cover, Mickey as circus ringmaster on back cover **50.00**

Bookends, pr, 3" x 5" x 7-1/4" painted plaster, red, white, blue, and yellow Donald, red books slung over his shoulder, metallic green grass base, incised Disney copyright and "U.S.A" on each, 1950s, pr, very fine **250.00**

Bottle, 4" x 4-1/2" x 9-1/2" h, *Donald Duck Orange Juice,* 64 oz glass bottle, Donald Duck tin lid, foil label on front.......... **35.00**

Charm, 1-1/2" h, celluloid, three-dimensional, deep metallic blue hat and jacket, bright orange accent on long bill, deep red-pink tie, pale yellow on jacket collar, small hanging loop on hat, mkd "Japan" on side, c1935 .... **20.00**

Comic Book

Donald Duck, Dell, #54, July-Aug 1957, Carl Barks cover art **35.00**

Uncle Scrooge, Dell, #5, March-May 1954, Carl Barks cover art **30.00**

Figure

2" x 2-1/2" x 5-1/2" h, ceramic, under and over glaze colors, Disney copyright and WD-26 and Dan Brechner foil sticker **35.00**

3" h, bisque, holding red rifle, mkd "Made in Japan," incised "S1335" on back, 1930s, some wear to paint **65.00**

Lamp, ceramic, 4" x 4" x 6-1/2", ceramic, Donald in western attire, cowboy hat, neckerchief, holster belt, pastel yellow, deep pink, green, and brown, Leeds, base incised "Donald Duck" and copyright.. **165.00**

Pencil, 5-1/2" l, red, white, and blue, Donald Duck Bread, loaf of bread, imprint of Ungles Baking Co, 1950s **25.00**

Pencil sharpener, 1-3/4" h, Catalin plastic, butterscotch yellow, image of Donald, c1938.. **150.00**

Pinback button, 1-3/4" d, dark green on bright yellow, Donald in football uniform, reaching out to catch football, mascot for Oregon college, text "Homecoming 1950 Oregon vs W.S.C," no back paper as issued **50.00**

Thermometer, 6" x 6" ceramic Sportsman plaque, Donald as bowler, black text, Kemper-Thomas Co., 1940s........... **35.00**

Toy, car, 2-1/2" x 6-1/2" x 3-1/2", red, silver accents, moveable head, Pluto seated behind him, mkd "Viceroy Sunroco, Made in Canada," 1940s **85.00**

Viewmaster set, 4-1/2" x 4-1/2" envelope, color photo, three reels, single inner sleeve, orig story booklet, Donald, Chip n' Dale and Uncle Scrooge, 1960s **25.00**

Dumbo

Card game, 2-1/2" x 3-1/2" x 3/4" deep blue and white box, 45 cards and instructions, English, marked "Pepy Series," c1941 .... **125.00**

Cookie jar, 7" x 9" x 13" h, glazed white china, over glaze green, orange, blue, and dark brown paint, turnabout type, Leeds China, late 1940s **100.00**

Puzzle, Jaymar, 1950s, orig 7" x 10" box **15.00**

Goofy

Book, *Story of Dippy the goof,* 4-3/4" x 5-1/2", Whitman 1066 series, copyright 1938, 96 black and white pages, full-page story illus on ever other page, full-color cover **50.00**

Magazine, *Mickey Mouse Magazine,* Vol. 3, #10, July 1938, full-color front cover with Goofy, firecrackers pinned to the seat of his pants, first issue with solo Goofy cover, very good condition............. **50.00**

Paint box, 2-1/2" x 6-1/4", tin litho, characters in band outfits, "Goofy's Paint Box" on flag, mkd "Made in England," late 1940s **55.00**

Johnny Tremain, hat, tricorn, starched black felt, yellow vinyl trim, black, yellow, and red synthetic fabric patch with photo of Johnny on front, Benay Albee Novelty Co., c1957, 10" x 10" x 5-3/4", $35.

Johnny Tremain

Costume, Ben Cooper, 8-1/4" x 11" x 3-1/2" black, white, and orange box with display window, thin molded plastic mask, one-pc synthetic fabric costume, c1957 ...... **25.00**

Hat, 10" x 10" x 5-3/4" tricorn, starched black felt, yellow vinyl trim, black, yellow, and red synthetic fabric patch with photo of Johnny on front, Benay Albee Novelty Co., c1957 .... **35.00**

Premium coin, 1-1/2" d, silvered raised plastic, issued in cereal boxes, set of three **10.00**

Record, 6-3/4" x 7-1/2", 78 rpm yellow vinyl Golden record, Simon & Schuster, full-color illus on sleeve, black and white scene on back **15.00**

Lady and the Tramp

Book, *Lady,* Whitman Tell-a-Tale, 1954 copyright, 5-1/2" x 6-1/2", 28 pgs, color art **20.00**

Jock, 2-1/2" x 3-1/2" stiff plastic sheet, punch-out figure of Jock, issued by Scotch Brand tape, c1955 .... **25.00**

Sheet music, Hanson Publications, copyright 1955 Walt Disney Music Co., 9" x 12" folio **40.00**

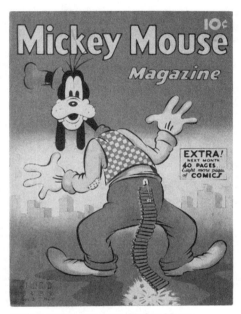

Mickey Mouse, magazine, *Mickey Mouse Magazine,* Vol. 3, #4, January 1938, K. K. Publications, 36 pages, **$75**.

Mickey Mouse, greeting card, *Mickey Mouse Baby's First Birthday,* diecut design, Hall Brothers, Inc., 1930s, 3-1/2" x 4-1/2", **$65**.

Mickey Mouse

Belt, 45" l, Hickok, black leather, 1-1/2" d cast metal buckle with full-figure image of Mickey in center, 1970s **50.00**

Better Little Book, #1451, *Mickey Mouse and the Desert Palace,* Whitman, copyright 1948 .... **48.00**

Book, *The Adventures of Mickey Mouse Book!,* David McKay Co., copyright 1931, hardcover, 5-1/2" x 7-1/2", 32 pgs, shows wear, good condition **55.00**

Doll, 4-1/2" x 7-1/2" x 12" h, Knickerbocker, stuffed cloth and composition, oilcloth eyes and thick felt ears, 1930s, some fading, played-with condition **250.00**

Figure, 2" h, painted and glazed ceramic, one hand raised, other behind his back, Shaw, yellow and black copyright sticker, 1950s **125.00**

Greeting card, *Mickey Mouse Baby's First Birthday,* 3-1/2" x 4-1/2", diecut design, Hall Brothers, Inc., 1930s **65.00**

Hair barrette, 2" l, brass, black, white, and red accent paint of figures of Mickey and Donald, each with one hand on hip, other hands joined, 1950s, some loss of paint **30.00**

Lapel stud, 9/16" d, Disney Licensees, Mickey with blue enamel ears and highlights on silver luster, on brass finished circular plate, threaded post, screw-on cap, c1960 .... **45.00**

Magazine, *Mickey Mouse Magazine,* Vol. 3, #4, Jan 1938, K. K. Publications, 36 pgs **75.00**

Pinback button

7/8" d, black text on muted orange, surrounded by black rim "I Am A Member Of The J. C. Penney Publix-Princess Mickey Mouse Club," mid-1930s... **85.00**

1-1/4" d, *Mickey Mouse Globe Trotters, Eat Sweaney's Butter Krust,* back paper with Mickey, hand extended beneath copyright "Walt Disney Enterprises," 1938 .... **75.00**

Plate, 7" d, Mickey and Pluto, white, orange rim, large color center image, Salem China Co., mkd "Patriot China" and Disney name, 1930s **150.00**

Pocket watch, 2" d, Bradley, goldtone metal case designed to look like vintage 1930s pocket watch, black, white, and red image of pie-cut eye Mickey, Art Deco design on base, 1970s **75.00**

Sand pail, 8" h, 8-1/4" d, tin litho, Ohio Art Co., copyright 1938, Mickey, Minnie, and Goofy, Donald carrying groceries in wagon pulled by Pluto, very fine condition **350.00**

Sheet music, *Dream of Mickey Mouse,* 9-1/4" x 12-1/4", Piano Solo, Bach Music Co, copyright 1933, image of sleeping Mickey on cover **45.00**

Sign, *Mickey Mouse Pencil Boxes,* 4" x 5", diecut cardboard, black, white, red, and yellow, text "Have You Seen The Mickey Mouse Pencil Boxes At The Big School Sale? Yours Truly, Mickey Mouse," 1930s **80.00**

Mickey Mouse Club, Mouseketeer dolls, matched pair, jointed vinyl boy and girl, black and white outfit, mouse ear's hat, Mickey Mouse Club logo on chest, 1950s, 11-3/4" h, **$95**.

Mickey Mouse Club

Loony-Kins boxed set, 11-1/2" x 15-1/2" x 1-1/2" h box, Hasbro, mid-1950s, hard plastic heads and bodies for Mickey, Minnie, Goofy, and Pluto, pipe cleaner arms and legs **80.00**

Lunch box, 7" x 8" x 4", emb metal, Aladdin, c1963 .... **75.00**

Magic slate, 8-1/4" x 13-1/2", diecut cardboard, Whitman, copyright 1964, full-color illus **40.00**

Membership certificate, 8-1/2 x 11", tan parchment-like paper, black text, repeated gold Mickey portrait, facsimile Mickey signature and seal design, unused **30.00**

Mouseketeer doll, 11-3/4" h, matched pair, jointed vinyl boy and girl, black and white outfit, mouse ear's hat, Mickey Mouse Club logo on chest, 1950s **95.00**

Viewmaster set, 4-1/2" x 4-1/2", Mickey Mouse Club Mouseketeers, Mickey's Magic Visit, Ghost Town, Mountain Rescue, copyright 1956 .... **25.00**

Minnie Mouse

Marionette, 10" h, Pelham, painted composition head, hands, and feet, wood segment arms and legs, red and white fabric dress, felt ears, 1950s, played-with condition **165.00**

Cigarette holder, 1-1/2" x 3-1/4" x 2-1/2" h, white china, gold trim, Minnie images on both sides, one side brushing hair, other side with finger point in the air **225.00**

Figure, bisque

3-1/4" h, nurse, yellow dress, dark orange polka dots, gold hat, orange shoes, silver case with orange cross, 1930s **80.00**

3-1/2" h, light blue dress, green hat, yellow shoes, holding tan and gold mandolin, 1930s, incised "C69" on back **75.00**

Pinback button, 13/16" d, black, white, and red image of Minnie on white ground, black text "Donald Duck Peanut Butter" on silver reverse **48.00**

Pinocchio, bank, painted composition, metal trap, Pinocchio leaning against tree stump, Crown Mfg Co., professional touch-up to stump, 1940, 2-3/4" x 3" x 5-1/4", **$75**.

Pinocchio

Bank, 2-3/4" x 3" x 5-1/4", painted composition, metal trap, Pinocchio leaning against tree stump, Crown Mfg Co., 1940, professional touch-up to stump **75.00**

Book, *Pinocchio,* 7" x 9", Grosset & Dunlap, copyright 1939, hardcover, 48 pgs, black and white as well as full-color illus . **75.00**

Bookmark, 1-1/4" x 4-3/4", off-white celluloid, design in black, portrait of Pinocchio at top, full figure Jiminy on bottom, their names and "The Foster Shop" in center, copyright, c1940 .. **25.00**

Pinback button, *I've Seen Pinocchio At Hudson's,* 1-1/2" d, black, white, and red with shaded red portrait on white, black text, premium from Detroit dept store, 1960s or earlier.............................. **50.00**

Toy, Pinocchio Pop Pal, 3" h, hard plastic push button, Kohner, c1970, dark brown, tree stump opens to review three-dimensional Pinocchio, squeaks.... **15.00**

Valentine, mechanical, 3-1/4" x 5" h, diecut stiff paper, full color, Geppetto carving heart out of wood, copyright 1939 . **24.00**

Whistle, 1-1/2" h, Jiminy Cricket, aluminum, name, image, and Disney copyright stamped on stem, c1960 .... **10.00**

Pluto, perfume bottle holder, 1-1/2" w, 1-1/2" h, hard plastic, raised front design of Pluto sniffing orange, red, black, and green flowers, marked "Potter & Moore, England," 2-1/2" h perfume bottle with plastic cap, label "Mitcham Lavender," 80 percent full, **$100**.

Pluto

Book, linen-like, 9-1/4" x 12-3/4", *Pluto the Pup,* Whitman #894, copyright 1937, 12 pgs, full color, very fine **85.00**

Candle, 1-1/2" x 2" x 3-1/2", figural, green base, red and brown dog dish, black and white eye stickers, 1960s, unused . **12.00**

Card game, 5" x 6-1/2" box, 35 playing cards, Whitman, 1939 copyright, black, white, and red illus......................... **50.00**

Figure, 1-1/2" x 2-1/2", yellow painted and glazed body, black, white, and red over glaze accents, c1970 .... **20.00**

Perfume bottle holder, 1-1/2" w, 1-1/2" h, hard plastic holder, raised front design of Pluto sniffing orange, red, black, and green flowers, mkd "Potter & Moore, England," 2-1/2" perfume bottle with plastic cap, label "Mitcham Lavender," 80% full **100.00**

Toy instruction sheet, *Fisher Price Pluto,* 4-1/2" x 12" l, black, white, and red one-sided paper, 1930s........................ **25.00**

Snow White, figurine set, bisque, 4-1/8" h Snow White, 3" h dwarfs, painted outfits, marked "Japan," 1938, three with well-done repairs, **$150**.

Snow White

Cake decoration figure, 1-5/8" h, Dopey, bisque, deep pink hat, yellow coat, green pants, tan shoes, c1938 .... **35.00**

Charm, 7/8" h, sterling, Happy, reverse stamped "Sterling," hanging rim, c1940
.... **30.00**

Figurine set, bisque, 4-1/8" h Snow White, 3" h dwarfs, painted outfits, mkd "Japan," 1938, three with well-done repairs **150.00**

Newspaper flyer, 11-1/4" x 17-1/2", *Snow White and the Seven Dwarfs Welcome You to Toytown* (spelled out in signs carried by the Dwarfs), eight black, white, and red pages, imprint for Georgia five and dime stores on front, copyright 1938
.... **60.00**

Mask, diecut stiff paper, premium from Stroehmann's Bread, ad for Snow White Cake, marked "Part-T-Mask/Eison-Freeman Co, Inc.," poem on back, 1937 copyright
Doc, 9-1/4" x 11" **25.00**
Grumpy, 9-1/4" x 13"...................... **25.00**
Snow White, 7-3/4" x 8-1/4" **30.00**
Witch, 8" x 10-1/4"............................ **45.00**

Paint book, 10-3/4" x 15", Whitman #696, 1938 copyright, 40 pgs, one pg crayoned, four painted.................. **75.00**

Sheet music, 9" x 12", *Whistle While You Work, The Dwarfs Marching Song Heigh-Ho,* Irving Berlin, copyright 1937 ... **25.00**

Three Little Pigs, playing cards, deck of 52 cards, plus Joker and scoring cards, black, white, red, and green design of Big Bad Wolf breaking down door to find two Pigs hiding under rug, Western P & L Co., 1930s, 2-1/2" x 3-1/2" x 3/4" deep box, $60.

Three Little Pigs

Greeting card, 4" x 5", parchment-like paper, black, white, red, blue, yellow, pink, and silver art, Hall Brothers, 1930s, Fiddler and Fifer behind sign that Practical Pig paints as birthday greeting for two-year old................................. **35.00**
Pendant, Fifer Pig, 1" h, diecut straw house, Fifer in center with fife in mouth, raised hands, silver lustered, blue accent on hat, blue jacket, dark red lower body, tiny loop on top... **40.00**
Playing cards, 2-1/2" x 3-1/2" x 3/4" deep box, deck of 52 cards, plus Joker and scoring cards, black, white, red, and green design of Big Bad Wolf breaking down door to find two Pigs hiding under rug, Western P & L Co., 1930s **60.00**

Winnie The Pooh

Game, 9" x 17" x 1-1/2" deep colorful box, Parker Brothers, 1964 copyright, 16-1/2" x 16-1/2" board, fabric "grab-bag," plastic disks, four figural playing pieces.... **30.00**
Glass, 4-3/4" h, black design, Canadian, text on back reads "Inspired by Walt Disney's Winnie The Pooh and The Honey Tree," 1965 copyright **40.00**
Viewmaster set, 4-1/2" x 4-1/2" envelope, color photo, three reels, color booklet and catalog, copyright 1964.................. **20.00**

Zorro

Comic book, *Walt Disney Presents Zorro,* Dell, #882, copyright 1957.............. **25.00**
Gloves, 4-1/2" x 7-1/2", vinyl cuff section, black fabric fingers, black, white, and red, Zorro image and name, orig staple, red and blue Disneyland Gloves tag, late 1950s, unused................................ **25.00**
Hat, 12" x 12-1/2" x 3", black starched straw, thin felt trim, orig black and white fabric chin strap, black and white patch, c1940 .... **60.00**
Pinback button, 3-1/2" d, black and white, block letters, c1958........................ **25.00**

Zorro, school table, mask cover, lined writing paper, unused, c1958, 8" x 10", $85.

School tablet, 8" x 10", mask cover, lined writing paper, c1958, unused **85.00**
Toy, wind-up, 4-1/4" h hard plastic, built-in key, Zorro and horse Tornado, Durham Industries, copyright 1975 .... **40.00**
Viewmaster set, 4-1/2" x 4-1/2" envelope, color photos, three reels, black and white booklet, copyright 1958 .... **30.00**

Dog Collectibles

History: Dogs, long recognized as "Man's Best Friend," have been associated with humans since the early cavemen. The first dogs probably were used for hunting and protection against the wilder animals. After man learned that dogs could be taught to provide useful services, many types of dogs were bred and trained for specific purposes. More than 100 breeds of dogs have evolved from the first dog, which roamed the earth more than 15 million years ago. Today, dogs are still hunters, protectors, and herders, and are trained to see, hear, and perform routine tasks for handicapped people.

Man has continued to domesticate the dog, developing today's popular breeds. The American Kennel Club has divided the breeds into seven classifications: herding, hounds, sporting, non-sporting, terriers, toy breeds, and working dogs.

The first modern dog show was held in Newcastle, England, in 1859. Its success spawned many other shows. The breeding of prize dogs became popular, and the bloodlines of important dogs were established and recorded. Today, the dogs with the most impressive pedigrees command the highest prices.

As dogs' popularity grew, so did the frequency of their appearance on objects. They became popular in literature, paintings, and other art forms.

Collecting Hints: A collection of dog-related items may be based on one particular breed or may be composed of items picturing a dog or even dog-shaped objects. With millions of dog owners in the United States, dog collectibles are very popular.

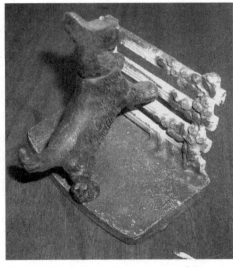

Bookend, black Scottie leaning against flower covered fence, painted cast iron, $20.

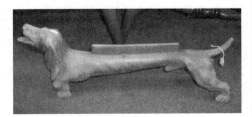

Boot scraper, Dachshund, cast iron, $35.

Ashtray, Scottish Terrier, sq, porcelain, center black terrier, images of hounds and rabbits, green and white ground, Hermes **50.00**

Bank

RCA Nipper **120.00**

Scottie, Hubley **115.00**

St. Bernard, cast iron, painted black and gold **130.00**

Bookends, pr

3-3/4" h, 2-1/2" w, 3-1/4" l, yellow dog, mkd "Made in Japan" **35.00**

5-1/2" h, Cocker Spaniels, chalkware **48.00**

6-1/4" h, Scottie, black satin glass **215.00**

Book

Lassie Come Home, Eric Knight, John Winston Co., 1944, illus by Marguerite Kirmse **6.00**

Secrets of Show Dog Handling, M. Miglorina, Arco, 1982, 127 pgs **7.00**

The Complete Lap Retriever, It's History, Development & Function As A Sporting Dog, H. Warwick, Howell, 1969, 304 pgs **7.00**

Bowl, 10" d, "DOG" written on side, yellow ware **55.00**

Brush

Bulldog, ceramic face, leather collar, full brush, 9" l **70.00**

Dalmatian, Norcrest, Japan, 1960s, 6-1/4" l **17.50**

Calendar, 1959, Texaco, Scottie and girl on telephone **20.00**

Calendar plate, 1910, black and white Bulldog, white china, gold trim **45.00**

Candy dish, cov, glass, Bulldog **75.00**

Cigarette box, large emb Borzoi heads **35.00**

Cigarette lighter, English Setter, Zippo, painted, 1950 .... **125.00**

Cocktail glasses, Scottie dec, set of six **55.00**

Cookie jar, tourist dog, wearing sunglasses, camera around neck, blue and white striped shirt **25.00**

Creamer, large, dog and child, mkd "Teplitz, Stellmacher" **65.00**

Doorstop, original gold-colored paint, **$175**.

Doorstop, painted cast iron
    Setter, on point, side view, black and
    white, Hubley................................. **300.00**
    Terrier **175.00**
Dresser jar, cov, satin glass, dog on top
    .... **45.00**
Dresser tray, four French Poodles doing
    can-can, sgd "Clement" **125.00**

Dog license, Stephenson Co., 1919, #378, figural
dog center, **$12**.

Figure
    Basset Hound, Napco................... **40.00**
    Beagle, #1072, Llardo **190.00**
    Bonzo Dog, 3" h, bisque, mkd
    "Germany," c1920 .... **45.00**
    Borzoi, Mortens Studios, #749..... **125.00**
    Collie, bisque, black and brown **40.00**
    Dachshund, Beswick, #1469........ **50.00**
    German Shepherd, Royal Dux, porcelain
    .... **85.00**
    Jack Russell Terrier, bisque, puppy **35.00**
    Poodle, sitting, Goebel, matte finish
    .... **90.00**
    Pug, Mortens Studios, #738......... **125.00**
    Spaniel, 4-1/2" h, china, gold trimmed
    collar with locket, Staffordshire **135.00**
Hooked rug, 26" x 43-1/2", black dog, dark
    green detail, black ground, multicolored
    borders, wear, holes **360.00**
Jewelry, pin
    Cocker spaniel, sterling silver, emb detail,
    mkd "Cini" **90.00**
    Terrier, carved wood, painted red collar,
    c1940 .... **50.00**
Magazine, *Dog*, 1941.......................... **24.00**
Nodder
    Dalmatian.. **80.00**
    German Shepherd........................... **75.00**
Patch, Rin Tin Tin insignia, set of seven
    .... **25.00**
Pen tray, Labrador, bronze **45.00**
Pipe rack, Terrier and Bulldog peeking over
    fence **35.00**
Planter, ceramic
    Cocker Spaniel, white, Royal Copley
    .... **40.00**
    Spotted Dog, McCoy.................... **145.00**

Print, large black and white dog with small curly
headed child, wood frame, **$85**.

Salt and pepper shakers, pr
    Poodle, heads, Rosemeade **165.00**
    RCA Nipper, Lenox......................... **75.00**

Snack set, Lassie, Melmac, three pcs **75.00**
String holder, Scottie, figural **125.00**
Stuffed dog, Lassie, vinyl collar **75.00**
Tape measure, bulldog, brass, glass eyes
.... **85.00**
Toy
   Fisher-Price, #240, boy with dog on
   tractor, gong bell **70.00**
   Snoopy, pull toy, ears move **40.00**
Vase, Poodle, Sascha Brastoff **75.00**
Wall plaque, Collie, Mortens Studio.... **24.00**

Dolls

History: The history of modern doll manufacturers is long and varied. Competition between companies often resulted in similar doll-making procedures, molds, and ideas. When Effanbee was successful with the Patsy dolls, Horsman soon followed with a Patsy look-alike named Dorothy. Vogue's Ginny doll was imitated by Cosmopolitan's Ginger. Some manufacturers reused molds and changed sizes and names to produce similar dolls for many years.

Dolls have always been popular with Americans. The early Patsy dolls with their own wardrobes were a success in the 1930s and 1940s. During the 1950s, the popularity of Vogue's Ginny Doll generated the sales of dolls, clothes, and accessories. The next decade of children enjoyed Mattel's Barbie. Doll collecting has become a major hobby, and collectors will determine what the next hot collectible will be.

Collecting Hints: The most important criteria in buying dolls are sentiment and condition. The value of a particular doll increases if it is a childhood favorite or family heirloom.

When pricing a doll, condition is the most important aspect. Excellent condition means that the doll has all original parts, a wig that is not soiled or restyled, skin surface free of marks and blemishes, the original free-moving sleep eyes, and mechanical parts that are all operational. Original clothing means original dress, underclothes, shoes, and socks—all in excellent and clean condition, and preferably with original tags and labels.

A doll that is mint in the original box is listed as "MIB." Many modern collectible doll prices depend on the inclusion of the original box. Mattel's original Barbie doll, for example, is valued at more than $1,000 MIB. However, without the original box, the doll is worth much less. Another pricing consideration is appeal. How important and valuable a particular doll is depends on the individual's collection.

Modern and 20th-century dolls are highly collectible. They offer many appealing features to collectors, one of which is an affordable price tag. Modern dolls are readily available at flea markets, garage sales, swap meets, etc.

Other determinants for collectors is whether the size of a doll is such that it can be artfully displayed and whether it is made of materials that can be easily cleaned and maintained.

Additional Listings: Barbie.

Note: All dolls listed here are in excellent condition and have their original clothes, unless otherwise noted.

Cameo Doll Co., Giggle Doll, No. 9613, composition, 12" h, **$375.**

Duck House Heirloom Dolls, dark green velvet dress, white fur trim, NRFB, $10.

Advertising

Advertising dolls come in many shape and sizes. They range from composition, vinyl, and plastic to stuffed cloth. Value is enhanced when the original mailing envelope, packaging, or box is included.

Allied Van Lines, 18" h, 7" w, soiled.... **10.00**

Blue Bonnet, 12" h, 5" w, 1986 mail-in premium... **25.00**

Chlorox, Lots of Legs, 12" l, 4" w, 1985 .... **25.00**

Coco Wheat, Gretchen, 1949, 12-1/2" h, cloth, stuffed.................................. **25.00**

Dutch Boy Paints, porcelain, limited edition, cloth costume, paint can and brush **125.00**

Johnson Wax, Minnie Mouse, 11-1/2" h, 6" w, Applause, 1988 mail-in premium, mint in orig envelope....................... **20.00**

Jolly Green Giant, 16" l, 6 w, 1969 mail-in premium, mint in orig envelope **50.00**

Little Debbie, 12" h, 4" w, 1985 mail-in premium, mint in orig envelope **50.00**

Lysol, Squeaky Clean, 7" h, 5" w, 1988 mail-in premium, mint in orig envelope .. **25.00**

Northern Tissue, 16" h, 6-1/2" w, 1987 mail-in premium, mint in orig envelope .. **60.00**

Planters Peanut, Mr. Peanut, 17" h, 6" w, monocle on left eye, 1960s............. **40.00**

American Character

The American Character Doll Company was founded in 1918 and made high-quality dolls. When the company was liquidated in 1968, many molds were purchased by the Ideal Toy Company. American Character Dolls are marked with the full company name, "Amer. Char." or "Amer. Char" in a circle. Early composition dolls were marked "Petite."

Baby, 16" h, composition head, stuffed cloth body and limbs, molded painted brown hair, brown sleep eyes, c1925 ..... **125.00**

Betsy McCall, 8" h, hard plastic, jointed knees, brunette rooted hair, sleep eyes, orig red and white striped skirt, white organdy top, red shoes, c1960...... **45.00**

Bottle Tot, 13" h, composition head, body mark, orig tagged clothes **175.00**

Sweet Sue, 15" h, blond wig, blue sleep eyes, rose dec white taffeta dress, pearl pin, silver dance shoes, all orig ... **200.00**

Tiny Tears, 12" h, hard plastic head, five-pc rubber body, blue sleep eyes, open nurser mouth, rooted hair, orig pink and white dress, unplayed with condition, orig clothing and accessories, NRFB . **550.00**

Toni, 10" h, collegiate outfit, orig booklet **70.00**

Arranbee

This company was founded in 1922. Arranbee's finest dolls were made in hard plastic. Two of Arranbee's most popular dolls were Nancy, and later, Nanette. The company was sold to Vogue Dolls, Inc., in 1959. Marks used by this company include "Arranbee," "R&B," and "Made in USA."

Angel Skin, 13" h, stuffed soft vinyl head, stuffed magic skin body and limbs, molded, painted hair, inset stationary blue eyes, closed mouth, mkd R & B on head, orig tag: The R & B Family/Rock Me/Nanette/Little Angel, Dream Baby/ Baby Bunting, Angel Skin/Taffy, c1954, MIB... **85.00**

Baby Bunting, 15" h, vinylite plastic head, stuffed magic skin body, molded, painted hair, pink fleece bunting, mkd 17BBS/R & B/D6 on head, orig tag reads: Head is of Vinylite Plastic by Bakelite Company **60.00**

Dream Baby, 20" h, composition shoulder-head, cloth body, painted hair, redressed, c1925 .... **110.00**

Little Dear, 8" h, stuffed vinyl body, rooted hair, blue sleep eyes, c1956 .... **80.00**

Littlest Angel, 11" h, vinyl head, hard plastic body, jointed, rooted dark brown hair, mkd R & B on head, 1959 .... **60.00**

Nancy, 21" h, composition, blue glass eyes, orig dress and cut-out shoes **395.00**

Nancy Lee, 14" h, composition head, five-pc composition child body, brown sleep eyes, closed mouth, orig mohair wig in orig set, orig long yellow dress with gold polka dots, matching bonnet, orig yellow taffeta underclothing, socks and shoes, mkd "R & B" faintly on back of head
.... **250.00**

Nanette, 15" h, all hard plastic, glued on wig, sleep eyes, walker, cotton pinafore, straw hat, 1952, MIB **250.00**

Character and personality

Many doll companies made dolls to resemble popular characters found in the funnies, the movies, radio, and later television.

Alf the Alien **30.00**

Beany, Mattel **95.00**

Bert, Sesame Street, Knickerbocker, 1981, MIB **25.00**

Brooke Shields, MIB **30.00**

Captain Caveman, stuffed, 30" h **65.00**

Carrie, Little House on the Prairie, © 1975, Knickerbocker, MIB **50.00**

Cher, 12" h, © 1975 Mego, MIB **50.00**

ET, fuzzy, brown, marble eyes **30.00**

Farrah Fawcett, 12" h, Mego, MIB **125.00**

General Douglas MacArthur, composition
.... **225.00**

Gizmo, squeaker **30.00**

Grinch Who Stole Christmas, Santa hat
.... **75.00**

Kristy McNichol, 8" h, MIB **45.00**

Little Lulu, MIB **125.00**

Mary Poppin, c1964, MIB **35.00**

Smokey the Bear, Ideal, talking, MIB
.... **350.00**

Sunbonnet Baby, Molly, Mandy or May, © 1975, Knickerbocker, MIB, each **25.00**

Tony Tennille, 12-1/4" h, © 1977 Mego, Moonlight & Magnolias, MIB **45.00**

Wizard of Oz, Cowardly Lion, © 1974 Mego, MIB **35.00**

Cosmopolitan Doll Company

Little recorded history is available about this company. Dolls dating from the late 1940s through the 1960s are found with the mark of CDC. It is believed that the company made many unmarked dolls. One of its most popular dolls was Ginger, made in 1955-1956, which was a take-off of Vogue Doll's Ginny. Many of these Ginger dolls are found with original clothes made by the Terri Lee Doll Company.

Ginger, 7-1/2" h

Hard plastic, glued on wig, walker, head turns, 1955, ice skating outfit **45.00**

Vinyl head, hard plastic body, arms, and legs, rooted medium blond hair, closed mouth, mkd Ginger on head, 1956 **35.00**

Little Miss Ginger, 8-1/2" h, vinyl head, hard plastic body, rooted ash blond hair, closed mouth, high heel feet, mkd Little Miss Ginger, 1956 .... **20.00**

Merri, 14" h, plastic, rooted blond hair, high heel feet, red gown, white fur trim, mkd AE1406/41, backward AE on lower back, 1960 .... **20.00**

Deluxe Reading, Deluxe Topper,

Topper Corporation, Topper Toys

Deluxe Reading, Deluxe Topper, Topper Corporation, Topper Toys, and Deluxe Toy Creations are all names used by Deluxe Toys. This company specialized in dolls that can do things. The company went out of business in 1972.

Baby Party, 10" h, vinyl head and arms, hard plastic body and legs, rooted blond hair, painted eyes, blows whistle and balloon, redressed **35.00**

Dawn and Friends, 6" h, vinyl, jointed at neck, shoulders, waist, hips, poseable legs, rooted hair, mkd "© 1970/Topper Corp/Hong Kong" on lower back, additional mark on head

Angie, black hair, brown eyes, mkd 51/D10 .... **10.00**

Dale, negro, black hair, brown eyes, mkd 4/H86 .... **12.00**

Dawn, blond hair, blue eyes, mkd 343/S11A **15.00**

Sweet Amy School Girl, 23" h, vinyl head, one pc latex body, mkd "A-!" on head, MIB **50.00**

Eegee Doll Mfg. Company

The owner and founder of this company was E. G. Goldberger. He began his company in 1917, marking his dolls "E.G." Other marks used by the company include "E. Goldberger" and "Eegee." This American doll company is one of the longest lasting doll manufacturers.

Dimples, 11" h, vinyl head, cloth bean bag type body, rooted blond hair, painted eyes, dimples, music box, key wind on back, mkd "148D/Eegee Co." **24.00**

Granny, 14" h, vinyl head, plastic body, long white hair in bun, hair grows, mature face, mkd "Eegee/3" **65.00**

Karne Ballerina, 21" h, hard plastic and vinyl, rooted h air, sleep eyes, jointed at knees, ankles, neck, shoulders, and hips, ballet shoes, satin and net ballet dress, c1958, MIB **45.00**

Layette Baby, 14" h, hard plastic head, latex body, molded, painted hair, glassine sleep eyes, orig layette, c1948, MIB **65.00**

My Fair Lady, 19" h, vinyl head and body, blond hair, black net, orig costume, c1958 .... **55.00**

Dolls from many time periods and manufacturers awaited doll collectors at Dawn Herlocher's booth at the March 2004 Atlantique City Antiques Show.

Effanbee Doll Corp.

The Effanbee Doll Corporation was founded in 1912 by Bernard E. Fleischaker and Hugo Baum. Its most successful line was the Patsy Doll and its many variations. Patsy was such a success that a whole wardrobe was designed and it also sold well. This was the first successful marketing of a doll and her wardrobe. Effanbee experimented with materials as well as molds. Rubber was first used in 1930; the use of hard plastic began in 1949. Today vinyl has replaced composition. Effanbee is still making dolls and has become one of the major manufacturers of limited-edition collector dolls.

Anne Shirley, 15" h, composition head, five-pc composition body, blue sleep eyes, closed mouth, orig mohair wig, orig black velvet dress with gold and red stars, mkd on back, Effanbee Durable dolls on metal heart bracelet **200.00**

Baby Dainty, 14" h, composition shoulder head, painted blue eyes, closed mouth, painted teeth, molded and painted hair, cloth body, composition arms and legs, orig blue print dress, matching bonnet and underclothing, orig socks and shoes **150.00**

Barbara Lou, 21" h, composition head, five-pc composition body, brown sleep eyes, open mouth, four upper teeth, orig human hair wig, orig blue jumper dress, white blouse, matching romper, white apron, socks, black leatherette flange tie shoes, mkd "Effanbee, Ann-Shirley" on back, clothing pale, lips repainted **350.00**

Bobbsey Twins, Flossie or Freddie, © 1982 Stratemeyer Syndicates, MIB, each **50.00**

Candy Kid, 12" h, composition head, blue sleep eyes, closed mouth, molded and painted hair, five-pc composition toddler body, orig red and white gingham sun-suit and bonnet, orig socks, red leatherette tie shoes, mkd "Effanbee" on back of head and back, "An Effanbee Durable Doll, The Doll with Satin-Smooth Skin" in heart on label on end of orig box **375.00**

Dy-Dee Baby, 12" h, hard plastic head, five-pc rubber baby body, blue sleep eyes, open nurser mouth, orig skin wig, orig pink dotted Swiss dress, matching bonnet, orig Effanbee Dy-Dee Baby case with orig clothing, accessories, Mennon products, mkd "Effanbee Dy-Dee Baby (patent numbers)" on back, "Dy-Dee Baby, The Almost Human Doll, An Effanbee Play Product" on inside of case, lightly played with condition **525.00**

Lovums, 25", composition head, composition shoulder plate, brown sleep eyes, open mouth with two upper and two lower teeth, molded tongue, molded and painted hair, cloth mama doll body with non-working crier, composition arms and lower legs, orig white organdy baby dress and bonnet, slip, undershirt, socks, leatherette baby shoes, pink baby jacket with embroidered collar, mkd "Effanbee Lovums, © Pat No. 1,283,558" on back of shoulder plate, "Lovums Trademark-Reg An Effanbee Durable Doll The Doll With the Golden Heart 6022" on box label, orig box **675.00**

Marilee, 30", composition shoulder head, composition arms and legs, blue tin sleep eyes, open mouth with four upper teeth, orig blond mohair wig, cloth body, orig pale green organdy ruffled dress, matching underclothes and bonnet, mkd "Effanbee, Marilee, Copyr. Doll" on back of shoulder plate, fine crazing **350.00**

Patsy-Ann, 19" h, composition head and child body, bent right arm, green sleep eyes, closed rosebud mouth, orig mohair wig over molded hair, orig white dress with green dots and trim, matching romper and hat, orig socks, black straps shoes, mkd "Effanbee, Patsy-Ann," with copyright and patent numbers, some play wear...................................... **325.00**

Patsyette, 9" h, composition head, painted brown eyes glance to side, closed mouth, molded and painted hair, composition five-pc body, bent right arm, orig pink dress, other underclothing, socks, pink leatherette shoes, mkd "Effanbee Patsyette Doll" on back, "A New Playmate Patsyette An Effanbee Durable Doll" on panel inside orig box, orig paper heart tag, contained in orig labeled wardrobe box with pale green dress, bonnet, pink dress, pajamas, red and white romper, red cape, brush, mirror, shoes, socks.................................. **550.00**

Patsy-Lou, 22" h, composition head, five-pc composition body, bent right arm, green sleep eyes, closed mouth, molded and painted hair, well-made copy of Patsy style dress, orig socks and snap shoes, orig blue-green felt coat with gold appliqué and trim, matching tam hat, mkd "Effanbee Patsy-Lou" on back
.... **375.00**

Patsy-Mae, 30" h, composition head, cloth body, composition arms and legs, composition shoulder plate, brown sleep eyes, closed mouth, orig human hair wig, tagged orig white organdy dress with red trim and print, metal heart bracelet, mkd "Effanbee, Patsy-Mae" on back of head, "Effanbee Lovums, ©, Pat. No. 1,383,558" on shoulder plate **800.00**

Storybook Doll, Little Bo Peep, MIB .. **40.00**

Hasbro

Hasbro is primarily a toy manufacturer founded by Henry and Hillel Hassenfeld in Pawtucket, RI, in 1923. One of its most popular dolls was GI Joe and his friends. Hasbro is also noted for their advertising and personality dolls.

Amanda, Sweet Dreams, 17" h, stuffed gingham head and body, yarn hair, black felt eyes, button nose, embroidered smile, eyelet lace trimmed night cap, orchid print dress, 1974.................. **10.00**

Lookin' Smart Maxine, © 1987, MIB . **25.00**

Maxine's Friend, Kristen, © 1987, MIB
.... **35.00**

Horsman Dolls Company, Inc.

The Horsman Dolls Company, Inc. was founded in 1865 by E. I. Horsman, who began importing dolls. Soon after the founding, Horsman produced bisque dolls. It was the first company to produce the Campbell Kids. Horsman invented "Fairy Skin" in 1946, "Miracle Hair" in 1952, and "Super Flex" in 1954. The Horsman process for synthetic rubber and early vinyl has always been of high quality.

Alice In Wonderland, MIB.................. **95.00**

Baby Bumps, 12" h, negro, cloth body, arms, legs, painted hair, eyes, large well molded ears, orig romper, c1912 **250.00**

Baby Dimples, 14" h, composition flange head, child torso, composition arms and lower legs, blue tin sleep eyes, open mouth with two teeth, molded and painted hair, orig tagged dress, leatherette baby shoes, mkd "© E.I.H. Co. Inc." **200.00**

Bye-Lo, 14" h, vinyl head, arms, and legs, cloth body, molded straight hair, painted eyes, christening outfit, mkd "Horsman Doll/1972" on head, MIB **50.00**

Joyce, 18" h, composition shoulder, head, arms, and legs, cloth body, glued on bright red mohair hair **50.00**

Peterkin, 11" h, composition, character face, molded hair, painted side glancing eyes, watermelon smile, c1915 .... **215.00**

Pram Baby, 19" h, vinyl, jointed head, glass sleep eyes, closed mouth, coos **65.00**

Ruthie, 12-1/2" h, all vinyl rooted black hair, Oriental hair style, long straight legs, dimpled knees, mkd 12-6aa on upper legs, B-1 on upper arms **30.00**

Rosebud, 20" h, composition head, arms and legs, cloth body, painted eyes, human hair wig **100.00**

Ideal, Tammy and her Friends, original dolls in carrying case, Ideal, $45.

Ideal Toy Co.

The Ideal Toy Company was formed in 1902 by Morris Michtom to produce his teddy bear. By 1915, the company had become a leader in the industry by introducing the first sleep eyes. In 1939, Ideal developed "Magic Skin." It was the first company to use plastic. Some of its most popular lines include Shirley Temple, Betsy Wetsy, and Toni dolls.

Bonny Braids, 14" h, orig toothbrush, 1951
.... **180.00**

Clapping, 15" h, composition flange head, cloth body with clapping mechanism in torso, composition hands, blue sleep eyes, closed mouth, molded and painted blond hair, white baby dress, mkd "Ideal" in diamond, rub on nose, some flaking and soil **115.00**

Dennis the Menace, cloth, MIB **55.00**

Harriet Hubbard, 21" h, vinyl head, blue sleep eyes, closed mouth, saran wig, hard plastic body, vinyl arms, orig flowered pique dress, white organdy pinafore, orig socks and shoes, orig cardboard tag with three plastic curlers, orig Stern Brothers price tag, mkd "MK 21, Ideal Doll" on back of head **225.00**

Jody the Country Girl, © 1976, MIB ... **45.00**

Miss Ideal, 25" h, Photographer's Model, vinyl head, rigid vinyl body, jointed at shoulders, waist, hips, and ankles, blue sleep eyes, rooted nylon hair, orig clothes, mkd "© Ideal Toy Corp SP-25-S: on head, © Ideal Toy Corp P-25" on back orig box with promotional paper, Playwave Kit in orig hatbox, Styling Hints wrist tag, some water stains to orig box **350.00**

Shirley Temple

15" h, vinyl head, five-pc vinyl body, hazel sleep eyes, open-closed mouth, six upper teeth, dimples, rooted hair in orig set, orig dress with red velvet bodice, white taffeta skirt with nylon overlay, lace trim, orig underclothes, pearl crown, mkd "Ideal Doll ST-15-N" on back of head, c1941 .... **325.00**

18" h, composition head, five-pc composition child body, hazel sleep eyes, open mouth with six upper teeth, orig mohair wig, orig tagged flower print dress, orig underclothing, socks and shoes, mkd "Shirley Temple" on head and body **600.00**

Suntan Dodi and her Suntan Doodles, © 1977, MIB **75.00**

Taylor Jones, 12" h fashion doll, hair changes color, © 1976, MIB **75.00**

Thumbelina, 18", vinyl flange head, cloth body with vinyl arms and legs, painted blue eyes, open-closed mouth, rooted synthetic hair, large wooden knob on back for winding to operate baby wiggling mechanism, orig blue and white knit outfit, mkd "Ideal Toy Corp. 77-16" on back of head, orig box **225.00**

Tony, 14-1/2" h, hard plastic head, five-pc hard plastic walker body, blue sheep eyes, closed mouth, orig brunette wig, orig dotted organdy dress, orig underclothes and shoes, mkd "90W Ideal Doll" on head and "Ideal Doll 90W" on back, orig Play Wave set with some orig contents, partial orig box **625.00**

Madame Alexander, Jo, hard plastic, bent knee, 8" h, no box, $225.

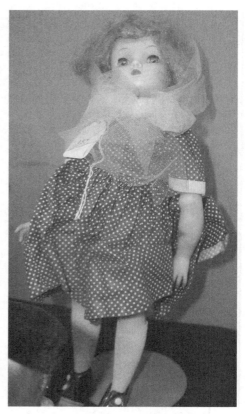

Madame Alexander, Elise, jointed knees and ankles, hard plastic, vinyl arms, tagged "Elise" dress, McGuffy Ana shoes, played with condition, 14" h, $200.

Madame Alexander

The Madame Alexander Doll Company was started in 1923 by Bertha Alexander. The dolls made by this company are beautifully designed with exquisite costumes. They have made hundreds of dolls, including several series, such as the International Dolls and the Americana Dolls. Marks used by this company include "Madame Alexander," "Alexander," "Alex," and many are unmarked on the body but can be identified by clothing tags. Today Madame Alexander continues to make dolls, which are very collectible. Many dolls are made for a limited time period of one year. Others are offered for several years before being discontinued.

Madame Alexander, Poor Cinderella, vinyl, missing scarf and broom, 1967-1992, played with condition, 13" h, $200.

American Girl, 8" h, hard plastic head, blue sleep eyes, closed mouth, orig synthetic wig, hard plastic body jointed at shoulders, hips, and knees, walking mechanism, orig red and white gingham dress, white eyelet pinafore, straw hat with flowers, white cotton socks, black suede shoes, 1962, mkd "Alex" on back of doll, "American Girl by Madame Alexander" on dress tag and gold wrist tag, orig box **285.00**

Binnie Walker, 17" h, hard plastic, blond hair, black striped dress, yellow pinafore, and straw hat, MIB, c1950 .... **500.00**

Bride, 20" h, composition head, blue sleep eyes, closed mouth, orig mohair wig in orig set, five-pc composition body, tagged bride dress, orig underclothes and veil, flowers in hand, factory paint and finish flaws, mkd "Madame Alexander, New York, U.S.A." on dress tag **525.00**

Bridesmaid, 17" h, composition, composition head, brown sleep eyes, closed mouth, orig mohair wig in orig set, five-pc composition body, tagged pink taffeta dress, orig underclothes, flowers in hair, mkd "Mme Alexander" on head "Madame Alexander, New York, U.S.A." on dress tag, unplayed with condition **675.00**

Coco Godey #2063, 21" h, vinyl head, blue sleep eyes, closed smiling mouth, rooted synthetic hair, vinyl body jointed at shoulders and waist, unjointed legs, bent right leg, orig red taffeta gown, trimmed with black lace, black velvet jacket and bonnet with red flower trim, red ruby necklace, diamond ring, 1966, mkd "Alexander 19©66" on back of head, "Madame Alexander All Rights Reserved" on dress tag, replacement box **500.00**

Coco Madame #2060, 21" h, vinyl head, blue sleep eyes, closed smiling mouth, rooted synthetic hair in long curls, vinyl body jointed at shoulders and waist, unjointed legs with bent right leg, orig pink brocade dress with lace and ribbon trim, matching cap, pearl necklace and earrings, diamond ring, 1966, mkd "Alexander 19©66" on back of head, "Madame Alexander All Rights Reserved, New York USA" on dress tag, replacement box **425.00**

Emelie, 7" h, composition head, painted brow eyes, closed mouth, molded and painted brow hair, five-pc composition toddler body, orig tagged lavender dress, matching bonnet, socks, center snap leatherette shoes, mkd "Alexander" on back of head, "Dionne Quintuplets, Madame Alexander, New York" on dress tag, name on pin **200.00**

International Series, 8" h

Germany, © 1975, MIB **50.00**

Greek Boy, jointed knees, 1968 ... **275.00**

Morocco **225.00**

Norway, #584, © 1975, MIB **50.00**

Thailand, © 1970 .... **135.00**

Little Women Series

#412, Beth, © 1975, MIB **50.00**
#416, Laurie, © 1975, MIB............. **50.00**
#1320, Amy, MIB **65.00**

Madeline, 17" h, vinyl head, blue eyes, open-closed smiling mouth, orig rooted wig, hard plastic body jointed at shoulders, elbows, wrists, hips, and knees, orig nightgown, replaced panties and slippers, mkd "Alexander" on back of head, "18" Tall Madame Alexander Reg U.S. Pat. Off Fashions New York USA" on tag on nightgown, clothing has been washed **475.00**

Madame Alexander, France, #590, hard plastic, straight legs, 8" h, MIB, **$200**.

Madame Alexander, Lucinda, #1535, vinyl, 1971-82, 13" h, MIB, **$225**.

Queen #2185, 21" h, vinyl head, blue sleep eyes, closed mouth, pierced ears, rooted synthetic hair, hard plastic body jointed at shoulders, hips, and knees, vinyl arms, high heel feet, orig white brocade dress, red sash of the Order of the Bath, orig underclothing, stockings, and satin shoes, tiara, earrings, bracelets, and gloves, diamond ring, mkd "Alexander 19©61" on back of head, "Madame Alexander All Rights Reserved" on dress tag **225.00**

Sonja Henie, 17" h, composition head, brown sleep eyes, open mouth with six teeth, orig blond human hair wig in orig set, five-pc composition body, orig pink rayon skating dress, gold skates, mkd "Genuine Sonja Henie, Madame Alexander NY USA, All Rights Reserved" on tag on dress, bottom half of orig box **750.00**

Wendy Bride, 17" h, hard plastic head, blue sleep eyes, closed mouth, orig wig in orig set, five-pc hard plastic body jointed at shoulders and hips, orig white satin wedding gown with rhinestones, veil with flower head pc, orig box with comb and curlers, mkd "Alexander" on head, "Madame Alexander All Rights Reserved, New York USA" on dress tag, "Fashion Academy Award" wrist tag, orig box with old repairs **550.00**

Mary Hoyer

The Mary Hoyer Doll Manufacturing Company was named for its founder, in 1925. Mary Hoyer operated a yarn shop and soon began designing doll clothes. She then wanted a perfect doll and approached well-known sculptor Bernard Lipfert, who designed the popular doll. The Fiberoid Doll Company, New York, produced composition Mary Hoyer dolls until 1946, when hard plastic production began. Mary Hoyer continued until the 1970s, when all production of these popular dolls ceased. Mary Hoyer's family has recently released a vinyl version of the vintage Mary Hoyer doll.

Cowgirl, 14" h, hard plastic, five-pc hard plastic body, blue sleep eyes, orig set brunette wig, cowgirl outfit, one orig felt boot, mark: Original Mary Hoyer Doll **360.00**

Girl, 14" h, composition head, five-pc composition body, blue sleep eyes, closed mouth, mohair wig, three-pc navy blue knit outfit, orig socks and black center snap leatherette shoes, mkd "The Mary Hoyer Doll" on back **325.00**

Walker, 14" h, hard plastic, five-pc hard plastic body, blue sleep eyes, closed mouth, orig saran wig in braids, peach knit two-pc outfit, matching cap and panties, gold sandals, trunk with five complete Mary Hoyer outfits, mkd "Made in U.S.A., Mary Hoyer" in black ink on back, circular mark **240.00**

Elsie Massey Originals, pink satin outfit, original tags, **$15**.

Irwin, polystyrene plastic, banner trademark with "Made in USA," 1960, 6-1/2" h, **$10**.

Mattel, Inc.

Mattel, Inc. was started in 1945. First production of this toy company was in the dollhouse furniture line. The toy line was expanded to include music boxes, guns, and several character-type dolls. The most celebrated doll they make is Barbie, which was designed by one of the company's founders, Ruth Handler, in 1958.

Bozo the Clown, 16" h, vinyl head, cloth body, pull talk string, c1962 .... **65.00**

Cheerful Tearful, 12" h, vinyl head and body, orig clothes, 1966 .... **35.00**

Charmin Cathy, 25" h, vinyl head and arms, plastic body and legs, rooted blond hair, blue side glancing sleep eyes, closed mouth, original clothes and metal trunk, 1961 .... **100.00**

Chatty Cathy, 18" h, soft vinyl head, hard plastic body, rooted blond dynel hair, blue sleep eyes, open mouth, two teeth, voice box, MIB, c1965 .... **65.00**

Chicken of the Sea Mermaid, 14" h, long blond yarn hair, diamond patterned green body, yellow tail fin with green polka dots, orig box, 1974 .... **45.00**

Truly Scrumptious, Chitty Chitty Bang Bang, 11-1/2" h, vinyl, straight legs, blond hair, pink and white gown, matching hat, mkd "Mattel, #1108," c1969.......... **90.00**

Sun Rubber Co.

The Sun Rubber Company produced all rubber or lasloid vinyl dolls. Many have molded features and clothes.

Betty Bows, 11" h, rubber, fully jointed, molded hair, blue sleep eyes, drinks and wets, mkd "Betty Bows/copyright The Sun Rubber Co/Barberton, OH USA/ 34A," c1953 .... **35.00**

Gerber Baby, 11" h, all rubber, molded, painted hair, open nurser mouth, dimples, crossed baby legs, mkd "Gerber Baby/ Gerber Products Co" on head **45.00**

Happy Kappy, 7" h, one-piece rubber body, molded painted hair, painted blue eyes, open/closed mouth, yellow hat, mkd "The Sun Rubber Co/Barberton, OH/Made in USA/Ruth E. Newton/New York/NY" **25.00**

Tod-L-Dee, 10-1/2" h, one-piece rubber body, molded painted hair, open nurser mouth, molded diaper, shoes, and socks **25.00**

Nancy Ann Storybook Doll, plastic, movable legs, original striped satin dress, pantaloons, painted shows, holds package and flowers, **$35**. Photo courtesy of Wells Memorial Library.

Terri Lee Dolls

The founder and designed of the Terri Lee family was Mrs. Violet Lee Gradwohl of Lincoln, Nebraska. She made the first Terri Lee doll in 1948. Jerri Lee, a brother, was trademarked in 1948. Connie Lee joined the family in 1955. Mrs. Gradwohl issued lifetime guarantees for each doll, which were honored until the demise of the company in 1958.

Baby Linda, 9" h, all vinyl, molded painted hair, black eyes, c1951 .... **95.00**

Jerri Lee, 16" h, hard plastic, jointed at neck, shoulders, and hips, orig curly wig, painted eyes, orig clothing and accessories, mkd "Jerri Lee" **225.00**

Patty Jo, 17" h, hard plastic, swivel head, jointed hard plastic body, black styled wig, painted brown eyes, closed mouth, orig dress, c1946 .... **450.00**

Terri Lee, 10" h, hard plastic head, five-pc hard plastic body, walking mechanism, brown inset eyes, closed mouth, tagged long blue taffeta dress, mkd "©" on head and back, "Terri Lee" on dress, "Tiny Terri Lee, Manufactured by Terri Lee, ® Apple Valley, Calif" on red box **225.00**

Terri Lee, 16" h, hard plastic head, painted brown eyes, closed mouth, black synthetic wig, five-pc hard plastic body jointed at shoulders and hips, blue and white floral sun suit, skirt, halter top, matching hat, no tags on clothing **250.00**

Terri Lee, 16" h, hard plastic head, painted brown eyes, closed mouth, auburn wig, five-pc hard plastic body jointed at shoulders and hips, tagged red plaid dress with white bodice and collar, tagged new nylon romper, socks, leatherette shoes, black jointed pool with red leather collar, reproduction Steiff tag with red coat trimmed with gold, mkd "Terri Lee" on back and dress tag **500.00**

Tiny Jerri Lee, 10" h, hard plastic, fully jointed, blond curly wig, brown sleep eyes, closed mouth **175.00**

Vogue

Vogue Dolls, Inc. was founded by Mrs. Jennie H. Graves. She began a small doll shop, which specialized in well-made costumes. The original business of doll clothing lead to a cottage industry which employed more than 500 home sewers in 1950. This branch of the industry peaked in the late 1950s with more than 800 home workers plus several hundred more at the factory. During World War II, the shortages created a market for an American doll source. Mrs. Graves created the Ginny Doll and promoted her heavily. The Ginny Doll was the first doll created with a separate wardrobe and accessories. For many years, Vogue issued 100 new outfits for Ginny alone. The company continued to produce its own dolls and clothing for other doll manufacturers. Ginny Dolls reached their heyday in the 1950s and are still being made today.

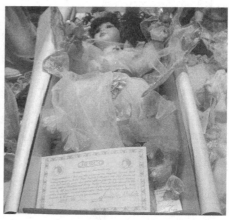

Jesco, fairy princess, original box, $15.

Alpine Lady, 13" h, blond, ethnic costume, 1930s, mkd **200.00**

Baby Dear, 12" h, all composition, bent baby limbs, 1961 .... **40.00**

Betty Jane, 12" h, all composition, bent right arm, braided pigtails, red plaid woven cotton dress, white eyelet trim; orig tag Vogue Dolls Inc., 1947 .... **85.00**

Crib Crow Baby, 7-1/2" h, all hard plastic, curved baby legs, painted eyes, blond synthetic ringlets wig, orig tagged dress, rubber pants, c1949 .... **425.00**

Ginny, 8" h, all hard plastic, painted eyes, molded hair, mohair wig, mkd "Vogue" on head, "Vogue Doll" on back, Springtime, c1948 .... **115.00**

Hug a Bye Baby, 22" h, pink pajamas, MIB **40.00**

Toodles, Bride, 8" h, composition head, five-pc composition child body, painted blue eyes to side, closed mouth, orig blond mohair wig, orig organdy bride dress with flocked design, orig underclothes, lace trimmed veil, orig white flowers, mkd "Vogue" on back of head, "Doll Co." on back **185.00**

Toodles, Julie, #8-10B, 8" h, composition head, five-pc composition body, painted blue eyes to side, closed mouth, orig mohair wig, orig tagged dark green knit bib pants, red felt squirrel trim, multicolored striped knit shirt and matching hat, orig socks and leatherette shoes, silver hoe with wooden handle, mkd "Vogue" on back, "Vogue Dolls, Inc., Medford, Mass" on pants tag **165.00**

Walking Ginny, 8" h, ballerina, poodle cut wig, 1954, walking mechanism, mkd "Ginny Vogue Dolls, Inc., Pat. Pend., Made in USA" **110.00**

Drugstore Collectibles

History: The increasing diversity of health-related occupations has also encouraged an awareness of pharmaceutical materials, items that appeared in drugstores from the turn of the century through the 1950s. Products manufactured before the Pure Food and Drug Act of 1906 are eagerly sought by collectors. Patent medicines, medicinal tins, items from a specific pharmaceutical company, dental items, and shaving supplies are a key collecting specialties.

The copyright date on a package, graphics, style of lettering, or the popularity of a specific item at a particular period in history are clues to dating a product. Pharmacists who have been in the business for a number of years are good sources for information, as are old manufacturing directories available at regional libraries.

Collecting Hints: There are several considerations when starting a drugstore collection: 1) Buy the best that you can afford. 2) Look for excellent graphics on the packaging of items. 3) Do not buy anything that is rusty or damp. 4) Before purchasing an item, ask the dealer to remove price tags or prices written on the piece. If this isn't possible, determine how badly you want the item. 5) Buy a variety of items. Consider placing several similar items together on a shelf for increased visual effect. 6) Purchase examples from a variety of time periods.

Bank, *Pepto Bismol 24 Hour Bug,* soft vinyl, 4" x 6", green, dark green spots, four legs, two crossed arms, white eyes, orange closure mkd "Niagara Plastics, Erie, Pa" **25.00**

Book, *Yellow Magic, The Story of Penicillin,* J. D. Ratcliff, Random House, 1945, 1st ed. **8.50**

Calendar, 1959, Santa with bag of toys, Merry Christmas and Happy New Year, St. Joseph's Aspirin, Blue Mound Pharmacy, weather chart and almanac, 8" w, 15" l **32.00**

Catalog, Merrell, J. S., Drug Co., St. Louis, MO, 1919, 103 pgs, 9-1/2" x 12-1/4", drug store fixtures, fountain supplies, pencil marks on front wrap **150.00**

Charm, 1-1/4" h, Boyd's Battery, narrow silver metal ring surrounds larger central metal segment with text surrounded by 12 individual circles in brass, silver, or copper luster, opposite side with inscription "Patented Jan 17, 1878," small brass loop on top **24.00**

Container, Little Imps, For All Who Breathe...Little Imps Throat Ease, Breath Perfume, The American Confection Co. (Inc.) Boston, 1-1/2" d celluloid top with center red devil's face, yellow horns, black hair, face surrounded by red and yellow flames on cream ground shading to gray at top, _" thick container, Whitehead & Hoag 1901 patent date **90.00**

Display, Blue-Jay Corn Plasters, cardboard, two drawers, "Make hard roads easy," displays two hobos walking along railroad tracks while passing billboard for Blue-Jay Plasters, © 1903, 6-1/2" h, 9-1/4" l, 10-1/4" d **50.00**

First Aid cabinet, Bauer & Black, #8, wall hung type, some orig contents, first aid book published in 1927, 18" x 15" x 4-1/4" **100.00**

First Aid kit

Bauer & Black, 5-1/2" x 3-1/2" tin box, orig contents **12.00**

Mine Safety Appliances, six little boxes with bandages, tincture of iodine, ammonia inhalants, torniquet, forceps, bandaids, instructions, 8" x 5" metal box with two latches **15.00**

First day cover, George Papanicolaou, first day of issue, May 18, 1978 .... **5.00**

Magazine or newspaper advertising tear sheet

Bauer & Black, Blue Jay Corn Ender, tri-color ad showing map on soap box with doctor's bag, guaranteeing to cure corns, also shows Blue Jan Corn Ender product, *Saturday Evening Post*, Aug. 16, 1919, 11" x 14" **8.00**

Bauer & Black, First Aid, tri-color ad for shows woman administering First Aid to man, *Saturday Evening Post*, 1926, 11" x 14" **9.00**

Bauer & Black, Wet-Pruf Adhesive Tape, black and white, newspaper ad, "Enjoy your swim my darling daughter, Wet-Pruf can't be hurt by water," 1935 .... **2.50**

Rexall Orderlies Laxative, aqua, orange and dark blue, dated Aug. 1, 1924, 3-1/4" x 1-3/4", **$10**.

Pain reliever tin

ADS Apsirin Highest Purity, green, red, and white **7.50**
BC Headache Neuralgia, blue and white **6.00**
Genuine Saleto Headache Tablets, black, white, and pink **8.50**
Laymon's 5¢ Aspirin Tablets, gray and silver **6.00**
Miles Anti-Pain Pills, blue and white . **5.00**
Nebs Pain Reliever, light blue, black, and white **7.50**
Stand Back Analgesic Tablets, red, white, and blue **6.00**

Pinback button, 1-1/4" d

Flushing Hospital Are You With Us, red on white, bright gold rim with diagonal red, white, and blue flag, issued for new building campaign, Whitehead & Hoag back paper, c1910 .... **15.00**
Fox Drug Co. Business is Good, dark blue on white, bright red running fox in center "Follow the Fox!," St Louis back paper, 1940s **12.00**
Jack's Friend Dentist-Clean Teeth-Chewing Exercise-Right Food, red, white, and blue, young boy in center **12.00**

Pocket mirror, 2" d, Ex Lax A Chocolate Laxative, full-color product tin, gold, black, and white against cream ground
.... **35.00**

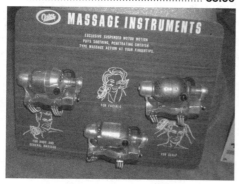

Oster Massage Instruments, store display, actual models mounted to board, white instructional text, **$195**.

Powder tin

A.D.S. Rose Talc, 5" h, rose graphic, text "American Druggist Syndicate Laboratories, New York, Made in U.S.A.," bottom "Patented March 4, 1914," same graphic and text on both sides, letters "A.D.S." on swivel closure, light blue, pink rose and rosebuds, green leaves .. **20.00**
Babcock's Corylopsis of Japan Talcum Powder, 4-1/2" h, multicolored graphic of Japanese lady kneeling by plants and flowers, birds in upper left, surrounded by gilt, green tin, top with branches and leaves and "Corylopsis" on either side, swivel closure, full, c1920 .... **18.00**
Bauer & Black Baby Talc, sample size; 2-1/4" h, some wear to rim **155.00**
Deodo, The Pleasant Deodorant Powder, 3" x 5-1/2", gold, white, and gray graphics on powder blue.............................. **25.00**
Dream Girl Talcum Powder, 2" x 6", black and white on red **25.00**
Johnson & Johnson, baby powder **20.00**
Massatta, 4-1/2" h, text "Massatta The Talcum With The True Oriental Odor," emb graphic on both sides of Oriental woman and child, flowers, and birds on top, full, 1920s **15.00**
Pond's Oeilletvleu Blue Carnation Talcum, 3" x 4-1/2", name and floral design on both sides **15.00**
Pond's Talc Dream Flower, 2-1/2" x 4", repeating text and pastel floral design
.... **18.00**
Velvet Night Talcum Vi-Jon Laboratories, St. Louis, 3" x 5-1/2", moonlight scene, 1930s **20.00**
Violet Jergen's Miss Dainty Talcum Borated, 4-3/4" h, graphic of four curly-haired girls in each corner surrounded by gold leaves and flowers, yellow filigree swivel closure, full, c1920 .... **24.00**
White Witch For The Skin, 2-1/2" x 5", blue and white graphic of kneeling nude on light gray ground **28.00**
Yardley's Old English Lavender Talc Powder, 4-3/4" h, oval graphic with lady in dress and bonnet carrying basket, two children followed by dog, gold cap, slide closure, text "33, Old Bond St London, Established 1770," reverse "For Nursery, Toilet & General Use," bottom "Invaluable For Use In Hot Climates, General Use," c1930 .... **24.00**

Prescription form, US Treasure Department Bureau of Industrial Alcohol Duplicate Form for Medicinal Liquor, 1930s, pink paper, issued, 4-1/2" x 5-1/2" **5.00**

Stamp case, book shape, By-Lo Breath Perfume, black, white, and red celluloid, spine lettered "Stamp And Court Plaster Edition" and sponsor's name, early 1900s
.... **55.00**

Store display box, Feen-A-Mint, The Chewing Laxative, cardboard box, 1930s, 4-1/2" x 6" **25.00**

Tape measure, celluloid canister, Dr. Caldwell's Syrup Pepsin Cures Constipation, reverse slogan "Cures All Stomach Troubles," yellow product box on both sides **40.00**

Prosser's Queen Corylopsis Talcum Powder, Borated, multicolored paper label with children, Christmas stockings over ends of beds, 4-5/8" h, **$25**.

Throat lozenge tin

Allenbury's Glycerine & Black Currant Pastilles, Made From The Fresh Ripe Fruit, Manufactured In England, colorful lid with flowers **7.50**

Asche's Bronchial Pastillen Seit 1877, red, white, and black........................ **6.00**

DeWitt's Throat Lozenges, blue, white, and black, 60 orig lozenges **5.00**

Huyler's Glycerine Tablets, bottom of tin shows bird flying to nest, blue, white, and light blue **5.00**

La Pate Kope, green, white, and gold floral design **5.00**

Pastilles Valda Antiseptiques, gold, black, white, and blue **5.00**

Robert J. Pierce's Empress Brand Tansy, Rootcotton Penny Royal and Apio Tablets, gold, black, green, and light green **7.50**

The Owl, Throat Pastilles, red, gold, yellow, and brown............................ **6.00**

Tin, Bauer & Black, Handi-Tape, orange, 1-7/8" w, 3-3/4" h **10.00**

Toothpick, 1-3/4" l, diecut celluloid, bottle shape, blue, white, yellow, red, white, and blue label "Bouvier Buchu Gin," brass grommet, pair of pointed flat celluloid arms fold out to serve as toothpicks, back with product name and "For The Kidneys & Bladder," Bastian, early 1900s ... **24.00**

Toy, Nature's Remedy Tablets, celluloid, center wooden spinner dowel, brown and white, c1920................................... **20.00**

Tray, tin litho

Heck's Capudine Medicine.......... **215.00**

Kaiser Willhelm Bitters Co., oversized bottle with trademark label, "For Appetite and Digestion" **70.00**

E

Electrical Appliances

History: The first all electric-kitchen appeared at the 1893 Chicago World's Fair and included a dishwasher that looked like a torture device and a range. Electric appliances for the home began gaining popularity just after 1900 in the major eastern and western cities. Appliances were sold door-to-door by their inventors. Small appliances did not gain favor in the rural areas until the late 1910s and early 1920s. However, most people did not trust electricity.

By the 1920s, competition among electrical companies was keen and there were many innovations. Changes occurred frequently, but the electric servants were here to stay. Most small appliance companies were bought by bigger firms. These, in turn, have been swallowed up by the huge conglomerates of today.

By the 1930s, it was evident that our new electric servants were making life a lot easier and were here to stay. The American housewife, even in rural areas, was beginning to depend on the electric age, enthusiastically accepting each new invention.

Some firsts in electrical appliances are:

1882	Patent for electric iron (H. W. Seeley [Hotpoint])
1903	Detachable cord (G.E. Iron)
1905	G.E. Toaster (Model X-2)
1905	Westinghouse toaster (Toaster Stove)
1909	Travel iron (G.E.)
1911	Electric frying pan (Westinghouse)
1912	Electric waffle iron (Westinghouse)
1917	Table Stove (Armstrong)
1918	Toaster/Percolator (Armstrong "Perc-O-Toaster")
1920	Heat indicator on waffle iron (Armstrong)
1920	Flip-flop toasters (many companies)
1920	Mixer on permanent base (Hobart Kitchen Aid)
1923	Portable mixer (Air-O-Mix "Whip-All")
1924	Automatic iron (Westinghouse)
1924	Home malt mixer (Hamilton Beach #1)
1926	Automatic pop-up toaster (Toastmaster Model 1-A-1)
1926	Steam iron (Eldec)
1937	Home coffee mill (Hobart Kitchen Aid)
1937	Automatic coffee maker (Farberware "Coffee Robot")
1937	Conveyance toaster ("Toast-O-Lator")

Collecting Hints: Small electric appliances are still readily available and can be found at estate and garage sales, flea markets, auctions, antiques malls, and best of all, in the back of your mom's upper cabinets or even in Grandma's attic! Most can still be found at antique malls, etc. for a reasonable price. However, in recent years, due to collectors, decorators, and the foreign market, some appliances, mostly toasters that are "high-style" Art Deco have been commanding an almost unbelievable and dramatic rise in value. Porcelain and porcelain insert appliances have risen sharply as well as some electric irons.

Most old toasters, waffle irons, and other appliances still work. When buying an old appliance, ask if it works and ask the *seller* to plug it in to see if it heats.

Note: use extreme caution; there could be a short due to many factors (dirt, bare wires, etc.). On "flip-flop" type toasters (the most numerous kind) check to see if the elements are intact around the mica and not broken.

Most appliances used a standard-size cord, still available at hardware stores. Some of the early companies had appliances that would only accept cords peculiar to that company. In such an instance, buy the appliance only if the cord accompanies it.

Unless you plan to use an appliance for display only or for parts, don't buy it if it doesn't work or is in rusted or poor condition.

Dirt does not count! With a little care, time, and diligence, most of old appliances will clean up to a sparkling appearance. Aluminum mag-wheel polish, available at auto parts stores, used with a soft rag will yield wonderful results. A non-abrasive kitchen cleanser can also be a great help. *But do not use steel wool!*

As with most collectibles, the original box or instructions can add 25 percent to 50 percent to the value of the piece. Also, beware of brass or copper appliances (usually coffee pots) because these were originally chrome or nickel. Devalue these by 50 percent.

Portable oven, Eureka, 1930s, $80.

Blenders

Berstead Drink Mixer, 1930s, Eskimo Kitchen Mechanic, Berstead Mfg. Co., domed chrome motor, single shaft, lift-off metal base with receptacle for tapered ribbed glass, 12" **60.00**

Chronmaster Mixall, 1930s, Chronmaster Electric Corp., NY & Chicago, chrome and black motor, single shaft on hinged black base, orig silver-striped glass **45.00**

Dorby Whipper, 1940s, Model E, chrome motor with black Bakelite handle, off/on toggle, clear, measured Vidrio glass **45.00**

Electromix Whipper, 1930s, Chicago, ivory colored, offset metal motor housing with push-down break, filler hole in lid, measured glass base, 7-1/2" **40.00**

Gilbert Mixer, Polar Cub, 1929, A.C. Gilbert Co., New Haven, CT, 10" h, lift-off gray painted metal, rear switch, blue wood handle, premium for Wesson-Snowdrift, orig box **125.00**

Hamilton Beach Malt Machine, forerunner to home malt maker, mid-1920s, Cyclone #1, 19" h, heavy nickel housing, sq stand on marble base, int push-down switch **350.00**

Kenmore Hand Mixer, 1940s, Sears, Roebuck & Co., Chicago, small, cream-colored plastic, single 4-1/2" beater, orig box, booklet, warranty and hanger plate **40.00**

Kenmore Whipper, 1940s, Sears, Roebuck & Co., Chicago, cream-colored metal domed top, large blue Bakelite knob, clear glass bottom, 8-1/2" h **30.00**

Knapp Monarch Whipper, mid-1930s, St. Louis, 9-1/2" h, white metal motor, red plastic top handle, round mild glass base with reeded, fin feet, white plastic beater **65.00**

Kwick Way, St. Louis, 7-1/2" h, white metal motor top over angular clear glass base, no switch, decal label **35.00**

Made-Rite Drink Mixer, 1930s, Weinig Made Rite Co., Cleveland, light-weight metal, cream and green motor, single shaft, no switch, stamped, permanent support, no glass **30.00**

Silex Blender, 1940s, NY, sq, white cast base, push-button switch, silver foil, Art Deco label, clear glass four-cup top with vertical "Silex" on black stripe, plastic lid **35.00**

Unmarked whipper, late 1920s-early 1930s, 7-1/2" h, green metal motor housing, green Depression glass "Vidrio" cup, unusual serpentine shaft **25.00**

Chafing dishes

American Beauty, c1910, American Electrical Heater Co., Detroit, MI, three-part, nickel on copper, base serves as hot-water container and has sealed element, separate plugs mkd "fast" and "slow," black painted wood handles and knob **50.00**

Chase Chrome Supper Set, 1930s, 11" x 18" Art Deco chrome body, chamfered corners, four white porcelain inserts with chrome lids, black plastic handles & knobs **215.00**

Manning Bowman, 1930s, Meriden, CT Chafing dish, bright chrome Art Deco design, reeded edges, two-part top on hot-plate base, black Bakelite knob and handles **75.00**
Supper set, 19" l oval, chrome, Art Deco body, reeded decoration, two large round Hall Porcelain inserts with chrome lids, black knobs **195.00**

Universal, c1910, Landers, Frary & Clark, New Britain, CT, nickel on copper faceted three-part body, sealed element in base hot-water pan, three-prong heat adjuster in base, large black wood handle and knob **50.00**

Coffee makers and sets

Coleman, percolator, "Electric Brew" model 70, high Art Deco, spherical, glass body, applied glass handle, chrome lid, black knob all mounted on black bakelite base, four vertical, silver fins...................... **95.00**

Farberware Coffee Robot, coffee set, 1937, S.W. Farber, Brooklyn, NY, coffee maker #500, set #501, two-part coffee dripolator, creamer, open sugar and tray, nickel chrome, walnut handles, orig booklet, price for set.................................... **125.00**

Manning Bowman, Meriden, CT

Percolator, 1930s, set #636, tall graceful Art Deco design, bright chrome, reeded decoration around neck and base, 12"h
.... **60.00**
Percolator urn, late 1920s, article #250, 3-part aluminum body, unique design prevents re-perking, front spigot, out-turned handles, clear glass insert in domed lid, 12-1/2" h........................ **50.00**

Meriden Homelectrics percolator set, 1930s, set #636, Manning Bowman Co., Meriden, CT, catalog #32, ser. #4-30, 15" h percolator/urn, creamer, open sugar, nickel chrome vertically faceted bodies, urn on short cabriole legs, up-turned black wood handles, glass knob insert on top, set.. **95.00**

Porcelier, breakfast set, 1930s, Greensburg, PA, all-porcelain bodies accented by basketweave design, floral transfers, silver line dec
Coffee urn....................................... **450.00**
Cream and sugar, cov **50.00**
Percolator #5007 .... **125.00**
Sandwich grill #5004..................... **195.00**
Toaster #5002................................ **850.00**

Royal Rochester percolator, Robeson Rochester Corp., Rochester, NY, percolator
c1912, round chrome body, shaped, clear glass basket, chrome lid, spigot and attached base, out-turned feet **75.00**
1930s, #D-30, almost-white porcelain, slight greenish luster around shoulder and spout, spring bouquet floral transfer, chrome lid and base, clear glass insert
.... **125.00**
1930s, model D-33, 1930s, high Art Deco design in chrome, cylindrical body with wide black stripe, stepped glass lid with black knob, open, vertical handle, ding timer.. **85.00**

Sunbeam Dripolator, 1930s, Model 14, high Art Deco design, cylindrical chrome body with horizontal black stripes, three-part, serving container with hinged lid, large chrome basket, short hot plate with rotating temperature control, matching creamer and sugar **150.00**

Universal

Breakfast set, 1930s, Landers, Frary & Clark, New Britain, CT, cream-colored porcelain, blue and orange floral transfers, waffle iron on pierced chrome base has porcelain insert, front drop handle
Creamer and sugar, cov..... **45.00**
Percolator #E6927............ **125.00**
Syrup, chrome cov............ **60.00**
Waffle iron E6324 .... **195.00**
Coffee set
14" h, squat cabriole legs, large wood ear-shaped handles; nickel bodies, oval tray, price for four-pc set..................................... **125.00**
1920s, Landers, Frary & Clark, New Britain, CT, urn #E9119-1, 16-1/2" h, chrome, chrome handles, swirl glass insert, octagonal body, handled tray, price for four-pc set.......... **150.00**

Egg cookers

Hankscraft Co., 1920s, Madison, WI, Model #599, yellow china base, large dish on top of domed chrome serves as knob and filler with hole in bottom, instructions on metal plate on bottom **35.00**

Rochester Stamping Co., c1910, Rochester, NY, egg-shaped, four-part chrome on small base, interior fitted with skillet with turned black wood handle, six-egg holder with lift-out handle, enclosed heating element **65.00**

Magazine tear sheet showing Westinghouse electric Ware for the home, $30

Food cookers

Eureka Portable Oven, 1930s, Eureka Vacuum Cleaner Co., Detroit, MI, 15" x 13" x 19", Art Deco-style, cream-colored painted body, black edges, sides fold down and contain hot plates on chrome surfaces, int fitted with wire racks, controls across bottom front **200.00**

Everhot, 1920s, Swartz Baugh Mfg. Co., Toledo, OH, EC Junior 10, 13" h, large chrome and black cylindrical body, aluminum cov, Art Deco design, "Everhot" embossed on front, int. fitted with rack, two open semicircular pans, one round cov pan, three-prong heat control **50.00**

Hankscraft, 1920s, Madison, WI, green enamel pan, detachable hinge-pin chrome cov, green ceramic lusterware knob, chrome base, black wood handles flare from sides of body **95.00**

Nesco Electric Casserole, early 1930s, National Enamel & Stamping Co., Inc., Milwaukee, WI, 9" d, forerunner of crock pot, cream-colored body with green enamel cov, high/low control, 3-prong plug **35.00**

Quality Brand, 1920s, Great Northern Mfg. Co., Chicago, IL, model #950, 14" h, cylindrical body, insulated sides and cov, fitted int. with cov aluminum pans, brown with red stripe body, lift-out rods **40.00**

Westinghouse, roaster oven, 1940s, white metal painted body, aluminum top with window of top, gray plastic handle, includes lift-out gray graniteware pan, three clear glass dishes with lids, matching stand with clock timer and storage door **50.00**

Hot plates

Edison-Hotpoint, c1910, Edison Electric, NY, Chicago and Ontario, CA, solid iron surface, clay-filled int., very heavy pierced legs, ceramic feet, copper control with ceramic knob **35.00**

El Stovo, c1910, Pacific Electric Heating Co., sometimes mkd "G.E. Hotpoint," solid iron surface, clay-filled int, very heavy pierced legs, pad feet, no control **25.00**

Volcano, 1930s, Hilco Engineering Co., Chicago, IL, slightly conical nickel body, black wood handle, slide lever as control on side that lifts grate...................... **40.00**

Westinghouse, 1920s, Mansfield, OH, 7-1/2" d top with green porcelain-metal top surrounding element, hollow legs, no control **25.00**

Miscellaneous

Angelus-Campfire Bar-B-Q Marshmallow Toaster, 1920s, Milwaukee, WI, 3" sq, flat top, pierced pyramid top piece, base on loop, wire legs with rubber-encased feet, flat wire forks, orig box **125.00**

Buffet warming oven, Chase Chrome and Brass **130.00**

Clock/timer, late 1930s, made for Montgomery Ward & Co., cream body, silver and red face, curved glass, body swivels on weighted base, clock mechanism winds up manually, cord at back with appliance receptacle..... **40.00**

Coffee grinder, Kitchen Aid, Hobart, Troy, OH, model #A-9, heavy cream-colored cast base with motor, course/fine adjustment on neck, clear glass jar container with screw-off top serves as storage for beans **75.00**

Miracle flour sifter, c1934, Chicago, IL, electric, cream body, blue wood hold-down button handle at base, vibrates flour through wire strainer.............. **35.00**

Sunkist juicer, 1930s, 9" h, opaque green Depression glass top, int. metal strainer, chrome body/motor housing with dark green painted center, metal "Sunkist" plate on front................................... **85.00**

Universal

Griddle, late 1930s, large 23" x 15" white porcelain body on short porcelain legs, full aluminum griddle top w/drain spout, two large red indicator lights, two front round controls with porcelain handles **175.00**

Tea kettle, c1910, Landers, Frary & Clark, New Britain, CT, model #E973, bright nickel one-pc squat body and base, long spout, black painted wood high curved handle on pierced vertically curved mounts **45.00**

Vita-Juicer, 1930s, Kold King Distributing Corp., Los Angeles, Hoek Rotor Mfg. Co., Reseda, CA, 10" h, heavy, cream-painted cast metal, base motor, container and lid fitted with lock groove and lock-down wire handle, aluminum pusher fits in top holder **35.00**

White Cross, oven 1920s, black steel body, 34" h on short legs, 14" x 12" vertical, small oven and warming compartment, larger top with two hotplates three front, round porcelain and chrome controls **175.00**

Mixers

General Electric, 1938, G.E. Corp., upright housed motor, no speed control, three synchronized beaters in a row, work light shines in handle, two white glass bowls, black Bakelite handle, ser. #10-A .. **50.00**

Hamilton Beach, 1930s, Racine, WI, model G, cream-colored metal, black Bakelite handle, on/off lever control, "Mix Guide" in window below handle, mixer lifts off base to become portable, two white glass bowls.................... **35.00**

Sunbeam Mixmaster

Attachments, fit most models

Bean slicer.........................	**20.00**
Can opener	**15.00**
Churn..............................	**50.00**
Coffee grinder....................	**25.00**
Drink mixer........................	**15.00**
Grater, slicer, shredder, three blades	**35.00**
Grinder/chopper	**25.00**
Juicer, mayonnaise maker .	**20.00**
Knife sharpener	**15.00**
Pea sheller	**10.00**
Potato peeler......................	**35.00**
Power unit	**10.00**
Ricer................................	**20.00**
Silver polisher and buffer ...	**10.00**

Cabinet, 60-1/2" x 24"................... **295.00**
Mixmaster, early 1930s, Chicago Flexible Shaft Co., model K, cream-colored body, fold-over black wood handle, rear speed control, light green opaque Depression glass bowls, juicer and strainer, orig booklet................... **65.00**

Popcorn poppers

Berstead, 1930s, model #302, sq, chrome, body with circular int., Fry Glass lid, large black knob on top, rod through lid for stirring.................................. **45.00**

Excel, 1920s, Excel Electric Co., Muncie, IN, one-pc cylindrical nickel body, metal handles form legs, lock-down levers, hand crank, black wood knob, top vent holes **25.00**

Manning Bowman, early 1940s, Meriden, CT, model #500, detachable large aluminum container, fits chrome hot plate, glass lid emb with floral motif, black Bakelite knob, never used **15.00**

Rapaport, 1920s, Rapaport Bros., Inc., Chicago, 5-1/2" sq black base, metal legs, round aluminum upper part with attached lid and red knob, chrome handle squeezes through slot in side to agitate corn **25.00**

U.S. Mfg. Corp., 1930s, Decatur, IL, #10, body and lid separate from hot plate base, top crank handle................... **15.00**

White Cross, c1918, National Stamping & Electrical Co., Chicago, IL, tin can base with heater and cord, wire basket fits onto can, metal top with stirrer mounted through handle, woo handle to side, primitive **30.00**

Marshmallow toaster, **$125**; three toasting forks, **$15**; and original campfire marshmallows tin, **$45**

Toasters

Edison Appliance Co., c1918, NY, cat. #214-T-5, open nickel body with free-swinging tab closures at top, single side knob, removable toast warming rack......... **95.00**

General Mills, early 1940s, Minneapolis, MN, cat. #GM5A, two-slice pop-up chrome body, wheat dec on side, black Bakelite base, A.C. or D.C., red knob, light/dark control **45.00**

Heat Master, 1923-35, sq chrome body, rounded corners, end opening, two-slice, manual operation, black Bakelite handle and feet **60.00**

Kenmore, early 1940s, Sears, Roebuck & Co., Chicago, mechanical, two-slice pop-up, chrome body, rounded edges and sides, black Bakelite handles, mechanical clock mechanism, light/dark control **30.00**

Knapp Monarch Reverso, 1930, cat. #505, light-weight rect nickel body, rounded corners, black painted base, flip-flop doors with tab handles, no mica, wires stretched across............................ **60.00**

Montgomery Ward & Co., mid-1930s, Chicago, IL, model #94-KW2298-B, flip-flop type, solid nickel-chrome body, Bakelite handle on end opens both doors simultaneously **50.00**

Steel Craft, late 1920s, open, painted green wire construction, flip-flop type, red painted wood knobs and feet........ **65.00**

Sunbeam, early 1920s, Chicago Flexible Shaft Co., model B, 5" x 9", flat, rect dec chrome body, round, reeded legs, hexagonal Bakelite feet, double wire cages flip over horizontally, small drop bail handles for carrying **125.00**

Toastmaster, 1927, Waters-Genter Co., Minneapolis, MN, model 1-A-1, recognized as first automatic pop-up, chrome Art Deco body, louvered sides, rounded end, manual clock timer mechanism, light/dark control from A to G, panic button............................ **250.00**

Universal, 1913-15, Landers, Frary & Clark, nickel body, flat base, tab feet, pierced concave spring-loaded doors, permanent warming rack **60.00**

Westinghouse

Toaster stove, 1909, Mansfield, OH, flat rect body, four flat strip plates, removable cabriole legs, tray and wire rack, orig box and paper guarantee, never used **175.00**

Turnover toaster, 1920s, Mansfield, OH, cat. #TT3, nickel body, pierced doors and top, flat tab handles, pierced, flat warming rack top **45.00**

Waffle irons and sandwich grills

The most popular are porcelain insert waffle irons. These are by most manufacturers in various transfer designs; any one worth at least $125.

Armstrong Waffle Iron, 1920, model W, first example with heat read/thermometer light on top, 7" round nickel body, black wood handles, distinctive prongs, with cord **45.00**

Coleman Waffle Iron, early 1930s, Coleman Lamp & Stove Co., Wichita, KS, high Art Deco style, chrome, low profile, small black and white porcelain top impala insert, black Bakelite handles **85.00**

Dominion Electric Co., double waffle iron, 1940s, Mansfield, OH, chrome rect stepped body, two round waffle grills, separate temperature controls, red light heat indicator, walnut handles, top circular dec, special two-headed cord **35.00**

Electrahot Double Waffle Iron, 1940s, Mansfield, OH, two 6" sets of plates mounted on oval base, heat indicators with surrounding dec on top **30.00**

Excelsior Waffle Iron, 1930s, Perfection Electric Co., New Washington, OH, 6" round white porcelainized iron body, four little stamped legs, plug in front, turned painted wood handle **25.00**

Fitzgerald Star Waffle Iron, 1920s, Torrington, CT, 7", solid flared base, unique handle design locks in position for raising or carrying **35.00**

General Electric Waffle Iron, early 1940s, 8" round chrome body, ivory Bakelite handles and heat control/off front lever, top dec of circle of stars surrounding stripes and leaves **35.00**

Hostess Sandwich Grill, 1930s, All Rite Co., Rushville, IN, 5" sq cast-aluminum body, angled at bottom to form feet, screw-off wood handle, orig box and booklet of suggestions **65.00**

Hotpoint Waffle Iron, 1920s, Edison, General Electric, Chicago, IL and Ontario, CA, "Automatic" below front handle, rotating cold/hot in small front window, round chrome body, top dec, ivory Bakelite handles, scalloped base dec **35.00**

Lady Hibbard Sandwich Grill, 1930s, Hibbard, Spencer, Bartlet & Co., Chicago, IL, nickel rect body, cast cabriole legs, black wood side handles, front handle swivels to form foot for top plate enabling use of both plates as grills, drip spout **25.00**

Manning Bowman, Meriden, CT, Twin-O-Matic Waffle Iron, late 1930s, Art Deco design, top heat indicator with rotating knob, chrome body flips over in brown Bakelite stand mounted on chrome base **125.00**

Sampson Waffle Iron, 1930s, Sampson United Corp., Rochester, NY, Art Deco design, chrome boy with wing-like flared Bakelite side handles set asymmetrically, stationary front handle **40.00**

Westinghouse Waffle Iron, 1905-21 patent date, rect chrome body, mechanical front handle with wood hand-hold, removable cabriole legs slip into body slots, off/on switch **80.00**

Elephant Collectibles

History: Elephants were unique and fascinating when they first reached America. Early specimens were shown in barns and moved at night to avoid anyone getting a free look. The arrival of Jumbo in England, his subsequent purchase by P. T. Barnum, and his removal to America brought elephant mania to new heights.

Elephants have always been a main attraction at American zoological parks. The popularity of the circus in the early 20th century kept attention focused on elephants.

Hunting elephants was considered "big game" sport, and President Theodore Roosevelt was one well-known participant. The hunt always focused on finding the largest known example. It is not a surprise that an elephant dominates the entrance to the Museum of Natural History of the Smithsonian Institution in Washington, D.C.

Television, through shows such as "Wild Kingdom," has contributed to knowledge about all wild animals, including the now quite-commonplace elephant.

Political convention souvenirs, "GOP June Kansas City" on backs, left: red and blue blanket; right, pink and blue blanket, viscoloid, American made, each **$35**.

Collecting Hints: There are vast quantities of elephant-shaped and elephant-related items. Concentrate on one type of object (toys, vases, bookends, etc.), one substance (china, wood, paper), one chronological period, or one type of elephant (African or Indian). The elephants of Africa and India do differ, a fact not widely recognized.

Perhaps the most popular elephant collectibles are those related to Jumbo and Dumbo, the Disney character who was a circus outcast and the first flying elephant. GOP material associated with the Republican party is usually left to the political collector.

Because of the large number of items available, stress quality. Study the market carefully before buying. Interest in elephant collecting is subject to phases, is and is currently at a modest level.

Advertising trade card, 4-7/8" x 3", Clark's Spool Cotton, Jumbo's Arrival, sepia, white, adv on back............................. **7.50**

Ashtray, elephant foot, silver-plate, 3-1/2" d
.... **25.00**

Bank

Cast iron, painted gold, A. Williams, USA, some wear to orig paint **110.00**

Chalk, 12" h, orig paint, c1930 ..... **125.00**

Battery operated toy, 3-1/4" x 4" x 6", playing cymbal and drum, made by M & M, Japan, c1960 .... **45.00**

Book, Edward Allen, *Fun By The Ton* . **20.00**

Bookends, pr, Ronson, sgd "L. V. Aronson, copyright 1923"

Elephant Country, black painted metal, elephant against landscape, back emb with design, 4-3/4" w, 4" h............. **195.00**

Howdah, black finish, verdigris accents, ivory painted tusks, orig felt, 4-1/2" h
.... **160.00**

Bottle opener, figural, cast iron, sitting, trunk raised

Brown, pink eyes and tongue, 3-1/2" h
.... **55.00**

Pink, "GOP" on base, 3-1/4" h........ **55.00**

Brooch

2" l, 1-1/2" h, rhinestones, pink tusks, black enamel trim, trunk up........... **95.00**

3" w, 3" l, faux jet stones, crystal rhinestones, Butler & Wilson logo on back
.... **135.00**

Child's book, *Travels of Babar*, Jean De Brunhoff, Randon House, 1962 ..... **12.00**

Christmas ornament

3" h, silver emb cardboard, Dresden, Germany **140.00**

3-1/2" l, blown glass, gray body, red blanket **95.00**

Cigarette dispenser, cast iron, orig paint dec **115.00**

Clothes sprinkler bottle, figural **165.00**

Creamer and sugar, 4-1/4" h creamer, 5-1/2" h sugar, blue Lusterware, black man riding on back as finial, mkd "Made in Japan," 1940s.............................. **195.00**

Decanter, 11" l, 9-1/2" h, heavy metal, painted gold, tube to feed liquor through elephant, mkd "Elephant Scotch C.T.S." on both sides **150.00**

Advertising trade card, Clark's O.N.T. Spool Cotton, Jumbo at Coney Island, sepia, 4-3/4" x 3", **$7.50**.

Figure

1-1/2" h, 2" l, ceramic, shaded gray glaze **8.00**

3" h, 2-1/2" l, glass, trunk raised **12.00**

Lamp, elephant with girl, hand painted, Japan, 14" h..................................... **45.00**

Letter opener, 7-1/2" l, celluloid, marked "Depose-Germany," c1900............. **40.00**

Mug, Frankoma, 1970s........................ **20.00**

Napkin ring, Bakelite, navy blue, c1940 .... **65.00**

Nodder, 3-1/2" l, 1-3/4" h, celluloid, gray back and head, pink ears, white belly, silver painted tusks **35.00**

Pie bird, 3-1/2" h, ceramic, white, mkd "Nutbrown Pie Funnel, Made in England, Reg. No. 880220," 1940s 185.00

Pinback button, Rub-No-More, gray and black image of elephant in household attire, using trunk as shower for baby elephant standing in washing pan . **25.00**

Pitcher, 6-1/2" h, figural elephant, black man as handle, incised "5020" **175.00**

Planter, 8" x 5-1/2", figural, pottery, unmarked **20.00**

Postcard, Elephant Hotel, Margate City, NJ, 1953 .... **7.50**

Poster, 47" x 58", Lil Nil Cigarette Papers, litho, trumpeting elephant, linen backing . **250.00**

Salt and pepper shakers, pr, figural, mkd "Japan" **27.50**

Sign, 15" x 13", Brown's Jumbo Bread, diecut tin, elephant with trunk curled down, blanket on back, c1930 .... **150.00**

Tobacco tag, tin, diecut, Red Elephant Tobacco **7.50**

Toothbrush holder, 5" h, mkd "Made in Japan," 1940s-50s **165.00**

Toy

3-1/2" h, 4-1/4" l, Jumbo, litho tin wind, mkd "U. S. Zone Germany" **85.00**

5" h, Elmer Elephant, gray, bow tie and hat, rubber, Sieberling **185.00**

Vase, figural handle, ivory matte finish **125.00**

F

Farm Collectibles

History: Initially, farm products were made by local craftsmen—the blacksmith, wheelwright, or the farmer himself. Product designs varied greatly.

The industrial age and the golden age of American agriculture go hand in hand. The farm market was important to manufacturers between 1880 and 1900. Farmers demanded quality products, capable of withstanding hard use. In the 1940s, urban growth began to draw attention away from the rural areas, and the consolidation of farms began. Larger machinery was developed.

The vast majority of farm models date between the early 1920s and the present. Manufacturers of farm equipment, such as John Deere, International Harvester, Massey-Ferguson, Ford, and White Motors, issued models to correspond to their full-sized products. These firms contracted with America's leading toy manufacturers, such as Arcade Company, Dent, Ertl, Hubley, Killgore, and Vindex, to make the models.

Collecting Hints: The country look makes farm implements and other items very popular with interior decorators. Often items are varnished or refinished to make them more appealing but, in fact, this lowers their value as far as the serious collector is concerned.

Farm items were used heavily; collectors should look for signs of use to add individuality and authenticity to the pieces.

When collecting farm toys, it is best to specialize in a single type, e.g., cast iron, models by one specific company, models of one type of farm machinery, or models in one size (1:16 scale being the most popular). Farm collectibles made after 1940 have not yet achieved great popularity.

Calendar top, P. L. Gross, Raw Milk, Richlandtown, PA, scene of boy picking apples, girl holding basket, farmyard scene, 1950s, no calendar pages, **$10**.

Ashtray, John Deere, deer jumping over log, galvanized metal, 3-1/4" d............. **35.00**

Bank

Allis-Chalmers, 3" x 5-1/2" x 4" h thin steel, mailbox shape, orange, cream-colored flag, black, white, and orange Allis-Chalmers logo sticker, lock and keys, 1970s **15.00**

Iowa Farmers Trust, tin canister, capped top and bottom by celluloid, yellow, black, and white, savings slogans on sides, 1920s, some wear **60.00**

Barn hinge, 27" l, wrought iron, strap type **75.00**

Book

Come Back to the Farm, Jesse Stuart, McGraw Hill, 1971, 1st edition **25.00**

Market Milk, Ernest Kelly & Clarence Clement, Wiley & Sons, 1923, 445 pgs **20.00**

Starting Right with Turkeys, G. T. Klein, MacMillan, 1947, 129 pgs............. **15.00**

Branding iron, Lazy B, wrought iron.. **40.00**

Card, Olds Patent Wheel Wagon, celluloid, multicolored, white ground, black letters, reverse with detailed aerial factory scene of Fort Wayne, IN............................ **80.00**

Catalog

B. F. Avery & Sons, Louisville, KY, 1938, 139 pgs, 5-1/4" x 9-1/4", Avery Agency Goods, Southern Price List No. 21, illus **35.00**

Colorado Bit & Spur Co., Denver, CO, 1948, 20 pgs, 5-1/2" x 8-1/4", cuts of bits, spurs, boot jacks, etc...................... **18.00**

Empire Drill Co., Shortsville, NY, 1886, 13 pgs, 5-3/4" x 6" **24.00**

Marugg Co., Tracy City, TN, 24 pgs, 1939, 6" x 9", company letter laid-in, illus of scythes, sickles, potato diggers, cultivating hoes, shears, etc. **24.00**

Montgomery Ward & Co., Chicago, IL, c1900, 12 pgs, 7-3/4" x 10-1/4", Special Vehicle Catalogue #, cuts and prices of Elliptic Spring, Corning, Texas side spring buggies, Phaetons, surries, pony carts, wagons, rakes, plows, loaders, etc. **26.00**

W. D. Allen Mfg Co., Chicago, IL, 1929, 472 pgs, 7-1/2" x 10-1/2", Allen's Red Book to Retailers, No. 69 .... **42.00**

Clip, Moline Wagon Co., red wagon wheel, orange background, silver lettered inscriptions "Light Running and Durable," insert brass pencil clip.................... **75.00**

Corn dryer, hanging, wrought iron...... **27.50**

Egg candler, 8" h, tin, kerosene burner, mica window.. **30.00**

Egg crate, Star Egg Carrier and Tray, wooden, Rochester, NY, minor wear, $35.

Egg crate, tin.. **15.00**

Feed bag, cotton

Black illus of sheet **12.00**

Floral print, washed.......................... **5.00**

Geometric print, yellow and green ... **7.00**

Flax comb, 17-1/2" l, wrought iron, ram's horn finials **135.00**

Flicker tag, Dairylea Milk, cardboard keychain tag, full color image of Miss Dairylea, flicker image "Look Both Ways Before Crossing," c1960 .... **12.00**

Flipper pin, diecut thin celluloid, 1-3/4" h Blue Valley Creamery, milk can shape, scenes titled "The Old Way" and "Our Way," back text "Blue Valley Butter/ Churned Fresh kin Chicago Every Day" **18.00**

Dain Hay Machinery, multicolored image of Great Dane dog, red and white sponsor name on back **50.00**

Grain shovel, wood, carved dec **300.00**

Hay rake, 48-1/2" l, varnished............. **65.00**

Implement seat, Hoover & Co., cast iron **115.00**

Magazine ad, 6" x 10", A. W. Stevens & Son Farm Machinery, little boy and dog, mkd "Gies & Co. Lith, Buffalo, NY," 8-3/4" x 12-3/4" frame....................................... **25.00**

Meat inspection stamp, US Dept of Agriculture, Bureau of Animal Industry, eagle, shield and E Pluribus Unum banner vignette, yellow paper, black text, ornate black border, 3" x 5" **18.00**

Medallion, 1-3/4" d, pair of brass loops at top, tin back, dark metal frame with fancy accents holding center of colored celluloid featuring farmer in yellow hat, red shirt, brown pants, suspenders, black boots, holding his hay scythe, using sharpening stone on blade, water jug and hay rake, cream and pale blue sky, "Hay Maker, Fun and Good Fellowship," Whitehead & Hoag, 1894.............. **40.00**

Milk bottle, Martin Century Farms, quart size, brown pryro, $85.

Memo booklet, Superior Drill Co., Springfield, OH, celluloid cover, full-color illus, tan leather piping, 1907 calendar, four pgs describing farm products, other illus **45.00**

Name tag, Grain Dealers Convention, diecut celluloid, full color illus of train at grain elevator, corn husk background **35.00**

Painting, 17" x 25", Delores Hackenberger, oil on canvas, old home, gray stone barn, covered bridge, orig owner's handwriting, name, and town on back, orig frame, 1940s **200.00**

Paperweight, Brown's Tested Seeds, Alfred J. Brown Seed Co., Grand Rapids, MI, clear glass, tinted color real photo of seed packets, patent dated June 14, 1917, 7/8" thick, 3" d........................ **55.00**

Pendant, celluloid, Agriculture Fair, Richfield, NY, 1898, diecut, multicolored horse heads, white ground, black lettering, inserted at top by red, white, and blue striped fabric bow, reverse has celluloid insert centered by multicolored image of various harvest fruit.......... **25.00**

Pinback button

1" d, Squire Land & Loan Co., Farms and Homes, Aberdeen, SD, 1" d, black and white, yellow wheat shock in center, Western Badge back paper, c1903-11 .... **15.00**

1-1/4" d, Dandy, Unriveled Unequaled Simplest And Strongest Challenge Windmill And Feed Co., Batavia, Illinois, detailed blue image of windmill on cream, red text, Whitehead & Hoag back paper, c1900-12 .... **250.00**

1-1/4" d, Peerless Separator, Waterloo Cream Separator Co., Waterloo, IA, sepia image of cream separator, brown text on cream, tin back, horizontal bar pin, light overall oxidation **85.00**

1-1/4" d, Sharples Cream Separator, multicolored, farm woman pouring milk into device as young child cranks handle, Whitehead & Hoag back paper **45.00**

1-1/2" d, Annual Corn Roast, Loveland, Sept 3-4-5, 1906, giant ear of yellow corn, shaded green and dark brown husk, tin back, St Louis Button Co. **25.00**

1-1/2" d, John Deere, Inventor Of The Steel Plow, gold bust on cream, blue text, Whitehead & Hoag back paper, c1900-12 .... **45.00**

1-1/2" d, The Huber, Marion, Ohio, detailed black and white steam tractor, red accents **65.00**

1-3/4" d, Meet Me At The Stockmen's Ball, East Turner Hall Thursday Jan 21 '09, steer in center, tin back, bar pin **30.00**

Paper bag, blue and white, Half Gallon, Milk, The Peak of Quality, Produced and Sold in NJ, designed to hold two quarts, unused, **$15**.

Pin holder, Success Spreader, celluloid, two-sided multicolored celluloid centered by thin wafer cardboard insert for holding straight pins, one side figural globe plus iron head logo, ed and black lettering for Kemp & Burpee Mfg. Co., Syracuse, multicolored graphic design of manure spreader on reverse, traces of wear **65.00**

Pocket mirror

Empire Cream Separator, multicolored celluloid, blond milkmaid, ethnic outfit, soft dark green background, slogan "Nothing Else Will Do," early 1900s **150.00**

Horlick's Malted Milk, multicolored milkmaid and cow in wooded setting, gold rim **55.00**

Seed dryer, chestnut frame, pine spindles, 21" x 43" **85.00**

Shovel, cast iron, wood handle **30.00**

Stickpin

Anchor Buggy Co., brass, miniature diecut naval anchor symbol........... **18.00**

Harber Farm Equipment, dark bronze luster finish, ships in harbor trademark, rim design of three spaced sppols of binding twine, inscription "Harber Bros. Of Bloomington, Ill," back inscription "If It's From Harber's It's Good Farm Machinery, Binder Twine, Buggies & Wagons" **18.00**

J. I. Case Co., figural, brass logo, eagle poised on world globe, early 1900s **20.00**

Moline Wagon Co., diecut brass, sprinting greyhound dog over spoked wheel, inscribed "Moline Wagon C., Light, Running, and Durable" **18.00**

Racine-Sattley Line, brass pin, red enameled, early 1900s **25.00**

Sechler Buggy, dark charcoal luster finish diecut, inscribed "Our Reputation Your Protection, The Sechler Buggy, Cincinnati, O/Sechler & Company" **30.00**

Stud

Detroit Disc, illus of American Harrow Co., Detroit, black in ivory-white celluloid, metal lapel stud fastener................. **25.00**

Sharples "The Russian," white porcelain, blue and black letters, slogan "The Bowl Alone Revolves" of cream separator, c1898.. **60.00**

Puzzle, Milton Bradley Co., #4146, Farmyard Puzzle, three-puzzle set, complete, original box, **$125.**

Tape measure, McCormick Harvesting Machine, celluloid canister, finely detailed black and white aerial illus of Chicago factory, titled "Largest Works in the World," early 1900s harvester machine **80.00**

Testimonial circular, Eureka Mower Co., Towanda, PA, 1883, for new model, testimonials from customers, 44 pgs, 5-3/4" x 8-3/4" **24.00**

Toy

Combine, Case, diecast, 1:16 scale, plastic reel, Ertl, 1974..................... **90.00**

Corn picker, pressed steel, 1:16 scale, John Deere, Carter, 1952.............. **135.00**

Dairy delivery van, Tootsietoy, cream-white body, white rubber tires, 1933 .... **110.00**

Disc, diecast, 1:16 scale, International Harvester, Ertl, 1965........................ **65.00**

Garden roller, Dinky, 1948-54......... **25.00**

Grain drill, pressed steel, 1:16 scale, John Deere, Carter, 1965 .... **150.00**

Hay rake, Dinky, 1954-71 .... **40.00**

Plow, McCormick-Deering, cast iron, red, yellow wheels, Arcade, 1932 .... **95.00**

Tractor, Caterpillar, Tootsietoy, cast driver, 1931 .... **45.00**

Tractor, Ford, Tootsietoy, rubber wheels **45.00**

Tractor, Huber Star, Tootsietoy, metal wheels, 1927.................................. **65.00**

Tractor, International Harvester, nickel-plated man, rubber wheels, c1940 .... **325.00**

Tractor, Massey-Harris, Dinky **75.00**

Tractor, Tru-Scale, Carter, diecast, 1:16 scale, 1975 .... **75.00**

Tractor magneto, K-W Ignition Co., Cleveland, OH, four-cylinder brass cover **80.00**

Tray, Success Manure Spreader, 3-1/4" x 4-3/4", litho tin, sponsor Kemp & Burpee Mfg Co., Syracuse, early 1900s, light wear.. **140.00**

Wagon seat, 42" l, wood, wrought iron trim, hinged compartment................... **250.00**

Fast Food Memorabilia

History: During the period just after World War II, the only convenience restaurants were the coffee shops and diners located along America's highways or in the towns and cities. As suburbia grew, young families created a demand for a faster and less-expensive type of food service.

Ray A. Kroc responded by opening his first McDonald's drive-in restaurant in Des Plaines, Illinois, in 1955. By offering a limited menu of hamburgers, french fries, and drinks, Kroc kept his costs and prices down. This success-ful concept of assembly-line food prep-aration soon was imitated, but never surpassed, by a myriad of competitors.

By the mid-1960s, the race was on, and franchising was seen as the new economic frontier. As the competition increased, the need to develop adver-tising promotions became imperative. A plethora of promotional give-aways entered the scene.

Collecting Hints: Premiums, made primarily of cardboard or plastic and of recent vintage, are the mainstay of today's fast food collector. Other collectible items are advertising signs and posters, character dolls, promotional glasses, and tray liners. In fact, anything associated with a restaurant chain is collectible, although McDonald's items are the most popular.

Collectors should concentrate only on items in mint condition. Premiums should be unassembled or sealed in an unopened plastic bag.

Collecting fast food memorabilia has grown rapidly, and, more than ever before, the fast food chains continue to churn out an amazing array of collectibles.

A & W

Doll, Root Beer Bear, plush **32.00**

Mug, glass, A & W logo **5.00**

Pitcher and glasses, Root Beer Bear and A & W logo, 1970s, seven-pc set **60.00**

Puppet, hand, Root Beer Bear, cloth .. **12.00**

Big Boy

Ashtray, 3-1/2" d, heavy glass, orange image and inscription "Frisch's Big Boy," 1968 .... **12.00**

Bank, 5" x 9", Big Boy, soft vinyl, red, white, blue, and black, imp "Big Boy Is A Reg U.S. Trademark" **48.00**

Menu, punch-out puppet, kiddie menu **45.00**

Nodder, papier-mâché head, 5" h **10.00**

Patch

1-1/2" x 4" stitched fabric bar, "Frisch's Big Boy," boy below tacked stitching, 1950-60s **40.00**

2-3/4" x 4-1/4", stitched fabric, employee type, black and white figure with red stripe accent on trousers and double burger on tan bun, 1950-60s **40.00**

Puzzle, 6-1/2" x 9-1/2" orig envelope, 6-1/4" x 9-1/4" frame tray puzzle, printed in color on both sizes, one side with Big Boy image and "Fritsch's," other with double cheeseburger on blue background, "R. C. W." copyright on both envelope and puzzle, c1960 .... **120.00**

Pinback button, Big Boy Club, red, white, blue, and brown hair, c1950 .... **65.00**

Salt and pepper shakers, pr, china, 1960s **125.00**

Tee shirt, white ground, red, white, and black trademark **10.00**

Ronald McDonald doll, stuffed, 1978, $35.

Burger Chef

Character ring, expandable band, large thin plastic sheet on top, mkd "Made In USA," c1970

Angel, yellow plastic **30.00**
Fang, blue plastic **30.00**
Jethro, white plastic **30.00**
Seymore, orange plastic **30.00**

Drinking glass

Collectors Series, Cincinnati Bengals, 1979 .... **3.00**
Collectors Series, Cleveland Browns, 1979 .... **4.00**
Endangered Species, Bald Eagle, 1978 .... **3.50**

Burger King

Bicycle clip, colorful wheel spokes, 1981 .... **6.00**

Card game, Burger King Rummy, orig box, 1978 .... **12.00**

Doll, 16" h, King, cloth, printed red, yellow, flesh, black, and white **7.50**

Drinking glass

Detroit Tigers, Rangers, bat, Aren't You Hungry? **4.50**
Dr Pepper, Dallas Cowboys, Charlie Waters **6.50**
Star Wars, RD-D2, C3PO, 1977 .... **3.50**

Frisbee, 9-1/2" d, R2-D2, C3PO, and Darth Vader, Empire Strikes Back, 1981 .. **17.50**

Glider, King Glider, Styrofoam, 1978 .... **2.50**

Lid, 3-1/4" d, red and white, cartoon of Burger King sitting on hamburger, 1970s, unused **8.00**

Pinback button

Happy face, Burger King logo eyes. **6.00**
Smiley Face, black on yellow litho, two
small Burger King symbols, c1970 .. **3.00**

Toy

Ball launching catapult unit, red plastic,
copyright 1980, 2" x 4" x 1" h **5.00**
King's Magic Pipe, hard red plastic pipe,
white Styrofoam ball, 1980s, 6" l **5.00**
King Spinner, soft plastic, orig cellophane
bag, copyright 1978-79, 3" x 4-1/2".. **7.50**
Saucer launcher, blue plastic, hand-held
launching unit, one saucer, copyright
1979, 2" x 5"..................................... **10.00**
Super pitcher, soft plastic and cardboard,
orig cellophane bag, copyright 1978-79,
3" x 3"... **7.50**
Trading cards, The Empire Strikes Back,
complete set of 36.......................... **37.50**
Yo-Yo, Yum Yum, Duncan Yo-Yo, 1979 . **5.00**

Dairy Queen

Diecut, House of Fun Mirror, 4-1/2" x 6-1/2"
stiff paper, diecut image of smiling clown,
3" x 3-1/4" diecut opening holding silver
accent aluminum foil, copyright 1960
.... **5.00**
Meal box, Hot Doggity, Dennis the Menace
.... **3.50**
Salt shaker, chocolate dip ice cream cone,
4-1/4" h... **22.00**
Spoon, red plastic, long handle, ice cream
cone top... **1.00**
Sundae dish, 3-1/2" x 8-1/4" x 1-1/4" deep,
green molded plastic, designed like boat,
curlicue of simulated ice cream scoop for
handle, diecut Dairy Queen name, Lynn-
Sign Molded Plastic Co., Boston, early
1960s **12.00**
Whistle, plastic, figural ice cream cone,
metal chain **3.50**

Denny's

Menu, plastic coated, c1960................. **2.50**
Puppet, hand, Deputy Dan, 1976......... **3.00**
Ring, brass, expansion bands, trace of orig
yellow paint, center brown "D," 1970s
.... **60.00**

Howard Johnson

Ashtray... **30.00**
Bank **35.00**
Drinking glass, multicolored logo, 4-1/4" h,
2-1/2" d **32.00**
Ice cream cup, sample size, paper, 1-1/2" h,
1-1/2" d **12.00**
Menu, ice cream cover......................... **2.00**
Pinback button, Vote for Howard Johnson's,
black lettering on orange, c1950 ..... **8.00**
Postcard, Howard Johnson's Motor Lodge,
Middletown, NJ, unused.................. **3.50**

Kentucky Fried Chicken

Bank, Colonel Sanders, vinyl, turns, Japan,
1960s **250.00**
Box, 1969.. **35.00**
Mug, 5-1/2" h, ceramic, high gloss white,
crisp black portrait above inscription in
red lettering, mkd "Hall, 1272" **18.00**
Pinback button, Vote for Col. Sanders, KFC,
blue and white, c1972, 1-1/2" d **24.00**
Salt and pepper shakers, pr, Col. Harland
Sanders, figural, 4-1/4" h, smiling full
figures, one on white base, one on black
base, incised name, Starting Plastics
Ltd., London, Canadian premium, c1970
.... **36.00**

Ronald McDonald, life size, fiberglass, red,
yellow, white, and black, **$1,800**.

McDonald's

Action figure, MOC
Big Mac, blue fabric police uniform,
plastic whistle **42.00**
Mayor McCheese, fuchsia coat, yellow
vest, purple pants........................... **40.00**
Ronald McDonald, footed red hair, yellow,
red, and white outfit....................... **35.00**
Ashtray, 3-1/2" x 6", metal, green, 1970 logo
in yellow, street address in silver ... **18.00**
Bank, 6" vinyl figure, made for Canton store
opening **20.00**

Bowling ball, 9" d, 9 lb, red Ebonite, drilled for child's fingers, Ronald McDonald image, 1970s.................................. **45.00**

Button, 1-1/2" d, McDonald's Hamburgers, bright red on bright yellow litho, smiling character with hamburger head, chef's hat, captioned "I'm Speedee" **75.00**

Coloring book, *Ronald McDonald Giant Story Coloring Book*, 17" x 22", 1978 copyright, unused **25.00**

Cup

Captain Cook, yellow plastic, copyright 1978.. **10.00**

Slogan, "McDonald's is your kind of place," red, white, blue, and yellow, 4-3/4" h, 1970s............................... **20.00**

Cup holder, dark blue, orig packaging **3.50**

Doll

Hamburglar, played with condition **15.00**

Ronald McDonald, stuffed, 1978.... **35.00**

Drinking glass

Action series, 1977, price for set of six, 5-1/2" h.. **15.00**

Canadian Disney Movie Series, Peter Pan **3.50**

Mac Tonight, 4" h............................... **4.00**

Ronald McDonald, Mayor McCheese, Grimace, Hamburglar, Big Mac, and Captain Cook, bright graphics, 1977 copyright, price for set of six, 5-3/4" h **20.00**

Employee cap, 12-1/2" x 11-1/2", flattened unused service cap, blue cardboard headband with yellow arch symbol on each side, white mesh open crown, mid-1960s.. **15.00**

Figure, Halloween series, McDonald's, set of four, sealed in orig bags **10.00**

Game sheet, 9" x 12" folded sheet opens to 17-1/2" x 24", full-color figures to be cut out, full color photo scene, unused **130.00**

Happy Meal box proof sheet, 18-1/4" x 23-3/4" white stiff paper printer's proof, full color image in center, four sided box design, unfolded

American Tail, Mouse in the Moon puzzle, finger puppets, characters flying away on pigeon Henri, ©1988 McDonald's Corp **18.00**

Muppet Babies characters, Egyptian theme, ©1986 McDonald's Corp.... **20.00**

Happy Meal display, Marvel Super Heroes **95.00**

Happy Meal prize, Genie and Building 5, from Aladdin and the King of Thieves, MIB.. **4.00**

Hat, 8-1/2" x 15", Captain Cook, glossy thin cardboard pirate hat, copyright 1978, unused.. **18.00**

McDonald Happy Meal prize, Hot Wheels Nascar, #7, MIB, $7.50.

Iron-on, 5" x 9-1/2" white tissue sheet with 4-1/2" x 6" black, white, red, and yellow transfer of Ronald and porpoise, early 1970s **20.00**

Lunch box, orig thermos, 1982......... **20.00**

Map, Ronald McDonald Map of the Moon, 1969 .... **7.50**

Mug, glass, Toledo Zoo panda series, set of three **9.00**

Patch, 2-1/2" x 3-1/4", stitched fabric, employee type, yellow arches, red McDonald's name, white ground, blue border, c1960, used **48.00**

Photoball, commemorating Mark McGwires 70 HR season, McDonald's, mint in back **12.00**

Plate, Spring, Melmac, 1977 .... **25.00**

Pokemon cards, 1999, complete set **24.00**

Puppet, hand, plastic, Ronald McDonald, c1977 .... **2.00**

Record, Ronald's Christmas, 45 rpm, dark red and silver label, late 1950s, 7" d **24.00**

Ring, Polly Pocket Doll, green vinyl base, pink flower petal design top, clear plastic dome with miniature doll in ballerina skirt, mkd "Copyright 1994 Bluebird Toys/ China" **12.00**

Ruler, Ronald McDonald, cardboard, early 1970s **12.00**

Sandwich wrapper, 10-1/2" x 14", thin paper, silver foil outer surface, 4-1/2" d center design, gold arch symbol on blue ribbons, "McDonald's Quality" ribbon badge in red and gold, inscribed "New-Juicy" in blue lettering about black "roast beef" title lettering on white, unused, may be test wrapper **45.00**

Teenie Beanie Babies, 1997, set of 10, MIP, complete set **35.00**

Toy train, wind-up train engine, passenger car, animal cage car, eight sections of railroad track, single golden arch bridge, round café table, happy tree with swing, Ronald, Mayor McCheese and Hamburglar dolls by Remco, some wear and repairs...................................... **75.00**

Valentines, strip of six different valentines, 1978 .... **3.00**

Pizza Hut

Drinking glass, Underdog flying, CB lingo text **35.00**
Mug, glass, Buffalo Bills, 1984 .... **5.00**
Paper napkin, logo .... **.50**
Puppet, hand, Pizza Pete **2.00**

Taco Bell

Banner, full color, Batman & Robin, 1997, full cast, 2" x 25", unused **150.00**
Drinking glass, Star Trek III, complete set of four **35.00**
Store display, Godzilla, 18" h, 18" w, holds six premiums, one missing **75.00**
Straw, monster eye, 1997, set of six ... **20.00**
Toy, Godzilla, sealed, 1977, set of seven
.... **20.00**

Wendy's

Flying ring, Fun Flyer, plastic, 3-1/2" d. **3.50**
Meal box, The Good Stuff Gang, 1988 . **3.00**
Mug, glass
   Wendy's Old Fashioned Hamburgers, ceramic, red, white, and black trademark, 1970s **6.50**
   Where's the Beef, 5-1/2" h **8.50**

Fiesta Ware

History: The Homer Laughlin China Company introduced Fiesta dinnerware in January 1936 at the Pottery and Glass Show in Pittsburgh, Pennsylvania. Frederick Rhead designed the pattern; Arthur Kraft and Bill Bensford molded it. Dr. A. V. Bleininger and H. W. Thiemecke developed the glazes. A vigorous marketing campaign took place between 1939 and 1943.

Fiesta ware was redesigned in 1969 and discontinued about 1973. In 1986, Fiesta was reintroduced by Homer Laughlin China Company. The new china body shrinks more than the old semi-vitreous and ironstone pieces, thus making the new pieces slightly smaller than the earlier pieces. The modern colors are also different in tone or hue, e.g., the cobalt blue is darker than the old blue. Other modern colors are black, white, apricot, lilac, persimmon, chartreuse, pearl gray, juniper, cinnabar, sunflower, plum, shamrock, and tangerine.

Collecting Hints: Whenever possible, buy pieces without any cracks, chips, or scratches. Fiesta ware can be identified by bands of concentric circles.

Colors: Homer Laughlin has produced some new colors in its popular Fiesta pattern. It's important for collectors to understand when different colors were made.

Color Name	Color palette	Years of Production
Red	Reddish-orange	1936-43 1959-72
Blue	Cobalt blue	1936-51
Ivory	Creamy yellow-white	1936-51
Yellow	Golden yellow	1936-69
Green	Light green	1936-51
Turquoise	Sky blue	1937-69
Rose	Dark dusky rose	1951-59
Chartreuse	Yellow-green	1951-59
Forest green	Dark hunter green	1951-59
Gray	Light gray	1951-59
Medium green	Deep bright green	1959-69
Antique gold	Dark butterscotch	1969-72
Turf green	Olive green	1969-72
Cobalt blue	Very dark blue, almost black	1986-
Rose	Bubblegum pink	1986-
White	Pearly white	1986-
Black	High gloss black	1986-
Apricot	Peach-beige	1986-98
Turquoise	Greenish-blue	1988-
Yellow	Pale yellow	1987-2002
Periwinkle blue	Pastel gray-blue	1989-
Sea mist green	Pastel light green	1991-
Lilac	Pastel violet	1993-95
Persimmon	Coral	1995-
Sapphire	Blue	1996-97
(Bloomingdale's exclusive)		1997-99
Chartreuse	More yellow than green	1977-99
Pearl gray	More transparent gray	1999-2001
Juniper green	Dark blue-green	1999-2001
Cinnabar	Brown-maroon	2000-
Sunflower	Bright yellow	2001-
Plum	Rich purple	2002-
Shamrock	Grassy green	2002-
Tangerine	Bright orange	2003-

Note: Prices listed here are for the original colors. The secondary market is not yet established for the post 1986 colors.

Grouping, four small rose plates, **each $5**, one small red plate, **$8**, stacked on top of turquoise chop plate, **$80**; green cup, **$15**, on left in front, red, **$24**, and yellow cup, **$20**, on right.

Ashtray, 5-1/2" d
Cobalt 45.00
Red 55.00
Yellow... 30.00
Bud vase, 6-1/2" h
Ivory 85.00
Red 175.00
Turquoise 115.00
Calendar plate, ivory, 1954, 10" d....... 55.00
Candleholders, pr, bulb
Ivory 115.00
Light green 90.00
Red 110.00
Turquoise 115.00
Carafe, cov
Light green 185.00
Red, 10" h 350.00
Casserole, cov, 7-3/4" d, 6" h
Gray 350.00
Rose... 295.00
Yellow.. 150.00
Chop plate, 14-1/4" d
Chartreuse...................................... 65.00
Cobalt 100.00
Gray 70.00
Ivory 60.00
Yellow... 30.00
Coffeepot, cov
Cobalt 300.00
Green.. 225.00
Ivory 245.00
Rose... 850.00
Yellow... 135.00

Comport, low, 12" d
Cobalt... 80.00
Turquoise, 12" d 100.00
Yellow 125.00
Creamer
Chartreuse, ring handle 40.00
Cobalt, stick handle....................... 50.00
Medium green, ring handle........... 80.00
Rose, ring handle 35.00
Turquoise, stick handle................ 115.00
Yellow, stick handle 50.00

Grouping, three luncheon plates in front (cobalt blue, **$7.50**; medium green, **$6.50**; and red, **$8.50**); stack of five saucers in back (yellow, **$5**; red, **$6.50**; medium green, **$4**; cobalt blue, **$4**; yellow, **$5**); four dessert bowls (medium green, **$65**; yellow, **$25**; red, **$70**; cobalt blue, **$35**).

Cream soup
Cobalt... 90.00
Light green..................................... 50.00
Red... 50.00
Rose... 95.00
Turquoise....................................... 30.00
Yellow 30.00
Cup and saucer
Chartreuse 28.00
Gray.. 26.00
Ivory... 24.00
Light green 20.00
Medium green 60.00
Red... 30.00
Rose 30.00
Turquoise.. 24.00
Yellow... 24.00
Deep plate
Chartreuse 50.00
Gray.. 50.00
Ivory... 40.00
Red... 50.00
Demitasse cup and saucer, stick handle
Chartreuse 495.00
Cobalt 100.00
Ivory... 60.00
Turquoise.. 70.00
Yellow 85.00

45 stars, 3-1/2" x 2-1/4", child's parade type, pattern of 8, 7, 7, 7, 7, 8 and five-point star **55.00**
45 stars, 32" x 47", 1896-1908, printed on silk, bright colors, black heading and no grommets **125.00**
46 stars, 4" x 5", 1908-1912, stars sewn on, Oklahoma **175.00**
48 stars, 5-3/4" x 4-1/2", 1912-1959, printed on heavy canvas-type material, used on D-Day in Infantry invasion, men wore them under the camouflage net on their helmets **195.00**

Handkerchief, World War I, flags of US and France, embroidered
A Kiss from France **15.00**
To My Dear Sweetheart **25.00**

Lapel stud, red, white, and blue enamel flag, white ground, Harrison/Morton 1888, enameled brass **35.00**

Letterhead, 11" x 8-1/2", Independence Hall, Liberty Bell, two crossed American flags, Sesquicentennial International Exposition **25.00**

Magic lantern slide, 42 star flag, c1889, hand tinted, mounted in wood **35.00**

Magnifying glass, pocket, 3/4" x 1-1/4", oval, Voorhees Rubber Mfg Co adv, American flag artwork **45.00**

Pinback button

Colorado Statehood, For Governor Henry R. Wolcott, black and white photo, red, white, and blue flag, 1898 .... **27.50**
Confederate Flag, white background, seven white stars, American Pepsin Gum, c1900 .... **35.00**
Welcome to Our President, Roosevelt, cloth flag below, 1-1/2" d pinback with bluetone photo **75.00**

Plate

St. Louis World's Fair, Washington, Jefferson, Lafayette and Napoleon's faces, very colorful, 1904 .... **120.00**
Washington's Headquarters, Newburg, NY, 1783-1883, crossed flags under house, 10" d **95.00**

Postcard, printed semblances of Stars and Stripes covering address side, picture of Wm H. Taft for president, July 4, 1908, 46 stars, used **27.50**

Poster, 14" x 29", lithograph, "History of Old Glory," Babbitt soap giveaway **145.00**

Print, 11-1/4" x 15-1/2", Currier and Ives, "The Star Spangled Banner," #481
.... **195.00**

Scarf, numerous multicolored flags and expos name and dates in center, sailing ships border, white ground **95.00**

Sheet music

Miss America, two step by J Edmund Barnum, lady with stars, red and white striped dress, large flowing flag **20.00**

Stars and Stripes Forever March, John Phillip Sousa portrait in upper left hand corner, Old Glory in center, published by John Church Co. **25.00**

Spoon, 4-1/2" l, Jefferson, eagle, two flags, globe, "1904, St. Louis" on handle, Electric Building in bowl, Louisiana Monument and Cascade Gardens on back, US Silver Co. **65.00**

Stevensgraph, postcard, "Hands Across the Sea," embroidered English and American flags, hands shaking, mkd "Woven in Silk, R. M. S. Aquitana," used
.... **65.00**

Stickpin

Celluloid, American flag, 48 stars, advertising, S A Cook for US Senator
.... **20.00**
Metal, 1-3/4" h, red, white, and blue painted furling flag at half staff, sign at left "Vietnam 1961," orig cardboard box with clear plastic window inscribed "Wear This Pin For Peace," Pace Emblem Company, New York, NY, c1970 .... **40.00**

Token, 3-3/4" d, "The Dix Token Coin," Civil War, commemorates the order of General John Adams Dix, Jan. 29, 1861, "If anyone attempts to haul down the American flag, shoot him on the spot," copper-colored coin, picture of "The Flag of Our Union" on one side and quote on the other **10.00**

Tray, 13" d, West End Brewing Co., American flag draped over Lady Liberty, standing next to keg of West End Brewing Co. Beer, Kaufmann & Strauss Co. litho **265.00**

Watch fob, Sesqui-Centennial, Liberty Bell and American flags, dates 1776-1926, crossed rifles at bottom **60.00**

Flow Blue China, American

History: When imported Flow Blue china, i.e., English, German, etc., became popular, American manufact-urers soon followed suit. There is great variation in quality. Compared to European makers, the number of U.S. manufacturers is small. The most well known are the French China Co., Homer Laughlin China Co., Mercer Pottery Co., Sebring Pottery Co., Warwick China, and Wheeling Pottery Co.

Collecting Hints: As with any Flow Blue china, value for American-made pieces depends upon condition, quality, pattern, and type. Avoid those pieces with flaws that cannot be repaired unless you plan to use them only for decorative purposes.

Additional Listings: See *Warman's Antiques and Collectibles Price Guide.*

Adviser: Ellen G. King.

Advertising
Ashtray, Sebring China, cherub decal in center, 4-1/2" **95.00**
Calendar plate, La Francaise, 9" d, c1910 .... **50.00**
Souvenir, German, pipe rest, horseshoe shape, 6" **75.00**

Argyle, J&E Mayer
Bone dish **55.00**
Butter pat **48.00**
Gravy boat **95.00**
Milk pitcher, 7" **165.00**
Plate, 8" d **65.00**

Autumn Leaves, Warwick
Jardinière, 8" x 7-1/2" **450.00**
Plate, 10-1/2" **135.00**
Relish, 8" **125.00**
Syrup pitcher, squat, silver plate lid **275.00**

Balmoral, Burgess & Campbell
Butter pat **55.00**
Plate, 8" **60.00**
Platter, 12" x 14" **225.00**

Bathing Beauty, The French Company
Plate, 8", colorful decal of woman in bathing suit, c1915 .... **75.00**

Colonial, Homer Laughlin
Dessert bowl, 4-3/4" **45.00**
Plate, 10" **95.00**
Soup bowl, 9" **60.00**
Teacup and saucer **95.00**
Vegetable bowl, round, 10" **125.00**

Calico, Warwick
Creamer, squat, 4-1/2" **250.00**
Tray, 9" x 6-1/2" **145.00**
Tea set, cov teapot, cov sugar, creamer, round large undertray **1,750.00**

Cracked Ice, International Pottery
Bowl, round, open, 10" **165.00**
Cake plate, round, open handles, 10-1/2" **225.00**
Chocolate pot with lid **450.00**
Plate, 9-1/2" **85.00**
Posset cup **75.00**

Delph, Sebring Pottery
Butter pat **45.00**
Cake plate, round, 10", with handles **150.00**
Plate, 9" **65.00**
Soup bowl, 8" **55.00**
Vegetable bowl, 10" **225.00**
Wash basin, 17" **450.00**

Fernery, Knowles, Taylor, Knowles
Hot water pitcher, 8" **135.00**
Relish, small, oval, 8" **65.00**
Soap dish, insert, lid **225.00**

Hawthorne, Mercer Pottery
Plate, 8" **65.00**
Platter, 13" **210.00**
Vegetable tureen with lid **295.00**

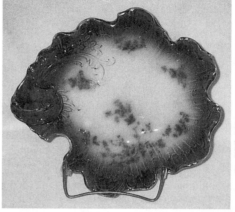

La Belle/Blue Diamond, bowl, leaf shape, with handle, 10" l, $395. All Flow Blue photos courtesy of adviser Ellen King.

LaBelle/Blue Diamond, Wheeling Pottery
Biscuit jar with lid, 8-1/2" **495.00**
Bone dish **85.00**
Bowl, helmet shape, footed, 8" **426.00**
Bowl, helmet shape, footed, 10" .. **550.00**
Bowl, leaf shape with handle, 10" **395.00**
Bowl, oval, with handle **375.00**
Bread tray, 14-1/2" x 6-1/8" **350.00**
Butter dish, insert, lid **575.00**
Butter pat **85.00**
Cake plate, closed handles **265.00**
Charger, round, 11-1/2" d **350.00**
Charger, round, 14" d **465.00**
Chocolate pot with lid **550.00**
Chocolate cup **350.00**
Creamer and sugar with lid **450.00**
Dessert bowl, 4-1/2" d **60.00**
Ice cream tray, oblong, 13-5/8" **450.00**
Plate, 7-1/2" d **60.00**
Plate, 9" d **75.00**
Plate, 10" d **95.00**
Punch cup, footed **450.00**
Relish, 8" l **275.00**
Soup bowl, 9" d **75.00**
Syrup pitcher with silver-plated lid **475.00**
Teacup and saucer **135.00**
Vegetable bowl, open, 9-1/2" **250.00**
Vegetable tureen with lid **375.00**

LaFrancaise, butter pat, gold tracing, $45.

LaFrancaise, child's toy cup and saucer, gold heart, $55.

LaFrancaise, vegetable tureen with lid, floral ivy pattern, $325.

LaFrancaise, The French China Co.

Butter dish, insert, lid, worn gold .. **150.00**
Butter pat, gold tracing **45.00**
Child's toy cup and saucer, gold heart
.... **55.00**
Creamer, 5", gold curtain tracing around
top **85.00**
Dessert bowl, 4-1/2" d, floral decal in
center
.... **35.00**
Plate, 8" d, floral decal in center **45.00**
Plate, 9" d, floral decal in center **55.00**

Plate, 9" d, gold curtain tracing around
edge **40.00**
Patter, 14" l, gold snowflake pattern **95.00**
Salt and pepper shakers, pr round, squat
.... **125.00**
Soup bowl, 9" d, floral decal in center
.... **45.00**
Teacup and saucer, gold snowflake
pattern **85.00**
Vegetable tureen with lid, floral ivy pattern
.... **325.00**

Luzerne, Mercer Pottery

Butter pat **50.00**
Cake stand, pedestal base, 10" d,
4-3/4" h **225.00**
Plate, 10" d, heavy gold **110.00**
Platter, 18" l **465.00**
Soup bowl, 6-1/8" d **60.00**
Soup bowl with rim, 9-1/2 d **75.00**
Teacup and saucer **110.00**
Teacup with lid **495.00**
Vegetable tureen with lid **395.00**

Paisley, Mercer Pottery

Butter pat **65.00**
Creamer, squat **150.00**
Plate, 6" d **65.00**
Plate, 9" d **75.00**
Soup bowl with rim, 8-7/8" d **75.00**

Pansy, Warwick

Cake plate with handles, 10" d **225.00**
Charger, 14" d **375.00**
Creamer, 6" **225.00**
Relish dish, 12-1/2" **150.00**

Poppy, tray, 6" x 9", $225.

Poppy, Warwick

Dessert bowl, 6" d **55.00**
Syrup pitcher with silver-plated lid **375.00**
Tray, 6" x 9" **225.00**

Royal Blue, Burgess & Campbell

Butter pat **45.00**
Plate, 9" d, church scene, gold sponge
edge **110.00**
Platter, 12-5/8" l **325.00**
Soup bowl with rim, 9" d **65.00**

Royal Blue, plate, church scene, gold sponge decoration, 9" d, **$110**.

Thistle, milk pitcher, 6-1/2" h, **$225**.

Snowflake, Knowles, Taylor, Knowles
    Plate, 9" d... **65.00**
    Vegetable bowl, oval, open, 9" l **70.00**

The Sebring, Sebring Pottery
    Charger, 14" d, polychromed green trim
    .... **375.00**

Thistle, Burroughs & Mountford
    Chocolate pot with lid, 8" **350.00**
    Milk pitcher, 6" **225.00**
    Tray, squared with handles, 6" **95.00**

U.S.S. Brooklyn, The French China Co.
    Vegetable bowl, open, round, 10" **350.00**

U.S.S. Maine, The French China Co.
    Vegetable bowl, open, oval, 9-1/2" x
    12-3/4".. **375.00**

Wild Rose, Warwick
    Berry set, 10" d bowl, six dessert bowls
    .... **450.00**
    Chocolate set, chocolate pot, five cups
    and saucers............................... **1,500.00**

Windmill, The French China Co.
    Butter pat **45.00**
    Plate, 9" d **50.00**
    Platter, 13" l.................................. **135.00**
    Relish, oval, 10" l........................... **65.00**
    Soup bowl, 8" d.............................. **55.00**
    Vegetable bowl, open, round, 9" d **95.00**

Winona, The French China Co.
    Pitcher, 5" h **125.00**
    Plate, 6" d **45.00**
    Platter, 14" l................................. **120.00**
    Teacup and saucer......................... **65.00**
    Toothbrush holder, upright........... **135.00**

Football Cards

History: Football cards have been printed since the 1890s. However, it was not until 1933 that the first bubble gum football card appeared in the Goudey Sport Kings set. In 1935, National Chickle of Cambridge, Massachusetts, produced the first full set of gum cards devoted exclusively to football.

Both Leaf Gum of Chicago and Bowman Gum of Philadelphia produced sets of football cards in 1948. Leaf discontinued production after its 1949 issue; Bowman continued until 1955.

Topps Chewing Gum entered the market in 1950 with its college-stars set. Topps became a fixture in the football card market with its 1955 All-Amer-

Thistle, chocolate pot, lid, 8-3/4" h, **$350**.

ican set. From 1956 thorough 1963 Topps printed card sets of National Football League players, combining them with the American Football League players in 1961.

Topps produced sets with only American Football League players from 1964 to 1967. The Philadelphia Gum Company made National Football League card sets during this period. Beginning in 1968 and continuing to the present, Topps has produced sets of National Football League cards, the name adopted after the merger of the two leagues.

Collecting Hints: Condition is critical—buy cards that are in very good condition, i.e., free from any creases and damaged corners. When possible, strive to acquire cards in excellent to mint condition. Devise a collecting strategy, such as cards related to one year, one player, Heisman trophy winners, or one team. A large quantity of cards is available and a novice collector can be easily overwhelmed, so all collectors can find everything they need to know in *Tuff Stuff® 2005 Standard Catalog of® Football Cards*, 8th edition, Krause Publications.

Bowman Card Company

1951

Complete set (144)	**1,500.00**
Common player (1-144)	**20.00**

1952, large

Complete set (144)	**12,000.00**
Comon player (1-72)	**25.00**
Common player (73-144)	**35.50**

1952, small

Complete set (144)	**5,500.00**
Common player (1-72)	**18.50**
Common player (73-144)	**24.00**

1954

Complete set (128)	**1,600.00**
Common player (1-64)	**6.50**
Common player (65-96)	**15.00**
Common player (97-128)	**5.50**
#102 Tunnel, SGC 92-8.5	**115.00**

1955, All American

#18 Heffelfinger, SGC 88-8	**80.00**
#36 Edwards, SGC 88-8	**65.00**
#41 Alexander, SGC 88-8	**65.00**
#42 Tryon, SGC 92-8.5	**100.00**
#53 Green, SGC 88-8	**50.00**
#54 Dooley, SGC 88-8	**65.00**
#55 Merritt, SGC 88-8	**65.00**
#57 Hanson, SGC 88-8	**65.00**

#64 Friedman, SGC 88-8	**50.00**
#86 Booth, SGC 88-8	**65.00**
#87 Schultz, SGC 92-8.5	**100.00**

1958

#2 Layne, SGC 88-8	**85.00**
#16 Marchetti, SGC 88-8	**45.00**
#18 Lary, SGC 92-8.5	**55.00**
#57 Morrall, SGC 92-8.5	**55.00**
#90 Jurgensen, SGC 92-8.5	**350.00**
#93 Perry, SGC 92-8.5	**75.00**
#120 Berry, SGC 92-8.5	**150.00**

1965

#24 Bass, SGC 92-8.5	**50.00**
#66 Appleton, SGC 88-8	**40.00**
#71 Burrell, SGC 88-8	**40.00**
#109 Robinson, SGC 88-8	**40.00**

1998, chrome

Complete set (220)	**550.00**
Common player	**.30**
Common rookie	**3.50**
Minor star	**.80**

Bowman Gum, 1950, top: Y.A. Tittle Jr., #5, **$22**; bottom: Glen Davis, #16, **$12**

Fleer

1960

Complete set (132)	**750.00**
Common player (1-32)	**3.25**

1961

Complete set (220)	**1,625.00**
Common player (1-132)	**4.25**

Common player (133-220)............... **4.75**
Uncut, 132 cards........................... **650.00**
#187 Otto, SGC 92-8.5 .... **125.00**
1963
Complete set (89)...................... **1,800.00**
Common player (1-88).................... **7.50**
1990, hand-collated set **10.00**

Leaf
1948
Complete set (98)...................... **6,000.00**
Common player (1-49)................... **22.00**
Common player (1-98)................ **100.00**
1949
Complete set (49)...................... **2,000.00**
Common player (1-49)................... **25.00**
1998
Complete set (300) **450.00**
Common player................................. **.15**
Common rookie **2.00**
Minor stars...................................... **.30**

Philadelphia
1964
Complete set (198) **950.00**
Common player (1-198)................... **2.00**
1966
Complete set (198) **950.00**
Common player (1-198)................... **2.75**

Pro Set, 1990
Factory sealed set............................ **5.00**
Hand collated set **18.00**

Score
1989
Complete set (330) **220.00**
Common player (1-330).................... **.10**
Minor star.. **.20**
Wax box....................................... **500.00**
1990, factory sealed set...................... **10.00**

Stadium Club
1991
Complete set (500) **90.00**
Common player................................. **.20**
Hand collated set........................... **90.00**
Minor star.. **.40**
Wax box.. **90.00**
1992
Complete set (700) **150.00**
Common Series 1 (300)................. **15.00**
Common Series 2 (300)................. **15.00**
Common player................................. **.10**

Topps
1956
Complete set (121) **1,100.00**
Common player (1-120)................... **3.75**
1958
Complete set (132) **1,350.00**
Common player (1-132)................... **3.75**

1962
Complete set (176).................... **1,825.00**
Common player (1-176).................. **3.65**
1964
Complete set (176).................... **1,450.00**
Common player (1-176).................. **3.50**
Common player SP **3.00**
1970
Complete set (263).................... **2,500.00**
Common player (1-132)..................... **.75**
Common player (133-263)............... **.85**
1975
Complete set (528)...................... **355.00**
Common player (1-528)..................... **.25**
1977
Complete set (528)...................... **225.00**
Common player (1-528)..................... **.15**
1981
Complete set (528)...................... **250.00**
Common player (1-528)..................... **.20**
1985
Complete set (396)........................ **80.00**
Common player (1-396)..................... **.05**
Wax pack, unopened **90.00**
1990
Complete set (528)........................ **15.00**
Common player (1-528)..................... **.03**
1997, chrome
Complete set (165)...................... **180.00**
Common player .... **.40**
Minor star .... **.75**
Wax box **220.00**

Upper Deck
1991
Factory sealed set **18.00**
Hand collated set **15.00**
1996, game jersey
Complete set (10)...................... **4,000.00**
Common player **150.00**
1997, game jersey
Complete set (10)...................... **3,000.00**
Common player **150.00**
1998, super powers
Complete set (30)......................... **45.00**
Common player .... **.50**
Minor stars **1.00**

Football Collectibles

History: The first American college football match was held between Princeton and Rutgers in New Brunswick, New Jersey, in 1869.

Harvard documents a more rugby-type game in the 1870s. A professional football association was founded in 1920 and renamed the National Football League (NFL) in 1922. Football really took off after World War II and grew to 28 teams in two conferences by the 1980s. Expansion continued until 30 teams were playing by 1995.

The Super Bowl was created in 1967 and has become the exciting termination of the season for many fans. The Canadian Football League (CFL) was created in 1959 and oversees a professional circuit.

Collecting Hints: Collectors of football items may decide to specialize in one team, one conference, or one type of collectible, i.e., helmets or pennants. Collectors should not overlook the wealth of items generated by colleges, high schools, and even younger participants.

Autographed artwork, scene of Bugs Bunny and friends, *The Jet Set,* signed by Joe Namath, matted and framed, official Jets logo and seal, $600.

Action figure, Starting Line-Up, Kenner
Bledsoe, Drew, 2002, MOC **12.00**
Esiason, Boomer, 1994, MOC **5.00**
Manning, Peyton, 2002, MOC **20.00**
Meggett, David, near mint **5.00**
Montana, Joe, 1993, MOC **35.00**
Plummer, Jake, 2002, MOC **5.00**
Rison, Andre, rookie, MOC **10.00**
Sanders, Barry, MOC **45.00**
Smith, Emmett, 1992, MOC **60.00**
Spikes, Takeo, rookie, 2002, MOC ... **5.00**
Testaverde, Vinny, 2000, MOC **12.00**
Autograph, NFL footballs
Allen, Marcus **250.00**
Bradshaw, Terry **245.00**

Culpepper, Daunte **180.00**
Dent, Richard, Super Bowl 20 ...... **200.00**
Elway, John **250.00**
Favre, Brett **250.00**
James, Edgerin **180.00**
Owens, Terrell **200.00**
Marino, Dan **300.00**
Montana, Joe **300.00**
Rice, Jerry **200.00**
Simpson, O. J. **200.00**
Smith, Emmitt **210.00**
Young, Steve, Super Bowl 29 ...... **215.00**
Autograph, jersey
Aikman, Troy, pro-cut, Nike **285.00**
Csonka, Larry, Dolphins, aqua, Wilson
.... **250.00**
Farve, Brett, Packers, green, Nike **300.00**
Griese, Bob, Dolphins, Champion **250.00**
Marino, Dan, Dolphins, white, Starter
.... **380.00**
Montana, Joe, Notre Dame **325.00**
Namath, Joe, University of Alabama
.... **300.00**
White, Reggie, Packers, green and white,
Starter **230.00**
Autographed mini helmet, accompanied by certificate of authenticity and security decal
Alstoff, Mike, Tampa Bay Bucks **80.00**
Banks, Carl, New York Giants **50.00**
Baugh, Sammy, Washington Redskins
.... **100.00**
Bradshaw, Terry, Pittsburgh Steelers
.... **150.00**
Brown, Willie, Oakland Raiders **80.00**
Brunell, Mark, Jacksonville Jaguars
.... **100.00**
Buchanan, Ray, Atlanta Falcons **40.00**
Campbell, Earl, Houston Oilers **80.00**
Clayton, Mark, Miami Dolphins **50.00**
Culpepper, Daunte, Minnesota Vikings
.... **80.00**
Curtis, Mike, Indianapolis Colts **40.00**
Davis, Stephen, Washington Redskins
.... **60.00**
Dawson, Len, Kansas City Chiefs . **70.00**
Dayne, Ron, New York Giants **85.00**
Dorsett, Tony, Dallas Cowboys **80.00**
Dugans, Ron, Cincinnati Bengals.. **40.00**
Elway, John, Denver Broncos **200.00**
Favre, Brett, Green Bay Packers . **200.00**
Ferguson, Joe, Buffalo Bills **60.00**
Hart, Jim, Arizona Cardinals **45.00**
Hornung, Paul, Green Bay Packers **60.00**
James, Edgerin, Indianapolis Colts
.... **120.00**
Jones, Ed Too Tall, Dallas Cowboys
.... **50.00**
Jones, Thomas, Arizona Cardinals **60.00**
Kelly, Jim, Miami Hurricanes **90.00**
King, Shawn, Tampa Bay Bucks.... **60.00**
Kosar, Bernie, Cleveland Browns .. **60.00**
Lewis, Jamal, Baltimore Ravens **60.00**
Marino, Dan, Miami Dolphins **170.00**

McNabb, Donovan, Philadelphia Eagles **80.00**
Moon, Warren, Houston Oilers **80.00**
Namath, Joe, New York Jets **150.00**
Pennington, Chad, New York Jets .. **60.00**
Pruitt, Greg, Oakland Raiders **45.00**
Reed, Andre, Buffalo Bills **80.00**
Sayers, Gale, Chicago Bears **90.00**
Sims, Billy, Detroit Lions **50.00**
Starr, Bart, Green Bay Packers **190.00**
Tarkenton, Fran, Minnesota Vikings **90.00**
Taylor, Fred, Jacksonville Jaguars .. **80.00**
Torreta, Gino, Miami Hurricanes **60.00**
White, Dez, Chicago Bears **40.00**
White, Reggie, Green Bay Packers **100.00**
Woodson, Rod, Baltimore Ravens .. **50.00**
Zorn, Jim, Seattle Seahawks **50.00**

Autograph, photograph
Blades, B., R. Crockett, K. Scott, and W. White **45.00**
Crockett, Ray, Detroit, 8" x 10" **5.00**
Eliss, Luther, Detroit, 8" x 10" **5.00**
Howard, Desmond, Washington, 8" x 10" **10.00**
Mitchell, Pete, Jaguars, 8" x 10" **4.00**
Moore, Herman, NFL Official **80.00**
Parcells, Bill and Jerry Jones, Dallas Cowboys, pennant with helmet, white lettering, silver and gray ground, orig header card, folded twice, sgd on front in silver sharpie **20.00**
Schembechler, Bo, Univ of Michigan, 8" x 10" **20.00**
White, William, Detroit, 8" x 10" **4.00**

Autograph, program
Montana, Joe, Super Bowl 24 ...... **175.00**
Rice, Jerry, Super Bowl 23, sgd "MVP" **150.00**

Autograph, ticket, Joe Paterno, Penn State, 9-4-99 .... **45.00**

Bobbing head
Cleveland Browns, sq brown wood base **75.00**
Portland Trailblazers, MIB **55.00**
Seattle Supersonics, MIB **55.00**
St. Louis Cardinal, 6-1/2" h **130.00**

Book
Backfield in Motion, A Full-Length Photo-Guide to Playing Quarterback, Running Back and Pass Receiver, Don Smith, Gallahad Books, 1973, 1st ed. **12.00**
The Big One, Michigan vs Ohio State, A History of America's Greatest Football Rivalry, Bill Cromartie, Rutledge Press, Nashville, 1988, 399 pgs, dj **10.00**
University of Toledo 1970 Football Dope Book, press guide, 64 pgs **17.50**

Card, Bowman
Ford, T. J., rookie **10.00**
Gilmer, #27, 1953 .... **250.00**
James, Lebron, #123, rookie **40.00**
Milicic, Darko, #130, rookie **15.00**

Sweetney, Mike, #ff-MS, jersey **15.00**
Drinking glass, Seagram V.O. Golden Quarterback Challenge 1990, football player on one side with facsimile signature, VO decal on other, 8 oz, set of eight **24.00**
Football, leather, Wilson, NFL **25.00**
Game, Tom Hamilton's Pigskin Football Game, 1935 .... **265.00**

Hartland figurine
Arnett, MIB **300.00**
Browns, MIB **125.00**
Giants, MIB **150.00**
Helmet, Wilson, red, white stripes, youth, large, heavy plastic, leather chinstrap, some wear **15.00**

Jersey, game used
Collins, J, LA Rams, white mesh, 1980s **225.00**
Reeves, Eagles, white mesh, 1990s **110.00**
Selman, D, Tampa Bay, white mesh, 1970s **325.00**
Warren, Univ of Miami, white mesh, Fiesta Bowl, 1990s **245.00**
Williams, T, Dallas Cowboys, white mesh, name plate restored, 1980s **145.00**

Lunch box, NFL/AFC, 1978 Broncos Bengals, helmets on side, NFL logo on back, some wear, orig thermos...... **30.00**
Magazine tear sheet, Wilson football, ball with "grip-ability," Paul Hornung, *Boy's Life*, 1967 .... **5.00**
Matchbook, *Gino Marchetti, Everybody Goes to Gino's,* 2" h, brown on white, cartoon football player with text "The Giant Sandwich, It's A Banquet On A Bun," c1950 .... **18.00**
Patch, Super Bowl V, 1970, Baltimore and Dallas **60.00**

Pennant
Chicago Bears, 11-1/2" x 28-1/2" black felt, "Bears" in orange, orange, green, and red football art, orange felt trim strip, late 1940s.................................... **25.00**
Cincinnati Bengal's Super Bowl 16 AFC Champions, orange........................ **65.00**
Denver Broncos 1987 AFC Champions, blue, orange, and white, Super Bowl, XXII Jack Murphy Stadium, San Diego, Sunday, January 31, 1998, 29-1/2" l **15.00**
Norte Dame, 1957 Conference Champions, gold filled, football shaped, chain... **75.00**
Pinback button, NFL Teams Official Booster Series, mail premium from H. J. Heinz, c1967, 1-5/8" d, litho
Atlanta Falcons, red and black helmet, white ground, black letters **18.00**
Baltimore Colts, blue and white, light surface wear **15.00**
Detroit Lions, blue and silver, white letters **20.00**

New York Giants, black and white helmet, orange ground, white letters **20.00**

Philadelphia Eagles, green and silver **18.00**

Pinback buttons, 4" l, representing, Rutgers, Xavier, and Syracuse, **each $45**.

Pinback button, Official Booster Philadelphia Eagles, 1-5/8" d, green on silver litho, extension text, H. J. Heinz Foods promotion, 1967 .... **15.00**

Pinback button, Super Bowl XV/ABC Sports, 1981, black and white, gray rim, black letters, Superdome, New Orleans, Oakland Raiders and Philadelphia eagles **30.00**

Playset, Bob Griese, Gale Sayers, orig box **245.00**

Postcard, young boy with football and turkey, postmarked Nov. 23, 1909 .... **5.00**

Press badge, U.S.C., blue lettering, taupe gray cello, "Camera" operator at Nov. 1, 1924 game, Los Angeles Coliseum, freshmen teams from Univ of Southern CA and Univ of CA **80.00**

Print, 1996 Superbowl XXX, patented chromium collector's edition, matted, certificate of authenticity, 14" x 11" ... **5.00**

Program

Martins Ferry and Brideport, Ohio, Sept. 26, 1941, line-up includes young Lou Groza **40.00**

New York Giants-Chicago Bears Playoff, 7-3/4" x 10-1/2", Dec. 30, 1956 .... **30.00**

Notre Dame vs Wisconsin, 1953 .... **50.00**

Penn Highlands, Hollidaysburg Game, 1972 .... **5.00**

Penn State-Navy Homecoming Game, 8" x 10-1/2", Oct. 15, 1955, Beaver Field, Penn State Centennial celebration . **40.00**

Radio, NFL 50th Anniversary, Chiquita **45.00**

Soda bottle, Dr Pepper, 1972 Commemorative, Miami Dolphins, unopened **95.00**

Stickpin, Army, diecut stiff cardboard replicating brown leather football, overprinted in black text, movable stickpin, 1930s **18.00**

Telephone, figural, NFL, NRMIB **30.00**

Ticket stub

American Football League Championship, 1967, Oakland and Houston **25.00**

NFC Division, 1977, Minnesota and LA Rams **12.00**

Notre Dame vs Stanford, 1964 .... **15.00**

Super Bowl I, 1966, Green Bay and Kansas City **125.00**

Window flag, Penn State, Collegiate Licensed Product, unused **10.00**

Wire service photo, Dallas Cowboys owner Jerry Jones and Jimmy Johnson, 1989 .... **3.50**

Yearbook, Greenbay Packers, 1974, autographed by coaches and players **35.00**

Franciscan Dinnerware

History: Gladding, McBean and Company, Los Angeles, California, produced the Franciscan dinnerware patterns at its Glendale, California, pottery. The company began in 1875 as a manufacturer of sewer pipe and terracotta tile. In 1922, Gladding, McBean and Company acquired Tropico Pottery in Glendale, and in 1933 the West Coast properties of American Encaustic Tile.

In 1934, the company began producing and marketing dinnerware and art pottery under the name Franciscan Ware. Franciscan dinnerware had talc (magnesium silicate) rather than clay as a base. Early lines, which used bright primary colors on plain shapes, include Coronado, El Patio, Metropolitan, Montecito, Padua, and Rancho. As the line developed, more graceful shapes and pastel colors were introduced.

Three patterns are considered Franciscan classics. The Apple pattern with its embossed body, hand decoration, and underglaze staining was introduced in 1940. The Desert Rose pattern (1941) is the most popular dinnerware pattern ever manufactured in the United States. Ivy, the last of the big three, was first made in 1948.

There are three distinct types of Franciscan products: 1) masterpiece china, a high-quality translucent ceramic; 2) earthenware, a cream-colored ware found in a variety of decal- and hand-decorated patterns; and 3) whitestone or white earthenware.

Gladding, McBean and Company became Interpace Corporation in 1963. In 1979 Josiah Wedgwood and Sons, Ltd., acquired the company. In 1986 the Glendale plant was closed, marking the end of American production.

Collecting Hints: The emphasis on Franciscan art pottery and dinnerware has overshadowed the many other collectible lines from Gladding, McBean and Company. Keep your eye open for Tropico Art Ware, made between 1934 and 1937. This company also made some high-style birdbaths, florists' vases, flowerpots, garden urns, and hotel cigarette snuffers. Catalina Art Ware (1937-1941) also is attracting collector attention.

Most buyers of Franciscan's big three patterns (Apple, Desert Rose, and Ivy) are seeking replacement pieces for sets currently in use. As a result, prices tend to be somewhat inflated, especially for hollow pieces. Keep in mind that these patterns were popular throughout the country.

Early Franciscan lines, which are similar to Bauer designs and Homer Laughlin's Fiesta, can be distinguished from their more popular counterparts by differences in shape and color. These pieces are more commonly found on the West Coast than the East.

Soup plate, Apple pattern, green leaves, brown twigs, $20.

Apple

Introduced in 1940. Embossed earthenware body, hand decorated and under the glaze stain.

Ashtray	25.00
Beer mug, 17 oz.	85.00
Bowl, ftd.	22.00
Bread and butter plate	18.00
Butter dish, cov, 8" l	95.00
Casserole, cov, individual	55.00
Chop plate, 14" d	195.00
Coaster	65.00
Cocoa mug	125.00
Compote, 8" d	175.00
Cookie jar, 6-1/4" d, 10" h	285.00
Creamer and sugar	60.00
Cup and saucer	
Coffee	9.50
Jumbo	70.00
Dinner plate	20.00
Grill plate	140.00
Gravy and underplate	42.00
Jam jar	135.00
Juice tumbler	37.50
Marmalade, apple shape, 4-1/4" d, 4-1/4" h	600.00
Mixing bowls, nested set, three pcs	400.00
Pepper mill, 7-3/8" h	150.00
Platter, 12-3/4" d	50.00
Salad plate	18.00
Salt and pepper shakers, pr, small	36.00
Snack plate, 10-1/2" d, round, indent for cup	250.00
Syrup pitcher	85.00
Teapot, cov	75.00
Tray, 8-3/8" sq	180.00
Tumbler	20.00
Turkey platter	320.00
Tureen, 13" w	385.00
Vegetable bowl, 7-1/2" l	65.00

Arcadia

Gravy boat, green, gold trim	145.00

Carmel

Vegetable, platinum trim, oval	80.00

Coronado

Dinnerware line produced from 1936 until 1956. Made in 15 different colors with both satin and glossy glazes.

Bowl, turquoise, 7-1/2" d	17.50
Bread and butter plate, turquoise	4.25
Butter dish, cov, turquoise	32.00
Candlesticks, pr, ivory satin	48.00
Chop plate, 12" d, yellow	20.00
Creamer, yellow	12.00
Cup and saucer, coral, matte	9.50
Demitasse cup and saucer, white	37.50
Dinner plate	
Coral, glossy	9.50
Turquoise	12.00

Nut cup
Maroon... **70.00**
Turquoise, glossy, orig box **120.00**
Platter, 15" l, oval, yellow **17.50**
Sugar, cov, coral, glossy **13.00**
Vegetable bowl, yellow **35.00**

Daisy
Milk pitcher................................. **80.00**
Vegetable bowl.................................. **40.00**

Del Monte
Gravy boat................................. **135.00**

Denmark
Coffeepot, blue, ... **110.00**

Set, Dawn, green, cream, silver trim, 60 pieces, **$85**.

Desert Rose
Introduced in 1941. Embossed earthenware with hand-painted under-the-glaze decoration. Known for its rosebud-shaped finials.
After dinner cup and saucer **50.00**
Ashtray, individual size **18.00**
Baking dish, 1-1/2 qt, 13-1/2" l, 8-3/4" w
.... **225.00**
Bowl, 9" d **45.00**
Bread and butter plate, 6-1/2" d **5.00**
Butter dish, cov................................... **30.00**
Candlesticks, pr **75.00**
Candy dish, cov, egg shape, 6" w, 3-1/2" h
.... **475.00**
Casserole, cov, 2-1/2 qt, 11-1/2" w, 6-1/2" h
.... **400.00**
Celery tray, 4-1/2" x 10-1/2"................ **35.00**
Cereal bowl, 6" d **10.00**
Child's plate...................................... **175.00**
Chop plate
12" d **75.00**
14" d **95.00**
Cigarette box, cov, 4-1/4" w, 2-1/2" h **150.00**
Coffeepot, cov **115.00**
Compote **75.00**
Cookie jar, 6-1/2" w, 10-1/2" h **300.00**
Creamer and sugar **40.00**
Cup and saucer **15.00**
Dessert plate, coupe **75.00**

Dinner plate, 10-1/2" d...................... **20.00**
Eggcup **35.00**
Fruit bowl **6.00**
Ginger jar, cov, insert, 3-1/4" d, 4-3/4" h
.... **425.00**
Gravy, underplate.............................. **65.00**
Grill plate.. **95.00**
Hurricane candle, 7-1/4" d, 9-1/4" h **435.00**
Luncheon plate, 8-1/2" d **12.00**
Milk pitcher **75.00**
Mixing bowl, 9" d, 5" h **150.00**
Mug, 16 oz **40.00**
Party plate, coupe **200.00**
Pickle dish **45.00**
Platter, 19" l....................................... **225.00**
Relish, three parts............................ **90.00**
Salad bowl **95.00**
Side salad **32.00**
Sherbet **20.00**
Snack plate **195.00**
Soup bowl **18.00**
Soup tureen, 12" w, 7-3/4" h **600.00**
Tea cup and saucer **10.00**
Tea jar, cov **150.00**
Tea tile, square.................................. **50.00**
Toast cover **155.00**
Vegetable bowl, 9" l **35.00**
Water pitcher, 2-1/2 quart **95.00**

Fremont
Gravy boat **145.00**
Platter, large **175.00**
Vegetable, oval.................................. **80.00**

Fresh Fruit
Tile, 6" **50.00**

Granville
Gravy boat **120.00**

Hacienda, green
Bread and butter plate **8.00**
Cup and saucer.................................. **20.00**
Dinner plate **25.00**
Platter, 14" l....................................... **65.00**
Salad plate **10.00**
Soup bowl **18.00**

Indian Summer
Bread and butter plate **4.50**
Cereal bowl, some wear....................... **3.00**
Dinner plate, few knife marks............ **12.00**
Fruit bowl **5.00**
Salad plate **7.50**
Salt shaker **5.00**
Saucer **4.00**

Ivy
Introduced in 1948. Embossed earthenware with hand-painted under-the-glaze decoration.
Bowl, 7-1/4" d..................................... **40.00**
Bread and butter plate, 6-1/2" d........ **15.00**
Cereal bowl.. **22.00**
Creamer... **30.00**

Cup and saucer 24.00
Fruit bowl, 5-1/4" d 17.50
Gravy, underplate 80.00
Platter, 12" l 70.00
Relish, 11" l 60.00
Salad bowl, 11" d, ftd 150.00
Salt and pepper shakers, pr, small.... 35.00
Sugar bowl, cov 50.00
Teapot, 10" w, 6-1/4" h 290.00
Tumbler, 10 oz 48.00
Turkey platter, 19" l........................... 325.00
Vegetable bowl, divided 40.00

Larkspur

Bread and butter plate 6.00
Bread bowl 24.00
Cup 5.00
Dinner plate...................................... 12.00
Saucer.. 5.00
Shaker 10.00

Magnolia

Creamer and sugar 75.00

Mariposa

Salt and pepper shakers, pr............. 90.00
Teapot, cov 200.00

Meadow Flower

Teapot, 10" w, 6" h............................ 185.00

Partial set, yellow and green florals, green
border, 37 pieces, $40.

Meadow Rose

Bowl, 6" d 9.00
Butter dish, cov................................. 65.00
Cereal bowl.. 20.00
Goblet... 175.00
Luncheon plate, 8" d.......................... 14.00
Side salad 45.00
Snack plate.. 170.00
Teapot 200.00

October

Baking dish, rect, 13-5/8" l, 8-13/16" w, 2-1/
8" h 190.00
Olympic, white violets, gold trim
Platter, medium................................. 120.00
Platter, large 175.00
Sugar bowl, cov................................. 80.00
Vegetable, oval.................................. 75.00

Palomar

Jasper, cov vegetable bowl 190.00

Poppy

Cup and saucer................................. 32.00
Dinner plate 37.50
Fruit bowl 30.00
Gravy, underplate.............................. 175.00
Platter, oval 170.00
Salad plate, 8" d................................ 35.00
Salt and pepper shakers, pr 60.00
Tumbler 148.00
Vegetable bowl.................................. 130.00

Renaissance

Platter, 15-5/8" l, 12" w, 1962........... 280.00
Vegetable bowl, oval, 9" l, 6-1/2" w, 1962
.... 250.00

Rosemore

Demitasse cup and saucer.............. 45.00
Platter, round.................................... 110.00

Starburst

Introduced in 1954. Designed by
George James, utilizing the eclipse
shape.

Ashtray 60.00
Bon bon dish..................................... 45.00
Butter dish, cov 45.00
Casserole, cov, large........................ 265.00
Chop plate... 60.00
Cup and saucer................................. 25.00
Dinner plate 18.00
Fruit bowl 12.00
Jelly dish 45.00
Nappy 35.00
Side salad plate, crescent shape...... 27.50
Soup bowl 20.00
TV plate 75.00

Sundance

Creamer... 22.00
Cup and saucer................................. 15.00
Dinner plate 16.00
Platter, large 42.00
Salad plate 9.00
Set, service for eight, creamer, sugar, platter,
vegetable bowl, 1972.................... 395.00
Soup bowl 12.00
Sugar bowl 27.00
Vegetable bowl.................................. 35.00

Westwood
Platter, round, light green band **120.00**

Wildflower
Plate, 9-1/2" d **80.00**

Willow
Chop plate, 14" d **275.00**

Woodside
Gravy boat **140.00**
Vegetable, oval **95.00**

Frankoma Pottery

History: John N. Frank founded a ceramic art department at Oklahoma University in Norman and taught there for several years. In 1933, he established his own business and began making Oklahoma's first commercial pottery. Frankoma moved from Norman to Sapulpa, Oklahoma, in 1938.

A fire completely destroyed the new plant later the same year, but rebuilding began almost immediately. The company remained in Sapulpa and continued to grow. Frankoma is the only American pottery to have pieces on permanent exhibit at the International Ceramic Museum of Italy.

In September 1983, a disastrous fire struck once again, destroying 97 percent of Frankoma's facilities. The rebuilt Frankoma Pottery reopened on July 2, 1984. Production has been limited to 1983 production molds. All other molds were lost in the fire. John Frank's daughter Joniece became president and chief executive officer upon his death in 1973. She ran the business until 1991 when she sold it. The new owners still make some of the original dinnerware patterns and have also added some computer-generated lines.

Prior to 1954, all Frankoma pottery was made with a honey-tan-colored clay from Ada, Oklahoma. Since 1954, Frankoma has used a brick-red clay from Sapulpa. During the early 1970s, the clay became lighter and is now pink in color.

Collecting Hints: There were a number of early marks. One most eagerly sought is the leopard pacing on the "Frankoma" name. Since the 1938 fire, all pieces have carried only the name.

Sugar and creamer, Ada clay, $35.

Ashtray, Texas state shape, pink, mkd "459"
.... **20.00**

Batter pitcher
Barrel, two qts, Prairie Green glaze **60.00**
Mayan-Aztec, Desert gold glaze, two qts, two mold flaws in base **55.00**

Bookends, pr, 6" x 3-1/2" x 6-1/2" h, horses, black, leopard mark **385.00**

Bowl, 11" l, 5" w, 3-1/2" h, blue with green, mkd "Frankoma 202" **95.00**

Bud vase
5-1/4" h, 2-3/4" d top, cornucopia, #56K, Ada clay, bluish-green glaze, c1942
.... **75.00**
8" h, crocus, Ada clay, White Sand glaze int. and ext., mold #43, c1942-43 .. **62.50**
8" h, crocus, Ada clay, Brown Satin glaze int. and ext., mold #43 .... **60.00**

Candlesticks, pr, 9" w, 3-1/4" h, three candle sockets on each, gray, mkd "Frankoma 306" **50.00**

Canister set, Desert Gold, Ring Band design, four pcs **160.00**

Christmas plate
1968, Flight into Egypt, semi-translucent Della Robbia white glaze, sgd "John Frank" in script on back, copyright 1968, 8-1/2" d **60.00**
1969, Laid in a Manger, mkd "Frankoma FP John Frank," 8-1/4" d **50.00**

Cornucopia, 12" l, #222, Desert Gold glaze
.... **60.00**

Deviled egg tray, 12" d, green glaze, mkd "Frankoma #819" **335.00**

Dish, 9-1/4" x 4-1/2", leaf shape, green and brown, mkd "225" **18.00**

Figure
Garden Girl, #700, yellow hair, white bandanna, unglazed face and arms, Prairie Green glazed skirt, c1942-52, 6" h
.... **165.00**
Indian maiden, brown glaze, 12-1/2" h
.... **95.00**

Coffee server, two cup size, Ada clay, **$48**.

Juice set, 5" w, 6-3/4" h carafe, six 3" h juice tumblers, metal frame **95.00**

Masks, pr, 6-3/4" h happy face, 8-3/4" sad face, black glaze **150.00**

Mint bowl, 3-3/4" d, Prairie Green glaze **70.00**

Mug, political, 5" w, 4" h, GOP, Nixon and Agnew, 1973, Desert gold glaze **70.00**

Pitcher
    7" h, 8-1/4" w, #91, Osage Brown, mottled brown, hint of orange, c1933-42 .... **85.00**
    7-1/4" h, flame red, mkd "8 Frankoma"
    .... **115.00**
    8" h, Prairie Green, red clay, mkd "Frankoma 835" **65.00**

Planter
    Cactus, #5, 5-3/4" l, 3-1/2" w, 7" h, Ada clay, incised "Frankoma 5" **65.00**
    Duck, brown, 4-3/4" h **40.00**

Soup tureen, cov, Plainsman Gold, orig ladle **65.00**

Souvenir plate, Kansas Centennial, 1861-1961 .... **25.00**

Teapot, cov, Wagon Wheels, Prairie Green glaze, six-cup size **80.00**

Trivet, 6-1/4" d
    Rooster **50.00**
    Sequoyah, Cherokee alphabet **65.00**

Vase
    7-5/8" h, 8" d top, 5-1/2" d base, #198
    .... **75.00**
    8" h, Wagon Wheels, Prairie Green glaze, Ada white clay **65.00**

Wall pocket
    Phoebe, 5" w, 3" d, 7" h, 1948-49 .. **240.00**
    Phoebe, 5" w, 3" d, 7" h, white glaze, reissue, 1973-75 .... **75.00**
    Woodland Moss, 8" l, incised "Frankoma 197," 1964-66 .... **85.00**

Furniture, Modernism Era

History: The Modernism Era 20th Century furniture designers were heavily influenced by the International Movement and the events that were changing the attitudes of the world immediately after World War II. This period of furniture starts roughly in the 1940s and extends up to the 1960s when designers of the Pop culture are included. Another influence was the architectural style and type of homes and spaces they for which they were designing. Sleek modern homes and office buildings demanded sleek furnishings. Designers were encouraged to incorporate different materials, such as steel, laminates, and chrome. Clean lines were desirable, easily maintained surfaces were demanded by a lifestyle that was changing.

Collecting Hints: When buying American 20th furniture, learn to recognize a particular designer's style. Blending several designers can lead to an interesting look and add texture and color to any decorating scheme. This sampling of Modernism Era furniture has been taken from prices realized by several major American auction houses. This is an area of furniture collecting that is becoming of interest to collectors. As more examples enter the secondary marketplace, prices may fluctuate, depending on availability and condition.

Blanket chest, Lane, cedar lined, interior shelf, Chippendale-style, original labels, **$100**.

Bar

Paul Evans, wall mounted, disc, two semi-circular sculpted bronze doors finished with gold patina, unmarked, 71" d, 18" h
.... **3,000.00**

Bed

Dunbar, **Berne**, IN, single size, post war, head and foot board comprised of bent wood in zigzag pattern between slender crest rail and two wide cross rails, leather capped feet, light brown finish, metal tag, single size, 41-1/2" w, 37" h **300.00**

Nelson, **George**, Thin Edge, manufactured by Herman Miller, birch frame, orig woven caned headrest, white enameled metal legs, 77" l, 38" w, 34" h **4,750.00**

Robsjohn-Gibbings, T. H., manufactured by Widdicomb, headboard only, walnut veneer frame, rattan and brass wrapped edge, 80" w, 36" h........................ **200.00**

Corner cabinet, wicker, glass door, interior shelves, **$35**.

Cabinet, side

Eames, Charles, manufactured by Herman Miller, ESU 400, c1954, primary colored masonite panels in chrome angle iron frame, two drawers, perforated metal panel, X-stretchers, replaced sliding dimple doors, some wear, 47" w, 17" d, 48" h.. **6,500.00**

Knoll, Florence, manufactured by Knoll, credenza, rectangular white marble top over four drawers, two doors, rosewood veneer, chrome base, roughness to drawers, 75" w, 18" d, 26" h....... **4,250.00**

McCobb, Paul, manufactured by Calvin, from Erwin Collection, bleached mahogany, four drawers, brass base, orig label, refinished, price for pair, 36" w, 19" d, 34" h................. **1,450.00**

Nelson, George, manufactured by Herman Miller

Birch veneer, four drawers, silver-plate pulls, ebonized wood legs, 36" w, 19" d, 30" h **1,750.00**

Rosewood veneer, three doors, lift-up top sections, white-coated pulls, cast aluminum legs, interior shelves, 56" w, 20" d, 41" h............................ **7,700.00**

Walnut veneer, four drawers, one door, orig forest green lacquer, silver-plate pulls, 34" w, 19" d, 30" h **2,100.00**

Rhode, Gilbert, manufactured by Herman Miller, pickled veneer, two doors with cutout pulls, tubular metal legs, 36" w, 13" d, 29" h................................. **1,200.00**

Robsjohn-Gibbings, T. H., manufactured by Widdicomb, walnut veneer, rattan wrapped handles, cast brass legs, four drawers, refinished, 35" w, 21" d, 41" h
.... **850.00**

Wormley, Edward, manufactured by Dunbar, dark mahogany, three drawers, three sliding doors, woven fronts, nickel plated base, 62" w, 18" d, 38" h **3,000.00**

Chair, arm

Bertoia, Harry, manufactured by Knoll, bird, chrome wire frame, red wool cover, unmarked, minor pitting to frame, 38" x 38" x 36" **900.00**

Cassina, after a design by Frank Lloyd Wright, barrel style, cherry, flared and spindled back, gray fabric-upholstered circular seat pad, Cassina paper tag, 31-3/4" x 21-1/2" x 20-1/2"................. **950.00**

Cherner, Norman, manufactured by Plycraft, molded plywood, walnut veneer, bentwood legs, price for pr, one with Plycraft label, 30-3/4" x 24-1/4" x 17"
.... **1,000.00**

Eames, Charles, low Wire, manufactured by Herman Miller, black naugahyde upholstered fiberglass shell, zinc struts, 26" w, 26" d, 24" h **600.00**

Frankl, Paul, manufactured by Directional, c1966, sculptural bronze exterior in abstract design, orig gray fabric, price for pair, 28" w, 29" d, 26" h **2,520.00**

Nakashima, George, solid walnut, Windsor back, plank seat, price for pair, 25" w, 18" d, 27" h **1,000.00**

Platner, Warren, manufactured by Knoll, 1966, bronze wire construction, orig orange fabric, label, 25" w, 22" d, 30" h
.... **325.00**

Chair, dining

Bertoia, Harry, manufactured by Knoll, set of four, white plastic wire construction, blue seat pads, label, 21" w, 20" d, 30" h
.... **500.00**

Cherner, Norman, manufactured by Plycraft, Lawrence, MA, c1960, set of four, armchair and three side chairs, molded walnut arms, wedge-shaped back, plywood seat, tapered legs, repair to one leg, wear, nicks, price for set of four, 24" w, 22" h, 31" h **920.00**

Komal, Ray, manufactured by J. G. Furniture, 1949, Model #939, set of four, one-piece molded plywood frame, nickel connector, tubular metal frame, 21" w, 19" d, 28" h.. **2,200.00**

Rhode, Gilbert, manufactured by Herman Miller, set of eight, pickled bentwood frames, reupholstered in black wool, some wear, 18" w, 20" d, 30" h **265.00**

Robsjohn-Gibbings, T. H., manufactured by Widdicomb, set of six, two arm and four side chairs, curved slat backs, orig orange upholstery curved legs, 23" w, 20" d, 35" h.. **1,650.00**

Saarinen, Eero, manufactured by Knoll, c1948, set of six, black fiberglass back, orig tan naugahyde seat, satin chrome base, 22" w, 21" d, 22" h............. **3,750.00**

Wormley, Edward, manufactured by Dunbar, set of six, two arms and four side chairs, dark mahogany frames, orig Jack Larsen patterned fabric, big "D" label, some fading to fabric, 19" w, 20" d, 39" h
.... **1,750.00**

Chair, side

Cherner, Norman, manufactured by Plycraft, set of four, molded walnut plywood seat and back, bentwood legs, label, 17" w, 19" d, 32" h **800.00**

Eames, Charles, manufactured by Herman Miller, DCM, molded ash plywood back and seat, metal frame, 19" w, 19" d, 29" h
.... **120.00**

Gehry, Frank, Easy Edges, c1972, corrugated cardboard construction, masonite edge, water stain, 16" w, 21" d, 32" h.. **850.00**

McCobb, Paul, dowel ladder back, plank seat, wrought iron frame, price for pair, 18" w, 20" d, 34" h.......................... **600.00**

Nelson, George, manufactured by Herman Miller, caned seat and back, wood frame, white metal base, set of four, c1956, 18" w, 19" d, 33" h....................... **1,700.00**

Chair, recliner, possibly Knoll, black leather and wood, $350.

Chest of drawers

Dunbar, Berne, IN, manufactured by mid-20th C, rectangular top, case with five graduated drawers, recessed handles, platform base, light finish, metal tag, scratches, wear, 28" l, 18" d, 31-1/4" h
.... **865.00**

McCobb, Paul, for Winchendon, Planner Group, blond wood, black laminate drawer fronts and aluminum ring pulls, resting on a blond-wood bench, unmarked, 39-1/4" x 48" x 18" **550.00**

Nakashima, George, c1957, walnut, block dovetail top, dowel construction, eight drawers, two walnut slab legs, orig finish, 72" w, 20" d, 32" h **6,000.00**

Nelson, George Nelson for Herman Miller Thin Edge, rosewood veneer, eight drawers, conical porcelain knobs, tapering brushed chrome legs, from collection of a George Nelson associate designer, orig foil label, 30-1/2" x 46-1/2" x 18-1/2".. **5,500.00**
Walnut veneer, three drawers, wooden cupcake pulls, ebonized plank leg base, foil label, 29-3/4" x 34" x 20" **500.00**

China cabinet

Frankl, Paul, manufactured by Johnson Furniture Co., mahogany top with three glass shelves, above seven drawers and two doors, mahogany and lacquered cork, 72" w, 21" d, 74" h, some wear
.... **1,000.00**

Marx, Samuel, manufactured by Quigley, c1940, eight doors with parchment wrapped front, 62" w, 24" d, 87" h **5,500.00**

Parzinger, Tommi, manufactured by Charak, 1940s, contrasting light and dark mahogany, two doors, brass pulls, upper cabinet with lattice glass doors, 36" w, 17" d, 81" h.................................... **950.00**

Rhode, Gilbert, manufactured by Herman Miller, checkerboard walnut veneers, two doors beneath sliding glass top, refinished, 36" w, 14" d, 50" h........ **750.00**

Desk

Baughman, Mylo, manufactured by Milo Baughman, 1950s, walnut veneer, two banks of drawers, floating top, dowel legs, wear, 60" w, 28" d, 31" h **1,980.00**

Dunbar, Berne, IN, rectangular top, cream-colored laminated writing surface, curved face front with center drawer flanked by shallow and deep drawers, tapered shaped legs, light finish, metal tag, wear, stains, scratches, 50" w, 21" d, 29-1/4" h **4,160.00**

Frankl, Paul, manufactured by Johnson Furniture Co., kneehole, two-tone, brass pulls, tapered legs, 1940s, 36" w, 24" d, 30" h **950.00**

Maloof, Sam, oak, rectangular top over two drawers, dowel detail to top and sides, branded "Design/Made Maloof," 60" w, 25" d, 29" h.............................. **5,000.00**

Knoll, Florence Knoll for Knoll, single pedestal, overhanging rect top, three blind drawers on tapering dowel leg frame, unmarked, 28-3/8" x 50" x 27-1/2", later contact paper added to tops, sides, and drawer fronts **350.00**

Nelson, George, manufactured by Herman Miller, drop leaf, hinged rectangular top, three drawers, brushed chrome base, refinished, 40" w, 24" d, 30" h........ **825.00**

Robsjohn-Gibbings, T. H., c1940, burled wood, fleur-de-lis inlay, two doors, interior drawers, refinished, 56" w, 22" d, 29" h **3,850.00**

Unknown designer, 1950s, rectangular formica top above two drawers, ebonized V-base, 40" w, 24" d, 30" h **100.00**

Sideboard/buffet

Evans, Paul, custom designed, wavy front, 1972, slat top, two welded steel doors with enameled and patinated textured ground, high relief biomorphic wave patterns with applied gold leaf, rect black wood base, sgd "Paul Evans," 38" x 76" x 21-1/2"............................... **9,500.00**

Unknown designer, 1940s custom made, orig finish, Chinese red lacquer, two doors, brass trim, Lucite handle, 60" w, 21" d, 37" h............................ **2,200.00**

Wormley, Edward, manufactured by Dunbar, light mahogany, central compartment flanked by two doors with ebony and walnut fronts, hinged corner doors, plinth base, brass "D" pulls and keys, orig "D" tag, 80" w, 18" d, 31" h **1,800.00**

Sofa

Frankl, Paul, manufactured by Directional, c1966, sculptural bronze exterior in abstract design, orig gray fabric, 60" w, 36" d, 24" h **850.00**

Heywood Wakefield, three seat bentwood maple frame, cushions reupholstered in vintage fabric, refinish, 73" w, 33" d, 30" h **650.00**

Harcourt, Geoffrey, manufactured by Artifort, c1973, Cleopatra, foam and metal frame, orig purple wool upholstery, casters, 74" w, 34" d, 26" d........ **3,500.00**

Matta, manufactured by Knoll, c1968, Malitte seating system, five piece stackable upholstered foam cushions, black and orange, wear to fabric, 62" w, 25" d, 61" h **2,000.00**

Nelson, George, manufactured by Herman Miller, Steel Frame, reupholstered seat and back, blue fabric, white laminate table, steel frame, 46" w, 30" d, 27" h **375.00**

Saarinen, Eero, manufactured by Knoll, c1948, Womb Settee, organically molded fiberglass shell, reupolstered in blue wool, chrome metal legs, 52" w, 34" d, 36" h **2,500.00**

Unknown designer, 1940s custom made, rectilinear upholstered form, orig blue lacquered wood base, needs to be reupholstered, 91" w, 32" d, 26" h **900.00**

Wormley, Edward, manufactured by Dunbar, V-form, reupholstered in light blue ultra-suede, walnut base, 108" w, 48" d, 32" h **1,750.00**

Table, coffee

Aalto, Alvar, manufactured by ICF, plate glass top, bentwood birch frame, 27" sq, 18" h **100.00**

Brown Saltman, 1960s, black and white laminate top, lift-up compartments, walnut frame, minor wear to wood, 41" sq, 16" h **500.00**

Butler, Lew, manufactured by Knoll, c1950, black and white laminate top, walnut base, 38" w, 34" d, 16" h **375.00**

Eames, Charles, manufactured by Herman Miller, surfboard, elliptical form, black formica, wire strut base, 89" w, 29" d, 10" h **3,550.00**

La Verne, Phillip, New York, c1962, "Creation of Man" design in bas-relief on rectangular top, two round fluted bronze legs, signed, some wear and corrosion, 65" l, 23-5/8" d, 17-1/2" h **2,760.00**

McCobb, Paul, manufactured by Calvin, circular white glass top, brass base, 42" d, 15" h **450.00**

Mont, James, circular red lacquer top, silver-leaf edge, ebonized base, refinished, 48" d, 14" h **50.00**

Nelson, George, manufactured by Herman Miller, round walnut veneer top, brushed steel frame, 41" d, 14" h **770.00**

Noguchi, Isamu, manufactured by Herman Miller, triangular glass top with early pale green edge, ebonized wood base, 50" w, 36" d, 16" h.................................. **1,300.00**

Platner, Warren, manufactured by Knoll International, c1966, steel rod hourglass shape, circular glass top, 16" d, 18" h **550.00**

Robsjohn-Gibbings, T. H., manufactured by Widdicomb, plate glass top with polished corners, light walnut and brass base, 45" sq, 12" h **2,100.00**

Schultz, Richard, manufactured by Knoll, c1960, Petal, white lacquered segmented top, metal prong base, some wear to top, 42" d, 15" h **550.00**

Unknown designer, 1940s custom made, circular white marble top, orig blue lacquered wood base, 40" d, 15" h **100.00**

Wegner, Hans, manufactured by Andr. Tuck, Denmark, rectangular top, chrome base, impressed mark, 47" w, 22" d, 15" h **300.00**

Wormley, Edward, manufactured by Dunbar
Black laminate top, light mahogany triangular frame, green tag, 34" sq, 17" h **500.00**
Flip-top, dark mahogany, white laminated shelf, two drawers, 40" w, 17" d, 26" h **850.00**
Rectangular dark mahogany top, perforated magazine holders on bentwood legs, green tag, 64" w, 23" d, 20" h... **1,300.00**
Walnut, sectioned burlwood veneer top, shaped legs, brass capped feet, gold metal tag, 16" w, 58" x 30-1/2".... **1,000.00**

Table, dining

Eames, Charles, manufactured by Herman Miller, rectangular walnut plywood top, folding chrome legs, refinished, 54" w, 34" d, 29" h.................................... **950.00**

Juhl, Finn, manufactured by Bovirke, 1953, rectangular top, two pop-up leaves, oval teak legs, 59" w, 35" d, 29" h......... **250.00**

Knoll, Florence, manufactured by Knoll, elliptical plywood top, chrome pedestal base, 78" w, 49" d, 29" h............. **1,500.00**

Nakashima, George, elliptical, cherry, two matched planks joined by four rosewood butterfly joints, trestle base, two 17" leaves for ends, excellent original finish, unmarked, from orig owner, c1950, 29" x 84" x 41-1/2".................................. **7,500.00**

Noguchi, Isamu, manufactured by Knoll, white laminated top, chrome struts, black enamel base, 48" d, 29" h **2,400.00**

Rhode, Gilbert, manufactured by Herman Miller, circular pickled veneer top, tubular metal legs, two leaves, minor wear, 48" d, 28" h ....'..... **1,540.00**

Robsjohn-Gibbings, T. H., manufactured by Widdicomb, radiating walnut veneer top, dowel legs, three leaves, label, 48" d, 29" h **2,310.00**

Saarinen, Eero, manufactured by Knoll, circular white laminate top, white cast aluminum pedestal base, 36" d, 29" h **775.00**

Woodard, 1960s, circular glass top, extruded aluminum base, 44" d, 29" h **550.00**

Wormley, Edward, manufactured by Dunbar, circular dark mahogany top, tapered legs, three leaves, 50" w, 29" h **1,900.00**

Table, suites with chairs

Frankl, Paul, manufactured by Johnson Furniture Co., game table and chairs, five-piece set, clover-shaped cream lacquered cork top, tapered mahogany legs, four arm chairs with striped gold and black fabric, table: 36" sq, 28" h, chairs: 25" w, 24" d, 32" h **385.00**

Mendini, Alessandro, and Alessandro Guerriaro, manufactured by Studio Alchimia, 1984, Ollo table and four inset chairs, black and white geometric patterned laminate, orange top, 42" sq, 29" h **5,500.00**

Nakashima, George, manufactured by Widdcomb, 1959, seven-piece set, rectangular walnut veneer dining table, dovetailed detailed to sides, tapered oval legs, six chairs, two arm and four sides, solid walnut frames, hickory dowel backs and seats, orig label, two leaves for table, table: 72" w, 42" d, 29" h, chair: 25" w, 23" d, 36" h................................. **4,950.00**

Robsjohn-Gibbings, T. H., seven pieces, drop-leaf dining table, two arm and four side chairs, all light walnut, table: 40" w, 28" d, 29" h, chairs: 22" w, 20" d, 33" h **775.00**

Saarinen, Eliel, manufactured by Johnson Furniture, 1950s, five-piece set, rectangular birch veneer top, molded birch legs, four side chairs with curved sets and backs, birch legs, table: 66" w, 40" d, 30" h, chairs: 19" w, 21" d, 33" h **2,350.00**

Vanity

George Nelson, manufactured by Herman Miller, blond wood, leather-covered case, center compartment with frosted glass lift-top and illuminated interior, flanked by side compartments with black enameled hinged lids and leather tab pulls, tapering legs, stenciled "4660," 27-1/4" x 48" x 19-3/4" **400.00**

G

Games

History: A board game dating from 4000 B.C. was discovered in ruins in upper Egypt. Board games were used throughout recorded history but reached their greatest popularity during the Victorian era. Most board games combine skill (e.g., chess), luck and ability (e.g., cards), and pure chance (dice). By 1900, Milton Bradley, Parker Brothers, C. H. Joslin, and McLoughlin were the leading manufacturers.

Monopoly was invented in 1933 and first issued by Parker Brothers in 1935. Before the advent of television, the board game was a staple of evening entertainment. Many board games from the 1930s and 1940s focused on radio personalities, e.g., Fibber McGee or The Quiz Kids.

In the late 1940s, the game industry responded to the popularity of television, and TV board games were at their zenith from 1955 to 1968. Movies, e.g., James Bond features, also led to the creation of games but never to the extent of television programs.

Collecting Hints: Make certain a game has all its parts. The box lid or instruction booklet usually contains a list of all pieces. Collectors tend to specialize by theme, e.g., Western, science fiction, Disney, etc. The price of most television games falls into the $10 to $25 range, offering the beginning collector a chance to acquire a large number of games without spending huge sums.

Don't stack game boxes more than five deep or mix sizes. Place a piece of acid-free paper between each game to prevent bleeding from inks and to minimize wear. Keep the games stored in a dry location; but remember, extremes of dryness or moisture are both undesirable.

Board

Acquire, Avalon	25.00
Action Man, English	45.00
Addams Family Reunion, Pressman, 1991, MISB	20.00

Alien	25.00
Amazing Dr. Nim Game	5.00
Apple's Way, Milton Bradley, 1974	25.00
Are You Being Served, English	30.00
Around the World in 80 Days, Transogram, copyright 1957	20.00
Arrest and Trial, Chuck Connors	35.00
Barney Miller, Parker Bros, 1977	24.00
Batman Returns, Parker Bros, 3-D, 1992, MISB	25.00
Beat the Clock, Lowell, 1954, 1st ed.	65.00
Beat the Drum Game of Skill, Rosebud Art, copyright 1942	40.00
Beetle Bailey	25.00
Ben Hur, C. Heston photo box, British	110.00
Blondie	25.00
Boots and Saddles, Gardner, 1958	48.00
Bozo the Clown Circus Game, Transogram	15.00
Branded, Milton Bradley, 1956	65.00
Camelot Game, Parker Brothers, 1955	15.00
Candid Camera	30.00
Candy Land, Milton Bradley, 1949, 1st ed.	45.00
Captain Action, Milton Bradley, 1977	30.00
Captain Caveman, MISB	40.00
Captain Gallant Adventure Board Game, Transogram, 1950s	48.00
Captain Video, Milton Bradley, 1950	115.00
Carrier Strike, Milton Bradley, 1977	35.00
Casey Jones, Saalfield, 1960s	8.00
Casper the Ghost	75.00
Charge Account, Lowell, 1961	12.00

Ellery Queen Mystery Game, Ideal, $15.

Cheyenne, photo box, British	100.00
Chicago Great Blizzard, C. P. Marino, 1978	85.00
Chutes and Ladders, 1956, 1st ed.	20.00
Circus Boy	70.00
Clash of the Titans	50.00
Clue, Parker Bros., 1949, 1st ed.	35.00
Contack, Parker Bros, 1939	45.00

Cootie, Schaper, 1966, unplayed-with condition **20.00**
Dark Towers, Milton Bradley, 1981 ... **150.00**
Dennis the Menace.............................. **20.00**
Dick Tracy Crime Stopper, MIB **100.00**
Doc Holiday.. **40.00**
Doctor Dolittle, 3-D action game, Mattel, MISB **125.00**
Donn Prairie Race **30.00**
Dracula, figural **50.00**
Dragnet, Transogram, 1955 .... **60.00**
Dream House **25.00**
Dr. Ruth's Game of Good Sex, 1985. **15.00**
Dynamite Shack, Milton Bradley, 1968
.... **35.00**
Easy Money, Milton Bradley **7.50**
Escape from New York **40.00**
Ewoks... **25.00**
Family Ties... **20.00**
Fantastic Voyage............................... **25.00**
Fess Parker's Trail Blazers Game **60.00**
Finance, Parker Brothers.................... **45.00**
Flintstone Kids, 1967 .... **25.00**
Fox Hunt, E. S. Lowe Co., 1940s........ **20.00**
Frankenstein, Jr.................................. **50.00**
Fugitive, Ideal, 1964........................... **280.00**
Funky Phantom **25.00**
Gas Crisis, 1979, factory seal, MIB.... **12.00**
General Hospital, Cardinal, 1982....... **18.00**
Gentle Ben, Mattel, 1968 .... **250.00**
Get Smart, time bomb, Ideal, 1965 .... **75.00**

How About a Game of Barney Miller with the 12th Precinct Gang, Parker Bros, complete, $24.

G-Men, Melvin Purvis, Parker Bros, 1930s
.... **200.00**
Gilligan's Island **225.00**
Goodbye Mr. Chips............................ **35.00**
Gray Ghost **95.00**
Green Hornet, Milton Bradley, 1966... **90.00**
Hands Down, Ideal, 1964 .... **15.00**
Hangman, Milton Bradley, 1976........... **8.00**
Happy Days, Parker Brothers, 1976, MISB
.... **45.00**
Hardy Boys, 1959................................ **35.00**
Have Gun Will Travel.......................... **70.00**
Hollywood Squares, Ideal, Peter Marshall, 1974... **10.00**
Howdy Doody, 1950s......................... **125.00**

Huckleberry Hound Bumps, Transogram, 1961 .... **50.00**
I'm Garry Moore...and I've Got a Secret, Lowell Toy Co., 1956 .... **30.00**
I Spy **50.00**
It's About Time.................................... **200.00**
Jackie Gleason, Away We Go, 1956 **165.00**
King Oil, Milton Bradley, 1974........... **45.00**
Knight Rider **25.00**
Kooky Chicks Magnetic Game, Milton Bradley, 1964.............................. **10.00**
Land of the Lost, 1975....................... **40.00**
Lassie, Whiting, 1955.......................... **25.00**
Leave It To Beaver Ambush Game, Hasbro, 1969 .... **120.00**
Let's Face It, Hassenfield Bros., four plastic Mr. Potato Heads, 15" sq box, 1950s
.... **140.00**

Lotto, J. Pressman & Co., suitcase-type box with travel labels, complete, $35.

Little House on the Prairie............... **25.00**
Little Lulu **180.00**
Looney Tunes, 1968.......................... **45.00**
Lost In Space..................................... **135.00**
Lucky Town the Build-A-Happy Home Game, Milton Bradley, 1946.......... **24.00**
Mad's Spy vs Spy, Milton Bradley, #4600, 1986 .... **12.00**
M*A*S*H, Milton Bradley, 1981........... **20.00**
Matchbox Traffic Game, 1967 .... **50.00**
Meet the Presidents Quiz Game, Selchow & Righter, 1950 .... **18.00**
Midway, Avalon Hill Co., Baltimore, 1965, play wear...................................... **20.00**
Mighty Comics, Super Heroes, Transogram, 1966 .... **60.00**
Mighty Mouse Rescue, 1950s **45.00**
Mod Squad.. **150.00**
Monopoly, Parker Bros., modern **5.00**
Mostly Ghostly **30.00**
Mr. T, A-Team, Milton Bradley, 1983.... **35.00**
My Fair Lady, Standard Toykraft, late 1950s
.... **15.00**
Mystery Date...................................... **125.00**
Name That Tune, Milton Bradley, 1959 **20.00**
Nancy Drew Mystery Game, Parker Bros, 1959 .... **100.00**
New Avengers **60.00**
No Time for Sergeants...................... **25.00**

Nurses, Ideal, 1963 .... **25.00**
Perry Mason, Transogram, 1959 .... **45.00**
Pinky Lee, Who Am I, 1950s **60.00**
Pit, Parker Bros. **7.50**
Pivot Game of Action, Milton Bradley, 1958
.... **10.00**
Play Hookey Go Fishin!, Cadaco, Inc.,
1974 .... **12.00**
Prisoner of Zenda, Milton Bradley, 1930s
.... **25.00**
Quick Draw McGraw Private Eye Game,
Milton Bradley, 1960 .... **45.00**
Raggedy Ann, 1954 .... **25.00**
Raiders of the Lost Ark, Kenner, 1981
.... **48.00**
Return A Putt, Bing Crosby, 1950s, MIB
.... **50.00**

Superman Game and Superboy Game, Milton
Bradley, some wear to box, **$10**.

Road Runner, © Warner Bros., Milton
Bradley, 1968 .... **70.00**
Ruff and Ready, Transogram, 1962 ... **35.00**
Sea Hunt, Lowell, 1961 .... **35.00**
Sgt. Preston, Milton Bradley, 1956 ..... **32.00**
Shotgun Slade **40.00**
Sigmund and the Sea Monsters, MISB
.... **40.00**
Silly Sidney, Transogram, 1963 .... **55.00**
Six Million Dollar Man, Bionic Crisis, Parker
Bros, 1976 .... **24.00**
Snagglepuss **35.00**
Space Angel, Transogram, © 1965 .... **75.00**
Spot A Car Bingo **10.00**
Spoutsie Hot Potato, Ohio Art, MIB... **25.00**
Star Trek, Ideal **60.00**
Stocks & Bonds, Avalon Hill Game Co.,
1978 .... **7.50**
Stock Market Deluxe, Whitman, 1963 **30.00**
Sub Search, Milton Bradley, 1973 ...... **35.00**
Superboy, Hasbro, 1950s **50.00**
Surfside Six, Lowell, 1959 .... **65.00**
S.W.A.T. **20.00**
Swayze, Milton Bradley, 1954 .... **40.00**
Swoop Space Game, 1969 .... **30.00**
Tank Command, Ideal **48.00**
Terry Toons, Ideal **45.00**
The Children's Hour, Parker Bros, 1958
.... **8.00**
The Godfather Game, Family Games, Inc.,
1971 .... **12.00**
The Rebel, Ideal, 1961 .... **60.00**

Sunset Limited, Milton Bradley, wear to original
box, **$25**.

Three Stooges, Lowell, 1959 .... **200.00**
Thunderbirds, Parker Bros., 1968 ..... **55.00**
Tic-Tac-Dough TV Quiz Game, 1960s
.... **20.00**
Titanic, Ideal...................................... **40.00**
Tom Hamilton's Pigskin Football Game,
Parker Bros., 1946 .... **175.00**
Treasure Hunt, Milton Bradley **7.50**
Twenty One TV Quiz Game, Lowell Toy Mfg.
.... **50.00**
Twiggy **40.00**
Twilight Zone **175.00**
Uncle Wiggily, 1930s **35.00**
Untouchables, Transogram **55.00**
Virginian, Transogram, 1962.............. **40.00**
Watergate Scandal, American Symbolic,
1973 .... **15.00**
Wolfman, 1960s **195.00**
Woody Woodpecker **25.00**
Zorro, Whitman, 1958 .... **30.00**

Card game, Touring, Parker Brothers, **$30**.

Card

Beverly Hill Billies Set Back Card Game,
Milton Bradley, MIB........................ **12.00**
Carol Burnette **25.00**
Dallas.. **20.00**
Davy Crockett, Castell Bros., Ltd., c1955
.... **90.00**
Dick Tracy... **45.00**
Doctor Dolittle, Whitman.................... **40.00**
Dukes of Hazzard **15.00**

E. T. **25.00**
F-Troop **70.00**
Howdy Doody **48.00**
I-Spy **75.00**
Llya Kurykakin **35.00**
Mork & Mindy **15.00**
Munsters **50.00**
Panic the Great Wall Street Game, Panic
    Card Co., copyright 1903 .... **20.00**
Shazam **15.00**
Twelve O'Clock High **40.00**
Welcome Back Kotter, Milton Bradley, MIB
    .... **10.00**

Gardening

History: Gardeners have long enjoyed the beauty of flowers and landscaping. Today whole outdoor rooms and spaces are being created just as gardeners did decades ago. Today antique collectors are fortunate to have a wide range of antiques and collectibles to chose from when creating their unique spaces. Many gardeners also include heirloom plants along with the vintage antiques and find they are perfect companions.

Other collectors are content to decorate with a garden theme, incorporating prints, small garden accessories, such as decorative flower pots and watering cans, into their room-scapes.

Collecting Hints: A collecting category has truly arrived when antique shows of the same name are happening events. The Antique Garden Show in New York is just the place to find vintage garden accessories of all types and price ranges.

Bench, wood, mortise and tenon joints
    through top, weathered green paint, 72" l
    .... **90.00**
Bird bath
    19" d, 45" h, cast stone, form of Atlas
    supporting stylized flower formed basin
    on his back, socle base **1,760.00**
    20-1/2" d, 33" h, cast stone, lotus shape
    base, circular leaf molded standard,
    octagonal base **460.00**
Book
    *An English Country Lady's Book of Dried
    Flowers*, Amanda Docker, Doubleday,
    1990 .... **12.00**
    Crockett's Tool Shed, Gardening
    Equipment, James Crockett, Little Brown,
    Boston, photos by Lou Jones, 1989. **7.00**
    Daylilies and How to Grow Them, Ben
    Arthur Davis, Tupper & Love, 1954, 1st
    ed, some wear to dj **8.00**

Birdhouse, white clapboard construction, shingled roof, six stories high, **$165**

Flower Arrangements to Copy, Tat
Shinno, Doubleday, 1966, 246 pgs,
author illus, soiled dj **12.00**
*How To Tell The Birds From The Flowers
And Other Woodcuts*, A Revised Manual
of Fornithology for Beginners, Robt
Williams, Wood, Dood Mead, 1917, 27th
ed. **8.00**
No-Work Garden Book, Ruth Stout and
Richard Clemence, Rodale Press, 1972,
3rd printing, dj **9.00**
*Soiless Growth of Plants-Use of Nutrient
Solutions, Water, Sand, Cinder, Etc.*,
Carlton Ellis & Miller W. Swaney, 1938,
Reinhold Publishing Co., 155 pgs ... **7.00**
Successful Gardening with Perennials,
Helen Van Pelt Wilson, Doubleday, 1976,
1st edition, worn dj **12.00**
*Taylor's Guide to Gardening, Techniques,
Planning, Planting & Caring For Your
Garden*, Houghton Mifflin Co., 1991, 1st
ed. **7.00**
*Terrific Tomatoes, How to Grow and Enjoy
Them*, Catherine O. Foster, Rodale Press,
1975, 1st printing, dj **8.00**
*The Complete Book of Dried
Arrangements*, Raye Miller Underwood,
Bonanza Books, 1952, dj **8.00**
What Kinda Cactus Izzat?, Reginald
Manning, black and white illus, A Who's
Who of Strange Plants of SW America, J.
J. Augustin Publ, 1949 .... **15.00**
Brooch, 1-3/8" h, watering can, goldtone
watering can, flowers, faux pearls on
handle **22.00**

Garden statues, concrete, boy and girl, pair, $125

Catalog

Bobbink & Atkins, Rutherford, NJ, 1926, *Hardy Herbaceous Plants*, some color illus, 68 pgs, 7" x 10" **15.00**

Erkins Studios, Inc., New York, NY, c1933, Cat No. 54, garden ornaments, pools, fountains, benches, etc., 32 pgs, 8" x 9-1/4" **24.00**

Johnson Cactus Gardens, Paramount, CA, 1957, 36 pgs, 7-3/4" x 10-1/2", illus **10.00**

Mathes Mfg Co., Cleveland, OH, 48 pgs, 10" x 12-1/2", cypress wood garden craft products **32.00**

Tom Craig, Escondido, CA, 1955, 32 pgs, 4" x 9", mail-out catalog, *Rancho De Las Flores*, iris and daylily breeder......... **6.00**

Walter Marx Gardens, Boring, OR, 1957, 64 pgs, 8-1/4" x 10-3/4", color illus of flowers **5.00**

Child's watering can, Mistress Mary, Cohn Toys, Brooklyn, NY, 8" w, 6-1/2" h, wear **115.00**

Creche, 16" w, 32" h, weathered wood and slate **275.00**

Fernery, 32" w, 13" d, 37" h, tôle peinte, molded rect planter inset in arched wirework frame, raised on elaborate cabriole-shaped legs ending in scrolled toes, painted pale yellow with blue accents, French Provincial, fourth quarter 19th C **775.00**

Folding chair, orig green and white cotton striped seat and back, some wear. **95.00**

Fountain

23-1/2" d, 45" h, cast iron, putto struggling with large fish, lattice edged basin with

reeded body, floral pedestal ending with three applied swans, concave triangular base **750.00**

26" d, 46-3/4" h, cast iron, attributed to J. W. Fiske, NY, 19th C, basin with cast leaf exterior, cranes and cat o'nine tails base, molded circular platform, old white paint, weathered **2,875.00**

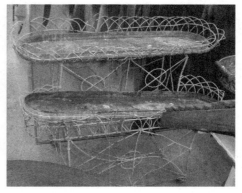

Planter, wire-work, two levels, some original white paint, rust, $45.

Fountain figure

17" l, 9" h, bronze, frog **360.00**

23-1/2" d, 48-1/2" h, patinated bronze, putto kneeling with one leg on acanthus-like form, holding hand on grapevine, other supporting shell form basin atop his head, circular base molded with clusters of grapes spilling out of barrel .. **1,320.00**

32" w, 42" h, patinated bronze, kneeling boy playing with frog, naturalistically molded base, applied lotus leaves **1,210.00**

35" h, bronze, naked boy holding goose, socle surrounded by four goslings with open beaks as fonts, greenish gold patina, 20th C **6,325.00**

Garden armillary sphere, Victorian, third quarter 19th C, 38" w, 64" h, later patinated bronze sphere raised on heavily molded cast iron base, fruit, floral and paw designs, plinth base... **3,520.00**

Garden bench

49" l, 14" d, 27" h, cast iron, polychromed, out-scrolling slatted back, conforming seat, rope-twist arms, molded klismos base, price for pr **750.00**

49" l, 41-1/2" d, 29" h, cast iron, slatted construction, naturalistically formed arms, interlocking snake and grapevine legs, leaf shaped feet, price for pr **1,650.00**

61-1/2" l, 20" d, 32" h, cast iron, out-scrolling slatted back, conforming seat, scrolled arms, interlocking acanthus legs, plinth feet, price for pr **275.00**

Garden chair, cast iron, painted and gilded, backrest with drapery and masks above two warriors, openwork frieze, cabriole legs, two painted black, four painted red, gilt highlights, price for assembled set of six.. **4,350.00**

Garden gate, 42-1/2" w, 70-1/2" h, cast iron, domed form, centered scrolling design, price for four-pc set.................... **3,500.00**

Garden seat, 32-1/2" h, painted arrow-back, curving crest above arrow-back spindles, shaped arm supports, plank seat, sq splayed legs with stretchers, orig green paint, 19th C, repairs.................. **1,725.00**

Garden suite, cast iron, two 38" h arm chairs, 49" l, 14-1/2" d, 38" h bench, each with arched back, centered armorial within a rosette, surrounded by interlacing branches, topped by trefoils, slatted seat, down-swept scrolling arms and legs, Victorian, price for three-pc set **1,760.00**

Garden urn, cast iron

16" d, 29" h, egg and dart molded lip above neck dec with spray of flowers and wheat over fluted body, circular molded standard, applied scrolling handles, price for pair... **750.00**

16" d, 31" h, campana form, egg and dart molded lip, partially reeded body on circular pedestal, pyramidal molded base, price for pr........................... **425.00**

16-1/2" d, 25-1/2" h, campana form, egg and dart molded lip, basketweave molded body, conforming circular base standard, socle, price for pr **825.00**

21-1/2" d, 24" h, campana form, egg and dart molded lip, body dec with scrolling arabesques, circular reeded standard, socle base, applied lion head centered handles, price for pr...................... **500.00**

25" w, 12" d, 12-1/2" h, rect, rococo manner, serpentine lip above garland and floral motifs dec body, splayed scroll feet, price for pr.............................. **350.00**

31-1/2" h, three-piece construction, scrolled borders with flowers beneath, swallows on wells, scrolled cast detail around base, old worn white repaint, one with welded repair, price for pr **550.00**

Garden urn

Cast stone, 18" d, 27" h, everted lip above a partially reeded bulbous body, circular standard, socle base, Italian **650.00**

Terra cotta, 27" d, 52" h, campana form, crested molded lip above body with two Bacchic masks among grapevines, lower fluted part with two rams heads, raised on reeded circular standard, socle base, price for pr.................................. **1,100.00**

Table and chairs, cast iron, repainted white, $250.

Table, cast iron, painted white, floral decoration, $90.

Gate, 29" w, 41" h, cast iron, vine cresting manner "Edward R. Dolan" above willow tree with doves in branches, flanking lambs and flowers below on grassy mound, old black, green, and white paint, America, c1860 .... **1,380.00**

Glider, metal, repainted turquoise, working condition **500.00**

Hand tool, normal wear, average price **5.00**

Hoe, wooden handle, well used **7.50**

Patio chair, metal, repainted white, c1950, some wear **125.00**

Pendant, celluloid, Agriculture Fair, Pope County, Greenwood, Minn, 1899, diecut, multicolored horse heads, white ground, black lettering, inserted at top by red, white, and blue striped fabric bow, reverse has celluloid insert **25.00**

Pinback button, Nebraska Seed Co., multicolored, "Seeds that Grow" .. **200.00**

Print, Garden of Allah, Maxfield Parrish, House of Art edition, 1918........... **500.00**

Rack, metal, well used **10.00**

Shears, long wooden handle, wear ... **25.00**

Shovel, wooden handle, well used **8.00**

Tumbler, 3-1/4" d, 3-1/2" h, glass, maroon-red image of Miss Dairylea scurrying while holding pail and spade, 1950s
.... **15.00**

Watering can

Brass, 9-1/2" l, 4-3/8" h, few small dents
.... **8.00**

Metal, 12" h, painted black, orig sprinkler attachment...................................... **25.00**

Porcelain, 8-1/2" h, painted flowers **17.50**

Tin, 9" h, sprinkler attachment missing
.... **25.00**

Toleware, 9-3/4" d base, 16" h, some rust and surface abrasion.................... **115.00**

Wheelbarrow, wooden, removable sides, wear **150.00**

Gasoline Collectibles

History: The selling of gasoline has come full circle. The general store, livery stable, and blacksmith were the first to sell gasoline. Gas stations, so prevalent from the 1930s to the 1960s, have almost disappeared, partially due to the 1973 gas crises. The loss of independently owned stations is doubly felt because they also were centers for automobile repair. Today gas sales at mini-markets are common.

The abolition of credit cards by ARCO marked another shift, as did price reduction for cash sales by other brands. The growing numbers of "pay-at-the-pump" stations will also influence the marketplace. Elimination of free maps, promotional trinkets, and other advertising material already is a factor. As more and more stores in shopping centers sell oil, parts, and other related automobile products, it is doubtful if the gasoline station will ever recover its past position.

Collecting Hints: There still is plenty of material stored in old garages; try to find cooperative owners. If your budget is modest, concentrate on paper ephemera, such as maps. Regional items will bring slightly more in their area of origin.

Reproduction Alert: Small advertising signs and pump globes have been extensively reproduced.

Ink blotter, Sunoco Oil, Nu-Blue Sunoco, Donald Duck illus, unused, 1940s, 4" x 7", **$40**.

Ashtray, Esso, clear glass, red and blue dealer inscription, 1950s, 4-1/4" sq **38.00**

Banner

8" l, Texaco Havoline, plastic.......... **65.00**

36-1/2" h, 60" h, Sunoco Winter Oil and Grease, heavy cloth, Mickey Mouse illus, © Walt Disney 1939...................... **650.00**

Blotter, Nu-Blue Sunoco Gas, Donald Duck, M. C. Sparks & Son, Ronton, OH, 1948, 4" x 7".. **40.00**

Book, *Gould Storage Battery Co.*, NY, NY, 1921, 54 pgs, 6" x 9"...................... **15.00**

Booklet, *Cities Service Refining*, Lake Charles, LA, 1944, spiral bound, 26 black and white photographs of construction progress, bird's eye views, 27 pgs, 8-1/4" x 10-1/4" **48.00**

Car attachment, Shell Oil, 3-3/4" x 5-1/2" metal domed image of Shell symbol, three colorful International Code Flags, late 1930s.................................... **190.00**

Catalog

Buick Motor Division, Flint, MI, 1953, 16 pgs, 11" x 13-1/2", color illus of 1953 Buick Roadmaster, Skylark, Estate Wagon, Buick Super, 56C Super ... **20.00**

Chrysler Motors Corp., Detroit, MI, 1954, 30 pgs, 6-1/2" x 12", color illus of 1954 Belvedere, convertible coupe, sports coupe, etc....................................... **15.00**

Cushman Motor Works, Lincoln, NE, 1949, two pgs, 8-1/2" x 11", Cushman Model 64 and 64A, cuts of scooter and parts **32.00**

Ford Motor Co., Dearborn, MI, 1961, 16 pgs, 11" x 14", color illus of 1962 Thunderbird **30.00**

General Motors Corp., Detroit, MI, 8 pgs, 11" x 12", Cadillac Eldorado........... **12.00**

Rootes Motors, Inc., New York, NY, c1940, 12 pgs, 7-1/2" x 10-1/2", color illus **24.00**

United Motor Service, Detroit, MI, 1955, 30 pgs, Delco Batteries, 8-1/4" x 11" **21.00**

Charm, Mobil Oil Co., Pegasus, red, plastic, 1-1/2" l, 1" h **15.00**

Child's hat, Texaco Fire Chief, bull horn speaker system, battery operated **135.00**

Coaster/ashtray, Mobil Safe Driving Award, 1953, metal, shield logo, 4" dia **25.00**

Coffee cup, milk glass

Cities Service, Burl S. Watson **38.00**

Sinclair Oil, Sinclair Dinosaur on each side **15.00**

Stark Oil, Phillips 66, logo on both sides of cup... **12.00**

Coloring book, Esso Happy Motoring, unused... **25.00**

Dashboard memo, Harry's Auto Service, Auto Repairing of All Kinds, Bernard, OH, use to record dates, car servicing info **55.00**

Decal sheet, Esso, 3-1/2" x 3-1/2", white, red letters, beige ground, Palm Brothers, Decalomania Co., NY, c1950 .... **3.00**

Doll, Texaco Cheerleader, 11-1/2" h, 1960s, MIB... **125.00**

Employee badge, Goodyear - Akron, initials, wingfoot logo, silver with blue enamel, 1" x 1/2" **20.00**

Fan, 10-1/2" l, 7-5/8" w, Sinclair Opaline Motor Oil, adv on back.................... **75.00**

Gas pump, electric, orig hose, nozzle missing, 16" w, 10" d, 36" h **325.00**

Good luck penny, 1953, Souvenir of Amoco Dealer Convention, 1953 penny....... **6.50**

Key chain, flicker

Amoco, As You Travel Ask Us, back side has place for name and address with please return to **12.00**

Chevron Supreme, Love That Chevron Supreme, man running towards gas pump, kissing it and throwing his arms around pump, back reads Chevron Supreme Gasoline Now At Calso Stations, Vari-Vue, USA................... **24.00**

Key ring

Gulf, Second Triangle Gulf Service Station, Miami, FL, round, orig plastic bag, 1960s **5.00**

Phillips 66 Philgas, plastic with metal holder.. **8.00**

Kit, Amoco Word Building Contest, 4-1/4" x 8-3/4", black and white envelope, instruction and blank folder, perforated card spelling "American Oil Company," contest dated Jan. 31, 1934, unused **20.00**

Lighter, flat style, Atlantic logo one side, Imperial shield reverse, made by Penguin **15.00**

License plate attachment, Sunoco, 1940 .... **100.00**

Magazine, The Autocar, London, Diamond Jubilee, 1955, 162 pgs, 8-1/2" x 11-1/2" **10.00**

Measuring can, Be-Sure Gasoline, side pouring spout **12.00**

Measuring stick, Southern, used to measure in tank, numbered on four sides, 55" l.. **25.00**

Mechanical pencil, Walter's Service Station, Mobil pegasus logo on top of cream-color pencil **15.00**

Neon sign, 48-1/2" l, 23" h, Chevrolet Corvette Approved Service....... **1,000.00**

Oil cans, left to right: Tru-Test Household Lubricant Oil, yellow, red, and black can; Texaco Home Lubricant, black and red label with cottage and trees; Bardahl Top Oil Valve Lubricant, black and green label, red block says "World's No. 1 Seller," **each $10**.

Oil cans, left: WOW Motor Oil, Waverly Oil Works, 100% Pure Pennsylvania, red, white, and blue paper label, **$25**; Atlantic Quality Motor Oil, litho tin, orange, white, and blue, considerable rust, **$5**

Oil can

D-A Speed Sport Oil, yellow full quart with old cars, checkered flags logo, "Racing Division," D-A Lubricant, Indianapolis, Indiana, C9+ **50.00**

Farmers Pride Household Oil, Hulman Co., lead spout, 5-3/4" x 2-1/8" x 1-1/4" oval base..................................... **365.00**

Paper cup, Gulf Oil, We Enjoy Serving You - Drop In Again **4.00**

Paperweight, American Oil Products, Somerville, Mass, "We Want To Do Business With The Man On The Other Side," domed glass with silvered reverse, red on white design of elephant within circular title, 1920s, 3" d **55.00**

Patch, cloth, Esso, 6" l, 4" w **24.00**

Pencil, lead, unused

Gulf Oil **5.00**

Marathon Gasoline - Lubricants, Best in the Long Run, Compliments of Your Marathon Dealer **5.00**

Pin

Phillips 66, 10-year pin, 10k gold, screw back, maker's mark **45.00**

Pure Safe Driver Pin, two years, Be Sure with Pure, screw back **35.00**

Shell, red cloisonné, gold Shell emblem, marked "NBG, #78, Tuckey S.F.," 1920s **95.00**

Sun Oil Company Service Pin, 15 years, 14k gold **75.00**

Pinback button

7/8" d, *I'm The Guy That Put The Gas In Gasoline,* white text on red, from 1912 cigarette series, back paper with product name "Clix," c1912 .... **18.00**

1" d, *Derby Refining Co.*, Petroleum Products, star, red, white, and blue, c1930 .... **15.00**

1" d, *Socony Motor Gasoline,* red, white, and blue **15.00**

1-1/4" d, *Keystone Grease World's Greatest Lubricant,* red and white text, red keystone design, dark blue ground, c1920 .... **18.00**

Pocket calendar, 1957, Esso, You get Something MORE at Your Happy Motoring Store **5.00**

Postcard, Firestone Tire & Rubber Company, 1933, R.R. Donnelly & Sons, Chicago, The Firestone Singing Color Fountain and Multiplane Shadow Sign, A Century of Progress **12.00**

Pump sign, Texaco Sky Chief, 12" x 18", porcelain, dated 3/11/62 .... **195.00**

Puzzle, Sohio Ethyl Gasoline, Mickey Mouse, plastic, 1950s, adv on back **72.00**

Radio, figural

FS Super Lube Oil Can, unused **40.00**

Marathon Ultra-D SW-40, oil can shape **45.00**

Sign, litho tin, Fire Chief Gasoline, Texaco, large red fireman's helmet in center, Texaco logo, some rust around hanging holes, **$185**.

Sign, porcelain, "Oilzum Motor Oils and Lubricants," orange, black, and white, 12" d, **$195**.

Salt and pepper shakers, pr, Texaco, figural gas pumps, some crazing to decals **50.00**

Score book, Amoco Gin Rummy Score and Bridge Score, 42 sheets, adv, unused **20.00**

Shirt, Texaco **45.00**

Sign

Esso Elephant Kerosene, porcelain **875.00**

Fisk Tires, porcelain, 1930s **425.00**
Good Gulf Gasoline, porcelain, flange
.... **550.00**
Goodyear Service Station, Goodyear
means Goodwear, porcelain, 1920s
.... **895.00**
Sinclair Gas, porcelain **100.00**
Tape measure, Shell Oil, A. C. McLoon &
Co., metal **24.00**
Thermometer
Shell Anti-Freeze **85.00**
Sunoco, 6-3/4" h, 3-3/4" w, tin, raised
finish, diecut, emb airplane in flight, adv
below, blue and white, black lettering
.... **275.00**
Tie bar, Esso, smiling tiger's head, goldtone,
no makers' marks 20.00
Token, Shell Safe Driver Award, 1 3/8" dia,
brass, 1929, name **50.00**

Toy, Hess Truck, helicopter, motorcycle and jeep
version, MIB, $25.

Toy truck
Hess, 1989, MIB **110.00**
Texaco #7, 1930 Diamond T Tanker, red
and black, MIB **90.00**
Texaco #12, 1910 Mack Texaco Tanker,
MIB **40.00**
Texaco #17, 1919 GMC Tanker Truck
.... **25.00**
Tumbler, Sinclair Gasoline, 1916, 5-1/2" h
.... **10.00**
Visor hanger, Sohio-X-70 - Brings Your Car
Up To Standard, mileage records, metal,
orig envelope **38.00**

G. I. Joe Collectibles

History: Hasbro Manufacturing Company produced the first G.I. Joe 12-inch posable action figures in 1964. The original line consisted of one male action figure for each branch of the military service. Their outfits were styled after uniforms from World War II, the Korean Conflict, and the Vietnam Conflict.

In 1965, the first Black figure was introduced. The year 1967 saw two additions to the line—a female nurse and Talking G.I. Joe. To keep abreast of changing times, Joe received flocked hair and a beard in 1970.

The creation of the G.I. Joe Adventure Team made Joe a prodigious explorer, hunter, deep-sea diver, and astronaut, rather than just an American serviceman. Due to the Arab oil embargo in 1976, and its impact on the plastics industry, the figure was renamed Super Joe and reduced in height to eight inches. Production was halted in 1977.

In 1982, G.I. Joe staged his comeback. A few changes were made to the character line and to the way in which the figures were presented. The Great American Hero line now consists of three-and-three-quarter-inch posable plastic figures with code names that correspond to the various costumes. The new Joes deal with contemporary and science fiction villains and issues.

Collecting Hints: It is extremely important to determine the manufacturing date of any G.I. Joe doll or related figure. The ideal method takes discipline—do a point-by-point comparison with the dolls described and dated in the existing reference books. Be alert to subtle variations; you do not have a match unless all details are exactly the same. It also is helpful to learn the proper period costume for each doll variation.

Accessory pieces can be every bit as valuable as the dolls themselves. Whenever possible, accessory pieces should be accompanied by their original packaging and paper inserts.

G.I. Joe dolls and accessories were produced in the millions. Rarity is not a factor; condition is. When buying dolls or accessories as collectibles, as opposed to acquiring them for play, do not purchase any items in less than fine condition.

Accessories pack, made for sale in Spain, Hasbro, c1975
#1 .... **18.00**
#2 .... **20.00**
#3 .... **15.00**
#4 .... **12.00**

Doll, Basic Training Grunt, Hall of Fame, NRFB, $35.

Action figures and dolls

Action Man Africa Corp, complete **450.00**
Action Man Black Soldier, complete **895.00**
Action Man Canadian Mountie, complete **495.00**
Action Man French Foreign Legion, complete **450.00**
Action Man German Tanker, complete **425.00**
Action Man Luffwaffe, complete ... **425.00**
Action Man Red Devil, complete .. **495.00**
Action Man SAS Key Figure, complete **395.00**
Action Man SAS Parachute Attack, complete **495.00**
Action Man SAS Underwater Attack, complete **425.00**
Action Man Soldier, 30th Anniversary **150.00**
Action Man Underwater Explorer, complete **425.00**
Action Marine, 12" h, 1964-1994, NRFB **150.00**
Action Marine Medic, equipment . **300.00**
Action Marine, parade dress uniform **150.00**

Action Navy Attack, orange vest . **195.00**
Action MP, incomplete uniform **195.00**
Action Navy, deep sea diver **295.00**
Action Navy, shore patrol **295.00**
Action Pilot, talking, complete **695.00**
Action Sailor, talking, complete **595.00**
Action Soldier, combat field jacket and gear **225.00**
Action Soldier of the World, British Commando **500.00**
Action Soldier of the World, Japanese Imperial Soldier, no medal, no bayonet **550.00**
Action Soldier, orig box, some paperwork **300.00**
Action Soldier, talking, red head .. **175.00**
Action Soldier, West Point Cadet . **275.00**
Adventure Team Commander, 12" h, talking **135.00**
Airborne Military Police, Kay-Bee Exclusive **50.00**
Air Adventurer, 1976, MIP **200.00**
Air Cadet, complete, painted head **595.00**
Arctic Joe Colton, mail order, 12" h **200.00**
A.T.A.A. Adventurer, Kung Fu grip, orig box **225.00**
Australian Jungle Fighter, complete **495.00**
Baroness, 1984, loose **45.00**
Big Red One, D-Day Salute Figure, unfolding decorating collectors box **25.00**
Black Adventurer, life-like body, Kung Fu grip, 1976 .... **125.00**
Bulletman, 1976 .... **75.00**
British 8th Army, 12" h, NRFB **40.00**
British Gunner, 12" h, NRFB **40.00**
Capture of the Pygmy Gorilla, complete **395.00**
Challenge at Hawk River **15.00**
Classic, Historical Commanders Edition, #4, General Colin Powell, MIB **50.00**
Cobra Commander, 1992, first issue, Japanese, 3" h, MOC, C-9 .... **40.00**
Cobra Officer, 1983, 3" h, carded, C-6 .... **80.00**
Cobra, straight arm, 1982, 3" h, carded, C-7.5 .... **140.00**
Combat Engineer, complete **995.00**
Construction Jack Hammer, complete **895.00**
Cover Girl, 1983, loose **18.00**
Crash Crew Fire Fighter, complete **475.00**
Croc Master, 1987, 3" h, MOC, C-8 **30.00**
Danger of the Depths, complete . **495.00**
Deep Freeze, complete, painted head **495.00**
Deep Sea Diver, complete, painted head **550.00**
Duke, 1983, loose **20.00**
Eagle Eye Black Commando, 1976, MIP **250.00**

Eight Ropes of Danger, complete **495.00**
Falcon, 1987, loose **8.00**
Fantastic Freefall, complete.......... **495.00**
Fighter Pilot, complete, painted head
.... **850.00**
French Resistance Fighter............ **495.00**
German Fallschrimjager Sniper, 12" h,
NRFB **40.00**
German Storm Trooper, complete **550.00**
G. I. Joe, 50th Anniversary, WWII limited
commemorative, Target exclusive, MIB
.... **40.00**
Green Beret, all accessories **495.00**
Heavy Weapons, complete, painted head
.... **550.00**
Hidden Missile Recovery, complete
.... **395.00**
Hurricane Spotter, complete......... **375.00**
Iceberg, 1986, loose **6.00**
Intruder Commander, 1976, MIP.. **150.00**
Intruder Warrior, 1976, MIP **175.00**
Japanese Imperial Soldier, complete
.... **695.00**
Land Adventurer, 1976, MIP......... **180.00**
Landing Signal Officer, complete . **475.00**
Man of Action, life-like body, Kung Fu
grip, 1974 .... **75.00**

G.I. Joe Action Marine, lunch box, metal, **$35**.

Marine, Masterpiece Edition, Vol. III,
black hair, camouflage fatigues, large
cardboard box with illus G. I. Joe book,
1996, NRFB **85.00**
Marine Raider, 12" h **16.00**
Mike Powers/Atomic Man, atomic
flashing eye, arm spins hand-held
helicopter, 1975 .... **75.00**
Military Police, complete **495.00**
Navajo Code Talker, 12" h **36.00**
Navy Attack, yellow life jacket, complete
.... **795.00**
Navy Seal, FAO, 12" h **200.00**
Pilot, blond, Masterpiece **100.00**
Police State Trooper, complete .. **1,495.00**

Range Viper, 1990, 3" h, MOC, C-9 **20.00**
Recsue Diver, complete **850.00**
Roadblock, 1984, loose **15.00**
Russian Soldier, complete............ **550.00**
Russian Spetznaz Solider, 12" h, NRFB
.... **40.00**
Sailor, black, Masterpiece **75.00**
Scarlett, 1992, loose, C-8.5........... **24.00**
Scramble Pilot, al accessories, painted
head figure................................... **595.00**
Sea Adventurer, clothing, shoulder
holster, pistol, 1970 .... **85.00**
Set, 1994, pilot, Marine, Navy, Soldier, 3-
1/4" h, MIB.................................... **100.00**
Short Fuse, 1992, loose................. **20.00**
Smoke Jumper **375.00**
Sneak Peek, 1987, 3" h, MOC, C-8 **18.00**
Snow Job, 1983, loose **18.00**
Soldier, black, painted black hair, green
fatigues, green plastic cap, black boots,
metal tags, Counter-Intelligence Manual,
Hasbro, 1964, slight age discoloration to
box **500.00**
Spetznaz Sniper, 12" h, NRFB........ **40.00**
Talking Adventure Team Black
Commander, 1973, MIP **600.00**
Thunder, 1984, loose..................... **10.00**
US Tank Commander, 12" h, NRFB **40.00**
Vietnam Veterans Memorial, three 12"
poseable figures with stand........... **50.00**
West Point Cadet, complete, painted
head **550.00**
White Tiger Hunt, complete **395.00**
Coloring book, 48 pgs, Spanish text, 1989
.... **15.00**
Foot locker, 20th Anniversary **200.00**
Gear, Classic Collection
Mission gear, M-60 gunner's pit, MOC
.... **15.00**
US Coast Guard, MIB..................... **30.00**
Kite, 42" l, keel-style, plastic, 1980s, sealed
in orig package............................... **20.00**
Outfit
Action Soldier, scuba bottom, orig card,
some tape..................................... **175.00**
A. T. Dangerous Mission, action outfit,
MOC... **50.00**
A. T. Jungle Ordeal, MOC **50.00**
Marine Dress Parade Set, #7710, 1964
.... **565.00**
Pilot Scramble Set, #7807l 1965.. **450.00**
Playset, Atomic Man Secret Outpost, good
box **85.00**
Ring, 30th Anniversary, reddish-pink stone
.... **400.00**
Set, Home for the Holidays, Wal-Mart **50.00**
Thermos, Aladdin, plastic cup, 1985... **8.00**
Vehicle
Adventure Team Vehicle Set, #7005,
1970, NRFB.................................. **350.00**
Desert Patrol Attack Jeep Set, #8030,
1967 .... **3,350.00**

Doll, GI Jane, US Army Helicopter Pilot, NRFB, **$35**.

Fight for Survival Set, Polar Explorer,
#7982, 1969................................. **650.00**
Official Sea Sled and Frogman Set,
#8050, 1966................................. **600.00**
Space Capsule, Convention Exclusive
.... **200.00**
Weapon
Automatic rifle, with clip, 1960s, 5-3/4" l
.... **5.00**
Bayonet.. **15.00**
Flare pistol **2.00**
M-16... **30.00**
Night stick.................................... **20.00**
Rifle, 1960s, 7-1/4" l.......................... **5.00**
WWII weapons pack for 12" figures **12.00**

Golf Collectibles

History: Golf has been played in Scotland since the 15th century, and existing documents indicate golf was played in America before the Revolution. However, it was played primarily by "gentry" until the less expensive and more durable "guttie" ball was introduced in 1848. This development led to increased participation and play spread to England and other countries, especially where Scottish immigrants settled. The great popularity of golf began about 1890 in both England and the United States.

Collecting Hints: Condition is becoming more important as collectors' sophistication and knowledge grow. The newer the item, the better the condition should be.

It is extremely rare to find a club or ball made before 1800; in fact, any equipment made before 1850 is scarce. Few books on the subject were published before 1857.

Most equipment made after 1895 is quite readily available. Common items, such as scorecards, ball markers, golf pencils, and bag tags, have negligible value. Some modern equipment, particularly from the years between 1950 and 1965, is in demand, but primarily to use for actual play rather than to collect or display.

The very old material is generally found in Scotland and England, unless items were brought to America early in this century. Christie's, Sotheby's, and Phillips' each hold several major auctions of golf collectibles every year in London, Edinburgh, and Chester. Golf collectible sales often coincide with the British Open Championship each July. Although the English market is more established, the American market is growing rapidly, and auctions of golf items and memorabilia now are held in the United States as well as overseas.

The price of golf clubs escalated tremendously in the 1970s but stabilized in more recent years. For many years golf book prices remained static, but they rose dramatically in the 1980s. Art prints, drawings, etchings, etc., have not seen dramatic changes in value, but pottery, china, glass, and other secondary items, especially those by Royal Doulton, have attracted premium prices.

Ashtray, 6" d, 1-1/4" h, crystal, silver deposit dec of golfer, silvered rim............... **90.00**
Ball
Advertising, imprinted company logo, used **2.00**
Haskell, bramble, patent 1899....... **50.00**
Lynx, rubber core **18.00**
Mitchell, Manchester, gutty **60.00**
Spring Vale Hawk, bramble **35.00**
Book
Arnold Palmer-A Personal Journal, Thos. Hauser, 1994, 1st ed., 192 pgs, photos, dj... **18.00**
Golf-A New Approach, Lloyd Mangrum, Whittlesey House, 1949, 127 pgs, illus of golf swings **10.00**

Caddie ID button, yellow ground, red, white, and black lettering, Rock Manor Golf Club, #113, **$15.**

Golf In The Sun All Year Round, Robert H. K. Browning, 1931 .... **38.00**
Golf, The History of An Obsession, David Stirk, Price-Stern Sloan, 1987, 1st ed., 190 illus, dj **12.00**
How To Play Your Best Golf All The Time, Tommy Armor, Simon & Schuster, 1953, 151 pgs **10.00**
Secrets of Accurate Putting and Chipping, Phil Galvano, c1957 .... **4.50**
Understanding Golf, John Gordon, 1926. .... **40.00**

Club

Burke, juvenile, mashie, wood shaft **30.00**
Burr Key Bilt, hickory shaft, hand forged, chrome coated, leather grips, 1920s, Niblick; Mashie Niblick, Mashie, Mid Iron, set of four **250.00**

C. S. Butchart, scare-head driver, stamped shaft **48.00**
E Foord Special Mashie Niblick, straight hickory shaft, initials "C.A.W." added to back of clubhead, well used leather grip, loose at bottom, chrome on face worn **75.00**
Fleetwood, Draper Maynard Co., Plymouth, NH, #4, stainless steel... **25.00**
Fleetwood, Draper Maynard Co., Plymouth, NH, #10 .... **25.00**
Hagen, iron-man sand wedge, wood shaft **190.00**
L Brownlee Special, 33-1/4" l wooden shaft **125.00**
McGregor, Tourney 693W driver, c1953, steel shaft **150.00**
Meadowlark, wood shaft, brass faceplate stamped "Brassie" **60.00**
Morristown iron, 33" l wood handle, wrapped in black tape part way, stamped "Morristown" on face of head **175.00**
Pro Made, H16, Heather Downs, Masie Niblick, 33-1/2" l wood shaft, other markings **145.00**
Scioto, leather-wrapped handles, wood heads, 40" l hickory wood shafts, stamped center mounted aluminum sole plate "Driver" and "Brassie," some wear, pr **225.00**
Spaulding, Cash-in Putter, steel shaft **65.00**
T. Stewart St. Andrews Mashie Niblick, hand forged hickory shaft, made in Scotland, initials "EB" etched into club face, leather grip repaired, additional rubber wrap at top **85.00**
Wilson, wedge, staff model, c1959, steel shaft.. **60.00**

Golf-themed teapot, ceramic, multicolored golfing theme, base reads "A Round Of Golf," clock face in chimney, gold trim, **$25.**

Jardinière

    Basketweave, white ground, brown speckles **24.00**
    Dripping color, 10" h, 11" d, used, some glaze chips, etc. **165.00**

Lamp, baluster, blue, 22" h **125.00**

Pitcher

    6" h, 60-3/4" w, #RG-28, pink, braided handle **55.00**
    18-1/2" h, handle, blended agate glaze, #408 .... **55.00**

Planter, Oriental girl, green blouse, yellow hat, $24

Pitcher and bowl set, 6" h pitcher, 7-1/2" d bowl, yellow glaze, raised brown and gold leaves and flowers, incised Haeger #934, pitcher stamped Royal Haeger, number not legible **35.00**

Planter

    Blue, 18" l, 8" w **55.00**
    Fawn, green, 9" l, 7-3/4" h, mkd "Royal Haeger, R-1913" **25.00**
    Green, 11" h, 7-1/2" w, 3-1/2" h **20.00**
    Horse **145.00**
    Hounddog Shoes, white, mkd "Hounddog Shoes" **55.00**
    Koala Bear, Bennington Brown Foam **45.00**
    Lion, Bennington Brown Foam, slight nick **45.00**
    Madonna and Cherub, #3264, blue, orig paper label, 4-1/2" w, 11" h **35.00**
    Melon ribbed, light green, 9" l, 3-3/4" **18.00**
    Sunbonnet Girls, 9" w, girls, yellow, c1946, 9" w **130.00**

Serving dish, 16", Gold Tweed, mkd "Royal Haeger" **32.00**

Store display, 6-1/2" l, figural green garden house, plaque "Gardenhouse by Haeger," orig label **24.00**

Television lamp

    Boxer dog, wood block base **150.00**
    Cocker spaniel, 6" x 10" x 10" **130.00**
    Horse, 12" **325.00**
    Leaping deer, Chestnut style, #160, orig tag "Phil-Mar Corp, Cleveland 3, Ohio" **65.00**
    Mother and young antelope, brown agate, #160 .... **65.00**
    Panther, high gloss chartreuse and yellow, 20" l **20.00**

Vase

    7" h, orange peel, cylindrical, imp mark, 1976 .... **125.00**
    7" h, 6-1/2" d, fluted, green **30.00**
    7" h, 8" w, Art Deco style, blended light pearl gray to darker pearl gray **25.00**
    8" h, mottled white and dusty rose pink glaze, 1930s **60.00**
    10" h, #R1919, white, concentric black, green, and orchid rings around base, mkd "Royal Haeger USA R1919" .. **25.00**
    10-1/4" h, 7-3/4" d, matte green sponge, Arts & Crafts style design, mkd "Haeger USA 4998" **225.00**
    11" h, Madonna with Cherub, #3264, blue, orig sticker **35.00**
    12" h, art deco-style, pale blue, leaf, mkd "Royal Haeger, made in USA" **42.00**
    12" h, baluster, peacock glaze, #4030 .... **150.00**
    12-3/4" h, 4" d, deco-style, gray-green textured surface............................. **30.00**
    13" h, lime peel, designed by Alrun Guest, 1976, mkd "Royal Haeger #4170" **225.00**
    14" h, lily, designed by E. Royal Hickman, blues, greens, and pinks, c1935 . **100.00**
    14-1/2" h, 9" d, ivory, small chip on base **30.00**
    16" h, cobra, white **135.00**
    17" h, 13-1/2" w, glossy black, orig paper label... **175.00**
    22" h, cream **265.00**

Wall pocket, fish, blue **40.00**

Hall China

History: Hall China Company was formed as a result of the dissolution of the East Liverpool Potteries Company. Robert Hall, a partner in the merger, died within months of establishing the new company. Robert T. Hall, his son, took over.

At first the company produced the same semi-porcelain dinnerware and toiletware that was being made at the other potteries in East Liverpool, Ohio. Robert T. Hall began experiments to duplicate an ancient Chinese one-fire process that would produce a non-crazing vitrified china, with body and glaze fired at the same time. He succeeded in 1911 and Hall products have been made that way ever since.

Hall's basic products—hotel and restaurant institutional ware—are sold to the trade only. However, the firm also has produced many retail and premium lines, e.g. Autumn Leaf for Jewel Tea and Blue Bouquet for the Standard Coffee Co. of New Orleans. A popular line is the gold-decorated teapots that were introduced for retail sale in 1920. In 1931 kitchenware was introduced, soon followed by dinnerware. These lines were made in both solid colors and with decals for retail and premium sales.

Collecting Hints: Hall China Company identified many of its patterns by name, but some of these are being gradually changed by dealers. A good example is the Silhouette pattern, which is also known as Taverne. Many shapes are also referred to by more than one name, i.e., Radiance is also known as Sunshine, Terrace as Stepdown, and Pert as Sani-Grid.

Because of their high quality, most Hall China pieces are still in wonderful condition. There is no reason to pay full price for imperfect pieces.

Mixing bowl, medium, Autumn Leaf pattern, gold backstamp, 8-3/4" d, $45.

Autumn Leaf pattern, ball shape jug, $60, resting on cake plate, $35.

Autumn Leaf pattern, coffee pot, $60.

Dinnerware patterns

Autumn Leaf

Premium for the Jewel Tea Company. Produced 1933 until 1978. Other companies made matching fabric, metal, glass, and plastic accessories.

Baker, two pint, 6-1/4" d 175.00
Bean pot, two handles 180.00
Berry bowl, 5-1/2" d 5.00
Butter dish, cov, 1 lb 255.00
Coffeepot, cov, rayed, 8 cup, gold double circle mark "Tested and approved by Mary Dunbar, Jewell Homemaker's Institute" 60.00
Cookie jar, cov 175.00
Creamer and sugar, cov, ruffled-D 35.00
Cream soup 35.00
Cup and saucer, St. Denis 50.00

Custard cup	24.50
Dinner plate, 9" d	6.50
Gravy boat	20.00
Hot pad, tin back, 7-1/4"	35.00
Jug, ball	60.00

Mixing bowl

7-1/2" x 4"	35.00
8-3/4" x 4-1/2"	45.00
Platter, 9" x 5-1/2"	25.00
Range salt and pepper shakers, pr	35.00
Salt and pepper shakers, pr	15.00
Serving tray, metal	55.00
Stack Set, three stacking containers, one lid	150.00
Teapot, cov, Aladdin, 6-1/2" h	95.00

Tumbler, glass, frosted

3-3/4" h	40.00
5-1/2" h	22.00
Vase	210.00
Vegetable bowl, oval, divided	175.00

Teapot, Boston shape, dresden blue, gold decoration, 5" h, $24.

Crocus

Dinnerware pattern produced during the 1930s. This decal has multicolored stylized crocuses and green and black leaves. It is also found on a wide array of kitchenware shapes.

Bowl, Radiance

6-1/8" d, 3" h	45.00
7" d	30.00
9" d	45.00
Bread and butter plate, 7-1/4" d	12.00
Cake plate	25.00
Casserole, cov	60.00
Cereal bowl, 6" d	15.00
Coffeepot, Terrace	110.00
Dinner plate	38.50
Gravy boat	32.00
Jug, ball	195.00
Luncheon plate, 9" d	15.00
Salad plate, 8-1/4" d	12.00
Platter, 13-1/4" l	35.00
Salt and pepper shakers, pr, teardrop shape	45.00
Soup tureen	395.00
Teapot, banded	175.00
Tidbit, three tier	50.00

Orange Poppy

Premium for the Great American Tea Company. Introduced in 1933 and discontinued in the 1950s. Dinnerware was made in the C-style shape. Metal accessories are available, though scarce.

Bean pot	115.00
Cake plate	20.00
Casserole, 8" l, oval	65.00
Coffee canister	325.00
Coffeepot	80.00
Custard	6.00
Hot plate, 9-1/2" d	36.00
Platter, 13" l	18.00
Salad bowl	12.00
Salt and pepper shakers, pr, handled	35.00
Sugar, Great American mark	30.00
Teapot, Boston	350.00
Vegetable bowl, round	25.00

Pastel Morning Glory

Dinnerware line produced in the late 1930s and readily found in northern Michigan, Wisconsin, and Minnesota. Design consists of large pink morning glories surrounded by green leaves and small blue flowers on white ground. The pattern was also used on kitchenware items.

Bread and butter plate, 6" d	6.00
Casserole, cov	48.00
Cereal bowl, 6" d	20.00
Cup and saucer	18.50
Custard	15.00
Dinner plate, 10" d	25.00
Drip jar, ink	20.00
Fruit bowl, 5-1/2" d	9.00
Gravy boat	25.00
Jug, ball, pink	165.00
Luncheon plate, 9" d	12.00
Pie baker	30.00
Salad plate, 8-1/4" d	9.00

Mixing bowl set, graduated, Poppy pattern, $120.

Red Dot (a.k.a. Eggshell Polka Dot)

This pattern is found on the Eggshell Buffet Service. Red is the most commonly found Dot color, but the pattern was also produced in blue, green, and orange.

Baker, 13-1/2" l, fish-shape	45.00
Bean pot, small, #1	95.00

Bowl, 8-1/2" d.. 25.00
Casserole, cov, oval or round 40.00
Cocette, 4" d, handle 25.00
Drip jar, tab handle, #1188.................. 45.00
Jug, cov, #2 or #4 .... 125.00
Mustard, cov, slotted lid 95.00
Onion soup, cov................................... 45.00
Pitcher, Baron 95.00
Range shakers, salt, pepper, flour, sugar
.... 150.00
Shirred egg dish, 6-1/2" d 25.00
Tom and Jerry punch bowl set, bowl and
  12 mugs.. 250.00

Red Poppy

Premium for Grand Union Tea Company. Produced from mid-1930s until mid-1950s. Complete line of D-style dinnerware and kitchenware in various forms. The design features red poppies and black leaves on a white background. Glass, metal, wood, and cloth accessories were also marketed.

Bowl... 10.00
Cereal bowl, 6" d 18.50
Coffeepot, Daniel, metal dropper 40.00
Cup and saucer 15.00
Custard cup, Radiance........................ 17.50
Dinner plate, 10" d 17.50
Drip jar 30.00
Salt and pepper shakers, pr, egg shape
.... 45.00
Soup plate, flat 20.00
Stack set 75.00

Taverne

This popular pattern was used as a premium for Hellick's Coffee in Pennsylvania. Other mediums are found with this pattern.

Bowl, medallion
  6" d.. 20.00
  7" d.. 25.00
Casserole, medallion............................ 75.00
Coffeepot, 10 cup, metal drip, gold mark
.... 115.00
Drip jar, cov.. 40.00
French baker, 8" d 30.00
Iced tea glass 50.00
Jug, #3.. 45.00
Leftover, cov
  4" x 8" 70.00
  8" x 8" 85.00
Pretzel jar, cov 165.00
Salad bowl, 9" d.................................. 25.00
Salt and pepper shakers, pr, five-band
.... 75.00
Saucer... 10.00

Kitchenware Patterns

Blue Garden/Blue Blossom

This 1939 pattern is a silk-screen decal on a cobalt blue glaze. Hall claims that this was the first time that cobalt blue had been used successfully for vitrified kitchen cooking items.

Batter jar 250.00
Butter, cov, Radiance........................ 475.00

Casserole, cov, sundial handle, cobalt
  blue, mkd "#2068"........................... 50.00
Cookie jar, cov 375.00
Jug, loop handle................................ 245.00
Leftover, loop handle 195.00
Mixing bowl, 6" d 85.00
Mixing bowl, 7-1/2" d, thick rim.......... 60.00
Range shakers, handle...................... 90.00
Refrigerator bowl, cov, loop handle 155.00
Syrup pitcher, banded 395.00

Batter pitcher, Chinese Red, gold mark, $75.

Chinese Red

This pattern name refers to the bright red color found on various shapes of solid-colored kitchenware. Chinese red is the most commonly found color.

Ashtray, triangular.............................. 30.00
Batter bowl, Five Band...................... 75.00
Bean pot, #5...................................... 155.00
Casserole, cov, 8-1/5" d, thick rim, mkd
  "Hall's Superior Quality Kitchenware
  Made in USA" 60.00
Creamer and sugar, cov, Morning..... 95.00
Drip jar, open, #1188.......................... 35.00
Jug, donut, 1-1/2 quarts, 6-7/8" h, mkd
  "Hall's Superior Quality Kitchenware
  Made in USA" 185.00
Leftover, Zephyr................................ 165.00
Pretzel jar, cov 125.00
Ramekin 50.00
Teapot, streamline............................ 275.00
Water bottle, Zephyr.......................... 90.00

Golden Glo

Casserole, three qt 30.00
Creamer, 4-7/8" h................................ 30.00
Sugar, 2-1/4" h 30.00

Rose White

Kitchenware pattern with Hi-White body and pink rose decal.

Bean pot, cov.................................... 115.00
Bowl.. 10.00
Casserole, cov, tab handles............... 27.50
Jug, 7-1/2" h, Perk 40.00
Pitcher, small 30.00
Salt and pepper shakers, pr 35.00

Wild Poppy (a.k.a. Poppy and Wheat)

Kitchenware line introduced in the late 1930s and sold by Macy's.

Bean pot **225.00**
Bowl, Radiance, set of four, 6", 7-1/2", 9", and 10" **140.00**
Casserole, cov, round, #76 .... **110.00**
Coffee canister, cov, 7-7/8" h, mkd "Hall's Superior Quality Kitchenware Made in USA" **250.00**
Custard, Radiance **20.00**
Flour canister, cov, 7-7/8" h, mkd "Hall's Superior Quality Kitchenware Made in USA" **225.00**
Salt shaker, Radiance **80.00**

Shirred egg dish

5-1/4" d **40.00**
6" d **40.00**
Stack set, Radiance **175.00**
Sugar, handle **75.00**
Tea canister, cov, 7-7/8" h, mkd "Hall's Superior Quality Kitchenware Made in USA" **250.00**
Teapot, cov, six cups, Manhattan **400.00**
Tea tile, 6" sq **85.00**

Mixing bowl, large, Tavern pattern, black silhouettes, impressed "Hall" and gold backstamp, **$120.**

Refrigerator ware and commercial ware

Dealer sign, cobalt blue **35.00**
Game bird percolator, gold trim **100.00**
General Electric Adonis, water server
    Blue and yellow **50.00**
    Gray and yellow **50.00**
Hotpoint, leftover, rect **60.00**
Interprise Drip-O-Later, 10 cup, orig instruction book **175.00**
Jolly Green Giant, mug **15.00**
Lipton Tea, creamer **135.00**
Montgomery Ward, mixing bowl, 7" d, 3" h, blue, mkd "Made Exclusively For Montgomery Ward & Co. By The Hall China Co., Made in USA, #5121" ... **30.00**

Quartermasters Corps, sauce boat, 10" l, white, emb logo on both sides, blue circle mark "Hall, Made in USA," 1940s .. **25.00**
Spittoon, 7-1/4" d, 4-1/4" h, green ext., white int. **90.00**

Westinghouse

Bowl, blue **45.00**
Butter Dish, cov, yellow, Hercules.. **30.00**
Leftover
    Delphite **16.00**
    Yellow, Hercules **30.00**
Pitcher, cobalt blue, Art-Deco styling, 9" h
    .... **125.00**
Water Server, delphinium blue, 8-1/4" h
    .... **85.00**

Teapot, blue, streamline shape, gold mark, **$65.**

Teapots

Airflow, orange, six cups **100.00**
Aladdin, yellow, gold trim, infusor **55.00**
Albany, brown, gold trim **70.00**
Baltimore, yellow **60.00**
Basket, canary yellow, gold trim **110.00**
Boston, Dresden Blue, gold mark **95.00**
Doughnut, cobalt blue **165.00**

Globe
    Canary Yellow **80.00**
    Cobalt Blue, gold trim **225.00**
    Emerald Green, gold trim **95.00**
    Light Green, gold trim **80.00**
Hollywood, green, gold trim, four cups, wear **70.00**
Manhattan, blue **65.00**
McCormick, turquoise, two cups, emb
    .... **110.00**
Melody, maroon and gold, c1939 .... **550.00**
Morning Glory, Aladdin, infuser, mkd "Hall's Superior Quality Kitchenware, Tested and Approved by Mary Dunbar, Jewel Homemakers Institute" **160.00**
Parade, yellow, six cups **60.00**
Philadelphia, green, gold trim, c1920 **75.00**
Royal, ivory **150.00**
Sundial, yellow, safety handle **75.00**
Teamster, double spout, yellow and gold
    .... **110.00**
Twin Spout, emerald green **80.00**
Windshield, gold dot dec, gold label **65.00**

Handkerchiefs

History: The world has not lost its interest in the handkerchief, even after more than a half-century has passed since the invention of the paper tissue. In the first half of the 20th century, department stores devoted hundreds of square feet of display cases full of handkerchiefs. Today, thousands of those vintage hankies are offered each day on Internet auctions, as well as in basket after basket in flea market and antique malls.

Handkerchiefs were designed for much more than just wiping noses and brows. Decorative lace and embroidered ones were made as wedding keepsakes. Printed ones celebrated everything imaginable: cartoon characters, nursery rhymes, political causes, and souvenirs of every major city or country across the globe.

Handkerchiefs are being bought up for several reasons. Collecting has become easier, with the wide variety offered on the Internet. Those who recognize high-quality workmanship in embroidery and lacemaking are beginning to snap up the truly fine works of art dating from the 19th century. Finally, crafty types are recognizing old handkerchiefs to be a wonderful source of fine quality linen and cotton, the raw materials for endless doll dresses, quilts, and other fiber arts.

The handkerchiefs bringing the highest prices at auction are the very old printed ones with stories to tell through great colorfully printed designs. Excellent condition is necessary to draw bidders over the $200 mark.

Designer handkerchiefs of the 1940s to 1960s are gaining notice, and dozens are appearing on the Internet. Only the most innovative designs with the wittiest personalities—dancing zebras, playful animals and figures, great graphic souvenir handkerchiefs of hot tourist scenes like San Francisco, New York and Los Angeles—are bringing prices of from $20 to $50. Because the handful of collectors are cherry picking the best designs in the best condition, it is too soon to tell if the name of the designer, such as Tammis Keefe or Carl Tait, or the superb graphics are the draw.

Designers like Tammis Keefe, Pat Pritchard, Faith Austin, and Carl Tait were unbelievably prolific. No comprehensive list has surfaced, but a review of handkerchiefs offered on the Internet show Tammis Keefe alone produced more than 20 series: Christmas, Easter, Valentines Day, souvenir cities, florals, geometrics, witty animal scenes, and exotic harem designs. Perhaps a dozen different designs, each produced in up to a half dozen color combinations, were produced in each series. Although Tammis Keefe designed handkerchiefs for a relatively brief period, from 1944 until her death in 1960, the thousands of Keefe designs should accommodate many more collectors before prices really skyrocket.

Among the lace and embroidered handkerchiefs, the 19th and early 20th century French handkerchiefs are starting to gain a bit of attention. Do your shopping in the United States for these embroidery-encrusted beauties. Handkerchiefs that sell for $100 to $300 in the U.S. bring well over a thousand in France, where their masterful handwork truly is appreciated.

Those offering the best quality early 20th century Chinese embroidered and drawn-work handkerchiefs on the Internet are wisely sticking to reserve prices well over $100. Although China is again producing brand new white-on-white embroidered and drawn-work handkerchiefs, these do not have the subtle details of scrollwork and shaping on flower petals, the heavy crusting of embroidery, and the elaborate needle lace insertions of the early examples.

Decorative embroidered monograms, especially those with highly decorated white-on-white lettering, are popular as wedding and other presents.

Collecting Hints: Collecting handkerchiefs has again become popular with collectors. Perhaps it's the affordability of vintage handkerchiefs, or their cheerful nature. Those shopping for handkerchiefs can still find the best bargains at garage sales, or by patiently rummaging through every basket offered at flea markets and antique malls. For collectors of centuries-old, high-end handkerchiefs, Phillips auction house in London offers three auctions of lace and vintage textiles each year. Shop by catalog or on the Internet at www.phillips-auction.com/uk.

Children's

Days of the Week, Monday, little girl and dog washing clothes, little boy and dog hanging them out, "Monday" in two corners, artist sgd "Tom Lamb," 8-3/4" x 9" **28.00**

Donald Duck, 8-1/4" sq, cotton, Donald in center about to set sail with his three nephews, mkd "© W.D.P" **30.00**

Raggedy Ann and Andy, c1920-30, Anne and Andy and animal characters playing around a maypole **228.00**

The Indian Hunter, c1900-10, children dressed as cowboys and cowgirls, shooting at cigar store Indian, 12-1/2" square... **66.00**

Designer printed

Faith Austin

Large old-fashions keys bordering center of foliage **10.00**
Small stylized owls in a tree **3.00**

Tammis Keefe

Design of whimsical lady scarecrows in a geometric cornfield **15.00**
Geometric pattern of leaves **5.00**
Stylized mermaids playing musical instruments **26.00**

Carl Tait

"Be My Valentine" motto printed in central field with large heart, cupids arrows and ribbons, surrounded by red and pink hearts 14-1/2" x 14-1/2" **36.00**
Colorful stylized zebras in bright primary colors **60.00**

Emily Whaley, Williamsburg, VA, motif on dark taupe, 13-3/8" sq, linen, machine stitched hem.................................... **20.00**

Assorted printed cotton handkerchiefs, each $5-$10.

Embroidered

11-1/2" sq, drawnwork, embroidery, filet lace, tatting, linen.......................... **24.00**
15" d, round, celadon green, white floral appliqué and embroidery **24.00**

Lace

Chinese embroidered handkerchief, late 20th C, floral design outlined in padded satin stitch, some drawn-work, scrolling embroidery.................................... **15.00**

Crochet-edged handkerchief, 1" of white crochet lace in unusual scallop design **15.00**

French embroidered handkerchief, heavily encrusted with embroidery in floral design, needle lace insertions in flower centers, 18" square...................... **185.00**

Monogram handkerchiefs

Elaborate scrolling monogram with three scrolling letters intertwined with floral design, white embroidery on white linen **25.00**

Simple monogram worked in satin stitch in bright color thread on white linen **5.00**

Souvenir and printed

Alaska, 12-3/4" sq, cotton, hand rolled edges, orig foil label "Foard Print".. **22.50**

China, Red Guard from Beijing Opera, uniform, 1965, unused **110.00**

Chicago theme, Mrs. O'Leary's cow and other city sights, Tammis Keefe **35.00**

Dayton, Ohio scenes, central airplane and sq vignettes as border, Carl Tait **38.00**

Florida, state map in center, gold with purple accents, green trimmed scalloped edge, white palm frond border design, 13" x 13-1/2", 1940s-50s................. **24.00**

Gone with the Wind theme, Scarlet in four different gowns, 13" square............ **55.00**

Hollywood Premiere scene, with klieg lights and palm trees, Tammis Keefe **25.00**

Niagara Falls, six views of falls, border of red and yellow roses, 10-1/2" square **3.75**

Strawberries, 14-1/4" d, round, scalloped edge, gray background, large red and pink strawberries tied in bunches with white ribbon **24.00**

Violets, 14" d, round, scalloped edge **24.00**

Harker Pottery

History: The Harker Company began in 1840 when Benjamin Harker, an English slater turned farmer in East Liverpool, Ohio, built a kiln and began making yellowware products from clay deposits on his land. The business was managed by members of the Harker family until the Civil War, at which time David Boyce, a brother-in-law, took over the operation. Although a Harker resumed management after the war, members of the Boyce family also assumed key roles within the firm; David G. Boyce, a grandson of David, served as president.

In 1879, the first whiteware products were introduced. The company was able to overcome severe financial problems caused by a disastrous flood in 1884. In 1931, the company moved to Chester, West Virginia, to escape repeated flooding. In 1945, Harker introduced Cameoware made by the engobe process in which a layered effect was achieved by placing a copper mask over the bisque and then sand blasting to leave the design imprint. The white rose pattern on blue ground was marketed as White Rose Carv-Kraft in Montgomery Ward stores.

In the 1960s, Harker made a Rockingham ware line which included the hound-handled pitcher and mugs. The Jeannette Glass Company purchased the Harker Company and the plant was closed in March 1972. Ohio Stoneware, Inc., utilized the plant building until it was destroyed by fire in 1975.

Collecting Hints: In 1965, Harker China had the capacity to annually produce 25 million pieces of dinnerware. Hence, there is a great deal of Harker material available at garage sales and flea markets.

Shapes and forms changed through the decades of production. Many patterns were kept in production for decades, and the same pattern was often made using different colors for the background. Patterns designed to have mass appeals include those like Colonial Lady, which was popular at "dish nights" at the movies or other businesses.

Between 1935 and 1955, Columbia Chinaware, which was organized to market Harker products in small towns across the country, promoted enamel ware, glass, and aluminum products.

Production of Cameo line at Harker began in 1940. The process was perfected by George Bauer and after the Bauer pottery closed, production began at the Harker Pottery Company. Dinnerware was added in 1941. Bauer continued to own the rights to the process and

received a royalty. It was made in blue and pink. Several distinct patterns exist in this line, including Dainty Flower, Shell Ware, Virginia, and Zephyr.

The Harker Company used a large variety of backstamps and names. Hotoven cookware featured a scroll, draped over pots, with a kiln design at top. Columbia Chinaware had a circular stamp showing the Statue of Liberty.

Collectors should consider buying Harker patterns by famous designers. Among these are Russel Wright's White Clover and George Bauer's Cameoware. Or an interesting collection could focus on one object, e.g., a sugar or creamer, collected in a variety of patterns from different historical periods. Watch for unusual pieces. The Countryside pattern features a rolling pin, scoop, and cake server.

Cameo pattern, teapot, peach, white lily of the valley decoration, 5-1/4" h, $65.

Amy
Rolling pin, 15" l 145.00
Scoop, 6" l 65.00

Cameo
Bowl, 8" d, Zephyr, blue 18.00
Casserole, cov, square, blue 50.00
Cheese box, cov, Zephyr, blue 44.00
Creamer, Gem, blue 35.00
Cup and saucer, Shell Ware, blue 15.00
Dish, lug handle, Shell Ware, blue 10.00
Jug, cov, pink, 6-1/2" h 60.00
Mixing bowl, pink, 9" d, mkd "Cameoware by Harker Pottery Co., Patented USA" 36.00

Pie baker
   Cameoware, Pie Baker, pink, 10" d, mkd "Harker Cameoware By Harker Pottery, Patented USA" 45.00

Plate
   7-1/2" d, Shell Ware, blue 10.00
   9-3/4" d, Virginia, pink 12.00
Platter, blue, 9" x 11-7/8", mkd "Cameoware by Harker Pottery, Patented USA" . 40.00

Rolling pin, 15" l **165.00**
Salad bowl, 6-1/2" w, square, blue **15.00**
Sugar, Virginia, blue............................ **20.00**
Teapot, cov, four cups **65.00**
Vegetable bowl, blue, 9" d, mkd
"Cameoware by Harker Pottery Co.,
Patented USA" **30.00**

Cattail
Dinner set, service for six, 43 pcs, 1960
.... **85.00**

Colonial Lady
Platter, 12" sq, mkd "Bakerite Oven Tested
Made in USA" **30.00**

Country Charm
Dinner set, 36 pcs **70.00**

Deco Dahlia
Jug, cov, 7" h **55.00**
Stack set, three pcs **65.00**

Fruit
Cake server **35.00**
Range set, peach motif, three pcs **80.00**
Salad fork **25.00**

Ivy Vine
Platter, 12" l **35.00**
Platter, 16" l **45.00**
Range drip jar, cov **47.50**
Teapot, cov **135.00**

Kelvinator
Casserole, cov, Hotoven Ware, black
bands, white body, emb, ftd, sq finial,
some crazing, 7-1/2" d **50.00**
Rolling pin, 14-3/4" l **160.00**

Mallow
Casserole, cov, 1 qt **55.00**
Fork **35.00**
Rolling pin, 15" l **145.00**
Utility bowl, 10" 3 .... **45.00**

Modern Tulip
Casserole, cov, 8-5/8" **45.00**
Cookie jar, cov **85.00**
Rolling pin, gold trimmed **125.00**

Monterey
Jug, cov, 5" h **70.00**
Jug, cov, 7" h **95.00**
Pie baker, 10" d, mkd "Hotoven Cooking-
ware Harker The Oldest Pottery In
America" **65.00**

Petit Point Rose
Batter bowl **60.00**
Bowl, 8-1/2" d **15.00**
Cake plate **20.00**
Cake server **15.00**
Canister, cov, 6" h, 5-3/4" d **125.00**
Casserole, cov, 8-1/2" d **50.00**
Casserole, cov, quart, platinum trim ... **40.00**
Coffeepot **45.00**
Cup and saucer **18.00**

Plate, gray border, 8-1/4" d, $3.

Dinner plate, 8-1/2" d.................... **12.00**
Fork, 8-3/4" **75.00**
Pie baker **25.00**
Rolling pin, 14-3/4" l **140.00**
Snack set, three pcs **48.00**
Spoon, 8-1/2" l **75.00**
Sugar, cov **15.00**

Red Apple
Cheese plate, 11" d **50.00**
Custard **8.50**
Dinner plate, 10" d **15.00**
Fork **40.00**
Mixing bowl, 9" d **30.00**
Pie baker, 9" d **30.00**
Range set, three-pc set, Hotoven **145.00**
Rolling pin **150.00**
Salad bowl, 9" d, swirl **24.00**
Spoon **40.00**
Utility tray, 11" l **24.00**
Vegetable bowl, 9" d **30.00**

Tulip
Pitcher, 9" h **95.00**
Rolling pin, 15" l............................. **150.00**

Holiday Collectibles

History: Holidays are an important part
of American life. Many have both
secular and religious overtones such as
Christmas, St. Patrick's Day, Easter,
Valentine's Day, and Halloween.
National holidays such as the Fourth of
July and Thanksgiving are part of one's
yearly planning. Collectors usually
consider President's Day, Memorial Day,
Flag Day, and the Fourth of July as part
of the general category of patriotic
collectibles.

Each holiday has its own origins and background and owes its current face to a variety of legends, lore, and customs. Holiday decorations were popularized by German cottage industries at the turn of the century. Germany dominated the holiday market until the 1920s when Japan began producing holiday items. Both countries lost their place during World War II and U.S. manufacturers filled the American appetite for holiday decorations.

Collecting Hints: Collectors often start with one holiday and eventually branch out and collect all the holidays. Reasonably priced items can still be found—especially items from the 1950s and 1960s.

Reproduction Alert.

Additional Listings: Christmas Items, Flag Collectibles, Patriotic Collectibles, Santa Claus, Valentines.

Advisers: Lissa Bryan-Smith and Richard Smith.

Easter, papier-mâché egg, interior marked "Germany," $95. All holiday photos courtesy of Advisers Richard Smith and Lissa Bryan-Smith.

Easter

Basket

Germany, painted red, Germany paper label, footed, 6" h............................ **45.00**
Japan, dyed and natural reed splints, square, 10" h................................. **15.00**
Mexico, splint, dyed and natural, stamped "Mexico," 16" h................ **10.00**

Candle

Easter Bunny holding up top hat, mkd "Gurley Novelty Co.," 3-1/2" h........ **10.00**
Easter Lily, green base, white and yellow flower, paper label on base, mkd "Gurley Novelty Co.," 3" h............................ **5.00**
Rabbit, sitting, off-white, mkd "Tavern Novelty Co.," 5" h............................ **10.00**

Candy container

Birdhouse, egg shape, papier-mâché, yellow egg bird house with orange cardboard roof, mkd "Easter Greetings," script, chicks and flowers all embossed paper attached to birdhouse, mkd "Germany," 7" h............................ **95.00**
Chicken on nest, pressed cardboard, opens at nest, USA, 7" d, 6-1/2" h.. **65.00**
Easter Bunny, pressed cardboard, light blue, opening in base, USA, 10" h.. **35.00**
Easter Bunny, pressed cardboard, white, green colored basket on back, USA, 9" h
.... **30.00**
Egg and chick, papier-mâché, blue half eggshell with yellow chenille chick coming out of top, 1950s, USA, 3" h
.... **12.00**
Rabbit, cotton batting with pink paper ears and pink composition eyes, holding orange cotton batting carrot attached to green reed basket that held candy, mkd "Japan," 4" h.................................. **35.00**
Rabbit, crouching on all fours, papier-mâché, removable head, mkd "Made in Germany, U.S. Zone," 4" x 4"......... **45.00**
Rabbit, standing in basket, side view, glass, opening in base, 3" h........ **90.00**

Decoration, cardboard and tissue paper honeycomb, unfolds to set-up, rabbit sitting among lilacs, surrounded by honeycomb eggs and basket, USA, 8-1/2" l **20.00**

Egg

Cardboard, violets dec, gold Dresden trim, Germany, 3" l...................... **25.00**
Metal, litho, purple and yellow, 3" l. **18.00**
Milk glass, white, gilded lettering "Easter Greetings," painted purple spring flowers, 6" h.................................. **45.00**

Figure

Chick, chenille, paper covered wire feet, paper label attached to foot mkd "Made in Occupied Japan," 1" h................ **5.00**
Duck, hard plastic, yellow, flat base **4.50**
Rabbit, chalk, standing, white with pink tipped ears, mkd "Japan," 3-1/2" h.. **6.00**

Postcard

A Peaceful Easter, girl and rabbit looking at Easter eggs, 1911 .... **5.00**

Easter Greetings, Victorian child cradling rabbit with a nest of colored eggs at her feet, mkd "Series D, No 12," Germany **3.00**

Rattle, rabbit, hard plastic, mkd "Irwin"
Dancing, pink with blue jacket and holding a blue carrot, 4" h **4.00**
Standing, pink with blue overalls, 6" h **8.00**

Sheet music, "Easter Parade," Bing Crosby **12.00**

Toy
Musical Easter Basket, cardboard, plastic handle, orig box, mkd "Mattel, 1952," 4" x 6" **65.00**
Rabbit pulling egg buggy with chick, celluloid and metal, wind-up **110.00**

Halloween, candy container, pressed cardboard, witch on pumpkin, USA, **$110.**

Halloween

Candle, cat, orange and black, base mkd "Gurley Novelty Co.," 3-1/2" h
Holding pumpkin and tipping hat..... **5.00**
Sitting on fence................................. **5.00**

Candy container
Cat, hard plastic, standing, paws on hips, wearing tee shirt, orange, black and green, pouch in back for lollipops, 5-1/4" h... **65.00**
Scarecrow, hard plastic, orange and black, opening on back, 5-3/4" h ... **85.00**
Witch, papier-mâché, 7" h, orange and black, opening on back, 7" h **135.00**

Clicker, litho tin, orange and black, frog shape, mkd "T. Cohn, USA".......... **12.50**

Costume, Battling Bunny, child's size, bunny wearing boxing gloves, cloth mask, sateen cloth costume, litho trim, 1940s **20.00**

Decoration
Pumpkin man, cardboard, 1960s, jointed arms and legs, jack o'lantern head, mkd "Beistle Co.," 29" h......................... **22.00**
Set of eight cardboard figures, orig pkg, Beistle Co, mkd "One Assortment of 6 Decorations – Halloween Standups," range in size from 7" to 10-1/2" **40.00**

Favor, soufflé cup covered with orange crepe paper, paper bale, black paper cat trim, USA, 3" h................................. **5.00**

Figure, cat, black
Cardboard, flat, moveable legs and tail, Beistle Co., USA, 9" h **20.00**
Cardboard, flat, USA, 2-3/4" h........ **15.00**
Hard plastic, jack o'lantern on back, 3-1/8" h... **35.00**

Hat, cardboard and crepe paper, Germany
Black and orange, 4" h................... **17.50**
Black and orange, gold and black cardboard band, 10" h **25.00**

Horn
Cardboard, orange and black, cat, witch, and moon litho figures, USA 9" h ... **15.00**
Paper, orange and black, wood mouthpiece, Germany, 8" h............ **12.00**
Pressed cardboard, wood mouthpiece, turnip, Germany, 1920-30s **95.00**

Lantern
Painted glass, pumpkin, scary face, wire handle, metal screw-on lid, 4" h... **125.00**
Papier-mâché, pumpkin, cutout eyes and mouth with tissue paper, wire handle, candleholder in base, Germany, 7" h **85.00**
Pressed cardboard, black cat head, cutout eyes and mouth, wire handle, metal candle holder in base, Germany, 4" h **115.00**

Mask
Boy, papier-mâché, painted face, cloth ties, stamped "Germany".............. **35.00**
Devil, rubber, red, black, and white, rubber ties...................................... **18.00**
Duck, buckram, molded bill, cloth ties **40.00**

Noisemaker, rattle, tin
Litho, round, three litho pumpkin heads, long black handle, mkd "Made in USA, TC," 9" l... **25.00**
Painted black, wood and metal noise prongs... **40.00**

Halloween, mask, buckram cloth, $40.

Postcard

Girl scared by pumpkin in mirror, Raphael Tuck **30.00**
The Witch's Dance, postmarked 1909, witch dancing with pumpkin man, mkd Germany... **25.00**
Witch riding broom.......................... **25.00**
Pumpkin, metal, 6" d **55.00**
Tambourine, cat head, metal, 6" d **35.00**
Trick or treat bag, brown, litho picture of children trick or treating, 11" x 9" **4.00**

St. Patrick's Day

Candy box, cardboard, green shamrock, 8-1/2" h.. **18.00**

Candy container

Hat, cardboard, green and gold, base label "Loft Candy Corp," 3" h.......... **25.00**
Potato, pressed cardboard, brown, green and gold velvet shamrock, Germany, 4" l **45.00**
Irish Girl, composition, holding harp, standing on box, Germany, 4-1/2" h **75.00**

Figure

Leprechaun, celluloid, holding pig, Japan, 7" h...................................... **32.00**
Man, composition, green felt coat, spring legs, beer stein, 6" h........................ **65.00**
Pig, composition, flocked green, Germany, 4" l **50.00**
Magazine cover, *Life*, March 15, 1923, cherub wearing Irish hat, playing harp **15.00**
Nodder, Irish boy, bisque, Germany, 3" h **45.00**

Postcard

Ireland Forever, scenes of Ireland, shamrock, green, and gold **4.00**

On March 17 May You Be Seen A Wearing Of The Green, Irish man standing on "17," Quality Cards, A. M. Davis Co., Boston, 1912.................. **4.50**
Shamrock, green silk floss-wrapped wire, small bisque hat attached to center, 2-1/2" l **5.00**

Thanksgiving

Advertisement, Pepsi, 1956, woman and man carving turkey in 1950s setting, 11" x 14" **10.00**

Candle

Swirl candle, autumn leaves and acorns, mkd "Gurley Novelty Co.," 7" h **5.00**
Turkey, iridescent green and purple, paper label, 4-1/2" h **7.00**

Candy container

Pigeon, composition, removable head, metal feet, Germany, 4" h **95.00**
Pheasant, composition, removable head, metal feet, Germany, 7" h **150.00**
Rooster, composition, removable head, metal feet, Germany, 6" h **85.00**
Turkey, gobbler, composition, removable head, horsehair beard, Germany, 8" h **125.00**
Turkey, gobbler, glass, red painted trim, USA, 8" h **65.00**
Decoration, honeycomb tissue paper, table top decoration, two-sided lithographed cardboard turkey, mkd USA, 8-1/2" h **15.00**

Figure, turkey

Bisque, green base, mkd Japan, 1" h **7.00**
Chalk, green base, black, white and red, USA, 2-1/4" h.................................... **12.00**
Papier-mâché, cardboard bottom, mkd "Western Germany," 4" h **25.00**
Greeting card, The Mayflower, With Joyful Thanksgiving Wishes **8.00**
Place card holder, turkey, standing, celluloid, holder at base of metal spring legs, 2-1/2" h **20.00**

Postcard

A Joyous Thanksgiving, boy carving pumpkin, 1913................................. **5.00**
I don't care, that turkey was good while I was eating it, pictures two girls one holding her stomach sitting by empty plate, 1917 postmark, USA **3.00**
Thanksgiving Greetings, boy sitting on fence feeding turkey, 1928 postmark, USA **4.00**
Seals, turkeys, orig pkg, Dennison, 12 seals and envelops **3.00**
Sheet music, "Guffy, The Goofy Gobbler," M. Witmark & Sons, NY, 1950 .... **11.00**
Tin, litho, Turkey on lid, black, USA, 4" d **110.00**

Homer Laughlin

History: Homer Laughlin and his brother, Shakespeare, built two pottery kilns in East Liverpool, Ohio, in 1871. Shakespeare resigned in 1879, leaving Homer to operate the business alone. Laughlin became one of the first firms to produce American-made whiteware. In 1896, William Wills and a Pittsburgh group led by Marcus Aaron bought the Laughlin firm.

Expansion followed. Two new plants were built in Laughlin Station, Ohio. In 1906, the first Newall, West Virginia, plant (#4) was built in. Plant #6, which was built at Newall in 1923, featured a continuous-tunnel kiln. Similar kilns were added at the other plants. Other advances instituted by the company include spray glazing and mechanical jiggering.

Between 1930 and 1960, several new dinnerware lines were added, including the Wells Art Glaze line. Ovenserve and Kitchen Kraft were cookware products. The colored-glaze lines of Fiesta, Harlequin, and Rhythm captured major market shares. In 1959 a translucent table china line was introduced. Today, the annual manufacturing capacity is over 45 million pieces.

Collecting Hints: The original 1871 to 1890 trademark used the term "Laughlin Brothers." The next trademark featured the American eagle astride the prostrate British lion. The third mark, which featured the "HLC" monogram, has appeared, with slight variations, on all dinnerware since about 1900. The 1900 version included a number that identified month, year, and plant at which the product was made. Letter codes were used in later periods.

So much attention has been given to Fiesta that other interesting Homer Laughlin patterns have not achieved the popularity they deserve, and prices for these less-recognized patterns are still moderate. Some of the patterns made during the 1930s and 1940s have highly artistic contemporary designs.

Virginia Rose is not a pattern name but a shape on which several different decals were used. Delicate pink flowers are the most common.

Reproduction Alert: Harlequin and Fiesta lines were reissued in 1978 and marked accordingly.

Additional Listings: Fiesta.

American Provincial, Rhythm shape
  Berry bowl... **4.00**
  Bread and butter plate **5.00**
  Cereal bowl.. **8.00**
  Luncheon plate, 8" d **8.00**
  Platter **16.00**
Amsterdam, Nautilus shape, creamer and
  sugar **24.00**
Apple Blossom, Eggshell Nautilus shape,
  salt and pepper shakers, pr...... **125.00**
Best China
  Bread and butter plate, 6-1/4" d **4.50**
  Coffee mug **5.00**
  Platter, 9" x 11-1/2" **5.00**
  Salad plate, 7-1/4" d **5.00**
  Saucer.. **4.00**
Brittany Majestic, Nautilus Eggshell, sugar,
  cov.. **12.00**
Calendar plate, 1953, zodiac symbols
  .... **25.00**
Cavalier
  Cup and saucer............................... **10.00**
  Dinnerware set, service for four, plus
  serving pieces **80.00**
Flowers of the Dell, casserole, cov, jade
  .... **125.00**
Georgian Eggshell, dinnerware set, service
  for 9 plus serving pcs.................. **900.00**

Plate, Georgian pattern, pale blue border, multicolored floral center, gold fleur-de-lis trim, eggshell, gold backstamp, **$18**.

Harlequin
  Baker, oval, spruce......................... **22.00**
  Berry bowl
    Maroon **6.50**
    Yellow **6.50**
  Candlestick, red............................... **17.00**

Creamer, individual size
    Mauve **28.00**
    Spruce **25.00**
Cream soup, mauve **22.00**
Cup, rose **6.50**
Cup and saucer, spruce **10.00**
Deep plate
    Gray **45.00**
    Mauve **28.00**
    Medium Green **95.00**
Dinnerware set, marigold yellow and
spruce, service for six **900.00**
Eggcup, double
    Chartreuse **20.00**
    Maroon **22.00**
Eggcup, single
    Maroon **30.00**
    Orange **25.00**
Nappy, 9" d, turquoise **18.50**
Nut dish, orange **15.00**
Platter
    11" l, maroon **18.00**
    13" l, oval, rose **15.00**
Relish insert
    Maroon **50.00**
    Mauve **75.00**
    Red **35.00**
    Rose **90.00**
    Yellow **75.00**
Salad bowl, individual
    Chartreuse **45.00**
    Light Green **45.00**
    Medium Green **175.00**
    Yellow **25.00**
Salt and pepper shakers, pr
    Gray **10.00**
    Maroon **10.00**
    Mauve **8.00**
    Yellow **12.00**

Kitchen Kraft

Cake server, cobalt blue **145.00**
Casserole, cov, individual
    Cobalt Blue **200.00**
    Light Green **150.00**
    Red **255.00**
    Yellow **110.00**
Casserole, cov, 7 1/2" d, cobalt blue
.... **70.00**
Cream soup bowl, double handle, pink
.... **6.00**
Fork, cobalt blue **150.00**
Mixing bowl, 6" d, red **110.00**
Pie baker, cobalt blue, 10" d **32.00**
Spoon, red, 8-3/4" l **125.00**
Kwaker, salad server, 8-1/2" d, two handles
.... **110.00**
Magnolia, plate, gold trim, 6-1/4" **6.00**

Marigold

Creamer and sugar **20.00**
Cup and saucer **11.50**
Dinner plate, 10" d **18.00**
Platter, 13-1/2" x 10-7/8" **30.00**
Vegetable bowl, 8-1/2" d **25.00**

Cereal bowl, Mexicali, blue backstamp, **$10.**

Mexicana

Baker, oval **25.00**
Batter jug, cov **80.00**
Bowl, 5" d **20.00**
Cake server **30.00**
Fruit bowl, individual **18.00**
Jar, cov, orig paper label **90.00**
Pie baker **35.00**
Soup, flat **24.00**
Nautilus, plate, 9-1/4" d, eggshell **8.00**
Oven Serve, Handy Andy, 8" cream-colored
bowl, red and platinum lines, chrome
holder, black handles **45.00**

Priscilla

Cup and saucer **8.00**
Dinner plate **10.00**
Gravy boat **12.00**
Mixing bowl, 8-1/4" d **36.00**
Vegetable bowl, divided **18.00**

Rhythm

Bread and butter plate, 6" d, yellow. **6.50**
Creamer, gray **8.50**
Gravy boat, gray **12.00**
Sauce boat, chartreuse **7.50**
Vegetable bowl, 9" l, chartreuse **8.00**

Riviera

Baker, oval, ivory **15.00**
Bowl, 5-1/2" d, ivory **8.00**
Bread and butter plate, 6" d
    Ivory **6.00**
    Red **12.00**
Butter dish, cov, 1/4 lb, Century, red or
yellow **125.00**
Casserole, cov
    Blue **140.00**
    Green **125.00**
    Ivory **125.00**
    Mauve **110.00**
    Red **125.00**
Cup
    Blue **7.50**
    Green **7.50**

Ivory	**7.50**
Light green	**12.00**
Red	**8.50**
Yellow	**8.00**

Dinner plate, 9" d
Blue	**15.00**
Green	**15.00**
Ivory	**12.00**
Red	**18.00**
Yellow	**18.00**

Dinnerware set, Century shape, mauve-blue, yellow, green, and ivory, 1938, service for eight ... **1,000.00**

Juice tumbler
Green	**85.00**
Ivory	**95.00**
Yellow	**85.00**

Oatmeal bowl, Century
Green	**65.00**
Ivory	**65.00**
Yellow	**65.00**

Platter
Ivory	**12.00**
Yellow	**22.00**

Sauce boat, attached underplate, ivory, 6-5/8" sq ... **145.00**
Syrup, Dripcut type, red, 5-7/8" h . **490.00**
Teapot, cov, yellow ... **185.00**

Tumbler, handle, Century
Green	**55.00**
Mauve	**110.00**
Red	**95.00**

Silver Patrician, Virginia Rose
Bowl, 8-1/2" d	**25.00**
Cup and saucer	**10.00**
Dinner plate, 10" d	**15.00**
Platter, 9-3/4" x 11-3/4"	**25.00**
Salad plate, 8" d	**18.00**
Saucer	**5.00**
Tray, 6" x 9-1/2"	**37.50**
Vegetable bowl, 7-1/4" x 10"	**27.50**

Skytone Stardust, coffeepot ... **40.00**
Song of Spring, bowl, 6-1/2" x 9" oval, 1929 Sears ... **18.00**

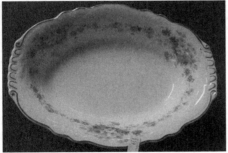

Vegetable dish, Virginia Rose, oval, gold backstamp, hand lettered V. R. 271, **$18**.

Virginia Rose
Baker, oval, 8" l	**20.00**
Butter, cov, jade	**75.00**

Creamer and sugar, cov	**35.00**
Cup and saucer	**4.00**
Dinner plate, 9" d	**8.50**
Fruit bowl, 5-1/2" d	**5.00**
Mixing bowl, large	**48.00**
Nappy, 10" d	**20.00**
Pie baker	**25.00**
Platter, 13"	**25.00**
Soup bowl	**20.00**
Tray, handles	**25.00**
Vegetable, cov	**45.00**

Horse Collectibles

History: Horses are not indigenous to the United States but were brought here by various means. The wild horses of the American Southwest are descended from Spanish Mustangs brought here by the Conquistadors. Later, English stock would arrive with the settlers on the East Coast, where they were used for farming and transportation and even as foods source. In those days, a person's social status was determined by the quantity and quality of the horses he owned. Remember the condescending phrase, "one-horse town?"

Daily life in the early days of the United States would have been much harder on humans were it not for the horse. They were used for transportation of products, pulling plows on farms, rushing a country doctor to his patients and later, for recreational sports like racing and rodeo. Even in the early days of the automobile, horse-drawn tankers normally transported gasoline to the local service station from the distributor.

As our means of transportation gradually shifted from the horse to automobiles, trains and airplanes, the horse was no longer a necessity to folks, especially those living in cities and suburbs. Today, horses still earn their keep by rounding up stray cattle, looking for lost people in remote areas, and in competition. For the most part, today's horses are pampered family pets living a sheltered life that the hard-working draft animal of the 1800s could only dream about.

Collecting Hints: The hottest area in equine memorabilia continues to be figures. Early Breyer plastic horse figures, are especially sought after. You can tell the early models by their glossy finish, although those with faux woodgrain finish or the unrealistic Wedgewood blue or Florentine gold "decorator" finish are harder to find. Breyers are designed by artists familiar with equine anatomy and are as close as possible as the "real thing." Hartland horses remain popular especially those representing Western movie and television characters, like Roy Rogers and Trigger or Dale Evans and Buttermilk. Historical characters, especially General Robert E. Lee on his horse, Traveler, are in demand as well. The ears of plastic figures are especially vulnerable, so check the ear tips. Paint rubs greatly reduce the value of plastic model horses.

Ceramic figurines, whether of English origin like Wades and Beswick, German like Goebel or American manufactures like Hagen-Renaker of California, remain a strong part of the market. Well-detailed ceramic Japanese horse figures made in the 1950s and 1960s have risen in popularity and price. Check ceramic figures carefully for chips, cracks and repairs, especially on legs and tails.

There are few categories of collecting that do not feature some sort of equine image. Advertising featuring the horse has always been popular, especially early memorabilia featuring the famous trotter Dan Patch. Saddle and tack catalogs, Wild West show posters, movie posters, and even Anheuser-Busch advertising featuring its beloved Clydesdale team are all avidly collected by horse lovers.

Kentucky Derby glass prices have leveled off somewhat, except for examples from the '50s and before. Carousel horses remain a high-ticket item but beware of imported hand-carved imitations. These are well done and nice as a decorator item, but don't be fooled into paying the price demanded of a Mueller, Loof or Denzel figure. It is best to find these figures at auctions where you can obtain a written guarantee of their origin.

Horse-drawn toys, whether cast iron or lithographed tin, seem to be a real bargain these days, especially when compared with automobile toys of the same era. Their performance at auctions and sales is just starting to improve, and they still provide a nice, affordable find for the horse enthusiast. The most popular horse-drawn toys remain the circus vehicles, an attraction for circus collectors along with horse lovers. Do be careful buying cast iron as many of the vehicles have been reproduced. Gaudy paint, ill-fitting parts, and a surface that feels rough to the touch should cause the warning lights to flash. Reproductions are worth maybe $25 as a decorative item, but have no value as a collectible. If you are not sure, it is best to do all your buying from a dealer you trust.

Horse brasses, English, assorted brasses, top left: London, lower left: England (leather back); two embossed "Tower of London," top right: King George VI, lower right: Scottish thistle, each $20-$45.

Horse equipment and related items

Bells

8" I metal strap, 4 graduated cast bells affixed, attaches to wagon or sleigh shaft **125.00**
84" I leather strap, 40 identical nickel bells, strap shows wear, tug hook **200.00**

Bit

Calvary, Civil War era, "US" spots at cheeks... **200.00**
Eagle figure, mkd "G.S. Garcia" .. **950.00**
Silver overlay, floral design, mkd "Crockett" **125.00**

Blanket

Canvas with straps, 1930s............. **75.00**
Carriage robe, buffalo **875.00**
Saddle, Navajo weaving, early 1900s, some wear **750.00**

Bridle

Calvary, mule bridle, brass "US" spots
.... **225.00**
Horsehair, woven, prison made. **2,500.00**

Bridle rosette

Brass, military, eagle motif **50.00**
Glass with rose motif inside, mkd
"Chapman"...................................... **40.00**

Brush, Calvary, stamped "US," patent date
1850, Herbert Brush Mfg. Co., never
used.. **95.00**

Catalog

Chicago, 1929, polo saddles and
equipment **75.00**
Kelly Brothers, 1960s, bits, spurs, etc.
.... **60.00**

Collar, draft horse, leather-covered wood,
brass trim.. **150.00**

Curry Comb, tin back, leather handle, early
1900s... **45.00**

Harness decorations (horse brasses)

Lion, rampant in center, England ... **40.00**
Rearing horse in center, backstamped
"England" **55.00**

Hobbles, chain and leather, sideline type
.... **150.00**

Hoof pick, bone handle, Wastenholm,
Germany, patent date 1885............ **55.00**

Horse drawn vehicle

Creators Popcorn Wagon, unrestored
.... **7,500.00**
Stagecoach, Half-scale detailed,
excellent condition **3,500.00**
Watkins Products Delivery Wagon,
restored..................................... **2,500.00**

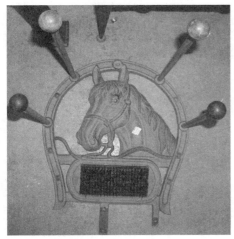

This contemporary cast iron boot rack may be new, but it appeals to those who collect horse-related items, **$20**.

Horsehide rug, 48" by 72", black & white
.... **250.00**

Lasso

Braided rawhide, Mexican reata.. **250.00**
Horsehair....................................... **175.00**

Mane and tail comb, Oliver Slant Tooth,
1940s **40.00**

Newspaper, *Horse & Stable Weekly*, Boston,
Jan. 2, 1891 .... **35.00**

Pinback button

7/8" d, *Luse Land Co., St. Paul,*
multicolored, rider on horseback looking
over homestead and farm lands,
sunburst in background, dark red rim,
Bastian back paper, c1910........... **15.00**
1-7/8" d, *Lafayette Stock Farm, Lafayette,
Ind.,* black horse and brown horse with
cropped tails facing opposite directions,
colored green hillside scene, water,
mountains, shaded sky, text "Largest
Importers of Percheron, Belgian, German
Coach, Shire & Hackney Stallions &
Mares," Bastian Bros back paper, c1905-
07 .... **90.00**

Saddle, McClelland military type, large
fenders, early 1990s..................... **950.00**

Spurs, Buermann, star mark and "Hercules
Bronze," old leathers **450.00**

Stud book

*American Quarter Horse Stud Book and
Registry*, 1959 .... **50.00**
Palomino Progress, Stud Book & Registry,
1966 .... **75.00**

Wagon seat, springs, padded seat,
replaced leather upholstery **250.00**

Watering trough, hollowed-out log, tin liner,
24" by 72"....................................... **225.00**

Horse theme items

Bank, Ertl, horse and tank wagon, Texaco
adv **50.00**

Blanket, brown and tan wool, Roy Rogers
and Trigger,1950s, twin size......... **350.00**

Book

American Trotting and Pacing Horses,
Henry V. Coats, 1st ed., 1902, 8 volumes
.... **400.00**
*Boots and Saddles, or Life in Dakota with
General Custer,* Elizabeth B. Custer, 1995
.... **38.00**
*Horse Power, A History of the Horse and
Donkey in Human Societies,* Brock **38.00**
The Black Stallion, Walter Farley, 1st ed.,
dust jacket...................................... **25.00**
The Horse in Art, John Baskett, NY
Graphic Society, Boston, 1980 ...... **50.00**
Understanding and Training Horses,
James Ricci, 1964 .... **9.50**

Calendar plate, 1911, two horse heads in center, horseshoe shaped calendar, gold text "Compliments of H. B. Schanley, Jeweler, Quakertown, Pa," 7" d, **$85**.

Calendar, 1907, cardboard, Dousman Milling, cowgirl and horse **75.00**
Carousel horse, jumper, flag on side, C. W. Parker, American, 1918............. **6,500.00**
Clock, United, brass horse, Western saddle, wood base.................................... **125.00**
Cookie cutter, prancing horse, bobtail, flat back, 6 1/2" by 7 1/2" **75.00**
Cookie jar, McCoy, Circus Horse........ **50.00**
Decanter, Avon, brown glass thoroughbred **10.00**
Decanter, Man O'War, Ezra Brooks..... **25.00**
Doorstop, racehorse, stamped "Virginia Metalcrafters," 1949...................... **195.00**
Fan, fold-out, paper and wood, painted horse racing scene with horse and jockey, Japan, c1960 .... **15.00**

Figure

Beswick, reclining foal, 3", brown, white blaze on forehead **75.00**
Breyer, glossy black rearing horse **125.00**
Hagen-Renaker Pegasus, 1985, mini **35.00**
Hartland, Roy Rogers and Trigger, near mint **225.00**
Heisey Clydesdale, amber glass ... **95.00**
Rookwood, #6140, 1939............... **400.00**
Summit Art Glass, blue, short legs . **25.00**
Vernon Kilns, Disney, unicorn, black "Fantasia" **600.00**
Wade, Tom Smith pony **45.00**

Fruit crate label, Bronco, bucking horse **25.00**
Jewelry, pin, figural, celluloid **35.00**
Magazine, *Western Horseman*, Volume 1 #1, 1935... **50.00**
Mug, Clydesdales, 1st in Series, Certamarte Brazil for Anheuser-Busch **45.00**

Nodder

Donkey in suit, carrying US flag **5.00**
Horse, celluloid, mkd "Occupied Japan" **75.00**

Platter, oval, two riders leading horses, marked "Royal Doulton, Made In England," **$80**.

Paperweight, James Hartley Brewing Co., Providence, RI, Prince Albert Race Horse, glass, black and white photo of horse, red lettering "Prince Albert 1.57/ The World's Champion Harness Gelding," 3/4" x 2-1/2" x 4" l............ **75.00**

Pinback button

7/8" d, *Bergen, Celebrated American Jockey,* full color, pink cap, yellow circles on light pink jacket, Whitehead & Hoag back paper with patent dates, "Compliments of High Admiral Cigarette" **24.00**
7/8" d, *E. H. Carrison Jockey, J. Ruppert Colors,* full color, Whitehead & Hoag back paper with patent dates, "Compliments of High Admiral Cigarette" **24.00**
7/8" d, *Sims Celebrated American Jockey,* full color, jockey in white uniform, light blue sash, Whitehead & Hoag back paper with patent dates, "Compliments of High Admiral Cigarette" **24.00**
1" d, *Black Bill, Easter Monday Frolic,* St. Louis back paper, c1930 .... **15.00**
1-1/2" d, *Dan Patch Fastest Harness Horse In The World M. W. Savage, Owner, He Eats International Stock Food Every Day,* black and white photo of Dan hitched to sulky, driver holding whip, Whitehead & Hoag back paper **85.00**

Tin, Arabian Scratches and Gall Salve, Manufactured and Sold by "Our Husbands' Company," Lyndon, VT, black and white graphics, 2" x 2-1/4" x 1-1/2", **$15**.

Trivet, metal, jockey riding race horse, marked "Germany" and also a triangle with "Ph," **$20**.

Postcard
Bucking Bronco, Prescott AZ Rodeo, 1920s **20.00**
Three draft horses, German, pre-1920, used **15.00**

Poster
Berry Exhibitions, Dayton, OH, Saddle Horse Contest, 1913 .... **350.00**
Studebaker Wagons, multiple tears and tape, 1909 .... **175.00**

Program, Kentucky Derby, 1964, signed by artist "Shoofly" **75.00**

Rocking horse, white, black spots, horsehair mane and tail, 75% original paint, handmade, one rocker split **450.00**

Sheet music, *Dan Patch March*, famous trotter on cover **65.00**

Sign, Hunter Cigars, tin, 19" by 27", fox hunter with horse **300.00**

Snowdome, Budweiser Clydesdales, 1988 limited edition **75.00**

Toy
Circus Wagon, 14" long, cast iron, mkd "Kenton" **1,200.00**
Fire pumper, three horses, cast iron, Hubley **1,750.00**
Hay cart, Gibbs, paper lithographed **495.00**

Tray, Genessee Twelve Horse Ale, 12" d **125.00**

Valentine, cowboy on horse, 1910, unused **30.00**

Windmill weight, Dempster, bobtail horse, 17" l **950.00**

Hot Wheels

History: Harry Bradley, an automotive designer, Howard Newman, a Mattel designer, Harry LaBranch, a Mattel designer, Elliot Handler, chairman of Mattel, and Jack Ryan, head of research and development for Mattel, joined forces to produce the first diecast Hot Wheels cars in 1968.

The first 16 diecast cars released featured thin axles and lightweight "mag" wheels that could zoom down bright orange tracks. The original cards were marketed as "Red Stripe Slicks" and are known to collectors as "redlines" because of the stripe around the tires.

Collecting   Hints: Collecting Hot Wheels is one of the fastest growing areas in collectibles. Mattel offers a quality product. However, it has also changed its packaging, re-issued numbers, and developed new series to keep collectors coming back for more. Learning the packaging variations adds to the excitement of the hobby for many collectors. For the best information about Hot Wheels and their variations, consult Michael Zarnock's books, *Hot Wheels Variations, the Ultimate Guide*, and *Warman's Hot Wheels Field Guide,* Krause Publications.

The listings here are for Hot Wheels in mint condition and that have never been removed from their original package. Deduct 50 percent for cars taken out of the package and another 25 percent for cars that have playtime wear.

Aeroflash, #444 .... **2.00**
Ailen, #62, dark red and silver **6.50**
Altered State, #6 .... **3.00**
Ambulance, #71 .... **5.00**
American Hauler, redline, 1976 .... **70.00**
American Tipper, redline, 1976 .... **65.00**
Assault Crawler, #624 .... **5.00**
Auburn 852, #94 .... **20.00**
Audi Avus, #453, red **10.00**
Baja Bug, #36 .... **125.00**
Beach Bomb, green **75.00**
Beatnik Bandit, redline, 1968 .... **45.00**
Big Bertha, #79, olive **11.00**
Blazer 4 x 4, #6, black **60.00**
BMW 323, #150 .... **8.00**
BMW 850i, #149 .... **5.00**
Buick Stocker, #472, Dayglo yellow **3.00**
Bugs & Bues, four-car set **40.00**
Bulldozer, #34 .... **28.00**
Buzz Off, redline, 1973 .... **500.00**
Bywayman, #220, pearl white **12.00**
Cadillac '59, #154 .... **6.00**

Deora, 1968, $375.

Camaro Wind, #599, white enamel 3.50
Camaro Z28, red, chrome base, #33 . 42.50
Chaparral 2G, redline, 1969 .... 45.00
Chevy, '57, Ultra Hots, #47 .... 110.00
Chevy 1500, #1121.............................. 3.00
Chevy Stocker, #170........................... 6.50
City Police, #622, black enamel........... 3.00
Classic '36 Ford Couple, redline, 1969
.... 60.00
Classic Packard, #625......................... 5.00
Command Tank, #27........................... 25.00
Computer Warrior, #479 .... 3.00
Cool One, redline, 1976 .... 60.00
Corvette, billionth.............................. 10.00
Corvette Couple, #499 .... 5.00
Custom Corvette, #66, metallic dark red
.... 45.00
Custom Firebird, blue 40.00
Custom T-bird, redline, #1968 .... 165.00
Custom VW Bug, redline, 1968........ 125.00
Delivery Truck, #52 .... 32.00
Digger, #643.................................... 5.00
Double Vision, redline, 1973 .... 400.00
Dragon Wagon, #478, Dayglow yellow 2.50
Dump Truck, steel bed, #38................. 7.00
Earthmover, #16................................ 85.00
Ed Big Daddy Roth four-car set 40.00
Evil Weevil, #485 .... 3.00
Express Lane, #1067, orange, "Floyd's
Market" 3.00
Fat Fendered '40, #216, purple.......... 20.00
Ferrari, #312, red enamel.................... 50.00
Ferrari, #175, pearl white 15.00
Fire Engine, redline, 1970................ 100.00
Fire Truck, 1980 .... 2.00
Fleetside, purple............................... 35.00
Flame Stopper, #761.......................... 2.00
Ford Aerostar, #151 .... 5.00
Ford Bronco, turquoise, #56.............. 18.00
Ford GT-90, #1073.............................. 2.00
Ford Stake Bed Truck, #99.................. 8.00
Ford Transit Wrecker, #620 .... 5.00
Forklift, #642..................................... 5.00
Funny Money, redline, #1972 .... 335.00
Gleamer Patrol, #189, dark chrome texture
.... 8.00
GM Ultralite, #594, 1995..................... 3.00
GT Racer, #598, 1995.......................... 3.00
Hood, redline, #1971 .... 110.00
Hot Bird, #178................................... 10.00

Ice T, redline, 1971............................ 200.00
Jaguar XJ40, #609, dark blue.............. 3.00
Lakester, #1064 .... 2.00
Light My Firebird, redline, 1970 .... 75.00
Limozeen, #112 .... 15.00
London Taxi, #619 .... 6.00
Lumina Van, #702, dark green metallic 4.00
Masarati Mistral, brown 55.00
Mazda MX-5 Miata, #116................... 10.00
McDonald's, Key Force Car, 1993 .... 3.00
McDonald's, Tattoo Machine, 1993...... 3.00
Mean & Green Passion, #263 .... 15.00
Mercedes 300TD, #606 .... 3.00
Mercedes 500 SL, 1997 .... 26.00
Mighty Maverick, redline, 1970 .... 130.00
Mod-Quad, redline, 1970................... 60.00

Bugeye, 1971, $140.

Mongoose Funny Car, redline, 1970 160.00
Monto Carlo Stocker, #440 .... 3.00
Moving Van, redline, 1970.............. 125.00
Mustang Cobra, #623, pearl dark pink 2.00
Mustang Convertible '65, #455........... 3.50
Neet Streeter, #526, yellow enamel 5.00
Nissan Custom "Z," #600 .... 3.50
No Madder What, #10 .... 3.00
Oldsmobile Aurora, #265 .... 15.00
Open Fire, redline, 1972................... 400.00
Oshkosh Cement Mixer, #144 .... 6.00
Peterbilt Dump Truck, #100, red 5.00
Pipe Jammer, #206, yellow 5.00
Poison Pinto, redline, #1976.............. 65.00
Pontiac Banshee, #457, 1995 .... 3.00
Pontiac Salsa, #596, 1995 .... 3.00
Porsche 930, #148.............................. 70.00
Porsche 959, #80, metallic red........... 15.00
Power Plower, #40.............................. 80.00
Probe Funny Car, #84, Motorcraft 30.00
Propper Chopper, #185....................... 6.50
Ramp Truck, #1060.............................. 4.00
Ratmobile, #81, white.......................... 5.00
Recycling Truck, #143........................ 10.00
Rescue Ranger, #45............................ 20.00
Rig Wrecker, #46.............................. 225.00
Roll Patrol, #12, olive, tan, green, and
brown camouflage.......................... 400.00
Road Roller, #55, yellow.................... 25.00
Rodzilla, #156 .... 15.00
Sand Crab, redline, 1970................... 60.00
School Bus, #72, yellow 8.00
Scooper, redline, 1971..................... 325.00
Set, 25th anniversary, 1993, five cars. 38.00

Shock Factor, #700 .... **3.00**
Side Splitter Funny Car-#2, #409, splatter paint **5.00**
Silhouette II, #212, metallic purple **6.50**
Snake II, redline, 1971 .... **275.00**
Spoiler Sport, redline, 1971 .... **50.00**
Sting Rod, #488 .... **3.00**
Street Beast, #473, pearl teal **3.00**
Street Roader, #73, white **15.00**
Suzuki Quadracer, #165, bright pink body
.... **8.00**
Swingfire, #214 .... **6.00**
Tail Gunner, #29 .... **75.00**
Talbot Lago, #22, white **25.00**
Tall Ryder, #481 .... **4.00**
Tank Truck, #147 .... **6.00**
Tantrum, #2 .... **3.00**
Team Trailer, redline, 1971 .... **225.00**

Swoopy-Do, 2004 First Editions #3, $2.

Thunderstreak, #153 .... **6.00**
Tipper, #712 .... **2.00**
Tow Truck, redline, 1970 .... **80.00**
Toy Fair, Cart, race car, 2002 .... **50.00**
Toy Fair, Maelstrom, 2002 .... **100.00**
Toy Fair, NASCAR, #99, J Burton, 2002
.... **50.00**
Toyota MR2 Rally, #122 .... **20.00**
Tractor, #145, yellow **10.00**
Turboa, #155, yellow **5.00**
Turbo Streak, #104 .... **75.00**
Twang Thang, #1104, pearl orange **3.00**
Van de Kamps, mail in premium, Deora, 1997 .... **20.00**
Van de Kamps, mail in premium, Hiway Hauler Truck, 1996 .... **24.00**
Vega Bomb, redline, 1975 .... **85.00**
VW Golf, #106, white **50.00**
Waste Wagon, redline, 1971 .... **325.00**
Wheel Loader, #641, orange and black
.... **4.00**
Whip Creamer, redline, #1870 .... **60.00**
Zender Fact 4, #125 .... **15.00**
Z Whiz, redline, 1977, gray **70.00**
Zombot, #53, gold chrim **15.00**

Hull Pottery

History: In 1905, Addis E. Hull purchased the Acme Pottery Co. in Crooksville, Ohio. In 1917, A. E. Hull Pottery Co. began to make a line of art pottery for florists and gift shops. The company also made novelties, kitchenware, and stoneware. During the Depression, the company primarily produced tiles. Hull's Little Red Riding Hood kitchenware was manufactured between 1943 and 1957 and is a favorite of collectors, including many who do not collect other Hull items.

In 1950, the factory was destroyed by a flood and fire, but by 1952 it was back in production, operating under the Hull Pottery Company name. At this time Hull added its newer glossy finish pottery, plus the firm developed pieces sold in flower shops under the Regal and Floraline trade names. Hull's brown House 'n' Garden line of kitchen and dinnerware achieved great popularity and was the main line being produced prior to the plant's closing in 1986.

Collecting Hints: Distinctive markings on the bottom of Hull Pottery vases help the collector to identify them immediately. Early stoneware pottery has an "H." The famous matte pieces, a favorite of most collectors, contain pattern numbers. For example, Camelia pieces are marked with numbers in the 100s, Iris pieces have 400 numbers, and Wildflower a "W" preceding their number. Most of Hull's vases are also marked with their height in inches, making it easy to determine their value. Items made after 1950 are usually glossy and are marked "hull" or "Hull" in large script letters.

Hull collectors are beginning to seriously collect the glossy ware and kitchen items.

Adviser: Joan Hull.

Pre-1950 Patterns

Bow Knot

    B3, 6" vase **250.00**
    B7, 8-1/2" vase **325.00**
    B10, 10-1/2" vase **500.00**
    B13, double cornucopia **295.00**
    B15, 13-1/2" pitcher **1,300.00**
    B28, 10" d plate **1,200.00**

Dogwood (Wildflower)

    501 7-1/2" basket **300.00**
    504, 8-1/2" vase **150.00**
    506, 7" pitcher **275.00**
    507, 5-1/2" teapot **350.00**
    511, 11-1/2" cornucopia **275.00**
    514, 4" jardinière **110.00**
    519, 13-1/2" pitcher **800.00**

Iris

401-8" pitcher		275.00
405, 4-3/4" vase		85.00
406, 7" vase		155.00
409 12" console bowl		260.00
412, 7" hanging planter		175.00
413, 9" jardinière		375.00
414, 16" floor vase		700.00

Jack-In-The-Pulpit/Calla Lily

500/32, 10" bowl		185.00
500/33, 8" vase		145.00
505, 6" vase		125.00
550, 7" vase		140.00
560/33, 13" vase		350.00

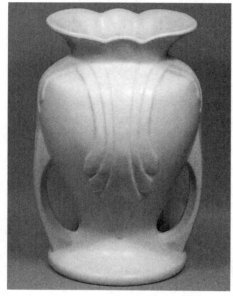

Vase, Mardi Gras, cream matte glaze, embossed "U.S.A. 49 9," 9-1/4" h, **$80**.

Magnolia

2, 8-1/2" vase		125.00
4, 6-1/4" vase		75.00
5, 7" pitcher		125.00
6, 12" double cornucopia		175.00
8, 10-1/2" vase		200.00
10, 10-1/2" basket		350.00
14, 4-3/4" pitcher		75.00
17, 12-1/2" winged vase		325.00
20, 15" floor vase		500.00
22, 12-1/2" vase		325.00
23, 25, 55, tea set		400.00

Magnolia (Pink Gloss)

H2, 5-1/2" vase		45.00
H5, 6-1/2" vase		45.00
H15, double cornucopia		125.00
H17, 12-1/2" vase		250.00
H23, 24, console and candleholders set		225.00

Open Rose (Camelia)

104, 10-1/2" mermaid planter		3,500.00
105, 7" pitcher		225.00

Magnolia, ewer, #18-13-1/2, $300.

110, 111, 112, tea set		550.00
114, 8-1/2" jardinière		375.00
115, 8-1/2" pitcher		350.00
120, 6-1/2" vase		150.00
125, 8-1/2" wall pocket		375.00
140, 10-1/2" basket		1,300.00
141, 8-1/2" cornucopia		225.00

Orchid

301, 10" vase		350.00
302, 4-3/4" vase		95.00
303, 7" vase		195.00
306, 6-3/4" bud vase		175.00
309, 6-1/2" vase		195.00
310, 9-1/2" jardinière		450.00
311, 13" pitcher		700.00
316, bookends		1,200.00

Pinecone, 55, 6" vase 175.00

Poppy

601, 9" basket		800.00
602, planter		300.00
604, 8" cornucopia		175.00
606, 6-1/2" vase		200.00
607, 4-3/4" vase		175.00
607, 8-1/2" vase		275.00
609, 9" wall planter		450.00
610, 4-3/4" pitcher		200.00
612, 6-1/2" vase		200.00

Rosella

R1, 5" vase		35.00
R8, 6-1/2" vase		75.00
R9, pitcher		75.00
R10, hanging planter		85.00

R12, 7" basket **185.00**
R15, 8-1/2" vase **85.00**

Stoneware

25H, 5-1/2" vase **75.00**
26H, vase **95.00**
492H, pretzel jar **275.00**
492H, stein **45.00**
492H, tankard **225.00**
536H, 9" jardinière **135.00**

Vase, Tulip, blue ground, pink and yellow
flowers, green leaves, embossed "USA 107-33-6,"
6" h, **$125**.

Tulip

101-33, 9" vase **245.00**
106-33, 6" basket **350.00**
108-33, 6" vase **125.00**
109-33, 8" pitcher **235.00**
110-33, 6" vase **150.00**
115-33, 7" jardinière **350.00**

Wildflower series, tea set, #72, 73, 74, **$550**.

Waterlily

L-1, 5-1/2" vase **75.00**
L-4, 6-1/2" vase **95.00**
L-8, 8-1/4" vase **165.00**
L10, 9-1/2" vase **225.00**
L14, 10-1/2" vase **350.00**
L-18, 6" teapot **225.00**
L-19, 5" creamer **75.00**
L-20, 5" sugar **75.00**

Wildflower

54, 6-1/2" vase **175.00**
66, 10-1/2" basket **2,000.00**
76, 8-1/2" vase **350.00**
W-3, 5-1/2" vase **55.00**
W-5, 6-1/2" vase **85.00**
W-8, 7-1/2" vase **95.00**
W-9, 8-1/2" vase **145.00**
W-12, 9-1/2" vase **175.00**
W-14, 10-1/2" vase **195.00**
W-18, 12-1/2" vase **350.00**
W-19, 13-1/2" pitcher **450.00**

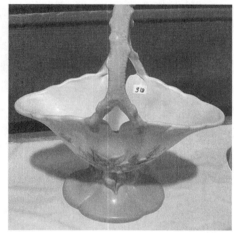

Woodland, basket, #W22-10-1/2, **$225**.

Woodland (matte)

W1, 5-1/2" vase **95.00**
W4, 6-1/2" vase **125.00**
W8, 7-1/4" vase **125.00**
W10, 11" cornucopia **195.00**
W18, 10-1/2" vase **185.00**
W23, 14" double cornucopia **475.00**
W25, 12-1/2" vase **425.00**
W31, 5-1/2" hanging basket **145.00**

Post-1950 Patterns (Glossy)

Blossom Flite

T1, 6" honey jug **65.00**
T8, basket **125.00**
T9, 10" low basket **135.00**
T10, 16-1/2" console bowl **125.00**
T11, candleholders, pr **75.00**
T14, 15, 16, tea set **200.00**

Butterfly

B1, 6" pitcher 45.00
B4, 6" bonbon dish 50.00
B7, 9-3/4" rect bowl 50.00
B10, 7" vase 55.00
B13, 8" basket 150.00
B14, 10-1/2" vase 100.00
B15, 13-1/2" pitcher 200.00
B23, 11-1/2" relish serving tray 200.00
B24, 25, lavabo set 200.00

Ebbtide

E2, 7" bud vase 95.00
E3, 7-1/2" mermaid cornucopia 225.00
E5, 9-1/8" basket 150.00
E7, 11" fish vase 175.00
E8, ashtray with mermaid 225.00
E12, 15-3/4" console 200.00
E13, console and pr candleholders
.... 325.00
E14, 15, 16, tea set 325.00

Figural Planters

27, Madonna, standing 65.00
74, bandana duck 50.00
80, swan 40.00
82, clown 125.00
95, twin geese 50.00

Parchment & Pine

S-1, 5" vase 50.00
S-5, 10-1/2" scroll planter 95.00
S-6, 12" cornucopia 125.00
S11, 12, 13, tea set 250.00
S-15, 8" coffeepot 175.00

Serenade (Birds)

S3, 5-3/4" pedestal planter 55.00
S7, 8-1/2" vase 65.00
S10, 11" cornucopia 100.00
S15, 11-1/2" ftd fruit bowl 125.00
S20, 9" cov casserole 125.00
S22, 8 oz mug 55.00

Sunglow

51, 7-1/2" cov casserole 50.00
53, grease jar 60.00
55, 7-1/2" beverage pitcher 85.00
80, wall pocket, cup and saucer 75.00
83, iron wall pocket 85.00
95, 8-1/4" vase 45.00
98, 7-1/2" flower pot 45.00

Tokay/Tuscany (Grapes)

4, 8-1/4" vase 95.00
6, 8" basket 95.00
8, 10" vase 150.00
12, 12" vase 125.00
14, 15-3/4" consolette 165.00
19, large leaf dish 95.00
20, 15" vase 225.00

Tropicana

T54, 12-1/2" vase 600.00
T55, 12-3/4" basket 750.00
T56, 13-1/2" pitcher 750.00

Woodland, double cornucopia, #W23, $475.

Woodland, tea set, #W26, 27, 27, $500.

Woodland

W-2, 5-1/2" cornucopia 40.00
W-6, 6-1/2" pitcher 65.00
W-8, 7-1/4" vase 60.00
W-9, 8-3/4" basket 110.00
W011, 6-1/2" flower pot, saucer 65.00
W-13, 7-1/2" shell wall pocket 95.00
W-19, 10-1/2" window box 95.00

Woodland, vase, #W25-12-1/2, $425.

Calendar, 1891, Gus Becht Butcher's Supply, full pad, lithograph by Gast, St. Louis and New York, 10" w, 14" l, **$950**.

Poster, Mayo's Plug, linen, 17-3/4" w, 30" h, **$700**. Photos courtesy of Past Tyme Pleasures Auction.

Poster, Red Belt 5¢ Cigar, professionally framed, 15" w, 20" h, **$750**.

Life and Adventures of Buffalo Bill, stone litho by Riverside Printing Co., Milwaukee, 29" w, 43" h, **$1,650**.

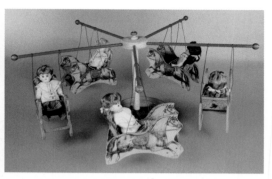

Carousel, Converse five wooden seats with lithographed horses, five matching 10" h German dolls in original clothing, 15" h, 36" w, **$1,500**. Photo courtesy of McMasters Doll Auction.

Battery-operated Dentist Bear, 19", **$450**. Photo courtesy of McMasters Doll Auction.

Ocean liner, Fleishman-painted tin wind-up, minor flakes, two lifeboats missing, 18" l, **$1,250**. Photo courtesy of Richard Opfer Auctioneering, Inc.

Battery-operated Barber Bear, 9-1/2", **$495**. Photo courtesy of McMasters Doll Auction.

Toy trains, American Flyer, railway set, engine, three cars, restoration, **$275**. Photo courtesy of Richard Opfer Auctioneering, Inc.

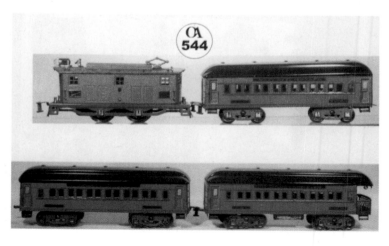

Doll, Poupee Pea, original clothing, 17" h, **$3,000**. Photos courtesy of McMasters Doll Auctions.

Effanbee, Skippy Policeman, rare original outfit and accessories, 14" h, **$1,950**.

Dolls, Huret, lady, 17" h, wooden body, **$7,000**; man, 17" h, gutta-percha body, **$17,500**.

Doll, Jumeau, 31" h, bisque head, brown sleep eyes, open mouth, human-hair wig, **$2,900**.

Dolls, Door of Hope, Bride, 11" h, **$1,350**; Groom, 11" h, **$1,100**.

Figure,
Revolutionary
War soldiers,
four of a set of
six, mid-1960s to
early 1970s,
7" h, each **$60**.

Japanese naval officer's cap, World War II, **$275**. Photo
courtesy of Jackson's Auctioneers & Appraisers.

First German transistor radio, Telefunken TR-1, 1955,
$3,197. Photo courtesy of Auction Team Breker.

Radio, Atwater Kent Type TA, 1924, **$1,465**. Photo
courtesy of Auction Team Breker.

Radio receiver, German Armed Forces,
designed to top and determine enemy
frequencies, 1944, **$5,230**. Photo
courtesy of Auction Team Breker.

Sports collectibles, pin, Lehigh University, brown and gold ribbon, 4-1/2" l celluloid football player, c1950, $40. Photo courtesy of Julie Robinson.

Painting, oil on canvas, created for King's Powder Quickshot, c1890, original frame, professionally cleaned and revarnished, 20" w, 28" h, $9,100. Photo courtesy of Past Tyme Pleasures Auction.

Holiday collectibles, McCoy Pottery cookie jar, Pumpkin Face, $375. Photo courtesy of House in the Woods Auction Gallery.

Holiday collectibles, postcard, Santa Claus and little girl, artist A. Tekauz, $100. Photo courtesy of Postcards International.

Holiday collectibles, Viscoloid Santa Express, blow-molded toy, Santa engineer on train, celluloid, $125. Photo courtesy of Julie Robinson.

Bank, Paddy and the Pig, J & E Stevens Co., **$1,110**.

Elephant, parade or circus, not marked, carnival chalkware, 10" h, **$85**. Photo courtesy of Thomas Morris.

Cartoon characters, Maggie and Jiggs, marked "Armistice," 11-1/4" h, **$285**. Photo courtesy of Thomas Morris.

Black memorabilia, Mammy, full figure, one-piece hollow casting, white scarf and apron, dark blue dress, red kerchief on head, 10" h, **$325**. Photo courtesy of Craig Dinner.

Hummel, Harmony in Four Parts, #471, trademark 6, **$1,155**. Photo courtesy of Jackson's Auctioneers & Appraisers.

Unusual coin-operated tall case clock, Polyphon No. 63, uses 11-1/4" metal discs to produce music, c1900, **$13,300**. Photo courtesy of Auction Team Breker.

Furniture, desk, Eastlake, walnut, center mirror plate surmounted by gallery, side shelf brackets with decorative banding, turned columns, slant front with embossed decoration on lid, brass escutcheon, galleried lower shelf, **$3,000**. Photo courtesy of Jackson's Auctioneers & Appraisers.

Furniture, music stand, Victorian, musical devices carved on single door, shelved interior, hairy paw front feet, late 19th C, 39" h, **$2,688**. Photo courtesy of Jackson's Auctioneers & Appraisers.

Furniture, linden press, Chippendale, poplar, reeded quarter columns, top dental molding, two arched top drawers, secret compartment, base with three drawers over two drawers, replaced ogee bracket feet, 56" w, 23-1/4" d, 81" h, **$4,125**. Photo courtesy of Alderfer Auction Company, Inc.

Morton Pottery Company, night-light, praying child, prayer in wall hanging shadow box, **$40**.

Morton Pottery Company, Santa, punch bowl, **$150**. Photos courtesy of Doris and Burdell Hall.

Morton Potteries, Cliftwood Art Potteries, waffle set, covered batter pitcher, covered syrup pitcher, matching tray, Old Rose drip over white, **$150**.

Morton Pottery Company, planter, rooster, natural colors, 9" h, **$30**.

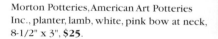

Morton Potteries, American Art Potteries Inc., planter, lamb, white, pink bow at neck, 8-1/2" x 3", **$25**.

Children's books, *The Pop-up Book of Trucks*, Random House, ©1974, **$12**.

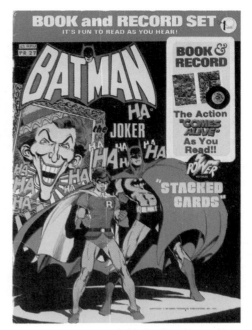

Super heroes, Batman, child's book and record set, ©National Periodical Publications, Inc., 1975, **$15**.

Cartoon characters, book and record set, child's, *Beep Beep The Road Runner, A Very Scary Lesson,* Peter Pan Records, Looney Tunes, Warner Bros., 45 rpm, **$12**.

Little Golden Books, *Three Little Kittens,* #381, ©1942, well read, **$5**.

Label, Silver Tip, Strathmore Grape Growers Assn., brown bear and mountains, black ground, **$.50**. Labels courtesy of Lorie Cairns.

Label, Valley Queen, regal young lady wearing crown, red grapes, vivid colors, 1950s, **$.25**.

Label, Piggy Pears Brand, Medford, Oregon, Highcroft Orchards, Product of U.S.A., cartoon pink pig, wearing clothes and bonnet, carrying basket of pears, maroon background, 10-1/4" x 7-1/4", **$3**.

Vending machine, coin-operated, Rosebud Matches, by Northwestern, 13-1/2" h, 5-1/2" w, **$525**. Photo courtesy of Past Tyme Pleasures Auction.

German chocolate vending machine, Schokoladen-Fabrik, c1900, **$3,150**. Photo courtesy of Auction Team Breker.

Coin-operated music box, Kalliope Panorama Automata, 1905, with rare horse game, **$24,046**. Photo courtesy of Auction Team Breker.

Gambling machine, "Bajazzo," approximately 1904 (#548), **$2,877**. Photo courtesy of Auction Team Breker.

Space adventurers and explorers, child's book and record set, *Star Trek, Passage to Moauv,* **$15**.

Coloring book, *Walt Disney Productions' The Black Hole,* Whitman, ©1979, used, **$3**.

Space adventurers and explorers, astronaut Donald K. Slayton, autographed color photo, U.S. Govt. Printing Office, 1974, **$15**.

Star Wars, book and record set, *Star Wars, Droid World, The Future Adventures,* ©MCMLSSSIII Lucasfilm Ltd., 33-1/3 rpm, **$18.50**.

Horse collectibles, carousel horse, carved and painted wood, repaint, 51" l, **$1,300**. Photo courtesy of Richard Opfer Auctioneering, Inc.

Horse collectibles, Breyer, Proud Arabian Mare, glossy alabaster, 1956-60, **$55**. Photo courtesy of Jim and Nancy Schaut.

Horse collectibles, mug, Famous Clydesdales, first in series, **$45**. Photo courtesy of Jim and Nancy Schaut.

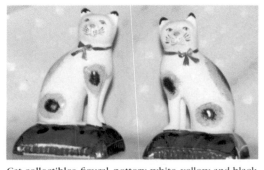

Cat collectibles, figural, pottery, white, yellow and black spots, blue bases, stamped in blue "Staffordshire, England," 4" h, pair, **$35**. Photo courtesy of Don Dipboye.

Cat collectibles, TV lamp, ceramic, two Siamese cats, incised "©1958 Lane & Co., Van Nuys, CA, U.S.A.," **$85**. Photo courtesy of Don Dipboye.

Motorbike, tin toy, "BMW500," approximately 1952 (#970), very original-like model by Bandai Japan, **$1,119**. Photo courtesy of Auction Team Breker.

Bicycle, Veliopede, New York, referred to as "Boneshaker," **$7,670**. Photo courtesy of Auction Team Breker.

World's fairs and expositions, New York, 1964-65, Flash Card Set, original box, **$5**.

TV memorabilia and personalities, book and record set, *Knight Rider, Highway to Danger,* Kid Stuff, ©1982, 1984 University City Studios, Inc., 33-1/3 rpm, **$7.50**.

Model kits, Revell, VW Pickup with ATV, 1:32 scale, partially put together, **$5**.

Lamp, Consolidated Glass Company, blown-out floral shade, silvered base, 10" h, **$660**. Photo courtesy of Jackson's Auctioneers & Appraisers.

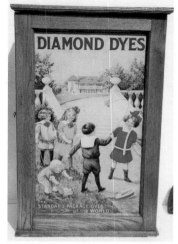

Advertising, cabinet, Diamond Dyes, wooden, counter top, embossed tin litho, 15-1/2" w, 9" d, 24-1/2" h, **$1,750**. Photo courtesy of Past Tyme Pleasures Auction.

Political and campaign items, Patriotic Order Sons of America, top pin printed celluloid, center portrait of George Washington, gold trim, center medallion with image of Washington kneeling in prayer, made by Whitehead & Hoag, 7" l, **$125**. Photo courtesy of Julie Robinson.

Political and campaign items, postcard, Teddy Roosevelt and Asians, newspaper headline reads, "Protestional, Californienne," satire, **$300**. Photo courtesy of Postcards International.

Postcard, Japanese woman, H. Nakazauwa, **$150**. Photo courtesy of Postcards International.

Plastics, autograph album, celluloid cover, ocean scene with seagulls, c1907, 5-1/2" x 4", **$75**. Photo courtesy of Julie Robinson.

Flow Blue, unknown pattern, Warwick, tea set: teapot, creamer, sugar and tray, **$1,100**. Photo courtesy of Ellen King.

Flow Blue, Weir, sauce tureen, four pieces, **$495**. Photo courtesy of Ellen King.

Royal China, Fair Oaks, platter, oval, 11" l, **$35**. Photo courtesy of David Folckemer.

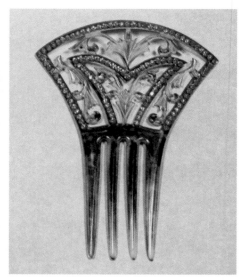

Plastics, comb, celluloid to imitate tortoiseshell, filigree ornamentation, set with blue rhinestones, 6-1/4" l, **$45**. Photo courtesy of Julie Robinson.

Clothing and accessories, Cocktail Dress, Christian Dior, periwinkle blue silk taffeta, large bow at center front bodice, original label, **$690**. Photo courtesy of Skinner, Inc.

Hummel Items

History: Hummel items are the original creations of Berta Hummel, who was born in 1909 in Massing, Bavaria, Germany. At age 18, she was enrolled in the Academy of Fine Arts in Munich to further her mastery of drawing and the palette. Berta entered the Convent of Siessen and became Sister Maria Innocentia in 1934. While in this Franciscan cloister she continued drawing and painting images of her childhood friends.

In 1935, W. Goebel Co. in Rodental, Germany, began producing Sister Maria Innocentia's sketches as three-dimensional bisque figurines. The Schmid Brothers of Randolph, Massachusetts, introduced the figurines to America and became Goebel's U.S. distributor.

In 1967, Goebel began distributing Hummel items in the United States. A controversy developed between the two companies, the Hummel family, and the convent. Law suits and counter-suits ensued. The German courts finally effected a compromise: the convent held legal rights to all works produced by Sister Maria Innocentia from 1934 until her death in 1946 and licensed Goebel to reproduce these works; Schmid was to deal directly with the Hummel family for permission to reproduce any pre-convent art.

Collecting Hints: A key to pricing Hummel figures is the mark. All authentic Hummel pieces bear both the signature "M. I. Hummel" and a Goebel trademark. Various trademarks were used to identify the year of production:

Crown Mark (trademark 1)
           1935 through 1949
Full Bee (trademark 2)
           1950-1959
Stylized Bee (trademark 3)
           1957-1972
Three Line Mark (trademark 4)
           1964-1972
Last Bee Mark (trademark 5)
           1972-1979
Missing Bee Mark (trademark 6)
           1979-1990

Current Mark or New Crown Mark (trademark 7)   1991 to the present.

Collectors are advised to buy pieces with the early marks whenever possible. Since production runs were large, almost all figurines, no matter what the mark, exist in large numbers.

Prices fluctuate a great deal. Antiques newspapers, such as *The Antique Trader*, often carry ads by dealers offering discounts on the modern pieces. The slightest damage to a piece lowers the value significantly.

Before World War II and for a few years after, the Goebel Company made objects, such as vases, for export. These often had the early mark. Prices are modest for these items considering the workmanship that went into their creation.

Angel, Festival Harmony, #172/II, with mandolin **140.00**

Anniversary plate

1975, Stormy Weather, #280, FE . **125.00**
1979, Singing Lesson..................... **40.00**

Ashtray

Boy With Bird, #166 .... **80.00**
Happy Pastime, #62, trademark 3 . **20.00**
Joyful, #33....................................... **75.00**
Let's Sing, #114 .... **75.00**

Bank, Little Thrifty, c1972.................... **50.00**

Bell, MIB

1975 .... **65.00**
1980 .... **60.00**

Collector plate, 1980, 2nd Anniversary plate and original box, $60.

Calendar, 1955, 12 illus **15.00**
Candleholder, Angel Lights, plate base, orig bees wax candles, #241, trademark 5
.... **150.00**

Collector plate, Happy Pastime, 1978, plate and original box, **$75.**

Christmas plate

1971, Heavenly Angel, #264 .... **700.00**
1972, Hear Ye, Hear Ye, #265 ...... **125.00**
1973, Globe Trotter, #266............... **70.00**
1974, Goose Girl, #267 .... **100.00**
1975, Ride Into Christmas, #268 .... **90.00**
1977, Apple Tree Boy, #270........... **95.00**
1978, Happy Pastime, #271 .... **75.00**
1979, Singing Lesson, #272.......... **85.00**
1980, School Girl, #273 .... **100.00**
1981, Umbrella Boy, #274 .... **100.00**
1983, Postman, #276 .... **110.00**
1984, A Gift From Heaven, #277 .. **100.00**
1985, Chick Girl, #278 .... **100.00**
1986, Playmates, #279 .... **100.00**
1987, Feeding Time, #283............. **100.00**
1988, Little Goat Herder, #284...... **100.00**
1989, Farm Boy............................. **100.00**

Bell, 1979, bas relief, second in series, MIB, **$60.**

Doll

Carnival, porcelain........................ **160.00**
Chimney Sweep **80.00**
Easter Greetings, porcelain **160.00**
Gretel.. **60.00**
Hansel... **60.00**
Little Knitter **65.00**
Postman, porcelain....................... **160.00**
Rose, pink **50.00**

Figure

Adoration, #23/111, trademark 5 . **375.00**
Artist, #304, trademark 6................ **90.00**
Barnyard Hero, #195/2/0, trademark 2
.... **115.00**
Be Patient, trademark 3................ **145.00**
Builder, #305, trademark 4............ **80.00**
Carnival, #328, trademark 6.......... **80.00**
Doll Bath, #319, trademark 5 .... **75.00**
Doll Mother, trademark 3.............. **135.00**
Duet, #130, trademark 1 .... **300.00**
Eventide, trademark 3 .... **135.00**
Farm Boy, #66, trademark 3......... **350.00**
Feather Friends, #344, trademark 1
.... **365.00**
Friend or Foe, #434, trademark 1 **285.00**
Gay Adventure, #356, trademark 6 **75.00**
Girl with Doll, #239, trademark 6.... **25.00**
Good Hunting, #307, trademark 4 **130.00**
Goose Girl, #47/0, trademark 2.... **200.00**
Happy Birthday, #176/0, trademark 3
.... **245.00**
Happy Pastime, #69, trademark 3
.... **190.00**
Hear Ye, #15/0, trademark 1 .... **300.00**
Herald Angels, #37, trademark 2... **80.00**
Just Resting, #112/I, trademark 1 **300.00**
Kiss Me, #311, trademark 5 .... **200.00**
Little Fiddler, #4, trademark 5....... **160.00**
Little Gardener, #72, trademark 2 .. **60.00**
Little Scholar, #80, trademark 3 ..... **55.00**
Lot Sheep, #68/0, trademark 3 ..... **72.00**
Merry Wanderer, #7/II, trademark 1
.... **500.00**
Out Of Danger, #56B, trademark 3
.... **290.00**
Photographer, trademark 2 .... **225.00**
Retreat to Safety, #201/2/0, trademark 4
.... **90.00**
School Girl, #81/2/0, trademark 3 .. **60.00**
Sensitive Hunter, trademark 2...... **240.00**
She Loves Me, She Loves Me Not,
trademark 2 .... **225.00**
Sweet Music, #186, trademark 1 . **125.00**
Telling Her Secret, #196/0, trademark 2
.... **235.00**
Tuneful Angel, #359, trademark 6.. **45.00**
Village Boy, #51/2/0, trademark 1 **115.00**
Waiter, #154/0, trademark 5 .... **200.00**
Wash Day, #321, trademark 4........ **80.00**
Weary Wanderer, #204, trademark 6
.... **80.00**
Worship, #84/0, trademark 1........ **250.00**

Collector plate, Singing Lesson, 1979, Hummel #272, boy playing horn, original box, $45.

Dolls, Gretel on left, Hansel on right, Goebel marks, MIB, **each $125**.

Font

Angel Cloud, #206, trademark 4 .... **25.00**
Angel Sitting, #167, trademark 4 .... **40.00**
Angel with Birds, #22/0, trademark 6
.... **20.00**
Angels At Prayer, #91B, trademark 3
.... **70.00**
Child With Flowers, #36/0, trademark 2
.... **48.00**
Good Shepherd, #35/0, trademark 6
.... **25.00**
Madonna and Child, #243, trademark 6
.... **25.00**
Worship, #164, trademark 2 .... **120.00**
Inkwell, With Loving Greetings, blue **135.00**
Lamp

Apple Tree Boy, #M/230, trademark 5
.... **165.00**
Good Friends, #M/228, trademark 5
.... **165.00**
Just Resting, #M/225/11, trademark 5
.... **175.00**
Loves Me, Loves Me Not, #M/227,
trademark 2, c1970 .... **190.00**
Out of Danger, trademark 2 .... **275.00**
Music box

Chick Girl **235.00**
Ride Into Christmas **240.00**

Nativity figures

Angel Serenade, #214/D/11 .... **40.00**
Donkey, #214/J/11 .... **35.00**
Infant Jesus, #260 .... **80.00**
King, kneeling on one knee, #214/M/11
.... **100.00**
Lamb, #214/0/11 .... **20.00**
Little Tooter, #214/H/11 .... **65.00**
Madonna, #214/A/M/11 .... **110.00**
Stable, 3 pc, #214/S11 .... **45.00**

Hunting Collectibles

History: Hunting became a necessity as soon as man discovered it could end hunger pains. Hunting collectibles, also known as sporting collectibles, encompass those items used for hunting, whether fox or big game. Today's hunters often choose to use binoculars and cameras in lieu of rifles, arrows, or caveman's clubs.

Collecting Hints: Sporting-minded collectors can easily find more and more items to add to their collections. Most flea markets yield everything from big-game trophy heads to canoes to hunting licenses.

Knife, original green sheath, unmarked, metal hanging bracket, as found, $5.

Award badge, NRA
Marksman, dark silver luster, hanger bar, First Class on center bar **12.00**
Marksman, First Class, NRA 50 Ft Award, 2" l **18.00**
Pro-Marksman, Junior Division, 1-3/4" l
.... **16.00**
Sharpshooter, brass link badge on hanger bar, Junior Division **10.00**
Book

Hunting, Fishing, and Camping, L. L Bean, 1942, 103 pgs, illus.............. **11.50**
The Complete Book of Hunting, Clyde Ormond, 1962, 467 pgs, illus......... **11.50**
The Sportsman's Almanac: A Guide to the Recreational Uses of America's Public Lands, with Special Emphasis on Hunting and Fishing, Carley Farquhar, Harper & Row, 1963, 1st ed., 453 pgs, small tear to dj... **9.50**

Broadside, litho
14-1/2" h, 12" w, DuPont Powders, two anxious duck hunters pecking out of camp, "Just look at 'em," image by Edmund Osthaus, c1910 .... **50.00**
42" h, 28" w, Western-Winchester, hunter preparing to shoot red squirrel, autumn foliage, Weimer Pursell litho, © 1955 .... **70.00**

Call
Crow, Charles Perdew, Henry, IL, fair condition **175.00**
Duck, Herter's, orig box **35.00**
Turkey Hooter Owl, Olt, orig box **35.00**

Catalog
Dave Cook Sporting Goods, 48 pgs, 1968 .... **5.00**
Edw Tryon Sporting Goods, 72 pgs, 1923 .... **27.50**
Kirtland Bros Sporting Goods, 16 pgs, 1924 .... **15.00**
Winchester Rifle, John Wayne cover, 16 pgs, 1982 .... **8.50**

Counter felt
Dead Shot Powder, "Kill Your Bird Not Your Shoulder," multicolored on black, trimmed **90.00**
Winchester, "Shoot Where You Aim" **175.00**

Decoy basket, clam-style **200.00**
Handbook, *Winchester Ammunition*, 112 pgs, 1951 .... **13.50**
Head, mounted, fine condition
Alaskan Wolf **350.00**
Antelope, head turned **150.00**
Auerhahn, German wild turkey **200.00**
Cape Buffalo, black horns **750.00**
Caribou **300.00**
Curly horn goat, brown **225.00**
Curly horn sheep **475.00**
Elk **600.00**
European red stag **200.00**
Fallow Deer **85.00**
Greater Kudo, curly horns **250.00**
Ibex **200.00**
Jacob's sheep, dark brown, ... **400.00**
Moose **450.00**
Mouflon, dark brown, two curly horns, one with natural damage, base with brass plaque reading "Het Loo 24, Sept 1970" **300.00**
Russian boar **200.00**
Water Buffalo, black **275.00**
White-tailed deer, 6-point antlers, head turned slightly **75.00**
White-tailed deer, 6-point antlers, head straight **90.00**
Wild boar **250.00**
Wildebeest **75.00**

License
New Jersey, 1928, for resident hunting/ fishing, black, white and blue **70.00**

Knife, original sheath, blade embossed "Cub Hunter, Colonial, Prov. R.I., USA," $16.

New Jersey, 1933, blue and white, black serial number, minor rust on back . **50.00**
New York, 1921, hunting and fishing, 1-1/2" d, bright yellow shading to cream, NY state seal, Bastian Bros back paper **25.00**
New York, 1924, for resident hunting and trapping, buff, black, and white **85.00**
New York, 1932, for resident hunting, trapping, and fishing, peach, black, and white **38.00**
North Carolina, 1929-30, pale blue and white, black serial number **80.00**
Ontario Guide, 1935, black and white, red numerals, worn **20.00**
West Virginia, 1934, blue and black, non-resident, black serial number on white band **80.00**
Wisconsin, 1932, black and white, some wear **25.00**

Magazine
American Rifleman, August 15, 1924 .... **10.00**
Hunting and Fishing, February 1938, Myrna Loy and Lucky Strike back cover color ad **12.00**
Magazine tear sheet, half page size, 1949 Western World Champion Ammunition, "Even bull strength is no match for the New Silver Tip" **3.50**
Winchester, "Bag A Buck," model 94, 70, and 12 .... **3.50**

Pamphlet, *Stoeger's Gun Stock*, black and white, 16 pgs, 8-1/2" x 11", c1930 .... **8.00**

Pinback button

Daisy Air Rifle, blue and white, red center text "Shoot Safe Buddy," text on rim "World-Wide Safety League," 1940s, 7/8" d... **25.00**

Dead Shot Smokeless Powder, mallard duck being shot out of air, Ehrman back paper, 7/8" d **30.00**

Ducks Unlimited, multicolored, 1948 .... **95.00**

Dupont Smokeless Powder, multicolored, fall hunting scene, pair of black and white pointer dogs, black lettering "Dupont Smokeless-The Champion's Powder" **100.00**

Experts Use Peters Cartridges, silvery bullet in brass casing, deep red ground, white text, Pulver back paper, c1904, 7/8" d... **70.00**

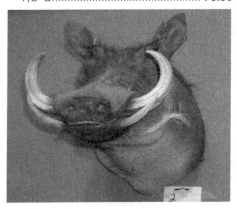

Trophy head, Warthog, South African, plaque with hunter's name, bronze award, and date, **$200.**

Nanty Glo Rod & Gun Club, blue lettering on white... **10.00**

Peters Cartridges, multicolored, silver bullet in brass casing, pale green ground, black letters.................................... **45.00**

Remington UMC, red and white center, white rim, blue text "Shoot Arrow Or Nitro Club Shells," Phelps & Sons, Newark back paper, 7/8" d **90.00**

Use Peters Referee Shells, cut-away view of purple shotgun shell overprinted with red letter "P," Bastian back paper, 7/8" d **80.00**

Winchester Crosby, multicolored, portrait of W. R. Crosby, The Champion Shot of the World, and the Shell He Shoots **150.00**

Winchester Shotgun & Shells, silver and navy blue, red letter "W" outlined in white, rim inscription "Shoot Winchester Shotgun Shells and Shotguns," back paper defaced............................... **35.00**

Winchester Topperweins, husband and wife sharpshooter team, black lettering inscriptions, red circle accent...... **100.00**

Shooter's box, fired brass shells, 24 **280.00**

Skiff, gunning, canvas covered, Harve de Grace, MD, tidewaters, c1910..... **500.00**

Stickpin, Smith Guns, celluloid, multicolored, oval, brass insert back, inscribed "The Hunter Arms Co, Fulton, NY" **120.00**

Target ball, glass

Amber, Bogardus **255.00**

Green, basketweave, shooting figure **185.00**

Tintype, 2-3/8" x 3", three young hunters, seated and holding rifles, stack of three more rifles in foreground, late 1800s **18.00**

▋

Ice Cream Collectibles

History: During the 1st century A.D. in ancient Rome, nearby mountains provided the Emperor Nero with snow and ice, which he flavored with fruit pulp and honey. This fruit ice was the forerunner of ice cream. The next development occurred in the 13th century. Among the many treasures that Marco Polo brought back from the Orient was a recipe for a frozen milk dessert resembling sherbet.

In the 1530s, Catherine de Medici, bride of King Henry II of France, introduced Italian ices to the French court. By the end of the 16th century, ices had evolved into a product similar to today's modern ice cream. By the middle of the 17th century, ice cream became fashionable at the English court.

Ice cream changed from being a luxury food for kings and their courts to a popular commodity in 1670 when the Cafe Procope (rue de l'Ancienne) in Paris introduced ice cream to the general populace, and by 1700 the first ice cream recipe book appeared. Ice cream was the rage of 18th-century Europe.

Ice cream appeared in America by the early 18th century. In 1777, an advertisement by Philip Lenzi, confectioner, appeared in the *New York Gazette* noting that ice cream was available on a daily basis. George Washington was an ice cream enthusiast, spending more than $200 with a New York ice cream merchant in 1790. Thomas Jefferson developed an 18-step process to make ice cream and is credited with the invention of baked Alaska.

By the mid-19th century, ice cream "gardens" sprang up in major urban areas, and by the late 1820s the ice cream street vendor arrived on the scene. However, because ice cream was still difficult to prepare, production remained largely in commercial hands.

In 1846, Nancy Johnson invented the hand-cranked ice cream freezer, allowing ice cream to enter the average American household. As the century progressed, the ice cream parlor arrived on the scene and homemade ice cream competed with commercial products from local, regional, and national dairies.

The arrival of the home refrigerator/freezer and large commercial freezers in grocery stores marked the beginning of the end for the ice cream parlor. A few survived into the post-World War II era. The drugstore soda fountain, which replaced many of them, became, in turn, a thing of the past in the 1970s when drugstore chains arrived on the scene.

America manufactures and consumes more ice cream than any other nation in the world. But Americans do not hold a monopoly. Ice cream reigns worldwide as one of the most popular foods known. In France it is called *glace*; in Germany, *eis*; and in Russia, *marozhnye*. No matter what it is called, ice cream is eaten and enjoyed around the globe.

Collecting Hints: The ice cream collector has many competitors. Those who do not have a specialty collection are sometimes hampered by the regional collector, i.e., an individual who exclusively collects ice cream memorabilia related to a specific manufacturer or area. Many ice cream collectibles are associated with a specific dairy, thus adding dairy collectors to the equation. Since most ice cream was made of milk, milk and milk bottle collectors also hover around the edge of the ice cream collecting scene, and do not forget to factor in the cow collector (ice cream advertising often features cows). Advertising, food mold, kitchen, and premium collectors are secondary considerations. The result is fierce competition for ice cream material, often resulting in higher prices.

When buying an ice cream tray, the scene is the most important element. Most trays were stock items with the store or firm's name added later. Condition is critical.

Beware of reproductions. They became part of the ice cream collectibles world in the 1980s. Many reproductions are introduced into the market as "warehouse" finds. Although these items look old, many are poor copies or fantasy pieces.

Advertising displays from the 1950s, the flashing neon sign on right sold for **$2,750** and the plastic cone displays on the left sold for **$550 each.**

Advertising trade card, Lightning Blizzard Freezers, diecut, girl giving dish of ice cream out window, mother hand cranking ice cream freezer on reverse.......... **15.00**

Book, *Snow Ice Cream Makers Guide,* B. Heller & Co., 1911............................ **15.00**

Carton, Hershey's Ice Cream, one pint, orange and blue.............................. **18.00**

Catalog, *Ice Cream Maker's Formulary & Price List*, Frank A Beeler, 1910-15 **30.00**

Christmas decoration, 6-1/2" x 10" diecut stuff paper string hanger, front illus of Santa making deliveries on foot, holding Christmas wreath under one arm, Merry Christmas placard in other hand, Bartholomay Ice Cream inscription in black on white snow, 1930s.......... **125.00**

Clock, Breyer's Ice Cream, wood, sailboat, chrome sails **50.00**

Cone dispenser, glass, copper insert **350.00**

Cup, 8-1/2" h, red plastic mug and removable red cap, 4" d brim, Tastee-Free clown, jiggle eyes, c1960....... **20.00**

Doll, Eskimo Pie **12.00**

Film, "Ice Cream Face," Our Gang Comedy, 1930s, 16 mm, 2-1/4" orig sq box .. **25.00**

Freezer box, Breyers Ice Cream green and red logo, half gallon size, white plastic, clear lid **24.00**

Ice cream fork, sterling silver, set of 12
   Debussy, Towle.............................. **480.00**
   Rose Point, Wallace **325.00**

Ice cream knife, sterling silver, repoussé dec, Kirk **85.00**

Ice cream maker
   Alaska, four qt **40.00**
   Unknown maker, tin, hand crank, used
   .... **80.00**
   White Mountain, triple motion **45.00**

Ice cream mold, pewter
   Cherub.. **95.00**

   Cupid on heart............................. **40.00**
   Ear of corn, mkd "E & Co. NY"....... **65.00**
   Grape cluster **30.00**
   Heart, Eppelsmeier........................ **40.00**
   Indian **45.00**
   Lady's shoe **25.00**
   Potato **45.00**
   Question nark................................. **50.00**
   Star in circle **40.00**
   Turkey... **45.00**

Ice cream scoop rest, Hendler's Ice Cream, molded brass, inscription "Friendship of Hendler's The Velvet Kind," 1930-40 .... **45.00**

Ice cream spoon, sterling, set of six
   Chantilly pattern, Gorham **95.00**
   Etruscan, Gorham **365.00**
   Naturalistic, Gorham.................... **260.00**

Menu board, Eat Longacre's Delicious Ice Cream, slots for eight changeable flavors, chrome frame, **$40**.

Ice cream tray, cut glass, American Brilliant Period, hobstars, dandelions, and parallel cuts, sawtooth edge, few chips **150.00**

Key chain, 1-7/8" l, clear plastic case, attached silver luster key chain, center with red and white flasher "Symbol of Quality" with company logo, changes to ice cream scoop in dish with text "Tween Emulsifiers," reverse is red text on white cardboard listing two Tween products, address of Atlas Powder Co., Wilmington, Delaware, c1960............................ **15.00**

Menu clip, Fairmont Ice Cream, 1930-40 .... **18.50**

Pennant, Tellings Ice Cream, felt, children making ice cream............................ **90.00**

Pinback button

Artic Rainbow Ice Cream Cones, rainbow and ice cream cone image, 7/8" d . **75.00**
Boston Ice Cream, red lettering on white ground **15.00**
Good Humor Safety Club, blue and white, orange accents, 1930s series **18.00**
Melorol Ice Cream, Slim Timblin, bluetone portrait of caricature Black youngster, portrait flanked by name in blue lettering, red inscription, early 1930s **25.00**

Pocket mirror, Better Made Ice Cream
.... **35.00**

Record brush, Abbotts Ice Cream, celluloid, soft bristles, mkd "Sixth Anniversary, pale red brick left and right, pale blue sky, red lettering, pale blue rim, 3-1/2" d...... **40.00**

Sign, light-up, Dolly Madison Deliciously Different Ice Cream, yellow background, white center, blue lettering and silhouette, $95.

Scoops, left to right: wood and brass, mechanical, round scoop, lever on side, $55; white metal, mechanical, detacher in cone-shaped scoop, $75; brass, squeeze type handle; tin, mechanical, wide handle, detacher in cone-shaped scoop, $60; tin, mechanical, loop handle, detacher in cone-shaped scoop, $65; tin, wide handle, loop on cone-shaped scoop, $70.

Scoop

Baskins-Robbins, name emb on front, back emb "Pat. No. 471-449-NSF C2 Buildit Engineering Co., #A-25, Burbank, California, USA"................................ **25.00**

Gilchrest #31................................... **95.00**
Gilchrest #33................................. **125.00**
No-Pak, #31, hole in scoop............ **85.00**
Williamson, conical, squeeze auction, inside blade mkd "12," chromed steel or brass, black hard plastic handle . **175.00**

Sign

Borden Dutch Chocolate Ice Cream, Elsie the Cow, paper, 13-1/2" w...... **50.00**
Hancock County Ice Cream, places for seven flavors, 10" w, 20" h, framed **95.00**
Jack & Jill Ice Cream Cake Roll, 8-1/2" x 19-1/2", full color, paper, image of housewife holding slice of ice cream cake, © Newly Weds Baking Co., c1940
.... **35.00**

Song brochure, Hendler's Ice Cream, 1950s **2.00**

Tape measure, Abbotts Ice Cream, black, white, and red illus......................... **20.00**

Thermometer, Abbottmaid Ice Cream, 2" x 6-1/4", 1920s................................. **45.00**

Toy

2" x 4-1/4 x 2", litho tin, Mister Softee Truck, red, white, and blue, silver and black accents, Mister Softee image on three sides, friction, marked "Made in Japan," 1960s............................... **40.00**
2-1/2" l, diecast metal truck, Commer Ice Cream Canteen, Lyons Maid decals in black, white, red, and yellow, white 3-D figure, Matchbox, c1963 .... **35.00**
4" h, ice cream vendor, litho tin wind-up, Depose France, 1930s................. **795.00**

Tray

13" d, Furnas Ice Cream, titled "In Old Kentucky," young girl caressing horse, © 1912, American Art Works litho, some inpainting, bottom rim repainted and relettered **175.00**
13" l, 10-1/2" w, Pangburns Pear Food Ice Cream, animated scene of Palmer Cox Brownies and huge dish of ice cream
.... **350.00**

Truck driver's manual, Jack & Jill, 4-1/2" x 6", black and white, 20 pgs, red accent cover, some scattered spots on cover, late 1930s..................................... **18.00**

Whistle, Puritan Dairy Ice Cream, yellow tin litho, black letters, c1930 .... **35.00**

Irons

History: Ironing devices have been used for many centuries, with the earliest references dating from 1100. Irons from medieval times, the Renaissance, and the early industrial eras can be found in Europe but are rare. Fine engraved brass irons and hand-wrought irons predominated prior to 1860. After 1860, the iron underwent a series of rapid evolutionary changes.

Prior to 1860, irons were heated by three different methods. 1) a hot metal slug was inserted into the body of the iron; 2) a burning solid, e. g. coal, charcoal, or wood, was placed into the body and the heat controlled with dampers, bellows, or other methods to simulate air flow into the burning chamber; and 3) the iron was placed on a hot stove top or over hot coals and by conduction gained heat. After about 1860, liquid and gaseous fuels, such as gasoline, kerosene, alcohol, and natural gas, were introduced into the body and burned.

By the early 1900s, electricity was introduced as a means to heat irons and the evolution changes of different types of irons continued using all the heating techniques for another twenty or thirty years. Finally only electric irons were being manufactured in the developed countries. In the under-developed countries, slug, coal, and conductive heating techniques continue even today.

Collecting Hints: Heavy rusting, pitting, and missing parts detract from an iron's value. More advanced collectors may accept some of these defects on a rare or unusual iron. However, the beginning collector is urged to concentrate on irons in very good to excellent condition.

Many unusual types of irons came from Europe and the Orient. These foreign examples are desirable, especially since some models were prototypes for later American-made irons.

Irons made between 1850 to 1910 are plentiful and varied. Many models and novelty irons still have not been documented by collectors.

Electric irons are just beginning to find favor among collectors but are not being added to older collections. Those with special features (temperature indicators, self-contained stands, sets) and those with Deco styling are the most desirable.

Reproduction Alert: The most frequently reproduced irons are the miniatures, especially the swan's neck and flat irons. Reproductions of some large European varieties have been made, but poor construction, use of thin metals, and the unusually fine condition easily identifies them as new. More and more European styles are being reproduced each year. Construction techniques are better than before and aging processes can fool many knowledgeable collectors. Look for heavy pitting on the reproductions and two or more irons that are exactly alike. Few American irons have been reproduced at this time, other than the miniatures.

Charcoal, box

European, cut work sides, hand made **250.00**
European, soldier's head for latch, sawtooth top edge... **150.00**
Improved Progress Iron, 1913........ **180.00**
Mexican, Paqoel, 1900 .... **50.00**
The Marvel, 1924 .... **125.00**

Charcoal, tall chimney

Double chimney, Ne Plus Ultra, 1902 .... **190.00**
E Bless, R. Drake, 1852................... **100.00**
Husquarna, Swedish, monster head is chimney.. **400.00**

Children's

Cross rib, one pc cast, 2-3/4" **40.00**
Dover sad iron, two pcs, #912, 4-1/8" **35.00**
English box, brass slug, 2-3/4" **180.00**
Enterprise, Pat. iron, holes in handle, 2-1/2" **100.00**
European ox tongue, brass, "L" handle, 4-1/8" **200.00**

French
    Cap iron, decorative casting over base **500.00**
    Oval base, 3-7/8" **80.00**
    Rooster design, 4" **130.00**
Goffering iron, all iron, "S" standard, 2-1/4" barrel.. **130.00**
Ober, No. 15, 4-3/8" **125.00**
Ober, removable handle, 1895 .... **150.00**
Rocker fluter, cast, 1-7/8"................. **300.00**
Swan, no paint, 2-1/4" **110.00**
Tri bump, one pc cast, 3-1/4" **40.00**
Wood grip, The Gem, #2.................. **180.00**

Flat irons

Belgium round back, "L" handle..... **100.00**
Cast, double point............................ **130.00**
Cast, ribbon-folded posts **200.00**
Dover sad iron, cold handle **40.00**
European, green enamel, detachable handle **130.00**
French, Le Gaulois #5 .... **90.00**
Hood's Patent 1867, soapstone top **190.00**
Over, detachable handle, size 3......... **70.00**

Belgium drop-in-the-back slug iron with trivet, $400. Photo courtesy of Sue and David Irons.

Sensible, NRS & Co., flat back, detachable handle... **110.00**
Union, Pat. 1892, detachable handle **130.00**
Wapak #4 .... **35.00**
Wrought, one pc, bell in handle **130.00**

Fluter, combination

Fluter inside, wire clip latch............. **125.00**
Hewitt 1873, revolving, fluter plate removable................................... **350.00**
Streeters Magic, three pcs, 1876..... **700.00**

Fluter, machine type

American, American Machine Co., Philadelphia, PA **130.00**
Companion, clamp-on **300.00**
Dudley, 1876 .... **500.00**

Fluter, rocker type

Geneva, most common **85.00**
The Globe **140.00**
The Star... **140.00**

Fluter, roller type

Clark's 1879, script markings **300.00**
J. Johnson crosswise fluter........... **300.00**
Shephard Hardware, Buffalo, NY **120.00**

Hat

Brass Tolliker, curved shape............ **130.00**
McCoys Patent, raised bottom......... **140.00**
Shackle, curved, movable side **130.00**

Goffering

Single, paw feet, all iron **300.00**
Single "S" wire, standard **110.00**
Single, wrought, monkey tail spiral in standard **450.00**

Electric, General Electric, chrome body, late 1930s, $15.

Liquid fuel, gasoline

Coleman, Model 4A, blue................ **100.00**
The Diamond Iron, Akron Lamp Co. . **65.00**
The Monitor, 1903............................. **85.00**
Wards Quick Lighting Gasoline Iron 80.00

Liquid fuel, natural gas

Central Flat Iron Mfg Co.................. **100.00**
The Perfect Gas Iron, 1913 .... **140.00**
Uneedit Gas Iron **100.00**
Wrights, 1911................................... **100.00**

Polishers

French, round nose, grid bottom **180.00**
Gleason, round back **110.00**
MAB Cook, 1848.............................. **100.00**
Mrs. Streeters #2, Gem Polisher...... **300.00**
Suffolk Polisher, all cast **150.00**
Sweeney Iron, 1894.......................... **190.00**
Troy, round nose, grid bottom............. **85.00**

Miniature, smoothing iron, 3" l, $20.

Slug

Empire Co., box, top lifts off **270.00**
English, box, all iron, lift gate **90.00**
European
    Ox tongue, all iron, china handle. **200.00**
    Ox tongue, brass, "L" handle....... **225.00**
Figural, swan, 1877, rare.............. **5,000.00**
French, wrought, "S" posts............... **250.00**
Scottish, box, turned brass posts.... **700.00**

Special purpose

Billiard table, English...................... **150.00**
Egg, on stand **250.00**
Leaf iron, G. Molla **110.00**
Seam iron, Ames, odd form............ **450.00**
Sleeve
    Asbestos, sad iron, two pcs......... **100.00**
    Sensible, No. 5, two pcs **85.00**

J

Jewelry, Costume

History: The term "costume jewelry" was not used until the 1920s, when Coco Chanel made the wearing of frankly faux jewels an acceptable part of *haute couture*. Prior to the Jazz Age, manufacturers mass-produced imitation jewelry—exact copies of the real thing. Fine jewelry continued to exert its influence on costume jewelry in the 20th-century but, because they were liberated from the costly constraints of valuable gemstones and metals, designers could be more extravagant in producing pieces made of non-precious materials.

By the 1930s, when more cost-effective methods were developed, casting superseded die-stamping in mass-production. The Great Depression instigated the use of the first entirely synthesized plastic, trade named "Bakelite," for colorful and inexpensive jewelry. During World War II, restrictions and shortages forced manufacturers to turn to sterling silver as a replacement for base white metals, and to experiment with new materials such as Lucite (DuPont's trade name for acrylic). Today, Lucite and sterling vermeil (gold-plated) animals and other figurals of the period, known as jelly bellies, are highly collectible. Other World War II novelty items were made of make-do materials such as wood, ceramic, textiles, and natural pods and seeds.

In the prosperous 1950s, high-fashion rhinestone, faux pearl, and colored-glass jewelry signed with the names of well-known couturiers and other designers, was sold in elegant department stores. A matching suite—necklace, bracelet, earrings, brooch—was the proper complement to the ensemble of a well-groomed 1950s' woman.

Collecting Hints: Scarcity and demand drive the market for costume jewelry. Demand is greatest for pieces marked with a recognizable and sought-after designer's or manufacturer's name. Name alone, however, does not guarantee high value. Collectors should also consider quality of design and manufacture, size, and color. Condition is of primary importance because costume jewelry is easily damaged and difficult to repair well. Certain types of unsigned pieces, particularly those made of Bakelite and other plastics, generate collector interest. Because costume jewelry is wearable, pieces should be chosen with personal style and wardrobe in mind.

Reproduction Alert: Recasts and knockoffs are widespread. Copies of high-end signed pieces—e.g., Trifari jelly bellies, Eisenberg Originals, and Boucher—are common. New Bakelite (sometimes called "fakelite") and marriages of old Bakelite parts are also cropping up in many areas.

Beads, casein plastic, often mistaken for celluloid, coral colored, one strand with round and molded beads, **$15**; other strand longer with oval beads, **$12**.

Bracelet

Ciner, hinged bangle, zebra motif, black and white painted enamel, green cabochon glass eyes, colorless rhinestone accents, sgd, c1960 .. **150.00**
Coro, goldtone, pressed glass scarabs, 7" l, 1950s **18.00**

Lane, Kenneth Jay, bangle, snake, hinged goldtone, rhinestones, green glass cabochon eyes, sgd "KJL" **155.00**

Eisenberg

Linked clusters of marquise-cut colorless rhinestones, v-spring and box clasp, block letters mark, safety chain, c1950, 7-1/2" l **70.00**

Original, links of large cushion-cut aqua-colored rhinestones alternating with rows of three small circ colorless rhinestones, sgd "Eisenberg Original," c1935-40, 7" l **210.00**

Haskell, Miriam, strand of large textured faux pearls flanked by two strands of small textured faux pearls, ornate multi-loop bow motif front clasp of faux seed pearls and colorless rhinestones, sgd on oval plate, c1950, 7-1/2" l **145.00**

Hollycraft, sq links set throughout with multi-colored rhinestones, variety of shapes, goldtone metal, foldover clasp, safety chain, sgd "Hollycraft," 7-1/2" l x 1-1/4" w **135.00**

Bracelets, bangle, Catalin plastic, nicely carved and polished, each 1" wide, black, **$65**; red **$75**.

Jomaz, hinged bangle, domed oval hinged at the sides, with irregularly-shaped cells of translucent blue and green painted enamel, central crossover design pavé-set with small colorless rhinestones, rhinestone-set thumbpiece on V-spring, c1965, 2-1/4" inside dia **175.00**

Lisner, goldtone

Olive green plastic stones, 7" l, 1" w **10.00**

Pearly pink Lucite beads, faux pearls, pink glass beads **18.00**

Renoir, copper cuff, openwork block design, sgd "Renoir," c1950, 2" w .. **35.00**

Stein, Lea, bangle, layered rhodoid, dark green and red swirled peppermint stick swirls **95.00**

Tortolani, hinged bangle, goldtone, three-dimensional zodiac figures interspersed with stars, sgd "© Tortolani" in script, snap clasp at center opening, c1960, 2-1/2" w at center **200.00**

Trifari, rhodium, clear rhinestones, oval cluster-type plaques interspersed with rectangular set rhinetones **185.00**

Unknown maker, Bakelite
"Apple juice" colored Bakelite encasing wood Scarab-type ornament **325.00**
Bangle, butterscotch, carved flower design, 2-1/2" d **325.00**
Bangle, pineapple motif, orange and yellow **245.00**

Unknown maker, pot metal, bangle, filigree
Amethyst rhinestones **145.00**
Blue rhinestones **110.00**
Blue and clear rhinestones **115.00**
Green and clear rhinestones **165.00**

Unknown maker, pot metal, clear rhinestones, black cabochon, and three strands of black beads **110.00**

Unknown maker, sterling silver, snake, clear and green rhinestones **165.00**

Charm bracelet, gold tone, four-leaf clover, Channel No. 5 bottle, shoe, cupid, Gucci-type handbag, turtle, unmarked, **$18**.

Brooch/pin

Artisan, floral spray with ribbon, nine faux pearl flower buds, three with colorless baguette rhinestone stems, small colorless rhinestones. throughout, all stones replaced, mkd "ARTISAN N.Y.," safety catch, c1945, 3-7/8" w x 2-3/4" **100.00**

Avon, acorn, gold wash, pearl trim, sgd, 1-1/2" x 1-1/2" **20.00**

Boucher

Bunch of three radishes with leaves, red and green enamel, pavé colorless rhinestones around bottom of each, rhodium-plated roots and stems, sgd "MB" with symbol for Marcel Boucher, c1940, 2-1/2" w x 3" **750.00**

Flower head, six petals pavé-set with small yellow rhinestones, each bisected by a line of colorless baguette rhinestones, cluster of small blue rhinestones in center, turned edges of petals pavé-set with colorless rhinestones, textured gold-toned finish on rev, mkd "© Boucher" (block letters) # 7713, c1950-60, 2-3/8" **230.00**

B.S.K.

Gingo Tree Leaf, gold wash, 2" x 2" **25.00**

Floral, goldtone, marquise shapes bezel set, pave rhinestone accents, 2-3/4" x 1-1/2" **18.00**

Sunflowers, pale yellow double layer flower petals, amber colored faceted stones in center, green enameled leaf, gold washed metal, 2-1/2" x 2-1/2". **45.00**

Caslecliff, goldtone, fish, frosted glass jelly belly, green rhinestone eye, 2-1/4" . **60.00**

Corocraft

Bow, sterling vermeil, clear rhinestone accents, 3" x 2" **345.00**

Crown, three dimensional, clear rhinestones **185.00**

Fish, jelly belly, sterling, clear and pink rhinestones and enameling **495.00**

Flamingo, enameled, clear rhinestones at neck **295.00**

Leaf, goldtone Florentine finish, center silvertone spray of pave rhinestones, 2-1/4" x 2-1/2" **22.00**

Rose, sterling vermeil, rhinestone accents, 2-1/2" x 2" **195.00**

Sunburst type flower, silvertone, 2" h **45.00**

Stylized rooster with large faceted rect red glass center, painted enamel tail and features in red, green, black and white, c1940, 2-1/4" w x 2-1/8" **185.00**

DeNiccola, textured goldtone, cupid, clear rhinestones **90.00**

Eisenberg

Eagle, spread wing figural, clear rhinestones and enameling **650.00**

Original, opposed C-scrolls tapering down to point forming fancy shield shape, set throughout with large and med oval, emerald-cut and marquise-shaped pink rhinestones, oulined with small colorless rhinestones, prong-set in gold plated white metal, mkd "Eisenberg Original," c1935-40, 3-1/4" w x 3-1/2" **250.00**

Overlapping open circles of colorless circ rhinestones and opaque white circ cabochons, outlined with a row of marquise-shaped opaque white cabochons along one side, block letters mark, c1950, 2" x 2" **50.00**

Tiger motif, top view, textured goldtone metal set throughout with small colorless rhinestones, sgd "Eisenberg Ice ©," c1970, 3-1/4" x 1-1/2" **85.00**

Emmons, circular motif, faux coral cabochons, emerald green and tangerine rhinestones, 2-1/4" d....... **35.00**

Giavonni, leaf shape, silver toned, sgd, 2-1/2" l, 2" w **22.00**

Haskell, Miriam, gold-plated brass wreath of ivy leaves and vines intertwined with opaque green glass seed beads around

large central opaque green glass circ cabochon, appl oval plate on rev sgd "Miriam Haskell," c1950, 2" d....... **105.00**

Hollycraft

Floral wreath design, large center circ red rhinestone encircled by goldtone floral and foliate motifs set with small red rhinestones, sgd "Hollycraft, Copr 1954," 1-1/2" w x 3/8" **40.00**

Pinwheel design of pale to dark green circ and marquise-shaped rhinestones, sgd "Hollycraft, Copr 1952," 2" d. **100.00**

Jomaz, mallard, enameled, rhinestone wing trim **145.00**

Julianna, floral wreath, tiny gold leaves, green, gold, blue, clear, and rose-colored rhinestones, 2-3/4" d....................... **40.00**

Kramer of New York

Rhodium, bar pin with criss-cross clear rhinestone dangles ending in emerald stones, 2-3/4" w, 1" h....................... **95.00**

Silvertone, pave set clear rhinestones, circle with floral dec, 1-3/4" d, slight discoloration to one stone **10.00**

Lane, Kenneth J.

Butterfly motif, prong-set throughout with multicolored marquise-shaped and circ rhinestones, sgd "KJL," c1970, 3" x 3" **55.00**

Maltese cross of large green oval cabochons and circ green rhinestones around center circ blue rhinestone, outlined in marquise and sq-cut colorless rhinestones, sgd "KJL," c1965, 3" x 3" **35.00**

Pins, man and woman, yard motif, gold plated, 1-1/2" h, **$12.**

Mazer

Apple with leaves, sterling vermeil, rhinestone accents, 2-1/2" x 2"..... **195.00**

Bow, sterling, blue glass cabochon and clear rhinestones, 3" x 1-3/4"........ **185.00**

Monet, goldtone, clown, red rhinestone eye for one eye, star on other, openwork collar, 1970s, 1-7/8" x 1-1/4" **12.00**

Rader, Pauline, large oval royal blue center stone surrounded by turquoise and royal blue stones, 2-1/2" h, 2" w **165.00**

Schreiner

Circ cluster of mottled orange and dark green cabochons interspersed with aurora borealis rhinestones and faux pearls, sgd "Schreiner New York," c1955-60, 2-1/4" d **100.00**

Domed triangular cluster, center circ dark blue rose-cut rhinestone encircled by small circ pale blue rhinestones, three small opaque turquoise cabochons prong-set around circle, large oval and circ light and dark blue rose-cut rhinestones prong-set around outer edges, sgd "Schreiner New York," c1960, 2-1/4" x 2-1/4" **85.00**

Staret, cluster of tulips and foliage, trembler, clear rhinestones **395.00**

Stein, Lea, layered rhodoid, signature Lea Stein-Paris V-shaped pin back

Bacchus, cat, pearly silver and black, 2-3/8" w, 1-1/8" h **65.00**

Bee, transparent wings with gold edge, faux ivory body and head, topaz colored glass edge eye, 2-3/8" wingspan ... **80.00**

Blueberries, peach lace, 2-7/8" l **65.00**

Bowl, purple lace and black, 2-5/8" w, 7/8" h **75.00**

Cat, standing, magenta lace, faux-mother-of-pearl ears and eyes, 3-3/4" l, 1-3/4" h... **75.00**

Flower pot, two flowers, one aqua lacy turquoise, other purple lacy, dark blue leaves, turquoise lacy pot, 1-1/2" w, 2-1/2" h.. **85.00**

Fox, red tones............................... **100.00**

Sailor, faux ivory face, neck, hands and feet, pearly purple suit and cap, pearly gray collar, 1-5/8" w, 2-3/8" h........... **80.00**

Trifari

Crown, clear, blue, and green rhinestones **155.00**

Faux pearl spray, green enamel leaves with colorless rhinestone accents, sgd "Trifari ©," c1950, 2-1/8" w x 1-1/4". **55.00**

Feather forming circle, gold tone, mkd, 2" d... **10.00**

Flower, retro, enameled and clear rhinestone accents, 1-3/4" x 2-1/2", minor wear **185.00**

Unknown maker, Aurora Borealis, gold wash, Aurora Borealis, champagne, and topaz colored faceted prong set stones, 1-1/2" x 2".. **45.00**

Unknown maker, Bakelite

Anchor, red anchor, red, white, and blue dangling plastic anchors, 2-3/4"... **295.00**

Bar, inlaid orange, red, green, and brown, 3-3/4" l... **525.00**

Greyhound, deep blue Bakelite, 4" l **365.00**

Unknown maker, goldtone

Basket of Flowers, faceted blue prong set stones, faux pearl centers **35.00**

Flower, goldtone wirework flowers, pale green rhinestones, 3" w, 1-3/4" h **16.00**

Flower, prong set blue and green faceted rhinestones, 3-D enameled leaves, 3-1/4" l **45.00**

Flower, prong set bright pink and green marquis-cut rhinestones, orange center surrounded by white faceted rhinestones, 3-1/4" x 2" **45.00**

Unknown maker, pot metal

Bow, clear rhinestones **85.00**

Grasshopper, enameled, clear rhinestones **95.00**

Trembler, clear and blue rhinestones, pansy and leaves **95.00**

Unknown maker, rhodium, flower, light blue and milky blue glass cabochons, clear rhinestone accents, worn signature, 1-3/4" x 3", 1940s **210.00**

Unknown maker, sterling vermeil

Flower, retro-style, clear and light blue rhinestones **40.00**

Flower, retro-style, clear rhinestones, green glass cabochons, 2" x 2", minor wear... **185.00**

Rose, 3-D, rhinestone accents, 2-1/2" x 3-1/2" **185.00**

Warner, Joseph, circle pin, black japanned metal with prong set scarlet red rhinestones, 1-3/4" d...................... **32.00**

Weiss

Star-shaped cluster of large pear-shaped and smaller marquise-shaped colorless rhinestones prong-set in rhodium-plated wm, sgd "Albert Weiss New York," c1950, 1-1/2" dia **40.00**

Pins, all unknown makers, left to right: wooden bird, brown wings, orange breast, green branch, **$5**; lady's hat, gold plated, pink, purple, and blue foil trim, **$7.50**; violin, silvertone, **$5**.

Clip

Eisenberg Original

Retro Modern, goldtone floral spray with large emerald-cut green rhinestone at base, smaller emerald-cut green rhinestone encircled by circ-cut green rhinestones forming flowerhead, marquise-cut green rhinestones in center of second flowerhead, sgd "Eisenberg Original," c1940-45, 3-1/4" w x 2-1/2" **155.00**

Sterling, large foliate spray, multiple "branches," each with a line of small colorless rhinestones terminating in a large oval rhinestone, sgd "Eisenberg Original," mkd "sterling," c1940, 2-1/4" w x 4" **250.00**

Staret, openwork shield shape set throughout with large oval and small circ colorless rhinestones (3 small stones missing), c1935-40, sgd "Staret," 2-1/8" w x 2-1/2" **115.00**

Trifari, painted enamel floral spray, red flowers, colorless rhinestone centers and accents, green leaves, brown stems on rhodium-plated white metal, c1935-40, sgd "Trifari," 1-1/2" w x 2-1/2" **90.00**

Cuff links, pair

Christian Dior, gold filled, textured ovals, orig box, c1960 .... **40.00**

Georg Jensen, sterling, rect checkerboard pattern, c1950, sgd "Georg Jensen" in dotted oval, mkd "sterling Denmark, #113" **170.00**

Duette, Coro, sgd
"Jelly belly" fish, sterling vermeil, Lucite centers, colorless rhinestone accents, red glass cab eyes, blue glass cab mouths, c1940, sgd "Coro Duette," mkd "sterling," 1931 pat no., 2-1/2" w x 1-3/4" **300.00**
Retro, opposed goldtone swirls set with colorless rhinestones, sgd "Coro Duette," 1931 patent no., 2-1/2" w x 1-1/2" ... **75.00**

Earrings, pair

Alice, gold plated, four leaf clover design, screw backs, 1940s **35.00**

Avon, silver double circles set with marquisettes, pierced, c1970 .... **20.00**

Chanel, faux pearl "puffy" heart suspended from circ faux pearl surmount, in textured goldtone setting, orig box, c1965-70, sgd "© Chanel," clip backs, 2" l **75.00**

Ciner, textured goldtone circ domes, small faux pearls in star-cut settings, c1960, clip backs sgd "Ciner," 1" d **32.50**

Eisenberg, clusters of prong-set cobalt blue marquise and circ rhinestones, small colorless rhinestone accents, c1950, block letter mark, clip backs, 3/4" w x 1-1/4" **55.00**

Haskell, Miriam, gold tone filigree, seven Japanese simulated pearls set in a flower form with decorative wire loops between each pearl, hinged screw-back findings, mkd **40.00**

Hollycraft, large multicolored clusters of circ, oval, marquise and baguette rhinestones prong-set in goldtone metal, sgd "Hollycraft Copr 1955," screwbacks, 1-1/2" l **145.00**

Matisse, circ domed red-enameled disk with appl copper dome at bottom and appl copper wires at top forming an abstract eye, c1952, one clipback earring mkd "Matisse" in script, 3/4" d **20.00**

Rebajes, copper, oval swirls around central domes, c1950, clip backs sgd "Rebajes," 1" x 1-1/4" **65.00**

Robert, flowerhead clusters of green rhinestones, faux pearl centers, c1950, clip backs mkd "Robert," 7/8" d **36.00**

Stein, Lea, layered rhodoid, clip, bright green swirls on pearly white, stamped on back, 1-3/8" d **95.00**

Unknown maker, antiqued gold finish, foil bead with four smaller green glass beads, glove of 10 faceted prong set white rhinestones, wire strung on antique design clip back, 1-1/2", 1950s **35.00**

Weiss, flowerhead clips, large dark blue circ rhinestone encircled by marquise-cut light blue rhinestones, c1950, sgd "Weiss" on clipback, 1" d **37.50**

Necklace, unknown maker, blue rhinestones, **$27.50**.

Necklace

Carnegie, Hattie, goldtone, double strand, peridot green aurora borealis crystals, 20" l **40.00**

Caslecliff, three strands, red glass beads, goldtone leaf closure, 22" l **45.00**

Coventry, Sarah
Goldtone links, 11 faceted aurora borealis crystals, 16" l **18.00**
Silvertone, composed of eight thin chain link chains, mid-1960s **12.00**

Eisenberg, double row torsade of emerald-cut colorless rhinestones surmounted by two short rows of circ colorless rhinestones at center, continuing to a small rhinestone-set chain and keyhole clasp mkd "EISENBERG," c1950, 1" w (at center), 17-1/4" l **250.00**

Florenza, goldtone, Victorian-style, filigree
.... **20.00**

Haskell, Miriam, clusters of three molded red glass and brass bead flowerheads with red rhinestone centers, suspended from red molded flowerhead beads, brass and colorless faceted glass rondels, alternating with red faceted glass beads, continuing to a hook clasp, c1960, mkd "MIRIAM HASKELL" on attached oval hang tag, 20" l........................ **420.00**

Trifari

Double strand, goldtone fittings, peridot colored glass beads, 18" l **40.00**

Silvertone, Egyptian abstract style, 21" l, 2-1/2" l drop, 1970s **18.00**

Unknown maker, Bakelite, yellow carved cherries.. **395.00**

Vendome, a row of paired circ-cut aurora borealis alternating with single circ-cut amber-colored rhinestones, suspending clusters of small and large circ-cut and emerald-cut green, orange, aurora borealis and amber-colored rhinestones, fancy pronged wm settings, terminating in a rhinestone-set chain and hook clasp mkd "© VENDOME," appl plaque rev center mkd "Vendôme," c1960, 1-7/8" w x 18" l **125.00**

Pearls

Hagler, Stanley, NYC, rhinestone clasp, 29" l **250.00**

Haskell, Mariam, pearls with brass drop of pearls surrounded by clear rhinestones, 14" l, 3-1/4" l drop **225.00**

Hobe, "potato" pearls, rhinestone and emerald clasp, 25" l, 1965 .... **175.00**

Pendant

Coventry, Sarah, goldtone flower sections connected together to form diamond, no chain, 2-3/4" x 3-1/8", 1970s **15.00**

Eisenberg, owl on a branch in dark, medium, and light green, and black painted enamel, suspended from a gold-plated wm snake chain, pendant rev mkd "EISENBERG," c1970, 1-1/4" w x 2-1/2" pendant, 20-1/2" l chain.................. **50.00**

Joseff of Hollywood, stamped gold-plated brass in a design of three overlapping circ disks with open scroll and geometric motif, suspending by two outside and two inside crossing chains a large circ disk with geo design, c1950, hook and ring clasp on gold-plated brass foxtail chain, 3" w x 5" pendant, 16" l chain........ **200.00**

Unknown maker, red Lucite heart pendant surmounted by applied sterling silver Air Force emblem, suspended from red celluloid chain, c1945, 1-3/4" w x 1-3/4" pendant, 19" l **165.00**

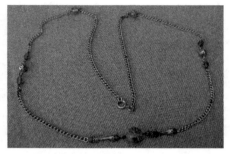

Necklace, unknown maker, gold toned chain, blue glass beads, $20.

Suite

Boucher, brooch and earrings, rhinestones, 2-1/4" x 2-1/4" pin, 1" x 1-1/2" earrings, 1940s **285.00**

Coro, necklace and earrings
Necklace of 10 linked foliate motifs, each with large central oval blue alternating with green faux moonstone cab framed by smaller circ blue faux moonstones and blue rhinestones set in silvertone metal branches, matching clip earrings, c1950, all pcs mkd "© Coro," necklace with adjustable hook closure, 17-1/2" l, earrings 1/2" w x 3/4" **85.00**

Rhodium plated necklace with 5/8" pear shaped prong set blue moonglow cabochon drop surrounded by facet cut rhinestones, smaller pear shaped moonglow stones, round faceted rhinestones and rhodium leaves along length of necklace, matching screw-clip earrings with large faceted center rhinestone surrounded by large pear shaped cabchon blue moonglow stones and rhodium leaves, all pcs mkd "© Coro" **35.00**

Coventry, Sarah, pin and earrings, smooth and textured silvertone swirls, 2-1/4" d pin, 1" d clip-on earrings **24.00**

Eisenberg, brooch and earrings, foliate clusters of circ and marquise large and med rhinestones, shades of green with small colorless accents, c1950, block letter mark, brooch 2-1/4" w x 2-3/4", clip earrings 1" w x 1-1/4".................... **225.00**

Florenza, necklace and earrings, 2-1/4" l drop with plastic insert with transfer printed flowers, 25" l paperclip chain............. **18.00**

Haskell, Miriam, bracelet, brooch, and earrings, floral clusters of pastel pink and blue glass beads, pale blue seed beads, and pale blue enameled petals on brooch and earrings, bracelet a floral cluster at the top of a double-hinged gold-plated bangle, clipback earrings a single flowerhead, c1960-65, all pieces mkd "MIRIAM HASKELL" on oval plate, bracelet 1-1/3" w x 2" (at top), 2-1/2" inside dia, brooch 2-3/4" w x 1-1/2", earrings 3/4" d.............................. **335.00**

Hobé, necklace and earrings, lariat-style necklace of goldtone metal mesh with circ central ornament and terminals set with marquise-cut citrine- and topaz-colored rhinestones, hook closure, matching clip earrings of clustered marquise rhinestones, c1950, sgd "Hobé," necklace 26-1/2" l, center 1-3/4" w, earrings 1" w x 1-1/2"...... **100.00**

Hollycraft, brooch and earrings, triangular openwork Christmas tree of intersecting ropetwist textured lines forming lozenge pattern, set with red, blue, yellow and green circ rhinestones in centers, surmounted by a rhinestone-set star, matching clipback earrings, c1955-60, mkd "© HOLLYCRAFT," brooch 1-1/4" w x 2-3/8", earrings 3/4" w x 1-1/8" **150.00**

Kramer of New York, collar and bracelet, flexible openwork rows of large and small circ gray and aurora borealis rhinestones, c1950, sgd "Kramer of New York," collar with adjustable hook closure, 16" l, bracelet 7" l, both 1" w................... **100.00**

Mazer Bros., necklace and bracelet, Retro Modern, necklace of open gold-plated links alternating with colorless rhinestone-set links suspending a central gold-plated and rhinestone-set scrolled ribbon bow with two large molded clear glass cherries and three grad clear glass cabs, mkd "Z" on rev, matching bracelet of linked molded glass cherries alternating with clear glass cab and rhinestone-set scrolls, mkd "K" on rev, both pcs mkd "Mazer," c1940, fold-over clasps, necklace 16" l, center 2-1/4" w x 2-1/2, bracelet 1" w x 7-1/2".................... **175.00**

Pin, circle type, gold and silver-toned leaves set with small rhinestones, larger round "jelly belly"-type white opaque cabochons, unmarked, **$25**.

Rebajes, necklace and bracelet, linked pairs of copper leaves, c1950, sgd "Rebajes," 7/8" w, necklace 15" l, bracelet 7-1/2" l, can be joined to form longer necklace **80.00**

Regency, bracelet, brooch and earrings, clusters of champagne-colored, aurora borealis and colorless marquise and circ rhinestones, c1955, mkd "Regency," bracelet 7-1/4" l, brooch 2" d, clip earrings 1-1/2" l.............................. **80.00**

Renoir, Matisse, bracelet and earrings, hinged copper bracelet with abstract enameled design, matching earrings with enameled disc................................. **75.00**

Trifari

Brooch and earrings, clear and red baguette rhinestones, 2-3/4" x 3" brooch with three swirls, 1" x 2" earrings, 1940s **325.00**

Necklace and clip-on earrings, heavy goldtone, hanging charms of swirled aqua glass leaves, mkd with crown above Trifari **50.00**

Unknown maker

Brooch and earrings, sterling vermeil, clear rhinestone accents, 2" x 2-1/2" apple-shaped pin, 1" x 1-12" clipback earrings, 1940s............................. **245.00**

Necklace, bracelet, and earrings, large dark blue rhinestones with surrounding lighter blue rhinestones, chrome setting, 1950s **175.00**

Weiss, necklace, bracelet, and brooch, light blue circ, pear-shaped and marquise glass cabochons and circ rhinestones, necklace of large pear-shaped cab flanked by four smaller pear-shaped cabs alternating with marquise cabs and circ rhinestones, continuing to a chain of circ rhinestones, hook closure, sgd "Weiss," flexible bracelet of alternating circ and marquise cabs between two rows of small circ rhinestones sgd "Weiss," brooch a large star shape of five pear-shaped cabs encircling circ cabs and rhinestones, c1950, necklace 18" l, bracelet 7" l, brooch 2-3/8" d **75.00**

Johnson Brothers China

History: Johnson Brothers was founded in 1883 by three English brothers. The business originated in the historic English Staffordshire district. By 1896, the business flourished and a fourth Johnson brother joined the firm. He was charged with establishing a stronghold in the American market, which he did quite successfully. The company's dinnerware business because so large that it opened additional factories in England, Canada, and Australia. By

1968, Johnson Brothers had become part of the Wedgwood Group. Because Johnson Brothers spanned such a long period of success, expect to find decorating techniques that reflect what was popular with consumers of the day. Its wares include flow blue patterns and plain patterns, as well as its most popular transfer patterns. Johnson Brothers used a variety of backstamps, many of which contain the name and give clues as to the production date.

Collecting hints: Johnson Brothers China is durable and features several decorating styles. Most patterns feature a decoration created by using transfers. This technique involves placing a very thin transfer on the still wet clay body. Careful examination of shaped pieces often shows tiny areas where the transfer is adjusted to fit the shape. The transfers can be one color or multicolored.

Bread and butter plate, 6-1/4" d

Coaching Scenes, ruffled edge **8.00**
Old Britain Castles, blue on white .. **12.00**

Breakfast set, Lily of the Valley, five pcs
.... **155.00**

Butter dish, cov, Eternal Beau............ **72.00**

Butter pat, Olde English Countryside, 4" d, set of six... **65.00**

Cereal bowl, Old Britain Castles, blue on white... **18.00**

Christmas tree dish, tree shape, Christmas dec, mkd **25.00**

Coffee pot

Blue Nordic..................................... **75.00**
Golden Dawn, yellow, 1930s, 9" h.. **30.00**
Hearts & Flowers............................ **200.00**
Old Britain Castles, castle on body is Bolsover Castle, 1792, lid with Kidwelly

Castle, red transfer, white ground, 1950s
.... **300.00**

Creamer, Blue Nordic **30.00**

Creamer and sugar

Floral pattern, 3-3/4" h creamer, 6-1/2" w sugar... **45.00**
Friendly Village **35.00**

Cup and saucer

Bouquet **10.00**
Brooklyn, flow blue, mkd "Royal Semi Porcelain, Johnson Brothers, England," c1900... **100.00**
Christmas theme, 1980s................. **30.00**
Countryside **55.00**
Harvest Time **55.00**
Old Britain Castles **20.00**

Dinner service, Hearts & Flowers pattern, 44 pieces, $75.

Dessert set, Exeter, Chinoiserie pattern, cream pitcher, relish and two each cup and saucer, dessert bowl, dessert plate, c1913 .... **160.00**

Dinnerware set

Bouquet, service for four, 20 pcs... **70.00**
The Friendly Village, service for six plus serving pcs, 119 pcs..................... **250.00**

Expresso cup and saucer set, eight 2" h cups and saucers, cream relief swirl pattern... **70.00**

Fruit bowl, Old Britain Castles, blue on white **10.00**

Gravy boat, attached underplate

English Chippendale, red on white
.... **250.00**
Old Britain Castles, pink on white **185.00**

Mug, Olde English Countryside, 3-1/4" h
.... **7.50**

Pitcher, Rose Chintz, 6-1/2" x 6" **200.00**

Plate

Brooklyn, flow blue, mkd "Royal Semi Porcelain, Johnson Brothers, England," c1900, 8-3/4" d............................. **100.00**
Devon Sprays, rose bouquets, scalloped rim, c1960-80, 10" d **15.00**
Friendly Village, Covered Bridge, 7-1/2" sq **6.00**
Old Britain Castles, blue on white.. **22.00**
Pareek, gold rim, gold filigree over yellow border, 1" green band, 1" yellow band, center colorful floral bouquet, 10-1/2" d
.... **30.00**
Regency, Snow White, ironstone, scalloped, swirled, 7-1/2" sq **9.00**
Rose Chintz, 8" sq **20.00**

Platter

Albany, 12-3/4" l **225.00**
Blue Nordic, medium...................... **65.00**

Blue Nordic, small **48.00**
Glenwood, flow blue, 14" x 10-1/2". **95.00**
Hearts & Flowers, 14" l **200.00**
Historic America, large **265.00**
Lindsey, small **250.00**
Old Britain Castles, brown on white, 12" l
.... **165.00**
Partridge, Game Birds series, c1950-80,
11-1/4" x 10-1/2" **24.00**
Relish, Friendly Village, three parts **40.00**
Saucer
Cherry Thieves, mkd "Staffordshire Old
Granite Made in England by Johnson
Brothers".. **5.00**
Coaching Scenes, ruffled edge, 5-3/4" d
.... **5.00**
Fruit Sampler, browns, center apple with
flowers, buds, and leaves................ **4.50**

Plate, Friendly Village, multicolored transfer
scene, **$15**.

Soup bowl, Old Britain Castles, blue on
white... **22.00**
Soup tureen, cov
Balmoral, blue transfer, gold trim,
11-1/2" w, 6-1/4" h.......................... **45.00**
Friendly Village, 10" x 7-1/2"......... **235.00**
Souvenir plate
Canadian coat of arms, gold stenciled
scalloped edge, Regency mold,
decorated in Canada, 1960s.......... **45.00**
Mt. Rushmore, imported for Sunset
Supply, Keystone, 10-3/4" d............ **15.00**
Sugar bowl, cov
Blue Nordic..................................... **40.00**
Crab Apple, Old Flower Print series, 7" x
2-1/2"... **25.00**
Teapot, cov
Hearts & Flowers, five cups.......... **270.00**
Old Britain Castles, pink on white. **250.00**
Pareek, two-cup size, white and yellow,
floral dec, c1930, 8-1/2" w, 3" h **128.00**
Turkey platter, Friendly Village, 20" l **190.00**
Vegetable bowl, cov
Blue Nordic.................................... **110.00**
Hearts & Flowers **185.00**
Vegetable bowl, open, Lindsey, oval,
10-1/4" l.. **250.00**

Jukeboxes

History: First came the phonograph.
When electrical amplification became
possible, the coin-operated phonograph,
known as the jukebox, evolved.

The heyday of the jukebox was the
1940s. Between 1946 and 1947, Wurlitzer produced 56,000 model-1015
jukeboxes, the largest production run
of all time. The jukebox was the center
of every teen-age hangout, from drugstores and restaurants to pool halls and
dance parlors. They even invaded
some private homes.

Styles changed in the 1960s. Portable radios coupled with "Top 40" radio
stations fulfilled the desire for daily repetition of songs. Television changed
evening entertainment patterns, and
the jukebox vanished.

Collecting Hints: Jukebox chronology
falls into four distinct periods:

In the pre-1938 period, jukeboxes
were constructed mainly of wood and
resembled a radio or phonograph cabinet. Wurlitzer jukeboxes from this era
are the most collectible, but their value
usually is under $600.

From 1938 to 1948, the addition of
plastics and animation units gave the
jukebox a gaudier appearance. These
jukeboxes played 78-RPM records.
Wurlitzer jukeboxes are king, with
Rock-Ola the second most popular.
This era contains the most valuable
models, e.g., Wurlitzer models 750,
850, 950, 1015, and 1080.

The 1940 to 1960 period is referred
to as the Seeburg era. Jukeboxes of
this vintage are collected for the
"Happy Days" feeling (named for the
TV show): drive-in food, long skirts,
sweater girls, and good times. The
jukeboxes, which play 45-RPM
records, rate second in value to those
of the 1938-1948 period, with prices
usually are under $2,500.

The 1961 and newer jukeboxes often
are not considered collectible because
the record mechanism is not visible,
thus removing an alluring quality.

Prices for vintage jukeboxes have
become soft during the last few years
as the higher quality reproduction juke-

boxes featuring CDs have appealed to the newer buyers entering this market.

There are exceptions to these generalizations. Collectors should have a price and identification guide to help make choices. Many original and reproduction parts are available for Seeburg and Wurlitzer jukeboxes. In many cases incomplete jukeboxes can be restored. Jukeboxes that are in working order and can be maintained in that condition are the best machines to own.

Do not buy any jukebox without taking time to thoroughly educate yourself, making sure you know how collectible the particular machine is and how missing components will affect its value.

Note: The following prices are good condition, grade #3.

AMI

Model A	**3,000.00**
Model B	**2,000.00**
Model C	**1,500.00**
Model E	**1,200.00**
Continental	**1,800.00**

Mills

Model Empress	**2,750.00**
Throne of Music	**2,250.00**
Packard, Manhattan	**4,500.00**

Rock-Ola

Model 418	**2,200.00**
Model 1422	**3,700.00**
Model 1426	**3,900.00**
Model 1428	**2,000.00**
Model 1432	**2,300.00**
Model 1436	**2,500.00**
Model 1438	**1,300.00**
Model 1465	**1,000.00**

Seeburg

Model 147	**2,300.00**
Model HF100G	**2,300.00**
Model HF100R	**2,500.00**
Model M100B	**2,000.00**
Model M100C	**3,000.00**
Model V-200	**5,000.00**

Wurlitzer

Model 412	**1,750.00**
Model 600	**1,400.00**
Model 700	**4,000.00**
Model 750	**4,000.00**
Model 800	**6,000.00**
Model 1015	**6,000.00**

Seeburg, black body, chrome trim, purple circle motif, push button selection, **$2,500**.

K

Keen Kutter

History: Keen Kutter was the trade name developed for quality hardware, tools, and other goods by businessman E. C. Simmons. Edward Campbell was born in Maryland in 1839. By 1846, he and his father, who was a hardware wholesale distributor, moved to St. Louis. At the age of 17, Edward also started working in the wholesale hardware business. By 1859, he started with the form of Wilson, Levery & Walters, as a clerk. He eventually became the owner of that firm, which he renamed "E. C. Simmons Co." By 1898, he retired while his company maintained its divisions in Sioux City, Ogden, Toledo, Wichita, New York, Minneapolis, and St. Louis. Its tools were made by factories in New Hampshire and its pocket knives were made in New York. All its products became well known household names as they represented quality tools, household products, and all sorts of things to be used in the workshop, the kitchen, or the garden. E. C. Simmons Company was bought by Shapleigh Hardware in 1940. That company continued to use the name until it closed in the early 1960s.

What E. C. Simmons did well was to promote his products through the use of advertising and his vivid yellow and red Keen Kutter logo. Ordinary packing boxes told about the contents of the box, plus also usually contained the trademark logo as well as other advertising about the company.

Collecting hints: Collecting Keen Kutter items has begun to take off as many collectors realize the quality and quantity of Keen Kutter material. At the present time, one of the hottest areas is ephemera related with cross-over collectors searching for Keen Kutter kitchen collectibles or quality Keen Kutter tools.

Advertising puzzle, Keen Kutter logo, orig envelope....................................... **775.00**

Cutlery set, original box with labels, service for four, **$95**.

Box, 10" l, 2-1/2" w, 1-3/4" h, wood, lid, lap joints at each corner, orig label "1/2 Doz. Special Auger Bits Simmons Hardware Co. Keen Kutter," Keen Kutter logo on label.. **35.00**
Can opener, patent Sept 20, 93 .... **25.00**
Carpenter pencil, slight use................ **5.00**
Catalog
   E. C. Simmons Keen Kutter Cutlery and Tools, Mail Order Book, #2764, name and logo on each page, distributed by Edw K. Tyron Company, Philadelphia, red cover, 6" x 9".. **65.00**
   Shapleigh Hardware, *#477 House Furnishing Goods*, 1951, green and red cover **55.00**
Chicken waterer, stoneware, blue label "Oak Leaf, E. C. Simmons" **85.00**
Food mill, 10-1/2" h, 8" w, cast iron, hardwood handle, mkd "E. C. Simmons Co., USA, Keen Kutter, Pat May 29, 1906" **50.00**
Gasoline can.................................... **50.00**
Letterhead, E. C. Simmons Co., 1911 **12.00**
Lock, brass, 3-3/4" h.......................... **75.00**
Magazine ad
   6-1/2" x 9-1/4", tool cabinet ad, 1910, black and white **8.50**
   6-3/4" x 9", tools and cutlery, black and white, 1916.................................... **10.00**
   6-3/4" x 9-3/4", Simmons Hardware Co., St Louis and NY, Keen Kutter Saw, black and white, Munsey's Magazine, NY, early 1900s **5.00**
   11" x 14", Keen Kutter Quality to Millions, 1921, two black and white pages.... **6.00**
Maple sugar tree tap.......................... **30.00**
Painter's hat, white, blue lettering for E. S. Simmons, unused........................... **50.00**
Pencil clip, 1950s............................... **17.50**
Pocket knife
   KK860, three blades, 3-7/8" l **65.00**
   KS 130.. **115.00**
   Mother of pearl handles **300.00**

Padlock, E. C. Simmons on top, two original keys, $25.

Postcard

Boardwalk in Atlantic City, NJ, Keen Kutter lighted sign on Hotel Traymore, 1914 .... **25.00**
The Dog Won't Mind, back with adv for Wm Chattin & Bros, Glenwood, Mo, and Keen Kutter tools **175.00**
Razor hone, 5-1/2", 2" w, slight wear from use **10.00**

Safety razor

Junior, 3-3/4" l, Keen Kutter logo on head, orig mkd blade, orig 4" x 2" green box, c1905-08 .... **25.00**
Red Bakelite handle, 4" l, orig paper label, orig box.................................. **60.00**

Straight razor

Black handle, inside of blade with Keen Kutter mark, with "Simmons Hdw Co. Inc., St. Louis, Mo," other side of blade mkd "Germany K11," orig box labeled "E. C. Simmons Barbers' Pet, Simmons Hardware Co. Manufacturers and Distributors USA" **40.00**
Cast aluminum, Art Nouveau woman admiring her reflection in mirror, scrolling flowers and foliage, blades marked, orig box.. **250.00**
Scissors, 6-3/4" l................................. **20.00**

Tool

Caliper rule, K302, 1 foot, arch joint, four folds, boxwood, mkd "Keen Kutter K320," company logo following mark **95.00**
Chisel, socket butt, beveled, mkd "E. C. Simmons Keen Kutter" on steel, Keen Kutter logo, 1-1/4" w, 9" l **22.00**
Draw knife, logo, 9" l blade, 15" l handle to handle....................................... **125.00**
Hatchet **30.00**
Mallet, wood **32.00**
Monkey wrench, 15" l, wood handle, mkd "E. C. Simmons Keen Kutter B J," and "Solid Bar Jan 14 96 Made in USA" **45.00**
Rule, #K680, 2 foot, four folds, boxwood, mkd... **12.00**

Puzzle, original box, incomplete, $65.

Spade.. **125.00**
T-square, mkd **45.00**
Wood plane, K-35, 10" l, 2" w cutter, solid handle and knob, mkd "E. C. Simmons Keen Kutter" on blade, Keen Kutter logo on toe **75.00**

Kitchen Collectibles

History: The kitchen was a focal point in a family's environment until frozen food, TV dinners, and microwaves changed both meal preparation and dining habits.

Many early kitchen utensils were handmade and prized by their owners. Next came a period of utilitarian products made of tin and other metals. When the housewife no longer wished to work in a sterile environment, enamel and plastic products added color, and their unique design served both aesthetic and functional purposes.

The type and style of kitchen products has changed through the past decades. Learning more about these changes whether through studying vintage kitchen tools, catalogs, vintage trade publications or magazines can give collectors a deeper insight into this specialized collecting area.

Collecting Hints: Today's homes are being built with large kitchens that offer interesting areas in which to display vintage kitchen collectibles. By being able to display the colorful items that a kitchen collector covets, they are often able to derive much pleasure from their collections. With careful handling, many vintage kitchen collectibles can be used as accent pieces in almost any décor.

Additional Listings: Advertising, Cookbooks, Griswold, Kitchen Glassware, Reamers.

Angel food cake pan, 10" d................ **28.00**
Angel food cake server, pale green Bakelite with swirls of yellow, metal tines **18.00**
Apple peeler, Turntable No. 98 .... **85.00**
Apple slicer-corer, Ludwig Mfg. Co., Racine, WI, copyright 1960, stainless steel blades, mint on card **12.00**
Basket, 4-1/2" d, 5-1/2" h, wire, folding, tulip form.. **45.00**
Basting spoon, granite, cobalt blue handle **15.00**
Biscuit cutter, 1-12" d, tin, bail............ **10.00**
Bowl
　Treasure Craft, green, large, fruit edged handles **10.00**
　Walnut, 10" w, 11" l, 3" h **65.00**
Bread board, 12" d, 7-1/2" l, pine handle **90.00**
Bread box, tin, 12" l, white, red top **20.00**
Breadstick pan, nickeled cast iron, Wagner Ware.. **35.00**
Bundt pan, iron, scalloped, 4-1/2 x 10-1/2" **45.00**
Butter fork, 7 x 2-1/2", hand carved maple **25.00**
Butter mold, 1-3/4 x 3-1/2", turned maple, carved floral design **45.00**
Butter paddle, wood, 10" l, 4-1/2" w... **48.00**
Cake carrier, aluminum, copper brushed color... **27.50**
Cake mold, 13-3/8" l, 4-3/8" w, 8" h, lamb, cast aluminum **45.00**
Cake pan, tin
　8" d, Swans Down Cake Flour **15.00**
　12", black, wire loop handle, Fries.. **12.00**
Can opener
　Cast Iron, bull's head holds blade, curved tail as handle, 2-1/4" w, 6-1/2" l **55.00**
　Cast Iron, fish figure, c1865.......... **140.00**
　Metal, red wood handle.................. **15.00**
Canister set
　Brushed and polished aluminum, flour, sugar, coffee, and tea, black plastic finials, mkd "AC Heller Hostess Ware, Made in Italy," eight pcs.................. **40.00**
　Copper over aluminum, flour, sugar, coffee, and tea, Lincoln Beauty Works, 1950s, 8 pc....................................... **24.00**

Bread box, metal, white enamel exterior, decal decoration with flowers in cart, **$35**.

　Copper, Wear-Ever, flour, sugar, coffee, tea, cookies, grease jar with orig strainer, orig lids with some touch-up to black paint, 13 pcs **60.00**
Catalog
　Aluminum Cooking Utensil, New Kensington, PA, 1920s, 44 pgs, 5-1/4" x 8", Cat No. 33, Wearever Specialities **26.00**
　Calumet Baking Powder Co., Chicago, IL, 1923, 24 pgs, 5" x 8".................. **12.00**
　Oscar G. Thomas Co., Taunton, MA, 1913, 32 pgs, 3-3/4" x 8-1/4", net trade price list, Herald ranges, parlor stoves, etc. **28.00**
　Revere Copper & Brass Co., Rome, NY, 1936, eight pgs, 3" x 6", cooking utensils **15.00**
　Rochester Stamping Co., Rochester, NY, 64 pgs, 4-1/2" x 7", chafing dishes **30.00**
　Savory, Inc., Newark, NJ, 1939, 55 pgs, 81/2" x 11", Cat No. 39A, galvanized, japanned, enameled, tin, dippers, baskets, buckets, funnels, etc. **28.00**
　Standard Electric Stove, Toledo, OH, 1927, 32 pgs, 8-1/2" x 11"............. **30.00**
Cheese grater, hanging, white china, gold trim, enameled blue forget-me-not dec **70.00**
Cheese slicer, enameled wood handle, marked "Unsco-Germany"............. **10.00**
Cherry seeder, Dandy 50A, orig damaged box **42.50**
Chopping knife, 61/2" l, Henry Disston & Sons, curved steel blade, wood handle **20.00**
Cleanser, Guardian Service, unopened, black and silver Art Deco design .. **35.00**
Clothes sprinkler, ceramic, figural, Chinese Man, Shawnee Pottery **110.00**
Coffee grinder, Olde Thompson, wooden base with dovetailed drawer and sides, iron hopper and handle, wood knob, mkd "Olde Thompson Coffee Mill, The Georges Thompson Corporation, 500 Mission Street, South Pasadena, Calif," 6-3/4" sq base, 8" h **95.00**

Colander, aluminum, cone shaped, mkd "Wear-Ever, Made in USA, #4," hand-held type.. **30.00**

Cooler, 23" h, 10 gallon size, aluminum, Igloo, solid holding handles.......... **75.00**

Cornstick pan, Junior Krusty Korn Kobs, italic "Wagner Ware" trademark **85.00**

Creamer and sugar, 3-3/4" w x 4-1/2" h creamer, 3-1/2" w x 2-3/4" h sugar, porcelain, pigs, white body, red-orange mouth, bowties, noses, and ears, black eyes and feet, some wear to glaze, unmarked **35.00**

Cake set, porcelain cake plate and matching server, cream ground, multicolored orchids, blue forget-me-nots, green foliage, gold grim, marked "Germany," $45.

Decorating tools, cylindrical tube, wooden pusher, changeable disks, mkd "Tala" **75.00**

Dipper, graniteware, 14-1/4" l, 5-1/2" x 3" dipper, white, fine speckled black and blue trim, heavy use **30.00**

Dish pan, enamel, gray **15.00**

Dish set, Tupper, service for six, pastels, three sizes of serving bowls, cups, plates, cups and saucers, desert dishes, sugar and creamer, salt and pepper shakers, mkd "Tupperware" **18.00**

Double boiler, cov, Porcelier, Sprig, pink, orange, and blue flowers, white ground **40.00**

Dough mixer, Universal, #8 .... **125.00**

Drink mixer, Ovaltine, aluminum, 8" h **18.00**

Drip-O-Later, Enterprise Aluminum, cream colored, green trim, mkd "Fraunfelter" **30.00**

Dust pan and broom, Kitchen Prayer Lady **245.00**

Dutch oven, enameled cast iron, aqua, mkd "DRU Made in Holland #82" **165.00**

Egg beater

9" l, H-L Beater, Tarrytown, NY, No. 0, cast wheel, gears, loop type handle, wood knob, wavy beaters...................... **50.00**

9-1/2" l, tin and iron, no markings, wavy beaters.. **85.00**

10-3/4" l, Taplin Mfg Co., red wooden handle, mkd "Made in USA Pat Oct 9, 1923" **12.00**

Eggcup

Baby Bird **45.00**

Bonzo, figural, Germany, 1920s .. **125.00**

Charlie McCarthy, lusterware, Canadian, 1930s **60.00**

China, blue and white floral design **20.00**

Popeye, 1930s, multicolored **110.00**

Canning funnel, tin, shaped iron handles, marked "The Butler Mfg Co., Chicago," 4" d top, $48.

Egg poacher, red enamel, gray enamel insert, 3-3/4" x 8" **24.00**

Egg separator, aluminum, 9" l **7.00**

Egg timer

Chef... **50.00**

Girl on phone **50.00**

Winking Chef, timer on back........ **195.00**

Egg whip, spring-type, enameled wood handle **10.00**

Electric mixer, Montgomery Ward, orig small white glass mixing bowl, 8" h **15.00**

Flour sifter, Bromweld's, side crank, red wood knob **15.00**

Food chopper

Aluminum shaft and blades, red wooden handle, Hazel Atlas measuring cup base **20.00**

Double blades, wood handle, some rust, 5-7/8" blade, 6-1/4" h **185.00**

Wrought iron horse shaped shaft, wooden handle, 19th C **250.00**

Frypan, Sunbeam Controlled Heat Automatic, c1950, used, orig box.. **25.00**

Funnel, Elliptical, gray graniteware **30.00**

Grease jar, 4-3/8" h, 4-3/8" w, teapot shape, aluminum, strainer fits between lid and pot, mkd "Grease" on front, side mkd "Japan" **30.00**

Grill plate, graniteware, 11-1/4" d, green and white, large swirl, black trim, c1960 .... **42.50**

Jelly mold, 3-1/2" d, 3-1/2" h, tin, Madeline, stamped "Of 539" **25.00**

Kettle, graniteware, 14-1/4" d, 8-3/4" h, blue and white, lid missing **55.00**

Knife cleaner, cast iron, painted black, lettering highlighted in white "Spong & Co., Umeek, Patent, Knife Cleaner" **85.00**

Lazy Susan, 17" d, aluminum metalware, Art Deco styling, mkd "Wilson Specialities of Brooklyn" **50.00**

Colorama Sherbet Set, Heller Hostess Ware, colored aluminum sherbet dishes, original box, $65.

Lemon squeezer

6-1/2" l, tin-plated iron **20.00**
11" l, hinged maple **65.00**

Match box holder, ironware, striker bar mkd "C. Parker," also mkd "Pat. Sept 14, 1869, May 3, 1870," 4-1/4" w, 1-5/8" d, 5-3/4" h **210.00**

Mayonnaise maker, 8-1/4" h, Wesson, glass base, aluminum top and mixer, orig directions **60.00**

Meat grinder

Sargent & Co, Patent March 8, 1892 .... **40.00**
Universal, bolts onto table, name and "Made in the USA" on side, wooden handle, used **15.00**

Meat tenderizer, 2 x 2-1/2 x 3", rect, iron, heavy handle **40.00**

Meat thermometer, 6" l, hanging, Taylor **10.00**

Mixing bowl, graniteware

10" d, 4" h, blue and white speckle, darker blue rim trim, some wear, few dings **45.00**
11" d, 5-1/4" h, green, black trim, dull int., some wear **30.00**

12-1/4" d, 5-1/4" h, green, black trim, flat rim, some wear **35.00**

Mixing spoon, wood handle, slotted bowl, Androck, Made in USA **18.50**

Mouli-Julienne, rotary cutter, three interchangeable cutting and shredding discs, orig box, c1950 .... **30.00**

Oats crusher, English Pat. No. 448339, white ceramic body, wooden handles, 18" l **125.00**

Pea sheller, 12" h, screw clamp, black wood handle, Vaughans **40.00**

Pencil clip, Driekorn's Bread, cello on silvered tin, orange, blue, white, and yellow wrapped loaf of bread, white ground, c1930 .... **15.00**

Coffeepot, nickel over copper, gooseneck spout, $45.

Pie bird

Blue and gray, long neck **90.00**
Yellow and brown, long neck **90.00**

Pitter, aluminum, hand squeeze type, 1920s **38.00**

Potato masher

9" h, zig zag wire end, red catalin handle **10.00**
10-1/2" l, red wooden handle **10.00**
12" l, all wood, well worn handle **15.00**

Pot holder, Kriebel's Dairies, Hereford, PA, muslin, 4-1/4" sq **7.50**

Relish tray, 15" l handle to handle, gold-colored aluminum tray, three-part 8-1/2" l, 7" w glass insert **25.00**

Rolling pin, 10" l, 3-1/2" handles, aluminum **40.00**

Tap-Icer, 9" l flexible hand held ice crusher, Williamsport, PA, maker, orig box **5.00**

Salt box, 8 x 17-1/2", rect, pine, hinged lid **120.00**

Scale, Salter #50, green enameled base, orig 12" d round, 2" deep pan, 8-1/2" w, 14-1/2" h... **175.00**

Scoop, brass, wood handle, 6-1/2" l... **50.00**

Sherbet set, Heller Hostess Ware Colorama, forest green scalloped dishes, anodized gold aluminum bases, set of 12 ... **135.00**

Sifter, three screens, colorful litho tin .. **20.00**

Skillet, cast iron, Wagner Ware No. 3, italic trademark "Wagner Ware, Sidney-O" **15.00**

Spice set, spun aluminum, copper-colored tops, marked with name of spice, cayenne, allspice, nutmeg, ginger, cinnamon, cloves, mustard, paprika **35.00**

Springerie rolling pin, 16" l, flag, owl, rabbit, cat, duck, leaf, florals **75.00**

Strainer, wire mesh bowl, twisted wire and wood handle.................................. **10.00**

Strawberry huller, Nip-It, 1906............ **4.00**

Stringholder, 6-1/2" h, table top type, cast aluminum, orig discolored paint, c1900 .... **65.00**

Sugar nippers, 9" l, c1800 .... **145.00**

Tea caddy, 8-1/2" h, tin, painted, red fruit, yellow leaves, orig cap **265.00**

Tea kettle

Aluminum, painted handle, Mirro ... **30.00**

Copper, gooseneck, dovetailed, sgd "JMWE" and hallmark **175.00**

Teapot and salt and pepper shakers, aluminum, four cup teapot, cov with red finial, orig strainer with red handle, orig box, mkd "Highly Polished Aluminum, Made in Japan" **25.00**

Tin, rect, Krispy Crackers **35.00**

Water set, Colorama, colored aluminum, copper colored pitcher with ice lip, seven ice tea tumblers in assorted colors, gold colored oval tray with handles, $35.

Tom & Jerry Set

9-1/2" d, 4" h white ceramic bowl, eight 3" h x 3" d mugs, gold trim, Homer Laughlin, mkd "USA, E6NS"........................... **75.00**

9-1/2" d x 5-3/4" h bowl, eight footed 3-1/2" d cups, white milk glass, green and red dec. unmarked **35.00**

11-1/4" d, six 3-1/2" h cups, white milk glass, multicolored scene of young couple in horse drawn sleigh, base mkd "McK," minor wear to decals **75.00**

Tomato slicer, enameled wood handle, orig litho sleeve **18.00**

Toothpick holder, Kitchen Prayer Lady, white **15.00**

Vegetable basket, 7" d, 5" h, wire, tapered, bale handle, 1870........................... **55.00**

Vegetable grater, Schroeter, tin, iron back, wood handle, old blue paint **40.00**

Vegetable slicer, Morris Metric, adjusting knob on side, metal, MIB **8.00**

Waf-L-Ette and Patty Shell Molds, Handi Hostess Kit, Bonley Products, 1950s, orig box **5.00**

Wall plaque

Fruit, paint scuffed, 1950s............... **8.00**

Parrot, chalkware, 10" x 6", chips... **12.00**

Water pitcher, aluminum

8" h, 6" d, deep red, mkd "Perma-Hues," missing small brad from ice lip **20.00**

10" h, cast, black plastic handle **18.00**

Kitchen Glassware

History: The Depression era brought inexpensive kitchen and table products to center stage. The companies in the forefront of production included Hocking, Hazel Atlas, McKee, U.S. Glass, and Westmoreland.

Kitchen glassware complemented Depression glass. Many items were produced in the same color and style. Because the glass was molded, added decorative elements included ribs, fluting, arches and thumbprint patterns. In order to be durable, the glassware had to be thick. This resulted in forms that were difficult to handle at times and often awkward aesthetically. After World War II, aluminum products began to replace kitchen glassware.

Collecting Hints: Glassware for the kitchen was made in quantity. Although collectors do tolerate signs of use, they will not accept pieces with heavy damage. Many of the products contain applied decals; these should be in good condition. A collection can be built inexpensively by concentrating on one form, such as canister sets, measuring cups, or reamers.

Ashtray
Butterfly, crystal, Jeannette.............. **7.00**
Green, fluted, Federal **12.00**
Banana split dish, Jeannette, oval, crystal
.... **5.00**
Bowl
5-1/2" d, red, platonite, Criss-Cross **12.50**
6" d, jade-ite, Jeannette **18.00**
7-1/2" d, cobalt blue, Hazel Atlas ... **45.00**
8" d, green, Hocking **15.00**
8" d, Orange Dot, custard.............. **32.00**
8-1/2" l, oval, Pyrex, beige, two handles,
blue dec, 1-1/2 quart **15.00**
9" d, Delphite, Pyrex....................... **19.00**
10" d, emerald glo........................... **50.00**
Butter churn, Dazy, No. 40, wood paddles
.... **125.00**
Butter dish, cov, one-pound size
Criss Cross, crystal **24.00**
Federal, amber............................... **35.00**
Hazel Atlas, green.......................... **60.00**
Hocking, crystal **25.00**
Cake plate, Snowflake, pink................ **35.00**
Canister
3" h, jade-ite, Jeannette, allspice, ginger,
nutmeg, or pepper, each **60.00**
5-1/2" h, sq, coffee, jade-ite, Jeannette
.... **175.00**
6" h, green, screw-on lid, smooth ... **40.00**
16 oz, tea, jade-ite, round **175.00**
28 oz, sugar, jade-ite..................... **300.00**
40 oz, coffee, Delphite, round **450.00**
Coffee measuring cup, Kitchen Aid
advertisement, coffee measurement
indicators, red and black, 4-3/8" h . **18.00**
Coffeepot, cov, Pyrex, Model #7759, nine
cups **60.00**
Cruet, stopper, Hocking, transparent green
.... **25.00**
Curtain tiebacks, pr, 3-1/2" d, flat, floral,
green and pink **25.00**
Double boiler, Pyrex, orig paper instruction
insert **30.00**
Drawer pull, green or pink
Double type.................................... **12.00**
Knob **5.00**
Egg cup
Black... **12.00**
Blue opaque................................... **20.00**
Epsom salt container, ribbed, jade. **150.00**
Fish bowl, 6" d, transparent green **22.00**
Flour shaker, Deco, ivory, black lettering
.... **45.00**
Grease jar, Seville Yellow, black trim... **35.00**
Hand beater, 32 oz measuring cup base,
green, stippled texture................... **45.00**
Knife
Dur-x, three-leaf, pink..................... **53.00**
Pinwheel, crystal **22.00**
Rose Spray, pink, orig box.............. **28.00**
Star, crystal **19.00**
Star, pink.. **54.00**
Thumbguard, crystal, dec, Westmoreland
.... **52.00**

Bottle, Genuine Three Crow Brand Warranted
Pure Made, The Atlantic Spice Company,
Rockland, Maine, conical glass, aluminum lid,
c1940, **$28**.

Lemon reamer, Delphite, Jeannette .. **80.00**
Match holder, Jeannette, Delphite, round,
black lettering "Matches" **145.00**
Mayonnaise ladle, amber, flat.............. **9.75**
Measuring cup
2 oz, 1/4 cup, jade-ite, Jeannette .. **40.00**
8 oz, Delphite, one spout **110.00**
8 oz, Fire-King, one spout **18.50**
16 oz, cobalt blue, Hazel-Atlas **175.00**
16 oz, green, stick handle, US Glass
.... **28.50**
16 oz, white milk glass **24.00**
Mixing bowl
5-3/4" d, Gold and Black Stripped
Ovenware, Pyrex **25.00**
6-1/2" d, amber, Federal................ **10.00**
7-1/4" d, yellow banded dot, Pyrex **10.00**
7-1/2" d, cobalt blue, Hazel-Atlas .. **42.00**
8-1/2" d, Criss-Cross, blue **100.00**

Chip and dip set, Anchor Hocking, Aqua Marine, original foil label, $30.

9-1/2" d, amber, Federal **18.00**
11" d, Vitrock, white **15.00**
Mixing bowl set, nested, Pyrex
  Butterprint, four pcs **75.00**
  Primary colors, 5-3/4" x 3-1/4" blue, 7-1/4" x 3-3/4" red, 8-5/8" x 4-1/4" green, 10-3/8" x 4-1/2" yellow **95.00**
Napkin holder, Nar-O-Fold, white, mkd "Napkin Company, Chicago, reg. U.S.A."
  .... **50.00**
Percolator lid, green, Hocking **12.00**
Pie lifter, Pine Cone **15.00**
Pie plate, individual size, heart shape, Cupid & Arrow **25.00**
Pitcher
  Delphite, two cups **150.00**
  Jade-ite, sunflower in base **40.00**
Refrigerator dish, cov, 4-1/2" x 4-1/2" sq, pink, Jennyware **35.00**
Refrigerator set, Pyrex, Early American pattern, ... **65.00**
Rolling pin
  13-1/4" l, colorless and white, blue and red speckles, bulbous hand holds, England, 19th C, imperfections **300.00**

14" l, black, white speckles, small button knop ends, England, 19th C, imperfections **175.00**
14" l, dark amber, white speckles, small button knop ends, England or eastern US, 19th C, imperfections **225.00**
14-1/2" l, pale translucent green, small button knop ends, England, 19th C, imperfections **155.00**
14-3/4" l, colorless, white, and amethyst loop design, bulbous hand holds, England or eastern US, 19th C, imperfections **245.00**
15" l, pale aqua, white marbrie, elongated bulbous hand holds, England, 19th C, imperfections **225.00**
Salt and pepper shakers, pr
  Cobalt blue, red lids, Hazel-Atlas .. **30.00**
  Jade-ite **150.00**
  Jennyware, ftd, pink **55.00**
  Ribbed, jade-ite, Jeannette **22.00**
  Roman Arches, black **65.00**
  Ships, red trim, red lids **55.00**
Sugar jar, slanted, clear glass, base emb "Pat. apl. 1.1924," orig lid **45.00**
Sugar shaker, cov, Hex optic, green **250.00**

Serving dish, oval, divided, white, blue floral trim, marked "Glassbake," $5.

Sundae, ftd, pink, Federal **12.00**
Tray, sq, Jeannette, handle, pink **18.00**
Trivet, 9" d, round, Pyrex, crystal **12.00**
Water dispenser, 17" h, black base, crystal bowl, silver trim **95.00**

L

Labels

History: The first fruit-crate art was created by California fruit growers about 1880. The labels became very colorful and covered many subjects. Most depict the type of fruit held in the box. Cardboard boxes replaced fruit crates in the 1940s, making the labels collectible.

Over the last decade, label collectors have begun to widen their collecting range. Today, can, luggage, and wine labels are sought as well as cigar, fruit crate, and other household-type labels.

Collecting Hints: Damaged, trimmed, or torn labels are less valuable than labels in mint condition. Collectors prefer labels that can be removed from the product and stored flat in drawers or albums.

Adviser: Lorie Cairns.

Apple, 10-1/2" x 9"

Appleton, Art Nouveau lady sniffing pink roses, apples, ranch scene **5.00**
Big J, red and green apples, blue official seal, aqua ground **1.00**
Bird Valley, big blue crow perched on shield, orange ground **2.00**
Blue Winner, cowboy in arena on horseback, reaching down to pick up apple from ground **3.00**
Buddy, grinning baby, two apples, dated 1920, blue ground **6.00**
Butler's Price, large red apple, blue ground **1.00**
Chelan Beauty, mountain scene, lake, trees, two red apples................................... **2.00**
Cliff, gorge and river scene, old car approaching bridge **4.00**
Color Guard, V-shaped rainbow, black ground **1.00**
Dainty Maid, little girl holding apple, blue ground **2.00**
Family Choice, cartoon family standing behind small house, red ground, Topeka, KS **2.00**
Golden Rod, sprays of golden rod flowers, black ground **2.00**
Golden Spur, name in rope script encircles huge spur, navy blue ground............ **2.00**
Heart of Washington, arrow points to Malaga... **1.00**

Hi-Buv-All, two red apples on branch, blue ground.. **1.00**
Jackie Boy, little boy in sailor suit, holding apple, blue ground **6.00**
Land O'Lakes, bird's eye view of town and river, big red apple, WI **3.00**
Mountain Goat, white goat standing on cliff, snow capped mountains and forest, turquoise sky.................................... **2.00**
North Country, three colorful apples, red ground.. **1.00**
Orchard Boy, redheaded boy's face, three red applies, blue ground................. **2.00**
Paradise, bird of paradise blossom, black ground.. **6.00**
Red Winner, Indian lady riding white horse **4.00**
Silver Spur, rope script words encircle spur, red ground **2.00**
Skookum, smiling Indian looking at lettering, blue ground **3.00**
Spinner, big red apple, curved red swirls emanating from it **4.00**
Swan, graceful white swan, black ground **6.00**
Tell, red apple with arrow through it, gray ground.. **2.00**
Trout, rainbow trout **5.00**
Uncle Sam, sad Uncle Sam, hat in hand, red ground.. **6.00**
Violet, big bunch of violets, black ground **7.00**

Mountain Goat, snow white mountain goat standing on cliff, snow capped mountains and forest in background, turquoise sky, 10-1/2" x 9", $2. All label photos courtesy of Adviser Lorie Cairns.

Cosmetics

Amber Lion, snarling lion's face, "Triple Action" germicidal dandruff remover, black ground, 3-3/4" x 2" .... **.75**
Aunt Doris Colonial Rose Sachet Powder, cherubs, flying bird, flowers, green and white, 2-1/2" d .... **.25**

Azure Violet Toilet Water, Art Nouveau, fancy shape, violets, 1-3/4" x 4-3/8".. **1.00**
Benzo Almond Cream, red and navy, white ground, 4-1/4" x 3-1/8"......................**.25**
Cream of Almond Lotion, Art Nouveau designs, trees, gilt, pointed arch shape, 3-3/4" x 1-1/2" ....**.75**
Edelweiss Disappearing Cream, "Flesh builder, removes wrinkles and develops the bust," fancy shape, red roses, dark green leaves, 3-5/8" x 2" ....**.50**
Fatima The Favorite Complexion Cold Cream, cherubs, flying bird, flowers, green and white, 2-1/2" d...................**.25**
La Bella Hair Tonic, Art Nouveau flowers, fancy shape, gilt, 1-3/4" x 4"..............**1.00**
Lady Marion Perfume, blond lady, pink flowers, 1-1/4" d.................................**.75**
Little Fairies Claro-Derm, The Irresistible Depilatory, 1-1/2" x 6-1/8" ....**.25**
Mirabeau Lipstick, green and white, emb, 1-3/8" x 1"...**.15**
Royal Bouquet Face & Body Cooling Lotion, gold foil, green and red, 2" x 4" ....**.50**
Salko Sachet, lady in white frilly cap, white flowers, 1-3/8" d................................**.75**
Shave Rite, shaving cream, striped blue, 3-1/2" x 4-1/2"..**.25**
Universal Cucumber Cream, lady, designs, orange, blue, and white, 3-1/2" x 1-3/4" ....**.50**
VJC Foundation Cream, gold foil, green scalloped border, 4" x 2-1/2"...............**.50**
White Top Liquid Shampoo, smiling lady, green and white, 3-1/4" x 1-1/2"..........**.25**

Grape, 13" x 4"

American Eagle, huge Bald Eagle, wings spread over entire label, sunset colors background **2.50**
American Pride, eagle, shield, orange, blue, and white....................................**.25**
Bear Mountain, two bears, scenic farm, mountains, house...........................**1.50**
Black Joe, smiling elderly black man, blue ground **2.00**
Buck Rock, buck standing near big rock **1.50**
Deer Valley, pink mountains, big farm, desert sky, inset deer's head, red letters ....**.50**
E.F.A., red and green grape bunches, lilac and yellow ground..............................**.25**
Elkhorn, big elk's head, brown ground .. **.75**
Exclusive, shield, lion, crown.................**.25**
Fantasia, dancing senorita, basket of fruit, blue ground ....**.50**
Gold Trout, leaping trout **4.00**
Grapeland, big castle, pennants, picture of grapes on easel, smiling bunch grapes ....**.25**
Halloween, grinning Jack-O-Lantern, witch on broom stick, cat...........................**6.00**

Horseshoe, blue horseshoe, red ground **.75**
Jo-Vista, red and green grapes, blue ground...**.25**
King's Ruby, red ruby gemstone, aqua ground...**.25**
Lady Rowena, lady riding sorrel horse, two brave knights jousting, castle, blue ground...**.50**
Million Dollar, stacks of shiny coins, yellow letters, blue ground ....**.25**
Miss Seedless, laughing little girl, vineyard scene, grape clusters......................**.25**
Mont Elisa, girl holding big bunch of purple grapes, yellow ground......................**.50**
Our Pick, white rooster pecking at bowl of fruit, red ground **1.25**
Paul Dobson, bunch of red grapes, scenic vineyard, river, mountains ....**.25**
Pia, smiling girl holding big basket of fruit ....**.50**
Rayo, sunrise scene over planted fields, colorful mountains, yellow grapes .....**.25**
Rosa De Maggio, three red roses, bunch of purple grapes ....**.50**
Royal Tiger Brand, fierce snarling tiger in greenery, aqua ground....................**5.00**
Salute, two hands holding two glasses of red wine, making toast, map of Portugal, grape cluster......................................**.25**
Silver King, smiling silver king with crown, blue ground ....**.25**
Small Black, little black child, grapes, red ground...**2.00**
Star of Ivanhoe, big red star, dark blue ground...**.25**
Tommy Boy, smiling little boy in gold picture frame **1.50**
Try One, bunches of red and yellow grapes, blue ground ....**.25**
White Horse, galloping white horse, black ground...**.50**
Zephyr, big green grape leaf, reddish-brown ground...**.25**

Lemon, 12-1/2" x 8-3/4"

All Year, orchard scene, mountains, cacti, desert vegetation, black border, Fillmore **2.00**
Cambria, brown eagle, two torches, blue ground, brown border, Placentia **1.00**
Estero, estuary scene, clipper ships near sheer rocky coastline, palm trees, dark green ground, Goleta **2.00**
Exposition, certificate of Alaska Yukon Pac Expo in Seattle, 1909, showing diploma for grand prize won for lemon exhibit, black ground...................................**2.00**
Fallbrook, rushing mountain stream, pine trees, lemons, leaves, blossoms, black ground...**1.00**
Gateway, two horseback riders in redwood forest, sprig of lemon blossoms, dark blue ground, Lemon Cover **3.00**
Keeper, pair of fancy keys, Santa Paula **2.00**

La Patera, big blue pond, grove scene **1.00**
OH-CEE, circle "C" in center, lemons, leaves, blossoms, brown ground **1.00**
Pacific, large lemon in center with Hawaiian Islands on it, maps of Asia, Austrialia, Pacific coast with trade routes, blue ocean ground **2.00**
Panama, map of USA and Mexico showing trade routes from Santa Barbara through Panama Canal, Santa Barbara **2.00**
Rough Diamond, large "L" in diamond, lime green ground.................................... **1.00**
Santa Rosa, man and burro, Spanish style home overlooking lemon grove **2.00**
Sespe, mountain scene, river, trees, rocks, black ground **2.00**
Superb, two lemons, blossoms, leaves, orange and brown ground............... **2.00**

Mustang Brand California Vegetables, Western Packing Co., Packers, Shippers, Guadalupe, Calif., white mustang horse, black ground, 7" x 9", **$1**.

Orange, 11" x 11"

Annie Laurie, Scottish lassie, bright plaid, Strathmore **6.00**
AR-SAR-BEN, orange, bright colors, blue ground, Lemon Cove **1.00**
Athlete, three runners reaching finish line, stadium setting, Claremont............... **7.00**
Blue Goose, blue fowl, orange ground, Los Angeles.. **2.00**
Coed, smiling graduate, purple ground, Claremont **2.00**
Daisy, large white flower, green leaves, black ground, Covina........................ **4.00**
Gold Buckle, gilt outline of buckle, orchard scene, two large oranges, royal blue ground, East Highlands **3.00**

Good Year, two oranges on leafy branch, blossoms, blue ground, Rayo **2.00**
Have One, hand holding partially peeled orange, royal blue, Lemon Cove **2.00**
Hi Tone, green musical notes, black ground, Upland **1.00**
Juciful, huge orange and leaves, light blue ground, Redlands........................... **2.00**
La Reina, pretty Spanish senorita holding black fan, hacienda scene, Rialto ... **2.00**
Lily, two large white calla lilies, green leaves, black ground, Exeter **4.00**
Marvel, brass looking letters on wood sign ground... **1.00**
Metropolitan, big city street scene, large orange, brown ground, Orange Cove **1.00**
Miracle, genie holding tray with three oranges, orchard and mountain scene, dated 1928, Placentia **4.00**
Orbit, meteor in shape of an orange, streaking thru starry evening skies, royal blue ground, Exeter **10.00**
Pala Brave, large Indian Chief, wearing headdress, maroon ground, Placentia **5.00**
Pine Cone, arrowhead on mountain framed inside huge pine cone on bough, orange adjacent **10.00**
Polo, polo player and bay pony, red and green ground **6.00**
Royal Knight, knight in armor on horseback, castle, yellow ground, Redlands...... **2.00**
Scotch Lassie Jean, Scottish lassie in kilts, castle, thistle, blue, green, and black ground, slight damage **3.00**
Shamrock, shamrock in sky over orange groves, Placentia **2.00**
Sierra Vista, scenic groves, snowy mountains, Porterville **12.00**
Star of California, red star, Exeter, CA, on map of California, Exeter **2.00**
Strength, large gray elephant with tusks, yellow ground, Santa Paula............ **35.00**
Sun Prince, smiling sun, blue ground, Orange Cove **2.00**
T.E.A., citrus blossoms and leaves, red lettering, blue ground, allover design of flowers in black............................... **1.00**

Pear, 10-3/4" x 7-1/4"

A-Plus, American girl athlete............... **2.00**
Boy Blue, little boy blowing horn.......... **3.00**
Capital Park, California State Capitol building and grounds, blue ground. **2.00**
Don't Worry, cute little boy, black ground **2.00**
Duckwall, colorful wood duck standing by brick wall **4.00**
Gold Wing, pair of gilt wings over golden pears, black ground **2.00**
High Hand, hand holding four aces, blue ground... **2.00**

Keystone Fruit Co., big red Keystone, navy ground **1.00**
Lake Ridge, scene of lake, orchard, forest, mountains, two big pears **2.00**
Maltese Cross, big Maltese cross on white ground, gilt dec **1.00**
Quail, CA quail walking through grass . **5.00**
Rancheria, Indian village by lake, Indians, white horse **3.00**
Repetition, orchard, home, snowy mountains, two big pears **1.00**
Sno-Gem, snow laden lettering, blue ground **2.00**
Snow Owl, fierce snow owl, blue ground **2.00**
Stagecoach, stagecoach scene........... **3.00**
Sun Smile, smiling sun, rays fill background **2.00**
Wonder-Ful, psychedelic blue rainbows emanating from big pear, black ground **2.00**

Miscellaneous

Betty Ann Baking Powder, little redhead girl, pink dress, skipping rope, white ground, gilt border, Hastings, NE..... **3.00**
Blue Hill, white corn, house by river, conifers **3.00**
Boyer's Oil Polish, boots and shoes, 3-1/8" x 1-1/8"... .**25**
Campfire Coffee, bubbling granite ware coffee pot on campfire, 3-3/8" x 17" . **4.00**
Capn John Clam Nectar Bouillon, captain, whole clams, stylized dolphins, Canada **1.00**
Clabber Girl Baking Powder, girl carrying plate of biscuits, family scene **1.00**
Ellendale, forest, stream, mountains, limes in pods, Ellendale, DE...................... **1.00**
Farmer's Pride, catsup, 2" x 2-3/4"........ .**25**
Green Mountain Syrup, cabin, ox team, man making syrup, black family boiling cane syrup in iron kettle, 3-3/4" x 3-1/2" **1.00**
Happy Day Soda, rising sun and rays, sailboat on lake, PA............................ .**25**
Hillview, farm scene, melons, 4-1/4" x 9-3/4" **75**
Hi Plane, pancake flour, aqua plane flying over stack of pancakes on plate, recipe, 9" x 12-3/4"...................................... **2.00**
Home Packed Beef, woodcut picture of Hereford cow, T.B. Tested, New York, black and white, c1910, 12" x 4-1/4" **3.00**
Imperial Tooth Wash, oval, Art Nouveau florals **75**
M & M, juicy strawberries, leaves, blossoms, black ground, 6" sq............................ .**50**
Mermaid, long haired topless mermaid seated beside sea shell...................... .**25**
New England, map of 6 New England states, ginger ale................................ .**25**
Pearson's Red Top Snuff, Victorian lady, deep red and black, 2-3/8" x 5-1/2".... .**50**

Popover, plate of biscuits, white ground **1.00**
Rondo, long haired pianist playing grand piano **25**
Royal Blue Stores Coffee, steaming cup of coffee, emb, gilt, 5" x 14"................. **6.00**
Vikings Choice, two Viking ships, gulls. .**25**
Wisk Shaving Cream, man's face, black, blue, and silver, 3" x 5"........................ .**25**

Tin can

Alpine, mountain climber figure, bowl with white kidney beans............................. .**50**
Bob White, bird surveying farm scene, big tomato **2.50**
Butterfly, Telephone Peas, emb, gilt.... **2.00**
Defender, clipper chip, tomato, Art Nouveau designs **1.00**
Fairfax Hall, big white mansion and grounds **1.00**
Isaacs, forest, stream, mountains, asparagus on plate **1.00**
Jonesport, lighthouse, ship, and fish, fish flakes, 9-7/8" x 4-1/4" **1.00**
Memory, two pictures of granny, bowl of mixed fruit **1.00**
Miriam, red apples, dish of applesauce, white ground **1.00**
Orchard Fresh, red whole and half apples, applesauce, blue ground.................. .**75**
Pride of Virginia, two gladiators, two tomatoes, black round..................... **1.00**
Rosefruit, cluster of raspberries, leaves, two tone blue border, 6-1/4" x 8" **50**
Sinatra's, picture of Frank singing, black ground, dated 1990, 4" x 11"............... **4.00**
Teacup, teacup and saucer, evaporated milk **2.00**
Velvet Rose, red roses and buds, red rose garlands around big pumpkin **2.00**
Woodlake, images of big lake and grove scene **25**

Vegetables

Bear, big brown bear with map of CA between paws **1.00**
Blue Mink, blue mink, colorful background, 6-1/2" x 5-1/2" **1.00**
Champ, two football players, blue ground, 9" sq **2.00**
Conestoga, covered red wagon and ox team, desert ground, 7" x 9"............. **2.00**
Deer Mark, stag's head over two sweet potatoes, red ground, 9" sq **1.00**
Deer Valley, russet buck, ranch scene, 4-1/4" x 6-1/2" **75**
Don't Cry, black youth shooting dice, yams, 9" sq **5.00**
Hillview, farm scene, yams, 4-1/2" x 7" .. .**50**
Joe Sammy's, little black boy displaying crate of yams, 9" sq........................ **2.00**
Nob Hill, San Francisco skyscrapers, navy **75**

Sky Path, small plane sky writing name, blue ground **1.00**

Smoky Jim's, smiling black man displaying crate of yams, 9" sq........................... **2.00**

Treasure, pirates treasure chest full of jewels, tropical island, four big yams **1.00**

White House, vegetables in splint basket, white mansion, 7" x 9" **1.00**

Lamps

History: The kerosene lamp was the predominant lighting device during the 19th century and the first quarter of the 20th century. However, its death knell was sounded in 1879 when Thomas A. Edison developed a viable electric light bulb.

The success of the electric lamp depended on the availability of electricity. However, what we take for granted today did not arrive in many rural areas until the 1930s.

Most electric lamps were designed to serve as silent compliments to period design styles. They were meant to blend, rather than stand out. Pairs were quite common.

Famous industrial designers did lend their talents to lamp design, and their products are eagerly sought by collectors. Bradley and Hubbard and Handel are two companies whose products have attracted strong collector interest.

Collecting Hints: Be aware that every lamp has two values—a collectible value and a decorative value. Often the decorative value exceeds the collectible value, in part because most lamps are purchased as decorative accessories, often as accent pieces in a period room setting.

In the 1990s, the hot lamp collectibles were the odd-shaped examples from the 1950s. Some of these were abstract; some figural. While 1950s lamps continue to sell well as part of the 1950s/1960s revival, prices have stabilized primarily because of the market saturation resulting from the large quantity of lamps of this era that survived in attics and basements.

Within the past five years, collector interest is spreading to other manufacturers and into electric lamps, although Aladdin is still one of the most sought after names in lamps.

Just as post-World War II collectors discovered figural transistor and character radios, so also are they discovering motion lamps, many of which are character related. Look for a growing interest in character lamps and a corresponding rise in prices.

Bedroom, Depression-era glass, English Hobnail pattern, pink, 9" h, **$115**.

Akro Agate, lavender and blue marbled shade **350.00**

Aladdin, Alacite, electric

#25 .... **50.00**

#236 .... **65.00**

#266 .... **50.00**

#351, round wall **75.00**

#354, rect wall................................ **75.00**

Bedroom

Art Deco, Chase Chrome, round base, conical shade, c1930.................... **90.00**

Southern Belle, blue, orig shade ... **80.00**

Character

Dick Tracy, painted ceramic bust of Dick, black coat, yellow hat, red tie, 1950s **1,500.00**

Fred Flintstone, 13-1/4" h, painted vinyl, black metal base, orig shade **75.00**

Howdy Doody, orig Howdy shade, figure of Howdy seated on base **500.00**

Mickey Mouse, 4" d, 6-1/2" h, globular metal base, beige ground, three Mickey decals around sides, Soreng-Manegold Co.. **85.00**

Jolly Scotsman holding on top lamp post, **$15**.

Children's

ABC Blocks, wood and plastic, linen over cardboard shade **20.00**
Bambi, plastic, 1950s **30.00**
Cookie Monster, figural, Sesame Street characters on shade **45.00**
Elephant, figural, ceramic, carousel beaded shade.............................. **195.00**
Football player, 14-1/2" h, hollow plaster, football player standing next to figural football standard, linen over cardboard shade, WK, Japan, Sears, Roebuck, 1978... **25.00**
Mountain goat, brown and green spatter glaze over white, American Art Potteries, 15" h... **50.00**
Dresser, Black Cameo, silhouette of young woman, surrounded by ribbon, Porcelier **48.00**
Floor lamp, Lightolier, three arms, adjustable enameled salmon, ivory and dark brown shades, circular black enameled metal base, stamped cipher and numbers on bottom, 33" d, 63" h **200.00**
Headboard, pink, chrome **65.00**
Lava, Lava Simplex Corp, c1968........ **80.00**

TV lamp and planter, deer and fawn, brown spray glaze, American Art Potteries, 7" h, $35.

Motion

Antique Cars, Econolite, 1957, 11" h **120.00**
Cheers Bar, sexy girls, MIB **125.00**
Fireside Peanut Vendor, dancing devil graphics, 1930s............................ **375.00**
Forest Fire, Econolite, 1955......... **115.00**
Fountain of Youth **150.00**
Goldfish, green satin glass, 1931 **300.00**
Niagara Falls, Goodman, extra wide style **150.00**
Snow Scene, bridge, Econolite.... **165.00**

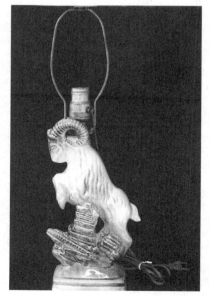

Table, figural, mountain goat, brown and green spatter over white, American Art Potteries, 15" h, $145. Photo courtesy of Doris and Burdell Hall.

Motion lamp, train, gold tone base, original wiring, $95.

Radio, Michael Lumitone.................. **200.00**
Stenographer's, Emeralite, clamps onto desk **395.00**
Television
    Flamingo, planter base, back incised "Lane & Co., Van Nuys, Calif, No. 1081," 16" w, 14-1/2" h.............................. **495.00**
    Gondola, ceramic, brown with gold trim, marked "Copyright Premco Mfg Co, Chicago, IL, 1954," 16" w, 7" h **45.00**
    Horse head, ceramic, 12" x 10-3/4" **25.00**
    Panther, black, 8-1/2" x 6-1/2"......... **35.00**
    Ship, 11" x 10-1/2", gold trim........... **35.00**
Wicker, floor, watermelon slice shaped shade, painted red........................ **300.00**
Wicker, table, Heywood Wakefield, latticework panels, two light bulbs, c1920, orig label, 26" h **525.00**

Limited Edition Collectibles

History: Limited edition plate collecting began with the advent of Christmas plates issued by Bing and Grondahl in 1895. Royal Copenhagen soon followed. During the late 1960s and early 1970s, several potteries, glass factories, and mints began to issue plates, bells, eggs, mugs, etc., which commemorated special events, people, places, or holidays. For a period of time these items increased in popularity and value, but in the late 1970s, the market became flooded with many collectibles and prices declined.

There are many new issues of collector items annually. Some of these collectibles can be found listed under specific headings, such as Hummel, Norman Rockwell, etc.

Collecting Hints: The first item issued in a series usually commands a higher price. When buying a limited edition collectible be aware that the original box and/or certificates increase the value of the piece. The values given below are for collectibles mint in their original box with all certificates of authenticity, etc. Deduct 50 percent if no box is present.

Abbreviation: FE = First Edition.

Department 56, Snow Village, Toy Shop, 1986, original box, $95.

Cottages

Cooper, Malcom, The Falstaff Canterbury
.... **50.00**

Department 56, Christmas in the City

1987, Bakery **100.00**
1987, Cathedral............................. **325.00**
1987, Palace Theatre **500.00**
1987, Toy Shop and Pet Store **175.00**
1988, Chocolate Shoppe.............. **100.00**
1988, City Hall **90.00**
1988, Hank's Market **80.00**
1988, Park Avenue Townhouse **60.00**
1989, Dorothy's Dress Shop **200.00**
1989, Mail box, fire hydrant **10.00**
1989, Ritz Hotel **20.00**
1989, wrought iron fence with gate **10.00**
1990, Fire Station............................ **60.00**
1990, Wong's in Chinatown **40.00**
1991, All Saints Corner Church **60.00**
1991, Arts Academy **65.00**
1991, Hollydale's Department Store
.... **80.00**
1991, Little Italy-Ristorante.............. **75.00**
1992, City Clockworks, Uptown Shoppe
.... **60.00**
1993, West Village Shops **70.00**
1994, Brokerage House................... **50.00**
1995, Beekman House, Brownstones
.... **35.00**
1995, Ivy Terrance Apartments **80.00**
1996, Café Caprice, French Restaurant
.... **40.00**
1996, Grand Central Railway Station
.... **150.00**
1997, City Globe **45.00**
1997, Hi-De-Ho Nightclub **50.00**
1998, Grand Movie Theater............ **60.00**
1998, Johnson's Grocery & Deli **50.00**
1999, Parkview Hospital **50.00**
1999, Wintergarten.......................... **75.00**
2001, 42nd Street Fire Co. **80.00**
2001, Foster Pharmacy................... **80.00**

Department 56, Dickens Village

1984, Bean and Son Smithy Shop **135.00**
1984, Candle Shop **145.00**
1984, Green Grocer **115.00**

Department 56, Victoria Station, original box, $125.

Department 56, The Old Globe Theatre, original box, $75.

1984, Jones & Co. Brush/Basket Shop
.... **125.00**
1985, Thatched Cottage **300.00**
1985, Tudor Cottage.................... **200.00**
1985, Village Church **100.00**
1986, Cottage of Bob Cratchit and Tiny
Tim... **45.00**
1986, Fezziwig's Warehouse......... **20.00**
1986, Scrooge & Marley Counting House
.... **80.00**
1987, Dickens Village sign............. **10.00**
1987, Old Curiosity Shop **30.00**
1988, Booter and Cobbler **60.00**
1988, George Weeton Watchmaker
.... **65.00**
1988, Ivy Glen Church................... **75.00**
1988, Nicholas Nickleby Cottage .. **45.00**
1989, Kings Road Cab................... **30.00**
1989, Peggotty's Seaside Cottage, tan
.... **90.00**
1989, Ruth Marion **175.00**
1989, Victoria Station...................... **90.00**
1990, King's Road **30.00**
1990, Tutbury Printer **35.00**
1991, Ashbury Inn **35.00**
1991, Fagin's Hide-A-Way.............. **30.00**
1992, King's Road Post Office **15.00**
1992, Lionhead Bridge................... **15.00**
1993, Dashing through the Snow .. **40.00**
1993, Pump Lane Shoppes **90.00**
1994, Boarding & Lodging School **40.00**
1994, Chelsea Market Mistletoe **30.00**
1994, Mr & Mrs Pickle **40.00**
1994, Whittlesbourne Church **75.00**
1995, Brickston Road Watchmen .. **20.00**
1995, Chelsea Market Hat Monger & Cart
.... **25.00**
1995, The Chop Shop **35.00**
1996, Grapes Inn............................ **40.00**
1996, Quilly's Antiques **40.00**
1997, Canadian Trading Co. **125.00**
1997, Leacock Poulterer **45.00**
1997, Tower of London................. **200.00**
1998, Heathmoor Castle **75.00**
1998, Lynton Point Tower **60.00**

1999, Little Women, The March
Residence **80.00**
2000, Fezziwig's Ballroom **65.00**
2001, Burwickglen Golf Clubhouse **75.00**
2001, Old Curiosity Shop Starter Set
.... **35.00**

Department 56, Heathmoor Castle, 1998,
original box, **$75**.

F. J. Designs, Cat's Meow, F. Jones
1983, Antique Shop **90.00**
1984, Attorney **115.00**
1984, Music Shop **100.00**
1985, Allen Coe House **60.00**
1985, Opera House **50.00**
1986, Canal Company **50.00**
1986, Golden Lamb Buttery **50.00**
1987, Jared Coffin House **30.00**
1988, Buckeye Candy and Tobacco
.... **20.00**
1988, County Courthouse.............. **20.00**
1989, Thorpe House Bed & Breakfast
.... **20.00**
1989, Winkler Bakery **15.00**
1990, FJ Jones Realty Co. **15.00**
1990, Noah's Ark Veterinary **15.00**
1990, Rising Sun Tavern **65.00**
1991, All Saints Chapel.................. **12.00**
1991, Christmas Rocky Mountain Set
.... **175.00**
1992, August Imgard House **45.00**
1992, Bank Barn **9.00**
1992, City News **9.00**
1992, Vermont Barn **9.00**
1993, Johann Singer Boots & Shoes **5.00**
1994, Craig Jeweler **15.00**

1995, St. Marks in the Bowery **12.00**
1996, Green Gables House **10.00**
1998, Black Dog Tavern................ **10.00**
1998, Father Flanagan's Home...... **10.00**
1998, New London Harbor Light ... **12.00**
1998, Statute of Liberty **12.00**
Harbour Lights, lighthouses
1991, Burrows Island, WA............ **300.00**
1991, Fort Niagara, NY................. **145.00**
1992, Nauset, MA......................... **225.00**
1993, Hilton Head, SC.................. **400.00**
1994, Assateague, VA **185.00**
1994, Barnegat, NJ **125.00**
1995, Marblehead, OH.................. **60.00**
1995, Round Island, MI **75.00**
1996, Pemaquid, ME..................... **125.00**
1997, Morris Island, SC **125.00**
1997, Yaquine Bay, WA **75.00**
1998, Cape Florica, FL **70.00**
1998, Execution Rock, NY **70.00**
Sheila's Collectibles, S. Thompson
1993, Amish buggy **25.00**
1993, Citadel................................. **40.00**
1994, Pennsylvania Dutch Barn **30.00**
1994, Trotman House **20.00**
1995, Banta House......................... **60.00**
1995, Casey Barn........................... **40.00**
1995, Capitol, Williamsburg **50.00**
1995, Dragon House **45.00**
1995, Magnolia Parlor House......... **20.00**
1995, Raleigh Tavern..................... **50.00**
1996, Cinnamon Hill **35.00**
1996, Silhouette **20.00**
1998, Night Before Christmas........ **40.00**
1999, Blanche & Ethel's Tea Room **40.00**
1999, Miller House.......................... **40.00**

Winter, David

Arches Thrice, autographed by David
Winter, orig certificate and box **200.00**
Astrotogue's Castle....................... **200.00**
Beekeepers, 1992 .... **125.00**
Buttercup Cottage, 1995................ **85.00**
Copae Chapel **110.00**
Daresbury Castle........................... **140.00**
Dower House **45.00**
Friendship Collage, 1994............. **100.00**
Guild Village Scene Display, 1987 **175.00**
Gunsmith's Cottage **80.00**
Hogmanay, 1988 Christmas........... **85.00**
Horatio Pernickety's Amorous Intent,
autographed by David Winter, orig
certificate and box........................ **350.00**
Hotspur's Keep **80.00**
Myton Tower.................................. **110.00**
Old Distillery.................................. **400.00**
Scrooges School, 1992 Christmas
.... **115.00**
St. Christopher's Church **100.00**
The Bird Cage................................ **100.00**
The Tickled Trout **115.00**
Thornill Chapel............................... **90.00**
Witch's Castle **75.00**

Lenox, The Spring Bunny Easter Egg, 2002, $15.

Eggs

Anri, 1979, Beatrix Potter 5.00
Cybis Studios, 1983, FE.................. 300.00
Ferrandiz
  1978, FE.. 15.00
  1979... 12.00
  1980... 9.50
  1981... 9.00
  1982... 8.00
  1983... 8.00
Franklin Mint, 1979, porcelain........... 35.00
Goebel
  1978, Easter 10.00
  1979, Easter 8.00
  1980, crystal 7.50
  1981, Easter 8.00
  1982, Easter 8.00
  1983, Easter 8.00
Gorham, bone china, pink rose, 4-1/4"
  .... 18.00
Noritake, Easter
  1971, FE.. 60.00
  1972... 35.00
  1973... 18.00
  1974... 18.00
  1975... 10.00
  1976... 10.00
  1977... 10.00
  1978... 10.00
  1979... 10.00
  1980... 10.00
  1981... 10.00
  1982... 10.00
  1983... 10.00
  1984... 10.00
Royal Bayreuth
  1975... 8.50
  1976... 6.50
  1977... 5.50
  1979... 5.00
  1980... 5.00
Wedgwood
  1977... 35.00
  1978... 25.00
  1979... 18.00
  1983... 15.00

Mugs

Bing & Grondahl, 1978, FE 50.00

Franklin Mint, 1979, Father's Day...... 40.00
Gorham, 1981, Bugs Bunny................ 8.00
Lynell Studios, 1983, FE, Gnome Series
  Gnome Sweet Gnome..................... 6.50
  Mama Gnome 7.00
Royal Copenhagen
  1967, large.................................. 200.00
  1968, large.................................... 24.00
  1972, large.................................... 24.00
  1976, large.................................... 24.00
  1979, small................................... 24.00
  1980, small................................... 24.00
  1981, large.................................... 24.00
  1982, small................................... 24.00
  1983, small................................... 24.00
Schmid, Zemsky, musical, 1981,
  Paddington Bear 20.00
Wedgwood
  1971, Christmas............................. 35.00
  1972, Christmas............................. 30.00
  1973, Christmas............................. 30.00
  1974, Christmas............................. 30.00
  1975, Christmas............................. 30.00
  1976, Christmas............................. 30.00
  1977, Father's Day......................... 25.00
  1978, Father's Day......................... 25.00
  1979, Christmas............................. 25.00
  1980, Christmas............................. 25.00
  1981, Christmas............................. 25.00
  1982, Christmas............................. 25.00

Plates

Anri, Christmas, J. Ferrandiz, 12" d
  1972, Christ in the Manger........... 230.00
  1974, Holy Night............................ 90.00
  1977, Girl with Flowers 80.00
  1979, The Drummer 80.00
  1980, Rejoice 80.00
  1983, Peace Attend Thee 80.00
Anri, Mother's Day, J. Ferrandiz
  1973, Alpine Mother & Child........ 150.00
  1975, Dove Girl............................ 150.00
  1977, Alpine Stroll........................ 125.00
  1980, Spring Arrivals 125.00
  1982, With Love 125.00

Bing & Grondahl, Christmas plate, Pheasants in the Snow at Christmas, 1970. $20.

Bing and Grondahl, Christmas, various artists, 7" d

1895, Behind the Frozen Window **3,400.00**
1897, Christmas Meal of the Sparrows **725.00**
1900, Church Bells Chiming in Christmas **800.00**
1902, Interior of a Gothic Church . **285.00**
1904, View of Copenhagen from Frederiksberg Hill **125.00**
1906, Sleighing to Church on Christmas Eve **135.00**
1909, Happiness Over the Yule Tree **100.00**
1911, First It Was Sung by Angels to Shepherds in the Fields **80.00**
1913, Bringing Home the Yule Tree **90.00**
1914, Royal Castle of Amalienborg, Copenhagen **75.00**
1916, Christmas Prayer of the Sparrows **85.00**
1918, Fishing Boat Returning Home for Christmas **85.00**
1920, Hare in the Snow **70.00**
1921, Pigeons in the Castle Court.. **55.00**
1923, Royal Hunting Castle, The Hermitage **55.00**
1925, The Child's Christmas **70.00**
1927, Skating Couple **80.00**
1928, Eskimo Looking at Village Church in Greenland **60.00**
1930, Yule Tree in Town Hall Square of Copenhagen **85.00**
1932, Lifeboat at Work **90.00**
1934, Church Bell in Tower **70.00**
1936, Royal Guard **70.00**
1939, Ole Lock-Eye, The Sandman **150.00**
1941, Horses Enjoying Christmas Meal in Stable **345.00**
1943, The Ribe Cathedral **155.00**
1945, The Old Water Mill **135.00**
1947, Dybbol Mill **70.00**
1948, Watchman, Sculpture of Town Hall, Copenhagen **80.00**
1950, Kronborg Castle at Elsinore **150.00**
1952, Old Copenhagen Canals at Wintertime with Thorvaldsen Museum in Background **85.00**
1954, Birthplace of Hans Christian Andersen, with Snowman **100.00**
1956, Christmas in Copenhagen . **140.00**
1959, Christmas Eve **120.00**
1961, Winter Harmony **115.00**
1963, The Christmas Elf **120.00**
1965, Bringing Home the Christmas Tree **65.00**
1968, Christmas in Church **45.00**
1970, Pheasants in the Snow at Christmas **20.00**
1972, Christmas in Greenland **20.00**
1974, Christmas in the Village **20.00**
1976, Christmas Welcome **25.00**

1981, Christmas Peace **50.00**
1983, Christmas in Old Town **55.00**
1985, Christmas Eve at the Farmhouse **55.00**
1987, The Snowman's Christmas Eve **60.00**
1989, Christmas Anchorage **65.00**
1990, Changing of the Guards **60.00**
1992, Christmas at the Rectory **65.00**
1994, A Day at the Deer Park **80.00**
1996, Winter at the Old Mill **70.00**
1997, Country Christmas **65.00**
1998, Santa the Storyteller **65.00**
1999, Dancing on Christmas Eve .. **65.00**

Bing & Grondahl, Christmas plate, 1967, Sharing the Joy of Christmas, $45.

Bing and Grondahl, Mother's Day, Henry Thelander, artist, 6" d

1969, Dog and Puppies **325.00**
1971, Cat and Kitten **25.00**
1973, Duck and Ducklings **20.00**
1975, Doe and Fawns **20.00**
1977, Squirrel and Young **20.00**
1978, Heron **20.00**
1980, Woodpecker and Young **20.00**
1982, Lioness and Cubs **20.00**
1984, Stork and Nestlings **20.00**
1986, Elephant with Calf **20.00**
1988, Lapwing Mother with Chicks **20.00**
1990, Hen with Chicks **20.00**
1991, The Nanny Goat and Her Two Frisky Kids **20.00**
1993, St. Bernard Dog and Puppies **20.00**
1995, Hedgehog with Young **20.00**
1996, Koala with Young **20.00**

Franklin Mint, Audubon Society Bird

1972, Goldfinch **115.00**
1972, Wood Duck **110.00**
1973, Cardinal **110.00**
1973, Ruffled Grouse **110.00**

Franklin Mint, Christmas, Norman Rockwell, artist, sterling silver, 8" d
1970, Bringing Home the Tree...... **275.00**
1972, The Carolers....................... **125.00**
1974, Hanging the Wreath............ **100.00**
1975, Home for Christmas............ **100.00**

Haviland & Parlon, Tapestry series, Marked "Ch Field Haviland Limoges, Limoges France, label, La Chasse a la Licorne, Robert Haviland & C. Parlon, 1976, Edition Limited N'6," original box, $70

Haviland & Parlon, Lady and the Unicorn Series, artist unknown, 10" d
1977, To My Only Desire, FE **60.00**
1978, Sight **40.00**
1979, Sound **40.00**
1980, Touch **40.00**
1981, Scent **40.00**
1982, Taste **40.00**
Edwin M. Knowles, Gone with the Wind Series, Raymond Kursar, artist, 8-1/2" d
1978, Scarlett, FE **300.00**
1979, Ashley................................. **75.00**
1980, Melanie................................ **75.00**
1981, Rhett **60.00**
1982, Mammy Lacing Scarlett........ **60.00**
1983, Melanie Gives Birth.............. **60.00**
1984, Scarlett's Green Dress **60.00**
1985, Rhett and Bonnie **60.00**
1985, Scarlett and Rhett: The Finale
.... **60.00**
Edwin M. Knowles, Wizard of Oz Series, James Auckland, artist, 8-1/2" d
1977, Over the Rainbow, FE.......... **65.00**
1978, If I Only Had a Brain **30.00**
1978, If I Only Had a Heart............. **30.00**
1978, If I Were King of the Forest ... **30.00**
1979, Wicked Witch of the West..... **30.00**
1979, Follow the Yellow Brick Road **30.00**
1979, Wonderful Wizard of Oz........ **30.00**
1980, The Grand Finale (We're Off to See The Wizard) **30.00**
Lenox, Boehm Bird Series, Edward Marshall Boehm, artist, 10-1/2" d
1970, Wood Thrush, FE **125.00**
1972, Mountain Bluebird................. **40.00**

1973, Meadowlark.......................... **50.00**
1974, Rufous Hummingbird........... **55.00**
1976, Cardinal **55.00**
1977, Robins.................................. **55.00**
1978, Mockingbirds........................ **55.00**
1979, Golden-Crowned Kinglets ... **55.00**
1981, Eastern Phoebes.................. **55.00**
Lenox, Boehm Woodland Wildlife Series, Edward Marshall Boehm, artist, 10-1/2" d
1973, Raccoons, FE **80.00**
1974, Red Foxes **50.00**
1975, Cottontail Rabbits................. **60.00**
1976, Eastern Chipmunks.............. **60.00**
1977, Beaver.................................. **60.00**
1978, Whitetail Deer **60.00**
1979, Squirrels............................... **60.00**
1980, Bobcats................................ **60.00**
1981, Martens................................ **60.00**
1982, River Otters.......................... **60.00**
Lladro, Christmas, 8" d, undisclosed artists
1971, Caroling **65.00**
1973, Boy & Girl............................. **50.00**
1975, Cherubs................................ **50.00**
1976, Christ Child........................... **50.00**
1978, Caroling Child....................... **50.00**
1979, Snow Dance **50.00**
Llardo, Mother's Day, undisclosed artists
1972, Birds & Chicks...................... **35.00**
1974, Nursing Mother..................... **35.00**
1975, Mother & Child...................... **35.00**
1977, Mother & Daughter.............. **35.00**
1979, Off to School........................ **35.00**
Reco International Corp., McClelland's Children's Circus Series, John McClelland, artist, 9"d
1981, Tommy the Clown, FE.......... **85.00**
1982, Katie the Tightrope Walker... **40.00**
1983, Johnny the Strongman......... **40.00**
1984, Maggie the Animal Trainer... **35.00**
Reco International Corp., McClelland's Mother Goose Series, John McClelland, artist, 8-1/2" d
1979, Mary, Mary, FE.................... **250.00**
1980, Little Boy Blue...................... **100.00**
1981, Little Miss Muffet.................. **30.00**
1982, Little Jack Horner **30.00**
1983, Little Bo Peep **30.00**
1984, Diddle, Diddle Dumpling **30.00**
1985, Mary Had a Little Lamb **30.00**
1986, Jack and Jill......................... **30.00**
Reed & Barton, Christmas Series, Damascene silver, 11" d through 1978, 8" d 1979-1981
1970, A Partridge in a Pear Tree, FE
.... **200.00**
1971, We Three Kings of Orient Are
.... **65.00**
1972, Hark! The Herald Angels Sing
.... **60.00**
1973, Adoration of the Kings **60.00**
1974, The Adoration of the Magi ... **60.00**
1975, Adoration of the Kings **60.00**
1976, Morning Train....................... **60.00**
1977, Decorating the Church......... **60.00**

1978, The General Store at Christmas
Time **60.00**
1979, Merry Old Santa Claus **60.00**
1980, Gathering Christmas Greens **60.00**
1981, The Shopkeeper at Christmas
.... **60.00**
Rosenthal, Christmas, various artists,
8-1/2" d
1910, Winter Peace **550.00**
1912, Shooting Stars **250.00**
1914, Christmas Song **350.00**
1916, Christmas During War **235.00**
1917, Angel of Peace **210.00**
1921, Christmas in the Mountains **200.00**
1923, Children in the Winter Wood
.... **200.00**
1926, Christmas in the Mountains **175.00**
1928, Chalet Christmas **175.00**
1930, Group of Deer Under the Pines
.... **225.00**
1933, Through the Night to Light .. **190.00**
1935, Christmas By the Sea **185.00**
1937, Berchtesgaden **195.00**
1940, Marien Church in Danzig **250.00**
1942, Marianburg Castle **300.00**
1944, Wood Scape **275.00**
1946, Christmas in an Alpine Valley
.... **250.00**
1948, Message to the Shepherds **850.00**
1949, The Holy Family **185.00**
1951, Star of Bethlehem **450.00**
1953, The Holy Light **185.00**
1955, Christmas in a Village **190.00**
1957, Christmas by the Sea **195.00**
1959, Midnight Mass **195.00**
1961, Solitary Christmas **225.00**
1962, Christmas Eve **185.00**
1964, Christmas Market in Nürnberg
.... **225.00**
1966, Christmas in Ulm **250.00**
1968, Christmas in Bremen **190.00**
1970, Christmas in Cologne **165.00**
1971, Christmas in Garmisch **100.00**
1973, Christmas in Lubeck-Holstein
.... **110.00**
1974, Christmas in Wurzburg **95.00**
Royal Copenhagen, **Christmas**, various
artists, 6" d 1908, 1909, 1910; 7" d 1911
to present
1909, Danish Landscape **150.00**
1911, Danish Landscape **135.00**
1913, Spire of Frederik's Church,
Copenhagen **125.00**
1915, Danish Landscape **150.00**
1917, Tower of Our Savior's Church,
Copenhagen **90.00**
1918, Sheep and Shepherds **80.00**
1920, Mary with the Child Jesus **75.00**
1922, Three Singing Angels **70.00**
1924, Christmas Star Over the Sea and
Sailing Ship **100.00**
1926, View of Christmas Canal,
Copenhagen **75.00**

Royal Copenhagen, Christmas plate,
Winterskumring, Winter Twilight, 1974, **$30**.

Royal Copenhagen, Christmas plate, The Old
Farmyard, 1969, original box, **$35**.

1928, Vicar's Family on Way to Church
.... **75.00**
1931, Mother and Child **90.00**
1933, The Great Belt Ferry **110.00**
1935, Fishing Boat off Kronborg Castle
.... **145.00**
1937, Christmas Scene in Main Street,
Copenhagen **135.00**
1939, Expeditionary Ship in Pack-Ice of
Greenland **180.00**
1940, The Good Shepherd **300.00**
1942, Bell Tower of Old Church in Jutland
.... **300.00**
1944, Typical Danish Winter Scene
.... **160.00**
1946, Zealand Village Church **150.00**
1948, Nodebo Church at Christmastime
.... **150.00**
1950, Boeslunde Church, Zealand
.... **175.00**
1951, Christmas Angel **300.00**
1953, Frederiksborg Castle **120.00**

1955, Fano Girl **185.00**
1957, The Good Shepherd **115.00**
1959, Christmas Night **120.00**
1960, The Stag **125.00**
1962, The Little Mermaid at Wintertime
.... **200.00**
1964, Fetching the Tree **75.00**
1966, Blackbird **55.00**
1968, The Last Umiak **40.00**
1970, Christmas Rose and Cat **40.00**
1971, Hare in Winter **40.00**
1973, Train Homeward Bound for
Christmas **30.00**
1975, Queen's Palace **30.00**
1977, Immervad Bridge **25.00**
1979, Choosing the Christmas Tree **50.00**
1981, Admiring the Christmas Tree **55.00**
1982, Waiting for Christmas............ **60.00**
1984, Jingle Bells **55.00**
1986, Christmas Vacation **55.00**
1988, Christmas Eve in Copenhagen
.... **55.00**
1990, Christmas at Tivoli............... **130.00**
1991, The Festival of Santa Lucia **100.00**
1993, Christmas Guests **95.00**
1996, Lighting the Street Lamp **70.00**
1997, Roskilde Cathedral **80.00**
1999, The Sleigh Ride..................... **60.00**

Rosenthal, Christmas In Denmark
1991, Bringing Home the Tree........ **48.00**
1992, Christmas Shopping **45.00**
1993, The Skating Party.................. **45.00**
1994, The Sleigh Ride..................... **45.00**
1995, Christmas Tales..................... **45.00**
1996, Christmas Eve **45.00**

Rosenthal, Mother's Day, various artists,
6-1/4" d
1971, American Mother **125.00**
1972, Oriental Mother **60.00**
1973, Danish Mother........................ **60.00**
1974, Greenland Mother.................. **55.00**
1975, Bird in Nest............................ **50.00**
1976, Mermaids **50.00**
1977, The Twins **50.00**
1978, Mother and Child **25.00**
1979, A Loving Mother..................... **30.00**
1980, An Outing with Mother **35.00**
1981, Reunion **30.00**
1982, The Children's Hour **30.00**

**Royal   Doulton,   Beswick   Christmas
Series**, various artists, earthenware in
hand-cast bas-relief, 8" sq
1972, Christmas in England, FE **40.00**
1973, Christmas in Mexico **40.00**
1974, Christmasin Bulgaria **40.00**
1975, Christmas in Norway............. **40.00**
1976, Christmas in Holland **40.00**
1977, Christmas in Poland.............. **40.00**
1978, Christmas in America **40.00**

Royal Doulton, Valentine's Day Series,
artists unknown, 8-1/4" d
1976, Victorian Boy and Girl **60.00**
1977, My Sweetest Friend **40.00**

1978, If I Love You **40.00**
1979, My Valentine **40.00**
1980, On a Swing **40.00**
1981, Sweet Music **40.00**
1982, From My Heart....................... **40.00**
1983, Cherub's Song....................... **40.00**
1984, Love in Bloom....................... **40.00**
1985, Accept These Flowers **40.00**

Schmid, Christmas, J. Malfertheiner, artist
1971, St. Jakob in Groden, FE **125.00**
1973, Alpine Horn........................... **120.00**
1975, Christmas in Ireland **100.00**
1977, Legend of Heligenblut **100.00**
1979, Moss Gatherers.................. **100.00**
1980, Wintry Churchgoing **100.00**
1982, The Star Singers................ **100.00**
1984, Yuletide in the Valley **100.00**
1986, A Goreden Christmas **75.00**

Schmid,   Disney   Christmas   Series,
undisclosed artists, 7-1/2" d
1974, Decorating the Tree............ **175.00**
1976, Building a Snowman **25.00**
1978, Night Before Christmas........ **25.00**
1980, Sleigh Ride **25.00**
1981, Happy Holidays..................... **25.00**
1982, Winter Games....................... **25.00**
1987, Snow White Golden Anniversary
.... **25.00**
1989, Sleeping Beauty 30th Anniversary
.... **25.00**
1990, Fantasia Relief **25.00**

Schmid, Disney Mother's Day Series
1974, Flowers for Mother, FE.......... **80.00**
1975, Snow White and the Seven Dwarfs
.... **45.00**
1976, Minnie Mouse and Friends .. **25.00**
1977, Pluto's Pals............................ **25.00**
1978, Flowers for Bambi **25.00**
1979, Happy Feet............................ **25.00**
1980, Minnie's Surprise **25.00**
1981, Playmates **25.00**
1982, A Dream Come True............. **25.00**

Schmid,   Peanuts   Christmas   Series,
Charles Schulz, artist, 7-1/2" d
1972, Snoopy Guides the Sleigh, FE
.... **90.00**
1974, Christmas Eve at the Fireplace
.... **65.00**
1976, Woodstock's Christmas........ **20.00**
1977, Deck the Doghouse **20.00**
1979, Christmas at Hand **20.00**
1981, A Christmas Wish **20.00**
1982, Perfect Performance **20.00**

Schmid, Peanuts Mother's Day Series,
Charles Schulz, artist, 7-1/2" d
1972, Linus, FE **50.00**
1974, Snoopy and Woodstock on Parade
.... **40.00**
1976, Linus and Snoopy **35.00**
1977, Dear Mom............................. **30.00**
1979, A Special Letter **20.00**
1981, Mission for Mom **20.00**
1982, Which Way to Mother? **20.00**

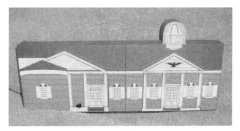

Cat's Meow, Harleysville National Bank,
Montgomery County, PA, $30.

Schmid, Peanuts Valentine's Day Series,
Charles Schulz, artist, 7-1/2" d
1977, Home Is Where the Heart Is, FE
.... **25.00**
1979, Love Match **20.00**
1980, From Snoopy, With Love **20.00**
1982, Love Patch **20.00**
Schmid, Raggedy Ann Annual Series,
undisclosed artist, 7-1/2" d
1980, The Sunshine Wagon **65.00**
1981, The Raggedy Shuffle **25.00**
1982, Flying High **20.00**
1983, Winning Streak **20.00**
1984, Rocking Rodeo **20.00**

Wedgwood, Calendar Series
1971, Victorian Almanac, FE **25.00**
1973, Bountiful Butterfly **20.00**
1975, Children's Games **20.00**
1977, Tonatiuh **20.00**
1979, Sacred Scarab **20.00**
1980, Safari **20.00**
1982, Wild West **20.00**
1984, Dogs **20.00**
1985, Cats **20.00**
1988, Sea Birds **20.00**

Wedgwood, plate, Bicentennial Series, Paul
Revere, 1976, blue and white jasper, original
box, $45.

Wedgwood, Christmas Series, jasper
stoneware, 8" d

1969, Windsor Castle, FE **225.00**
1971, Piccadilly Circus, London **40.00**
1973, The Tower of London **40.00**
1975, Tower Bridge **40.00**
1976, Hampton Court **40.00**
1977, Westminster Abbey **45.00**
1978, The Horse Guards **55.00**
1980, St. James Palace **45.00**
1982, Lambeth Palace **45.00**
1984, Constitution Hill **45.00**
1986, The Albert Memorial **45.00**
1987, Guildhall **45.00**
Wedgwood, Mothers Series, jasper stoneware, 6-1/2" d
1972, The Sewing Lesson **20.00**
1974, Domestic Employment **20.00**
1976, The Spinner **20.00**
1978, Swan and Cygnets **25.00**
1981, Mare and Foal **25.00**
1983, Cupid and Butterfly **25.00**
1985, Cupids and Doves **25.00**
1986, Anemones **25.00**
1987, Tiger Lily **25.00**

Linens

History: Vintage lace and linens always
have been important accessories.
Brides-to-be stitched and embroidered
sheets, tea towels, and all kinds of
linens for their hope chests. The linens
created right after World War II are now
being eagerly collected for their bright
colors and interesting designs.

Collecting hints: Many vintage linens
have a lot of use left in them. Handle
them carefully, wash gently, and store
rolled whenever possible.

Bed sheet
Homespun, double size, c1900 ..... **45.00**
Linen, white, eyelet lace and white satin
embroidered flowers and butterflies,
1930s, 74" x 96" **35.00**
Linen, white, red cross-stitch monogram
and lace edging, early 1900s, top sheet
and pr pillow cases **45.00**
Raw silk, ivory, beige lace insertion,
1920s, twin size **35.00**
Collar, Duchesse bobbin lace, roses,
daisies, and scrollwork design, 5" at
center back, 32" l, c1870 .... **125.00**
Curtain, machine made lace, ecru, 36" x 72"
.... **75.00**

Doily
Crocheted, pineapple design, white **8.00**
Crocheted, pink and cream, 7" sq... **5.00**
Embroidered, round, holly dec, scalloped
edge **12.00**

Linen toweling material, unused, ivy, floral, fruit, and garden cart motif in chartreuse, red, and black, 72" l piece, **$10**.

Needle lace, rose design, round, 6" d **20.00**

Dresser scarf
Embroidered, white cotton, fall foliage, browns, reds, oranges, and greens, tatted edge **10.00**
Embroidered, white cotton, flower basket embroidery in bright colors, white crochet edge, c1930 .... **12.00**
Embroidered, white cotton, red nursery rhyme characters, c1940 .... **15.00**

Hand towel
Damask, linen, white, drawn work, paper label "All Linen, Made in Ireland," 1920s **20.00**
Damask, linen, white, shamrock design, lace insert, early 1900s **25.00**
Linen, white, lace insert, early 1900s **20.00**

Napkins
Bastite, white, blue border design, luncheon size, 1940s, set of six...... **20.00**
Cotton, polished, peach, edged in blue and gold grosgrain ribbon, 1920s, dinner size, 19" x 20-1/2", set of 18 .... **40.00**
Damask, linen, white, three initial white monograms, dinner size, early 1900s, set of 11 .... **45.00**
Linen, white, embroidered white garland and three initial monogram, 28" x 29", 1900s, set of four............................. **20.00**
Voile, white, orange, pink, green, and yellow floral pattern, pink border, luncheon size, set of 12, 1940s **36.00**

Bureau scarf, beige linen, cross-stitched red ivy motif, fringed, **$20**.

Pillow case
Cotton, white, plain, home made, crocheted edge, pr **10.00**
Cotton, white, red and blue monograms, crocheted edge, pr **20.00**
Muslin, white, lace edge, 1930s **5.00**

Place mat
Cotton, woven, rect shape, fringe, orange and brown, mid-1940s, set of six... **35.00**
Linen, white, Battenberg lace edge, elaborate needle weaving, 36" d, late 1800s **40.00**
Linen, white, embroidered edge, early 1940s, set of 16, some stains **48.00**
Linen, white, lace edge, early 1940s, set of six **36.00**
Sewing bag, printed cotton, mauve, green, lilac, and beige floral design, late 1920s **25.00**

Hand towel, homespun, red embroidered "A," fringed, **$15**.

Table cloth

Cotton, hand crocheted, cream, lacy design, 1930s, 58" x 82" **40.00**

Cotton, printed, red and green poinsettias, 62" x 120", laundered, stains **20.00**

Cotton, printed, rust, red, blue, yellow Mexican motif, 48" sq, laundered ... **25.00**

Damask, linen and silk, green and gray, leaf pattern, 1930s, 62" x 100" **45.00**

Damask, linen and silk, white and blue, fruit and flowers design, unused, 1940s, 50" x 48" **40.00**

Damask, white linen, eight matching 16" sq napkins, orig box and paper tags "Pure Irish Linen Damask, Made in Ireland," never used, orig gift card, 64" x 84" **85.00**

Damask, white line, rose design, paper label "All Pure Linen, Made in Ireland," 1930s, 70" sq................................... **35.00**

Lace, Battenburg, beige, early 1900s, 52" d round **125.00**

Lace, net darning, large areas of cloth stitched accented with lace stitch, 1930s, 64" x 74", some discoloration and loose threads... **35.00**

Linen, beige, satin scrolling, twelve 22" x 33" napkins, unused, orig paper label "Made in Ireland," early 1940s, 106" x 72" **90.00**

Linen, cream, cutwork, embroidery, and lace insertion, 13" edge of net darning, 1940s, 62" x 92"............................... **65.00**

Linen, cream, cutwork and tan embroidery, 10 matching napkins, some stains, 1940s **20.00**

Doily press, floral printed cotton, shades of rose, green, and cream, lace edging, holding several white linen mats and doilies, 1920s, **$45**.

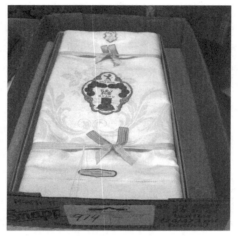

Tablecloth, white linen damask, original box, original tags "Pure Irish Linen Damask, Made in Ireland," 64" x 84", eight matching 16" square napkins, late 1930s, original gift card, **$85**.

Table runner

Damask, gold silk, metallic braid and lace edging, late 1800s, 28" x 7-1/2" **20.00**

Linen, white, straight bobbin lace insertion and edging, early 1900s . **40.00**

Teapot warmer, blue, tan, and ivory cotton floral and pineapple print, padding, blue linen lining, early 1900s, 13" x 10".. **20.00**

Yardage

Cotton, printed, horses, buggy with one horse, inn in background, green, brown, tan, red, and gold, brown and pink edging, 1930s................................. **12.00**

Damask, linen, white, Swedish, 50" x 73" **15.00**

Lace, machine made Valenciennes lace, all cotton, floral and scrollwork design, 4" d, yard length................................. **10.00**

Little Golden Books

History: Simon & Schuster published the first Little Golden Books in September 1942. They were conceived and created by the Artists & Writers Guild Inc., which was an arm of the Western Printing and Lithographing Company. More than 1.5 million copies of the initial 12 titles (each 42 pages long and priced at 25¢) were sold within the first five months of publication. By the end of World War II, 39 million Little Golden Books had been sold.

A Disney series was begun in 1944, and Big and Giant Golden Books followed that same year. In 1949, the first Goldencraft editions were introduced. Instead of side-stapled cardboard, these books had cloth covers and were sewn so that they could withstand school and library use. In 1958, Giant Little Golden Books were introduced, most combining three previously published titles into one book. In that same year, Simon & Schuster sold Little Golden Books to Western Printing and Lithographing Company and Pocket Books. The titles then appeared under the Golden Press imprint. Eventually, Western, now known as Western Publishing Company, Inc., bought out Pocket Books' interest in Little Golden Books.

In 1986, Western celebrated the one-billionth Little Golden Book by issuing special commemorative editions of some of its most popular titles, such as *Poky Little Puppy* and *Cinderella*.

Collecting Hints: Little Golden Books offer something for everybody. Collectors can pursue titles according to favorite author, illustrator, television show, film, or comic strip character. Disney titles enjoy a special place with nostalgia buffs. An increasingly popular goal is to own one copy of each title and number.

Books published in the forties, fifties, and sixties are in the most demand at this time. Books from this period were assigned individual numbers usually found on the front cover of the book except for the earliest titles for which the title must be checked against the numbered list at the back of the book.

Although the publisher tried to adhere to a policy of one number for each title during the first 30 years, numbers were reassigned to new titles as old titles were eliminated. Also, when an earlier book was re-edited and/or re-illustrated, it was given a new number.

Most of the first 36 books had blue paper spines and a dust jacket. Subsequent books were issued with a golden-brown mottled spine, which was replaced in 1950 by a shiny gold spine.

Early books had 42 pages. In the late 1940s, the format was gradually changed to 28 pages, then to 24 pages in the mid-1950s. Early 42- and 28-page books had no price on the cover. Later the 25¢ price appeared on the front cover, then 29¢, followed by 39¢. In the early 1950s, books were produced with two lines that formed a bar across the top of the front cover. This bar was eliminated in the early sixties.

Little Golden Books can still be found at yard sales and flea markets. Other sources include friends, relatives, and charity book sales, especially if they have a separate children's table. Also attend doll and book shows—good places to find books with paper dolls, puzzles, or cutouts. Toy dealers are also a good source for Disney, television, and cowboy titles.

Look for books in good or better condition. Covers should be bright with the spine paper intact. Rubbing, ink and crayon markings, or torn pages lessen the value of the book. Unless extensive, pencil marks are fairly easy to remove by gently stroking in one direction with an art-gum eraser. Do not rub back and forth.

Notes: Prices are based on a mint condition book from the first printing. The printing edition is determined by looking at the lower right-hand corner of the back page. The letter found there indicates the printing of that particular title and edition. "A" is the first printing, "B" the next, and so forth. Occasionally the letter is hidden under the spine or was placed in the upper right-hand corner, so look closely. Early titles will have their edition indicated in the front of the book.

Any dust jacket, puzzles, stencils, cutouts, stamps, tissues, tape, or pages should be intact as issued. If not, the book's value suffers a drastic reduction of up to 80 percent off the listed price. Books that are badly worn, incomplete, or badly torn are worth little. Sometimes they are useful as temporary fillers for gaps in a collection.

The Animals of Farmer Jones, #11, Leah Gale, author, Rudolf Freund, illustrated, 1942, wear, **$20**.

Amanda's First Day at School, #204-56, 1985, A **4.00**
Animal Daddies and My Daddy, #576, 1968, A... **5.00**
Animals on the Farm, #573, 1968, A **4.50**
Bunny's New Shoes, #204-60, 1987, A . **4.00**
Buster Bunny and The Best Friends Ever, #111-76, 1991, A............................... **4.50**
Buster Cat Goes Out, #302-57, 1989, A **5.00**
But You're A Duck, #206-58, 1990, A.... **3.00**
Cinderella's Friends, #D115, 1950, F edition **7.50**
Dick Tracy, 1962 .... **30.00**
Donny and Marie: The Top Secret Project **5.00**
Home for a Bunny, 1979 .... **4.00**
Hop, Little Kangaroo, #558 .... **5.00**
Heidi, 1st ed., 1954 .... **6.00**
Hopalong Cassidy and the Bar 20 Cowboy, 1952, unused **40.00**
Howdy Doody's Circus, 1st ed., 1950 . **15.00**
Hush, Hush, It's Sleepytime, #577, 1968, A **6.50**
I Have A Secret, #495, 1962, A **8.50**
Lassie and the Big Clean-Up Day, #572, 1971, A **6.00**
Little Golden Book of Dinosaurs, #355, penciled name on front page, some rubs **4.00**
Little Golden Book of Dogs, #532, some cover damage................................... **4.00**
Little Golden Book of Wild Animals, #499, 1960.. **3.00**
Little Golden Dictionary, 18th printing, 1969 .... **4.00**
Little Mommy, #569, 1967, A................ **75.00**
My Little Dinosaur, #571, 1971, A **6.00**
My Little Golden Calendar for 1961, illus by Richard Scarry **10.00**
Ookpik, The Artic Owl, #579, 1968, A . **20.00**
Pluto and the Adventure of the Golden Scepter, #D124, 1972, A.................... **6.50**
Rumpelstiltskin and the Princess and the Pea, #498, 1962, A........................... **8.00**

Saggy Baggy Elephant, No Place For Me, #305-59, 1989.................................... **4.50**
Seven Dwarfs Found a House, 6-1/2" x 8", Simon & Schuster, 1952 copyright, fourth printing, 1957, 25 pgs, color illus... **20.00**
So Big, #574, 1968, red spine, A **15.00**
Supercar, #492, 1962, A...................... **25.00**
The Cold Blooded Penguin, 6-3/4" x 8", Simon & Schuster, 1946 second printing, 24 pgs, full color **60.00**
The Emerald City of Oz, L. Frank Baum, adapted by Peter Archer, 1952..... **25.00**
The Friendly Book, 2nd ed. **6.00**

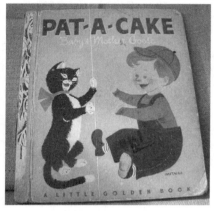

Pat-A-Cake, Baby's Mother Goose, illustrated Aurelius Battaglia, 1948, wear, **$5**.

The Gingerbread Man, 6th ed. **5.00**
The Golden Egg, #486, illus by Lillian Obligado **7.50**
The Happy Little Whale, 3rd ed. **5.00**
The Little Red Caboose, 13th ed. **5.00**
The Monster at the end of this Book, Starring Lovable, Furry Old Grover, Sesame St., 2nd ed.. **4.00**
The Taxi That Hurried, 1946 .... **17.50**
The Tiny Tawny Kitten, 1st ed., 1969 .. **15.00**
The Wonderful School, 1st ed.............. **8.00**
Things in My House, #570, 1968, A...... **6.50**
Tottle, 1945... **12.00**
Tweety Plays Catch the Puddy Kat, 1975 .... **4.00**
Underdog... **20.00**
Walt Disney's Goofy—Movie Star, 1956, red spine... **27.50**
Walt Disney's Old Yeller, 3rd ed., 1950s **12.00**
Walt Disney's Uncle Remus, #D85, 1945 .... **45.00**
Walt Disney's Winne-the-Pooh and Tigger, 4th ed. **5.00**
When I Grow Up, #578, 1968, A **5.00**
Winnie-The-Pooh the Honey Tree, #D116, 1965, A.. **8.00**
Wizard of Oz, 1st edition **22.00**
Who Comes To Your House, #575, 1973, A **5.00**

M

Magazines

History: In the early 1700s, general magazines were a major source of information for the reader. Literary magazines, such as *Harper's*, became popular in the 19th century. By 1900, the first photo-journal magazines appeared. *Life*, the most famous example, was started by Henry Luce in 1932.

Magazines created for women featured "how to" articles about cooking, sewing, decorating, and childcare. Many of the publications were entirely devoted to fashion and living a fashionable life, such as *Harper's Bazaar* and *Vogue*. Men's magazines were directed at masculine interests of the time, such as hunting, fishing, and woodworking, supplemented with appropriate "girlie" titles.

Collecting Hints: A rule of thumb for pricing general magazines with covers designed by popular artists is the more you would enjoy displaying a copy on your coffee table, the more elite the publication, or the more the advertising or editorial content relates to today's collectibles, the higher the price. *Life* magazine went into millions of homes each week, *Harper's Bazaar* and *Vogue* did not. Upper-class families tended to discard last month's publication, while middle-class families found the art on the *Saturday Evening Post* and *Collier's* irresistible and saved them. The greater the supply, the lower the price.

Notes: General magazine prices listed here are retail prices. They may be considerably higher than what would be offered for an entire collection filling your basement or garage. Bulk prices for common magazines such as *Life*, *Collier's*, and *Saturday Evening Post* generally range between 50¢ and $1 per issue. Magazine dealers have to sort through many issues to find those which may be saleable; some protect individual issues, covers, or tear sheets with plastic covering, etc. before they can realize a profit for more common magazines.

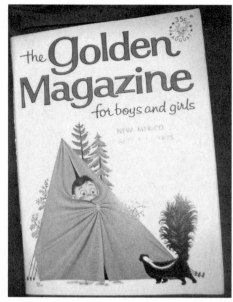

The *Golden Magazine for Boys and Girls*, August, **$.50**.

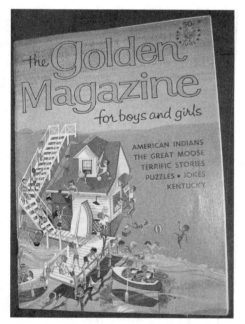

The *Golden Magazine for Boys and Girls*, June, **$.50**.

Alfred Hitchcock Mystery **5.00**

Amateur Photographer's Weekly, June 6, 1919 .... **3.00**

Amazing Stories, July 1943, Ziff-Davis Publishing Co., 208 pgs, 7" x 10" **5.00**

American Golfer, December 1932....... **10.00**

American Heritage, October 1958, Pocahontas cover **6.00**

American Rifleman, 1929.................... **15.00**

Aviation, 1928 .... **15.00**

Better Homes and Gardens, December 1942.. **6.00**

Billiard's Digest.................................... **1.00**

Boy's Life, June 1955, Boy Scout Statue cover, Coca-Cola ad **5.00**

Child's Life, 1930 .... **4.00**

Collier's, Maxfield Parrish cov, rows of soldiers, Nov. 16, 1912 .... **50.00**

Confidential, August 1966, Sammy Davis cover **8.00**

Cosmopolitan, 1910 .... **6.00**

Crime Detective, Steve McQueen on cover, 1950s **65.00**

Dare-Devil Aces, September 1937, Fredrick Blakeslee cover, 112 pgs, 7" x 10" . **48.00**

Elle, July 1997, Cindy Crawford.......... **20.00**

Ellery Queen Mystery Magazine, 1950s **5.00**

Esquire Magazine, July 1935, Ernest Hemingway story **50.00**

Family Circle, 1954.............................. **5.00**

Fantastic Adventures, October 1945, vivid cover art by J. Allen St. John, 178 pgs, 7" x 9-3/4" **10.00**

Fantastic Novels, November 1948, New Publications, Inc., 128 pgs, 7" x 9-1/2" **2.00**

Farm & Fireside, March 1923, boy and dog cover **6.00**

Farm Journal, March 1940, sheep and lion cover **5.00**

Fate, 1953, Atlantis............................. **7.50**

Film Culture, John Ford cover, #25, Summer 1982.. **4.00**

Fortune, April 1941 .... **32.00**

Front Page Detective, August 1952 ...... **3.00**

Gayety Magazine, Alex Schomberg pin-up cover, 1942...................................... **45.00**

Golf Journal Magazine, May 1967, Jack and Barbara Nicklaus............................. **18.00**

Good Housekeeping, 1965 .... **4.00**

Hit Parade, September 1947, Jane Greer cover 7.00

Horse Lovers Magazine, 1956.............. **1.00**

Horticulture, December 1959, poinsettia cover **3.50**

Jewelers' Weekly, 1889, New York, 88 pgs, 7" x 10" **18.00**

Junior Natural History, April 1954, goat cover **4.00**

Ladies Home Journal, June 1960......... **5.00**

Life

July 13, 1953, Hillary Climb, Mt Everest, adv with stars **12.00**

May 23, 1963, Gordon Cooper's Space Flight **12.00**

March 13, 1964, series on World War I **7.00**

Bound copy of *Weekly Philatelic Era*, 1900, $25.

April 12, 1968, Martin Luther King Jr., ... **18.00**

July 7, 1972, George McGovern cover, Pandas in DC article........................ **5.00**

1973, The Year in Pictures............. **10.00**

Literary Digest, May 1, 1937, Princess Elizabeth cover **7.00**

Look, Davy Crockett, Walt Disney cover **35.00**

MAD, #170; October 1974; Exorcist cover **15.00**

Mature Outlook Magazine, September/ October, 1987, Charles Schulz and Peanuts cover **12.00**

McCall's, 1961, Christmas Make-It Ideas **4.00**

Mechanix Illustrated, 1974 .... **2.00**

Motion Picture Classic, August 1927, 9-1/4" x 12" **12.00**

Motor Trend, 1978.................................. **1.00**

National Future Farmer, 1956................ **1.00**

Newsweek, 1974, August 19, Pres Ford cov, special issue **6.00**

Photon, #22F, The Thing from Another World **12.00**

Photo Screen, July 1973, Waltons cover **7.00**

Popular Aviation, 1933........................ **10.00**

Popular Science, Steve McQueen on cover, 1966 .... **40.00**

Quick, July 24, 1950, Princess Elizabeth cover **8.00**

Quilter's Newsletter **2.50**

Radio and TV Mirror, 1950.................. **10.00**

Redbook, June 1925 .... **5.00**

Rexall, June 1939, Nan Gray cover, Judy Garland article **5.00**

Saturday Evening Post, Nov. 5, 1955, Nehru, Rockwell cover **12.00**

McCall's Book of Fashions, Quarterly, Summer, 1916, large format, **$20**.

Scouting, September 1973, Soap Box Derby cover **3.00**

Secrets, January 1959 .... **3.00**

Seventeen Magazine, June 1970, Susan Dey cover **45.00**

Silver Screen, June 1973, Bunkers cover **8.00**

Sky Birds, October 1933, full-color art by Tinsley, 7" x 10" **4.00**

Sports Illustrated, July 29, 1963, Sonny Liston **15.00**

Successful Farming, May 1941 .... **5.00**

Ten Detective Aces, May 1949, Ace Periodicals, 7" x 10" **6.50**

The Granite State (NH) Magazine, Volumes 1-6, bound **30.00**

The Magazine Antiques, June 1972.... **15.00**

Time
      1933, Dec. 11, 1933, General Chiang **75.00**
      1944, June 19, Eisenhower cover **8.00**
      1987, December 7, *Shirley Maclaine* **4.50**

True Detective, Volume 37, #1, October 1941, Bob Hope cover, 120 pgs, 8-1/2" x 11-1/4" **10.00**

True Story, January 1938, 8-1/2" x 11" ... **2.50**

Today's Health, June 1960, Kate Smith cover **4.00**

TV Dial, Roy Rogers, Hopalong Cassidy, Gene Autry on cover **140.00**

TV Digest, Lucille Ball and Ricky in motorboat, Philadelphia, 1952...... **135.00**

TV Guide
      Beverly Hillbillies **60.00**
      Lawman **25.00**
      Lil'Abner... **50.00**

The Delineator, October 1904, elegantly dressed lady with Borzoi on cover, some wear, **$15**.

      Lost in Space **65.00**
      Maverick, James Garner **30.00**
      Paladin **25.00**
      Wild Wild West **30.00**
      Zorro, Guy Williams **45.00**

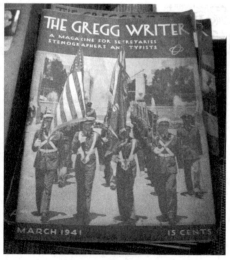

The Gregg Writer, The Magazine for Secretaries, Stenographers, and Typists, March, 1941, patriotic cover, **$5**.

TV People, Bonzana cover................. **40.00**

TV Radio Mirror, photo of Honeymooner's Art Carney and others on cover, article on Honeymooners, April 1960 .... **24.00**

TV Week, Dick Tracy, 1960s................. **35.00**
Venture Magazine, April 1971, 3D picture on cover.. **5.00**
Vogue, Dec 1986, Paloma Picasso on cover
.... **15.00**
Wee Wisdom, July 1939......................... **7.50**
Western Horseman, 1950 .... **8.00**
Woman's World, March 1936................. **2.00**
Wonder Story Annual, Volume 1, #1, 1950, 194 black and white pages, 6-1/2" x 9-1/2"... **25.00**
Workbasket, whole year, 1965.............. **5.00**

Marbles

History: Marbles date back to ancient Greece, Rome, Egypt, and other early civilizations. In England, Good Friday is known as "Marbles Day" because the game was considered a respectable and quiet pastime for the hallowed day.

During the American Civil War, soldiers carried marbles and a small board to play solitaire, a game whose object was to jump the marbles until only one was left in the center of the board.

In the last few generations, school children have identified marbles as "peewees," "shooters," "commies," and "cat's eyes." A National Marbles Tournament has been held each year in June since 1922.

Collecting Hints: Handmade glass marbles usually command higher prices than machine-made glass, clay, or mineral marbles. There are a few notable exceptions, e.g., machine-made comic strip marbles were made for a limited time only and are highly prized by collectors. Care must be taken in purchasing this particular type since the comic figure was stenciled on the marble. A layer of glass was to be overlaid on the stencil, but sometimes this process was not completed. In such cases, the stencils rub or wear off.

Some of the rarer examples of handmade marbles are Clambroth, Lutz, Indian Swirls, Peppermint Swirls, and Sulphides. Marble values are normally determined by their type, size, and condition. Usually, the larger the marble, the more valuable it is within its category.

A marble in mint condition is unmarred and has the best possible condition with a clear surface. It may have surface abrasions caused by rubbing while in its original package. A marble in good condition may have a few small surface dings, scratches, and slight surface cloudiness. However, the core must be easily seen, and the marble must be free of large chips or fractures.

Reproduction Alert: Comic marbles and some machine-made marbles are being reproduced, as are some polyvinyl packages, mesh packages, and original boxes.

Notes: Handmade marbles listed here are common examples in mint condition. Unusual examples command prices that are two to 20 times higher. Mint condition machine-made marbles priced here have a diameter between 9/16 and 11/16 inch, unless otherwise noted.

Bennington, blue, 3/8" d, $2.

Handmade marbles

End of Day

Onionskin

 Confetti onionskin, 2-3/8".......... **1,575.00**
 Onionskin with mica, 3/4" d **975.00**
 Suspended mica **1,200.00**

Lutz

 Amber glass ribbon...................... **475.00**
 Banded, 1" **265.00**
 Black glass **525.00**
 Cranberry ribbon, 1-1/16" d **325.00**
 Pink onionskin.............................. **200.00**

Mica

 3/4" d, peppermint........................ **300.00**
 1-1/2".. **200.00**

Other

Clambroth, black and white, 11/16" d **250.00**
Opaque, red on pink banded **250.00**
Translucent, Butterfly **3,650.00**

Sulphide

Bird, white, 1-1/2" d, played-with condition **150.00**
Duck, tri-color paint **1,100.00**
Pair of kissing love birds **750.00**

Swirl

Banded, 1" **75.00**
Divided Core, 1-3/4" **150.00**
End of cane double ribbon **350.00**
Indian Swirl, 1-1/6" d, blue bands, translucent **3,550.00**
Joseph, multicolored **300.00**
Latticino Core, bright red swirl **325.00**
Green Mist, 1" d, with mica **650.00**
Ribbon Core, 3/4" **80.00**
Solid Core
    1-7/8", red **2,350.00**
    2-5/16", lobed **1,150.00**

Machine-made marbles

Akro Agate

Boxed set, No. 00, 60 black, red, yellow, blue, white, and green, orig box **50.00**
Helmet Patch **3.00**
Lemonade corkscrew **17.50**
Moonstone **12.00**
Popeye
    5/8" d, purple, yellow, and white **85.00**
    2-1/32", green and yellow, pr .. **40.00**

Christensen Agate Co.

American Agate **50.00**
Cobra/Cyclone **750.00**
Electric Swirl **75.00**
Guinea **350.00**
Slag **30.00**

Marble King Co.

Color Matrix, multicolor opaque Bumblebee **2.00**

Cub Scouts, 26 blue and yellow marbles in orig package, blue and white label with saluting young Cub Scout and two flags, reads: "10 cents Cub Scouts American Made Marbles" **24.00**
Girl Scout, package of 20 green and yellow marbles, orig label: "Made in U.S.A. 10 cents Girl Scouts Premium Quality Marbles" **30.00**
Two-Color, white matrix .... **.25**
White Matrix .... **.45**

Master Marble Co.

Patch **1.25**
Sunburst, clear **22.00**

M. F. Christensen & Son

Brick, 9/16" to 11/16" **75.00**
Opaque, set of eight, orig box .. **1,600.00**
Slag, 1-7/8" d **375.00**

Peltier Glass Co.

Boxed set, five comics **525.00**
Christmas Tree, shooter size **220.00**
Peerless Patch **5.50**
Slag **20.00**
Sunset, Muddy, Acme Reefer, Tri-Color, 7-Up **1.50**
Superman, mint, wet **175.00**
Two-color Rainbo, old type **20.00**

Transitional

Chocolate-brown Navarre transition, resembles a banded agate **1,200.00**
Ground pontil hand gathered, green, white, red, and pink **325.00**
Horizontal swirl Navarre, 1-1/8" .. **1,350.00**

Vitro Agate/Gladding Vitro Co.

All red .... **.45**
Blackie .... **.65**
Conqueror **1.20**
Hybrid Cat's Eye **2.50**
Patch and Ribbon Transparent .... **.45**
Victory **3.50**

Matchcovers

History: The book match was invented by Joshua Pusey, a Philadelphia lawyer, who also was a chemist in his spare time. In 1892, Pusey put 10 cardboard matches into a cover of plain white board and sold 200 of them to the Mendelson Opera Company which, in turn, hand-printed messages on the front.

The first machine-made match-book was made by the Binghamton Match Company, Binghamton, New York, for the Piso Company of Warren, Pennsylvania.

Few covers survive from the late 1890s to the 1930s. The modern craze for collecting matchcovers was started when a set of 10 covers was issued for the Century of Progress exhibit at the 1933 Chicago World's Fair.

The golden age of matchcovers was the mid-1940s through the early 1960s when the covers were a popular advertising medium. Principal manufacturers included Atlas Match, Brown and Bigelow, Crown Match, Diamond Match, Lion Match, Ohio Match, and Universal Match.

The arrival of throwaway lighters, such as BIC, brought an end to the matchcover era. Today, manufacturing costs for a matchbook can range from less than 1¢ to 8¢ for a special die-cut cover. As a result, matchcovers no longer are an attractive free giveaway, and, therefore, many of the older, more desirable covers are experiencing a marked increase in value. Collectors have also turned to the small pocket-type boxes as a way of enhancing and building their collections.

Collecting Hints: Matchcovers generally had large production runs; very few are considered rare. Most collectors try to obtain unused covers. They remove the matches, flatten the covers, and mount them in albums arranged by category.

Trading is the principal means of exchange among collectors, usually on a one-for-one basis. At flea markets and shows, beer or pinup art ("girlie") matchcovers frequently are priced at $1 to $5. Actually those interested in such covers would be best advised to join one of the collector clubs and get involved in swapping.

Special covers

Airliner Showbar–"Chicago's brilliant new intimate rendezvous–the Airliner, phone Del 1169," Art Deco graphics of plane in blue cloud on cov, couple sitting at bar with cocktails on back, each match is airplane propeller, 13 orig matches, two missing **18.00**

Apollo Flights, 8-18, Cameo **8.00**

Basketball Schedule, U.S.C., 1953-54 season **20.00**

Beverly Flower Shop ~ Your Downtown Florist, Ft. Wayne, Indiana, A-3401, A.E. Koeneman, Prop., 30 matches make up floral arrangement, inside cover: "Send Your Mother Flowers on Your Birthday," front strike "Made by Lion Match Company," 4" x 2" **12.00**

Bob's Seasoning Salt, 1" x 3-3/4" opened, 1960s, unused **5.00**

Bonat's French-American Café, In the Heart of the Nation's Capitol, 1022 Vermont Ave., N.W., Washington, DC, Eiffel Tower on cover, French Chef head on 21 matches, front strike "Made by Lion Match Company," unused **20.00**

Chicago & Southern Airlines, "The Valley Level Route" uses Shell Aviation Gasoline- Now flying 21 Passenger Douglas Planes-Serving Chicago, Memphis, Jackson, New Orleans, Pine Bluff, Shreveport & Houston, cover Shell Oil wings, S & S logo and passenger plane, each match features a stewardess with serving tray, front strike "Made by Lion Match Co." **65.00**

Food Fair, Serve Yourself, The Best, Pay Less, America's Food Department Stores, Safety Matches, red, white, and blue box, original matches, **$.50**.

Chicago Cubs, Diamond Match Co., complete first set, 1934 .... **175.00**

Dentyne Gum, matches intact **4.00**

Dwight D. Eisenhower, Five-Star General **17.50**

Economy Blue Print, girlies, set of six, 1950s **48.00**

F & F Lozengers, Soothes your Throat, Cleans the Breath, matches intact... **4.00**

Hawaiian Mermaid **2.25**

Hillbilly, set of five

1950 .... **5.00**
1953 .... **5.00**
1954 .... **7.50**
1556 .... **40.00**

Hog's Breath Inn, San Carlos, CA....... **1.00**

Jas T Mullins, Wilmington on ext., inside: Hickey-Freeman Clothes, Johnston & Murphy Shoes, Manhatten Products, Interwoven Hosiery, Cavanagh Hats, some matches missing **4.00**

Jour et Nuit, French restaurant on "M" and 30th St., NW, Georgetown, Washington, D.C., 30-match strike, made by Maryland Match Corp., Washington, DC......... **1.00**

KFC, Colonel Sanders, Tampa, FL....... **2.00**

Las Vegas Casino, Jewelite................. **2.50**

Linton's Friendly Restaurants, "Hold Your War Bonds," listing of Pennsylvania restaurants inside cover, one match missing **4.00**

Marcy Drug Stores 16th & Market Sts., 15th & Locust Sts. Philiadelphia, matches intact **4.00**

Martian Boyd Spring Works, L. St., N.W., Wahsington D.C., phone ME.6667 & ME.3173, car inside a garage, inside cover advertises Auto-Springs - Cars-Trucks-Buses, Front-end and wheel alignment, Frames and Axles straightened, front strike "Made by Lion Match Co.," some matches missing **7.00**

Mike Palm's Restaurant, Washington, DC, inside cov with Jewel Match insignia and "Served Capitol Hill for over a quarter of a century," Universal Match, Washington, DC, 1970s, unused **1.00**

Milder Oil Co., Omaha, NE, Skelly Oil, few matches missing **4.00**

New Port Authority Bus Terminal, One block from Times Square, 4th Street & Eighth Avenue, crowd walking toward the port authority building, Deco red bus parked outside, inside cover locations of Port Authority Bus Terminal New York-New location opening Dec. 15, 1950 at 41st and 8th Ave., Manhattan, front strike "Made by Lion Match Co.," some matches missing **7.00**

Old Gold Cigarettes, P. Lorillard Co., each match with "Old Gold" on it, front strike "Made by Lion Match Co.," two matches missing, 4" x 2" **14.00**

Presidential Helicopter, Marine One . **12.00**

Presidential Yacht, Patricia................. **12.00**

Pull for Wilkie, Pullquick Match **30.00**

Safety Edge Waxed Paper, matches intact **4.00**

Stoeckle Select Beer, Giant, Stoeckle Brewery... **7.50**

Temple National Bank, TX, blue and white matchbook, bank services listed inside cover, 1970s, 28 unused matches ... **1.00**

The Captain's Table, TX restaurant, gold toned matches with white heads, made by Atlas Match Corp., Arlington, TX, 1970s **2.00**

Trader Vic's, Washington, D.C., "For reservations at Hilton Hotels and Inns Around the World Call the Local Hilton Reservation Service in your City," Universal Match, Los Angeles, 1979, matches intact **2.00**

Transport Motor Express, "Transport with Transport," map and routes inside cover, red and black ext. with company truck, 40 matches with various trucking company locations, front strike "Made by Lion Match Company," 4" x 3"........ **22.00**

Victory Shoe Repair 109 Fairfield Ave., Upper Darby, Pa, fishing scene on back, matches intact **4.00**

French Casino, Chicago's Finest All Girl Revue, $4.50.

Topics

Americana..	.25
Atlas, four color	.20
Barber shop...	.75
Beer and Brewery	.75
Best Western, stock design	.25
Bowling alleys	.25
Cameo's, Universal trademark...............	.45
Canadian, four color	.60
Chinese restaurants	.25
Christmas..	.25
Classiques	.50
Colleges	.25
Contours, diecut....................................	.50
Conventions	.15
Country Clubs	.15
Dated	.15

Diamond Quality .... .50
Fairs .... .25
Features .... .20
Follies, Universal trademark .... .25
Foreign .... .15
Fraternal .... .25
Full Length .... .60
Giants .... .50
Girlies, stock design .... .50
Group One, non-advertising, old .... .50
Holiday Inns, stock design .... .25
Jewelites .... .25
Jewels .... .25
Knot Holes .... .50
Matchorama's, Universal trademark ...... .25
Matchtones, Universal trademark .... .25
Midgets .... .25
Navy Ships .... .45
Odd Strikers .... .75
Patriotic .... .25
Pearltone .... .20
Personalities 1.00
Political 1.00
Pull Quick 1.00
Radio and Television .... .45
Railroads .... .55
Rainbows, Universal trademark .... .25
Restaurants .... .25
Savings & Loans .... .25
Service, old .... .25
Ship Lines .... .45
Signets, Universal trademark .... .25
Small towns .... .25
Soft Drinks .... .85
Souvenir .... .25
Sports, old 1.00
Ten Strikes .... .25
Transportation .... .45
Truck Lines .... .65
U. S. Air Force, 1940s 1.50
U. S. Army, 1940s 1.00
VA Hospitals .... .25
Whiskey .... .35
World War II 1.00

McCoy Pottery

History: The J. W. McCoy Pottery Co. was established in Roseville, Ohio, in September 1899. The early McCoy company produced both stoneware and some art pottery lines, including Rosewood. In October 1911, three potteries merged creating the Brush-McCoy Pottery Co. This firm continued to produce the original McCoy lines and added several new art lines. Much of the early pottery is not marked.

In 1910, Nelson McCoy and his father, J. W. McCoy, founded the Nel-son McCoy Sanitary Stoneware Co. In 1925, the McCoy family sold their interest in the Brush-McCoy Pottery Co. and started to expand and improve the Nelson McCoy Co. The new company produced stoneware, earthenware specialties, and artware.

Collecting Hint: Several marks were used by the McCoy Pottery Co. Take the time to learn the marks and the variations. Pieces can often be dated by according to the mark.

Most of the pottery marked "McCoy" was made by the Nelson McCoy Co.

Reproduction Alert: Unfortunately, Nelson McCoy never registered his McCoy trademark, a fact discovered by Roger Jensen of Tennessee. As a result, Jensen began using the McCoy mark on a series of ceramic reproductions made in the early 1990s. While the marks on these recently made pieces copy the original, Jensen made objects never produced by the Nelson McCoy Co. The best-known example is the Red Riding Hood cookie jar originally designed by Hull and also made by Regal China.

The McCoy fakes are a perfect example of how a mark on a piece can be deceptive. A mark alone is not proof that a piece is period or old. Knowing the proper marks and what was and was not made in respect to forms, shapes, and decorative motifs is critical in authenticating a pattern.

Ashtray, Seagram's VO, Imported Canadian Whiskey, black, gold letters **15.00**
Baker, oval, Brown Drip, 9-1/4" l **12.00**
Bank, Centennial Bear, sgd, numbered
.... **110.00**
Basket, black and white, emb weave ext., double handle **25.00**
Bean pot, brown
    #2 .... **35.00**
    #22 .... **60.00**
Bird bath **48.00**
Bowl and flower frog, Onyx pattern, greens, blues, black, and rust, 7" d
.... **130.00**
Canister, vegetable dec, white ground, mkd "McCoy #216M," 10" h **25.00**
Casserole, open, Brown Drip **5.00**
Center bowl, 5-1/2" h, Classic Line, pedestal, turquoise, brushed gold **35.00**
Cookie jar, cov
    Caboose, 7-1/2" h, #182 .... **250.00**
    Coffee Grinder **50.00**

Vase, brown shading to green, tall leaves and flowers at base, two handles, 9" h, **$45**.

Colonial Fireplace	**150.00**
Cottage	**120.00**
Covered Wagon	**150.00**
Elephant, 1943, 11" h	**175.00**
Kookie Kettle, black	**55.00**
Log Cabin	**175.00**
Mammy	**195.00**
Mr. and Mrs. Owl	**155.00**
Oaken Bucket	**40.00**
Potbelly stove, black	**50.00**
Puppy, with sign	**135.00**
Rooster	**225.00**
Sad Clown	**125.00**
Schoolhouse	**225.00**
Squirrel	**225.00**
Strawberry, white	**35.00**
Tea Kettle, black	**40.00**
Touring Car, 6-1/2" h	**155.00**
Train, black	**150.00**

Cornucopia, yellow **20.00**

Creamer

Brown Drip, 3-1/2" h **6.00**
Elsie the Cow **20.00**

Custard cup, vertical ridges, green **5.00**
Decanter, Apollo Mission **45.00**
Dog food dish, emb Scottie **15.00**
Figurine, lion, ... **65.00**
Flower bowl, Grecian, 12" d, 3" h, 24k gold marbling **24.00**
Hanging basket, stoneware, marked "Nelson McCoy," 1926 .... **20.00**
Jar, panda standing on his head, Avon heart-shaped label on one foot **150.00**

Jardinière, Pine Cone pattern, light green, $80.

Jardinière

7" d, swallows, brown and green matte glaze **85.00**
8" h, Springwood, white, lilac colored flowers **95.00**

Jug, 10" h, Onyx, brown, orig stopper **150.00**
Lamp, Cowboy Boots, c1956 .... **150.00**

Mug

Davy Crockett, cream and brown glaze **65.00**
Surburbia, yellow **10.00**
Willow Ware, brown, c1926 .... **15.00**

Pitcher

Brown, Drip, 5" h, 16 oz **10.00**
Elephant, figural, tan glaze, c1940 **32.00**
Kolor Kraft, #331, dark green glaze **85.00**
Water Lily, c1935 .... **20.00**

Planter, mail box shape, "Letters" across top, pink glaze, $45.

Planter, Humpty Dumpty, pink glaze, **$28**.

Planter
Duck and egg, yellow **30.00**
Frog, green, 5-1/2" l **40.00**
Mums, 8" h, pink flowers, green leaves,
mkd "McCoy" **155.00**
Wishing Well **40.00**
Salt and pepper shakers, pr, figural,
cucumber and mango, 1954 .... **20.00**

Spoon rest
Butterfly, dark green, 1953 .... **15.00**
Penguin, black, white, and red, 1953
.... **20.00**
Strawberry jar, 12" h, stoneware **150.00**
Sugar, cov, emb face and scrolls, red
glazed cover **12.00**

Teapot
Brown Drip, short spout **20.00**
Grecian, 1958 .... **30.00**
Sunburst Gold, 1957 .... **25.00**
Tea set, Ivy, cov teapot, creamer, open
sugar, beige, brown highlights, green
flowers and stems, sgd "McCoy USA"
.... **150.00**

Vase, cream glaze, embossed "U.S.A.," 5" h, **$35**.

Vase
6-1/2" h, cylindrical, applied pink flower
.... **40.00**
7-1/2" h, lily, single flower, three leaves
.... **48.00**
8" h, double handles, green, 1948. **60.00**
8" h, Ringed, #508, white **40.00**
12-1/2" h, swan emerging from swirled
foliage, yellow glaze, mkd **25.00**
14-1/2" h, white, purple grapes dec,
green leaves **235.00**

Wall pocket
Basketweave **80.00**
Butterfly, white **150.00**
Dog and doghouse, 8" h **90.00**
Iron Trivet **50.00**
Lily **70.00**
Wren house **150.00**

Model Kits

History: The plastic scale-model kit originated in England in the mid-1930s with the manufacture of 1/72 Frog Penguin kits. The concept caught on during World War II when scale models were used in identification training. After the war companies such as Empire

Vase, aqua ground, white dogwood decoration,
black highlights, 10" h, **$24**.

Plastics, Hawk, Lindberg, Renwal, and Varney introduced plastic model kits to American hobbyists. The 1950s witnessed the arrival of Aurora and Monogram in the United States, Airfix in the United Kingdom, Heller in France, and Hasegawa and Marusan in Japan.

The 1960s was the golden age of the plastic kit model. Kits featured greater detail and accuracy than the early examples, and three scale sizes dominated: 1/48, 1/72, and 1/144. The oil crisis in the 1970s caused a temporary set back to the industry.

A revival of interest in plastic scale-model kits occurred in the late 1980s. At the same time, collector interest began to develop. The initial collecting focus was on automobile model kits from the 1950s and early 1960s. By the end of the 1980s interest had shifted to character and monster kits.

Collecting Hints: Model kits, assembled or unassembled, are one of the hot collectibles of the 1990s. Even assembled examples, provided they are done well, have value.

In many cases, a kit's value is centered more on the character or object it represents than on the kit itself. The high prices paid for monster-related kits is tied directly to the current monster collecting craze, which means a portion of the value is speculative.

Box art can influence a kit's value. When individual boxes sell in the $40 to $100 range, it becomes clear that they are treated as *objets d'art*, a dangerous pricing trend. The value of the box is easily understood when you place an assembled model beside the lid. All too often, it is the box that is more exciting.

Accurate Miniatures B25-G, #3432, Mitchell, 1:48 scale, unassembled. **12.00**
Apollo Saturn Rocket, Monogram, 1968, MIB.................... **35.00**
Batman, Aurora, MIB........................ **270.00**
Bell AH-1G Assault Copter, Aurora, MIB **60.00**
Black Night, series 2, Aurora, MIB **35.00**
Bonzana, Revell, MIB........................ **150.00**
Buck Rogers Marauder, Monogram, sealed, MIB **30.00**
Camaro, T-top, AMT............................ **20.00**
Captain Kidd Bloodthirsty Pirate, Aurora **150.00**
Cherokee Sports Roadster, Hawk, 1964, MIB.. **25.00**

Chevy, 51, Fleetline, AMT **45.00**
Corvette, 57, MPC, 1:16 scale, sealed, MIB **65.00**
Custom T-Bird, Aurora, 1963 .... **40.00**
Dick Tracy Space Coupe, Aurora, NRFB **235.00**
Double Whammy, Henri Studebaker, 1953, AMT, NRFB.................................... **85.00**
Dracula, Aurora, NRFB **350.00**
Drag Strip, accessory pack, AMT, MIB **40.00**
Flying Saucer, Aurora....................... **150.00**
Ford, Fairlane, 1956, customizing kit, Revell, 1958, MIB.................................... **80.00**
Ford, Model T pick-up, Monogram, 1975, MIB.. **35.00**
Forgotten Prisoner **150.00**
Frankenstein, Aurora, 1961, 3" x 7-1/2" x 9-1/4", assembled **30.00**
George Washington, Aurora, 1965, MIB **125.00**
Godzilla, glow, Monogram, 1978 ..... **250.00**
H.M.S. Bounty, Pyro, 1966, unassembled **30.00**
Hunchback of Notre Dame, Aurora, Anthony Quinn box, MIB **275.00**

Jaymar's Wild and Weird picture puzzle, left, $20; Lindy Loony's Road Hog Kit, $45.

Invaders UFO, Aurora....................... **250.00**
Jaguar CC120 Roadster, Aurora, 1961 .... **35.00**
Japanese Submarine, Aurora, Young Models Builder's Club box, MIB..... **38.00**
Knight Rider **25.00**
Lockhead U-2 Spy Plane, Hawk, NRFB **55.00**
Mark II Ford GT, AMT **40.00**
Masarati Auto, Aurora, 1966, MIB **40.00**
MASH Camp Swampy, NRFB........... **20.00**
Mister Mulligan Plane, Hawk **15.00**
Monkees, Monkeemobile, MPC, No. 605, 1967, unassembled.................... **150.00**
Monogram Relic Kothuga, Revell, NRFB **25.00**
Munster Koach, AMT, 1964, neatly built **100.00**
My Mother The Car, AMT, 1965 copyright, 1:25 scale, unassembled.............. **25.00**
Mustang, 1:16 scale, AM, NRFB........ **45.00**

ODS Infantry Fighting Vehicle, #264, Tamiya, 1:35 scale, unassembled.. **12.00**

Old Ironsides, *USS Constitution*, "S" kit, Revell, 1956, MIB **48.00**

Paul McCartney, Revell, 1964 .... **300.00**

Phantom of the Opera, Aurora, #428, © 1963 Universal Pictures, MIB **300.00**

Pilgrim Observer, MPC Space Station, NRFB **25.00**

Polaris Nuclear Sub Ethan Allan, Renwall **40.00**

Predicta Futuristic Car, Monogram, 1964, MIB.. **75.00**

Prehistoric Scenes, Cro-Magum Woman, Aurora, NRFB **85.00**

Ranch Wagon Western, Revell, horse drawn, 1950s.................................. **35.00**

Rat Fink, Revell, MIB **115.00**

International Off-road Scout II, Ertl, #8024, 1:25 scale, MIB, $30.

Return of the Saint, Jaguar CJ, Revell, 1:25 scale **25.00**

Smokey and the Bandit, Ertl, unbuilt in box **45.00**

Sopwith Camel, Aurora, unassembled **45.00**

Spider-Man, Aurora, orig box **200.00**

Star Trek, Klingon Battle Cruiser, AMT, MIB **120.00**

Street Fever Vette, MPC, 1978, NRFB **30.00**

Supecharged 56 Chevy, Monogram.. **40.00**

Superman, Aurora, 1963, MIB **375.00**

Talos anti-aircraft missile, Revell, 1957, MIB.. **45.00**

The Creature, Aurora, assembled and painted, 6" x 7-1/2" x 8-1/2", copyright 1963 **Universal Pictures Co.**, Inc., missing skeleton hand from base .. **35.00**

The Invisible Pigeon, Renwal **75.00**

The Saint's Jaguar XJS, Revell, copyright 1979, MIB **48.00**

The White House, Empire.................. **75.00**

Twin Mustang, F-82G, Monogram, MIB, $20.

Time Tunnel, Lunar, 1989 .... **250.00**
TransAm, 10th, MPC, MIB................. **25.00**
US Army MB Munitions Carrier, Aurora, 1/4 scale, plastic, NRFB **75.00**
US Navy F4J-4 Corsair Fighter-Bomber, Monogram, some parts assembled, orig instructions, most decals present.... **5.00**
Wacky Back Wacker Machine, Aurora, 1965, MIB.................................... **350.00**
Warlord TransAm, MPC, MIB............. **30.00**

Morton Potteries

History: Pottery was produced in Morton, Illinois, for 99 years. In 1877, six Rapp brothers, who emigrated from Germany, began the first pottery, Morton Pottery Works. Over the years, sons, cousins, and nephews became involved, and the other Morton pottery operations were spin-offs from this original Rapp brothers' firm. When it was taken over in 1915 by second-generation Rapps, Morton Pottery Works became the Morton Earthenware Company. Work at that pottery was terminated by World War I.

The Cliftwood Art Potteries, Inc., which operated from 1920 to 1940, was organized by one of the original founders of the Morton Pottery Works and his four sons. They sold out in 1940, and the production of figurines, lamps, novelties, and vases was continued by the Midwest Potteries, Inc., until a disastrous fire in March 1944 brought an end to that operation. By 1947, the brothers who had operated the Cliftwood Art Potteries, Inc., came back into the pottery business. They established the short-lived American Art Potteries. The American Art Potteries made flower bowls, lamps, planters, some unusual flower frogs, and vases. Their wares were marketed by florists and gift shops. Production at American Art Potteries was halted in 1961. Of all the wares of the Morton potteries, the products of the American Art Potteries are the most elusive.

Morton Pottery Company, which had the longest existence of all of the potteries in Morton, was organized in 1922 by the same brothers who had operated the Morton Earthenware Company. The Morton Pottery Company specialized in beer steins, kitchenwares, and novelty items for chain stores and gift shops. They also produced some of the Vincent Price National Treasures reproductions for Sears Roebuck and Company in the mid-1960s. The Morton Pottery closed in 1976, thus ending almost 100 years of pottery production in Morton.

Collecting Hints: The potteries of Morton, Illinois, used local clay until 1940. The clay fired out to a golden ecru color, which is quite easy to recognize. After 1940, southern and eastern clays were shipped to Morton, but these clays fired out white. Thus, later wares are easily distinguishable from the earlier ones.

Few pieces were marked by the potteries. Incised and raised marks for the Morton Pottery Works, the Cliftwood Art Potteries, Inc., and the Morton Pottery Company do surface at times. Occasionally, the Cliftwood, Midwest, Morton Pottery Company, and American Art Pottery affixed paper labels, and some pieces have survived with these intact.

Glazes from the early period, 1877 to 1920, usually were Rockingham types, both mottled and solid. Yellow-ware also was standard during the early period. Occasionally, a dark cobalt blue was produced, but this color is rare. Colorful drip glazes and solid colors came into use after 1920.

Advisers: Doris and Burdell Hall.

Morton Pottery Works, Dutch jugs, three pint, left: brown Rockingham, $60; right: cobalt blue, $90.All Morton Potteries photos by advisers Doris and Burdell Hall.

Morton Pottery Works, teapot, pear shape, six cups, brown Rockingham, $90.

Morton Pottery Works, Morton

Earthenware Co., 1877-1917

Bank, acorn, green, Acorn Stove Co. adv, 3-1/2" h **60.00**
Butter churn, brown Rockingham, 4 gallon **250.00**
Coffeepot, drip-o-later, 3 pc, 8 cups, brown Rockingham................................... **60.00**
Dutch jug, three pints
    Brown Rockingham **60.00**
    Cobalt blue **90.00**
Jardinière, leaf dec, 5" d, 4" h
    Brown **20.00**
    Cobalt blue **50.00**
    Green **45.00**
Milk pitcher, bulbous body, tree bark design, yellow ware, green and brown spatter, 1-3/4 qt............................. **150.00**
Miniature
    Coffeepot, brown Rockingham, 3-1/2" h
    .... **75.00**
    Jug, 3" h, brown Rockingham........ **50.00**
    Milk pitcher, cobalt blue, 3-3/4" h... **60.00**
Mixing bowls, yellow ware, white slip lines, nested set of five **280.00**
Mug, one pint, brown Rockingham **60.00**
Pie baker, yellow ware, 10" d............ **125.00**

Teapot, acorn shape, 3-3/4 cup, brown
Rockingham **80.00**
Urinal, shovel shape
Brown Rockingham......................... **50.00**
Yellow ware.................................... **65.00**

Cliftwood Art Potteries, Inc., chocolate set,
pitcher and six mugs, Tree Trunk line, chocolate
drip glaze, **$175**.

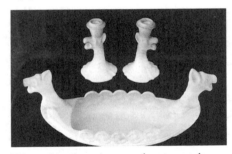

Cliftwood Art Potteries, console set, console
bowl, pairr matching candlesticks, Viking ship
bowl, dragon head candleholders, matte ivory/
turquoise, **$225**.

Cliftwood Art Potteries, Inc.,

1920-1940

Bookends, pr, tree trunk with woodpeckers,
chocolate brown drip glaze, 6" x 5" x
3-1/2".. **100.00**
Compote, four-dolphin base, Old Rose high
gloss, 6" h, 8-1/2" d **90.00**
Console bowl, four-dolphin base, matte
ivory ext., Old Rose high gloss int., 6" h,
12" l **100.00**
Console set, bowl and candleholders
Petal-shaped bowl, apple green **75.00**
Viking ship bowl, dragon heads at each
end, dragon head candleholders, matte
ivory/turquoise **225.00**
Figure
Billiken, brown, 11" h..................... **100.00**
Bulldog, Nero, gray grip, 11" h **95.00**
Elephant trumpeting, Blue Mulberry
.... **75.00**
German Shepherd, reclining, white drip,
8-1/2".. **70.00**

Lamp
Boudoir, #18, 6-1/2" h, cobalt blue. **30.00**
Desk, elephant figure, natural colors, 8" h
.... **80.00**
Donut shape, clock insert, Blue Mulberry,
8-1/2" h **150.00**
Mint compote, ftd, 3-1/2" h, 6-1/2" d, matte
blue **30.00**
Vase, 9" h
Handled, red and white drip over white
.... **60.00**
Tree trunk, Herbage Green **70.00**
Waffle set, covered batter pitcher, covered
syrup pitcher, on tray, Old Rose drip over
white **150.00**
Wall pocket, 8" x 5", handled, cone shape,
matte ivory/turquoise **50.00**

Midwest Potteries, Inc., 1940-1944

Bookends, pr, Art Deco-style base with
deer, Turquoise, 8" h **40.00**
Bud vase, hand, 6-1/2" h
Flesh color..................................... **18.00**
14k gold **25.00**
Figure
Baseball player, batter, gray uniform,
7-1/4" h **300.00**
Baseball player, catcher, white uniform, 6-
3/4" h **300.00**
Baseball player, umpire, black suit and
cap, 6-1/4" h................................. **300.00**
Crane, drip colors, 11" h................. **35.00**
Deer, stylized, looking back, white, gold
dec, 12" h.. **50.00**
Deer, stylized, with antlers, blue-brown
spray glaze, 12" h **30.00**
Ducks, three in a row, 6-1/2" l, 2-1/2" h,
white, yellow dec **24.00**
Giraffe, looking over back, yellow/green
drip on white, 12" h **35.00**
Heron, blue-yellow spray glaze, gold dec
.... **40.00**
Tiger, natural colors, 7" h, 12" l **40.00**

Midwest Potteries, Inc., bookends, pair, Art-Deco
style base with deer, turquoise, 8" h, **$40**.

Miniature

Dog, brown drip, 2" x 2" **14.00**
Frog, green drip, 1" h **12.00**
Kissing rabbits, white/gold, 2-1/2" x 3-1/4"
.... **25.00**
Lion, brown drip, 2-1/2" x 1-3/4" **14.00**
Rabbit, white and pink, 1-1/2" h **14.00**
Sailboat, blue/tan drip, 2" x 2" **45.00**
Squirrel, brown drip, 2" h **14.00**
Swan, matte white, 2" h **14.00**
Turtle, green drip, 1" h **12.00**
Pitcher, duck, figural, cattail handle, brown/
gray spray glaze, 10" h **40.00**

Morton Pottery Company, 1922-1976

Bank, hen, hand painted dec, 4" h **50.00**
Bean pot, cov, blue and white sponge ware,
Sears Vincent Price National Treasures,
four qts... **55.00**

Cookie jar

Basket of fruit, green, naturally colored
fruit **40.00**
Hen, chick finial, white, black wash
.... **135.00**
Panda, black and white **75.00**
Turkey, chick finial, brown **150.00**
Turkey, chick finial, white.............. **200.00**

Flowerpot soaker

Bird, blue and yellow...................... **20.00**
Calla lily, yellow and green............. **18.00**
Hound dog, brown and white........ **24.00**

Lamp

Kerosene, brass fixture with glass
chimney, cylindrical body with ribbed
base, white **50.00**
TV, buffalo figure atop rock base,
openings at top of rocks allow animal to
be lighted...................................... **100.00**
Mixing bowls, Woodland glaze, yellow and
green spatter over yellow clay, nested set
of four.. **175.00**

Morton Pottery Company, mixing bowls, red,
white, and blue spatter over white clay, nested
set of three, **$225**.

Nightlight

Old women in shoe, yellow house, red
roof **30.00**
Praying child, prayer in wall hanging
shadow box **40.00**
Teddy bear, brown spray glaze, hand
painted dec, heart-shaped nose ... **40.00**

Planter

Covered wagon, unattached oxen team,
price for set.................................... **55.00**
Davy Crockett as boy, bear beside open
stump **50.00**
Rabbit, female, with umbrella, beside
blue egg... **24.00**

Salt shaker, chick, white, black wash,
1-3/4" h **75.00**

Santa Claus head

Ashtray **15.00**
Mug **18.00**
Nut cup **14.00**
Plate, 6" d **45.00**
Plate, 12" d **55.00**
Punch bowl **150.00**
Punch bowl set, bowl, 12 mugs, white,
rare **360.00**
Toothpick holder, chick, white, black wash,
1-3/4" h **75.00**

American Art Potteries, 1947-1963

Candleholder, donut shape, three candle
cups, green, 6" x 7-1/2" **40.00**
Console set, petal design, 10" l x 6-1/2" h
bowl, pr 1-3/4" h candleholders, pink and
gray spray glaze............................. **30.00**
Creamer, bird, tail as handle, black and
green spray glaze........................... **24.00**
Flower bowl, Art Deco style, tan with brown
spackling, 10" x 4" x 1-1/2" **20.00**
Lamp, mountain goat figural, brown and
green spatter over white, 15" h **55.00**

Planter

Baby buggy, white, hand decorated,
5-1/2" x 7" **20.00**
Elephant, trumpeting, white, 7-1/2" x
2-1/2" **30.00**
Lamb, white, pink bow at neck, 8-1/2" x 3"
.... **25.00**
Pheasant, natural colors, spray glaze, 8-
1/2" h, 18" l **40.00**
Swan, orchid/pink, gold dec, 11" x 7"
.... **25.00**

TV lamp

Afghan hounds, black, 15" h.......... **75.00**
Conch shell, yellow and green spray
glaze, 6" h **35.00**
Double fish planter, pink-purple spray
base, 6" x 9" x 3-1/2" rect base **40.00**

Vase

Feather shape, gray and yellow spray
glaze, 10-1/2" h............................... **35.00**

Ruffled tulip, ivory, pink, and blue spray glaze, 9" h **35.00**

Wall pocket

Apple, red and green, three leaves, 5" h **24.00**

Chrysanthemum blossom, mauve and green spray glaze, 7-1/2" h **28.00**

Movie Personalities

History: The star system and Hollywood are synonymous. The studios spent elaborate sums of money promoting their stars. Charlie Chaplin, Rudolph Valentino, and Mary Pickford gave way to Greta Garbo and Clark Gable.

The movie magazine was a key vehicle in the promotion. *Motion Picture*, *Movie Weekly*, *Motion Picture World*, and *Photoplay* are some examples of this genre, although *Photoplay* was the most sensational.

The film star had no private life and cults grew up around many of them. By the 1970s, the star system of the 1930s and 1940s had lost its luster. The popularity of stars is usually much shorter lived today.

Collecting Hints: Focus on one star. Today, the four most popular stars are Humphrey Bogart, Clark Gable, Jean Harlow, and Marilyn Monroe. Many of the stars of the silent era are being overlooked by the modern collector.

Remember that stars have big support staffs. Not all autographed items were or are signed by the star directly. Signatures should be checked carefully against a known original.

Many stars had fan clubs and the fans tended to hold on to the materials they assembled. Collectors should be prepared to hunt and do research. A great deal of material rests in private hands.

Additional Listings: Autographs, Cowboy Heroes, Magazines.

Abbott & Costello, game, Who's On First, 9-1/2" x 19", Selchow & Righter Co., © ZIV International **50.00**

Allen, Woody, magazine, *Life*, March 21, 1969 .... **9.00**

Astaire, Fred

Magazine, *Life*, Dec. 30, 1940 .... **7.00**

Sheet Music, *My Shining Hour* **7.50**

Bacall, Lauren, magazine, *Life*, April 3, 1970 .... **7.00**

Bardot, Brigitte

Book, *Brigitte Bardot*, Francoise Sagan, 1976, 100 pgs, 12-1/2" x 9-1/2" **10.00**

Magazine, *Life*, July 28, 1961 .... **15.00**

Bergmann, Ingrid, magazine

Life, Oct. 13, 1967 .... **8.00**

Look, Nov. 11, 1958 .... **12.00**

Blair, Linda, autographed photo, 8" x 10", Exorcist, Reagan Possessed **40.00**

Bow, Clara, arcade card, black and white portrait, tan background **2.50**

Brando, Marlon

Book, *Brando*, Charles Highman, hard back **10.00**

Magazine, *Life*, Dec. 14, 1962 .... **12.00**

Bushman, Francis X., silent star, pennant, Metro **25.00**

Cantor, Eddie

Big Little Book, *Eddie Cantor In An Hour With You*, Whitman, #774, © 1934, 4-3/4" x 5-1/4" **40.00**

Pin, Eddie Cantor Magic Club, 1-1/2" d, brass, black facial features, red, background, tall hat, Pebeco Toothpaste, 1935 .... **50.00**

Chaplin, Charlie

Cartoon book, Charlie Chaplin in the Movies, 1917 .... **65.00**

Figure, 2-1/2" x 8", stuffed leather, full-length portrait image, inked in black on natural tan leather, black felt back, 1920s **70.00**

Postcards, set of five, 3-1/2" x 5-1/2", Courtesy Essaney, copyright 1918 **50.00**

Sheet music, Charlie Chaplin Walk, © 1915 Rossiter Music Co., Chicago **20.00**

Coogan, Jackie

Arcade card, black and white portrait, tan background **2.00**

Clicker, metal, adv for peanut butter **24.00**

Pencil box, red litho tin, black and white portrait on cover, 2-1/4" x 8" **28.00**

Cooper, Jackie, big little book, *Jackie Cooper in Peck's Bad Boy*, Saalfield, #1084, © 1934, 4-/4" x 5-1/4", some wear **35.00**

Crawford, Joan

Photograph, black and white, 14" x 17", black and white, facsimile signature **15.00**

Pocket mirror, black and white photo, mid-1920s, tiny facsimile signature **65.00**

Bing Crosby, diecut stand-up, Bing ready to play golf, cream colored sweater, brown slacks, pipe in mouth, **$225**.

Crosby, Bing

Game, Call Me Lucky, Parker Bros, 1954, black and white portrait on box lid, 19-1/2" sq playing board **30.00**
Magazine, *Look,* June 7, 1960, Bing and family cover **13.00**

Davis, Bette

Coloring Book, 10" x 13", Merrill, 1942 .... **24.00**
Movie Poster, *Hush Hush Sweet Charlotte,* 27" x 41" **35.00**
Press Book, *The Catered Affair,* 20 pgs **30.00**

Davis, Sammy, Jr., bobblehead **12.00**

Dean, James

Bobblehead.................................... **12.00**
Scrap book of press cuttings and photographs, anniversary book, and 1955 magazine................................ **80.00**

Elvira

Autographed photo, color 8" x 10", sexy pose **40.00**
Video, "Dead of the Night Hosted by Elvira," VHS Thriller Video **15.00**
Farnum, William, silent star, pennant, Fox **25.00**

Fields, W. C.

Lighter, W. C. Fields, figural, painted heavy white metal, 1930s, 4" x 4" x 5-1/4", ... **70.00**
Record album, 10-1/2" x 12", Variety Records, United Artist label, © 1946 .... **60.00**

Ford, Clint, cigar box label, portrait on wood grained background, unused **3.00**

Funicello, Annette, magazine, *Teen Screen* **22.00**

Gable, Clark, photograph, black and white, 14" x 17", black and white, facsimile signature **15.00**

Garland, Judy, photograph, black and white, 8" x 10", black and white, checkered Wizard of Oz dress, 1940s **8.00**

Garson, Greer, photograph, black and white, 14" x 17", black and white, facsimile signature.......................... **15.00**

Grable, Betty, photograph, black and white, 8" x 10".. **5.00**

Gleason, Jackie, magazine
Life, Nov 2, 1959............................. **15.00**
Look, Nov 15, 1966, with Art Carney on cover **12.50**

Harlow, Jean, post card, 3-1/2" x 45-1/2", glossy, small facsimile signature, fan card, 1930s, unused **30.00**

Bob Hope, comic book, *The Adventures of Bob Hope,* DC Comics, September, **$9**.

Hope, Bob

Book, *I Never Left Home,* Simon & Schuster, 8-1/2" x 11" glossy paper softcover, 1944, 80 pgs **45.00**
Magazine, *Post,* Nov. 9, 1963 .... **20.00**
Karloff, Boris, magazine cover, *Life*, Sept. 1964 .... **10.00**
Kelly, Grace, coloring book, Whitman, 1956, few pages colored **45.00**
Lake, Arthur, arcade card, Educational Pictures, black and white, tan background **2.50**

Laurel & Hardy

Arcade card, Stan Laurel, Paramount Pictures, black and white, tan background **2.25**
Figure, flat metal, Mignot, Stan wearing gray suit, blue stripes on pants, holds Oliver with one hand, Oliver in dark blue suit, red tie, cane, both hold derby in one hand, 1930s **48.00**
Movie poster, *Four Clowns,* 27" x 41" **45.00**
Salt and pepper shakers, pr, 1/2" x 2-1/2" x 4" white china tray, 4" h Laurel with black derby, 3" h Hardy with brown derby, Beswick, England, three pcs **115.00**
Lee, Christopher, autographed photo, sgd "Dracula" **35.00**
Leigh, Janet, magazine, *Motion Picture,* August 1959 .... **10.00**

Lloyd, Harold

Beanie, The Freshman, 6-1/2" d, Pathe Picture **75.00**
Mechanical eyeglasses, Movie Crazy, 5-1/4" w **75.00**

Buster Keaton, lobby cards for *The Buster Keaton Story,* three different cards shown, **each $20**.

Nutcracker, 5-3/4" h, cast iron, English, 1930s **150.0**
Loren, Sophia, magazine, *Life,* Nov. 14, 1960 .... **15.00**

Liberace bear, black tuxedo, aqua-colored plush bear, original tags, $35.

Marx, Groucho, sheet music, *Copacabana,* 9" x 12", 1947 copyright **20.00**
Marx, Zippo, arcade card, black and white portrait, tan background **2.50**
Mayo, Virginia, pencil tablet, 12 lined sheets, full-color cover, 1950s, unused **3.00**
Midler, Bette, magazine, *Time,* March 2, 1987 .... **5.00**

Monroe, Marilyn

Cologne spray, 1983, MIB **45.00**
Doll, Tristar, 11-1/2" h **45.00**
Newspaper Supplement, New York, Sunday, 1982 .... **20.00**
Novak, Kim, fan club kit, wallet, photos, and Christmas card, 1966 .... **25.00**

Our Gang

Figure, bisque, 2" h, Pete the Pup, painted brown body, 1930s **75.00**
Premium card, Yuengling's Ice Cream, black and white or color tinted image, set of ten, 1-1/4" x 3", c1930 .... **125.00**
Puzzle, 11" x 14" brown envelope, 80 pcs, sponsored by McKesson's Milk of Magnesia, scene of Our Gang characters in a soda fountain **135.00**

Pickford, Mary

Magazine, *Photoplay,* September 1914, full-color cover, article with photos. **45.00**
Pennant, Famous Players Film Co. **35.00**
Photograph signed, 1930 .... **55.00**

Price, Vincent, autographed book, *Crimefantastique,* Jan, 1989......... **100.00**

Redford, Robert, magazine, *Argosy,* cover story, August 1974 .... **5.00**

Rogers, Ginger

Magazine, *Life,* Nov. 5, 1951 .... **15.00**

Photograph signed, 5" x 7", color, Alhambra Theatre 1940 roster on back **15.00**

Rooney, Mickey, photograph, black and white, 14" x 17", black and white, facsimile signature **15.00**

Skelton, Red, lobby card, Lovely to Look At, 8" x 10", autographed, 1952, with certificate of authenticity **40.00**

Sinatra, Frank, magazine

Life, April 23, 1965 .... **15.00**

TV Guide, May 14, 1954, New England edition, full-color cover photo **45.00**

Sparks, Ned, arcade card, black and white portrait, tan background **2.00**

Stanwyck, Barbara

Box, Vita-Sert Chocolates 1940s, illus on lid **150.00**

Press book, Gambling lady, 11" x 17", 1934, Warner Bros, some wear **30.00**

Streisand, Barbara, set of eight lobby cards for "Funny Girl," 27 black and white stills, "Funny Girl" program, two "Funny Girl" records.................................... **120.00**

Taylor, Elizabeth, photograph, black and white, facsimile signature, 3" x 5"...... **8.00**

Taylor, Robert, photograph, black and white, 14" x 17", black and white, facsimile signature **15.00**

Temple, Shirley

Arcade Card, Educational Pictures, black and white **2.50**

Book, *Shirley Temple, My Life & Times,* 1936 .... **50.00**

Figure, 8-1/2" h, rubber, black Scottie dog under one arm, marked "Made in Czechoslovakia," mid-1930s **90.00**

Pinback button, 1" d, enamel on brass, "Sunday Referee/Shirley Temple League," English newspaper issue **110.00**

Scrapbook, 11" x 15", Saalfield, 1937 copyright....................................... **25.00**

Three Stooges

Fan photo, 5" x 6", full color, Three Stooges on flying carpet, steering wheel gripped by Larry, facsimile signatures, c1960 .... **20.00**

Pinback button, Carter is Doing the Work of 3 Men, black on yellow, cartoon images, c1980 .... **8.00**

Punch-out book, 7-1/2" x 13", Golden Press, 1962 .... **75.00**

Trading cards, eight-card sticker set, black and white, peel of stickers, 1970s, mkd "Norman Maurer Productions, Inc., Columbia Pictures" **15.00**

Valentino, Rudolph, movie folder, Son of the Sheik **25.00**

West, Mae

Magazine, *Life,* April 18, 1969 .... **10.00**

Photograph, 7" x 10" black and white, glamour pose.................................. **15.00**

Stage play program, Come On Up, 1946 .... **20.00**

White, Pearl, silent star, pennant, Pathe **20.00**

N

NASCAR

History: Man's quest for speed is as old as time. If it moves, it will and can be raced.

Automobile racing began before the turn of the century. Many of the earliest races took place in Europe. By the first decade of the 20th century, automobile racing was part of the American scene.

The Indianapolis 500 began in 1911 and was interrupted only by World War II. In addition to Formula 1 racing, the NASCAR circuit has achieved tremendous popularity with American racing fans. Cult heroes such as Richard Petty have become household names.

Collecting Hints: This is a field of heroes and also fans. Collectors love the winners; a household name counts. Losers are important only when major races are involved. Pre-1945 material is especially desirable because few individuals were into collecting prior to that time.

The field does have problems with reproductions and copycats. Check every item carefully. Beware of paying premium prices for items made within the last 20 years.

Auto racing items are one of the hot collectible markets of the 1990s. Although interest in Indy 500 collectibles remains strong, the market is dominated by NASCAR collectibles. In fact, the market is so strong that racing collectibles have their own separate show circuit and supporting literature.

Advertising display, Tide, Darrell Waltrip, life-size, full color, heavy hardboard, unused... **45.00**

Ashtray, Indy Speedway, bronze, Indy car emb on front, made by Bastin Bros. Co., 6-1/2" w, 5" h **125.00**

Autograph, photo signed, 8" x 10", color
Austin, Pat, Top Fuel Dragster, Top Alcohol Funny Car, 1994................. **10.00**
Force, John, AA Fuel Funny Car, 1994 .... **10.00**
Gordan, Jeff, #24, 1995 NASCAR Winston Cup Champion, 1996 .... **10.00**

Autograph, postcard, Red Farmer, front with Farmer beside his F97, post card produced by Bill Wilson Studios,

#270187, divided back reads "Red Farmer, Hueytown, Alabama, 1969 National Sportsman Champion winner 31 features 1968; votes Nascar most popular modified driver winner; 34 features 1956; National Modified Champion"....................................... **20.00**

Autograph, promotional card with photo of car and drivers in front, bios and stats on back, sgd in black sharpie, 8-1/2" x 11"
Force, John **10.00**
Skuza, Dean, Matco Tools............. **10.00**
Willard, Jessica, Queen of Diamonds **12.00**

Autograph, trading card, Knight Quest, Dale Earnhardt, #57, sgd on front of card in blue sharpie, with Dale Earnhardt Incorporated Certificate, 1996..... **150.00**

Bank, Super Truck Series, Craftsmen, Tobey Butler, Ortho, #21, 1:24 scale, 1995 Premier Edition, NRFB, **$18.**

Bank
Kellogg's Corny Bank, Monte Carlo, Terry Labonte, 1:24 scale, made by Action, 1998, NRFB..................................... **65.00**
Texaco Davey Allison, #28, helmet, Texaco logo, made by Racing Champions, 1994 .... **55.00**

Book
NASCAR: The Thunder of America! NASCAR 50th anniversary, hardcover, orig dj, illus..................................... **30.00**
Unfair Advantage, Mark Donohue, hard cover, orig dj **350.00**

Calendar, 1995, Winston Cup Series, different driver and car for each month **8.00**

Cap
Indianapolis Motor Speedway Inaugural Race, limited edition, Aug. 6, 1994, blue, gold lettering, orig hang tag, never worn **15.00**
McDonald's Racing Team, embroidered Bill Elliot signature and "94" on side, red, unused **9.00**

Christmas ornament, NASCAR 2001, Trevco, 3" d, 3" h, NRFB
#17, Matt Kenseth, 2000 Rookie of the Year **10.00**
#18 Bobby Labonte, 2000 Winston Cup Champion, Interstate Batteries, slight damage to package......................... **8.00**

Diecast car, Action Racing, 1:24 scale
   Dallenbach, Wally, #75, Power Puff Girls,
   2000, MIB **15.00**
   Labonte, Terry, #5, Rice Krispies Treats,
   1999, MIB **18.00**
   Nadeau, Jerry, #9
   Cartoon Network, Power Puff Girls, 1998,
   MIB.. **18.00**
   Scooby Doo on Zombie Island, 1998,
   MIB.. **18.00**
   Cartoon Network, The Jetsons, 1999
   .... **15.00**

Toy, truck, Terry Labonte, driver, Kellogg's Corn
Flakes tractor trailer, original box, Racing
Champions, Inc., 1994, NRFB, **$30.**

Diecast car, Racing Champions, 1:24 scale,
   Zerex, numbered edition, certificate of
   authenticity, NRFB **45.00**
Diecast car, Revell Club, 1:18 scale, NRFB
   Coca-Cola, #1, #1 of 504, plaque on
   back window of car with number . **100.00**
   John Deere #97, #1 of 504, plaque on
   back window of car with number . **100.00**
   Skoal, #33, #1 of 504, plaque on back
   window of car with number........... **100.00**
   Tide, #10, #1 of 504, plaque on back
   window of car with number........... **100.00**
   Winn Dixie, #60, Mark Martin driver **90.00**
Diecast car, Revell Club, 1:24 scale,
   advertising logo on hood, numbered
   edition, orig certificate of authenticity,
   NRFB
   CAT, #96, David Green, 1997 Chevrolet
   Monte Carlo, black and yellow **48.00**
   Citgo, #21, Michael Waltrip, 1997 Ford
   Thunderbird, white and red **48.00**
   Kodak, #4, Sterling Martin, 1997 Chevy
   Monte Carlo, yellow........................ **48.00**
Doll, Barbie, NASCAR 50th Anniv, 1998,
   MIB.. **100.00**
Game, Daytona 500, Milton Bradley, 1990,
   officially licensed by NASCAR........ **35.00**
Helmet, miniature, facsimile signature,
   Simpson, made in China, 2-1/2" x 3"
   Earnhardt, Dale, fair condition **18.00**
   Gordan, Jeff, #24............................. **12.00**
   Labonte, Bobby, San Francisco 49er's,
   Shell, Interstate Batteries, and Max Tools
   "Getting the job done" **12.00**
   Labonte, Terry, 1996 NASCAR Winston
   Cup Champion, Kellogg's Corn Flakes
   and rooster logo **12.00**
   Wallace, Rusty, Penske Auto Center PPG,
   Fleetwood's RV's, Miller, Bosch, Mobile 1
   sponsor logos................................. **12.00**

Ingot, Franklin Mint, The Greatest Racing
   Cars, first edition proof set, Panhard 70
   hp on front, copyright 1977, orig
   packaging....................................... **50.00**
Key chain, Kelloggs, plastic, car-shape
   .... **8.00**
License plate, plastic, Bill Elliott, Ford
   Taurus, #94, sponsored by McDonald's,
   1998, 19" l, 8" h **8.00**
Limited edition plate, Dale Earnhardt,
   issued by Hamilton Collection, 1999, orig
   box, 6-1/2" d
   Always A Champion **40.00**
   D-Day **40.00**
   Hot Property.................................. **40.00**
   Ready To Race **40.00**

Magazine ad

Champion Spark Plugs, Daytona 500
   Marvin Panch, shows two race cars,
   black and white, March, 1961, 10" x 13"
   .... **15.00**
Champion Spark Plugs, Indianapolis 500
   scene, Pagoda tower in background,
   Collier's Magazine, 1938, tri-color, 11" x
   14" **10.00**
Champion Spark Plugs, Jim Rathmann,
   Monza, Italy, in his winning #5 race car,
   after winning 500-mile race, full color,
   1959, 5" x 7" **18.00**
Champion Spark Plugs, shows
   Cunningham, Austin-Healey, Jaguar,
   Lancia, and Ferrari, Saturday Evening
   Post, 1954, tri-color, 11" x 14" **10.00**
*Champion Spark Plugs, The Results Are
   In, Champion Spark Plugs Powered 100
   Out of 105 Stock Winners In 1957,* small
   score box of 1957 NASCAR winners, full
   color, 10" x 14".............................. **15.00**
Get Champion Spark Plugs Today, Sam
   Hanks, 1953 Driving Champion, in his
   race car, black and white, 1954, 10" x 12"
   .... **18.00**
Goodyear Tires, Bobby Unser,
   Indianapolis 500, full color, June 1960,
   two 10" x 13" pages **25.00**
Mobil Oil and Mobilgas, endorsement by
   Indianapolis 500 Winner Bill Vukovich,
   Mobil's 50th anniversary, black and white,
   1953, 8" x 12" **15.00**
Mobil Oil and Mobilgas, endorsement by
   Indianapolis 500 Winner Pat Flaherty, also
   by Don Campbell, speedboat racer,
   black and white, 1956, 10-1/2" x 14"
   .... **18.00**
*Pyroil Additive, Another Indianapolis
   Speedway Record For Pyroil, Ronny
   Householder,* black and white, 1938, 3"
   x 8" **8.50**

Toy, truck, Circuit City Racing, #8, Racing
Champions, Inc., 1996, NRFB, $25.

Mug
Avon Gift Collection, 50th anniversary
commemorative, ceramic, 3-D, Jeff
Gordan, #24, MIB............................ **10.00**
Jeff Gordan, #24, ceramic, Hunter Corp,
Kentucky, 4-3/4" d, 6-3/4" h............. **25.00**
Slim Jim Racing Team, glass, Busch
Series Champions 1991 & 1994, c1996,
6-1/2" h....................................... **10.00**
Patch, Indianapolis Motor Speedway,
multicolored, 4-1/4" w, 2-1/2" h, unused
.... **10.00**
Pennant, Indianapolis Speedway, some
wear and discoloration, 22" w, 11" h
.... **75.00**
Photo, framed
Earnhardt, Dale, Sr., black metal frame,
16" x 20"...................................... 10.00
Gordan, Jeff, 1990 winner of Bellvile
Midget Nationals, taken night before 500,
driving for Diet Pepsi Racing Team **15.00**
Pinback button
American Bowling Congress 36th
Internat'l Tournament March-April 1936
Indianapolis, 2-3/4" d, blue, red text,
cream ground, bluetone aerial view of
Indianapolis race course in progress
.... **24.00**
Indianapolis Speedway, 1-1/4" d, shaded
blue and white ground, judges stand with
two bright yellow racing cars, overprinted
with large black and white checkered
flag, c1950................................... **12.00**
Press pass
Racing 2000, Optima Cool, Jeff Gordan,
#2... **18.00**
Racing 2000, VIP, Jeff Gordon #X32
.... **15.00**
Racing 2001, Optima Up Close, Keven
Harvick, #UC 3.............................. **15.00**
Print, framed, 3rd Indy 500 Line-Up,
31-1/4" w, 9-1/4" h......................... **150.00**
Program
Brickyard 400 NASCAR, Aug. 2, 1997, all
pullouts intact, mint **45.00**
Die Hard 500, 27th The Ultimate in
Competition, July 23, 1995, Talladega,
with 4-1/4" x 3" patch on front cover
"Talladega Superspeedway Die Hard 500
1995 NASCAR'S Most Competitive Track"
.... **18.00**

Ft Miami Mile Track, Sept. 12, 1926, nine
adv, pencil notations, creased in half
.... **75.00**
*Grand Prix Circuit Car Races, Brands
Hatch,* Sept. 19, 1968, lists races, racers,
cars, records, etc........................... **15.00**
Indianapolis 500, 1927, Lap Fund Prize,
features past racers, many ads ... **320.00**
Indianapolis 500, 1990, 74th Running,
May 27, 1990, 195 pgs **10.00**

Toy, Watkins Glen Grand Prix, Jackie Stewart HO
scale, Aurora, complete, some damage to
original box, $35.

Seat cushion, Indy 700, orange and black,
officially licensed product of Indianapolis
Motor Speedway **8.00**
Stein, Winston Cup 25th Anniversary, 1995,
limited edition, pictures of Kulwicki,
Wallace, Earnhardt, Elliott, Allison, Petty,
Yarborough, Parson, Waltrip, LaBonte, 5-
1/2" h **10.00**
Stickpin, Indianapolis 500 Speedway, 1-1/4"
wide figural enameled white race car
.... **10.00**
Textiles, curtains, pr, pinch pleated, late
1960's Dodge Charger, #10, #12 with
Coca-Cola adv, #93 with STP adv,
NASCAR International, Grand National,
Winston 500, World 600, Champion
Spark Plugs, Sears Steel-Belted Tires,
Union 76, 72" w, 45" l **80.00**
Tin, Winston 25th Anniversary, contains 50
book matches with assorted race drivers
and statistics, 7-1/2" x 4-1/2" x 2" ... **15.00**
Toy train set, Dale Earnhardt, limited
edition, certificate of authenticity
#3 Goodwrench Service, Olympic
Games, HO scale, #3114, Revell, six pcs
.... **150.00**
#3 Wrangler, #2 Mike Curb Tender,
Revell, four pcs............................. **125.00**
#98, Bass Pro Shops, seven pcs. **100.00**
Wall plaque, Dale Earnhardt, inset Nitro 2
card, c1990, 9" l, 7" h..................... **30.00**

New Martinsville-Viking Glass

History: The New Martinsville Glass Manufacturing Company, founded in 1901, took its name from its West Virginia location. Early products, made from opal glass, were decorative and utilitarian. Later, pressed crystal tableware with flashed-on ruby or gold decorations was made. In the 1920s, innovative color and designs made vanity, liquor, and smoking sets popular. Dinner sets in patterns such as Radiance, Moondrops, and Dancing Girl, as well as new colors, cuttings, and etchings were produced. In the 1940s, black glass was formed into perfume bottles, bowls with swan handles, and flower bowls. In 1944, the company was sold and reorganized as the Viking Glass Company.

The Rainbow Art Glass Company, Huntington, West Virginia, was established in 1942 by Henry Manus, a Dutch immigrant. This company produced small, hand-fashioned animals and decorative ware of opal, spatter, cased, and crackle glass. Rainbow Art Glass also decorated for other companies. In the early 1970s, Viking acquired Rainbow Art Glass Company and continued the production of the small animals. By 1979, it had developed a black glass formula.

The Viking Glass Company was acquired by Kenneth Dalzell in 1986. The company's name was changed to Dalzell-Viking Glass. Production included items made with Viking molds, some animal figures were reintroduced, and other items were made using new colors. In late 1998, Dalzell-Viking closed.

Collecting Hints: Before 1935, New Martinsville glass was made in a wide variety of colors. Later glass was only made in crystal, blue, ruby, and pink.

Look for cocktail, beverage, liquor, vanity, smoking, and console sets. Amusing figures of barnyard animals, sea creatures, dogs, and bears were produced.

Both Rainbow Art Glass and Viking Glass hand made their products and affixed a paper label. Rainbow Art Glass pieces are beautifully colored, and the animal figures are more abstract in design than those of New Martinsville. Viking made plain, colored, cut, and etched tableware, novelties, and gift items.

Basket, Janice
9-1/2" h, 12" w, 7" d, black, crystal handle
.... **200.00**
9-3/4" h, 12" w, blue **250.00**
Bookend, flat back, Viking
4-1/2" h, Shaggy dog, pink............ **15.00**
5-1/4" h, squirrel, frosted **10.00**
Bowl
Meadow Wreath, crimped, 10" d ... **35.00**
Radiance, amber, 12" d................. **40.00**
Teardrop, ftd, 11" d, 4" h.............. **45.00**
Butter dish, cov, Moondrops, 6" d, cobalt blue base, 3-1/2" h clear dome cover
.... **250.00**
Candlesticks, pr
Figural, squirrel, 4-3/4" l, 3-1/2" w, 6-3/4" h
.... **120.00**
Moondrops, pink, 5-1/8" h, 4-1/2" w
.... **165.00**
Candle vases, pr, Janice, 5-3/8" h, 9" h, red
.... **400.00**
Creamer and sugar, Addie pattern, #4004, ruby, c1930 .... **65.00**
Creamer and sugar on tray, Radiance, blue, 4-7/8" w, 3-1/4" h creamer, 5" w, 2-7/8" sugar, 10-3/8" l tray............ **100.00**
Cup and saucer
Fancy Square, jade **18.00**
Hostmaster, ruby............................ **15.00**
Moondrops, amber......................... **20.00**
Decanter
Moondrops, beehive style stopper, emerald green, 10-1/2" h.............. **150.00**
Nice Kitty, green............................ **65.00**
Volkstead Pup, crystal.................... **85.00**
#606, ruby, tilted, 9" h **145.00**
Dresser set, Tapered Spiral pattern, 4" sq x 3" h powder box, pr 5-1/2" perfume bottles with orig daubers............. **190.00**
Figure
Angel sitting on the moon, frosted and clear, Viking, orig label **45.00**
Baby bear with cart, 3" h, 5-1/2" l. **130.00**
Dog, 8-1/2" l, orange, Viking, #1316
.... **40.00**
Praying boy, frosted and clear, Viking, orig label, 6" h **45.00**
Seal, ball on nose, clear, 7-1/4" h, 1930s
.... **75.00**
Woodsman, clear, 7-1/4" h, 4" w... **120.00**
Flower bowl, flowerlite frog, evergreen, 5-1/2" w, 4-1/2" h, 3-1/2" frog, Viking. **90.00**
Guest set, three pcs
Blue, 2-5/8" d x 2-7/8" h tumbler, 5-1/2" w x 6-1/8" h pitcher, 9-1/4" l x 5-7/8" w tray
.... **125.00**

Fairy lamp, two pieces, orange, diamond point type pattern, original Viking label, **$17.50**.

Pink satin, 2-3/4" h tumbler, 5-1/2" w x 6" h pitcher, 6" l tray, pink satin, hand painted floral dec **325.00**

Handkerchief bowl, 5" x 5-1/2", crimped, deep orange, orig red and gold "Hand Made Viking" sticker **25.00**

Iced tea tumbler, ftd, Prelude etching, crystal **17.50**

Plate

Fancy Square, jade, 7-1/2" w **8.00**
Florentine, clear, 14" d **25.00**
Moondrops, red, 8-1/2" d **20.00**
Radiance, red, 8" d **15.00**

Relish

Epic, bluenique, three-part, 12" w, Viking
.... **26.00**
Radiance, three-part, amber, 9" d .. **18.00**

Swan

Amber, 5" x 6" x 5-1/4" **45.00**
Clear, 10" l, 8" w, 10" h to top of head, Janice pattern **80.00**

Tidbit tray, 7-1/4" d, 2-1/4" h, White Rose etch, silver trim, center handle, orig gold Viking label **15.00**

Vase

Art Deco style, black, 8-1/2" h, 4-1/2" d
.... **90.00**

Epic, sapphire blue, Viking, 17-1/2" h
.... **25.00**
Radiance, Meadow Wreath, blue, 9-3/4" h, 6" d **165.00**
Radiance, red, 10-1/8" h, 5-1/2" d **170.00**
Shell, leaded crystal, 5" h, pr **125.00**

Whiskey, Moondrops, amethyst **20.00**

Wine set, amethyst, 11-1/2" h decanter, four 4-5/8" h wine glasses **190.00**

Newspapers, Headline Editions

History: America's first successful newspaper was *The Boston Newsletter*, founded in 1704. The newspaper industry grew rapidly and reached its pinnacle in the early 20th century. Within the last decade, many great evening papers have ceased publication, and many local papers have been purchased by the large chains.

Collecting headline-edition newspapers has become popular during the last 20 years, largely because of the decorative value of the headlines. Also, individuals like to collect newspapers related to the great events they have witnessed or which have been romanticized through the movies, television, and other media. Historical events, the Old West, and the gangster era are particularly popular subjects.

Collecting Hints: All newspapers must be complete with a minimum of chipping and cracking. Post-1880 newsprint is made of wood pulp and deteriorates quickly without proper care. Pre-1880 newsprint was composed of cotton and rag fiber and has survived much better than its wood-pulp counterpart.

Front pages only of 20th-century newspapers command about 60 percent of the value for the entire issue, since the primary use for these papers is display. Pre-20th-century issues are collectible only if complete, as banner headlines were rarely used. These papers tend to run between four and eight pages in length.

Major city issues are preferable, although any newspaper providing a dramatic headline is collectible. Banner headlines, those extending completely across the paper, are most desirable. Those papers from the city in which an event happened command a substantial premium over the prices listed below. A premium is also paid for a complete series, such as all 20th-century election reports.

Twentieth-century newspapers should be stored away from high humidity and out of direct sunlight. Issues should be placed flat in polyethylene bags or in acid-free folders that are slightly larger than the paper.

Although not as commonly found, newspapers from the 17th through the 19th centuries are highly collectible, particularly those from the Revolutionary War, War of 1812, Civil War, and those reporting Indian and desperado events.

Two of the most commonly reprinted papers are the *Ulster County Gazette*, of Jan. 4, 1800, dealing with Washington's death and the *N.Y. Herald*, of April 15, 1865, concerning Lincoln's death. If you have either of these papers, chances are you have a reprint.

Adviser: Tim Hughes.

Notes: The following listing includes prices of issues dating more than 200 years old, but concentrates on newspapers of the 20th century. The date given is the date of the event itself; the newspaper coverage usually appeared the following day.

1778, Average Revolutionary War newspaper **275.00**
1795, Typical late 18th century newspaper **28.00**
1813, Typical War of 1812 newspaper **18.00**
1836, March 6, Battle of the Alamo ... **400.00**
1863, July 4, Battle of Gettysburg **380.00**
1865, April 14, Lincoln is assassinated at Ford's Theater............................... **875.00**
1876, June 25, Custer's Massacre, but not reported in newspapers until July 7 and later **345.00**
1881, Oct. 26, Gunfight at the O.K. Corral.... .... **650.00**
1886, Sept. 1, final surrender of Geronimo **95.00**
1895, Feb. 19, death of Frederick Douglas **90.00**
1898, Feb. 15, battleship *Maine* is sunk **80.00**
1901, Sept. 6, President McKinley is shot **75.00**

1903, Dec. 17, the Wright Bros. first flight in their airplane **550.00**
1904, Nov. 8, Teddy Roosevelt elected **40.00**
1906, April 18, San Francisco earthquake **75.00**
1908, Nov. 3, President Taft is elected **25.00**
1912, April 15, the Titanic hits an iceberg and sinks.................................... **600.00**
1914, July 11, Babe Ruth's first Major League game (Boston) **60.00**
1915, May 7, the *Lusitania* is sunk.... **425.00**
1917, April 6,War is declared: the U.S. enters WW1.. **55.00**
1918, Nov. 11, Armistice is signed, ending WW1.. **70.00**
1919, Jan. 6, Teddy Roosevelt dies.... **30.00**
1920, Aug. 26, Suffrage: women get right to vote.. **65.00**
1921, Oct. 25, death of Bat Masterson in N.Y. **100.00**
1923, Feb. 16, opening of King Tut's tomb **45.00**
1924, Feb. 3, President Wilson dies ... **65.00**

July 10, 1925, Scopes,Trial, City Journal, $48.

1925, July 10, Scopes trial begins...... **48.00**
1926, May 8, Byrd reaches the North Pole **40.00**
1926, Aug. 22, Rudolph Valentino dies **60.00**

May 22, 1927, Lindbergh Does It, New York Times, **$375**.

1927, Sept. 30, Babe Ruth hits his 60th homerun **210.00**

1928, Nov. 6, Hoover elected **38.00**

1929, May 16, first Academy Awards held, Hollywood **45.00**

1929, Oct. 28, Stock Market crash (report of Monday's closing) **345.00**

1930, Oct. 31, "Bugs" Moran is arrested **55.00**

1931, June 5, Al Capone prosecuted for tax evasion **55.00**

March 1, 1932, Lindbergh baby kidnapping, Kidnap Rendezvous Reported: Woman Mails Lindbergh Note, $110.

1932, March 1, Lindbergh baby is kidnapped **110.00**

1933, Jan. 31, Hitler becomes Chancellor of Germany.. **40.00**

1933, March 4, Franklin D. Roosevelt is inaugurated **57.00**

1933, April 7, end of Prohibition......... **115.00**

1933, July 6, the First All Star game ... **48.00**

1933, Sept. 22, Dillinger is captured in Dayton, Ohio.................................. **38.00**

1933, Dec. 5, Prohibition is repealed .. **92.00**

1934, Jan. 26, John Dillinger is captured **85.00**

1934, May 23, Bonnie and Clyde are killed in Louisiana **225.00**

1935, May 26, Babe Ruth hits home run #714, also his final game **85.00**

1935, Aug.16, Will Rogers and Wiley Post are killed **63.00**

1936, Aug. 3, Jesse Owens captures the 100 meter gold at the Berlin Olympics **40.00**

1937, May 6, *Hindenburg* disaster at Lakehurst, New Jersey................. **210.00**

1937, July 3, Amelia Earhart disappears **130.00**

July 3, 1937, US Planes Speed to Aid Ships in Amelia Search, $130.

1938, Oct. 30, "War of the Worlds" broadcast on radio **75.00**

1939, May 2, Lou Gehrig's consecutive-name streak ends........................... **69.00**

1939, Sept. 1, Germany attacks Poland beginning WWI **47.00**

Dec. 8, 1941, Japan Declares War After Attacking US, $65.

1941, May 27, *Bismark* is sunk **48.00**

1941, July 17, Joe DiMaggio's last game of hitting streak (56th)....................... **44.00**

1941, Dec. 7, Pearl Harbor attack **65.00**

1942, June 5, Battle of Midway........... **44.00**

1943, Typical World War 11 newspaper **7.00**

1943, Jan. 5, death of George Washington Carver **50.00**

1944, June 6, D-Day invasion of France **60.00**

April 12, 1945, American Journal, Roosevelt Dies, $45.

1945, Feb. 18, Battle of Iwo Jima **48.00**
1945, April 12, President Franklin D. Roosevelt dies **45.00**
1945, May 8, Germany surrenders: V-E Day **60.00**
1945, Aug. 9, atomic bomb is dropped on Nagasaki, Japan **57.00**
1947, April 11, Jackie Robinson breaks the color barrier & signs with the Dodgers **57.00**
1947, July 8, Roswell, New Mexico, UFO crash **35.00**
1948, May 14, Israel is given statehood **80.00**
1950, June 28, Korean War begins **40.00**
1952, Sept. 24, Marciano new boxing champion **37.00**
1953, Oct. 5, Yankees win the World Series **50.00**
1954, Jan. 14, Joe Dimaggio marries Marilyn Monroe.. **35.00**
1955, Oct. 4, Brooklyn Dodgers win the World Series **45.00**
1959, March 13, Hawaii joins union..... **35.00**
1960, Nov. 8, John F. Kennedy is elected **50.00**
1961, Oct. 1, Roger Maris hits his 61st home run, breaking Babe Ruth's record} **145.00**

1963, June 17, Supreme Court rules that reading the Bible in public schools is unconstitutional **35.00**
1963, Aug. 28, Civil Rights march on Washington: "I have a dream..." speech by Martin Luther King, Jr. **37.00**

Nov. 22, 1963, Kennedy Slain on Dallas Street, $35.

1963, Nov. 22, John F. Kennedy is assassinated.................................. **35.00**
1964, Feb. 9, Beatles come to America; perform on the Ed Sullivan Show in New York.. **38.00**
1965, Feb. 21, Malcolm X is assassinated in New York City................................ **70.00**
1967, Jan. 16, First Superbowl – Green Bay Packers defeat Kansas City Chiefs **35.00**
1968, April 15, Martin Luther King is assassinated.................................. **53.00**
1969, July 21, Man walks on the moon **38.00**
1973, Jan. 26, Vietnam war ends........ **32.00**
1977, Aug. 17, Elvis Presley dies in Memphis **25.00**
2001, Sept. 11, terrorists attack the United States, issue must be dated Sept. 11

O

Occupied Japan

History: The Japanese economy was devastated when World War II ended. To secure necessary hard currency, the Japanese pottery industry produced thousands of figurines and other knickknacks for export. The variety of products is endless—ashtrays, dinnerware, lamps, planters, souvenir items, toys, vases, etc. Initially, the figurines attracted the largest number of collectors; today many collectors focus on other types of pieces.

Collecting Hints: Buyers should be aware that a rubber stamp can be used to mark "Occupied Japan" on the base of objects. Fingernail polish remover can be used to test a mark. An original mark will remain intact since it is under the glaze; fake marks will disappear. This procedure should not be used on unglazed pieces. Visual examination is the best way to identify a fake mark on an unglazed item.

Damaged pieces have little value unless the item is extremely rare. Focus on pieces well made and nicely decorated. There are many inferior examples.

From the beginning of the American occupation of Japan until April 28, 1952, objects made in that country were marked "Japan," "Made in Japan," "Occupied Japan," or "Made in Occupied Japan." Only pieces marked with the last two designations are of major interest to Occupied Japan collectors. The first two marks also were used during other time periods.

Ashtray, frog, ceramic, sitting on lily pad, 5" l, 3" w, 2-1/2" h **30.00**
Basket, china, miniature, floral dec **9.00**
Box, cov, inlaid, dog motif **15.00**
Children's play dishes, Blue Willow, 18-pc set **375.00**
Cigarette box, cov, china, rect, blue floral dec, gold trim **15.00**
Cigarette set, plated metal, cov box, Scottie dog dec, matching lighter **20.00**
Clicker, beetle, silver colored **5.00**
Clock, bisque, dancing couple in colonial garb, floral encrusted case, 10-1/2" h **250.00**

Box, covered, round, black ground, pink and white florals, row of orange flowers, green foliage, multicolored bird in center, 10" d, **$15**.

Coaster set, papier-mâché box, floral dec, price for six-pc set **18.00**
Coffee set, 7-3/4" h coffee pot, creamer, sugar, six cups and saucers, white ground, pink flowers **165.00**
Compass, pocket-watch shape **20.00**
Cornucopia, china, white, pink roses, gold trim **35.00**
Crumb tray, metal, emb New York scenes **10.00**
Demitasse cup and saucer, white, yellow and red flowers **10.00**
Dinnerware set
Royal Embassy Wheeling, mkd "Made in Japan Royal Embassy China Wheeling, Made in Occupied Japan," 55 pcs, never used **400.00**
Rutland pattern, 83 pcs **900.00**
Doll, celluloid, baby wearing snowsuit, jointed **40.00**
Figure
1-1/4" x 5", farm girl with scarf, egg basket beside her, red mark **15.00**
3" h, Colonial lady, red stamped mark **12.00**
3-3/4" h, metal, cowboy on rearing horse **15.00**
4-1/4" h, girl with milk pails **17.50**
4-3/4" h, ballerina, bisque.............. **35.00**
5" h, jumping horses..................... **12.00**
5-1/2" h, lady seated in chair, reading sheet music................................... **15.00**
6" h, 2" w, man............................. **25.00**
7" x 4-1/2", couple........................ **35.00**
8" h, 3-1/2" w, man holding flower.. **40.00**
9" h, Colonial lady, sitting on bench, holding fan, multicolored clothing, base mkd **125.00**
9-1/2" h, Colonial gentleman playing violin, base mkd........................... **120.00**

9-1/2" h, Colonial woman playing accordion, base mkd **120.00**
Harmonica, Butterfly, orig box **17.50**
Head vase, Oriental girl, china **18.00**
Honey jar, bee hive, bee finial **25.00**
Incense burner, woman **20.00**
Lantern, 4-1/2" h, owl motif **35.00**
Mat, hooked, 4-1/4" d, cream center, brown, teal, and green border with three daisy-like flowers, orig label **20.00**

Figure, three puppies in basket, tan, gray and brown, 2-7/8" w, 2-1/2" h, **$12**

Miniature, cups and saucers, 1-5/8" h quatrefoil cup, hand painted cobalt blue, peach, and iron red Imari type design, gilt Imari flower and fan dec, 1-1/8" h saki cup, quatrefoil saucer, each pc stamped with cursive black H, curved green twig, iron-red cursive Hokutosha, black manuscript "Made in Occupied Japan," c1945 .... **135.00**
Napkin, damask, orig paper labels, price for set of six **45.00**
Necklace, pearls, double strand, orig paper label **12.00**
Nodder, celluloid, figural, elephant, white body, green and gold trim, 3-1/2" l, 2-1/2" h **25.00**
Noise maker, horn, gold **25.00**
Perfume bottle, glass, blue, 4" h **15.00**
Piano baby, hp **65.00**
Pincushion, metal, grand-piano shape, red velvet cushion **15.00**
Planter, figural
Baby booties, blue trim **9.00**
Cat, sitting up **15.00**
Dog, with basket **18.00**
Donkey pulling cart **12.00**
Dragon with cherub riding its back, peach and lime green on white ground, bisque, mkd **95.00**
Regal Carriage **22.50**
Plate
Cabin Scene, chickens in yard **18.00**
Cherries, lacy edge **25.00**
Gold Castle pattern, set of six .. **165.00**
Platter, Courley pattern, heavy gold trim
.... **30.00**

Powder jar, cov, Wedgwood style, blue and white, 3" d **15.00**
Range set, figural red tomatoes, 3-5/8" h salt and pepper shakers, 5-1/4" h cov grease jar, applied leaf handles, mkd "Made in Occupied Japan," and a circle with "K" **125.00**
Salt and pepper shakers, pr
Boy and girl sitting on bench, orig cork stoppers, mkd **95.00**
Coolies, orig box **25.00**
Hat, one brown, one black **20.00**
Mammy and Chef **185.00**
Pigs, large ears **18.00**
Shelf sitter, Little Boy Blue **18.00**
Silent butler, metal **15.00**
Stein, man and woman with dog, 8-1/2" h
.... **40.00**
Tape measure, pig, stamped "Occupied Japan" **45.00**
Teapot, 6-3/4" h, individual size, chocolate brown mirror glaze **20.00**
Tea set, china
Black high gloss ground, delicate gold, pink, and black rose dec, angular handles, 5" h teapot, 3-1/4" h creamer, 3-1/2" h cov sugar, mkd "Made in Occupied Japan" and M with T superimposed over circle **125.00**
Moriage Dragonware, 7-1/2" h teapot with dragon head spout, dragon head finial, body curves down side of pot, three 2" h cups with lithophane of Geisha girl in bottom, three 5-1/4" d saucers, six 7" d dessert plates **225.00**
Toby mug, General Douglas MacArthur, 4" h, mkd **100.00**
Toothpick holder, puppy in barrel **20.00**
Toy
Clown, litho tin wind-up, celluloid face and shoes, walks on hands, non-working
.... **110.00**
Hopping dog, windup **27.50**
Walrus, wind-up black plush fabric, white plastic tusks, black beaded eyes, 4-1/2" l, 3-1/2" h **90.00**
Tray, rect, papier mâché, black ground, gold floral dec **8.00**
Vase, 9-1/4" h, 4-3/4" w, brown ground, lighter brown leaves and bulbs, greenish-blue shading and swirls, mkd "Made in Occupied Japan" **125.00**
Wall plaque, 5" w, 6-1/2" h, unglazed, pastel scene of man holding musical string instrument, woman dancing **135.00**
Writing set, 7-1/2" l, 5-1/4" w, 2-1/4" h, painted metal box, two small lacquered wood box inside, stone wrist rest, metal box mkd "Made by Hand in Occupied Japan, Basuni, Patented Lacquerware, Metal Base" **400.00**

Ocean Liner Collectibles

History: Transoceanic travel falls into two distinct periods—the era of the great Clipper ships and the era of the diesel-powered ocean liners. The latter craft reached their golden age between 1900 and 1940.

An ocean liner is a city unto itself. Most have their own printing rooms to produce a wealth of daily memorabilia. Companies, such as Cunard and Holland-America, encourage passengers to acquire souvenirs with the company logo and ship's name. Word-of-mouth is a principal form of advertising.

Certain ships acquired a unique mystic. The *Queen Elizabeth, Queen Mary,* and *United States* became symbols of elegance and style. Today the cruise ship dominates the world of the ocean liner.

Collecting Hints: Don't concentrate only on ships of American registry, although many collectors try to gather material from only one liner or ship line. Objects associated with ships involved in disasters, such as the *Titanic,* often command higher prices.

Reverse painting on glass, Titanic, some mica and foil highlights, ornate gold frame, **$75.**

Advertisement, framed, *Normandie* and *Ile de France,* Lafayette, Paris, and Champlain, NY Times May 31, 1936 color adv describing arrival of ships, 16" x 21" **250.00**

Ashtray, 5" d, *Normandie,* porcelain, transatlantic map view, crackle finish **275.00**

Baggage tag, French Line, first class, unused **7.50**

Belt buckle, *RMS Queen Elizabeth II,* Cunard Line, chrome plated solid brass, black outline of ship, name in red .. **15.00**

Birthday candle holder set, *SS Pleasure Cruise,* 5" l boat, three 2" l boats, hand carved, hand dec, each mkd "Japan," c1950 .... **5.00**

Booklet

Independence, American Export Lines, 1966 Gala Springtime Cruise, itinerary and deck plan inserts **24.00**

White Star Line, sailing list, 1933 ... **40.00**

Bottle opener, *RS Queen Mary,* ship floats in handle **30.00**

Brochure

Cunard and Anchor-Donaldson Line, Canadian Service, *The Historic St. Lawrence River Route to Europe,* late 1920s **7.50**

Cunard Line, *Getting There is Half the Fun,* 16 pgs, 1952 .... **6.00**

Empress of Japan, Transatlantic sailings, 1930-31 .... **10.00**

Italian Line, *Six Cruises to the Mediterranean and Egypt,* 1934 .... **12.00**

Cigarette lighter, *RMS Queen Mary* .. **32.00**

Coffee cup, *SS United States* **32.00**

Compact, *Empress of Canada,* Canadian Pacific Line, Stratton, line flag logo, ship's name in enameled front medallion **40.00**

Cruise book, *Scythia,* 1929 .... **40.00**

Deck card, Concordia Lines, *Norway* **18.00**

Dish, *RMS Queen Mary,* Cunard Line, ceramic, 5" l, oval, color portrait, gold edge, Staffordshire **37.50**

Display, Mediterranean *Americhe,* 1927, easel back, artwork by Riccobaldi **165.00**

Excursion announcement, SS Cuba **20.00**

Goblet, *RMS Queen Elizabeth II,* Cunard Line, souvenir, etched image and name, manufactured by Stuart Crystal, #1305 .... **225.00**

Illustration, framed

Le Paquebot Normandie Le Harve, engineering specs given in French, 1936, 11-1/2" x 24" **250.00**

Nord-Lloyd Bremen, at sea, 1932, 5-1/2" x 7-1/2" image, acid free mat, orig tourist class stateroom sticker on reverse, dated 12/9/32 .... **125.00**

R.M.S. Queen Elizabeth, stern view, 12" x 15-1/2" image with slight wrinkling to upper portion, 1940s vintage 18-1/2" x 22-1/2" frame **150.00**

Key chain, *Carnival,* Lucite, ship photo **4.00**

Letter opener, *HMS Liverpool,* silver, enamel dec, 1921 .... **75.00**

Medal, *Normandie CGT,* bronze, given to passengers on maiden voyage, Le Harve to New York, June, 1935, designed by Jean Vernon, 2-1/2" d **300.00**

Puzzle, Victory Constructional Puzzle of Union Castle Liner, 100+ pieces, complete, original box, **$175**.

Menu

Grace Line, *SS Santa Rose,* dinner, June 18, 1964 .... **5.00**
Ile de France, July 12, 1938, dinner . **5.00**
RMS Caronia, breakfast, Aug. 2, 1950, one-page card **6.00**
SS Leonardo Da Vinci, January 1973 .... **6.00**
SS Lurline, Matson Lines, Commodore's Dinner, March 3, 1959, 12" x 9" **20.00**
SS Manhattan, United States Lines, 6" x 10", four pgs, 1933, dinner, cream-colored cover with Arch of Triumph, deckled edges **7.50**

Newspaper

RMS Caronia, Ocean Times, Aug. 1, 1950, four pgs **10.00**
RMS Queen Mary, May 10, 1950, 12 pgs **15.00**

Note paper

Cunard *White Star,* blue **5.00**
M/S Osloofjord, two color views of ship **6.00**
RMS Queen Mary, beige **6.50**

Passenger list

RMS Aquitania, full-color illus of ship **50.00**
SS Leviathan, 1924 .... **15.00**
St. Louis, American Line, eastbound trip, Feb. 10, 1906 .... **35.00**
Passport cover, Red Star Line, fabric, ship illus **27.50**
Photograph, *Normandie,* sepia, engineering specifications in French, 9-1/4" x 18-1/2" custom frame **300.00**

Pinback button

Cunard Line Servia, 7/8" d, black and white ship, pale green ocean, pale blue and white skies, black text, Whitehead & Hoag back paper, c1896-98 .... **15.00**

Cunard Line Steamship Campania, 7/8" d, black and white ship, pale green ocean, pale blue and white skies, black text, Whitehead & Hoag back paper, c1896-98 .... **15.00**
French Line La Normandie, 7/8" d, black and white ship, pale green ocean, pale blue and white skies, black text, Whitehead & Hoag back paper, c1896-98 .... **15.00**
French Line Steamship La Bretagne, 7/8" d, black and white ship, pale green ocean, pale blue and white skies, black text, Whitehead & Hoag back paper, c1896-98 .... **15.00**
Great Eastern, 7/8" d, black and white ship, pale green ocean, pale blue and white skies, black text, no back paper, c1896-98 .... **12.00**
Great Lakes, C & B Line, 1-3/4" d, multicolored steamship, wavy lake waters, red and white loco, black smoke from single stack, blue and white clouds, red text "The Flyer Of The Lakes Connecting Cleveland And Buffalo While You Sleep," Whitehead & Hoag back paper, c1900-12 .... **100.00**
Hamburg American Line Normannia, 7/8" d, black and white ship, pale green ocean, pale blue and white skies, black text, no back paper, c1896-98 .... **12.00**
White Star Line Britannic, 7/8" d, black and white ship, pale green ocean, pale blue and white skies, black text, Whitehead & Hoag back paper, c1896-98 .... **12.00**
White Star Line Majestic, 7/8" d, black and white ship, pale green ocean, pale blue and white skies, black text, American Pepsin Gum Co. back paper, c1896-98 .... **15.00**
Pocket mirror, *Queen Mary,* sepia photo, New York harbor scene, c1930 ...... **75.00**

Postcard

Berengaria, Cunard Line, color horizontal view **12.00**
California, twin screw steamship, pre-1930 color **10.00**
Caronia, Cunard Line, color horizontal view, 1967, used **8.00**
City of Washington, Wilson Line Steamer, black and white, pre-1930, descriptive paragraph on reverse, unused **10.00**
Europa, North German Lloyd Line, color, reverse with stats, 1966, used **7.50**
Italia, color horizontal, at sea, pre-1950, unused **15.00**
Leviathan, leaving New York City, color horizontal, pub by Union News Co., pre-1940, unused **10.00**
Malolo/Matson, Oceanic Route from California to Hawaii, color linen, 1935, used **10.00**

New Amsterdam, Holland America Line, color horizontal, postally used, 1957 **8.00**
New Mauertenia, Cunard White Star Line, color horizontal, reverse with stats, launched 1938, maiden voyage 1939 .... **12.00**
Normandie/Queen Mary/Queen Elizabeth, linen, bird's eye view of ships docked in New York City harbor **12.00**
Panama Line, Frederick Hopstz illus, "Short Route" cancellation, 1950s.... **7.50**
Saxoma Ocean Liner, real photo, stamped "Copyright & published by Real Photograpgrahs Co., Ltd.," unused . **8.00**
Steamer Eastern States, D & C Navigation Co., horizontal black and white, pre-1920................................ **12.00**
Steamer Peter Stuyvestant, Hudson River Day Line, black and white, 1947, used **7.00**
Steamship America, black and white, pre-1920, imprinted "Issued By The Jewish Welfare Board To Soldiers & Sailors Of the US Army & Navy," unused **18.00**
Steamship Columbia, color, shows single stack, pre-1920 .... **8.00**
Steamship Santa Clara, Grace Lines, real photo.. **10.00**
Steamship Tionesta, Anchor Line, private mailing card, used **10.00**
Poster, Grace Line, Caribbean, 1949 C Evers, illus of tourists, ship, cars, and boats, 23" x 30"............................ **200.00**
Race card, Cunard White Star
RMS Caronia **8.00**
RMS Queen Mary........................... **10.00**
Razor towel, Cunard White Star, paper **5.00**

Ashtray, SS Argentina, Moore-McCormick Lines, brass, marked "Made in Switzerland," 5-1/2" d, $38.

Stationery

RMS Queen Mary, Cunard Line, note paper, matching envelope, color portrait, line, and ship name, 5" x 7"............. **15.00**

Royal Mail Steamer, two sheets of paper, matching envelope......................... **20.00**
Sylvania, Cunard Line, beige, color portrait, line, and ship name, 5-1/4" x 6-3/4"... **8.00**
Steamer directory, Clyde-Mallory Lines, c1920 .... **12.00**
Tea set, Cunard steamship, Art Deco cube shape, cov teapot, two salts, two sugars, creamer, sherbet, two teacups, cereal bowl, two salad plates, luncheon plate, three saucers, two demitasse saucers **850.00**
Ticket folio, Cunard Line, c1928........ **50.00**
Tie clasp, Cunard Line *RMS Queen Mary,* gold tone, red, white, and blue enameled ship.. **20.00**
Timetable, Monticello Steamship Co, "On the Bay of San Francisco," 1907 ... **65.00**
Tin, *US Bremen* at sea on front panel, 1930s **50.00**

Olympics Collectibles

History: Organized amateur sports games originated in ancient Greece. The games were held every four years beginning about 776 B.C. At first running events were the only type held, but many different events have been added over the years. The Olympics as we know them were revived in Athens about 1896. After that date the games were held in a different city around the world every four years. The number of participants, competing nations, and events have increased steadily.

Women were first allowed to participate in the games in 1912. The winter games began in 1924 and were held on a four-year schedule until 1992 when they were rescheduled so that they would alternate at a two-year interval with the more traditional summer games.

Collecting Hints: Collectors of Olympic materials should remember that the Olympic Games have been a multi-language event. Collectors may not wish to limit their collections to English-only examples. The other important fact to remember is that the more recent the Olympiad, the greater the number of items that have survived. Items from the 1996 Olympics have not yet reached the secondary market, but things from 1988 are beginning to surface. More collectibles tend to enter the antiques and collectibles marketplace during the years the games are scheduled, creating more interest in this fast-growing field.

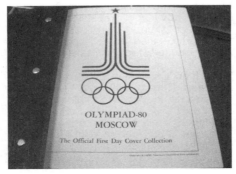

Olympics Stamp book, red and black cover, titled "Olympiad-80 Moscow, Official First Day Cover Collection," copyright 1978, Paramont International Coin Co., $95.

Badge
>   1980 Winter Olympics, 2-1/2" d, celluloid, color image of mascot raccoon as hockey player, white ground, black letters **20.00**
>   Los Angeles 1984 Olympics, 1-1/8" x 2-1/4", red, white, and blue star.. **10.00**

Barbie, Mattel
>   Barbie as Olympic gymnast, 1995, NRFB **20.00**
>   Barbie and Ken as African-American Olympic skaters, #18727, released 1998 .... **25.00**

Beer can, 1996 Summer Olympic Set, Budweiser, sports include biking, baseball, soccer, boxing, and basketball, Olympic facts and history, cans carefully opened, price for five-can set **20.00**

Book, *Sarajevo 1984 Winter Olympics* **12.00**

Bowl, Campbell Kids, 1984 Sarajevo **12.00**

Cabbage Patch doll, 1996 Olympic set, tennis player with black hair and green eyes, four smaller female athletes, price for set of five in orig box.................. **30.00**

Calendar, 1992, Coca-Cola................... **5.00**

Cigarette lighter, 1976, Montreal........ **12.00**

Cookie jar, cov, Olympic Tunes, Warner Brothers, 14" h, MIB **100.00**

Doll, 1980 Winter Olympics raccoon mascot, Chiquita, 14" h, stuffed cloth, gray, black, and white face, blue body, orange gloves, skating boots, separate white vinyl racing bib pullover vest, orig stitched tag with licensing authorization, Chase Bag Co. **40.00**

Fan, Tenth Olympic Games/1932/Los Angeles, folding paper type, balsa sticks, chapel building illus, Olympic symbol, Japan **40.00**

Gasoline truck, Texaco, 1996 Olympics dec, MIB.. **30.00**

Glass, 5-1/2" h, 1932 Olympics, clear, frosted white picture **50.00**

Key chain, 1984, Los Angeles **6.50**

License plate holder, 1932, aluminum, two athletes holding the world, "Los Angeles" in raised letters **150.00**

Magazine, *Sports Illustrated*, Sept. 5, 1960, Rome Olympics Ceremonies........... **7.50**

Map, 1960, Rome Olympics, 6" x 10" folder opens to 10 x 35", eight color maps on both sides, Automobile Club of Italy sponsor **15.00**

Pamphlet, 1936 Berlin **80.00**

Paperweight, 1992, Coca-Cola McDonald's **12.00**

Pennant, 1968 Mexico, felt................. **24.00**

Pin
>   1928, Olympic Fund, red, and white enameled brass, miniature shield, sold for 50¢ to help defray expenses of American team, orig card **25.00**
>   1932, Los Angeles Xth Olympiad 1932, 3/8" h, silver luster, red, and blue enamel shield.. **24.00**
>   1964, Innsbruck Winter Olympics, Austrian made, black, white, and red accent enamels, gold finish **65.00**
>   1980, Moscow Olympics, figural mascot bear as soccer player, blue, white, and brown enamels, gold luster............ **20.00**
>   1980, Moscow Olympics, official symbol flanked by deep red porcelain enamel under Russian inscription, gold luster **15.00**
>   1980 Summer Olympics, 23 kt yg 1980 Olympic postage stamp replicas of swimming, issued by Westport Mint, orig card, MOC **10.00**
>   1984, Calgary Winter Olympics, official symbols in five colors, white ground, double needle post and clutch fasteners **8.00**
>   1984, Los Angeles Olympics, Fuji, domed acrylic on metal, symbolic cartoon US eagle holding Olympic torch, needle post and clutch fastener **10.00**
>   1988, Seoul Summer Olympics, domed acrylic, three enamel colors, gold luster, needle post and clutch fastener **5.00**
>   1992, Albertville Winter Olympics, CBS, domed acrylic, gold luster, white enamel, tiny Olympic rings in five colors **5.00**
>   1996, Atlanta Olympics pre-event promotion pin, cartoon baseball player, four colors, gold above bar inscription "Atlanta 1996/1000 Days/October 23, 1993" **10.00**
>   1996, Balfour................................. **20.00**

Page from Olympics stamp book, showing FDC for Judo and accompanying text card, **$95.**

Pinback button

Barcelona '92, 1-1/2" d, color accents at top, Olympic rings in five colors, 1988 copyright.. **10.00**
Swimming-Games-Athletics, 1-1/4" d, real photo of children's class, white uniforms, text "YMCA West Side Department 1515 W Monroe St., Chicago, Ill," early 1900s
.... **50.00**

Pin display, 1988 Olympics, 1-3/4" x 6" x 8" cover box, wooden display frame, high gloss finish, very dark mahogany enamel, frame holds recessed glass over gold luster metal title plate identifying Jeep as official sponsor of U. S. Olympic team, five different jeep pins comprising limited edition set **30.00**

Plate, 7" d, 1968, gold leaf, Mexico and torch dec **60.00**

Postcard

1912 Stockholm Olympics, black and white photo **30.00**
1936, view of Berlin Olympics, Olympic cancel **15.50**
1988, Korea, Coca-Cola, set #1 .... **7.50**

Program, 1996 Centennial Olympic Games, July 19-Aug. 4, 1996, 10-1/2" l, 9" w **32.00**

Smurf, Olympic outfit.......................... **40.00**

Souvenir dish, 7-1/4" d, Munich 72, porcelain, mkd "Made in Denmark, #8000/9472, First Issue" **40.00**

Stadium cushion, 11" x 13-1/2", 1956 Summer Olympics, red vinyl, yellow, white, and blue Olympics logo **48.00**

Statue, 5" h, bronzed white metal with patina, 1900-20 athlete **75.00**

Stickpin

1940, sterling-like silvered metal, Helsinki, Finland, torch flame under Olympics rings symbol, above 1940 date
.... **80.00**
1964, silvered metal, Tokyo, rings above Olympic symbol **35.00**

1972, gold luster, Sapporo, winter, red, white, and blue enamels **30.00**
1978, gold luster, Innsbruck, winter, red and blue enamels, blue ground..... **25.00**
1980, Moscow Olympics, miniature Gold Olympics rings under miniature image of Soviet flag, dark red porcelain enamel accents **18.00**

Sweater, shooter's, NRA International Team Tryouts, 1972 Olympics, light green ribbed wool, zipper front, shoulder shooting pad, deep pockets, red, yellow, blue, and white NRA patches **60.00**

Token, 1984 Olympiad, Los Angeles, transit fare set, designed by N. Harris, orig 7" x 11" case **30.00**

Toy, 1992 Olympic Bobsled Run, wooden replica, 1-1/2" h x 2" w x 8-1/2" l, wire handgrip rail and bumper bar, two front skis swivel left and right, driver unit inscribed "U.S.A.," thumb tack steering wheel, Olympic symbols on riding surface **200.00**

Tray, 1976 Olympics, Montreal, litho metal, Coca-Cola adv............................... **40.00**

Venue guide, staff, 1996.................... **12.00**

Owl Collectibles

History: Owls have existed on earth for more than 60 million years. They have been used as a decorative motif since before Christ. An owl and Athena appeared on an ancient Greek coin.

Every culture has superstitions surrounding the owl. Some believe the owl represented good luck, others viewed it as an evil omen. The owl has remained a popular symbol in Halloween material.

Of course, the owl's wisdom is often attached to scholarly pursuits. Expanding this theme, the National Park Service uses Woodsey to "Give A Hoot, Don't Pollute."

Collecting Hints: If you collect the "creature of the night" or the "wise old owl," any page of this book might conceivably contain a related object since the owl theme can be found in hundreds of collectible categories, including advertising trade cards, books, buttons, and postcards, to name a few.

Don't confine yourself just to old or antique owls. Owl figurines, owl themes on limited edition collectors' plates, and handcrafted items from modern artisans are plentiful. There are many examples available in every price range.

Limited edition collector's plate, Screech Owls, 1977, Hutschenreuther, Germany, John A. Ruthorn, artist, **$7.50**.

Ashtray, 3-1/2" d, crystal, gold top edge trim, multicolored owl in center, Viking Glass paper label, 1960s.................. **5.00**

Bank, bright green plastic applied eyes, log base titled "Be Wise Save," mkd "Logsdon," 6" h, orig stopper missing **10.00**

Blotter, "Whoo? Oswald, I told you we couldn't get away with that bone!," two puppies under a tree, owl sitting on branch, Harry N. Johnson, Real Estate & Insurance, Highlands, NJ **10.00**

Book

An Owl Came To Stay, Clair Rome, Crown Pub., NY, 1980.................... **7.50**

Owls in the Family, Farley Mowat, Little, Brown & Co., 1961 .... **10.00**

Bookends, pr

Brass, Frankart............................. **135.00**

Bronze, head, sgd "M Carr" **120.00**

Book rack, expanding......................... **55.00**

Box, cov, Limoges, France, owl on cover, small rocks painted on inside **175.00**

Calendar plate, 1912, owl on open book, Berlin, NE....................................... **45.00**

Calling card tray, 8-1/2" x 7", quadruple plate, emb music staff and "Should Owl's Acquaintance Be Forgot," two owls sitting on back of tray................................ **85.00**

Candy container, owl on branch **50.00**

Clock, 6-1/2" h, wood, hand carved . **100.00**

Coal hood, brass, figural.................. **300.00**

Desk set, metal, letter holder, book rack, note spike, letter opener, envelope holder, inkwell, blotter, four blotter corners, sgd "CV" **650.00**

Figure

3" h, pottery, Winnie the Pooh owl, Beswick Walt Disney series, 1968-1990 .... **125.00**

4" h, porcelain, Karl Ens Factory.... **80.00**

4-1/2" h, porcelain, Cybis **90.00**

7-1/2" h, 6" w, porcelain, pair of naturalistic colored owls perched upon books **75.00**

Jigsaw puzzle, child's, Milton Bradley, 25 pieces, **$4**.

Inkwell, figural, Noritake **125.00**

Lamp, candle, 5-1/4", snow white china, owl shaped shade, stump shaped base, fitted candleholder, mkd "R S Germany" **225.00**

Letter opener, brass......................... **25.00**

Limited edition plate, Goebel, Wildlife Series, barn owl, 1976................... **25.00**

Mask, papier-mâché, c1915.............. **90.00**

Match holder

2-/12" h, dark green, Wetzel Glass Co **8.00**

8" h, 3" w, metal, hanging type....... **18.00**

Medal

Leeds International Exhibition, 1890, 2-1/4", metal, white bust of Queen Victoria on one side **25.00**

Natural History Society of Montreal, 1-3/4", bronze, cast, owl with branch in beak **20.00**

Mustard jar, cov, 5" h, milk glass, screw top, glass insert, Atterbury **165.00**

Napkin ring, standing owl, silver-plated **150.00**

Owl Drug Co.

Bottle, 3-1/2" h, cork top, clear, Oil of Sweet Almond label, 1 oz................. **5.00**

Shot Glass, one wing..................... **17.50**

Soda Bottle, 9-1/2" h, blob top, teal green, two wings, San Francisco **50.00**

P

Paper Dolls

History: The origin of the paper doll can be traced back to the jumping jacks (pantins) of Europe. By the 19th century, boxed or die-cut sheets of paper dolls were available featuring famous dancers, opera stars, performers such as Jenny Lind, and many general subjects. Raphael Tuck began to produce ornate dolls in series form in the 1880s in England.

The advertising industry turned to paper dolls to sell products. Early magazines, such as *Ladies' Home Journal*, *Good Housekeeping*, and *McCall's*, used paper doll inserts. Children's publications, like *Jack and Jill*, picked up the practice.

Cardboard-covered paper doll books first appeared and were mass-marketed in the 1920s. Lowe, Merrill, Saalfield, and Whitman were the leading publishers. The 1940s saw the advent of paper doll books featuring celebrities drawn from screen and radio, and later from television. A few comic characters, such as Brenda Starr, also made it to paper doll fame.

By the 1950s, paper doll books were less popular and production decreased. Modern books are either politically or celebrity oriented.

Collecting Hints: Most paper dolls that are collected are in uncut books, on intact sheets, or in boxed sets. Cut sets are priced at 50 percent of an uncut set, providing all dolls, clothing, and accessories are still present.

Many paper doll books have been reprinted. An identical reprint has just slightly less value than the original. If the dolls have been redrawn, the price is reduced significantly.

Ancient Egyptian Costumes **12.00**
Archie, boxed set, played with condition
.... **45.00**
Baby Sister and Baby Brother Dolls, Merrill, uncut **10.00**
Baby Sparkle Plenty, Saalfield, 1948, uncut
.... **60.00**
Ballerina Barbie, Whitman, uncut **12.00**

Ballet, Nanceie Swanberg................... **8.00**
Barbie, uncut book............................ **15.00**
Betsy McCall, Easter Surprise, uncut magazine page **14.00**
Cara & Curtis, Mattel, 1975, 10" dolls, cut, played with condition **6.00**

Esther Williams, Merrill Co., 1953, $25.

Children from Other Lands, Whitman, 1961, unused................................ **20.00**
Cinderella Steps Out, Lowe, 1948, uncut
.... **20.00**
Crissy, Whitman, 1970, uncut, mint.... **65.00**
Deanna Durbin, Merrill, 1940, uncut, mint
.... **375.00**
Dionne Quintuplets, cut **75.00**
Dollies to Paint, Cut Out, and Dress, Saalfield, 1920s, six dolls, some pages neatly colored **85.00**
Doris Day, Whitman, 1956, uncut....... **60.00**
Drayton Paper Doll, uncut
   Alice, two outfits............................ **12.00**
   Anna, three outfits........................ **10.00**
   Baby and Baby Doll, three outfits
   .... **15.00**
   Betty, two outfits............................ **12.00**
   Fido, five outfits............................ **10.00**
   Fred, two outfits **15.00**
   Harriet, three outfits **15.00**
   Jane, four outfits **15.00**
   Kitty, six outfits **12.00**
   Phyllis, four outfits **10.00**
Dude Ranch, Saalfield, 11" x 14", unused
.... **18.00**
Family Affair, 1968, orig box............. **12.50**
Fun Farm, #1729, Saalfield, Dime Line, c1940, unpunched, orig envelope
.... **18.00**
Girl Friends, Whitman, 1944, uncut, mint
.... **150.00**

Girl Scouts, Brownies, c1950, MIB **.... 40.00**
Happy Bride, Whitman, 1967, uncut
.... **20.00**
Heidi and Peter, Saalfield, 1960s, six pgs, 8-1/4" x 11-3/4", uncut **15.00**
Indians, Artcraft series, Saalfield, 10-1/2" x 12-1/2", uncut **18.00**
Janet Leigh, Lowe, album #2405, 1957, some pages neatly cut **20.00**
Janet Lennon, Whitman, 1959, some uncut pages.. **45.00**
Judy Holiday Paperdolls, Saalfield, #159110, 1954, 11" x 12", uncut..... **45.00**
Laugh-In, uncut **35.00**
Lennon Sisters, Whitman, copyright 1958, 9" x 12", neatly cut **28.00**
Liberty Fair Dressing Doll, Miss Liberty cardboard doll, flags on wood stick, cut, c1900, 7" x 13" blue and white box
.... **65.00**
Little Lulu, boxed **25.00**
Little Miss America, Saalfield, uncut
.... **20.00**
Little Women, 1981, uncut.................. **12.00**
Loretta Young Paper Dolls and Coloring Book, uncut........................... **50.00**
Majorette Paper Dolls, Saalfield, 1957, uncut **10.00**
Malibu Francie, Whitman, uncut........ **12.00**
Malibu Skipper, Whitman, 1973 .... **17.50**
Mardi Gras, King and Queen Statuette Dolls and Costumes, Saalfield, 1955, cut, orig folder, repairs to Queen **50.00**
Mary Martin, Saalfield, #365, copyright 1944, 10-1/2" x 12-1/2", uncut........ **48.00**
Millie the Model................................. **10.00**
Nancy, Whitman, 1971, uncut **40.00**
Nanny and the Professor, Saalfield, 1970, uncut **15.00**

Ballet Dancers, Merrill Co., #3497, 1947, $22.

Nursery Rhyme, Hallmark, uncut **27.50**
Nutcracker Ballet, Tom Tierney, full color, 1981, uncut **15.00**
Pat and Pru, 1958............................. **15.50**
Pat Boone, Whitman, 1959, some pages uncut **45.00**
Patty Duke Paper Doll Book, punch-out type, 1964, partially used.............. **20.00**
Playhouse Dolls, Stephens Co., 1949, uncut **20.00**
Pope John Paul II, Tom Tierney, Dover, 1984, 9" x 12", uncut...................... **10.00**
Raggedy Ann & Andy Paper Dolls Book, Saalfield, 1944, Johnny Gruelle Co., four pgs of clothes **50.00**
Ricky Nelson, Whitman, 1959, uncut
.... **150.00**
Rosemary Clooney, Bonnie Book, 1958, uncut **70.00**
Roy Roger & Dale Evans, Roy Rogers Enterprises and Whitman Publishing, 1953, two Roys, two Dales, 40 outfits and accessories, cut, orig cover with some wear.. **150.00**
Secret Garden **15.50**
Shari Lewis, Saalfield, 1958, uncut
.... **20.00**
Shirley Temple, uncut....................... **18.50**
Skipper, Whitman, boxed, uncut **12.00**
Snow White, Whitman, 1972 copyright, 10" x 12-3/4", stiff paper full-color covers, six glossy pages of outfits, uncut
.... **30.00**
Sonny and Sue, Lowe Co., copyright 1940, 10-1/4" x 13-1/2", uncut **15.00**
Southern Belles **14.50**
Sports Time, Whitman, 1952, uncut
.... **20.00**
Storybook Kiddle, Mattel, Whitman
.... **15.75**
Tammy/Pepper Paper Dolls, Whitman, 1966, authorized by Ideal, uncut, mint
.... **125.00**
Teen Time Dolls, Whitman, early 1950s, 7" x 10-1/2" box, neatly cut................... **15.00**
That Girl Paper Doll, Saalfield, 1967 uncut
.... **135.00**
The Nutcracker Ballet, Cut and Assemble Toy Theater by Tom Tierney, 1981, Dover, unused **15.00**
Tiny Tots Paper Dolls, Whitma, 1959, uncut
.... **50.00**
Tru-Life Paper Dolls, Milton Bradley, 1914, one large and one small doll, orig folder and instruction booklet
.... **85.00**
Tubsy, Whitman, 1968........................ **35.00**
Tuesday Weld, Saalfield, 1960, orig box, unused **60.00**
Twins Around The World.................... **7.50**
Vivien Leigh, uncut............................ **15.00**
Walt Disney's Snow White, 1972 ...... **15.50**
Wedding Party, Saalfield, 1951, uncut
.... **20.00**

Pennsbury Pottery

History: In 1950, Henry and Lee Below established Pennsbury Pottery, named for its close proximity to William Penn's estate "Pennsbury," three miles west of Morrisville, Pennsylvania. Henry, a ceramic engineer and mold maker, and Lee, a designer and modeler, had previously worked for Stangl Pottery in Trenton, New Jersey.

Many of Pennsbury's forms, motifs, and manufacturing techniques have Stangl roots. A line of birds similar to those produced by Stangl were among the earliest Pennsbury products. The carved-design technique is also of Stangl origin; high bas-relief molds are not.

Most Pennsbury products are easily identified by their brown-wash background. The company also made pieces featuring other background colors so do not make the mistake of assuming that a piece is not Pennsbury if it does not have a brown wash.

Pennsbury motifs are heavily nostalgic, often farm- or Pennsylvania German-related. Among the most popular lines were Amish, Black Rooster, Delft Toleware, Eagle, Family, Folkart, Gay Ninety, Harvest, Hex, Quartet, Red Barn, Red Rooster, Slick-Chick, and Christmas plates (1960-1970). The pottery made a large number of commemorative, novelty, and special-order pieces.

In the late 1950s, the company had 16 employees, mostly local housewives and young girls. By 1963, at the company's peak, there were 46 employees. Cheap foreign imports cut deeply into the pottery's profits, and by the late 1960s, just over 20 employees remained.

Marks differ from piece to piece depending on the person who signed it or the artist who sculpted the mold. Some initials still have not been identified.

Henry Below died on Dec. 21, 1959, leaving the pottery in trust for his wife and three children with instructions that it be sold upon the death of his wife. She died on Dec. 12, 1968, and in October 1970 the Pennsbury Pottery filed for bankruptcy. The contents were auctioned off on Dec. 18, 1970. On May 18, 1971, a fire destroyed the pottery and support buildings.

Collecting Hints: Concentrate on one pattern or type. Since the wares were hand carved, aesthetic quality differs from piece to piece. Look for those with a strong design sense and a high quality of execution.

Buy only clearly marked pieces. Look for decorator and designer initials that can be easily identified.

Pennsbury collectors are concentrated in the Middle Atlantic states. Many of the company's commemorative and novelty pieces relate to businesses and events in that region, thus commanding the highest prices when sold within that area.

Look-Alike Alert: The Lewis Brothers Pottery, Trenton, New Jersey, purchased 50 of the Pennsbury molds. Although they were supposed to remove the Pennsbury name from the molds, this was not done in all instances. Further, two Pennsbury employees moved to Lewis Brothers when Pennsbury closed, helping to produce a number of pieces that are reminiscent of Pennsbury's products. Many of Pennsbury's major lines, including the Harvest and Rooster patterns, plaques, birds, and highly unusual molds, were not reproduced.

Glen View, Langhorne, Pennsylvania, continued marketing the 1970s Angel Christmas plate with Pennsbury markings. The company continued the Christmas plate line into the 1970s, utilizing the Pennsbury brown-wash background. In 1975, Lenape Products, a division of Pennington, bought Glen View and continued making Pennsbury-like products.

Creamer, Rooster pattern, marked "Pennsbury Pottery" on base, **$20**.

Ashtray

Don't Be So Doppish, 5" l............... **20.00**
Hex Sign, earthtones...................... **27.50**
Outen the Light.............................. **20.00**
Such Schmootzers......................... **20.00**
Bank, jug, pig, "Stuff Me" **100.00**
Bird, Nuthatch, blue and brown, artist initials, c1950-70 .... **250.00**
Bowl, rooster, 6-1/2" d...................... **24.00**
Bread tray, rect, wheat motif **45.00**
Cake stand, Amish **75.00**
Canister set, cov, Black Rooster dec, 9" h flour and sugar, 8" tea and coffee
.... **425.00**
Chamber stick, Rooster, 5-1/8" w, 1-6/7" h
.... **40.00**
Coaster, Shultz.................................... **17.50**
Coffeepot, cov, 8" h, Rooster **110.00**

Cream pitcher

Large, Hex Sign **55.00**
Medium, Distilfink........................... **45.00**
Small, Hex Sign **25.00**

Relish tray, Christmas tree shape, Rooster pattern, $35.

Cruet set, Rooster, 6-1/2" h **72.00**
Dealer sign, yellow bird perched on top of name plaque, c1950-70, 5" w, 4-3/4" h
.... **365.00**
Dinner plate, Hex pattern **17.50**
Egg cup, Red Rooster pattern **25.00**
Milk pitcher, Amish farm, 6-1/2" h..... **175.00**
Mother's Day plate, 1971, 8-1/2" d..... **50.00**
Motto bowl, 9" d, 2-1/4" h.................... **72.00**

Pie plate

Apple Tree pattern **37.50**
Rooster, 8" d **65.00**

Pitcher

Amish man, 2-1/2" h........................ **12.00**
Amish woman, 5" h.......................... **45.00**
Eagle pattern................................. **65.00**

Plate, Hex sign pattern, $20.

Christmas Plate, 1972, Countryside, red cardinal on top of lamp post, original tag, $20.

Plaque

Amish Family, 8" d **55.00**
B & O Railroad, Lafayette engine and coal car, 5-3/4" x 7-3/4" **65.00**
Pennsylvania RR 1888, Tiger Locomotive, 5-5/8" x 8" **60.00**

Plate

Black rooster, 10" d........................ **15.00**
Hex sign, 8" d................................ **20.00**
Pretzel bowl, large, Sweet Adeline.... **70.00**
Salt and pepper shakers, pr, Amish heads
.... **60.00**
Snack tray, matching cup, Red Rooster
.... **25.00**
Teapot, Red Rooster pattern **65.00**
Tea tile, 6" d, skunk "Why Be Disagreeable"
.... **60.00**
Tray, yellow rooster, 6" w, 8" l.............. **50.00**
Vase, Rooster, 5-1/4" w, 5" h............... **20.00**
Vegetable dish, divided, Red Rooster
.... **30.00**
Wall pocket, 10" h, bellows-shape, eagle motif... **60.00**

Pens and Pencils

History: The steel pen point, or "nib," was invented by Samuel Harrison in 1780. It was not commercially produced in quantity until the 1880s when Richard Esterbrook entered the field. The holders became increasingly elaborate. Mother-of-pearl, gold, sterling silver, and other fine materials were used to fashion holders of distinction. Many of these pens can be found along with their original velvet-lined presentation cases.

Lewis Waterman invented the fountain pen in the 1880s. Three other leading pioneers in the field were Parker, Sheaffer (first lever filling action, 1913), and Wahl-Eversharp.

The mechanical pencil was patented in 1822 by Sampson Mordan. The original slide-type action developed into the spiral mechanical pencil. Wahl-Eversharp was responsible for the automatic "click," or repeater-type, mechanism which is used on ballpoints today.

The flexible nib that enabled the writer to individualize his penmanship came to an end when Reynolds introduced the ballpoint pen in October 1945.

Collecting Hints: Price is lessened dramatically by any defects such as scratches, cracks, dents, warping, missing parts, bent levers, sprung clips, nib damage, or mechanical damage. Engraved initials or names do not seriously detract from the price.

Desk set

Cross
Chrome ballpoint pen, 0.5 mm pencil, orig box.. **20.00**
No. 6601, Gold filled, 12kt, Ertl Employee, engraved "10 year service," NRFB **75.00**
Epenco, fountain pen and pencil, 5-1/4" l
.... **30.00**
Moore, gray and black marble base, black pen, 12 carat nib, side lever fill....... **75.00**
Sheaffer, Balance, fountain pen and pencil, hard case, black and gray pearl marble barrel, silver nickel trim, clips with flattened gall, gold Sheaffer #3 nib, 1930-40s **150.00**
Sinclair, butterscotch Bakelite base, black glass inkwell, butterscotch Bakelite pen, tag on bottom "Sinclair & Company, Factory Representative, 1385 Greenwich St., San Francisco, Prospect 7185," orig box, 4" x 3" x 2-1/2"...................... **225.00**

Stanhope, metal squared enameled burgundy case, dip pen, propelling pencil, "A Memory of Kirkby Lonsdale" Stanhope set in nip holder of pen, six views **310.00**

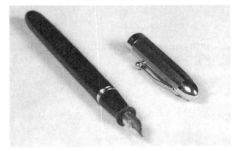

Morrison Fountain Pen Co., NY, black pen with chrome plated cap, 14kt tip, lever fill, marked "USA," $20.

Pen

Advertising
Coca-Cola, 1996, polar bear, Coca-Cola bottle clip **8.00**
Westinghouse, emblem in window, Garland, maroon and silver............. **8.00**

Character
Mickey Mouse, mid "Walt Disney Mickey Mouse," nib marked with Mickey's face, manufactured by Inkograph Co., New York, mkd "Ink-O-Gator"............... **470.00**
Playboy, red ink.............................. **7.50**
Roy Rogers, Stratford, unused..... **145.00**
Taz, Looney Toons, Stylus Pen, Tax on clip.. **9.00**
Columbia, Safety Fountain Pen, three engraved designs on cap top, professionally restored **300.00**

Conklin
Model 25P, lady's, filigree cap ribbon, black, crescent filler, 1923 .... **70.00**
Model 30, black hard rubber, 1903
.... **75.00**
Symetrick, self filing, Pat 5-28-1918 and 11-17-1925, green and black, Conklin nib
.... **150.00**

Cross
Black, center leaf design **8.00**
Silver, engraved band of seashells
.... **8.00**
Dunn, black, red barrel, gold-plated trim, c1920 .... **40.00**
Epenco, black case, gold-plated trim
.... **25.00**

Eversharp
CA Model, ball point pen, black, gold filled cap, 1946.............................. **42.00**
Presentation, fountain pen, Dubonnet red, 14k nib **95.00**

Combination, pencil turns out, pen pulls out, gold plated, point marked "E. J. Johnson & Co., New York, No. 4," 2-3/8" l closed, $80.

Hallmark, wood, dark colored.............. **9.00**
Marvel, black chased hand rubber, eyedropper, 1906........................... **75.00**
Moore, black, lady's ribbon pen, three narrow gold bands on cap, lever fill, patent nib #2 .... **70.00**
Onoto, 18k yg, fountain, 6" l, engraved "R. D. Charman" **190.00**
Osmiroid, black, name on clip, tip mkd "Osmiroid, England," medium........ **20.00**
Parker
Blue-Diamond-51, black, goldplated cap, button filled, 1942.......................... **70.00**
Duofold, Deluxe, pen and pencil set, black and pearl, three narrow gold color bands on cap, push button fill, 1929
.... **575.00**
Duofold, marbleized jade green, point mkd "Indium Tipped," button filler, 5-5/8" l, bladder dried out......................... **42.00**
Duofold, pearlized white, black lines, barrel pearlized brown with black lines, "Parker" on clip, point mkd "Parker Duofold, 6-3/8" l, ... **45.00**
Junior Lucky Curve, lapis blue, "Parker 5-16" on clip, replaced Parker nib with arrow design, button filler, 5-5/8" l, bladder dried out **45.00**
Model 48, ring top, gold filled barrel and cap, button filled, 1915 .... **150.00**
Parker 51, brown, jewel on cap, Vacumatic filler, mkd "Made in USA"
.... **75.00**
Political
Bush-Quayle '92, bluetone bald eagle, red, white, and blue stars and strips design **7.50**
George Bush for President in '88, elephant emblem, red lettering, white ground **9.00**
Mike Dukakis for President in '88, donkey emblem, blue lettering, white ground
.... **8.00**
Reynolds, Model 2, orig ball point, c1945
.... **75.00**
Sanford, black, soft rubber grip, 5-1/2" h
.... **5.00**
Security, check protector, red hard rubber, gold filled trim, 1923........................ **85.00**
Sheaffer
Model #875, lady's, White Dot, Sovereign model #875, marine green striated celluloid body, visulated body section, plunger style vacuum fill, streamline no

hump clip with small flat ball, body imprted with Sheaffer name and model #875, two-tone (gold/silver) nib with heart shaped breathing hole, nib mkd with Lifetime imprint **75.00**
Model #1000, yellow and brown stripe, white dot on top of cap, gold tone band and clip, 14K Lifetime #79 writing tip
.... **70.00**
White Dot, green jade, gold-plated trim, lever filled, 1923............................ **95.00**
Wahl, store display, oversized fountain pen, solid brass and wood, 24" l, 1-1/2" d, c1930 .... **500.00**
Wahl-Eversharp, gold seal, black, gold filled trim, lever filled, 1930.......... **125.00**
Waterman
Ideal, gold filled engraved filigree overlay, lever filler mkd "Ideal," globe on clip cap, nib mkd "Waterman's Ideal," c1915, 5-1/4" l............................. **250.00**
Ideal, marbled gray-green, silver stripe, stepped barrel and cap, small gold button on cap, 14k gold Waterman gold nib, 1930s, orig blue box **85.00**
Ideal 3V, level fill, marbleized green, red, and mother of pearl barrel and cap, nickel silver lever, military style clip and cap ring, gold Waterman's nib, clip broken **100.00**
Ideal #52 1/2V, lever fill, nickel plated trim, orig blue box and directions for use
.... **110.00**
Sterling silver filigree, black hard rubber, unrestored, 1905 patent date on clip, orig Waterman nib, 6-1/2" l **45.00**
Taperite, black, gold filled metal mounted cap, gold filled trim, lever filled, c1949
.... **75.00**

Pencil

Advertising
A. J. Spaulding Brothers, NY, silver lettering "Put Importance to the History and Tradition," Reimei **8.00**
Broadman Supplies, red logo, 23rd Psalm printed in blue...................... **8.50**
Planter's Peanuts, mechanical, blue and yellow, Mr. Peanut on top, 1950s
.... **28.00**
RCA, gold-colored Cross, "RCA" on clip
.... **8.00**
Eversharp, lady's, silver-plated, c1920
.... **25.00**

Souvenir, "1898-1948 - Golden Anniversary, New York City" emb on side, blue and orange stripes, brass sq eraser head, 12" l **8.50**
Wahl-Eversharp, gold filled, metal mounted, 1919 .... **35.00**
Zippo, black, gold trim **10.00**

Pepsi-Cola Collectibles

History: Pepsi-Cola was developed by Caleb D. Bradham, a pharmacist and drugstore owner in New Bern, North Carolina. Like many drugstores of its time, Bradham provided "soda" mixes for his customers and friends. His favorite was "Brad's Drink," which he began to call "Pepsi-Cola" in 1898. Its popularity spread, and in 1902 Bradham turned the operation of his drugstore over to an assistant and devoted all his energy to perfecting and promoting Pepsi-Cola. He sold 2,008 gallons of Pepsi-Cola syrup his first three months and by 1904 was bottling Pepsi-Cola for mass consumption. He sold his first franchise within a short time.

By the end of the first decade of the 20th century, Bradham had organized a network of more than 250 bottlers in 24 states. The company's fortunes sank shortly after World War I when it suffered large losses in the sugar market. Bankruptcy and reorganization followed. Roy Megargel, whose Wall Street firm advised Bradham, helped keep the name alive. A second bankruptcy occurred in 1931, but the company survived.

In 1933, Pepsi-Cola doubled the size of its bottle but held the price at 5 cents. Sales soared. Under the direction of Walter Mack, 1938 to 1951, Pepsi challenged Coca-Cola for market dominance. In the 1950s, Pepsi advertising featured slogans such as "Pepsi Cola Hits the Spot, Twelve Full Ounces That's a Lot."

Collecting Hints: Items advertising Pepsi, Hires, and a number of other soft drink companies became hot collectibles in the 1980s, fueled in part by the pricey nature of Coca-Cola items. The Pepsi market is still young; and, some price fluctuations occur.

Pepsi-Cola enjoys a much stronger market position in many foreign countries than it does in the United States.

Reproductions, copycats, and fantasy items are part of the Pepsi collecting scene. Be on the alert for the Pepsi and Pete pillow issued in the 1970s, a 12-inch-high ceramic statue of a woman holding a glass of Pepsi, a Pepsi glass-front clock, a Pepsi double-bed quilt, and set of four Pepsi glasses. These are just a few of the suspect items, some of which were done under license from Pepsi-Cola.

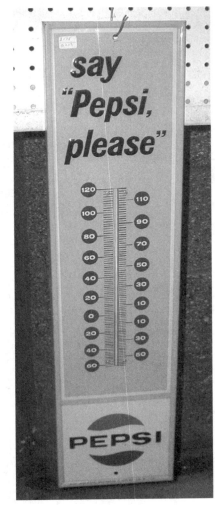

Thermometer, litho tin, yellow ground, "say Pepsi please" logo, red, white, and blue trademark, **$175**.

Bottle cap, 1910, never crimped **50.00**
Bottle opener, slight rust **20.00**
Calendar, 1955, card stock, 12" x 20"
.... **400.00**
Carrier, metal, 8-1/2" w, 10-1/2" h **30.00**
Cigarette lighter, 4" l, metal, bottle cap illus
on side, 1950s **150.00**
Clock, wall type **40.00**
Cooler, metal, blue and white, 1950s, slight
rust **100.00**
Cookie jar, 8" d, 15" h, limited edition
.... **70.00**
Crate, wooden
Four compartments, wear, 18" x 6" x 12"
.... **48.00**
Six compartments, bright markings,
1940s **145.00**
Twenty-four compartments, mkd
"Pittsburgh, Pa.," c1940 .... **30.00**
Door push, wrought iron, 1960s **65.00**
Drinking glass
Boris and Natasha, 1970s **30.00**
Uh-Huh Diet Pepsi **4.00**
Fan, 10" sq, cardboard, wood handle, c1940
.... **75.00**
Figure, 5-1/2" h, 30 Anniversary, pewter,
billboard center with bottle cap and
"Cool" and cat figure leaning on it with
one elbow, feet crossed, limited edition of
250 .... **60.00**
Fountain glass, 5" h, syrup line, double dot
.... **45.00**
Key chain, Pepsi Beach Club, 1960s
.... **35.00**
Letterhead, 8-1/2" x 11", Pepsi-Cola Bottling
Works, Greensboro, NC, 1916 ..... **100.00**
Magazine tear sheet, full color
1958, 10" x 12", rolling skating theme, girl
in short skating outfit, reads "Slim Figures
Go With The Light Refreshment" **14.00**
1964, 10" x 12", two page ad, couple
playing pool in recreation room **14.00**
Napkin, 19" sq, cloth, c1940 .... **25.00**
Notepad, 2-1/2" x 4-1/2", cardboard cov, red
and black logo, 1914 calendar **35.00**
Paper cup and cup holder, Pepsi Double
Dot, cone shape, made by Paper
Container Mfg. Co., Chicago **75.00**
Pinback button, 2" d, red, white, and blue
bottle cap design, slogan "More Bounce
to the Ounce," 1950s **25.00**
Radio, transistor, 10" l **55.00**
Record, 78 rpm, *The Voice Of Your Man In
The Service,* courtesy of Pepsi-Cola,
1942, orig 7" l cardboard envelope
.... **25.00**
Salt and pepper shakers, pr, 4-1/2" h, bottle
shape, glass, plastic lids **25.00**
Sign
3-1/2" x 10", emb tin, dark green, white,
and red, mkd "Crown Cork & Seal Co.,
Baltimore, USA" c1910 .... **650.00**
9" d, celluloid and tin, "Ice Cold Pepsi-

Cola Sold Here," 1930s **300.00**
12" x 8", plastic, "Take Home Pepsi," light-
up type, bottle cap illus, 1950s.... **160.00**
13" d, bottle cap, double-sided, Pepsi
Double Dot, painted emb metal, late
1940s or early 1950s, some yellowing to
white **250.00**
16" w, 15" h, double sided, Pepsi-Cola,
masonite, red, white, and blue..... **200.00**
22" x 7", paper, "Have A Pepsi," man,
woman, and bottle cap illus, 1950s
.... **35.00**
24" x 28", tin, "Drink Pepsi-Cola," bottle
cap illus, 1950s **55.00**

Tray, red, white, and blue litho, Enjoy Pepsi-Cola,
Hits the Spot, slight wear, $35.

Thermometer, 27-1/4" h, 7-1/8" w, double
dot, some wear and stains **365.00**
Thimble, plastic, red and blue on yellow,
"America's Choice," Pepsi logo **7.50**
Toy
Car, diecast, #38, 1993, 1:64 scale, MOC
.... **6.50**
Delivery truck, 2-1/2" x 7-1/2" x 2", white
plastic body, black wood wheels, red,
white, and blue Pepsi decal, three white
plastic cases with 24 plastic bottles, Marx
Toys, c1940 .... **95.00**
Dispenser, 6" x 12" x 12", red, white, and
blue plastic, 2" h scaled Pepsi plastic
cups, some play wear, c1970 .... **30.00**
Tray
Bottle cap shape, round, 1940 .... **325.00**
Coney Island, 1955 .... **50.00**
Uniform patch, 7".............................. **15.00**
Walkie-talkie, bottle shape **25.00**

PEZ

History: Vienna, Austria, is the
birthplace of PEZ. In 1927, Eduard
Haas, an Austrian food mogul, invented
PEZ and marketed it as a cigarette
substitute, i.e., an adult mint. He added

peppermint oil to a candy formula, compressed the product into small rectangular bricks, and named it PEZ, an abbreviation for the German word *Pfefferminz*. Production of PEZ was halted by World War II. When the product appeared again after the war, it was packaged in a dispenser that resembled a BIC lighter. These early 1950s' dispensers had no heads.

PEZ arrived in the United States in 1952. PEZ-HAAS received United States Patent #2,620,061 for its "table dispensing receptacle," but the public response was less than overwhelming. Rather than withdraw from the market, Haas repositioned his product to appeal to children by adding fruit flavors. PEZ's success was assured when it became both a candy and a toy combined into one product. In some cases, the shape of the dispenser mimics an actual toy, e.g., a space gun. Most frequently, appealing heads were simply added to the tops of the standard rectangular containers.

PEZ carefully guards its design and production information. As a result, collectors differ on important questions such as dating and numbers of variations. Further complicating the issue is PEZ production outside the United States. A company in Linz, Austria, with PEZ rights to the rest of the world, including Canada, frequently issues PEZ containers with heads not issued by PEZ Candy, Inc., an independent privately owned company which by agreement manufactures and markets PEZ only in the United States. PEZ Candy, Inc., is located in Connecticut.

The American and Austrian PEZ companies use a common agent to manage the production of dispensers. The result is that occasionally the same container is issued by both companies. However, when this occurs, the packaging may be entirely different.

PEZ Candy, Inc., issues generic, seasonal, and licensed-character containers. Container design is continually evaluated and upgraded. The Mickey Mouse container has been changed more than a dozen times.

Today PEZ candy is manufactured at plants in Austria, Hungary, Yugoslavia, and the United States. Previously, plants had been located in Czechoslovakia, Germany, and Mexico. Dispensers are produced at plants in Austria, China, Hong Kong, Hungary, and Slovenia.

Collecting Hints: PEZ became a hot collectible in the late 1980s. Its rise was due in part to the use of licensed cartoon characters as heads on PEZ dispensers. Initially, PEZ containers were an extremely affordable collectible. Generic subjects often sold for less than $5, character containers for less than $10.

Before investing large amounts of money in PEZ containers, it is important to recognize that: 1) they are produced in large quantities—millions, 2) PEZ containers are usually saved by their original buyers, not disposed of when emptied, and 3) no collecting category stays hot forever. PEZ prices fluctuate. Advertised price and field price for the same container can differ by as much as 50 percent, depending on who is selling.

Alpine Boy, purple hat and shoes, loose **6.50**
Ant, green stem, loose **8.00**
Barney, Flintstones **3.00**
Boy with Hat, Pez Pal, 1960 .... **12.00**
Captain Hook, 4-1/4" h **125.00**
Charlie Brown, frown, MIP **8.00**
Donald Duck, no feet, MIP **27.50**
Dumbo, Disney, no feet, yellow base and hat, blue trunk and mouth, turquoise head and ears, loose **65.00**
Fozzie Bear, 1991 .... **3.00**
Frankenstein, 1960s, mint **250.00**
Icee **5.50**
Inspector Clouseu, yellow stem, loose **6.00**
Kermit, mkd "Made in Hungry" **7.50**
Lamb, mkd "Made in Yuglosavia" **6.00**
Mickey Mouse **5.00**
Panda, Pony Go Round sticker, no feet, two packages of Pez Candy, MOC **150.00**
Parrot, Merry Melody Maker, MOC **8.50**
Pebbles, Flintstones **3.00**
Penguin, Melody Maker, MOC **12.00**
Pilot, white hat, black shoes, loose **6.00**
Pink Panther, pink stem, loose........... **12.00**
Pluto **4.00**
Practical Pig, no feet, two packages of Pez Candy, MOC **150.00**
Rabbit **7.50**
Santa, mkd "Made in Yuglosavia" **8.00**
Sheep **3.00**
Shell Gas, yellow hat, red shoes, loose **7.00**

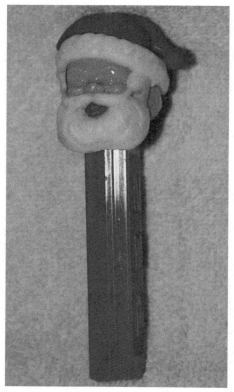

Santa, $8.

Smurf

Boy, blue stem.................................... 3.00
Papa, red stem................................. 3.00
Smurfeette, yellow stem.................. 14.00
Snowman.. 3.00
Tom... 6.00
Tuffy... 7.50
Tweety Bird... 4.00
Whistle, 1960s..................................... 4.00
Yosemite Sam....................................... 5.00

Pfaltzgraff Pottery Dinnerware

History: The company known as Pfaltzgraff today got its start in the early 1810s as Germany immigrant George Pfaltzgraff and a few other family members started a stoneware and redware pottery in the York area of Pennsylvania. They produced utilitarian wares such as crocks, jugs, and pots until 1913. The natural clay deposits found in Pennsylvania helped them create gray salt glaze and redware vessels so necessary for food storage at that time. Some art pottery was made by Pfaltzgraff during 1931 to 1937. During this time, kitchenwares were introduced.

Pfaltzgraff began to produce dinnerware in 1940. Using stoneware formulas, they created patterns that quickly caught on. Today collectors are recognizing the value in collecting these early patterns.

Collecting hints: Most Pfaltzgraff is marked. Over the years, its mark has changed slightly but usually includes a castle outline. Stoneware manufacturing often creates seconds, pieces with a slight flaw or something that causes them to be slightly less desirable. These seconds have been sold at Pfaltzgraff factory stores for decades. Most are marked, but not all. If buying Pfaltzgraff dinnerware to use, check for signs of damage from previous use. Many matching services are now also stocking Pfaltzgraff dinnerware, making finding an odd piece much easier.

Folk Art

Bowl, 12" d...................................... **45.00**
Bread and butter plate, 6-3/4" d **10.00**
Dinner plate, 10-1/4" d.................. **15.00**
Soup plate, 8-1/4" d...................... **12.00**

Ash tray, brown and white, marked "The Pfaltzgraff Pottery, USA, AT22," $3.50.

Gourmet Royal, Brown Drip

Bean pot, cov, two qt..................... **35.00**
Coffeepot, drip, 64 oz, 8" h........... **50.00**
Coffee server, metal and wood stand,
warmer candle............................. **150.00**
Creamer and sugar **15.00**
Cup and saucer............................. **5.00**
Mixing bowl, 8" d **18.00**
Salt and pepper shakers, pr, 4" h
.... **25.00**

Teapot, 10" w, 5-1/2" h **55.00**
Vegetable bowl, 9" d **15.00**
Heirloom, beige, sculptured gray leaves, white flowers
Cereal bowl, 6" d **7.50**
Cup and saucer **6.00**
Dinner plate, 10-1/2" d **10.00**
Fruit bowl, 5" d **6.50**
Platter, 14-1/2" l **37.50**
Vegetable bowl, 8-3/4" d **15.00**

Miscellaneous

Mug, Jester, Norman Rockwell, stamped "The Saturday Evening Post Co., 1979 Dave Grossman Designs, Inc., NRM-4, Feb. 11, 1939" **100.00**
Mug, Sleepy Sam, 5-1/4" w, 4-3/4" h
.... **45.00**
Snowbear, 2002
Cake plate, 12-1/4" d, 7" h **55.00**
Napkin rings, 4" x 2-1/2", set of four
.... **30.00**
Platter, five-part, 16" l **50.00**

Tea Rose

Bread tray, 12-1/2" l **12.00**
Creamer **7.50**
Cup and saucer **5.00**
Dinner plate, 10-1/2" d **12.00**
Dinnerware, 36 pcs **150.00**
Salad plate, 7-1/2" d **5.00**
Salt and pepper shakers, pr **15.00**
Soup bowl, 9" d **7.50**
Sugar **7.50**

Village, brown dec on beige
Bank, piggy **55.00**
Casserole, cov **25.00**
Coffeepot, 10" h **38.00**
Dinner plate, 10-1/2" d **15.00**
Platter, 14" l, 10" w **30.00**
Soup tureen, cov **35.00**

Tidbit tray, two-tier, Brown Drip Glaze, marked "Pfaltzgraft, (castle mark) USA," 6-3/4" d top plate, 10" d bottom plate, 9-1/2" h, **$35**.

Wyndham, gray band, pink and gray floral border
Baker, 14-1/8" l **50.00**
Breakfast plate, 9-3/8" d **10.00**
Cake plate, 13" d **25.00**
Canister, cov, 8" h **55.00**
Casserole, cov, 9" d **75.00**
Cereal bowl, 6-1/2" d **10.00**
Cup and saucer **9.00**
Dinner plate, 10-1/2" d **12.00**
Heart box, cov, 4-1/4" w, 2" h **12.00**
Luncheon plate, 8-7/8" d **11.50**
Mug, ftd, 5" h **12.00**
Napkin holder **13.00**
Pie baker, 10-1/2" d **16.00**
Soup tureen, cov, ladle **120.00**
Vegetable bowl, round, 8-1/4" d **34.00**
Yorktowne, blue dec on gray
Au gratin dish, 11-1/2" l **12.00**
Bean pot, 6-3/4" d, 7-1/8" h **30.00**
Candleholders, 3-5/8" h, finger rings, pr
.... **30.00**
Clock, 10-1/4" d, battery **35.00**
Coffeepot, 40 oz **37.50**
Cup and saucer **8.50**
Dinner plate, 10-1/2" d **12.00**
Luncheon plate, 8-7/8" d **10.00**
Pitcher, 72 oz, 8-1/4" h **40.00**
Platter, medium **30.00**
Salt and pepper shakers, pr, figural rabbits **40.00**
Teapot, cov, two-cup size **25.00**
Vegetable bowl, round **36.00**

Phoenix Bird China

History: The manufacture of the Phoenix Bird design began in the late 19th century, and pieces were marked "Nippon" from 1891 to 1921. Large quantities of this ware were imported into the United States from the 1920s through the 1940s. A smaller amount went to a few European countries and are so marked, each in their own way. The vast majority of Phoenix Bird was of the transfer-print variety, but its hand-painted pieces with Japanese characters underneath are rare.

The pattern was primarily sold, retail, through Woolworth's 5 & 10¢ stores. It could also be ordered, wholesale, from the catalogs of Butler Brothers and the Charles William Stores in New York. However, only the most basic shapes were offered through the catalogs. The pattern was also carried by A. A. Vantine Company, New York. These products, exported by Morimura Brothers, Japan, were known at that time as "Blue Howo Bird China." Morimura used two different marks: "Japan" below a convex "M" inside of two crossed branches or "Made in Japan" beneath a concave "M" inside a wreath. Unlike Noritake's wreath that opens at the top, Morimura's wreath opens at the bottom.

There are several other patterns which are considered to be in the phoenix family: Flying Turkey (an all-over pattern that was hand-painted and/or transfer-printed), Twin Phoenix (a Noritake border-only pattern), Howo (a Noritake allover pattern), Flying Dragon (available in blue and white and green and white, and usually marked with six Japanese characters), and Firebird (the bird's tail flows downward; usually hand-painted and character-marked). Most Japanese potteries were destroyed during World War II making it difficult to trace production of these related patterns.

Identification of these intricate patterns can be added by consulting the four books written and published by Adviser Joan Collett Oates, *Phoenix Bird Chinaware*, I-V, 1984-2002.

Collecting Hints: Within this particular design of primarily blue and white Japanese chinaware, more than 500 different shapes and sizes, and more than 100 different factory marks have been cataloged. The pieces vary greatly, not only in the quality of chinaware itself—from very thick to eggshell thin—but also in design execution, even the shades of blue vary from powder blue to deep cobalt. All of these factors, as well as condition, should be considered when determining prices. Especially important is the border width of the design: "superior" widths are preferred over the more common, narrower border. Another important consideration is that pieces with "Japan" appearing below the cherry blossom mark generally have a better-quality print and came in some of the more unique shapes in this pattern.

Note that the Phoenix Bird's body is facing *forward*, while its head is facing *back over its wings*, that is, the head looks opposite the direction the body is facing. Occasionally, on one side of a rounded piece, such as a creamer, sugar, or teapot, the phoenix's stance is reversed, but this is not the norm. Note, too, the phoenix always has at least four and no more than seven spots on its chest, and its wings are spread out and upward.

Green and white pieces are *very rare*. However, do not confuse the Phoenix Bird pattern with the Flying Dragon design that does, in fact, come in either green and white or blue and white.

E-bay has taken its toll on Phoenix Bird pattern. Values for Phoenix Bird and the low dollars bid and/or paid for most of its commonly-shaped pieces today, is because there seems to be more "supply" out there then there is "demand." Why the supply? A lot of Phoenix Bird collectors are slowly growing older and giving-in to downsizing or giving-up for various reasons. With so many collections becoming so readily dispersed and the common, everyday shapes becoming more available, values will, and have, declined. However, no matter how many pieces in a collection, collectors are always looking for the unusual and those are the pieces that will claim the dollars. Today though, it seems that the common shapes are more "valuable" staying in one's cupboard and/or passed on to friends and relatives to enjoy. Hopefully, in time, kept off the market, they will one day return to be "wanted" items and the "demand" will be there again.

Adviser: Joan Collett Oates.

Note: Since there are several different shapes within some categories of Phoenix Bird, the various shapes are given a style number in the listings below. This numbering system corresponds to that used in the books by Joan Collett Oates.

Cup and saucer, blue "M" in wreath over Japan mark, **$35**.

Bouillon, cup with two handles **8.00**
Butter pat.. **10.00**
Cereal bowl, 6" d **9.00**
Chocolate pot.................................... **95.00**
Coffee pot.. **55.00**
Creamer, adult size, common shape
.... **18.00**
Demitasse cup and saucer, gold rims, no
mark **10.00**
Dessert plate, 7-1/2" d **8.00**

Tea set, child size, three pieces, **$85**.

Dinner plate, 9-3/4" d **25.00**
Luncheon plate, 8-1/2" d **12.00**
Platter, oval
    10" l **20.00**
    12" l **30.00**
    14" l **45.00**
    17" l **90.00**
Rice tureen, cov, #2 .... **55.00**
Sauce bowl, 5-1/2" d **6.00**
Soup bowl, 7-1/4" d **10.00**
Soup plate, 9" d **15.00**
Sugar bowl, cov, adult size, common shape
.... **22.00**
Sweetmeat dish, scalloped, #5.......... **27.00**

Standard reference guide for *Phoenix Bird Chinaware*, Book 5, by adviser Joan Collett Oats, **$17.50**.

Teapot, cov, steam hole in cover, round
.... **35.00**
Tile, round.. **25.00**
Tureen, cov
    Eight-sided, English, #2 .... **125.00**
    Oval, large...................................... **65.00**
    Round, large **65.00**
Vegetable bowl, open, oval, 8" x 6".... **45.00**

Pig Collectibles

History: Historically, the pig has been important as a source of food and has also been an economic factor in rural areas of Europe and America. It was one of the first animals imported into the American colonies. A fatted sow was the standard gift to a rural preacher on his birthday or holiday.

As a decorative motif, the pig gained prominence with the figurines and planters made in the late 19th century by English, German, and Austrian potters. These "pink" porcelain pigs with green decoration were popular souvenir or prize items at fairs and carnivals or could be purchased at five-and-dime stores.

Many pig figurines were banks, and by the early 20th century "Piggy Bank" became a synonym for coin bank. When tourist attractions became popular along America's coasts and in the mountain areas, many of the pig designs showed up as souvenir items with gilt decals identifying the area.

The pig motif appeared on the advertising items associated with farm products and life. Movie cartoons introduced Porky Pig and Walt Disney's "Three Little Pigs."

In the late 1970s, pig collectibles caught fire again. Specialty shops selling nothing but pig-related items were found in the New England area. In a 1981 issue, *Time* magazine devoted a page and a half to the pig phenomena.

Collecting Hints: Bisque and porcelain pig items from late 19th-century European potters are most widely sought by collectors. Souvenir items should have decals in good condition; occasionally the gilding wears off from rubbing or washing.

Reproduction Alert: Reproductions of three German-style painted bisque figurines have been spotted in the market. They are pig by outhouse, pig playing piano, and pig poking out of large purse. The porcelain is much rougher and the green is a darker shade.

Additional Listings: Cartoon Characters, Disneyana.

Adviser: Mary Hamburg.

Figure, ceramic, mother pig and three piglets, high glaze, European, marked #E1593, 5-1/2" w, 7-1/4" l, 2-1/2" h, **$85**.

Advertising

Cutting board, Arnold Kent Feeds, wood, pig shape, 14" x 19-1/2" **22.00**
Trade card, Try Wright's Little Liver Pills, five pigs **10.00**

Bank

Heart, green, two pigs on each side of sheet music, mkd "Germany" **85.00**
My System, money bag, pig along side, 3-3/4" h... **125.00**

Barometer, pig shape **125.00**

Bottle, Benedictine Liqueur, pig popping out of bottle, orange seal, 5-3/4" h...... **120.00**

Cork, Heidisieck Dry Champagne, two pigs, 3" h.. **85.00**

Crock, orange pig along side, 3" h **85.00**

Dice, with large pig **110.00**

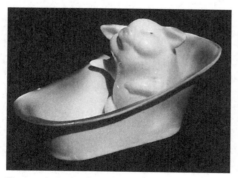

Figure, pig in small wash tub, **$95**.

Figure, baby pig inside well with orange roof, large pig looking in, 3-1/2" h, **$120**.

Figure

Black bisque pig jumping over fence, 4-1/2" l, 3-1/2" h............................. **110.00**
Black cook holding frying pan, pink pig in basket, 4-1/4" h............................. **450.00**
Good Old Annual, water pump with piglet inside, mkd "Made in Germany," 3-3/4" h **100.00**
Hearts are Trumps, two pigs playing cards, 3-1/2" h, 3-3/4" h **105.00**
Let Me Also Have Some Mother, Mother pig and piglet, 2" h, 3" w.............. **110.00**
Lobster, pulling leg of red pig **125.00**
Mammy, spoon and bandanna, pink pig in basket, 4-1/4" h **450.00**
Money Bag, large pig with binoculars, brown and green coat and hat, 5" h **125.00**
Pig beside large basket, 3" h **125.00**
Pink pig with devil, pulling on hose **200.00**
Purse, green, black bisque pig sitting on top, 2-1/4" h.................................... **80.00**
Shoe, two pigs inside looking out .. **85.00**
Souvenir of Chicago, IL, gold pig, orange top, wishing well, mkd "Made in Germany," 1930s, 3" h.................... **75.00**
The Heavenly Twins, mother pig wheeling two piglets, incised "Made in Germany," 3-3/4" l, 3" h **115.00**
Typewriter gentlemen, pink pig.... **125.00**
Water Trough, bisque, surrounded by four pigs, 4" l, 3-3/4" h **110.00**

Inkwell, pink pig sitting on top of green inkwell, 3" h **125.00**

Match holder, pig holding flag, 2 black kids in boat, striker on match holder ... **450.00**

Nodder, china, dressed as man and woman **90.00**

Pin dish

Good Luck, horseshoe, large yellow and green horseshoe, pink pig, stamped "Made in Germany," 5" w **85.00**

Figure, large pink pig crashing through fence,
Souvenir of Canada, **$125**.

Older couple pink pigs, top hat, green
bow tie, umbrella, yellow bonnet and
bow, "Grandma" on dish, 4-3/4" w,
3-1/2" h,.. **135.00**
Pitcher, figural, dressed in tie and tails,
brown, 4" h...................................... **30.00**
Salt dish, chef pig with shamrocks, salt
cellars on each side, 4-1/4" h **150.00**

Toothpick holder

2-1/2" h, small and large pig in front of
open mushroom **95.00**
2-3/4" h, two little pigs in front of egg
.... **75.00**
3" h, pig with mug in hand, leaning on
fence **75.00**
3-3/4" h, pig with racquet, "Lawn Tennis".
.... **100.00**
4" h, three large pigs in front of water
trough.. **100.00**

Tray, Three Little Pigs, enamel, dark green
decoration on white, **$130**.

Toy

Squeak, painted papier-mâché, 5" h
.... **350.00**
Wind-up, tin litho, Porky Pig, cowboy
outfit, yellow hat, Marx, MIB.......... **200.00**
Vase, 7-1/4" l, red devil's arm around pink
pig, sitting on log........................... **110.00**
Weather vane, metal **130.00**

Pinback Buttons

History: Pinback buttons are small buttons with a back holding a straight pin. The front surface served as an instant billboard for early advertisers. Because the front advertising surface was so small, many advertisers added a paper insert, known as a back paper, which further exclaimed the values of the product. Many times the pinback button maker used the back paper to add his name to the creation, if it was not included on the rim or in the design. Politicians soon learned the value of these small advertisements as did those organizations, which had a cause to promote or protest. Newspapers and cigarette companies issued pinbacks in series, sometimes for contests, as well as other types of promotions. Event promoters also issued buttons to help promote their fairs and expositions.

Collecting hints: Look for pinback buttons that show great design and bright colors. Any discoloration or rust will deter from the value.

Additional listings: Advertising, Political, as well as many other topics.

3/4" d

Calif Dairy Industries Assn 1935, white on red, St. Louis back paper............... **10.00**
I'm A Chicken Dinner Candy Kid, blue text over red center chicken on yellow, c1930 .... **12.00**
Votes for Women, black text on gold, Whitehead & Hoag back paper, c1912 .... **35.00**

Favorite Stoves & Ranges, "We Guarantee Best in the World," celluloid, multicolored, orange ground, Baltimore Badge & Novelty Co., 1-1/4" d, **$15**.

7/8" d

Boost East St. Louis, dark blue building with yellow windows, chimney stacks belching smoke against orange ground, light blue text "Get It At Kaminer's," Bastian back paper, c1907-20 .... **12.00**

Bread and Milk, multicolored, sliced loaf, knife on table next to milk bottle, blue text on light blue ground, Bastian back paper, c1920 .... **18.00**

Compliments Of The Woman's Benefit Association Port Huron, Michigan, portrait of women in black on silver, c1920
.... **20.00**

Conn Pomological Society, 1912, designed as shaded yellow apple on cream, black text, 2" yellow ribbon
.... **15.00**

Falcon Flour Grocers Picnic, flour sack with company logo in cream, blue, and brown accents, 1899 .... **15.00**

For Mayor, James M. Curley, young photo of Boston mayor candidate
.... **45.00**

I Will C U At The (flower) Show, yellow flower, green leaves, cram ground, Whitehead & Hoag back paper, 1896
.... **18.00**

Newsboys Home, Sept. 23rd for Our Boys, red text, Whitehead & Hoag back paper, c1901-12............................. **18.00**

U of T, full-color Texas flag on cream, Whitehead & Hoag back paper, 1901-12
.... **18.00**

13/16" d

Business and Booze Are Out, white on dark blue, Bastian back paper, c1910
.... **25.00**

Friend of The Abraham Lincoln Battalion, red, blue, cream, Lincoln profile and soldiers, 1930s **20.00**

I Gave To Save A Life In Spain-Medical Bureau To Aid Spanish Democracy, green on cream, black and white photo of nurse in center................................. **20.00**

1" d

Member Michigan Milk Producers Ass'n, Quality Dairy Products-The Cooperative Way, red and white, milk cow over printed by shape of Michigan in bright yellow, c1940... **15.00**

Night and Day Club, black and white, world globe with half in black, right half in black and white, Whitehead & Hoag back paper, c1920 .... **15.00**

Victory Over Communism In Vietnam, dark blue on white, bright red "Communism," made by Emress ... **18.00**

You Need Vitamin H, red upper area, blue base, white and bright yellow text, letter "H" outlined in yellow with a blue shadow, c1930, St. Louis back paper **18.00**

Old Boatmen's Reunion, Capt Chas G Montague, Port Treverton, Pa, Aug 29, '42, 1-1/4" d celluloid button, red, white, and blue striped ribbon, $20.

1-1/8" d

Maccabee Heroes of Palestine, blue on cream litho, soccer player, small Star of David at center, few Hebraic letters, late 1940s **30.00**

The Freshest Thing in Town, Johnny Lawrence wearing a derby on bright yellow, red text, 1930s **12.00**

Thorola, purple sound amplifying horn superimposed over black and white early radio set against bright yellow ground, black product name **30.00**

1-1/4" d

Acid Indigestion? Check Your Source, green text on pale blue, Greenwich Village underground store address on curl, late 1960s **25.00**

Annual Summer Suit Sale, black and orange sweating man next to thermometer reading over 90 degrees, price at right is $13.75, c1930 .... **15.00**

A Winning Harvest Hand, Four Jacks And A Queen Not In The Trust, wheat field with four brown mules pulling large hay cutter reading "Acme Queen," farmer in blue and white outfit, yellow hat, yellow mower blades **100.00**

Ban the Bra, black on green, late 1960s
.... **18.00**

Colorado National Apple Exposition Jan. 3-8, 1910, Denver, ornate black and white building overprinted by deep red apples, dark green leaves, surrounded by white text on blue rim, Whitehead & Hoag back paper **25.00**

Disarm Now! No More Hiroshimas, red and white bomb cloud, blue ground, white text, Australian issue, 1960s . **20.00**

Dr. Spock Brought Me Up, black text on blue, late 1960s **15.00**

Lauson Frost King, green gasoline engine in center, Jack Frost with flowing beard and crown on head, wide red rim with black and white text enclosed in narrow yellow outer rim "Manufactured By The John Lauson Mfg Co. New Holstein, Wis," maker "J. B. Carroll, Chicago" name on curl **65.00**

Lincoln Centennial, black and white, beardless photo in center, rim text "100th Anniversary Feb. 12 1909," St. Louis back paper **30.00**

LSD Legalize Spiritual Discovery, red text on pale pink, late 1960s **25.00**

Member Junior Humane Society, red on white, bird, cat, and dog, tin back, bar in, c1940 .... **12.00**

Sharples Cream Separator, multicolored, farm woman pouring milk into device as she cranks handle, c1900-10 .... **35.00**

The Real Issue, The Saloon Or The Boys And Girls, multicolored young boy and girl with American flag below red text, c1910 .... **125.00**

Today East Village-Tomorrow The World, red text on bright yellow, late 1960s **18.00**

Vietnam Love It Or Leave It, blue text on white panels, bright red ground, 1970 copyright on curl **15.00**

Welcome Arch, The Struby-Estabrook Merc Co. Stands For Quality At A Moderate Price, Denver, CO, street scene, black and red text on white, Bastian back paper, c1910 .... **30.00**

Pinback button, McKinley, commemorates assassination, black and white portrait, black ribbon, original paper insert, Whitehead & Hoag Co., Newark, NJ, c1896, 1-3/16" d, **$85**.

1-1/2" d

Brooklyn College Women's Liberation, bright red on cream, female with clenched fist, 1970s **30.00**

Come Together At Headquarters, black and white, peace symbol in center **35.00**

I'm A Peanuts Pal, red, white and blue clown, white ground, blue type, c1970 .... **15.00**

Join the Sexual Revolution, Come Home With Me Tonight, orange on white, late 1960s **25.00**

Royal Typewriter Entrant, blue and white typewriter on white, blue text on dark red rim "Dawson Company Photo Contest," name repeated on curl plus "Cleve Mfrs" **25.00**

S.A.M. Wants You, Students Against Militarism To End The Viet Nam War, red on white **95.00**

Stewardesses for Women's Rights, bright red on cream, female symbol, single wing design, NY City address on curl with group initials "SFWR" **35.00**

Teach Peace, black text, black mortarboard hat design, orange and white world globe **80.00**

Vancouver BC, bright green leaf on dark red ground, narrow black and white ribbon accents, c1940 .... **20.00**

You Don't Have To B Jewish To Oppose The War In Vietnam, black on white, Greenwich Village underground store name on curl **30.00**

1-3/4" d

Gay March Against The War, dark red text, matching male and female symbols on light purple, dark purple text **40.00**

Parade Every Sunday, Virginian Pilot, red, white, and blue, red and blue text, image of drum majorette, 1960s **24.00**

Republican William Scranton Harrisburg, PA, Jan. 15 1953, black on cream. **15.00**

Tiger Cage Fast and Vigil, Summer 1974 Washington, D.C., black and cream **35.00**

2" d

Bring All The GI's Home-Out Now, March on Washington, Nov. 6, dove illus, WATAC, made by Horn **35.00**

May Day, '80, Peace, Jobs Equality, Communist, yellow lettering on purple, white rim **12.00**

Take Brooklyn Out Of The War, black text and illus of bridge on day-glo yellow **45.00**

Pinback button, For Willkie President, union logo on front, red, white, and blue, "Phila Badge Co., Phila, Pa." on curl, 7/8" d, **$12**.

2-1/2" d

Cut Off War Funds Ring Around Congress, bright red text on bright yellow surrounded by cut-out human figures forming circle with black and white US Capitol in center **150.00**

Meck in '82, flasher, black and white photo of man wearing heavy black eyeglass frame, opposite view black in shape of Florida with text, Vari-Vue **25.00**

Vote DFL '56 and *Re-elect Gov Freeman,* flasher, white lettering, Minnesota, made by Pictorial Productions **30.00**

Pinball Machines

History: Pinball machines can be traced back to the mid-1700s. However, it was not until Gottlieb introduced Baffle Ball in 1931, during the Depression, that pinball machines caught on and became a popular and commercial success because people were hungry for something novel and for the opportunity to make money. Pinball machines offered both. The first games were entirely mechanical, cost about $20, and were produced in large numbers—25,000 to 50,000 machines of the same model were not uncommon.

Pinball developments include:
- 1932—addition of legs
- 1933—electric, at first using batteries
- 1936—addition of bumpers
- 1947—advent of flippers
- 1950—kicking rubbers
- 1953—score totalers
- 1954—multiple players
- 1977—solid-state electronics

The size of the machines changed over the years. The early countertops were 16 by 32 inches. Later models were freestanding with the base measuring 21 by 52 inches and the back box, 24 by 30 inches.

Most pinballs were made in Chicago. Major manufacturers were Gottlieb, Williams, and Bally.

The total number of pinball models that have been manufactured has not been precisely determined. Some suggest more than 10,000 different models from 200-plus makers. After 1940, most models were produced in quantities of 500 to 2,000; occasionally, games had production figures as high as 10,000. Pinball machines have always enjoyed a high attrition rate. New models made the most money and were introduced by several of the major manufacturers at the rate of one entirely new model every three weeks during the mid-1940s and 1950s. Today new models are introduced at a slower rate, averaging four to six new games per year.

Pinball art is part of the popular culture and the kinetic art movement. The strength of its pinball playfield design made D. Gottlieb & Co. the premier maker through the 1950s and into the 1970s. During the 1960s, the company's fame grew because of its animated backglasses, which both amused and attracted players. The combination of animation and availability make the 1960s' machines a target for collectors.

The advent of solid-state games in 1977, coupled with the video-game boom, dramatically changed the pinball-machine market. Solid-state game production increased as manufacturers attempted to replace all obsolete electromechanical games. Initially, Bally was the predominant maker, but Williams has since attained this position. Although solid-state games made electromechanical ones commercially obsolete, collectors who are rediscovering the silver ball are helping the pinball machine recover some of its popularity.

Collecting Hints: Cosmetic condition is of paramount importance. Graphics are unique to specific models, especially backglass and playfield plastics, making replacements scarce. Because they are complex, graphics are difficult, if not impossible, to repair. Prices in this listing are for games in working condition that are considered cosmetically good and have 95 percent or more of backglass decoration present.

Some wear is expected in pinballs as a sign that the game was a good one, but bare wood detracts from overall condition. Watch for signs of loose ink on the rear of the glass. Unrestorable games with good cosmetics are valuable because they can be used to help restore other games. A non-working game is worth 30 to 40 percent less than a working one.

Add 10 percent if the paper items, such as score card, instruction card, and schematic, are present and in good condition. It is fair to suggest that regardless of mechanical condition, a game in good cosmetic condition is worth roughly twice that of the same game in poor cosmetic condition.

Prices for specialty games and newer high tech theme machine have aroused new interest and better prices in certain categories. Collecting has also bee helped by newer homes having bigger sized gamerooms.

Notes: Pinballs are listed by machine name and fall into various classifications: novelty with no awards, replay which awards free games, add-a-ball which awards extra balls instead of games, and bingo where players add additional coins to increase the odds of winning. Some payout games made in the mid- to late-1930s paid out coins for achieving scoring objectives. After the first add-a-ball games in 1960, many game designs were issued as both replay and add-a-ball, with different game names and slight modifications to the game rules, but similar art work.

Adviser: Bob Levy.

Bally
1933, Airway, first mechanical scoring
.... **350.00**
1951, Coney Island, bingo **400.00**
1963, Moon Shot, replay **400.00**
1968, Rock Makers, replay, unusual playfield **500.00**
1972, Fireball **1,500.00**
1975, Bon Voyage, replay **350.00**
1978, Lost World, electronic **475.00**
Chicago Coin, 1948, Spinball, spinner action **175.00**

Game, Smith, front only, **$65**.

Exhibit, 1941, Big Parade, patriotic theme, classic art **450.00**
Genco, 1936, Daily Races, 1-ball **375.00**
Gottlieb
1936, Daily Races, one-ball **375.00**
1948, Buccaneer, replay, mirrored graphics **700.00**
1950, Knockout, playfield animated **2,500.00**
1951, Mermaid, backglass animated **3,000.00**
1956, Auto Race, replay **800.00**
1960, Flipper, first add-a-ball **1,000.00**
1965, Cow Poke, animation classic **1,750.00**
1966, Subway, backglass animation **1,500.00**
1967, King of Diamonds, replay, roto **1,100.00**
1977, Target Alpha, multiplayer ... **500.00**
1981, Black Hole, electronic, multi-level **800.00**
Mills Novelty Co., 1932, Official, push-button ball lift................................. **350.00**
Pacific Amusement, 1934, Lite-A-Line, first light-up backboard **400.00**
Rock-Ola
1932, Juggle Ball, countertop, road ball manipulator **300.00**
1934, World Series, desirable sports theme **1,000.00**
United, 1951, ABC, first bingo **400.00**

Williams

1948, Yanks, baseball theme, animated..
.... **600.00**
1951, Jalopy, mechanical car race
.... **1,000.00**
1953, Army-Navy, replay, reel scoring
.... **750.00**
1958, Gusher, disappearing bumper
.... **900.00**
1958, Turf Champ, playfield animation
.... **1,500.00**
1961, Metro, replay **400.00**
1964, Palooka, add-a-ball............. **600.00**
1973, Travel Time, timed play....... **300.00**
1977, Grand Prix, replay.............. **350.00**
1980, Firepower, electronic **610.00**

Planters Peanuts

History: Amedeo Obici and Mario Peruzzi organized the Planters Nut And Chocolate Company in Wilkes-Barre, Pennsylvania, in 1906. Obici had conducted a small peanut business for several years and was known locally as the "Peanut Specialist."

At first, Spanish salted red skins were sold for 10 cents per pound. Soon after, Obici developed the whole, white, blanched peanut, and this product became consumers' favorite.

In 1916, a young Italian boy submitted a rough version of the now-famous monocled and distinguished Mr. Peanut as an entry in a contest held by Planters to develop a trademark. A wide variety of premium and promotional items were soon based on this character.

Planters eventually was purchased by Standard Brands, which itself later became a division of Nabisco.

Collecting Hints: Planters Peanuts memorabilia is easily identified by the famous Mr. Peanut trademark. Items made between 1906 and 1916 have the "Planters Nut And Chocolate Company" logo.

Papier-mâché, die-cut, and ceramic pieces must be in very good condition. Cast-iron and tin pieces should be free of rust and dents and have good graphics and color.

Reproduction Alert.

Ashtray, 4-3/4" h, center figural Mr. Peanut, 1906-1956, mkd "Made in the USA by Diecasters Inc., Ridgefield, NJ" **30.00**

Counter jar, large, colorless glass, $90.

Bowl, 2" d, blue on bright yellow, Mr. Peanut holding tennis racquet, "Helps Easter Seals Serving the Handicapped," c1970
.... **15.00**

Bracelet, metal, 8" l, five plastic 1" charms, 1960s **30.00**

Burlap sack, 16" h, Mr. Peanut Roasted Peanuts, 1 lb, 8 oz, c1970.............. **18.00**

Can, tin

2-3/4" h, Mr. Peanut Cashew Nuts, Planters Nut and Chocolate Co., orig lid with wear, 1944 .... **32.00**

2-3/4" d, 3" h, Planters the Name for Quality, Mr. Peanut, recipe on back for Pecan Coffee Cake and Pecan Meringue Frosting, 4 oz, key wind lid, mkd "Canco," C-9.. **45.00**

Charm, 2-1/8" h, hard plastic, figural Mr. Peanut, emb "Mr. Peanut," 1950s.. **15.00**

Charm bracelet, 8" l, brass link bracelet, six colorful plastic charms, dark blue peanut, beige peanut, two beige Mr Peanut figures, two red Mr Peanut figures. **30.00**

Coloring book, Mr. Peanut American Ecology Coloring Book, 1970, unused
.... **15.00**

Cookbook, *Cooking The Modern Way*, Planters Peanut Oil, 1948, 40 pgs
.... **12.00**

Counter jar, 7" d clear heavy glass, orig lid, 8" x 8" x 9-1/2", corrugated cardboard shipping carton, c1960s................ **90.00**

Dish set coupon, 6-3/4" x 8-1/2", shows single serving dish and four individual smaller dishes, mail-in premium offer on back, expiration date of Sept. 30, 1939, folds **14.00**

Front: jar top to crush peanuts for salads, recipes, etc., **$18**; rear: nut set, serving bowl and four individual bowls, litho design with Mr. Peanut in center, **$75**.

Figure, 6" h, flexible vinyl, black and white with yellow/orange body, cane in hand, Russ sticker on back, 1991 copyright **20.00**

Jacket, Racing Team, dark blue, yellow lining, Mr. Peanut on front, larger one on back, unworn.................................. **30.00**

Lapel pin, hard plastic, figural Mr. Peanut **15.00**

Limited edition plate, 6" d, Wilton, pewter, 75th anniversary.............................. **60.00**

Mug, 4-1/4" d, 5" h, pewter, engraving of Mr. Peanut on side with date 1983 .... **15.00**

Olympic coin, 2" d, 1980, incised with Mr. Peanut, Winter Games, Lake Placid mascot on other side **15.00**

Paint book, Planters Seeing the USA, 1950, Mr. Peanut's trip through 48 states, Alaska, Hawaii, and Puerto Rico, unused **38.00**

Pen, 5-1/4" l, "Planters Snacks, Cheese Curls, Corn Chips, Pretzels" written on barrel, Mr. Peanut top, 1970s **20.00**

Pencil, mechanical, blue and yellow, Mr. Peanut on top, 1950s...................... **28.00**

Statue, 17" h, Mr Peanut **85.00**

Straw, 8" l, plastic, figural Mr. Peanut **15.00**

Tray, 15-5/8" x 11-5/8", tin................... **18.00**

Whistle, 2-1/2" h, figural plastic, Mr. Peanut, light blue plastic............................. **18.00**

Plastics

History: The word plastic is derived from the Greek *plastikos,* which literally translates to mean *pliable.* Therefore, any natural or artificial substance which can be shaped or formed by the application of heat and pressure is technically a plastic material. Natural plastics are organic compounds harvested from the animal and plant kingdoms; these include horn, tortoise shell, shellac, wax and latex. Semi-synthetic plastics are man made substances—combinations of natural materials that have been treated with chemicals; these include Vulcanite or Hardened Rubber, Casein, Celluloid, Cellulose Acetate and Beetleware. Synthetic plastics are made totally from chemical ingredients; these include Bakelite, Acrylic, Ethylene, Styrene and Vinyl.

All plastics fall into two distinct categories: they are either thermoplastic or thermoset plastic. Thermoplastics are materials molded by the application of heat, which then harden into shape—however, they are not heat resistant and may be reformed by subsequent application of heat. Thermoplastics are often recyclable. Thermoset plastics are those which, once molded, retain their original shape regardless of temperature. Thermoset plastics are durable and heat resistant.

Semi-synthetic man-made plastics

Celluloid

When celluloid was first commercially manufactured in the 1870s, its greatest virtue was as an imitative material for expensive natural substances that were becoming scarce. The introduction of faux ivory, tortoise shell, coral, amber and jet had a great impact on both society and industry as it made for a wide variety of inexpensive and easily manufactured goods that rivaled the genuine articles at a fraction of the cost. Eventually celluloid gained acceptance as a waterproof alternative to paper and textile in the manufacture of detachable collars. Furthermore, celluloid sheet was artfully decorated by lithograph and embossing techniques, then fashioned into some of the most fanciful objects of the Victorian and Edwardian Eras: highly desirable photograph albums and storage boxes. Advertising novelties and pinback buttons were also popular applications for sheet celluloid and are just as collectible today as they were 100 years ago.

Perhaps one of the most prolific uses for celluloid was in the manufacture of lightweight, unbreakable dolls and toys for children. Today it is not unusual for small holiday themed toys, which were once mass-produced and sold for pennies, to command hundreds of dollars as collectibles. Unfortunately the high content of nitric acid used in the recipe for celluloid rendered it highly inflammable and by the late 1920s modern non-flammable plastics were being developed to replace it.

Casein

Casein is a milk-based plastic that was accidentally discovered in 1890 by a German scientist, who had for some time been trying to develop a "white" black board with little success. It seems that one day his curious cat jumped upon the laboratory work table and tipped over a flask of formaldehyde, spilling the contents into a saucer of milk, resulting in a waxy solid substance. Realizing his good fortune, Adolph Spittler began to experiment by chemically treating casein curd, eventually finding success and patenting his material as Galalith, which translated means "milk stone." Later casein plastics became widely manufactured under trade names like Erinoid, Syrolit, Ameroid and Alladinite. Casein plastics found their greatest niche in buttons and beads, jewelry components, pen barrels, fan sticks and knitting needles. A word of caution to collectors: Casein easily breaks down with exposure to water and light, and care must be taken to prevent exposure which causes surface crazing and eventual

cracking. Furthermore, because casein is a protein-based plastic, it is also susceptible to parasitic infestation.

Beetle

Beetleware was a durable light-colored thermoset plastic material developed by British Cyanide in 1928. Hailed as the "great white hope," it was just as durable as Bakelite, but could be produced in pure white and pastel colors. Made from cellulose fiber that had been chemically treated with urea formaldehyde, it was introduced to American markets as Plaskon in 1929 when American Cyanamide began to manufacture the molding powder. Other trade names followed including Linga Longa and Bandalasta. Picnic sets, table wares, small novelty items and personal accessories, clock and radio cases are most often found in Beetle. Collector tip: Beetle is often mis-identified as celluloid because they are similar in color.

Synthetic plastics

Bakelite

Bakelite was the world's first completely synthetic thermoset plastic material, introduced in 1909 by Leo Baekland of Yonkers, New York. Made from coal tar distillates, phenol formaldehyde (carbolic acid and formaldehyde) and a variety of fillers, Bakelite was a dark brownish black, practically indestructible moldable material used primarily for electrical components, radio cases, car distributors, telephones and other objects that required heat resistance and durability. Eventually Bakelite recipes were refined and the colors red, green and amber were introduced to the molding process. By the 1930s, colorful radios, kitchen novelties, jewelry items and personal accessories were being cast and carved from the popular resin. When the statute of limitations ran out on Baekland's original patents in 1927, American Catalin Corporation and then the Marblette Corporation were organized for the production of cast and molded phenolic resin objects. Eventually these firms proved to become competitive rivals of Bakelite. Overall these three firms manufactured a wide variety of funky jewelry items, novelties and handsome radio cases in a range of 20 different translucent, opaque and mottled colors. Collector tip: Look for Bakelite objects that have a distinct artistic flare or exhibit Art Deco or Art Moderne design styles. Heavily carved jewelry items and multi colored examples are more valuable than plain or single colored objects. Vintage Bakelite has a mellow aged patina, and surface dirt or scratches can be polished away with a high quality plastic cream like Novus or Semi-chrome.

Acrylic

Acrylic resin is a crystal clear thermoplastic resin that was introduced in Germany by Rhom and Haas in 1931. Dupont introduced its brand of acrylic plastic in 1936 under the trade name Lucite. The beauty and durability of translucent acrylic resin made it a fine choice for molding a variety of fashion accessories, jewelry, novelty items and household wares. During the years after World War II, some furniture manufactures used acrylic resin to mold small tables, shelves and stands, lamps, telephones and even pianos. Today vintage acrylic jewelry, purses and small accessories are gaining momentum as a plastics collectible.

Polystyrene

Introduced in 1938, polystyrene thermoplastic became the stuff toys were made of after World War II. Inexpensive, lightweight and versatile, polystyrene could be produced in an array of mottled, opaque and translucent colors with its greatest applications being toys, advertising premiums and kitchen wares. By 1960, there were 6,000 firms in the U.S. making plastics materials, with 2,000 of those molding one billion pounds of polystyrene into toys annually.

Collecting Hints: A word of caution to collectors--thermoplastics can be irreparably damaged by a hot pin test. Almost any type of damage to plastic is non-reversible, so collectors should concentrate on examples in mint or good condition.

Adviser: Julie P. Robinson.

Acrylic

Bar stool, swivel with clear back, chrome legs **450.00**

Bedside stand, three-pc twisted acrylic rod base, round glass top **250.00**

Bracelet, 3/4" bangle, green, opaque, orig tag "Genuine Lucite" **12.00**

Brush and comb, translucent pink set, nylon bristles, mkd "Dupont Lucite," orig box **18.00**

Business card holder, rose inclusion, rect base **6.00**

Buttons, pearlescent pink squares, metal loop, set of eight on orig card **4.00**

Clock, electric, chrome and lucite, cylinder shaped, rotating disc that changes color, pink, yellow, purple, and green reflect in fact, 1970s **65.00**

Compact, 4" sq translucent case, applied sunburst medallion gold glitter acrylic, Roger & Gallet, mfg by Donmark Creations, Co, 1946 .... **150.00**

Cufflinks, pr, Krementz, toggle findings, paperweight style, fishing fly suspended in Lucite **35.00**

Drafting tools, Rhom & Haas Plexiglass, set of two rulers, two triangles, and semi-circle, c1940 .... **20.00**

Étagère, 60" h, free-standing triangular-shape shelf, clear acrylic with four mirror shelves, pointed finial **550.00**

Hand mirror, beveled acrylic handle and frame, U-shaped mirror, sterling floral ornament, c1946 .... **55.00**

Lamp, floor, faceted clear lucite balls alternating with chrome tubing, three twisted lucite arms for light bulbs, no shade **350.00**

Lamp, table, chrome cylinder base, 3" d solid Lucite ball top, flickering red, white, and blue lights in base reflect through bubbles in acrylic globe, c1976 .... **22.00**

Napkin ring, translucent lucite, square shape, rounded edges, circular center, c1960, price for four-pc set **10.00**

Paperweight, 3" cube, translucent lucite, suspended JFK 50 cent piece, c1965 .... **12.00**

Pin

Apple, pink lucite, gold-plated stem and leaf, Sarah Coventry, c1970 .... **20.00**
Dragonfly, pearlescent green lucite wings, enamel paint over pot metal, c1960 .... **8.00**
Turtle, jelly belly, aqua lucite center, pot metal, red painted eyes, c1950 ..... **12.00**

Purse

Basketweave chrome, 8" x 4", clear lucite bottom, black lucite hinged to and handle, c1955 .... **65.00**
Clutch, smoky gray lucite, camera case shape, hinge opening, c1950 .... **55.00**

Vanity, 4-1/2" x 4-1/2", envelope type front, white marbleized, Elgin American **100.00**

Shoe clips, pr, 2" oval shape, set with rhinestones **18.00**

Tumbler, clear 8 oz octagonal shape, chevron design, Art Deco revival, Norse Products, price for four-pc set
.... **25.00**

Bakelite

Ashtray, 8" d, black and white **45.00**

Bar pin, dangling heart, bright red catalin
.... **150.00**

Bracelet

1/2" w, bangle, carved leaf design, red catalin **65.00**
3/4" w, reverse carved floral design, translucent amber **150.00**

Buckle, circular, interlocked red, yellow, green, and blue rings...................... **25.00**

Button, one large, four small, oval, two holes, translucent amber and brown swirl, price for five-pc set............... **12.00**

Cake server, green handle.................. **12.00**

Chess set, butterscotch and marbleized brown... **400.00**

Clock, 12" h, Western Electric, Gothic shape, dark brown **65.00**

Crib toy, amber, green, and orange opaque catalin, shape of girl doll, 17 separate pieces strung together
.... **125.00**

Dress clip, catalin, triangular, chevron grooves, translucent green, price for pr
.... **65.00**

Manicure box, Cleopatra, mfg by GE, black and red Art Deco.......................... **165.00**

Napkin ring, figural
Bird, green, black bill **45.00**
Rabbit, butterscotch **65.00**
Scottie dog, red.............................. **65.00**

Pie crimper, marbleized butterscotch handle... **6.00**

Pin, figural, cat, yellow catalin, chrome
.... **95.00**

Poker chips, black, maroon, butterscotch, maroon holder **130.00**

Rattle, barbell shape, five rings, red, green, and butterscotch............................ **90.00**

Ring

Dome top, floral carving, butterscotch
.... **75.00**
Square, starburst carving, brown ... **65.00**

Ring box

Clamshell-style, streamline modern grooves, orange and butterscotch swirl
.... **85.00**
Semi-circular, hinged lift top, square base, mottled green and yellow **75.00**

Salt and pepper shakers, pr, figural
Amber shakers, brown bird shaped holder... **120.00**

Marbleized caramel, gear shape, chrome lids, 2" h... **95.00**

Serving tray, oval dark blue, inlaid strips of chrome, Art Deco style................ **350.00**

Souvenir

Washington Monument, obelisk shape, cream colored................................. **65.00**
World's fair, Trylon and Perisphere, orange, green, red, and yellow, price for pr **75.00**

Stationery box, 7" x 8", molded brown, Art Deco winged horse design, American Stationery Co., 1937 .... **75.00**

Toothpick holder, dachshund, green
.... **95.00**

Utensil set, knife, fork, spoon, marbleized red and yellow handles, three pcs
.... **18.00**

View-Master stereoscope, orig box
.... **65.00**

Yo-yo, mottled green, mkd "Regal PDC"
.... **30.00**

Beetleware: candlesticks, chartreuse green and black, very Art Deco, 6" h, **$85**. All plastics photos courtesy of adviser Julie Robinson.

Beetleware: Coty make-up clutch fitted with three cosmetics made from gold tone metal and green Beetleware plastic, 2-1/8" h lipstick with hinged top, 2-1/2" x 1-1/2" compact with mirror and original puff, 2-1/4"h perfume flask marked "Emeraude," **$36**.

Beetleware

Cups, cov, graduated, set of four, 1 oz, blue; 2 oz green; 3 oz, red; 4 oz, yellow, mkd "Beetle".. **24.00**

Mixing bowl set, three graduated sizes, Bandalasta Mottled, gray with speckled orange, yellow, red, black, green ... **28.00**

Razor, Kewtie Miniature, pink beetleware clamshell type holder with small razor inside **18.00**

Shake-up mug, Ovaltine premium, Little Orphan Annie, cream colored, orange lid, decal of Annie with dog Sandy **55.00**

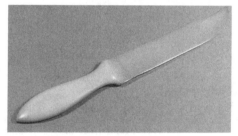

Casein: knife, unmarked, 8" l, $12.

Casein: dress clips, chevron shaped Alladinite Plastic, lozenge-shaped rims set with rhinestones, metal clips marked "Pat 1852188," pair, $28.

Casein

Beads

10" graduated length, creamy white imitation ivory, heavily molded to resemble carving **12.00**

12" double strand, imitation coral, plain, only a few molded beads **12.00**

Button set, original card, four mottled brown buttons shaped like flowers
.... **4.00**

Dress clips, 2-1/4" l, chevron shaped with rhinestones, pr................................ **28.00**

Letter opener, stamped metal handle with casein plastic blade, overall 8" l, some surface crazing, imitation tortoise **8.00**

Celluloid

Animal

Cow, 6", laying down, mkd "VCO" .. **35.00**

Dog, St. Bernard, 5" h, mkd "VCO - Made in USA".. **14.00**

Duck, 3" l, cream colored, gray highlights, mkd "VCO - Made in USA" **12.00**

Horse, 7" l, cream color, brown highlights, hp eyes, intertwined VCO mark..... **45.00**

Scottie Dog, 3", mkd "Made in USA" **18.00**

Bar pin, 2-3/4" l, ivory grained, orange and brown-layered pearlescence, hp rose motif... **12.00**

Bookmark, 4-1/2" l, cream-colored diecut, poinsettia motif, Psalm 22, printed by Meek Co... **15.00**

Celluloid: photo album, girl with cat decoration, $100.

Bracelet, bangle, translucent amber celluloid, double row of green rhinestones
.... **25.00**

Collar box, 6" x 6", olive colored, emb celluloid with floral motif, picture of beautiful woman on top.................. **45.00**

Doll

4-1/4" h, girl holding horse, Irwin.... **32.00**

5" h, Jackie Cogan **45.00**

Dresser set, comb, brush, mirror, tray, powder, box, and hair receiver, marked "Ivory Pyralin," price for six-pc set. **65.00**

Dresser tray, 8" oval, imitation amber rim, embossed and painted with black and gold trim, glass and lace center **35.00**

Fan box, 12-1/2" x 3-3/4", reverse painted Art Nouveau design, cream, with green, black, yellow and gold fan motif **85.00**

Hair comb, 6" l, pale amber, blue rhinestones, painted blue bird motif..................... **55.00**

Ink blotter booklet, 8-1/2" l, 1-1/2" Christmas premium with colorful manger scene and three wise men offering gifts, marked 1917 Whitehead & Hoag, Newark, NJ **55.00**

Match safe, 2-1/4" x 1-1/2", color photo scenes from Atlantic City, NJ **18.00**

Celluloid: toy, roly poly, Halloween witch, made by Viscoloid, trademark, c1927, 3-3/4" h, **$375**.

Picture frame, 8" x 10", oval, ivory grained, easel back **25.00**

Pinback button, 1-1/4" d, dangling 1" celluloid camel, Shriner's logo **55.00**

Pocket mirror, 2-1/2" oval, souvenir of Niagara Falls, printed colored drawing of Falls... **38.00**

Purse, 4-1/4" d, clam shell-type, imitation tortoise with pearlized clasp, leather strap **85.00**

Roly-Poly

2-1/2" d, realistic chicken, weighted base **45.00**

4" h, witch sitting on pumpkin roly poly base with cat, VCO, Made in USA **350.00**

Polystyrene: salesman's premium bank, Electrolux vacuum cleaner, detailed, marked "Electrolux, Automatic, Model G," 1950s, 5-1/2" l, **$35**.

Polystyrene: party favor, witch's basket, orange base, black handle, made by Best USA, 1950s, 3" w, 3" h, **$8**.

Polystyrene

Bank, 5-1/2" l, novelty premium, Electrolux Vacuum Cleaner, aqua blue, mkd "Electrolux, Automatic, Model G"... **24.00**

Doll, 2-1/4" h, baby, movable arms and legs, Renwal No. 5................................... **20.00**

Party favor, 3" x 3"
Basket, figural stork handle, blue and pink, Best, USA................................. **4.00**
Basket, figural witch handle, Halloween, orange and black, Best, USA **8.00**

Toy, violin, orig bow, Duraltone Toy Co., two tone green and pink mottled polystyrene, orig box, NY, USA........................... **18.00**

Political and Campaign Items

History: Since 1800, the American presidency always has been a contest between two or more candidates. Initially, souvenirs were issued to celebrate victories. Items issued during a campaign to show support for a candidate were widely distributed beginning with the William Henry Harrison campaign of 1840.

There is a wide variety of campaign items—buttons, bandannas, tokens, pins, etc. The only limiting factor has been the promoter's imagination. The advent of television campaigning has reduced the quantity of individual items, and modern campaigns do not seem to have the variety of materials that were issued earlier.

Modern collectors should be aware of reproduction button sets issued as promotional items by companies such as Kleenex Tissues and American Oil in the 1970s.

Collecting Hints: Items priced below $100 sell frequently enough to establish firm prices. Items above that price fluctuate according to supply and demand. Many individuals now recognize the value of acquiring political items and holding them for future sale. As a result, modern material has a relatively low market value, unless few examples were produced.

Knowledgeable collectors also keep in touch with Presidential libraries to find out what type of souvenir items they are offering for sale. This information is helpful in determining which items on the market originated at the time of actual campaigns, and these are the ones collectors should concentrate on acquiring.

The pioneering work on the identification of political buttons has been done by Theodore L. Hake. His three-volume *Encyclopedia of Political Buttons* pictures 12,000 items from 1789 through 1976. Each volume, and the just completed "Revised Prices 2004," are available at Hake's Auction Web site, www.hakes.com. Joining the hobby group American Political Items Collectors (APIC) is recommended and applications are available by email from APIC@hakes.com. Two other books have greatly assisted in the identification and cataloging of pre-1896 campaign materials: Herbert R. Collins's *Threads of History* and Edmund B. Sullivan's *American Political Badges and Medalets 1789-1892*.

Adviser: Ted Hake.

William Howard Taft, mechanical postcard, "Pull My Tail and See the Next President," 1908, postally used, **$50**.

William Howard Taft, badge, brass top bar with celluloid insert "Captain" in blue on white, purple ribbon with gold lettering "West Side Businessman's Taft & Sherman Association Oct. 31, 1908," 7/8" jugate attached to 2-1/4" x 4-1/2", **$75**.

William Howard Taft

Badge, 2-1/4" x 4-1/2", 7/8" jugate attached, brass top bar with celluloid insert "Captain" in blue on white, purple ribbon with gold lettering "West Side Business-men's Taft & Sherman Association Oct. 31, 1908" **75.00**

Pinback, 7/8" d, real photo, sepia, reverse with paper from Weber Badge and Novelty, Reading **60.00**

Postcard, mechanical, Pull My Tail and See the Next President, 1908, postally used **50.00**

Stickpin, 2" brass pin, 3/4" diecut embossed oval plate, black and white photo in center, 1912 .... **25.00**

Teddy Roosevelt

Bank, 5" h, cast iron, bust, inscribed below uniform "Teddy," gold paint, silver eyeglasses **200.00**

Button, rebus

For President, rebus, large full-color design of red rose, green stem, center above lettering "Velt," no back paper **200.00**

Vote For Roosevelt Use Maple City Soap, dark red, cream lettering, 1904 .... **210.00**

Sheet music, 10-3/4" x 13-1/2", *Marche de Triomphe Roosevelt March,* six pgs, full color, 1902 .... **95.00**

Theodore Roosevelt, bank, cast iron, bust, inscribed "Teddy" below uniform, gold paint, silver eyeglasses, 5" h, $200.

Woodrow Wilson, 1912, 1916

Button, 7/8", real profile portrait photo, shades of gray and cream, black ground, reverse paper from Phila Badge Co **65.00**

Calendar, 1918, 15" w, 25" l, full-color image of Uncle Sam with his arm over Wilson's shoulder, who is steering ship wheel, "Ship of State," fleet of battleships and biplanes in background, orig calendar pad **65.00**

Campaign ribbon, 3" x 6", red, white, and blue, Democratic ticket, above and below crossed flags, Wilson/Marshall **35.00**

Jugate, 13/16", cream and dark brown, "Gardner and Wilson," slogan below "Peace and Prosperity," Bastian back paper **85.00**

Postcard, 3-1/4" x 5-1/2", "Our Next President," black on pale green, "Magic Moving Pictures Card," push/pull black and white flicker of Teddy Roosevelt, Taft, or Wilson, 1912 .... **40.00**

Warren G. Harding, 1920

Button, "For President Warren G. Harding," 7/8" d, photo center, white rim, blue lettering **15.00**

Stereoscopic card, set of five, showing Harding and wife at visits, speeches, and vacations, c1920 .... **20.00**

Herbert Hoover, 1928, 1932

Button, 13/16", litho tin, black and white photo on black, "Hoover for President" **35.00**

Campaign ring, Hoover 1928, non-adjustable silvered brass, ornate enameled designs **30.00**

Franklin D. Roosevelt, 1932, 1936, 1940, 1944

Button

7/8", large bluetone photo, accent stars surrounded by white lettering on bright red rim, "Re-elect Roosevelt" **12.00**

13/16", black on cream, "For President Franklin D. Roosevelt," 1932, made by Green Duck.................................... **20.00**

3-1/2" d, black and white photo, "Re-Elect Our President, Franklin D. Roosevelt" **45.00**

Campaign Ribbon, 2" x 6-1/2", blue and white, imprinted "Roosevelt Reception/Los Angeles/September 24th 1932" **20.00**

Inauguration program, 8-1/2" x 11", 65 pgs, blue, white, and black cover, *Official Inaugural Program, March 4, 1933,* cover artwork by Newman S. Sudduth **50.00**

Jugate, 1-1/4", Roosevelt/Garner, red, white, and blue, star and stripe design, blue illus portraits................................... **40.00**

Menu, pair of 6" x 9" menu folders, both titled *The President Of The United States of America and Party,* gold logo for Atlantic Coastline Railroad, one from Washington to Jacksonville, March 27-28, 1934, other from Miami to Washington, April, 1934 .... **35.00**

Mug, Happy Days Are Here Again, 3" d, 5" h, green glazed ceramic, c1933........ **24.00**

Pillow Cover, 16" x 18", large black photo of FDR in wicker chair on front, navy border, blue piping, bright orange fabric back, c1932-36 .... **60.00**

Ribbon, 1-1/2" x 5", white and blue striped fabric, gold type "We Want Roosevelt," 1938 .... **25.00**

Sheet music, 9" x 12", *On With Roosevelt*, red, white, and blue, four pgs, words and music by Louise Graeser, 1938 ...... **20.00**

Tab, 15/16" litho tab, "Roosevelt/Truman," Green Duck **60.00**

Alfred Landon, 1936

Button, 7/8" d, red, white, and blue panels, white and blue text "Landon for President," Bastian **12.00**

Campaign card, 2-1/4" x 4" heavy paper card for election day, 1936 .... **10.00**

Napkin, 13-1/2" sq brown on white in paper, Landon's sunflower art in center as compass, folds to 7" sq, c1936
.... **18.00**

Sheet music, *G.O.P. March*, 9" x 12", four pgs, red, white, and blue cover with elephant beating bass drum, images of Landon and Knox in blue and white, text at bottom "Sold to Help Finance the 1936 Campaign," red, white, and blue text on back listing contracts between FDR and Landon, lists Republican candidates for US Senate and House of Rep **90.00**

Wendell Willkie, 1940

Banner, 5" w, 6" l, red, white, and blue fabric, blue and white Willkie portrait, red and white "God Bless America," red "Our Next President," blue and white "Wendell Willkie," orig brass hanger at top ... **45.00**

Button

7/8" d, black on bright gold, "Willkie Contributor," St Louis backpaper
.... **18.00**

1-1/4" d, black and white graphic photo on white, red, white, and blue rim .. **10.00**

1-1/4" d, white text on red panel at top "Caution," white text on blue below "We Need Willkie Not Dictatorship"
.... **15.00**

3-1/2" d, black and white real photo, eagle on either side, rim text "For President, Wendell L. Willkie" **35.00**

Car attachment, 3-1/2" h, black and white, 1940 .... **50.00**

Coaster, 3-1/8" d, pair, blue and white image, name "Wendell L. Willkie" below, each has eight tiny embossed stars, red rim and back **35.00**

Stickpin, 7/8" h, six-sided white plastic frame with real photo, 1" vertical pin on back **8.00**

Harry S. Truman, necktie, oval portrait, burgundy background, 1948, 48" l, **$125**.

Harry S. Truman, 1948

Autograph, 8" x 10" matte finish photo, inscribed in black fountain pen "To Hon. George L. Peck Kind Regards from Harry Truman, 4-64" **200.00**

Booklet, *The Democratic Digest, June-July 1950*, 7-1/2" x 10-3/4", 32 pgs, black and white, photos, text of Democratic stand
.... **20.00**

Bottle stopper, 3-1/2" h, hollow plaster, full dimensional likeness head, 7/8" l cork stopper, c1948 to 1952 .... **75.00**

Button, 1-1/2" d, black text on light blue, "Harry S. Truman Good Neighbor Award Foundation" **12.00**

Inauguration button, 3-1/2" d, red, white, and blue, black and white center photo
.... **90.00**

Necktie, 48" l, oval portrait, burgundy background, 1948 .... **125.00**

Tab, 1" wide, litho tin, dark blue text on white, "Truman Barkley," returned to unfolded position **45.00**

Thomas E. Dewey

Booklet, 3-1/2" x 11", 10 unused Dewey-Warren dollar certificates, each with oval portraits, dated 1948...................... **25.00**

Button, 7/8" d, red, white, and blue, white and blue text "Dewey for President," pair of union bugs on curl **5.00**

Jugate, 3-1/2" d, Vote Republican for Dewey Warren, red, white, and blue, black and white photos **60.00**

Lapel stud, 7/8" d, celluloid, profile diecut elephant with name on side............. **5.00**

Dwight Eisenhower, poster, "Back 'Em Up," red, white, and blue portrait of General Eisenhower, "Buy Extra Bonds, Official US Treasury Poster," 1944, 28" x 20", folds as issued, $85.

Dwight Eisenhower, 1952, 1956

Button

5/8" d, red, white, and blue rim surrounding young black and white photo in military uniform, "Get Right with Ike," St. Louis back paper........................ **25.00**

1" d, red, white, and blue litho, white and blue text "I Like Mamie" **12.00**

Inaugural paperweight, 2-3/4" x 3-3/4", glass, black on silver image of Ike, date "January 20, 1953" in upper left corner, facsimile signature "With Best Wishes Dwight D. Eisenhower," copyright Fabian Bachrach **35.00**

Inauguration button, brown and white photos of Ike, Mamie, Dick, and Pat, "43rd Inauguration 1957 Consent of the Governed," inauguration logo about photos **50.00**

Jugate

1-3/8" d, litho, bluetone photos on white, red accents, white text and panel, "Let's Back Ike & Dick," 1952.................. **25.00**

4" d, red, white, and blue celluloid, Ike and Nixon dark blue tone photos, names in red, elephant above pictures **60.00**

License plate, 3" x 5", black on orange steel, Ike.. **35.00**

Matchbook, *Citizens for Eisenhower*, red, white and blue pack, Reading, PA, hotel sponsor, used **12.00**

Pocket mirror, 2-1/4" x 3-1/2", "I Like Ike," c1952 .... **30.00**

Poster

10" x 13-1/2", black and white jugate of Eisenhower and Nixon, "You Win When You Vote For Ike and Dick," text at bottom in white on blue............................... **35.00**

28" x 20", "Back 'Em Up," red, white, and blue portrait of General Eisenhower, "Buy Extra Bonds, Official US Treasury Poster," 1944, folds as issued **85.00**

Sign, 9" x 11", cardboard, 2-3/4" x 3-1/2" color paper image of Ike, facsimile signature, dark blue, metallic highlights of dove, stars, and text "May God Bless Our President".. **35.00**

Tab, 2-1/8" h, litho tin, unbent stem, bright red, white and blue design, "Sweep Clean-Vote · Republican," sweeping broom image, c1956 .... **20.00**

Richard Nixon, jugate, "Peace Experience Prosperity Vote Republican," photos of Nixon and Lodge, red, white, and blue, 3-1/2" d, $25.

Richard Nixon, door hanger, orange, brown, and white diecut pumpkin shape, "Even the Great Pumpkin is Voting for Nixon/Agnew," 7-1/2" x 9", $30.

Richard M. Nixon, 1960, 1968, 1972

Bendee, 4" h, painted rubber figure of Nixon, jointed swivel arms, hands giving victory sign, 1" d suction cup attached to top of head, c1972 .... **20.00**

Bubble gum cigars, 4-1/2" x 5", red, white, and blue box, 22 cigars, "Win with Dick" on labels, black and white photo of Nixon on box lid **35.00**

Button

1", dark blue on white litho, red center accent stripe, "I'm A Democrat for Nixon Lodge" **20.00**

1-1/4" d, blue text on white, "Nixon for President" **15.00**

1-1/4" d, Watergate Bugger, black and white, Nixon head, holding ear trumpet, louse body **12.00**

1-3/4" d, Nixon Lodge Experience Counts, white names, bright red elephant and slogan **15.00**

Car antenna flag, 4" x 9-1/2", Pat for First Lady, plastic, 1960 .... **25.00**

Clicker, 1-3/4", Click with Dick, dark blue on white litho tin **12.00**

Door hanger, 7-1/2" x 9", orange, brown, and white diecut pumpkin shape, "Even the Great Pumpkin is Voting Nixon/Agnew" **30.00**

Hat, 5-1/2" x 11", paper, "Experience Counts! Vote Nixon Lodge," red, white, and blue, two sided, adjustable, telescoping, unused **25.00**

Jugate

2-3/4" h, red and white stripes, names in blue, black and white photos of Nixon and Lodge **20.00**

3-1/2" d, red, white, and blue, "Peace Experience Prosperity Vote Republican," photos of Nixon and Lodge **25.00**

Poster, 14" x 20", "Welcome President Nixon to Pekin," dark blue on bright orange on white, made for 1973 visit to Everett Dirkson Congressional Research Center and Pekin (Illinois) Public Library... **25.00**

Ticket, 3-1/2" x 6", Nixon/Lodge Campaign Breakfast, Oct. 5, 1960, Hotel Commodore, New York City, 7/8" d red, white, and blue "Nixon/Lodge" button attached **30.00**

Wristwatch, orig black glossy leather strap, 1-1/2" d brass luster case, red, white, blue, and fleshtone carton of Nixon in baseball uniform, holding bat, mkd "E. K. O. Mfg CO., 1970," working **75.00**

John F. Kennedy, hand-out, diecut paper, red, white and blue, "Give Me Your Hand Pull The First Lever for Jack Kennedy and his Team," 6" x 10-1/2", $35.

John F. Kennedy, 1960

Ashtray, 4" x 4-1/2", smoked glass, black and white photos of JFK and RFK at center, gold trim, birth and death dates, gold stars, famous quotes, c1968 . **25.00**

Button

7/8", black on bright orange, black donkey, "Young Americans for Kennedy" **20.00**

7/8", white on dark blue, "OK Oregon for Kennedy" **25.00**

1-3/4", picture button, bluetone photo, bright red text on white "On The Right Track With Jack" **75.00**

Delegate badge, 1960 Democratic National Convention, Los Angeles, orig box **40.00**

Hand-out, 6" x 10-1/2", red, white and blue, "Give Me Your Hand Pull The First Lever for Jack Kennedy and his Team," diecut paper **35.00**

Jugate, 1-3/4" x 2-3/4", rect, black and white photos, blue rim, red eagle, "Kennedy Johnson" **50.00**

Magazine

Photoplay, March 1964, full-color cover of Pres and First Lady, special section titled "Jack & Jackie - Their Courtship," seven-page article on "JFK, the Assassin Was Not Alone," black and white and color photos **15.00**

US News & World Report, Nov. 21, 1960, full-color photo of Kennedy on cover **25.00**

Paper cup, 2-3/4" d, 3-1/8" h, Coffee with Kennedy, red on white **25.00**

Pin, 1" l, brass luster diecut initial "K" at left, arrow design pointing to left, forming part of K, 1960 .... **20.00**

Sheet music, *Massachusetts, My Home State,* 9" x 12", Special Kennedy Version, text "Souvenir Copy John F. Kennedy Received The Nomination For The Presidency of The United States At The 1960 Democratic National Convention Held At Los Angeles, California," cartoon donkey holds picture of JFK **40.00**

Souvenir plate, 6-1/2" d, President and Mrs. John F. Kennedy, painted full-color illus, c1961 .... **20.00**

Lyndon Johnson, 1964

Button

1-1/2" d, LSD NOT LBJ, dark red, day-glow yellow, curl with imprint of Greenwich Village underground shop, c1967-68 .... **40.00**

2" d, bright red on bright yellow, "Young Texans for Johnson" **75.00**

Flasher, 2-1/2" d black and white flasher with picture and slogan "All The Way With LBJ," 6" white on purple ribbon reading "Welcome President L. B. Johnson, Inauguration, Jan. 20, 1965" **35.00**

Glass, 5-1/2" h, clear glass, Kosygin Summit, Glassboro State College, NJ, June, 1967, black and white illus of meeting place **20.00**

Hat, 4" x 11", plastic, campaign style, red, white, and blue stripes, black and white illus of Johnson on right, "LBJ for the USA" **10.00**

Pen, give-away, gold presidential logo, facsimile signature on black plastic, gold metal top and clip, felt tipped pen frayed **15.00**

Program, 9" x 12", 'Congressional Secretary's Club," 1965, 100 pgs, cover features "Man of the Year, Lyndon Johnson" **30.00**

Barry Goldwater, 1964

Autographed jugate, 3-1/2" d, red, white, and blue, black and white photo of Goldwater and Miller, "The Best Men for the Job Goldwater Miller," black ink autograph "William Miller" **25.00**

Autographed photo, 8" x 10", black and white glossy, 2-1/2" l blue inked Goldwater autograph **40.00**

Barry Goldwater, jugate, red, white, and blue photo of Goldwater and Miller, "The Best Men for the Job Goldwater Miller," black ink autograph "William Miller," 3-1/2" d, **$25**.

Badge, 2-3/4" x 3", diecut cardboard, Liberty Bell, yellow, red, white, and black, text "Ring Freedom In With Goldwater For President" **45.00**

Button, 1-1/4", black, gold text and elephant, "Goldwater for President". **8.00**

Rebus, 7/8", black and white, glass filled with gold liquid, black imprint "H2O" formula, by Trimble **8.00**

Ring, orig 3-1/2" x 5-1/2" red, white, and blue card, "Official National Kids for Goldwater Club Ring, stars and stripes motif, black and white photos of Goldwater, blue plastic flasher ring with picture of Goldwater and "I'm For Barry" **40.00**

Stickpin, elephant, diecut plastic, wearing Goldwater-style eyeglasses **5.00**

Tie tac, diecut letters, brass luster, needlepost and clutch back **5.00**

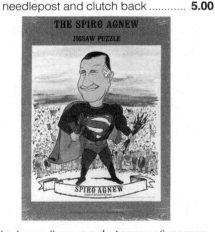

Spiro Agnew, jigsaw puzzle, Agnew as Superman, copyright 1970 Game Ophiles Unlimited Inc., color caricature "Friend of the Silent Majority," 500 pieces, unopened, 9-1/4" x 13", **$15**.

Spiro Agnew

Jigsaw puzzle, 9-1/4" x 13", 500 pcs, Agnew as Superman, copyright 1970 Game Ophiles Unlimited Inc., color caricature "Friend of the Silent Majority," unopened **15.00**

Wristwatch, glossy red bands, 1-1/2" silver luster case, red, white, blue, and fleshtone cartoon of him, large red hands in "V" gesture, dial reads "Peace Time Company," working **50.00**

Gerald Ford

Button

1-1/2" d, white text, panels of dark red and dark blue, "Republican and Proud 1976" **7.00**
2-1/4" d, blue on white, red "'76," "Ford in '76 Makes Sense for America" **15.00**
2-1/2" d, blue lettering, gray elephant on white, "Remember Republicans Eat Peanuts" **35.00**

Pin

1" h, brass, stylized elephant, accented by red, white, and blue on brass enamel, "Ford" in white, orig plastic bag **8.00**
1-1/4" x 1-1/2", blue text "Wear an 'F' Support Ford for President," orig white card with diecut brass letter "F," needle post and clutch back **8.00**

Gerald Ford, button, blue lettering, gray elephant on white, "Remember Republicans Eat Peanuts," 2-1/2" d, **$35**.

Jimmy Carter, 1976

Bandanna, 28" sq, Carter-Mondale, white and green, 1980 .... **25.00**
Inauguration medal, 5" x 6" x 2" white cardboard box, blue presidential seal on top, solid bronze medal, antique finish, diecut repository lined in dark blue felt, parchment authenticity certificate, "Sculptured by Julian Harris/Minted by the Franklin Mint" **30.00**

Button

1-1/4" d, green, white text "Carter for President/Keep Brown Governor," 1976 .... **10.00**
1-1/4" d, white and bright green, "Jimmy Carter for President in '76" **8.00**
1-3/4" d, bright green on white, "Carter by a Country Smile," Music City, USA, Nashville, Tennessee **10.00**
2-1/4" d, red, white, and blue, cartoon of Carter as Planters Peanut Man, blue text "I'm Working for Peanuts," on white, maker's name "Mac Donald Associates" on curl, 1976 .... **15.00**

Jugate

2-1/4" d, black and white, Carter shaking hands with man (may be Abe Beame, NY City), dated Dec. 5, 1978 .... **12.00**
2-1/2" d, green and white, "Iowans For 1976 Carter-Mondale" **15.00**
License plate, 6" x 12", red, white, and blue, "District of Columbia 10526 Inauguration 1977" **35.00**
Press badge, ABC News, Democratic National Convention, black on pink **5.00**
Watch, 1-1/4" d. dial with brown, rd, gray, and blue caricature figure, reads "Official Jimmy Cater from Peanuts to President," Goober Time Company, 1976, stainless steel back, gold colored metal bezel **50.00**

Ronald Reagan, button, black and white photo of Reagan dressed as cowboy, "I Shot JR, I Despise Bleeding Heart Liberals," 1980, 4" d, **$20**.

Ronald Reagan, 1980, 1984

Button

2-1/4" d, purple on black, "That's All Folks" **15.00**
2-3/4" d, black, white, red, fleshtone, dark blue background, cartoon of Nancy, "Let Them Eat Cake," c1984 .... **15.00**

4" d, black and white photo of Reagan dressed as cowboy, "I Shot JR, I Despise Bleeding Heart Liberals," 1980 ...... **20.00**

Christmas card, 1982, unused, 6" x 8", orig envelope **15.00**

Inaugural attendance package, 7" x 10-1/2", used admission ticket, invitation folder, set of Reagan and Bush black and white photos with tissue sheets, events program with gold presidential emblem, 1985, with 6-1/2" x 14" card stock inaugural parking sign with gold seal **50.00**

License plate, Presidential Inauguration, red, white, and blue aluminum, 1981 .... **17.50**

Poster, 17" x 22", Reagan for President, blue text, red and blue border around picture, c1976 .... **20.00**

George Bush, 1980, 1984, 1988

Bumper sticker, 3-1/2" x 9-1/2", "Bush/Quayle '88," red, white, and blue **2.50**

Button, 2-13/16" d, black and white cartoon, blue accent, red text "No Bush in '92!" **20.00**

Inaugural mug, 3-1/2" h, blue, gold printing "Staff" **20.00**

Jugate, 2-1/8" d button, red, white, blue, and gold, attached red, white, blue, and gold ribbon, "Peace Prosperity Progress Bush Quayle, Inauguration of George Bush and Dan Quayle, January 20, 1989" **20.00**

Bill Clinton, campaign card, black and white photo of Clinton talking to farmers, reverse with black and white button of Governor Clinton," "Bill Clinton Knows That To Put Our State On The Road To Growth And Prosperity, We Need More Jobs, Controlled Utility Rates, And A Better Education System, We Need Bill Clinton In The Governor's Office," 1982, 2" x 4", **$30**.

Bill Clinton, 1992, 1996

Button, 3" d, blue and white picture of Clinton wearing shades and playing sax, white on black text "Clinton A Cure For The Blues Young Democrats," PA Young Democrats **35.00**

Campaign card, 2" x 4", black and white photo of Clinton talking to farmers, reverse with black and white button of Clinton Governor, "Bill Clinton Knows That To Put Our State On The Road To Growth And Prosperity, We Need More Jobs, Controlled Utility Rates, And A Better Education System, We Need Bill Clinton In The Governor's Office," 1982..... **30.00**

Inaugural, 2-3/16" d, color photos of Clinton and Gore against light pink tone background, full color over printing of presidential seal, names in white on blue rim, "January 20, 1997 Inauguration".............................. **15.00**

Presidential give-away, memo pad holder, 4" sq, polished silver finish, Presidential seal upper left, facsimile signature "Bill Clinton" upper right corner, plain gray box, late 1990s **65.00**

George W. Bush, Toby mug, full color, flag handle, text "Bairstow Manor Pottery Enduring Freedom George W. Bush Ltd. Edition of 500, This is No. 88, Modelled by Ray Nobie," produced in England, spring 2003, original plain box with "88" inked on top, 7" h, **$150**.

George W. Bush, 2000

Button, 3-1/2" d, "2001 Black Tie & Boots Inaugural Ball," red, white, and blue, black and white photos, "Texas State Society of Washington DC," Clint Black & Lisa Hartman, Tanya Tucker, Beach Boys, Asleep at the Wheel, Mark Chestnut, Lee Greenwood, January 19, 2001 .... **25.00**

Toby mug, 7" h, full color, flag handle, text "Bairstow Manner Pottery Enduring Freedom George W. Bush Ltd. Edition of 500 This is No. 88, Modelled by Ray Nobie," produced in England, spring 2003, orig plain box with "88" inked on top **150.00**

Postcards

History: The golden age of postcards dates from 1898 to 1918. Cards printed earlier are collected for their postal history. Postcards prior to 1898 are called "pioneer" cards.

European publishers, especially in England and Germany, produced the vast majority of cards during the golden age. The major postcard publishers are Raphael Tuck (England), Paul Finkenrath of Berlin (PFB-German), and Whitney, Detroit Publishing Co., and John Winsch (United States). However, many American publishers had their stock produced in Europe, hence, "Made in Bavaria" imprints. While some Tuck cards are high priced, many are still available in the "10¢" boxes.

Styles changed rapidly, and manufacturers responded to every need. The linen postcard, which gained popularity in the 1940s, was quickly replaced by the chrome cards of the post-1950 period.

Collecting Hints: Concentrate on one subject area, publisher, or illustrator. Collect cards in mint condition, when possible.

The more common the holiday, the larger the city, the more popular the tourist attraction, the easier it will be to find postcards on the subject because of the millions of cards that were originally available. The smaller runs of "real" photo postcards are the most desirable of the scenic cards. Photographic cards of families and individuals, unless they show occupations, unusual toys, dolls, or teddy bears have little value.

Stamps and cancellation marks may sometimes affect the value of cards. Consult a philatelic guide.

Postcards fall into two main categories: view cards and topics. View cards are easiest to sell in their local geographic region. European view cards, while very interesting, are difficult to sell in America.

It must be stressed that age alone does not determine price. A birthday postcard from 1918 may sell for only 10 cents, while a political campaign card from the 1950s may bring $10. The price of every collectible is governed by supply and demand.

Although cards from 1898 to 1918 are the most popular with collectors, the increasing costs of postcards from this era have turned attention to postcards from the 1920s, 1930s, and 1940s. Art Deco cards from 1920-1930 are the most desirable. The 1940s "linens," so called because of their textured linen-like paper surface, are the most popular cards of that time period.

Cards from 1950 to 1970 are called "Chromes" because of their shiny surface.

Notes: The following prices are for cards in excellent to mint condition— no sign of edge wear, no creases, untrimmed, no writing on the picture side of the card, no tears, and no dirt. Each defect reduces the price given by 10 percent.

Advertising

Adv on linens, large product image .. **12.00**
Adv on chromes, large product image
.... **7.50**

Automobile adv
    American prior to 1920 .... **28.00**
    European prior to 1920 .... **17.50**
    Oldsmobile 88 Super, four-door sedan, 1952 .... **18.50**
    Pontiac Streamliner, four-door sedan, 1949 .... **18.50**

Campbell Soup adv
    Horizontal format **32.00**
    Vertical format **100.00**

Coca-Cola adv
    Duster girl in car **450.00**
    Hamilton King **250.00**
Diner Adv, linen era **12.50**

DuPont Gun
    Dogs.. **100.00**
    Zeppelin **150.00**
Elgin Watch Co **8.00**
Formica, chrome era **3.50**
Heinz, Ocean Pier, Atlantic City, NY, 1910s
.... **6.00**

Hotel-Motel
Chrome **3.50**
Linen era **8.50**
Kellogg Co., Toasting Ovens, Battle Creek, Michigan, black and white, some color tinting, 1920s **7.50**
McDonald's chrome era **4.00**
Michelin Tire Company, featuring Michelin man **30.00**
R. J. Reynolds, chrome era **10.00**
Rockford Watch, calendar series **18.50**
Wood's Boston Coffees, black and white oval portraits of George and Martha Washington **8.50**
Zeno Gum, mechanical **35.00**

Animals
Bears of the Week, D Hillson, set of four, chalk-like illus on dark green, bears doing domestic chores, 1907 copyright ... **25.00**
Panda **4.00**
Polar bear **5.00**
Seasonal set, titled "Winter, Summer, Spring," Porter, illus by St. John, pre-1920 .... **18.00**

Artist signed, Mabel Lucie Attwell, child in cradle and mice, titled "Visitors!," $24.

Artist signed
Atwell, Mabel Lucie
Early by Tuck **20.00**
Regular, comic **15.00**
Bertiglia, children **18.00**
Boileau, Philip
By Reinthal Neuman **20.00**
By Raphael Tuck **100.00**
Boulanger, Maurice, cats
Large images **25.00**
Many, in action **15.00**

Browne, Tom
American Baseball series, green background **15.00**
English comic series **8.00**
Brundage, Frances
Children **15.00**
Early Tuck Chromolithograph **40.00**
Caldecott
Early **15.00**
1974 reprints **3.00**
Carmichael, comic **8.00**
Carr, Gene, comic **19.50**
Chiostri, Art Deco **24.00**
Christy, Howard Chandler **35.00**
Clapsaddle, Ellen Hattie
Children **25.00**
Floral, sleds, crosses **18.00**
Unsigned, Wolf Publishing Co **15.00**
Valentine, mechanical **65.00**
Corbella, Art Deco **17.50**
Corbett, Bertha, sunbonnets **20.00**
Curtis, E., children **10.00**
Daniell, Eva, Art Nouveau, Tuck **95.00**
Drayton/Weiderseim, Grace (Campbell's Kids) **55.00**
Dwig
Comic **9.50**
Halloween **20.00**
Fidler, Alie Luella, women **15.00**
Fisher, Harrison **35.00**
Gear, Mabel
Cairn Terrier, Pekingese, Sealyham Terrier, and Cocker Spaniel, published by Valentine & Sons, Ltd., unused **30.00**
Cocker Spaniel and Scottish Terrier, published by Valentine & Sons, Ltd., unused **30.00**
Gibson, Charles Dana, sepia **35.00**
Golay, Mary, flowers **17.50**
Greiner, M
Blacks **27.50**
Children **15.00**
Molly and Her Teddy **17.50**
Gutmann, Bessie Pease **27.50**
Hays, Margaret **12.00**
Humphrey, Maud, sgd **85.00**
Innes, John, western **16.00**
Johnson, J., children **17.50**
Kirchner, Raphael
First period **125.00**
Second period **75.00**
Third period **60.00**
Klein, Catherine
Floral **9.50**
Alphabet **20.00**
Alphabet, letters X, Y, Z **25.00**
Koehler, Mela, early **65.00**
Mauzan, Art Deco **25.00**
May, Phil, English comic series **25.00**
McCay, Winsor, "Little Nemo" **25.00**
Mucha, Alphonse
Art Nouveau, months of the year . **225.00**
Slavic period, murals **95.00**
Women, full card design **600.00**

O'Neill, Rose

Ice Cream adv 100.00
Kewpies 35.00
Suffrage, Babies 200.00
Suffrage, Kewpies 125.00
Opper, Frederick, comic 22.00
Outcault 25.00
Parkinson, Ethel, children 22.00
Patella, women 25.00
Payne, Harry 20.00
Phillips, Cole, fade-away style 45.00
Price, Mary Evans 18.00
Remington, Frederic 45.00
Robinson, Robert 20.00
Rockwell, Norman 35.00
Russell, Charles 25.00
Sager, Xavier 25.00

Schmucker, Samuel

Halloween greetings 75.00
New Years 35.00
St. Patrick's Day greetings 25.00
Valentine greetings 30.00
Shinn, Cobb 18.00
Smith, Jessie Wilcox, seven different
images 25.00

Thiele, Arthur

Blacks, large faces 35.00
Blacks, on bikes 65.00
Cats, in action 25.00
Cats, large heads 30.00
Pigs, large heads 35.00
Twelvetrees, Charles, comic, children
.... 30.00
Underwood, Clarence 24.00
Upton, Florence, Golliwoggs, Tuck 55.00

Wain, Louis

Cat 65.00
Dog 60.00
Frog 55.00
Paper doll, cat 225.00
Santa and cat 150.00
Wall, Bernhardt, sunbonnets 30.00
Wood, Lawson 30.00

Blacks

Bill Cosby, Las Vegas Hilton, "Now at the
world famous Las Vegas Hilton," names
of stars on back, 11" w, 4-1/2" l, fold-up
type, unused 8.00
Cotton Pickers in the Field, #11277, Post
Tint Card, Detroit Publishing Co. 12.00
Greetings from Mann, S. C., cotton pickers
at work, #90473, published by The
Asheville Post Card Co., Asheville, N.C.,
linen, unused 12.00
King Cotton at Home on A.B. & A.R.R.,
#C5837, published by The A.B.& A. R.R.
Line, Atlanta, Georgia, litho chrome,
made in Germany, slight wear 15.00
Old Slave Market, St. Augustine, FL, Duy
News Company, Jacksonville, FL, #5A-H,
Curtech-Chicago, unused 15.00

Picking Cotton in the South, unused
.... **14.00**
Seven-Up in Dixieland, #E-5405, published
by The Asheville Post Card Co.,
Asheville, N.C., linen, unused **12.00**

Special occasion, Happy Birthday, 1908, Dutch
children feeding cats, silver gilding, marked
"Depose," and "B.K.W.I. 840-9," **$9.50**.

Greetings

April Fools

American comic **12.50**
French litho with fish **15.50**

Birthday

Floral **10.00**
Children **12.50**
Christmas, no Santa **15.00**
Christmas, Santa
Artists signed **25.00**
German, highly embossed **25.00**
Hold to light type **120.00**
Installment, unused **100.00**
Kirchner **200.00**
P.F.B. Publishing Company **50.00**
Red suit, in automobile, pre-1920,
horizontal format, pine cones in left
border, unused **15.00**
Santa, red suit, picture card, 1920, vertical
format **20.00**
Red suits **25.00**
Silk appliqué **80.00**
Suits other than red **25.00**
Easter, printed in Germany
Boy in sailor suit, holding chick, high top
boots, hens and roosters, "Best Easter
Wishes," postmarked Grand Rapids, MI,
1912 .... **15.00**
Boy on egg cart, wheels of forget-me-
nots, pulled by two chicks, "Happy
Easter-Tide," postmarked Kalamazoo,
MI, 1913 .... **20.00**
Boy with arm full of pussy willows and
forget-me-nots, three lambs, "Easter
Greetings," postmarked Columbus, Ohio,
1910 .... **18.00**
Children playing in open egg, "Happy
Easter" **12.00**
Victorian boy and girl gathering Easter
eggs, "Easter Greeting," unused ... **32.00**

Victorian boy pushing egg entwined with roses, "Easter Greeting," unused ... **35.00**
Victorian child pushing egg buggy filled with forget-me-nots and back chick, "A Very Happy Easter To You," postmarked 1903 .... **30.00**

Fourth of July

Children **24.00**
Uncle Sam **36.00**
Others **15.50**

Ground Hog Day, after 1930 .... **24.00**

Halloween

Children **24.00**
Children, extremely colorful or artists sgd **85.00**
Winsch Publishing **65.00**

Labor Day

Lounsbury Publishing **125.00**
Nash Publishing **95.00**

Leap Year **20.00**

Mother's Day, early **24.00**

New Year

Bells **17.25**
Children or Father Time **15.00**
Winsch Publishing, beautiful women **45.00**

St. Patrick's Day

Children **24.00**
No children **17.50**

Thanksgiving

Children **24.00**
No children **17.50**
Uncle Sam **36.00**

Valentines

Children, women **24.00**
Hearts, comic **35.00**
Winsch Publishing, beautiful women **65.00**

Real photo, Bates College, Maine, labeled "Bates College Band," black and white, 1914, $20.

Photographic

Atlantic City Boardwalk, postmarked 1919 .... **9.00**

Children under Christmas trees **19.50**

Children with animals or toys **20.00**

Christmas trees **18.00**

Circus performer, identified and close-up **25.00**

Constitution Mall, government area, theme center, used **9.00**

Diamond Green Ramblers, Silver City **7.00**

Exaggerations

Conrad Publishing, after 1935 .... **20.00**
Martin Publishing **22.50**
Martin Publishing, US Coin **75.00**

Indian chiefs, five chiefs in full regalia, emb, postmarked 1910 .... **22.00**

Lincoln Statue on Lincoln Memorial Bridge, Milwaukee, WI, used **6.50**

Main Streets

Large cities **17.50**
Unidentified towns **9.50**
With trains or trolleys **24.50**

Men peeling potatoes, Co. B, 311th Inf. Kitchen Mechanics, Camp Dix, unused **15.00**

People

Military with flags **20.00**
Occupation, American **35.00**
Portraits, instant relatives **5.00**
Unusual studio backdrops **10.00**

Railroad Depots **30.00**

Railroad Depots, with trains **35.00**

Shop Exteriors, identified **40.00**

Shop Interiors, identified location **50.00**

The Belles of California, three elderly Indian women sitting in field, color, postmarked 1907 CA **15.00**

The Old Indian Whale Hunter of Puget Sound, kneeling on the shore and leaning against dug-out **20.00**

Visit Backstage at Radio City, NBC Studio Tour, black and white, postmarked 1937 .... **17.50**

Political and social history

Blacks **25.00**

Campaign

1900 .... **100.00**
1904 .... **65.00**
1908 .... **45.00**

Col. Roosevelt's Home, Oyster Bay, Long Island, NY, postmarked 1922 .... **15.00**

McKinley Monument, Buffalo, NY, needlework type emb, postmarked 1907 .... **19.00**

McKinley Monument, Canton, OH, emb, muted gray and pink **12.00**

Muriel Humphrey, portrait and facsimile signature, reverse with Muriel Humphrey's Beef Soup recipe **24.00**

President Franklin Roosevelt

Posing with rangers in front of giant CA redwoods **24.00**

Speaking at dedication of Great Smoky Mountains National Park, linen finish **30.00**

President and Mrs. Woodrow Wilson, tinted **20.00**

Prohibition **18.00**

Richard Nixon, Vote Republican, 1960, colored **12.50**

School Delinquency, fill-in the blank 1932 post card, mailed in Baltimore, MD .. **9.50**

Suffrage

Cargill publisher **32.00**
Clapsaddle **50.00**
General **17.50**
Kewpie **125.00**
Parades **35.00**

Taft and Sherman, oval portraits with facsimile signatures, Capitol building in background **20.00**

Washington DC, The New White House Sideboard designed by Mrs. Roosevelt, large marble top sideboard with two eagles **24.00**

William H. Taft, dark sepia tone photo **24.00**

William Jennings Bryan

Addressing his Sunday School Class, Miami, Florida, huge crowd in amphitheater, palm trees, color tinted, used **20.00**
Home of F. R. Rogers, Dayton, Tenn. Where Wm. Jennings Bryan died July 26, 1925, unused **36.00**
Sepia tone photo **18.00**

Willkie, "Think! Who Nominated Hitler? -- Hitler. Who Nominated Mussolini? - Mussolini. Who Nominated Stalin? -- Stalin. Who Nominated Roosevelt? -- Roosevelt. Who Nominated Willkie? -- The People. Vote for Willkie" **32.00**

States

Florida

Floronton Hotel, linen **2.00**
Moonlight on Mirror Lake, linen **2.50**
St. Petersburg, Augusta Memorial Hospital & Shell Mount, linen **2.00**

Maine, Old Orchard Beach, pre-1930, by Portland Candy Co. **3.00**

Michigan, City of Detroit, steamship pre-1920, Detroit Publishing Co., horizontal, color **2.50**

New Jersey, Bridgeton, hospital, postally used, 1939 postmark, black and white photo **5.00**

New York

Elmira, Chemung River near Mt. House, pre-1920 linen **5.00**
Elmira, State Reformatory, pre-1920 linen **3.50**
Hornell, Main Street Looking East, street scene with early autos **8.00**

Lake George, Steamer Sagamore, pre-1930, unused, J S Wooley, Bailston Spa, NY **15.00**
New York City, Hotel Lexington, 1940s **5.00**
New York City, Normandy Sightseeing Cruises, schedule, Statue of Liberty, color, 1940s **8.00**
Schenectady, Entrance to Forest Park, pre-1920 linen **5.00**
Sidney, silk mill, pre-1920, used **7.00**

Ohio

Cincinnati, Hotel Gibson, Roof Dining Room, pre-1940 .... **6.00**
Cincinnati, Union Terminal, pre-1950 linen **5.00**
Toledo, Dreher's Simplex Street & House Number Guide, pre-1920 .... **20.00**

Oklahoma, Fort Sill, Theatre exterior, 1943, used **10.00**

Pennsylvania

Allentown, Center Square, Hamilton St, unused **8.00**
Harrisburg, Dining Room, Wm Penn Hotel, unused, pre-1950 .... **5.00**

Virginia

Norfolk, passenger and car ferry **10.00**
Norfolk County, real photo, gates opened from shore **12.00**

Washington DC, Mayflower Hotel, Harvey's Famous Restaurant, horizontal exterior pre-1950 view **6.00**

World War II

Man of the Time, Adolf Hitler, #91, Hindenburg postage stamp, postmarked 1939 .... **35.00**

Mortars at Fort Wright, No. 19, published by American Colortype Co., Chicago, Photo International Film Service Inc., unused **26.00**

U.S.S. Utah rescues torpedo, No. 13, published by American Colortype Co., Chicago, Photo International Film Service Inc., unused **26.00**

Punchboards

History: Punchboards are self-contained games of chance made of pressed paper half an inch or so thick that has holes that coded tickets have been folded inside. For the amount stated on the board, the player uses a "punch" to extract the ticket of their choice. Prizes are awarded to the winning tickets. Punch prices can be 1 cent, 2 cents, 3 cents, 5 cents, 10 cents, 20 cents, 50 cents, $1, or more.

Not all tickets were numbered. Fruit symbols were used extensively as well as animals. Some punchboards had no printing at all, just colored tickets. Other ticket themes included dice, cards, dominoes, and words. Some dropped small colored balls. Punchboards come in an endless variety of styles. Names reflect the themes of the boards: Barrel of Winners, Break the Bank, Dangling Duckets, JAR O DO, Easy Fins, and Take It Off are just a few.

At first punchboards winners were awarded cash. As a response to attempts to outlaw gambling, prizes were switched to candy, cigars, cigarettes, jewelry, radios, clocks, cameras, sporting goods, toys, beer, chocolate, etc. Push Cards are cardboard thin versions of punchbords.

The golden age of punchboards was from the 1920s to the 1950s. Attention was focused on the keyed punchboard in the film "The Flim Flam Man." This negative publicity hurt the punchboard industry. Other forms of gambling also helped the demise of the punchboards. Legal State lotteries were the final blow. It is much easier to play state-sanctioned games than risk the chance of an illegal punchboard.

Collecting Hints: Punchboards that are unpunched are collectible. A board that has been punched has little value unless it is a rare or special design. Like most advertising items, price is determined by graphics subject matter and rarity.

The majority of punchboards sell in the $8 to $30 range. At the high end of the range are boards such as Golden Gate Bridge ($85) Baseball Classic ($100) and some boards with coins in them go for as much as $500.

Adviser: Clark Phelps.

Ace High, 13" x 17", deck of cards for jackpot **90.00**
Barrel of Cigarettes, 10" x 10", Lucky Strike Green **44.00**
Bars & Bells, 13" x 8-1/2", deck of cards, fruit symbols **135.00**
Baseball Push Card, 7" x 10", 1¢, candy prize **10.00**
Basketball Push Card, 6" x 9", thin, 1¢, candy prize **10.00**
Beat the Seven, 10" x 10", card tickets determine winners **35.00**

Best Hand, poker hand tickets, 6-1/2" x 11", 1-1/4" thick, pays out in cigarettes . **40.00**
Big Game, 8" x 10-1/2" **30.00**
Buck-A-Roo, silver dollars **500.00**
Candy Special, 4-1/2" x 7-1/2", penny candy board **24.00**
Cash In, 8-1/2" x 9", sack of money.... **18.00**
Double of Nothing, 9" x 10", trade stimulator **36.00**
Extra Bonus, 13" x 12" **40.00**
Fin Baby, 19" x 6", folding pull tab **32.00**
Five on One, 11" x 11" **18.00**
Five Tens, 10" x 13" **18.00**

Professor Charley, Superior Company, Chicago, 1946, 12-1/4" x 10", **$18**. All punchboard photos courtesy of adviser Clark Phelps.

Glades Chocolates, 7" x 9", set of three boards, factory wrapped **75.00**
Good Punching, 9-1/2" x 10", cowboy motif **36.00**
Hang It, factory paper **95.00**
Home Run Derby, 10" x 12", baseball theme, green baseball park **75.00**
Jackpot Bingo, 10" x 8", thick card jackpot **10.00**
Joe's Special, 11" x 14" **20.00**
Johnson's Chocolates, 9" x 11", Elvgren girl **35.00**
Lu Lu Board, 10" x 11", colored tickets **28.00**
McCoy, six cutouts, old lighters and sterling silver bolo tie **100.00**
More Smokes, 10-1/2" x 10-1/2", red, white, and blue tickets **24.00**
Nestle's Chocolate, 9" x 8-1/2", 2¢ board **45.00**
Nickel Fins, 12" x 15", cash board, colorful jackpot **40.00**

Odd Pennies, 6-3/4" x 11", small change, 2¢ and 3¢ board **45.00**
Palm Chart, 20" x 11-1/2", 1936, orig envelope **8.00**
Perry's Prizes, 9-1/2" x 13" **60.00**
Pocket Board, 2" x 2-3/4", great action cartoon graphic **8.00**
Positive Prizes, 12" x 17", diecut field for prizes of your choice **25.00**
Pots A Plenty, 11" x 17-1/2" **26.00**
Premium Prizes, 10" x 12" **20.00**
Professor Charley, 1946, Superior Mfg. Typical 25¢ cash board **18.00**
Race Track, Pimlico and Churchill Downs, minor shelf wear **50.00**
Section Play, 8-1/2" x 10" **18.00**
Select Your Smokes, 9-1/2" x 7-1/4" ... **55.00**
Ship Ahoy, factory wrapped, 9" x 15" **95.00**
So Sweet, 13-1/2" x 13" **40.00**
Speedy Tens, 10" x 13" **18.00**
Stars & Stripes, 9" x 14", red, white and blue, jackpot card **26.00**
Take It Off, minor shelf wear **45.00**
Tavern Maid, 9-1/2" x 13-1/2", cans of beer prize **55.00**
Three Sure Hits, 10" x 13" **24.00**
Tropics, diecut, hula dancer **110.00**
Tu Pots, 12" x 18" **44.00**
Win A Buck, 4-1/2" x 7-1/2" **12.00**
Win A Seal, 1920s, wooden puncher, six numbers on a ticket, colored foil **70.00**
Win Twice, quarters and dimes, orig wrapper present but torn **175.00**

By A Nose, horse race theme, 10" x 7", $36.

Purinton Pottery

History: Bernard Purinton founded Purinton Pottery in 1936 in Wellsville, Ohio. This pilot plant produced decorative dinnerware as well as some special-order pieces. In 1940, Roy Underwood, President of Knox Glass Company, approached Purinton about moving his operation to Knox's community, Shippenville.

In 1941, the pottery relocated to a newly built plant in Shippenville, Pennsylvania. The company's first product at the new plant, a two-cup premium teapot for McCormick Tea Company, rolled off the line on December 7, 1941.

Dorothy Purinton and William H. Blair, her brother, were the chief designers for the company. Maywood, Plaid, and several Pennsylvania German designs were among the patterns attributed to Dorothy Purinton. William Blair, a graduate of the Cleveland School of Art, designed the Apple and Intaglio patterns.

Initially slipware was cast. Later it was pressed using a Ram Press process. Clays came from Florida, Kentucky, North Carolina, and Tennessee.

Purinton Pottery did not use decals as did many of its competitors. Greenware was hand painted by locally trained decorators who then dipped the decorated pieces into glaze. This demanded a specially formulated body and a more expensive manufacturing process. Hand painting also allowed for some of the variations in technique and colors found on Purinton ware today.

Purinton made a complete dinnerware line for each pattern, plus a host of accessory pieces ranging from candleholders to vases. Dinnerware patterns were open stock. Purinton's ware received national distribution, and select lines were exported.

The plant ceased operations in 1958, reopened briefly, and finally closed for good in 1959. Cheap foreign imports were cited as the cause of the company's decline.

Collecting Hints: The most popular patterns among collectors are Apple, Intaglio (brown), Normandy Plaid (red), Maywood, and Pennsylvania Dutch. Variations, e.g., Intaglio with a green ground, are known for many of these patterns.

Purinton also made a number of kitchenware and specialty pieces. These should not be overlooked. Among the harder-to-find items are animal figurines, tea tiles, and the Tom and Jerry bowl and mug set.

Baker, Apple, 6" x 4"............................ 30.00
Bank, Raggedy Andy, 6-1/2" h............ 80.00
Canister
Flour, Intaglio, square, wooden lid
.... 95.00
Set, Pennsylvania Dutch.............. 195.00
Sugar, Intaglio, square, wooden lid
.... 95.00
Cereal bowl
Apple 18.00
Intaglio 12.00
Pennsylvania Dutch 15.00
Coffee mug, Plaid................................. 3.00
Coffeepot, cov, Apple 60.00
Cornucopia... 20.00
Cookie jar, cov
Howdy Doody............................... 250.00
Pennsylvania Dutch 55.00
Creamer
Apple, double spout, 1-1/2" h......... 12.00
Normandy Plaid 40.00
Cup and saucer
Apple 24.00
Estate... 12.00
Normandy Plaid 17.50
Dinner plate
9" d, Normandy Plaid..................... 20.00
9-3/4" d, Plaid 15.00
10" d, Intaglio, brown 16.00
Drip jar, cov
Apple 20.00
Daisy.. 80.00
Plaid... 20.00
Dutch jug, Apple, 6" h, 8" w 35.00
Fruit bowl, Estate 6.00
Grill plate, Apple, 12" d 25.00
Honey jug, Ivy, 6-1/2" h....................... 45.00
Jug
Intaglio, 5 pint, 8" h......................... 75.00
Normandy Plaid, two quarts, 7-1/2" h, 10-
1/2" w 90.00
Tulip & Vine, 5-1/2" h 35.00
Lazy Susan, Fruits, apple finial, painted
pear, plum, pineapple, and cherries
.... 250.00
Luncheon plate, Apple, 8-1/2" d 24.00
Marmalade, cov, Maywood................. 32.00

Oil and vinegar bottle set, Fruits,
9-3/8" h 80.00
Pitcher
Apple, 6" h...................................... 45.00
Fruits.. 32.00
Roll tray, Intaglio, brown, 11" l............ 35.00
Salad plate, First Love 6.00
Salt and pepper shakers, pr
Apple... 18.00
Palm Trees 100.00
Plaid 15.00
Shake and Pour, 4-1/4" h................ 65.00
Snack set, Intaglio, brown 20.00
Soup and sandwich set, Rubel, bowl and
plate 17.50
Tea and toast set, Apple, plate and cup
.... 30.00
Teapot, cov
Apple.. 35.00
Fruit, individual, apple on one side, pear
on other, 4" h 50.00
Maywood, six cups......................... 35.00
Red Ivy, 5" h 35.00
Tea tile trivet 115.00
Tid-bit serving plate, Fruit, two tiers, 8" d
and 10" d plate, 14" h wooden handle
.... 45.00
Tumbler, Apple.................................... 20.00
Vase, 5-3/4" h, 5" w, hand painted 20.00
Vegetable
Apple, oval...................................... 20.00
Intaglio, brown, 8-1/2" d 25.00
Normandy Plaid, 10-1/2" l, divided
.... 50.00

Fruits, salt and pepper shakers, miniature jugs,
original corks, $18.

R

Radio Characters and Personalities

History: The radio show was a dominant force in American life from the 1920s to the early 1950s. "Amos 'n' Andy" began in 1929, "The Shadow" in 1930, and "Chandu the Magician" in 1932. Although many of the characters were fictional, the individuals who portrayed them became public idols. A number of figures achieved fame on their own—Eddie Cantor, Don McNeill of "The Breakfast Club," George Burns and Gracie Allen, Arthur Godfrey, and Jack Benny.

Sponsors and manufacturers were quick to capitalize on the fame of the radio characters and personalities. Premiums were offered as part of the shows' themes. However, merchandising did not stop with premiums. Many non-premium items, such as bubble gum cards, figurines, games, publicity photographs, and dolls, were issued. Magazine advertisements often featured radio personalities.

Collecting Hints: Many items associated with radio characters and personalities were offered as premiums. This category focuses mostly on the non-premium items. Radio premiums are listed separately in this book.

Don't overlook the vast amount of material related to the radio shows themselves. This includes scripts, props, and a wealth of publicity material. Many autographed photographs appear on the market. Books, especially Big Little Books and similar types, featured many radio-related characters and stories.

Radio characters and personalities found their way into movies and television. Serious collectors exclude the products, which spun off from these other two areas.

Additional Listings: Big Little Books, Comic Books, Radio Premiums, Super Heroes.

Amos and Andy, sign, Rexall Value Spot, metal, double-sided, orange, white, and dark blue, adv for *Life, Look, Post, Collier's* and *Country Magazine*, $125.

Amos 'n' Andy

Book, *Amos 'n' Andy*, Rand McNally & Co., © 1929, hardcover, autographed **265.00**

Game, Card Party, M. Davis Co., two score pads, eight tallies, orig box, 1938.. **75.00**

Photo, 5" x 7", browntone, matte finish, Pepsodent Co., 1929 .... **30.00**

Pinback button, 13/16" d, "Howdy Boys," Amos 'n' Andy Fresh Air Candy, black on bright yellow, 1930s....................... **35.00**

Record set.. **50.00**

Don Winslow

Bank, 2-1/4" h, Uncle Don's Earnest Saver Club, oval, paper label, photo and cartoon illus, Greenwich Savings Bank, New York City, 1930s...................... **40.00**

Pinback button **15.00**

Salt and pepper shakers, pr, full color, plaster **75.00**

Edgar Bergen and Charlie McCarthy

Bubble gum wrapper, Bergen's Better Bubble Gum **15.00**

Game, Charlie McCarthy Radio Party Game, orig envelope **65.00**

Pencil sharpener, figural, diecut plastic, color decal, 1930s.......................... **72.00**

Pinback button, 1-1/4" d, Charlie McCarthy Goldwyn Follies Club, black, white, and red, red accent on Charlie's face... **25.00**

Soap, 4" h, figural, orig box, Kerk Guild, 1930-40.. **75.00**

Fibber McGee and Molly

Fan card, 8" x 10", black and white glossy, 11 cast members, Kolynos Dental Cream, © 1933 .... **60.00**

Menu, 9-1/2" x 12-1/4", Brown Derby, autographed **120.00**

Record, 10-1/4" x 12", four 78 RPM records, live broadcasts, colorful cover, 1947 .... **55.00**

Jack Armstrong

Bomb sight kit, MIB **525.00**
Photo, Blackstar, 1933 .... **20.00**
Ring, baseball **500.00**
Sound effects kit, mint in orig mailer **300.00**

Laurel & Hardy, Transfer Co. moving truck, bank, wooden, $8.50.

Jack Benny

Booklet, Zenith Radios, Burns & Allen, Boswells, 1930s **45.00**
Magazine, Jack Benny and Rochester, *Look* **20.00**
Program, 9" x 12", black and white photos, Phil Harris signature, 12 pgs, late 1930s **32.50**

Jimmie Allen

Badge

1-1/2", Jimmie Allen Squadron Commander, diecut, 1939 .... **295.00**
1-3/4" l, Jimmie Allen Pilot Leader, Canadian issue, 1939, high gloss copper luster lettering on silvery-white background **295.00**
Bracelet, silvered links, 1-1/2" center plate with airplane in flight, text panel accented in dark red, lower accented in dark blue, reads "Jimmie Allen Air Races Skelly 1935," reverse with maker's name "Hirschfeld, K.C. Mo." **220.00**

Little Orphan Annie

Book, *Little Orphan Annie and the Circus*, Cupples & Leon, 1927, 7" x 9", hardcover **60.00**
Coloring book, Little Orphan Annie, McLaughlin, 10" x 13" **120.00**
Decoder, Lil Orphan Annie, Secret Society, brass, silver outer rim, 1935 .... **65.00**
Game, Little Orphan Annie, Milton Bradley, 1927 .... **125.00**
Manual, Secret Society, orig mailer... **125.00**
Puzzle, 9" x 12-1/2", Tucker County Horse Race, orig instruction sheet and mailing box, Ovaltine, c1933 .... **75.00**
Ring, secret message **335.00**
Shake-up mug, vintage, brown **130.00**

Sheet music, *Little Orphan Annie's Song*, Harold Gray illus cov, Ovaltine, 1931, four pgs **27.50**

The Shadow

Book, *The Living Shadow*, Maxwell Grant, c1931 .... **10.00**
Figure, 7" h, china, glossy black cloak and hat, c1930 .... **265.00**
Ring, secret agent, MIB **130.00**
Rubber stamp **40.00**
Toy, super jet, plastic, orig package... **45.00**

Radios

History: The radio was invented more than 100 years ago. Marconi was the first to assemble and employ the transmission and reception instruments that permitted electric messages to be sent without the use of direct connections. The early name for radio was "Wireless," and its first application was to control ships in 1898. Early wireless equipment is not generally considered collectible since its historic value makes it important for museum display.

Between 1905 and the end of World War I, many technical advances, including the invention of the vacuum tube by DeForest, increased communication technology and encouraged amateur interest. The receiving equipment from that period is desired by collectors and historians but is rarely available.

By 1920, radio technology allowed broadcasts to large numbers of people simultaneously and music could be brought directly from concert halls into living rooms. The result was the development of a new art that changed the American way of life during the 1920s. The world became familiar through the radio in an average listener's home.

Radio receivers changed substantially in the decade of the 1920s, going from black boxes—with many knobs and dials—powered by expensive and messy batteries, to stylish furniture, simple to use, and operated from the house current that had become the standard source of home energy. During the '20s, radios grew more complicated and powerful as well as more ornate. Consoles appeared, loudspeakers were incorporated into them, and sound fidelity became an important consideration.

In the early 1930s, demand changed. The large expensive console gave way to small but effective table models. The era of the "cathedral" and the "tombstone" began. By the end of the '30s, the midget radio had become popular. Quality of sound was replaced by a price reduction, and most homes had more than one radio.

Shortly after World War II, the miniature tubes developed for the military were utilized in domestic radios. The result was further reduction in size and a substantial improvement in quality. The advent of FM also speeded improvements. Plastic technology made possible the production of attractive cases in many styles and colors.

The other development that drastically changed the radio receiver was the invention of the transistor in 1927. A whole new family of radio sets that could be carried in the shirt pocket became popular. Their popularity grew as they became less and less expensive, but their low cost meant that they were frequently thrown away when they stopped working. Today they are not easy to find in good condition and are, therefore, quite collectible.

Collecting Hints: Radio collectors divide into three groups: those who collect because of nostalgia, those interested in history and/or acquiring radios that represent specific periods, and collectors of personality and figural radios. Most collectors find broadcasting, and therefore broadcast receivers, of primary interest.

Broadcast receivers can be divided into these significant categories:
- Crystal sets and battery-powered receivers of the early 1920s
- Rectangular electric table models of the late 1920s
- Cathedrals, tombstones, and consoles of the '30s
- Midget plastic portables and wood-cabinet table models built before and after World War II
- Shaped radios with cases made of Bakelite or other plastic

- Personality and figural radios made between the 1930s and the 1960s.

Because the prime nostalgic period seems to be the decade of the '30s, the cathedral-style, socket-powered radios (e.g., the Philco series) have become sought after items. Recently young collectors have exhibited interest in the plastic-cabinet radios built between 1945 and 1960.

Newer radio collectors are influenced by novelty, with the outside appearance the most important feature. The radio must play; but shape, color, decoration, and condition of the case far outweigh the internal workings of the set in determining desirability and, consequently, price. Enclosures that resemble things or figures (e.g., Mickey Mouse) command premium prices. The square table models of the later 1930s and the midget sets of the late 1930s and 1940s have recently attracted the attention of collectors.

The value of a radio is directly proportional to its appearance and its operating condition. Minor scratches are to be expected as is alligatoring of the surface finish, but gouges, cracks, and delaminated surfaces adversely affect prices, as will a crack, a broken place where plastic closures belong, or missing parts, tubes, or components. If major repairs are required to make the set work, the price must reflect this potential expense.

Very rare radios usually go directly to major collectors, seldom appearing in the general market. Wireless equipment and radios used commercially before World War I are considered rare and are not listed here.

Adviser: Lewis S. Walters.

Notes: The prices listed are for sets in average to good condition and are based upon an electrically complete receiver that operates when powered.

Admiral

Portable
#33	**30.00**
#37	**30.00**
#218, leatherette	**40.00**
#909, All World	**85.00**
Y-2127 - Imperial 8, c1959	**45.00**
Transistor, 1960s	**15.00**

www.primeaumusic.com offered a whole booth full of vintage radios at the March Atlantique City Show.

Arvin
Hoppy with lariatenna **585.00**
Table, #444 .... **100.00**

Atwater Kent
Breadboard Style, Model 12 ...... **1,250.00**
Cathedral, 80, c1931 .... **200.00**
Table, 55 Keil **200.00**

Bulova, clock radio
#100 .... **25.00**
#110 .... **25.00**
#120 .... **30.00**

Crosley
Pup, with box **450.00**
Sheraton, cathedral **225.00**
Super Buddy Boy **115.00**
#4-28 battery operated **120.00**
Dashboard **100.00**

Emerson, BT-245, tombstone Catalin, broadcast band (AM), six tubes, three-section grill, three knobs, louver grill, AC/DC, 1939, **$1,800**.

Emerson
AU-190 Catalin Tombstone **1,200.00**
BT-245 .... **1,100.00**
Patriot **700.00**
#274 Brown Bakelite **150.00**
#409 Mickey Mouse **1,200.00**
#570 Memento **100.00**

Federal
#58DX **500.00**
#110 .... **550.00**

General Electric
#400 .... **30.00**
#515, clock radio **30.00**
K-126 .... **125.00**
Tombstone **225.00**
#81, c1934 .... **150.00**

Motorola
#68X11Q Art Deco **75.00**
M logo **25.00**
Pixie **45.00**
Ranger #700 .... **30.00**

Reproduction Philco, brass plate on front reads: "Special Edition Built for True Value, Baby Grand, Originally Produced by Philco 1930-36" Philco Ford Corp., **$65**.

Philco
T-7 126, transistor **50.00**
T1000, clock radio **80.00**
#551, 1928 .... **165.00**
#17, cathedral **225.00**
#46 – 132, table **20.00**
#52 – 544, Transitone **40.00**
#49 – 501, Boomerang **400.00**

Radio Corporation of America – RCA
LaSiesta **550.00**
Radiola
#17 .... **75.00**
#28 console **200.00**

#33 .... 60.00
40X56 Worlds Fair **1,000.00**

Silvertone - Sears

#1, table 75.00
#1582, cathedral - wood **200.00**
#9205, plastic transistor 45.00
Clock Radio – plastic 15.00

Transistor, Coca-Cola Bottle, plastic, marked
"Made in Hong Kong," 8" h, **$40.**

Sony - transistor

TFM-151, 1960 .... 50.00
TR-63, 1958 .... **145.00**

Sparton

#506 Blue Bird -art deco **3,200.00**
#5218 .... 95.00

Zenith

#500 transistor - owl eye 75.00
#750L transistor w/leather case 40.00
Trans-Oceanic 100.00
#6D2615, table w/boomerang dial. 95.00
Zephyr, multiband 95.00

Railroad Items

History: It was a canal company, the Delaware and Hudson, which used the first steam locomotive in America. The Stourbridge Lion moved coal from the mines to the canal wharves. Just as America was entering its great canal era in 1825, the railroad was gaining a foothold. The Commonwealth of Pennsylvania did not heed William Strickland's advice to concentrate on building railroads instead of canals.

By the 1840s, railroad transportation was well-established. Numerous private companies were organized although many remained in business for only a short time.

During the Civil War, the effectiveness of the railroad was demonstrated. Immediately following the war the transcontinental railroad was completed, and entrepreneurs such as Gould and Vanderbilt created financial empires. Mergers generated huge systems. The golden age of the railroad extended from the 1880s to the 1940s.

After 1950, the railroads suffered from poor management, a bloated labor force, lack of maintenance, and competition from other forms of transportation. Thousands of miles of track were abandoned. Many railroads failed or merged together. The 1970s saw the federal government enter the picture with Conrail and Amtrak. Today railroads still are fighting for survival.

Collecting Hints: Most collectors concentrate on one railroad as opposed to one type of object. Railroad material always brings a higher price in the area in which it originated. Local collectors tend to concentrate on local railroads. The highest prices are paid for material from railroads, which operated for only a short time. Nostalgia also influences collectors.

There are many local railroad clubs. Railroad buffs tend to have their own specialized swap meets and exhibitions.

Hat, conductor's, 698 in gold laurel wreath, navy blue, black brim, gold braid and trim, **$65.**

Baggage check, Texas Central RR, 1-5/8" x 2", brass, Poole Bros, Chicago....... **38.50**
Blanket, Canadian Pacific.................. **85.00**
Blotter, Soo Line, 1920s, unused......... **5.00**
Book

Norfolk & Western Second Generation Diesels, Withers & Bowers, 256 pgs, hardcover **35.00**
Southern Pacific Color Guide to Freight & Passenger Equipment, Vol. 1, Anthony Thompson, 128 pgs, hardcover **30.00**
Box, tin, black, paper attached to handle reads "Pittsburgh, Cincinnati, Chicago, St. Louis Railway Co., June 15, 1901"
.... **40.00**

Brochure

Eastern Summer Trips, B & O........ **12.00**
Florida East Coast Railway & Steamship Co., January 1900, 39 pgs **150.00**
Holiday Haunts, Adirondacks & 1,000 Islands, NYC, 1940, 63 pgs........... **20.00**
Caboose marker, Atlantic Coast Line RR Co., 1900, four-way lamp............. **385.00**

Calendar

1943, Burlington Zephyr **90.00**
1961, PA RR Transportation Center, Six Penn Center Plaza, Philadelphia, plastic, wallet size **5.00**
Catalog, Hibbard Spencer Barlett & Co, Railway and Manufacturer's Supplies, 1907, 632 pgs **55.00**
Car inspector's record, D & RGW, Ridway, filled in, 1928 .... **10.00**
Car seal, Pittsburgh & Lake Erie (P & LE)
.... **10.00**
Cereal premium, tin sign, set of ten ... **35.00**
China

Bouillon cup, WP, feather Friver, top logo, Shenango **75.00**

Celery dish, Union Pacific, 10" l, oval, blue and gold pattern, backstamped "Scannel China"............................ **40.00**
Coffee cup, Illinois Central, Coral pattern
.... **24.00**
Creamer, B & O, Centenary pattern, Scammell's Lamberton China, 3-1/2" d, 3-3/4" h **210.00**
Cup and saucer, B & O, Capital **60.00**
Cup and saucer, Southern Pacific. **75.00**
Demitasse cup and saucer, CMSTP & P, Traveler, Syracuse, backstamped **. 85.00**
Dinner plate, B & O, Shenango, 10-1/2" d
.... **120.00**
Dinner plate, Missouri Pacific, state flowers.. **275.00**
Dish, Santa Fe Super Chief........... **65.00**
Mustard container, cov, small, white china, red PR RR keystone logo **45.00**
Platter, Union Pacific, 8" l, oval, Challenger pattern, top mkd "The Challenger," backstamped Union Pacific RR... **95.00**
Sauce dish, NYNH & H, Indian Tree pattern, Buffalo China backstamp . **35.00**
Sherbet, PRR, Keystone, Buffalo China
.... **65.00**
Soup plate, PRR, Purple Laurel, 6-1/2" d, broad lip, Sterling China............. **60.00**
Coaster, Central RR, New Jersey, Statue of Liberty logo, set of six................... **15.00**
Coloring book, Union Pacific RR give-away, 29 pgs, 1954, 8" x 10".............. **20.00**
Commemorative plate, 10-1/2" d, B & O Railroad, blue transfer scene of Harper's Ferry, Lamberton China, 13-1/4" d turned wood frame................................. **165.00**
Conductor's report, Wiscasset, Waterville & Farmington Railway, CO, filled in, 1920s
.... **5.00**
Creamer, Canadian Pacific, SP, mkd "England"................................... **25.00**
Freight receipt, NY, Lake Erie & Western RR, dated 1883............................. **8.00**
Hat rack, overhead type, coach, wood and bras, six brass double-sided hooks
.... **200.00**
Head rest cover, PRR, tan ground, brown logo, 15" x 18"............................ **15.00**
Kerosene can, tin, AT & SFRY, spout cap missing, 11" h............................. **75.00**
Label .

Double A, train on trestle supported by two large "A's" as foundations, East Highlands.................................. **2.00**
General Wm J. Palmer, portrait of General flanked by Antlers Hotel & Colorado RR train scene, unused inner cigar box label
.... **6.00**
Golden Spike Centennial, color, 1-1/2" x 2".. **5.00**
Seven Thirty Express, speeding train, clock, gilt, unused whiskey bottle label
.... **.50**

Print, framed, Pennsylvania RR, #9604 locomotive, **$125**.

Stamp case, book shape, North-Western Line, black and white illus of railway line, spine lettered "Postage And Revenue Stamps/Court Plaster/Nick Nacks," 1900 .... **60.00**

Stock certificate
Baltimore & Ohio Railroad, vignette of Tom Thumb style engine and cars with freight and passengers, ornate olive green border, International Bank Note Co., NY, 1950s **20.00**
Sharon Railway, Sharon, PA, 1908, train yard vignette with yard shifter engine **15.00**

Ticket, Pennsylvania Railroad Co, identification check, exchange ticket, and passenger's ticket **15.00**

Timetable
Erie Railroad, 1907 .... **32.00**
L&N Kansas City Southern, 1955 ..... **8.50**
Southern Pacific RR, 1915 .... **22.00**

Towel, 24" x 16", Property of the Pullman Company, white, red and blue stripe **12.00**

Voucher, Union Pacific, Denver and Gulf Railway, 1890s **5.00**

Watchman's station box, iron **25.00**

Reamers

History: Devices for getting the juice from citrus fruit have been around almost as long as the fruit itself. These devices were made from all types of material—from wood to glass and from nickel plate and sterling silver to fine china.

Many different kinds of mechanical reamers were devised before the first glass one was pressed around 1885.

Very few new designs have appeared since 1940, when frozen juice first entered the market. Modern-day ceramists are making clown and teapot-shaped reamers.

Collecting Hints: Reamers are seldom found in mint condition. Small cone and rim nicks are usually acceptable, but cracked pieces sell for considerably less. Ceramic figurals and American-made glass examples are collected more than any other types.

Reamer collecting, which can be an endless hobby, first became popular as a sideline to Depression glass collecting in the mid-1960s. It may be impossible to assemble a collection that includes one of every example made. One-of-a-kind items do exist, as some examples were never put into mass production.

Reproduction Alert: Many glass reamers are being reproduced at this time. Some are American reissues from original molds, while others are made from old reamers in Asia. The Asian reamers are usually easy to spot since they are made from poor quality glass that feels greasy and is generally thicker than that used in the originals. Many reproductions are being made in colors never used originally, but some of the reamers being made from the original molds are the same colors as the originals, making them harder to detect. There are also several new ceramic reamers being made. One series looks like an old piece of flow blue or English china, and is marked with a crested "Victoria Ironstone" on the bottom.

An old 5-inch Imperial Glass Co. reamer, originally made in clear glass, was reproduced for Edna Barnes in dark amethyst; 1,500 were made. The reproduction is marked "IG" and "81."

Mrs. Barnes has also reproduced several old 4-1/2-inch Jenkins Glass Co. reamers in limited editions. The reproductions are also made in a 2-1/4-inch size. All Jenkins copies are marked with a "B" in a circle. These limited editions have become collectible in their own right and should not be considered or valued the same as the reproduction reamers described above.

Collectors should consult Gene Florence's book *Kitchen Glass of the Depression Era* for information about glass reproductions. Also, the National Reamer Collectors Association, www.reamers.org keeps its members up to date on the latest reproductions via its newsletter and members' area on its Web site.

The first book on reamers, now out of print, was written by Ken and Linda Ricketts in 1974. Their numbering system was continued by Mary Walker in her first two books, *Reamers (200 Years),* 1980 and *More Reamers (200 Years)* 1983, both published by, Muski Publishers, Sherman Oaks, CA, and both now out of print, and in her newest book, *And Many More Reamers* (http://www.reamers.org/andmore.html). The Ricketts-Walker numbers will be found in the china and metal sections listed here. The numbers in parentheses in the glass section are from Gene Florence's *Kitchen Glassware of the Depression Years,* and indicate the page number, row number and item number to be referenced

Adviser: Judy Smith.

Cottage, F5670, beige walls, blue window, green grass, Japan, two pieces, $75.

China and ceramic

Austria, 3-3/4" h, white, pink flowers, green trim (D-106) **95.00**

Bavaria, 3-1/2" h, white, red, yellow and green flowers, gold trim, two pcs (E-119) **110.00**

Czechoslovakia, 6" h, orange shape, white, green leaves, mkd "Erphila," two pcs (L-17) **65.00**

England, 3-1/2" h, white, orange and yellow flowers (D-107) **90.00**

Germany, 5" d, Goebel, yellow (E-108) **95.00**

Japan

3" h, saucer-type on pedestal, loop handle fruit dec (D-59) **65.00**
8-1/2" h, pitcher and tumbler, blue and white windmill dec (P-87) .... **\80.00**

United States

Red Wing (A-7) **145.00**
United States Ade-O-Matic Genuine, 8" h, green (A-11) **145.00**
Universal Cambridge, 9" h, beige w/pink flowers (A-28) **195.00**

Elegant reamer, Austrian, white with pink flowers, royal blue and gold trim, E-36, 3-1/4" h, **$125**. Photo courtesy of Judy Smith.

Glass

(Measurements indicate width, not including spout and handle.)

Anchor Hocking Glass Co., 6-1/4" d, lime green, pouring spout (155-4-3) **35.00**

Federal, transparent green, pointed cone (151-3-4) **30.00**

Fluted ruffle, rose (149-5-3) **275.00**

Fry, 6-5/16" d, opalescent, pouring spout (149-6-1) **55.00**

Hazel Atlas

Criss-Cross, orange size, pink (153-2-2) **350.00**
Criss-Cross, crystal, tab handle, small (153-5-3) **25.00**
Indiana Glass Co., green, horizontal handle (151-5-3) **35.00**

Jeannette Glass Co.

Delphite Jennyware, small, (159-3-1) **110.00**
Pink Jennyware, small (159-4-4) .. **145.00**
Light Jadite, two-cup, two pcs (159-2-3) **45.00**

McKee

White, embossed Sunkist (163-1-4) **15.00**
Vaseline green embossed Sunkist (162-5-4) **60.00**
Chalaine blue, embossed Sunkist (162-3-3) **245.00**

U.S. Glass Co., light pink, two-cup pitcher set (167-2-1) **55.00**

Figural reamer, house, Japanese, tan with brown and green trim, blue windows, pink door, 5-3/4" h, **$110**. Photo courtesy of Judy Smith.

Metal

Aluminum, Pat, 8" 1, 161609, Minneapolis, MN **5.00**

Bernard Rice & Sons, Apollo EPNS, 3-3/4" h, two pcs (PM-70) **134.00**

Cocktail Shaker set, Kinsway Plate, German, one pint (PM-49) **95.00**

Derby S.P. Co., International Co., 1923 EPNS W.M. Mounts (PM-74) **235.00**

Dunlap's Improved, 9-1/2" l, iron hinge (M-17) **45.00**

Nasco-Royal, 6"1, scissors type, (M-265) **8.00**

Presto Juicer, metal stand, porcelain juicer (M-112) **145.00**

Wagner Ware, 6"d, cast aluminum, skillet shape, long rect. seed dams beneath cone, hole in handle, two spouts (M-96) **45.00**

Williams, 9-3/4" l, iron , hinged, glass insert (M-60) **50.00**

Yates, EPNS, 4-3/4" d, two pcs (PM-73) **195.00**

Records

History: The first records, which were cylinders produced by Thomas Edison in 1877, were played on a phonograph of his design. Edison received a patent in 1878, but soon dropped the project in order to perfect the light bulb.

Alexander Graham Bell, Edison's friend, was excited about the phonograph and developed the graphaphone, which was marketed successfully by 1889. Early phonographs and graphaphones had hand cranks to wind the mechanism and keep the cylinders moving.

Around 1900, Emile Berliner developed a phonograph which used a flat disc, similar to today's records. The United States Gramophone Company marketed his design in 1901. This company eventually became RCA Victor. By 1910, discs were more popular than cylinders.

The record industry continued to develop as new technology improved processes and sound quality. Initially 78-RPM records were made. These were replaced by 45 RPMs, then by 33-1/3 RPMs, compact discs, and finally DVDs.

Collecting Hints: Collectors tend to focus on one particular music field, e.g., jazz, the big bands, or rock 'n' roll, or on one artist. Purchase records with original dust jackets and covers whenever possible.

Also check the records carefully for scratches. If the sound quality has been affected, the record is worthless.

Proper storage of records is critical to maintaining their value. Keep stacks small. It is best to store them vertically. Place acid-free paper between the albums to prevent bleeding of ink from one cover to the next.

Note: Prices are for first pressings in original dust jackets or albums.

Additional Listings: Rock 'n' Roll.

Frampton Comes Alive, picture record, clear plastic sleeve, **$12**.

Baby Blue, 45 rpm **1.00**

Badfinger, 45 rpm, picture sleeve **2.00**

Bye Bye Birdy, Columbia, orig cast, 1980 .... **17.50**

Christmas with Glen Campbell, Capitol, black label, pink colorband **8.00**

Country Music Time, Kitty Wells, Decca, black label, rainbow band through center **8.00**

Collection of Favorite Hawaiian Songs by Dorothy Lamour with Dick Mcintire and His Harmony Hawaiians, book style color cover with photo of Dorothy in strapless dress, black and white photo of her on inside cover **12.00**

Crazy, Who Can I Count On, Patsy Cline, Decca, 1951, 45 .... **3.00**

Day after Day, 45 rpm **1.00**

Dumbo, Disneyland, record and book, 1968 .... **10.00**

Empire State Observatory Voiceogram, 6-1/8" sq printed envelope, 1930s **20.00**

Firestone Presents, Your Favorite Christmas Carols, Julie Andrews, Andre Previn and the Firestone Orchestra and Chorus, Vol. 5 .... **15.00**

Glenn Miller Store, LP, Decca, 1954 . **22.00**

Glorious Night Blues, Allen Brothers, Victor **50.00**

Mario Lanza, The Toast of New Orleans, RCA Victor, Red Seal Records, pink cover with black and white photo, **$10**.

Johnny B Goode, Chuck Berry, 78 rpm **10.00**

Josie & the Pussycats, Capitol, soundtrack, 1970.................................... **300.00**

Limbo Party, Chubby Checker, Parkway, 1962, LP.. **20.00**

Maryland Vietnam Veterans Memorial Concert 1968, 12" sq album, unused record **20.00**

Mighty Hercules................................. **95.00**

Rapunzel from the Brothers Grimm, RCA Victor Youth Series, book style, attached sleeves for two records, story with colorful pictures on inside front and back cover, black and white photo for Dame May Whitty, narrator among litho **12.00**

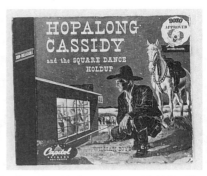

Hopalong Cassidy, Square Dance Hold-Up, 78 rpm, two-record set, Capitol, 1950, **$35**.

Reflections of Those Who Loved Him, Hank Williams, three LPs, promotional box set, 1975 .... **60.00**

She Came Rolling Down the Mountain, Blue Ridge Mountain Girls, Champion **12.00**

The Big Gun, 33-1/3 rpm, blue and white record jacket, from Revell model kit **10.00**

The Stars Are Out Tonight, Teardrops **30.00**

The Thing, soundtrack, John Carpenter's **15.00**

This is Andy Griffith, LP **100.00**

Touch of Gold, Elvis Presley, Vol. 2, maroon label.. **85.00**

Zorro, by The Chardettes, promo....... **40.00**

Red Wing Pottery

History: The category of Red Wing Pottery covers several potteries started in Red Wing, Minnesota. The first pottery, named Red Wing Stoneware Company, was started in 1868 by David Hallem. The primary product of this company was stoneware. The mark used by this company was a red wing stamped under the glaze. The Minnesota Stoneware Company was started in 1883. The North Star Stoneware Company opened a factory in the same area in 1892 and went out of business in 1896. The mark used by this company included a raised star and the words "Red Wing."

The Red Wing Stoneware Company and the Minnesota Stoneware Company merged in 1892. The new company was called the Red Wing Union Stoneware Company. The new company made stoneware until 1920 when it introduced a line of pottery.

In 1936, the name of the company was changed to Red Wing Potteries Incorporated. It continued to make pottery until the 1940s. During the 1930s, it introduced several lines of dinnerware. These patterns, which were all hand painted, were very popular and sold through department stores, Sears Roebuck and Company, and gift stamp centers. The production of dinnerware declined in the 1950s. The company began producing hotel and restaurant china in the early 1960s. The plant closed in 1967.

Collecting Hints: Red Wing Pottery can be found with various marks and paper labels. Some of the marks include a stamped red wing, a raised "Red Wing U.S.A. #___," or an impressed "Red Wing U.S.A. #___." Paper labels were used as early as 1930. Some pieces were identified only by a paper label that was easily lost.

Many manufacturers used the same mold patterns. Study the references to become familiar with the Red Wing forms.

Bowl, Brush Ware, daisy-type embossed decoration on exterior, green-glazed interior, marked "Red Wing Union Stoneware, Red Wing, Minn," **$75**.

Ashtray, horse's head, ochre **75.00**
Beverage server, cov, Tampico **130.00**
Box, cov, 4-1/2" l, 3-1/2" w, 3-1/4" h, #1272, matte pink, white int., applied leaf dec, mkd "Red Wing USA 1272" **120.00**
Bread and butter plate, 6-1/2" d
   Bob White **12.50**
   Pepe **8.00**
   Pompeii.. **7.50**
   Random Harvest **7.50**
Bulb bowl, 9" d, 2-3/4" h, Brush Ware, green glossy int., mkd "Red Wing Union Stoneware Co., Red Wing, Minn," pre-1936 .... **75.00**

Butter dish, cov, Bob White **48.00**
Cake plate, Fleck Zephyr, pink, 11-1/4" d, 3-1/2" h....................................... **95.00**
Candleholders, pr, #397, Sylvan, 5-1/2" h, 4" d base **95.00**
Candy dish, three parts, hexagon, gray, semi-gloss..................................... **18.00**
Chip and dip set, Tampico, 12" d serving bowl and six 8" d plates, 1950s **95.00**
Chop plate, Capistrano, 12" d **26.00**
Compote, orchid, cherub **65.00**
Console bowl, 12" d, Renaissance, brown dec **45.00**
Cookie jar, cov
   Katrina, beige **145.00**
   Monk, yellow, mkd "Redwing Pottery, Hand painted Patent D-130,328, C-130,329, G-130,330," imp "Redwing" **85.00**
Cornucopia, #442, 12" l, 9" d
   Blue ext., pink int. **95.00**
   Tan ext., coral pink int.................... **95.00**

Dinnerware service, Tampico pattern, 80 pieces, **$500**.

Dinnerware set, Bob White, **$525**.

Custard cup, Fondos, green and pink **18.00**
Dinner plate, 10" d
   Bob White **15.00**
   Lotus **12.50**
   Town and Country, blue **12.50**
Figure, Bird on stump, #1033, 6" h .. **90.00**
Flower frog, 10" h, Deer, white........... **25.00**
Hanging planter, Brush Ware, brown
   gloss int., 3 hanging holes, c1910-30
   .... **150.00**
Mixing bowl, 7" d, 4-1/4" h, blue and rust
   spongeware, 1930s **175.00**
Mustard jar, Town & Country, Eva Zeisel,
   sand, 4-1/4" d, 5-3/4" h................. **400.00**
Nappy, Lotus **9.50**
Pitcher
   Blue Deco, #768, orig paper tag, 5-1/8" h
   .... **325.00**
   Bob White, 12" h, 1855 .... **75.00**
   Bob White, 15" h, 124 oz.............. **350.00**
   Stoneware, blue Dutch boy and girl
   kissing, windmill, 7" h **295.00**
Planter
   Bamboo, #407, 12" l, 3-1/4" w, 4" h, rust
   ext., light green int., orig label "Minnesota
   75th Anniversary, 1878-1853," mkd "Red
   Wing USA 407"............................... **95.00**
   Boy, #1344, white glaze, 6-1/4" h . **100.00**
   Cart, #M1531, 8-1/2" w, 12" l,
   butterscotch **75.00**
   Giraffe, #896, 12" h, 8" x 5" base .. **385.00**
   Lamb, #1343, white......................... **30.00**
   Urn, #852, white glaze, two scrolled
   handles **95.00**
Platter, Town & Country, Eva Zeisel,
   chartreuse **24.00**
Salad bowl, Pheasant, blue and green
   .... **48.00**

Plate, Bob White, **$15**.

Salt and pepper shakers, pr
   Bob White **30.00**
   Brittany, Provincial **18.00**
Sugar bowl, bronze lid, Town & Country, Eva
   Zeisel **65.00**
Syrup, Town & Country, Eva Zeisel, forest
   green, 3-1/4" d, 5-3/4" h **325.00**

Teapot
   Mediterranean **65.00**
   Town & Country, Eva Zeisel, chartreuse,
   11-1/2" l, 7" w, 4-3/4" h **625.00**
Trivet, 6-5/8" d, Minnesota Centennial,
   1958 .... **95.00**

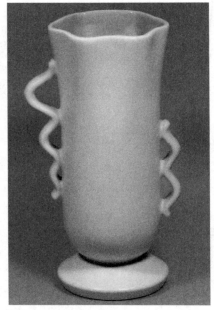

Vase, matte white exterior, green glazed interior, embossed "1352 Redwing USA," **$65**.

Vase
   #896, bulbous tulip shape, blue-gray
   ext., pink int., mkd "Red Wing USA
   896," 6-1/2" h, 8" d **95.00**
   #897, Gypsy Trail, semi gloss white
   glaze, 4-1/2" **90.00**
   #954, Adobe, bisque ext., apricot
   glazed int., c1939, 6" h **125.00**
   #1151, Art Dec lady and deer in relief,
   turquoise semi gloss glaze, white
   crackle glaze int., asymmetric handles,
   8" h **65.00**
   #1169, Ribbon, soft green, 7" h, 6" w
   .... **85.00**
   #1481, Castle Series, glossy pink fleck
   glaze, Murphy design, mkd "M-1481,"
   c1955, 10-3/4" h.......................... **145.00**
Vegetable bowl, divided, Bob White,
   boomerang shape, 14" l............. **75.00**
Wall pocket, Colonial style, white .. **200.00**

Rock 'n' Roll

History: Rock music can be traced back to early rhythm and blues. It progressed and reached its golden age in the 1950s. The current nostalgia craze for the 1950s has produced some modern rock 'n' roll, which is well received. Rock 'n' roll memorabilia exists in large quantities, with each singer or group having had many promotional pieces made.

Collecting Hints: Many rock 'n' roll collections are centered around one artist. Flea markets and thrift shops are good places to look for rock 'n' roll items. Prices depend on the singer or group, and works by stars who are no longer living usually command a higher price.

Glossy, non-authographed 8-by-10-inch photographs of singers are generally worth $3.

Action figure
> Dave Clark Five, Remco, Rick, Mike, Dennis **95.00**
> KISS, © 1978 Mego, 12" h, set of Ace, Gene, Peter, and Paul, MIB, price for set **500.00**

Badge, 1-1/2" h, Devo, red plastic, 1980s **20.00**

Ballot, official US Postal Service ballot for 1993 commemorative Elvis stamp . **12.00**

Bobbleheads
> Grateful Dead **70.00**
> KISS, set of four **50.00**
> Rolling Stones, set of four **50.00**

Book cover, orange and red title paper, three black and white book covers, one with Pat Boone, one with Sal Mineo, third generic signer, 1958 Cooga Mooga Products, Inc., NY, unused in clear plastic bag **18.00**

Bracelet, gold chain link, burnished gold disc with raised Monkees guitar symbol, orig retail card, © 1967 .... **27.50**

Bubblegum cards
> Donruss, The Osmonds, 1973, 15 cards **10.00**
> Elvis Presley, series one, 1992, unopened pack, 12 cards **85.00**

Colorforms, KISS, MIB **27.50**

Comic book
> *Elton John,* #62, 1993 .... **15.00**
> *Frank Zappa,* #32, 1991 .... **20.00**
> *Janis Joplin* #63, 1993 .... **15.00**
> *Kiss,* #9, March, 1990 .... **7.00**
> *Metallica,* 1990 .... **10.00**
> *Queen, Night at the Opera,* #9, 1992 .... **15.00**
> *The Who,* 1992 .... **8.00**

Cuff links, pr, Dick Clark, MIB **35.00**

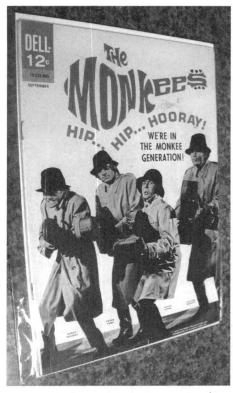

Comic book, The Monkees, Dell, September, $3.

Decanter, Elvis Presley, McCormick Dist. Co., musical, plays Love Me Tender **120.00**

Finger doll, Remco, Monkees, Davey or Peter **40.00**

Flicker button, 2-1/4" d, black and white photos of Elvis playing guitar, titled "Love Me Tender," © 1958 Elvis Presley Enterprises **25.00**

Flicker ring, Monkees, plastic, bright silver luster, "Official Member Monkees Ring Club," four portraits within red heart designs on yellow background, Kellogg's cereal premium **25.00**

Game, Elvis Presley, King of Rock, Santa Clara, CA, copyright 1979 .... **80.00**

Gumball charm, Elvis Presley, 7/8" h gray plastic, bright yellow celluloid-like sticker with name and portrait illus on both sides in bright red, loop at top, 1956 .... **95.00**

Handkerchief, Buddy Holly, silk, red and gold paisley, authenticity card **450.00**

Pendant, 1-5/8" h, The Beatles, white metal frame finished with brass luster, beetle shape, back inset with 1" glossy oval photo, English, c1965 .... **50.00**

Pez container, Elvis Presley, stem gold outfit, hand-painted **85.00**

Lobby cards, set of three, Hey Let's Twist, black and white image, red and white lettering, each $20.

Pinback button

Berkeley Rock and Roll Revival April 18, 1-1/4" d, blue text on bright yellow, c1970 .... **15.00**

Bette Mindler, 1-3/4" d, black and white photo, black text on bright yellow "Do You Want To Dance," c1973 .... **30.00**

Grateful Dead, 1-1/4" d, black and white portraits of six group members **30.00**

Jerry Garcia, 1-1/4" d, black and white **20.00**

Herbie Mann, 1-1/4" d, stylized purple and red on white, image of him playing flute **12.00**

David Peel, 1-1/2" d, first record album promo, "Have a Marijuana," black and white photo on white surrounded by bright red record title, NYC street musician and political activist **30.00**

Elvis Presley, 7/8" d, "You're Nothin' But A Houn' Dog," red, white, and blue litho, 1956 .... **24.00**

Rock-Ola, 3" d, red, white, and blue illus c1950 .... **17.50**

Rolling Stones 1981 Tour DC-101, 1-1/2" d, black and gray on white **35.00**

Springsteen, 1-3/4" d, black text on white, red heart surrounding "RCA," rebus slogan "I (Love) The Boss" **25.00**

The Doors, 1-1/4" black and white photo **20.00**

Pocket calendar, Elvis, 1968, RCA Records, Elvis in red and blue silk shirt **5.00**

Pop-up book, Elvis, *Graceland,* $35.

Poster

Barry Manilow, Dec 1979 .... **185.00**

Bobby "Blue" Bland, March 1973, Fort Worth, TX **295.00**

Bob Dylan, Nov 1978, Oakland ... **115.00**

Charlie Pride, April 1971, Waterloo, IA **200.00**

Conway Twitty, July 1973, Wellsville, OH **300.00**

Elton John, performing at piano, red, white, and blue glasses, musical note jacket, 1974 Pace International, 24" w, 36" h, rolled **20.00**

Elvis Presley, Tenth Anniversary Tribute Poster, 1977-1987, shows Elvis singing into microphone, 1987 Zorcom Licensed **24.00**

Eric Clapton, Delaney & Bonnie, German tour, 1970 .... **295.00**

Everly Brothers, Aug 1966, Colorado Springs **395.00**

Fats Domino, Gerry & Pacemakers, March 1967, London **245.00**

Fleetwood Mac, Sept 1972, Wilmington NC **225.00**

Grateful Dead, June 1966, Filmore West (Bill Graham) **375.00**

Joan Baez, April 1962, Santa Monica **400.00**

Johnny Cash, May 1965, Des Moines, IA **495.00**

John Prine, Oct 1976, Portland, OR **245.00**

King Crimson, May 1971, Plymouth, UK **295.00**

Led Zeppelin, Jethro Tull, Aug 1969, San Antonio, TX.................................... **995.00**

Lovin' Spoonful, Nov 1966, Houston **395.00**

Ray Charles, May 1967, Santa Barbara, CA **225.00**

Sly & The Family Stones, Dec 1972, San Francisco **345.00**

Steve Miller Band, May 1973, Geneva, NY.. **125.00**

Stevie Wonder, Beach Boys, Nov 1972, Greenville SC **365.00**

Tanya Tucker, June 1975, Portlane, OR **265.00**

Tony Bennett, Duke Ellington, March 1963, Philharmonic Hall, NY **395.00**
Who, Nov. 1973, Cow Palace **295.00**
Radio, KISS, 1977 .... **100.00**
Salt and pepper shakers, pr, ceramic feet, mkd "Rock-N-Roll Indiana," mkd "Japan," 2-3/4" l **12.00**
Ring, Monkees, club, flicker **50.00**
Store display, Jackson 5, Meagus, 27" x 22" **295.00**
Tab, 2" d, litho tin, blue, gold lettering, "I Love Elvis," metallic gold background, 1970s **15.00**
Thermos, Bee Gees, plastic, King Seeley, 1978 .... **27.50**
Tie clip, Dick Clark American Bandstand, gold-tone metal **18.00**
Tour book, Bob Dylan, 28 pgs, c1977 **30.00**
Vending machine insert, showing Monkee pinback buttons, 1967 .... **75.00**
Viewmaster reel, Last Wheelbarrow to Pokeyville, Monkees, orig booklet .. **12.00**

Roseville Pottery

History: In the late 1880s, a group of investors purchased the J. B. Owens Pottery in Roseville, Ohio, and made utilitarian stoneware items. In 1892, the firm was incorporated, and George F. Young became general manager. Four generations of Youngs controlled Roseville until the early 1950s.

A series of acquisitions began: Midland Pottery of Roseville in 1898, Clark Stoneware Plant in Zanesville (formerly used by Peters and Reed), and Muskingum Stoneware (Mosaic Tile Company) in Zanesville. In 1898, the offices also moved from Roseville to Zanesville.

In 1900, Roseville developed its art pottery line—Rozane. Ross Purdy designed a line to compete with Weller's Louwelsa. Rozane became a trade name to cover a large series of lines by designers such as Christian Neilson, John J. Herold, and Gazo Fudji. The art lines of hand-decorated underglaze pottery were made in limited quantities after 1919.

The success of Roseville depended on its commercial lines, first developed by John J. Herald and Frederick Rhead in the early decades of the 1900s. Decorating techniques included transfers, pouncing (a method which produced the outline of a pattern which could then be used as the basis for further decorating), and air brushing or sponging over embossed motifs. Dutch, Juvenile, Cameo, and Holland are some of the lines from this early period.

George Young retired in 1918. Frank Ferrell replaced Harry Rhead, who had replaced Frederick Rhead, as art director. Ferrell developed more than 80 lines, the first being Sylvan. The economic depression of the 1930s caused Roseville to look for new product lines. Pine Cone was introduced in 1935, made for 15 years, and issued in more than 75 shapes.

In the 1940s, a series of high-gloss glazes were used to try to revive certain lines. Other changes were made in response to the fluctuating contemporary market. Mayfair and Wincraft date from this period. In 1952, Raymor dinnerware was produced. None of these changes brought economic success back to Roseville. In November 1954, Roseville was bought by the Mosaic Tile Company.

Collecting Hints: The prices for Roseville's later commercial ware are stable and unlikely to rise rapidly because it is readily available. The prices are strong for the popular middle-period patterns, which were made during the Depression and produced in limited numbers. Among the most popular patterns from this middle period are Blackberry, Cherry Blossom, Falline, Ferella, Jonquil, Morning Glory, Sunflower, and Windsor.

The Art Deco craze has increased the popularity of Futura, especially the more angular-shaped pieces. Pine Cone pieces with a blue or brown glaze continue to have a strong following as do the earlier lines of Juvenile and Donatello.

Desirable Roseville shapes include baskets, bookends, cookie jars, ewers, tea sets, and wall pockets.

Most pieces are marked. However, during the middle period paper stickers were used. These often were removed, leaving the piece unmarked.

Roseville made more than 150 different lines or patterns. Novice collectors will benefit from reading one of the several books about Roseville and should visit dealers who specialize in art pottery. Collections generally are organized around a specific pattern or shape.

Reproduction Alert: Reproductions of several Roseville patterns began to plaque the marketplace in the late 1990s.

Console bowl, Bushberry, c1948, marked "414-10 Roseville," 10" w, **$350**. Photo courtesy of Wellscroft Lodge.

Basket
    Clematis, #389, 10" h **275.00**
    Mock Orange, No. 911-10, white blossoms, green leaves, green ground, 10" h **180.00**

Bookends, pr
    Burmese, green, raised marks **255.00**
    Iris, book shape, blue **290.00**

Bowl
    Blueberry, blue, 412-6 .... **130.00**
    Lombardy, dark teal **85.00**
    Moss Blue, high sides, #294-12 ... **275.00**
    Nursery Rhyme **150.00**
    Peony, yellow, 428-6 .... **95.00**
    Rosecraft Panel, rolled rim, brown, 8" d
    .... **140.00**

Bowl and flower frog, Clematis, mkd "Roseville USA 458-10," c1944 .... **195.00**

Bud vase, double
    Dahl Rose **175.00**
    Foxglove, green with peach blush **375.00**

Candlesticks, pr
    Columbine, blue, #1145 .... **90.00**
    Ixia, #1125, green **75.00**
    Snowberry, mauve **75.00**

Child's feeding plate, rolled edge
    Duck with Hat, c1916 .... **395.00**
    Nursery Rhyme **150.00**
    Tom Tom **90.00**
Compote, Magnolia, 13" h **110.00**
Conch Shell, Peony, blue **185.00**
Console bowl, Cremona, pink **95.00**
Cookie jar, cov
    Clematis, blue **395.00**
    Freesia, No. 4-8 .... **440.00**
    Magnolia, No. 2-8 .... **425.00**
Cornucopia, #190, 6" h **220.00**
Cup and saucer, Zephyr Lily, blue.... **125.00**

Double bud vase, Clematis pattern, #194-5, blue ground, white flower, green leaves, **$140**.

Floor vase, Gardenia, 689, green, matte finish, int. rim chip **550.00**
Flower frog, Clematis, 50 .... **90.00**
Hanging planter, Zephry Lily, green **275.00**
Jardinière
    Florentine, cream and green **325.00**
    Fuchsia, blue **350.00**
Lamp, Rozane Royal, c1905, 17" h .. **600.00**
Mug
    Duck with boots **150.00**
    Dutch **110.00**
    Rabbit **140.00**

Pitcher, Pinecone, ball jug shape, ice lip, shaded green to ivory ground, brown twig handle, **$495**. Photo courtesy of Wellscroft Lodge.

Pitcher
    Blended Landscape, 7-1/2" h **140.00**
    Flute Player and Jester, c1915, small crack **400.00**
Planter, Florentine, brown **290.00**
Tea set, Zephr Lily, teapot, creamer, sugar, small manuf defect on sugar lower rim
    .... **495.00**

Jardinière and pedestal, Pinecone, **$550**. Photo courtesy of Wellscroft Lodge.

Vase, Bittersweet, embossed "Roseville, USA 874-7," 7-1/4" h, **$45**.

Vase

Blackberry #572, 6" h.................... **635.00**
Gardenia, gray, 14" h **320.00**
Ming Tree, #581, 6" h **175.00**

Rosecraft Vintage, RV ink mark, 8-1/2" l
.... **295.00**

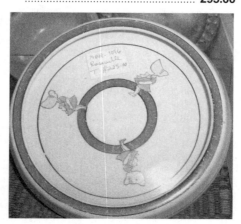

Children's feeding dish, sunbonnet girl decoration, **$225**.

Wall pocket

Apple Blossom, green.................. **550.00**
Cosmos, blue............................... **375.00**
Foxglove, brown, 1296-8"............ **190.00**
Green, matte, 8" l **120.00**
Maple Leaf, 8-1/2"......................... **75.00**
Snowberry, blue, 1WP-8.............. **180.00**
Tulips, emb flowers, white **60.00**
White Rose, pink........................... **325.00**

Royal China

History: The Royal China Company manufactured dinnerware in Sebring, Ohio, from 1934 to 1986. The original officers were Beatrice L. Miller, William H. Hebenstreit, and John Briggs. Miss Miller became known as the "Queen of China" and sold Royal in 1969 upon retiring. She passed away in 1979. John Briggs passed away in 1980. Bill Habenstreit retired from Royal in 1946, moved to California, and passed away in 1964. They started the company with $500, six months free rent, and a handful of employees working without pay in the depths of the Depression. Four months later, they had 125 people on their payroll. At the height of Royal's popularity in 1970, the company had 700 employees, seven acres under roof, and annual sales of around $16 million. It was the largest manufacturer of popular-priced dinnerware in the United States.

Royal produced a large variety of dinnerware patterns, well over 600, the most popular being the blue and white Currier and Ives. Other patterns made by the company include Bucks County, Colonial Homestead, Fair Oaks, Memory Lane, Old Curiosity Shop, and Willow Ware. The blue Currier & Ives and blue Willow Ware were continued through the years, while most of the other patterns were discontinued when Royal sold to Jeannette in 1970 which as probably a mistake. Bucks County, with a matte finish, Fair Oaks, and Memory Lane were reintroduced in 1985, but too late to save the company. These popular dinnerware patterns were made in four basic colors: blue, pink, green, and brown. Some were also made in black and multicolored.

Royal China was sold through retail department stores, catalog mail-order houses, and supermarket chains. They were also given as premiums. Numerous serving pieces as well as advertising and decorative items to compliment the dinnerware were available.

In the last few years that they were in business, Royal made many different cake plates, pie bakers, coasters, and holiday related items, including Christmas items. Royal Holidays and Royal Holly were two such patterns. These items are becoming very collectible and sought after.

The company had various owners including the Jeanette Glass Corporation from 1969 to 1976. In 1970, the building and records were destroyed by fire and the operation was moved to the French Saxon China Company building. In 1978 the company was purchased by Coca-Cola and was operated by them until 1981, when it was sold to the J. Corporation. It was sold for the last time in 1984 to Nordic Capital, who filed for bankruptcy in 1986 and ceased production in March of that year.

Collecting Hints: The dinnerware has become very collectible and increasingly popular. It can be found at flea markets and antiques malls across the country. There are no known reproductions of Royal China dinnerware. The backstamps usually contain the name of the pattern. In addition to many variations of company backstamps, Royal China also produced objects with private backstamps. All records of these markings were lost in a fire in 1970.

The following are some of the items that are considered scarce: Charles Denning clocks, grill plates, snack/soup and sandwich plates, tab handled items, and some beverage/juice sets and tumblers. Items that are more sought after by collectors are items with decorated handles such as: cups, sugar bowls, creamers, teapots, and casseroles. Also items with backstamps such as the ashtray and the gravy underplate.

Advisers: David J. and Deborah G. Folckemer.

Bucks County, coffee mug, 2-3/4" x 3-3/4", $40.
All Royal China photos by advisers David and Deborah Folckemer.

Bucks County

Introduced c1950; prices given are for yellow pieces with a dark brown printed farm scene. Also made in a green and white version.

Accessories

Hostess table tidbit, two tiers, 10" d and 13" d plates, wood legs	**100.00**
Juice tumbler, 3-1/2"	**15.00**
Promotional jug, 2" x 2-3/4"	**100.00**
Tidbit, three tiers, 6" d, 9" d, and 12" d plates	**50.00**

Dinnerware

Bread and butter plate, 6-3/8" d	**3.00**
Butter dish, cov, 1/4 lb	**40.00**
Casserole, cov, angle handles	**75.00**
Creamer	**4.00**
Cup and saucer, 6" d	**4.00**
Dinner plate, 10-1/4" d	**4.00**
Fruit bowl, 5-3/4" d	**3.00**
Gravy boat	**15.00**
Gravy ladle, white	**40.00**
Grill plate, three sections	**15.00**

Lug soup/cereal bowl **15.00**
Rim soup bowl, 8-3/8" d................... **9.00**
Salad plate, 7-3/8" d......................... **8.00**
Salt and pepper shakers, pr.......... **20.00**
Teapot, cov **75.00**
Vegetable bowl
　9" d... **15.00**
　10" d... **20.00**

Colonial Homestead, tab handle gravy boat, **$85**.

Colonial Homestead

Introduced c1950. Design consists of colonial home scenes of about 1750. Prices given are for white pieces with a green print. Also made with black and pink prints.

Accessories

Ashtray, 5-1/2"................................. **10.00**
Beverage set, frosted pitcher and six
tumblers... **200.00**
Beverage tumbler, 5-1/2" **14.00**
Clock, electric, Charles Denning, 10" d,
spinning wheel **350.00**
Hostess table tidbit, two tiers, 10" d and
13" d plates, wood legs................. **100.00**
Juice set, frosted pitcher and six tumblers
.... **150.00**
Juice tumbler, 3-1/2"....................... **14.00**
Tile and rack, 6" x 6", Wheeling **70.00**
Water tumbler, 4-3/4" **14.00**

Dinnerware

Bread and butter plate, 6-3/8" d **2.50**
Breakfast plate, 9" d **12.00**
Butter dish, cov, 1/4 lb **25.00**
Casserole, cov
　Angle handles......................... **65.00**
　Tab handles **200.00**
Cereal bowl, 6-1/4" d...................... **10.00**
Coffee mug..................................... **15.00**
Cup and saucer, 6" d **4.00**
Dinner plate, 10-1/4" d **4.00**
Fruit bowl, 5-3/4" d **3.00**
Gravy boat, regular **15.00**
Gravy ladle, white........................... **40.00**
Gravy underplate, tab handle......... **15.00**
Lug soup/cereal bowl **15.00**
Pie plate, 10" d **20.00**
Platter
　Lug, meat, 11-1/2"................... **20.00**

Oval, 10" x 13" **25.00**
Round, 13" d............................. **25.00**
Rim soup bowl, 8-3/8" d **8.00**
Salt and pepper shakers, pr
　Angle handles........................ **20.00**
　Round handles....................... **25.00**
Snack plate with cup, 9-1/4" d **65.00**
Soup and sandwich plate, with mug,
10"d, coupe.................................. **100.00**
Sugar bowl, cov, angle handles..... **10.00**
Teapot, cov **90.00**

Currier and Ives

Introduced late 1940s; prices given are for white pieces with a blue print. Also made in pink, green, black, brown, and multicolored.

Accessories

Beverage set, frosted pitcher and six
tumblers **425.00**
Beverage tumbler, 5-1/2"............... **10.00**
Calendar plate
　1969, light blue, coupe **25.00**
　1973 through 1986, each........ **12.00**
　Candle lamp, with globe, Grist Mill,
　mid-1980s **300.00**
Clock plate, electric, Charles Denning
　10-1/4" d, Old School House. **500.00**
　12" d, Grist Mill **650.00**
Juice set, frosted pitcher, Star of the Road
and six tumblers **350.00**
Juice tumbler, 3-1/2" **10.00**
Old fashion tumbler, 3-1/4" **10.00**
Placemats, vinyl, foam back, Marcrest,
set of four **100.00**
Tile and rack, Snowy Morning, Wheeling,
6" x 6".. **150.00**
Wall plaque, Rocky Mountains, 5-1/4" x
6-3/4" **500.00**
Water tumbler, 4-3/4" **10.00**

Currier and Ives, tile and rack, Wheeling, Snowy Morning, 6" x 6", **$150**.

S

Salt and Pepper Shakers

History: The Victorian era saw the advent of elaborate glass and fine-china salt and pepper shakers. Collectors were attracted to these objects by the pioneering research work of Arthur Goodwin Peterson that was published in *Glass Salt Shaker*. Figural and souvenir shakers, most dating from the mid-20th century and later, were looked down upon by this group.

This attitude is slowly changing. More and more people are collecting the figural and souvenir shakers, especially since prices are lower. Many of these patterns were made by Japanese firms and imported heavily after World War II.

Some forms were produced for decades; hence, it is difficult to tell an early example from a modern one. This is one of the factors that keeps prices low.

Collecting Hints: Collect only sets in very good condition. Make certain the set has the proper two pieces, and base if applicable. China shakers should show no signs of cracking. Original paint and decoration should be intact on all china and metal figurals. All parts should be present, including the closure.

Collectors compete with those in other areas, e.g., advertising, animal groups, Blacks, and holiday collectors. Many shakers were stock items to which souvenir labels were later affixed. The form, not the label, is the important element.

Coffee grinders, ceramic, marked "Made in Japan," original box, **$12**.

Advertising

Budweiser, miniature bottles **27.50**
Coca-Cola, miniature bottles **25.00**
Dairy Queen.. **32.00**
GE Refrigerators, 1930 style refrigerator, milk glass **36.00**
Hormel, hash and egg........................ **24.00**
Nipper, 3" h, white china, black ears, eyes, and noses, base inscribed "His Master's Voice/RCA Victor," orig cork stoppers, c1930 .... **36.00**
Pillsbury Dough Boy **20.00**
Planters Peanuts.............................. **36.00**
Schlitz Beer, miniature bottles........... **27.50**
Tappan Baker, glossy finished glass, black on pale yellow salt, pale blue pepper, inscribed "Tappan Kitchen Ranges" on one, black threaded plastic caps, c1940 .... **24.00**

Ceramic

Bell Bottom Gobs, sailors, Holt Howard **40.00**
Bellhop, ceramic, each wearing orange jacket and hat, black accents, gray pants with blue pin stripe, black shoes, green base, orig cork stoppers, mkd "Made in Japan," 1930s, 3-3/4" h **24.00**
Birds, standing, white, gold trim, mkd "Made in Japan" **9.50**
Bugs Bunny and Taz with football **18.00**
Chattercoons, Peppy and Salty, Holt Howard... **38.00**
Cozy Kittens, Holt Howard................ **20.00**
Donald Duck and BBQ **25.00**
Feet **12.00**
Frogs.. **15.00**
Goose n' golden egg, Holt Howard... **35.00**
Indian chief and squaw, 3-1/4" h, composition wood, both mkd "1947 copyright, Multi Products" **27.50**
Kitchen Prayer ladies, pink **30.00**
Monkeys, nodders, c1940, mkd "Made in Japan".. **175.00**
Penguins, black and white body, orange bill and webbed feet, mkd "Japan," c1930s, 3" h **12.00**

Birds, white, gold trim, marked "Made in Japan," 3" h, **$9.50**.

Pluto and doghouse......................... **20.00**
Rabbits, yellow, snuggle type, Van Telligen **42.00**

Red Rooster, Holt Howard.................. **45.00**
Rock 'n' Roll Santas, on springs, Holt Howard **75.00**
Rooster and hen................................ **12.50**
Sailor and anchor, figural glass shakers, wrought iron tray holder that has anchor and ships wheel, 2" h, most orig paint missing **48.00**
Skunks, Enesco................................ **18.00**
Snow Babies, Holt Howard................ **35.00**
Telephone and directory, 1-1/2" x 2" x 2" black cradle telephone, 1-1/2" h brown telephone directory, SC souvenir decal, stoppers missing............................ **15.00**
Thread and thimble.......................... **30.00**
Toilets... **10.00**
Tomatoes... **20.00**
Wall telephone, pink plastic phone, two small containers slip out of front, Party Line, orig box, 4-1/2" h **7.50**

Scouting

History: The Boy Scout movement began in America under the direction of William D. Boyce, inspired by a helping hand he received from one of Baden-Powell's English scouts when he was lost in a London fog in 1909. Other American boys' organizations, such as the one organized by Dan Beard, were quickly brought into the Boy Scout movement. In 1916, the Boy Scouts received a charter from the United States Congress. Key leaders in the movement were Ernest Thompson-Seton, Dan Beard, William D. Boyce, and James West. One of Norman Rockwell's first jobs was editor of *Boys' Life* in 1913, and this began the famous American illustrator's lifelong association with the Boy Scouts.

The first international jamboree was held in England in 1920. America's first jamboree was held in 1937 in Washington, D.C. Manufacturers, quick to recognize the potential for profits, issued a wealth of Boy Scout material. Local councils and Order of the Arrow lodges have added significantly to this base, especially in the area of patches. Around the time of the 1950 National Jamboree, everything from patches to lizards were traded.

The Girl Scout movement began on March 12, 1912, under the direction of Juliette Gordon Low of Savannah, Georgia. The movement grew rapidly, and in 1928 the Girl Scout manual suggested cookies be sold to raise funds. The Girl Scout movement received wide recognition for its activities during World War II, selling over $3 million worth of bonds in the fourth Liberty Loan drive.

Girl Scout material is about five to ten years behind Boy Scout material in respect to collecting interest. A Girl Scout collection can still be assembled for a modest investment. While Boy Scout uniforms have remained constant in design throughout time, the Girl Scout uniform changed almost every decade. This increases the number of collectibles.

Collecting Hints: Nostalgia is one of the principal reasons for collecting Scouting memorabilia; individuals often focus on the period during which they themselves were involved in the Scouting movement. Other collectors select themes, e.g., handbooks, jamborees, writings by scout-movement leaders or Eagle Scout material. Jamboree ephemera is especially desirable. The greatest price fluctuation occurs in modern material and newly defined specialized collecting areas.

Scouting scholars have produced a wealth of well-researched material on the Scouting movement. Many of these pamphlets are privately printed and can be located by contacting dealers specializing in Scouting items.

Adviser: Richard Shields.

Reproduction Alert: Boy Scout jamboree patches, rare Council Shoulder patches, and rare Order of the Arrow patches.

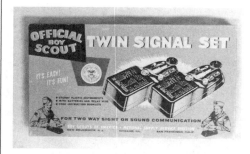

Official Boy Scout Twin Signal set, Catalog No. 1098, complete, **$38**

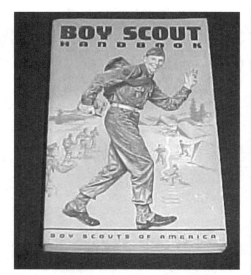

Boy Scout Handbook, 6th ed, Norman Rockwell illustrated cover, **$5**.

Boy Scouts

Bear Cub Scout Book, 1960-80 .... **1.00**
Bolo tie, 1977 National Jamboree **6.00**
Booklet, *Philadelphia Enquirer*, National Jamboree, 1950 .... **8.00**
Campaign hat (Smokey Bear), felt, leather band, chin strap **50.00**

Handbook

Boys, 6th ed, Rockwell cover **5.00**
Scoutmaster, 5th ed **8.00**
Key chain, Cub Scout, "Be Square" in promise **3.00**

Medal, Ben Franklin Historical Trail, **$6**.

Medal

Historical Trail medals **6.00**
Eagle, blue casket-shaped box... **100.00**
Eisenhower War Service **20.00**
Mug, ceramic, white **2.50**
Neckerchief, National Jamboree, 1953 .... **30.00**
Neckerchief slide, New York World's Fair, 1964-65 .... **25.00**
Pamphlet, *Merit Badge*, full picture, 1950-60s **1.00**
Paperback, *The Scout Oath in Action*, MacPeek **5.00**

Patch

Fifty Miler Award, cloth **1.00**
Meet Me at The Hill, 2001 Jamboree dome shaped patch with various names **5.00**
National Jamboree, 1960, inch round **20.00**
New York World's Fair, 1964-5........ **25.00**
Scouting Rounds A Guy Out............ **1.00**

Pocket coin, 1952 Get Out the Vote, Freedoms Foundation silver painted, **$2**.

Neckerchief, National Jamboree, Washington, DC, 1935, blue, white emblem. The 1935 Jamboree was canceled due to the polio epidemic so the first jamboree was in 1937. But, neckerchiefs and patches were sold before the Scouts got there so they could wear them to the jamboree. Some of the Scouts got as far as the train station in Washington before they received the word that the jamboree had been canceled, **$90**.

Plate, Csatri, BSA 75th Anniversary.... **25.00**
Pocket coin, 1952 Get Out the Vote, Freedoms Foundation silver painted **2.00**
Shampoo bottle, Snoopy Beagle Scout, plastic **20.00**
Shirt, Explorer, dark green, circle v design emblem... **8.00**
Toy, Matchbox, NASCAR, BSA **15.00**
Utensil set, three pcs, fits together, plastic case **5.00**
Wolf Cub Scout Book, 1960-80 .... **1.00**

Book, *Worlds to Explore*, 1980s, $3.

Girl Scouts

Belt, dark green web, trefoil emblem, metal buckle **15.00**
Beret, dark green wool, with patch **8.00**
Book, *Worlds to Explore*, 1980s............ **3.00**
Camera, Herbert George Co., model 620 .... **50.00**
Guide book, leader's, nature, 1942 .... **12.00**
Handbook, *Brownie*, 1964 .... **3.00**
Photo album, dark green cover, small size **25.00**
Pin, World Association, crude clasp **2.00**

Sewing Items

History: Sewing was considered an essential skill of a young woman of the 19th century. The wealth of early American samplers attests to the talents of many of these young seamstresses.

During the Victorian era, a vast assortment of practical, as well as whimsical, sewing devices appeared on the market. Among these were tape measures, pincushions, stilettos for punchwork, and crochet hooks. The sewing birds attached to tabletops were a standard fixture in the parlor.

Many early sewing tools, e.g., needle holders, emery holders and sewing boxes, were made of wood. However, the sterling silver tool was considered the height of elegance. Thimbles were the most popular of these, although sterling silver was used in other devices, particularly the handles of darning eggs, stilettos, and thread holders.

Needle cases and sewing kits were important advertising giveaways in the 20th century. Plastic sewing items are available, but they have not attracted much collector interest.

Collecting Hints: Collectors tend to favor sterling silver items. However, don't overlook pieces made of metal, ivory, celluloid, plastic, or wood. Before buying anything metal-plated, be sure the plating is in very good condition.

Advertising and souvenir items are part of sewing history. Focus on one of these aspects to develop a fascinating collection. Other collectors may specialize in a particular instrument, i.e., tape measures. Figural items of any sort have a high value because of their popularity.

Most collectors concentrate on material from the Victorian era. A novice collector might look to the 20th century, especially the Art Deco and Art Nouveau periods, to build a collection.

Dress pattern, Vogue, lady's vests, $15.

Basket, wicker, round, beaded lid **27.50**

Book

American Needlework, 1776-1976, Leslie Tillett, NY Graphic Society, 1975 .... **15.00**

Crewel Embroidery in England, Joan Edwards, Wm Morrow, NY, 1974, 248 pgs, color and black and white drawings **36.00**

Gloria Vanderbuilt designs for your Home, 1977, 1st edition, dj **10.00**

Sewing for Babies, 1943 .... **12.50**

Terrace Hill Needlepoint Designs, Orig Designs from Iowa Governor's Mansion, Billie Ray, 1980, sgd **10.00**

Button display card, The Ball & Socket Manufacturing Co., for Uniform Buttons, including buttons of Cardin, Paris; American Airlines; Western Union Pacific Railroad; Fire Department, etc., consisting of card and 25 buttons .. **70.00**

Button hole cutter, pliers type, mkd "F. C. Leypoldt, Phila, Pa, 2, Pat'd 1860 & 1865" **150.00**

Calendar, perpetual, Singer **300.00**

Catalog

Davis Sewing Machine Co., Watertown, NY, 1881, 64 pgs, 5-1/2" x 8-3/4", cover wear **24.00**

United Thread Mills, New York, NY, c1930, 7 pgs, 6-3/4" x 10" **18.00**

Wilson Sewing Machine Co., Chicago, IL, pre-1900, 26 pgs, 6" x 9" **38.00**

Charm, sewing machine on stand, gold, 14k **150.00**

Clamp, wood, painted, pin cushion, cupid decal **115.00**

Crochet hook, metal, capped **15.00**

Crochet needles, pr **10.00**

Darner, Titus, orig box **25.00**

Darning egg, 4-1/4" l, 1-1/2" w egg, ebony, sterling silver handle, stamped "Sterling" on both sides **95.00**

Folder, full color, 4" x 5"

Singer/Mother's Helper, The Handy Extension Leaf, copyright 1899, int. describes "The Light-Running Singer Sewing Machine No. 28," lightly browned **12.00**

The Refinement of Needlework, The Singer Automatic, c1900, describes "The Singer Automatic" and "The Singer Cabinet-Table," lightly browned **12.00**

Hem gauge, 4-3/4" l, poinsettias dec, mkd "Sterling" **95.00**

Magazine

McCalls, 1969, 8-1/4" x 11-1/4" **8.00**

Workbasket and Home Arts Magazine, 1976, 12 issues **10.00**

Singer sewing machine, ornate carved case, working condition, **$200**.

Needle book

Knight Life Insurance, colonial style characters on front **5.00**

Sears Fine Needlework **15.00**

Sewing Circle, four ladies sewing, six needle packets and threader **10.00**

Sewing Susan, Japan, four needle packets and threader, Japan **10.00**

Sew Smart, Japan **12.00**

Worcester Ivory Salt **10.00**

Needle case

Adv, Formamint, metal, adv "Wulfing's Formamint for Sore Throat" on side, mkd "Germany" on bottom, 2" h **10.00**

Barrel Shape, Piccadilly, wood, 3" h, 1-1/4" d **85.00**

Needle gripper, Nimble Thimble, orig package **20.00**

Needle sharpener (emery)

Cat **50.00**

Strawberry **9.00**

Needle threader, Witch, orig box **15.00**

Pin cube, 1-1/2" sq, 1-1/2" h, mkd "Toilet Pins, No. 1660," orig flat jet black pins **35.00**

Pin cushion, shoe shaped, bronze-colored metal, purple velvet cushion, image of Niagara Falls, Prospect Point, 3" w, **$25**.

Pincushion, star shaped, made by Julia Jensen, Grand Forks, ND, c1930, from flour sack scraps, 4-1/2" d, **$35**.

Pin cushion

2-1/2" w, 3" h, bisque, seated man, dressed in Colonial attire, barrel-shaped pin cushion with gold velvet top, mkd "Occupied Japan" **40.00**

3" d, 2-1/2" h, apple, satin, red and yellow, green leaves and stem **65.00**

3" w, 5" h, strawberry, red velvet, green felt leaves, c1870 .... **90.00**

3-1/4" l, 2" w, nodding turtle, wagging tail, off-white body with goldtone highlights, rhinestone eyes, gray pin cushion, Florenza **60.00**

4" l, 3" h, cast metal, figural Victorian high-heeled shoe, gold finish............... **125.00**

4-7/8" d, 5-3/4" h, porcelain and fabric, half doll, crocheted skirt............... **130.00**

5" l, porcelain, multicolored chicken, tape measure and thimble holder........... **25.00**

5-3/8" w, 5-7/8" h, ceramic, black cat, pin cushion on back, tape measure tongue mkd "Japan"................................... **135.00**

6" l, 2-1/4" w, wood, hand painted flowers, shoe, orig velvet pin cushion, orig silk hanging cord **65.00**

Pinking shears, Weiss, orig box and instructions **25.00**

Scissors, emb florals on handle, German **30.00**

Sewing bird, hand held, sgd "Turner" **80.00**

Sewing caddy

4" x 3-1/2", wood, red stain, three spools **28.00**

11" l, 8" w, 9" h, fabric, shape of upholstered couch, seat lifts up to reveal wood storage compartment, 1940s......... **145.00**

Sewing machine, full size, working condition, Minnesota Model D, hand crank, carved wood carrying case **350.00**

Sewing machine, toy, working condition

Casige **200.00**

German, 6-1/2" l, 5" h, tin, stencil dec **155.00**

Little Mother, 8" l, 8" h, tin, stenciled name and dec... **155.00**

Singer, 7" l, 6" h **85.00**

Spool cabinet, oak, gold lettering "Corticelli," glass, oak, original spool holders, **$825**.

Spool cabinet, JP Coats, metal, black, glass slant front..................................... **175.00**

Tailor's clamp, cast metal, emb lettering "Alburger, Stoer & Co., Tailors Trimmings, Chicago, Philadelphia, Patented 1886," leaf with spring operated clamp .. **200.00**

Tailor's crayons, Gilt Edge Tailors Crayons, American Crayon Co., white crayons, orig box **4.00**

Tape measure, figural

Apple, hard plastic, red, leaf pull... **24.00**

Clock, metal, hands turn, mkd "Germany" **125.00**

Dress form **50.00**

Little Boy, clown hat, mkd "Germany" **45.00**

Thimble

Gold, 14k, monogram **195.00**

Sterling silver, English, daisy motif, hallmarked for Chester, 1896, mkd "H.G.& S.," 7/8" h **100.00**

Sterling silver, English, Dorcas, size 6, hallmarked for Chester, 1905, mkd "C.H.," 11/16" d, 13/16" h **75.00**

Sterling silver, English, engraved band, faceted bottom rim, size 11, hallmarked for Chester, 1899, mkd "J.F.," 15-16" h.. **85.00**

Sterling silver, Simons, cupid and garlands, stamped "Nov 21, 1905" on side, Simons shield, and "Sterling" on inside, 7/8" h................................ **155.00**

Thread holder, 3-1/2" h, thimble top, red celluloid top, hand painted floral pattern **38.00**

Tie-tac, men's, goldtone, zipper pull, mkd "Talon" **5.00**

Tracing paper, Singer, unopened back, c1960 .... **4.00**

Zipper pull, 1-1/8" h, tassel, Bakelite, butterscotch, orig metal attachment **8.50**

Sheet Music

History: Sheet music, especially piano scores, dates to the early 19th century. The early music contains some of the finest examples of lithography. Much of this music was bound into volumes.

The covers of sheet music chronicle the social, political, and historical trends of all eras. The golden age of the hand-illustrated cover dates to around 1885. Leading artists such as James Montgomery Flagg used their talents to illustrate sheet music. Cover artwork was critical to helping a song sell.

Once radio and talking pictures became popular, covers featured the stars. A song sheet might be issued in dozens of cover versions, each picturing a different personality. By the 1950s, piano playing no longer was popular and song sheets failed to maintain a high quality of design.

Collecting Hints: Pick a theme for your collection: show tunes, songs of World War I, Sousa marches, Black material, songs of a certain lyricist or composer—the list is endless.

Be careful about stacking sheets on top of one another because the ink on the covers tends to bleed. The ideal solution is to place acid-free paper between each cover and sheet.

Unfortunately, tape was often used to repair tears in old sheet music, resulting in discoloration. This detracts from value. Seek professional help in removing tape from rarer sheets.

America I Love You, 1915, Tom Ward and Dolly McCue on cover with sketches of Statue of Liberty, Indian chief, covered wagon, Liberty Bell, pilgrims, farmer, New York City **12.00**

A Precious Little Thing Called Love, Lou Davis and J. Fred Coots, 1928 .... **8.00**

Carioca, 1933, movie "Flying Down to Rio," Fred Astaire and Dolores Del Rio cov **9.00**

Chariot Race or Ben Hur March, E. T. Paull Music Co., Richmond, VA, c1894. **175.00**

Childhood Days Are Dear to Me, 1910, man looking into mirror with reflection as young boy, insert oval photo of Paulina Parks **10.00**

Loves Golden Star, Louis A. Drummeller, Jos Morris Co., Philadelphia, **$12**

Over the Rainbow, Wizard of Oz, E.Y. Harbur, lyrics, Harold Arlen, music, cast photos and drawings, 1939, **$25**.

Comin' In On A Wing And A Prayer, 1943, Eddie Cantor and plane on cover.. **10.00**

County Kerry Mary, words and music by Ed Nelson and Harry Pease, Louis Hersher, copyright 1920 by A. J. Stasny Music Co, NY, Rolf Armstrong type dark-haired flapper with head band on cover... **48.00**

Country Style, Bing Crosby, Joan Caulfield, and Barry Fitzgerald on cover, 1947, Paramount, "Welcome Stranger"... **10.00**

Dance of the Paper Dolls, Johnny Tucker, Joe Schuster, Jon Siras, copyright 1927 by M Whitmark & Sons, cover art by Hap Hadley **5.25**

Doin' The Raccoon, Raymond Klages, music by J. Fred Coots, cover with dancing couple in raccoon coat, orange and blue background, 1928............................ **8.00**

For Once in My Life, Stevie Wonder on cover, 1965... **9.00**

Happy Go Lucky, Mary Martin, Dick Powell, Betty Hutton, Eddie Bracken, and Rudy Vallee **18.00**

Harold Teen Songsheet, movie poster graphics cover, 1934 .... **45.00**

Humpty Dumpty Heart, 1941, Kay Kyser, John Barrymore, Lupe Velez, Ginny Simms on cover dancing................ **15.25**

If I Could Live Life Over, words by Jack Wells, music by Ted Snyder, copyright 1919 by Waterson, Berlin & Snyder, NY, cover art of sultry looking brunette holding fan, sgd "Rolf Armstrong," penciled owner's signature............ **80.00**

It Takes A Long Tall Brown-Skin Gal to Make A Preacher Lay His Bible Down, lyrics by Marshall Walker, music by W. E. Skidmore, Skidmore Music Co., Kansas City, MO, 1917, cover design by E. H. Pfeiffer, **$35**.

Just You, Just Me, 1929, soldiers and Marion Davies on cover, MGM "Marianne" .. **9.00**

Kiss Waltz, from Dancing Sweeties, Al Dubin, music by Joe Burke, 1930 .... **8.00**

Lincoln Centennial Grand March, E. T. Paull Music Co., detailed litho portrait of Lincoln surrounded by birthplace, memorial, tomb, and emancipation statue, c1909.................................. **90.00**

Ma Riza Love, The Warmest Yet-A Rag-Time Sensation, Frank S. Snyder, published 1899 by Norwood Publishing Co., Minneapolis **42.00**

Muddy Waters, A Mississippi Moan, 1926, Nora Baves on cover, lagoon background **10.00**

My Garden of Love, words by Ella M. Smith, music by W. C. Polla, copyright 1919 by C. C. Church & Co., Hartford, Unusual Rolf Armstrong cover art of short-haired beauty holding bouquet with monarch butterfly on her finger, sgd "Rolf Armstrong," inked owner's signature **55.00**

Old Black Joe, Beaux Arts edition, 1906 .... **12.00**

Pick Yourself Up, 1936, RKO "Swing Time," Fred Astaire and Ginger Rogers cov **12.00**

Plantation Echoes, "Respectfully Dedicated to the Misses Drisiane," Otto M. Heinzman, c1899, cover with Southern river plantation, young dancing couple, banjo player, figures sitting around cotton bales, river boat............................. **90.00**

Please, 1932, by Leo Robin and Ralph Ringer, Paramount "The Big Broadcast," cover montage with Bing Crosby, Burns & Allen, Cab Calloway, Boswell Sisters, Mills Brothers, Vincent Lopez, Kate Smith, Leila Hyams, Stuart Erwin, and Arthur Tracy... **15.00**

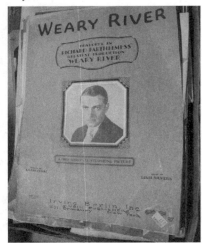

Weary River, words by Grant Clarke, music by Louis Silvers, **$3.50**.

Queen of Beauty, written by Otto Heinzman, E. T. Paull Music Co., front cover dedication "Respectfully inscribed to Miss Alma Kremer New York City," cover with group of roses surrounding ornate framed photo of Alma Kremer wearing feather boa, published 1898 .... **225.00**

Ringgold March Two-Step, Chas C Sweeley, published by Vandersloot Music, Williamsport, PA, 1911, front with black and white photo of 41-member band, drum reads "Ringold Reading PA" .. **8.00**

Roaring Volcano, E. T. Paull Music Co., erupting Mt. Vesuvius with Pompeii on cover, c1912 .... **95.00**

Silver Bell, Edward Madden, music by Percy Wenrich, 1910, color litho of 2 Native American lovers standing on cliff high above plains, moonlight night **8.00**

Take Me, words by Harry Edelheit, music by Clarence Senna & Monte Carlo, copyright 1920 by A. J. Stasny Music Co, NY, H. E. Musselman cover art with figure wearing large spring bonnet......................... **48.00**

The Army Air Corps, Official Song of the United States Army Air Corps, 1939, logo, red, white and blue, "Buy War Bonds" stamp on cover **15.00**

The Leader of the German Band, Edward Madden, music by Theodore Morse, 1905, orange cover with cartoon like band characters................................ **8.00**

There Must Be a Way To Love You, words by Harry Hoch, music by Ted Snyder, A. J. Stasny & Co, NY, cover with young flapper image sgd "Rolf Armstrong," c1919... **90.00**

The Royal Vagabond, lyrics by William Cary Duncan, music by Ansley Goetz, Cohan & Harris Presents The Cohanized Opera Comique in Three Acts, light stamp mark on cover, **$5**.

The Triumphant Banner, E. T. Paull Music Co., 45-star flag in center of cover with eagle seal, 1907 .... **60.00**

The Waltz In Swing Time, 1936, RKO "Swing Time," Fred Astaire and Ginger Rogers on cover.. **15.00**

Uncle Josh's Huskin Dance, E. T. Paull Music Co., front cover dedication "Respectfully dedicated to Denman Thompson... and the Old Homestead Company," black fiddler and group of people watching, c1898.. **150.00**

United Nations March and Two-Step, E. T. Paull Music Co., two women version cover, 1900, owner's inked signature **65.00**

Will You Remember, 1944, Nelson Eddy & J. McDonald **12.00**

Slot Machines

History: The Liberty Bell, the first three-reel slot machine, was invented in 1905 by Charles Fey in San Francisco. Only three of these can be accounted for, and one of them is housed at the Liberty Bell Saloon, the inventor's grandson's restaurant in Reno, Nevada.

In 1910, the classic fruit symbols were copyrighted by Mills Novelty Company. They were immediately copied by other manufacturers. The first symbols still are popular on contemporary casino machines. The wood cabinet was replaced by cast iron in 1916. By 1922, aluminum fronts were the norm for most machines, and in 1928, the jackpot was added.

Innovations of the 1930s included more reliable and improved mechanisms with more sophisticated coin entry, and advanced slug detection systems. In the 1940s, drill-proof and cheat-resistant devices were added. Electronics, including electronic lighting, were introduced in the 1950s.

Although the goosenecks of the 1920s and 1930s often are more intricate and rarer than the models of the 1930s and 1940s, the gimmickry and beauty of machines of the latter period, such as Rolatop, Treasury, Kitty or Triplex, bring more money.

Collecting Hints: Check the laws in your state. Some states permit the collecting of slot machines manufactured prior to 1941, while other states allow the collecting of all machines 25 years old or older provided that they are not used for gambling. A few states prohibit ownership of any gambling machine.

A complete slot machine is one that is in working order, has no wood missing on the case and no cracked castings. Restoration work to improve appearance can cost from $100 to more than $1,000. The average restoration includes plating of all castings, refinishing the cabinet, repainting the castings to the original colors, rebuilding the mechanism, tuning up the operation of the mechanism, and adding new reel strips and award card. A quality restoration will increase the value of a machine by $400 to $800. A guarantee usually is given when a restored machine is purchased from a dealer.

Most collectors stay away from foreign machines, primarily because foreign coins are hard to find. Machines that have been converted to accept American coins frequently jam or do not pay out the correct amount.

Condition, rarity, and desirability are all very important in determining the value of a machine. Try to find one that is in as close to new condition as possible since "mint original" machines will resell for at least the same amount as restored machines.

The past few years have shown how the age of collectors and their interests can change a collecting field. The Baby Boomers surely desire the '40s and '50s and not the earlier style slots.

Notes: All machines listed are priced as if they are in good condition, meaning the machine is complete and working. An incomplete or non-working machine is worth only 30 percent to 70 percent of the listed price.

Machines listed are those that accept nickels or dimes. Quarter and 50¢-piece machines can run several hundred dollars more. A silver-dollar machine, if you are lucky enough to find one, can cost $400 to $800 more than those listed.

Adviser: Bob Levy.

Bally, Double Bell, 1936, only all mechanical unit produced **5,000.00**
Bones, 1937, very desirable auto payout dice machine **11,000.00**
Buckley, Criss-Cross, c1948, revamp of 1946 Mills "Golden Falls," Art Deco styling, guaranteed jackpot window
.... **1,500.00**
Caille

Cadet, c1934, Art Deco style **700.00**
Centaur, c1904, single wheel upright floor model, superb cast iron feet and dec
.... **15,000.00**
Superior Jackpot, c1928, first countertop machine during Depression to make a jackpot **1,500.00**

Mills, FOK, Future Pay, 1926, **$3,000**. All photos courtesy of adviser Bob Levy.

Mills, Black Cherry, 1946, **$2,000**.

Dewey, 1896, upright single wheel payout
.... **10,000.00**

Jennings

Little Duke, c1932, most unusual in that
reels spin concentrically, Art Deco style
.... **2,000.00**
One Star Chief, c1936, large bronze
Indian head on front, hunting Indian
scene at bottom **1,800.00**
Standard Chief, c1946, chrome face, first
basic slot after WWII **1,500.00**
Sun Chief, c1948, illuminated colored
front panels, introduced for the glitz of
Las Vegas.................................. **2,500.00**

Pace, Comet, 1946, **$1,800**.

Mills, Puritan Bell, 1926, **$1,200**.

Mills

Black Cherry, c1946, silver and black
painted, raised red cherries **1,500.00**
Castle front, c1939, golden age machine
.... **1,800.00**
Diamond front, c1938, 10 raised
diamonds on chrome front......... **1,600.00**
Golden Falls, c1946, gold and black
painted, raised red cherries **1,600.00**
Jewel Hightop, c1948, colorful, bright,
wringle-painted design in car-like style
.... **1,700.00**
Operator Owl, c1925, classic gooseneck
coin entry................................... **1,400.00**
War Eagle, c1931, very colorful, often
reproduced, price for vintage model
.... **1,800.00**

Pace, Fancy Comet, 1935, **$1,800**.

Pace

Bantam, 1928, three-quarter size counter
machine **1,300.00**

Comet, c1935, fancy front, Art-Deco style
.... **1,600.00**
Harrahs Club Special, c1962, all chrome
plated **900.00**
Watling
Blue Seal, 1931 .... **1,200.00**
Rolatop Coin Front, c1937 .... **4,000.00**
Treasury, c1936, extremely ornate, raised
gold coins top and front castings
.... **4,000.00**

Soakies

History: "Soaky" is the common name for children's bubble bath containers. The name and concept were developed by Colgate-Palmolive in the late 1950s. By the 1960s, the idea really was popular with the buying public. Moms loved them as they were inexpensive and a great way to get kids to enjoy bath time more. The kids loved them as the Soakies represented their favorite cartoon characters. The term "Soaky" now means an upright figural plastic bubble bath container. The character's head hid the screw cap. Several styles of Soakies also contained a slot that could be cut out to turn the used container into a bank.

Because Soakies became so popular, Avon, Minnekota, and Purex also developed their own characters. Other characters that children could identify with, such as sports heroes or entertainment idols were added to the original cast of cartoon characters.

Collecting hints: The original Soakies are the most desirable. One reason is the attention to detail used for each character. Several modern manufacturers have revived the concept and are now making new character soakies, such as Batman, Superman, and the Simpsons. Whether these will become as collectible remains to be seen.

Most collectors want their Soakies in mint condition, with original tags and contents if possible. Soakies that have been converted to banks are usually less desirable.

Reproduction Alert: Reproduction Soakies have been reported. Of particular interest are reproductions of the Beatles, Ringo and Paul. The originals were made of colored plastic, blue for

Ringo and red for Paul. Today's reproductions are made of white resin and left unpainted. The original has a hole on top of the head where the head fits; the reproductions do not. The reproductions also do not have a cap that threads like the originals do.

The booth at What A Character! At the March 2004 Atlantique City Antiques Show offered many examples of Soakies. Shown here are a whole shelf full; representative prices are: the Dentist, **$10**; Mickey Mouse by Avon for **$20**, and Donald Duck was priced at **$24**.

Alvin the Chipmunk, mkd "1963 Ross Bagdasarian, Colgate Palmolive Co."
.... **24.00**
Augie Doggy, Purex **18.00**
Bozo the Clown **18.00**
Casper the Friendly Ghost **28.00**
Creature from the Black Lagoon, 10" h, Colgate-Palmolive, 1960s, mint ... **140.00**
Deputy Dog **15.00**
Dopey, Disney, 10" h **30.00**

Another shelf full at What A Character! These include Wicket the Ewok at **$22**; Jabba The Hutt, with original tag, **$21**; Bullwinkle ranged from **$45 to $115**; Secret Squirrel by Purex at **$50**, as well as many other examples.

Elmer Fudd, hooded red hunting outfit
.... **15.00**
Flintstones, Bam Bam, Purex **15.00**
Goofy, 11 oz **30.00**
Mr. Jinx and Pixie and Dixie, Purex .. **15.00**

Muskie	**20.00**
Pinocchio	**15.00**
Pluto, 11 oz	**30.00**
Popeye	**24.00**
Porky Pig, Colgate-Palmolive, 9-1/2" h	**32.00**
Ricochet Rabbit, Bubble Club, moveable arm, 1964	**35.00**
Smokey The Bear, 8-3/4" h	**50.00**
Snow White, 10" h	**30.00**
Superman, 1965	**45.00**
Sylvester the Cat, racquet behind back	**15.00**
Theodore the Chipmunk	**15.00**
Thumper	**15.00**
Top Cat, 10 oz	**45.00**

Soda Fountain Collectibles

History: From the late 1880s through the end of the 1960s, the local soda fountain was the social center of small-town America, especially for teenagers. The soda fountain provided a place for conversation and gossip, a haven to satisfy the mid-afternoon munchies, and a source for the most current popular magazines.

Collecting Hints: The collector of soda fountain memorabilia competes with collectors in many other categories—advertising, glassware, ice cream, postcards, food molds, tools, etc. Material still ranges from 25 cents to $200.

When buying a tray, the scene is the most important element. Most trays were stock items with the store or firm's name added later. Always look for items in excellent condition.

Blackboard, Frostie Root Beer, tin, 1950s **75.00**

Booklet, Moxie Menu Book, 4-3/4" x 7", 12 pgs, some wear, c1910 .... **32.00**

Bottle, Breyers, milk bottle shape, clear **30.00**

Brochure, Brummel's, "What is Soda Water?," four pgs, 5-1/2" x 7" **24.00**

Calendar, Squirt, 1947, 25" h **300.00**

Can, Abbott's Ice Cream, half gallon, Amish girl, c1940 .... **15.00**

Catalog

Bastian-Blessing Co, Chicago, IL, Soda Fountain Parts & Carbonators, 1955, 65 pgs, 8-1/2" x 11" **30.00**

Bottle advertising, diecut cardboard, orange and white, Try the Monstrously Delicious Taste of Nesbitt's, **$15**.

National Licorice Co, New York, NY, early 1900, 19 pgs, 3-1/4" x 6-1/4", licorice specialties, lozenges, penny sticks, cigars, pipes, etc. **65.00**

Stanley Knight Corp, Chicago, IL, Soda Fountains, Instructions and Specifications, c1944, 52 pgs, 7" x 10" **32.00**

Dispenser, white ceramic body

13-1/2" h, Drink Dr. Swett's The Original Root Beer, On The Market Seventy Five Years," picture of boy holding glass of root beer, silhouette shows older profile, picture on front and back, replaced pump **3,200.00**

14" h, Birchola, birch leaves around "Drink Birchola" on front and back, not orig pump **1,800.00**

14-1/2" h, Fowler's Root Beer, bulbous, "Drink Fowler's Root Beer The Best" on two sides, orig pump mkd "Fowler's Root Beer" **700.00**

14-1/2" h, Ward's Orange-Crush, orange shape, porcelain ball pump, some paint loss, hairline cracks **950.00**

Menu board, wood, painted light green, red lettering, "Fresh-Up with 7-Up, You Like It...It Likes You," 19 aluminum slots, **$125**.

Drinking glass

Buddy-Ginger, 5" h, clear glass, red script and small boy with "B" and "G" initials on shirts, boy holds chain leash which extends around to radio microphone and monkey wearing fez, c1930.. **10.00**
Grapette.. **10.00**
Vernors Ginger Ale, Deliciously Different. 4" h **40.00**

Festoon, diecut cardboard, Hires
11" h, 49-1/2" l, full bottles of Hires on each end, logo in center **800.00**
14"h, 52" l, lady in winter scene reaching for bottle, c1940 .... **600.00**

Hat, soda-jerk style **10.00**

Ice chipper, Gilchrist, 1930s **95.00**

Ice cream scoop

Dover, brass **70.00**
Erie, round, size 8, aluminum **180.00**
Gilchrist, #30, size 8, polished........ **70.00**

Jar, Borden's Malted Milk, glass label
.... **175.00**

Magazine cover, *Saturday Evening Post*, young soda jerk talking to girls at counter, Norman Rockwell, Aug. 22, 1953... **15.00**

Malt machine

Arnold #15 .... **145.00**
Dairy Bar, metal, white Bakelite canister, logo **115.00**

Milkshake machine

Gilchrist, orig cup, c1926.............. **100.00**
Hamilton Beach, push-down type **150.00**

Mug

Belfast Root Beer, Tepco China, price for pr... **65.00**
Rochester Root Beer, 6" h, 3-1/2" d, clear heavy glass, tankard style, c1940.. **30.00**

Soda fountain syrup containers, stainless steel, chrome, and white ceramic bases, tags to describe flavors, three-syrup pump tops, **$65**

Pinback button

1" d, Cherry Smash, George Washington, Whitehead & Hoag **95.00**
1" d, Cleo Cola Knothole Gant, red and white litho, figural baseball, 1939 Red Birds **15.00**
1" d, Sanderson's Drug Store, blue and white, soda fountain glass illus, "Ice Cream, Soda/Choice Cigars/Fine Candies," 1901-12......................... **28.00**
2-1/4" d, Hi-Hat Ice Cream Soda, 10¢, McCory's, c1940............................ **15.00**

Postcard

Bodie's Ice Cream Store, diecut **15.00**
Gunther's Soda Fountain, Chicago **18.00**

Pretzel jar, 10-1/2" h, Seyfert's Original Butter Pretzels, glass, orig lid......... **60.00**

Seltzer bottle, Sun Shine, 11" h........ **150.00**

Set, black and chrome, Art-Deco styling, price for 11 pcs............................ **495.00**

Sign, litho tin, Drink Canada Dry Beverages, black and red lettering on cream ground, **$90**.

Sign

Orange County Fountain, porcelain on steel, yellow oval center, blue and white lettering, dark blue ground........... **110.00**
Purity Brand Pretzels, diecut cardboard, easel-back, multicolor, smiling blond boy carrying giant pretzel, white lettering, black, red, and gold ground, Harrisburg, PA, early 1930s.............................. **75.00**

Syrup jug, Cherry Smash, paper label with George Washington, glass, one gallon
.... **45.00**

Sign, Ice Cold Birch-O Served Here, celluloid, tan, black, and red, $95.

Table, square white marble top, four fold-out seats with wooden backs and seats, cast iron base.. **900.00**
Table and chairs, child size, pr cast iron chairs with wood seats, matching table **350.00**
Tin, Schraftt's Marshmallow Topping, 25 lbs **35.00**
Toy, Kool-Ade Soft Drink Kooler, plastic dispenser holds inverted glass jar, 12 orig waxed paper cups, Trim Toys of Trim Molded Products Co., 1970s, 7-1/2" x 8-1/2" x 9" h orig box **24.00**
Tray, 13" x 11", Schuller's Ice Cream, ice cream sodas and cones **200.00**
Wafer holder, Reliance..................... **175.00**

Soldiers, Dimestore

History: Three-dimensional lead, iron, and rubber soldier and civilian figures were produced in the United States by the millions before and after World War II. These figures are called dimestore soldiers because they were sold in the "five and dime" stores of the era, and usually cost a nickel or dime. Although American toy soldiers can be traced back to the early 20th century, the golden age of the dimestore soldier lasted from 1935 until 1942.

Four companies—Barclay, Manoil, Grey Iron, and Auburn Rubber—mass-produced the three-inch figures. Barclay and Manoil dominated the market, probably because their lead castings lent themselves to more realistic and imaginative poses than iron and rubber.

Barclay's early pre-war figures are identifiable by their separate glued-on and later clipped-on tin hats. When these are lost, the hole in the top of the head identifies the piece as a Barclay.

The Manoil Company first produced soldiers, sailors, cowboys, and Indians. However, the younger buyers of the period preferred military figures, perhaps emulating the newspaper headlines as World War II approached. Manoil's civilian figures were made in response to pacifist pressure and boycotts mounted before the war began.

Figures also were produced by such companies as All-Nu, American Alloy, American Soldier Co., Beton, Ideal, Jones, Lincoln Log, Miller, Playwood Plastics, Soljertoys, Tommy Toy, Tootsietoy, and Warren. Because most of these companies were short-lived, numerous limited production figures command high prices, especially those of All-Nu, Jones, Tommy Toy, and Warren.

From 1942 through 1945, the wartime scrap drives devoured tons of dimestore figures and the molds that produced them.

In late 1945, Barclay and Manoil introduced modernized military figures, but they never enjoyed their pre-war popularity. Military operations generally were phased out by the early 1950s. Similarly, the civilian figures could not compete with escalating labor costs and the competition from plastic products.

Collecting Hints: Figures of soldiers are preferred over civilians. The most valuable figures are those that had short production runs, usually because they were less popular with the youthful collectors of the period.

Condition, desirability, and scarcity establish the price of a figure. There are many style and color variations in which these soldiers were made, and these variations often affect the price. Repainting or the presence of rust severely reduces the value.

Auction and Internet prices often mislead the beginning collector. While some rare figures have sold in the $150 to $300 range, most sell between $10 and $25.

Notes: Prices listed are for figures in original condition with at least 95 percent of the paint remaining. Unless otherwise noted, uniforms are brown.

Adviser: Barry L. Carter.

Borbur Enterprises, three-piece horse set, lead, original paint, original box, $75.

Civilian figures

Auburn Rubber
Baseball	30.00
Football	30.00

Barclay
Cowboy
Mounted, firing pistol	22.00
With lasso	18.00

Indian
Standing, bow and arrow	9.00
Tomahawk and shield	9.00

Miscellaneous
Girl Skater	10.00
Newsboy	10.00
Pirate	12.00
Policeman, raised arms	10.00
Woman passenger with dog	10.00

Barclay, 11 pod-foot lead soldiers, two unidentified lead soldiers, price for set, $120.

Grey Iron
American Family Series, 2-1/4" h
Average	5.00
More elaborate figure	25.00

Western
Bandit, hands up	55.00
Cowboy, hold-up man	25.00
Cowboy, standing	9.00

Manoil
Happy Farm Series
Blacksmith, horseshoes	20.00
Farmer sowing grain	18.00
Man chopping wood	18.00
Watchman with lantern	25.00
Woman with pie	20.00

Western
Cowboy, arms raised	16.00
Cowboy, one gun raised	14.00
Cowgirl riding horse	25.00
Indian with knife	10.00

Military figures

Auburn Rubber
Charging with tommy gun	15.00
Grenade thrower	15.00
Machine gunner, kneeling	12.00
Marching with rifle	15.00
Motorcycle with sidecar	55.00
Searchlight	25.00

Barclay
Podfoot Series, 2-1/4" h
Bugler	7.00
Flag bearer	10.00
Gunner, prone	8.00
Nurse	18.00
Officer standing	8.00
Sailor, blue	10.00
Soldier, marching, with rifle	7.00

Post War, pot helmet
Flag bearer	18.00
Officer with sword	18.00
Rifleman, standing	18.00

Pre-War
AA gunner	18.00
At attention	14.00
Aviator	15.00
Bugler, tin helmet	15.00
Cameraman, kneeling	35.00
Dispatcher with dog	38.00
Doctor, white, with bag	16.00
Lying wounded	12.00
Machine gunner, kneeling	15.00
Marine officer, marching	35.00
Mortar, two-man	20.00
Nurse, kneeling, cup	18.00
Parachutist	18.00
Prone with binoculars	18.00
Releasing pigeons	18.00
Running with rifle	18.00
Sailor, marching	12.00
Sailor with signal flags	22.00
Searchlight	25.00

Stretcher bearer **15.00**
Telephone operator **15.00**
Wounded crutches................. **18.00**
Wounded, sitting, arm in sling **15.00**

Barclay, 10 different lead soldiers, price for set, **$110**.

Grey Iron

Cavalryman **25.00**
Colonial soldier............................... **20.00**
Doctor, white, with bag................... **20.00**
Drum Major.................................... **18.00**
Drummer.. **15.00**
Ethiopian
    Charging **25.00**
    Marching **28.00**
Kneeling, with rifle **15.00**
Machine gunner
    Kneeling **10.00**
    Prone................................... **15.00**
Marching.. **10.00**
Nurse **18.00**
Radio operator **45.00**
Sailor marching **14.00**
Sentry.. **15.00**

Manoil

Post-War
    Bazooka **25.00**
    Marching with rifle.................. **18.00**
    Mine detector......................... **30.00**
    Tommy-gunner, standing **22.00**
Post-War, 2-1/2" h, mkd "USA"
    Aircraft spotter **25.00**
    Aviator with bomb **28.00**
    Bazooka **18.00**
    Flag bearer............................. **20.00**
    Machine gunner, seated **20.00**
    Observer, with binoculars **27.00**
Pre-War
    At searchlight......................... **20.00**
    Bicycle rider **30.00**
    Bomb thrower, with three grenades
    .... **14.00**
    Boxer **70.00**
    Cameraman with overhead flash
    .... **45.00**
    Charging with bayonet **28.00**
    Cook's helper with ladle **30.00**

Barkley, messenger boy, $10.

Deep-sea diver **15.00**
Firefighter, Hot Papa, gray **75.00**
Flag bearer............................. **18.00**
Hostess, green **45.00**
Machine gunner, prone **15.00**
Marching **16.00**
Navy deck gunner.................. **30.00**
Nurse, white, red dish **16.00**
Observer with periscope **30.00**
Radio operator, standing........ **35.00**
Rifleman, standing **15.00**
Sailor **18.00**
Sharpshooter, camouflage **20.00**
Stretcher carrier, with medical kit
    .... **18.00**
Wounded............................... **15.00**
Writing letter **50.00**

Soldiers, Toy

History: The manufacture of toy soldiers began in the late 18th century by individuals such as the Hilperts of Nuremberg, Germany. The early figures were tin, pewter, or composition. By the late 19th century, companies in Britain (Britain, Courtenay), France (Blondel,

Gerbeau, and Mignot), and Switzerland (Gottschalk, Wehrli) were firmly established. Britain and Mignot dominated the market into the 20th century.

Mignot established its French stronghold by purchasing Cuperly, Blondel, and Gerbeau who had united to take over Lucotte. By 1950, Mignot had 20,000 models representing soldiers from around the world.

Britain developed the hollow cast soldiers in 1893. Movable arms also were another landmark. Eventually bases were made of plastic, followed finally by the entirely plastic figures. Production ceased in the 1980s.

Between 1930 and 1950, the English toy soldier was challenged in America by the dimestore soldiers made by Barclay, Manoil, and others. Nevertheless, the Britains retained a share of the market because of their high quality. The collecting of toy soldiers remains very popular in the United States.

Collecting Hints: Consider three key factors: condition of the figures and the box, the age of the figures and the box, and the completeness of the set.

Toy soldiers were meant to be playthings. However, collectors consider them an art form and pay premium prices only for excellent to mint examples. They want figures with complete paint and intact parts, including the moving parts.

The box is very important, controlling 10 percent to 20 percent of the price of a set. The style of the box is a clue to the date of the set. The same set may have been made for several decades; the earlier the date of manufacture, the more valuable the set.

Sets have a specific number of pieces or parts. These must all be present for full value to be realized. The number of pieces in each set, when known, is indicated in the listings below.

Beware of repainted older examples and modern reproductions. Toy soldiers still are being manufactured, both by large companies and private individuals. A contemporary collection may prove a worthwhile long-term investment, at least for the next generation.

Reproduction Alert: Ertl has acquired Britains, Ltd., and are now reproducing some old hollow cast soldiers.

Adviser: Barry L. Carter.

Authenticast, Russian Infantry, advancing with rifles at the ready, two officers, carrying pistols and swords, eight pcs **75.00**

Bienheim, sets only, mint, orig excellent box
B2, Coldstream Guards Colors, 1812, two color bearers, escort of four privates, six pcs **115.00**
B17, Royal Marines, 1923, marching at the slope, officer, sword at carry, six pcs **75.00**
B63, Royal Co of Archers Colors, two color bearers, escort of four privates, six pcs **100.00**
C13, 17th Lancers, 1879, foreign service order, officer, bugler and trooper with lance, six pcs **130.00**

Britain mounted horse brigade, assorted figures, each figure, $20.

Britains, sets only
28, Mountain Gun of the Royal Artillery, with gun, gunners, mules, and mounted officer, 14 pcs, mint, orig good box **250.00**
33, 16th/5th Lancers, mounted at the half in review order, officer turned in the saddle, excellent orig illus box **175.00**
44, 2nd Dragoon Guards, The Queen's Bays, mounted at the gallop, lances and trumpeter, c1940, five pcs, excellent, good orig Whisstock box **135.00**
117, Egyptian Infantry, at attention in review order, c1935, eight pcs, good, orig Whisstock box **150.00**
136, Russian Cossacks, mounted at the gallop with officer, five pcs, excellent, orig box **145.00**

138, French Cuirassiers, mounted at the walk, review order with officer, five pcs, excellent, orig box.......................... **120.00**

190, Belgian 2nd Regiment Chasseurs a Cheval, mounted in review order, officer, five pcs, good, orig box................ **140.00**

201, Officers of the General Staff, comprising Field Marshal, General officer and two Aides-de-Camp, four pcs, good **120.00**

1343, The Royal Horse Guards, mounted in winter cloaks, officer, c1940, five pcs, good orig "Armies of the World" box **150.00**

1631, The Governor General's Horse Guards of Canada, mounted in review order, officer on prancing horse, five pcs, mint, orig excellent box................. **120.00**

2009, Belgian Grenadier Regiment, marching in review order, officer, eight pcs, excellent, orig box................. **180.00**

2035, Swedish Life Guard, marching at the slope, officer, eight pcs, mint, tied in excellent, orig box.......................... **200.00**

2059, Union Infantry, action poses, with officer holding sword and pistol, bugler and standard bearer, 87 pcs, excellent, orig box... **90.00**

9217, 12th Royal Lancers, mounted in review order, officer, five pcs, mint, good orig window box **85.00**

9291, Arabs of the Desert on Horses, with jezalls and scimtars, excellent, good orig window box **80.00**

9402, State Open road Landau, drawn by six Windsor Grays, with three detachable positions, attendants, Queen Elizabeth and Prince Philip as passengers, 13 pcs, mint, tied in excellent orig box...... **375.00**

Mixed set of eight Britain Medial Knights and soldiers, two dimestore figures on bench also included. Note how the scale of the Britain's is much smaller and more precise than the dimestore figures, **$165**.

Elastolin/Lineol

Flak Gunner, blue and gray uniform, kneeling with shell, very good........ **40.00**

Medic, walking, helmet, backpack with red cross **35.00**

Nurse, attending wounded, kneeling, olds foot of soldier sitting on keg, excellent... **40.00**

Staff Officer, pointing, field glasses, aristocratic pose **35.00**

Heyde

Chicago Police, 1890s, on foot, with billy clubs, policeman with dog, standard bearer, and mounted policeman, very good.. **225.00**

French Ambulance Unit, horse-drawn ambulance, two-horse team, rider with whip, stretcher bearers, stretchers, casualties, mounted and foot medical officers, medical orderly, very good, fair orig box **275.00**

German Infantry, World War I, attacking with fixed bayonets, officer with extended sword, very good........................... **90.00**

Mignot

15, French Muskeeters Period of King Louis XIII, marching with muskets at shoulder arms, officer and standard bearer, c1960, 12 pcs, excellent, orig box **275.00**

28/C, Napoleon's Imperial guard Band, 1812, marching will full instrumentation, band director with baton, 12 pcs, excellent.. **350.00**

36, French Napoleonic Skirmishers of the 17th Line Regiment, 1809, marching in blue and white uniforms, faced in red, tall plumed shakos, gloss paint, c1965, mint four-piece set in excellent orig window box and outer cardboard box...... **110.00**

39, Italian Light Infantry, Regiment de Beauhamais, 1810, marching at the slope, green uniforms, pale blue facings, plumed shakos, drummer and officer, 12 pcs, excellent, orig box................ **275.00**

45/A, Bavarian Infantry, 1812, marching at the slope, blue and white uniforms, yellow facings, plumed light infantry caps, standard bearer and bugler, excellent eight-pc set in orig box. **250.00**

Cherilea, set, hand painted H. M. Lifeguards, original box, **$175**.

200, Ancient Gaul Cavalry, mounted with swords, spears, and shields, five pcs, excellent, orig box **275.00**
255, Spanish Hussars, 1808, mounted in green uniforms, red facings, tall plumed shakos, officer, trumpeter, and standard bearer, mint, excellent orig box **375.00**
1016, Drum Majors of the Empire, French Napoleonic regiments, including Orphans of the Guard, Marines of the Guard, St. Cyr Academy and various line infantry regiments, special limited edition, all mint, excellent orig boxes **475.00**
Nostalgia, mint, excellent orig box
1st Gurkha Light Infantry, 1800, red and blue uniforms, marching with slung rifles, officer with sword at the carry **95.00**
Kaffrarian Rifles, 1910, gray uniforms, plumed pith helmets, marching at the trail, officer with sword at the carry, mint **125.00**
New South Wales Lancers, 1900, marching, carrying lances on the shoulder, khaki uniforms, trimmed in red and plumed campaign hats, officer holding swagger stick **85.00**
S.A.F., mint, excellent orig box
1358, Royal Horse Guards, 1945, mounted at the halt, officer **80.00**
1761, French Cuirassiers, mounted at the walk **95.00**
3310, 1st Bengal Lancers, mounted at the half **125.00**

Souvenir and Commemorative Items

History: Souvenir and commemorative china and glass date to the early fairs and carnivals when a small trinket was purchased to take back home as a gift or remembrance of the event. Other types of commemorative glass include pattern and milk glass made to celebrate a particular event. Many types of souvenir glass and china originated at the world's fairs and expositions.

The peak of souvenir spoon collecting was reached in the late 1800s. During that time two important patents were issued. One was the December 4, 1884, patent for the first flatware design, and it was issued to Michael Gibney, a New York silversmith. The other important patent was the one for the first spoon design which commemorated a place. That patent was given to Myron H. Kinsley in 1881 for his spoon which showed the suspension bridge at Nia-

gara Falls. This was the first of many scenic views of Niagara Falls which appeared on spoons over the years.

Spoons depicting famous people soon followed, such as the one of George Washington which was issued in May 1889. That was followed by the Martha Washington spoon in October 1889. These spoons, made by M. W. Galt of Washington, D.C., were not patented but were trademarked in 1890.

During the 1900s, it became popular to have souvenir plates made to memorialize churches and local events such as centennials and homecomings. These plates were well received in their respective communities. Collectors search for them today because they were made in a limited number. They are especially interesting as an indication of how an area changed architecturally and culturally over the years.

Collecting Hints: Most collectors of souvenir and commemorative china and glass collect items from a region particularly interesting to them—their hometown or birthplace, or place of special interest such as a President's home. This results in regional variations in price because a piece is more likely to be in demand in the area it represents.

When collecting souvenir spoons be aware of several things: condition, material, subject, and any markings, dates, etc. Damaged spoons should be avoided unless they are very rare and are needed to complete a collection. Some spoons have enamel crests and other decoration. This enameling should be in mint condition.

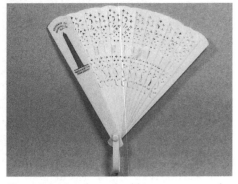

Fan, celluloid, embossed gold imagery on guard stick, Washington Monument, Washington, DC, souvenir, 5-1/4" h, **$12**.

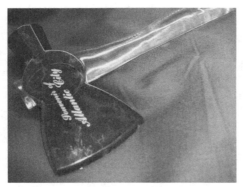

Hatchet, glass, ruby stained blade, marked "Souvenir of Atlantic City" in gold letters, clear handle, **$70**.

Ashtray, Wrigley Building, clear glass, center image of Chicago building, 4-1/2" d, c1940 .... **15.00**

Booklet

Souvenir of Coney Island, Brighton, and Manhattan Beaches, 1904, 40 pgs with black and white illus, 8" x 5" **65.00**

Steel Pier, Atlantic City, NJ, summer program, 32 pgs, pictures and ads **45.00**

Bottle opener, San Diego, 1912 ...... **25.00**

Box, 1-3/4" sq, 1-3/4" h, brass, glass insert, building on front, mkd "Souvenir Corner Stone, United Benefit Life Ins Co., Mutual Benefit Health Assoc," bottom mkd "Grammes, Allentown, Pa" **15.00**

Card game, Excursion to Coney Island, Milton Bradley, c1885 .... **20.00**

Franconia Notch, NH, Cannon Mountain, aerial passenger tramway, brown and white, marked "Aerial Tramway in the heart of the picturesque White Mountains," Old English Staffordshire Ware, (Jonroth mark)...Imported for the State of New Hampshire, Forestry and Recreation Dept...," **$20**.

Cup and saucer, "Souvenir of Wildwood-By-The-Sea, NJ," multicolored scenes, marked "Hand Painted Japan," **$30**.

Condiment set, Gettysburg, 1863, hp china, salt and pepper shakers, condiment jar with lid and spoon, 5-1/4" x 5-1/2" base, orange, yellow flowers, green leaves, gold, irid slate blue, and white accents, mkd "Nippon," 1930s **35.00**

Creamer and sugar, Washington, DC, fall scenes, bright colors, mkd "Silberne Japan," 4-1/4" h **12.00**

Cup, china, white, St. Charles Hotel, New Orleans **15.00**

Cup and saucer, Niagara Falls, marked "Carlsbad, Austria" **18.00**

Demitasse cup and saucer, Hotel Roosevelt, New Orleans **35.00**

Doll, Icey the Ice Man, 9" h, Ice Capades 1950s tour, plastic, soft vinyl head, glued flannel felt Deutch boy cap, turquoise flannel jacket, blue flannel trousers, name and "Ice Capades" marks **45.00**

Egg cup, Macclesfield Parish Church, pottery, 2-1/2" h, black and white image of church, pink luster and gold trim, c1930 .... **28.00**

Hatchet, 6" l, Hazelton, PA, white milk glass, red letters **40.00**

Medal, Souvenir of Wisconsin, green with gold **30.00**

Money clip, Empire State Building, gold toned metal, clear dome over design with building, 1940s **12.00**

Mug

Hardwick, VT, custard glass, gold trim **35.00**

Lincoln Hotel, Reading, PA, white ceramic **10.00**

New Rockford, ND, custard glass . **35.00**

Mustard, cov, Central School, Owosso, MI, mkd "Made in Germany," 3-1/2" h . **35.00**

Paperweight, glass, Mathewson Hotel, glass, detailed view of "The New Mathewson Narragansett Pier, RI,

Grandest Hotel Plaza in the World, maker American P. W. Co., Pittsburgh, 1890s," 1" x 2-1/2" x 4" **60.00**
Pencil, mechanical, 3-7/8" l, Odessa, TX **20.00**

Pennant, felt
Coney Island, maroon, white title, yellow, green, orange, and white scene of Steeplechase Pool, amusement rides, Luna Mill Sky Chaser building, c1930 .... **30.00**
Great Allentown Fair, black ground, white and yellow letters **27.50**
Hershey Park, brown ground, white letters, c1950 .... **25.00**
Photo album, New Orleans, various scenes, 1885 .... **45.00**

Pennant, Allentown Fair, Sept. 22-27, 1919, red and blue felt, girl with horse in heart shape, $30.

Pinback button, 1-1/4" d
Asbury Park, black and white, bathing beach scene, c1900 .... **12.00**
Coney Island, multicolored, bathing beauty scene, rim reads "Citizens Committee of Coney Island," c1915 .... **35.00**
Dorney Park, Allentown, PA **12.00**
Hershey Park, multicolored, child emerging from cocoa bean, c1905 **35.00**
Wonderland Stamford, CT, multicolored, c1900 .... **90.00**
Pinback button name tag, attached ribbon Charter Day Celebration, July 5-6-7, MCMIX, 1884-1909, North Plainfield, Plainfield, Member of Citizen Committee,

1-3/4" d **42.00**
18th Annual Saengerfest, Philadelphia, Pa, June 21-24, 1897, Aurora Singing Society, New Brunswick, NJ, double sided, 1-1/2" d **45.00**
Pitcher, Bar Harbor, ME, custard glass, gold trim, beaded base **95.00**

Plaque
New York, Empire State Building, Rockefeller Center, Statue of Liberty, Arrow Ware, pre-1960, 10-1/2" h, 11-3/4" w **25.00**
Washington DC, Capitol Building, center tinted postcard-type image, chased silverplate frame with scrolls and florals, mkd "WMFM" **25.00**

Plate, Plymouth Rock, Plymouth, MA, brown and white, marked "Old English Staffordshire Ware, Made in England, (Jonroth mark) (Adams mark) Imported Exclusively for Plymouth Rock Gift Shop, Plymouth, Mass," $25.

Plate, America's Playground, Florida Sunshine Flowers, The Singing Tower, brown and white, marked "Florida State Plate, brief history of Florida, (Jonroth mark), Old English Staffordshire Ware, Made in England, state seal and portrait of Ponce de Leon, Imported for the Mountain Lake Sanctuary, Lake Wales, Florida," 6" d, $25.

Plate

Alabama, state capital in center, blue, Vernon Kilns.................................. **28.00**

Along 101 The Redwood Highway, maroon, Vernon Kilns...................... **25.00**

Birmingham, AL, The Industrial City, maroon, Vernon Kilns...................... **25.00**

Boston, MA, Filene's, brown, Vernon Kilns **25.00**

Delaware Tercentenary Celebration, 1938, black and white, Spode........ **35.00**

Denver, CO, state capital in center, blue, Vernon Kilns.................................. **25.00**

Exxon Building, heavy smoke colored glass, gold image and title "Exxon Building at Rockefeller Center-1972," maroon felt protective bag, orig box, 6-1/4" x 8-3/8" **30.00**

Jacksonville, FL, Gateway to Florida, maroon... **25.00**

Laguna Beach, CA, Festival of Arts **25.00**

Maine, state capital in center, multicolored, Vernon Kilns **30.00**

Mississippi, blue, Vernon Kilns....... **20.00**

Missouri Sesquicentennial, Capitol dome in Jefferson City, First State Capitol Building in St Charles, 150 years of Statehood 1821-1971, gold on white, Tri-State Arts & China Davenport, Iowa **12.00**

Nevada, The Silver State, Hoover Dam in center, brown, Vernon Kilns **28.00**

Northwestern University, multicolored, Vernon Kilns.................................. **35.00**

Our West, Vast Empire, maroon, Vernon Kilns **35.00**

Portsmouth Virginia Bicentennial, 1752-1952, light brown, Vernon Kilns **28.00**

Saint Augustine, FL, brown, Vernon Kilns **25.00**

San Diego County Fair, Delmar, CA, Don Diego Welcomes You, blue............. **35.00**

SE Missouri State College, Diamond Jubilee, brown, Vernon Kilns **25.00**

Sonoma, CA, Cradle of California, maroon, Vernon Kilns...................... **35.00**

South Dakota, state capital in center, maroon, Vernon Kilns...................... **25.00**

Spokane, Washington, The Inland Empire, blue, Vernon Kilns.............. **25.00**

St. Louis, Union Station, World's Largest Bird Cage, War Memorial Building, Washington Univ, gold trim, green border, 6" d.. **10.00**

Vermont, Green Mountain State, brown, Vernon Kilns.................................. **30.00**

Washington, state capital in center, brown, Vernon Kilns **25.00**

West Virginia, state capital in center, brown... **25.00**

Woolworth Building, New York City, 4" d, back mkd "Made in Germany" **40.00**

Salt and pepper shakers, pr

Alscar de Segovia, emblem, Limoges **32.00**

Lafayette, TN, black maid and butler, white uniforms, c1940 .... **125.00**

Penn State, ceramic, blue logo........ **8.00**

Poster, Earl Held's All Girl Band, annual church picnic, Spinnerstown, PA, black and white, 1940, framed, $30.

Spoon, sterling silver (unless otherwise specified)

Battleship *Iowa,* raised design of ship in bowl, ornate handle, 4-1/2" l........... **10.00**

Battleship *Maine,* Captain Sigsbee, raised design of ship in bowl, ornate handle, 4-1/2" l................................ **10.00**

Boston, emb sites and scenes on front and back, mkd "Watson," 5-7/8" l .. **35.00**

Brooklyn, NY, 13th Regiment **35.00**

Calumet, MI, mining, Helco Shaft #2 .... **35.00**

Canadian Railroad Terminal, Vancouver British Columbia, 1901, gold wash bowl with building, enamel shield with maple leaf on handle, crown on top, "Canada" in banner, flowers and leaves on front and back of handle, 5-1/4" l........ **30.00**

Detroit Skyline **70.00**

Fisheries Building, Columbian Expo, Chicago, 1892, silver plate, Leonard Manufacturing Co, building and sam pam in bowl, 5-7/8" l.................... **45.00**

Flagship *Brooklyn,* raised design of ship in bowl, ornate handle, 4-1/2" l....... **10.00**

Flagship *New York*, Admiral Sampson, raised design of ship in bowl, ornate handle, 4-1/2" l.............................. **10.00**

Flagship *Olympia,* raised design of ship in bowl, ornate handle, 4-1/2" l....... **10.00**

Halifax, 3-1/2" l **24.00**

Minneapolis, 4" l **12.00**
Missouri State Building, inscription in
bowl, floral design on front and back of
handle, early 1900s, 5-1/2" l **20.00**
Morro Castle, Cuba Libre, raised design
of castle in bowl, ornate handle, 4-1/2" l
.... **10.00**
Newtown, demitasse, hallmarked .. **12.00**
New York, colorful litho of city with Empire
State building, Galaxy, silver plate, 4-1/2" l
.... **8.00**
New York and Empire State Building,
mkd "Made in Germany," demitasse,
4" l **20.00**
Niagara Falls, fleur-de-lis bowl with
engraved view of Falls, mkd "Sterling,"
4-1/2" l **20.00**
Pikes Peak, train and building, US
Silver Co., silver plate, 4-3/8" l **24.00**
Statue of Liberty, statue on end of handle
which reads "Centennial Celebration,"
bowl engraved "Keep the Torch Lit,"
nickel silver, 4" l **12.00**
Womens Building, Columbian Expo,
Chicago, 1893, bust of Columbus,
dates "1492-1893" on handle, bowl with
Womens Building, back mkd
"Standard," 4-3/8" l **20.00**
Yellowstone Park, etched falls bowl, bear,
stag's head, and buffalo head on handle
.... **45.00**

Trinket box, cast metal, celluloid medallion with
Capitol, Washington, DC, blue velvet lining, 4" l,
2-1/2" h, **$65**.

Tape measure, New York City, celluloid, pig
.... **25.00**
Teapot, Morrison Hotel, Chicago **35.00**
Thermometer, Florida, figural flamingo, 6" h,
c1940-50 .... **60.00**
Tip tray, Hotel Coronado, china **18.00**
Toothpick holder
Lewistown, ME, Georgia Gem pattern,
custard glass, gold trim **45.00**
Providence, Shamrock pattern, ruby
stained glass **40.00**
Vase, china
Camp Lake View, Lake City, MN **20.00**
Catalina Island, two handles, blue,
dragon dec, gold accents, 2-1/2" h.. **5.00**
High School Building Elkhart, Indiana,
3-1/4" d, 5" h, bottom stamped "Made in
Germany" **40.00**

Space Adventurers and Exploration

History: In January 1929, "Buck Rogers 2429 A.D." began its comic strip run. Buck, Wilma Deering, Dr. Huer, and the villain Killer Kane, were the creation of Phillip Francis Nowlan and John F. Dille. The heyday of Buck Rogers material was 1933 to 1937 when premiums were issued in conjunction with products such as Cream of Wheat and Cocomalt.

Flash Gordon followed in the mid-1930s. Buster Crabbe gave life to the character in movie serials. Books, comics, premiums, and other merchandise enhanced the image during the 1940s.

The use of rockets at the end of World War II and the beginning of the space research program gave reality to space travel. Television quickly capitalized on this in the early 1950s with programs such as "Captain Video" and "Space Patrol." Many other space heroes, such as Rocky Jones, had short-lived popularity.

In the 1950s, real-life space pioneers and explorers replaced the fictional characters as the center of the public's attention. The entire world watched on July 12, 1969, as man first walked on the moon. Although space exploration has suffered occasional setbacks, the public remains fascinated with its findings and potential.

"Star Trek" enjoyed a brief television run and developed a cult following in the early 1970s. "Star Trek: The Next Generation" has an established corps of watchers. "Star Wars" (Parts IV, V, and VI) and "ET" also initiated a wealth of merchandise which already is collectible.

Collecting Hints: There are four distinct eras of fictional space adventurers: Buck Rogers, Flash Gordon, the radio and television characters of the late 1940s and 1950s, and the Star Trek and Star Wars phenomenon. Because Buck Rogers material is rare, condition is not as much of a factor as it is for the other three areas. Beware of dealers who break apart items, especially games, and sell parts separately.

In the early 1950s, a wealth of tin, battery-operated, friction, and windup toys not associated with a specific Space Adventurer were marketed. The popularity of these robots, space ships, and space guns is growing rapidly.

Trekkies began holding conventions in the early 1970s. They issued many fantasy items that must not be confused with items issued during the years the TV show was broadcast. The fantasy items are numerous and have little value beyond the initial selling price.

The American and Russian space programs produced a wealth of souvenir and related material. Beware of astronaut-signed material; it may have a printed or autopen signature.

Additional Listings: Robots, Space Toys, Star Wars.

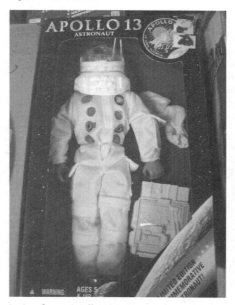

Action figure, Apollo 13 Astronaut, limited edition, NRFB, **$25**.

Buck Rogers Sonic Ray Gun, **$125**.

Battlestar Galactica

Comic book, 1978, large size format **15.00**
Electronic game, working condition.. **50.00**
Figure, Cylon Centurian, Mattel, MIB **150.00**
Magazine, glossy periodical unfolds to 33" x 22"
   #2, Battlestar Spacecraft poster **25.00**
   #3, Cyclon Warriors poster............ **25.00**
Model, Cylon Base Star, Revell Monogram, copyright 1997, MIB **25.00**
Script, 1970s **20.00**

Buck Rogers

Atomic pistol, Daisy, silvered metal, C-8.5
   .... **240.00**
Badge, Solar Scouts **100.00**
Battle cruiser.................................... **100.00**
Book, *Buck Rogers Solar Scouts Handbook*, © 1936 .... **275.00**
Comics, orig Sunday Funnies **100.00**
Figure, lead **15.00**
Membership kit
   1938, Rocket Rangers, card, letter, orig mailer.. **200.00**
   1945, letter, card, and ship poster, envelope **500.00**
Photo, Buck Rogers, Buck and Wilma, 7-1/2" x 10", black and white, facsimile signatures, Cocomalt, c1934 .... **85.00**
Rocket fighter, Wyandotte, 1936, 6" l
   .... **295.00**
Thermos, plastic, Aladdin, 1979 .... **35.00**
Whistle badge, Spaceship Commander
   .... **275.00**

Space Ranger badge, some play wear, **$25**.

Flash Gordon

Bank, metal, rocket **35.00**
Better little book, *Flash Gordon and the Perils of Mongo*, Whitman, 1940 .... **45.00**
Comics, Sunday Comics Page, 1935 **15.00**
Book, pop-up, *Tournament Of Death,* Blue Ribbon Press and Pleasure Books, © 1935, 20 pgs................................. **145.00**
Figure, Defender of the Earth
   Flash Gordon, MIP......................... **15.00**
   Ming, MIP....................................... **15.00**
Pencil case, 1951 .... **120.00**

Playset, Tootsietoy, figures, 1978, MIB
.... **100.00**
Water pistol, holster, King Features, 1975,
MOC **45.00**

Lost in Space

Blueprint set.................................. **20.00**
Comic album, 7-3/4" x 10-1/4", Space
Family Robinson/Lost In Space, stiff
cover comic album, English reprints of
Western Publishing Co. full-color comic
book stories, ©1965 by World
Distributors Ltd, 64 pgs **18.00**
Gum wrapper, US Gum, C-9.5 .... **100.00**
Lunch box, dome **35.00**
View Master, unopened **250.00**

Outer Limits

Bubble gum cards, complete set, 1960s
.... **250.00**
Model, 6th Finger, vinyl, MIB **150.00**
Television poster **20.00**

Magazine cover, *Time*, July 25, 1969, $12.

Space Cadet, Tom Corbett

Binoculars **125.00**
Book, *Tom Corbett Space Cadet/Sabotage
In Space,* Grosset & Dunlap, hardcover,
212 pgs, dj **15.00**
Decoder, 2-1/2" x 4", Tom Corbett Space
Cadet Code, black, white, and red
cardboard, membership card printed on
back **45.00**
Flashlight, 7" l, Space Cadet Signal Siren
Flashlight, full color illus, orig box, c1952
.... **65.00**
Lunch box, red **185.00**

Membership kit fan photo, 3-1/2" x 5-1/4",
glossy black and white photo, Tom with
Space Rangers, facsimile blue ink
signature, c1952 .... **28.00**
Patch, 2" x 4", cloth, Space Cadet, red,
yellow, and blue, Kellogg's premium
.... **35.00**
Photo, 3-1/2" x 5-1/2", black and white
glossy, blue signature "Spaceman's Luck/
Tom Corbett/Space Cadet," early 1950s
.... **45.00**
Thermos, tin litho, Space Cadet **75.00**
View master reel, set of three, orig story
folder and envelope **45.00**
Wrist watch **250.00**

Space Patrol

Belt and buckle, 4" brass buckle, rocket,
decoder mounted on back, glow-in-the-
dark belt, Ralston premium, early 1950s
.... **175.00**
Coin album, 3" x 7-3/4", thin cardboard
black, white, and blue folder, spaceship
landing and men rushing toward it, diecut
slots for plastic Ralston premium or
Schwinn Bicycle dealer coins, c1953
.... **175.00**
Film projector, pocket **185.00**
Gun, Satellite **40.00**
Handbook **165.00**
Microscope, orig slides **195.00**
Paper cup, package of six, rocket ships,
stars, and planets motif, orig cellophane
and company label......................... **70.00**
Premium card, 2-1/2" x 3-1/2", full-color
scene on front and back, text, ad for
Wheat and Rice Chex Cereal, Rockets,
Jets, and Weapons Series, seven cards
from 40-card set, early 1950s **135.00**
Watch, silvered chrome, stainless steel
back, black leather straps, "Space Patrol"
inscription on dial, black numerals, US
Time, early 1950s **165.00**

Star Trek

Action figure

Borg Queen, loose **20.00**
Captain Kirk, Tholian Suit, loose **10.00**
Chekov, 9" h, loose **15.00**
Cheron, 8" h, MOC **250.00**
Gorn Captain, loose **10.00**
Guian, 9" h, MOC **50.00**
Jem Hadar, 9" h, MOC.................... **25.00**
Keeper, loose **75.00**
Kirk, City on the Edge of Forever, loose
.... **10.00**
Kirk and Spock, #1, Piece of the Action,
Kaybee Set, MIB **200.00**
Klingon, 8" h, MOC **60.00**
Lt. Commander La Froge Interstellar,
loose **10.00**
McCoy, 8" h, MOC **125.00**

Comic book, *Star Trek*, DC Comics, April, 1984, **$6.50**.

Mugato, loose................................. **300.00**
Neptuneman, loose........................ **100.00**
O-Brien, 9" h, loose **15.00**
Professor Data, All Good Things, loose
.... **10.00**
Riker, 9" h, loose **50.00**
Scotty, 8" h, MOC **125.00**
Spock, City on the Edge of Forever, loose
.... **10.00**
Talos, 8" h, MOC............................ **400.00**
Talos, 8" h, loose............................ **200.00**
Ulhura, 8" h, MOC **125.00**
Warrior Worf, 9" h, loose................. **50.00**
Bike scout and bike, Target Exclusive, MISB **60.00**
Children's book, *The Truth Machine*, hardcover, 1977 .... **10.00**
Cup, plastic, Deka, 1701 ship and crew, 1975.. **30.00**
Doll, Commander Sulu, 15" h, MIB ... **135.00**
Drinking glasses, set of four, orig Taco Bell display, Star Trek 3 .... **60.00**
Halloween costume, Mr. Spock, 1975
.... **85.00**
Inflatable Enterprise, Star Trek 5, Kraft Foods promo, 24" l......................... **15.00**
Limited edition figure, Franklin Mint, pewter, orig stand, MIB
  Borg Ship............................... **125.00**
  Space Station **125.00**
  U. S. S. Enterprise........................ **150.00**
Lunch box, Borg, head, talking, 1992 **40.00**
Manual, *Star Fleet Technical Manual*, hardcover, 1975 .... **60.00**
Model
  AMT Enterprise, promo diecast TNG
.... **100.00**
  Galileo 7 Space Ship, AMT, 1974, orig contents sealed in box................. **150.00**

Klingon Battle Ship, AMT, 1968, orig contents sealed in box **150.00**
Mr. Spock, AMT, 1968, orig contents sealed in box **250.00**
USS Enterprise, AMT, 1968, orig contents seated in box **200.00**
USS Enterprise Command Bridge, AMT, 1975, orig contents sealed in box **150.00**
Playset, Mego
  Bridge, 1975, sealed, MIB **300.00**
  Combat Klingon Warrior, 9" **25.00**
  Communicators, MOC **200.00**
  Galileo, shuttlecraft........................ **35.00**
  Gorn, 12" **30.00**
  Insurrection Captian Picard, 12" **30.00**
  Mission to Gamma VI, MOC **400.00**
  Seven of Nine, 9" **30.00**
  Sulu, 12" **30.00**
  Trekulator, MOC **250.00**
Playset, Playmates, Bridge, NRFB... **100.00**
Puzzle, boxed, Canadian **20.00**
Stamp cachet, Trek Artwork, Shuttle, 1991, limited edition............................. **50.00**
Record, book and record, MIP............ **5.00**
Towel, Voyager Promo, Fritts Candy, full color **50.00**

Vehicle and accessories

Borg Cube **50.00**
Communicators, pr........................ **85.00**
Enterprise B **140.00**
Excelsior....................................... **140.00**
Insurrection Phaser........................ **15.00**
Klingon Disruptor............................ **25.00**
Pikes Laser Pistol.......................... **20.00**
Romulan Warbird............................ **50.00**
Spacecraft Galileao, Galoob, 1989, MIB
.... **45.00**
Voyager **140.00**
Wall clock, 1701-E Ship, Wesco **50.00**
Watch, Timex, Cloaking Romulan, 1993, orig case... **75.00**

Space Exploration

Autograph, envelope, inked Jack Swigert signature on back, Man on Moon stamp, canceled Kennedy Space Center, April 11, 1970 .... **50.00**
Badge, 4" l, black, white, and orange, "First Man on The Moon," for Astronaut Armstrong's hometown observance in Wappeukeneta, OH, after July 19-20, 1969 flight **40.00**
Bank, Apollo Astronaut in Space Suit, ceramic **40.00**
Candy container, 2-3/4" h, hard plastic, moon module, red, blue, and green, Triumph Candy, 1970s, one black plastic wheel missing **12.00**
Children's book, *The Conquest of Space*, Willy Ley, illus by Chesley Bonestell, Viking, 1952, 7th printing................. **9.00**

Toy, Mars Attack, Supreme Mars Ambassador,
1996 Warner Bros copyright, battery operated,
NRFB, **$18.**

Dish, 8" d, Apollo II Commemorative,
iridescent glass, raised design,
inscription "One Small Step," 1970s
.... **18.00**
Figure, 5" h painted composition wood
figure of child astronaut on 2" x 3" globe
base, helmet inscribed "U.S.A.," United
Fund Campaign, Multi Products, Inc.,
1960s **30.00**
Globe, 9" d, tin, "John Glenn's First
American In Orbit, Feb. 20, 1962,"
octagonal tin base, J. Chein & Co.,
Burlington, NJ **20.00**
Gyroscope, Gemini, plastic, 1960s, MOC
.... **30.00**
Letter opener, 7" l, Apollo 11, gold colored
metal, insignia on handle, grained black
leather-like scabbard **30.00**
Magazine, *Life*
1966, July 1, Moon Shot cover **5.00**
1969, July 25, Leaving for Moon cover,
article on Armstrong........................ **10.00**
1969, Aug. 8, On the Moon with Flag
cover, color photos......................... **12.00**
Magazine, *Newsweek*
1969, Jan. 6, Apollo, Anders, Lovell,
Borman cover.................................. **8.00**
1969, July 28, Moonwalk cover, black
and white **9.00**
1969, Aug. 11, Moonwalk cover, color
.... **9.00**
Magazine, *Time*
1962, March 2, John Glenn cover **6.00**
1962, Aug. 24, Russian Astronauts cover
.... **5.00**
1969, Jan. 3, US Astronauts cover ... **5.00**

Map
15" x 25", Rand McNally, Moon Globe
offer, 1969 .... **10.00**
19" x 25", Esso, map of the moon, 1969
.... **8.00**
27" x 42", National Geographic, map of
the moon **12.00**
37" x 42", Babcock & Wilcox Beaver Falls
Plant Open House, Sept. 20, 1969 .. **8.00**

Helmet, Col. McCauley Space Helmet, red,
white, and blue box, **$65**

Model, Space 1999
MPC, Moonbase Alpa, MIB **300.00**
MPC, Eagle, MIB **100.00**
Mug, 3" h, china, black St Louis Globe-
Democrat newspaper design of July 20,
1969, moon landing....................... **35.00**
Newsletter, Baltimore News-Post, Feb. 20,
1962, Glenn In Orbit, black and white
photo of Glenn entering hatch of
Friendship **15.00**
Pennant, 29" l, felt, red and white, blue trim,
First Man On Moon **20.00**
Photograph, Space Program, 1965/66, set
of 5 UPI and WW photos **20.00**
Pinback button
1-1/2" d, Salute Of The 1st Manned
Space Flight To The Moon By Borman
Anders & Lovell, Dec. 21 to 27, 1968, NY
Welcomes Astronauts Jan. 10th, 1969-
The Chrome-Post-Card Collectors Club,
blue on white, hand lettered, cartoon art
of Apollo 8 headed towards the cratered
surface of the moon........................ **15.00**
3-1/2" d, America's First Orbital
Spaceman/Astronaut John Glenn, black
and white, red text **18.00**
3-1/2" d, Welcome Astronaut Gordon
Cooper 22 Orbits-May 15-16, 1963, red,
blue, and blue, blue and white photo of
cooper, red and white images of Mercury
capsule on both sides **30.00**
Postcard, 3-1/2" x 5-1/2", glossy color, "US
Astronaut John H. Glenn Jr.," bio on
back, unused **5.00**
Poster, Apollo Astronaut, set of three, large
.... **35.00**

Press pass, 3" x 4-1/4", laminated, ABC News, June 18-24, 1983, Challenger Mission, black and white photos, blue, white, and orange design **60.00**

Universe Car, battery operated, original box marked "Made in China," $45.

Puzzle, Apollo 11, 1969, MIB **25.00**
Record, America's First Man In Orbit, John Glenn, 33-1/3 rpm, orig envelope .. **35.00**
Ring, Astronaut, adjustable aluminum ring, mkd inside band "Copyright Uncas Mfg Co., top with atom symbols surrounding rocketships, large raised image of astronaut wearing helmet and oxygen mask, 1960s, slight wear **18.00**
Rug, 19-1/2" x 37-1/2", woven, full-color moon landing scene, red, white, and blue stars and stripes motif border, made in Italy, orig label **60.00**
Salt and pepper shakers, pr, 3" h, china, blue symbol and Columbia shuttle design, inscription "Johnson Space Center, Houston, TX," early 1980s.. **20.00**
Tie clip, 1-1/2", Apollo 11, brass, black accents, raised moon landing design, landing date and astronaut names on rim, orig plastic display case **42.00**
View Master pack, America's Man in Space, 4-1/2" sq paper pack, five color images relating to 1962 space flight, each with protective sleeve, foldout booklet, c1962 .... **18.00**

Sports Collectibles

History: Individuals have been saving sports-related equipment since the inception of sports. Some material was passed down from generation to generation for reuse. The balance occupied dark spaces in closets, attics, and basements.

In the 1980s, two key trends brought collectors' attention to the sports arena. First, decorators began using old sports items, especially in restaurant decor. Second, card collectors began to discover the thrill of owing the "real" thing. Although the principal thrust was on baseball memorabilia, by the beginning of the 1990s all sport categories were collectible, with automobile racing, boxing, football, and horse racing especially strong.

Collecting Hints: The amount of material is unlimited. Pick a favorite sport and concentrate on it. Within the sport, narrow collecting emphasis to items associated with one league, team, individual, or era, or concentrate on one type of equipment. Include as much three-dimensional material as possible.

Each sport has a hall of fame. Make a point to visit it and get to know its staff, an excellent source of leads for material that the museum no longer wants in its collection. Induction ceremonies provide an excellent opportunity to make contact with heroes of the sport as well as with other collectors.

Additional Listings: Baseball Collectibles, Basketball Collectibles, Boxing Collectibles, Fishing Collectibles, Golf Collectibles, Hunting Collectibles, Olympics Collectibles, Racing Collectibles; Wrestling Collectibles.

Autograph
    Augassi, Andre, photograph.......... **40.00**
    McEnroe, John.............................. **40.00**
    Navrailova, Martina....................... **40.00**
    Sabatina, Gabriella........................ **42.00**
    Witt, Katarina, photograph **40.00**
Bank, 4-1/2" d, metal, emb enameled fishing, golf, and travel scenes, changing date feature, 1950s, Cada Co., Chicago **60.00**
Bowling shirt, woman's, white, red trim, name "Betty" stitched on pocket, numerous bowling related patches on back and shoulder, c1950 .... **48.00**
Calendar plate, 1967, bowling, football, water skiing, tennis, gold trim, 10" d **5.00**
Cigarette card, John Player and Sons, Imperial Tobacco Co., Great Britain, showing tennis stars, set of 50 cards **150.00**
Cigarette lighter, Scripto VU, bolwing motif **30.00**
Counter display sign, 17-1/2" h, Budweiser, scoring soccer player, MLS soccer logo **8.00**
Decanter, tennis player, Ezra Brooks, Heritage China, 1973 .... **20.00**

Dexterity game, 2-1/4" d, soccer motif, sgd "D.R.G.M. in US Zone Germany" ... **25.00**

Figure, 6-1/2" h, caricature, zealous lady bowler who rocks back and hits male bowler, © 1941 L. Ritgers, painted plaster **195.00**

Game, Bowling-A Board Game, Parker Bros, orig box, 1896 .... **60.00**

Mug, 5" h, gentleman playing with balls, two ladies shaking hands on reverse, Arthur Wood, Royal Bradwell, England, c1945 .... **45.00**

Necklace, 16" l twisted rope cord, 1-3/4" l wood bowling pins, brass clasp, c1925 .... **125.00**

Magazine, *National Geographic World*, January 1982, article about special young adult skiers, $1.50.

Nodder, 6" h, "You're Right Down My Alley," composition, man holding bowling ball, mounted on wood block base **50.00**

Pencil sharpener, 1-1/4" x 1-3/4" x 2", green had plastic, portable TV shape, full-color flicker as screen, Kohner Products, c1950.. **25.00**

Pennant, 9" l, soccer ball and shoe, Sportvyroba Bardejov **20.00**

Pinback button, Floyd Patterson, Punch With Patterson Polo Grounds, July 29, 1-3/4" d, bright red, yellowish-cream ground, redtone photo of Patterson **70.00**

Pocket mirror, 2-1/2" d, Wilkinson College of Swimming Exclusive Ladies Plunge, bright orange rim, black and white text surrounds black and white photo of

proprietor of Los Angeles establishment, text includes address and five-digit phone number **35.00**

Sculpture, 14-7/8" h, metal, tennis player holding racquet, sgd by Mexican artist **85.00**

Soccer ball, Always Coca-Cola, 1997 **12.00**

Stuffed toy, bear wearing Philadelphia Flyers emblem on felt outfit, $10.

Telephone, Centra II, soccer motif, orig owner's manual, MIB **60.00**

Tennis balls, Wilson Match-point, c1945, orig can never opened **30.00**

Tennis racket

Dayton, 1923 patent date, 26-1/2" l **70.00**
Magnan, vintage............................ **80.00**
Maureen Connolly, full-color portrait on handle, Wilson Sporting Goods, 1950s **20.00**
Wright & Ditson Championship, 26" l **50.00**

Tie tac, 14k yg, bowling ball and pin, patchwork Florentine texture, c1960 .... **135.00**

Trophy, 3-1/4" h, crystal soccer ball on pedestal, sgd "Val St. Lambert"... **125.00**

Wire service photo, Chicago Bulls Scottie Pippen and Detroit Pistons Vinnie Johnson, 1989 .... **3.50**

Stangl Pottery

History: The origins of Fulper Pottery, the predecessor to Stangl, are clouded. The company claimed a date of 1805. Paul Evans, a major American art pottery researcher, suggests an 1814 date. Regardless of which date is correct, by the middle of the 19th century an active pottery was located in Flemington, New Jersey.

When Samuel Hill, the pottery's founder, died in 1858, the pottery was acquired by Abraham Fulper, a nephew. Abraham died in 1881, and the business continued under the direction of his sons, Edward, George W., and William.

In 1910, Johann Martin Stangl began working at Fulper as a chemist and plant superintendent. He left Fulper in 1914 to work briefly for Haeger Potteries. By 1920, Stangl was back at Fulper serving as general manager. In 1926, Fulper acquired the Anchor Pottery in Trenton, New Jersey, where a line of solid-color dinnerware in the California patio style was produced.

William Fulper died in 1928 at which time Stangl became president of the firm. In 1920, Johann Martin Stangl purchased Fulper, and Stangl Pottery was born. During the 1920s production emphasis shifted from art pottery to dinner and utilitarian wares.

A 1929 fire destroyed the Flemington pottery. Rather than rebuild, a former ice cream factory was converted to a showroom and production facility. By the end of the 1930s production was concentrated in Trenton with the Flemington kiln used primarily for demonstration purposes.

Stangl's ceramic birds were produced from 1940 until 1972. The birds were made in Stangl's Trenton plant, then shipped to the Flemington plant for hand painting. During World War II, the demand for these birds and Stangl pottery was so great that 40 to 60 decorators could not keep up with it. Orders were contracted out to private homes. These pieces were then returned for firing and finishing. Different artists used different colors to decorate these birds.

On August 25, 1965, fire struck the Trenton plant. The damaged portion of the plant was rebuilt by May 1966. On February 13, 1972, Johann Martin Stangl died. Frank Wheaton Jr., of Wheaton Industries, Millville, New Jersey, purchased the plant in June 1972 and continued Stangl production. In 1978 the Pfaltzgraff Company purchased the company's assets from Wheaton. Production ceased. The Flemington factory became a Pfaltzgraff factory outlet. One of the original kilns remains intact to commemorate the hard work and to demonstrate the high temperatures involved in the production of pottery.

Collecting Hints: Stangl Pottery produced several lines of highly collectible dinnerware and decorative accessories, including the famed Stangl birds. The red-bodied dinnerware was produced in distinc-tive shapes and patterns. Shapes were designated by numbers. Pattern names include Country Garden, Fruit, Tulip, Thistle, and Wild Rose. Special Christmas, advertising, and commemorative wares also were produced.

Bright colors and bold simplistic patterns make Stangl pottery a favorite with Country collectors. Stangl sold seconds from a factory store long before outlet malls became popular. Large sets of Stangl dinnerware currently command high prices at auctions, flea markets, and antiques shops.

As many as 10 different trademarks were used. Dinnerware was marked and often signed by the decorator. Most birds are numbered; many are artist signed. However, signatures are useful for dating purposes only and add little to value.

Several of the well-known Stangl birds were reissued between 1972 and 1977. These reissues are dated on the bottom and are worth approximately half as much as the older birds.

Additional Listings: See *Warman's Antiques and Collectibles Price Guide* for prices of bird figurines.

Bittersweet pattern, plate, decorator's initials on back, 9" d, $20.

Golden Blossom, platter, $20.

Dinnerware

Amber Glo, pitcher, pint **40.00**
Arbor, dinner plate **22.50**
Bachelor Button, teapot **40.00**
Bittersweet, tidbit tray, 10" d **45.00**
Blueberry
    Coffeepot **100.00**
    Creamer **15.00**
    Platter, 14" d **75.00**
    Salt and pepper shakers, pr **24.00**
    Vegetable bowl, 8" **50.00**
Brittany, dinner plate, 10-1/2" d **125.00**
Colonial, #1388
    Candleholders, pr, blue **40.00**
    Carafe, pottery stopper, wooden handle
    .... **65.00**
    Cigarette box **60.00**
    Cup and saucer, green **12.00**
    Dinner plate, 10"d, yellow **12.00**
    Salad bowl, Round, 10" d **35.00**
    Teapot, individual **45.00**
Country Garden, dinner plate, 10-1/4" d
.... **35.00**
Festival, vegetable bowl, open, round **45.00**
Fruit
    Casserole, 8" d **85.00**
    Chop plate, 14" d **65.00**
    Creamer, individual **25.00**
    Cup and saucer **18.00**
    Dinner plate, 10" d **25.00**
    Eggcup **18.00**
    Platter, round, 12-1/2" d, green **35.00**
    Salt and pepper shakers, pr **24.00**
    Sherbet **20.00**
    Teapot **100.00**
    Teapot, individual **60.00**
    Vegetable bowl, divided **38.00**
Fruit and Flowers, cake stand, 10" d,
4-3/8" h **60.00**
Garland, 1959-63
    Butter dish, cov, 8-1/2" l **45.00**
    Dinner plate, 10-1/2" d **24.00**
    Sugar bowl, light gray, maroon flowers
    and trim, 6-1/2" d, 3-1/2" h **35.00**

Golden Harvest
    Cup and saucer **12.00**
    Dinner plate, 10" d **12.00**
    Gravy boat **15.00**
    Platter, 13-3/4" l, casual shape **25.00**
    Salt and pepper shakers, pr **12.50**
    Vegetable bowl, open, 8" d, round **28.00**
Harvest, dinner plate, 10" d **18.00**
Holly, pitcher, pint **38.00**
Jeweled Christmas Tree
    Chop plate, 14" d **175.00**
    Cigarette box **250.00**
    Creamer **40.00**
    Cup and saucer **50.00**
    Dinner plate, 10" d **65.00**
    Pitcher, two qt. **100.00**
    Punch bowl, 12" d **200.00**
    Punch cup **25.00**
    Sugar **40.00**
Kiddieware
    Bowl, Goldilocks **150.00**
    Child's feeding dish, three compartments
        Ducky Dinner **125.00**
        Kitten Capers **160.00**
        Playful Pups.......................... **125.00**
    Cup
        ABC cup, 4-3/16" w, 2-5/8" h .. **55.00**
        Goldilocks **150.00**
        Kitten Capers **75.00**
        Little Bo Peep **150.00**
        Little Boy Blue **50.00**
        Ranger Boy **100.00**
    Plate
        Little Quakers **110.00**
        Mary Quite Contrary **200.00**
        Peter Rabbit **175.00**
        Pony Trail **200.00**
    Set, Little Boy Blue, bowl, cup, and plate
.... **550.00**
Magnolia
    Berry bowl **30.00**
    Cereal bowl **35.00**
    Chop plate, #3870, coupe shape, 1952,
14-1/2" d **40.00**
    Coffeepot, individual size **100.00**

Creamer and sugar **20.00**
Cup and saucer **12.50**
Fruit bowl **30.00**
Platter, round, 14" d **40.00**
Salad plate **30.00**
Soup bowl **30.00**
Vegetable bowl, cov **60.00**

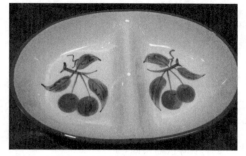

Orchard Song, divided vegetable dish, **$25**.

Morning Blue, tid-bit server, small gold-colored handle, 6" d, **$45**.

Orchard Song

Chop platter, 14-1/2" d **45.00**
Creamer and sugar, cov **24.00**
Gravy boat and underplate **28.00**
Salad bowl, 12" d, 4" h **50.00**
Vegetable bowl, divided **25.00**
Vegetable bowl, round, 8" d **17.50**

Thistle

Coffeepot, cov **100.00**
Cup and saucer **13.50**
Dinner plate, 10" d **20.00**
Eggcup **15.00**
Fruit dish **12.00**
Gravy boat **20.00**
Pitcher, one qt **35.00**
Platter, oval **35.00**

Town and Country

Bowl, blue, 10"d **60.00**

Butter dish, cov **60.00**
Coffeepot, 6-1/2" h **38.00**
Creamer **20.00**
Cup and saucer **20.00**
Mug, blue **40.00**
Platter, 14-3/4" x 10-1/8" **145.00**
Salad plate, 8-1/2" d, brown **15.00**
Soap dish **75.00**
Spoon rest **35.00**
Sugar, cov **30.00**
Toothbrush holder **75.00**
Wash pitcher and basin, large, blue
.... **175.00**

Tropic, # 3338

Carafe, wood handle **5.00**
Cup and saucer **15.00**
Dinner plate, 10"d **25.00**
Salad plate, 7" d **12.00**
Salt and pepper shakers, pr, figural **60.00**
Vegetable bowl, oval **40.00**

Water Lily pattern, plate, 6" d, **$15**.

Miscellaneous and Artware

Antique Gold, giftware line
Ashtray, 10" d, 2-3/4" h, mkd "Stangl Pottery Trenton NJ 3972 pat. pend."
.... **48.00**
Bowl, 14" l, 6-1/2" w **40.00**
Vase, 5-1/2" h, orig sticker **45.00**
Vase, 9-3/4" h, #3060610 .... **50.00**
Ashtray, Pheasant, Sportsman Giftware, teardrop shape, hand painted, 10-1/2" l, 8" w **65.00**

Christmas coasters

Carolers **125.00**
Holly & Bells **125.00**
Snowman **125.00**

Cigarette boxes, cov
Daisy, #3666 .... **50.00**
Pagoda Lid, Marsh Rose, #3799 ... **75.00**

Freeform, vase, 5-1/2" h, 3-7/8" w, blue and
purple glaze, orig label **125.00**

Sunburst Artware ("Rainbow")

Planter, swan, large **400.00**
Vase, Acanthus Leaf, #1540 .... **125.00**
Vase, Deco, #1185, 9" h **150.00**
Vase, Twist, #1124, three handles **125.00**

Terra Rose Artware

Box, cov, hand painted, sgd, 5-1/2" l,
4-1/2" w **45.00**
Bowl, Lily of the Valley, green, #3620
.... **75.00**
Candy jar, cov, bird finial, #3676 .... **60.00**
Nautilus Shell, blue #3705 .... **75.00**
Teapot, cov **60.00**
Watering can, yellow tulip, #3511. **150.00**
Watering pitcher, blue tulip, #3211 **50.00**

Star Wars

History: "Star Wars," 1977; "Empire
Strikes Back," 1980, and "Return of the
Jedi," 1983, have delighted movie-
goers with special effects and stunning
music as George Lucas has created a
classic for all times. The most recent
releases, "Episode I, The Phantom
Menace," and "Episode II, Attack of the
Clones," successfully take the story line
back in time to reveal, among other
things, the origins of Anakin Skywalker
who later becomes that dastardly villain,
Darth Vader. Episode III is due for
release in 2005.

While most collectors know the
details of each of the movies, hopefully
they will not be disappointed with the
wide range of collectibles being
offered. The first three movies have
yielded many collectibles and rare
items now going to auction and are
showing signs of high prices and keen
collector interest.

Besides the toys and collectibles
licensed by Hasbro and Kenner, the
fast food companies have also created
items which collectors eagerly seek. So
strap yourself down in the old Land
Speeder and enjoy the collecting ride
of the millennium.

Collecting Hints: Look for completeness when collecting vintage toys and
figures. When Kenner originally introduced Star War figures in 1977, the line
contained only 12 figures. One way to
identify those early figures when mint on

the card is by the 12 photographs on
the back. Collectors have nicknamed
these "12 backs" to be able to tell the
difference from "20 backs" and later
issues.

If buying new release items, be
aware their value is speculative and
also be prepared to store them carefully for several years. Remember that
the anticipated revenue from the new
release is estimated to be $4 billion in
sales. That should give collectors many
buying opportunities.

Note: Loose, mint condition (LMC)
means accompanied by all small
accessory pieces, but not in original
package.

Action figures

Anakin Skywalker, loose, mail away
premium figure, 1983 .... **35.00**
AT-AT Commander, MOC **15.00**
Ben Kenobi, AFA 85, 12 back, MOC
.... **900.00**
Ben Kenobi, clothing, boots, no light
saber, 12" h, loose **100.00**
Ben Obi-Wan Kenobi, *Power of the Force*,
glowing light saber, 1995, MOC ... **15.00**
Blue Snaggletooth, Kenner, 1977, only
issued with playset **150.00**
Boba Fett, orig backpack, belts missing
Wookie scalps, 12" h, loose **125.00**
Chewbacca, bandolier and crossbow,
12" h, loose **65.00**
C-3PO, 12" h, loose **60.00**
Chief Chirpa, Return of the Jedi, MOC
.... **35.00**
Darth Vader, orig cape, 12" h, loose
.... **60.00**
Darth Vader with Interrogation Droid
.... **10.00**
Death Squad Commander, Kenner, 1977,
3-3/4" h, MIP **175.00**
Death Star Droid, 3" h, 1978, MIP **155.00**
Duros **12.00**
Emperor's Royal Guard, loose **14.00**
Emperor's Wrath Death Vader **12.00**
FX-7, Kenner, 1980
LMC **8.00**
MIP **55.00**
Gammoran Guard, Return of the Jedi,
MOC **75.00**
Greedo, Kenner, 1977
LMC **15.00**
MIP **135.00**
Greedo, JC Penney **45.00**
Greedo, with COM chip **10.00**

Doll, Princess Leia Organa, Epic Force, NRFB, $30

Hammerhead, Kenner, 1977
    LMC **15.00**
    MIP... **135.00**
Han & Tauntaun, Kenner, 1997, Toys R'
Us exclusive
    LMC **65.00**
    MIP... **185.00**
Han Solo, Kenner, 1980, Hoth outfit
    LMC **10.00**
    MIP... **80.00**
Hans Solo, 12 back, small head, MOC
.... **700.00**
Han Trench, *Return of the Jedi*, MOC
.... **60.00**
Hoth Snowtrooper, *Empire Strikes Back*,
MOC **150.00**
Imperial Commander, loose **8.00**
Jawa, Kenner, 1977, 3-3/4" h
    Cloth cape, MIP **220.00**
    Vinyl cape, MIP **3,200.00**
Ketwol.. **12.00**
Lando Calrissian, Kenner, 1980
    LMC **10.00**
    MIP... **40.00**

Leia Bespin, turtleneck, C-9.5...... **295.00**
Leia Combat, Return of the Jedi, MOC
.... **65.00**
Luke Skywalker, Kenner, 1977, 3-3/4" h,
MIP **320.00**
Luke Skywalker, shirt, pants, boots,
blaster with sling, 12" h, loose........ **70.00**
Obi-Wan, Kaybees Exclusive, 12" h,
MISB.. **60.00**
Obi-Wan Kenobi, Kenner, 1977
    LMC **30.00**
    MIP **300.00**
Power Droid, loose **10.00**
Princess Leia, Kenner, 1977, Benspin
outfit
    LMC **70.00**
    MIP **100.00**
Red Snaggletooth, Kenner, 1977
    LMC **24.00**
    MIP **140.00**
Ree Yees, *Return of the Jedi*, MOC **25.00**
Romba, *Power of the Force*, MOC. **50.00**
R2-B1 Droid, MOMC **12.00**
R2-D2, Kenner, 1980, retractable sensor-
scope
    LMC **10.00**
MIP **50.00**
R2-D2, loose, 12" h....................... **65.00**
R2-D2, holding Leia **20.00**
R5-D4, 3" h, 1978, MIP **130.00**
Sand Person, 12 back, MOC **325.00**
Sand Trooper, Diamond Exclusive, 12" h
.... **75.00**
Shmi Skywalker.............................. **12.00**
Snaggletooth, 3" h, 1978
    Blue body, Sears Exclusive, MIP
.... **200.00**
    Red body, MIP...................... **160.00**
Snow Trooper, loose **10.00**
Stormtrooper, laser rifle, 12" h, loose
.... **75.00**
Stormtrooper with battle damage, COM
ship.. **10.00**
Swimming Jar Jar **15.00**
TC-14 Droid, MOMC **12.00**
Tie Pilot, MOC **185.00**
Tusken Raider, Kenner, 12" h
    With blaster rifle...................... **50.00**
    With gafi stick **50.00**
Walrus Man, Kenner, 1977
    LMC.. **25.00**
    MIP **135.00**
Wequay, loose **7.50**
Wicket, loose.................................. **25.00**
Yak Face, *Power of the Force,* MIP
.... **1,700.00**
Yoda, loose **25.00**
Zuckuss, loose................................ **12.00**

Darth Maul, life size, red and black face, black outfit, $200.

Dewback and Sandtrooper, NRFB, $20.

Child's school desk, *Star Wars Return of the Jedi,* American Toy & Furniture Corp, 1983, 22" l, 15" w, 26" h **35.00**
Coat rack, Jedi **400.00**
Costume and mask, child's, Ben Cooper
   Darth Vader, 1977 .... **45.00**
   Princess Leia, medium, orig blue box, 1977 .... **20.00**
   Robot C-3PO, small, orig black box, 1980 .... **20.00**
   Stormtrooper, 1973 .... **50.00**
Doll, 7-1/2" h, RD-D2, plush and plastic, 1977 .... **12.00**
Doll, 12" h, sealed in orig box
   Ben Kanobi **550.00**
   Chewbacca **150.00**
   Darth Vader **450.00**
   Han Solo **800.00**
   Jawa **350.00**
   Lea **450.00**
   Luke Skywalker **550.00**
   R2D2 .... **300.00**
Frisbee, Star Wars The Empire Strikes Back, Burger King, 1980, white **15.00**
Game, board
   Star Wars Adventures of R2-D2, orig rules missing **5.00**
   Star Wars Destroy The Death Star Game, Kenner, MIB **25.00**
   Star Wars Escape From The Death Star Game, Kenner, 1977, MIB **25.00**
   Star Wars Return Of The Jedi Wicket The Ewok and Friends Adventure Game, Parker Bros, 1983 .... **12.00**
   Star Wars The Empire Strikes Back, Hoth Ice Planet Adventure Game, Kenner, orig box, 1980, one Millennium Falcon playing piece missing **15.00**
   Star Wars The Empire Strikes Back, Yoda The Jedi Master Game, near mint, orig box **15.00**
   The Ultimate Space Adventure Game, Parker Bros, MIB **20.00**
Game, electronic, *Star Wars Electric Laser Battle Game,* Kenner, orig instructions and box, some play wear **90.00**
Jigsaw puzzle
   Ailens of Star Wars, Return of the Jedi, Craftmaster, 70 pcs, 12" x 16", 1983, near mint, orig box **10.00**

Bandolier strap, Chewbacca, Kenner, MIB **18.00**
Belt buckle, metal, Yoda **8.00**
Book, hard cover
   Star Wars Episode I: The Phantom Menace, Terry Brooks, based on screenplay and story by George Lucas, Ballantine Pub, orig dj **20.00**
   Star Wars Return of the Jedi Storybook, Random House **10.00**
   The Star Wars Question & Answer Book About Space, Random House **8.00**
Bowl and mug, blue and white, Vader, Stormtroopers, Leia, Luke, and druids, Deka, plastic, 1977 .... **15.00**
Bubble bath container, Darth Vader, 1982, plastic, empty, 9" h **5.00**
Carrying case
   Empire Strikes Back
      Darth Vader, 1982 .... **35.00**
      Mini figure, 1980 .... **30.00**
      R2-D2, Droid **14.00**
   Return of the Jedi
      C-390, 1983 .... **40.00**
      Darth Vader, 1983 .... **210.00**
      Laser rifle shape, for 3-3/4" figures, Kenner **35.00**
   Star Wars **45.00**

Attack of the Sand People, Kenner, 140 pcs, 14" x 18", 1977, near mint, orig box **12.00**
Han and Chewbacca, Parker Bros, 140 pcs, 14" x 18", near mint, orig box .. **12.00**
RD-D2 and C-3PO, Kenner, 140 pcs, 14" x 18", 1977, near mint, orig box **10.00**
Star Wars Adventure, Kenner, 1,000 pcs, 19-3/8" x 26-3/4", 1977, near mint, orig box **15.00**
The Selling of the Droids, Kenner, 500 pcs, 15-1/2" x 18", near mint, orig box **12.00**
Trapped In The Trash Compactor, Kenner, 140 pcs, 14" x 18", near mint, orig box **10.00**

Halloween costume, C-3PO, Ben Cooper, child size, used, original box, $20.

Model kit
Authentic C-3PO, MPC, #1-1913, 1977, unassembled, MIB **15.00**
Authentic Darth Vader Tie Fighter, MPC, unassembled, MIB **20.00**
Luke Skywalker Van, MPC, glow-in-the-dark decals, 1:32 scale, MIB **24.00**
Mug, figural, Applause, 1996, 5" h, MIB
Gamorrean Guard **10.00**
Tusken Raider **12.00**
Necklace, by Factors
C-3PO, gold colored chain, gold metal C-3PO with moveable arms, orig retail bag **20.00**
R2-D2, silver colored chain, silver metal R2-Da with moveable legs, orig retail bag **20.00**
Photograph, autographed, certificate of authenticity
Fisher, Carrie **65.00**
Ford, Harrison **95.00**

Guiness, Alex **95.00**
Hamill, Mark **65.00**
Jones, James Earl **95.00**
Lloyd, Jake **55.00**
McGregor, Ewan **60.00**

Playset
Dagobah, Star Wars The Empire Strikes Back, NRFP **70.00**
Darth Vader's Star Destroyer, Star Wars The Empire Strikes Back, instructions, orig box **65.00**
Endor Ambush, 1997 .... **20.00**
Ewok Village, Kenner, 1983
LMC **30.00**
MIP **90.00**
Hoth Ice Planet, *Star Wars The Empire Strikes Back,* near mint, orig box ... **75.00**
Ice Planet Hoth Action Fleet, Galoob, 1996
LMC **10.00**
MIP **25.00**
Jabba The Hutt, Star Wars Return of the Jedi, MIB **45.00**
Land of the Jawas, Kenner, 1978
LMC **50.00**
MIP **200.00**
Snowspeeder, Action Fleet, Galoom, 1995
LMC **8.00**
MIP **16.00**

Star Wars Lego Ultimate Collector Series Tie Interceptor, $125.

Poster
Boba Fett, 10th anniversary **195.00**
Burger King, 1978-80 .... **10.00**
Empire Strikes Back
Advance **100.00**
Re-release, 1981-82 .... **35.00**
Nestea, 1980 .... **10.00**
Revenge of the Jedi
With date **150.00**
Without date **200.00**
Return of the Jedi
1986 re-release **80.00**
Special edition **20.00**
Star Wars
Advance, mylar **1,200.00**

Second advance................... **175.00**

Radio controlled

Imperial Speeder Bike, 1997, MIB . **30.00**
R2-D2, Kenner, wireless control, 1977,
8" h... **95.00**

Record tote, Star Wars 33-1/3 RPM record
and booklet, Disney, 1982 .... **20.00**

Robot, Talking R2-D2, Palitoy, battery
operated, four different sounds, 1977,
8" h... **295.00**

Soap, Princess Leia, 1981, MIB **8.00**

Trading card, *A New Hope Metallic Images
Collector Cards, Series I*, 1994, sealed in
cello, collectible metal box **35.00**

Vehicle, diecast, *Millenium Falcon*, three
landing stands, 1979, 5-3/4" l **25.00**

Millennium Falcon Vehicle, micro collection,
NRFB, $40.

Vehicle, Kenner, for 3-3/4" h figures

Anakin's Jedi Starfighter **30.00**
At-AT All Terrain Armored Transport,
missing one clear plastic cannon. **110.00**
B-Wing... **40.00**
Darth Vader Tie Fighter, orig box and
instructions, wear to box................. **65.00**
Empire Rebel Transport, MIB **150.00**
Federation Tank............................... **30.00**
Geonasian Fighter............................ **30.00**
Halifire Droid................................... **35.00**
Imperial Tie Fighter, no instructions, orig
box **80.00**
Jawa Sandcrawler, contents sealed, MIB
.... **1,000.00**
Jedi AT-AT Walker, MIB **325.00**
Jedi Millennium Falcon **250.00**
Jedi Speederbike, MIB **35.00**
Landspeeder, unopened box with special
collectors series logo on top........... **75.00**
Millennium Falcon **80.00**
Rebel armored snowspeeder, Star Wars
The Empire Strikes Back, orig box . **45.00**
Sith Attack Speeder with Darth Maul
.... **15.00**
Snowspeeder, MIB......................... **85.00**
Speeder Bike, 1983, MIB............... **30.00**

Taun Taun.. **75.00**
Tie Fighter **25.00**
Tie Interceptor................................. **55.00**
Twin-Pod Cloud Car, Star Wars The
Empire Strikes Back, orig box........ **45.00**
X-Wing Fighter, white, 1978
LMC... **50.00**
MIP **320.00**
Y-Wing, MIB **185.00**

Watch, digital, Official Star Wars
Microelectronic, Texas Instruments, orig
packaging, 1977 .... **75.00**

Weapon

Laser pistol, The Empire Strikes Back,
Kenner, MIB **75.00**
Tripod laser cannon, Star Wars Return of
the Jedi, MIB................................. **10.00**

Stock and Bond Certificates

History: The use of stock to raise
capital and spread the risk in a business
venture began in England. Several
American colonies were founded as
joint-venture stock companies. The New
York Stock Exchange on Wall Street in
New York City traces its roots to the late
18th century.

Stock certificates with attractive
vignettes date to the beginning of the
19th century. As engraving and printing techniques developed, so did the
elaborateness of the stock and bond
certificates. Important engraving
houses which emerged include the
American Bank Note Company and
Rawdon, Wright & Hatch.

Collecting Hints: Some of the factors
that affect price are: 1) date (with pre-
1900 more popular and pre-1850 most
desirable), 2) autographs of important
persons (Vanderbilt, Rockefeller, J. P.
Morgan, Wells and Fargo, etc.), 3)
number issued (most bonds have the
number issued noted in text), and 4)
attractiveness of the vignette.

Stocks and bonds are often collected for the appeal of their graphics
or as a record of events or people that
have impacted American history, such
as gold and silver mining, railroad
development, and early automobile
pioneers.

Canal Department, State of New York, cancelled, Draper, Toppan & Co., NY, engravers, 1842, 10-1/2" x 8", **$15**.

Bonds

Central San Cristobal, Inc., CT, 1910, First Mortgage $1000 Gold Bond, at 7 percent, Connecticut state seal at top center, ornate green border, "promises to pay to the bearer in gold coin of the United States," 34 coupons attached
.... **5.00**

City of Los Angeles, 1911, Street Improvement Bond Series 1, Blake Ave, California state seal on title panel in blue and gray, black printing, orange border, punch canceled, no coupons **12.00**

New York City, 1858, city seal, signed by Mor.. **45.00**

Pennsylvania Canal Company, issued and canceled, 1870, canal and surrounding area vignette, two revenue stamps
.... **125.00**

Southern Indiana, 1908, $1,000, issued and canceled, green...................... **28.00**

Sovereign Gold Mining, issued and canceled, $5,000, Canadian, 1903, peach borders, coupon **10.00**

Union Pacific RR, 1946, $1,000, issued and canceled, two engraved angels and company logo **15.00**

West Shore Railroad, $10,000 First Mortgage Bond, 1948..................... **20.00**

Stocks

Alpha Portland Cement Co., NJ, common, allegorical maids Industry and Agriculture with Alpha Seal in center, ornate orange-red border, punch canceled, hand stamped "Cancelled," American Bank Note Co. **15.00**

Baldwin Co., Ohio, 1919, orange, common, odd shares, no vignette, fancy border, punch cancel **8.00**

Buffalo Niagara & Eastern Power Co., NY, 1926, common, less than 100 shares, blue and black, vignette at top of Niagara Falls, 2nd vignette of workman with oil

can standing beside giant turbine, issued, punch, cancelled, American Bank Note Co. **18.00**

Butte Carriage Works, Butte, Montana, black, wavy gold sunray, gold seal, vignette top center of allegorical male riding winged Wheel of Progress, common, odd shares, GOES......... **20.00**

Chico Gold & Silver Mining Co., 1867, sgd by company president John Bidwell
.... **310.00**

Custer Channel Wing Corp, MD, 1969, common, less than 100 shares, green, vignette top of aircraft with unusual wing design, issued, perforation cancel, Security-Columbian Bank Note Co. **25.00**

Deer Lodge Investment Company, Deer Lodge, MT, common, unissued, black, violet border, violet seal, low issue number, vignette of elk, shares $10 each, GOES **12.00**

Durant Motors, Inc., DE, issued, thirty-sixteenth of one share, capital stock, no vignette, green border, American Bank Note Co.. **70.00**

Engineers Petroleum Co., DE, 1921, 100 shares, eagle on rock vignette, orange green border design, Security Bank Note Co., Phila.. **18.00**

Essex County Building & Loan Assoc, Bloomfield, NJ, 1909-13, common, issued, black, fancy arched title above vignette of Victorian era two-story home, cancelled, M. Plum, Newark, NJ, flaws
.... **5.00**

General Foods, issued and canceled, green, brown, or orange, engraved, vignette scene on right.................... **2.50**

Great Atlantic & Pacific Tea Company, MD, common, less than 100 shares, angels touching hands over company logo, ornate company border, 1925 corporate seal, American Bank Note Co........ **10.00**

Great Divide Oil Co., Colorado, 1930s, oil field, gushers, train, and buildings, common, odd shares, green, unissued
.... **8.50**

Helena National Bank of Helena, Montana, common, odd shares, issued, fancy script, gold seal lower left, red hand-written cancel, fold lines................ **18.00**

Isabella, Gold Mining Co., Colorado, 1890s, issued and canceled, engraved, eagle vignette **8.00**

Jantzen Knitting Mills, 1930s, issued and canceled, engraved, swimmer vignette, orange or green............................. **20.00**

Kaiser-Frazer Corp, brown, mid-1940s, common, 100 shares, vignette of auto in center, issued and cancelled, Security Banknote Co. **24.00**

Laclede Gas Light Co., MO, 1890s, rust, preferred, 100 shares, horse drawn wagon and pedestrians pass by Gas Light Works, issued, punch cancel, Franklin Back Note Co. **20.00**

Mt. Tamalpais Muir Woods Railway, H.S. Crocker Co., 1914, 7-3/8" x 10-1/2", **$195**.

Midland Grange No. 27 Co., Georgetown, DE, common, black, arched title over small circular vignette of State Arms, uncanceled, printed by C. P. Thomas & Co., Wilmington, DE, "Incorporated April 1885" printed on bottom, 7-1/2" x 9-1/2" **10.00**

Nelson Mining Co., Anaconda, MT, common, unissued, green and black, green sunray and seal, large vignette of five miners working underground, six smaller mining related vignettes, reverse in orange, GOES **15.00**

Pan American World Airways, Inc., NY, 1978, common, odd shares, aqua, large eagle with spread wings over twin world hemispheres, flanked by two allegorical men, issued, perforation cancel, American Bank Note Co**.** **10.00**

Pan Handle Consolidated Coal Co., Indiana, 1903, large eagle with flag vignette, gold rays, gold seal, green back with eagle and shield, punched "Cancelled," Bankers Supply Co, Chicago **15.00**

PRR common, 100 shares, Horseshoe Curve vignette, green and black, shows three long trains, printed by American Bank Note Co. **10.00**

Susa Corp, Co., 1972, corporate logo at top center, green border, corporate seal, Rocky Mt Bank Note Co. **7.50**

Tamarack & Custer Consolidated Mining Co., Wallace, Idaho, 1913, 100 shares, mining scene vignette, ornate brown border, hand stamped "Cancelled," Spokane Litho, 10" x 12" **35.00**

Tarentum Light & Heat Co., Tarentum, PA, c1880, common, unissued, fancy arched title, State Arms with two rearing black stallions just below arched title, uncanceled, Wm Mann Philadelphia, stud attached **10.00**

Universal Motors Co., Delaware, 1916, orange "Temporary Stock Certificate," issued, Common, ornate border, no vignette, uncanceled, emb company seal lower left corner, sgd by officers.... **10.00**

Vose Mining Co, Townsend, MT, c1890, common, odd shares, unissued, arched title, black, fancy gold border, green diamond shaped vignette of mining scene, very thin paper, 11-1/4" x 7-1/8" **20.00**

Washington Gas Light Co., Washington, DC, 1987, 19th C style vignette, company works at top center, men on horses, man with wheelbarrow, bystanders, and blacksmith, Washington Monument at right, American Bank Note Co. **15.00**

Washoe Mercantile Co, Deer Lodge, MT, c1890, common, odd shares, low issue number, unissued, black on green, top vignette of Christopher Columbus landing in new world, brown reverse with State Arms **15.00**

Western Union Mining Co., Wallace, ID, common, odd shares, unissued, black and gold seal, gold sunray, two small circular vignettes with miners flanking larger center vignette of mining scene, river, train, and mountains, green reverse, GOES **12.00**

Willys-Overland Motors, Inc., DE, 1946, full share subscription warrant, common, orange, no vignette, "Right to Subscribe" appears in upper right, issued and canceled, American Bank Note Co. **24.00**

Wisconsin Edison Company, NY, 100 shares, allegorical females seated with dynamo, gas lights, and street cards, ornate purple border with medallion for corporate seal, hand stamped "Cancelled," American Bank Note Co., folds and wrinkling........................ **20.00**

Yellowstone Boat Co., MT, c1910, common, odd shares, low issue number in red, unissued, green on white, sunray above title, two small US shields with allegorical figure in each upper corner, larger US shield bottom center, Pioneer **15.00**

Super Heroes

History: The super hero and comic books go hand in hand. Superman made his debut in 1939 in the first issue of *Action Comics,* six years after Jerry Siegel and Joe Shuster conceived the idea of a man who flew. A newspaper strip, radio show, and movies followed. The popularity of Superman spawned many other super heroes, among them Batman, Captain Marvel, Captain Midnight, The Green Hornet, The Green Lantern, The Shadow, and Wonder Woman.

These early heroes had extraordinary strength and/or cunning and lived normal lives as private citizens. A wealth of merchandising products surround these early super heroes. Their careers were enhanced further when television chose them as heroes for Saturday morning shows as well as for prime time broadcasts.

The Fantastic Four—Mr. Fantastic, The Human Torch, The Invisible Girl, and The Thing—introduced a new type of super hero, the mutant. Other famous personalities of this genre are Captain America, Spiderman, and The Hulk. Although these characters appear in comic form, the number of secondary items generated is small. Television has helped to promote a few of the characters, but the list of mutant super heroes is close to a hundred.

Collecting Hints: Concentrate your collection on a single super hero. Because Superman, Batman, and Wonder Woman are the most popular, new collectors are advised to focus on other characters or on one of the modern super heroes. Nostalgia is the principal motivation for many collectors; hence, they sometimes pay prices based on sentiment rather than true market value.

Comics are a fine collectible but require careful handling and storage. An attractive display requires inclusion of a three-dimensional object. Novice collectors are advised to concentrate on these first before acquiring too much of the flat paper material.

Additional Listings: Action Figures, Comic Books, Radio Characters and Personalities.

Aquaman

Action figure, MOC............................ **35.00**
Bathtub toy, Burger King Kids Meal
    premium... **12.00**
Comic book, DC, #4, August, 1962 ... **40.00**
Costume, Ben Cooper, 1967 .... **200.00**
Glass, 1973... **15.00**

Puzzle, Whitman, action scene, 1967 **40.00**
Tattoo, 1967, unused, orig wrapper... **50.00**

Batman, metal carrying case, oval, black plastic handle, **$10**.

Batman & Robin

Action figure, diecast, fully jointed, Mego,
    5-1/2" h, C-9, orig box **115.00**
Batcopter, Batman the Dark Knight, Kenner,
    1990, MIB....................................... **65.00**
Bank, plastic, full color, arms crossed **75.00**
Batmobile
    Animated.. **90.00**
    Radio controlled, Richman's Toys, 1989,
    some damage to remote **350.00**
Batmobile Gift Pack, batmobile and boat,
    Corgi, 1979, MOC **395.00**
Battery operated, Batwing, Blue-Box Toys,
    copyright 1989.............................. **40.00**
Binder, 10" x 12" vinyl colored cardboard,
    Standard Plastic Products Co., copyright
    1966 NPP **50.00**
Coloring book, 1963, used **20.00**
Cosmetics, Robin goes to a Weekend,
    Travel Time Cosmetics, Hasbro, 1960s,
    unused, MIB.................................... **65.00**
Costume, Switch & Go, orig box...... **150.00**
Desk set, calendar, stapler, and pencil
    sharpener, MIB **150.00**
Doll, Batman, 15" h, 1992, DC Comics **85.00**
Figure, McDonald's Happy Meal, never
    removed from plastic bag
    Batman, press and go car, © 1991 . **6.00**
    Ridler, © 1993 .... **5.00**
Halloween mask
    Batgirl, 1977, Ben Cooper, unworn, orig
    elastic.. **25.00**
    Batman, 1960s, tears on lower chin
    section.. **36.00**
Joker cycle, Batman the Dark Knight,
    Kenner, 1990, MIB **25.00**
License plate, Batmobile, 1966 .... **45.00**
Lunch box, Batman & Robin, C-8.75 **225.00**
Model, MPC Super Powers, Aurora.... **75.00**
Movie viewer, cassette, Galoob, 1984, MIB
    .... **20.00**

Night light, 4" x 5-1/2" blister card, 2-1/2" long hard plastic light, Cable Electric Products, Inc., copyright 1966 .... **75.00**

Pencils, 1-3/4" x 7-1/22" sealed pack, six Batman pencils, Eagle Pencil Co., copyright 1966 NPP **45.00**

PEZ dispenser, European, Dark Knight, TAS, MOC **20.00**

Plane, friction, plastic, MIB **65.00**

Puppet

    Hand, Robin, vinyl, Ideal, 1966 .... **185.00**

    Marionette, hard plastic, Hazelle, c1966

        Batman................................. **195.00**

        Robin.................................... **195.00**

Puzzle, Batman Returns, 1992, MIB ... **10.00**

Ring, sterling silver, batwing logo, DC Comics, MIB................................... **90.00**

Sneakers, 3-1/2" x 8-1/2" x 3" orig box, 8" l child's shoes, text on box in Japanese, copyright 1966, Manga-style art on box with Batman and Robin, shoes unworn **275.00**

Statue, WB Resin, Batgirl **100.00**

Watch, Fossil, MIB **60.00**

Original cartoon art, Batman and Robin, signed "Best Always, Bob Kane," inscribed "To My Friend, Harry Pollack, 1976," **$1,650**.

Bionic Woman

Bank, figural, wearing running suit, pile of rocks base **42.00**

Card set, 44 color cards, colorful wrapper with Jamie.. **40.00**

Doll, Kenner, 1977 .... **45.00**

Game, The Bionic Woman Board Game, Parker Bros. **35.00**

Model, Repair Kit, Jamie on operating table, computerized medical equipment, Oscar Goldman, snap together, 1976 .... **30.00**

Buck Rogers

Action figure, 12" h, Mego, NRFB **30.00**

Diecast, Buck Rogers Starfighter, Corgi, 4" x 5-1/4" blister card **20.00**

Press book, 10-3/4" x 17", Planet Outlaws, Universal, 1939, Buster Crabbe **75.00**

Rubber stamp kit, MIB..................... **35.00**

View Master set, Battle of the Mon, cartoon version, 1978, MISP....................... **24.00**

Captain Action

Doll, red shirt, fully dressed, complete accessories, orig box **225.00**

Outfit, cap, chains **95.00**

Captain America

Action figure, 12" h, Mego, MIB **125.00**

Boomerang, Ideal............................. **12.00**

Comic book, Marvel

    #27 .... **195.00**

    #217 .... **3.00**

    #264 .... **3.00**

Game, Captain America game, Milton Bradley, 1977 .... **30.00**

License plate, 2-1/4 x 4", metal, full color graphics, green background, © 1967 Marvel Comics Group, Louis Marx & Co, Japan **28.00**

Pop-on ring, pale green plastic base, top with diecut brown plastic head, charm loop on to, copyright symbol and "MC," c1966 .... **30.00**

Tricycle, worn **95.00**

Wrist watch, figural, digital, MIP **30.00**

Captain Marvel

Christmas card................................. **150.00**

Code wheel...................................... **350.00**

Figure, lead, British, set of Captain Marvel, Captain Marvel Jr., and Mary Marvel **275.00**

Magic flute, MOC............................. **125.00**

Membership kit, card, pin, letter, code sheet... **300.00**

Pencil clip... **75.00**

Pinback button, club......................... **100.00**

Power siren...................................... **250.00**

Shoulder patch, multicolored **150.00**

Slurpee cup, 7-11 .... **15.00**

Toy, Captain Marvel Buzz Bomber, Fawcett Publications, 1945 .... **22.00**

Transfer iron-ons, 4" x 9-1/2" red, white, and blue envelope, 20 original comic iron-ons **135.00**

Wrist watch, Mary Marvel, Shazam, wear **140.00**

Fantastic Four

Action figure, Mego, set of four figures, MOC.. **200.00**

Comic book, Marvel, #375 .... **4.00**

Figure, 5" h

    Human Torch...................................... **5.00**

    Thing.. **5.00**

Lunch box **50.00**

Puzzle, Marvel, 1970s...................... **120.00**

Green Hornet

Annual, British, hardbound, 1966, some ink marks **75.00**
Cutlery set, MOC **85.00**
Halloween costume, Ben Cooper, c1966, MIB.. **275.00**
Magic rub-of slate, Whitman, 1966.. **200.00**
Membership card.............................. **15.00**
Pennant, orange and green, felt, 28" l
.... **185.00**
Puzzle, frame tray, 1966, set of four.... **95.00**
Ring, seal/secret compartment......... **850.00**
Spoon... **20.00**
Trading card **8.00**

Incredible Hulk

Figure, jointed, flat, litho, 1978, MIP.... **27.50**
Lunch box, C-8.................................... **85.00**
Playing cards, MIB............................. **15.00**
Premium ring, white, expansion bands, metallic green raised image, 1960s **20.00**
Sunglasses, child's, 6" x 7" diecut head shape card, plastic sunglasses positioned over eyes, Nasta Industries, copyright 1978 .... **12.00**
Utility belt, Remco, 1978, MIB............ **45.00**

Spider-Man

Action figure

Dr. Octopus, Toy Biz, 10" h, MIB..... **50.00**
Spider-Man, 9-1/2 x 14-3/4", diecut card, Spider-Man on rope, red, blue, and black costume, Fly Away Action version sticker, Mego, © 1979 Marvel Comics, MOC
.... **90.00**
Doll, Energized Spider-Man, Mego, copter, trap, accessories........................... **165.00**
Game, Spider-Man Web Spinning Action Game, Ideal, 1979, factory sealed **130.00**
Halloween candy container, plastic, black and white eyes, AJ Renzy Corp, Leominster, MA, 1979 Marvel Comic copyright... **20.00**
Model kit, MPC, 1978.......................... **50.00**
Motorcycle, Super Moto, MIP **40.00**

Patch, iron-on, set of six different poses, Marvel **5.00**
Premium ring, red plastic, black and white face on to, mkd "Hong Kong," 1970s
.... **18.00**
Race-car, Ricochet, 1974 .... **85.00**
Sign, adv Spider-Man comic strip in Bee Comics, autographed by Stan Lee, 1977
.... **150.00**
Toy, Helicopter, NRMIB **95.00**
Wrist watch, figural, digital, MIP **35.00**

Super Heroes, DC Comics

Activity set, Prestofix, Tarco, 1977, MIB
.... **50.00**
Plaster set **25.00**

Comic book, *Super Team Family*, DC Giant Comics, $9.50.

Superman

Animation art, cel, Superman with three lava monsters, flying to left, matted and framed.. **300.00**
Birthday card, 5" x 6", Quality Art & Novelty Co., early 1940s, Superman Inc. copyright, for seventh year **125.00**
Cake topper, Wilton, set in orig box, 1979
.... **20.00**
Coloring book, Saalfield, 11" x 15", 1940, 52 pages, some colored **120.00**
Comic book, *Amazing World of Superman, Official Metropolis Edition*, 14" x 12", 1973, NPP **30.00**
Cookie jar, ceramic, brown telephone booth
.... **595.00**
Figure, rubber, flexible, Ben Cooper, 1978
.... **65.00**
Game, Superman Match Game, Ideal, 1978, MIB... **85.00**
Membership card, 1940.................... **24.00**

Movie viewer, cassette, Galoob, 1984, MIB
.... **20.00**

Newspaper ad, Krypto Ray Gun, 15" x 21-1/2" four page Sunday comics section dated Jan 12, 1941 .... **40.00**

Record player, child's, 1970s **40.00**

Ring

Logo, DC Comics, sterling silver .. **100.00**

Superman of America, silver, diamond, metal tin container, membership kit
.... **375.00**

Squirt gun **65.00**

Toy, roll-over tank, C9 .... **650.00**

Wallet, vinyl, 1966, unused **45.00**

Wonder Woman

Action figure, MOC **25.00**

Animation art, cel, Wonder Woman and Firestore, 3/4 poses, matted and framed
.... **50.00**

Bath sponge, unopened package **70.00**

Book and record set, 33-1/3 rpm, Peter Pan, 16 pg comic story, 1977, orig cardboard sleeve **20.00**

Cake pan set, Wilton, 16" h figural aluminum pan, orig plastic Wonder Woman face, MIB **40.00**

Card game, Superhero Color-A-Deck, 1977, MIP with colored pencils, unused .. **90.00**

Collector drinking glass, Pepsi **30.00**

Doll, Mego, Nubia, 1981, 8-1/2", MIB **200.00**

Greeting card, orig envelope, unused, risqué verse **16.50**

Light switch cover **15.00**

Lunch box, vinyl, C8-8.5 .... **95.00**

Pencil case, vinyl, C-9.5 .... **72.00**

Playing cards, MIB **15.00**

Puzzle, 130 pcs, 10-3/4" x 5-1/2" **15.00**

Set, mask, cloak, wrist band, lasso, MIB
.... **15.00**

Skates **20.00**

Sticker, 3-D, unused sheet **3.00**

Sunglasses **4.00**

T

Taylor, Smith and Taylor

History: W. L. Smith, John N. Taylor, W. L. Taylor, Homer J. Taylor, and Joseph G. Lee founded Taylor, Smith, and Taylor in Chester, West Virginia, in 1899. In 1903, the firm reorganized and the Taylors bought Lee's interest. In 1906, Smith bought out the Taylors. The firm remained in the family's control until it was purchased by Anchor Hocking in 1973. The tableware division closed in 1981.

Taylor, Smith, and Taylor started production with a nine-kiln pottery. Local clays were used initially; later only southern clays were used. Both earthenware and fine-china bodies were produced. Several underglaze print patterns, e.g., Dogwood and Spring Bouquet, were made. These prints, made from the copper engravings of ceramic artist J. Palin Thorley, were designed exclusively for the company.

During the 1930s and through the 1950s, competition in the dinnerware market was intense. Lu-Ray was designed to compete with Russel Wright's American Modern. Vistosa was Taylor, Smith, and Taylor's answer to Homer Laughlin's Fiesta.

Collecting Hints: Collector interest focuses primarily on the Lu-Ray line, introduced in 1938 and named after Virginia's Luray Caverns. The line actually utilized forms from the Empire and Laurel lines. Lu-Ray was made from the 1930s through the early 1950s in coordinating colors, which has encouraged collectors to mix and match sets.

Pieces from the Coral-Craft line are very similar in appearance to pink Lu-Ray. Do not confuse the two.

Vistosa, introduced in 1938, is another example of the California patio dinnerware movement that featured bright, solid-color pieces. Unfortunately, the number of forms was restricted. As a result, many collectors shy away from it.

Pebbleford, a plain colored ware with sandlike specks, can be found in gray, dark blue-green, light blue-green, light tan, and yellow. When in production, it was the company's third most popular line, but it is only moderately popular among today's collectors.

Taylor, Smith, and Taylor used several different backstamps and marks. Many contain the company name as well as the pattern and shape names. A dating system was used on some dinnerware lines until the 1950s. The three-number code identifies month, year, and crew number.

Autumn Harvest, Ever Yours
Butter dish, cov.............................. **30.00**
Casserole, cov, 10-3/8" x 7"........... **38.00**
Coffeepot, cov **30.00**
Vegetable bowl, cov........................ **40.00**
Vegetable bowl, open, round, 7-1/2" d
.... **38.00**
Autumn Leaves, coffeepot, Conversation
shape, 7" h...................................... **45.00**
Beverly, platter **12.00**
Bonnie, sugar, cov **30.00**
Boutonniere, Ever Yours
Gravy boat, with underplate........... **35.00**
Platter, 13-1/2" l, medium................ **35.00**
Break O' Day
Creamer, ivory, deep orange int., pecking
chicken dec **25.00**
Sugar, cov....................................... **30.00**
Vegetable bowl, round **30.00**
Cape Cod, breakfast set, rooster, horse and
carriage dec, toast plate, creamer, sugar,
salt and pepper shakers, pr.......... **35.00**
Chateau Buffet, skillet, cov, 10" d, aqua int.
.... **45.00**
Classic Heritage, sugar bowl, cov **35.00**
Corinthian, vegetable bowl, round, blue,
gray, and black snowflake dec, 9-1/2" d
.... **30.00**
Dawn Treasure, carafe, pink dogwood
flowers, turquoise leaves, gold colored
metal ring, wood handle................. **65.00**
Dianthus, nut set, 11-3/8" l x 4-1/16" w
master bowl, four 5-1/8" l x 1-7/8"
individual bowls **35.00**
Dwarf Pine, dinnerware set, service for
eight, Versatile shape **150.00**
Empire
Butter dish, cov.............................. **20.00**
Dinner plate, 10" d **12.00**
English Abbey
Cup and saucer.............................. **30.00**
Gravy boat and underplate........... **95.00**
Fairway
Casserole....................................... **20.00**
Dinner plate, 9-1/2" d...................... **8.50**

Indian Summer

Gravy boat, underplate, orig ladle . **45.00**
Platter, large...................................... **35.00**
Vegetable bowl, round, open **30.00**

Laurel

Cake plate, 10-1/4" d **12.00**
Creamer... **27.50**
Teapot, chain of leaves dec............ **32.00**
Lazy Daisy, platter, 13-5/8" x 11" **30.00**

Dinnerware set, #8401, yellow daisies, blue
forget-me-nots, green leaves, creamy
background, **$35**.

Lu-Ray

Berry bowl, Chatham Grey **14.00**
Bowl, c1936
    Persian Cream **60.00**
    Surf Green.............................. **60.00**
    Windsor Blue........................... **60.00**
Bread and butter plate, 6" d, Windsor
Blue... **6.00**
Breakfast plate, 9" d, Persian Cream
.... **17.50**
Bud vase
    Surf Green............................ **150.00**
    Windsor Blue......................... **135.00**
Butter dish, Persian Cream............. **35.00**
Casserole, cov
    Sharon Pink.......................... **150.00**
    Surf Green............................ **140.00**
    Windsor Blue......................... **140.00**
Creamer, Persian Cream................. **22.50**
Cup and saucer
    Sharon Pink........................... **22.50**
    Windsor Blue.......................... **22.50**
Demitasse creamer, Sharon Pink ... **50.00**
Dinner plate, 10" d
    Persian Cream **28.00**
    Sharon Pink........................... **20.00**
    Surf Green.............................. **20.00**
Eggcup
    Persian Cream **20.00**
    Surf Green.............................. **20.00**
    Windsor Blue........................... **20.00**
Fruit bowl, Persian Cream................. **8.00**
Juice pitcher, Windsor Blue **225.00**

Nappy, Sharon Pink........................ **15.00**
Pickle dish, Persian Cream **45.00**
Platter, 12" l, Surf Green................. **20.00**
Relish, four sections, Surf Green . **220.00**
Salad bowl, Sharon Pink **45.00**
Soup, flat, Windsor Blue................. **15.00**
Teapot, Sharon Pink........................ **50.00**
Tumbler, Windsor Blue.................... **98.00**
Marsh Violets, chop plate, Conversation
shape, 13" d.................................... **36.00**

Marvel

Cup and saucer................................ **6.00**
Salad bowl **17.50**
Modern Star, dinnerware set, service for 10,
Versatile shape **165.00**
Paramount, gravy boat..................... **12.50**
Pebbleford, dinner plate, 10" d **10.00**
Plymouth Petit Point, chop plate, lug
handles, 12-1/4" d........................... **22.00**
Ranchero, platter, large **32.00**
Rita, casserole, cov, 8-1/4" x 11"........ **40.00**
Scroll Border, sauceboat, attached
underplate, Laurel shape, ivory border,
1942 .... **30.00**

Sea Shell

Casserole, cov, 8" d........................ **50.00**
Platter, 13-1/2" l **30.00**
Shasta Daisy, gravy boat, 8" l **22.50**
Silhouette, vegetable bowl, cov......... **95.00**
Stagecoach, designed by J Palin Thorley,
1934-41, chop platter, round well, 11" x
11-3/4" **35.00**

Summer Rose

Casserole, cov, 10" d, three quarts **45.00**
Place setting, eight pcs.................. **42.00**

Vistosa

Bowl, 8" d, Cobalt Blue.................. **65.00**
Chop plate, 12" d, Light Green **85.00**
Creamer
    Cobalt Blue............................ **20.00**
    Light Green **20.00**
Cup and saucer
    Deep Yellow **15.00**
    Light Green **17.50**
Demitasse cup and saucer, Deep Yellow
.... **45.00**
Dinner plate, Cobalt Blue **20.00**
Eggcup, Cobalt Blue....................... **25.00**
Luncheon plate, 9" d, Light Green . **17.50**
Salad bowl, 12" d, ftd, Light Green
.... **195.00**
Sauceboat, Light Green.............. **145.00**
Sugar bowl, cov, Light Green or Mango
Red... **25.00**
Teapot
    Deep Yellow **85.00**
    Light Green **95.00**
    Mango Red.............................. **85.00**
Vegetable bowl, Cobalt Blue.......... **45.00**
Water pitcher, Mango Red **85.00**
Vogue, cup and saucer **6.50**

Wheat, starter set, four each berry bowls, cups and saucer, dinner plates, MIB
.... **95.00**

Wood Rose
Gravy boat and underplate **25.50**
Sugar bowl, cov, coupe shape, solid brass finial **22.50**

Teapots

History: The origin of the teapot has been traced back to the Chinese province of Yixing in the late 16th century. The teapots, similar to ones still being produced today, were no bigger than the tiny teacups used at that time.

By the 17th century, tea drinking had spread throughout the world. Every pottery or porcelain manufacturer from the Asia, Europe and America has at one time produced teapots. Forms range from the purely functional, such as the English Brown Betty, to the ornately decorative and whimsical, such as individual artist renditions or popular figurals depicting shapes of people, animals, or things. The majority of teapots available in today's market date from 1870 to the present.

Collecting Hints: Most collectors focus on pottery, porcelain or china examples. Much attention has been given recently to the unglazed pottery teapots referred to as Yixing. These teapots are small in size and feature earthy designs such as lotus flowers, handles of twig, and insects shaped on the body or lid finial. Yixing (traditionally Vis-Hsing or I Hsing) is a Chinese province that has been known for these artistic wares since the 16th century. Since they are still being produced, collectors need to learn to differentiate the antique from the modern.

Limited-edition teapots have become popular. As with any limited edition, make sure to get as much original documentation about the teapot as possible, including the original box, tag, information about the artist and company.

Reproduction Alert: New and modern Yixing teapots mimicking the vintage pots. This category requires extra study. Watch for teapots and other porcelain with a celadon color and cobalt design

similar to flow blue. These reproduction teapots often have a blurred mark, including a lion, unicorn and shield, which is similar to many pottery marks from England.

China, individual size, dark brown, orange and white dot decoration, gold trim, unmarked, $15.

Brass
Gooseneck spout, dents **125.00**

Ceramic, pottery or porcelain
Belleek, Shamrock dec, 2nd black mark
.... **295.00**
Fraunfleter, ribbed body, marked "Ohio" in diamond **32.00**
Harker, Royal Gadroon pattern, floral. **25.00**
Mammy, 4-1/4" h, mkd "Made in Japan," c1940 .... **195.00**
Mulberry China, Washington's Vase, mismatched lid **195.00**
Rockingham Glaze, sterling silver appliqué design **145.00**
Royal Winton, Chintz **195.00**
Staffordshire, coralene raised decoration, black ground, lion and Staffordshire knot mark, made as fund raiser for wartime efforts, c1948 .... **40.00**
Torquay, motto ware, small, Watcombe, England **65.00**
Vernon Kilns, Linda, mkd on bottom **125.00**
Villeroy & Boch, Rusticana, red transferware, 9" h, 9" w **148.00**
Wade, Scottie, 51/2" h, 8" w handle to spout
.... **300.00**
Wedgwood, deep green, 4-3/4" h, 8" w handle to spout **400.00**

Chinese
Brass, hammered design, matching warming stand, mkd "China" **85.00**
China, white, large eight-cup teapot, rattan handle, no mark **18.00**
Floral, tiny spout, unmarked **25.00**
Set, teapot and two cups, in padded basket, mkd "China" **125.00**

Figural

Captain Pooh, Cardew Design, limited edition, large size, 40 oz
.... 175.00
Colonial man and woman, Tony Wood, England **40.00**
Dickens characters, Beswick, England
.... **75.00**
Dog holding newspaper, upright, mkd "Sunshine Ceramics," 1987, England, 9-1/2" h **150.00**
Gardener's bench, Cardew Design, limited edition, large size, 40 oz **220.00**
House, Cottage Ware, Price, Kensington, England **32.00**
Jim Bean Club, collector's edition, Wade, 1995 .... **50.00**
Santa, white glaze, Price Bros, England, 1960s **30.00**
Sewing machine, Cardew Design, limited edition, large size, 40 oz **220.00**

China, white, red flowers, green leaves, marked "Germany," wear to gold trim, **$25**.

Sherlock Holmes, Hall China, 1988, 12" h
.... **125.00**
Snow White, dwarves around base, holds 1-1/2 cups, music box base plays "Hi Ho, Hi Ho," c1940, 6" h **130.00**
Top-U-Up, figural gas pump, England, 10-1/2" h **150.00**
Ye Daintee Ladyee, 7-1/2" w, 7-1/2" h, peach-colored glaze, figural lady in crinoline, name inscribed underglaze on bottom, English 1937 registry mark
.... **150.00**

Miniature

Aluminum, Swans Brand, two cups, England, 4" h **15.00**
China
   Hand painted, dragonflies, Chinese mark, 2-1/2" h **12.00**
   Peking Duck, teapot on stand, 2" h **18.00**
Copper, mkd "Italy," 1-3/4" h **10.00**

Porcelain

   Children playing dec, no mark, attributed to Germany, 4" h **25.00**
   Floral, lid screws on, Germany, 3" h **25.00**
   Relief flowers, white porcelain, England, 2" h **15.00**
   Precious Moments, Taiwan, 1992, 2" h
   .... **12.00**
   Thimble, pewter mouse peaks out of teapot, 1" h **10.00**
Pewter
   5-3/4" h, 10" w handle to spout, mkd "M209" with diamond shape **145.00**
   6" h, 10" w handle to spout, Richard Franklin & Sons, Sheffield **175.00**

Television Personalities and Memorabilia

History: The late 1940s and early 1950s was the golden age of television. The first TV programming began in 1948. Experimentation with programming, vast expansion, and rapid growth marked the period. Prime-time live drama series were very successful, and provided the start for many popular stars, such as Paul Newman, Steve McQueen, Rod Steiger, Jack Lemmon, and Grace Kelly. The stars signed autographs and photographs to promote the dramas. These items, plus scripts and other types of articles, have become very collectible.

When the period of live drama ended, the Western assault began. In 1959, there were 26 Western series, many of which were based on movie or radio heroes. The Western era continued until the early 1960s when it was replaced by the space adventure series and science fiction.

The 1970s are remembered for their situation comedies, including "All In The Family" and "M*A*S*H*." The collectibles resulting from these series are numerous.

Collecting Hints: Collectors of television memorabilia fall into two categories. One includes those who specialize in acquiring items from a single television series. "Star Trek," "Hopalong Cassidy," "Howdy Doody," "Roy Rogers," or "Leave It To Beaver" are the most popular series. The other category of collector specializes in TV memorabilia of one type such as *TV Guides*, model kits, films, or cards.

There have been more than 3,750 series on television since 1948. Therefore, an enormous number of artifacts and memorabilia relating to television are available. Premiums from the early space shows and cowboy adventure series are eagerly sought by pop-culture collectors. As a result, these items are beginning to command high prices at auction.

Systematic scheduling of television programs developed a new type of publication called *TV Guide*. The early guides are avidly sought. The first schedules were regional and include titles such as *TV Today in Philadelphia*, *TV Press in Louisville*, and *Radio-Television Life in Los Angeles*. The first national *TV Guide* was published on April 3, 1953. Collectors enjoy these older magazines because they are good sources for early stories about the stars of the time.

Additional Listings: Cowboy Heroes, Space Adventurers & Explorers, Super Heroes, Western Americana.

Action figure

Father McHalhee, priest, M*A*S*H*, 3-3/4" h, 1981 .... **5.00**

Poncho, CHIPS, Mego, 8" h, MOC . **25.00**

Second Banana, Warner Bros, Dankin, 6" h **24.00**

Advertising flyer, *Six Gun Territory Between Ocala and Silver Springs Florida,* black and white photo of Darby Hinton who played Israel Boone on Daniel Boone TV series, announces his appearance at Six Gun over Easter weekend in mid-1960s, other attractions on back **7.50**

Alarm clock, Mr. T., A-Team, metal, blue, silvered metal bells, Zeon, © 1973 Ruby-Spears Enterprises.......................... **27.50**

Autograph, Morey Amsterdam, letter, hand written, 8-1/2" x 11" sheet of personal stationery, portrait in black at top, 1956 .... **35.00**

Bobbing head, Dr. Kildare, 6-1/2" h, painted composition, MGM copyright sticker, 1960s **125.00**

Book cover, *Welcome Back Kotter,* Horshak, rolled, 1976, unused **8.50**

Comic book, *The Beverly Hillbillies*, Dell, July-September, **$4.50**.

Book

Dragnet, Richard Deming, Whitman Auth TV edition, 1970.............................. **10.00**
Ironsdies, The Picture Frame Frame-up, William Johnston, Whitman Auth TV edition, 1969 .... **8.00**
Voyage to the Bottom of the Sea, Raymond Jones, Whitman Auth TV edition, 1965 .... **15.00**
Cereal box, Rice Krispies, Howdy Doody **150.00**
Coloring book, Green Acres, Whitman, © 1967, few pages neatly colored..... **20.00**
Cookie jar, Howdy Doody, Purinton Pottery, 9-3/4" h **900.00**

Doll

Bart Simpson **35.00**
Happy Days, Fonzie, Mego, 8" h, 1976, MOC... **150.00**
Happy Days, Potsy or Ralph, Mego, 8" h, 1976, MOC....................................... **75.00**
Happy Days, Ritchie, Mego, 8" h, 1976, MOC... **100.00**
I Dream of Jeannie, Remco, poseable, 1977, MIB...................................... **125.00**
John Wayne, 1981, MIB **185.00**
Jughead, Mattel, 7" h, 1977 .... **50.00**
Ricky Jr., 1950s............................ **275.00**
Finger puppet, Shari Lewis, set of four, Quaker Oats cereal premiums....... **20.00**

Doll, Urkle, Family Matters, NRFB, **$20**.

Fire helmet, child's, Emergency, color photo on front with show stars **50.00**

Game

I Dream of Jeannie, Milton Bradley, 1965
.... **50.00**
Knight Rider, 1983........................... **65.00**
Kukla, Fran & Ollie........................... **27.50**
Leverne and Shirley **27.00**
Perry Mason, Missing Suspect, 1959
.... **42.00**
The Gomer Pyle Game, Transogram
.... **120.00**
The New Zoo Revue Game, Kontrell Industries, © 1973.......................... **25.00**
Guitar, Shaun Cassidy As Joe Hardy, Hardy Boys, 12" x 23" cardboard display card, shrink wrap sealed 29-1/2" l hard plastic guitar, Carnival Toys, © 1978.......... **40.00**

Halloween costume

Alf.. **10.00**
Banana Splits **85.00**
Big Bird... **5.00**
Captain Kangaroo........................... **85.00**
Dukes of Hazzard, Bo, 1982........... **40.00**
Howdy Doody................................. **125.00**
I Dream of Jeannie, 1960s............. **125.00**

I Love Lucy **300.00**
Little House on the Prairie, Laura... **10.00**
Miss Piggy **12.00**
Mr. Ed **110.00**
Six Million Dollar Man, Ben Cooper, 1974, C-9... **40.00**
Thunderbirds **325.00**
Zorro, Ben Cooper, 1981, MIB **75.00**
Hat, Robin Hood, suede-like green cloth, brown brim.................................. **35.00**
Hat box, Buffy, Family Affair, 10" d, pink plastic, 1969 .... **48.00**
Kite, Knight Rider, 1982 .... **28.50**

Lunch box, Muppets, metal, wear, **$5**.

Lunch box

Bonzana, brown, C-8.................... **180.00**
Fall Guy, box and thermos, C7 ...... **40.00**
Family Affair, King-Seeley, © 1969, no thermos **95.00**
Happy Days, orig thermos............. **85.00**
Land of the Giants, C-8.5 .... **250.00**
Super Friends, box and thermos, C-7
.... **80.00**
Thundercats, box and thermos, C-9
.... **90.00**
Wagon Train, King Seeley, © 1964, no thermos **160.00**
Welcome Back Kotter, C-8 .... **90.00**
Magazine, *TV Fan,* Vol. 1, #1, June 1953, 20th Century Books, 76 pgs **20.00**
Newspaper ad, Sky King, Name-A-Plane Contest, 1950s.............................. **25.00**
Night light

Church Lady, Saturday Night Live, 1991
.... **30.00**
Howdy Doody, figural, Leadworks, Inc., 1988, 8" h **150.00**
Paint by Number, Dukes of Hazzard, acrylic, MIB **50.00**
Paint set, Winky Dink, 1950s, 12" x 18" x 2" box, slight use................................. **70.00**
Paperback, *Man from UNCLE*, #2, Ace **6.50**
Paper dolls

New Zoo Revue, Saalfield, © 1974, orig box, mint **25.00**

Welcome Back Kotter, © 1976 Wolper Organization, Toy Factory, diecut figure, orig box **50.00**
Party hat, A-Team, mint in orig bag **5.00**
Pinback button, 3-1/2" d, Ben Casey, black and white photo of Vince Edwards, 1960s **20.00**

Limited-edition plate, Star Trek, Commander Kirk, original box, **$15.**

Poster, Partridge Family, unopened pack **30.00**
Postcard, The Rebel, Johnny Yuma, fan club **40.00**
Puppet, Rootie Kazootie, 8-1/2" h, fabric and soft vinyl **20.00**
Puzzle
  Beany & Cecil, frame tray, c1960 ... **95.00**
  Charlie's Angels, Farrah, sealed, orig box **25.00**
  Chicken Charlie, Jaymar, boxed **90.00**
  Dukes of Hazzard, boxed, Canadian **25.00**
  Flipper, frame tray, 1965 .... **20.00**
  Gumby, frame tray.......................... **20.00**
  Six Million Dollar Man, British.......... **50.00**
  Super Six, Whitman, 1959, boxed.. **27.00**
  Zorro, Whitman No, 4417, 1957, frame tray **40.00**
Record
  Checkmate, 12-1/4" sq, Columbia label for CBS **20.00**
  Merry Christmas From Kukla, Fran and Ollie, 12-1/4" sq, 33-1/3 rpm Decca record, 1950s **48.00**
  Rawhide, Clint Eastwood, Cameo #C-1056, autographed **245.00**
Sheet music, theme song, Neil Diamond, c1972... **10.00**
Sneakers, Howdy Doody **250.00**
Slippers, Howdy Doody **40.00**
Souvenir book, Neil Diamond, 1972.. **10.00**
Sweatshirt, child's, Pee Wee Herman, Penny... **75.00**

Store display featuring Philco televisions, featured at March 2004 Atlantiques City Antiques Show.

Star Trek Barbie & Ken, NRFB, **$80**.

Toy
  A-Team Great Escape Stunt Set, motorized van, Lin, 1983, played with condition **30.00**
  Howdy Doody Power Tools, MIB ... **20.00**
  Knight Rider, K.I.T.T. dashboard, MIB **175.00**
  Yogi, squeeze toy **35.00**
TV repair shop sign, 11-3/4" x 15-3/4", cardboard, black, white, and red image of Jackie Gleason, text: "Get Our Special TV-Tune-Up/Get Star Performance," 1950s **115.00**
View master reel
  Fantastic Voyage **75.00**
  Flying Nun, three reel set **20.00**
  Six Million Dollar Man, talking, 1970s, MISB.. **10.00**

Walkie talkie, Six Million Dollar Man Porta Communicator Set, Kenner, 1975, unused **48.00**

Wallet, Howdy Doody **40.00**

Wrist watch, Dukes of Hazzard, Unisonic, 1981, orig case, unused **25.00**

Writing tablet, Hogan's Heroes **35.00**

Tobaccoania

History: Collectors have coined a new term for the collecting of tobacco-related items. These items can be things related to the tobacco industry from its beginnings and items that developed as smoking and its accruements became part of the fabric of every day life.

Although the tobacco industry dates back to the late 19th century, it was during the decades of the 1930s and 1940s that cigarettes became the primary tobacco product. The cigarette industry launched massive radio advertising and promotional campaigns. In the 1950s, television became the dominant advertising medium.

The Surgeon General's Report, which warned of the danger of cigarette smoking, led to restrictions on advertising and limited the places where cigarettes could be smoked. The industry reacted with a new advertising approach aimed at 20- to 40-year olds and at females. Recent government regulations and changes in public opinion towards smoking in general have altered the style and quantity of tobacco-related collectibles.

Collecting Hints: Don't overlook advertising that appeared in the national magazines from the 1940s to 1960s. Many stars and public heroes endorsed cigarettes and tobacco products. Modern promotional material for brands such as Marlboro and Salem has been issued in large quantities, and collectors have put much aside. Most collectors tend to concentrate on the pre-1950 period.

Lamp, National Cigar Stand, red and white stained glass top, long white beaded fringe, black trim, **$475**.

Ashtray, *Pittsburgh Bicentennial 1958-59,* white glass, center litho of Skyline, Golden Triangle, Liberty Bridge, Airport, 5" d **7.50**

Banner, 12" h, 9-1/2" w, Seminola 5¢ Cigar, painted velvet, Indian princess in center **350.00**

Book, *Lorillard and Tobacco 200th Anniversary,* 7-1/2" x 10-1/2", 61 pgs, 1960 .... **20.00**

Catalog, Ferguson Bros Mfg Co., Hoboken, NJ, 1911, 36 pgs, 7-1/2" x 10-1/2", Cat No. 10, humidors, combination cigar and cigarette cabinets, poker sets, game chests, etc....................................... **24.00**

Cigar box

Chancellor, wood and litho paper, blue and gold labels, c1900-20, 5" x 8" ... **4.00**

Kenwood Club, wood and litho paper, full color, c1900-20, 5" x 8" **5.00**

Little Chancellor, wood and litho paper, blue and gold labels, c1900-20, 5" x 8" **4.00**

Little Tom, wood and litho paper, inside with full color graphic of man dressed in turn-of-century frock, wear, 2" x 5" x 8" **10.00**

Seal of Minneapolis/Lafayette, wood and litho paper, full color, c1900-20, 5" x 8" **5.00**

Cigar label, inner lid type, unused

Abe Martin, three views of famous cartoon character, scenes of Martin's farm **2.00**

Banker's Bouquet, colorful lettering on lace-like border **2.00**

Big Five, bright fancy lettering and designs **2.00**

Calsetta, redhead in green bodice, gilt coins **3.00**

Canadian Club, fall colored maple leaf, orange, gold background **2.00**

Cranes Imported, gilt frame on inn sign **2.00**

Dolly Madison, brunette in red gown, 4-3/4" x 6-3/8" **3.50**

El Producto, senorita in red dress, playing lyre, on patio with peacock, sea vista, 6-1/4" x 4-7/8" **2.00**

Engagement, man seated at oak desk with candlestick phone, gazing at fiancé in cameo **5.00**

Five Grand, fancy monogrammed design **1.50**

Flor Fina, fancy leaf and floral garlands **1.00**

General Wm J. Palmer, portrait of General flanked by Antlers Hotel & Colorado RR train scene **6.00**

Have Crook, fancy bold gilt beaded letters **2.00**

Judge Ross, judge, gilt coins **3.00**

La Credencia, six fancy gilt coins, colorful ribbons **2.00**

La Flor De Victor, city cigar factory, gilt statute, people, gilt dolphins **6.00**

Mark Twain, portrait of Twain, boy fishing, boy carrying bucket **6.00**

Montebello, fancy colorful shield, gilt coins, crowns, and leaves **2.00**

Old Well, stone well **2.00**

Prime Minister, bold letters, gilt crown and leaves **1.50**

Radford, word diagonally, gilt leaves **1.50**

Red Tips, horses head in horseshoe, white ground **1.00**

Sea Robin, fishing catch on grass, rod, flask, wicker creel **7.00**

Tavern, red lion on gilt shield, Tudor style tavern **2.50**

White Cat, fluffy white cat lying on cigar **3.00**

Cigar cutter, figural

Boar's tusk **245.00**

Pelican, cast iron **75.00**

Cigarette card, American

Allen & Ginter, Pirates of the Spanish Main, 1888 .... **15.00**

Kinney Tobacco Co, military and naval uniforms, 1887 .... **5.00**

Wing Cigarettes, first series of fifty . **50.00**

Cigarette card album

Allen & Ginter, Napoleon **60.00**

W Duck & Sons, Terrors of America **65.00**

Cigar holder

Amber, solid gold band **65.00**

Tortoiseshell **10.00**

Tin, Rainbow Cut Plug Tobacco, Smoke-Chew, Frishmuth Bro & Co, Philadelphia, green, gold lettering, **$55**.

Cigarette holder, 4" l, 2-3/4" base, bellhop, ceramic, orange painted hat, hair, suit, and base, black highlighted eyes and hair, red mouth, eight vertical cylinders to hold cigarettes upright, German, 1930s **24.00**

Cigarette case

2-1/2" x 3", tan leather and cardboard, Fatima, veiled lady in gold, "Ninth Annual Convention/A.A.C. of A./Baltimore, June 1913" on reverse **35.00**

3" x 4", enameled, woman's, black, envelope style, red stone dec **35.00**

Cigar piercer, 3" l, silvered brass, celluloid wrapper band inscribed "Westchester County Bar Association, Annual Dinner, 1995," sharp metal point **60.00**

Cigarette tin

Elmas Gold Tips, 50 Cigarettes, 1" x 3" x 5-3/4", black, white, red, and gold, multicolored graphic of Egyptian lady and symbols, hinged lid with sphinx logo **35.00**

Murad The Turkish Cigarette, 3/4" x 4-1/4" x 5-1/2", multicolored hinged lid with Cleopatra style lady lounging among symbols of Egyptian style looking dogs, red text "Sanagyros Calital Stock Owned by P Lorillard Co.," ends printed "50 Murad 50 Turish Cigarettes," tax stamp, 1930s **40.00**

Cigar tin

Cinco Handy Humidor, 4-1/2" x 5", hinged, wire handle, hook latch, red and black lettering, two full-color oval panels on either side, simulated wood, full-color 4-1/4" x 4-1/2" paper label on inside with same graphics of well dressed man on left, lady in bonnet and apron on right, ostrich in middle, top reads "Cinco Otto Eisenlohr & Bros, Incorporated, Manufactuers, Philadelphia," 1920s **45.00**

Oricico, 4-1/2" x 6", multicolored images of Indian, bow, arrow, peach pipe, horses, buffalo, teepees, sunrise, side panel reads "Orrison Cigar Co., Inc., Manufacturers, Bethseda, Ohio," interior of hinged lid cream with black text "Oricico 2 for 5¢, Cigar, Quality Guaranteed, Superior Workmanship," 1919.. **115.00**
Phillies Only 5¢, 3-1/4" x 3-1/4" x 5", red, white, blue, black, and gold, same graphic and text "Phillies For Years America's Largest Selling 10¢ Brand, Only 5¢," lid text "Vayuk's Guarantee," c1940... **25.00**
White Owl Squires, yellow, red, black, white, and tan, removable top reads "Milder White Oil Squires," owl perched on cigar logo on four panels, text "That Wonderful 10¢ Cigar With New HTL Makes The Big Difference, Blended With Havana," 4-1/2" x 6", c1950 .... **25.00**
Yocum Brothers-Y-B Quailty, 3-1/2" x 5", red, yellow, gold, black, blue, and beige, color portraits of Y-B on simulated wood, hinged lid, side panels read "Pocket Size, Dollar Pack, Mild, Mfg by Yocum Brothers, Reading, PA," c1920....... **30.00**
Lighter, Zippo, engraved "Otto Cream Thru Milk Oscar Otto," orig box with red and white striped lid........................ **15.00**

Clock, Vantage Cigarettes, battery operated **40.00**

Dexterity puzzle, Camel Lights, clear styrene plastic key chain case, miniature replica of cigarette pack, small square opening in top to capture nine miniature filter tip cigarettes in filter ends up, c1980 .... **25.00**

Dish, 7-1/8" d, all over multicolored cigar bands, diecut beautiful woman in center, green felt back **35.00**

Display sign, 7" x 8", molded hard plastic, Ronson Table Lighters, full-color photo of lighter being used over cocktails by young couple, raised image of cigarette, easel back, c1950........................... **18.00**

Humidor, silver-plated, bottle shaped, holds matches, cigars, cutter **400.00**

Tin, Chancellor, Humidor Packed, Liberty Size, 10 cigars, 4-1/2" x 2-3/4", slight wear, **$25**.

Lighter
ASR, Ascot hidden watch, swivels **85.00**
Beatti Jet, pipe lighter, chrome **35.00**
Canon Camera, Zippo................... **45.00**
Consolidated Amusement Co........ **12.00**
Corona, gun shape, chrome, black **35.00**
Counter type, cast iron, bulldog-shape, 4-1/2" h **90.00**
Crestline, musical, Colonel Reb & Confederate flag............................ **50.00**
Dunhill, with ruler **70.00**
Dupont, 1950s, silver plated, slight wear **50.00**
Dupont, 1960s, gold plated butane **175.00**
Flaminaire, Limoges, cobalt blue and gold, table model, 3-1/2" h **30.00**
Jet 200, torpedo shape, black plastic and aluminum, MIB............................... **15.00**
MEB, Austrian, pull part, patent April 2, 1912 .... **22.00**
Playboy, brass, engraved bunny, MIB **30.00**
Rexxy, chrome, 1930s, four-hinge mechanism, Swiss........................ **37.00**
Rite Point, pocket clip, pen shape... **9.50**
Ronson, Standard, England, hallmarked sterling silver, picture of Queen...... **85.00**
Stankyo, musical, brass, large....... **45.00**
Zippo
1959, Boston, ME RR, MIB...... **42.50**
1966, pin-up girl in collector's tin **30.00**
1968, slim submarine, Tullibee, SSN **35.00**

Matchbook holder, blued metal, c1920
1-1/8" x 1-5/8", Muriel Cigars, celluloid insert, woman in multicolored portrait, small gold frame, dark red ground **65.00**
1-1/2 x 2-1/4", 1-1/2" oval celluloid, multicolored insert inscribed "For Gentlemen Of Good Taste," well dressed gentleman seated in wicker chair, smoking cigar **75.00**

Match safe/cigar cutter, 1-3/8" x 2-3/8" x 5", brass, one side with hinged lid to hold matches, other side with raised match striker, pull-out metal slide cutter, 1920s **40.00**

Medallion, 1-1/4" d, Tobacco Merchants Association of the US, brass, wreath design surrounding diamond-shaped raised center, blue and white enamel, brass lettering, 1920s.................... **15.00**

Notepad, 2" x 3", Hemmeter Cigar Co, floral and cigar design on cover, calendar, unused **25.00**

Pinback button
1" d, Recruit Little Cigars, military cadet, red ground, white letters "Join The Army of Recruit Little Cigar Smokers," short product slogan on back paper, early 1900s **40.00**

1-1/4" d, Napoleon All Tobacco, full color portrait of lady with shades of cream and gray shading to brown at outer edge, orig back paper **24.00**
1-1/4" d, *Smoke Maine Cigar,* multicolored, Spanish-American war battleship on ocean waters, cigar text, 1898 W&H copyright on curl, orig back paper **48.00**

Tin, Zippo Lighters, black and white illustration, founder Blandell and Zippo Guarantee in center, $15.

Pipe rack, wood
5-1/2" l, 7" h, holds three pipes, star design at top of raised pillar, shelf for pipe tips **8.00**
8" l, 6-1/2" h, crescent shape, holds six pipes, felt bottom **10.00**
11-1/8" l, 5-1/4" h, solid walnut, holds six pipes, two pillars at each end hold top shelf, 1950s **10.00**
15" l, 10" h, wall mounted, holds six pipes, two shelves...................................... **12.00**

Pocket mirror
2" d, Mascot Crushed Cut Tobacco, multicolored, small dog in center, blue and tan shaded ground surrounded by narrow green circle, bright red rim, tiny center text "5¢ In Pouch, In Tins It Would Cost You Double-For Pipe And Cigarette" **65.00**
2-1/8" d, Union Made Cigars, celluloid, detailed union label, light blue, black lettering, c1900............................... **65.00**

Poster, 14" x 10", Smoke 54 In Your Pipe-No Flavoring Better Taste, smoking man, yellow and brown on white **15.00**

Radio, figural
Chester Cheetah, MIB **35.00**
Marlboro Cigarette Pack................ **45.00**

Sign
10" h, 13-1/2" w, Imperial Club Cigars, emb self-framed tin, full box of cigars, Sentenne & Green litho................. **150.00**
12" h, 10" w, Roi-Tan Cigars, self framed tin over cardboard, oval, raised frame, couple looking at each other as lady lights his fire, c1910 .... **650.00**

Sign, Fatima, A Sensible Cigarette, tin litho, multicolored pack of cigarettes, green background, 12" x 8-1/2", $165.

12" x 18", high gloss paper, model in negligee, glamour pose, Brown & Williamson Co., c1940s, two archival tape repairs on back............................... **65.00**
14-1/2" d, Bill Dugan, cardboard, image of Dugan, framed **175.00**
17-1/2" h, 13-1/2" w, three-dimensional emb paper and cardboard, Seminola Cigars, cameo of Indian princess, framed **700.00**
19-1/2" h, 11" w, Mecca Cigarettes, paper, Art Deco lady with hat, Earl Christy artist, orig frame stenciled "Mecca Cigarettes" **275.00**
30-1/2" h, 20-1/2" w, Egyptienne Straights, paper, titled "Absolutely Pure," Mormon-type lady in bonnet over full pack, framed **200.00**
38" h, 24-1/2" w, El Principal Cigars, diecut cardboard, two full boxes of cigars, titled "The taste pleases - it really does" **60.00**

Silk
1" l, Wm Randolph Hearst for Governor **10.00**
3-3/4" l, Wm McKinley.................... **25.00**

Stamp case, book shape, Tom Moore Cigar, black and white portrait on front, red and gold spine and corners, black and white portrait for "Henry George Cigar" on back, spine lettered "Postage And Revenue Stamps/Court Plaster/Nick Nacks," early 1900s **60.00**

Stock certificate, United Cigar-Whelan Stores, 1945, 100 shares, vignette **15.00**

Stud
All Tobacco Cigarettes, red, white, and blue celluloid, metal lapel stud, inscribed "Morgan Marshall's Red White & Blue All Tobacco Cigarettes," 1896, some yellowing **25.00**
High Admiral Cigarettes, multicolored celluloid, metal lapel stud, young girl dancer, ethic outfit, inscribed "Smoke High Admiral Cigarettes And Dance For Joy," early 1900s............................ **40.00**

Tray lot, top: sign, red and white, Pig-Tail Crooks, handmade cigars, **$20**; bottom: left: Friends Smoking Tobacco, papers to roll cigarettes, **$15**; center: Harp Hand Cut Tobacco, cloth pouch, **$15**; right: assorted tobacco cards, **$1 each**; assorted tobacco related pinback buttons, **$10 each**.

Thermometer

Marlboro, Marlboro Man **40.00**
Winston Taste Good...Like a Cigarette Should, 9" d, round, metal **60.00**

Toys

History: The first cast iron toys began to appear in America shortly after the Civil War. Leading 19th-century manufacturers include Hubley, Dent, Kenton, and Schoenhut. In the first decades of the 20th century, Arcade, Buddy L, Marx, and Tootsie Toy joined these earlier firms. Wooden toys were made by George Brown and other manufacturers who did not sign or label their work.

Nuremberg, Germany, was the European center for the toy industry from the late 18th through the mid-20th centuries. Companies such as Lehman and Marklin produced high-quality toys.

Collecting Hints: Condition is a critical factor. Most collectors like to have examples in very fine to mint condition. The original box and any instruction sheets add to the value.

Sophisticated collectors concentrate on the tin and cast iron toys of the late 19th and early 20th centuries. However, more and more collectors are specializing in products made between 1940 and 1970, including those from firms such as Fisher-Price.

Many toys were characterizations of cartoon, radio, and television figures. A large number of collectible fields have some form of toy spin-off. The result is that the toy collector is constantly competing with the specialized collector.

Additional Listings: Battery Operated Automata, Cartoon Characters, Diecasts, Disneyana, Dolls, Games, Hot Wheels, NASCAR, Paper Dolls, Radio Characters, Dimestore Soldiers, Toy Soldiers, Toy Trains, and many other categories.

American Metal Specialties, doll accessories, bottle sterilizer, bottles, funnel, bottle brush, glass jar marked "Sterilized Nipples," original box with some damage, **$20**.

Acme Toys

Several toy companies used the name "Acme." These companies all had slight variations in their names, but some only marked their toys "Acme." The factories were located in Bridgeport, Chicago, Cleveland, Columbus, and Philadelphia.

Fire chief car, 4-1/4" l **45.00**
Police car, 4-1/4" l **45.00**

Alps

Alps Shoji Ltd, located in Tokyo, Japan, was founded in 1948. The company manufactured windup and battery-powered toys made from tin and plastic. Toys are marked "ALPS."

Butterfly, litho tin friction, 1950s, 4" l **100.00**
Chimpee The One Man Drummer, 1970s, orig box **45.00**
Donkey Clown, litho tin wind-up, orig box **75.00**

Juggling clown, tin litho, fabric outfit, orig box **435.00**

Merry Go-Round, windup, litho tin, four cars and celluloid balls rotate around base, child rider in each car, orig box, 10" l **265.00**

Mr Sudo the Sleepy Pup, wind-up, 9-1/2" h, orig box.. **155.00**

School bus, battery operated, doors open and close, flashing headlights, MIB **125.00**

Television car, 1950s, 6-1/4" l **125.00**

Andy Gard, Brink's Armored Car, battery operated, blue, yellow, white, and gray box, NRFB, **$65**.

Arcade

The Arcade Manufacturing Company first produced toys in 1891. In 1919, the firm began to make the yellow cabs for the Yellow Cab Company of Chicago. The exclusive advertising rights were sold to the cab company with Arcade holding the right to make toy replicas of the cabs. This idea was popular and soon was used with Buick, Ford, etc., and McCormack and International Harvester farm equipment. The company remained in business until 1946 when it was sold to Rockwell Manufacturing Company of Pittsburgh.

Allis-Chalmers tractor and dump trailer, #2657 .... **460.00**

Austin delivery truck, #173, 1932 ... **100.00**

Avery wrecker, #177X, 1932............. **225.00**

Car transport, #2977, 1937, two sedans and two trucks **850.00**

Caterpillar tractor, #266X, 1931....... **100.00**

Chevrolet couple, #1150X, 1936 ..... **200.00**

Chevrolet stake truck, #2610, 1936 **200.00**

Express truck, #209X, 1929 .... **500.00**

Fire ladder truck, mkd "Mack," worn old paint, mismatched accessories, 18" l **115.00**

Ford sedan, #1620X, 1933 .... **800.00**

Ice truck, #1933, 1941 .... **450.00**

Oliver plow, 1923............................. **500.00**

Auburn Toys

Car, yellow, rubber............................. **20.00**

Farm tractor, red, orig driver, 7" l........ **75.00**

Fire truck, red, rubber **25.00**

Pick-up truck, red, rubber................. **20.00**

Pistol, black vinyl, western-type........ **15.00**

Take-apart hot rod, 1960s, unplayed with, orig bag on header card **35.00**

Telephone repair truck, rubber......... **25.00**

Truck, rubber.................................... **22.00**

Colorforms, The Color Kittens, A Golden Book Game, original box with some damage, **$10**.

Bandai Co.

Bandai Co., one of the many toy manufacturers that began production in Japan after World War II, started with tin toys and later changed to plastic and steel. Bandai Toys have friction action or are battery operated. They are often marked "Bandai Toys, Japan." Bandai still produces toys and is a major Japanese exporter to the U.S. and other foreign countries.

Cessna airplane, plastic and tin, battery operated, 13" l, 10" fuselage, orig box **125.00**

Citreon D5-19, friction, tin, detailed litho tin int., "DS" on hubs, 8-1/4" l **120.00**

Family house trailer, 1950s, 12" l, 7" h **195.00**

Ford Taurus, 3" x 8" x 2" blue litho tin friction car, c1960, wear **18.00**

Isetta 700, litho tin friction, 1950s **185.00**

Jeep and Trailer, battery operated, 1970s, MIB.. **45.00**

MG Magnetta convertible................. **90.00**

Ocean boat, litho tin, crank handle, driver wearing goggles, orig box, 12" l... **165.00**
Rocket racer, 7" l **175.00**
Tumbling series, 1970s, MIB
    Fire Truck **40.00**
    Police Wagon **40.00**
    Train Engine.................................... **40.00**
Vespa Scooter, friction, tin, Vespa license plate, 9" l **275.00**
Volkswagen Beetle, friction, tin, plastic steering wheel and windshield, 6" l **125.00**

Buddy L

The Buddy L Company was founded in 1921 by Fred Lundahl. It produced high-quality, finely detailed toys. Many were large enough to ride on. Production changed from steel to lighter-weight, smaller toys in the 1930s. A limited number of wooden toys were made during World War II. The firm still operates today.

Airplane, orange wings, 2" d aluminum propeller, decals, c1930 .... **95.00**
Baggage truck.................................. **165.00**
Dairy transport truck, Duo-Tone slant design paint, red and white, opens in back, orig decal, 26" l **75.00**
Dump truck, winch, A-frame............ **500.00**
Fast freight truck, pressed steel, white cap, orange truck, black rubber tires, c1940, 20" l **150.00**
Flat tire wrecker, yellow **125.00**
Merry go round truck........................ **95.00**
Repair-it wrecker, 1957 .... **200.00**
Steam shovel, orig red and black paint, orig decals **150.00**
Texaco tanker, red, white letters........ **75.00**

Duraltone Toy Co., Inc., NY, two-tone green and pink polystyrene violin and bow, original box with red and blue graphics, c1960, 10" l, $18.

Chein

The Chein Company was in business from the 1930s through the 1950s. Most of its lithographed tin toys were sold in dimestores. Chein toys are clearly marked.

Alligator, windup, native on back..... **315.00**
Bear, litho tin wind-up, 1938, 4" h **65.00**
Clown, litho tin wind-up, black, white, red, yellow, and blue............................. **75.00**
Disney top, litho tin, Walt Disney Productions, c1950, 5-1/2" d........ **100.00**
Duck, litho tin wind-up, 1930, 4" h **45.00**
Ferris wheel, Hercules, 1930s **350.00**
Roller coaster, two repro works cars **495.00**
Sand pail, tin litho, Fish at the Sea, 8" d, 8" h **150.00**
Skin diver, red flippers, 12" l, MIB.... **365.00**
Three Little Pigs wringer washer, crank, litho tin tub, wood and tin ringer attachment, 1930s, 8" h................ **225.00**
Troop transport **450.00**
Truck, Hercules Motor Express, red and green, 1936, 15" l.......................... **575.00**
Windmill sand toy, litho tin................ **90.00**

Corgi

Playcraft Toys introduced Corgi miniature vehicles in 1956. This popular line soon became Corgi Toys. The first cars were made on a scale from 1:45 to 1:48. Corgi cars were the first miniature cars to have clear-plastic windows. Other design features included doors that opened and interiors. In 1972, the scale of 1:36 was introduced. This scale was more durable for play but less desirable to collectors. Finally, the company added other types of cars and trucks, including character representations.

Austin Cambridge Saloon, #201, MIB **100.00**
Buick Riviera, #245, MIB **100.00**
Bus, Burlington, Way of the Zepher, MIB **45.00**
Captain American jet mobile, #263, MIB **85.00**
Charlie's Angels van, MIB................ **75.00**
Chevrolet Caprice, #325, MIB **55.00**
Circus land rover and animal trailer, #30 MIB.. **220.00**
Citreon DS 19, #210S, MIB **70.00**
Construction set, #GS-24, MIB....... **250.00**
Corgi Motor School car, #238, MIB .. **90.00**
Dodge Kew Fargo Tipper, #483 .... **65.00**
Ford Consol Saloon, #200M, MIB .. **100.00**
Ford Cortina police car, #402, MIB... **15.00**
Ford T-Bird, #214, MIB........................ **70.00**

Ford tractor, #67, MIB......................... **80.00**
Hyster 800 Stratcatruck, #1113, MIB **75.00**
Jacguar XJ12C, #286 .... **200.00**
James Bond, Aston Martin D.B. **300.00**
Kennel Service Wagon, #486, MIB.... **75.00**
London Routemaster Bus, #468, MIB
.... **80.00**
Massey Ferguson 65 Tractor, #50, MIB
.... **135.00**
Mazda Camper, #415, MIB **40.00**
Mercedes Benz 220 SE coupe, #230 **75.00**
Monkee Mobile, #277, MIB............... **250.00**
Renault 16TS, #202, MIB.................... **50.00**
Rice's Pony trailer with pony, #102, MIB
.... **75.00**
Rover 90 Saloon, #204, MIB **100.00**
US Racing Buggy, #167, MIB **35.00**
Vegas T-Bird, #348, MIB.................... **85.00**
Yardley McLaren M19A, #151, fair..... **30.00**

Cragston, Japan

Buick, dashboard remote, all tin, 11-3/4" l,
C-9.5 toy, C-7.5 box **355.00**
Crap shooter, battery operated, vinyl face,
MIB... **150.00**
Jet transport, two fighter escorts, friction,
10" wingspan, orig box **385.00**
Pet shop truck, litho tin, friction, swivel bed
doors, black rubber tires, orig box, 11" l
.... **125.00**
Police chief car, battery operated, fires
caps, Chevrolet, 12" l, never used **545.00**
Shuttling freight train, train set with shuttle,
switcher, load and unload action, 8"
engine, near mint, C-8.5 box **145.00**
Star of the Circus Clown, litho tin, friction,
clown driving red and yellow car, 6-1/2" l
.... **190.00**

Elephant Push, litho tin wind-up, marked "Made
in China," NRFB, **$15**.

Dinky

Dinky Toys, made by the Meccano Toy
Company of England, were first created
by Frank Hornby in 1933. The Dinky
series of die-cast cars and trucks continued until World War II precluded the
use of metal for toys. In 1945, production of die-cast metal toys again began
with the introduction of a military line, as
well as new cars and trucks. Production
continued in factories in England and
France until competition from Corgi,
Tootsietoy, and Matchbox caused a
decline in sales. The Dinky line was discontinued in 1979.

Airport fire tender, #276, MIB........... **90.00**
Austin Somerset Saloon, #161, MIB **70.00**
Bently coupe, #194, MIB **125.00**
Brinks truck, #275, MIB **100.00**
Bristol helicopter, #715, MIB........... **65.00**
Caravan, #117, MIB **60.00**
Cinderella's coach, #111, MIB **55.00**
Coles Hydra truck, #980, MIB **100.00**
Engineering staff, #4, MIB............... **450.00**
Farm produce wagon, #343, MIB **75.00**
Fire chief's land rover, #195, MIB **50.00**
Ford Consul Corsair, #130, MIB **65.00**
Happy Cab, #130, MIB **50.00**
International road signs, #771, MIB **180.00**
Jaguar Mark X, #142, MIB **100.00**
Jeep, #405, MIB **40.00**
London taxi, #284, MIB...................... **50.00**
Mercury Cougar, #174, MIB.............. **95.00**
Michigan tractor dozer, #976 .... **100.00**
Passengers, #3, MIB **350.00**
Plymouth Stockcar, #201, MIB......... **50.00**
Range Rover ambulance, #268, MIB **60.00**
Refuse wagon with cars, #978, MIB **75.00**
Rover 75 Saloon, #156, MIB............. **100.00**
Sam's car, #108, MIB....................... **120.00**
Shovel dozer, #977, MIB **100.00**
Telephone service van, #261, MIB . **100.00**
Train and hotel staff, #5, MIB......... **270.00**
Triumph Spitfire, #114, MIB **100.00**
UFO Interceptor, #351, MIB............. **125.00**
VW Beetle, #181, MIB........................ **95.00**

Doepke, Charles William, Mfg. Co.

This company is known for well made
pressed steel toys. It used the "Model
Toys" trademark.

Airport tractor................................... **125.00**
Baggage trailer, yellow or green........ **50.00**
Farm conveyor, sheet steel, wear to orig
paint, labeled "Barber Greene," 24" l
.... **160.00**
Fire ladder wagon, sheet steel, minor wear
to orig paint, 36" l **100.00**
MG.. **75.00**
Mining conveyor, sheet steel, wear to orig
paint, labeled "Barber Greene," 17-1/2" l
.... **110.00**
Road grader, orange **275.00**
Unit crane.. **250.00**

Ertl, Transtar truck, blue cab, white body, original box with damage, $8.

Ertl

Fred Ertl Sr., founded Ertl in 1945. Blueprints obtained from companies such as John Deere and International Harvester were used as patterns, thus ensuring a high level of similarity to the originals. Ertl produces a fill line of wheeled vehicles and is recognized as the world's largest manufacturer of toy farm equipment.

Car, Dukes of Hazzard, General Lee, 1981, MOC **25.00**
Chevy Bel Air, 1/18 scale, 1957, hard-top, green and ivory **30.00**
Coke beverage truck, 1/64 scale **15.00**
Farmall tractor, 1586, MIB **55.00**
Ford F150 pickup truck, 1/16 scale.. **24.00**
Manure Spreader, New Holland, high sides **65.00**
Papa Smurf car, MIP **10.00**
Rumley #6 tractor, 1/16 scale **50.00**
Smurfette car, MIP **10.00**
Tractor, diecast, 1/16 scale, Agri King, Case, white, 1974...................... **185.00**
Truck, semi, American Hardware...... **100.00**
Wagon, diecast, 1/16 scale, John Deer, metal wheels, 1960 .... **95.00**

Fisher Price, television, cow jumps over the moon, $20.

Fisher Price, #573, Merry Mutt, pull toy, play wear, $40.

Fisher-Price

Fisher-Price Toys was founded in East Aurora, New York, in 1930. The original company consisted of Irving L. Price, retired from F. W. Woolworth Co., Herman G. Fisher, who was associated with the Alderman-Fairchild Toy Co. in Churchville, New York, and Helen M Schelle, a former toy store owner. Margaret Evans Price, wife of the company president, was the company's first artist and designer. She had been a writer and illustrator of children's books. The company began with sixteen designs. Herman Fisher resigned as president in 1966. In 1969, the company was acquired by the Quaker Oats Company. Black and white rectangular logos appeared on all toys prior to 1962. The first plastic part was used after 1949.

Donald Duck Xylophone **65.00**
Dr. Doodle, #132, 1940, 10" h............ **95.00**
Hickory Dickory Dock, radio and clock **30.00**
Jalopy, #724, car, wood body, plastic accessory pieces and wheels, wood clown head, copyright 1965, 4-1/2" x 7" x 6-1/2", scattered wear **18.00**
Little Snoopy, wood and plastic **18.50**
Magic Key Mansion, six rooms, furnishings, 125-pc set.................................... **245.00**
Mickey Mouse Drummer **60.00**
Miss Piggy, puppet, 1978 .... **25.00**

Fisher-Price Play Family, Sesame Street, play house, played-with condition, $10.

Molly Mop, #190 .... **250.00**
Music Box, #795 .... **10.00**
Puppy, #365, wood, paper labels, built-in key, orig fabric ears, tongue missing, replaced tail, 3-1/2" x 8" x 8" h, some wear **245.00**

Gabriel

Bozo the Clown, Tricky Trapeze **25.00**
Disney Dancer, Tricky Trapeze, 1975. **20.00**
Donald Duck, Tricky Trapeze **25.00**
Mickey Mouse, Tricky Trapeze **25.00**
Monster Machine, orig molds, 1970, C-9 .... **80.00**
Santa Claus, Tricky Trapeze **20.00**

Gama/Schuco,
US Zone Germany

Mirako Car, #1001 .... **95.00**
Sedan, red, wind-up with key, 6-1/2" l, near mint **135.00**

Gilbert, Erector set, No. 8-1/2, All Electric Set, MIB, $110.

Gilbert

Mysto Magic Set, late 1930s, some items missing, orig box **130.00**
Telescope, #13214, 80 Power, reflecting, 26" steel tripod, heavy diecast base, orig instructions, orig case **50.00**

Hasbro

Hasbro Industries, Inc., an American toy manufacturer, is well known for several lines. One of the most popular toys produced by this company is Mr. Potato Head. It was introduced in 1948 and is still being made today. Another popular Hasbro line is GI Joe, along with all the accessories made for this series of action figures.

Brothers Grimm school kit, 1962..... **48.00**
Buick Century, Amaz-A-Matics, 1969, MIB **48.00**
Casper Stitch a Story, 1967, sealed, MOC **48.00**
Junior police kit, cars, plastic scenery, 1960s, MOC **48.00**
Mr. And Mrs. Potato Head Kit, 1960s, colorful 10-1/4" x 14" x 2-1/4" orig box **20.00**
Transformer Mircomaser Patrols, Military Patrol, 1989, MIP **35.00**
Wacky Wheel, 1960s, MOC **40.00**

Hubley

The Hubley Manufacturing Company was founded in 1894 in Lancaster, Pennsylvania, by John Hubley. The first toys were cast iron. In 1940, cast iron was phased out and replaced with metals and plastic. By 1952, Hubley made more cap pistols than any other type of toy. Gabriel Industries bought Hubley in 1965.

Bell Telephone truck, light rust to orig paint, marked inside, 5-1/4" l **220.00**
Boat Tail racer, cast iron, 6-1/2" l **200.00**
Bus, cast iron, 5-3/4" l, new tires **125.00**
Coupe, very worn orig paint, deteriorated white rubber tires, 6-1/4" l **300.00**
Delivery truck, worn old repaint, label on side of panel, deteriorated white rubber tires, 4-3/4" l **100.00**
Duck, very worn orig paint, rust, 9-1/2" l **110.00**
Earth mover, #354, plastic, automatic dumping auction, spare tire, orig box, 14" l **110.00**
Fire truck, ladder wagon, worn old paint, some touch-up repair, mismatched driver, accessories missing, 13-1/2" l **80.00**

Kiddie toy race car, metal, nickel plated driver, red, black rubber tires, 1950s, 7" l **30.00**

Motorcycle, cast iron, replaced handle bars, 60 percent orig paint **200.00**

Police Department motorcycle, Kiddietoy, 5" l, 1950s **165.00**

Racer, driver, old worn paint, some rust, labeled inside body, 7" l **165.00**

Surf 'n' Sand, jeep and boat with trailer, blue and white, orig window box, 15" l ... **95.00**

Wonder Cement Mixer, cast iron, nickel plated, 3-1/2" l **155.00**

Wrecker, sprayed painted orange **50.00**

Ideal

The Ideal Toy Company was owned by Lewis David Christie. It was located in Bridgeport, Connecticut. Among the toys it produced were dolls, cars, trucks, and even a line of toy soldiers produced for a short time span in the 1920s.

Atomic rocket launching truck, 1955, 12" l **135.00**

Bomber, B-25 Mitchell, plastic, 9" wing span **65.00**

Cadillac, fix-it convertible, hard plastic, one pc missing, 13" l **195.00**

Car, XP-600 fix-it **75.00**

Evel Knievel Precision Miniature, Formula 5000 race car replica, diecast metal, white, orig box, 1977 .... **24.00**

Flintstone Cave House, 1964 .... **65.00**

Harbor Launch, 1950s, C-8 .... **65.00**

Jeep, plastic, brown, star stick, 1950s, 4" l **24.00**

King Zor, battery operated, orig balls **295.00**

MG, beige hard plastic, silver/blue foil sticker on dash, repairs, c1960, 3-1/2" x 9-1/2" x 3" **5.00**

Mickey Mouse pirate ship playset, missing several figures **365.00**

Out West-Monkey Stix, complete set .. **5.00**

Race car, battery operated, hard plastic body, metal chassis, mkd "Chaparrel D2" in white, red, yellow, green, and black accents, 3-1/2" l **10.00**

Roy Rogers jeep and trailor set, NMIB **395.00**

Washing machine, windup, MIB **50.00**

Fun Factory, Play-Doh Modeling Set, eight pieces, original box, $12.

Japanese, post war

Following World War II, a huge variety of toys produced in Osaka and the Koto District of Japan flooded the American market. The vast majority of these toys are marked only with the country of origin and a trademark, usually consisting of a two- or three-letter monogram. It is virtually impossible to trace these trademarks to a specific manufacturer. Also, many toys were assembled from parts made by several different factories. To make matters even more confusing, names found on boxes are often those of the agent or distributor, rather than the manufacturer.

Air Force mobile hospital, friction, light blue, nurses and doctors litho at windows, late 1950s, 8" l **115.00**

American Airlines Boeing 727, chrome litho, friction, 10" wingspan, TT Toys, 1960s, orig box **70.00**

Continental Trailways bus, Golden Eagle, friction, 7" l **125.00**

Convertible warship/cruise liner, friction, 1950s, 12" l **115.00**

Frankie the Roller Skating Monkey, Frankonia Toys, battery operated, tin removed, orig box **140.00**

Koko the Sandwich Man, TN, 1950s, 7" h, orig box **95.00**

Laughing clown robot, 14" h, hard plastic, battery operated, 1960s **135.00**

Mary Open Television Car, Asahi Toys, tin litho, friction, MIB **225.00**

Police Department, three-wheeled Harley motorbike, KO, crank wind **245.00**

Propeller driven race car, S & E, tin fiction **160.00**

Rocket ship, Winner #23, tin litho, battery operated **140.00**

Space car, SS-18, tin litho friction, yellow dome over tin driver, orange, silver, and red, S & E, 9" l.................................. **80.00**

Stunt car, pop-up driver, SY, friction, orig box... **285.00**

United States liner passenger ship, K Toys, tin litho friction, 6-1/2" l.......... **75.00**

Venus #27 speedboat, tin litho, crank wind-up, 1950s, 6" l............................... **105.00**

Kenner

This Cincinnati, OH, based toy manufacturer is a familiar name to Baby Boomers.

Easy Bake oven, orig box and orig Betty Crocker mixes, c1960.................. **140.00**

Easy Show, six movies, orig box, c1960 .... **140.00**

Girder and Panel Building Set, #8.. **110.00**

Give-A-Show projector set, Frankenstein Jr., Hanna-Barbera, orig slides with other Hanna-Barbera characters, working projector, orig box, 1967 .... **175.00**

Mold Master road builder set, 1964, unused, MIB................................. **115.00**

Sky Rail girder and panel set, #17, 1963, MIB... **65.00**

Spiroman, #432, 1968........................ **25.00**

Knickerbocker

This New York City-based toy maker is well known for teddy bears and stuffed toys, but they also made quality puppets and toys.

Dukes of Hazzard, finger racer crash car, General Lee or Sheriff, 1981, MOC, each **25.00**

Fred Flintstone, pushbutton marionette, 1960s.. **185.00**

Pixie and Dixie, stuffed, pair............. **300.00**

Snooper and Blabber Mouse, stuffed, pair **180.00**

Spare darts, two per card, MOC **6.00**

Lionel, raceway set, original box, complete, $75.

Line Mar (Linemar)

Line Mar is a subsidiary of Marx. Linemar toys are manufactured in Japan.

Animal Set, #134 seal, #135 moose, #136 gorilla, #137 giraffe, #138 hippo, Elegant Miniatures, yellow box **20.00**

Fire chief car, battery operated, orig box, 1950s **225.00**

G-Man Machine Gun, green metal gun, black perforated barrel, 1950s, 13" l, MIB **100.00**

Hopping bluebird, litho tin wind-up, built-in key, 1960s...................................... **45.00**

Jumping Squirrel, tin litho, remote control, 1950s, 2" x 7" x 4-1/2" h.................. **30.00**

Mechanical Cat, litho tin wind-up, ribbon collar, swirling rubber tail, 1950s, orig box, 3-1/2" h................................. **160.00**

Patsy the Pig, litho tin wind-up, pink, blue, and yellow, 1960s, orig box, 4" h ... **65.00**

Pick up truck, Chevy, 6-1/2" l, orig box **90.00**

Pluto Drum Major, 1950s, 6-1/2" h .. **645.00**

Pointer, #25, Elegant Miniatures set, brown/ blue box **5.00**

Popeye lantern, litho tin battery operated, 1950s, 7-1/2" h............................. **245.00**

Pull Back Donald Duck and Huey, litho tin, orig box, 5-1/2" h.......................... **895.00**

Sleeping baby bear, battery operated, 9" l, orig box **285.00**

Touchdown Pete, the Football Player, litho tin wind-up, 1950s, 6" l **240.00**

Marusan, Japan

Ford, 1953, friction, burgundy, chrome detailing, 10" l, C-9...................... **255.00**

Greyhound Lines Red Ribbon bus, 1950s, friction, detailed litho 11 passengers, driver, red, green, orange, gray, silver, chrome bumper, jeweled chrome lights, five top lights, 12-1/2" l, 4" w, C.8+ **485.00**

Main Street Bakery van, tin litho **395.00**

Marx

Louis Marx founded the Marx Toy Company in 1921, stressing high quality at the lowest possible price. His popular line included every type of toy except dolls. The company was sold to Quaker Oats Company, who sold it in 1976 to the European company of Dunbee-Combex-Marx.

Archie & Veronica's Jalopie, litho tin wind-up, 1960s, 7-1/2" l.......................... **600.00**

Automatic police station, tin litho police station and car, Dick Tracy, 1950s **1,200.00**

Batmobile, child's ride-on type, green, silver hubcaps, plastic, 1960s, 24" l...... **185.00**

B. O. Plenty walker, 1940s............... **450.00**

Cape Canaveral Missle Set, 1950s, nearly complete.. **225.00**

Cat, ramp walker, hard plastic, 1950s. **25.00**

Coca-Cola Truck, repainted, 20" l..... **225.00**

Combine, tin friction, MIB.................... **35.00**

Construction worker with wheelbarrow, ramp walker, 3-1/2" l....................... **20.00**

Dachsund, ramp walker, hard plastic, brown, black and white accents **25.00**

Dick Tracy Nora the Nursemaid, litho tin ramp walker, Baby Bonnie in carriage **345.00**

Dinosaurs, from Prehistoric Play Set, dark green, set of four, played with......... **10.00**

Dog and doghouse, tin litho, 1920s. **100.00**

Fire truck

Aerial ladder, plastic, wind-up, electric lights **125.00**

Hose and ladder **350.00**

Flame, brown, complete tack, 1970s, C-9 toy, C-8 box **90.00**

Fort Apache playset, 12" x 19" x 4" deep metal box, 11 cowboys, 12 Indians, 7 horses, other accessories, played with **20.00**

Friction car, tin litho, soft vinyl comical guitar driver, copyright 1968, 2-1/4" x 4" x 3-1/4" **15.00**

Dana's Hover Cycle, Matchbox Robotech, MIB, **$15**.

Great Garloo, 1960s, battery operated, 1960s, 24" h, C-9 toy, C-8 box **745.00**

Infantry soldier, tan outfit, plastic combat helmet, dark green plastic rifle, pistol in one hand **8.00**

Intercity delivery truck, 18" l, played-with condition **55.00**

International agent car, tin litho, vinyl head, 1966 .... **70.00**

Jaguar XKE, friction **45.00**

Jumping Jeep, litho tin wind-up, C-8 **175.00**

Kangaroo, ramp walker, hard plastic, brown **40.00**

Laser Rifle, two action sounds, 1970s, MOC **45.00**

Lightning racer, green car, black wheels, silver accents, "Marx Speed Wheels" sticker, copyright 1971, 5-1/2" x 11" x 2-3/4", orig display bag with header card **15.00**

Marx Presidents of the United States, seven 2-3/4" h white hard plastic figures, booklet with photos and text, 3-3/4" x 17" x 1-1/2" orig box............................ **15.00**

Mini Blazer, diecast, 2-1/4", MOC **25.00**

Pistol, Blue & Grey Civil War, caps sealed in orig plastic sleeve, NRFP **65.00**

Prehistoric Animals, 2" l yellow hard plastic Stegosaurus, 1-1/2" x 3" x 1" box, c1960 .... **15.00**

Racer, tin litho, built-in key, diecut tin driver, 2-12" x 5" x 2-1/4", scattered overall tiny paint nicks.................................... **145.00**

Race track, Action Plus, Classic 500, 29" x 63" figure-8 track, orig hand throttles, za-zoom noise unit, orig box, 1960s... **75.00**

Robin Hood, figure set, six painted plastic figures, c1960s **12.00**

Security pistol, two action sounds, 1970s, MOC... **35.00**

Sir Stuart the Silver Knight, late 1960s, C-9 box **110.00**

Skycruiser, friction plane, some rust **150.00**

Three Keys to Treasure, pinball/bagatelle, orig prizes, 1960s, MIB **75.00**

Tinykins, Flintstone Cop **45.00**

Tractor, orig white rubber treads, partial box, pre-war... **250.00**

Train Set, #532, 4 cars, 10 pcs of track, two keys, torn orig box **200.00**

Western Express, wind-up tin litho, train, western motif, wear **30.00**

Matchbox, 66, Greyhound bus, original box, **$18**.

Matchbox, 53, blue car with hood that exposes engine, original box $20.

Matchbox

Matchbox cars were first manufactured by Lesney Products, an English company founded in 1947 by Leslie Smith and Rodney Smith. Its first die-cast cars were made in 1953 on a scale of 1:75. The trademark "Matchbox" was registered in 1953. In 1979, Lesney Products Corp. made over 5.5 million toys a week. The company was sold to Universal International in 1982.

Austin Taxi, #17, 1960, MIB **60.00**
Beach Buggy, #30, 1971, MIB **9.00**
Blue Shark, #61, 1971, MIB **10.00**
Case Tractor Bulldozer, #16, 1969, MIB
.... **18.00**
Caterpillar Tractor, No. 8, 1955 .... **40.00**
Citreon DS19, #66, 1959 .... **30.00**
Coca-Cola truck, #37, 1956, MIB **80.00**
Daimler ambulance, #14, 1955 .... **25.00**
Dennis Refuge truck, #15, 1963 .... **20.00**
Disney car, 1989, Mickey or Donald... **45.00**
Flying Bug, #11, 1972, MIB **14.00**
Flat car and container, #25, 1979, MIB **8.00**
Formula I racing car, #34, 1971, MIB **15.00**
Ford pickup, #6, 1969 .... **15.00**
Ford Zephyr 6, MKIII, #33, 1963, MIB **38.00**
Freeway gas tanker, #63, 1973, MIB**. 20.00**
General Army lorry, #62, 1959, MIB .. **28.00**
Honda motorcycle with trailer, #38, 1968, MIB.. **24.00**
Horse box, #40, 1977, MIB **8.00**
House Trailer Caravan, #23, 1967, MIB
.... **40.00**
Jaguar XK 140 coupe, #32, 1956, MIB
.... **55.00**
Lamborghini Countach, #27, 1974, MIB
.... **10.00**
London Bus, #5, 1954, MIB **45.00**
Mark Ten Jaguar, No. 28, MIB **65.00**
Maxx FX, 1989, boxed set, MIB.......... **40.00**
Mercury Cougar, #62, 1969, MIB **15.00**
MGA sports car, #19, 1969, MIB........ **70.00**
Military scout car, #61, 1959, MIB **32.00**
Mobile home, #54, 1981, MIB **8.00**

Pontiac convertible, #39, 1962, MIB. **65.00**
Swamp Rat, #30, 1977, MIB **8.00**
Talking Freddy Krueger, 18" h, MIB.. **35.00**
Taxi Cab, Chevrolet Impala, #20, 1965, MIB
.... **35.00**
Tractor, #4, 1954 .... **45.00**
Truck, Ken Worth, made in Macau... **500.00**
Volkswagen 1500 Saloon, #15, 1968, MIB
.... **25.00**
Wild life Truck, #57, 1973, MIB **12.00**

Matchbox, Models of Yesteryear, c1985 Y-28/ 1907 Unic Taxi, Y-27/1922 Foden Steam Lorry, NRFB, $35.

Matchbox, Models of Yesterday, Colman's Mustard, 1912 Ford Model T, NRFB, $30.

Mattel

Mattel, formed by Harold Mattson and Ruth and Elliot Handler in 1945, originated in a garage in Los Angeles. From its humble beginnings as a manufacturer of picture frames, the company evolved into making dollhouse furniture, burp guns, and eventually the Barbie doll, its most-famous product.

Beany and Cecil, Beany Copter, 1950, MOC **150.00**
Beany and Cecil disguise kit **75.00**
Crackers, The Talking Parrot, 1960s, on stand **195.00**
Doctor Dolittle, talking, MIB **175.00**
Hot Birds collector's case, with airplanes, vinyl, inside storage tray missing, copyright 1970, 6" x 10" x 3", played with condition **10.00**
Incredible Edibles, 1966 .... **35.00**
Jack in the Box, tin, clown, 1971 .... **48.00**
Jack in the Box, tin, Winnie the Pooh
.... **100.00**
Mother Goose, pull string talker **150.00**
Outdraw the Outlaw, C-9 toy, C-8 box
.... **165.00**
Rocket Set, H20, MIB........................ **125.00**
Vic-A-Farm Set, 1962 .... **125.00**
V-Rrooom Racer, guide-whip, orig box
.... **125.00**

Mego

This New York City toy manufacturer is well known for its celebrity dolls and action figures.

Amazing Spider-Car, orig box **125.00**
Dukes of Hazzard Boss Hogg Caddy, 1981, 10-1/2" l................................ **385.00**

Modern Toys, Japan

BZ Porter, NMIB **300.00**
Comet jetliner, friction, rubber tires, 1950s
.... **70.00**
Donald Duck fire engine, plastic, large tin bell, wind-up, late 1960s, near mint, C-8 box **65.00**
Drive set, tin litho, 6" friction Ford Fairline 500, 3-1/2" gas pump with bear head insignia, six 4" h road signs, C-9+ toy, C-8 store display box **355.00**
Fork lift truck, battery operated, 11" l, orig box **255.00**
Planet Explorer Spaceship, battery operated, 9-1/2" l................................ **125.00**
South Pole snowmobile, battery operated, 1950s **190.00**
Space tank, battery operated, 8-1/2" l
.... **110.00**
Train engine, 2" x 13" x 4" h litho tin, friction motor, c1950, flint wheel no longer works
.... **24.00**

MTU, Korea

Happy Days, boy on tricycle, litho tin wind-up, built-in key, 3" x 4-1/2" x 6" h, orig box with slight wear, c1970.................... **15.00**

Happy Easter, white vinyl rabbit on tricycle, litho tin wind-up, built-in key, 3" x 4-1/2" x 6" h, orig box with slight wear, c1970
.... **15.00**
Police helicopter, tin wind-up, orig box
.... **20.00**

Nylint Tool & Mfg. Co.

Located in Rockford, IL, this company specialized in scale model toys with interesting mechanical elements.

ABC Olympic Truck........................... **75.00**
Ford Bronco, pressed steel, red, black plastic interior, silvered metal movable windshield frame, 1960s, 5" x 10-1/2" x 5" h **18.00**
Ford camper, with radio................... **250.00**
Grand Prix Special, racer and trailer **50.00**
Horse van.. **160.00**
Jungle wagon.................................. **135.00**

Occupied Japan, various unknown makers

Boy in row boat, red, white, yellow, and green painted tin boat, red, white, and blue boy with celluloid upper body
.... **125.00**
Clown, with cane, sad face **45.00**
Dancing Black man **395.00**
Dancing couple, celluloid wind-up, boy with dark blue suit, girl with pink dress . **65.00**
Friction car, Alps, red metal, white rubber tires, 5" l, box missing end flap **160.00**
Kitten with ball, celluloid, off-white and gray kitten, pink shirt and hair bow **35.00**
Merry car, Sinsei Toys, tin litho keywind, 5-1/2" l, MIB.................................. **300.00**
Stork, celluloid, figural, set of 12 in orig box, "Grade A, Made in Occupied Japan"
.... **500.00**

Marx, play set, Fort Apache, original box, complete, **$95**.

Playsets

Black Goucho, Zorro, Nadel & Sons Toy Corp, 1950s **35.00**
Block House, Marx, unassembled, orig bag **25.00**
Blue Knight, George Peppard, MOC. **15.00**
Charles Bronson's Commander, MOC **15.00**
CHiPs Highway Patrol, MOC............. **15.00**
Dr. Kildare Doctor Playset, 1960s, MIB **50.00**
Green Giant, Child Guidance, one truck missing **95.00**
Handy Dandy Mechanical Drawing Set, MIB... **85.00**
Johnny Astro................................. **135.00**
Los Angeles Invasion Set, 104 pcs, MIB **45.00**
Movieland Drive In Theatre, Remco, few pcs missing **235.00**
Prehistoric Dinosaurs, Marx, MIB... **225.00**
Shell Oil Playset, Playmobile, 1992 ... **35.00**
Walton's, Amsco, figures missing **125.00**

Pedal car, blue body, original wheels, as-found condition, $95.

Promo Car, various makers

Chevrolet Bel Air, 1957, plastic, four-door station wagon, metal base plate, working friction mechanism, two-tone green, silver accents, by Scale Model Products, 3" x 8" x 2-1/4" h.. **40.00**
Chevrolet Corvette, 1979, hard plastic, red, 2-3/4" x 7-1/2" x 1-3/4" **20.00**
Chrysler New Yorker, 1961, hard plastic, red, off-white roof, 3" x 8-1/2" x 2" h, some warping to front **25.00**
Ford Maverick, 1970-71, hard plastic, orange, by Jo-Han, 2-1/2" x 7" x 2", wear on silver accents **48.00**
Ford Thunderbird, 1964, hard plastic, pea green with silver accents, 3" x 8" x 2" **48.00**
Lincoln Continental, 1956, hard plastic, metal base plate, working friction mechanism, by AMT, 3" x 8-1/4" x 2" **28.00**

Manza, 1976, hard plastic, metallic green, by MPC, 2-1/2" x 7" x 2" **20.00**
Oldsmobile F-85, 1961, hard plastic, four-door station wagon, deep red, working friction mechanism, by Jo-Han, 2-3/4" x 7-1/2" x 2" h **58.00**
Oldsmobile Starfire, 1963, plastic, two-door hardtop, off-white, silver accent, by Jo-Han, 3" x 8-1/2" x 2", some defects **45.00**

Radio Flyer

Radio Steel & Mfg. Co., Chicago, IL, created wagons, sleds, and other riding toys.

Row cart, wood and metal, orig condition **225.00**
Scooter, orig emblem present, but very worn, late 1930s **75.00**
Super wagon/car, orig paint, c1960 **125.00**
Toddler tike, wood, metal, and plastic, orig colorful handlebar streamers **55.00**
Wagon
     1930s-40s, well used.................... **130.00**
     1940s-50s, 42" l, rolled edges, worn **175.00**

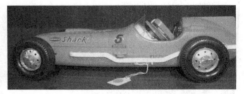

Remco, racer, Shark, red plastic body, $25.

Remco

Remco Industries, Inc., was founded by Sol Robbins and was the first company to advertise its products on television. A unique aspect of the firm was that many of its products were related to television and promotional character dolls. The company closed in January 1974.

I.C.B.M. Vanguard Satellite Launcher, battery operated, orig box, C-9 ... **275.00**
Lone Ranger Bazooka, shells, orig box, 1961 .... **75.00**
Mighty Magee aircraft carrier, hard plastic, gray and white ship, decals, black, white, red, and blue box, copyright 1963, 4" x 18" x 3-1/2" h, wear to box.............. **65.00**
Project Yankee Doodle, complete set **110.00**
Shark race car, 19" l........................... **70.00**
Swap mobile, 1970s, MIB **345.00**
Viking Ship, played with condition .. **225.00**

Gas stove, cast iron. Eagle, very worn orig paint, rust, 9" h **250.00**

Orchard tractor, cast iron, worn orig paint, worn rubber wheels, 5-1/2" l **175.00**

Police motorcycle, cast iron
Marked "Made in the U.S.A.," worn old paint with good color, black rubber tires, 4-1/4" l **85.00**
Marked "Patrol," worn orig paint, worn white rubber tires, 6-1/2" l **110.00**

Racer, hard plastic body, heavy metal weighted wheels, black rubber treads, gold "1" decal on both sides, 1950s, 2-1/2" x 5" x 1-1/2" **30.00**

Railway Express truck, cast iron, worn old green paint, very worn white rubber tires, 5" l **80.00**

Steam ship, cast iron, old repaint flaking, 7-1/2" l **165.00**

Williams, A. C.

This toy manufacturer specialized in cast iron toys. It was founded in Ravenna, OH, 1886 and continued until 1939.

Coupe, rumble seat, 4-3/4" l, c1930, small chip on bottom of seat **195.00**

Motorcycle cop, worn orig paint, rust, old replaced tires, 7" l **140.00**

Wolverine

The Wolverine Supply & Manufacturing Company was founded in 1903 and incorporated by Benjamin F. Bain in 1906. The first type of toys it produced was lithographed tin sand toys. It began to make girls' housekeeping toys and action games by the 1920s. Production of toys continued and expanded in 1959 to include children's appliances, known as "Rite-Hite." The name was changed to Wolverine Toy Co. in 1962. The company was originally located in Pittsburgh, Pennsylvania, but relocated to Booneville, Arkansas, in 1970 after being acquired by Spang and Company.

Arithmetic toy calculator, tin, 3-3/4" x 6-1/8" x 7-1/8" **24.00**

Camping trailer **95.00**

Express bus **315.00**

Farm wagon, plastic wind-up, orig box, 10" l **115.00**

Jet roller coaster, one car, orig box . **145.00**

Lunar landing, marble game **55.00**

Merry Masons, automatic sand toy, litho tin, building shape, three litho tin masons, 1950s, orig box, 16" h **145.00**

Mustang, white **75.00**

Wolverine, child's play cupboard, litho tin, green and white with multicolored decoration, original box, $35.

Snow White ironing board, tin, white ground, 8" x 27" l top, 21" h **150.00**

Submarine, blue and white, two brass cannons, ice cutter, 1930s, orig key, 13" l, near mint, C-8 box **290.00**

Wyandotte

All Metal Products Company, located in Wyandotte, Michigan, was in business by the early 1920s. The company, better known as Wyandotte Toys, originally produced wood and steel toy weapons. In 1935, it introduced an innovative line of streamlined wheeled vehicles. The firm ceased operations in 1956.

Chrysler Airflow, some damage to orig paint **100.00**

Coast to Coast Bus **315.00**

Giant construction dump truck, 1950s **195.00**

Log truck, three logs, plastic, 9-1/2" l **65.00**

Medical Corps truck, pressed steel, wood tires, c1939, 12" l **200.00**

Pickway pasture truck **95.00**

Sambo target, tin litho, attached metal easel, orig box, 1930s, 14" x 23" **95.00**

Steam shovel, pressed steel **150.00**

Tipper truck, 1950s **195.00**

Touring sedan, #220, 1930s, 6" l, professional restoration................... **45.00**

Water pistol, Thinjet Repeater, metal gun, plastic liner, mkd "Pat Appl'd For Wyandotte Toys, Made in USA," 1950s **25.00**

Yone and Yonezama, Japan

Boxing dog, wind-up, plush and litho tin, sign around neck reads "Next 4th Round," orig box, 6" h **115.00**

Circus drumming monkey, litho tin wind-up, built-in key, 1960s **65.00**

Happy n' Sad Magic Face Clown, battery operated, tin litho and cloth, 1960s, orig box... **145.00**

Helicopter, tin litho friction, mkd "PD Sky Patrol," black, white, red, white, blue, and orange, 2" x 6" x 3" h **20.00**

Helicopter, tin litho friction, mkd "Rescue," red, white, blue, black, and orange, 2" x 6" x 3" h **20.00**

Navy demon jet, friction, 9" l, 8" wingspan, 1950s.. **140.00**

Spin Turn Racer, wind-up, tin, plastic tires, orig box, 5" l.................................. **115.00**

Two-gun sheriff, battery operated, tin litho, vinyl head, cloth outfit, removable tin hat, orig box.. **165.00**

Trains, Toy

History: Railroading has always been an important part of childhood, largely because of the romance associated with the railroad and the prominence of toy trains.

The first toy trains were cast iron and tin; windup motors added movement. The golden age of toy trains was 1920 to 1955, when electric-powered units and high-quality rolling stock were available and names such as Ives, American Flyer, and Lionel were household words. Today train collectors look for these and other names, often off-shoots of the original train manufacturers. Many collectors specialize in one manufacturer or one gauge of train. Many collectors also specialize in securing train accessories and are as particular about the condition of those items as they are their trains. The advent of plastic in the late 1950s resulted in considerably lower quality.

Toy trains are designated by a model scale or gauge. The most popular are HO, N, O, and standard. Narrow gauge was a response to the modern capacity to miniaturize.

Collecting Hints: Prices do fluctuate—those from mail order houses and stores generally are higher than those found at train swap meets.

Condition is critical. Items in fair condition (scratched, chipped, dented, rusted or warped) and below generally have little value to the collector. Restoration is accepted and can enhance the price by one or two grades, provided it has been done accurately. Spare parts are actively traded and sold among collectors to assist in restoration efforts.

Exterior condition often is more important than operating condition. If you require a piece that works, you should test it before you buy it.

Collecting toy trains is a very specialized field, and collectors tend to have their own meets. A wealth of literature is available but only from specialized book, railroad, or toy-train dealers. Novice collectors should read extensively before buying.

American Flyer, HO gauge

Brochure, full color, 12 pgs, 1976........ **9.00**

Catalog

    1957, four pgs................................. **10.00**

    1959, four pgs................................. **15.00**

Locomotive, #426, B&O, blue and gray **150.00**

Rolling stock

    #33507, gondola, D&H, brown, canister load **60.00**

    33514, boxcar, Silver Meteor, brown **45.00**

    #33515, caboose, C&O, lighted, yellow, center cupola................................. **75.00**

American Flyer, O gauge

Instruction booklet, for 3/16" scale trains and equipment, 65 pgs, 5-1/4" x 8-1/2" **12.00**

Locomotive, #3020, electric, 4-4-4, c1922-25 .... **375.00**

Set

    Burlington Zephyr Streamliner, passenger, #9900 power car, coach, baggage car, #9900 tail car........ **700.00**

    Freight, 2-6-4 locomotive, eight-wheel tender, flat bed car, box car, derrick car, tank car, gondola, caboose, 1930s **450.00**

    Freight, #476 gondola, #478 boxcar, #480 tank car, #484 caboose **130.00**

    Passenger, Railway Post Office car, Paul Revere coach, Lexington observation, orange... **115.00**

Athearn, HO gauge, locomotive, #6707, light blue, white lettering, yellow "We Support Our Troops" ribbon, NRFB, $60.

American Flyer, S gauge

Accessories
Billboard, #566, whistling, 1951-55 **20.00**
Eureka Diner, #275, 1952-53 .... **45.00**
Gabe The Lamplighter, #23780, controller, orig decal, 1958 .... **585.00**
Hotel, #168, roof reattached, 1953 .... **225.00**
Log loader, #164, gray, vermilion roof, controller, wiring bad, 1940 .... **400.00**
Magnetic crane, #165, controller, 1940 .... **600.00**
Station and terminal, #795, 1954.. **400.00**
Transformer, Model #8B, 100 watts **50.00**
Trestle set, #26782, 20" l, orig box.. **90.00**
Truss bridge, #571, 1955-56 .... **7.50**

Locomotive
#303, 4-4-2, Atlantic, 1954-56, steam **25.00**
#316, 4-6-2, K-5, Pennsylvania, 1946, steam **45.00**
#345, 4-6-2, Pacific, 1954, steam... **50.00**
#405, Silver Streak, 1952, Alco PA **. 85.00**
#499, New Haven, 1956-57, GE Electric **150.00**
#21551, Northern Pacific, 1958, Alco PA **110.00**

Rolling stock
#607, caboose **10.00**
#653, pullman, 1946-53 .... **25.00**
#662, Vista dome, 1950-52 .... **27.50**
#719, hopper and dump car, CB & Q, 1950-54 .... **30.00**
#752, coal car, Seaboard, three-button controller, 1946 .... **475.00**
#907, caboose **18.00**
#935, caboose, 1957, brown **.......... 60.00**
#940, hopper and dump car, Wabash, 1953-56 .... **15.00**
#941, gondola, Frisco, 1953-57 ..... **40.00**
#944, crane car, Industrial Brown hoist, 1952-57 .... **95.00**
#961, passenger car, Jefferson, 1953-58 .... **30.00**
#24047, box car, GN, plug door **85.00**

#24191, reefer Canadian National, 1958 .... **250.00**
#24125, gondola, Bethlehem Steel, three rails, 1960 .... **40.00**
#24313, tank car, Gulf, 1957-60 ..... **20.00**
#24330, tank car, Baker's Chocolate, 1961-72 .... **25.00**
#24526, caboose, 1957 .... **15.00**
#24558, flat car, Canadian Pacific, Christmas tree load, 1959-60 .... **145.00**
#24773, passenger car, Columbus, 1957-58 .... **45.00**

Set
American Legion Ltd, #4019 locomotive, #4040 box car, American pullman, Pleasant View observation car, maroon litho and roofs **660.00**
Century, #9915, locomotive, integral tender, two #3178 coaches, #3179 observation car **850.00**
Eagle, #21920 MP Alco PA, #24856 combine, #24863 vista dome, #24866 observation car, 1963, MIB **1,600.00**
Minnie Ha-Ha, locomotive, three coaches, orange and gray, minor wear **295.00**
Nation Wide, #1093 locomotive, green and black, brass trim, combine and coach **575.00**
Northwestern Freight, #4677 diecast locomotive and tender, #3207 sand car gondola, #3025 wrecker car, #3211 caboose, 10 pcs curved track, 1938, some wear from use **400.00**
Passenger, #4331, #4331, #4332 **300.00**
Passenger, #4340, #4341, two-tone red, brass trim **320.00**
Passenger, #4653 electric locomotive, two Bunker Hill coaches, Yorktown observation car, orange, pre-war **. 865.00**
Passenger, #21927 engine, #24773, #24813, #24833 cars, 1960 .... **450.00**
Post Office, #1270 locomotive, coach, Railway Post Office car, eight pcs track, orig box, uncataloged, cars unnamed, 1927, some wear **250.00**
Washington, #21089 locomotive and tender, #24055 box car, #24565 flat bed car with replica cannon, #24750 coach **600.00**

Aristocraft, G gauge

Locomotive
#21403, Milwaukee Road, 4-6-2 Pacific, steam locomotive, coat tendering, NOB **250.00**
#22128, CSX GE U25-B, gray, blue, and yellow OB **165.00**
#22508, C&NW Alco RS-3, yellow and green, OB **185.00**
Rolling stock, #46211, Stewart's Root Beer, steel reefer box car, NOB **50.00**

Atlas, N gauge

Locomotive
EMD E8, diesel, Santa Fe **25.00**
Mikado, steam, MIB **70.00**

Rolling stock
#2204, box car, Great Northern **5.00**
#2601, Pullman car, Santa Fe **9.00**

Athearn, HO gauge, locomotive, brown, white lettering, silver streak, Delaware Valley Lines, 102, no box, **$30**.

Ives

Accessories
Bridge, three 10-1/2" l pieces, orig paint
.... **195.00**
Platform, cov, 119, 1905-14 .... **100.00**

Locomotive
#11, 0-4-0, 1910-13 .... **165.00**
#17, 0-4-0, 1908 .... **300.00**
#19, 0-4-0, 1917-25 .... **225.00**
#25, 4-4-2, 1906-07 .... **275.00**
#1118, 0-4-4-, 1913-14 .... **275.00**
#1661, 2-4-0, steam, 1932 .... **125.00**
#3200, 0-4-0, 1911 .... **250.00**
#3218, 0-4-0, 1917 .... **125.00**

Rolling stock
#25, tender, 1928-30 .... **150.00**
#50, baggage car, c1908-09 .... **150.00**
#52, passenger car, 1915-25 .... **45.00**
#57, lumber, 1915-30 .... **40.00**
#62, parlor car, 1924-30 .... **75.00**
#63, gravel car, 1913-14 .... **35.00**
#65, livestock car, 1918 .... **30.00**
#66, tank car, 1921-35 .... **25.00**
#67, caboose, 1918 .... **45.00**
#70, baggage car, US Mail **30.00**
#72, parlor car, 1910-15 .... **490.00**
#121, caboose, 1929 .... **75.00**
#130, buffet, 1930 .... **75.00**
#136, observation, 1926-30 .... **40.00**
#198, gravel car, 1930 .... **200.00**
#1813, baggage, 1931-32 .... **20.00**

Set
#3 cast iron stem locomotive, #1 tender, three #54 gravel cars, #56 caboose, c1910-14 .... **700.00**
#701, engine missing, Texas Oil tanker, PARR fenced car, SFRR ventilator and refrigerator car, #195 caboose, all mkd

"The Ives Railway Lines," curved track
.... **850.00**
#3250 tinplate locomotive with repainted body, #53 box car with white body, gray roof, #57 log car with brown body, 1908-30, assembled set, some wear **325.00**

Kato, N gauge

Locomotive
Amtrak GE P42 Genesis, phase III paint, OB **60.00**
BNSF EMD SD70MAC #9853, Heritage II scheme, NOB **60.00**
Burlington Road (CB&Q) EMD, painted silver, thin red stripes, NOB **90.00**
Conrail EMD SD-40 $6324, Conrail blue, OB **60.00**
Sante Fe EMD, blue and yellow, Warbonnet freight scheme, NOB... **18.00**
Union Pacific, EMD SD40-2 Snoot, lightly weathered, OB **60.00**

Rolling stock
Amtrak 4 car Superliner set, two coaches, sleeper, lounge, NOB **60.00**
CB&Q Chicago, Burlington & Quincy, passenger set, silver and black, NOB
.... **55.00**

K-Line, O gauge

Locomotive, #K3480-0001, PRR 0-6-0, switcher, steam, slant back coal tender, gunmetal gray smoke and tender, Tuscan paint on cab roof, OB **275.00**
Rolling stock, Canadian Pacific, two-car set, dome coach, café lounge car, extruded aluminum, 15" l, NOB ... **250.00**

Bachman, house, Master Craftsmen Series, early 20th C Catalog House, lighted, C-8 box, C-9 model, **$45**.

LGB, G gauge

Locomotive
#2061, Furka-Oberalp, two-axle diesel switcher, bright red, white horizontal stripes, OB **135.00**

#2090N, Kof, two-axle, BR 239 Diesel, yellowish-orange, OB.................... **120.00**
#3015, coach **75.00**
#3500, Electric Panagraph Trolley and Trolley Coach, 20th Anniversary, red and black, NOB................................ **215.00**
#20130, Grizzly Flats, 0-4-2 steam, Chloe #1, NOB.................................. **225.00**
#22171, 0-4-0 Porter style steam locomotive and coal tender, dark red, black, and silver, gold "LGB," both powered, NOB **225.00**
#22604, Schoema CFL-150DH, diesel, light gray and black chassis, green and white body, NOB **225.00**
#23570, Union Pacific F7A, yellow and gray, NOB **280.00**

Rolling stock

#3080, Denver Rio Grande Western, passenger coach, brown, gold trimmed windows.............................. **200.00**
#40919, Western Pacific boxcar, orange and silver, NOB **40.00**
#41390, Red Cross wagon car, Tuscan, Red Cross emblems, NOB **40.00**
#41490, Fire Dept, search light, water pumper, NOB **50.00**
#41760, Santa Fe two-bay cov hopper, painted Tuscan, NOB..................... **40.00**
#43760, Rio Grande two-bay coal hopper, coal load, painted black, white and orange logo, NOB.................. **40.00**
#46211, Grizzly Flats, passenger car, NOB **50.00**
#48913, Popsicle boxcar, NOB **50.00**

Lionel, O gauge

Accessories

Block signal, red base, #99N, 1932 .... **200.00**
Diesel fueling station, #415, 1955-57, MIB **250.00**
Light tower, 11" h **110.00**
Milk car platform............................ **75.00**
Power station, #435, mustard, terra cotta, and green, 1926........................ **275.00**
Railroad crossing station **125.00**
Street sign, Main Street/Broadway, 7" **60.00**
Trainmaster remote command controller, #6-12868 .... **40.00**
Catalog, *Lionel Trains and Toys*, 1965, 39 pgs, 8-1/2" x 11" **30.00**

Locomotive

#60, Lionelville, trolley type, aluminized paper reflector, 1955-58 .... **175.00**
#156, 4-4-4, electric, dark green, c1917-23 .... **265.00**
#203, 0-6-0, steam, 1940-42 .... **325.00**
#212, US Marine Corps, Alco A, 1958-59 .... **50.00**
#248E, locomotive and tender, 1936-39

.... **220.00**
#600, NW-2, 1955..................... **275.00**
#665, 41-6-4, steam, 1954-59........ **75.00**
#706, 0-4-0, Electric, 1913-16...... **250.00**
#3927, Lionel Lines, 1956-60......... **65.00**

Rolling stock

#50, gang car, MIB **75.00**
#175, rocket launcher................. **100.00**
#530, observation car, 1926-32 .... **17.50**
#605, pullman, 1925-32 .... **65.00**
#607, pullman, 1926...................... **45.00**
#754, observation car, 1934, streamliner **70.00**
#801, caboose, 1915-26 .... **17.50**
#638-2361, Van Camp's Pork & Beans, 1962 .... **20.00**
#1007, Lionel Lines, SP Die 3, 1948-52 .... **17.50**
#1514, Baby Ruth **35.00**
#1717, gondola, 1933-40 .... **25.00**
#1887, flat car, fence and horses, 1959 .... **125.00**
#2400, Maplewood, green and gray **25.00**
#2454, Sunoco tank car, 1946 .... **10.00**
#2533, pullman, 1952, mkd "Silver Cloud" **85.00**
#2602, baggage car, 1938.......... **100.00**
#2816, hopper and dump car, 1935-42 .... **50.00**
#3356, Santa Fe Railway Express, 1956-60 .... **35.00**
#3360, Burro crane, 1956, MIB.... **275.00**
#3413, Mercury capsule launching, 1962, MIB.. **325.00**
#3444, gondola, Erie, 1957-59....... **30.00**
#3461, flat car, log, dump, 1949-55 **25.00**
#3494-150, box car, MoPac, 1956, MIB **300.00**
#6025, tank car, Gulf, 1956-57....... **10.00**
#6454, boxcar.............................. **75.00**
#6456, hopper car, Lehigh Valley **150.00**
#6650, IRBM missile car, red frame, blue support.................................... **45.00**
#6814, Caboose rescue unit, 8-1/2" l **65.00**
#9116, hopper, Domino Sugar, dome tank car, blue, black vertical stripe and center dome, blue and white logo . **25.00**
#9422, box car, EJ & E, green, orange, black.................................... **20.00**
#9705, box car, D & RGW, orange and silver **27.50**
#9859, billboard reefer, Pabst Blue Ribbon Beer.................................... **85.00**
#16219, boxcar, True Value Hardware **75.00**
#16617, box car, C & NW, 10-3/4" l **30.00**
#17203, box car, Cotton Belt, double doors, red, large white letters **35.00**
#19835, box car, Fedex, animated, blue and white....................................... **40.00**

#6-16904, TTU NYC, articulated truck spine car, missing two trailer loads, NOB **25.00**

#6-19286, Warner Bros Sylvester & Tweety, boxcar, NOB...................... **25.00**

#6-19774, porthole caboose, LRRC, Railroader Club, 1999 MIB **55.00**

#6-19775, turkey stock, LRRC, Railroader Club, 1999, MIB **50.00**

#6-19966, gondola car, Railroader Club, 1998, MIB **50.00**

#6-19978, boxcar, Railroaders Club, 1999, MIB **85.00**

#6-19991, boxcar, Centennial Celebration, Railroader Club, MIB **100.00**

#6-26749, Alaska log dump, NOB . **24.00**

#6-36769, box car, Fourth of July, lighted, LRRC, Railroad Club, 2003, MIB.... **60.00**

Lionel, O gauge, #292 set, 153 locomotive, two #629 cars, one #630, original track and transformer, original box, $400.

Set

Blue Streak, #265, #265WX, #617 coach, #618 observation car, #619, 1936 **700.00**

City of Denver, #636W locomotive, two #617 coaches, #618 observation car, 1936... **550.00**

Flying Yankee, #616 locomotive, three #617 coaches, #618 observation car, gunmetal and chrome, 1935 .... **275.00**

L.A.S.E.R., #1150, chromed DC switcher locomotive, Ram-Jet A.C.L.M. car, glow-in-the-dark radar tracking car, survelliance helicopter car, glow-in-the-dark Laser Gun Security Car," DC power pack, orig tract, play mat, 36" x 54" set up, orig box **250.00**

Passenger, #252 electric locomotive,

#529 coach, #530 observation, olive green, c1926................................ **175.00**

Passenger, Union Pacific, #752E power unit, #753 coach, #754 observation, silver, c1934 .... **350.00**

Pennsylvania, red and yellow, decal worn, four pcs.............................. **185.00**

Lionel, S gauge

Accessories

Animated circus clown car, #16651, MIB **30.00**

Christmas car/Seasons Greetings

#7806, 1976, MIB.................... **75.00**

#7813, 1977, MIB.................... **75.00**

#7814, 1978, MIB.................... **80.00**

#9491, 1986, MIB.................... **50.00**

#9778, 1975, MIB.................. **145.00**

#19908, 1989, MIB................. **35.00**

#19929, 1994, MIB................. **30.00**

Passenger train station, Lionelville, c1923, some scratches and paint chips, chimneys missing........................ **175.00**

Catalog, accessories

1953, 9" x 6", 15 pgs...................... **35.00**

1959, 34 pgs................................. **15.00**

Catalog, consumers

1953, 8" x 5-1/2", 31 pgs **35.00**

1954 .... **35.00**

1955 .... **35.00**

1956 .... **30.00**

Catalog, dealer, 1955........................ **45.00**

Catalog, Super O Track, 1957, four pgs, 11" x 8"... **10.00**

Instruction sheet, giraffe car, four pgs, folded, 1961..................................... **4.00**

Locomotive

#5, 0-4-0, steam, c1910-18.......... **475.00**

#10E, electric **90.00**

#1912, square cab, 1910-12........ **250.00**

#2035, steam locomotive, tinplate, #6466W tender, sq firebox, high headlight, repainted, smoke, whistle in tender, c1950............................... **225.00**

Magazine tear sheet, Joe DiMaggio endorsing Lionel, 1950, 7" x 10"....... **7.00**

Manual, *How to Operate Lionel Trains and Accessories*, 1957, 64 pgs, 8-1/2" x 5-1/2" **15.00**

Rolling stock

#35, Pullman, c1915, orange......... **65.00**

#213, cattle car, c1926-50............ **450.00**

#214R, refrigerator car, ivory body, peacock roof.................................. **400.00**

#216, hopper car, Sunoco decal, 1926-40 .... **350.00**

#217, caboose, orange and maroon, 1926-40.. **150.00**

#322, observation car, 1924........... **95.00**

#6017, caboose, brown **10.00**

#6175, rocket car, 1958................. **20.00**

V

Valentines

History: Early cards were often handmade and included both hand-written verses and hand-drawn design or border. Many cards also had some cutwork and hand-colored designs.

Among the prettiest collectible cards found today are the early hand-done lace paper valentines made between 1840 and 1900. Lace paper cards are folded in half, the front is covered with one or more layers of lace paper—either white, silver, or gold—with colored scraps or lithos filling the center. A printed verse is found inside, and the card may come in a matching embossed lacy enve-lope. The older the paper-lace, the fine the quality of the paper. The period from 1840 to 1860 is consid-ered the golden age of lace paper valentines.

Most of the collectible valentines found today were made between 1900 and 1914 and are freestanding and consist of layers of die cuts. These include pull-downs, pullouts, pop-ups, and foldouts.

Pull-downs are made of cardboard die cut into fancy, lacy, colored shapes that create multi-dimensional images such as boats, ships, cars, planes, or gardens. Early examples pulled down from the middle; later pieces, which are not quite as elaborate as their prede-cessors, come down from the front.

Honeycomb tissue was used a great deal on pullouts, which open out and are free standing on a honeycomb base or easel back. Some of these open to form a whole circular design. The most valuable ones are those with a center column and a honeycomb base and canopy top. Tissue used on the early pieces was usually white, soft pink, blue, or green; during the 1920s, red or soft red tissue was used.

Along with tissue-paper valentines, we see lots of mechanical cards from the 1920s. Mechanicals have moving parts that are set in motion by pulling at tabs or moving wheels that are part of the card.

Two other popular styles are flats and hangers. Flats—easy to find and among the most reasonable to col-lect—often have fancy die-cut borders, embossing, and an artist-designed center of a pretty girl. Hangers are cards with silk ribbon at the top for hanging. A string of pretty die-cuts on a ribbon is called a charm string.

Bitter comic valentines were made as early as 1840, but most are from the post-1900 period. These cards make fun of appearance, occupation, or per-sonality, and also embraced social issues of the day. Comic character val-entines feature comic strip characters or the likes of Snow White, Mickey Mouse, Superman, or Wonder Woman.

Collecting Hints: Unless the design is unique, the very simple, small penny cards given by school children are not of interest to collectors. Most collectors tend to specialize in one type of card, e.g., transportation theme cards, lacy, or honeycomb.

Condition of the card is very impor-tant—watch out for missing parts, soil, etc.

Keep cards out of direct sunlight to prevent fading and to keep them from becoming brittle. Store them in layers with acid-free tissue between each one, and use moth crystals or silverfish packets to protect them from insect infestation.

Adviser: Evalene Pulati.

Fold-out, two children in 17th C dress, boy playing violin, basket of flowers with pink tissue fold-out at feet, **$35**.

Animated

Children with bear, seesaw, 1920s ... **20.00**
Girl playing piano, 1920s, 6" h.......... **15.00**
Walking Doll, small, 4" h, 1923 .... **15.00**
World War II sailor boy, in boat, 5" x 8"
.... **30.00**
World War II soldier boy, stand-up **22.00**

Comic

McLoughlin
4" x 6", old car................................. **10.00**
8" x 10", sheet, sgd CJH, 1914, old maid
.... **9.00**
10" x 15", sheet, occupational, butcher
.... **15.00**
Unknown maker, 8" x 10", sheet, 1925 **5.00**

Diecut, small

Brundage, artist sgd, child **12.00**
Clapsaddle, artist sgd, child **12.00**
Heart shapes, girls **7.50**

Flat

Art Nouveau, embossed
Fancy, 4" x 4", kittens........................ **8.00**
Girls, 3" x 5"..................................... **7.50**
Heart shape, child, 1920s.................... **3.50**

Folder

Fancy borders, birds, 1914 .... **7.50**
Lacy cutwork edges, verse............... **10.00**
Tied with silk ribbon, 1920 .... **7.50**

Hanger and string

Hanger
Art Nouveau, heart, silk ribbon, 5" x 5"
.... **12.50**
Cutwork edge, litho, 1910, 3" x 4"... **12.50**
Fancy, artist sgd, 8" x 8", 1905........ **25.00**

String
Artist sgd, 3" x 3", 4 pcs **35.00**
Sweet children, 2" x 4", five pcs...... **45.00**

Honeycomb tissue

Beistle
Early 1920s, pale red **12.50**
Honeycomb base and top, red, 1926
.... **22.50**

Temple Love
Honeycomb base only.................... **18.00**
Honeycomb base and top.............. **25.00**
Wide-eyed children playing house. **30.00**

Paper lace

American
McLoughlin, layered folder, 1890... **20.00**
3" x 5", orig envelope, c1900 .... **25.00**
6" x 9", two added lace layers **20.00**
8" x 10", two layers, c1910 .... **30.00**
Boxed, fancy scraps, ribbons............. **35.00**
Early, hand done, scraps, ribbons...... **45.00**

Simple lace folder

c1870, 5" x 7" **18.50**
c1885 .... **18.50**

Parchment

Children, umbrella **7.50**
Layered, ribbons **30.00**
Silk, cherubs..................................... **35.00**

Diecut, front folds down to show garden,
4-3/8" w, 7-3/8" h, **$15**.

Pull-down

Artist diecut, three layers, 1920s....... **35.00**
Auto, layered, large, c1910 .... **95.00**
Auto, large, cute children, 1920s **65.00**
Children,1930s
Fancy background, large.............. **20.00**
Two layers, large............................ **18.50**
Windmill background, large.......... **30.00**
Dollhouse, large, elaborate, 1920s ... **65.00**
Floral, large, children, four layers, 1920s
.... **55.00**
Flowers, three layers, 1920s **30.00**
Garden, large, layered, fancy, 1920s . **65.00**
German Auto, pre-World War I, 5" x 8" **75.00**
Hearts, 1930s................................... **35.00**
Horse-drawn wagon, 1910............. **110.00**

Pullout

Flowers in vase, opens out, 1920s.... **35.00**
Garden scene, children, 7" x 10"........ **35.00**
Gondola, children, honeycomb base, 1930s
.... **55.00**
Lighthouse, opens out, 1920s........... **45.00**
Sea plane, opens out, 1920s............. **65.00**
Ship, honeycomb base, 7" x 12"......... **75.00**

Tunnel of Love
Honeycomb base **25.00**
Honeycomb base and top **35.00**

Silk fringed

Prang

Double-sided, 1880s, 3" x 5" **25.00**
Fancy, padded front, 5" x 7" **35.00**

Tuck

Artist-signed, c1890, 5" x 7" **25.00**
Double-sided, c1900, 3" x 5" **25.00**
Unmarked, small, 1900 .... **10.00**

Standup with easel back

Airport scene, children traveling **15.00**
Automobile, windows open, small **25.00**
Cherub with heart **7.50**

Children

Diecut, fancy, house **12.50**
Dollhouse, 1925, large **15.00**
Figural **5.00**
School room scene **10.00**
Sledding, flat **15.00**
Fancy, silk inserts, 1900, 10" x 14" **15.00**
Flat, flapper, c1920, 8" **10.00**

Flower basket

Cherub **10.00**
Pasteboard, 1918, large **10.00**
Layered parchment, c1910, 5" x 8" **15.00**
Schoolroom scene, children at desks
.... **18.00**
Sports figure, 7" h **12.50**
World War I, doughboy, 6" h **20.00**
World War II, soldier and sailor boys, flat
pcs, 8" h **15.00**

Victorian novelty

Animated, doll, head reverses, large, rare
.... **95.00**

Diecut

Children, fancy, boxed **27.50**
Musical instruments, large **85.00**
Musical instruments, small **35.00**

Wood, telephone, boxed

Large 75.00
Small 45.00

Vending Machines

History: Some of us still remember the penny gumball or peanut machine of our childhood. Many such vendors still survive on location after 30 years or more of service, due in part to the strength and simplicity of their construction.

The years between 1910 and 1940 were the heyday of the most collectible style of vendor, the globe-type peanut or gumball machine. Throughout this period, machine manufacturers invested a great deal of money in advertising and research. Many new designs were patented.

The simple rugged designs proved the most popular with the operator who serviced an established route of vendors as a means of making a living. Many operators made their fortunes "a penny at a time," especially during the Depression when dollars were hard to come by. Fifty years later, the vendors that originally cost between $4 and $15 command a much higher price.

In addition to the globe-style variety of vendor, cabinet-style machines were also made. These usually incorporate a clockwork mechanism and occasionally mechanical figurines to deliver the merchandise. The earliest examples of these were produced in the 1890s.

Collecting Hints: Since individual manufacturers offered such a wide range of models, some collectors choose to specialize in a particular brand of machine. Variations are important. Certain accessories, porcelain finish, colors, or special mechanical features on an otherwise common machine can add greatly to value.

Original paint is important, but numerous machines, especially peanut vendors with salt-damaged paint, have been repainted. Most vendors were in service for 10 to 20 years or more. Repainting normally was done by the operator as part of routine repair and maintenance. Repaints, recent or otherwise, if nicely done, do not necessarily lessen the value of a desirable machine. However, original paint should be retained if at all possible.

Decals add substantially to the appearance of a vendor and often are the only means of identifying it. Original decals, again, are the most desirable. Reproduction decals of many popular styles have been made and are a viable alternative if originals are not available.

Some reproduction parts also are available. In some cases, entire machines have been reproduced using new glass and castings. Using one or two new parts as a means of restoring an otherwise incomplete machine is generally accepted by collectors.

Collecting vending machines is a relatively new hobby. It has increased in popularity with other advertising collectibles. Previously unknown machines constantly are being discovered, thus maintaining the fascination for collectors.

Adviser: Bob Levy.

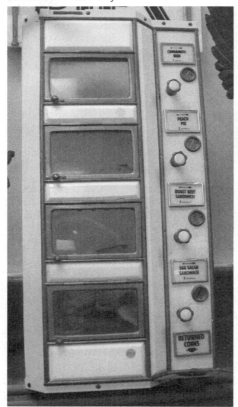

Horn & Harnardt, four-section cabinet, white enamel, black trim, original coin slot and labels, separate "Pies" sign, **$450**.

Arcade cards, Exhibit Supply, c1925, two columns, 1¢ **175.00**
Aspirin, Certified, c1950, 12 for 25¢ .. **50.00**
Candy/gum
Advance Junior, 1904 .... **250.00**
Ajax Deluxe Nut, c1947 .... **350.00**
Canteen, c1933 .... **425.00**
Columbus, Model K, c1917 .... **350.00**
Dean, c1972 .... **50.00**
Hershey, c1950, 1¢ **75.00**
Mansfield Automatic Clerk, c1902
.... **1,000.00**
Mills, automatic, c1936 .... **100.00**
Norris, Master Novelty, c1923 .... **175.00**
Northwestern, merchandiser, c1931
.... **175.00**
Oak, Acorn, c1947 .... **50.00**
Pulver, short, policeman **1,400.00**
Silverking Hunter, c1940 .... **300.00**
Victor, Topper, c1950 .... **90.00**

Ajax, hot nut vendor, with side cup holder, top lights up, 1940, **$800**.

Cigarettes, Dial-A-Smoke, Elde, Inc., c1940, circular **200.00**
Cigars, Roi-Tan, c1940 .... **125.00**
Combs, Advance, Unit-e, c1950, 10¢ **75.00**
Lighter fluid, Van-Lite, c1933 .... **900.00**
Matches, Diamond books, c1928 .... **350.00**
Novelty Card Vendor, c1930 .... **300.00**
Pens, Servend, c1960 .... **75.00**
Perfume, Bull's Head, 1905 .... **2,000.00**
Prophylactic, Advance, c1923 .... **125.00**
Stamps
American Postmaster, c1930 .... **125.00**
National Postage, c1940 .... **75.00**
Shipman Stamp, c1960 .... **45.00**
Victory Automatic, c1930 .... **100.00**

View-Master Products

History: The first View-Master viewers and reels were made available in 1939. Invented by William Gruber, View-Master products were manufactured and sold by Sawyer's, Inc., of Portland, Oregon. The early growth of View-Master was cut short by World War II. Shortages of film, plastic, and paper would have crippled the operation and possibly ended the existence of View-Master had not the Army and Navy recognized the visual training potential of this product. Between 1942 and the war's end, about 100,000 viewers and five to six million reels were ordered by the military.

After the war, public demand for View-Master products soared. Production barely satisfied the needs of the original 1,000-dealer network. The

Model C viewer, introduced in 1946, was practically indestructible, making it the most common viewer found by collectors today.

In October 1966, General Aniline & Film Corporation (GAF) bought Sawyer's and revamped the View-Master line. GAF introduced new 2-D projectors and the 3-D Talking View-Master.

In late 1980, GAF sold the View-Master portion of its company to a limited partnership headed by businessman Arnold Thaler. Further acquisition resulted in the purchase of Ideal Toys. Today the 3-D viewers and reels are manufactured by View-Master Ideal, Inc.

Collecting Hints: Condition is the key price determinant. Because this collecting category is relatively new and large quantities of material were made, viewers and reels in mint or near-new condition can still be found.

Original packaging is sought by collectors. Many viewers and reels were removed from boxes and envelopes, used excessively, and damaged.

Viewer, black Bakelite, Sawyers, Portland, OR, embossed "Reg US Pat Off, US Pat 2,189,285," original box, 4-1/2" x 3-3/4", **$65.**

Alaska Bound, Sawyer, 1948, #301 ... **15.00**
Alaska Ketchikan, Sawyer, 1948, #302 .... **15.00**
Alex **4.50**
Alf **8.50**
Annie **5.00**
Annie Oakley **15.00**
Archie **8.00**
Auto Racing, Phoenix 200, ABC Sports **35.00**
Badlands, GAF, #A-489 .... **17.50**
Bad News Bears, 1977 .... **15.00**
Banana Splits **10.00**
Barnaby In Space, GAF, 1972 .... **20.00**
Baseball Stars, Sawyer, 1953, #725, #726, #727 .... **60.00**
Batman **15.00**
Battle of the Planets **15.00**
Beautiful Cypress Gardens, FL, Sawyer, #A961, 1958 .... **20.00**
Beverly Hillbillies **15.00**

Big Blue Marble **10.00**
Birds of the World, GAF, 1968 .... **15.00**
Black Beauty **10.00**
Black Hole **15.00**
Bon Voyage Charlie Brown, GAF, 1980 .... **10.00**
Bonanza, GAF, B47, 1964 .... **34.00**
Bozo **15.00**
Brady Bunch, GAF, 1960s **38.00**
Brooklyn USA, three reels **40.00**
Buck Rogers, GAF, 1960s **10.00**
Buffalo Bill Jr **24.00**
Bugs Bunny **10.00**
Bugs Bunny and Tweety **4.00**
Bugs Bunny-Road Runner Show **4.00**
Bullwinkle **12.50**
Captain America **5.00**
Captain Kangaroo **10.00**
Care Bears **5.00**
Casper, GAF, 1961 .... **25.00**
Charles Dickens, Sawyer, A Christmas Carol, 1956, three reel set **24.00**
Charlie Brown, Bon Voyage **5.00**
Charlotte's Web **5.00**
CHiPs **15.00**
Christmas Story, Sawyer, 1948, three reel set **24.00**
Cisco Kid **5.00**
Columbia River, Sawyer, 1950, #151 **17.50**
Coronation of Queen Elizabeth II, Sawyer, three reel set **24.00**
Cowboy Stars **25.00**
Croquet Game and Trial, Alice in Wonderland, FT-20-C **10.00**
Daktan, GAF, 1968 .... **35.00**
Dale Evans **27.50**
Daniel Boone **15.00**
Dark Shadows **32.00**
Dennis the Menace **4.00**
Deputy Dawg **30.00**
Desert Cactus in Bloom, Sawyer, #289 .... **15.00**
Desert Wildflowers in Bloom, Sawyer, #290 .... **15.00**
Detroit, A583, three reels **18.00**
Dick Tracy **7.50**
Disneyland, Sawyers, 1962
    Adventureland **20.00**
    Fantasyland **25.00**
    Main Street USA **20.00**
    Tomorrowland **25.00**
Donald Duck, Sawyers, 1960s **25.00**
Dr. Who **35.00**
Dracula **15.00**
Duck Tales **5.00**
Dukes of Hazzard, MOC **15.00**
Dumbo **7.50**
Eight is Enough, 1980 .... **15.00**
Emergency **10.00**
E. T. **15.00**
Expo, 1967, three reels
    A071 .... **24.00**
    A073 .... **24.00**
    A074 .... **27.00**
Family Affair **24.00**

Fantastic Four................................ 10.00
Fantastic Voyage.......................... 75.00
Fat Albert & Cosby Kids.............. 10.00
Flintstones, View Master International, 1980
copyright, MOC............................. 15.00
Fraggle Rock.................................. 3.50
France, Sawyers, sealed pack........... 15.00
Frankenstein, GAF, 1976................ 15.00
Full House..................................... 3.00
Garden Flowers of Autumn, Sawyer, 1953,
#982.. 15.00
Garden Flowers of Summer, Sawyer, 1953,
#981.. 15.00
Gene Autry................................... 40.00
Germany, GAF, sealed pack............. 15.00
Ghostbusters................................ 5.00
GI Joe Adventures, GAF................ 20.00
Godzilla.. 14.00
Goonies.. 7.50
Great Muppet Caper...................... 4.50
Great Smokey Mountains National Park,
Tennessee, Sawyer, 1948, #336..... 15.00
Grizzly Adams............................... 10.00
Grotto of Redemption West Bend, IA, GAF
.... 10.00
Gunsmoke, GAF, 1972................... 30.00
Happy Days................................... 10.00
Hawaii Five-O............................... 20.00
Highway US 1, Daytona Beach, Sawyer,
#162.. 17.50
Hopalong Cassidy and Topper, 1950, #955
.... 12.00
Howard the Duck........................... 8.00
Huckleberry Hound & Yogi Bear........ 5.00
Inauguration of Pres Eisenhower, Sawyer,
#400.. 37.50
Incredible Hulk, three reels, booklet,
envelope, GAF Viewmaster Cartoon
Favorites, J26, 1981...................... 18.00
Inspector Gadget.......................... 6.00
International Swimming and Diving, ABC
Sports.. 60.00
Iowa, Sawyers................................ 15.00
Ironman.. 3.50
Isis, MIP....................................... 25.00
Italy, Sawyers, sealed pack.............. 15.00
Jasper Icefields, Canadian Rockies,
Alberta, Sawyer, 1948, #317......... 17.50
Jasper Parks, Canadian Rockies, Sawyer,
1948, #316.................................. 17.50
James Bond, Live & Let Die.............. 12.00
Jaws... 3.50
Jesus Turns Water Into Wine, Churchcraft
Pictures, Sawyer, 1947, #CH-15, maroon
sleeve.. 18.00
Jetson's, 1981, sealed pack............. 24.00
John Travolta, 1979, MIP................ 35.00
Julia, three reels, story booklet, no
envelope, 1969............................. 40.00
King Kong..................................... 12.00
Knight Rider.................................. 5.00
Korg, sealed.................................. 10.00
Kotter, sealed................................ 18.00
Kung Fu.. 10.00
Lake Tahoo, A161, three reels........... 14.00

Land of the Giants, Sawyer, #B484, three
reels, 1968................................... 45.00
Land of the Lost, GAF, #2, The Abominable
Snowman, 1971, orig booklet, damage to
envelope...................................... 15.00
Lassie and Timmy, GAF, 1958......... 20.00
Lassie Look Homeward, GAF, 1965. 20.00
Last Starfighter........................... 7.50
Laugh-In, GAF, three reels, orig envelope,
1968.. 45.00
Legend of the Lone Ranger.............. 7.50
Little Mermaid............................... 6.50
Los Angeles, CA, Sawyer, 1948, #221
.... 17.50
Love Bug....................................... 10.00
Mad Tea Party, Alice in Wonderland, FT-20-B
.... 10.00
Mannix, sealed.............................. 15.00
Maoris Natives of New Zealand, Sawyer,
1950, #5261................................ 15.00
Marine Studios, Marineland, FL, Sawyer,
1948, #166.................................. 17.50
Mary Poppins................................ 8.00
M*A*S*H....................................... 10.00
Mexico, GAF, 1973, sealed pack....... 18.00

Lassie & Timmy, $20

Miami, FL, Sawyer, 1949, #165.......... 17.50
Mickey Mouse Club........................ 25.00
Mickey Mouse in Clock Cleaners, GAF,
1971.. 20.00
Mighty Mouse............................... 20.00
Mission Impossible........................ 15.00
Mod Squad, B478, three reels........... 38.00
Monkees, talking, illus box.............. 80.00
Mount Lassen, Volcanic Natural Park,
Sawyer, #256............................... 17.50
Mount Rushmore, GAF, 1966........... 15.00
Movie Stars, one reel...................... 15.00
Muppets Go Hawaiian..................... 5.00
Naval Aviation Training, World War II, test
reel #13, hand lettered, plane
identification............................... 25.00
Natural Bridge, VA, Sawyer, 1949, #SP-
9012.. 15.00
NCAA Track & Field Championships, ABC
Sports.. 55.00
New Mickey Mouse Club.................. 4.50
New York City, Twin Towers, Sawyer, 1950,
#157.. 30.00

New Zoo Revue.................................. 12.00
Niagara Falls, Sawyer, 1948, #375..... 15.00
Niagara Falls In Winter, Sawyer, 1950, #82
.... 17.50
Niagara Falls, NY, Sawyer, 1950, #81 17.50
Old Mexico, Sawyer, #B206, three reels,
sealed.. 15.00
One of Our Dinosaurs is Missing..... 12.00
Painted Desert, Arizona, Sawyer, #177
.... 17.50
Partridge Family, talking, illus box, MIB
.... 50.00
Pee-Wee's Playhouse, Tyco, 1987, MOC
.... 15.00
Petrified Forest, Sawyer, #178.......... 17.50
Pete's Dragon...................................... 8.00
Pinocchio, Sawyer, #B311, three reels,
sealed.. 16.00
Planet of the Apes, master set, orig
envelope... 30.00
Pluto... 5.00
Polly in Venice.................................. 18.00
Popeye, Sawyers, 1962..................... 20.00
Poseidon Adventure......................... 24.00
Prodigal Son, Churchcraft Pictures, 1947,
#CH-55, maroon sleeve.................. 18.00
Quick-Draw McGraw, Sawyers, 1961 25.00
Red Riding Hood................................. 5.00
Return to Witch Mountain................. 7.50
Ringling Bros and Barnum & Bailey
Circus, 1952, three reels, red envelope
.... 35.00
Rin-Tin-Tin.. 15.00
Road Runner, GAF, 1967.................. 20.00
Robin Hood....................................... 24.00
Romper Room...................................... 8.00
Royal Gorge, Colorado, Sawyer, 1947, #238
.... 17.50
Roy Rogers....................................... 25.00
San Diego Zoo, Sawyer, #A173, three reels
.... 15.00
San Juan, Puerto Rico, Sawyer, 1946, #564
.... 15.00
Santa Catalina Island, CA, Sawyers, #201
.... 5.00
Scenic USA, GAF, sealed pack.......... 15.00
Scooby Doo... 9.50
Sebastian.. 28.00
Secret Squirrel & Adam Ant............. 10.00
Sesame Street, Follow That Bird.......... 4.50
Silver Dollar City, GAF, 1971.............. 15.00
Silverhawks... 5.00
Silver Springs, FL, Sawyers, #A962, 1958
.... 20.00
Smurf, Flying....................................... 3.50
Snoopy and the Red Baron................ 8.00
Snow White and the Seven Dwarfs.. 10.00
Snowman... 6.50
South Carolina, 1954, Sawyer, three reel set
.... 20.00
Space Mouse, Sawyer, 1964.............. 25.00
Space: 1999, GAF, 1975..................... 28.00
Spider-Man.. 10.00
Star Trek, Mr. Spock's Time Trek, GAF, 1974
.... 20.00
St. Augustine, Florida, Sawyer, #160 . 15.00

Strange Animals of the World, GAF, 1958
.... 18.00
Superman Movie, sealed................... 18.00
S.W.A.T., sealed 15.00
Tailspin... 5.00
Tarzan, Sawyer, #B444, three reels.... 48.00
Teenage Mutant Ninja Turtles............ 2.50
Texas, Sawyer, three-reel set............. 20.00
Thomas the Tank Engine................... 7.50
Thor.. 2.00
Thunderbirds..................................... 45.00
Time Tunnel, Sawyer, 1966.............. 165.00
Toby Tyler... 30.00
Tom & Jerry....................................... 10.00
Tom Sawyer....................................... 10.00
Top Cat, 1962, MIP........................... 40.00
Tournament of Thrills, ABC Sports... 35.00
TV Stars, one reel............................. 20.00
Tweety & Sylvester........................... 10.00
20,000 Leagues Under The Sea, Sawyers,
1962.. 30.00
U.N.C.L.E., three reels, story booklet, no
envelope, 1965................................. 36.00
U.F.O.. 40.00
United States Naval Academy, Sawyer,
1950, #139.. 17.50
Universal Studios Scenic Tour, GAF, 1974,
sealed pack...................................... 25.00
Upper Michigan, Sawyer, 1949, #248 15.00
US Spaceport, GAF............................ 15.00
Venice, Italy, Sawyer, 1949, #1606..... 15.00
Virgin Islands, Sawyers, #B036, three reels
.... 16.00
Voyage to the Bottom of the Sea, Sawyers,
1966.. 30.00
Waltons.. 10.00
Washington DC, Sawyers, sealed pack
.... 15.00
Water Ski Show, Cypress Gardens.. 15.00
Welcome Back Kotter, three reels, story
booklet, color photo cover, 1977 ... 24.00
Wild Animals of Africa, GAF, 1958... 15.00
Wild Animals of the World, GAF, 1958
.... 12.00
Wild Bill Hickcock & Jingles............ 30.00
Wind in the Willows............................ 8.00
Winnetou... 25.00
Wise Men Find Jesus, Churchcraft
Pictures, 1947, #CH-8, maroon sleeve
.... 18.00
Wizard of Oz, 4-1/2" sq envelope, set of
three, full color, orig booklet, 1957
copyright.. 24.00
Woody Woodpecker............................ 15.00
World Adventureland, GAF................ 20.00
World Bobsled, Championships, ABC
Sports... 60.00
Yellowstone National Park, Sawyer, 1948,
#126.. 17.50
Yellowstone National Park, Sawyer, 1948,
#127.. 17.50
Yellowstone National Park, Sawyer, 1948,
#128.. 17.50
Young Indiana Jones.......................... 7.50
Zorro.. 35.00

W

Watch Fobs

History: A watch fob is a useful and decorative item that attaches to a man's pocket watch by a strap and assists him in removing the watch from his pocket. Fobs became popular during the last quarter of the 19th century. Companies such as The Greenduck Co. in Chicago, IL, Schwabb in Milwaukee, WI, and Metal Arts in Rochester produced fobs for companies that wished to advertise their products or to commemorate an event, individual, or group.

Most fobs are made of metal and struck from a steel die. Enamel fobs are scarce and sought after by collectors. If a fob was popular, a company would order restrikes. As a result, some fobs were issued for a period of 25 years or more. Watch fobs still are used today in promoting heavy industrial equipment.

Collecting Hints: The most popular fobs are those related to old machinery, either farm, construction, or industrial. Advertising fobs are the next most popular group.

The back of a fob is helpful in identifying a genuine fob from a reproduction or restrike. Genuine fobs frequently have advertising or a union trademark on the back. Some genuine fobs do have blank backs; but a blank back should be a warning to be cautious.

Reproduction Alert.

Advertising

Anheuser-Busch, 1-1/2" d, diecut silvered brass, enameled red, white, and blue trademark **60.00**
Brown Gin and Liquors, 1-1/2" d, brass, raised moose head, reverse "Sold by H Obernauer & Co, Pittsburgh, PA" ... **60.00**
Buster Brown Blue Ribbon Shoes, silvered white metal oval, attached 3-3/4" long black leather strap with detailed image of Mary Jane looking at her new shoes, Buster and Tige smiling and waving **150.00**
Caterpillar, MacAllister Machinery Co., Ft. Wayne-Indianapolis, Plymouth, IN . 1-1/2" **45.00**
Engeman-Matthew Range, diecut range **85.00**

Bronze-colored metal, Viking-type ship in center, marked "KEPKYPA" on one side, other side with Olympic-type scenes, **$12.**

Evening Gazette, baseball shape, scorecard back, 1912 .... **95.00**
Gardner-Denver Co, jackhammer, silvered brass, tool replica, symbol and name on back, c1950 .... **25.00**
General Motors Diesel Engine, bronze luster metal, detailed engine image, block inscription "GM/General Motors Diesel Power," block logo on back, engraved dealer name.................. **15.00**
Green River Whiskey **45.00**
Huntingdon Pianos, dark white metal, 7/8" black, white, blue, and gold celluloid with Paderewski, inscription "Paderewski Bought One," early 1900s.............. **65.00**
Johnston's the Appreciated Chocolates, pretty woman offering platter full of candy, 2-1/8" **40.00**
Kellogg Switchboard & Supply Co/The Service Of The Telephone Proves The Worth Of The Line, dark copper luster brass, raised image of candlestick phone with receiver off the hook, "K" circular logo, 1920s **60.00**
Kelly Sprfingfield Tires, 2" d, white metal, raised illus of female motorist, "Kelly Springfield Hand Made Tires" on back **75.00**
Lima Construction Equipment, copper luster, large excavation tractor, world continents background, inscribed "Lima/ Move The Earth With a Lima," back text for shovels, draglines, clamshells, and cranes **25.00**
Lorain Construction Equipment, silvered brass, truck crane used to fill bed of pickup truck, inscribed "Loraine Cranes-Shovels/Draglines/Moto-Cranes," back inscribed "Freeland Equipment Co, Baltimore, orig strap **30.00**

Martin-Senour Paints, 1-1/2" d, silvered brass, 1" d multicolored celluloid insert, hand holding dripping paint brush, text on back... **65.00**
Moose Club Whiskey, silvered brass, center celluloid insert, inscribed "Moose Club Whiskey, The Best in The Land, The Adler Co., Cincinnati, O," early 1900s
.... **125.00**
Old Dutch Cleanser, porcelain center with Dutch lady **75.00**
Red Bird Coffee, silver luster finish, brass, black, white, and red celluloid disk, blank reverse **50.00**
Red Goose Shoes, enameled red goose
.... **95.00**
Rosenthal Bros, NY, Adamant Suit, boy holding knickers, sitting on box holding extra pants...................................... **40.00**
Schramm Tractors **60.00**
Sterling Has No Equal, Sterling Ranges, Sill Stove Works, Rochester, NY, 1-3/4" h diecut white metal, company logo stamped on back **40.00**
Studebaker, enameled tire design . **50.00**
Ward's Fine Cakes, white porcelain, bluebird, silvered beaded rim **45.00**
Zeno Means Good Chewing Gum, brass
.... **95.00**
Brass, mechanical cigar cutter, mkd "D B Patent" **275.00**
Bronze, emb United States Great Seal, back mkd "Genuine Bronze," 1-5/8" d **36.00**
Carnelian, carved mask, gold filled frame, 1-3/8" x 1".. **95.00**
Citrine, gold filled, engraved floral design, 1-1/2" x 1"...................................... **275.00**
Elk's tooth, bone engraved "1888 Deer" on one side "Feb 10" on other, replaced leather strap **60.00**

Gold filled/plated/tone

Coin, one cent, gold filled frame, 1-1/4" x 1-1/2"... **75.00**
Elk, mkd "St. Louis Button Co.," very worn, 1-1/2".................................... **20.00**
Horn, Victorian, c1870, 1-1/8" x 5".. **75.00**
Jitney, stamped, 1-5/8" h................. **55.00**
Oval bezel set amethyst, 3-3/4" x 1-1/2"
.... **100.00**

Political

Bryan, Our Next President............. **40.00**
Democratic National Convention, Baltimore, 1912, silvered brass, center shield with eagle standing atop...... **20.00**
Hughes, Charles E, 1908, silvered brass, head and shoulder portrait, from governor's campaign **60.00**
Republican National Convention, brass, 1920, bust of Lincoln...................... **40.00**
Taft and Sherman, 1-1/4" jugate portraits, leather fob, back paper from Rudolph Bros. Syracuse **45.00**

Laddie Athletic, white metal, $12.

Taft, brass, figural, padlock, "White House Lock, Taft 1908/Holds The Key"
.... **50.00**
Taft, brass, two sided, four sections, top section shows elephant with letters "G.O.P." on back, second section shows Teddy Roosevelt beating bass drum "Use TR's Nerve Tonic For Business Troubles," third section shows soldiers and rifles "Regular Army Should Be Increased," fourth section shows TR "No Man Is Above The Law and No Corporation So Wealthy That I cannot Be Called To Account," reverse top section crossed US flags, second section with battleship "Upbuilding of Navy Must Be Continued," third section "Look At The Doughnut Not The Hole" with "Big Crops Great Natural Resources" on doughnut, "Business Depression" inside doughnut, "Compliments of Judge Co., Copyrighted Judge Co. 1908," bottom section shows "Taft for President," 1-1/2" x 6" including chain and clasp **100.00**

Souvenir

Cleveland State Convention, American Legion, 1946, diecut brass **30.00**
Jennie Wade House, Gettysburg, PA, silvered brass, 1930s, 1-7/8" l........ **25.00**
Mormon Temple, Salt Lake City **50.00**
Municipal Pier, Chicago, emb scene, initials "MWA" and cross hatchet and mallet, back mkd "Souvenir Chicago Camp, June 19-23, 1917," 1-7/8" l. **30.00**
Princeton University, brass, 1908 .. **45.00**

World Championship Rodeo Contest, Chicago **45.00**
Sterling silver, Victorian, center shield, anchor, lion passant, "O" and "WHH" marks, English, c1850, 1" x 1-3/4" **145.00**
Vegetable ivory, carved face, mkd "Un Recuerdo," 7/8" x 1" **28.00**

Watt Pottery

History: Watt Pottery traces its roots back to W. J. Watt who founded the Brilliant Stoneware Company in 1886 in Rose Farm, Ohio. Watt sold his stoneware company in 1897. Between 1903 and 1921, W. J. Watt worked at the Ransbottom Brothers Pottery owned by his brothers-in-law.

In 1921, W. J. Watt purchased the Crooksville, Ohio, Globe Stoneware Company, known briefly as the Zane W. Burley Pottery between 1919 and 1921, and renamed it Watt Pottery Company. Watt was assisted by Harry and Thomas, his sons, C. L. Dawson, his son-in-law, Marion Watt, his daughter, and numerous other relatives.

Between 1922 and 1935, the company produced a line of stoneware products manufactured from clay found in the Crooksville area. The company prospered, exporting some of its wares to Canada.

In the mid-1930s, Watt introduced a kitchenware line with a background of off-white and tan earth tones. This new ware was similar in appearance to dinnerware patterns made by Pennsbury, Pfaltzgraff, and Purinton. It also can be compared to English Torquay.

Most Watt dinnerware featured an underglaze decoration. On pieces made prior to 1950, decoration was relatively simple, e.g., blue and white banding. Patterns were introduced in 1950; the first was a pansy motif. Red Apple began in 1952 and Rooster in 1955. Floral series, such as Starflower and Tulip variations, were made. New patterns were introduced yearly.

Watt sold its wares through large chain stores such as Kroger's, Safeway, and Woolworth, and grocery, hardware, and other retail merchants. Most of their output was sold in New England and New York. The balance was sold in the Midwest, Northwest, and South.

In the early 1960s, Watt was grossing over three-quarters of a million dollars. Future prospects were promising, but on October 4, 1965, fire destroyed the factory and warehouse. The pottery was not rebuilt.

Watt Pottery is collected by a well-organized collectors' club, Watt Collectors Association (WCA). This non-profit educational organization gathers yearly and has issued some Watt Pottery commemoratives. These commemoratives are now coming into the secondary market and are becoming collectible.

Collecting Hints: Since Watt pottery was hand painted, there is a great deal of variation in patterns. Look for pieces with aesthetically pleasing designs that have remained bright and cheerful.

Watt had a strong regional presence in New England and New York, where more than 50 percent of its production was sold. Little of the output made its way West. Beware of placing too much emphasis on availability as a price consideration when buying outside the New England and New York areas.

Watt made experimental and specialty advertising pieces. These are eagerly sought by collectors. In addition, Watt made pieces to be sold exclusively by other distributors, e.g., Ravarino & Freschi Company's "R-F Spaghetti" mark.

Reproduction Alert: A Japanese copy of a large spaghetti bowl marked simply "U.S.A." is known. The Watt example bears "Peeddeeco" and "U.S.A." marks.

Many forms of Watt's Apple pattern were included in Spotlight Antiques at the March 2004 Atlantique City show.

Apple

Baker, open
#95 .... **45.00**
#604, adv "A Little Thank You From
Cascade Oil Co." **35.00**
Beanpot, #76 .... **200.00**

Bowl
#04, ribbed **25.00**
#05, adv, "Stan Ferris Insurance,
Enterprise, Oregon" **40.00**
#05, ribbed **25.00**
#06, adv "John Roric Hardware, Home of
Frigidaire Maytag-Hamilton" **65.00**
#07, ribbed **25.00**
#08, adv for Hillsboro Farmers Co-Op
Warehouse," mkd "Watt 8, USA" **95.00**
#09 .... **75.00**
#63 .... **60.00**
#66 .... **95.00**
#73, adv for W. C. Keinas Markesan,
Wisconsin, mkd "Oven Ware 73 USA"
.... **125.00**
#96, mkd "Watt 96 USA Oven Ware,"
8-1/2" d **75.00**
Canister, cov, #72 .... **265.00**
Casserole, cov
#96 .... **65.00**
#2/48 .... **175.00**
#18, individual, handle **170.00**
#601, ribbed **135.00**
Cereal bowl, #74 .... **30.00**
Chip 'n' dip set, #119/#120, wire stand
.... **200.00**
Cookie jar, #21 .... **375.00**
Creamer, #62, adv "Farmers Lumber Co.,
Fontanelle, Iowa" **95.00**
Dinner plate, #29, 10" d **250.00**

Grease jar
#01 .... **350.00**
#47, adv "In Appreciation Rock Rapids
Co-op Creamery" **675.00**
Ice bucket, #59 .... **295.00**
Mixing bowl, #64 .... **50.00**
Mug **65.00**
Nappy, #64 .... **65.00**
Pie plate, #33, adv "Kanne's Our Own
Hardware, Brooten, Minn" **95.00**

Pitcher
#15, adv "Culligan Soft Water Service,
Oberlin, Kans," rub on spout **65.00**
#15, adv "Farmers Savings Bank,
Walford, Iowa" **165.00**
#16, turquoise leaves **60.00**
#17, ice lip, light crazing **120.00**
Platter, #49 .... **450.00**
Salad bowl, #73
Apple inside **65.00**
Apple inside, outside adv "Whitman,
N.D." **85.00**
Salad bowl, #106 .... **165.00**
Salt and pepper shakers, #45/46, barrel
.... **450.00**

Spaghetti bowl, #39 .... **95.00**
Sugar bowl, #98 .... **400.00**
Teapot, cov, #112, spout repaired. **1,900.00**
Vegetable bowl, cov **50.00**

Apple, spaghetti bowl, $95.

Autumn Foliage

Baker, cov **90.00**
Bean pot, #76 .... **50.00**
Cookie jar, #76 .... **95.00**
Creamer, #62 .... **200.00**
Grease jar, #01, some wear **85.00**
Salad bowl, #106 .... **45.00**
Salt and pepper shakers, pr, #117/118,
hourglass **95.00**
Spaghetti bowl, #39, crazing **20.00**
Sugar, cov, #98 .... **150.00**
Teapot, #505 .... **995.00**

Black Moonflower

Cup and saucer, cup damaged **10.00**
Plate, #101 .... **20.00**

Bleeding Heart

Bean pot **125.00**
Bowl, #7 .... **30.00**
Creamer **75.00**
Pitcher, #15 .... **55.00**

Cherry

Baker, #53 .... **100.00**
Berry bowl, #4 .... **25.00**

Bowl
#23 .... **100.00**
#89 .... **50.00**
Pitcher, #15 .... **60.00**
Platter **150.00**
Salt shaker **50.00**
Spaghetti bowl, #39 .... **85.00**

Cut-leaf Pansy

Bowl, #23 .... **25.00**
Creamer **30.00**
Lid, #18 .... **5.00**

Spaghetti bowl
#39 .... **40.00**
#44 .... **25.00**

Double Apple
Baker, cov, #96, wire stand **115.00**
Beanpot, #76 .... **325.00**
Bowl, #07, ribbed **65.00**
Cookie jar, #503 .... **650.00**
Creamer, #62 .... **250.00**
Salad bowl, #73 .... **60.00**

Dutch Tulip
Bowl, #68, small **80.00**
Creamer, #62 .... **195.00**
Mixing bowl, #63, deep **90.00**
Pitcher
#15 .... **195.00**
#16, nick on spout **105.00**
Refrigerator pitcher, #69 .... **225.00**

Pansy
Casserole, cov, individual, stick handle, mkd "Watt Oven Ware USA" **145.00**
Creamer, 3-1/2" h **100.00**
Pie plate, #33, adv **60.00**
Pizza plate **275.00**
Spaghetti bowl, #39 .... **95.00**

Rio Rose
Casserole, cov, #2/48 .... **40.00**
Plate, #28, 7-1/2" d **20.00**
Platter, #49 .... **40.00**
Spaghetti bowl
#24 .... **35.00**
#39 .... **25.00**

Rooster
Baker, cov
#66, repaired lid **40.00**
#67 .... **165.00**
Baker, open, #66, crazing **20.00**
Beanpot, #76 .... **375.00**
Bowl
#9, wide rim **35.00**
#58 .... **85.00**
Casserole, cov, #18 .... **425.00**
Cheese crock, #80 .... **1,500.00**
Creamer, #62 .... **275.00**
Ice bucket **125.00**
Mixing bowl
#5 .... **85.00**
#7, ribbed, "Random Lake Co-op, Chester E Stahl, mgr, 1963" **65.00**
Pitcher
#15, nick on spout **75.00**
#16 .... **185.00**
#16, adv "Compliment of the Beery's," stained **85.00**
Refrigerator pitcher, #69, small nick on spout **425.00**

Salt and pepper shakers, pr, #45/46, pepper cracked **145.00**
Spaghetti bowl, #39, slant sided **265.00**

Starflower
Baker, #67 .... **165.00**
Bowl
#4 .... **20.00**
#15, four petal flower **95.00**
#55 .... **45.00**
#60 .... **30.00**
#68 .... **50.00**
Casserole, cov, #18
Stick handle, nick on lid **30.00**
Tab handle, individual size **55.00**
Casserole, cov, #67 .... **110.00**
Cookie jar, #21 .... **165.00**
Creamer, #62 .... **185.00**
Dinner plate, 10" d **15.00**
Grease jug, #1 .... **350.00**
Mixing bowls, nesting, set of four, #4, #5, #6, #7 .... **185.00**
Mug, #501 .... **95.00**
Pitcher
#15, lavender flower **90.00**
#16 .... **85.00**
#17 .... **115.00**
Platter, #31 .... **65.00**
Salt and pepper shakers, #45/46, barrel **95.00**
Spaghetti bowl
#24, small **45.00**
#39, slant sides **50.00**
Tumbler **300.00**

Teardrop
Baker, cov, #66 .... **120.00**
Bean cup, #75, hairline **5.00**
Salad bowl, #73 .... **75.00**
Spaghetti bowl, #39 .... **165.00**

Daisy, bowl, marked "Ovenware," **$45.**

Tulip
Baker, ribbed
#600 .... **195.00**
#603 .... **145.00**
#604 .... **155.00**

Baker lid, ribbed, #600 .... **35.00**
Bean pot, #76 .... **100.00**
Bowl
    #62, mkd "Oven Ware 62 USA".... **150.00**
    #64, 5" h, 7-1/2" d, mkd "Oven Ware 64
    USA" **180.00**
    #65, 5-3/4" h, mkd "Oven Ware 65 USA"
    .... **190.00**
    #73 .... **115.00**
Casserole, cov, #600 .... **125.00**
Cookie jar, #503 .... **375.00**
Creamer, #62 .... **225.00**
Pitcher
    #15, small ground chip on rim **450.00**
    #16 .... **95.00**
    #17, ice lip, two rim chips **100.00**
Salad bowl, #73 .... **145.00**
Spaghetti bowl, #39 .... **100.00**

Two-Leaf Apple

Baker, cov, #3/19, wire stand **115.00**
Bowl
    #6, wide rim, hairline **25.00**
    #60 .... **75.00**
Canister, #72, buffed edge chip **350.00**
Casserole, cov
    #3/19 .... **105.00**
    #18, stick handle, individual size.... **75.00**
    #67 .... **85.00**
Ice bucket, #59 .... **175.00**
Salad bowl, #55 .... **85.00**
WCA commemorative
    1993, Apple, pie plate.................. **475.00**
    1994, Apple, creamer **85.00**
    1995, Apple, grease jar **30.00**
    1996, Apple, salt and pepper shakers
    .... **50.00**
    1997, Apple, refrigerator pitcher **25.00**
    1998, Apple, divided dinner plate.. **10.00**
    1999, Apple, beanpot **20.00**
    2000, Apple, knife sharpener **5.00**
    2002, Apple barrel mug.................. **20.00**

Westwood

Baker, #96, yellow, brown glaze drip, imp
    "Watt 96 Oven Ware USA" **45.00**
Mixing bowl, 7-1/2" d **45.00**

Weller Pottery

History: In 1872, Samuel A. Weller opened a small factory in Fultonham, near Zanesville, Ohio. There he produced utilitarian stoneware, such as milk pans and sewer tile. In 1882, he moved his facilities to Zanesville. Then in 1890, Weller built a new plant in the Putnam section of Zanesville along the tracks of the Cincinnati and Muskingum Railway. Additions to this plant followed in 1892 and 1894.

In 1894, Weller entered into an agreement with William A. Long to purchase the Lonhuda Faience Company, which had developed an art pottery line under the guidance of Laura A. Fry, formerly of Rookwood. Long left in 1895, but Weller continued to produce Lonhuda under the new name "Louwelsa." Replacing Long as art director was Charles Babcock Upjohn who, along with Jacques Sicard, Frederick Hurten Rhead, and Gazo Fudji, developed Weller's art pottery lines.

At the end of World War I, many prestige lines were discontinued and Weller concentrated on commercial wares. Rudolph Lorber joined the staff and designed lines such as Roma, Forest, and Knifewood. In 1920, Weller purchased the plant of the Zanesville Art Pottery and claimed to produce more pottery than anyone else in the country.

Art pottery enjoyed a revival when the Hudson Line was introduced in the early 1920s. The 1930s saw Coppertone and Graystone Garden wares added. However, the Depression forced the closing of the Putnam plant and one on Marietta Street in Zanesville. After World War II, inexpensive Japanese imports took over Weller's market. In 1947, Essex Wire Company of Detroit took control through stock purchases, but early in 1948 operations ceased.

Collecting Hints: Because pieces of Weller's commercial ware are readily available, prices are stable and unlikely to rise rapidly. Forest, Glendale, and Woodcraft are the popular patterns in the middle price range. The Novelty Line is most popular among the lower-priced items.

Novice collectors are advised to consider figurals. There are more than 50 variations of frogs, and many other animal shapes also are available.

Pieces made during the middle production period are usually marked with an impressed "Weller" in block letters or a half-circle ink stamp with the words "Weller Pottery." Late pieces are marked with a script "Weller" or "Weller Pottery." Many new collectors see a dated mark and incorrectly think the piece is old.

There are well more than 100 Weller patterns. New collectors should visit other collectors, talk with dealers, and look at a large range of pieces to determine which patterns they like and want to collect. Most collections are organized by pattern, not by shape or type.

Note: For pieces in the middle and upper price ranges see *Warman's Antiques and Collectibles Price Guide.*

Basket, Apple Blossom, green matte body, white flowers and green leaves at handle, marked, **$35**.

Ashtray
Coppertone, frog seated at end... **115.00**
Roma, 2-1/2" d.................................... **35.00**
Woodcraft, 3" d.................................. **75.00**

Basket
Florenzo, 5-1/2" **75.00**
Melrose, 10"..................................... **155.00**
Sabrinian.. **165.00**
Silvertone, 8"................................... **350.00**
Wild Rose, 6" h, 5" d........................ **65.00**

Bowl
Bonito, brown, green, and blue, int. crazing, 9" d **150.00**
Cameo, 6" d...................................... **95.00**
Claremont.. **325.00**
Claywood, 4" d **40.00**
Knifewood, swans, dark ground... **255.00**
Marbleized, 5-3/4" d, 1-5/8" d, shades of rose, pink and mauve **55.00**
Sabrinian, 6-1/2" x 3" h **240.00**
Scandia, 6-1/2" d.............................. **75.00**
Woodcraft, squirrel, 5-1/4" d, 3" h. **195.00**
Bud vase, Muskota, double, 5-1/4" h, small rim chip... **175.00**

Candlesticks, pr
Euclid, 12-1/2" h, orange luster **85.00**
Floraia, 11" h................................... **235.00**

Lorbeek, 2-1/2" h, shape #1 .... **125.00**
Pumila **65.00**
Silvertone **175.00**

Children's ware
Feeding Dish, Strutting Duck **125.00**
Milk Pitcher, 4" h, Zona **75.00**
Plate, Zona, 7" d............................. **70.00**
Cigarette holder, figural, frog, Coppertone
.... **200.00**
Compote, Bonito, 4" h........................ **75.00**
Console bowl, Syndonia, 17" x 6" **90.00**

Console set
Ardsley, c1928, 12" d bowl, pr 4-3/8" h candlesticks................................. **345.00**
Warwick, 10-1/2" d bowl, pr candlesticks
.... **175.00**

Cornucopia
Softone, light blue........................... **45.00**
Wild Rose... **75.00**

Ewer
Cameo, 10" h, white rose, blue ground
.... **65.00**
Etna, 9" h...................................... **150.00**
Forest, 8" h **175.00**
Greenbrier, 11-1/2" h **200.00**
Louwelsa, red and orange clover dec, 5-1/2" h, artist sgd........................... **190.00**
Panella **55.00**

Left: ewer, blue ground, pink flower, green leaves, **$45**; right: matching bud vase, both inscribed "Weller," **$25**.

Figure
Brighton Kingfisher...................... **350.00**
Elephant, bug-eyed, Cactus line, yellow
.... **145.00**
Turtle, Coppertone, 5-1/2" l **95.00**
Flask, Take a Plunge........................ **135.00**

Flower frog
Kingfisher, 6" **475.00**
Marvo, blue...................................... **55.00**
Silvertone, 1928 .... **100.00**
Woodcraft, figural lobster, c1917 . **120.00**

Hanging basket
Ivory Ware, marked with half kiln ink
stamp **110.00**
Marvo, 7" **145.00**
Woodcraft, 9" **225.00**

Jardinière
Claywood, 8", cherries and trees.... **95.00**
Fairfield, 6-3/4" h **175.00**
Ivory, 5" **45.00**
Marvo, rust, 7-1/2" **85.00**
Roma, cat chasing canary **175.00**
Jug, Louwelsa, small **140.00**
Lamp base, Louwelsa, artist sgd, 9" h
.... **350.00**

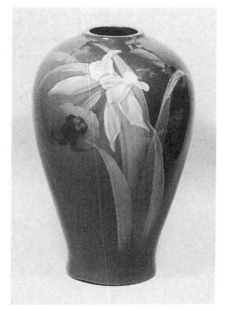

Vase, Louwelsa, Jonquil, hand-painted
decoration, c1900, 9-1/2" h, **$500**. Photo
courtesy of Wellscroft Lodge.

Mug
Aurelian, 4-1/2" h .....,.................... **375.00**
Claywood, star shaped flowers **75.00**
Dickensware, 5-3/4" h **375.00**
Ivory, brown accents, cream ground
.... **55.00**
Souevo, #30 .... **150.00**

Pitcher
Bouquet, 6" h, ruffled top, lavender flower,
white ground, artist sgd "M" **60.00**
Louwelsa, #750, 14" h, artist sgd. **600.00**
Pansy, 6-1/2" h **110.00**
Pierre, 5" h **50.00**
Zona, 8" h, kingfisher dec, green glaze,
c1920 .... **140.00**

Planter
Blue Drapery **60.00**
Duck **75.00**
Forest Tub, 4" **135.00**
Klyro, small **45.00**
Sabrinian, 5" x 5" **170.00**
Woodrose, 9" h **60.00**
Spittoon, Louwelsa, 7" d, 5-1/2" h **225.00**
Tub, Flemish, 4-1/2" d **75.00**
Tumbler, Bonito, multicolored flowers,
4-1/4" h **70.00**
Umbrella stand, Ivory, 20" h **225.00**
Urn, sculpted handles, matte blue, unmark-
ed, 5-1/2" h **50.00**

Vase, Louwelsa, square, hand-painted
raspberries, c1900, 8-1/4" h, **$435**. Photo
courtesy of Wellscroft Lodge.

Vase, spherical, aqua matte glaze, three pedestal feet, marked "Weller P-1," 5" h, $45.

Vase, spherical, cream matte glaze, daisy decoration, marked "Weller B-3," 5" h, $65.

Vase

Art Nouveau, 5" h	**160.00**
Atlas, yellow, white trim, mkd "C-3, Weller," 6-1/2" d, 4" h	**165.00**
Bonito, 9" h	**350.00**
Burntwood, pin-oak dec, 11" h	**150.00**
Chase, 9" h	**350.00**
Claremont, 5" h, 2 handles	**60.00**
Coppertone, 8-1/2" h	**265.00**
Dogwood, 9-1/2" h	**125.00**
Eocean, 10-1/2" h	**250.00**
Floretta, 7-1/2" h, grapes dec, high-gloss glaze	**175.00**
Forest, 6" h	**165.00**
Genova	**95.00**
Glendale Thrush	**250.00**
Hudson, floral dec, sgd "D England," 7" h	**200.00**
Ivory, peacocks, 11" h	**85.00**
Knifewood, 5-1/2" h, canaries, high glaze, nick on inside rim	**125.00**
Louella, gray, hp, nasturtiums	**220.00**
Louwelsa, #595, 6-5/8" h	**180.00**
Muskota, boy fishing, c1915, 7-1/2" h	**200.00**
Oak Leaf, 8-1/2" h	**185.00**
Paragon, gold, base chip, 6-3/4" h	**145.00**
Scenic	**65.00**
Souevo, 7" h	**115.00**
Turkis, deep red, yellow and green drip, script "Weller Pottery," 5" h	**195.00**
Tutone, 4" h, three-legged ball shape	**75.00**
Viola, fan shape	**65.00**
Woodcraft, 1917, smooth tree-trunk shape, molded leafy branch around rim, purple plums, 12" h	**195.00**

Wall pocket

Ardsley, double, 12" l	**190.00**
Blue, emb leaf, 7" l	**60.00**
Glendale, 9-1/2" l	**450.00**
Iris, blue, 8-1/2" l	**50.00**
Klyro, 8" l	**110.00**
Pearl, 8-1/2" l	**160.00**
Roma, 7" l	**130.00**
Squirrel	**375.00**
Souevo	**195.00**
Sydonia, blue	**225.00**
Tutone, 11" l	**170.00**
Woodcraft, 10" h	**300.00**
Woodland	**120.00**
Woodrose	**110.00**

Western Americana

History: Western American was sought out and preserved even before the turn of the century when astute historians saw their way of life disappearing before their eyes and made an effort to save all that they could through oral histories and artifacts. Much regional Western memorabilia is available in tiny local museums and historical societies. Early collectors were often ranchers, cowboys, and the descendants of early residents trying to keep their own family history intact. Today, collectors are more varied and you can find Western memorabilia on display in barns, high-class restaurants and attorney's offices. As the American West has become more popular, prices have risen and the fine line between the "real" old West and that of story, song and movie has blurred. Today, you can find a fine pair of wooly chaps displayed beside a vintage Gene Autry movie poster or a Red Ryder BB gun mounted on a gun rack right next to a Winchester.

Collecting Hints: The collecting category of Western Americana is as vast and as wide ranging as the West itself. Western art and books are collected, along with well-used cowboy gear like saddles and spurs. Western-theme furniture, decorative items, and dinnerware have become very collectible and are often priced as high as their antiques that are one hundred years older.

Western memorabilia has a strong regional following. For example, memorabilia from the early years of the Grand Canyon National Park has a stronger following in Arizona while "Let 'er Buck" souvenirs of the Pendleton Rodeo are more eagerly sought out by Oregon collectors.

Look for a hot spot in the market to be ethnic collectibles. Memorabilia from the black "Buffalo Soldiers" calvary units is sought after by Western and military collectors for its rarity as well as for the contribution to black Western history. Hispanic cultural influence in the settlement of the West cannot be overlooked. After all, it has been over four hundred years since the first Spanish settlers arrived in modern day New Mexico. Souvenirs from Mexico continue to be popular today, as more collectors come to recognize the fine craftsmanship involved in their manufacture of sterling silver jewelry, weavings and pottery.

Cowgirl memorabilia has long been a "sleeper" in this category and is now becoming a vibrant, exciting part of the Western Americana market. This is due, in part, to a growing number of books and short stories chronicling the role of women in settling the West. Just check out the auction prices for a signed Annie Oakley cabinet card! Posters, sheet music, or postcards featuring a cowgirl in vintage clothing is a hot item. Cowboy and cowgirl toys remain a good buy. Western-themed toys, especially Japanese tin lithographed toys from the 1950s and 1960s are relatively inexpensive and sure to appreciate.

With popularity comes imitation, and Western memorabilia is no exception. Beware of the many "new" items of Western memorabilia that are in reality cheaply made imports. Be especially wary of spurs marked "Korea" or those that have scratch marks where the country of origin has been ground off. Most contemporary Western artists, whether their medium is leather, metal or oils, market their products honestly, as a new work of art.

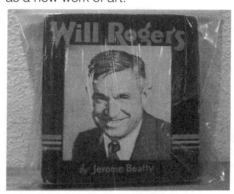

Book, *Will Rogers,* Jerome Beatty, $20.

Advertising

Banner, 19 1/2" by 29", Winchester horse and rider in center, "Headquarters for Winchester Rifles and Shotguns," fringed hem **250.00**
Figure, cowboy with saddle, rope, Stetson cologne, composition **35.00**
Sign, Moccasin Agency, fierce Indian with headdress, emb tin **95.00**

Artwork

Buffalo Bill, pyrography, drawn and burnt of Albert J.Seigfried, NY, 1907 ..... **150.00**
Wells Fargo Depot and Office Building, Moron Taft, CA, 1910, orig ink drawing, 20" by 30" framed **750.00**
Autograph, photo card, "Louise from W. F. Cody, 1906" (Buffalo Bill) **1,500.00**
Belt buckle, Heston, Rodeo, 1985 ..... **25.00**

Bit

Iron, rusted, marked "CSA," often used by former Confederate soldiers in the West **500.00**
Silver inlay spade bit, full engraving of kissing birds, J. F. Echaverria, minor restoration **2,000**
G. S. Garcia, silver inlay, curved snake cheeks, large 2" domed conchos **1,500.00**
Bolo, 3" diameter figural turtle, crushed turquoise inlay, marked ".925" (sterling silver) and "Taxco" **65.00**

Book

Cowboys North and South, Will James, 1924 .... **45.00**

Doctor at Timberline, Charles Fox Gardiner, Caxton Printers, Caldwell, Idaho, 1939, 3rd printing, 315 pgs. **10.00**

Famous Sheriffs and Western Outlaws, William MacLeod Raine, Doubleday, 1929, 1st ed., 294 pgs **12.00**

Hidden Trails, Wm Patterson White, color frontis, Ralph Coleman, A. L. Burt, 1920 .... **5.25**

Mark Turns West, A Western Story, Mary Imlay Taylor, Chelsea House, 1926, colorful dj **6.50**

Recollections of Persons and Places in the West, H. M. Brackenridge, 1868, 331 pgs **50.00**

The Frontier, A Frontier Town Three Months Old, Ward Platt, Jennings & Graham, Young People's Missionary Movement, 1908, color fold-out maps, illus **18.00**

The Keeper of Red Horse Pass, W. C. Tuttle, Grossett & Dunlap **7.50**

The Secret of Lonesome Cove, Samuel Hopkins Adams, b/w illus by Frank Schoonover, Bobbs Merrill, 1912 ..... **8.00**

The Snake Pit, Alex Knopf, 1929 ...... **8.00**

The Virginian, A Horseman of the Plains, Owen Wistler, Arthur Keller illus, Grossett & Dunlap, 1904 .... **8.50**

The Wild West: A History of the Wild West Shows, Don Russell, 1970, ex-lib ... **12.00**

Two on the Trail, A Story of the Far Northwest, Hubert Footner, Grossett & Dunlap, 1912 .... **7.50**

Bookends, pr, "End of the Trail," tired Indian on pony, cast metal **75.00**

Buckskin jacket, beaded, w/fringe, 1920s **250.00**

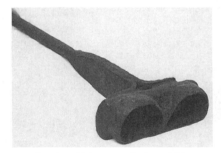

Branding iron, "B," wwrought iron, $90.

Catalog

Hamley & Co., Pendleton, OR, 1931, 176 pgs, 6" x 9", Hamley Cowboy Cat No. 32, color illus of saddles, ropes, hand woven Navajo blankets, bridles, etc. **250.00**

Stockman-Farmer Supply Co., Denver, CO, 1941, 56 pgs, 8-1/4" x 10-1/2", Spring & Summer Catalog No. 16, Miller Western Wear **35.00**

Chaps

Black woolies **500.00**

Edward Bohlin, batwing style, black, engraved sterling silver buckle mounted with eight 1878 silver dollars **2,800.00**

Shotgun (narrow leg) style, well-worn leather, initials "JS" **450.00**

Cowboy hat, Stetson, orig box **150.00**

Cowboy outfit, child's, Bat Masterson, size 4, unused, MIB **225.00**

Cuffs, pr

Plain leather, brass studs form star design, unmarked **250.00**

Tooled leather, fancy floral engraving, no maker's mark **150.00**

Dinnerware, Wallace China

Boots & Saddles, cup and saucer set **45.00**

Rodeo, salad plate, 7" d **75.00**

Westward Ho, ashtray **55.00**

Drinking glass, frosted, painted cowboy on bucking bronco, 1950s era **25.00**

Holster and belt, tooled leather, floral design, marked Mexico **95.00**

Holster w/running iron (portable branding iron), crudely handmade **75.00**

Broadside, Silver City Raiders, Russell Hayden, black and white, $45.

Label, unused

Big Chief, handsome Indian chief and tomatoes, strip label .... **.75**

Bronco, cowboy swinging lariat, riding galloping brown horse, western desert scene, Redlands oranges **3.00**

Conestoga, covered wagon and ox team, desert background, 7" x 9" **3.00**

Lazy G, cowboy branding a calf...... **2.00**

Mustang Vegetables, wild white mustang horse, black ground, 5" x 7" .... **.75**

Santa Rosa, man and burro, Spanish style home overlooking lemon orchard **2.00**
Tex-Rio, pretty senorita, black ground, lug size.. **1.00**
Texus, cowboy wearing cowboy hat, tomato label, lug size **2.00**
White Horse, galloping white horse, black ground .... **.50**
Magic lantern slides, set of 60, "Colorado by a Tenderfoot," shows mining towns, Pike's Peak, waterfalls, 1907 Denver **300.00**
Mug, steer head, Western Enamel, 4-3/4" h **22.50**
Neckerchief, bucking bronco motif, "Let 'er Buck" rodeo souvenir, 1920s........ **125.00**
Pennant, Grand National Livestock Show and Rodeo, San Francisco, 1960s. **35.00**
Pinback button, "Let 'er buck," celluloid, cowboy on bucking horse, 1" d...... **25.00**
Pitcher, plastic, figural cowboy with gun, 1950s.. **45.00**
Postcard, cowboys & cowgirls on picnic, by "Dude" Larsen................................ **15.00**
Poster, Yosemite National Park, 1931, Jo Mora... **200.00**
Program, Texas Prison Rodeo, 1970s **15.00**
Rope

Braided horsehair.......................... **225.00**
Braided rawhide, "riata"............... **150.00**
Rope box, tooled leather with initials "FS" **450.00**

Stereograph card, Round-up on the Sherman Ranch, Genesse, Kansas, Keystone View Co., #12475, **$10**

Saddle

Calvary, McClellan military issue .. **800.00**
Charo style, mother of pearl inlay, marked "La Moderna" **2,500.00**
Child's, Roy Rogers imprint **1,250.00**
Hamley, Pendleton, OR, exc condition **2,800.00**
Pack saddle, wood frame for burro **75.00**
Saddle bags

Embossed floral leather, black, marked "Garcia, Mexico" **125.00**
R. T. Frazier marked, wooly angora trim **2,000.00**
"US" military saddle bags, fair condition **250.00**

Saddle blanket

Navajo, densely woven, few stains, 1960s **475.00**
Pendleton, Indian style print, 1970s tag **125.00**
Scarf, horses motif, rayon, 28" sq....... **24.00**
Spittoon

Brass and iron turtle **650.00**
Copper, 13" d, saloon-type, 1870s **275.00**
Spurs

Buerman, marked "Hercules Bronze," gal leg, old leathers **650.00**
Child's, marked "Made in USA," good leather **40.00**
Mexican style, silver inlay, large rowels **450.00**
N & J, brass, horse heads, pr...... **225.00**
Tobacco felt, Indian rug design, "rolling logs" (swastikas) good luck motif .. **25.00**
Toy, Cortland, Rocking R Ranch, litho tin wind-up **295.00**
Toy chest, cowboy and Indian motif, burnt-wood designs, 1950s **250.00**
Vase, Wagon Wheel shape, stamped "Frankoma" **35.00**
Wall lamp, cast iron, silhouette of bronco buster **30.00**
Watch fob, sterling, 101 Ranch, shows the Miller Bros **650.00**

Westmoreland Glass Company

History: The Westmoreland Glass Company was founded in October 1899 at Grapeville, Pennsylvania. From the beginning, Westmoreland made handcrafted high-quality glassware. During the early years, the company processed mustard, baking powder, and condiments to fill its containers. During World War I, candy-filled glass novelties were popular.

Although Westmoreland is famous for its milk glass, other types of glass products were also produced. During the 1920s, Westmoreland made reproductions and decorated wares. Color and tableware appeared in the 1930s; but, as with other companies, 1935 saw production return primarily to crystal. From the 1940s to the 1960s, black, ruby, and amber objects were made.

In May 1982, the factory closed. Reorganization brought a reopening in

July 1982, but the Grapeville plant closed again in 1984.

Collecting Hints: The collector should become familiar with the many lines of tableware produced. English Hobnail, made from the 1920s to the 1960s, is popular. Colonial designs were used frequently, and accessories with dolphin pedestals are distinctive.

The trademark, an intertwined "W" and "G," was imprinted on glass beginning in 1949. After January 1983, the full name, "Westmoreland," was marked on all glass products. Early molds were reintroduced. Numbered, signed, dated "Limited Editions" were offered.

Covered dish, eagle on nest, aqua carnival glass, $35.

Animal, covered dish type, white milk glass
   Camel, kneeling **75.00**
   Cat, blue eyes **75.00**
   Chick on eggs, iridized................... **85.00**
   Fox, brown eyes, lacy base **75.00**
   Hen on nest, white milk glass, blue head, diamond basket weaved nest, 5-1/2" l, 4-1/4" w **65.00**
   Hen on nest, white milk glass, red painted top and eyes, 5-1/2" l, 4-1/2" h, WG mark **60.00**
   Swan, raised wing.......................... **115.00**
   Turkey, crystal, some Goofus glass dec remaining, 6-1/4" w, 5-1/4" d, 7" h. **125.00**
Appetizer canape set, Paneled Grape, milk glass **80.00**
Ashtray, 5" d, Beaded Grape.............. **15.00**
Basket
   Pansy, milk glass............................ **20.00**
   Princess Feather, 7-1/4" d **125.00**
   Thousand Eye, clear, 8-3/4" h **300.00**
Bonbon, Waterford, #1932, ruby stained, 6" d, heart shaped, handle **70.00**
Bowl, cov, 5" d, flared, Beaded Grape **55.00**

Bowl, open
   7" d, 2-3/4" h, English Hobnail, three legs **75.00**
   7-1/2" d, vaseline, crimped, round foil label... **55.00**
   8" d, Hobnail, blue, ftd, two handles **160.00**
   9" w, sq, ftd, Beaded Grape, milk glass **55.00**
   9" d, 6" h, ftd, Paneled Grape, milk glass **60.00**
   10-1/2" d, ftd, Paneled Grape, milk glass. **100.00**
Bud vase, 10" h, Paneled Grape, milk glass, orig label **30.00**
Butter dish, cov, 1/4 lb
   Old Quilt, milk glass........................ **28.00**
   Paneled Grape, milk glass............. **24.00**
Cake stand, Paneled Grape, milk glass **95.00**

Covered dish, Santa on sleigh, purple, $45.

Candlesticks, pr
   Dolphins, white opaque glass, 9" h **75.00**
   English Hobnail, green, 3-3/4" h **78.00**
   Old Quilt, milk glass........................ **30.00**
   Paneled Grape, milk glass, 4" h..... **25.00**
   Ring & Petal **22.00**
   Sleighs, cobalt blue, 4-1/4" h **75.00**
   Waterford, #1932, ruby stained, 6" h, 1-lite... **130.00**
Candy dish, cov
   Beaded Bouquet, blue milk glass.. **35.00**
   Beaded Grape, 9" d, ftd **40.00**
   Della Robbia, 7" h **100.00**
   Old Quilt, milk glass, high foot **30.00**
   Paneled Grape, milk glass, three legs, crimped... **35.00**
   Wakefield, crystal, low................... **45.00**
   Waterford, ruby stained, 9" d **35.00**
Cheese, cov, Old Quilt, milk glass...... **45.00**
Children's dishes
   Creamer, File & Fan, ruby carnival. **20.00**
   Mug, chick, milk glass, #603, dec, orig label... **30.00**
   Pitcher, Flute, cobalt blue, white floral dec **40.00**

Sugar, cov, File & Fan, ruby carnival
.... **30.00**
Table set, cov butter, creamer, cov sugar,
File & Fan, milk glass **45.00**
Tumbler, Flute, green, white floral dec
.... **15.00**

Compote
Vaseline, WG mark, 9" d, 7" h **145.00**
Waterford, #1932, ruby stained, ruffled,
ftd **120.00**

Console set
Crystal Wedding, milk glass, pr 4-1/2" h
candlesticks, orig label **150.00**
Dolphin, milk glass, three pcs **85.00**

Cordial, Waterford, #1932, ruby stained
.... **50.00**

Creamer, 6-1/2 oz, Paneled Grape, milk
glass, orig label **16.00**

Cruet, stopper
Old Quilt, milk glass **30.00**
Paneled Grape, milk glass **30.00**

Cup and saucer
Paneled Grape, milk glass **22.00**
Plain, beaded edge, milk glass **12.00**

Dinner plate, Daisy Decal, #1800, 10-1/4" d,
dark blue mist, scalloped edge...... **45.00**

Dish, heart shape, handle, Della Robia,
stained **70.00**

Dresser tray
Paneled Grape, milk glass, dec ... **125.00**
Sunflower, milk glass....................... **30.00**

Epergne, 8-1/2" h, Paneled Grape, milk
glass **70.00**

Flower pot, Paneled Grape, milk glass
.... **48.00**

Fruit cocktail, Paneled Grape, milk glass
.... **25.00**

Fruit cocktail underplate, Paneled Grape,
milk glass... **9.00**

Goblet, 8 oz
Della Robia, stained........................ **40.00**
Paneled Grape, milk glass **18.00**

Gravy boat and underplate, Paneled
Grape, milk glass **58.00**

Honey dish, cov, 5" d, Beaded Grape, milk
glass, roses and garland dec......... **45.00**

Ice tea tumbler
Old Quilt, milk glass, 5-1/4" d **18.00**
Paneled Grape, milk glass, 12 oz .. **25.00**

Jardinière, Paneled Grape, milk glass,
6-1/2" h, ftd **42.00**

Jelly, cov, Paneled Grape, milk glass . **30.00**

Mayonnaise set, Paneled Grape, milk
glass, three pcs............................... **65.00**

Mint compote, Waterford, #1932, ruby
stained, crimped **60.00**

Oil and vinegar cruets, English Hobnail,
crystal **65.00**

Pickle jar, Deco pattern, frosted, flower dec,
4-1/4" d, 12" h **85.00**

Paneled Grape pattern, white milk glass, covered
sugar, **$20**; creamer, **$15**, pair candlesticks, **$15**.

Pitcher
Old Quilt, milk glass......................... **40.00**
Paneled Grape, milk glass, 16 oz .. **45.00**

Planter, 5" x 9", Paneled Grape, milk glass
.... **48.00**

Plate
Beaded Edge, 7" d, goldfinch center
.... **15.00**
Old Quilt, milk glass, 8" d **32.00**

Puff box, cov, Paneled Grape, milk glass
.... **30.00**

Punch cup, Fruits, milk glass **6.00**

Punch set
Della Robbia, bowl, six cups **45.00**
Fruits, milk glass, 12-pc set **150.00**
Paneled Grape, milk glass, red hooks
and ladle, 13" d, 15-pc set **595.00**

Rose bowl, 4" d, Paneled Grape, milk glass,
ftd **30.00**

Salad plate, Della Robbia, dark stain... **22.00**

Salt and pepper shakers, pr
Della Robbia, stained **70.00**
Old Quilt, milk glass........................ **25.00**
Paneled Grape, milk glass............. **25.00**

Sauceboat and underplate, Paneled
Grape, milk glass............................ **70.00**

Saucer, Paneled Grape, milk glass **8.50**

Sherbet, 10-3/4" h, Della Robia, light stain
.... **26.00**

Sleigh, cobalt blue, 9" l, 5" h **175.00**

Slipper, figural, almond milk glass **20.00**

Spooner, Old Quilt, milk glass, 6-1/2" h
.... **28.00**

Sugar bowl, cov
Beaded Grape, milk glass, individual size
.... **10.00**
English Hobnail, ice blue, octagonal foot,
4-1/4" h **55.00**
Old Quilt, milk glass, large, open... **15.00**

Plate, rabbit at top, horseshoe and shamrock border, blue carnival glass, 6" d, **$15**.

Sweetmeat, Waterford, #1932, ruby stained, ftd, crimped **40.00**
Toilet bottle stopper, English Hobnail, green.. **55.00**
Torte plate, 14" d, Della Robbia, light stain **125.00**

Tray
    Heavy Scroll, gold dec.................... **25.00**
    Maple Leaf, 9" d **12.00**
Tumbler, flat
    Della Robia, dark stain, 8 oz.......... **28.00**
    Paneled Grape, milk glass **12.50**
Vase
    6" h, ftd, bell-shape, Paneled Grape, milk glass **15.00**
    7" h, horn-shape, Lotus, #9............. **35.00**
    9" h, Paneled Grape, milk glass, bell shape, ftd.. **30.00**
    10" h, Grape and Lattice, milk glass **115.00**
    15" h, swung-type, Paneled Grape, milk glass **20.00**
Water set, 1776 Colonial, amber, flat water pitcher, six goblets, price for seven-pc set **70.00**
Wedding bowl, Roses & Bows, milk glass, 10" d.. **130.00**

Whiskey Bottles, Collectors' Special Editions

History: The Jim Beam Distillery began the practice of issuing novelty (collectors' special edition) bottles for the 1953 Christmas trade. By the late 1960s, more than 100 other distillers and wine manufacturers followed suit.

The Jim Beam Distillery remains the most prolific issuer of the bottle. Lionstone, McCormick, and Ski Country are the other principal suppliers today. One dealer, Jon-Sol, Inc., has distributed his own line of collector bottles.

The golden age of the special edition bottle was the early 1970s. Interest waned in the late 1970s and early 1980s as the market became saturated with companies trying to join the craze. Prices fell from record highs, and many manufacturers dropped special edition bottle production altogether.

A number of serious collectors, clubs, and dealers have brought stability to the market. Realizing that instant antiques cannot be created by demand alone, they have begun to study and classify their bottles. Most importantly, collectors have focused on those special edition bottles which show quality workmanship and design and which are true limited editions.

Collecting Hints: Beginning collectors are advised to focus on bottles of a single manufacturer or to collect around a central theme, e.g., birds, trains, or Western. Only buy bottles that have a very good finish (almost no sign of wear), no chips, and intact original labels.

A major collection still can be built for a modest investment, although some bottles, such as the Beam Red Coat Fox, now command more than $1,000. Don't overlook miniatures if you are on a limited budget.

In many states it is against the law to sell liquor without a license; hence, collectors tend to focus on empty bottles.

Ballantine
Golf Bag, 1969 .... **9.50**
Mallard, 1969..................................... **12.00**
Zebra, 1970 .... **10.00**

Jim Beam
Ahepa, 1972..................................... **5.00**
Akron, Rubber Capital, 1973............. **24.00**
Barney's Slot Machine, 1978 .... **20.00**
Bing Crosby, 1970s........................... **15.00**
Buffalo Bill, 1970s **10.00**
Cable Car, 1983 .... **60.00**
Churchill Downs, Kentucky Derby.... **18.00**
Civil War, 1961, South......................... **50.00**
Cowboy, 1981 .... **12.00**
Ducks Unlimited.............................. **50.00**
Ernie's Flower Car, 1976 .... **35.00**
Evergreen State Club, 1974.............. **12.50**

Aeshetic Specialties Inc., 1909 Stanley Steamer, Model A, contains amaretto, original box, $45.

Harolds Club, Covered Wagon, green, 1969 .... **6.00**
Hawaiian Open **10.00**
Horse, brown, 1967-68 .... **18.50**
Kansas City Convention Elephant, 1976 .... **15.00**
Katz Cat, black, 1968 .... **12.00**
Key West, FL **6.00**
John Henry, 1972 .... **65.00**
London Bridge, Regal China, 1971 ..... **7.50**
Louisiana Superdome, 1975 .... **9.00**
Madame Butterfly, 1977 .... **120.00**
Marine Corps **35.00**
New Jersey **40.00**
New York World's Fair, 1964 .... **12.00**
Ohio, 1966 .... **18.00**
Pennsylvania Dutch Club, 1974 .... **12.00**
Pony Express **10.00**
Rabbit, 1971 .... **15.00**

Jim Beam, Model T Ford, original box, $45.

Jim Beam, States Series, South Carolina, $25.

San Diego, 1968 .... **7.00**
Saturday Evening Post, 1970s **15.00**
Stutz Bearcat **50.00**
Thomas Flyer, cream, brown roof **135.00**
Train Caboose **60.00**
Travelodge Bear **25.00**
Twin Bridges Club, 1971 .... **50.00**
Volkswagen **55.00**
Yellowstone **8.00**
Yosemite **8.00**
Zimmerman Liquors **10.00**

Beneagle
Alpine pitcher, 1969 .... **25.00**
Barrel, thistle **4.50**
Bell House, 1960 .... **12.00**
Chess Pawn, John Knox, black, miniature **12.00**
Fruit, canteen, 1969 .... **18.00**

Bischoff
Chinese Boy, 1962 .... **32.00**
Grecian Vase, 1969 .... **15.00**
Pirate **20.00**

Ezra Brooks
Basketball Players, 1974 .... **10.00**
Card, Jack of Diamonds, 1969 .... **10.00**
Casey at Bat, 1973 .... **15.00**
Clown with balloons, 1973 .... **20.00**
Club Bottle #1, Distillery, 1970 .... **12.50**
Clydesdale, 1974 .... **10.00**
Dummy Gallon, 1969 .... **60.00**
Elephant, Big Bertha, 1970 .... **8.00**
FOE Eagle, 179 .... **15.00**
Fresno Grape, 1970 .... **12.00**
Go Big Red #3, 1972 .... **12.00**
Greensboro Open, cup, 1975 .... **50.00**
Hereford, 1971 .... **12.00**
Iowa Farmers Elevator, 1978 .... **36.00**
Lion on Rock, 1971 .... **10.00**

Ezra Brooks, racing car and driver, white body, red, blue and black decoration, gold foil label, $35.

Masonic, fez, 1976 .... 10.00
Max "The Hat" Zimmerman, 1976..... 32.00
Mr. Merchant, 1970 .... 10.00
Motorcycle, 1971.............................. 17.50
Oliver Hardy, 1976 .... 17.50
Ontario Racer, #10, 1970.................. 24.00
Panda, 1972 .... 18.00
Penguin, 1973 .... 15.00
Phoenix Bird, 1975 .... 18.00
Spirit of St. Louis, 1977 .... 12.00
Stonewall Jackson, 1974.................. 32.00
Tank, 1972 .... 30.00
Train, Iron Horse, 1969 .... 12.00
Vermont Skier, 1973 .... 12.00
Whitetail Deer, 1974.......................... 20.00
Wichita Centennial, 1970.................... 7.50

Cyrus Noble

Buffalo Cow & Calf, Nevada, 1977.... 75.00
Burro, 1973...................................... 50.00
Carousel Series, pipe organ, 1980.... 45.00
Harp Seal, 1979............................... 50.00
Moose & Calf, 1977 .... 60.00
Sea Turtle, 1979............................... 50.00
Snowshoe Thompson, 1972............ 150.00
Whitetail Deer, 1979........................... 35.00

J.W. Dant

American Legion, 1968...................... 10.00
Boeing 747.. 12.00
Boston Tea Party 12.00
Field Bird, #2, 1969, Chukar partridge
.... 12.00
Mt. Rushmore, 1968 .... 12.00
Patrick Henry, 1969............................. 5.00

Early Times, 1976

Cannon Fire
Delaware... 24.00
Nevada.. 22.00
New Mexico..................................... 28.00

Drum and Fife
Florida... 18.00
Kansas.. 20.00

Minuteman
Alaska... 37.50
Oklahoma.. 24.00
Paul Revere, Arizona.......................... 21.00
Washington Crossing the Delaware, South
Dakota 18.00

Famous Firsts

Balloon, 1971.................................... 65.00
Bears, miniature, 1981 .... 36.00
Bucky Badger Mascot...................... 10.00
China Clipper, 1989......................... 100.00
Circus Lion, 1979 .... 20.00
Corvette, 1963 Stingray, white, miniature,
1979 .... 15.50
Fireman, 1980.................................... 50.00
Golfer, 1973..................................... 30.00
Hippo, baby, 1980.............................. 50.00
Hurdy Gurdy, miniature, 1979 .... 12.50
Minnie Meow, 1973 .... 17.50
National Racer, No. 8, 1972.............. 70.00
Panda, baby, 1980.............................. 50.00
Pepper Mill, 1978 .... 20.00
Phonograph, 1969 .... 36.00
Porsche Targa, 1979.......................... 44.00
Sewing Machine, 1979....................... 35.00
Swiss Chalet, 1974............................ 20.00
Winnie Mae, large, 1972.................... 85.00
Yacht America, 1978.......................... 25.00

Garnier (France)

Baby Foot, 1963 .... 15.00
Bullfighter 18.00
Cat.. 60.00
Christmas Tree, 1956 .... 65.00
Diamond Bottle, 1969....................... 15.00
Inca, 1969.. 15.00
Locomotive, 1969.............................. 18.00
Meadowlark, 1969 .... 12.00
Parrot.. 30.00
Soccer Shoe, 1962 .... 30.00
Trout... 24.00
Young Deer 28.00

Grenadier

American Revolution Series
Second Maryland, 1969................ 37.50
Third New York, 1970 .... 22.00
British Army Series, Kings African Rifle
Crops, 5th, 1970 .... 20.00
Civil War Series, General Robert E. Lee, 1/2
gal, 1977 .... 130.00
George Washington, on horseback .. 20.00
Jester Mirth King, 1977 .... 50.00
San Fernando Electric Mfg Co., 1976
.... 50.00
Santa Claus, blue sack 30.00

Hoffman

Aesop's Fables Series, music, six types,
1978 .... 30.00
Canada Goose Decoy 15.00
Cheerleaders, Rams, miniature, 1980 20.00
Doe and fawn.................................... 40.00
Fox and eagle, 1978.......................... 45.00
Kentucky Wildcats, football, 1979..... 35.00
Mr. Lucky Series, music
Barber, 1980 .... 35.00
Cobbler, 1973 .... 25.00

Bols, musical bottle, $20.

Fiddler, 1974	25.00
Mailman, miniature, 1976	12.50
Pistol, Dodge City Frontier, framed	25.00
Stage Coach Driver	30.00
Tennessee Volunteers	25.00
Wood Duck, decoy	15.00

Japanese Firms

House of Koshu

Geisha, chrysanthemum, 1969	20.00
Sake God, white, 1969	14.00
Kamotsuru, treasure tower, 1966	18.00

Kikukawa

Eisenhower, 1970	18.00
Royal couple, pr	32.00

Lewis and Clark

Clark, miniature, 1971	12.50
General Custer, 1974	70.00
Grandfather, 1978	10.00
Indian, 1978	65.00
Lewis, 1971	85.00
Major Reno	25.00
Sheepherder	40.00
Trader	50.00

Lionstone

Annie Oakley, 1969	60.00
Barber, 1976	40.00
Bartender, 1969	30.00
Baseball Player, 1974	24.50
Cherry Valley	20.00
Dance Hall Girl, 1973	60.00
Dove of Peace, 1977	40.00
Eastern Bluebird, 1972	20.00
Fireman, #8, fire alarm box, 1983	50.00
Hockey Player, 1974	20.00
Indian, squaw, 1973	25.00
Riverboat Captain, 1969	12.00
Stutz Bearcat, miniature, 1978	15.00
Telegrapher, 1969	20.00
Tennis Player, male, 1980	45.00
Turbo Car STP, red, 1972	27.50

Luxardo

Apple, figural	12.00
Apothecary Jar	20.00
Bizantina	20.00
Calypso Girl, 1962	15.50
Coffeepot	12.00
Mayan, 1960	50.00
Tower of Flowers, 1968	18.00
Venus, 1969	20.00
Zodiac, 1970	30.00

O.B.R., River Queen, transportation series, 1968, $12.

McCormick

Betsy Ross, miniature, 1976	48.00
Bluebird	20.00
Centurion, 1969	20.00
Chair, 1979	30.00
Eleanor Roosevelt	20.00
FOE, 1985	50.00
Henry Ford	30.00
Kit Carson, 1975	15.00
Mark Twain, 1977	32.00
Merlin	30.00
Nebraska Football Player, 1972	24.00
Oregon Duck	20.00
Robert E. Lee, 1976	40.00
Sir Lancelot	40.00
Texas Longhorn, 1974	32.50
Train Series, wood tender, 1969	20.00
Ulysses S. Grant, 1976	25.00
Victorian, 1964	20.00
Wood Duck, 1983	25.00

OBR

Caboose, 1973 .... 20.00
River Queen, 1967 .... 10.00
W.C. Fields, top hat, 1976 .... 15.00

Old Commonwealth

Apothecary Series, North Carolina University, 1979 .... 30.00
Coal Miners, #5, coal shooter, 1983 ... 40.00
Fireman, #5, Lifesaver, 1983 .... 70.00
Indian Chief Illini, University of Illinois, 1979 .... 60.00
Irish at the Sea, 1989 .... 24.00
Lumberjack, old time, 1979 .... 20.00
Kentucky Peach Bowl 30.00
Kentucky Thoroughbreds, 1977 .... 40.00
Sons of Erin 25.00
Symbols of Ireland, 1985 .... 12.00

Old Crow

Chess Set, 32 pcs 450.00
Crow, 1974 .... 15.00

Old Fitzgerald

America's Cup, 1970 .... 25.00
Blarney, Irish toast, 1970 .... 15.00
Candlelite, 1963 .... 10.00
Classic, 1972 .... 10.00
Davidson, NC, 1972 .... 40.00
Hospitality, 1958 .... 9.00
Old Ironsides 9.00
Rip Van Winkle, 1971 .... 32.50
West Virginia Forest Festival, 1973 .. 20.00

Old Mr. Boston

Black Hills Motor Club, 1976 .... 12.00
Concord Coach, 1976 .... 15.00
Dan Patch 25.00
Deadwood, SD, 1975 .... 12.00
Eagle Convention, 1973 .... 10.00
Hawk, 1975 .... 15.00
Lion, sitting 12.00
Nebraska, #1, gold, 1970 .... 20.00
Paul Revere, 1974 .... 12.50
Town Crier, 1976 .... 10.00
Wisconsin Football 25.00

Pacesetter

Camaro, Z28, yellow, 1982 .... 40.00
Coca-Cola Truck 135.00
Corvette, red, 1975 .... 40.00
Mack Pumper 120.00
Pontiac Firebird 35.00
Tractor Series, No. 2, Big Green Machine, International Harvester, 1983 .... 60.00
Vokovich, #2, 1974 .... 30.00

Ski Country

Antelope, pronghorn 70.00
Bassett, miniature, 1978 .... 20.00
Blackbird 40.00
Bull Rider 15.00

Ceremonial Indian, Falcon 90.00
Chickadee 50.00
Cigar Store Indian, 1974 .... 40.00
Clown, bust, 1974, miniature 18.00
Eagle, paperweight 175.00
Ebenezer Scrooge, 1979, miniature .. 24.00
Jaguar, miniature 30.00
Koala, 1973 .... 40.00
Labrador with mallard, 1977, miniature 40.00
Mallard Drake 40.00
Mill River Country Club, 1977 .... 40.00
Mountain Lion, 1973, miniature 30.00
Ringmaster, 1975, miniature 22.50
Salmon 40.00
Submarine, 1976, miniature 20.00
Tom Thumb 30.00
Woodpecker, ivory bill, 1974 .... 50.00

Ski Country, Lady Blue, $20.

Wild Turkey

Mack Truck 20.00

Series #1

No. 2, female, 1972 .... 150.00
No. 3, on wing, miniature, 1983 ..... 65.00
No. 5, with flags, 1975 .... 40.00
No. 8, strutting, 1978 .... 45.00

Series #2, No. 2, lore, 1980................ **30.00**
Series #3
    No. 5, with raccoon, 1984.............. **40.00**
    No. 7, with fox, 1984, miniature **30.00**
    No. 12, with skunk, 1986................ **90.00**
Series #4, No. 2, habitat, 1989........... **90.00**

World War I Collectibles

History: Power struggles between European countries raged for hundreds of years. As the 20th century dawned, leading European countries became entangled in a series of complex alliances, many sealed by royal marriages, and a massive arms race. All that was needed to set off the powder keg was a fire. The assassination of Austrian Archduke Franz Ferdinand by a Serbian national ignited the fuse on June 28, 1914. Germany invaded Belgium and moved into France. Russia, England, and Turkey joined the war. Italy and the United States became involved by mid-1917.

In 1918, Germany sued for peace. A settlement was achieved at the Versailles Conference, January-June 1919, during which time the United States remained in the background. President Wilson's concept for a League of Nations failed to gain acceptance in his own country, opening the door to the events which culminated in World War II.

Collecting Hints: Uniforms and equipment from World War I were stockpiled at the end of the war and reissued in the early years of World War II. Know the source of the items before you buy, and scrutinize all materials. Some research and investigation might be necessary to correctly identify an item as an actual war artifact.

Collectors' clubs and re-enactment groups are among the best sources of information. These groups also are very knowledgeable about reproductions, copycats, and fantasy items.

Advertising, drawing book, Old Reliable Coffee, patriotic edition..................... **8.00**

Badge
    American Red Cross-Military Welfare, cap, enamel..................................... **20.00**
    Rural Mail Carrier Award, brass, 1st place bar, profile bust of Benjamin Franklin **15.00**
Bayonet, orig case............................ **20.00**
Beanie, ribbon and charms, 7" d, 3" h, dark brown corduroy, yellow felt trim, red, white, and blue stars and stripes V-ribbon shown in place on top, three charms sewn in place around sides, silver accent double flag, clear plastic star, silver accent Police Commissioner, ribbon slightly frayed................................. **20.00**
Belt, web.. **250.00**
Book
    Building the Kaiser's Navy, Gary Weir, 289 pgs... **25.00**
    Granville: Tales and Tail Spins from A Flyer's Diary, Abingdon Press, 1919 .... **75.00**
Candleholder, Germany, sword handle fits into candleholder, silver inlay reads "To Mom & Dad from Gordon" just above handle, no blade............................. **85.00**
Canteen, Army **15.00**
Census badge, diecut brass shield, state seal of NY in center, 1917 .... **18.00**
Checkbook, 11 different patriotic designs, including Pershing facsimile, 3-1/2" x 7-1/2"... **5.00**
Easel plaque, 6" d, convex celluloid over metal, wire easel, colorful Allied flags **35.00**
Flip book, 2" x 2-1/2" x 1/4", soldier, sailor, and Uncle Sam presenting the colors, pledge of Allegiance, Liberty Bone promotion, © 1917.......................... **30.00**
Gas mask, carrying can, shoulder strap, canister attached to bottom, German **50.00**
Handkerchief, 11" sq, "Remember Me," soldier and girl in center, red, white, and blue edge....................................... **20.00**
Helmet, US, 3rd Army insignia **65.00**
Key chain fob, Kaiser Bill's Bones, 1-1/4" l replica of shell casing holding miniature celluloid die set, inscription on firing cap end of brass cartridge, removable silver bullet head, loop for key chain....... **70.00**
Medal, Iron Cross **45.00**
Paperweight
    Brass, hat replica, dark luster finish, adv plate "Bankers Loan & Trust Co., Frances Building, Sioux City, Iowa," narrow woven brass wire hatband........................ **25.00**
    Weighted celluloid, full-color image of 12 "Flags of the Allies-United For The Cause Of Liberty," white center, black letters, mirror base...................................... **40.00**

Pinback button

Australia Day, 1916, light sepia portrait of English naval officer Lord Kitchener, white ground, blue letters, 1916 Unley event **20.00**

Australia Day, 1918, red, white, blue, and black, aborigine young lady puffing pipe, wearing red bandanna, blue and black rim depiction of tiny boomerangs... **40.00**

French Orphans Fund, red, white, and blue, illus of woman holding two youngsters, inscribed "France Always Our Friend, Help the Orphaneliant Des Armees" **12.00**

Puzzle, Victory Constructional Puzzle of H.M.S. Warspite, British Warship, 100+ pieces, complete, original box, **$175**.

Jewish Relief, red, white, and blue, silver accents, Hebrew man holding youngster in one arm, upper rim inscription in Hebrew, lower "The Jews Look to America For Help," back paper inscription "Remember Relief Ball Wed March 15, 1916 at Symphony Hall-Boston" **15.00**

Liberty Loan Committee, blue lettering on white ground, gold rim, red, white, and blue patriotic shield, c1918 .... **12.00**

Lloyd George, black and gray portrait of British Prime Minister, Welsh rim inscription **30.00**

On Active Service, multicolored image of

English bulldog staunchly positioned on nationality flag, blue lettering **30.00**

Our Heroes Welcome Home, blue letters, white bordered by red victory wreath **20.00**

Port Pirie Repatriation, black cat on lower yellow ground, shaded blue top, black lettering, Australian, c1916 .... **35.00**

78th Division, red, white and blue, Welcome Home, issued for "The Fighting Demons" **35.00**

We Mourn Our Loss, black and gray photo celluloid of unidentified officer, spiked military helmet..................... **20.00**

World Peace, multicolored, Allied flags around white dove carrying olive branch **60.00**

Pin holder, 2-1/4" d, celluloid, full color image of 12 Allies flags around white center, blue letters, perimeter ring holds glass mirror **35.00**

Portrait, 5-3/4" x 8", full-color celluloid, sepia portrait, surrounding flags and patriotic symbols, inscription "Army and Navy Forever," single star service banner, black velveteen over metal back, wire easel stand **65.00**

Poster, 13" x 30", Your War Savings Pledge, brown and blue text on white, "Our Boys Make Good Their Pledge, Are You Keeping Yours," W.S.S. War Savings Stamps issued by the United States Government **75.00**

Ribbon, 2" x 5", Welcome Home 26th Division **25.00**

Sheet music

If We Had A Million Like Him Over There, George Cohan songwriter, 10-1/2" x 13-1/2", 1918 copyright **35.00**

Spirit of France, "Respectfully inscribed to Ferdinand Foch Marshall of France and Generalissimo of Allied Armies," cover shows French WWI troops, inset portrait of General Foch, some wear **45.00**

Tobacco jar, cov, 6-1/2" h, ceramic, brown glaze, General Pershing............... **145.00**

Uniform, US Army, Engineer, coat, belt, pants, cap, canvas leggings, wool puttees, and leather gaiters, canteen **400.00**

Watch fob, flag on pole, USA, beaded, blue **45.00**

World War II Collectibles

History: With the rise of the German Third Reich, European nations once again engaged in a massive arms race.

The 1930s Depression compounded the situation.

After numerous compromises to German expansionism, war was declared in 1939 following Germany's Blitzkrieg invasion of Poland. Allied and Axis alliances were formed.

Although neutral, Americans were very supportive of the Allied cause. The December 7, 1941, Japanese attack on the U.S. Naval Station at Pearl Harbor, Hawaii, forced America into the war. It immediately adopted a two-front strategy.

From 1942 to 1945, the entire world was directly or indirectly involved in the war. Virtually all industrial activity was war related. The resulting technological advances guaranteed that life after the war would be far different from prior years.

Germany surrendered on May 7, 1945. Japan surrendered on Aug. 14, 1945, after the atomic bombing of Hiroshima on Aug. 6, 1945, and Nagasaki on Aug. 9, 1945.

Collecting Hints: To the victors go the spoils, or so World War II collectors would like to think. Now that the Soviet Block has fallen, a large number of dealers are making efforts to import Soviet Block World War II collectibles into the United States. Be careful when buying anything that has a new or unused appearance. Many Soviet countries continued to use stockpiled World War II equipment and still manufacture new goods based on World War II designs.

The Korean Conflict occurred shortly after World War II. The United States and other armed forces involved in this conflict used equipment and uniforms similar to those manufactured during World War II. Familiarize yourself with model styles, dates of manufacture, and your buying sources.

If you locate a World War II item, make certain to record all personal history associated with the item. This is extremely important. Collectors demand this documentation. If possible, secure additional information on the history of the unit and the battles in which it was engaged. Also make certain to obtain any extras that are available, such as insignia or a second set of buttons.

Album picture, Hi-Speed Victory Club, 6-1/4" x 8-1/2", bluetone photo and text, Hi-Speed Gas, c1943....................... **2.00**

Arm band, Civilian Defense Air Raid Warden, 4" w, white, 3-1/2" blue circle, red and white diagonal stripes within triangle **10.00**

Bank, 3" d, 7-1/2" h, hollow plaster, gray paint, white letter "V," raised lettering "Bomb the Axis/Bonds Buy Bombs," red, white, and blue paper sticker **125.00**

Ration book, cover with children and dog sitting watching garden grow, titled "Looking into the Future," ©Shaw Barton, $5.

Better Little Book, *Fighting Heroes Battle For Freedom*, #1401, © 1942, 1943 **18.00**

Binoculars, Army, M-17, field type, 7-1/2" l, olive drab, 7 x 50 power, clear, fixed optics.. **95.00**

Book

Aerial Warfare, The Story of the Aeroplane as a Weapon by Hal Goodwin, New Home Library, 1943, 273 pgs, hard cover **10.00**

Baa Baa Black Sheep, War Memoirs of Pappy Boyington, Marine Corps Pilot Ace with Flying Tigers, Boyington, 1958 **38.00**

Blood and Banquets, A Berlin Social Diary by a Jewish Reporter and Witness to Nazi Rise, Fromm, 1942 .... **30.00**

Bunker's War-The World War II Diary of Colonel Paul D. Bunker, Barlow ed., 32-pgs **38.00**

Day of Infamy, Dec. 7, 1941, Walter Lord, 1957, Henry Holt, 243 pgs, illus, slightly worn dj **12.00**

Europe & the Mediterranean, Dept. of History, West Point Military Academy, 1978, 366 pgs................................. **35.00**

From Hell to Heaven Memoirs from Patton's Third Army in WWII, McHugh, 1980 .... **30.00**

Handbook of Hospital Corps, United States Navy, Government Printing Office, 1939 .... **18.00**

History of World War II, Armed Services Memorial Edition, Francis Trevelyan Miller, Reader's Service Bureau, war photos, official records, maps **18.00**

Pearl Harbor Story, Capt. Wm. T. Rice, 1973, 9th printing **12.00**

Semper Fi, Mac, Living Memories of the US Marines in WWII, Berry, 1982 ... **40.00**

Song & Service Book for Ship & Field, Army & Navy, Ivan L. Bennett, 1942, A. S. Barnes Pub **15.00**

Ten Thousand Eyes-Spy Network That Cracked Hitlers Atlantic Wall for D-Day, 1958, 300 pgs, plates, photos, maps **40.00**

The General Was a Spy-The Truth About German General Gehlen, Who Served Hitler, The CIA & West Germany, Heinzel-Hohne, H. Zolling, c1972, photos, dj **30.00**

World War II Operations in North African Waters, Oct 1942-June 1943, Samuel Eliot Morison, Atlantic, Little Brown, 1955, 297 pgs, dj **25.00**

Calendar, 6-3/4" x 10", Co-Operative Elevator Co, Gen Douglas MacArthur, 1943, cream-colored diecut sheet, red, and blue sword design at center, brown-tone portrait of general **45.00**

Cap, AAF Officer's, 50-Mission, crash cap, small gilded eagle, front and back straps, soft bill, gabardine, mkd "Fighter by Bancroft, O.D." **95.00**

Card game, Navy Aircraft Squadron Insignia, 1" x 4" x 5", 17 pairs of cards **35.00**

Elongated cent, Remember Pearl Harbor, FDR image, brass key chain, rolled penny, text below FDR, 1933-1945 **40.00**

Figure, 3-3/4" h, Kilroy Was Here, plastic, wistful pregnant girl **35.00**

Flight suit, Army Air Force, Type A-4, olive drab gabardine, matching belt, zipper front **95.00**

Guide book, *Aeronautics Aircraft Spotters Guide* **15.00**

Glass

4-1/2" h, flying white eagle, blue and red "V" symbol **24.00**

4-3/4" h 2-1/4" d, clear glass, applied red, white, and blue, "Remember Pearl Harbor, Dec 7, 1941," image of US aircraft **20.00**

Flag, Nazi, red, white, and black, **$175**

Gunpowder can, 18" h, 10" d, copper and brass, US Navy, hinged brass port hole opening with tie dogs (wing nuts) **225.00**

Hanger, 9-3/8" x 12-1/8", cardboard, Remember Pearl Harbor, Liberty Bell, red, white, and blue US flags, browntones, white text, silver border **75.00**

Helmet, MI, olive drab sand finish, olive drab chin strap, orig liner, thin mesh helmet net **175.00**

Jacket, A-2 Army Air Force, leather, cowhide, light brown, name tag... **495.00**

Knife, Camillus USN Mark 5 Sheath, black finish blade, light scabbard wear, USN and name marked on guard, gray web belt loop, gray fiber scabbard **65.00**

Lamp, 5" h base of painted figural plaster, 3-1/2" h figural soldier, flesh-tone face, brown uniform, garrison cap, 3" h tan cardboard shade with printed red, and blue aviation scenes, parachuting Air Force figure **75.00**

Magazine

Liberty, Aug. 24, 1940, 8-1/2" x 11-1/2", full-color cover art for Lighting in the Night, A Story of the Invasion of America **25.00**

Life, Occupation of Germany, Feb. 10, 1947 .... **12.00**

Pin-Up Parade, 8-1/2" x 11", black and white photo cov, purple and yellow accents, 48 pgs, full-page black and white pin-up photos of Hollywood stars such as Lucille Ball, Barbara Stanwyck, Lana Turner, Ginger Rogers centerfold, © 1944 Bond Publishers **45.00**

Steel Horizons, Allegheny Ludlum Steel Corp, Pittsburgh, 1941 .... **10.00**

War Planes, Dell, 8-1/4" x 11", full color cov, 28 black and white pgs, © 1942 .... **35.00**

Manual

The Bluejackets Manual, 1946, 13th ed., US Naval Institute, Annapolis, 622 pgs **15.00**

War Department Technical Manual Air Navigation, 1940, 296 pgs, U. S. Govt. Printing Office, maps, charts, illus.. **12.00**

Matchbox, 5/8" x 1-1/2" x 2-1/4", cardboard slipcase cover, wooden safety matches, red, white, and blue war bonds and slogans, "Keep Em Rolling" and "Keep Em Flying" **15.00**

Mirror and thermometer premium picture, 4-1/2" x 9-3/4", cream-colored cardboard mat, diecut opening, blue accent mirror, full-color 3" oval art of Gen MacArthur, 2-1/4" diecut opening with thermometer, c1943.. **65.00**

Notebook, spiral-bound, pocket-type, bald eagle perched on sword on cover, "The Pen and the Sword for Victory," red, white, and blue.................................. **9.00**

Patch

AAF, cloth, bombardier wings, embroidered silver and gray, tan cotton, unused... **20.00**
War Production Soldier, 3-1/4" x 7-1/2", red, white, and blue stitched fabric **75.00**

Pencil box, 1-1/4" x 5" x 8-1/2", "V for Victory," sturdy cardboard, snap fastener, early 1940s **75.00**

Pillow cover, 20" x 20", Armored Force, Keep 'Em Rolling Fort Knox, KY, red, white, and blue, red fringed border **20.00**

Pillow top, US Army Air Corps, Baer Field, Ind., tan ground, rose, silver, and black decoration, rose and silver fringe, **$45**.

Pin

Axe the Axis, hatchet shape, inscription on blade, marked "Sterling Silver" . **85.00**
Boston Paper Trooper, diecut white plastic, red and blue lettering "Salvage for Victory" **20.00**
Marine Civilian Corps, diecut circular plastic, red spoked wheel design, inscribed "Depot of Supplies-San Francisco" **25.00**
Remember Pearl Harbor, 2-1/8" stiff cream cardboard card, blue text, red and blue stripes, text "United For Victory

Keep 'Em Flying," 1-3/4" w metal pin mounted in center, diecut letters, with first word finished in dark red, center word in white, final word in dark blue **100.00**
Stage Door Canteen, red, white, and blue enamel, silver lettering "American Theatre Wing-Stage Door Canteen," mkd "Sterling" on bar pin **18.00**
US for Victory, bright luster brass frame, clear plastic insert cover over paper insert with red, white, and blue flag **20.00**
USO Camp Shows, diecut brass, white enamel eagle, red ground, "Camp Shows" **18.00**
Women's Service, diecut brass eagle and shield symbol, rim inscribed "National League for Woman's Service"........ **20.00**

Pinback button

Avenge Manila, red, white, and blue, on pale gray ground **40.00**
Battleship USS Washington, green on gold, June 1, 1940 launch from Philadelphia Navy Yard **45.00**
Beat the Schedule, red, white, and blue celluloid, Congress of Industrial Organizations................................. **25.00**
Buy A Liberty Bond School Childrens Corp, 7/8" d, dark blue text on cream **20.00**
Dry Dock Victory Club, 3/4" d, dark blue on white, red accent stripe, back with text on paper "I Hereby Resolve On Every Pay Day During 1942 To Set Aside Some Part Of My Pay For U. S. Defense Bonds" **15.00**
Eat To Beat The Devil, red, white, and blue litho, image of clenched fist belting head of devil **55.00**
Gen MacArthur Welcome Home, red, white and blue, bluetone portrait ... **60.00**
Gopher Ordnance Works, full-color war production cartoon of determined gopher **35.00**
I Am Bringing A Hero Home, R-U?, 7/8" d, blue on cream, question marks and letters "R-U" in red, Brunt back paper **18.00**
I Am Buying 10% Or More War Bonds, 1" d, dark blue, bright red text on white, red, white, and blue shield, American Badge **18.00**
I Am Making My Old Clothes Do, 7/8" d, dark blue on white, Whitehead & Hoag back paper **18.00**
I Buy Defense Saving Stamps, 1" d, blue text over bright red ground, large "V" for victory, Bastian............................... **18.00**
I've Subscribed For My Fourth Bond, 1" d, red, white, and blue, white text on red rim "Saco-Lowell Shops Payroll Allotment Plan," blue and white text in center, Whitehead and Hoag back paper . **18.00**
Mothers of World War II, blue and white image **40.00**

Pabst Breweries Bond Buyer, red, white, and blue, 10 percent salary contributor **30.00**
Victory Girls Earn and Give, 13/16" d, white text on red center shield surrounded by dark blue **20.00**
War Saver, 13/16" d, hand giving thumb's up gesture, cream ground, red text **18.00**
War Service League, Troy, NY, 13/16" d, brass frame, brass back, vertical pin holds red, white, and blue celluloid insert . **18.00**
Welcome Balto Co Soldiers & Sailors, 7/8" d, black and white rim, center circle with top half in black, bottom half in bright yellow, Torsch & Franz back paper . **15.00**
Plate, 10-1/2" d, General Mac Arthur, blue design on white, Vernon Kilns **50.00**
Postcard, 3-1/2" x 5-1/2", Just A Little Something To Remember Pearl Harbor, full-color cartoon showing Navy ship firing on and sinking Japanese ship, 1942 cancellation **18.00**

Poster, WAAC, This is My War Too!, $85.

Poster

Bunds-Bonds, 16-1/2" x 22", Hitler confusing German word "Bunds" for Bonds, discrepancy whispered by character representing Goebbels to Nazi cohort Herman Goering, government printing date 1942, #473829 .... **125.00**
Buy War Bonds, 22" x 28", vivid color beachhead assault scene, artist Ferdinand Warren, facsimile signature, government printing date 1942, #497775 .... **75.00**
Enemy Propaganda, 18" x 23" frame, art by Jack Betts, caricature images of Tojo and Hitler, sponsored by Veterans of Foreign Wars, early 1940s **120.00**

Fatso-Ratso-Japso, 15-1/4" x 18" rigid cardboard, caricature art of Mussolini, Hitler and Tojo as the blame for "Higher Prices and Shortages!," cardboard easel back, paper stick for sponsor Schnaley, Three Feathers Whiskey, and Coronet Brandy... **275.00**
US Cadet Nurse Corps, 20" x 28", color art by Edmundson, "Enlist in a Proud Profession, Join the US Navy Cadet Nurse Corps, A Life-Time Education-Free!" US Public Health Service, Federal Security Agency **95.00**
Welcome Home, "Join in the Celebration of June Dairy Month!" portrait of Elsie, smaller print reads "Looking forward to our future, we salute our past," 1942, 5" x 15" **15.00**
Premium, Navy Code Signal Flags, 5" x 12-1/2" brown paper mailer from Tootsie Rolls, pair of folded paper sheets, each opening to 12" sq........................... **60.00**
Prints, *Fighting Airplanes,* orig paintings by William Heaslip, set of 20 8-1/2" x 11" images on 12" x 14" paper sheets, each with text naming plane, nickname, branch of service, purpose, issued by Coca-Cola.................................... **250.00**
Record, "Remember Pearl Harbor," 10" d black wax, 78 rpm, RCA Victor Bluebird label.. **65.00**
Sheet music, *Rosie the Riveter,* 9" x 12", 1942 .... **25.00**
Shovel, fox-hole type **15.00**
Sign, 18" h, 12" w, Kool Cigarettes, full color, graphics showing Kool penguin as Army sentry on duty, text at top "Keep Alert-Smoke Kools" **135.00**
Stud, V symbol, white metal, gold luster finish, red, white and blue paint accents **18.00**
Toby mug, 4" h, Man of the Year, Winston Churchill, Royal Winton **25.00**
Vase, 6-1/4" h, 4" d base, letter "V," light blue glaze.. **40.00**
Wall plaque, 6-1/2" x 8-1/2", red, white, and blue painted plaster, brass hanging loop, 7" Uncle Sam holding arm around Lincoln Monument statue on pedestal, thermometer in upper right, light blue paper ad "Compliments of Christopher Quinn Green Mount Ave and Preston St., Beer, Wines, and Liquors, Vernon 5184," copyright 1937 U.I. Co., N.Y., made in USA, professional repair **45.00**
War stamp card, 1-1/2" x 2-3/4" red, white, and blue card slotted to hold 1945 Liberty head dime, text promises one dime buys four bullets **40.00**
Window hanger, 9" x 12", red, white, and blue, gold edge trim, cord, and tassels, single star.. **20.00**

World's Fairs and Expositions

History: The Great Exhibition of 1851 in London marked the beginning of the World's Fair and Exposition movement. The fairs generally featured exhibitions from nations around the world displaying the best of their industrial and scientific achievements.

Many important technological advances have been introduced at world's fairs, including the airplane, telephone, and electric lights. Ice cream cones, hot dogs, and iced tea were first sold by vendors at fairs. Art movements were often closely associated with fairs and exhibitions. The best works of the Art Nouveau artists were assembled at the Paris Exhibition in 1900.

Collecting Hints: Familiarize yourself with the main buildings and features of the early World's Fairs and Expositions. Much of the choicest china and textiles pictured an identifiable building. Many exposition buildings remained standing long after the fairs were over, and souvenirs proliferated. Prices almost always are higher in the city or area where an exposition was held.

There have been hundreds of local fairs, state fairs, etc., in the last 100 years. These events generally produced items of value mostly to local collectors.

Columbian Expo, Puzzle, McLoughlin Bros., The World's Columbian Exposition Picture Puzzles, complete, original box, **$175**.

1893, Columbian Exposition, Chicago

Belt buckle, brass, "Landing of Columbus," wheat husk tied with bow, 1492-1892, mkd "Made by Tiffany Studio, NY," 3-3/8" x 2-3/8" **100.00**

Book, *Harper's Chicago and the World's Fair*, Julian Ralph, NY, Harper and Brothers, 1893, clothbound, 244 pgs, 70 illus **45.00**

Brochure

Lundborg Perfuem, 8-1/2" x 6-1/2". **18.00**
Mammoth Redwood Plank, Owned By The Berry Bros, Ltd, four pgs, 4" x 5" **25.00**

Comb and case, 4-1/2" l, gold colored, top of case mkd "1934 Chicago World's Fair," Golden Temple of Jehol, US Building, and Dairy Building, other side shows General Exhibits Building, Travel & Transportation Building and Electrical Building, yellow comb **60.00**

Crumb tray and scraper, silver-plated **30.00**

Drinking glass, 2-1/2" d, 3-1/2" h, clear, frosted white "World's Fair, Electrical Building" **35.00**

Scarf, 17" x 15", silk, Chicago 1893, Expo, panorama of Expos overlaying American flag **45.00**

Souvenir book, *Official Guide To The World's Columbian Exposition*, 5" x 7", 192 pgs **50.00**

Souvenir spoon, profile of Columbus on handle, 1492 above, 1893 below sketch of ship, "Columbian Exposition" emb down handle, different scene and map on back **27.50**

Table cloth, 11" sq, Machinery Hall, fringed border, small stain and damage **70.00**

1901, Pan Am Exposition, Buffalo

Bandanna, 20" sq, silk, Electrical Tower illus **195.00**

Book, *The Pan American Exposition, Buffalo, N.Y., 1901*, softbound, green cover, gold lettering **25.00**

Elongated cent, 1-3/8" l, Indian head penny, text "Mfg & Liberal Arts Pan-Am 1901," back "Armour & Company Dainty Canned Meats-Delicious-Chicago," worn **20.00**

Fan, flowers on front, back "Japan Welcome, Beautiful, Battleship Game, Fishing Game, Lucky Co., On the Zone, Pan. Pac. Int. Expo, San Francisco, 1915" **70.00**

Match holder, hanging type **25.00**

Memo pad, 1-1/2" x 2-1/4", Mother's Oats, diecut celluloid covered tablet, grommet fastner, "A Souvenir of the Pan-American Exposition and Mother's Oats" **75.00**

Pinback button

Lion Brewery, multicolored cartoon of man falling upside down from hot air balloon over city, "Drop In Buffalo 1901" **35.00**
Pan-American Exposition Buffalo, NY, 1901, 1-1/4" d, curved color panels, red, white, and blue accents, blue and white text, Whitehead & Hoag back paper **40.00**
Temple of Music, 1-1/4" d, black and white photo of building, rim text "Where Our President Fell Buffalo Sept 6th, 1901," Keystone Badge back paper **30.00**

Pan-American Expo, 1901, celluloid tape measure, flag on obverse, Native and South Americans joining hands at the Panama Canal on reverse, made by Whitehead & Hoag Co., Newark, NJ, 1-3/4" d, $35.

Souvenir spoon, silver plated
4-1/2" l, Machinery & Transportation Building on bowl **18.00**
6" l, buffalo sitting on earth on top of handle, waterfalls on bowl **15.00**
Stud, diecut thin brass figural charging buffalo, silver luster finish, blue porcelain disk with North and South America continents **20.00**
Tip tray, King's Puremalt, woman holding tray with bottle, fair emblem at bottom, reads "Panama-Pacific International Exposition-Medal of Award," 6" l, 4-1/4" w, oval **165.00**

1904, Louisiana Purchase Exposition, St. Louis

Bowl, Grant log cabin **165.00**
Brooch, figural, diecut celluloid, apple applied on silvered tin backing, diecut opening at center for pin, Arkansas Exhibit Building, railroad train, floral motif **45.00**
Coffee tin, Hanley & Kinsella **30.00**
Letter opener, emb buildings on handle **45.00**

Napkin ring, aluminum, engraved "World's Fair, St Louis, 1904," engraved US flag **50.00**
Pinback button, Philadelphia's Souvenir St. Louis 1904, 1-1/4" d, Liberty Bell in gold on cream, cream letters on dark blue rim, blue and white back paper with Liberty Bell and slogan "Proclaim Liberty Throughout All The Land Until All The Inhabitants Thereof" **25.00**
Postcard, Art Palace, silver foil background, artist sgd "H. Wunderlich," mkd "Samuel Cupples Envelope Co., St. Louis, MO-Sole World's Fair Stationers," unused **10.00**
Souvenir book, *Souvenir Book of the Louisiana Purchase Exposition,* day and night scenes, published by the Official Photographic Company, 11" x 8-1/2" **45.00**
Tip tray, tin, multicolored image of blond child, "Have Some Junket, Chr. Hansens Laboratory, Little Fall, NY" **200.00**

1909, Hudson-Fulton Exposition

Pinback button

AYPE, 1-3/4" d, rim text "City of Seattle AYPE 1909 Washington," center scene with Indian maiden in three feather headdress flying over city buildings holding yellow "I Do" pennant, tiny text along harbor water edge "Onward And Upward" **70.00**
Hudson-Fulton Celebration 1909, 1-1/4" d, multicolored, portraits of explorer and steamboat inventor, shaded blue ground, W. F. Miller back paper **40.00**

1915, Panama-Pacific International Exposition, San Francisco

Badge w/ribbon, top pin "Guest-Los Angeles Produce Exchange," orange ribbon mkd "San Francisco Dairy Produce Exchange, Santa Barbara, May 6-8, 1910," attached hen charm reads "Laying For Panama-Pacific International Exposition" **95.00**
Booklet, *Panama-Pacific International Exposition,* compliments of Remington Typewriter, 30 pgs, 7-1/4" x 11" **40.00**
Handbook, *The Sculpture & Murals of the Panama-Pacific International Exposition,* Stella S G Perry, 1915, 104 pgs, 5" x 6-3/4", ex-library copy **45.00**
Print, 6" x 26-1/2", Panoramic View of Panama-Pacific International Exposition, San Francisco, 1915, Tower of Jewels in center, some aging, traces of moisture **20.00**
Tray, 3-1/2" x 5-1/2", hammered metal, bear figural, emb "Tower of Jewels, Panama Pacific International/San Francisco, Cal 1915," dark finish **45.00**

Watch fob, brass, orig black leather strap **95.00**

1934, Century of Progress, Chicago

Ashtray, 5-1/2", Firestone, black rubber tired, transparent amber glass insert inscribed "Firestone/Century of Progress/ Chicago 1934" **30.00**

Automobile Accessory, rear view mirror, no glare, orig box **90.00**

Bracelet, copper, scenic **35.00**

Brochure

Baltimore and Ohio Railroad World's Fair Exhibit 1934, 20 pgs, 4-1/2" x 9-3/4" **25.00**

57 At The Fair, Heinz 57 Exhibit, Agricultural Building, 16 pgs **22.00**

How! And Where! At Chicago and The World's Fair, Chicago and Northwestern (Railroad) Line, 16 pg guide to Chicago **20.00**

Official Pictures, Rueben H Donnelly, black and white, 7" x 10" **35.00**

Sky-Ride, See The Fair From The Air, four pg, 3-1/2" x 5-3/4" **12.00**

The Why-What-and When of A Century of Progress, 10 pgs........................... **10.00**

Certificate of attendance, Closing Day, Oct 31, 1934, 3" x 5-1/4" **15.00**

Coffee mug, Stewart's **50.00**

Coin, flattened
1-3/8" l, Fort Dearborn.................... **15.00**
1-1/2" x 3/4", General Motors Exhibit **15.00**

Good luck key, 2" l, Master Lock, pavilions on shank **20.00**

Handkerchief, 11" sq, painted silk, small stains.. **40.00**

Centennial, Book, *Centennial Philadelphia*, Richard A. Nicholai, Bryn Mawr Press, 1976, $12.

Hot pad, exhibits and fair themes, Federal Building in center, silvered overlay worn, 9-3/4" w, 6-1/2" h.............................. **12.50**

Lapel stud, A Century of Progress, 1/2" octagonal, diecut brass, black ground, comet design, threaded post and cap **18.00**

Magazine

Liberty, 8-1/2" x 11-1/2", June 9, 1934, full-color cover art by Carl Pfeufer of honeymooners arriving at fair, article about technical achievements and exhibits at fair.................................. **15.00**

Marshall Field & Co, 9-1/2" x 13", 44 pgs, photos and articles......................... **20.00**

Map, City of Chicago and Century of Progress fairgrounds, Shell Oil **16.00**

Medal, 1-1/4" d, A & P Carnival **45.00**

Needlecase, 6-3/4" x 4-1/2", A Century of Progress... **27.00**

Pin, Sharpshooter, vertical format, silvered brass, official 1933 symbol between inscription "Safety Glass" and "Sharp-shooter/Chicago"............................ **20.00**

Pinback button

Black and white litho image of symbol, reverse "Cardinelli Century/Official Photographers for Century of Progress 1933".. **15.00**

Blue lettering on white "Century of Progress Tour-New York Farm Bureau-Chicago, 1933"............................... **12.00**

I Have Seen The World Champion Log Rollers, 1" d, black text on tan paper **18.00**

Playing cards, gold leaf edges, orig red leather case **30.00**

Pocket mirror................................... **25.00**

Press pass, 2-1/2" x 4-1/4", Short Term Press Pass, typewritten name of user and "Postal Telegraph Co.," 1934 .... **20.00**

Puzzle, 16-1/2", aerial view of fair opening, 300 pcs **50.00**

Ring, silvered adjustable brass ring, image of Hall of Science, 1934 date in vertical letters on band.............................. **20.00**

Snow globe.................................... **50.00**

Souvenir book

1933 Century of Progress Souvenir Book, 8-1/2" x 11-1/2"............................. **20.00**

Official Guide Book of the Fair, foldout map and Firestone colored adv insert **25.00**

Souvenir bottle, 3-1/2" x 6" x 6" h, clear glass, threaded red enameled tin cap, emb image of skyscraper flanked by frontier log cabin and Indian teepee, inscribed "A Century of Progress, 1833-1933"... **35.00**

Souvenir spoon, silver-plate
Electrical Group on bowl, Fort Dearborn on handle, dated 1934 .... **10.00**
Travel & Transport on bowl, Hall of Science on handle, dated 1933....... **8.00**

Tie bar, 2-3/4" l, silvered brass, small front center plate with black enamel around silver comet logo **24.00**

Tray, Hall of Science, emb buildings, bridge **30.00**

View book, 9" x 12", *A Century of Progress Exhibition Official Book of Views*, watercolor views and painting reproductions, published by Donnelly **30.00**

Wings **25.00**

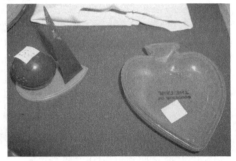

New York World's Fair, 1939, left: salt and pepper shakers, blue round ball and tall spike on orange base; right: club shaped dish, gold letters "Souvenir of the Fair," $60.

1939, New York World's Fair, New York

Album, 5" x 6-3/4", Snapshots, cardboard covers, 15 pages of black paper ... **30.00**

Ashtray

Aviation Building, 1939 NY World's Fair, scene in center, ceramic **30.00**

Trylon and Perisphere, Manuf by Almar, Point Marian, PA **60.00**

Badge, *USSR The New York World's Fair 1939*, 1-3/8" h, diecut brass, worker with raised arm standing on platform, deep red enamel flag **75.00**

Banner, 10" x 8", multicolored paint on blue felt **45.00**

Belt buckle, goldtone, enameled Trylon, and Perisphere **20.00**

Bookends, pr, alabaster, figural, Trylon and Perisphere **110.00**

Booklet

Around the Grounds, Greyhound, 2-1/2" x 5" opens to 9" x 12" sheet, orange and blue printing, white ground **18.00**

General Motors Highway & Horizons, 20 pgs **24.00**

The Foods of Tomorrow, Birdseye **8.00**

Bowl, 10" d, 2-1/5" h, pottery, color design of fair motifs, musical notes, mkd "Paden City Pottery, Paden City, W Va," and Union Made logo **95.00**

Brochure, *Compliments of Bullock Tours*, Kinston, NC, fold-out **35.00**

Cake server, 10" l, National Silver Co., view of man with five stars on handle "New York World's Fair 1939" with symbols and flags surrounding words **60.00**

Cane, 34" l, wood, blue, round wooden knob, Trylon and Perisphere decal **85.00**

Charm bracelet, brass link bracelet, five 3/4" brass disk charms, each with major exhibit building **40.00**

Clip, 7/8" h, brass, Trylon and Perisphere, sun-like accents showing across dark blue enamel, bright orange top and bottom panels, NYWF, copyright symbol, and "Pmeco" on back, brass clip for wearing **30.00**

Clock, travel, chrome silver case, Trylon, Perisphere, and fair buildings on cover, blue and orange enamel accents **125.00**

Coin, flattened, World of Tomorrow, Trylon and Perisphere **13.00**

Commemorative plate **150.00**

Compact, 2-3/4" d, metal, full-color celluloid insert, ivory white enameling **40.00**

Cuff links, pr, Trylon, and Perisphere. **45.00**

Cup **25.00**

Flashlight, 2-7/8" l, metal barrel, white plastic cap, blue finish, two orange and silver accent bands, fair emblem .. **55.00**

Fountain pen, 5" l, ivory white celluloid, matching cap, semi-iridescent, orange and blue Trylon and Perisphere symbols, mkd "Stratford" **85.00**

Glass, 4-1/4" h

Business Administration Building, dark blue top and center, orange base, NYWF 39 and row of stars at base **20.00**

Textile Building, yellow top and center, green base, center shows building **20.00**

Guide book, *Official Guide to World of Tomorrow*, first edition, 1939 .... **25.00**

Handkerchief, 10-1/2" x 11", sheer white silk-like fabric, printed images of 13 couples, each in different ethnic costume, red trim, mkd "Made in Hungary" **20.00**

Hat, employee, wool, navy, orange Trylon and Perisphere, and "1940" on front **42.00**

Hot plate, silver, engraved fair scenes **15.00**

Identification check, Greyhound Bus, Sightseeing Bus Trip Through Grounds **7.50**

Key ring **20.00**

Magazine

Band World, Summer, 1939 .... **18.00**

Life, Trylon, and Perisphere on cover **30.00**

Map, Transit Map of Greater New York, Compliments of Franklin Fire Insurance Co. **25.00**

Match case, 1-1/2" x 2", leather, Trylon and Perisphere **35.00**

Medallion, World's Fair NY 1939, 1-1/4" d, brass, raised image of passenger plane below circular metal piece depicting Trylon and Perisphere, brass loop on upper edge, worn **18.00**

Motion pictures reel, 1" x 3-3/4" x 3-3/4" boxed metal reel, black and white 16mm silent film for home projection use, black, white, and orange box dec, 1940 .. **70.00**

Music box **65.00**

Night light, ceramic, oval base with Trylon and Perisphere, ivory white finish, gold accents **100.00**

Photo, 25" x 20", American Jubilee, dry-mounted **55.00**

Pin

I Have Seen The Future **25.00**

Little Miss Junket, black and white litho of serving girl, Junket Food Products Exhibit **15.00**

Shield-shaped logo, 5/8" h, 3/8" w, 1-1/2" chain to "39" on smaller shield, blue enamel on brass............................. **25.00**

Trylon and Perisphere, diecut brass, orig luster **30.00**

Pinback button

Anthracite Booster New York World's Fair, 3/4" d, red, white, and blue Trylon and perisphere, center text "I Belong 1939" **18.00**

General Electric New York World's Fair 1940, 1-3/4" d, blue and bright gold, center GE logo **65.00**

Plate

7-1/4" d, Joint Exhibit of Capital & Labor, The American Potter, New York World's Fair, 1940, National Brotherhood Cooperative Potteries..................... **45.00**

9" d, Homer Laughlin Pottery, potter, turquoise.. **38.00**

10" d, Cronin, crazed **85.00**

Playing cards, two decks, orig box, US Playing Card Co **50.00**

Postcard

Jungland Jiggs, high gloss, sepia photo of costumed chimp riding tricycle, "Frank Buck's Jungleland At N. Y. World's Fair, Jiggs, The Mayor of Jungeland," unsed **15.00**

Set of 10 double faced cards, orig folder, unused.. **18.00**

Postage stamps, 54 licensed stamps in orig envelope, unused **25.00**

Pot holder, 7-1/2" x 8-1/2", woven terry cloth, blue and white design, inscribed "Macy's Pot Holder" **50.00**

Program, Opening Day, April 30, 1939 .... **150.00**

Ring

Brass, adjustable, oval disk with raised relief of Trylon and Perisphere **30.00**

Sterling silver, 5/8" d, 3/8 x 5/8" top with Trylon and Perisphere **45.00**

Rug, 9" x 13", woven Oriental-type, image of Trylon and Perisphere surrounded by flowers, shades of green, yellow, red, and orange highlights, Italian............... **95.00**

Salt and pepper shakers, pr, Trylon and Perisphere, 3" h, gold trim.............. **60.00**

Scarf, 18" x 17", white, orange, yellow, and maroon, blue ground, trees and buildings, Trylon and Perisphere around edge, clouds center **45.00**

Spoon

4-1/2" l, flags, Sphere and Trylon, date "1939" and two stars on handle, bowl with "New York World's Fair," tarnished silver **24.00**

6" l, Aviation Building, NY World's Fair, 1939 .... **15.00**

6" l, 3 stars, flags, Theme Bldg, date "1939" and two more stars on handle, bowl with "New York World's Fair," rim of stars, silver-plated......................... **30.00**

Swizzle stick, glass, amethyst, Brass Rail adv **8.00**

Table lighter, 2-1/2" d, 2-5/8" h, metal globe, gloss black baked enamel finish, chromed mechanism, applied 3/4" brass disk symbol emblems, orange and blue enamel accents **150.00**

Table mat, 11" x 21", red felt, yellow, green, and white graphics, Statue of Liberty, Fair Administration Bldg., Empire State Bldg, Trylon, and Perisphere **95.00**

New York World's Fair, card game, Official 1964/65 New York World's Fair Children's Card Game, original box and contents, slight play wear, $12.

Tape measure, 2-1/2" w, egg shape, metal, blue finish, bee figure on both sides, orange Trylon and Perisphere on one side, mkd "New York World's Fair 1939" **60.00**

Teapot, white glazed china, blue Trylon, and Perisphere....................................... **50.00**

Thermometer, 8-1/4" l, key shape, aerial view **32.00**

Thermos, 10" h, steel, threaded aluminum cap, orange Trylon and Perisphere, Universal Thermos **100.00**

Ticket, 3" x 4", black and white photo, starched black fabric holder **45.00**

Tie clip, 2-3/4" w, brass, raised center emblem of Trylon and Perisphere .. **25.00**

Valet holder, clothes brush holder and tie rack, syrocco wood, raised Trylon and Perisphere, orig brush **50.00**

View-Master, set of three reels, orig booklet and envelope **40.00**

1939, Golden Gate International Exposition, San Francisco

Ashtray, 1939 Golden Gate Expo, Homer Laughlin Pottery **125.00**

Belt buckle, silver colored metal, badge emblem in center, aerial view of Treasure Island, name at top, 1-1/2" l, 1" w ... **60.00**

Handkerchief, 12-1/2" sq, Treasure Island, minor stains **40.00**

Labels, set of five, 1-1/2" d, "1939 Golden Gate International Exposition 1939 - a Pageant of the Pacific" around edge, center with woman arms up, flags at her feet, sunset, Treasure Island in background **30.00**

Matchbook cover, Golden Gate Bridge scenes, pr...................................... **25.00**

Pinback button, 1-1/4" d, yellow, blue, and white.. **25.00**

Plate, 10" d, Homer Laughlin............. **125.00**

Stamps, set of six, San Francisco, Oakland and Bay Cities Invite the World in 1939, "1939 Golden Gate International Exposition 1939, A Pageant of the Pacific," one stamp stuck to another, orig packaging **45.00**

Ticket, 3-1/2" x 2-1/4", general admission, slight glue and paper on back **15.00**

1962, Century 21 Exposition, Seattle

Glass, set of eight **80.00**

Lobby card, 11" x 14", Elvis Presley, It Happened at the World's Fair, MBM copyright, 1963, #3, small tack holes **20.00**

Pinback button, 1-1/4" d, red, white, and blue, Space Needle scene **17.50**

Postal cover, 2-3/4" x 10", glossy cardboard self mailer, full color night photo of Space Needle **8.00**

Souvenir plate, 10-3/4" d, gray outer rim band, silver bands, white center with multicolor view of grounds, inscribed "Century 21-Seattle World's Fair, 1962," back mkd "Made Expressly for Frederick & Nelson-Seattle" **18.00**

Token, gold **10.00**

Tray, metal, Space Needle scene **12.00**

New York World's Fair, drinking glasses, New York World's Fair, 1964-1965, each showing different view, left: red and purple; center: green and blue; right: red and blue, frosted grounds, each **$10**.

1964, New York World's Fair, New York

Ashtray, 4" x 5", glass, white, orange, and blue graphics, two Fair Kids, Unisphere, 1964 .... **25.00**

Bank, dime register, orig card **40.00**

Bookmark, orig cello package.......... **35.00**

Change tray **12.00**

Coaster, 4" d, plastic, white, emb gold Unisphere, title and date, price for four-pc set... **32.00**

Comic Book, *Flintstones at the World's Fair* **22.00**

Doll, 8-1/2" h, © 1963 Sun Rubber, New York World's Fair, 1964-1965 .... **85.00**

Envelope, Unisphere as Christmas tree ornament, unused **10.00**

Flash card set, New York World's Fair Attractions, 3-1/2" x 6", 28 cards **25.00**

Fork and spoon display, 11" l, mounted on wooden plaque, Unisphere decals on handles **45.00**

Hat, black felt, Unisphere emblem, white cord trim, feather, name "Richard" embroidered on front..................... **25.00**

Lodge medallion, bronze luster finish, image of Unisphere and two exhibit buildings, brass hanger loop, inscribed "The Grand Lodge I.O.O.F. of the State of New York"....................................... **15.00**

Mug, 3-1/4" h, milk glass, red inscription **17.50**

Paperweight, panoramic scenes....... **40.00**

Placemat, 11" x 17-1/2", plastic, full-color illus, Swiss Sky Ride and Lunar Fountain, price for pr **25.00**

Postcard, 10 miniature pictures, 20 natural color reproductions, unused **20.00**

Puzzle, jigsaw, 2" x 10" x 11", Milton Bradley, 750 pcs, unopened **20.00**

Ring, silvered plastic, small clear plastic dome over blue and orange image of Unisphere, inscription "NY World's Fair 1964-1965" **10.00**

Salt and pepper shakers, pr, Unisphere, figural, ceramic **50.00**

Souvenir book, *Official Souvenir Book of the New York World's Fair, 1965* **25.00**

Stein, 6" h, ceramic, blue, German-style, emb Unisphere, German village scene **25.00**

Thermometer, 6" x 6", diamond shape, metal and plastic, full-color fair buildings and attractions............................... **25.00**

New York World's Fair, 1939, pillow, multicolored, blue fringe, fair scenes, **$45**.

Ticket

Belgian Village................................... **7.50**

General Admission, adult, unused. **20.00**

Pavilion of American Interiors, unused prepaid ticket, courtesy of International Silver Co **15.00**

Travelers Pavilion, The Travelers Insurance Companies stockholders courtesy card **12.00**

Tray, 10-1/2" x 11-1/2", oval, plastic, raised fair attractions................................. **42.00**

Tumbler, Science Hall, 6-1/2" h **17.50**

Videotape, Lowell Thomas, shows construction through models and pictures.. **20.00**

1967, Montreal Expo, Montreal

Bookmark, multicolored picture of sphere **8.00**

Lapel pin, brass, repeated motif around edge, threaded post fastener on back **12.00**

Tab, 1-1/2" l, litho tin, blue and white, US Pavilion, Compliments of Avis Car Rental **6.00**

Tray, 7" l, 5" w, metal, United States Pavilion **15.00**

1974, Expo '74, Spokane

Ashtray, luster scenes, unused............ **9.00**

Token, US Pavilion on one side, Expo '74, Spokane on other **15.00**

1982, World's Fair, Knoxville

Dish, 6" l, 3-3/4" w, leaf shape, dogwood blossoms, gold trim and title "World's Fair 1982 Knoxville, Tennessee," Lefton China **15.00**

Drinking glass

McDonald's, 5-1/2" h, clear, tapered, Energy Turns The World theme, trademark for McDonald's and Coca-Cola.. **8.00**

Wendy's, 5-1/2" h, set of four.......... **16.00**

Mug, ceramic...................................... **20.00**

Pencil sharpener, 4" h, metal, bronze finish, replica of Sunsphere, orig box....... **15.00**

Plate, 4" d, multicolored center scene **15.00**

Pocket knife, several different fair scenes **20.00**

Wright, Russel

History: Russel Wright was an American industrial engineer with a passion for the streamlined look. His influence is found in all aspects of domestic life. Wright and his wife, Mary Small Einstein, wrote *A Guide To Easier Living* to explain their concepts.

Russel Wright was born in 1904 in Lebanon, Ohio. His first jobs included set designer and stage manager under the direction of Norman Bel Geddes. He later used this theatrical flair for his industrial designs, stressing simple clean lines. Some of his earliest designs were executed in polished spun aluminum. These pieces, designed in the mid-1930s, include trays, vases, and teapots. Wright garnered many awards, among which were those he received from the Museum of Modern Art in 1950 and 1953.

Chase Brass and Copper, General Electric, Imperial Glass, National Silver Co., Shenango, and Steubenville Pottery Company are some of the companies that used Russel Wright designs.

Collecting Hints: Russel Wright worked for many different companies in addition to creating material under his own label, American Way. Wright's contracts with firms often called for the redesign of pieces which did not produce or sell well. As a result, several lines have the same item in more than one shape.

Wright was totally involved in design. Most collectors focus on his dinnerware; however, he also designed glassware, plastic items, textiles, furniture, and metal objects. He helped popularize bleached and blonde furniture. His early work in spun aluminum often is overlooked as is his later work in plastic for the Northern Industrial Chemical Company.

Chrome

Ice bucket, 7-1/4" d, 7" h, Antarctica, chrome, orig tongs, Chase Chrome, mkd **175.00**

Dinnerware

American Modern: Made by the Steubenville Pottery Company, 1939-1959. Originally issued in Bean Brown, Chartreuse Curry, Coral, Granite Grey, Seafoam Blue, and White. Later color additions were Black Chutney, Cedar Green, Cantaloupe, Glacier Blue, and Steubenville Blue.

Baker, small, Chartreuse Curry **25.00**
Bread and butter plate, 6" d
   Coral **4.00**
   Granite Gray **5.00**
Butter, cov
   Black Chutney **285.00**
   Chartreuse Curry **285.00**
   Coral **285.00**
   White **625.00**
Carafe, Granite Grey **175.00**
Casserole, cov, stick handle, Seafoam Blue
   .... **40.00**
Celery
   Bean Brown **24.00**
   Black Chutney **30.00**
   Granite Grey **20.00**
Children's tea set, Ideal, orig box **90.00**
Chop plate
   Black Chutney **50.00**
   Chartreuse Curry **20.00**
   Coral **20.00**
   Granite Grey **25.00**
   Seafoam Blue **25.00**
Coaster, White **24.00**
Cocktail, 2-3/4" h, 2-1/2 oz, Seafoam Blue, glass **20.00**
Creamer
   Chartreuse **18.00**
   Coral **20.00**
   Granite Gray **18.00**

Cups and saucers, green, pink, orange, and maroon, gold edges, marked "Steubenville," **each** $35.

Creamer and sugar bowl, Chartreuse Curry **20.00**
Cup and saucer
   Black Chutney **28.00**
   Chartreuse **25.00**
   Coral **25.00**
   Granite Gray **28.00**
   Oyster **20.00**
   Sea Foam **25.00**
Demitasse cup
   Chartreuse Curry **12.50**
   Granite Grey **19.00**
Demitasse pot, cov
   Coral **120.00**
   Granite Grey **150.00**
   Seafoam Blue **150.00**
Dinner plate, 10" d
   Bean Brown **20.00**
   Black Chutney **18.00**
   Cedar Green **15.00**
   Coral **24.00**
   Glacier Blue **30.00**
   Granite Gray **16.00**
   Seafoam Blue **18.00**
Fruit bowl, lug handle
   Bean Brown **20.00**
   Chartreuse Curry **12.00**
   Coral **15.00**
Hostess plate
   Chartreuse Curry **75.00**
   Granite Grey **85.00**
Iced tea tumbler, 5" h, Coral, glass, slight use **24.00**
Pickle
   Chartreuse Curry **15.00**
   Granite Grey **18.00**
Pitcher
   Chartreuse Curry **65.00**
   Coral **120.00**
   Seafoam Blue **185.00**
Platter, 13-1/2" l, 9" w, Glacier Blue **30.00**

Platter, 13" sq, Sea Foam Blue............ **60.00**
Refrigerator dish, cov
    Coral **225.00**
    Granite Grey **175.00**
Relish
    Chartreuse Curry, rosette.............. **145.00**
    Seafoam Blue................................ **28.00**
Salad bowl, 10-3/4" x 7" x 4-1/8" h
    Bean Brown................................. **125.00**
    Coral **115.00**
    Granite Grey **95.00**
    Seafoam Blue................................ **95.00**
Salad fork and spoon, Chartreuse Curry
and Granite Gray, 10" l **175.00**
Salad plate, 8" d
    Coral **18.00**
    Granite Grey **15.00**
Salt and pepper shakers, pr
    Black Chutney............................... **40.00**
    Cedar Green.................................. **45.00**
    Chartreuse.................................... **20.00**
    Coral **30.00**
    Granite Grey **20.00**
    Seafoam Blue................................ **25.00**
Sauceboat
    Black Chutney............................... **80.00**
    Coral **75.00**
Sherbet, 5 oz, Seafoam Blue, glass ... **20.00**
Soup bowl, lug handle
    Bean Brown................................. **24.00**
    Coral **18.00**
    Granite Grey **18.00**
Stack server, Cedar Green.............. **250.00**
Sugar bowl, cov
    Cedar Green.................................. **15.00**
    Chartreuse Curry............................ **20.00**
    Coral **30.00**
    Seafoam Blue................................ **15.00**
Teapot, cov
    Bean Brown................................. **200.00**
    Coral **125.00**
    Granite Grey **95.00**
    Seafoam Blue................................ **145.00**
Tumbler
    Black Chutney............................... **65.00**
    Cedar Green.................................. **72.00**
    Coral **60.00**
    Granite Grey **95.00**
Vegetable bowl
    Chartreuse Curry............................ **15.00**
    Coral **20.00**
    Granite Grey **22.00**
    Seafoam Blue................................ **20.00**
Vegetable bowl, divided, Chartreuse Curry
.... **80.00**

Highlight: Made in 1948 by the Paden City China Company and distributed by Justin Tharaud. Made in Blueberry, black, dark green, citron, nutmeg brown, white.

Bread and butter plate, 6-5/8" d
    Blueberry, matte.............................. **27.50**
    Nutmeg brown **8.50**
Cereal bowl, 6-3/4" d, coupe, Nutmeg
brown matte **14.00**
Chop plate, 13-1/2" d, white, glossy, wear
.... **40.00**

Cup and saucer
    Blueberry **28.00**
    Citron.. **26.00**
Dinner plate, 10-3/8" d
    Blueberry **75.00**
    White, matte **12.00**
Platter, 14-3/8" l, oval, Nutmeg brown, matte
.... **65.00**
Salad plate, 8-3/8" d, white, wear....... **18.00**

Iroquois Casual: Made by the Iroquois China Company and distributed by Garrison Products, 1946-1960s. Initially issued in Ice Blue, Lemon Yellow, and Sugar White. Later colors produced were Aqua, Avocado Yellow, Brick Red, Cantaloupe, Charcoal, Lettuce Green, Oyster, Nutmeg Brown, Parsley Green (later called Forest Green), Pink Sherbet, and Ripe Apricot Yellow.

Bread and butter plate, 6-1/2" d
    Avocado Yellow **6.00**
    Ice Blue **7.00**
    Ripe Apricot **9.50**
    Sugar White **8.50**
Butter, cov, 1/4 lb
    Avocado Yellow **115.00**
    Ice Blue **160.00**
    Lemon Yellow **95.00**
    Pink Sherbet................................. **125.00**
    Ripe Apricot **135.00**
    Sugar White **125.00**
Carafe
    Avocado Yellow **125.00**
    Ripe Apricot **175.00**
Casserole, cov, two qts
    Avocado Yellow **35.00**
    Oyster... **20.00**
Cereal bowl, 5-1/4" d
    Cantaloupe **18.00**
    Ice Blue **12.00**
    Oyster... **15.00**
Chop plate, 13" d
    Ripe Apricot **24.00**
    Sugar White **30.00**
Coffeepot, cov
    Ice Blue **135.00**
    Nutmeg Brown.............................. **125.00**
Coffee service, Nutmeg Brown, 10-pc set
.... **135.00**

Creamer and sugar, cov, stacking
    Avocado Yellow **45.00**
    Ice Blue **42.50**
    Oyster... **95.00**
    Sugar White **67.50**
Creamer, stacking, Lettuce Green **24.50**

Dinnerware set, American Modern, Seafoam green, 71 pieces, **$275.**

Cup and saucer
Charcoal **18.00**
Ice Blue, ear handle **15.00**
Lemon Yellow **15.00**
Pink Sherbet **15.00**
Sugar White **18.00**
Demitasse pot, cov
Avocado Yellow **95.00**
Nutmeg Brown **90.00**
Demitasse cup and saucer
Avocado Yellow **170.00**
Ice Blue **180.00**
Dinner plate, 10" d
Avocado Yellow **18.00**
Charcoal **18.00**
Lemon Yellow **15.50**
Lettuce Green **17.00**
Oyster **20.00**
Fruit bowl
Avocado Yellow **9.00**
Oyster **12.50**
Gumbo
Ice Blue **45.00**
Pink Sherbet **40.00**
Hostess plate, Ice Blue **95.00**
Luncheon plate, 9" d
Avocado Yellow **12.00**
Ice Blue **12.50**
Oyster **14.00**
Mug
Avocado **125.00**
Ripe Apricot **125.00**
Pitcher, cov
Parsley, 6-1/2" h **475.00**
Coral, 6" h **95.00**
Platter
12-1/2" l, Ice Blue **40.00**
12-3/4" l, Charcoal **60.00**
14-1/4" l, Pink Sherbet **55.00**

Salad plate, 7-3/8" d
Ice Blue **12.00**
Lemon Yellow **14.00**
Oyster **15.00**
Sugar White **14.00**
Salt and pepper shakers, pr, stacking
Avocado **35.00**
Oyster **28.00**
Sugar White **29.50**
Soup bowl, Cantaloupe **95.00**
Teapot, cov, Sugar White **385.00**
Vegetable dish, divided, Lettuce Green
.... **50.00**
Vegetable bowl, 8" d, open
Avocado Yellow **25.00**
Ice Blue **25.00**
Nutmeg Brown **25.00**
Pink Sherbet **27.50**
Vegetable bowl, 10" d, cov
Chartreuse, pinch lid, two pts **40.00**
Nutmeg Brown **65.00**
Pink Sherbet **60.00**

Iroquois Casual, Redesigned: In 1959, Iroquois Casual dinnerware was produced in patterns and offered in 45-piece sets. Cookware was another later addition in the redesigned style.

Butter, cov, 1/4 lb, Ripe Apricot **745.00**
Butter, cov, 1/2 lb
Charcoal **275.00**
Lettuce Green **225.00**
Pale pink **225.00**
Parsley **195.00**
Casserole, cov, pinch top, 8" d, Ripe Apricot
.... **125.00**
Creamer, Canteloupe **220.00**
Cup and saucer
Aqua Blue **125.00**
Ice Blue **70.00**
Gravy, Ice Blue **220.00**
Mug
Apricot Yellow **80.00**
Ice Blue **75.00**
Lemon Yellow **75.00**
Nutmeg Brown **85.00**
Pink Sherbet **70.00**
Ripe Apricot **70.00**
Sugar White, Christmas dec **85.00**
Platter, Pink Sherbet, 14-1/4" l **55.00**
Skillet, cov, Sugar White, 15" w, 4" h **325.00**
Teapot, Lemon Yellow **185.00**
Vegetable, divided, Sugar White, some mottling on interior **200.00**
Wine carafe, 10" h, Charcoal **550.00**

Z

Zeppelins

History: The terms "airship," "dirigible" and "zeppelin" are synonymous. Dirigible (from Latin) means steerable and the term originally applied to bicycles although it evolved into a synonym for airship. Zeppelin honors the name of Count Frederick Von Zeppelin, the German inventor whose first airship flew on July 2, 1900, its maiden flight lasting only eighteen minutes.

There are three types of dirigibles: 1) Rigid—a zeppelin, e.g., *Hindenburg*, *Graf*, *Shenandoah*; 2) Non-Rigid—a blimp, e.g., those flown by the Navy or bearing Goodyear advertising; and 3) Semi-Rigid—non-rigid with a keel, e.g., *Norge* and *Italia*. Only non-rigid and semi-rigid dirigibles were made prior to 1900. Hot-air balloons, barrage balloons, hydrogen balloons, and similar types are not dirigibles because they are not directable. They go where the wind takes them.

Zeppelins were made from 1900 to 1940, the last being the *LZ130*, sister ship to the *Hindenburg*. The *Graf* zeppelin was the most successful one, flying between 1928 and 1940. The *Hindenburg*, which flew in 1936 and 1937, was the most famous due to the spectacular fire that destroyed it in 1937.

America never used its four zeppelins for passenger travel; they were strictly for military use. The Naval Air Station at Lakehurst, New Jersey, where the well-known zeppelins docked, is still open, although its name has been changed to the Naval Air Engineering Center. The last Navy blimp flew from Lakehurst in 1962.

Collecting Hints: All types of zeppelin material remain stable. Specialize in one specific topic, e.g., material about one airship, models and toys, or postcards. The field is very broad, and a collector might exhaust his funds trying to be comprehensive. The most common collecting trend focuses on material relating to specific flights.

Reproduction Alert.

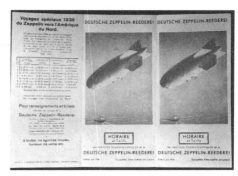

Timetable, *Hindenburg*, French, three folds, 1936, $24.

Badge, *Graf Zeppelin*, German, silver, mkd "800" **2,500.00**
Block set, litho paper on wood, hinged box with sea bi-plane, zeppelin, locomotive, tramp steamer, snow tractor, stake truck, orig glossy 6" x 8" finish prints, box lined with pink satin paper, mkd "Made in Germany," c1920, 9-1/4" x 8-3/4" x 2" **500.00**
Book
Aircraft Carrier: Graf Zeppelin, Breyer, 48 pgs **10.00**
Nations of Europe in Great War, Charles Morris, 1914, zeppelin on colorful cover **30.00**
The Story of the Airship, Hugh Allen, Goodyear Tire & Rubber Co. 84 pages, 1937 .... **40.00**
The Zeppelin in Combat, A History of the German Naval Airship Division, Douglas H. Robinson, 400 pgs, black and white photos, charges, drawings **50.00**
Candy mold, two part type **95.00**
Cocktail shaker, silver plated, figural **50.00**
Envelope, first flight, canceled
Graf Zeppelin, July 12, 1931, Austrian **65.00**
Vaduz St. Gallen, Liechtenstein, Switzerland, registered air mail cover sent to Zurich, St. Gallen arrival strike, 1930 .... **65.00**
Wein, Germany to Buenos Aires, Argentine, three stamps, 1938....... **45.00**
First day cover, "San Francisco Greets *U.S.A.S. Macon* Upon Arrival at Home Base," 8-cent airmail stamp, postmarked "Moffett Field, Oct. 15, 1933" **30.00**
Flight schedule, from Germany to America, c1936 .... **60.00**
Magazine cover
New Yorker Magazine, German *Graf Zeppelin* flying over NY skyscrapers, illus by Haupt, 1930, 8" x 11" image, acid-free mat **125.00**

Saturday Evening Post, black and white adv for Packard, showing US Navy Dirigible *Shenandoah* **8.00**

Needle book, Silver Flyer Needles, one fold cardboard, showing *Silver Flyer* over New York skyline, harbor with Statue of Liberty on back, 6-3/4" x 3-3/4", wear **2.00**

Newspaper, Pierce, SD, *Daily Capital Journal,* November 1928, "Jones Holds Milwaukee Railroad Pass," *Graf* Zeppelin in Home Port, Seventy-One Hours to Port **35.00**

Pennant, 8-1/2" l, *Hindenburg,* airship and swastika symbols, black and gold, 1936 .... **150.00**

Candy mold, #25647, Anton Reiche, Dresden, tin, two-piece clamp style, **$145**.

Photograph

3" x 7", zeppelin sinking in English Channel, March 31, 1916, half tone, by Collier **20.00**
5" sq, French officers examining zeppelin bombs, 1917, half tone, by Collier . **20.00**
8" x 6", *Graf Zeppelin,* Lakehurst, NJ, August 1929, by Keystone, German stamp on back **25.00**

Pinback button, Lakehurst Naval Air Station, red, white, and blue, attached ribbon and aluminum airship, 1930s **95.00**

Postcard

Airship Bodensee, 58th Anniv Exhibition of Akron, OH, Rubber City Stamp Club, #15 of series, reverse with ship stats **5.00**
Airship Hma R34, 54th Anniv Exhibition of Akron, OH, Rubber City Stamp Club, reverse with ship stats **5.00**
Airship LZ.7 Deutschland, 55th Anniv Exhibition of Akron, OH, Rubber City Stamp Club, reverse with ship stats . **5.00**
Airship Shenandoah, Rubber City Stamp Club, 1982, reverse with ship stats .. **5.00**
Graf L2127, real photo of zeppelin about to enter hanger **20.00**

Mooring scene, real photo, details about Dr. Z. Reederei, Frankfurt, unused. **45.00**
Zeppelin over Friedrichshafen, issued by Aubert Ulrich, Ravensburg, Wurtemburg, black and white, 1928, used.......... **15.00**
Zeppelin L. Z. 127, Graf Zeppelin, landing, real photo, German title, issued by Karl Cramer, Leipzig................. **22.00**
Zeppelin L. Z. 127, Graf Zeppelin, Oct. 10, 1928, first flight, clear cancellations **120.00**
Zeppelin L. Z. 129, Hindenburg, real photograph by Horn....................... **25.00**

Pull toy, *Graf Zeppelin,* Steelcraft, C-8 .... **490.00**

Stamp, *Graf Zeppelin,* on post card, postmarked Los Angeles, first European Pan-American round flight, C14 .. **325.00**

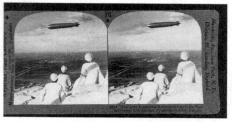

Stereograph, Keystone View Co., #7758632, The Great Zeppelin's Rendezvous with the Eternal Desert and Ancient Pyramids of Giza, historical information and facts on reverse, **$35**.

Tape measure, figural.................... **1,500.00**

Toy

Graf Zeppelin, 2-1/2" x 4-1/2", red, white, and blue diecut paper mounted to wood, rubber bands, toy whizzes when swung, Japanese, c1930.......................... **25.00**
Los Angeles, cast iron, unknown maker, worn old repaint, one cabin damaged, 11-1/4" l **275.00**
Pony Blimp, cast iron, unknown maker, old worn repaint, nickel finish wheels, light rust, 5-1/2" l **180.00**
Sky Rangers, litho tin, Unique Art, revolving planes and zeppelins, c1940, played with condition **70.00**
Zep, cast iron, unknown maker, old repaint, 5" l **100.00**

Whistle, 2" w, tin litho, dark red, blue, yellow, and green airship with gondola below, mkd "Japan" at top, c1930 .... **30.00**